Get connected
power of the Internet

McDougal Littell's online resources for students and parents provide motivating instruction, practice, and learning support.

Visit classzone.com for eEdition Plus Online purchasing information and a free demo

eEdition Plus ONLINE

This online version of the text encourages students to explore world geography through interactive features.

- Animated maps and infographics
- Onscreen notetaking
- Links to online test practice

classzone.com

With a click of the mouse, students gain immediate access to this companion Web site to *World Geography*.

- Links correlated to the text
- Web Research Guide
- Demographic data updates
- Self-scoring quizzes
- Interactive games and activities
- Links to current events
- Test practice

Now it all clicks!™

CLASSZONE.COM

McDougal Littell

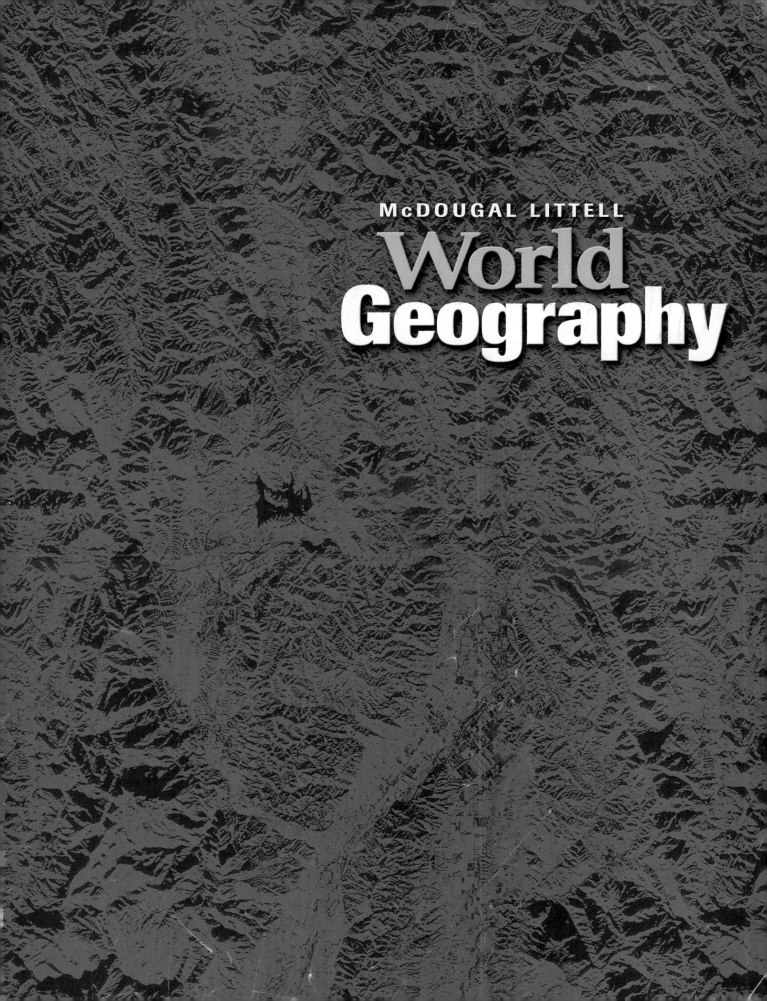

McDOUGAL LITTELL

World
Geography

Namche Bazaar, Nepal

Leaning tower, Pisa, Italy

Masai warriors, Kenya

Volcano, Honolulu, Hawaii

World Geography

Daniel D. Arreola

Marci Smith Deal

James F. Petersen

Rickie Sanders

McDougal Littell

A DIVISION OF HOUGHTON MIFFLIN COMPANY

Maps on pages A1–A37, 64, 102–115, 131, 179, 190–199, 206, 248, 262–271, 281, 322, 336–343, 357, 391, 402–413, 419, 464, 478–485, 494, 528, 542–549, 559, 596, 610–617, 624, 664, 678–687, 693, 733 © Rand McNally & Company. All rights reserved.

Acknowledgments begin on page R66.

ISBN 0-618-37760-3

Printed in the United States of America

X 2 3 4 5 6 7 8 9 – VEI – 09 08 07 06 05 04

Daniel D. Arreola is Professor of Geography and an affiliate faculty member of the Center for Latin American Studies at Arizona State University. He has taught world regional geography for more than a decade at universities in Arizona and Texas. Dr. Arreola has published extensively on topics relating to the cultural geography of the Mexican-American borderlands. He is co-author of *The Mexican Border Cities: Landscape Anatomy and Place Personality* and author of *Tejano South Texas: A Mexican American Cultural Province*.

Marci Smith Deal is the K-12 Social Studies Curriculum Coordinator for Hurst-Euless-Bedford Independent School District in Texas. She received the 2000 Distinguished Geographer Award for the State of Texas, and was one of the honorees of the 2001 National Council for Geographic Education Distinguished Teacher Award. She has served as president for the Texas Council for Social Studies Supervisors and as vice-president for the Texas Council for Social Studies. She currently serves as a teacher consultant for National Geographic Society.

James F. Petersen is Professor of Geography at Southwest Texas State University. He served as president of the National Council for Geographic Education in 2000. As a charter member of the National Geographic Society's Alliance, Dr. Petersen has directed summer institutes and national conferences for teachers and educational organizations. He is the author of many articles on geographic education, as well as media/book reviews, textbooks, and curricular materials.

Rickie Sanders is Professor and Chair of Geography/Urban Studies at Temple University. She recently served on the team that directed the National Science Foundation/National Council for Geographic Education's "Finding A Way" project, which produced learning modules for integrating gender into geography classrooms. Dr. Sanders has received numerous awards for teaching, including the NCGE Distinguished Teaching Award and the Temple University Distinguished Teaching Award. She has numerous publications and is co-author of *Growing Up in America: An Atlas of Youth in the U.S.A.*

Content Consultants

C. Cindy Fan
Department of Geography
UCLA
Los Angeles, California

Howard Johnson
Department of Physical and Earth
    Sciences
Jacksonville State University
Jacksonville, Alabama

Cheryl Johnson-Odim
Liberal Education Division
Columbia College
Chicago, Illinois

Charles Kovacik
Department of Geography
University of South Carolina
Columbia, South Carolina

Barbara McDade
Department of Geography
University of Florida
Gainesville, Florida

Inés Miyares
Department of Geography
Hunter College
New York City, New York

Joseph Stoltman
Department of Geography
Western Michigan University
Kalamazoo, Michigan

Donald Zeigler
Department of Political Science and
    Geography
Old Dominion University
Norfolk, Virginia

Multicultural Advisory Board

Betty Dean
Social Studies Consultant
Pearland, Texas

C. Cindy Fan
Department of Geography
UCLA
Los Angeles, California

Cheryl Johnson-Odim
Liberal Education Division
Columbia College
Chicago, Illinois

Barbara McDade
Department of Geography
University of Florida
Gainesville, Florida

Inés Miyares
Department of Geography
Hunter College
New York City, New York

Pat Payne
Office of Multicultural Education
Indianapolis Public Schools
Indianapolis, Indiana

Betto Ramirez
Region One Education Service
    Center
Edinburg, Texas

Jon Reyhner
Department of Education
Northern Arizona University
Flagstaff, Arizona

Teacher Consultants

The following educators reviewed manuscript or wrote classroom activities.

Deborah Althouse
Thomas J. Anderson High School
Southgate, Michigan

Jamie Berlin
South High School
Sheboygan, Wisconsin

Heather Berry
Hazelwood East High School
St. Louis, Missouri

Jewel Berryman
Kashmere High School
Houston, Texas

Deborah Bittner
Sandra Day O'Connor High School
Helotes, Texas

Dora Bradley
Lakewood Middle School
North Little Rock, Arkansas

Denise Butler
Hillcrest High School
Dallas, Texas

Deborah Canales
Austin High School
Houston, Texas

Fred Cibik
Brown Deer High School
Brown Deer, Wisconsin

Jim Curtis
Antioch High School
Antioch, Illinois

Sam Eigel
Cody High School
Detroit, Michigan

Jan Ellersieck
Ft. Zummalt South High School
St. Peters, Missouri

Thomas Figurski
Thomas J. Anderson High School
Southgate, Michigan

Karen Fletcher
Haltom High School
Haltom City, Texas

Kathy Gilbert
Mukwonago High School
Mukwonago, Wisconsin

Manuel Gomez
McAllen Memorial High School
McAllen, Texas

Richard Goodwin
Yvonne A. Ewell Township Center
Dallas, Texas

Craig Grace
Lanier High School
West Austin, Texas

David Haas
Waukegan High School
Waukegan, Illinois

Britin Hanson
Granite Hills High School
El Cajon, California

William Hoffman
Capistrano Valley High School
Mission Viejo, California

Alan Hunt
Coronado High School
El Paso, Texas

Amy Kiehl
Milwaukee Trade & Technical High
    School
Milwaukee, Wisconsin

Cliff Kinder
Bowie High School
Arlington, Texas

Korri Kinney
Meridian High School
Meridian, Idaho

Sherry Kusenberger
MacArthur High School
San Antonio, Texas

Rick Looze
Ft. Atkinson High School
Ft. Atkinson, Wisconsin

Jerome Love
Beaumont High School
St. Louis, Missouri

Kara Lukens
Dakota High School
Macomb, Michigan

Matt Lyons
Hastings Ninth Grade Center
Houston, Texas

Gene Mahurin
Western Hills High School
Ft. Worth, Texas

Joy McKee
Lamar High School
Arlington, Texas

Patricia Medina
Ray High School
Corpus Christi, Texas

Tim Murray
Plano Senior High School
Plano, Texas

Joseph Naumann
McCluer North High School
Florissant, Missouri

Phillip Owens
Ball High School
Galveston, Texas

Robert Parker
St. Margaret's High School
San Juan Capistrano, California

Cathy Probst
Nathan Hale High School
West Allis, Wisconsin

Dan Richardson
East Troy High School
East Troy, Illinois

Robert Schutt
Detroit High School for the Fine and
    Performing Arts
Detroit, Michigan

Martha B. Sharma
National Cathedral School
Washington, D.C.

Brenda Smith
Social Studies Instructional
    Supervisor
Colorado Springs School District #11
Colorado Springs, Colorado

Jody Smothers-Marcello
Sitka School District
Sitka, Alaska

Linda Tillis
South Oak Cliff High School
Dallas, Texas

Mark Van Hecke
Anchor Bay High School
New Baltimore, Michigan

Glenn Watt
Grayslake High School
Grayslake, Illinois

Alice White
Bryan Adams High School
Dallas, Texas

Sarah White
Dakota High School
Macomb, Michigan

Tom Wissink
Oshkosh West High School
Oshkosh, Wisconsin

Anne Woods
Orchard Farms High School
St. Charles, Missouri

Tom Wurst
Langham Creek High School
Houston, Texas

Unit 1

The Basics of Geography

Volcano in Costa Rica (p. 2)

Nanjing Road, Shanghai, China (p. 81)

For more information on the basics of geography . . .

CLASSZONE.COM

The United States and Canada

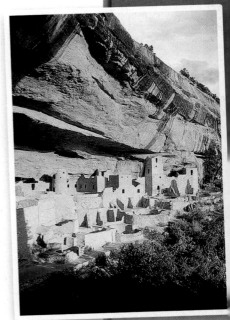

Mesa Verde National Park, Colorado (p. 135)

Parliament guards, Ottawa, Ontario (p. 158)

For more information on the United States and Canada . . .

CLASSZONE.COM

ix

Unit 3 Latin America

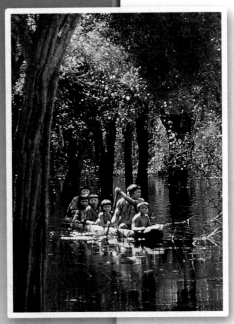

Chacobo Indians on the Amazon River, Bolivia (p. 186)

São Paulo, Brazil (p. 251)

For more information on Latin America . . .

CLASSZONE.COM

Europe

The Eiffel Tower,
Paris, France
(p. 259)

The Wetterhorn,
Switzerland
(p. 310)

For more information on Europe . . .

Frozen Lake
Baikal, Russia
(p. 350)

St. Basil's
Cathedral,
Moscow,
Russia
(p. 362)

For more information on Russia and the Republics . . .

 CLASSZONE.COM

Africa

Unit 6

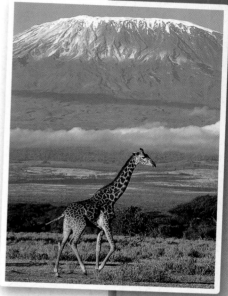

Mount Kilimanjaro, Tanzania (p. 399)

Masai Girl, Kenya (p. 434)

For more information on Africa . . .

CLASSZONE.COM

Sahara Desert, North Africa (p. 420)

xiii

Unit 7 Southwest Asia

Oasis on caravan route from Yemen to Palestine (p. 475)

Kurdish family, Turkey (p. 476)

For more information on Southwest Asia . . .

CLASSZONE.COM

South Asia

Unit 8

For more information on South Asia . . .

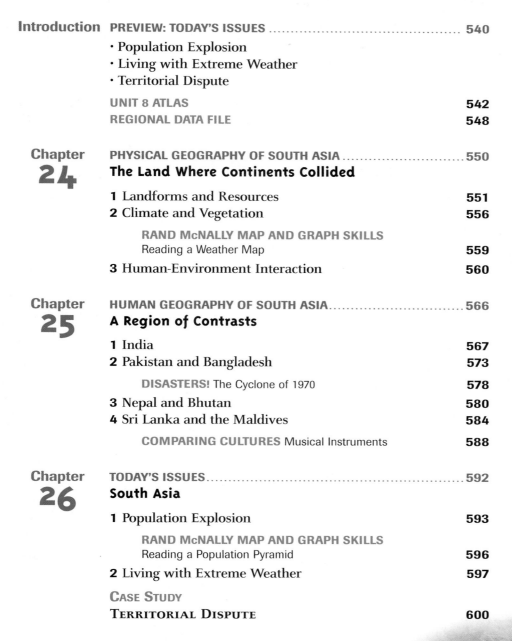

**Taj Mahal,
Agra, India**
(p. 538)

**Tea Plantation,
Sri Lanka**
(p. 586)

xv

Unit 9 · East Asia

Mount Fuji,
Japan (p. 607)

Potala Palace,
Tibet (p. 619)

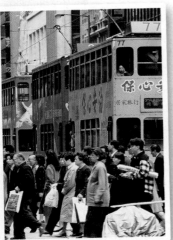

Crowded urban street,
Hong Kong (p. 668)

For more information on East Asia . . .

CLASSZONE.COM

Southeast Asia, Oceania, and Antarctica

Unit 10

Ice Cliffs, Antarctica (p. 674)

Fishing on Cook Island (p. 714)

Uluru, or Ayers Rock, Australia (p. 729)

For more information on Southeast Asia, Oceania, and Antarctica . . .

CLASSZONE.COM

xvii

Features

Comparing Cultures

Disasters!

RAND McNALLY Map and Graph Skills

growing up in

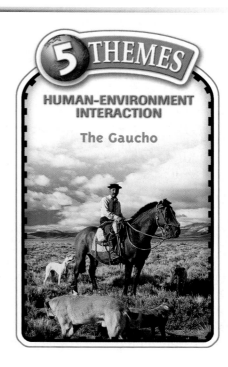

5 THEMES

HUMAN-ENVIRONMENT INTERACTION

The Gaucho

Geography TODAY

Maps

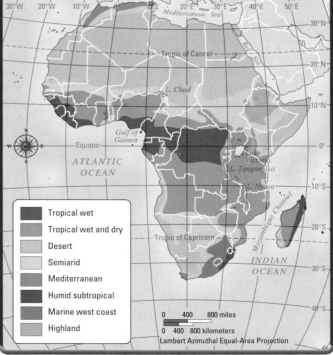

Climates of Africa

Maps

Graphs, Charts, and Tables

GRAPHS

CHARTS AND TABLES

World Population Growth

2050 9 billion

1999 6 billion

1975 4 billion

1 A.D. 200 million

1930 2 billion

1850 1 billion

SOURCE: *The World Almanac*, 2000

SKILLBUILDER: Interpreting Graphs

❶ **ANALYZING DATA** How long did it take for the population to reach one billion?

❷ **MAKING GENERALIZATIONS** How have the intervals between increases changed?

Infographics and Time Lines

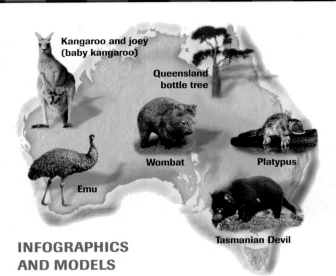

Kangaroo and joey (baby kangaroo)
Queensland bottle tree
Wombat
Platypus
Emu
Tasmanian Devil

INFOGRAPHICS AND MODELS

TIME LINES

Primary Sources

"My goodness, if I'd known how badly you wanted democracy I'd have given it to you ages ago."

Primary Sources/Videos

The Voyageur Experience in World Geography Videos

Student Guide to the
Sunshine State Standards

CONTENTS

Student Guide to the Grade 9–12 Sunshine State Standards

At the beginning of every section in this book, you will see a listing that contains combinations of numbers and letters (such as A.1.3.1). These combinations are codes that refer to standards and benchmarks developed by the state of Florida for its public schools. These standards and benchmarks describe the content and skills you are expected to have learned by the end of specific grades.

Standards labeled with "SS" are specific skills related to the study of social studies. Benchmarks labeled with "FCAT" are specific skills tested on the Florida Comprehensive Assessment Test.

The following chart contains the complete wording of these standards and benchmarks. When you see a list of codes at the start of a new section, you can use this chart to find out which skills you will be studying as you work through the chapter. In this way, you will be able to keep track of what you learn throughout the year.

SOCIAL STUDIES

Time, Continuity, and Change [History]

Standard 1	The student understands historical chronology and the historical perspective. **(SS.A.1.4)**
SS.A.1.4.1	The student understands how ideas and beliefs, decisions, and chance events have been used in the process of writing and interpreting history.
SS.A.1.4.2	The student identifies and understands themes in history that cross scientific, economic, and cultural boundaries.
SS.A.1.4.3	The student evaluates conflicting sources and materials in the interpretation of a historical event or episode.
SS.A.1.4.4	The student uses chronology, sequencing, patterns, and periodization to examine interpretations of an event.

Standard 2	The student understands the world from its beginnings to the time of the Renaissance. **(SS.A.2.4)**
SS.A.2.4.1	The student understands the early physical and cultural development of humans.
SS.A.2.4.2	The student understands the rise of early civilizations and the spread of agriculture in Mesopotamia, Egypt, and the Indus Valley.
SS.A.2.4.3	The student understands the emergence of civilization in China, southwest Asia, and the Mediterranean basin.
SS.A.2.4.4	The student understands significant aspects of the economic, political, and social systems of ancient Greece and the cultural contributions of that civilization.
SS.A.2.4.5	The student understands the significant features of the political, economic, and social systems of ancient Rome and the cultural legacy of that civilization.
SS.A.2.4.6	The student understands features of the theological and cultural conflict between the Muslim world and Christendom and the resulting religious, political, and economic competition in the Mediterranean region.

SS.A.2.4.7	The student understands the development of the political, social, economic, and religious systems of European civilization during the Middle Ages.
SS.A.2.4.8	The student understands cultural, religious, political, and technological developments of civilizations in Asia and Africa.
SS.A.2.4.9	The student understands significant social, cultural, and religious features of India, and India's conflict with the Moslem Turks.
SS.A.2.4.10	The student understands significant cultural, religious, and economic features of civilizations in Mesoamerica and Andean South America.
SS.A.2.4.11	The student understands political and cultural features of the Mongol Empire and the Empire's impact on Eurasian peoples.

▶**Standard 3**	The student understands Western and Eastern civilization since the Renaissance. **(SS.A.3.4)**
SS.A.3.4.1	The student understands the significant political and economic transformations and significant cultural and scientific events in Europe during the Renaissance.
SS.A.3.4.2	The student understands significant religious and societal issues from the Renaissance through the Reformation.
SS.A.3.4.3	The student understands the significant economic, political, and cultural interactions among the peoples of Africa, Europe, Asia, and the Americas during the Age of Discovery and the European expansion.
SS.A.3.4.4	The student knows the significant ideas and texts of Buddhism, Christianity, Hinduism, Islam, and Judaism, their spheres of influence in the age of expansion, and their reforms in the 19th century.
SS.A.3.4.5	The student understands the significant scientific and social changes from the Age of Reason through the Age of Enlightenment.
SS.A.3.4.6	The student understands transformations in the political and social realms from the Age of Absolutism through the Glorious Revolution to the French Revolution.
SS.A.3.4.7	The student understands significant political developments in Europe in the 19th century.
SS.A.3.4.8	The student understands the effects of the Industrial Revolution.
SS.A.3.4.9	The student analyzes major historical events of the first half of the 20th century.
SS.A.3.4.10	The student understands the political, military, and economic events since the 1950s that have had a significant impact on international relations.

▶**Standard 4**	The student understands U.S. history to 1880. **(SS.A.4.4)**
SS.A.4.4.1	The student understands the economic, social, and political interactions between Native American tribes and European settlers during the Age of Discovery.
SS.A.4.4.2	The student understands how religious, social, political, and economic developments shaped the settlement patterns of the North American colonies.
SS.A.4.4.3	The student understands the significant military and political events that took place during the American Revolution.
SS.A.4.4.4	The student understands the political events that defined the Constitutional period.

SS.A.4.4.5	The student understands the significant political events that took place during the early national period.
SS.A.4.4.6	The student understands the military and economic events of the Civil War and Reconstruction.

Standard 5	The student understands U.S. history from 1880 to the present day. **(SS.A.5.4)**
SS.A.5.4.1	The student knows the causes of the Industrial Revolution and its economic, political, and cultural effects on American society.
SS.A.5.4.2	The student understands the social and cultural impact of immigrant groups and individuals on American society after 1880.
SS.A.5.4.3	The student understands significant events leading up to the United States involvement in World War I and the political, social, and economic results of that conflict in Europe and the United States.
SS.A.5.4.4	The student understands social transformations that took place in the 1920s and 1930s, the principal political and economic factors that led to the Great Depression, and the legacy of the Depression in American society.
SS.A.5.4.5	The student knows the origins and effects of the involvement of the United States in World War II.
SS.A.5.4.6	The student understands the political events that shaped the development of United States foreign policy since World War II and knows the characteristics of that policy.
SS.A.5.4.7	The student understands the development of federal civil rights and voting rights since the 1950s and the social and political implications of these events.
SS.A.5.4.8	The student knows significant political events and issues that have shaped domestic policy decisions in contemporary America.

People, Places, and Environments [Geography]

Standard 1	The student understands the world in spatial terms. **(SS.B.1.4)**
SS.B.1.4.1	The student uses a variety of maps, geographic technologies including geographic information systems (GIS) and satellite-produced imagery, and other advanced graphic representations to depict geographic problems.
SS.B.1.4.2	The student understands the advantages and disadvantages of using maps from different sources and different points of view.
SS.B.1.4.3	The student uses mental maps of physical and human features of the world to answer complex geographic questions.
SS.B.1.4.4	The student understands how cultural and technological characteristics can link or divide regions.
SS.B.1.4.5	The student understands how various factors affect people's mental maps.

Standard 2	The student understands the interactions of people and the physical environment. **(SS.B.2.4)**
SS.B.2.4.1	The student understands how social, cultural, economic, and environmental factors contribute to the dynamic nature of regions.
SS.B.2.4.2	The student understands past and present trends in human migration and cultural interaction and their impact on physical and human systems.

SS.B.2.4.3	The student understands how the allocation of control of the Earth's surface affects interactions between people in different regions.
SS.B.2.4.4	The student understands the global impact of human changes in the physical environment.
SS.B.2.4.5	The student knows how humans overcome "limits to growth" imposed by physical systems.
SS.B.2.4.6	The student understands the relationships between resources and the exploration, colonization, and settlement of different regions of the world.
SS.B.2.4.7	The student understands the concept of sustainable development.

Time, Government and the Citizen [Civics and Government]

▶ Standard 1	The student understands the structure, functions, and purposes of government and how the principles and values of American democracy are reflected in American constitutional government. (SS.C.1.4)
SS.C.1.4.1	The student understands the nature of political authority and the nature of the relationship between government and civil society in limited governments (e.g. constitutional democracies) and unlimited governments (e.g. totalitarian regimes).
SS.C.1.4.2	The student understands the ideas that led to the creation of limited government in the United States (e.g., ideas of natural rights philosophy, and the concept of popular sovereignty).
SS.C.1.4.3	The student understands how the overall design and specific features of the Constitution prevent the abuse of power by aggregating power at the national, state, and local levels; dispersing power among different levels of government; and using a system of checks and balances (e.g., federalism).
SS.C.1.4.4	The student understands the role of special interest groups, political parties, the media, public opinion, and majority/minority conflicts on the developmentof public policy and the political process.

▶ Standard 2	The student understands the role of the citizen in American democracy. (SS.C.2.4)
SS.C.2.4.1	The student develops and defines his or her own political beliefs and tendencies.
SS.C.2.4.2	The student assesses the role that his or her own political behavior plays in determining the flow of power through our political system and for resolving conflicts in a pluralistic society.
SS.C.2.4.3	The student understands issues of personal concern: the rights and responsibilities of the individual under the U.S. Constitution, the importance of civil liberties, the role of conflict resolution and compromise, and issues involving ethical behavior in politics.
SS.C.2.4.4	The student understands the distinction between citizens and noncitizens (aliens) and the process by which aliens may become citizens.
SS.C.2.4.5	The student understands how personal, political, and economic rights are secured by constitutional government and by such means as the rule of law, checks and balances, an independent judiciary, and a vigilant citizenry.
SS.C.2.4.6	The student understands the argument that personal, political, and economic rights reinforce each other.
SS.C.2.4.7	The student knows the points at which citizens can monitor or influence the process of public policy formation.

Economics

Standard 1 The student understands how scarcity requires individuals and institutions to make choices about how to use resources. **(SS.D.1.4)**

SS.D.1.4.1 The student understands how many financial and nonfinancial factors (e.g., cultural traditions, profit, and risk) motivate consumers, producers, workers, savers, and investors to allocate their scarce resources differently.

SS.D.1.4.2 The student understands credit history and the positive and negative impacts that credit can have on an individual's financial life.

Standard 2 The student understands the characteristics of different economic systems and institutions. **(SS.D.2.4)**

SS.D.2.4.1 The student understands how wages and prices are determined in market, command, tradition-based, and mixed economic systems and how economic systems can be evaluated by their ability to achieve broad social goals such as freedom, efficiency, equity, security, and growth.

SS.D.2.4.2 The student understands how price and quantity demanded relate, how price and quantity supplied relate, and how price changes or controls affect distribution and allocation in the economy.

SS.D.2.4.3 The student understands how government taxes, policies, and programs affect individuals, groups, businesses, and regions.

SS.D.2.4.4 The student understands how United States fiscal policies and monetary policies reinforce or offset each other and how they effect levels of economic activity, the money supply of the country, and the well being of individuals, businesses, regions and the nation.

SS.D.2.4.5 The student understands basic terms and indicators associated with levels of economic performance and the state of the economy.

SS.D.2.4.6 The student understands factors that have led to increased international interdependence and basic concepts associated with trade between nations.

FCAT — Florida Comprehensive Achievement Test
Language Arts

Grade 9–10 Reading Benchmarks

LA.A.1.4.2	The student selects and uses strategies to understand words and text, and to make and confirm inferences from what is read, including interpreting diagrams, graphs, and statistical illustrations.
LA.A.2.2.7	The student recognizes the use of comparison and contrast in a text.
LA.A.2.4.1	The student determines the main idea and identifies relevant details, methods of development, and their effectiveness in a variety of types of written material.
LA.A.2.4.2	The student determines the author's purpose and point of view and their effects on the text. (Includes **LA.A.2.4.5** The student identifies devices of persuasion and methods of appeal and their effectiveness.)
LA.A.2.4.4	The student locates, gathers, analyzes, and evaluates written information for a variety of purposes, including research projects, real-world tasks, and self-improvement. (Includes **LA.A.2.4.6** The student selects and uses appropriate study and research skills and tools according to the type of information being gathered or organized, including almanacs, government publications, microfiche, news sources, and information services.)
LA.A.2.4.7	The student analyzes the validity and reliability of primary source information and uses the information appropriately.
LA.A.2.4.8	The student synthesizes information from multiple sources to draw conclusions.
LA.E.2.2.1	The student recognizes cause-and-effect relationships in literary texts. [Applies to fiction, nonfiction, poetry, and drama.]
LA.E.2.4.1	The student analyzes the effectiveness of complex elements of plot, such as setting, major events, problems, conflicts, and resolutions.

Grade 10 Writing Benchmarks

LA.B.1.4.1 The student selects and uses appropriate prewriting strategies, such as brainstorming, graphic organizers, and outlining.

LA.B.1.4.2 The student drafts and revises writing that
- is focused, purposeful, and reflects insight into the writing situation
- has an organizational pattern that provides for a logical progression of ideas
- has effective use of transitional devices that contribute to a sense of completeness
- has support that is substantial, specific, relevant, and concrete
- demonstrates a commitment to and involvement with the subject
- uses creative writing strategies as appropriate to the purpose of the paper
- demonstrates a mature command of language with freshness of expression
- has varied sentence structure
- has few, if any, convention errors in mechanics, usage, punctuation, and spelling

LA.B.1.4.3 The student produces final documents that have been edited for
- correct spelling
- correct punctuation, including commas, colons, and common use of semicolons
- correct capitalization
- correct sentence formation
- correct instances of possessives, subject/verb agreement, instances of noun/pronoun agreement, and the intentional use of fragments for effect
- correct formatting that appeals to readers, including appropriate use of a variety of graphics, tables, charts, and illustrations in both standard and innovative forms

This section of the textbook helps you develop and practice the skills you need to take the reading and writing sections of the Florida Comprehensive Assessment Test (FCAT). **Part 1, Introducing the FCAT**, provides some basic information on the FCAT and describes the types of questions you will find on the reading and writing tests.

    Part 2, FCAT Strategies and Practice, offers specific strategies for tackling the skills that are tested on the reading section of the FCAT. You will find a list of these skills on page S2. Strategies on how to handle the Writing FCAT are also provided. Each strategy is followed by a set of questions that you can use for practice.

CONTENTS

General Information About the FCAT

FCAT is short for the Florida Comprehensive Assessment Test. The FCAT measures your reading and writing skills against official **benchmarks**, or standards (listed below). On the reading section of the FCAT, you will be asked to read several passages. Then you will answer questions to show how well you understood the material. You will have one hour to complete the 9th grade FCAT, which consists only of multiple choice questions. However, a reading test usually will have:

- 6–7 reading passages
- 40–45 multiple choice questions
- 6–8 short-response questions
- 2–3 extended-response questions

On the writing section of the FCAT, you will be given a short writing assignment, called a **prompt** (topic). You will not be told the prompt beforehand, but it can be answered based on your own opinions and experience. You will be given 45 minutes to plan and write your response.

Grade 9 Benchmarks	
LA.A.1.4.2	Selects and uses strategies to understand words and text, and to make and confirm inferences from what is read, including interpreting diagrams, graphs, and statistical illustrations.
LA.A.2.2.7	Recognizes the use of comparison and contrast in a text.
LA.A.2.4.1	Determines the main idea and identifies relevant details, methods of development, and their effectiveness in a variety of types of written material.
LA.A.2.4.2	Determines the author's purpose and point of view and their effects on the text. (Includes **LA.A.2.4.5** Identifies devices of persuasion and methods of appeal and their effectiveness.)
LA.A.2.4.4	Locates, gathers, analyzes, and evaluates written information for a variety of purposes, including research projects, real-world tasks, and self-improvement. (Includes **LA.A.2.4.6** Selects and uses appropriate study and research skills and tools according to the type of information being gathered or organized, including almanacs, government publications, microfiche, news sources, and information services.)
LA.A.2.4.7	Analyzes the validity and reliability of primary source information and uses the information appropriately.
LA.A.2.4.8	Synthesizes information from multiple sources to draw conclusions.
LA.E.2.2.1	Recognizes cause-and-effect relationships in literary texts. [Applies to fiction, nonfiction, poetry, and drama.]
LA.E.2.4.1	Analyzes the effectiveness of complex elements of plot, such as setting, major events, problems, conflicts, and resolutions.

Types of Questions on the FCAT

There will be two types of questions on the reading portion of the FCAT: multiple choice questions and performance tasks. The majority of questions will be in the multiple-choice format.

Multiple-Choice Questions

Every multiple–choice question on the FCAT will have four possible answers, and only one of them will be considered the best answer. The four choices will be labeled A, B, C, D or F, G, H, I.

The following are some strategies for answering multiple-choice questions:

- Try to determine the answer to the question before examining the answer choices. Then look to see if your answer is one of the four choices.

- Eliminate answers you are certain are incorrect.
- Try to find a clue in the question that will lead you to the correct answer.
- Some questions are more difficult than others and will require more time. Do not panic if you feel that you have spent too much time on a question. Easier questions can be answered quickly and will help make up for lost time.
- If a question appears to be too difficult, skip it and proceed to other questions. After you finish answering the remaining questions, return to the one you skipped. Occasionally, later questions and answers will be helpful in answering the complicated ones that you skipped.

Performance Tasks

Performance tasks require you to respond to test questions in your own words. You will also be asked to support your answer with details and information from the passage. There are two types of performance tasks:

Short-Response Questions are identified by the following symbol:

A short response should take from three to five minutes to complete. Short responses are scored from 2 to 0 based on the following rubric:

Rubric for Short-Response Questions	
2 points	– Shows a complete understanding of the reading concept. – Response is accurate and complete. – Necessary supporting examples are included. – Information is clearly based on the text.
1 point	– Shows a partial understanding of the reading concept. – Includes information that is correct and based on the text but is too general or too simplistic. – Some of the supporting examples are incomplete or omitted.
0 Points	– Response is inaccurate. – Response is confused or irrelevant. – No response is given.

Extended-Response Questions are identified by the following symbol:

Extended-response questions require more thought and longer answers than short-response questions. Extended responses should take from 10 to 15 minutes to complete. Extended responses are scored from 4 to 0 based on the following rubric:

Rubric for Extended-Response Questions	
4 points	– Shows a complete understanding of the reading concept. – Response is accurate and complete. – Necessary supporting examples are included. – Information is clearly based on the text.
3 points	– Shows an understanding of the reading concept. – Response is accurate. – Supporting examples are not complete. – Supporting examples are not clearly based on the text.
2 points	– Shows a partial understanding of the reading concept. – Includes information that is essentially correct or based on the text but is too general or too simplistic. – Some supporting examples are incomplete or omitted.
1 point	– Shows a very limited understanding of the reading concept. – Response is incomplete and flawed. – Response may not address all the requirements of the task.
0 points	– Response is inaccurate. – Response is confused or irrelevant. – No response is given.

The following are some strategies for completing performance tasks:

- Read the question carefully. Look for key words that will help you write your answer.
- Sometimes a question may have two or more parts. Ensure that you answer every part.
- Include information from the passage in your answer.
- Write your answers on the writing lines provided.
- Do not skip any questions. Incomplete answers earn partial credit.

The Writing FCAT

The Writing FCAT consists of a short writing assignment, called a prompt. The prompt involves one of two kinds of writing: **expository writing**, which requires you to explain a topic, or **persuasive writing**, which requires you to convince someone of something. You will not be told the prompt beforehand, but you should be able to write a response based on your own opinions and experience. You will have 45 minutes to write your response.

The following are some strategies for answering writing prompts:

- Read the prompt carefully and focus your answer on what it asks.
- Plan your time. You will have 45 minutes to complete your writing. Allow yourself time for planning, writing, *and* proofreading.
- Jot down an outline to organize your writing before you start.
- Provide details that support your main ideas effectively.
- Conclude your response by summing up the main points of your explanation or the main reasons for the course of action you suggest.

Writing test responses are scored from 6 to 1 based on the following rubric:

Rubric for Writing Assessment Responses	
6 points	– **Focus:** clear, appropriate, and well maintained – **Organization:** logical and clear, with a beginning, a middle, and an end and good use of transitions – **Supporting details:** precise, related to the topic, and effective – **Conventions:** sophisticated vocabulary, mostly error-free standard English, and varied sentence structures
5 points	– **Focus:** clear and appropriate – **Organization:** sensible and obvious, with a beginning, a middle, and an end; some deviation from the logical progression of ideas; few transitions – **Supporting details:** generally appropriate and effectively expressed – **Conventions:** standard English and varied sentence structures
4 points	– **Focus:** basically clear despite some vaguely related material – **Organization:** occasional deviation from the logical progression of ideas – **Supporting details:** adequate but uneven – **Conventions:** some errors in grammar, usage, and mechanics; little variation in sentence structure
3 points	– **Focus:** appropriate but obscured by unrelated material – **Organization:** some unclear relationships between ideas – **Supporting details:** inadequate to support the topic – **Conventions:** errors in grammar, usage, and mechanics; little variation in sentence structure
2 points	– **Focus:** minimally related to the topic – **Organization:** little evidence of organizational planning – **Supporting details:** few, if any, logical details – **Conventions:** errors in grammar, usage, and mechanics; limited variation in sentence structure
1 point	– **Focus:** only minimally appropriate – **Organization:** little if any, evidence of organization – **Supporting details:** minimal or illogical details – **Conventions:** many errors; limited variation in sentence structure
Unscorable	A response may be considered unscorable for any of the following reasons: it is off topic; it is only a restatement of the prompt; it contains too little writing to be evaluated; it is in a foreign language; it is plagiarized; it is illegible; no response was written.

Understanding Texts and Making Inferences (LA.A.1.4.2)

Sometimes, understanding texts involves comprehending only what is directly stated. Often, however, understanding texts requires making inferences, which means reading between the lines to extend the provided information. Inferences are based on careful study of what is stated in the passage as well as the reader's own common sense and previous knowledge.

1 Examine word parts. The addition of a prefix and/or a suffix can change a word's meaning or its part of speech. (Here, the suffix *–graph* indicates an instrument that makes or transmits records or images.)

2 Rereading sentences before and after unfamiliar words may provide information or context clues needed to guess a word's meaning. (Here context clues suggest *dissipate* means "to grow weaker.")

3 Read the stated facts and ideas.

4 Recognize inferences that are already made. (Words such as "presumably" may indicate inferences already made by the author.)

5 Use your knowledge, logic, and common sense to make inferences. (You can infer from the information provided that, in a region hit by an earthquake, the most damage will often occur in areas closer to the epicenter.)

answers: 1 (B), 2 (H)

Scaling Earthquakes

In 1935, C. F. Richter devised a scale of earthquake *magnitude*. An earthquake is really a form of energy expressed as wave motion passing through the surface layer of the earth. Radiating in all directions from the earthquake focus, seismic[1] waves gradually *dissipate* their energy at **2** increasing distances from the *epicenter* (the point on the earth's surface directly above the focus). On the Richter scale, the amount of energy released during an earthquake is estimated by measurement of the ground motion that occurs. Seismographs record earthquake **1** waves, and by comparison of wave heights, the relative strength of quakes can be determined. Although Richter scale numbers run from 0 to 9, there is no absolute upper limit to earthquake severity. **4** Presumably, nature could outdo the magnitude of the most intense earthquakes recorded so far, which reached 8.5–8.6.

—Arthur and Judith Getis and Jerome D. Fellmann, *Introduction to Geography* (1998)

1 Which of the following is MOST likely to be related to the word *radiating*?

A. radical

B. radius

C. radish

D. eradicate

2 Comparing the amount of property damage caused by different earthquakes might be an unreliable measure of magnitude because

F. it is difficult to determine the exact time of a building's collapse.

G. local officials will exaggerate property damage to secure emergency relief funds.

H. earthquakes strike areas that are hard to compare because they have different amounts and/or types of property.

I. government officials are usually too far from regions with significant earthquake activity.

[1]**seismic**: caused by earth vibrations

Read this passage about Earth's physical geography before answering Questions 1 through 3.

Once Upon a Time

Today, the planet, still restless, consists of seven continents, or land masses, of light granite rock "floating" on a denser basalt layer and sustained largely by a sheet of soil derived from, and covering, the rock. Still, water makes up 70 percent of the total surface of the planet.

Tomorrow? Crete will probably knock into Libya. The Farallon Islands off San Francisco will continue to move up the West Coast of the United States. The Indian Ocean could rise a few inches and drown the 1,200 [Maldive Islands]. The Indo-Australian plate, or slab of rock, which is still colliding with the Eurasian plate, could lift the Himalayas even higher than their present 22,000-plus feet. Africa's Great Rift Valley could sink enough to let seawater pour in, flooding the valley and splitting the already-splintering continent in two. One of the planet's annual million earthquakes and its attendant shudders could send California, which already is breaking up, shuddering toward the Pacific Ocean. The "ring of fire," the zone with most of the world's active volcanoes and earthquakes, could ignite and reshape the entire Pacific basin, threatening Japan. The plates are always moving, always impacting on Earth's places.

—George J. Demko, *Why in the World: Adventures in World Geography* (1992)

❶ *Restless* probably means

    A. tired.

    B. stationary.

    C. continuously moving.

    D. floating.

❷ It is clear from the passage that

    F. Earth will become increasingly uninhabitable.

    G. Earth's plates are still in motion.

    H. Africa's Great Rift Valley will move toward the Pacific Ocean.

    I. geographers differ over the number of Earth's continents.

❸ In the passage, *attendant* means

    A. accompanying as a consequence or result.

    B. destructive.

    C. seismic.

    D. an employee who waits on customers.

Comparing and Contrasting (LA.A.2.2.7)

Writers compare and contrast a variety of things—including places, events, people, and institutions—in order to understand them thoroughly. Comparing involves finding both similarities and differences between two or more things. Contrasting means examining only the differences between them.

1 Note what is being compared. (Here, the author is comparing different landforms.)

2 Compare: Look for clue words indicating that two things are alike. Clue words include *all, both, like, as, likewise* and *similarly*.

3 Contrast: Look for clue words that show how two things differ. Clue words include *unlike, by contrast, however, except, different,* and *on the other hand*.

4 Compare: Look for features that two subjects have in common. (Both buttes and mesas are hills that rise sharply from the surrounding area and have sloping sides and flat tops.)

5 Contrast: Look for ways in which two things are different.

answers: 1 (D), 2 (I)

The Badlands is a reservation in South Dakota marked by intricate erosional sculpturing, scanty vegetation, and fantastically formed hills. **3**

What is a Butte?

First of all, say it like this: *beaut* as in *beautiful*, not like the body part you're sitting on.

This is the geographic word for what Bart Simpson's haircut looks like. Typical of the stark scenery of the Badlands, a butte is a hill that rises sharply from the surrounding area and has sloping sides and a flat top. A characteristic formation of the plateau region of the western United States, these flat-topped hills are formed when hard **1** rock sits on top of weaker rock like a helmet, keeping the weaker **2** rock beneath from being worn down by natural forces of erosion.

4 Sounds just like a mesa? Well, it is Except that the butte (from the **3** French word for a "mound behind targets") is smaller than a *mesa*, which is the Spanish word for "table." Buttes are often produced **5** from mesas that have been reduced in size through erosion. Going back a geological step, mesas are eroded forms of plateaus, which are large highland plains raised above the surrounding land.

—Kenneth C. Davis, *Don't Know Much About Geography* (1992)

Here you learn that buttes and mesas differ in terms of their relative size.

1 According to the passage, what process plays a role in the formation of buttes, mesas, and plateaus?

A. excavation

B. glaciation

C. convergence

D. erosion

2 Mesas and plateaus differ in that

F. plateaus are raised above the surrounding land.

G. mesas have a flat top and sloping sides.

H. plateaus are smaller than mesas.

I. mesas are smaller than plateaus.

Read this passage about the Ohio River before answering Numbers 1 through 3.

Along the Ohio River

   [T]hat [state] which follows the numerous windings of the Ohio [River]upon the left is called Kentucky; that upon the right bears the name of the river. These two states differ only in a single respect: Kentucky has admitted slavery, but the state of Ohio has prohibited the existence of slaves within its borders. Thus the traveler who floats down the current of the Ohio to the spot where that river falls into the Mississippi may be said to sail between liberty and servitude; and a transient[1] inspection of surrounding objects will convince him which of the two is more favorable to humanity.

   Upon the left bank of the stream the population is sparse; from time to time one descries[2] a troop of slaves loitering in the half-desert fields; the primeval forest reappears at every turn; society seems to be asleep, man to be idle, and nature alone offers a scene of activity and life.

   From the right bank, on the contrary, a confused hum is heard, which proclaims afar the presence of industry; the fields are covered with abundant harvests; the elegance of the dwellings announces the taste and activity of the laborers; and man appears to be in the enjoyment of that wealth and contentment which is the reward of labor.

—Alexis de Tocqueville, *Democracy in America*, Volume 1 (1835)

❶ The author of this passage contrasts

  A. slavery and socialism.

  B. the Ohio and Mississippi rivers.

  C. Kentucky and Mississippi.

  D. two states with different labor systems.

❷ The two states described by Tocqueville are comparable because

  F. they share a similar social system.

  G. they differ only in Kentucky's admittance of slavery.

  H. Ohio was admitted to the Union only 11 years after Kentucky.

  I. Kentucky eventually became heavily industrialized.

❸ Why does Tocqueville believe the state of Ohio is more favorable to humanity than the state of Kentucky? Support your answer with details from the passage.

[1]**transient**: brief

[2]**descries**: catches sight of

Determining the Main Idea (LA.A.2.4.1)

The main idea is a statement that sums up the most important point of a paragraph, a passage, an article, or a speech. Identifying the main idea will increase your understanding as you read. Main ideas are supported by details and examples.

1 To find the main idea of a passage, first identify the topic. Then, as you read, define the central idea about the topic that the many details explain or support. The source line can sometimes help identify the topic.

2 Looking at the beginning and ending sentences of each paragraph can also help you identify the topic and main idea. (Here, the first sentence indicates that the author is writing about Florida's natural environment.)

3 Read the entire passage. As you read, ask yourself questions such as "What is the most important point the author wants to convey about the topic?" The answer will help you identify the main idea. (After reading the entire passage, it becomes clear that the passage's focus is the significant impact of climate on the history of Florida.)

4 Look for details about the main idea. What central idea do they explain or support?

answers: 1 (C), 2 (G)

Natural Endowments and First Inhabitants

[T]he natural environment conditioned when it did not determine **2** what man's life in Florida would be. . . .

Perhaps nowhere in North America has climate been such a factor in the lives of people from the first comers to the present inhabitants. Major contemporary sources of livelihood such as tourism, the growing **4** of citrus fruits and winter vegetables, and some aspects of the aviation **3** industry depend upon the climate. And in spite of the marvels of modern technology and science, the warm, wet, and humid summers slow down much activity and create problems of control of insect pests and plant diseases as well as efforts to control climate in home, office, and factory. But climate is only one feature of the natural endowment of land, water, plants, birds, and fishes that help to explain man's life in the peninsular state.

—Charlton W. Tebeau, *A History of Florida* **1**

1 According to the passage, climate has had a positive impact on Florida by

A. facilitating the development of modern technology.

B. reducing the length of the growing season.

C. making the state attractive to tourists.

D. making climate control in office buildings less expensive.

2 Which of the following statements best describes the main idea of the passage?

F. Florida's climate has determined what people's lives in the state would be like.

G. Climate is one among several natural features that has had a powerful influence over Florida's inhabitants.

H. Climatic factors have had a largely negative impact on Floridians.

I. Modern technology has largely eliminated the negative effects of Florida's climate.

Read this passage about Florida before answering Numbers 1 through 4

Rising from the Ruins

Many people remember Florida in the 1930s and the early 1940s as a place where one could look across the lake or river or bay at fish leaping and birds soaring, where the fragrance of orange blossoms filled the air each spring, where woods or prairies were open for roaming or hunting in season. Near Miami or Tampa, Palm Beach or Orlando, one could drive to farms and groves for vegetables and fruit without passing through miles of suburban sprawl. Yet there were also days when Tampa Bay or Biscayne Bay smelled from raw sewage, when the skies over the lower east coast were darkened not by birds but by smoke from fires in the Everglades, when the pulp mills popping up around Jacksonville, Fernandina, Pensacola, and Port St. Joe spewed their stench into the air, their waste into the water, when there was no money and no work and the whole state appeared doomed beyond the worst nightmares of anyone.

Ravaged though Florida was in the eyes of those familiar with its more lush times, it was an exotic, new country to half of its residents, and compared with the present, the state fifty years ago was a remarkably scenic and rich blend of rural, urban, and wild areas, where a person could easily find companionship or escape.

—Mark Derr, *Some Kind of Paradise: A Chronicle of Man and the Land in Florida* (1989)

❶ It is clear from the passage that the author does not like

   A. the fragrance of orange blossoms.

   B. suburban sprawl.

   C. the people who moved to Florida after the 1930s and 1940s.

   D. Florida's urban areas.

❷ How does the author qualify his point that Florida was remarkably scenic and rich in the 1930s and 1940s compared to the present? Support your answer with details from the passage.

❸ According to the passage, in the 1930s and 1940s, the Tampa region

   F. was a wilderness area unspoiled by man.

   G. became the state's undisputed capital.

   H. was, unlike the rest of the state, a polluted industrial region.

   I. had both positive and negative features.

❹ Which statement best reflects the main idea of the passage?

   A. In many ways, Florida is far less attractive today than in was in the past.

   B. People who romanticize Florida are misguided.

   C. Florida's original inhabitants initiated the process that led to the ruination of the state.

   D. It is unlikely that the Everglades will survive much longer.

Identifying the Author's Purpose and Point of View (LA.A.2.4.2)

When an author writes, he or she has a purpose in mind. Authors often write to explain, to persuade, or to entertain. Understanding an author's purpose will help you to interpret what he or she has to say. In addition to a purpose, an author usually has a personal perspective. This perspective is called a point of view. Knowing an author's point of view is useful because it can influence the way he or she handles the facts in a piece of writing.

① Look at the source line to learn about the passage.

② Before reading the passage review the questions to identify information that you need to find.

③ Skim the passage to form an idea of what it is about. (It is only toward the end of the passage that you learn that automobiles are the primary source of Mexico City's air pollution.)

④ Use active reading strategies. As you read, ask yourself: "Why did the author write this?" (purpose) and "What is the author's personal perspective?" (point of view)

⑤ Use word structure and context clues to understand unfamiliar words. (The prefix *mega-* means "greatly surpassing others of its kind," suggesting that Mexico City is exceptionally large)

answers: 1 (C), 2 (G)

S12

Stories of Hope

Computer-generated models help visualize [Mexico City's] fundamental problem. Mexico City is located in a valley a mile and half above sea level. Surrounded by a wall of mountains, some as high as 12,000 feet, it's locked into what scientists call a closed eco-system. Unlike most other **⑤** mega-cities there is little wind to cleanse the air and no ocean or major river to exchange water and sewage.

The city's atmosphere is thick with smog; a toxic soup cooking airborne chemicals into ozone. Eight out of ten days are declared hazardous to human health. Just breathing is said to be the equivalent of smoking two packs of cigarettes a day. Adding to the problem are 35,000 factories **④** spewing tons of pollutants into the air.

But it's primarily the emissions from over three million cars that leave **③** the city gasping for breath. Mexico City is trapped between the limitations of its geography and a way of life shaped by the internal combustion engine. . . .

The lesson of Mexico City is simple. Despite all its history, all its efforts, the devastating consequences of uncontrolled growth serve as an environmental warning to the rest of the world.

—From *Journey to Planet Earth* "Mexico City, Mexico" **①**

① Which statement best expresses the author's purpose in writing this passage?

A. to explain how geographers use computer models

B. to list the main sources of air pollutants in Mexico City

C. to describe how Mexico City's geography concentrates pollutants, causing serious environmental problems

D. to compare sensible policies that limit population growth to the laissez-faire policies of Mexico

② **②** Based on this passage, which of the following BEST describes the author's point of view?

F. The author feels that Mexico City is a clean city.

G. The author believes it is important for governments to adopt policies that will protect the environment.

H. The author thinks that the automobile industry has helped Mexico City to grow and prosper.

I. The author is skeptical of the claim that automobiles could emit more pollutants than 35,000 factories.

① Mexico City is t capital of Mexic is home to over million citizens growing by 350,000 each y

These words signal that you have to make inferences from information in the passage.

Read this passage about Brasília, Brazil's capital since 1960, before answering Numbers 1 through 4.

Brasília

Brasília must have looked good on paper, and it still does in photos. In 1987 it was added to the UNESCO list of World Heritage Sites, being considered one of the major examples of this century's modern movement in architecture and urban planning.

But the world's great planned city of the 20th century is built for automobiles and air-conditioners, not people. Distances are enormous and no one walks. The sun blazes, but there are few trees for shelter.

Bureaucrats and politicians, who live in the model 'pilot plan' part of the city, were lured to Brasília by 100% salary hikes and big apartments in the 1960s. Even today, as soon as the weekend comes, they get out of the city—to [Rio de Janeiro], to São Paulo, to their private clubs in the country—anywhere that's less sterile.

—Nick Selby *et al.*, *Brazil* (Lonely Planet, 1998)

1 The authors' purpose in writing this passage was to

   A. caution tourists not to visit Brazil.

   B. describe the capital of Brazil.

   C. demonstrate a failure of urban planning.

   D. explain why Brasília is a good place to work, but not to live.

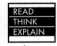

2 If the authors were to plan a city, what might be some of their goals? Support your answer with details from the passage.

3 Which of the following sentences BEST describes the authors' point of view?

   F. Brasília's nomination as a World Heritage Site was well-deserved.

   G. In spite of Brasília's shortcomings, building a capital there was a good idea.

   H. Brasília is a poorly designed city.

   I. São Paulo is equally unsuitable as a capital city.

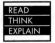

4 What evidence exists for accepting or rejecting the authors' opinion of Brasília? Support your answer with details from the passage. For a complete response, consider these points:

   • the authors' point of view

   • the opinions of Brazilians

   • the viewpoint of experts

Identifying Devices of Persuasion and Methods of Appeal (LA.A.2.4.5)

Persuasive devices and methods of appeal, such as propaganda techniques, are ways in which authors attempt to win readers to their point of view. Becoming knowledgeable about these techniques will help you recognize propaganda and differentiate between strong and weak arguments in a wide range of texts.

❶ Facts: Look for specific names, dates, statistics, and statements that can be proved. (The facts provided in the passage do little to reinforce the authors' argument about the Berlin Wall.)

❷ Opinion: Look for assertions, claims, hypotheses, and judgments.

❸ Opinion: Look for judgment words that the writer uses to describe people and events.

❹ Note any special punctuation. Ellipses, for example, indicate that words or sentences have been removed from the original.

❺ Identify the source. Does the author belong to a special interest group, social class, political party, or movement that might promote a one-sided or slanted viewpoint on the subject? (This passage originated in East Germany, which was attempting to justify the construction of the Berlin Wall.)

answers: 1 (C), 2 (I)

What You Should Know About the Wall

Berlin lies in the middle of the German Democratic Republic [East Germany], exactly 180 kilometers (112.5 miles) to the east of its western **❶** frontier. A quite normal locality for the capital of a state. Only one thing is not normal at all: that a hostile, undermining policy and disruptive acts **❸** have for years been carried on from the western part of this city against the surrounding state territory. West Berlin Mayor Willi Brandt called West Berlin a "thorn in the side of the GDR." Would you like to have a thorn in your side? . . . **❹**

We no longer wanted to stand by passively and see how doctors, engineers, and skilled workers were induced by refined methods **❸** unworthy of the dignity of man to give up their secure existence in the GDR and work in West Germany or West Berlin. These and other manipulations cost the GDR annual losses amounting to 3.5 thousand million marks. . . .

> The author doe not specify exactly what methods were used by West Germany to attract workers from the GDR.

—Excerpts from an East German brochure defending the Berlin Wall (1962) **❺**

❶ According to the passage, professionals were leaving East Germany because

A. they would enjoy more freedoms in West Germany, which was administered in part by the United States.

B. communists had taken control of the East German government.

C. West Germany was using undignified methods to attract East German workers.

D. they had few job opportunities in postwar East Germany.

❷ According to the author, the mayor of West Berlin

F. was cooperating with the Americans to rebuild the capital.

G. opposed the GDR's alliance with communist Russia.

H. refused to allow East Berliners into West Germany.

I. had called West Berlin a thorn in the side of East Germany.

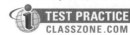
STRATEGIES FOR TAKING THE FCAT

Read the passage about political boundaries before answering Numbers 1 through 4.

Boundaries on the Map

[I]f you took a National Geographic world map and traced with a magic marker all political boundaries that correspond with physical features, you'd still be left with thousands of miles of boundaries *not* natural in origin. What caused the wiggles in those borders? In fact, we can witness the process in progress during the present decade, in the former Yugoslavia . . . and in many other places. Our world is a mosaic of ethnic and cultural groups, and human history is the story of struggles for territory. Those bends and turns in [European] boundaries . . . result from repeated, if not endless, clashes over turf. Even the smallest nations have battled over the tiniest fragments of land, resulting in boundaries that seem, in places, (may I use a subjective word?) ridiculous. A large-scale map of the border area between Belgium and the Netherlands reveals tiny, village-size pockets of one country encircled by the other. It all harks back to the days when religion and language and other cultural traditions provoked border conflicts that surged back and forth across what was then an unstable frontier.

—Harm de Blij, *Harm de Blij's Geography Book* (1995)

1 Which of the following details could you use to begin verifying or disproving the author's claims?

    A. the names of the three countries mentioned in the passage

    B. the name of the magazine, *National Geographic*

    C. the religious war between Yugoslavia and the Netherlands

    D. the turf clash of Serbians and Muslims in Belgium

2 The author suggests that

    F. political boundaries are only secondarily the result of natural features.

    G. Yugoslavia's boundaries were drawn after the first World War.

    H. human history is the story of struggles over territory.

    I. ethnicity has caused unnecessary political problems.

 3 What does the author's use of the word *ridiculous* suggest about his view of the topic? Support your answer with details from the passage.

 4 How might the meaning of this passage have been altered? Support your answer with details from the passage. For a complete response, consider these points:

• special punctuation

• missing information

S15

Locating, Gathering, Analyzing, and Evaluating Information

(LA.A.2.4.4)

Finding any amount of information, no matter how small, involves research. Research mean locating, gathering, analyzing, and evaluating information. Such skills will enable you to perform research projects, but they will also be useful for other purposes, including real-world tasks and self-improvement.

1 Determine the subject of your research, then identify the location of sources that you can use to gather information. (In this case, read the title to determine the subject and purpose of the map.)

2 Familiarize yourself with the major elements of your source. Different sources—Web sites, maps, tables, charts, or other type of graphics—will have different features. (Examine the labels and legend on the map to find more detailed information on the map's subject.)

3 Analyze the information. Ask yourself questions such as "How is the information organized?" (Study the legend, the symbols, and the colors on the map. Try to identify patterns.)

4 You will usually need to cite books, magazines, newspapers, electronic media, and other sources. Take care to record your sources of information.

answers: 1 (C), 2 (F)

Ethnic Diversity in the Former Yugoslavia

The map and legend show you nine distinct ethnic groups that reside in the former Yugoslavia, which is now eight republics or provinces.

1 According to the map, which of the following ethnic groups live in Serbia and Vojvodina?

   A. Macedonians, Slovenes, and Croats

   B. Bulgarians, Albanians, Italians, Romanians and Montenegrins

   C. Serbs, Muslims, Bulgarians, Hungarians, and Albanians

   D. Serbs, Macedonians, Croats, and Hungarians

2 Slovenia is a(n)

   F. republic.

   G. country.

   H. autonomous province.

   I. nation-state.

Examine the graph below before answering Numbers 1 and 2.

The graph below is from the International Data Base (IDB) of the U.S. Census Bureau. The IDB is a computerized data bank containing statistical tables of demographic and socio-economic data for over 200 countries and areas of the world. It is available on the World Wide Web at the U.S. Census Bureau's Web site. A "population pyramid" is a type of graph that shows the distribution of population by age and sex.

Population Pyramids for Georgia

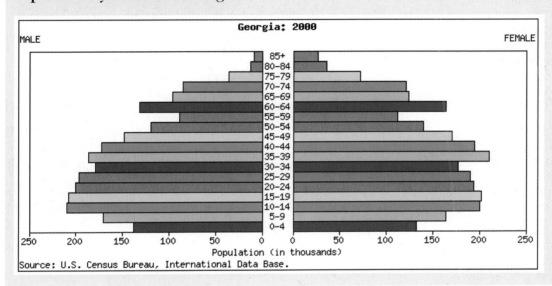

1 The different colors in the population pyramid

   A. represent gender.

   B. indicate specific age groups.

   C. are meant to make the chart easier to read.

   D. represent the relative size of each age group.

2 The information in the bar graph

   F. is not reliable.

   G. shows change over time.

   H. is for the year 2000.

   I. was gathered by members of U.S. Senate.

Using Appropriate Study and Research Skills (LA.A.2.4.6)

Using appropriate study and research skills means adapting techniques that are suitable for the type of information being gathered or organized.

① There are many sources from which you can gather and organize information including almanacs, government publications, microfiche, news sources, and information services. It is important to select an appropriate source.

② Evaluate the reliability of your sources. (In the second paragraph, Palin presents several facts, whose authenticity you could corroborate in an almanac or encyclopedia.)

③ In evaluating your source, also consider the context in which it was written or produced. (This sentence makes it clear that Palin is speaking from first-hand experience of the Sahara.)

④ Use comparisons, information from other sources, and your own knowledge to interpret your sources. (You might enrich your understanding of the Sahara by carrying out further research on the recent growth of the desert.)

⑤ Use standard formats when making citations of books, magazines, newspapers, and other sources.

answers: 1 (C), 2 (I)

Sahara

The Sahara is a potent, evocative reality. It is one of the world's great brands. No one name so completely epitomizes an environment. Oceans can be Atlantic or Pacific or Indian, mountains can be Himalayas or Andes or Alps, but if you want to convey desert, you only have to say Sahara.

It embodies scale and mystery, the thin line between survival and destruction, the power to take life or to transform it. A self-contained, homogenous, identifiable world, uncompromising and irreducible.

In other words, a challenge. And by no means an easy one.

As big as the United States, with a population the size of Norfolk[1], the Sahara is only 15 per cent sand, and though the great ergs, the sand seas, are among the most exquisitely beautiful landscapes I've ever seen, there is a dark side. The Sahara is also a killer, scorching the life out of crops, people, and all but the most tenacious living creatures. It's growing larger every year as drought turns pastures back into sand, which the remorseless desert wind carries into towns and villages until they die of suffocation.

—Michael Palin, *Sahara* (2002) **⑤**

① In the passage, Michael Palin suggests that

   A. the Sahara, though world-renowned, is not as impressive as Mount Everest in the Himalayas.

   B. the Sahara has a population density comparable to Norfolk, England.

   C. the Sahara has a very small population, considering the amount of territory it covers.

   D. 90 percent of the desert is something other than sand.

② Michael Palin's passage would be MOST useful to

   F. someone researching population density in the United States.

   G. scholars comparing the size of different landforms.

   H. the people of Norfolk, England.

   I. students seeking both factual details and subjective impressions of the Sahara.

[1]**Norfolk**: an English county; population 800,000

S18

Read this passage, written in November 1849 by the French novelist Gustave Flaubert, before answering Numbers 1 through 3.

From Alexandria to Cairo

Leave on a boat towed by a small steamer carrying only its engine. Flat, dead banks of the Mahmudiyeh; on the shore a few naked Arabs running, from time to time, a traveler trots by on horseback, swathed in white in his Turkish saddle. Passengers: . . . an English family, hideous; the mother looks like a sick old parrot . . . At 'Atfeh you enter the Nile and take a larger boat.

First night on the Nile. State of contentment and of lyricism: I gesticulate, recite lines from Bouilhet[1], cannot bring myself to go to bed; I think of Cleopatra. The water is yellow and very smooth; a few stars. Well wrapped in my [coat], I fall asleep on my camp-bed, on deck. Such rapture! . . .

On one side, the desert; on the other, a green meadow. With its sycamores it resembles from a distance a Norman plain with its apple-trees. The desert is a reddish-gray. Two of the Pyramids come into view, then a smaller one. To our left, Cairo appears, huddled on a hill; the dome of the mosque of Mohammed Ali; behind it, the bare Mokattam hills.

—Gustave Flaubert, *Flaubert in Egypt: A Sensibility on Tour* (1972)

1 Flaubert's account would be of MOST interest to someone

    A. researching the annual flooding of the Nile.

    B. seeking a literary impression of Egypt.

    C. looking for details about the Great Pyramids.

    D. interested in 19th-century English literature.

2 This passage can BEST be described as a(n)

    F. scientific report.

    G. objective account of 19th-century Cairo.

    H. first-hand account of a trip on the Nile River.

    I. critique of the Egyptian landscape.

3 In the passage, Flaubert

    A. seems depressed by his surroundings.

    B. is traveling by train.

    C. describes parts of the landscape between Cairo and Alexandria.

    D. is critical of Muslims.

[1]**Bouilhet**: a French poet and dramatist

Analyzing the Validity and Accuracy of Primary Sources (LA.A.2.4.7)

Analyzing the validity and accuracy of primary sources means making sure that a primary source is accurate and dependable.

1 Look at the source line to learn about the document and its author. Consider the reliability of the information in the document.

2 Skim the document to get an idea of what it is about.

3 Use active reading strategies. As you read, ask yourself questions, review sequence, and make predictions. (Based on your knowledge of Twain's writing style and your knowledge of geography, it might be safe to assume that the author has written an exaggerated description of Palestine.)

4 As you read, look for the main idea. This is the writer's most important point. Remember that supporting details or arguments will back up this idea.

5 Use context clues to help you understand unfamiliar words. (Here it is clear that "Shechem, Esdraelon, Ajalon" must be places in Palestine.)

6 Before re-reading the document, skim the questions. Previewing the questions will help focus your reading.

answers: 1 (B), 2 (I)

Present Palestine

Of all the lands there are for dismal scenery, I think Palestine must be the prince. **4** The hills are barren, they are dull of color, they are unpicturesque in shape. The valleys are unsightly deserts fringed with a feeble vegetation that has an expression about it of being sorrowful and despondent. The Dead Sea and the Sea of Galilee sleep in the midst of a vast stretch of hill and plain wherein the eye rests upon no pleasant tint, no striking object, no soft picture dreaming in a purple haze or mottled with the shadows of the clouds. **5** Every outline is harsh, every feature is distinct, there is no perspective—distance works no enchantment here. It is a hopeless, dreary, heart-broken land. **3**

Small shreds and patches of it must be very beautiful in the full flush of spring, however, and all the more beautiful by contrast with the far-reaching desolation that surrounds them on every side. I would like much to see the fringes of the Jordan in spring-time, and Shechem, Esdraelon, Ajalon and the borders of Galilee—but even then these spots would seem mere toy gardens set at wide intervals in the waste of a limitless desolation.

—Mark Twain, *The Innocents Abroad* (1996) **1**

The passage excerpted from a book, first published in 1869, that features a se of Twain's humorous tra letters.

1 Why might Mark Twain's description of Palestine be of questionable reliability?

A. because Palestine no longer exists

B. because Twain used humor and exaggeration to add interest to his writing

C. because Twain never visited Israel

D. because he didn't get to see Palestine during the springtime

2 It is MOST likely that Twain wrote this passage to

F. accurately describe Palestine for people who might want to travel there.

G. criticize and ridicule the people who lived in Palestine.

H. provide a precise description for geographers who wanted to study the region.

I. describe his travels and entertain his readers.

Read this passage, written by an English traveler in Iran in 1926, before answering Numbers 1 through 3.

Round Teheran

It would seem. . .that Persia [Iran] is a country made for wandering onward; there is so much room, and no boundaries anywhere, and time is marked only by the sun. Nor is it only in the open country that one wanders, but in the bazaars too. . . .

[The bazaars] ramble literally for miles. They are lined with little shops, less shops than stalls. It is impossible to say that one shop is larger than another, though it is possible to say that some are smaller than others. These, the smaller ones, are no bigger than cupboards, mere recesses in the wall. . . . Then there are bazaars devoted to one industry: the leather-workers' street, which is very quiet, industrious, and rich in tone; the coppersmiths' street, filled with the sound as of an army beating on gongs, and resplendent with huge copper trays hanging like shields on the wall, and shelves of silver ewers[1] of the lovely traditional shape seen in sixteenth century miniatures. . . .

Darkness is the keynote of this vaulted warren, darkness cleft with sudden beams. The round holes in the roof correspond to the round stains of sunlight on the floor. And it is a darkness not only of fact, but also of impression; a sense of obscure and pullulating[2] life, hurrying about unknown business.

—Vita Sackville-West, *Passenger to Teheran* (1990)

❶ Which of the following BEST describes the author's attitude toward Persia's bazaars?

    A. Persia's bazaars are too small for someone accustomed to shopping in England.

    B. The uniformity of the bazaars can be overwhelming.

    C. The bazaars are a telling and fascinating feature of Persia.

    D. Persia's bazaars are wonderful for the cheapness of their wares.

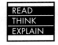

❷ Having read the author's account, do you think you have an accurate sense of what bazaars were actually like? Support your answer with details from the passage.

❸ Which statement BEST describes the degree to which the passage is reliable?

    F. The passage is not credible because it is secondhand.

    G. The author is merely recounting rumors and cannot be believed.

    H. The passage contains what appear to be the author's genuine impressions.

    I. The author is clearly biased against Iranians and is not trustworthy.

[1]**ewers**: decorative pitchers
[2]**pullulating**: swarming

Synthesizing Information to Draw Conclusions (LA.A.2.4.8)

Synthesizing is a skill that writers use to develop interpretations. Like detective work, synthesizing involves putting together clues, information, and ideas to form an overall picture. Drawing conclusions means analyzing what you have read and forming an opinion about its meaning. To draw conclusions, look closely at the facts, combine them with your own inferences, and then use common sense and experience to decide what the facts mean.

1 Read carefully to gain a clear understanding of the information presented.

2 Consider what you already know that could apply. (Your knowledge of history may tell you that Pakistan is a Muslim state that split from India in 1947.)

3 Ask questions of the material. (For example, "Why is there a dispute over Kashmir?")

4 Bring together, or synthesize, the information you have about a subject.

5 Draw conclusions after synthesizing the information from both passages. (The two passages suggest that radical nationalism among Indian Hindus could hurt India and Pakistan's efforts to resolve the dispute over Kashmir.)

answers: 1 (C), 2 (G)

India and Pakistan: A Break in the Clouds

The guns fell silent on the long border between India and Pakistan at **2** midnight on November 25th–26th, when the two nuclear powers marked the annual Muslim festival of Eid by beginning their first formal **1** ceasefire for at least 20 years. Proposed . . . by Pakistan's prime minister, **5** to apply to the line of control that divides the disputed territory of **3** Kashmir the ceasefire was extended at India's suggestion to cover the full border, including the remote Siachen Glacier in the Karakoram mountains, which has been a freezing battleground since 1984.

—*Economist* (November, 2003)

Headlines Over the Horizon: The Hindu-Muslim Divide

[India's] radical nationalists view [India's] secular political system as a threat to Hindu identity, largely because of the power it offers India's 140 million Muslims. Weakening, or even abolishing, the secular state **5** has therefore become part of the radical-nationalist agenda. This may force Indian Muslims—traditionally moderate and supportive of the secular state . . . —to shift their allegiance from the state to some sort of larger international Islamic movement. . . .

—*Atlantic Monthly* (July/August 2003)

1 The first pa discusses a recently dec ceasefire in Kashmir. Th second pass focuses on nationalism India.

4 India's inter conflicts, be Hindus and Muslims, co affect relatio its neighbor Muslim stat Pakistan.

1 What effect might radical nationalism have in India?

   A. It might result in greater religious harmony.

   B. It would lead most Indian Muslims to adopt Hinduism.

   C. It might cause Indian Muslims to support Muslim Pakistan's position on Kashmir.

   D. It would help improve India's human-rights record.

2 The dispute over Kashmir is of concern to the international community primarily because

   F. Kashmir possesses a wealth of natural resources.

   G. both India and Pakistan are nuclear powers.

   H. Kashmir has many potential markets.

   I. India cannot defend itself.

Read the passages about Bhutan before answering Numbers 1 through 3.

Bhutan: Druk-Yul

Sandwiched between the Assam Plain of India and the crest of the Himalayan range in Tibet, Bhutan long avoided contact with foreigners. Only in the 1960s did King Jigme Dorji Wangchuk permit a road to be constructed from the Indian frontier. His son, King Jigme Singye Wangchuk, continued his policies, trying to modernize the economy while protecting its special, Buddhist-dominated culture from the West.

—Peter Menzel, *Material World: A Global Family Portrait* (1994)

Country Profile: Bhutan

[Bhutan's king] has gone to great lengths to preserve the indigenous Buddhist culture of the majority Drukpa, who have a common culture with the Tibetans and other Himalayan peoples. . . .

But by the 1990s, attempts to stress the majority Buddhist culture and the lack of any political representation had led to deep resentment among the ethnic Nepali community in the south.

Violence erupted and tens of thousands of Nepali speakers fled to refugee camps in Nepal. [Their plight remains unresolved today and has led to criticism of Bhutan's government by human rights groups.]

—BBC News (December 2003)

1 According to both authors,

    A. Bhutan's leaders have tried, since the 1960s, to bring democracy to Bhutan.

    B. the Drukpa are Buddhists.

    C. Bhutan lies south of India and the Himalayan range in Tibet.

    D. the Drukpa have fled to Nepalese refugee camps.

2 Which of the following statements BEST describes a view held by both authors?

    F. Bhutan's policies have caused problems for Nepali speakers.

    G. Bhutan's leaders have sought to protect the indigenous Buddhist culture.

    H. Lack of political representation is the chief cause of ethnic violence in the south.

    I. Human rights groups have helped address Bhutan's problems.

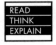

READ
THINK
EXPLAIN

3 Based on the two passages, how might Bhutan's policies have had both positive and negative effects on the country? Support your answer with details from both passages.

Recognizing Cause and Effect
(LA.E.2.2.1)

Causes are the events, conditions, and other reasons that lead to an event. Because causes exist before the event in time, they help to explain why it occured. Effects are the results or consequences of an event. One effect often becomes the cause of other effects, resulting in a chain of events. Causes and effects can be both short-term and long-term. Examining cause-and-effect relationships will help students see how events are related and why they took place.

1 Causes: Look for clue words that show cause. These include *because, due to, since,* and *therefore.*

2 Effects: Look for results or consequences. Sometimes these are indicated by clue words such as *brought about, led to, as a result,* and *consequently.*

3 Sometimes causes and effects are not signaled by clue words. Look for implied causes and effects.

4 Notice that an effect may be the cause of another event. This begins a chain of causes and effects.

5 Look for multiple causes and multiple effects. (Here three features of the environmental report caused Ecologist Hou Xueyu to refuse to sign it.)

The Three Gorges Dam Project

Sun Yatsen first proposed building a dam on the Yangtze River in 1919 for power generation purposes, but the idea was shelved due to unfavorable political and economic conditions. Major floods resurrected the idea and the government adopted it in 1954 for flood control. **1**

Vice minister of Electric Power Li Rui initially argued that the dam should be multipurpose, that smaller dams should be built first until China could afford such a costly project and that construction should proceed in stages to allow time to solve technical problems. . . .

Later, Li Rui concluded that the dam should not be built at all since it would be too costly. He added that the dam would also flood many cities and fertile farmland, subject the middle and lower reaches of the river to catastrophic flooding during construction and would not contribute much to shipping. Sichuan province officials also objected to the construction since Sichuan, located upstream, would shoulder most of the costs while downstream Hubei province would receive most of the benefits.

Lin Yishan, head of the Yangtze Valley Planning Office, which was in charge of the project, favored the dam construction, however. His optimism about resolving technical problems was further encouraged in 1958 by the favorable political climate and the support from the late chairman Mao Zedong, who wanted China to have the largest hydroelectric dam in the world. . . . Criticisms were suppressed. But depression resulted from the disastrous Great Leap Forward (a political campaign boasting China's economic development) and ended the preparation work in 1960. **2**

The idea resurfaced in 1963 as part of the new policies to build a "third front" of industry in southwest China. But the Cultural Revolution erupted in 1966, and in 1969 the fear that the dam would be sabotaged by the Soviet Union, now an enemy, resulted in a construction delay. . . .

The economic reforms introduced in 1978 underlined the need for more electric power to supply a growing industrial base, so the State Council approved the construction in 1979. A feasibility study was conducted in 1982 to 1983 to appease the increasing number of critics, who complained that the project did not adequately address technical, social, nor environmental issues. . . .

[L]eaders from Chongqing also demanded suddenly that the dam height be raised so substantially that it would cripple the project and free them from bearing the brunt of the costs. The new height and the demand for a more reliable study with the use of international standards resulted in a new feasibility study in 1986. But a few scientists dared to sign off on a project that had already been approved.

4 The economic ref introduced in 19 caused industrial growth, which ca a demand for mc electricity, which caused the State Council to appro construction in 1

Ecologist Hou Xueyu was among the few who refused to sign the environmental report because it falsely hyped the environmental benefits provided by the dam, failed to convey the real extent of environmental impact and lacked adequate solutions to environmental concerns.

Environmentalists at home and abroad began to protest more vociferously. Human rights advocates criticized the resettlement plan. Archeologists balked at the submergence of a huge number of historical sites. Many mourned the loss of some of the world's finest scenery.

Increasing numbers of engineers doubted whether the dam would actually achieve its stated purposes. Chinese journalist/engineer Dai Qing published a book of relentless critiques of the project by Chinese scientists. Yet many foreign construction companies continued to press their governments to financially support the construction in hopes of winning contracts.

3 Here it is clear that the promise of extremely profitable contracts caused foreign construction companies to put pressure on their governments to support the dam.

In the face of a lot of domestic and international pressure, the State Council agreed in March 1989 to suspend the construction plans for five years. After the Tiananmen Square massacre in June 1989, however, the government forbade public debate of the dam, accused foreign critics of ignorance or intent to undermine the regime, and imprisoned Dai Qing and other famous critics.

Former Premier Li Peng crusaded for the dam and pushed it through the National People's Congress in April 1992 despite the opposition or abstention from one-third of the delegates. Such actions were unprecedented from a body that usually rubberstamped all government proposals.

—*China Online* (October 2000)

1 According to the passage, what was the cause of the 1969 construction delay?

  A. domestic and international pressure

  B. discouraging ecological reports

  C. the skepticism of an increasing number of engineers

  D. fear that the dam would be sabotaged by the Soviet Union

2 According to the passage, what effect did the Tiananmen Square massacre have on the project?

  F. It led to the suspension of construction plans for five years.

  G. It led to demands that the dam height be raised substantially.

  H. It led the government to forbid public debate of the dam.

  I. It led environmentalists at home and abroad to begin protesting more vociferously.

answers: 1 (D), 2 (H)

Read this passage about Mongolia before answering Numbers 1 and 2.

On the Edge of the Gobi

All over the Communist world the collapse of the old regimes brought inevitable hardships. In Mongolia the transition to a market economy was exacerbated by the withdrawal of Russian subsidies. The Soviet Union's strategic interests in Mongolia had led to a level of financial subsidy that had allowed the country to live far beyond its means. For a poorly developed nomadic society with a subsistence economy and little hard currency, Mongolia enjoyed remarkable social services with education, health and pension systems that few Third World countries could aspire to. The Russian support that artificially maintained these systems amounted to as much as $800 million US dollars a year, about $400 for each Mongolian, a figure higher than the per capita GDP. By 1990, when the Russians went home, Mongolia's cumulative debt to the USSR was said to be six billion US dollars.

Within months of the end of the Russian subsidies Mongolia was broke. Inflation, devaluation, shortages, rationing all followed quickly on one another. Most state industries, centred around Ulan Batur, were crippled, and in the countryside everything from local power stations to medical clinics closed down. Their employees, most of them first and second generation townsfolk, returned to their family pastures. Mongolia became one of the only places in the world where the drift to cities, common in underdeveloped countries, was reversed. In their hour of need urban Mongolians were rescued by the self-sufficiency of the nomadic life to which the rest of their countrymen had clung tenaciously for millennia. The lesson was not lost on traditionalists. . . .

'I'm not a Marxist,' [Bold, the author's companion] said, 'I didn't support the Communist Party. In fact our KGB had a file on me. I was part of the pro-democracy movement. But now I am not so confident about the free market. Perhaps it is not suited to a country like Mongolia. How can a herdsman, a thousand miles from a market, be a part of a market economy in a country without roads or trains?'

'Sometimes I feel guilty,' he went on. 'When the Communists were in power, we thought only of the corruption . . . because we wanted choices. We wanted to vote, to read the truth in the newspapers, to travel abroad, to buy Western goods. But these were our concerns, the concerns of people with salaries in Ulan Batur. To the herdsman in the countryside what did they matter?'

He gestured to the empty window. 'Here in Dariv the medical centre is closed. There used to be doctors here who went out to the countryside, to the most remote *gers*[1] if they were needed. Now that is gone. There was a school here that was free for everyone. Now the herdsmen have to pay to send their children to school, and many of them cannot afford it.' He twisted his face into an expression of distaste. 'So now they get to vote every five years. Now they have a mayor of their choosing. So what? It doesn't bring the doctors back.'

'Change was inevitable,' I said.

'Of course,' he said. He turned his hands upward in some admission of reality. 'It is easy to forget how insane the old system had become. It was rotten. No one told the truth any more, about anything. We were living in a fantasy of lies. But the changes . . .' he drew a hand across his forehead. 'Everything happened too quickly. Everything seemed to collapse overnight and now we have to begin again. Everything that had become . . .' he searched for a word '. . . civilized—education, health—was lost and people here have gone back to an earlier time, fending only for themselves.' . . .

From the window came the sound of the wind keening[2] around the corners of the abandoned town. 'In this new world of the market there is no room for such idealism,' Bold said. 'Now we have economics. If we have doctors it is only because we can pay for them. Not because they are right or necessary. This is what is difficult to accept.' He looked across at me. His face was a troubled mask. 'The end of idealism. It feels like a kind of barbarism.'

—Stanley Stewart, *In the Empire of Genghis Khan: A Journey Among Nomads* (2002)

❶ According to the passage, what impact did Soviet subsidies have on Mongolia?

A. They forced Mongolians to return to their nomadic lifestyle.

B. They forced medical clinics to close down.

C. They allowed the country to live far beyond its means.

D. They enabled Mongolians to have faith in Marxism.

❷ According to Bold, doctors now take care of Mongolians

F. because medicine is subsidized.

G. because Mongolia has a free market.

H. because it is right and necessary.

I. when Mongolians can pay them.

[1]**gers**: Central Asians nomads' dwellings
[2]**keening**: wailing

Understanding Plot Development

(LA.E.2.4.1)

> Plot is the sequence of events in a narrative, which often has a beginning, a middle, and an end.

Many works of nonfiction tell a story. Therefore, developing an understanding of plot elements—such as setting, major events, problems, conflicts, and resolutions—will help you to cope with difficult reading selections.

1 Identify the narrative's setting—its time and place.

2 Note how writers use literary techniques to make nonfiction writing more interesting. (In the first paragraph, biologist Hamner uses expressive language to describe a jellyfish.)

3 Look for plot elements, such as sequence of events and conflict and resolution. (The author engages readers by vividly describing his own sensations after being stung by the venomous box jellyfish.)

4 Use active reading strategies. As you read, ask yourself, "What is the problem being dealt with?"; "How are individuals and groups interacting?"

5 Look for the narrative's theme—the primary message or insight about life that is revealed in the narrative. (Here the author attempts to evoke both the stunning beauty and terrible danger presented by the box jellyfish.)

answers: 1 (B), 2 (H)

Australia's Box Jellyfish: A Killer Down Under

2 Shimmering in the glow of flood lamps along the pier, two large ghostly shapes undulated just beneath the surface of the dark sea. Webs of long, almost invisibly thin tentacles swept out behind their box-shaped translucent bodies. We had spotted our quarry: *Chironex fleckeri*, the infamous box jellyfish found in the near-shore waters of Australia and southeastern Asia.

5 Difficult to see, these cubic phantoms have long cast a dreadful shadow over the sundrenched beauty of the north Australian coast. Known also as marine stingers or sea wasps, box jellies have killed at least 65 people in the past century.

"*Chironex fleckeri* is without question the most venomous animal on earth," says physician Peter Fenner, marine stinger officer for the Surf Life Saving association of Queensland. "No other animal's venom can kill a human in four minutes or less." Australia's most dangerous snake, the taipan, has enough venom to kill 30 adults, but its bite is not very painful, and it can take several hours for an untreated victim to die. A large box jellyfish, however, has enough venom to kill 60 adults, and the pain of its sting is instant and unbearable. Breathing may quickly become distressed as venom is absorbed into the circulatory and lymphatic systems; in some cases, the heart's pumping slows or stops almost immediately.

I knew *Chironex* were dangerous back in 1977 when my wife and research assistant, Peggy, and I were working as marine biologists at the newly founded Australian Institute of Marine Science in Townsville. Intrigued by box jellies, we collected several juveniles with nets and placed them in an aquarium. We put small live shrimp into the tank for them to eat, but they ignored the prey.

We then tried feeding them by hand—using rubber gloves, of course. Only one, whom we named Charlie, would eat the prawns we placed in its mouth. The other jellies died, while Charlie doubled in size within a month. Charlie died two months later when the aquarium sprang a leak, but the scientific literature indicated that we had accomplished something unique: No one had ever kept a *Chironex* alive in the lab before.

4 At times, animals, and even things, can take on the role of a "character." Here the box jellyfish is given such a role.

Peggy and I decided to try capturing full-grown *Chironex*. We knew that big jellyfish gathered at night beneath the institute's pier to feed on plankton and small fish attracted to the lights. We also knew that catching them would be tricky. The monsters we were after might have a bell, or body, as big as a basketball, only square, and 60 tentacles, each 15 feet long.

With colleague Martin Jones we loaded 55-gallon plastic buckets onto a truck. Wearing long pants, long-sleeved shirts, and gloves taped at the wrists over our sleeves, we looked like toxic-waste handlers.

Looking down from the pier, we saw two large *Chironex*. We watched, fascinated, as they maneuvered in and out of shadows, never touching the oyster-encrusted pilings that could easily tear their delicate tissue.

We used long-handled nets to prod them into the buckets, which we then lifted onto the dock. By then I had overheated, and I took off my shirt. While we were hoisting the buckets onto the truck, a breeze caught a single tentacle still dangling outside one of the buckets. It gently blew the tentacle against the inside of my upper arm.

I felt as if I had been branded by red-hot steel. My first instinct was to claw at my skin, but I knew that dropping the bucket would be too dangerous. Wincing with pain, I managed to help lift the bucket onto the truck. Then I examined the damage: a fiery welt, braided with the characteristic bands of the box jelly's tentacle. **3**

I was lucky. Only about an inch of tentacle had stuck to my arm. It takes ten feet or more to deliver a fatal dose of box jelly venom. An inch was enough for me. A hundred times that level of pain was unimaginable

—William M. Hamner, *National Geographic* (August 1994) **1**

1 Why does the author use the phrase "red–hot steel" to describe the sensation of a jellyfish tentacle touching his arm?

   A. It is the only way he could have described the stinging.

   B. It is a vivid description that makes the narrative more interesting.

   C. It is an example of scientific jargon.

   D. It is meant to help the reader understand the physiology of the *Chironex*.

2 Why does the author tell the story about the box jellyfish named "Charlie?"

   F. because a full-grown *Chironex* had never been captured

   G. because he had developed a special attachment to Charlie

   H. to explain to readers that no one had ever kept a *Chironex* alive in the lab before

   I. to set up the scene in which he is stung by Charlie

Read this story before answering Numbers 1 through 4.

How the Sun Was Made: An Aboriginal Tale

When the emu egg was hurled up to the sky it struck a great pile of wood that had been gathered by a cloud man named Ngoudenout. It hit the wood with such force that the pile instantly burst into flame, and flooded the earth with the soft, warm light of dawn. The flowers were so surprised that they lifted their sleepy heads to the sky, and opened their petals so wide that the glistening dewdrops which night had given them fell to the ground and were lost.

The little birds twittered excitedly on the trees, and the fairies, who kept the snow on the mountain tops, forgot their task, and allowed it to thaw and run into the rivers and creeks. And what was the cause of this excitement?

Away to the east, far over the mountains, the purple shadows of night were turning grey; the soft, pink-tinted clouds floated slowly across the sky like red-breasted birds winging their way to a far land. Along the dim sky-line a path of golden fire marked the parting of the grey shadows, and down in the valley the white mist was hiding the pale face of night.

Like a sleeper stirring softly at the warm touch of a kiss, all living things of the bush[1] stirred at the caress of dawn. The sun rose with golden splendor in a clear blue sky, and, with its coming, the first day dawned. At first the wood pile burned slowly, but the heat increased, until at noonday it was thoroughly ablaze. But gradually it burnt lower and lower, until at twilight only a heap of glowing embers remained. These embers slowly turned cold and grey. The purple shadows and white mists came from their hiding-places, and once again the mantle of night was over the land.

When Ngoudenout saw what a splendid thing the sun was, he determined to give it to us for ever. At night, when the fire of the sun has burnt out, he goes to a dark forest in the sky and collects a great pile, of wood. At dawn he lights it, and it burns feebly until noonday is reached, then it slowly burns away until twilight and night falls. Ngoudenout, the eternal wood gatherer, then makes his lonely way to the forest for the wood that lights the fire of the sun.

—Retold by William Jenkyn Thomas, *Some Myths and Legends of the Australian Aborigines* (1923)

[1]**bush**: Australia's dry backcountry

❶ What happened after the emu egg hit the woodpile in the sky?

    A. The earth was flooded.

    B. The first light of dawn came.

    C. The earth was set on fire.

    D. The first flowers came into existence.

❷ In the middle of the day,

    F. the fire was at its hottest.

    G. there was a terrible storm.

    H. the fire in the woodpile went out.

    I. purple shadows came over the land.

❸ The light of the sun is made by

    A. a god of night.

    B. a snow fairy.

    C. Ngoudenout.

    D. an emu.

❹ In what ways does the world change from the beginning of the story to the end of the story? Use information and details from the story to support your answer.

The Writing FCAT

During the writing FCAT, you will be given 45 minutes to plan and write a detailed response to a prompt. The first part of the prompt gives you the writing situation. The second part gives you more specific directions for writing. The writing test may feature an expository prompt (that asks you to explain something) or a persuasive prompt (that asks you to convince someone of something).

❶ You have only 45 minutes, so manage your time well. Make sure that you assign enough time for all of the tasks involved in writing—jotting down ideas, developing an outline, writing the response, and proofreading.

❷ Read the Writing Situation to get an idea of topic.

❸ Then read the Writing Directions carefully. Look for cue words. Are you being asked to explain or define something or to persuade or convince someone? Also, identify the audience to whom you must write your response. (Here, your principal is the audience you must convince.) Use an appropriate tone and language.

❹ Jot down ideas on a separate sheet of paper. Use these ideas to develop an outline for your response. (In the actual test, you will receive a separate booklet in which to plan your response.)

Carefully read the information below. Then write your response on a separate sheet of paper. Make sure to use correct spelling, grammar, and punctuation.

This clock shows about how much time you should spend on each part of the writing process.

Manage Your Time
- List major points to cover: 5 minutes
- Create outline: 5 minutes
- Write response: 30 minutes
- Proofread and correct: 5 minutes

❷ **Writing Situation:** The principal of your school has announced a plan to start school an hour earlier each morning so that students can do their homework in a supervised environment.

❸ **Directions for Writing:** Think about how an extra hour of school would change your routine and decide if you are for or against the plan. Now write to convince your principal to accept your point of view on the plan.

A top-scoring response will include the following elements:

- clear statement of your opinion on the proposed schedule change
- arguments supporting your position including specific details and logical development
- restatement of your position and appeal for action
- grammatical, legible presentation of your ideas

You will be graded on spelling, grammar, and punctuation. So, after you finish writing, proofread.

For more test practice online . . .

TEST PRACTICE
CLASSZONE.COM

Carefully read the information below. Then write your response on a separate sheet of paper. Make sure to use correct spelling, grammar, and punctuation.

Writing Situation: You have the opportunity to visit any location in the world.

Directions for Writing: Think about where you would like to visit.

Now explain to your reader which place you would choose and why.

RAND McNALLY
World Atlas

Contents

Complete Legend for Physical and Political Maps

Symbols

 Lake

 Salt Lake

 Seasonal Lake

 River

\ Waterfall

— Canal

△ Mountain Peak

▲ Highest Mountain Peak

Cities

■ Los Angeles   City over 1,000,000 population

▣ Calgary   City of 250,000 to 1,000,000 population

• Haifa   City under 250,000 population

✹ *Paris*   National Capital

★ **Vancouver**   Secondary Capital (State, Province, or Territory)

Type Styles Used to Name Features

CHINA   Country

O N T A R I O   State, Province, or Territory

PUERTO RICO (U.S.)   Possession

ATLANTIC OCEAN   Ocean or Sea

A l p s   Physical Feature

Borneo   Island

Boundaries

 International Boundary

Secondary Boundary

Land Elevation and Water Depths

Land Elevation

Meters		Feet
3,000 and over --		-- 9,840 and over
2,000 - 3,000 --		-- 6,560 - 9,840
500 - 2,000 --		-- 1,640 - 6,560
200 - 500 --		-- 656 - 1,640
0 - 200 --		-- 0 - 656

Water Depth

Less than 200 --		-- Less than 656
200 - 2,000 --		-- 656 - 6,560
Over 2,000 --		-- Over 6,560

A1

ARCTIC OCEAN

Baffin
Bay

Baffin
Island

Greenland

Jan Mayen

Arctic Circle

Iceland

Faroe Is.

Yukon

Mackenzie

Mt. McKinley △
20,320 Ft.
6,194m

NORTH

Canadian Shield

Hudson
Bay

British
Isles

London

Aleutian Islands

Vancouver

Great Plains

ROCKY MOUNTAINS

AMERICA

Newfoundland

St. Lawrence

Appalachian Mts.

Iberian
Peninsula

Azores

Los Angeles

Colorado

Mississippi

Washington D.C.

Cape Hatteras

ATLANTIC

Atlas
Mts.

Midway Is.

Tropic of Cancer

Baja
California

Gulf of Mexico

Canary
Islands

Yucatan
Peninsula

Cuba

Hispaniola

Puerto Rico

Cape
Verde
Islands

Hawaiian
Islands

Jamaica

Caribbean
Sea

Cape Verde

Niger

PACIFIC

Orinoco

Trinidad

OCEAN

Palmyra

Galapagos Islands

Amazon

Amazon

Equator

SOUTH

Kiribati

Basin

Marquesas Is.

Andes

AMERICA

St. Helena

Samoa
Islands

Mato Grosso
Plateau

Tonga
Is.

Cook
Islands

Tahiti

Rio de Janeiro

Tropic of Capricorn

Easter Island

Paraná

Andes

Mt. Aconcagua
22,831 Ft.
6,959m

Chatham Is.

Archipiélago
Juan Fernández

Buenos Aires

N

Patagonia

0   1000   2000 Miles

Falkland Is.

South
Georgia

0   1000   2000   3000 Kilometers

Copyright by Rand McNally & Co.
Robinson Projection

Tierra del Fuego

South
Sandwich Is.

Cape Horn

South
Orkney Is.

Antarctic Circle

South
Shetland Is.

Antarctic
Peninsula

Weddell
Sea

Ross
Sea

Marie
Byrd
Land

△ Vinson Massif
16,066 Ft.
4,897m

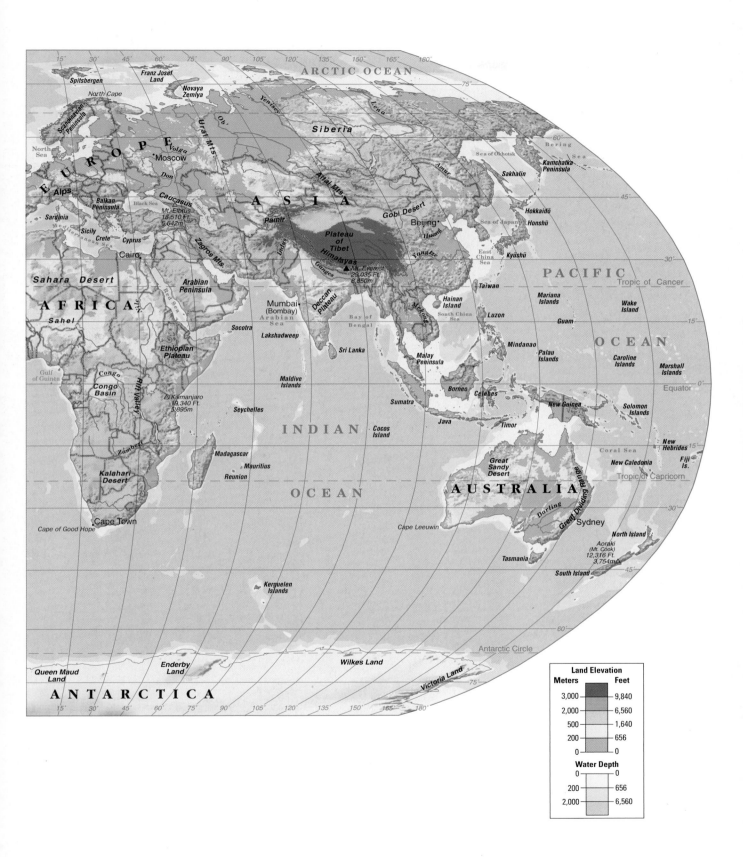

ARCTIC OCEAN

75°

Spitsbergen

Franz Josef
Land

North Cape

Novaya
Zemlya

Scandinavian
Peninsula

Yenisey

60°

Bering

Siberia

Sea of Okhotsk

Sea

Ob'

Ural Mts.

Lena

Amur

EUROPE

North
Sea

Volga

Moscow

Kamchatka
Peninsula

Sakhalin

45°

Don

Aral
Sea

Altai Mts.

Alps

Caucasus

Hokkaidō

Balkan
Peninsula

Black Sea

Mt. Elbrus
18,510 Ft.
5,642m

Pamir

Gobi Desert

Beijing

Honshū

Sea of Japan

Sardinia

A S I A

Sicily

Crete

Cyprus

Plateau
of
Tibet

Huang

Kyūshū

East
China
Sea

30°

Mediterranean Sea

Zagros Mts.

Indus

Himalayas

Yangtze

Cairo

Red Sea

Arabian
Peninsula

▲ Mt. Everest
29,035 Ft.
8,850m

Taiwan

PACIFIC

Tropic of Cancer

Sahara Desert

Nile

Mumbai
(Bombay)

Deccan
Plateau

Hainan
Island

Mariana
Islands

Wake
Island

AFRICA

Sahel

Arabian
Sea

Bay of
Bengal

South China
Sea

Luzon

Guam

15°

Socotra

Lakshadweep

OCEAN

Gulf
of Guinea

Ethiopian
Plateau

Sri Lanka

Malay
Peninsula

Mekong

Mindanao

Palau
Islands

Caroline
Islands

Marshall
Islands

Congo

Congo
Basin

△ Kilimanjaro
19,340 Ft.
5,895m

Maldive
Islands

Sumatra

Borneo

Celebes

0°

Equator

Rift Valley

Seychelles

Java

Timor

New Guinea

Solomon
Islands

Madagascar

Cocos
Island

New
Hebrides

15°

Zambezi

Mauritius

INDIAN

Coral Sea

Kalahari
Desert

Reunion

Great
Sandy
Desert

New Caledonia

Fiji
Is.

Tropic of Capricorn

OCEAN

AUSTRALIA

30°

Cape Town

Cape of Good Hope

Cape Leeuwin

Darling

Great Dividing Range

Sydney

North Island

Aoraki
(Mt. Cook)
12,316 Ft.
3,754m △

Tasmania

Kerguelen
Islands

South Island

45°

60°

Antarctic Circle

Queen Maud
Land

Enderby
Land

Wilkes Land

Victoria Land

75°

A N T A R C T I C A

Land Elevation		
Meters		Feet
3,000		9,840
2,000		6,560
500		1,640
200		656
0		0
Water Depth		
0		0
200		656
2,000		6,560

ARCTIC OCEAN

GREENLAND
(Den.)

Baffin
Bay

Arctic Circle

ICELAND

FAROE IS.
(Den.)

RUSSIA   ALASKA
Yukon (U.S.)
Anchorage

UNITED
KINGDOM

IRELAND

London

C A N A D A

Aleutian Islands

Vancouver

Newfoundland

FRANCE

Missouri

Montréal
Ottawa

Madrid
PORTUGAL   SPAIN

Chicago

New York
Washington D.C.

Azores
(Port.)

UNITED   S T A T E S

Los Angeles

Colorado

ATLANTIC

Casablanca

MOROCCO

Houston

Canary
Islands
(Sp.)

MIDWAY IS.
(U.S.)
Tropic of Cancer

MEXICO

Gulf of Mexico

BAHAMAS

W. SAHARA

CUBA
HAITI   DOM. REP.

MAURITANIA   MALI

Hawaiian
Islands
(U.S)

Mexico City

BELIZE
GUAT. HOND.

JAMAICA

PUERTO RICO (U.S.)

Caribbean
Sea

Niger

CAPE
VERDE

SENEGAL
GAMBIA
GUINEA-BISSAU   GUINEA

BURK.
FASO

EL. SAL.   NIC.

COTE
D'IVOIRE

GHANA

P A C I F I C

COSTA
RICA

PANAMA

Caracas

VENEZUELA

TRINIDAD AND TOBAGO

GUYANA

SIERRA LEONE

LIBERIA

COLOMBIA

SURINAME
FRENCH GUIANA

Equator

KIRIBATI

Galapagos Islands
(Ecuador)

ECUADOR

Amazon

O C E A N

SAMOA

AMERICAN
SAMOA
COOK
ISLANDS (N.Z.)

TONGA

O C E A N

PERU
Lima

B R A Z I L

O C E A N

ST. HELENA
(U.K.)

FRENCH POLYNESIA

BOLIVIA

Tropic of Capricorn

PARAGUAY

Rio de Janeiro

Easter Island
(Chile)

ARGENTINA

URUGUAY

Santiago

Buenos
Aires

CHILE

N

0   1000   2000 Miles

0   1000   2000   3000 Kilometers

Copyright by Rand McNally & Co.
Robinson Projection

FALKLAND IS.
(U.K.)

South
Georgia
(U.K.)

South
Orkney Is.
(U.K.)

Antarctic Circle

South
Shetland Is.
(U.K.)

Weddell
Sea

⊕ National Capital

• Major Cities

🌐 RAND MᶜNALLY

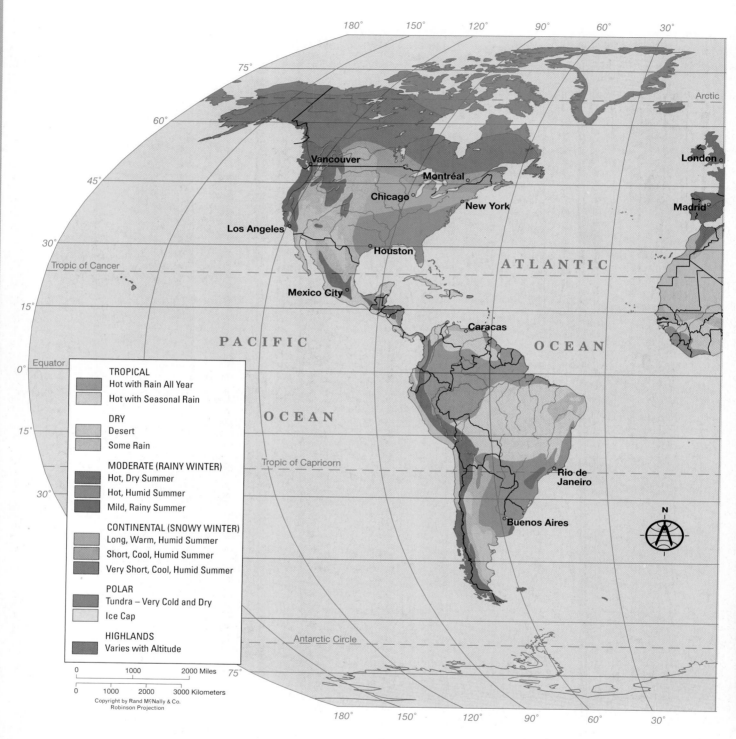

TROPICAL
Hot with Rain All Year
Hot with Seasonal Rain

DRY
Desert
Some Rain

MODERATE (RAINY WINTER)
Hot, Dry Summer
Hot, Humid Summer
Mild, Rainy Summer

CONTINENTAL (SNOWY WINTER)
Long, Warm, Humid Summer
Short, Cool, Humid Summer
Very Short, Cool, Humid Summer

POLAR
Tundra – Very Cold and Dry
Ice Cap

HIGHLANDS
Varies with Altitude

0   1000   2000 Miles
0   1000   2000   3000 Kilometers
Copyright by Rand McNally & Co.
Robinson Projection

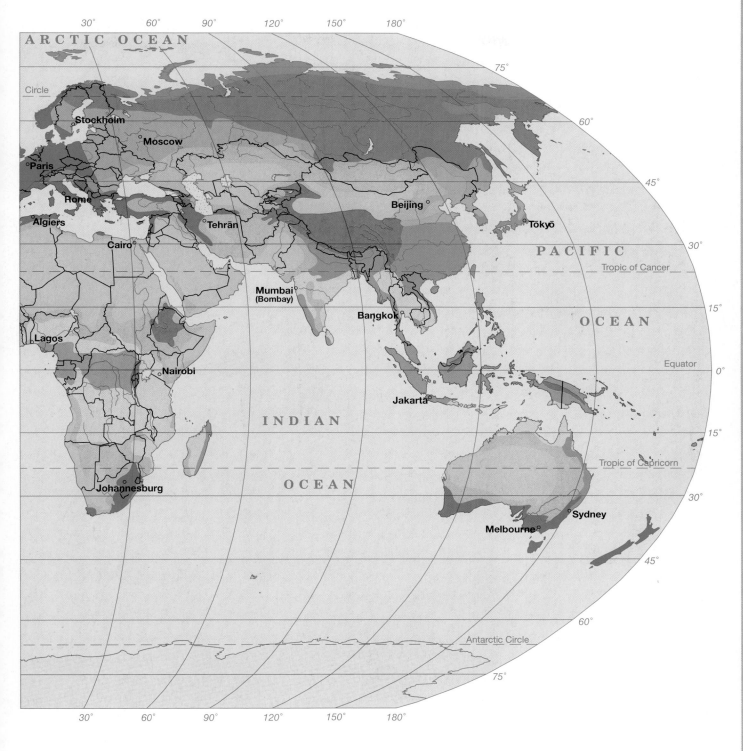

ARCTIC OCEAN

30° 60° 90° 120° 150° 180°

75°

Circle

60°

Stockholm

Moscow

45°

Paris

Rome

Beijing

30°

Algiers

Tōkyō

Tehrān

PACIFIC

30°

Cairo

Tropic of Cancer

15°

Mumbai
(Bombay)

OCEAN

Bangkok

Lagos

Equator 0°

Nairobi

Jakarta

INDIAN

15°

OCEAN

Tropic of Capricorn

Johannesburg

30°

Sydney

Melbourne

45°

60°

Antarctic Circle

75°

30° 60° 90° 120° 150° 180°

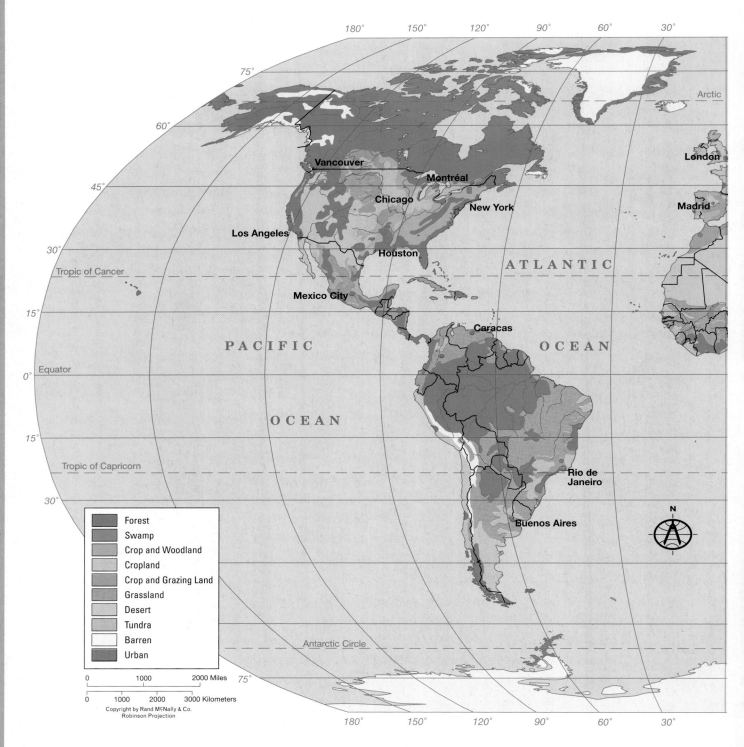

180° 150° 120° 90° 60° 30°

75°

Arctic

60°

London

45°

Vancouver

Montréal

Madrid

Chicago

New York

Los Angeles

30°

Houston

ATLANTIC

Tropic of Cancer

15°

Mexico City

Caracas

OCEAN

PACIFIC

0° Equator

OCEAN

15°

Tropic of Capricorn

OCEAN

Rio de Janeiro

30°

Buenos Aires

N

Forest
Swamp
Crop and Woodland
Cropland
Crop and Grazing Land
Grassland
Desert
Tundra
Barren
Urban

Antarctic Circle

75°

0   1000   2000 Miles

0   1000   2000   3000 Kilometers

Copyright by Rand McNally & Co.
Robinson Projection

180° 150° 120° 90° 60° 30°

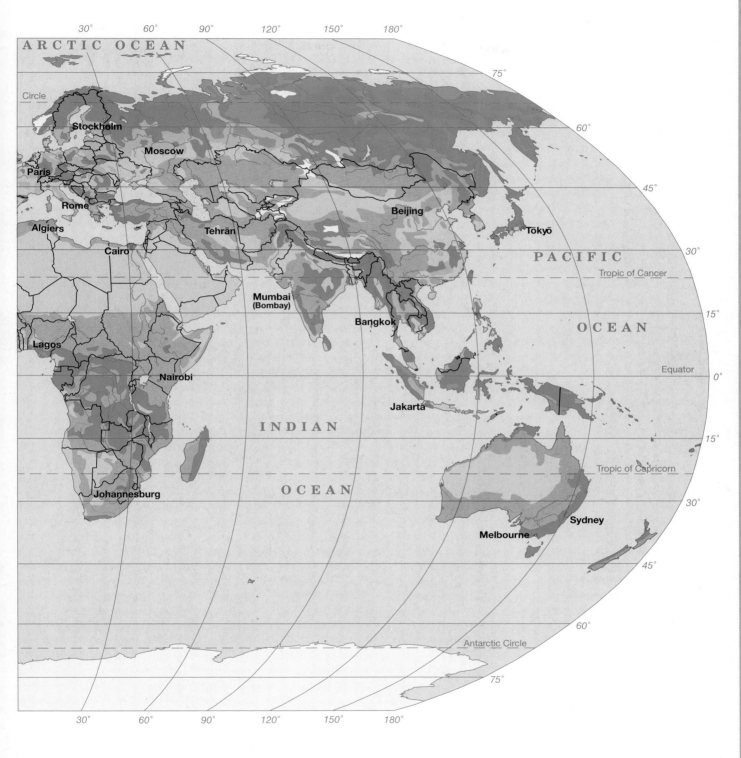

ARCTIC OCEAN

Circle

Stockholm

Moscow

Paris

Rome

Algiers

Cairo

Tehrān

Beijing

Tōkyō

PACIFIC

Tropic of Cancer

Mumbai
(Bombay)

Bangkok

OCEAN

Lagos

Nairobi

Equator

Jakarta

INDIAN

Johannesburg

OCEAN

Tropic of Capricorn

Melbourne

Sydney

Antarctic Circle

30° 60° 90° 120° 150° 180°

75°

60°

45°

30°

15°

0°

15°

30°

45°

60°

75°

RAND McNALLY

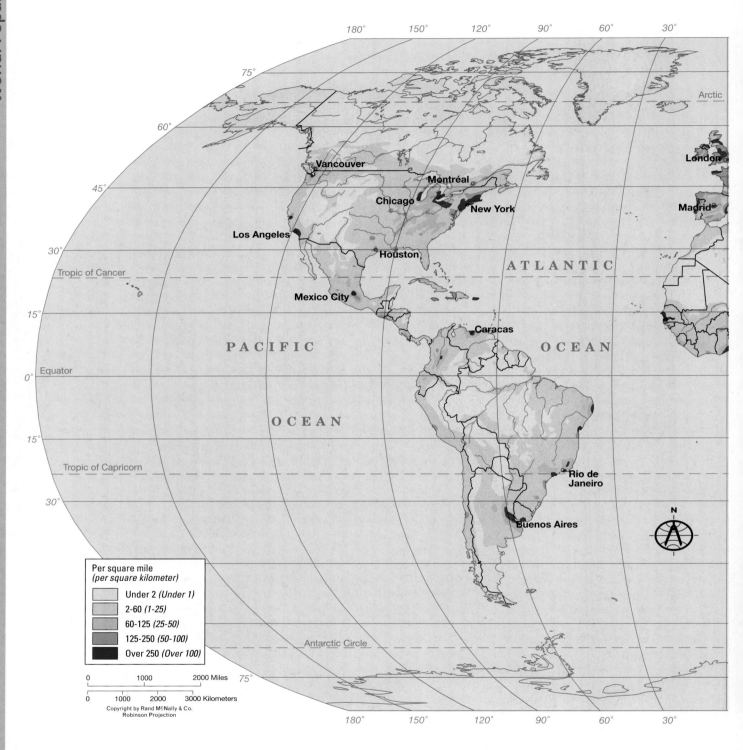

Arctic

London

Madrid

Vancouver
Montréal
Chicago
New York
Los Angeles
Houston
ATLANTIC
Mexico City
Caracas
OCEAN

PACIFIC

OCEAN

Rio de
Janeiro

Buenos Aires

N

Per square mile
(per square kilometer)

	Under 2 *(Under 1)*
	2-60 *(1-25)*
	60-125 *(25-50)*
	125-250 *(50-100)*
	Over 250 *(Over 100)*

Tropic of Cancer

Equator

Tropic of Capricorn

Antarctic Circle

0		1000		2000 Miles

0	1000	2000	3000 Kilometers

Copyright by Rand McNally & Co.
Robinson Projection

ARCTIC OCEAN

75°

Circle

60°

Stockholm

Moscow

Yekaterinburg

45°

Paris

Rome

30°

Algiers

Tehrān

Beijing

Tōkyō

Cairo

PACIFIC

Tropic of Cancer

Mumbai
(Bombay)

15°

Bangkok

OCEAN

Lagos

Equator

0°

Nairobi

Jakarta

INDIAN

15°

Tropic of Capricorn

OCEAN

30°

Johannesburg

Sydney

Melbourne

45°

60°

Antarctic Circle

75°

30°   60°   90°   120°   150°   180°

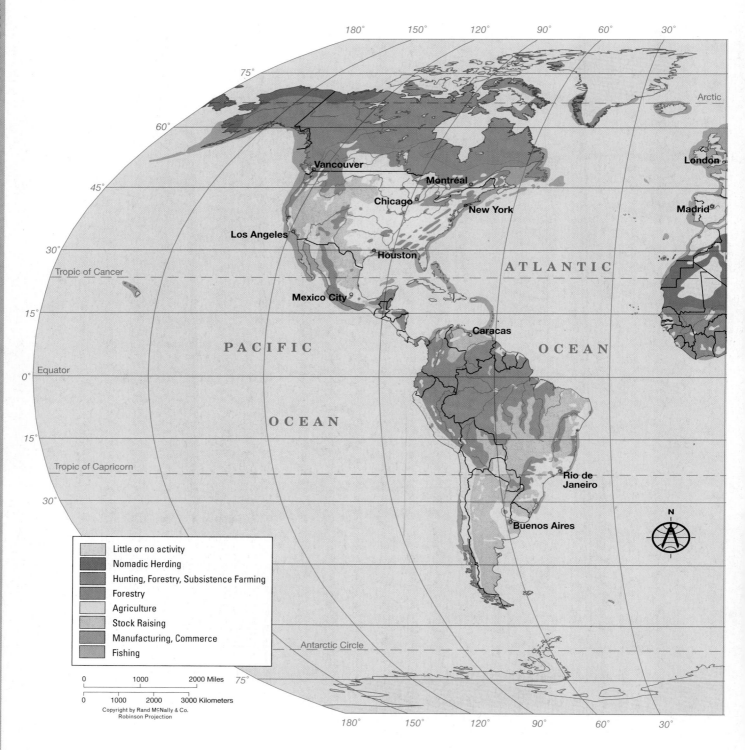

	Little or no activity
	Nomadic Herding
	Hunting, Forestry, Subsistence Farming
	Forestry
	Agriculture
	Stock Raising
	Manufacturing, Commerce
	Fishing

180° 150° 120° 90° 60° 30°

75°
60°
45°
30°
Tropic of Cancer
15°
Equator 0°
15°
Tropic of Capricorn
30°

Arctic

London
Madrid

Vancouver
Montréal
Chicago
New York
Los Angeles
Houston
Mexico City
Caracas

ATLANTIC
OCEAN

PACIFIC

OCEAN

Rio de Janeiro
Buenos Aires

N

Antarctic Circle
75°

0   1000   2000 Miles
0   1000   2000   3000 Kilometers
Copyright by Rand McNally & Co.
Robinson Projection

180° 150° 120° 90° 60° 30°

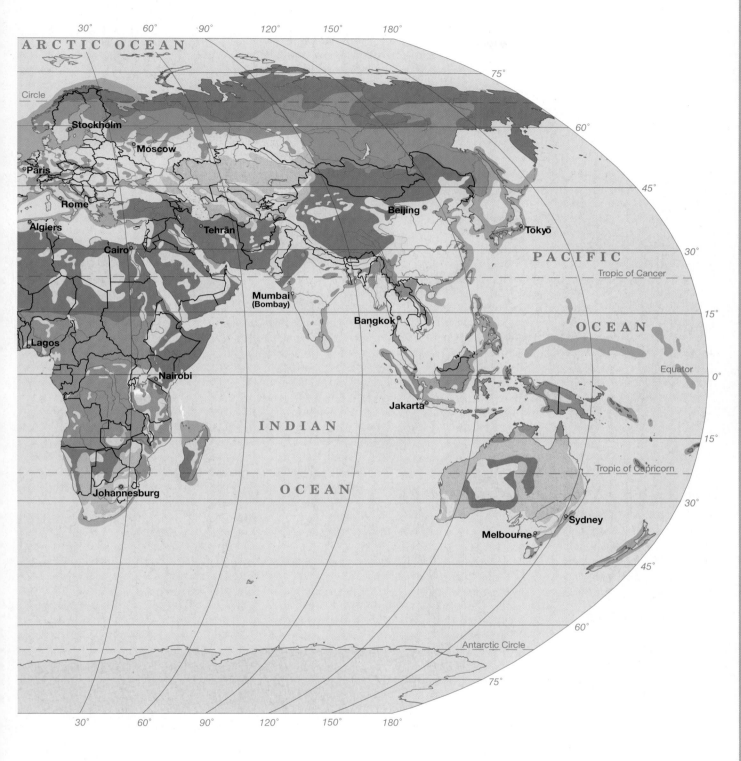

ARCTIC OCEAN

Circle

75°

60°

45°

30°

Stockholm

Moscow

Paris

Rome

Algiers

Cairo

Tehrān

Beijing

Tōkyō

PACIFIC

Tropic of Cancer

Mumbai
(Bombay)

Bangkok

OCEAN

15°

Lagos

Equator

0°

Nairobi

Jakarta

INDIAN

15°

Johannesburg

OCEAN

Tropic of Capricorn

30°

Sydney

Melbourne

45°

60°

Antarctic Circle

75°

30°   60°   90°   120°   150°   180°

30°   60°   90°   120°   150°   180°

Eurasian Plate

North Ameri[ca] Plate

Juan de Fuca Plate

Philippine Plate

Pacific Plate

Cocos Plate

Indo-Australian Plate

Nazca Plate

N

Antarctic Plate

Scale at Equator

0   500   1000   1500   2000   2500 Miles

0   1000   2000   3000   4000 Kilometers

Copyright by Rand McNally & Co.
Miller Cylindrical Projection

90° 105° 120° 135° 150° 165° 180° 165° 150° 135° 120° 105°

90° 105° 120° 135° 150° 165° 180° 165° '50° 135° 120° 105°

60°
45°
30°
15°
0°
15°
30°
45°
60°

ATLAS

Eurasian Plate

Caribbean
Plate

Arabian
Plate

African

Plate

Indo-
Australian
Plate

South
American
Plate

Antarctic
Plate

Scotia Plate

△ Volcanic eruptions since 1900

● Earthquakes of 7.7 magnitude
and above since 10 A.D.

➤ Directions of plate movement

RAND MCNALLY

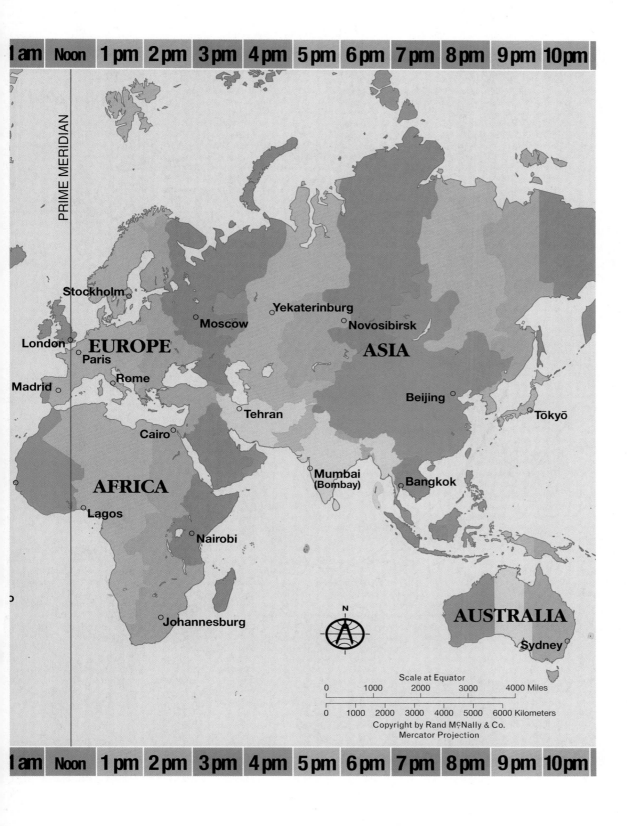

| 11 am | Noon | 1 pm | 2 pm | 3 pm | 4 pm | 5 pm | 6 pm | 7 pm | 8 pm | 9 pm | 10 pm |

PRIME MERIDIAN

Stockholm

Yekaterinburg

Moscow

Novosibirsk

London

EUROPE

ASIA

Paris

Rome

Madrid

Beijing

Tehran

Tōkyō

Cairo

Mumbai
(Bombay)

AFRICA

Bangkok

Lagos

Nairobi

AUSTRALIA

Johannesburg

Sydney

N

Scale at Equator

| 0 | 1000 | 2000 | 3000 | 4000 Miles |

| 0 | 1000 | 2000 | 3000 | 4000 | 5000 | 6000 Kilometers |

Copyright by Rand McNally & Co.
Mercator Projection

ATLAS

Land Elevation

Meters		Feet
3,000		9,840
2,000		6,560
500		1,640
200		656
0		0

Water Depth

0		0
200		656
2,000		6,560

0   100   200   300 Miles

0   100   200   300   400 Kilometers

Copyright by Rand McNally & Co.
Alber's Conic Equal Area Projection

PUERTO RICO (U.S.)

0   25   50 Miles

0   25   50 Kilometers

RAND McNALLY

A19

RAND McNALLY

A20

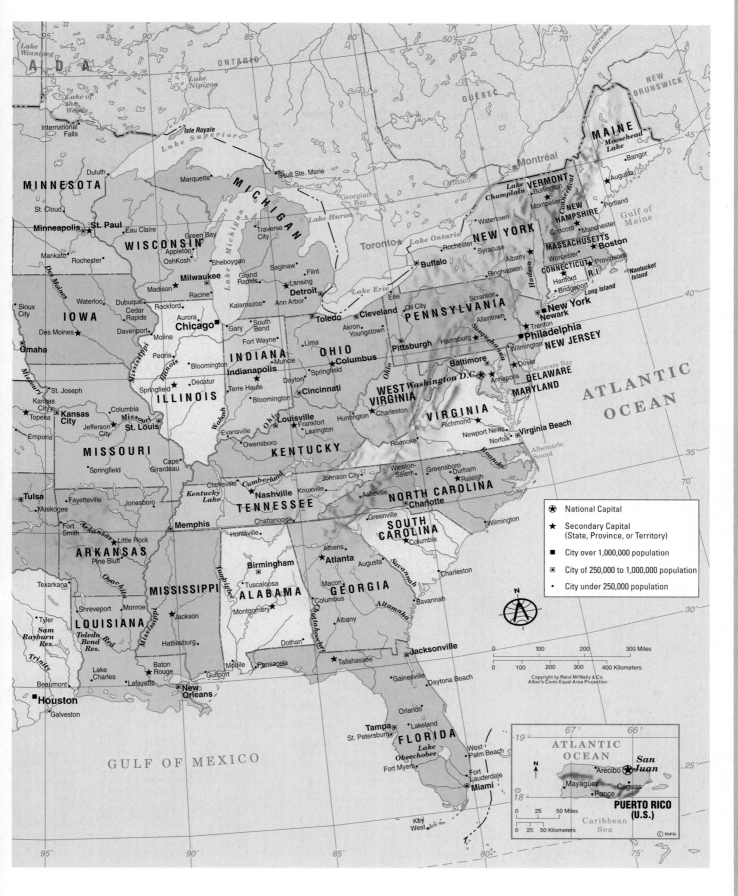

CANADA

Lake Winnipeg
Lake of the Woods
International Falls
Duluth
Isle Royale
Lake Superior
ONTARIO
Lake Nipigon
Marquette
Sault Ste. Marie

MINNESOTA
St. Cloud
Minneapolis
St. Paul
Eau Claire
Mankato
Rochester
WISCONSIN
Appleton
OshKosh
Green Bay
Sheboygan
Madison
Milwaukee
Racine
Rockford

MICHIGAN
Lake Michigan
Traverse City
Lake Huron
Saginaw
Flint
Grand Rapids
Kalamazoo
Lansing
Detroit
Ann Arbor

Georgian Bay
Lake Ontario
Toronto
Ottawa
QUÉBEC
Montréal
St. Lawrence

NEW BRUNSWICK

MAINE
Moosehead Lake
Bangor
Augusta
Portland
Gulf of Maine

VERMONT
Lake Champlain
Burlington
Montpelier
NEW HAMPSHIRE
Concord
Manchester
Watertown

NEW YORK
Rochester
Syracuse
Albany
Binghamton
Buffalo
Lake Erie
Erie

MASSACHUSETTS
Worcester
Boston
Providence
R.I.
CONNECTICUT
Hartford
Bridgeport
Nantucket Island
Long Island

Sioux City
Des Moines
IOWA
Waterloo
Cedar Rapids
Dubuque
Davenport
Moline
Omaha

Des Moines
Mississippi
St. Joseph
Kansas City
Topeka
Jefferson City
Emporia
Columbia
St. Louis
Missouri
MISSOURI
Springfield
Cape Girardeau

Chicago
Aurora
Gary
South Bend
Fort Wayne
Peoria
Bloomington
Decatur
Springfield
ILLINOIS
Terre Haute
INDIANA
Indianapolis
Muncie
Bloomington
Dayton
OHIO
Columbus
Springfield
Cincinnati
Toledo
Cleveland
Akron
Youngstown
Lima
Wabash

Oil City
Scranton
PENNSYLVANIA
Pittsburgh
Harrisburg
Allentown
Susquehanna
Trenton
Philadelphia
Newark
New York
NEW JERSEY
Dover
Wilmington
DELAWARE
Delaware Bay
Baltimore
Washington D.C.
Annapolis
MARYLAND

WEST VIRGINIA
Charleston
Huntington
VIRGINIA
Richmond
Roanoke
Newport News
Norfolk
Virginia Beach
Ohio
Louisville
Frankfort
Lexington
Owensboro
Evansville
KENTUCKY

ATLANTIC OCEAN

Albemarle Sound

Tulsa
Muskogee
Fayetteville
Jonesboro
Fort Smith
Little Rock
Pine Bluff
ARKANSAS
Arkansas

Clarksville
Kentucky Lake
Cumberland
Nashville
Knoxville
TENNESSEE
Chattanooga
Memphis
Huntsville
Johnson City
Winston-Salem
Greensboro
Durham
Raleigh
Asheville
NORTH CAROLINA
Charlotte
Greenville
SOUTH CAROLINA
Columbia
Wilmington
Charleston

Texarkana
Tyler
Sam Rayburn Res.
Toledo Bend Res.
Red
Ouachita
Shreveport
Monroe
LOUISIANA
Jackson
MISSISSIPPI
Tuscaloosa
Birmingham
ALABAMA
Montgomery
Tombigbee
Athens
Atlanta
Macon
Columbus
GEORGIA
Augusta
Savannah
Albany
Altamaha
Savannah
Chattahoochee

Hattiesburg
Beaumont
Lake Charles
Baton Rouge
Lafayette
Gulfport
Mobile
Pensacola
New Orleans
Dothan
Tallahassee

Houston
Galveston
Trinity

GULF OF MEXICO

Gainesville
Jacksonville
Daytona Beach
Orlando
Lakeland
Tampa
St. Petersburg
FLORIDA
Lake Okeechobee
West Palm Beach
Fort Myers
Fort Lauderdale
Miami
Key West

N

	National Capital
	Secondary Capital (State, Province, or Territory)
■	City over 1,000,000 population
▫	City of 250,000 to 1,000,000 population
•	City under 250,000 population

0   100   200   300 Miles
0   100   200   300   400 Kilometers
Copyright by Rand McNally & Co.
Alber's Conic Equal Area Projection

ATLANTIC OCEAN
San Juan
Arecibo
Mayagüez
Ponce
Caguas
PUERTO RICO (U.S.)
Caribbean Sea
N
0   25   50 Miles
0   25   50 Kilometers

RAND McNALLY

A21

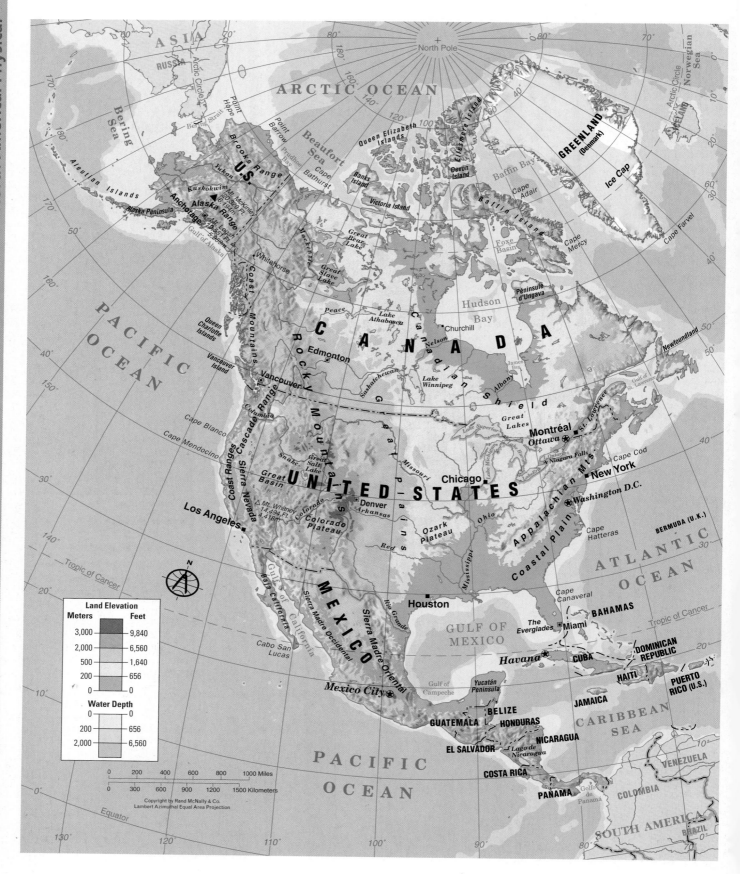

ASIA
RUSSIA
Arctic Circle

ARCTIC OCEAN

North Pole

Bering
Sea

Point
Hope

Beaufort
Sea

Queen Elizabeth
Islands

Ellesmere Island

GREENLAND
(Denmark)

Ice Cap

Aleutian Islands

Bering Strait

Point
Barrow
Prudhoe
Bay

Cape
Bathurst

Banks
Island

Devon
Island

Baffin Bay

Cape
Adair

Brooks Range

U.S.

Yukon

Alaska Peninsula

Kuskokwim

Mt. McKinley
20,320 Ft.
6,194m

Mt. Logan
19,551 Ft.
5,959m

Anchorage

Alaska Range

Gulf of Alaska

Whitehorse

Victoria Island

Great Bear
Lake

Mackenzie

Great
Slave
Lake

Baffin Island

Foxe
Basin

Cape
Mercy

Cape Farvel

PACIFIC

OCEAN

Cape Blanco

Cape Mendocino

Coast Mountains

Queen
Charlotte
Islands

Vancouver
Island

Vancouver

Columbia

Coast Ranges

Cascade Range

Sierra Nevada

Peace

Lake
Athabasca

Nelson

C A N A D A

Edmonton

Saskatchewan

Lake
Winnipeg

Rocky Mountains

Snake

Great
Salt
Lake

Great
Basin

Mt. Whitney
14,494 Ft.
4,418m

Los Angeles

Denver

Colorado

Colorado
Plateau

Arkansas

Churchill

Hudson
Bay

Péninsule
d'Ungava

James
Bay

Albany

Canadian
Shield

Lake Superior

Great
Lakes

Lake Michigan

Lake Huron

Missouri

G r e a t   P l a i n s

Chicago

Ontario

Niagara Falls

Montréal
Ottawa

St. Lawrence

Gulf of
St. Lawrence

Newfoundland

New York

Cape Cod

Appalachian Mts.

UNITED STATES

Ozark
Plateau

Red

Ohio

Mississippi

Coastal Plain

Cape
Hatteras

ATLANTIC

OCEAN

BERMUDA (U.K.)

Tropic of Cancer

N

Baja California

Gulf of California

MEXICO

Sierra Madre Occidental

Sierra Madre Oriental

Rio Grande

Houston

Cape
Canaveral

The
Everglades

Miami

BAHAMAS

Tropic of Cancer

Cabo San
Lucas

GULF OF
MEXICO

Gulf of
Campeche

Yucatán
Peninsula

Havana

CUBA

DOMINICAN
REPUBLIC

HAITI

PUERTO
RICO (U.S.)

Mexico City

JAMAICA

CARIBBEAN
SEA

BELIZE

GUATEMALA

HONDURAS

EL SALVADOR

NICARAGUA

Lago de
Nicaragua

VENEZUELA

COLOMBIA

COSTA RICA

PANAMA

Golfo
de
Panamá

PACIFIC

OCEAN

SOUTH AMERICA

BRAZIL

Equator

Land Elevation

Meters		Feet
3,000		9,840
2,000		6,560
500		1,640
200		656
0		0

Water Depth

0		0
200		656
2,000		6,560

0 200 400 600 800 1000 Miles
0 300 600 900 1200 1500 Kilometers

Copyright by Rand McNally & Co.
Lambert Azimuthal Equal Area Projection

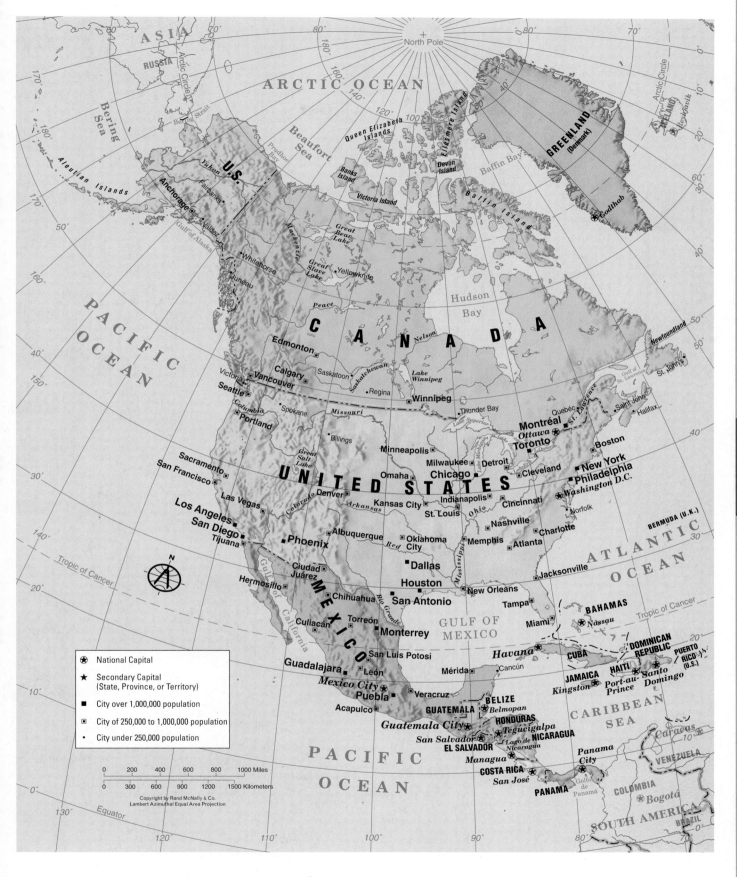

ASIA
RUSSIA
Arctic Circle
Bering Strait
Bering Sea
Aleutian Islands
PACIFIC OCEAN

North Pole
ARCTIC OCEAN
Beaufort Sea
Queen Elizabeth Islands
Banks Island
Victoria Island
Ellesmere Island
Devon Island
Baffin Bay
Baffin Island
Arctic Circle
GREENLAND (Denmark)
Godthåb
ICELAND
Reykjavik

U.S.
Yukon
Fairbanks
Anchorage
Valdez
Gulf of Alaska
Prudhoe Bay
Mackenzie
Great Bear Lake
Great Slave Lake
Yellowknife
Whitehorse
Juneau
Peace

Hudson Bay
Nelson
Newfoundland
Gulf of St. Lawrence
St. John's

C A N A D A

Edmonton
Calgary
Saskatoon
Saskatchewan
Regina
Lake Winnipeg
Winnipeg
Thunder Bay
Lake Superior
Québec
St. Lawrence
Saint John
Halifax

Victoria
Vancouver
Seattle
Columbia
Spokane
Portland
Billings
Missouri
Great Salt Lake

Minneapolis
Milwaukee
Omaha
Chicago
Detroit
Cleveland
Lake Michigan
Lake Ontario
Montréal
Ottawa
Toronto
Boston
New York
Philadelphia
Washington D.C.

Sacramento
San Francisco
Las Vegas
Denver
Kansas City
St. Louis
Indianapolis
Cincinnati
Nashville
Norfolk
Charlotte

U N I T E D   S T A T E S
Colorado
Arkansas
Ohio
Mississippi

Los Angeles
San Diego
Tijuana
Phoenix
Albuquerque
Oklahoma City
Dallas
Memphis
Atlanta
Red
BERMUDA (U.K.)

Ciudad Juárez
Hermosillo
Chihuahua
Rio Grande
Houston
San Antonio
New Orleans
Jacksonville
Tampa

ATLANTIC OCEAN
Tropic of Cancer

M E X I C O
Culiacán
Torreón
Monterrey
San Luis Potosí
Gulf of California

Miami
BAHAMAS
Nassau

Guadalajara
León
Mexico City
Puebla
Veracruz
Acapulco
Mérida
Cancún

GULF OF MEXICO
Havana
CUBA
JAMAICA
Kingston
HAITI
Port-au-Prince
DOMINICAN REPUBLIC
Santo Domingo
PUERTO RICO (U.S.)

CARIBBEAN SEA

BELIZE
Belmopan
GUATEMALA
Guatemala City
San Salvador
EL SALVADOR
HONDURAS
Tegucigalpa
NICARAGUA
Lago de Nicaragua
Managua
COSTA RICA
San José
PANAMA
Panama City
Golfo de Panamá

Caracas
VENEZUELA
COLOMBIA
Bogotá
SOUTH AMERICA
BRAZIL

PACIFIC OCEAN
Equator
Tropic of Cancer

Legend

⊛ National Capital
★ Secondary Capital (State, Province, or Territory)
■ City over 1,000,000 population
▣ City of 250,000 to 1,000,000 population
• City under 250,000 population

Scale
0 200 400 600 800 1000 Miles
0 300 600 900 1200 1500 Kilometers

Copyright by Rand McNally & Co.
Lambert Azimuthal Equal Area Projection

South America: Physical

RAND McNALLY

A24

NORTH AMERICA

GULF OF MEXICO

MEXICO
BELIZE
GUATEMALA
HONDURAS
EL SALVADOR
NICARAGUA
COSTA RICA
PANAMA

CUBA
JAMAICA
HAITI
DOMINICAN REPUBLIC
PUERTO RICO (U.S.)

Greater Antilles
Lesser Antilles

CARIBBEAN SEA

Gulf of Honduras
Gulf of Panama

TRINIDAD AND TOBAGO

ATLANTIC OCEAN

Cristóbal Colón Peak △ 18,948 Ft. 5,775m

Caracas ✪

VENEZUELA

Llanos

Orinoco

GUYANA

SURINAME

FRENCH GUIANA

Cape Orange

Magdalena

Bogotá ✪

COLOMBIA

Galapagos Islands (Ec.)

ECUADOR

△ Chimborazo 20,703 Ft. 6,310m

Putumayo

Japurá

Negro

Amazon

Ilha de Marajó

Belém ■

Equator

Manaus ■

Amazon

Tapajós

Tocantins

Amazon Basin

Juruá

Madeira

B R A Z I L

Selvas

Ucayali

P E R U

A n d e s

Mt. Huascarán 22,133 Ft. 6,746m

Lima ✪

Mato Grosso Plateau

Recife ■

Serra do Espinhaço

São Francisco

Mt. Illampu 21,066 Ft. 6,421m

Lake Titicaca

BOLIVIA

Brasília ✪

Cordillera Oriental

△ Mt. Sajama 21,463 Ft. 6,542m

Gran Chaco

PARAGUAY

Paraná

São Paulo ■

Rio de Janeiro ■

Tropic of Capricorn

Isla San Ambrosio (Chile)

Isla San Felix (Chile)

Atacama Desert

Mt. Ojos del Salado 22,615 Ft. 6,893m

A n d e s

C H I L E

A R G E N T I N A

Paraná

URUGUAY

PACIFIC OCEAN

Archipiélago Juan Fernández (Chile)

▲ Mt. Aconcagua 22,831 Ft. 6,959m

Santiago ✪

Buenos Aires ✪

Rio de la Plata

Pampas

San Matías Gulf

Península Valdés

Chiloé

Patagonia

San Jorge Gulf

Point Medanoso

ATLANTIC OCEAN

Grand Bay

West Falkland

East Falkland

FALKLAND ISLANDS (U.K.)

Strait of Magellan

Tierra del Fuego

Cape Horn

South Georgia (U.K.)

South Sandwich Islands (U.K.)

Drake Passage

South Shetland Islands (U.K.)

South Orkney Islands (U.K.)

Land Elevation

Meters		Feet
3,000		9,840
2,000		6,560
500		1,640
200		656
0		0

Water Depth

0		0
200		656
2,000		6,560

0 200 400 600 800 1000 Miles
0 300 600 900 1200 1500 Kilometers

Copyright by Rand McNally & Co.
Lambert Azimuthal Equal Area Projection

GULF OF MEXICO

Havana

CUBA

DOMINICAN REPUBLIC

HAITI

PUERTO RICO (U.S.)

Lesser Antilles

ATLANTIC OCEAN

NORTH AMERICA

MEXICO

BELIZE

JAMAICA

CARIBBEAN SEA

GUATEMALA

HONDURAS

EL SALVADOR

NICARAGUA

COSTA RICA

PANAMA

Barranquilla

Cartagena

Maracaibo

Barquisimeto

Caracas

Valencia

TRINIDAD AND TOBAGO

Cúcuta

Orinoco

Ciudad Guayana

Medellín

Bucaramanga

VENEZUELA

Georgetown

Paramaribo

GUYANA

Cayenne

Bogotá

Cali

COLOMBIA

SURINAME

FRENCH GUIANA

Macapá

Galápagos Islands (Ec.)

Quito

ECUADOR

Equator

Guayaquil

Putumayo

Japurá

Negro

Amazon

Manaus

Belém

São Luís

Santarém

BRAZIL

Fortaleza

Iquitos

Amazon

Juruá

Imperatriz

Teresina

Chiclayo

Madeira

Natal

Trujillo

PERU

Pôrto Velho

Recife

Maceió

Lima

Cusco

BOLIVIA

Cuiabá

Feira de Santana

Aracaju

Salvador

Lake Titicaca

La Paz

Cochabamba

Goiânia

Brasília

Arequipa

Sucre

Santa Cruz

Montes Claros

Campo Grande

Uberlândia

Belo Horizonte

Antofagasta

PARAGUAY

Paraná

Campinas

Rio de Janeiro

Vitória

Tropic of Capricorn

Isla San Ambrosio (Chile)

Salta

Asunción

São Paulo

Isla San Felix (Chile)

San Miguel de Tucumán

Curitiba

Caxias do Sul

Archipiélago Juan Fernández (Chile)

Córdoba

Santa Fe

Pôrto Alegre

PACIFIC OCEAN

Valparaíso

Rosario

URUGUAY

Santiago

Mendoza

Buenos Aires

Montevideo

CHILE

Concepción

ARGENTINA

La Plata

Río de la Plata

N

Bahía Blanca

Mar del Plata

ATLANTIC OCEAN

Chiloé

Archipiélago de los Chonos

Comodoro Rivadavia

National Capital

Secondary Capital (State, Province, or Territory)

City over 1,000,000 population

City of 250,000 to 1,000,000 population

City under 250,000 population

FALKLAND ISLANDS (U.K.)

West Falkland

East Falkland

Strait of Magellan

Punta Arenas

Tierra del Fuego

South Georgia (U.K.)

0   200   400   600   800   1000 Miles

0   300   600   900   1200   1500 Kilometers

Copyright by Rand McNally & Co.

Lambert Azimuthal Equal Area Projection

Drake Passage

South Shetland Islands (U.K.)

South Orkney Islands (U.K.)

South Sandwich Islands (U.K.)

RAND McNALLY

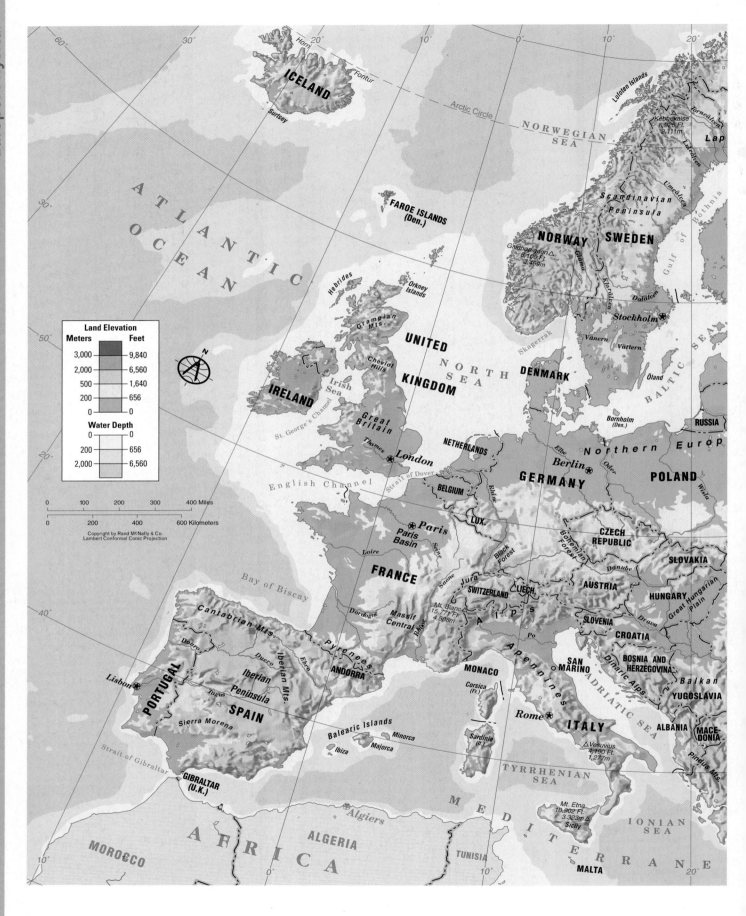

ICELAND

Horn

Fontur

Surtsey

ARCTIC OCEAN

NORWEGIAN SEA

Lofoten Islands

Tornealven

Kebnekaise 6,926 Ft. 2,111m

Lap

ATLANTIC OCEAN

FAROE ISLANDS (Den.)

Scandinavian Peninsula

NORWAY SWEDEN

Galdhøpiggen 8,100 Ft. 2,469m

Glomma

Klarälven

Dalälven

Gulf of Bothnia

Hebrides

Orkney Islands

Stockholm

Vänern

Vättern

Öland

BALTIC SEA

UNITED KINGDOM

Grampian Mts.

Cheviot Hills

NORTH SEA

DENMARK

Skagerrak

Land Elevation

Meters		Feet
3,000		9,840
2,000		6,560
500		1,640
200		656
0		0

Water Depth

0		0
200		656
2,000		6,560

Irish Sea

IRELAND

Great Britain

Bornholm (Den.)

RUSSIA

Northern Europ

St. George's Channel

Thames

London

NETHERLANDS

Elbe

Berlin

Oder

GERMANY

POLAND

Wisła

English Channel

Strait of Dover

BELGIUM

Rhine

LUX.

Black Forest

Bohemian Forest

CZECH REPUBLIC

SLOVAKIA

| 0 | 100 | 200 | 300 | 400 Miles |
| 0 | 200 | 400 | 600 Kilometers |

Copyright by Rand McNally & Co.
Lambert Conformal Conic Projection

Paris

Paris Basin

Seine

Loire

Danube

Saône

Jura

SWITZERLAND

LIECH.

AUSTRIA

HUNGARY

Great Hungarian Plain

FRANCE

Massif Central

Rhône

A l p s

SLOVENIA

Drava

Po

CROATIA

Bay of Biscay

Dordogne

Mt. Blanc 15,771 Ft. 4,808m

Apennines

SAN MARINO

Dinaric Alps

BOSNIA AND HERZEGOVINA

Balkan

Cantabrian Mts.

Pyrenees

MONACO

ADRIATIC SEA

YUGOSLAVIA

Douro

Iberian Mts.

ANDORRA

Corsica (Fr.)

ALBANIA

MACE- DONIA

Ebro

PORTUGAL

Lisbon

Duero

Tagus

Iberian Peninsula

SPAIN

Sierra Morena

Rome

ITALY

Pindus Mts.

Balearic Islands

Minorca

Sardinia (It.)

△Vesuvius 4,190 Ft. 1,277m

Ibiza

Majorca

TYRRHENIAN SEA

IONIAN SEA

Strait of Gibraltar

GIBRALTAR (U.K.)

Mt. Etna 10,902 Ft. 3,323m △

Sicily

MOROCCO

Algiers

AFRICA

ALGERIA

TUNISIA

M E D I T E R R A N E

MALTA

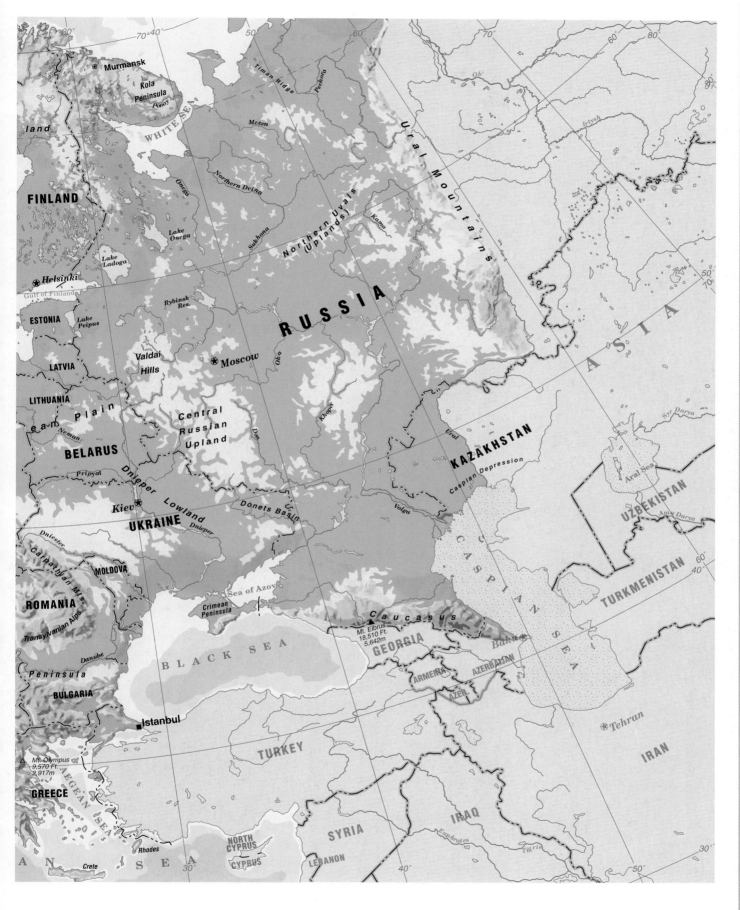

Murmansk
Kola
Peninsula
Ponoy

FINLAND

land

WHITE SEA

Timan Ridge

Pechora

Ural Mountains

Ob

Irtysh

Mezen

Northern Dvina

Onega

Lake
Onega

Sukhona

Northern Uvals
(Uplands)

Kama

ASIA

Lake
Ladoga

Helsinki

Gulf of Finland

ESTONIA

Rybinsk
Res.

RUSSIA

50°

70°

Lake
Peipus

LATVIA

Valdai
Hills

Moscow

Oka

Don

Khopër

LITHUANIA

e a m   P l a i n

Neman

Central
Russian
Upland

BELARUS

Pripyat

Dnieper

Ural

KAZAKHSTAN

Caspian Depression

Aral Sea

UZBEKISTAN

Syr Darya

Amu Darya

Kiev

Lowland

Dniester

UKRAINE

Donets Basin

Dnieper

Volga

CASPIAN SEA

TURKMENISTAN

60°

40°

MOLDOVA

Carpathian Mts.

Sea of Azov

Crimean
Peninsula

ROMANIA

Transylvanian Alps

Danube

Caucasus

Mt. Elbrus
18,510 Ft.
5,642m

Baku

Peninsula

GEORGIA

BLACK SEA

BULGARIA

ARMENIA

AZERBAIJAN

AZER.

Istanbul

Mt. Olympus
9,570 Ft.
2,917m

TURKEY

Tehran

IRAN

GREECE

AEGEAN SEA

Rhodes

Crete

SEA

30°

NORTH
CYPRUS

CYPRUS

SYRIA

LEBANON

IRAQ

Euphrates

Tigris

50°

30°

A N

RAND MCNALLY

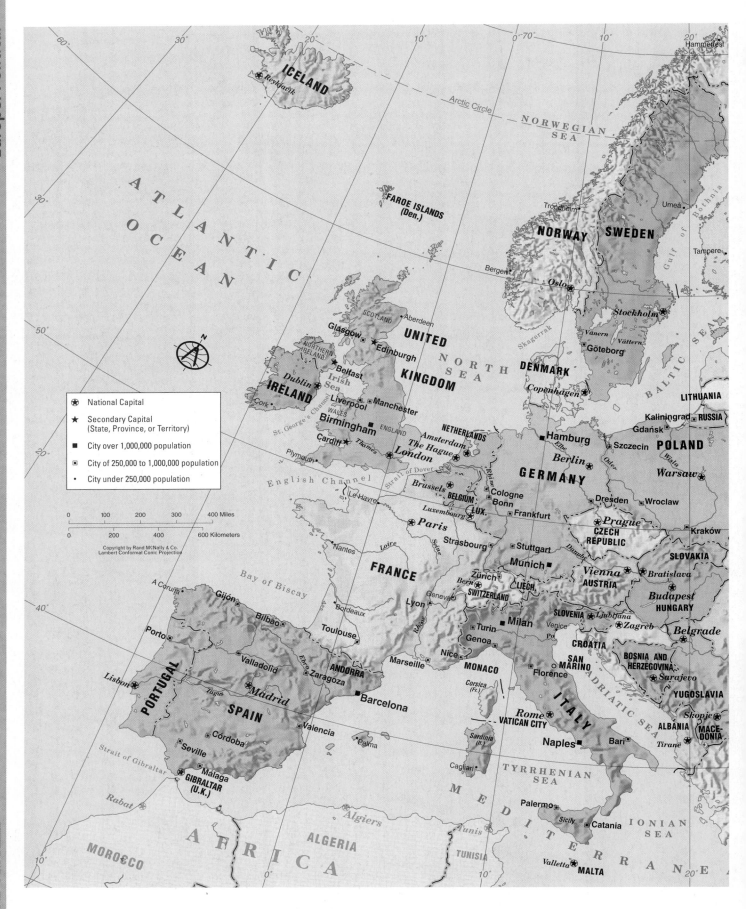

National Capital

Secondary Capital
(State, Province, or Territory)

■ City over 1,000,000 population

▣ City of 250,000 to 1,000,000 population

• City under 250,000 population

0   100   200   300   400 Miles

0   200   400   600 Kilometers

Copyright by Rand McNally & Co.
Lambert Conformal Conic Projection

ATLANTIC OCEAN

ICELAND
Reykjavík

NORWEGIAN SEA

Arctic Circle

FAROE ISLANDS
(Den.)

Hammerfest

NORWAY   SWEDEN

Trondheim   Umeå

Gulf of Bothnia

Bergen

Oslo   Tampere

Vänern   Vättern

Stockholm   Göteborg

Skagerrak

DENMARK

Copenhagen

BALTIC SEA

LITHUANIA

Kaliningrad   RUSSIA

Gdańsk

Szczecin   POLAND

Hamburg

Berlin   Warsaw

Odra

GERMANY

Dresden   Wroclaw

Cologne
Bonn
Frankfurt

Prague
CZECH REPUBLIC

Kraków

SLOVAKIA

Stuttgart

Munich   Vienna   Bratislava

AUSTRIA

Budapest
HUNGARY

Belgrade

SCOTLAND
Aberdeen

Glasgow
Edinburgh   UNITED KINGDOM

NORTH SEA

NORTHERN IRELAND
Belfast

Dublin   Irish Sea

IRELAND

Cork

Liverpool   Manchester

WALES   ENGLAND

Birmingham

Cardiff   Thames

London

Plymouth

St. George's Channel

English Channel

Strait of Dover

Le Havre

NETHERLANDS
Amsterdam
The Hague

Brussels   BELGIUM

Luxembourg   LUX.

Paris
Strasbourg

Zürich
Bern   LIECH.
SWITZERLAND

Geneva

Lyon

Turin   Milan

Genoa

Nice

Venice

SLOVENIA   Ljubljana

Zagreb

CROATIA

SAN MARINO

BOSNIA AND HERZEGOVINA

Sarajevo

YUGOSLAVIA

Skopje

ALBANIA   MACEDONIA

Tiranë

Nantes

Loire

Seine

FRANCE

Rhine

Danube

Po

ADRIATIC SEA

ITALY

A Coruña

Gijón

Bilbao

Porto

Valladolid

Bordeaux

Toulouse

Bay of Biscay

Ebro   Zaragoza
ANDORRA

Marseille

MONACO

Corsica (Fr.)

Florence

Rome
VATICAN CITY

Naples   Bari

PORTUGAL

Lisbon

Tagus

Madrid
SPAIN

Córdoba

Seville

Málaga

Valencia

Barcelona

Palma

Sardinia (It.)

Cagliari

TYRRHENIAN SEA

Palermo

Sicily   Catania

IONIAN SEA

Valletta   MALTA

MEDITERRANEAN

Strait of Gibraltar

GIBRALTAR (U.K.)

Rabat

Algiers

MOROCCO   AFRICA   ALGERIA

Tunis

TUNISIA

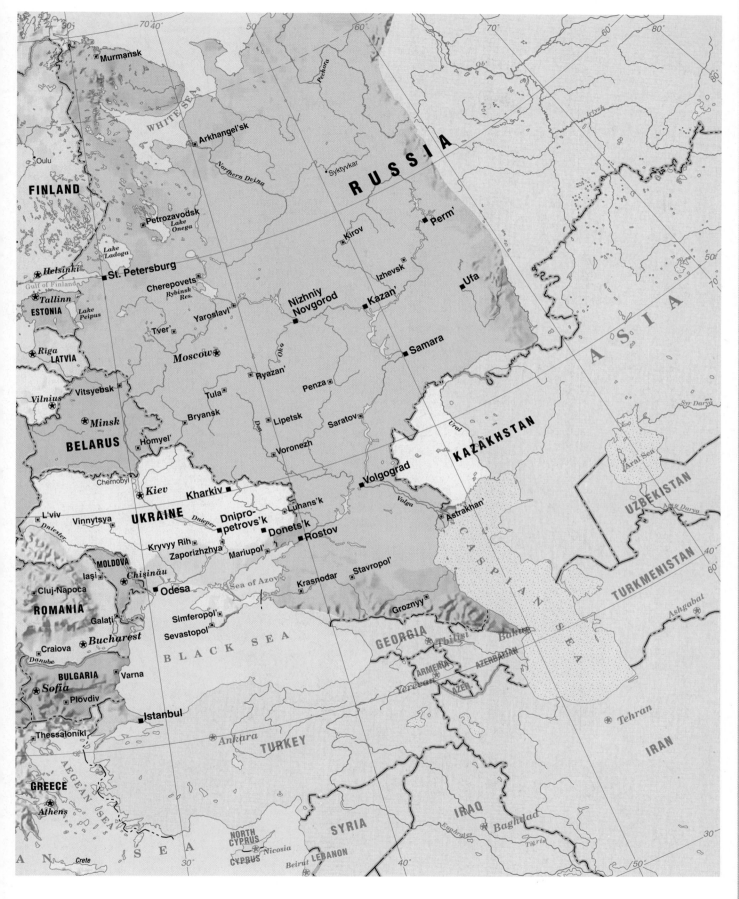

Murmansk

FINLAND

Oulu

WHITE SEA

Arkhangel'sk

Northern Dvina

Syktyvkar

Pechora

RUSSIA

Ob'

Irtysh

Petrozavodsk
Lake
Onega

Kirov

Perm'

Lake Ladoga

Helsinki

St. Petersburg

Cherepovets
Rybinsk Res.

Izhevsk

Ufa

Gulf of Finland

Tallinn

ESTONIA

Lake Peipus

Yaroslavl'

Nizhniy
Novgorod

Kazan'

Oka

ASIA

Riga

LATVIA

Tver'

Moscow

Ryazan'

Samara

Vilnius

Vitsyebsk

Tula

Penza

Volga

Syr Darya

Minsk

Bryansk

Lipetsk

Saratov

Ural

KAZAKHSTAN

Aral Sea

BELARUS

Homyel'

Don

Voronezh

Chernobyl

Kiev

Kharkiv

Volgograd

UZBEKISTAN

L'viv

Vinnytsya

UKRAINE

Dnieper

Dnipro-
petrovs'k

Luhans'k

Astrakhan'

Amu Darya

Dniester

Kryvyy Rih
Zaporizhzhya

Donets'k

Rostov

CASPIAN SEA

TURKMENISTAN

MOLDOVA

Iaşi

Chişinău

Mariupol'

Sea of Azov

Krasnodar

Stavropol'

Ashgabat

Cluj-Napoca

Odesa

ROMANIA

Simferopol'

Groznyy

Baku

Galaţi

Sevastopol'

BLACK SEA

GEORGIA

Tbilisi

AZERBAIJAN

Craiova

Bucharest

ARMENIA

AZER.

Danube

BULGARIA

Varna

Yerevan

Tehran

Sofia

Plovdiv

IRAN

Istanbul

Thessaloniki

Ankara

TURKEY

GREECE

Athens

AEGEAN SEA

SYRIA

IRAQ

Euphrates

Baghdad

Crete

NORTH
CYPRUS

Nicosia

CYPRUS

Beirut

LEBANON

Tigris

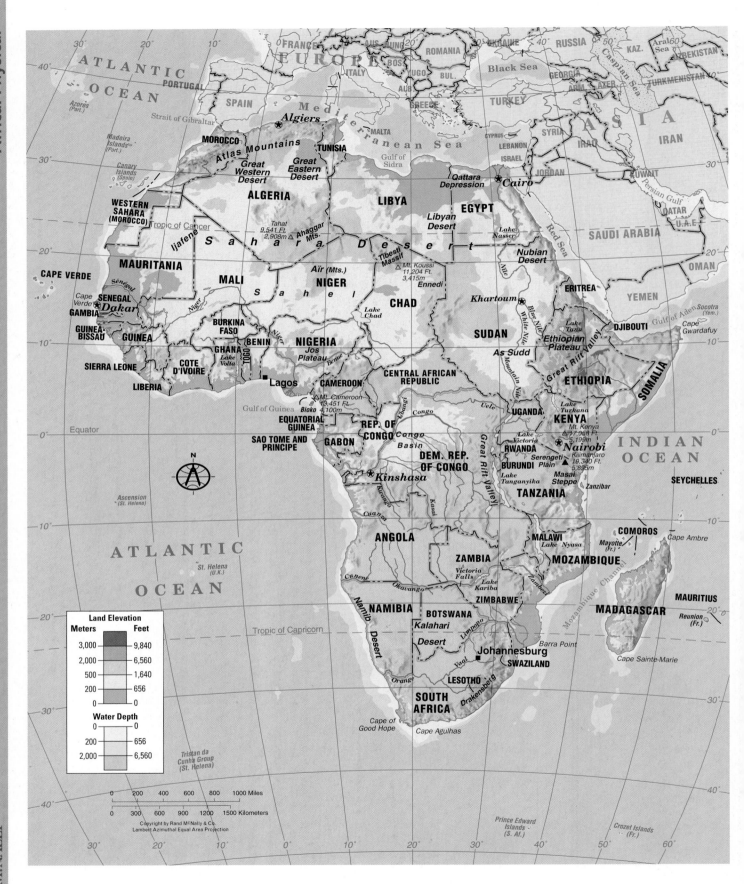

ATLANTIC
OCEAN

EUROPE

FRANCE
PORTUGAL
SPAIN
AUS. HUNG. ROMANIA
ITALY BOS. YUGO. BUL.
ALB.
GREECE
MALTA
Strait of Gibraltar
Azores
(Port.)
Madeira
Islands
(Port.)
Canary
Islands
(Spain)

Mediterranean Sea

RUSSIA
UKRAINE
Black Sea
GEORGIA
TURKEY
CYPRUS
SYRIA
LEBANON
ISRAEL
JORDAN
IRAQ
KUWAIT

KAZ.
Aral
Sea
UZBEKISTAN
TURKMENISTAN
ARM. AZER.
Caspian Sea
IRAN

MOROCCO
Atlas Mountains
TUNISIA
Algiers
Great
Western
Desert
Great
Eastern
Desert
Gulf of
Sidra
Qattara
Depression
Cairo
EGYPT
LIBYA

ALGERIA
Libyan
Desert

WESTERN
SAHARA
(MOROCCO)
Tropic of Cancer
Ijafene
Tahat
9,541 Ft.
2,908m
Ahaggar
Mts.
S a h a r a   D e s e r t
Nubian
Desert
Lake
Nasser
Red Sea
SAUDI ARABIA
OMAN

MAURITANIA
Aïr (Mts.)
Tibesti
Massif
Mt. Koussi
11,204 Ft.
3,415m
Ennedi
Nile
SUDAN
ERITREA
YEMEN
Gulf of Aden
Cape
Gwardafuy
Socotra
(Yem.)

MALI
NIGER
CHAD
Khartoum
DJIBOUTI

CAPE VERDE
Sénégal
Senegal
Cape
Verde
Dakar
GAMBIA
GUINEA-
BISSAU
GUINEA
SIERRA LEONE
LIBERIA
S a h e l
BURKINA
FASO
BENIN
GHANA
Lake
Volta
COTE
D'IVOIRE
Niger
NIGERIA
Jos
Plateau
Benue
Lake
Chad
CENTRAL AFRICAN
REPUBLIC
As Sudd
Blue Nile
White Nile
Mountain Nile
Lake
Tana
Ethiopian
Plateau
Great Rift Valley
ETHIOPIA
SOMALIA

Lagos
CAMEROON
Mt. Cameroon
13,451 Ft.
4,100m
Bioko
EQUATORIAL
GUINEA
Gulf of Guinea
Ubangi
Congo
Uele
UGANDA
KENYA
Mt. Kenya
17,058 Ft.
5,199m
Lake
Turkana

Equator

SAO TOME AND
PRINCIPE
GABON
REP. OF
CONGO
Congo
Basin
Congo
DEM. REP.
OF CONGO
Kwango
Kasai
Lake
Victoria
RWANDA
BURUNDI
Nairobi
Kilimanjaro
19,340 Ft.
5,895m
Serengeti
Plain
Masai
Steppe
Zanzibar
INDIAN
OCEAN

Ascension
(St. Helena)
Kinshasa
Cuanza
Great Rift Valley
Lake
Tanganyika
TANZANIA
SEYCHELLES

ATLANTIC
OCEAN
St. Helena
(U.K.)
ANGOLA
Cunene
Cuando
MALAWI
Lake Nyasa
ZAMBIA
Victoria
Falls
Lake
Kariba
Zambezi
MOZAMBIQUE
COMOROS
Mayotte
(Fr.)
Cape Ambre
MADAGASCAR
MAURITIUS
Reunion
(Fr.)

Okavango
NAMIBIA
Namib
Desert
BOTSWANA
Kalahari
Desert
ZIMBABWE
Limpopo
Barra Point
Mozambique Channel

Tropic of Capricorn

Johannesburg
SWAZILAND
Vaal
LESOTHO
Drakensberg
Orange
SOUTH
AFRICA
Cape of
Good Hope
Cape Agulhas
Cape Sainte-Marie

N

Land Elevation
Meters		Feet
3,000		9,840
2,000		6,560
500		1,640
200		656
0		0

Water Depth
0		0
200		656
2,000		6,560

Tristan da
Cunha Group
(St. Helena)

0   200   400   600   800   1000 Miles
0   300   600   900   1200 1500 Kilometers
Copyright by Rand McNally & Co.
Lambert Azimuthal Equal Area Projection

Prince Edward
Islands
(S. Af.)
Crozet Islands
(Fr.)

RAND McNALLY

ATLANTIC
OCEAN

30° 20° 10° FRANCE AUS. HUN. ROMANIA UKRAINE 40° RUSSIA 50° KAZ. Aral 60°
40° EUROPE BOS. YUGO. BUL. Black Sea GEORGIA Caspian Sea UZBEKISTAN
PORTUGAL ITALY ALB. TURKMENISTAN 70°
Madeira Rome GREECE TURKEY ARM. AZER.
Islands SPAIN Madrid Athens CYPRUS SYRIA IRAN
(Port.) Mediterranean Sea MALTA LEBANON IRAQ
Azores Strait of Gibraltar ISRAEL JORDAN KUWAIT
(Port.) Algiers Qacentina Tunis Persian Gulf QATAR
Rabat Oran TUNISIA Tripoli Gulf of Banghāzī QATAR U.A.E.
Casablanca Ghardaia Sidra Alexandria Cairo 30°
MOROCCO Suez SAUDI ARABIA OMAN
Marrakech Tropic of Cancer Riyadh
WESTERN El Aaiún ALGERIA LIBYA EGYPT Asyut
SAHARA In Salah Aswan
(MOROCCO) Sabhá Lake Red Sea
Tamanrasset Nasser Port Sudan 20°
MAURITANIA Nile YEMEN Socotra
CAPE VERDE Nouakchott MALI NIGER CHAD Omdurman ERITREA (Yem.)
Timbuktu Gao Agadez Khartoum Asmara Gulf of Aden
Dakar Senegal Lake Chad Abéché SUDAN Lake DJIBOUTI
SENEGAL Bamako Niger Niamey N'Djamena Blue Nile Tana Djibouti 10°
GAMBIA BURKINA FASO Kano DJIBOUTI
GUINEA- Ouagadougou ETHIOPIA Dire SOMALIA
BISSAU GUINEA BENIN NIGERIA Abuja Waw Addis Dawa
Conakry GHANA Lake Niger CENTRAL AFRICAN Ababa
Freetown Volta Benue REPUBLIC Mountain Nile
SIERRA LEONE COTE Cotonou Bangui Uele Mogadishu
Monrovia D'IVOIRE Lagos CAMEROON Ubangi Congo UGANDA Equator 0°
LIBERIA Accra Douala Yaoundé Kisangani Kampala Lake KENYA
Abidjan Malabo REP. OF Victoria Nairobi INDIAN
EQUATORIAL CONGO DEM. REP. Kigali RWANDA Mombasa OCEAN
GUINEA Libreville OF CONGO BURUNDI
SAO TOME AND GABON Bujumbura SEYCHELLES
PRINCIPE Brazzaville Lake Dodoma
Kinshasa Tanganyika TANZANIA Dar es Salaam 10°
Mbuji-Mayi COMOROS
Luanda Kolwezi Mayotte
Lobito Lubumbashi MALAWI (Fr.) Antsiranana
ATLANTIC Huambo Ndola Lake Nyasa
ANGOLA ZAMBIA Lilongwe MOZAMBIQUE
St. Helena Lusaka MADAGASCAR MAURITIUS
(U.K.) Lake Harare Beira Fianarantsoa Reunion
OCEAN Okavango Kariba ZIMBABWE Mozambique Channel (Fr.) 20°
NAMIBIA BOTSWANA
Windhoek Limpopo
Tropic of Capricorn Gaborone Pretoria Maputo
Johannesburg SWAZILAND
Orange Maseru LESOTHO Durban 30°
SOUTH Port Elizabeth
Cape Town AFRICA

National Capital
Secondary Capital (State, Province, or Territory)
City over 1,000,000 population
City of 250,000 to 1,000,000 population
City under 250,000 population

Tristan da
Cunha Group
(St. Helena)

0 200 400 600 800 1000 Miles
0 300 600 900 1200 1500 Kilometers
Copyright by Rand McNally & Co.
Lambert Azimuthal Equal Area Projection

Prince Edward
Islands
(S. Af.)

Crozet Islands
(Fr.)

RAND McNALLY

ATLANTIC OCEAN

ARCTIC OCEAN

ICELAND

Arctic Circle

Barents Sea

Severnaya Zemlya

Novaya Zemlya

Kara Sea

Yamal Pen.

FAROE ISLANDS (Den.)

IRELAND

UNITED KINGDOM

London

North Sea

DENMARK

NORWAY

SWEDEN

FINLAND

Ob

West Siberian Lowland

Ural Mountains

Novosibirsk

Yenisey

Irtysh

PORTUGAL

SPAIN

FRANCE

GERMANY

NETH.

BEL.

LUX.

SWITZ.

AUSTRIA

ITALY

MONACO

ANDORRA

ESTONIA

LATVIA

LITH.

POLAND

BELARUS

CZECH REP.

SLOVAKIA

HUNGARY

SLOVENIA

CROATIA

BOS.

YUGO.

UKRAINE

Moscow

Volga

Astana

KAZAKHSTAN

Ishim

MOROCCO

ALGERIA

TUNISIA

Mediterranean Sea

ALB.

MAC.

GREECE

BULGARIA

ROMANIA

Black Sea

Ankara

TURKEY

GEORGIA

Caucasus

Mount Ararat 16,940 Ft. 5,165m

ARM.

AZER.

Caspian Depression

Aral Sea

Syr Darya

Lake Balkhash

Tian Shan

N. CYPRUS

CYPRUS

LEBANON

SYRIA

ISRAEL

JORDAN

IRAQ

Tigris

Euphrates

Tehran

Caspian Sea

Ust-Urt Plateau

Kara Kum (Desert)

UZBEKISTAN

Amu Darya

TURKMENISTAN

KYRGYZSTAN

TAJIKISTAN

Pamirs

Tarim Basin

K2 (Qogir Feng) 28,250 Ft. 8,611m

Altun Shan

LIBYA

Cairo

Nile

EGYPT

Sinai Pen.

Red Sea

An-Nafud

SAUDI ARABIA

Arabian Peninsula

KUWAIT

Zagros Mts.

Dasht-e Kavir

IRAN

Persian Gulf

BAHRAIN

QATAR

U.A.E.

Gulf of Oman

AFGHANISTAN

Hindu Kush

HIMALAYA MTS.

Kunlun Mts.

PAKISTAN

Indus

Great Indian Desert

New Delhi

NEPAL

Mt. Everest 29,035 Ft. 8,850m

Ganges

CHAD

SUDAN

ERITREA

DJIBOUTI

ETHIOPIA

Rub Al-Khali

YEMEN

OMAN

Gulf of Aden

Socotra (Yem.)

Arabian Sea

Mumbai (Bombay)

Godavari

Deccan Plateau

Western Ghats

Eastern Ghats

INDIA

Bay of Bengal

DEM. REP. OF THE CONGO (ZAIRE)

UGANDA

RWANDA

BURUNDI

KENYA

SOMALIA

Lakshadweep (India)

SRI LANKA

TANZANIA

ZAMBIA

MALAWI

MOZAMBIQUE

MALDIVES

INDIAN OCEAN

N

| 0 | 200 | 400 | 600 | 800 Miles |

| 0 | 200 | 400 | 600 | 800 | 1000 Kilometers |

Copyright by Rand McNally & Co.
Lambert Azimuthal Equal Area Projection

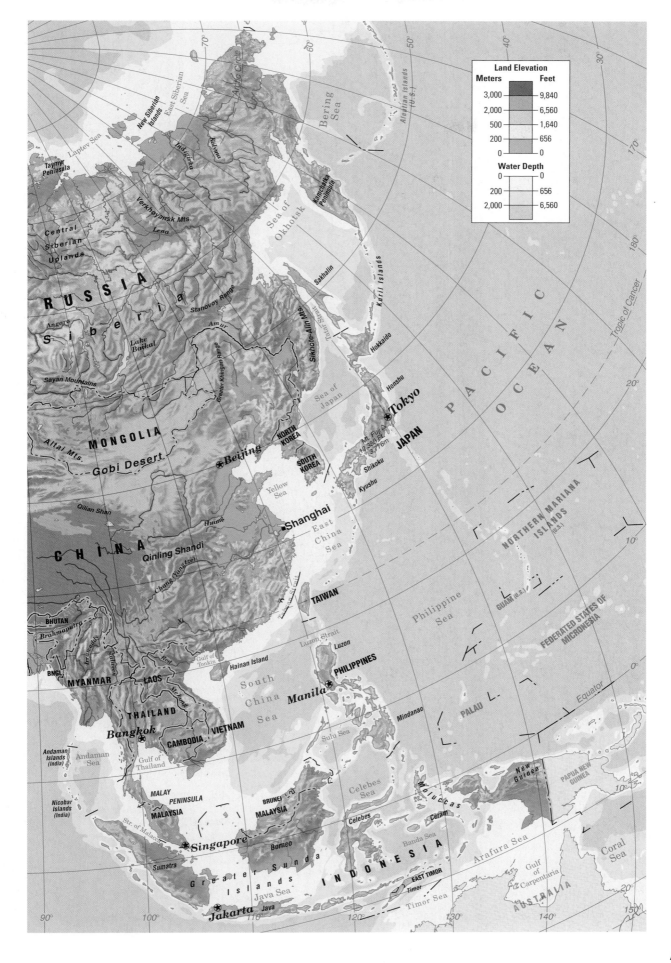

Land Elevation

Meters	Feet
3,000	9,840
2,000	6,560
500	1,640
200	656
0	0

Water Depth

0	0
200	656
2,000	6,560

New Siberian Islands

East Siberian Sea

Laptev Sea

Taymyr Peninsula

Indigirka

Kolyma

Bering Sea

Aleutian Islands (U.S.)

Verkhoyansk Mts.

Central Siberian Uplands

Lena

Kamchatka Peninsula

Sea of Okhotsk

RUSSIA

S i b e r i a

Angara

Stanovoy Range

Amur

Sakhalin

Kuril Islands

Lake Baikal

Sikhote-Alin Mts.

Tatar Strait

Arctic Circle

Sayan Mountains

Greater Khingan Range

Sea of Japan

Hokkaido

PACIFIC

OCEAN

Altai Mts.

MONGOLIA

Honshu

Tropic of Cancer

Gobi Desert

NORTH KOREA

Tokyo

Beijing

SOUTH KOREA

Mt. Fuji 12,388 ft. 3,776m

JAPAN

Shikoku

Qilian Shan

Yellow Sea

Kyushu

Huang

Shanghai

East China Sea

NORTHERN MARIANA ISLANDS (U.S.)

C H I N A

Qinling Shandi

Chang (Yangtze)

BHUTAN

Brahmaputra

Xi

TAIWAN

Philippine Sea

GUAM (U.S.)

FEDERATED STATES OF MICRONESIA

BNGL

Irrawaddy

Salween

Red

Gulf of Tonkin

Luzon Strait

Luzon

MYANMAR

LAOS

Hainan Island

PHILIPPINES

Mekong

South China Sea

Manila

PALAU

THAILAND

VIETNAM

Mindanao

Equator

Bangkok

CAMBODIA

Andaman Islands (India)

Andaman Sea

Gulf of Thailand

Sulu Sea

Celebes Sea

New Guinea

PAPUA NEW GUINEA

MALAY PENINSULA

BRUNEI

Moluccas

Nicobar Islands (India)

MALAYSIA

MALAYSIA

Celebes

Ceram

Str. of Malacca

Singapore

Borneo

Banda Sea

Arafura Sea

Coral Sea

Sumatra

G r e a t e r S u n d a I s l a n d s

EAST TIMOR

Gulf of Carpentaria

Jakarta

Java

I N D O N E S I A

Timor

AUSTRALIA

Java Sea

Timor Sea

RAND MCNALLY

ATLANTIC OCEAN

ARCTIC OCEAN

ICELAND

FAROE ISLANDS (Den.)

Arctic Circle

Norwegian Sea

SVALBARD (Nor.)

Spitsbergen

Franz Josef Land

Severnaya Zemlya

Barents Sea

Novaya Zemlya

Kara Sea

IRELAND
UNITED KINGDOM
London
PORTUGAL
SPAIN
MOROCCO
GIBRALTAR (U.K.)

North Sea
DENMARK
NETH.
BEL.
FRANCE
GERMANY
SWITZ.
NORWAY
SWEDEN
FINLAND
ESTONIA
LATVIA
LITH.
Kiev
Moscow
BELARUS
POLAND
UKRAINE
Volga

R U S

Noril'sk

Ob'
Yenisey

Yekaterinburg
Chelyabinsk

Ishim
Irtysh

Novosibirsk
Omsk
Barnaul
Ob'
Semipalatinsk
Öskemen

Astana
Karaganda

KAZAKHSTAN

Aral Sea

Lake Balkhash

Ürümqi

Almaty

ANDORRA
MONACO
ITALY
Adriatic Sea
BOS.
YUGO.
MAC.
ALB.
ROMANIA
Danube
BULGARIA
GREECE
Black Sea
Istanbul

ALGERIA
TUNISIA
Mediterranean Sea
LIBYA

Izmir
Ankara
TURKEY
N. CYPRUS
CYPRUS
LEBANON
SYRIA
Damascus
ISRAEL
Amman
JORDAN
GEORGIA
Tbilisi
ARM.
Yerevan
AZER.
Baku
Caspian Sea

Tabriz
Euphrates
TIGRIS
Baghdad
IRAQ
Tehran
IRAN
Mashhad
Esfahan

TURKMENISTAN
Ashgabat

UZBEKISTAN
Tashkent
Sir Darya

Bishkek
KYRGYZSTAN

Dushanbe
TAJIKISTAN

Kabul
AFGHANISTAN
Islamabad

Lahore
Amritsar
PAKISTAN
Indus

CHAD
EGYPT
Cairo
Nile

SUDAN
Red Sea
Nile

SAUDI ARABIA
Riyadh
Jiddah
Kuwait
KUWAIT
Persian Gulf
BAHRAIN
QATAR
Abu Dhabi
U.A.E.
Muscat
OMAN
Gulf of Oman

Karachi
Hyderābād
Delhi
New Delhi
Kānpur
Ganges
NEPAL
Kathmandu
Brahmaputra

Ahmadābād
INDIA
Nāgpur
Kolkata (Calcutta)
Godāvari
Ganges

ERITREA
DJIBOUTI
ETHIOPIA
Blue Nile
Gulf of Aden

YEMEN
Sanaá
Socotra (Yem.)

Arabian Sea

Mumbai (Bombay)
Hyderābād

Bay of Bengal

DEM. REP. OF THE CONGO (ZAIRE)
UGANDA
RWANDA
BURUNDI
KENYA
SOMALIA
TANZANIA

Bangalore
Lakshadweep (India)
Chennai (Madras)

N

Colombo
SRI LANKA

MALDIVES

I N D I A N   O C E A N

ZAMBIA
MALAWI
MOZAMBIQUE

0   200   400   600   800 Miles
0   200   400   600   800 1000 Kilometers
Copyright by Rand McNally & Co.
Lambert Azimuthal Equal Area Projection

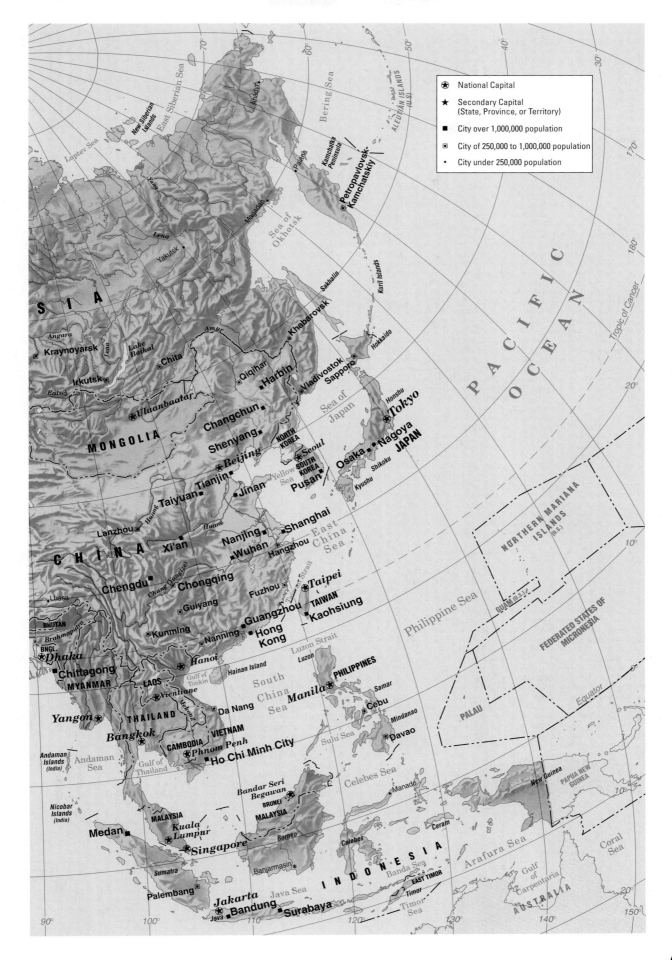

★ National Capital

★ Secondary Capital
(State, Province, or Territory)

■ City over 1,000,000 population

▣ City of 250,000 to 1,000,000 population

• City under 250,000 population

A S I A

New Siberian Islands

Laptev Sea

East Siberian Sea

Yana

Bering Sea

ALEUTIAN ISLANDS (U.S.)

Palana

Kamchatka Peninsula

Anadyr

Petropavlovsk-Kamchatskiy

Magadan

Sea of Okhotsk

Lena

Kraynoyarsk

Angara

Lake Batkal

Irkutsk

Yakutsk

Chita

Amur

Qiqihar

Harbin

Khabarovsk

Sakhalin

Kuril Islands

Hokkaido

Sapporo

Vladivostok

Sea of Japan

Honshu

Tokyo

Nagoya

JAPAN

Enisei

MONGOLIA

Ulaanbaatar

Changchun

Shenyang

NORTH KOREA

Beijing

Seoul

SOUTH KOREA

Pusan

Osaka

Shikoku

Kyushu

PACIFIC OCEAN

Tropic of Cancer

Tianjin

Taiyuan

Jinan

Yellow Sea

Lanzhou

Huang

Huang

Shanghai

East China Sea

NORTHERN MARIANA ISLANDS (U.S.)

C H I N A

Xi'an

Nanjing

Wuhan

Hangzhou

Chengdu

Chang (Yangtze)

Chongqing

Fuzhou

Taipei

TAIWAN

FEDERATED STATES OF MICRONESIA

Lhasa

Guiyang

Guangzhou

Kaohsiung

GUAM (U.S.)

BHUTAN

Brahmaputra

Kunming

Nanning

Hong Kong

Luzon Strait

Philippine Sea

BNGL.

Dhaka

Hanoi

Hainan Island

Luzon

Chittagong

Gulf of Tonkin

South China Sea

PHILIPPINES

MYANMAR

LAOS

Samar

Manila

PALAU

Vientiane

Da Nang

Mekong

Cebu

Yangon

THAILAND

VIETNAM

Mindanao

Davao

Bangkok

CAMBODIA

Phnom Penh

Ho Chi Minh City

Sulu Sea

Andaman Islands (India)

Andaman Sea

Gulf of Thailand

Celebes Sea

Manado

New Guinea

PAPUA NEW GUINEA

Bandar Seri Begawan

BRUNEI

Nicobar Islands (India)

MALAYSIA

Kuala Lumpur

MALAYSIA

Borneo

Ceram

Coral Sea

Medan

Singapore

Celebes

Sumatra

Banjarmasin

I N D O N E S I A

Banda Sea

Arafura Sea

Gulf of Carpentaria

Palembang

Jakarta

Bandung

Surabaya

Java

Java Sea

EAST TIMOR

Timor

Timor Sea

AUSTRALIA

A35

North Pole

Chukchi
Sea
Wrangell I.
East Siberian
Sea
New Siberian I.
New Siberian
Islands
Kotelny I.
Laptev Sea
Severnaya
Zemlya

ALASKA
(U.S.)
Brooks Range
Pt. Barrow
Point Barrow
CANADA
Inuvik
Norman Wells
Great Bear
Lake
Amundsen
Gulf
Banks
Beaufort
Sea
Prince Patrick
Island
Melville I.

ARCTIC OCEAN

North Magnetic
Pole
North Pole

VICTORIA IA
Kalukhuliak
Prince of
Wales I.
Gulf of
Boothia
Somerset I.
QUEEN ELIZABETH ISLANDS
Ellef
Ringnes I.
Axel
Heiberg I.
ELLESMERE I.
Alert
Lady
Eta
Thule
Bylot I.
BAFFIN
Baffin
Bay
Disko
Godhavn
Davis Strait
GREENLAND
(Den.)

RUSSIA
Verkhoyansk
Mts.
Verkhoyansk
Tiksi
Lena
Olenëk
Anabar
Taymyr
Peninsula
Lake
Taymyr
Khatanga
Kotuy
Kara
Sea
Dikson
Novaya
Zemlya
Franz
Josef
Land
SVALBARD
(Nor.)
SPITSBERGEN
Greenland Sea
Barents
Sea
Vorkuta
Pechora
North Cape
Jan Mayen
(Nor.)
Hammerfest
Murmansk
Kola
Peninsula
Arhangel'sk
NORWAY FINLAND

Godthåb
Angmagssalik
Gunnbjörn Fjeld
12,139 Ft.
3,700m

Srednekolymsk
Indigirka
Yana
Aldan

Greenland Sea
0   200   400   600 Miles
0   200 400 600 800 1000 Kilometers
Copyright by Rand McNally & Co.
Azimuthal Equidistant Projection

Land Elevation

Meters		Feet
3,000		9,840
2,000		6,560
500		1,640
200		656
0		0

Water Depth

0		0
200		656
2,000		6,560

South Pole

Strait of
Magellan
Cape Horn
FALKLAND ISLANDS
(U.K.)
Drake Passage
Scotia Sea
South Georgia
(U.K.)
South Shetland
Islands (U.K.)
Graham
Land
Adelaide I.
Alexander I.
Antarctic Peninsula
Larsen Ice
Shelf
South Orkney
Islands (U.K.)
South Sandwich
Islands (U.K.)

PACIFIC OCEAN
Antarctic Circle
Thurston I.
Bellingshausen
Sea
Amundsen
Sea
Ellsworth
Land
Mt. Sidley
13,717 Ft.
4,181m
Vinson Massif
16,066 Ft.
4,897m
Weddell Sea
Marie
Byrd
Land
Ronne Ice
Shelf
Berkner I.
Filchner Ice
Shelf
Rockefeller
Plateau
Pensacola
Mts.
Coats
Land
Cape Norvegia
Roosevelt I.
Mt. Kirkpatrick
14,856 Ft.
4,528m
Ross
Sea
Ross Ice
Shelf
Transantarctic Mountains
South
Pole
Queen Maud
Land
Mühlig
Hofmann
Mts.
Cape
Adare
Mt. Erebus
12,451 Ft.
3,785m
Victoria Land
ANTARCTICA
Ser Rondane
Mts.
George V Coast
Macquarie Island
(Austl.)
South
Magnetic
Pole
Wilkes Land
American
Highland
Lambert
Glacier
Amery Ice
Shelf
Enderby
Land
Napier
Mts.
Cape
Ann
Cape
Darnley
Cape
Poinsett
Antarctic Circle
Prince
Edward Is.
(S. Afr.)
Crozet
Archipelago
(Fr.)

INDIAN OCEAN
ATLANTIC OCEAN

0   200   400   600   800 1000 Miles
0   300 600 900 1200 1500 Kilometres
Copyright by Rand McNally & Co.
Polar Stereographic Projection

FLORIDA
STATE ALMANAC

CONTENTS

Florida State Information

Florida State Maps

FLORIDA
STATE ALMANAC

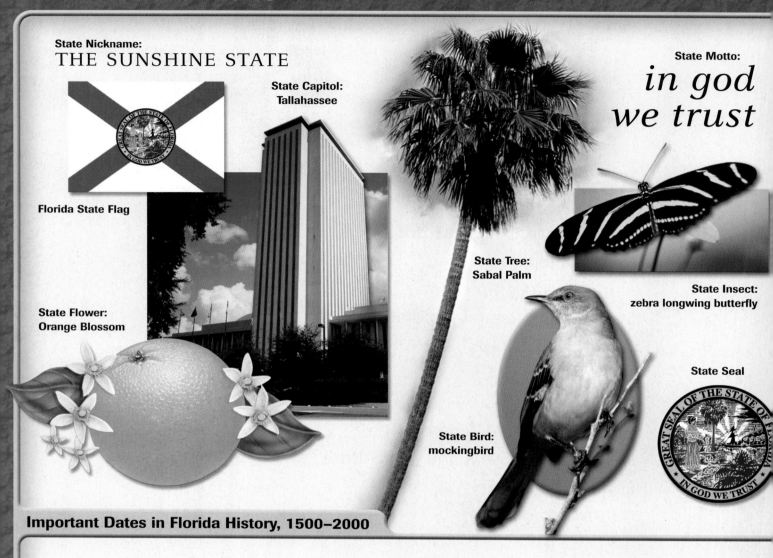

State Nickname:
THE SUNSHINE STATE

State Capitol:
Tallahassee

State Motto:
in god we trust

Florida State Flag

State Tree:
Sabal Palm

State Insect:
zebra longwing butterfly

State Flower:
Orange Blossom

State Seal

State Bird:
mockingbird

Important Dates in Florida History, 1500–2000

1513
Juan Ponce de Léon claims Florida for Spain.

1586
English admiral Sir Francis Drake plunders and burns St. Augustine.

1500 — 1600 — 1700

1565
Pedro Menéndez de Avilés establishes the first permanent European settlement at St. Augustine.

1763
Spain gives Britain Florida in exchange for Havana, Cuba, which Britain captured during the Seven Years' War.

GeoFunFacts

Landmass

Florida
58,681 sq mi

Continental United States
3,165,630 sq mi

Population

Florida
16,396,515

United States
284,796,887

Population (in millions)
0   75   150   225   300

Lakes

World's Largest
Caspian Sea
143,550 sq mi

U.S. Largest
Lake Superior
31,800 sq mi

Florida's Largest
Lake Okeechobee
680 sq mi

FunFact:
The name Florida probably comes from *Pascuar Florida,* the Spanish for Easter. Juan Ponce de Léon named the area *La Florida* shortly after he landed there during Easter of 1513.

1783
Before surrendering to American forces in the Revolutionary War, Britain gives Florida back to Spain to keep it out of American hands.

1861
Florida secedes from the United States to join the Confederacy on January 10.

1865
The Confederacy surrenders ending the Civil War. Florida's capital, Tallahassee, is the only Confederate capital east of the Mississippi not occupied by Union forces during the Civil War.

1937
Florida abolishes the poll tax as a requirement for voting.

1971
Walt Disney World opens near Orlando.

2000
Florida electoral votes are pivotal in the election of Texas Governor George W. Bush as president of the United States.

1800   **1900**   **2000**

1819
The United States and Spain negotiate the Adams-Onís Treaty, which gives the United States lawful claim to Florida.

1822
Congress creates the Territory of Florida.

1845
Florida becomes the 27th state in the Union on March 3.

1868
Florida is readmitted to the Union.

1880
Florida's first citrus nursery opens in Tampa.

1947
Everglades National Park is created.

1969
The first spacecraft to land humans on the moon, Apollo 11, is launched from Cape Canaveral.

1992
Hurricane Andrew strikes Florida, killing 54 people and causing $22 billion in property damage.

ATLANTIC OCEAN

ESCAMBIA · SANTA ROSA · OKALOOSA · HOLMES · JACKSON · WASHINGTON · WALTON · CALHOUN · GADSDEN · LEON · MADISON · HAMILTON · JEFFERSON · LIBERTY · WAKULLA · TAYLOR · GULF · FRANKLIN · BAY

Pensacola

Panama City

Tallahassee

Apalachicola R.

Suwannee R.

St. Johns R.

Jacksonville

NASSAU · DUVAL · BAKER · SUWANNEE · COLUMBIA · UNION · BRADFORD · CLAY · ST. JOHNS

St. Augustine

LAFAYETTE · DIXIE · GILCHRIST · ALACHUA · PUTNAM

Gainesville

FLAGLER

LEVY · MARION

Ocala

VOLUSIA

Daytona Beach

CITRUS · SUMTER · LAKE · SEMINOLE

Titusville

Cape Canaveral

HERNANDO · PASCO

ORANGE

Orlando

Kissimmee

OSCEOLA

POLK

Tampa

Clearwater

PINELLAS

Lakeland

BREVARD

St. Petersburg

HILLSBOROUGH

Tampa Bay

MANATEE

INDIAN RIVER

Bradenton

HARDEE

Fort Pierce

OKEECHOBEE

ST. LUCIE

Sarasota

SARASOTA

Peace R.

DE SOTO

HIGHLANDS

MARTIN

Lake Okeechobee

Port Charlotte

CHARLOTTE

GLADES

Caloosahatchee R.

West Palm Beach

Fort Myers

LEE

HENDRY

PALM BEACH

Fort Lauderdale

COLLIER

BROWARD

Miami

MONROE

MIAMI-DADE

MONROE

Key West

Gulf of Mexico

KEY

★ State capital

• Other city

95 Interstate

0   50   100 miles

0   50   100 kilometers

Albers Equal-Area Projection

GeoFunFact

In terms of land area, Collier County, located in the southwest of the state, is Florida's largest county. It covers more than 2,025 square miles, about 4 percent of Florida's total land area.

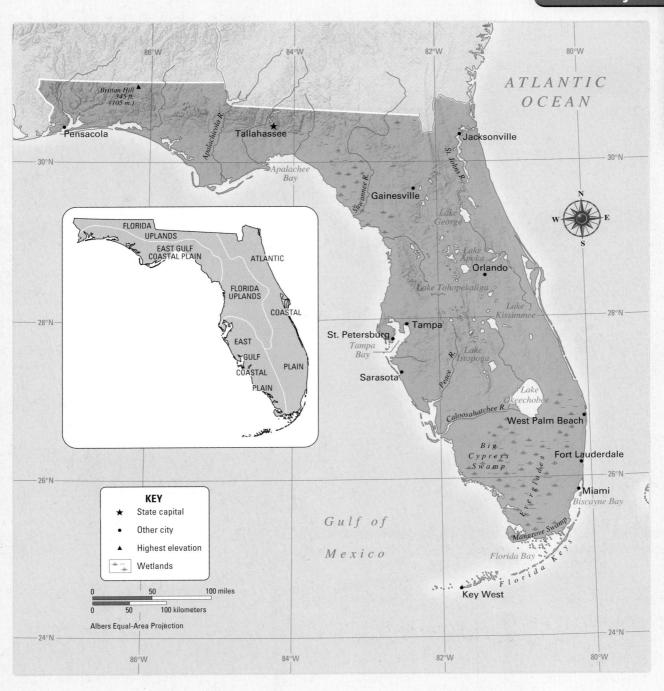

ATLANTIC OCEAN

Britton Hill
345 ft.
(105 m.)

Pensacola

Tallahassee

Apalachicola R.

Apalachee Bay

Jacksonville

Gainesville

Suwannee R.

St. Johns R.

Lake George

Lake Apoka

Orlando

Lake Tohopekaliga

Lake Kissimmee

Tampa

St. Petersburg

Tampa Bay

Sarasota

Peace R.

Lake Istopoga

Lake Okeechobee

Caloosahatchee R.

West Palm Beach

Big Cypress Swamp

Everglades

Fort Lauderdale

Miami

Biscayne Bay

Mangrove Swamp

Florida Bay

Florida Keys

Key West

Gulf of Mexico

FLORIDA UPLANDS

EAST GULF COASTAL PLAIN

ATLANTIC

FLORIDA UPLANDS

COASTAL

EAST GULF COASTAL PLAIN

PLAIN

KEY

★ State capital

● Other city

▲ Highest elevation

▬ Wetlands

0   50   100 miles

0   50   100 kilometers

Albers Equal-Area Projection

GeoFunFact

Some 24 percent of Florida's land area consists of wet-lands—swamps and marshes.

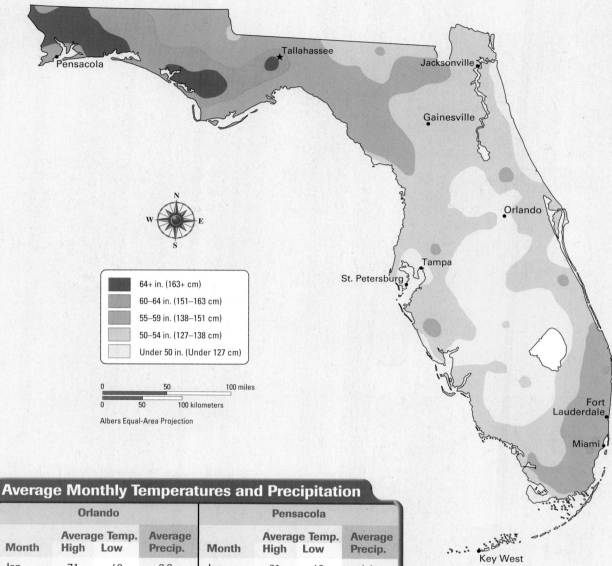

64+ in. (163+ cm)

60–64 in. (151–163 cm)

55–59 in. (138–151 cm)

50–54 in. (127–138 cm)

Under 50 in. (Under 127 cm)

0   50   100 miles

0   50   100 kilometers

Albers Equal-Area Projection

Average Monthly Temperatures and Precipitation

	Orlando				Pensacola		
Month	**Average Temp.** High	Low	**Average Precip.**	**Month**	**Average Temp.** High	Low	**Average Precip.**
Jan.	71	49	2.8	Jan.	61	43	4.4
Feb.	73	50	3.1	Feb.	63	46	4.9
Mar.	78	55	2.9	Mar.	68	52	5.5
Apr.	83	59	2.2	Apr.	75	59	4.2
May	88	66	3.5	May	82	66	3.9
June	91	72	6.0	June	87	73	5.1
July	92	73	5.4	July	89	75	6.8
Aug.	92	73	6.2	Aug.	89	75	6.1
Sept.	90	72	6.3	Sept.	86	71	6.5
Oct.	85	69	4.1	Oct.	79	60	4.3
Nov.	79	58	2.8	Nov.	69	51	3.5
Dec.	73	51	2.6	Dec.	63	45	3.9

 GeoFunFact

With annual average precipitation of 54 inches, Florida is the nation's second wettest state. Only Louisiana has a higher annual precipitation rate.

Florida: Industry, Agriculture, Resources

Cotton
Forest Products
Sugar Cane
Cotton
Peanuts
Hogs
Corn
Corn
Forest Products
Hogs
Fish
Forest Products
Fish
Fish
Tallahassee
Peanuts
Phosphate Rock
Corn
Corn
Jacksonville
Forest Products
Fish
Beef
Vegetables
Hogs
Poultry
Vegetables
Fish
Phosphate Rock
Vegetables
Fruits
Fish
Fruits
Fruits
Orlando
Fruits
Fish
Fruits
Fruits
Fruits
Tampa
Phosphate Rock
Fruits
St. Petersburg
Fruits
Fruits
Fish
Dairy
Beef
Beef
Fruits
Phosphate Rock
Fruits
Fruits
Fish
Poultry
Beef
Beef
Vegetables
Sugar Cane
Vegetables
Fort Lauderdale
Dairy
Miami
Vegetables

Major manufacturing areas
Major agricultural areas

0   50   100 miles
0   50   100 kilometers
Albers Equal-Area Projection

GeoFunFact

Florida is responsible for more than 75 percent of citrus production in the United States. The rest of the country's citrus fruit is produced in the states of California, Texas, and Arizona.

A45

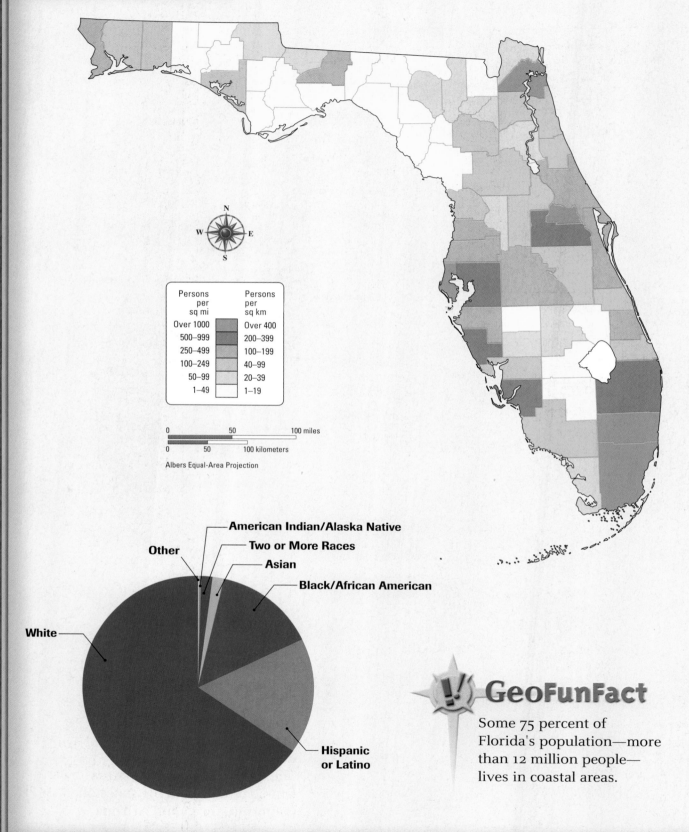

Persons per sq mi | Persons per sq km
Over 1000 | Over 400
500–999 | 200–399
250–499 | 100–199
100–249 | 40–99
50–99 | 20–39
1–49 | 1–19

0   50   100 miles
0   50   100 kilometers

Albers Equal-Area Projection

American Indian/Alaska Native
Two or More Races
Other
Asian
Black/African American
White
Hispanic or Latino

GeoFunFact

Some 75 percent of Florida's population—more than 12 million people—lives in coastal areas.

Florida National Parks

GULF ISLANDS
NATL. SEASHORE

Tallahassee

Jacksonville

Timucuan Ecological
and Historical Preserve

Fort Caroline
National Memorial

Castillo De San Marcos
National Monument

Fort Matanzas
National Monument

CANAVERAL
NATIONAL
SEASHORE

Tampa

St. Petersburg

De Soto
Natl. Memorial

Lake
Okeechobee

BIG CYPRESS
N. PRESERVE

Miami

EVERGLADES
NATL. PARK

BISCAYNE
N. PARK

DRY TORTUGAS
NATIONAL PARK

KEY

★ State capital

• Other city

95 Interstate

National parks, preserves,
and seashores

National monument

0 ——— 50 ——— 100 miles
0 ——— 50 ——— 100 kilometers

Albers Equal-Area Projection

GeoFunFact

The Everglades National Park is
the only subtropical nature preserve in North America. It also
is the only place in the world
where alligators and crocodiles
live side by side.

Unit 1

The Basics of Geography

The earth is a unique planet capable of supporting a wide variety of life forms. Human beings adapt and alter the environments on earth.

PHYSICAL GEOGRAPHY Internal and external forces constantly change the earth's surface. Here the volcano Arenal, located in Costa Rica, spews molten rock that will cool and alter the land.

GeoData

PHYSICAL GEOGRAPHY The earth is not round but is slightly flattened at the poles.

PHYSICAL GEOGRAPHY The total distance from the highest point on earth, Mt. Everest (29,035 ft.), to the lowest point on earth, Mariana Trench (35,840 ft. below sea level), is just over 12 miles.

HUMAN GEOGRAPHY The world's population growth in 1999 was an additional 84 million people, or about 230,000 people per day.

For more information on physical and human geography . . .

RESEARCH LINKS
CLASSZONE.COM

BASICS

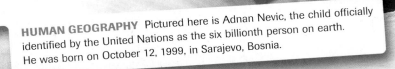

HUMAN GEOGRAPHY Pictured here is Adnan Nevic, the child officially identified by the United Nations as the six billionth person on earth. He was born on October 12, 1999, in Sarajevo, Bosnia.

The Basics of Geography **3**

PHYSICAL GEOGRAPHY
Looking at the Earth

Road Map

Heat Sensing Scan

Seneca Falls, New York,
is represented in a road
map, a heat sensing
(thermal) scan, and
a satellite image.

Satellite Image

Geo**Focus**

How do geographers view the world?

Taking Notes Copy the graphic organizer
below into your notebook. Use it to record
information about the work of geographers
and the themes of geography.

5 Themes:
Tools:

The Five Themes of Geography

Main Ideas
• Geographers view the world in terms of the use of space.
• Geographers study the world by looking at location, place, region, movement, and human-environment interaction.

Places & Terms
geography
absolute location
relative location
hemisphere
equator
prime meridian
latitude
longitude

A HUMAN PERSPECTIVE Between 1838 and 1842, Captain Charles Wilkes led an American expedition to the South Pacific and Antarctica. At one stop at a South Sea island, a friendly islander drew a map on the wooden deck planks of the ship. To Wilkes's amazement, the map accurately showed the location of the Tuamotu Archipelago—a chain of about 80 coral islands that stretches more than 1,000 miles across the South Pacific. The islander relied on personal experience sailing in the area and a mental map to accurately show the positions of the islands.

The Geographer's Perspective

Maps like the one that the islander drew are important tools in geography. The word *geography* comes from the Greek word *geographia,* which means "to describe the earth." Geographers study the world in a different way than do other social scientists. Historians look at events over time. Geographers, on the other hand, view the world by looking at the use of space on the earth and the interactions that take place there. They look for patterns and connections between people and the land that they live on. **Geography,** then, is the study of the distribution and interaction of physical and human features on the earth.

METHODS OF GEOGRAPHY Geographers use a variety of tools to study the use of space on earth. The most common one is a map. Maps are visual representations of a portion of the earth. Maps do not have to be written down to be useful. Since people began roaming the earth, they have created mental maps—maps that they carry in their minds. You use a mental map every day as you go to and from school.

The maps that you are probably most familiar with appear in printed form, such as in road atlases and books. In recent years, more maps have appeared in electronic media such as CD-ROMs and on the Internet.

Geographers also use photographs to gain visual evidence about a place. They organize information into charts, graphs, or tables to learn about geographic patterns and to understand changes over time. They may also construct scale models to make study of the real world easier. Sometimes they use graphic models to illustrate an idea.

Other basic tools used by geographers are the five themes of geography, which also describe patterns and connections in the use of space. These themes organize information about geography into five distinct categories, shown at right. These themes are important to geographic study. They help the geographer to describe the use of space.

SUNSHINE STATE STANDARDS
Key Standard SS.B.1.4.2 The student understands the advantages and disadvantages of using maps from different sources and different points of view.
Other Standards SS.B.1.4.1, B.1.4.4, B.2.4.1, B.2.4.2
FCAT LA.A.1.4.2 Reading: Strategies

The Five Themes

Location
Where is it?

Place
What is it like?

Region
How are places similar or different?

Movement
How do people, goods, and ideas move from one location to another?

Human-Environment Interaction
How do people relate to the physical world?

Latitude Lines (Parallels)

North Pole
90°N
60°N
30°N
Equator——0°
30°S
60°S
90°S
South Pole

Longitude Lines (Meridians)

North Pole
180°
150°W   150°E
120°W   120°E
90°W   Prime Meridian   90°E
0°
60°W   60°E
30°W   30°E

North Pole   **Northern Hemisphere**

Equator

Southern Hemisphere   South Pole   **Eastern Hemisphere**

Western Hemisphere

SKILLBUILDER: Interpreting Graphics

❶ **LOCATION** In which two hemispheres is the United States located?

❷ **LOCATION** How many degrees of latitude are there?

Theme: Location

The geographic question "Where is it?" refers to location. Geographers describe location in two ways. **Absolute location** is the exact place on earth where a geographic feature, such as a city, is found. **Relative location** describes a place in comparison to other places around it.

ABSOLUTE LOCATION To describe absolute location, geographers use a grid system of imaginary lines for precisely locating places on the earth's surface. (See the diagram at left.) Earth is divided into two equal halves. Each half of the globe is called a **hemisphere.** Because the earth is round, a hemisphere can be north and south, or east and west. The **equator** is the imaginary line that divides the north and south halves. The **prime meridian** is the imaginary line dividing the earth east and west. Sometimes this line is called the Greenwich meridian (GREHN•ich muh•RIHD•ee•uhn) line because the line runs through Greenwich, England. Ⓐ

LATITUDE LINES To locate places north or south, geographers use a set of imaginary lines that run parallel to the equator. These lines are called **latitude** lines. The equator is designated as the zero-degree line for latitude. Lines north of the equator are called north latitude lines, and lines south of the equator are called south latitude lines.

LONGITUDE LINES To complete the grid system, geographers use a set of imaginary lines that go around the earth over the poles. These lines, called **longitude** lines, mark positions in the east and west hemispheres. The prime meridian is the zero-degree line for longitude.

Each site on the earth can have only one absolute location. To find an absolute location using the grid system, you need to find the point where the latitude and longitude lines cross. For example, the absolute location of Melbourne, Australia, is 37° South latitude, 145° East longitude. To see how latitude and longitude lines cross and to learn more about absolute location, see page 17 in the Geography Skills Handbook.

RELATIVE LOCATION Relative location describes how a place is related to its surrounding environment. For example, you may tell a person that the library is three blocks west of the park. This helps the person find the library—if he or she knows where the park is located. Using relative location may help you become familiar with the specific characteristics of a place. Learning that Cairo, Egypt, is located near the mouth of the Nile River in Africa, for example, tells you something about Cairo, the Nile River, and even Africa itself.

Geographic Thinking

Making Comparisons
Ⓐ How is the equator different from the prime meridian?

Overlooking the entrance to Guanabara Bay, Sugarloaf Mountain is a prominent landform in the skyline of Rio.

Leisure boats rest in the harbor of Botafogo Bay. There is a large commercial shipyard industry in Rio.

Headquarters of corporations and expensive housing compete for space in the scenic part of the city.

PLACE Rio de Janeiro, once the capital of Brazil, lies on the western shore of Guanabara Bay. **How would location on a bay affect the economy of a city?**

Theme: Place

The question "What is it like?" refers to place. Place includes the physical features and cultural characteristics of a location. All locations on earth have physical features that set them apart, such as climate, landforms, and vegetation. Other features are the product of humans interacting with the environment, such as by building dams, highways, or houses. Still others are the result of humans interacting with animals or with each other. In the photograph above, you can see place features of Rio de Janeiro. Since a location's culture and its use of space may change over time, the description of a place may also change.

Theme: Region

The question "How are places similar or different?" refers to region. A region is an area of the earth's surface with similar characteristics. Regions usually have more than one characteristic that unifies them. These may include physical, political, economic, or cultural characteristics. For example, the Sunbelt in the southern United States is a physical region. Geographers categorize regions in three ways: formal, functional, and perceptual regions.

FORMAL REGIONS A formal region is defined by a limited number of related characteristics. For example, the Sahel region of Africa is a desert area characterized by specific climate, vegetation, and land use patterns. In this textbook, the regions you'll explore generally are defined by continental area and by similar cultural styles. The following are considered formal regions:

- The United States and Canada
- Latin America
- Europe
- Russia and the Republics
- Africa
- Southwest Asia
- South Asia
- East Asia
- Southeast Asia, Oceania, and Antarctica

Geographic Thinking

Using the Atlas
Refer to the U.S. map on pages A8–A9. What states might be included in the Sunbelt?

FUNCTIONAL REGIONS A functional region is organized around a set of interactions and connections between places. Usually a functional region is characterized by a hub, or central place, and links to that central place. For example, a city and its suburbs may form a functional region. Highways, commuter railroads, subways, and bus lines move people from the suburbs to the city for jobs and other activities. Because the city and its suburbs are connected by a great deal of movement back and forth, they form a functional region. ▶

PERCEPTUAL REGIONS A perceptual region is a region in which people perceive, or see, the characteristics of the region in the same way. However, the set of characteristics may not be precisely the same for all people. For example, although many people are familiar with the region called the American Midwest, they sometimes differ on how that region is defined. Some people believe the Midwest begins in Ohio. Others believe the region begins in the middle of Illinois.

Geographic Thinking

Seeing Patterns
▶ How might areas within a city form a functional region?

Theme: Human–Environment Interaction

The question "How do people relate to the physical world?" refers to the relationship between humans and their environment. People learn to use what the environment offers them and to change that environment to meet their needs. They also learn to live with aspects of the environment that they cannot control, such as climate.

People living in similar environments do not respond to them in the same way. For example, some people view a hot, sunny climate near a body of water as ideal for recreational activities. Others may see this as an opportunity for raising citrus, olives, or grapes. Human beings work to alter their environments to make them better places or to provide needed goods. People may drain swamps or dig irrigation ditches to grow crops in a particular environment. Sometimes the alterations create new problems, such as pollution. As you study geography, you will learn about many ways humans interact with their environment.

HUMAN–ENVIRONMENT INTERACTION
Neighbors and friends use sandbags to hold back floodwaters during the Great Mississippi Flood of 1993.
In what ways do floods alter the landscape?

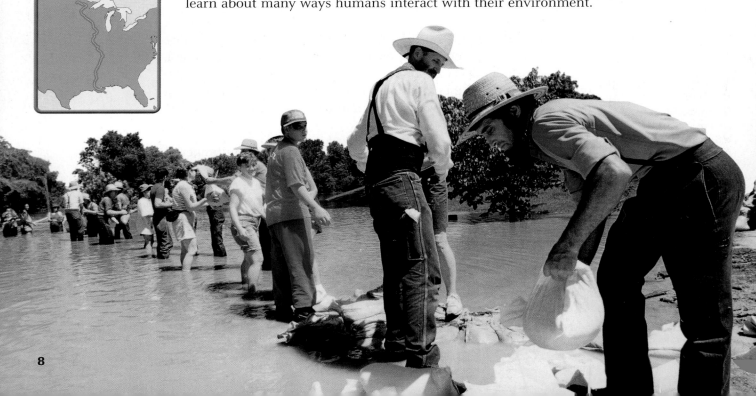

Theme: Movement

The question "How do people, goods, and ideas move from one location to another?" refers to movement. Geographers are interested in the ways people, goods, and ideas move from place to place. Think about the clothing you wear, the music you listen to, or the places you go for entertainment. All of these things involve movement from one place to another. Geographers analyze movement by looking at three types of distance: linear distance, time distance, and psychological distance.

LINEAR DISTANCE AND TIME DISTANCE Linear distance simply means how far across the earth a person, an idea, or a product travels. Physical geography can affect linear distance by forcing a shift in a route to avoid impassable land or water.

Time distance is the amount of time it takes for a person, an idea, or a product to travel. Modern inventions have shortened time distances. For example, in the 1800s, pioneers traveled up to six months to reach California. Today you can get there by airplane from almost any U.S. location in under six hours. With the use of the Internet, ideas can travel around the world in seconds. ◖D◗

PSYCHOLOGICAL DISTANCE Psychological distance refers to the way people view distance. When you were younger, some locations seemed very far away. As you grew older, the distance to these locations probably seemed to shrink. Studies show that, as we become familiar with a place, we think it is closer than it actually is. Less familiar places seem to be further away. Psychological distance may influence decisions about many different human activities.

Across the world, people make important choices based on linear distance, time distance, and psychological distance. These choices make up patterns that geographers can study. In the next section, you'll read about the tools they use to study these patterns.

Geographic Thinking

Seeing Patterns
◖D◗ How do interstate highways affect linear distance and time distance?

SECTION 1 — Assessment

❶ Places & Terms
Explain the meaning of each of the following terms.
- geography
- hemisphere
- equator
- prime meridian
- latitude
- longitude

❷ Taking Notes
REGION Review the notes you took for this section.

5 Themes:

- What is a region?
- What are three types of regions?

❸ Main Ideas
a. What are the five themes of geography?

b. How is place different from location?

c. Why do geographers study human-environment interaction?

❹ Geographic Thinking

Making Generalizations
How is the study of geography different from the study of history? **Think about:**
- use of space on earth
- relationships between people and the environment

See Skillbuilder Handbook, page R6.

EXPLORING LOCAL GEOGRAPHY Using the five themes of geography, develop a **brochure** describing your community. Use pictures or sketches, maps, and other data to complete your descriptions.

The Geographer's Tools

Main Ideas
- Geographers use two- and three-dimensional tools to learn about the earth.
- Geographers use computer-assisted technology to study the use of the earth's surface.

Places & Terms
globe
map
cartographer
map projection
topographic map
Landsat
Geographic Information Systems (GIS)

SUNSHINE STATE STANDARDS
Key Standard SS.B.1.4.1 The student uses a variety of maps, geographic technologies including geographic information systems (GIS) and satellite-produced imagery, and other advanced graphic representations to depict geographic problems.
FCAT LA.A.2.4.1 Reading: Identify Main Idea, Details, and Methods

A HUMAN PERSPECTIVE At noon on a sunny midsummer day, sometime around 255 B.C., Eratosthenes drove a stake into the ground at the mouth of the Nile River in Alexandria, Egypt. He then noted the angle of the shadow cast by the stake. Meanwhile at Syene (modern-day Aswan, Egypt), another person drove a stake into the ground—but it cast no shadow. Using the angle of the first shadow and the distance between Syene and Alexandria, Eratosthenes calculated the circumference of the earth. By today's measurements, he was off by about 15 percent, but he was remarkably accurate considering the simple tools he used. Eratosthenes was one of the earliest geographers to use tools and critical thinking to measure and describe the earth.

Maps and Globes

A geographer's tools include maps, globes, and data that can be displayed in a variety of ways. The oldest known map is a Babylonian clay tablet created about 2,500 years ago. The tablet is about four inches high and shows the Babylonian world surrounded by water. Over the centuries, mapmaking evolved into a very complex task. However, a map's function has remained the same—to show locations of places, landforms, and bodies of water, and where they are in relation to other parts of the earth.

TWO OR THREE DIMENSIONS A **globe** is a three-dimensional representation of the earth. It provides a way to view the earth as it travels through space. But since the earth is a sphere, we can see only one half of it at any time. For certain tasks, globes are not very practical because they are not easily portable.

People often prefer to use **maps,** which are two-dimensional graphic representations of selected parts of the earth's surface. Maps are easily portable and can be drawn to any scale needed. The disadvantage of a map is that distortion occurs as the earth's surface is flattened to create the map. A **cartographer,** or mapmaker, reduces some types of distortion by using different types of map projections. A **map projection** is a way of drawing the earth's surface that reduces distortion caused by presenting a round earth on flat paper. To learn more about map projections, see the Geography Skills Handbook, pages 18–19.

This globe, created circa 1492, is turned to show Africa and Europe.

TYPES OF MAPS The three types of maps are general reference maps, thematic maps, and navigational maps. One kind of general reference map is called a **topographic map,** which is a representation of natural and man-made features on the earth. Thematic maps emphasize specific kinds of information, such as climate or population density. Sailors and pilots use the third type of map—navigation maps. You can learn more about using different maps in the Geography Skills Handbook, pages 20–23.

The Science of Mapmaking

A cartographer decides what type of map to create by considering how the map will be used. Keeping that purpose in mind, he or she then determines how much detail to show and what size the map should be.

SURVEYING The first step in making a map is to complete a field survey. Surveyors observe, measure, and record what they see in a specific area. Today, most mapping is done by remote sensing, the gathering of geographic information from a distance by an instrument that is not physically in contact with the mapping site. These data are gathered primarily by aerial photography or by satellites.

The data gathered includes information such as elevation, differences in land cover, and variations in temperature. This information is recorded and converted to a gray image. Cartographers then use these data and computer software to construct maps. See the illustration below to learn more about satellite surveying.

How Satellites Gather Map Data

1. As the satellite orbits the earth, a scanner constantly records data from the earth's surface.

2. Instruments measure invisible electromagnetic waves emitted by each object on earth. Because these waves are unique for every object, computers can analyze and identify them.

3. The data collected is converted first to code and then to pixels—electronic dots. Computer software then converts the pixels into usable images.

The first step in mapmaking is collecting data. Remote sensors gather information for constructing maps.

Code

97	128	151
64	97	133
46	78	102

Pixels

Image

BASICS

11

SATELLITES Today, geographers rely heavily on satellites to provide geographic data. Two of the best-known satellites are Landsat and GOES. **Landsat** is actually a series of satellites that orbit more than 100 miles above Earth. Each time a satellite makes an orbit, it picks up data in an area 115 miles wide. Landsat can scan the entire Earth in 16 days.

Geostationary Operational Environment Satellite (GOES) is a weather satellite. This satellite flies in orbit in sync with Earth's rotation. By doing so, it always views the same area. It gathers images of atmospheric conditions that are useful in forecasting the weather.

Geographic Information Systems

Geographic Information Systems (GIS) allow geographers to solve problems by combining geographic information about a location from several sources.

1 A question or problem is posed. An example is, "In what general area near this town might an airport be located?" A section of land is identified for problem solving.

2 Computer databases hold geographic information about the location.

3 The user selects layers of information that answer the question "What geographic characteristics are important for a good airport site?"

4 A **terrain map** is selected to identify all areas flat enough for landing airplanes.

5 A **land use map** shows areas that have few homes.

7 The layers of information are combined to create a **composite map** showing possible sites for the airport.

6 The **base map** shows where roads are located so that the airport can be reached and safety concerns are handled.

Economic Activities of Southwest Asia

Activities
- Commercial farming
- Commercial fishing
- Forestry
- Nomadic herding
- Subsistence farming
- Little or no economic activity

Resources
- Chromium
- Coal
- Copper
- Hydroelectric power
- Iron ore
- Lead
- Natural gas
- Petroleum
- Phosphate

500 miles
500 kilometers
Lambert Conformal Conic Projection

ading a Map

maps have these elements, which are necessary to read and understand them.

1 TITLE The title explains the subject of the map and gives you an idea of what information the map conveys.

2 COMPASS ROSE The compass rose shows you the north (N), south (S), east (E), and west (W) directions on the map. Sometimes only north is indicated.

3 LABELS Labels are words or phrases that explain features on the map.

4 LEGEND A legend or key lists and explains the symbols and use of color on the map.

5 LINES OF LATITUDE These are imaginary lines that measure distance north or south of the equator.

6 LINES OF LONGITUDE These are imaginary lines that measure distance east or west of the prime meridian.

7 SCALE A scale shows the ratio between a unit of length on the map and a unit of distance on the earth.

8 SYMBOLS Symbols represent such items as capital cities, economic activities, or natural resources. Check the map legend for more details.

9 COLORS Colors represent a variety of information on a map. The map legend indicates what the colors mean.

Scale

A geographer decides what scale to use by determining how much detail to show. If many details are needed, a large scale is used. If fewer details are needed, a small scale is used.

Ratio Scale

This shows the ratio of distance on the map compared to real earth measurement. Here, 1 inch on the map equals 30,000,000 inches (500 miles) in actual distance on the earth.

Bar Scale

This bar shows the ratio of distance on the map to distance on the earth. Here, 1 inch equals 500 miles.

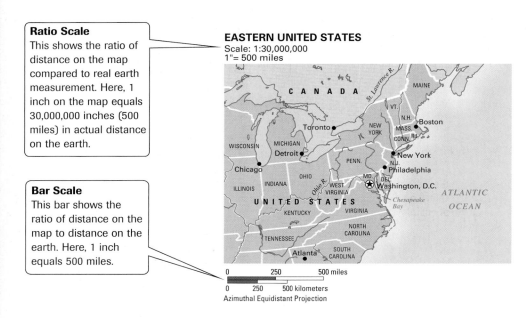

EASTERN UNITED STATES
Scale: 1:30,000,000
1"= 500 miles

0   250   500 miles
0   250   500 kilometers
Azimuthal Equidistant Projection

Small Scale

A small scale map shows a large area but without much detail. A small scale is used to see relative location in a region or between regions.

WASHINGTON, D.C., METRO AREA
Scale: 1:3,000,000
1"= 50 miles

0   25   50 miles
0   25   50 kilometers
Albers Equal-Area Projection

Large Scale

A large scale map shows a small area with much more detail. A large scale is used to see relative location within a region.

WASHINGTON, D.C.
Scale: 1:62,500
1"= 1 mile

0   .5   1 mile
0   .5   1 kilometer
Albers Equal-Area Projection

Using the Geographic Grid

As you learned in Chapter 1, geographers use a grid system to identify absolute location. The grid system uses two kinds of imaginary lines:

- latitude lines, also called parallels because they run parallel to the equator
- longitude lines, also called meridians because, like the prime meridian, they run from pole to pole

Latitude

There are 90° in North latitude and 90° in South latitude.

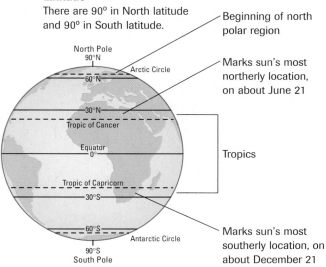

Beginning of north polar region

Marks sun's most northerly location, on about June 21

Tropics

Marks sun's most southerly location, on about December 21

Longitude

There are 180° in West longitude and 180° in East longitude. Lines also mark the hours of the day as the earth rotates. Every 15° east or west is equal to one hour.

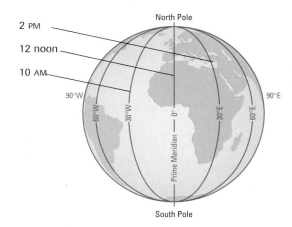

Global Grid

Absolute location can be determined by noting where latitude and longitude lines cross. For more precision, each degree is divided into 60 minutes.

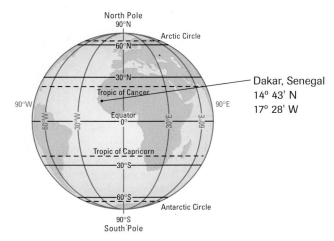

Dakar, Senegal
14° 43' N
17° 28' W

Projections

A projection is a way of showing the curved surface of the earth on a flat map. Because the earth is a sphere, a flat map will distort some aspect of the earth's surface. Distance, shape, direction, or area may be distorted by a projection. Be sure to check the projection of a map so you are aware of how the areas are distorted.

PLANAR PROJECTIONS

A planar projection is a projection on a flat surface. This projection is also called an azimuthal projection. It distorts size and shape. To the right is a type of planar projection.

The **azimuthal** projection shows the earth so that a line from the central point to any other point on the map gives the shortest distance between the two points. Size and shape are distorted.

CONICAL PROJECTIONS

A conical projection is a projection onto a cone. This projection shows shape fairly accurately, but it distorts landmasses at the edges of the map.

Conical projections are often used to show landmasses that extend over large areas going east and west.

COMPROMISE PROJECTIONS

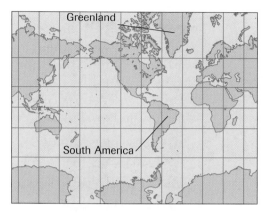

A compromise projection is a projection onto a cylinder. This projection shows the entire earth on one map. Included here are three types of compromise projections.

In the compromise projection called **Mercator,** the shapes of the continents are distorted at the poles and somewhat compressed near the equator. For example, the island of Greenland is actually one-eighth the size of South America.

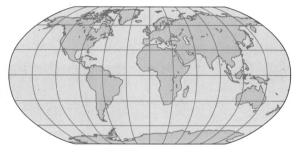

The compromise projection called **homolosine** is sometimes called an "interrupted map," because the oceans are divided. This projection shows the accurate shapes and sizes of the landmasses, but distances on the map are not correct.

A **Robinson** projection is a type of compromise projection, commonly used in textbooks. It shows the entire earth with nearly the true sizes and shapes of the continents and oceans. However, the shapes of the landforms near the poles appear flat.

 Map Practice

Use pages 14–19 to help you answer these questions. Look at the map on page 15 to answer questions 1–3.

1. How are colors used on this map?

2. Is the map a large-scale or a small-scale map? How do you know?

3. What is the approximate longitude of Buenos Aires?

4. What are the names of three lines of latitude besides the equator?

5. Which projections show shape of landmasses most accurately?

MAKING COMPARISONS Look at the maps in the atlas in this book. Create a **database** that shows the projection and scale of each map. Write a summary of your findings.

Using Different Types of Maps

PHYSICAL MAPS Physical maps help you see the types of landforms and bodies of water found in a specific area. By studying the map, you can begin to understand the relative location and characteristics of a place or region.

On a physical map, color, shading, or contour lines are used to indicate elevation or altitude, also called relief.

Ask these questions about the physical features shown on a map:

- Where on the earth's surface is this area located?
- What is its relative location?
- What is the shape of the region?
- In which direction do the rivers flow? How might the direction of flow affect travel and transportation in the region?
- Are there mountains or deserts? How do they affect the people living in the area?

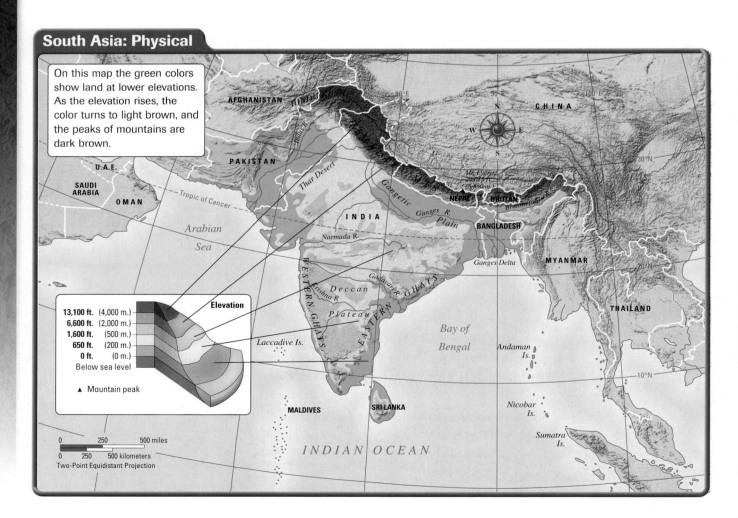

South Asia: Physical

On this map the green colors show land at lower elevations. As the elevation rises, the color turns to light brown, and the peaks of mountains are dark brown.

Elevation

13,100 ft. (4,000 m.)
6,600 ft. (2,000 m.)
1,600 ft. (500 m.)
650 ft. (200 m.)
0 ft. (0 m.)
Below sea level

▲ Mountain peak

0 250 500 miles
0 250 500 kilometers
Two-Point Equidistant Projection

POLITICAL MAPS Political maps show features on the earth's surface that humans created. Included on a political map may be cities, states, provinces, territories, or countries.

Ask these questions about the political features shown on a map:

• Where on the earth's surface is this area located?

• What is its relative location? How might the location affect the economy or foreign policy of a place?

• What is the shape and size of the country? How might shape or size affect the people living in the country?

• Who are the neighbors in the region, country, state, or city?

• How populated does the area seem to be? How might that affect activities there?

South Asia: Political

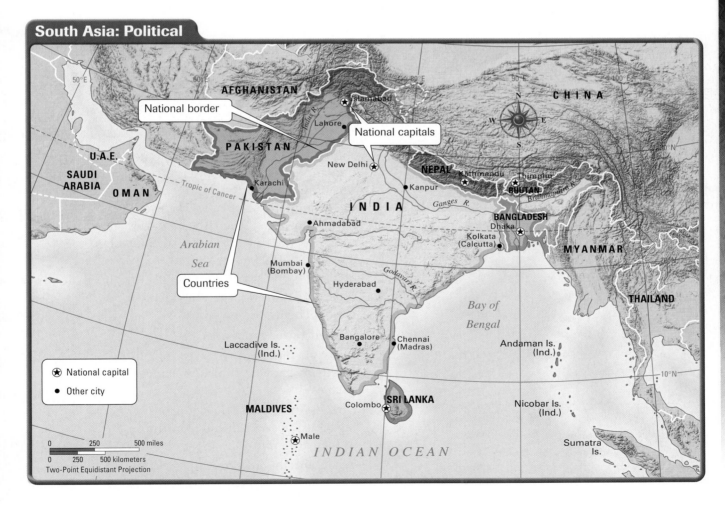

Thematic Maps

Geographers also rely on thematic maps, which focus on specific types of information. For example, in this textbook you will see thematic maps that show climate, vegetation, natural resources, population density, and economic activities. Some thematic maps illustrate historical trends, and others may focus on the movement of people or ideas. These maps may be presented in a variety of ways.

Cultural Legacy of the Roman Empire

Christian areas around A.D. 500

Romance language spoken, present-day

Boundary of Roman Empire A.D. 395

Estimated World Oil Reserves

1–10 Billion barrels
10–40 Billion barrels
40–100 Billion barrels
100+ Billion barrels
□ Each square equals 1 billion barrels

Source: *Oil and Gas Journal*, 1999

QUALITATIVE MAPS Qualitative maps use colors, symbols, dots, or lines to help you see patterns related to a specific idea. The map shown to the left shows the influence of the Roman Empire on Europe, North Africa, and Southwest Asia. Use the suggestions below to help you interpret a map.

• Check the title to identify the theme and data being presented.

• Study the legend to understand the theme and the information presented.

• Look at physical or political features of the area. How might the theme of the map affect them?

• What are the relationships among the data?

CARTOGRAMS In a cartogram, geographers present information about a country based on a set of data other than land area. The size of each country is drawn in proportion to that data rather than to its land size. On the cartogram shown to the left, the countries are represented on the basis of their oil reserves. Use the suggestions below to help you interpret a cartogram.

• Check the title and legend to identify the data being presented.

• What do sizes represent?

• Look at the relative sizes of the countries shown. Which is largest? smallest?

• How do the sizes of the countries on the physical map differ from those in the cartogram?

• What are the relationships among the data?

FLOW-LINE MAPS Flow-line maps illustrate movement of people, goods, ideas, animals, or even glaciers. The information is usually shown in a series of arrows. Location, direction, and scope of movement can be seen. The width of the arrow may show how extensive the flow is. Often the information is given over a period of time. The map shown to the right portrays the movement of the Bantu peoples in Africa. Use the suggestions below to help you interpret a flow-line map.

- Check the title and legend to identify the data being presented.
- Over what period of time did the movement occur?
- In what direction did the movement occur?
- How extensive was the movement?

Remember that the purpose of a map is to show a location and provide additional information. Be sure to look at the type of map, scale, and projection. Knowing how maps present the information will help you interpret the map and the ideas it presents.

Bantu Migrations

Legend:
- Desert
- Tropical rain forest
- Migration route

Original Bantu Area · 2000 BC · Congo River · CENTRAL AFRICAN RAINFOREST · Equator · 0° · Lake Victoria · Lake Tanganyika · AD 1–500 · Lake Nyasa · Zambezi R. · 20°S · NAMIB DESERT · AD 500–1000 · Tropic of Capricorn · KALAHARI DESERT · Limpopo R. · AD 500–1000 · Orange R. · ATLANTIC OCEAN · INDIAN OCEAN · 0° · 20°E

0   500   1,000 miles
0   500   1,000 kilometers
Azimuthal Equal-Area Projection

Map Practice

Use pages 20–23 to help you answer these questions. Use the maps on pages 20–21 to answer questions 1–3.

1. In what direction does the Ganges River flow?

2. China is the northern neighbor of which countries?

3. Which city is closer to the Thar Desert—Lahore, Pakistan or New Delhi, India?

4. Why are so few nations shown on the cartogram?

5. Which of the thematic maps would best show the location of climate zones?

EXPLORING LOCAL GEOGRAPHY Obtain a physical–political map of your state. Use the data on it to create two separate **maps.** One should show physical features only, and one should show political features only.

Chapter 1 Assessment

VISUAL SUMMARY
LOOKING AT THE EARTH

The Five Themes of Geography

Location
- **Absolute Location** uses latitude and longitude.
- **Relative Location** uses relationships to other places.

Place This explains the characteristics of an area.

Region This looks at a larger area with similar characteristics.

Movement People, plants, animals, and ideas move through time and across space.

Human–Environment Interaction Humans interact with the environment to adjust to it or to alter it.

The Geographer's Tools

Globe A three-dimensional representation of the earth

Map A two-dimensional representation of the earth

Mapmaking
- Area is surveyed.
- High-tech tools, including satellites, are used to gather data and create maps.

Geography Skills Handbook

Map Elements Maps have elements such as a legend to aid in interpreting them.

Scale This determines how much detail is shown on a map.

Grid Gridlines help to determine absolute location.

Projection This shows the earth's surface in two dimensions but distorts either size, shape, direction, or area.

Types of Maps These include physical, political, and thematic, such as qualitative, cartographic, or flow-line.

Reviewing Places & Terms

A. Briefly explain the importance of each of the following.

1. geography
2. hemisphere
3. equator
4. prime meridian
5. latitude
6. longitude
7. globe
8. map
9. cartographer
10. map projection

B. Answer the questions about vocabulary in complete sentences.

11. Which of the above terms indicate imaginary parallel lines that circle the earth?
12. Which term marks the beginning of longitude?
13. Which of the above terms has 180° in each hemisphere?
14. How may hemispheres be divided?
15. What imaginary line separates the Northern Hemisphere from the Southern Hemisphere?
16. Which term is also known as a meridian line?
17. Would a cartographer work on a map or a globe?
18. Why are map projections needed?
19. Which of the above terms are associated with the geographic grid?
20. Which term characterizes the study of the use of land space?

Main Ideas

The Five Themes of Geography (pp. 5–9)

1. How is absolute location different from relative location?
2. What are some examples of information that would be included in a place description?
3. How is place different from region?
4. Why do geographers study movement?

The Geographer's Tools (pp. 10–13)

5. What is the purpose of a map?
6. How do satellites aid in mapmaking?
7. Why is GIS a valuable tool for examining the geography of a place?

Geography Skills Handbook (pp. 14–23)

8. How is the use of small-scale maps different from the use of large-scale maps?
9. In what ways may relief be shown on a map?
10. What are three types of thematic maps?

Critical Thinking

1. Using Your Notes

Use your completed chart to answer these questions.

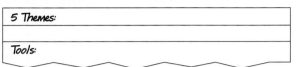

5 Themes:

Tools:

   a. How are relative location and place related?

   b. How do thematic maps help geographers understand the five themes?

2. Geographic Themes

   a. **REGION** Write a sentence describing a region that your community is a part of. Be sure to identify the region and give reasons for your answer.

   b. **MOVEMENT** How are linear and time distances related to the theme of movement?

3. Identifying Themes

Into which two hemispheres would an island at 50°S, 60°W be placed? Which of the five themes are reflected in your answer?

4. Drawing Conclusions

Why was it necessary for geographers to develop a grid system?

5. Seeing Patterns

Into which formal region, functional region, and perceptual region might your community be placed?

Additional Test Practice, pp. S1–S37

TEST PRACTICE
CLASSZONE.COM

Geographic Skills: Interpreting Maps

Continents of the World

Use the map to answer the following questions.

1. **LOCATION** What is the absolute location of the continent of Australia?

2. **LOCATION** What is the relative location of South America?

3. **PLACE** What body of water is located at 45° N, 45° W?

With a partner, choose and record the latitude and longitude of five locations on the map at left. Then trade your list with another set of partners. Have them search for the coordinates on your list, and do the same with their list. Then check the accuracy of the findings.

INTERNET ACTIVITY

Use the links at **classzone.com** to do research about GIS. Take notes on the ways GIS can be used to provide geographic information for mapmaking, site selection, and simulating environmental effects.

Creating a Multimedia Presentation Using the information you gathered about GIS, create a multimedia presentation explaining the various aspects of GIS and how it helps geographers and others solve problems.

PHYSICAL GEOGRAPHY
A Living Planet

Third planet from the Sun: Earth appears as a blue and white ball in the darkness of space.

GeoFocus

What forces shape the earth?

Taking Notes Copy the graphic organizer below into your notebook. Use it to record information from the chapter about the structure of the earth.

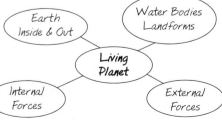

Earth Inside & Out

Water Bodies Landforms

Living Planet

Internal Forces

External Forces

The Earth Inside and Out

A HUMAN PERSPECTIVE A quick look at a world map will convince you that the <u>**continents,**</u> landmasses above water on earth, fit together like a huge jigsaw puzzle. South America and Africa are good examples. With imagination, you can see how other continents might fit together as well. The first person to suggest that the seven continents were once all one supercontinent was Englishman Francis Bacon in 1620. Bacon's idea received support in the early 1900s, when scientists found rocks in Africa that matched rocks in South America. Other evidence also supported the idea of a supercontinent millions of years ago.

The Solar System

The "home address" of the earth is the third planet in the solar system of the sun, which is a medium-sized star on the edge of the Milky Way galaxy. Its distance from the sun is 93 million miles. The <u>**solar system**</u> consists of the sun and nine known planets, as well as other celestial bodies that orbit the sun. The solar system also contains comets, spheres covered with ice and dust that leave trails of vapor as they race through space. Asteroids—large chunks of rocky material—are found in space as well. As you can see in the diagram, our solar system has an asteroid belt between the orbits of Jupiter and Mars.

LOCATION This not-to-scale illustration shows the nine planets and other objects in our solar system.
What is the earth's relative location in the solar system?

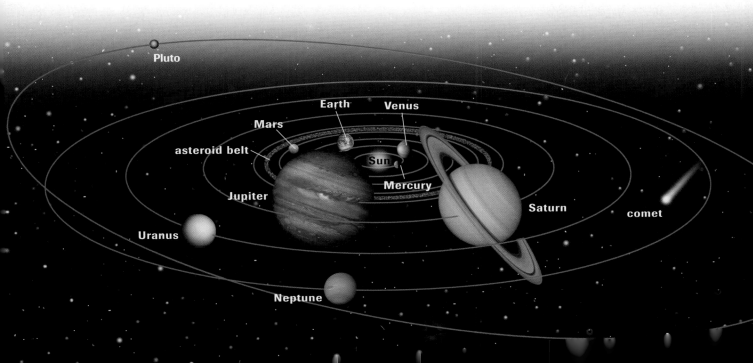

The Structure of the Earth

The earth is about 24,900 miles in circumference and about 7,900 miles in diameter. Although the earth seems like a solid ball, it is really more like a series of shells that surround one another.

INSIDE THE EARTH The <u>**core**</u> is the center of the earth and is made up of iron and nickel. The outer core is liquid, but the inner core is solid. Surrounding the core is the <u>**mantle,**</u> which has several layers. The mantle contains most of the earth's mass. <u>**Magma,**</u> which is molten rock, can form in the mantle and rise through the <u>**crust,**</u> the thin layer of rock at the earth's surface. Study the diagram below to learn more about the earth's interior.

ON AND ABOVE THE EARTH Surrounding the earth is a layer of gases called the <u>**atmosphere.**</u> It contains the oxygen we breathe, protects the earth from radiation and space debris, and provides the medium for weather and climate. The solid rock portion of the earth's surface is the <u>**lithosphere,**</u> which includes the crust and uppermost mantle. Under the ocean, the lithosphere forms the seafloor. The huge landmasses above water are called continents. There are seven continents: North America, South America, Europe, Asia, Africa, Australia, and Antarctica. The <u>**hydrosphere**</u> is made up of the water elements on the earth, which include oceans, seas, rivers, lakes, and water in the atmosphere. Together, the atmosphere, the lithosphere, and the hydrosphere form the <u>**biosphere,**</u> the part of the earth where plants and animals live.

BACKGROUND
Part of the upper portion of the mantle is known as the asthenosphere. It is the hot, but still mostly solid, rock below the cold, brittle rock of the lithosphere.

The Earth's Interior

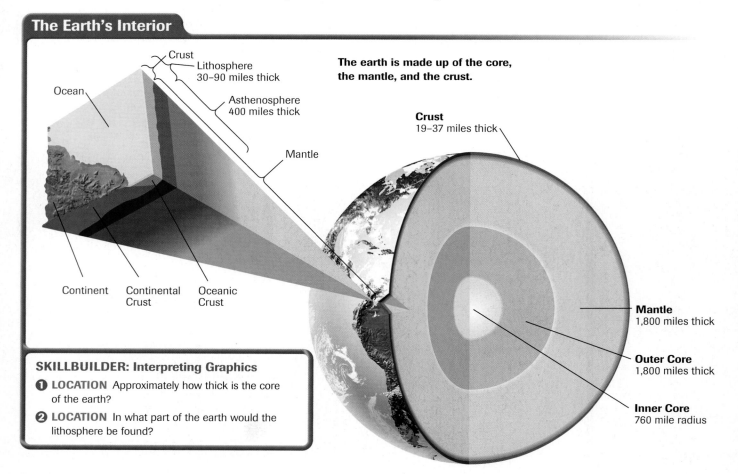

The earth is made up of the core, the mantle, and the crust.

Crust

Lithosphere
30–90 miles thick

Asthenosphere
400 miles thick

Ocean

Mantle

Continent

Continental Crust

Oceanic Crust

Crust
19–37 miles thick

Mantle
1,800 miles thick

Outer Core
1,800 miles thick

Inner Core
760 mile radius

SKILLBUILDER: Interpreting Graphics

❶ **LOCATION** Approximately how thick is the core of the earth?

❷ **LOCATION** In what part of the earth would the lithosphere be found?

CONTINENTAL DRIFT In 1912, Alfred Wegener of Germany presented a new idea about continents—the **continental drift** hypothesis. It maintained that the earth was once a supercontinent that divided and slowly drifted apart over millions of years. Wegener called the supercontinent Pangaea (from a Greek word meaning "all earth"). An ocean called Panthalassa surrounded it. The supercontinent split into many plates that drifted, crashed into each other, and split apart several times before they came to their current positions. This process occurred over millions of years.

In the 1960s, scientists studying the sea floor discovered that the youngest rocks were in the middle of the ocean, at long cracks in the crust. This suggested that the new sea floor was being added, pushing the continents apart. Later in this chapter, you will learn how the rocks of Earth's surface are broken into giant plates that move and continue to shape the earth.

Continental Drift Hypothesis

200 million years ago The supercontinent was named *Pangaea*. An ocean called Panthalassa surrounded it.

65 million years ago The supercontinent split apart and began moving in different directions. Notice that India broke away from Antarctica and Australia and drifted toward Asia.

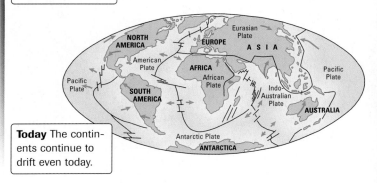

Today The continents continue to drift even today.

Assessment

1 Places & Terms

Identify and explain where on the earth these terms would be found.

- continent
- mantle
- magma
- crust
- biosphere

2 Taking Notes

PLACE Review the notes you took for this section.

- What are the three basic parts of the earth's interior?
- What are four basic spheres found on or above the earth?

3 Main Ideas

a. What makes up the interior of the earth?

b. What makes up the biosphere?

c. How can the presence of seven continents on the earth's surface be explained?

4 Geographic Thinking

Making Inferences How do the earth's spheres influence one another? **Think about:**

- the function of the atmosphere
- the makeup of the biosphere

 See Skillbuilder Handbook, page R4.

MAKING COMPARISONS Study the diagrams of continental drift on this page. Write a **description** of the location of the continents in the past in comparison with their current location.

Disasters!

Asteroid Hit!

For years, scientists speculated that the extinction of dinosaurs was due to one very large "environmental event." Today we know that event was most likely the impact of an asteroid about six miles wide. Sixty-five million years ago it slammed into the earth traveling a thousand times faster than a rifle bullet. Fallout from the asteriod impact changed the environment so drastically that 50 to 70 percent of all living species on earth were wiped out.

SUNSHINE STATE STANDARDS
Key Standard SS.A.1.4.4 The student uses chronology, sequencing, patterns, and periodization to examine interpretations of an event.
FCAT LA.B.1.4.3 Writing: Edit Final Documents

The asteroid hit near Chicxulub (CHEEK•shoo•loob) on the Yucatán Peninsula of Mexico. It dug a crater about 62 miles (100km) across.

The asteroid plows into the earth at 150,000 mph, vaporizing limestone and seawater. It creates an immense fireball that causes fires thousands of miles away.

The Earth's skies are darkened for several months by 25 trillion tons of rock, dust, and smoke from the impact. Acid rain created by vaporized minerals poisons lakes and rivers. Food chains collapse, and plants and animals die.

A thick layer of carbon dioxide is trapped in the atmosphere, creating a "greenhouse effect" for perhaps a thousand years or more. Ferns, burrowing mammals, and some freshwater animals survive. Some even thrive in the new climate.

GeoActivities

CREATING A FRONT PAGE
With a small group, use the Internet to research the Chicxulub event. Then create the front page of a **newspaper** describing the event.

- Create a map showing the impact area.
- Add an article describing the destruction caused by the asteroid.
- Write an interview with a scientist who predicts event results.

RESEARCH LINKS
CLASSZONE.COM

GeoData

ASTEROIDS
- Asteroids are small planetary bodies that orbit the sun.
- There are an estimated 50,000 asteroids in our solar system.
- Asteroids range in size from 20 feet to 580 miles in diameter.
- Fragments of asteroids that reach the earth are called meteorites.

TUNGUSKA EVENT
On June 30, 1908, at about 7:30 A.M., an explosion occurred over the Tunguska region of Siberia. This event might have been an asteroid hit.

- The force of the explosion was estimated at between 10 and 20 megatons of TNT.
- The fireball and explosion were seen and felt 500 miles away.
- Five hundred thousand acres of forest were flattened and burned.
- More than 600 grazing reindeer were roasted instantly.
- No crater could be found.

Bodies of Water and Landforms

Main Ideas
• Water covers about three-fourths of the earth's surface.
• The earth's surface displays a variety of landforms.

Places & Terms
hydrologic cycle
drainage basin
ground water
water table
landform
continental shelf
relief
topography

SUNSHINE STATE STANDARDS
Key Standard SS.B.1.4.3 The students uses mental maps of physical and human features of the world to answer complex geographic questions.
Other Standards SS.B.1.4.1
FCAT LA.A.1.4.2 Reading: Strategies

A HUMAN PERSPECTIVE In July 1971, astronaut James Irwin was lifted into space on the Apollo 15 mission. As he circled the earth, he was deeply moved by the beauty of our planet. Later he wrote this:

> Anyone passing through our solar system would be attracted to the blue planet. They would know that the blue color indicated water on Earth. They would know that where there is water there is probably life. They might try to meet us. We, the blue planet, stand out as a beacon to all.

The earth is unlike any other observable planet in our solar system. It is a living planet.

Bodies of Water

Without both freshwater and saltwater, life on this planet would be impossible. Water not only supports plants and animals, it helps distribute heat on the earth.

OCEANS AND SEAS The ocean is an interconnected body of salt water that covers about 71 percent of our planet. It covers a little more than 60 percent of the Northern Hemisphere and about 81 percent of the Southern Hemisphere. Even though it is one ocean, geographers divide it into four main parts: the Atlantic Ocean, the Pacific Ocean, the Indian Ocean, and the Arctic Ocean, which is sometimes considered part of the Atlantic. The largest of the oceans is the Pacific. The waters near Antarctica are sometimes called the Southern Ocean.

OCEAN MOTION The salty water of the ocean circulates through three basic motions: currents, waves, and tides. Currents act like rivers flowing through the ocean. Waves are swells or ridges produced by winds. Tides are the regular rises and falls of the ocean created by the gravitational pull of the moon or the sun. The motion of the ocean helps distribute heat on the planet. Winds blow over the ocean and are either heated or cooled by the water. When the winds eventually blow over the land, they moderate the temperature of the air over the land.

HYDROLOGIC CYCLE The **hydrologic cycle** is the continous circulation of water between the atmosphere, the oceans, and the earth. As you can see in

PLACE Iguaçu Falls at the Argentina-Brazil border has 275 separate waterfalls varying between 200 and 269 feet high. It is nearly three times wider than Niagara Falls in North America.

A total of approximately 119,000 cubic miles of water evaporates into the atmosphere every year and returns as precipitation—rain or snow.

Evaporation from the land pumps 17,000 cubic miles of water into the atmosphere every year. The water evaporates from the land itself and from plants.

Some water flows into the underground water table.

Evaporation from the oceans and other bodies of water sends 102,000 cubic miles of water into the atmosphere.

SKILLBUILDER: Interpreting Graphics

❶ **MOVEMENT** Does more water evaporate from the land or from the ocean?

❷ **MOVEMENT** How does precipitation falling on the land reach the ocean?

the diagram above, water evaporates into the atmosphere from the surface of the oceans, other bodies of water, and from plants. The water exists in the atmosphere as vapor. Eventually, the vapor cools, condenses, and falls to earth as precipitation—rain or snow. The water soaks into the ground, evaporates to the atmosphere, or flows into rivers to be recycled.

LAKES, RIVERS, AND STREAMS Lakes hold more than 95 percent of all the earth's fresh water supply. The largest freshwater lake is Lake Baikal in Russia. Its volume of water equals 18 percent of all freshwater on earth. Freshwater lakes like the Great Lakes of North America are the result of glacial action thousands of years ago. Saltwater lakes result from changes in the earth's surface that cut off outlets to the sea. Saltwater lakes are created when creeks and rivers carry salts into a lake, and there is no outlet to carry the salt away. The Great Salt Lake in Utah is the remnant of a large freshwater lake—Lake Bonneville. Its water outflows were cut off, causing the remaining water to become more salty as the water evaporated. The largest saltwater lake is the Caspian Sea in Western Asia.

Rivers and streams flow through channels and move water to or from larger bodies of water. Rivers and streams connect into drainage systems that work like the branches of a tree, with smaller branches, called tributaries, feeding into larger and larger ones. Geographers call an area drained by a major river and its tributaries a **drainage basin.**

GROUND WATER Some water on the surface of the earth is held by the soil, and some flows into the pores of the rock below the soil. The water held in the pores of rock is called **ground water.** The level at which the rock is saturated marks the rim of the **water table.** The water table can rise or fall depending on the amount of precipitation in the region and on the amount of water pumped out of the ground.

BACKGROUND
Rock layers that store water are called aquifers. The largest U.S. aquifer is the Ogallala Aquifer, which runs from South Dakota south to Texas.

Landforms

Landforms are naturally formed features on the surface of the earth. The diagram on pages 34–35 shows the different kinds of landforms.

Landforms at a Glance

VOLCANO
an opening in the earth, usually raised, through which gases and lava escape from the earth's interior

STRAIT
a narrow channel connecting two larger bodies of water

CAPE/PENINSULA
a point of land extending into an ocean or lake

SEA LEVEL
level of the ocean's surface, used as a reference point when measuring the height or depth of the earth's surface

BAY/GULF
part of an ocean or lake partially enclosed by land

HARBOR
a sheltered area of water deep enough for docking ships

(RIVER) MOUTH
the place where a river flows into a lake or an ocean

MARSH
soft, wet, low-lying, grassy land that serves as a transition between water and land

ISLAND
a body of land surrounded by water

DELTA
a triangular area of land formed from deposits at the mouth of a river

FLOOD PLAIN
flat land near the edges of rivers formed by mud and silt deposited by floods

SWAMP
a lowland region that is saturated by water

BUTTE
a raised, flat area of land with steep cliffs, smaller than a mesa

OASIS
a spot of fertile land in a desert, fed by water from wells or underground springs

PRAIRIE
a large, level area of grassland with few or no trees

MOUNTAIN
natural elevation of the earth's surface with steep sides and greater height than a hill

GLACIER
a large ice mass that moves slowly down a mountain or over land

STEPPE
a wide, treeless grassy plain

VALLEY
low land between hills or mountains

MESA
a wide, flat-topped mountain with steep sides, larger than a butte

PLATEAU
a broad, flat area of land higher than the surrounding land

CATARACT
a step-like series of waterfalls

CANYON
a narrow, deep valley with steep sides

CLIFF
the steep, almost vertical edge of a hill, mountain, or plain

5 THEMES

REGION

The Everglades

Native Americans called it Pa-May-Okee ("Grassy Water"). Today, we call it the Everglades. It is a region of wetlands, a marshy landform, that covers 4,000 square miles of Florida. Live oak, palms, and pines cover the region. Saw grass with tiny sharp teeth stands over 10 feet high among cypress. Swampy waters hide snakes, alligators, and turtles. Huge numbers of birds call the Everglades home.

Drainage projects have met with protest because they threaten the plants and animals that flourish there. Plans are now under way to restore the Everglades to its natural habitat.

Everglades National Park

OCEANIC LANDFORMS The sea floor has landforms similar to those above water. The earth's surface from the edge of a continent to the deep part of the ocean is called the **continental shelf.** The floor of the ocean has ridges, valleys, canyons, and plains. Ridges mark places where new crust is being formed on the edges of the tectonic plates. Mountain chains similar to those on the continents themselves cover parts of the ocean floor. The longest continuous range is the Mid-Atlantic Ridge, which extends for thousands of miles north to south through the middle of the Atlantic Ocean. Islands dot the ocean surface. Islands can be formed by volcanic action, deposits of sand, or deposits of coral skeletons.

CONTINENTAL LANDFORMS To understand the types of landforms, study the illustration on pages 34–35. The major geographic feature that separates one type of landform from another is relief. **Relief** is the difference in elevation of a landform from its lowest point to its highest point. There are four categories of relief: mountains, hills, plains, and plateaus. A mountain, for instance, has great relief compared with a plain, which displays very little difference between its high and low points. **A**

Topography is the combination of the surface shape and composition of the landforms and their distribution in a region. A topographic map shows the landforms with their vertical dimensions and their relationship to other landforms.

In the next section, you will learn how internal forces of the earth help to build and change the landforms on the earth—and how those forces affect humans.

 Geographic Thinking

Using the Atlas
A Use the map on page A10 to determine the relief of your state.

SECTION 2 Assessment

① Places & Terms

Explain the meaning of each of the following terms.

- hydrologic cycle
- ground water
- continental shelf
- relief
- topography

② Taking Notes

MOVEMENT Review the notes you took for this section.

Water Bodies Landforms

Living Planet

- How does the hydrologic cycle circulate water?
- How does ocean water circulate?

③ Main Ideas

a. How do the winds and the ocean distribute heat on the earth's surface?

b. How are relief and topography related?

c. How are islands formed?

④ Geographic Thinking

Making Comparisons How is the floor of the ocean similar to land above sea level? **Think about:**

- mountain chains
- other landforms

S **See Skillbuilder Handbook, page R3.**

GeoActivity

SEEING PATTERNS Study the Landforms at a Glance diagram on pages 34–35. Choose a part of it to reproduce in a three-dimensional **relief map.** Be sure to label the landforms clearly.

Internal Forces Shaping the Earth

Main Ideas
• Internal forces reshape the earth's surface.
• Internal forces shaping the earth often radically alter the lives of people as well.

Places & Terms

tectonic plate	Richter scale
fault	tsunami
earthquake	volcano
seismograph	lava
epicenter	Ring of Fire

BASICS

A HUMAN PERSPECTIVE Sally Ride, America's first female astronaut, wrote the following after one of her trips into space:

> I also became an instant believer in plate tectonics; India really is crashing into Asia, and Saudi Arabia and Egypt really are pulling apart, making the Red Sea even wider. Even though their respective motion is really no more than mere inches a year, the view from overhead makes the theory come alive.

From space, Ride was seeing evidence of the internal forces that have shaped the earth's surface.

SUNSHINE STATE STANDARDS
Key Standard SS.B.1.4.1 The student uses a variety of maps, geographic technologies including geographic information systems (GIS) and satellite-produced imagery, and other advanced graphic representations to depict geographic problems.
Other Standards SS.B.1.4.3
FCAT LA.A.1.4.2 Reading: Strategies

Plate Tectonics

The internal forces that shape the earth's surface begin beneath the lithosphere. Rock in the asthenosphere is hot enough to flow slowly. Heated rock rises, moves up toward the lithosphere, cools, and circulates downward. Riding above this circulation system are the **tectonic plates,** enormous moving pieces of the earth's lithosphere. You can see the position of the tectonic plates in the map below.

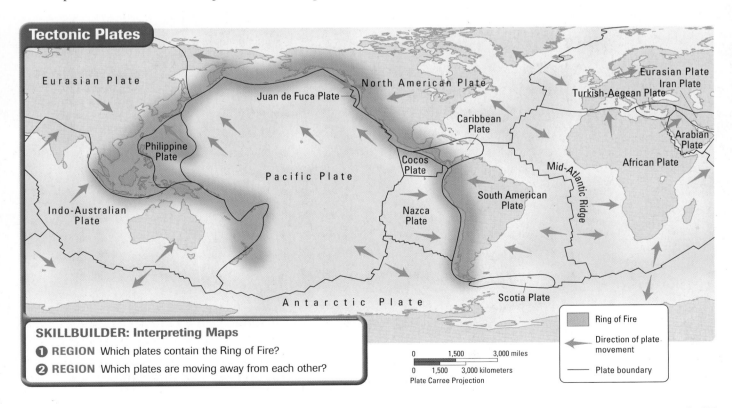

Tectonic Plates

Eurasian Plate
Juan de Fuca Plate
North American Plate
Eurasian Plate
Iran Plate
Turkish-Aegean Plate
Philippine Plate
Caribbean Plate
Arabian Plate
Cocos Plate
African Plate
Pacific Plate
Mid-Atlantic Ridge
Indo-Australian Plate
South American Plate
Nazca Plate
Scotia Plate
Antarctic Plate

Ring of Fire
Direction of plate movement
Plate boundary

0 — 1,500 — 3,000 miles
0 — 1,500 — 3,000 kilometers
Plate Carree Projection

SKILLBUILDER: Interpreting Maps

❶ **REGION** Which plates contain the Ring of Fire?

❷ **REGION** Which plates are moving away from each other?

Geographers study the movement of the plates and the changes they cause in order to understand how the earth is continually being reshaped—and how earthquakes and volcanoes occur.

PLATE MOVEMENT Tectonic plates move in one of four ways: 1) spreading, or moving apart; 2) subduction, or diving under another plate; 3) collision, or crashing into one another; 4) sliding past each other in a shearing motion. The diagrams below show details about plate movement.

When tectonic plates come into contact, changes on the earth's surface occur. Three types of boundaries mark plate movements:

- **Divergent boundary**—Plates move apart, spreading horizontally.
- **Convergent boundary**—Plates collide, causing either one plate to dive under the other or the edges of both plates to crumple.
- **Transform boundary**—Plates slide past one another. △

An example of a divergent boundary is the one between Saudi Arabia and Egypt. The two plates on which those countries sit are spreading apart, making the Red Sea even wider. The Red Sea is actually a part of the Great Rift Valley in Africa. If you look at the map of Africa on page A18, you will see a string of lakes along the eastern side of Africa, including Lake Tanganyika and Lake Nyasa. These lakes, along with the Red Sea, were formed in the spreading boundary.

An example of a convergent boundary can be found in South Asia. The plate where India is located is crashing into the Asian continent and building up the Himalayas. One of the most famous examples of a transform boundary is in North America—the San Andreas Fault in

Geographic Thinking

Making Comparisons
△ Which of the plate boundaries involves a collision of plates?

Plate Movement and Boundaries

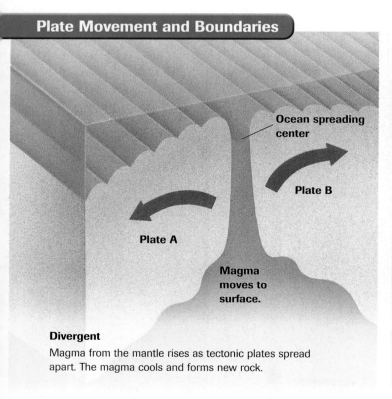

Ocean spreading center

Plate B

Plate A

Magma moves to surface.

Divergent
Magma from the mantle rises as tectonic plates spread apart. The magma cools and forms new rock.

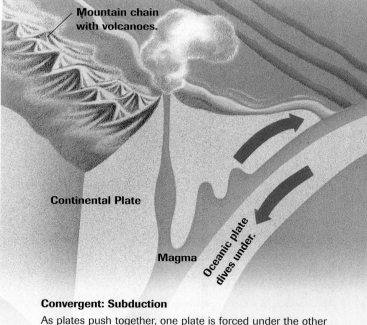

Mountain chain with volcanoes.

Continental Plate

Magma

Oceanic plate dives under.

Convergent: Subduction
As plates push together, one plate is forced under the other in a process called subduction. As the bottom plate starts to melt, magma rises and forms volcanoes at the surface.

California. Study the diagrams below to understand the movement of the plates and their effect on the surface of the earth.

FOLDS AND FAULTS When two plates meet each other, they can cause folding and cracking of the rock. The transformation of the crust by folding or cracking occurs very slowly, often only a few centimeters or inches in a year. Because the movement is slow, the rocks, which are under great pressure, become more flexible and bend or fold, creating changes in the crust. However, sometimes the rock is not flexible and will crack under the pressures exerted by the plate movement. This fracture in the earth's crust is called a **fault.** It is at the fault line that the plates move past each other.

Earthquakes

As the plates grind or slip past each other at a fault, the earth shakes or trembles. This sometimes violent movement of the earth is an **earthquake.** Thousands of earthquakes occur every year, but most are so slight that people cannot feel them. Only a special device called a **seismograph** (SYZ•muh•GRAF) can detect them. A seismograph measures the size of the waves created by an earthquake.

EARTHQUAKE LOCATIONS The location in the earth where an earthquake begins is called the focus. The point directly above the focus on the earth's surface is the **epicenter.** The map on page 37 outlines the major plate boundaries. Nearly 95 percent of all recorded earthquakes occur around those boundaries. Plate movement along the Pacific Rim

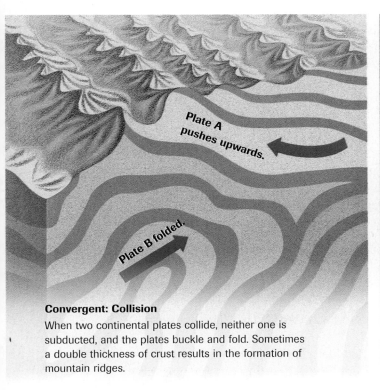

Convergent: Collision
When two continental plates collide, neither one is subducted, and the plates buckle and fold. Sometimes a double thickness of crust results in the formation of mountain ridges.

Transform
Plates slide past each other along a fault or fracture in the crust. Transform movement does not create new landforms but does cause earthquakes along the boundaries.

LOCATION Victims of the 1995 earthquake in Kobe, Japan, wait out aftershocks. More than 5,000 people died in this quake.
Why does the location of Japan make it vulnerable to earthquakes?

and from southern Asia westward to southern Europe makes this region especially vulnerable to quakes.

EARTHQUAKE DAMAGE Earthquakes result in squeezing, stretching, and shearing motions of the earth's crust that damage land and structures.

The changes are most noticeable in places where people live. Landslides, displacement of land, fires (from broken gas lines), and collapsed buildings are major outcomes of the ground motion. Aftershocks, or smaller-magnitude quakes, may occur after an initial shock and can sometimes continue for days afterward.

An earthquake is the sudden release of energy in the form of motion. C.F. Richter developed a scale to measure the amount of energy released. The **Richter Scale** uses information collected by seismographs to determine the relative strength of an earthquake. The scale has no absolute upper limit. Most people would not notice a quake that measured 2 on the scale. A 4.5 quake will probably be reported in the news. A major quake has a measurement of 7 or more. The largest quake ever measured was 8.9 in the Kermadec Islands of the South Pacific in 1986.

TSUNAMI Sometimes an earthquake causes a **tsunami** (tsu•NAH•mee), a giant wave in the ocean. A tsunami can travel from the epicenter of a quake at speeds of up to 450 miles per hour, producing waves of 50 to 100 feet or higher. The world record for a tsunami was set in 1971 off the Ryukyu Islands near Japan, where the wall of water reached 238 feet—more than 20 stories high. Tsunamis may travel across wide stretches of the ocean and do damage on distant shores. For example, in 1960 a quake near Chile created a tsunami that caused damage in Japan, almost half a world away. A tsunami from a quake near Alaska killed 159 people in Hilo, Hawaii, in 1946. **B**

Volcanoes

Volcanoes are among the most spectacular of natural events. Magma, gases, and water from the lower part of the crust or the mantle collect in underground chambers. Eventually the materials pour out of a crack in the earth's surface called a **volcano.** Most volcanoes are found along the tectonic plate boundaries.

VOLCANIC ACTION When the magma flows out onto the land slowly, it may spread across an area and cool. Magma that has reached the earth's surface is called **lava.** The most dramatic volcanic action is an eruption, in which hot lava, gases, ash, dust, and rocks explode out of vents in the earth's crust. Often a hill or a mountain is created by lava. The landform may also be called a volcano.

Volcanoes do not erupt on a predictable schedule; they may be active over many years and then stop. Sometimes they remain inactive for

Geographic Thinking
Using the Atlas
B Using the map on pages A2–3, calculate the distance these two tsunamis traveled.

long periods of time—as long as hundreds of years—before becoming active again.

RING OF FIRE The **Ring of Fire,** a zone around the rim of the Pacific Ocean, is the location of the vast majority of active volcanoes. You can see the zone on the map on page 37. Eight major tectonic plates meet in this zone. Volcanic action and earthquakes occur frequently there. Other volcanoes are located far from the margins of tectonic plates. They appear over "hot spots" where magma from deep in the mantle rises and melts through the lithosphere, as in volcanoes in the Hawaiian Islands.

Hot springs and geysers are indicators of high temperatures in the earth's crust. Hot springs occur when ground water circulates near a magma chamber. The water heats up and rises to the surface. The hot springs and pools of Yellowstone Park are examples of this type of activity. A geyser is a hot spring that occasionally erupts with steam jets and boiling water. Old Faithful, a geyser in Yellowstone, erupts regularly, but most geysers are irregular in their eruptions. Countries with hot springs and geysers include the United States, Iceland, and Japan. ◁

Not all volcanic action is bad. Volcanic ash produces fertile soil. In some parts of the world, the hot springs, steam, and heat generated by the magma are tapped for energy. In Iceland, for example, volcanic heat and steam are used for heating and hot water in the city of Reykjavik.

Internal forces have a major role in shaping the earth. In the next section, you will learn how external forces also change the landscape.

Geographic Thinking

Seeing Patterns
▷ Why do the United States, Iceland, and Japan have geysers?

Geography TODAY

An Island Is Born

On May 14, 2000, a team of scientists observed the birth of a new island in the South Pacific. On that day Kavachi, a volcano in the Solomon Islands, erupted for the first time since 1991. The volcano is located about 18 miles from the boundary of the Indo-Australian plate and the Pacific plate.

For at least 20 hours, the volcano erupted every 5 to 7 minutes, shooting ash and glowing lava blocks 230 feet into the air (shown below). The peak of the volcano is under water, about 2,100 feet above the sea floor. A sandy, ashen beach is forming about 6 feet below the surface of the ocean.

BASICS

SECTION 3 Assessment

❶ Places & Terms
Explain the meaning of each of the following terms.
- tectonic plate
- fault
- earthquake
- seismograph
- epicenter
- volcano

❷ Taking Notes
MOVEMENT Review the notes you took for this section.

- What are four types of plate movement?
- How are folds and faults created?

❸ Main Ideas
a. How does the movement of tectonic plates shape the earth's surface?

b. When does a volcano occur?

c. How do earthquakes cause damage?

❹ Geographic Thinking

Making Generalizations
Why do volcanoes and earthquakes occur along the Ring of Fire? **Think about:**
- tectonic plate movement
- movement of magma

RESEARCH LINKS
CLASSZONE.COM

GeoActivity

SEEING PATTERNS Use the Internet to find information on the top 10 most deadly volcanoes in history. Create a **database** showing the information by continent. Summarize your findings about the location of deadly quakes in two sentences.

External Forces Shaping the Earth

4

A HUMAN PERSPECTIVE In Egypt, a seasonal dry wind is called khamsin ("fifty") for the number of days the season occurs. During khamsin, wind-driven sandstorms kill and injure people, close businesses and airports, and strip topsoil and seed from the ground. Sandstorms are not limited to the desert areas of Africa and Southwest Asia. For instance, a five-hour storm recently blasted Jingchang, China, causing millions of dollars of damage and killing about 300 people. Sandstorms are among the external forces that change the shape of the earth and affect the lives of the people in their paths.

Weathering

In the last section, you learned about forces within the earth that changed the land. External forces, such as weathering and erosion, also alter landscapes and in some instances create the soil that is needed for plant life. **<u>Weathering</u>** refers to physical and chemical processes that change the characteristics of rock on or near the earth's surface. Weathering occurs slowly over many years and even centuries. Weathering processes create smaller and smaller pieces of rock called **<u>sediment.</u>** Sediment is mostly identifiable as either mud, sand, or silt, which is very fine particles of rock.

MECHANICAL WEATHERING Processes that break rock into smaller pieces are referred to as **<u>mechanical weathering.</u>** Mechanical weathering does not change the composition of the rock—only its size. For example, when ice crystals build up in the crack of a rock, they can actually create enough pressure to fracture the rock into smaller pieces. All sorts of agents can break apart rocks. Frost and even plant roots dig into crevices in the rock, splitting it. Human activities, like road construction or drilling and blasting in mining, are also mechanical weathering forces. Eventually, the smaller broken material will be combined with organic material to become soil.

Main Ideas

- Wind, heat, cold, glaciers, rivers, and floods alter the surface of the earth.
- The results of weathering and erosion change the way humans interact with the environment.

Places & Terms

weathering	delta
sediment	loess
mechanical weathering	glacier
	glaciation
chemical weathering	moraine
erosion	humus

SUNSHINE STATE STANDARDS
Key Standard SS.B.1.4.3 The student uses mental maps of physical and human features of the world to answer complex geographic questions.

Other Standards SS.B.2.4.1

FCAT LA.A.1.4.2 Reading: Strategies

MOVEMENT A natural arch frames a view of the Grand Canyon in Arizona. The canyon's depth was created by water erosion, and the width by rain and wind erosion. **What has happened to the sediment created by weathering in the canyon?**

CHEMICAL WEATHERING <u>**Chemical weathering**</u> occurs when rock is changed into a new substance as a result of interaction between elements in the air or water and the minerals in the rock. Decomposition, or breakup, can happen in several ways. Some minerals react to oxygen in the air and begin to crumble. That is what happens when iron rusts, for example.

Other minerals break down when combined with water or carbon dioxide, which form weak acids within the rock. When sulfur and nitrogen oxides mix with water, acid rain is formed. The increase of acid rain in the 20th century is believed to be speeding up some decomposition. The location and the climate in which the rocks are located have a great deal to do with how rocks decompose. Climates that are warm and moist will produce more chemical weathering than do cool dry areas. Rocks in cold dry and hot dry areas generally experience more mechanical weathering than chemical weathering. Ⓐ

🌐 **Geographic Thinking** ◂

Making Comparisons
Ⓐ Why would chemical weathering be rare in a desert area?

Erosion

<u>**Erosion**</u> occurs when weathered material is moved by the action of wind, water, ice, or gravity. For erosion to occur, a transporting agent, such as water, must be present. Glaciers, waves, stream flow, or blowing winds cause erosion by grinding rock into smaller pieces. Material moved from one location to another results in the lowering of some locations and increased elevation in others. For example, water might carry topsoil from a hill into a river and gradually cause the river to become more narrow. Erosion in its many forms reshapes landforms and coastal regions, as well as riverbeds and riverbanks.

WATER EROSION One form of water erosion occurs as water flows in a stream or river. The motion picks up loose material and moves it downstream. The greater the force of water, the greater the ability of the water to transport tiny rock particles, or sediment. Another form of erosion is abrasion, the grinding away of rock by transported particles. The heavier the load of sediment, the greater the abrasion on the banks and riverbed. A third eroding action of water occurs when the water dissolves chemical elements in the rock. The composition of the rock changes as a result.

Most streams erode both vertically and horizontally—that is, the valley cut by a stream gets deeper and wider, forming a V-shaped valley. As the water slows, it drops the sediment it is carrying. When a river enters the ocean, the sediment is deposited in a fan-like landform called a <u>**delta.**</u>

Wave action along coastlines also changes the land. Waves can reduce or increase beaches. Sediment deposited by wave action may build up sandbars or islands. Wave action is so powerful that in some locations, it erodes about three feet of beach per year. For some unfortunate people, a beach house with an ocean view

BACKGROUND
The term *delta* is used because the shape of the landform resembles the Greek letter delta (Δ).

Geography TODAY

Moving the Cape Hatteras Lighthouse

Coastal erosion led to one of the great moving projects of the 20th century. The Cape Hatteras Lighthouse (shown below), the tallest brick lighthouse in the nation, was dangerously close to disappearing into the sea. Built in 1870 on Hatteras Island off the coast of North Carolina, the lighthouse stood 1,500 feet from the sea. By 1987, it was only 160 feet away. The only way to save the historic lighthouse was to move it.

In the summer of 1999, the structure was slowly moved—10 to 355 feet per day—to a new location 1,600 feet from the sea. But erosion will also take beach from the new location, and by 2018, as much as 404 feet may be gone.

MOVEMENT At Chakachamna in Alaska, a glacier moves down a mountain.

What effect has the glacier had on the landform shown here?

may end up in the ocean as a result of wave action erosion.

WIND EROSION In many ways, wind erosion is similar to water erosion because the wind transports and deposits sediment in other locations. Wind speeds must reach 11 miles per hour before fine sediment can be moved. The greater the speed of the wind, the larger the particles moved. Dust storms are capable of carrying as much as 6,000 tons of sediment per cubic mile of air. As the wind slows, the sediment is dropped.

Depending on the type of wind-borne sediment, new landforms—such as sand dunes miles from seashores and rocks sculpted into fantastic forms—may be produced. Deposits of **loess** (LOH•uhs), wind-blown silt and clay sediment that produce very fertile soil, are found across the world. In northern China, for example, the deposits are several hundred feet deep. Extensive areas of loess are found in the Mississippi Valley in the United States and in the grasslands of Argentina. **B▸**

GLACIAL EROSION A **glacier** is a large, long-lasting mass of ice that moves because of gravity. Glaciers form in mountainous areas and in regions that are routinely covered with heavy snowfall and ice. In mountain regions, glaciers move downslope as a result of gravity. Glaciers such as ice caps and ice sheets move from the highest point on land toward the lowest point.

Glaciation is the changing of landforms by slowly moving glaciers. As a glacier moves, several types of erosion occur. Rocks caught underneath the glacier are ground into finer and finer particles. Some particles are so small that they are called rock flour, which is one component of soil. Massive glaciers also cut U-shaped valleys into the land. On top of or within the ice are other rocks carried by the glacier. When the glacier melts, these rocks are left behind. Rocks left behind by a glacier may form a ridge or a hill called a **moraine.** Moraines can be found on the sides, down the center, or at the leading edge of a glacier.

Inside or under the glacier may be tunnels formed by running water. These tunnels fill up with sediment dropped by the water. When the ice melts, it leaves a long snakelike ridge called an esker. Sometimes blocks of ice are trapped in the sediment. They melt slowly and leave behind a dent or a depression in the ground. These depressions are called kettles. The kettles may be filled with water forming a small lake.

Geographic Thinking◂

Making Comparisons

B In what ways are water and wind erosion similar? different?

Building Soil

Weathering and erosion are a part of the process of forming soil. Soil is the loose mixture of weathered rock, organic matter, air, and water that supports plant growth. Organic matter in the soil helps to support the growth of plants by providing needed plant food. Water and air share tiny pore-like spaces in the soil. When it rains, the pores are filled with water. As the water evaporates, drains away, or is used by the plants, the pores are filled with air. The texture of the soil, the amount of organic material called **humus,** and the amount of air and water in the soil all contribute to the soil's fertility—its ability to nurture plants.

SOIL FACTORS When geographers study soil, they look at five factors:

- **Parent material** The chemical composition of the original rock, or parent rock, before it decomposes affects its fertility.
- **Relief** Steeper slopes, such as mountainsides, are eroded easily and do not produce soil quickly.
- **Organisms** Organisms include plants, small animals like worms, ants, and bacteria that decompose material. They help to loosen soil and supply nutrients for plants.
- **Climate** Hot climates produce a soil different from that produced by cold climates. Wet climates and dry climates produce soils that are different from each other as well.
- **Time** The amount of time to produce soil varies, but a very rough average is about 2.5 cubic centimeters per century.

The variety of soils—and the climates in which they are found—determine the types of vegetation that can grow in a location. Agricultural activities, such as farming, ranching, and herding, depend on this complex relationship. In the next chapter, you will learn about the climate and vegetation on the earth and how it affects human life.

BACKGROUND
In some soils, as many as a million or more bacteria inhabit each cubic centimeter of soil.

SECTION 4 Assessment

1 Places & Terms

Explain the meaning of each of the following terms.

- weathering
- sediment
- erosion
- delta
- glaciation
- humus

2 Taking Notes

REGION Review the notes you took for this section.

- How does weathering vary according to climate?
- What are five factors affecting soil composition?

3 Main Ideas

a. What is the difference between mechanical weathering and chemical weathering?

b. What are three types of eroding action by water?

c. What factors contribute to soil fertility?

4 Geographic Thinking

Making Inferences In what ways does erosion affect the lives of humans? **Think about:**

- water, wind, and glacial action
- results of erosion

 See Skillbuilder Handbook, page R4.

EXPLORING LOCAL GEOGRAPHY Choose a type of erosion that occurs in your community. Do some research to find examples of that type of erosion. Make **sketches** or take **photographs** of the effects of the erosion. Write captions for the pictures describing the type of erosion and where it was found.

Chapter 2 Assessment

VISUAL SUMMARY
A LIVING PLANET

The Earth Inside and Out

- The earth's interior is made up of a series of layers that float on one another.
- The exterior of the earth is the crust.
- The presence of air and water make life on earth possible.

Bodies of Water and Landforms

- Almost three-fourths of the earth is covered with water.
- The hydrologic cycle circulates water.
- Landforms on the land and under the ocean are similar.

Internal Forces Shaping the Earth

- Huge plates on the earth's crust move because of the circulation of magma.
- Earthquakes and volcanoes are the results of plate movement.

External Forces Shaping the Earth

- Weathering and erosion cause changes in the earth's surface and build soil.
- Actions of wind, water, ice, and gravity shape the earth's surface.

Reviewing Places & Terms

A. Briefly explain the importance of each of the following.

1. continent
2. magma
3. hydrologic cycle
4. landform
5. relief
6. tectonic plate
7. earthquake
8. volcano
9. weathering
10. erosion

B. Answer the questions about vocabulary in complete sentences.

11. How are continents and tectonic plates related?
12. Where is magma found?
13. Lava is a form of which term listed above?
14. What is an example of a landform?
15. What does relief tell you about a landform?
16. What is the purpose of the hydrologic cycle?
17. What causes earthquakes?
18. How are magma and volcanoes related?
19. What are the two types of weathering?
20. What must be present for erosion to occur?

Main Ideas

The Earth Inside and Out (pp. 27–31)

1. What layers are found in the earth's interior?
2. What is the continental drift theory?

Bodies of Water and Landforms (pp. 32–36)

3. How does water reach a drainage basin?
4. What is topography?

Internal Forces Shaping the Earth (pp. 37–41)

5. What are three types of plate boundaries?
6. How are the Richter scale and a seismograph used?
7. What is the Ring of Fire?

External Forces Shaping the Earth (pp. 42–45)

8. What is the difference between weathering and erosion?
9. What are three transporting agents of erosion?
10. Why are there many different types of soil?

Critical Thinking

1. Using Your Notes

Use your completed chart to answer these questions.

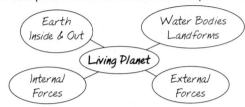

a. Why is water a critical element on the earth?

b. How do internal and external forces shape the earth?

2. Geographic Themes

a. **MOVEMENT** How does the movement of wind, water, or ice reshape the earth's surface?

b. **HUMAN–ENVIRONMENT INTERACTION** How do volcanoes and earthquakes affect human life?

3. Identifying Themes

What might be the hazards of living near the Ring of Fire? Which of the five themes apply to this situation?

4. Determining Cause and Effect.

What is the relationship between tectonic plates, earthquakes, and volcanoes?

5. Making Comparisons

How is a valley created by water different from a valley created by a glacier?

Additional Test Practice, pp. S1–S37

TEST PRACTICE
CLASSZONE.COM

BASICS

Geographic Skills: Interpreting Charts

Ten Most Deadly Earthquakes in the 20th Century

Use the information in the chart to answer the following questions.

1. **LOCATION** Which location suffered two deadly earthquakes in the 20th century?

2. **MOVEMENT** How is the magnitude of a quake related to loss of life?

3. **PLACE** What reasons might there be for so great a loss of life in Tangshan, China?

GeoActivity

Using a base map of the world and an atlas, plot the locations of the ten most deadly earthquakes. Write a sentence describing the pattern you see in the locations.

Date	Location	Deaths	Magnitude*
1976, July 27	Tangshan, China	255,000	8.0
1920, Dec. 16	Gansu, China	200,000	8.6
1927, May 22	Nan-Shan, China	200,000	8.3
1923, Sept. 1	Yokohama, Japan	143,000	8.3
1908, Dec. 28	Messina, Italy	83,000	7.5
1932, Dec. 25	Gansu, China	70,000	7.6
1970, May 31	Northern Peru	66,000	7.8
1935, May 30	Quetta, India	50,000	7.5
1990, June 20	Western Iran	40,000	7.7
1988, Dec. 7	Armenia	25,000	7.0

*Magnitude of earthquakes measured on the Richter scale developed in 1935.
SOURCES: Global Volcanism Network, Smithsonian Institution, U.S. Geological Survey, *World Almanac*

INTERNET ACTIVITY

Use the links at **classzone.com** to do research about volcanic action. Focus on a variety of volcanic activities, including eruptions, geysers, hot springs, and island formation.

Creating a Multimedia Presentation Put together a presentation about the variety of volcanic activity. Include diagrams of several different types of activity and give examples of locations where the activity takes place.

PHYSICAL GEOGRAPHY
Climate and Vegetation

A tornado roars through the countryside. Tornado winds may reach speeds up to 300 miles per hour.

GeoFocus

How do climate and vegetation affect life on earth?

Taking Notes Copy the graphic organizer below into your notebook. Use it to record information about weather, climate, and vegetation.

Seasons & Weather	
Climate	
World Climates	
Soils & Vegetation	

Seasons and Weather

A HUMAN PERSPECTIVE The smell of thousands of decaying corpses hung in the air in what was once the thriving seaport of Galveston, Texas. The day before, winds estimated at 130 miles per hour roared through the city. A storm surge of seawater more than 15 feet high pushed a wall of debris across the island of Galveston. Through this turmoil, Isaac Cline's family huddled in their home. A trolley trestle rammed the house until at last it collapsed, and the waves poured in. Cline survived, but some of his family did not. With a toll of 8,000 human lives, the "Great Galveston Hurricane" would be the deadliest hurricane to hit the United States. The storm date was August 8, 1900.

Seasons

Hurricanes occur frequently in the southern and eastern United States during summer and fall. During these seasons, storm systems with strong winds form over warm ocean water.

EARTH'S TILT Seasons have an enormous impact on us, affecting the conditions in the atmosphere and on the earth that create our weather. As the earth revolves around the sun, it is tilted at a 23.5° angle in relation to the sun. Because of the earth's revolution and its tilt, different parts of the earth receive the direct rays of the sun for more hours of the day at certain times in the year. This causes the changing seasons on the earth. Notice in the diagram to the right that the northern half of the earth tilts toward the sun in summer and away from the sun in winter.

Two lines of latitude—the tropic of Cancer and the tropic of Capricorn—mark the points farthest north and south that the sun's rays shine directly overhead at noon. The day on which this occurs is called a **solstice.** In the Northern Hemisphere, the summer solstice, or the beginning of summer, is the longest day of the year. Winter solstice, the beginning of winter, is the shortest.

Another signal of seasonal change are the equinoxes. Twice a year on the **equinox,** the days and nights all over the world are equal in length. The equinoxes mark the beginning of spring and autumn.

Seasons: Northern Hemisphere

The seasons are related to the earth's tilt and revolution. Some locations receive more direct sun rays because of the earth's tilt.

Vernal (Spring) Equinox
about March 21

N

Equator

Winter Solstice
December 22 or 23

Tropic of Cancer

N

N

S

Sun

N

S

S

Tropic of Capricorn

Summer Solstice
June 21 or 22

Equator

S

Autumnal Equinox
about September 23

Weather

Weather and climate are often confused. **<u>Weather</u>** is the condition of the atmosphere at a particular location and time. **<u>Climate</u>** is the term for weather conditions at a particular location over a long period of time. Northern Russia, for example, has a cold climate.

Geographic Thinking

Making Comparisons
Ⓐ Why might geographers be more interested in the climate of a place than its weather?

WHAT CAUSES THE WEATHER? Daily weather is the complex result of several conditions. For example, the amount of solar energy received by a location varies according to the earth's position in relation to the sun. Large masses of air absorb and distribute this solar energy, which in turn affects the weather. Other factors include:

- **water vapor** This determines whether there will be **<u>precipitation</u>**—falling water droplets in the form of rain, sleet, snow, or hail.
- **cloud cover** Clouds may hold water vapor.
- **landforms and bodies of water** Water heats slowly but also loses heat slowly. Land heats rapidly but loses heat quickly as well.
- **elevation** As elevation above sea level increases, the air becomes thinner and loses its ability to hold moisture.
- **air movement** Winds move the air and the solar energy and moisture that it holds. As a result, weather can change very rapidly.

PRECIPITATION Precipitation depends on the amount of water vapor in the air and the movement of that air. As warm air rises, it cools and loses its ability to hold water vapor. The water vapor condenses, and the water droplets form into clouds. When the amount of water in a cloud is too heavy for the air to hold, rain or snow falls from the cloud. Geographers classify precipitation as convectional, orographic, or frontal, as illustrated in the diagram below.

Types of Precipitation

Convectional Typical of hot climates, convection occurs after morning sunshine heats warm moist air. Clouds form in the afternoon and rain falls.

Orographic Associated with mountain areas, orographic storms drop more rain on the windward side of a mountain and create a rain shadow on the leeward side.

Frontal Mid-latitude frontal storms feature cold dense air masses that push lighter warm air masses upward, causing precipitation to form.

Convectional precipitation occurs in hot, moist climates where the sun quickly heats the air. The heated air rises, and by afternoon clouds form and rain falls. Orographic precipitation falls on the windward side of hills or mountains that block moist air and force it upward. The air cools and rain or snow falls. The land on the leeward side is called a **rain shadow** because it gets little rain from the descending dry air. Frontal movement causes most precipitation in the middle latitudes. A front is the boundary between two air masses of different temperatures or density. Rain or snow occurs when lighter, warm air is pushed upward by the colder, denser air. The rising air cools, water vapor condenses, and precipitation falls.

Weather Extremes

As air masses warm and cool and move across the earth's surface, they create weather. Sometimes the clashes between air masses cause storms, which can be severe. They disrupt the usual patterns of life and often cause major property damage and loss of human life. Hurricanes, tornadoes, blizzards, droughts, and floods are examples of extreme weather.

HURRICANES Storms that form over warm, tropical ocean waters are called **hurricanes**—also known as **typhoons** in Asia. These storms are called different names around the globe: tropical cyclones, willy-willies (Australia), *baguios* (Philippines), and *chubascos* (Mexico). Hurricanes are one way heat from the tropics is moved out of the region. Air flowing over an ocean with a water temperature of 80°F or higher picks up huge amounts of moisture and heat energy. As these water-laden winds flow into a low-pressure core, they tighten to form an "eye." The eye is usually 10 to 20 miles across and has clear, calm skies. But the winds moving around the eye may be as strong as 200 miles per hour.

The clouds and winds stretch over a vast area, sometimes as wide as 500 miles. Upper air currents blowing from the east steer the hurricanes in a westerly direction. As the hurricane hits land, it pounds the area with howling winds and very heavy rains. It may also cause a storm surge along coastal regions. This wall of seawater, pushed ashore by the winds, may rise to 16 feet or more. The low-lying coastal regions of Bangladesh in South Asia are especially vulnerable to storm surges from tropical cyclones. ◀B

TORNADOES Unlike hurricanes, which take days to develop, tornadoes form quickly and sometimes without warning. A **tornado,** or twister, is a powerful funnel-shaped column of spiraling air.

Geographic Thinking

Using the Atlas
B▸ Use the map on page A20. On which river delta is Bangladesh located?

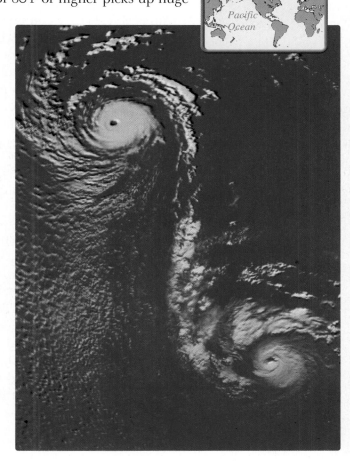

MOVEMENT A pair of typhoons move across the Pacific Ocean. Notice the "eye" in each storm. **What is the weather inside the "eye" like?**

Pacific Ocean

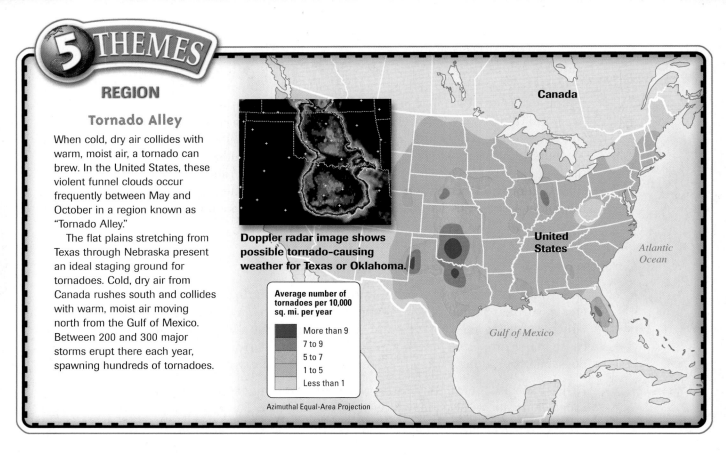

5 THEMES

REGION

Tornado Alley

When cold, dry air collides with warm, moist air, a tornado can brew. In the United States, these violent funnel clouds occur frequently between May and October in a region known as "Tornado Alley."

The flat plains stretching from Texas through Nebraska present an ideal staging ground for tornadoes. Cold, dry air from Canada rushes south and collides with warm, moist air moving north from the Gulf of Mexico. Between 200 and 300 major storms erupt there each year, spawning hundreds of tornadoes.

Doppler radar image shows possible tornado-causing weather for Texas or Oklahoma.

Average number of tornadoes per 10,000 sq. mi. per year

More than 9
7 to 9
5 to 7
1 to 5
Less than 1

Azimuthal Equal-Area Projection

Born from strong thunderstorms, tornadoes are capable of immense damage. In a tornado, winds swirl counter-clockwise around a low-pressure center. These winds may reach speeds of 300 miles per hour, blasting apart buildings and lifting objects as large as cars and mobile homes. Generally, tornadoes have small diameters (about 300 feet), travel about a mile, and last only a few minutes. However, the largest and most forceful can reach a mile across and stay on the ground for hours, hopscotching from one location to another. The largest outbreak of tornadoes in the United States occurred during a 16-hour period, April 3 and 4, 1974. A total of 148 tornadoes ripped through the Ohio and Tennessee valleys, killing 330 people. The largest share of tornadoes, about 3 of every 4, hit in the United States. On average, the U.S. National Weather Service counts 700 tornadoes each year.

BLIZZARDS A **blizzard** is a heavy snowstorm with winds of more than 35 miles per hour and reduced visibility. These weather conditions snarl traffic, endanger livestock, and trap travelers. The greatest snowfall for a 24-hour period was 76 inches (6 feet 4 inches) in Silver Lake, Colorado, in 1921. A snowstorm that lasted from February 13 to 19, 1959, dumped 189 inches (almost 16 feet) of snow on Mt. Shasta, California.

Because of their location, some areas of the country are frequently hit with snowstorms that produce huge amounts of snow. For example, the eastern and southern shores of the Great Lakes are snowbelts that experience days and days of heavy snow resulting in enormous snow depths. Around the Lake Erie and Lake Ontario areas, the annual snowfall can be as much as 450 inches (37.5 feet).

Geographic Thinking

Making Comparisons
◄ How are tornadoes different from hurricanes?

DROUGHTS A **drought** is a long period of time without rain or with very minimal rainfall. This lack of rain results in crop failures and drastically reduced levels in water storage facilities. In the early 1930s, a drought hit the Great Plains in the United States. Dust storms damaged farms across a 150,000-square-mile region that became known as the "Dust Bowl." Suffering the effects of a harsh climate, thousands of families were forced to leave their land to find work elsewhere. (See the Dust Bowl Disaster feature on pages 150-151.) In 2000, a large portion of the southern United States was struck with a long drought. Northern Texas was particularly hard hit, with 84 straight days of no rain and extremely high temperatures.

FLOODS When water spreads over land not normally covered with water, it is called a flood. Melting snow or rainwater fills streams or rivers until they reach flood stage, the point at which the banks can no longer contain the water. The water then flows into the surrounding area, called a floodplain.

Floods take lives every year, especially in low, flat places like Bangladesh, where millions of people live on the flood plains and the delta. In 1993, flooding along the Mississippi and Missouri rivers claimed 50 lives and caused about $15 billion in damage. Nearly 150 rivers and their tributaries were involved. It was the largest flood ever to hit the United States.

In the next section, you will learn about how climate affects people's lives and how humans adapt to changes in climate.

BACKGROUND
A series of droughts in Texas between 1996 and 2000 caused $5.3 billion in damages.

REGION Before the drought in Texas, this boat floated on the waters of a lake now barely visible in the background.
How is life affected by drought?

Assessment

1 Places & Terms

Explain the meaning of each of the following terms.

- solstice
- equinox
- weather
- climate
- precipitation

2 Taking Notes

MOVEMENT Review the notes you took for this section.

Seasons & Weather

- Which latitude lines mark the summer and winter solstices?
- How do moving air masses create weather?

3 Main Ideas

a. How do the earth's revolution and tilt affect the seasons?

b. What is the difference between weather and climate?

c. What are some examples of extreme weather?

4 Geographic Thinking

Determining Cause and Effect What must be present for any type of precipitation to occur? **Think about:**

- the cause of precipitation
- the types of precipitation

S **See Skillbuilder Handbook, page R9.**

GeoActivity

EXPLORING LOCAL GEOGRAPHY Using your local newspaper, television, or an Internet weather forecast, make a **chart** showing predicted temperature highs and lows and precipitation for several days. Then record the actual weather on those days. Write a summary of your observations of the accuracy of the weather forecast.

Climate

Main Ideas
- Climate reflects the seasonal patterns of weather for a location over a long period of time.
- Global climatic changes may be natural or human-made.

Places & Terms
convection
El Niño
greenhouse effect

SUNSHINE STATE STANDARDS
Key Standard SS.B.2.4.1 The student understands how social, cultural, economic, and environmental factors contribute to the dynamic nature of regions.
Other Standards SS.B.2.4.4
FCAT LA.A.1.4.2 Reading: Strategies

A HUMAN PERSPECTIVE Nineteenth-century fishermen along the Peruvian coast called the event El Niño—the Spanish name for the infant Jesus—because the event occurred near Christmastime. Every two to seven years, the waters off the Peruvian coast became warmer than usual, resulting in poor fishing. Eventually, 20th-century scientists studying worldwide climate changes confirmed the truth of this folk knowledge. They discovered that El Niño brought about changes in global weather patterns that disrupted not only fishing, but also other economic activities. Droughts and floods in Asia, Africa, and North America seemed to be related to El Niño. Scientists recognized that weather and climate conditions are not isolated but are connected parts of the global climate system.

Factors Affecting Climate

Four major factors influence the climate of a region: wind and ocean currents, latitude, elevation, and topography.

WIND CURRENTS Wind and ocean currents help distribute the sun's heat from one part of the world to another through **convection,** the transfer of heat in the atmosphere by upward motion of the air. As sunlight heats the atmosphere, the air expands, creating a zone of low air pressure. Cooler dense air in a nearby high-pressure zone rushes into the low-pressure area, causing wind.

Global wind patterns are caused by the same kind of circulation on a larger scale. The hot air flows toward the poles, and the cold air moves toward the equator. The winds would blow in straight lines, but since the earth rotates they are turned at an angle. In the Northern Hemisphere, they turn to the right. In the Southern Hemisphere, they turn to the left. This bending of the winds is called the Coriolis effect.

The map to the right shows that the wind patterns are mirror images of each other in the Northern and Southern Hemispheres. Winds are identified by the direction from which they blow; a north wind blows from the north to the south.

Global Wind Currents

North Pole
90°N
POLAR EASTERLIES
60°N / 60°N
WESTERLIES
30°N / 30°N
Tropic of Cancer
NORTHEASTERLY TRADE WINDS
0° / Equator / 0°
SOUTHEASTERLY TRADE WINDS
Tropic of Capricorn
30°S / 30°S
WESTERLIES
60°S / POLAR EASTERLIES / 60°S
90°S
South Pole

SKILLBUILDER: Interpreting Maps
❶ **MOVEMENT** From which direction do the wind currents blow near the equator in the Southern Hemisphere?
❷ **LOCATION** Between which latitudes do the westerlies blow?

Map labels:
60°N · Alaska · North Pacific · 30°N · NORTH AMERICA · California · North Equatorial · Equatorial Counter Current · 0° · PACIFIC OCEAN · South Equatorial · Tropic of Capricorn · 30°S · 60°S · West Wind Drift · 150°W · 120°W · 90°W · 60°W · 30°W · Labrador · Gulf Stream · North Equatorial · South Equatorial · Brazil · Peru · SOUTH AMERICA · ATLANTIC OCEAN · 0° · Arctic Circle · North Atlantic Drift · EUROPE · Canary · Guinea · AFRICA · Tropic of Cancer · Equator · Benguela · West Wind Drift · Antarctic Circle · ANTARCTICA · 30°E · 60°E · 90°E · ASIA · Oyashio · Japan · PACIFIC OCEAN · North Equatorial · INDIAN OCEAN · South Equatorial · AUSTRALIA · East Australian · West Australian · West Wind Drift · 120°E · 150°E

Robinson Projection

Legend: Warm current / Cool current

SKILLBUILDER: Interpreting Maps
❶ **MOVEMENT** What happens to the Peru Current as it reaches the equator?
❷ **LOCATION** Where does the West Wind Drift flow?

OCEAN CURRENTS Ocean currents are like rivers flowing in the ocean. Moving in large circular systems, warm waters flow away from the equator toward the poles, and cold water flows back toward the equator. Winds blowing over the ocean currents affect the climate of the lands that the winds cross. For example, the warmth of the Gulf Stream and the North Atlantic Drift help keep the temperature of Europe moderate. Even though much of Europe is as far north as Canada, it enjoys a much milder climate than Canada.

Ocean currents affect not only the temperature of an area, but also the amount of precipitation received. Cold ocean currents flowing along a coastal region chill the air and sometimes prevent warm air and the moisture it holds from falling to earth. The Atacama Desert in South America and the Namib Desert in Africa, for example, were formed partly because of cold ocean currents nearby. ◀A

ZONES OF LATITUDE Geographers divide the earth into three general zones of latitude: low or tropical, middle or temperate, and high or polar. Tropical zones are found on either side of the equator. They extend to the tropic of Cancer in the Northern Hemisphere and the tropic of Capricorn in the Southern Hemisphere. Lands in tropical zones are hot all year long. In some areas, a shift in wind patterns causes variations in the seasons. For example, Tanzania experiences both a rainy season and a dry season as Indian Ocean winds blow in or away from the land.

Geographic Thinking

Making Comparisons
Ⓐ How are wind and ocean currents similar in their effect on climate?

Latitude and elevation influence climate. Notice that as you move along the latitude line, the climates at the lower altitude change. However, the greater the altitude, the fewer the climate zones no matter what latitude a location may be.

SKILLBUILDER: Interpreting Graphics

❶ **LOCATION** At about what latitude and altitude would you find a desert climate?

❷ **REGION** How do the climate zones change as latitude gets higher?

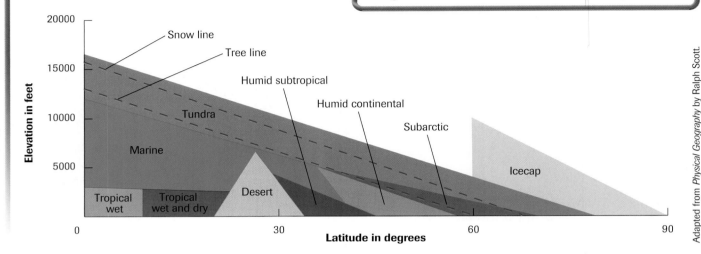

Adapted from *Physical Geography* by Ralph Scott.

The high-latitude polar zones, which encircle the North Pole and South Pole, are cold all year. Summer temperatures in the polar regions may reach a high of only 50°F.

The earth's two temperate zones lie at the middle latitudes, between the tropics and the polar regions. Within the temperate zones, climates can vary greatly, ranging from relatively hot to relatively cold. These variations occur because solar heating is greater in the summer than in the winter. So summers are much warmer.

ELEVATION Another factor in determining the climate of a region is elevation, or distance above sea level. You would think that the closer you get to the sun, the hotter it would become. But as altitude increases, the air temperature drops about 3.5°F for every 1,000 feet. Therefore, the climate gets colder as you climb a mountain or other elevated location. Climates above 12,000 feet become like those in Arctic areas—with snow and ice. For example, Mt. Kilimanjaro in east Africa is capped by snow all year long. The diagram above will help you see how latitude and elevation are related.

TOPOGRAPHY Landforms also affect the climate. This is especially true of mountain areas. Remember that moisture-laden winds cool as they move up the side of a mountain, eventually releasing rain or snow. By the time the winds reach the other side of the mountain, they are dry and become warmer as they flow down the mountain.

Changes in Climate

Climates change over time. Scientists studying ice-core samples from thousands of years ago have noted a variety of changes in temperature and precipitation. Some of the changes in climate appear to be natural while others are the result of human activities.

EL NIÑO The warming of the waters off the west coast of South America—known as **El Niño**—is a natural change in the climate. About every two to seven years, prevailing easterly winds that blow over the central Pacific Ocean slow or reverse direction, changing the ocean temperature and affecting the weather worldwide. Normally, these easterlies bring seasonal rains and push warm ocean water toward Asia and Australia. In El Niño years, however, the winds push warm water and heavy rains toward the Americas. This can cause floods and mudslides there, while Australia and Asia experience drought conditions.

When the reverse occurs—that is, when the winds blow the warmer water to the lands on the western Pacific rim—the event is called La Niña. La Niña causes increases in precipitation in places such as India and increased dryness along the Pacific coasts of the Americas.

El Niño and La Niña

El Niño and La Niña act to transfer the heat on the earth's surface and in the atmosphere to other parts of the globe.

SKILLBUILDER: Interpreting Graphics

❶ **MOVEMENT** In which direction do winds and water move in El Niño?

❷ **LOCATION** Where does flooding occur during La Niña?

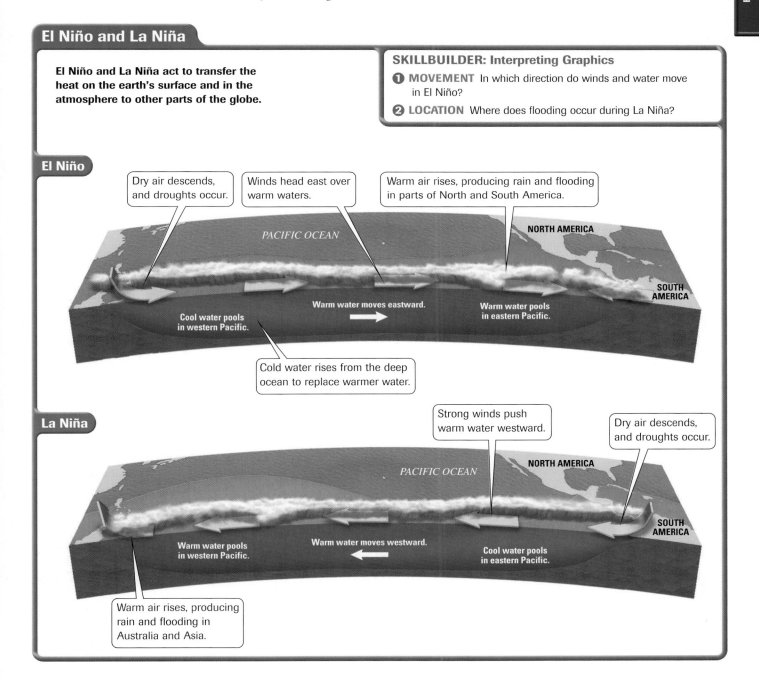

El Niño

Dry air descends, and droughts occur.

Winds head east over warm waters.

Warm air rises, producing rain and flooding in parts of North and South America.

PACIFIC OCEAN

NORTH AMERICA

SOUTH AMERICA

Cool water pools in western Pacific.

Warm water moves eastward.

Warm water pools in eastern Pacific.

Cold water rises from the deep ocean to replace warmer water.

La Niña

Strong winds push warm water westward.

Dry air descends, and droughts occur.

PACIFIC OCEAN

NORTH AMERICA

SOUTH AMERICA

Warm water pools in western Pacific.

Warm water moves westward.

Cool water pools in eastern Pacific.

Warm air rises, producing rain and flooding in Australia and Asia.

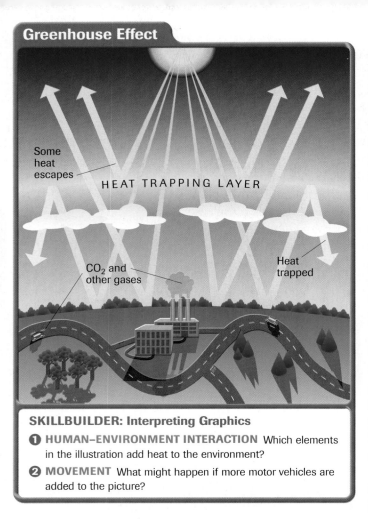

Some heat escapes

HEAT TRAPPING LAYER

CO_2 and other gases

Heat trapped

SKILLBUILDER: Interpreting Graphics

❶ **HUMAN–ENVIRONMENT INTERACTION** Which elements in the illustration add heat to the environment?

❷ **MOVEMENT** What might happen if more motor vehicles are added to the picture?

GLOBAL WARMING Although controversy exists over the causes of global warming, scientists agree that air temperatures are increasing. Since the late 1800s, the temperature of the earth has increased by one degree. However, estimates for the next century suggest that the increase will be almost 3.5 degrees.

Some scientists believe that this warming is part of the earth's natural warming and cooling cycles. For example, 18,000 to 20,000 years ago, the earth was in the last of several ice ages, when vast glaciers advanced over huge portions of the land mass.

Other scientists argue that global temperature increases are caused by the **greenhouse effect.** The layer of gases released by the burning of coal and petroleum traps some solar energy, causing higher temperatures in the same way that a greenhouse traps solar energy.

As more and more nations become industrialized, the amount of greenhouse gases will also increase. Scientists predict that, if global warming continues, ice caps will melt, flooding some coastal areas, covering islands, and changing the global climate. In the next section, you will learn about world climate regions.

BACKGROUND
The air temperature in the period between about 1500 and 1850 was so much cooler than today that it is known as a "Little Ice Age."

Assessment

❶ **Places & Terms**

Explain the meaning of each of the following terms.

• convection
• El Niño
• greenhouse effect

❷ **Taking Notes**

MOVEMENT Review the notes you took for this section.

Climate

• What are four factors that affect climate?

• What are examples of forces that produce climate changes?

❸ **Main Ideas**

a. What role do wind and ocean currents play in climate?

b. How do latitude and altitude affect climate?

c. How do El Niño and La Niña affect climate?

❹ **Geographic Thinking**

Drawing Conclusions
Which of the factors affecting climate has the greatest impact on the climate in your region? **Think about:**

• the four factors affecting climate

• the climate where you live

RESEARCH LINKS
CLASSZONE.COM

GeoActivity

SEEING PATTERNS Review the information and diagram about El Niño and La Niña on page 57. Use the Internet to find more information on these events. Create a **multimedia presentation** explaining one of the events and how it affects the world-wide weather conditions.

3 World Climate Regions

Main Ideas
- Temperature and precipitation define climate regions.
- Broad climate definitions help to identify variations in weather at a location over the course of a year.

Places & Terms
tundra

permafrost

SUNSHINE STATE STANDARDS
Key Standard SS.B.2.4.1 The student understands how social, cultural, economic, and environmental factors contribute to the dynamic nature of regions.
FCAT LA.A.1.4.2 Reading: Strategies

PLACE This highland climate zone in Patagonia, South America, has several different climate regions, including tundra and subartic.

A HUMAN PERSPECTIVE Songs have been written celebrating April in Paris. Springtime there is mild, with temperatures in the 50°F range. But no songs have been written about April in Winnipeg, Canada. Temperatures in April there are only slightly above freezing. If you look at the two locations on a map, you will find the cities are almost the same distance north of the equator. To understand why two cities at the same latitude are so different, you need to understand climate regions. When studying climate, one of the key words is location.

Defining a Climate Region

Climate regions act like a code that tells geographers much about an area without giving many local details. To define a climate region, geographers must make generalizations about what the typical weather conditions are like over many years in a location.

The two most significant factors in defining different climates are temperature and precipitation. A place's location on a continent, its topography, and its elevation may also have an impact on the climate.

Geographers use a variety of methods to describe climate patterns. The most common method uses latitude to help define the climate. There are five general climate regions: tropical (low latitude), dry, mid-latitude, high latitude, and highland. Dry and highland climates occur at several different latitudes. Within the five regions, there are variations that geographers divide into smaller zones. You can see the varied climate regions on the map on pages 60–61.

Although the map shows a distinct line between each of the climate regions, in reality there are transition zones between the regions. As you read about climate regions, refer to the climate map. You should see the latitude-related patterns that emerge in world climate regions.

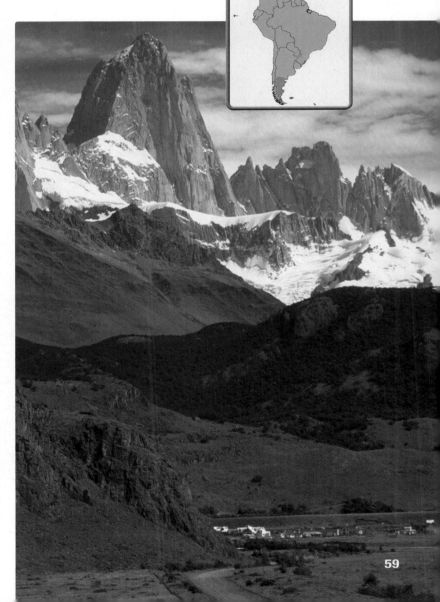

BASICS

59

Types of Climates

World climates are generally divided into five large regions: tropical, dry, mid-latitude, high latitude, and highland. The regions are divided into smaller subregions that are described below.

TROPICAL WET This subregion has little variation in temperature over the year—it is always hot, with an average temperature of 80°F. The days begin sunny but by afternoon have clouded up, and rain falls almost daily. The average amount of rain in a year is more than 80 inches. Tropical wet climates are found in Central and South America as well as Africa and Southwest Asia.

Climate Regions

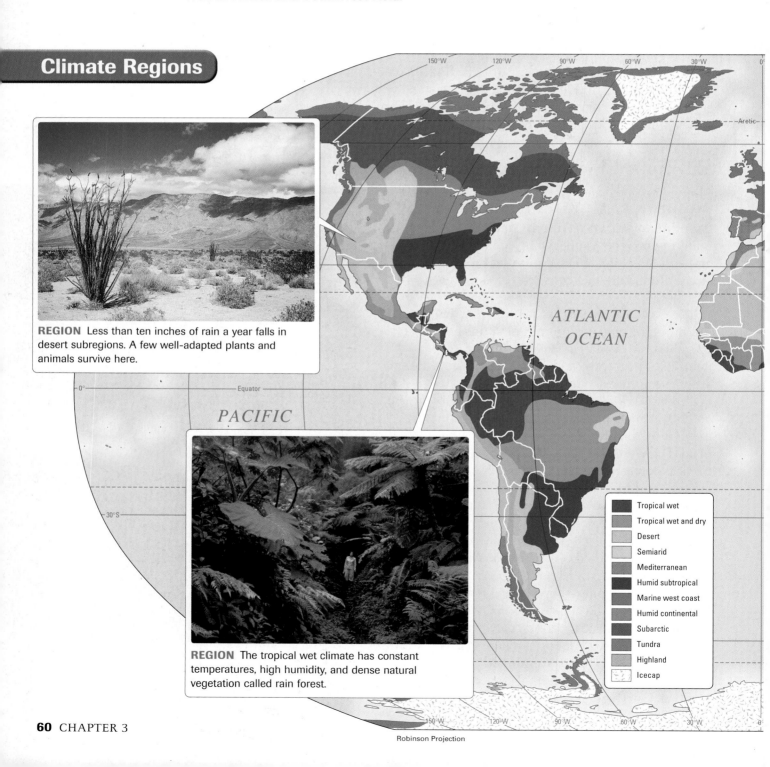

REGION Less than ten inches of rain a year falls in desert subregions. A few well-adapted plants and animals survive here.

REGION The tropical wet climate has constant temperatures, high humidity, and dense natural vegetation called rain forest.

ATLANTIC OCEAN

PACIFIC

Equator

Arctic

- Tropical wet
- Tropical wet and dry
- Desert
- Semiarid
- Mediterranean
- Humid subtropical
- Marine west coast
- Humid continental
- Subarctic
- Tundra
- Highland
- Icecap

Robinson Projection

TROPICAL WET AND DRY This climate is called "tropical wet and dry" because the subregion has a rainy season in summer and a dry season in winter. Temperatures are cooler in the dry season and warmer in the wet season. Rainfall is less than in the tropical wet climate subregion and occurs mostly in the wet season. Tropical wet and dry climates are found next to tropical wet climates in Africa, South and Central America, and parts of Asia.

SEMIARID This climate subregion does receive precipitation, just not very much: about 16 inches per year. Summers are hot. Winters are mild to cold, and some semiarid locations can produce snow. The climate is found in the interior of continents, or in a zone around deserts. The region contains some of the most productive agricultural lands in the world.

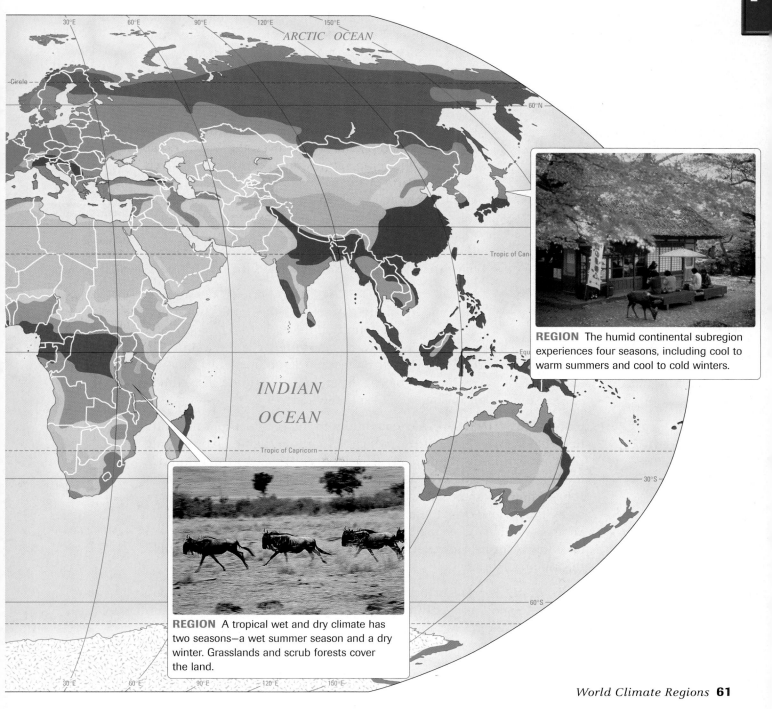

REGION The humid continental subregion experiences four seasons, including cool to warm summers and cool to cold winters.

REGION A tropical wet and dry climate has two seasons—a wet summer season and a dry winter. Grasslands and scrub forests cover the land.

DESERT Some people think a desert is nothing but sand dunes. However, deserts are categorized according to the amount of rainfall, rather than by landforms, and can be hot or cool/cold. Deserts receive less than ten inches of rain per year. Hot deserts, like the Sahara and the Arabian Desert, regularly have low humidity and high temperatures during the day. At night, temperatures drop because the dry air cannot hold heat well.

Cool/cold deserts are found in the mid-latitudes mostly in the Northern Hemisphere, often in the rain shadow of nearby mountain ranges. Summer temperatures are warm to hot, and winter temperatures range from quite cool to below freezing.

PLACE These Italian vineyards thrive in the hot dry summers and cool rainy winters of the Mediterranean climate. The climate also supports the cultivation of citrus fruit, olives, and vegetables.

MEDITERRANEAN This climate subregion is named for the land around the Mediterranean Sea where it is located. It also exists elsewhere, such as the west coast of the United States and parts of Australia. Its summers are dry and hot, and its winters cool and rainy. This climate region supports a dense population and rich agricultural activity.

MARINE WEST COAST This climate subregion, which is located close to the ocean, is frequently cloudy, foggy, and damp. The winds over the warm ocean moderate the temperatures and keep them relatively constant. Parts of the west coast of the United States and Canada and most of Western Europe experience this climate. Precipitation in marine west coast climate regions is evenly distributed throughout the year. Industrial regions with marine west coast climate may have smog (a mixture of smoke and fog).

HUMID SUBTROPICAL Long periods of summer heat and humidity characterize the humid subtropics. These areas are found on the east coast of continents and are often subject to hurricanes in late summer and autumn. The southeastern part of the United States and large areas of China are examples. Winters are mild to cool, depending on latitude. The climate is very suitable for raising crops, especially rice.

HUMID CONTINENTAL A great variety in temperature and precipitation characterizes this climate, which is found in the mid-latitude interiors of Northern Hemisphere continents. For example, Winnipeg, Manitoba, in Canada is located deep in the North American continent. It has a humid continental climate. Air masses chilled by Arctic ice and snow flow south over these areas and frequently collide with tropical air masses, causing changing weather conditions. These areas experience four seasons. However, the length of each season is determined by the region's latitude.

SUBARCTIC Evergreen forests called taiga cover the lands in the subarctic subregion, especially in Canada and Russia. Huge temperature variations occur in this subregion between summer and winter. Although the summers are short and cool, the winters are always very cold.

Geographic Thinking

Making Comparisons
◀A How are Mediterranean and marine west coast climates different?

Temperatures at freezing or below freezing last five to eight months of the year.

TUNDRA The flat, treeless lands forming a ring around the Arctic Ocean are called **tundra.** The climate subregion is also called tundra. It is almost exclusively located in the Northern Hemisphere. Very little precipitation falls here, usually less than 15 inches per year. The land has **permafrost**—that is, the subsoil is constantly frozen. In the summer, which lasts for only a few weeks, the temperature may reach slightly above 40°F. **B**

ICE CAP Snow, ice, and permanently freezing temperatures characterize the region, which is so cold that it rarely snows. These subregions are sometimes called polar deserts since they receive less than ten inches of precipitation a year. The coldest temperature ever recorded, 128.6°F below zero, was on the ice cap at Vostok, Antarctica.

HIGHLANDS The highlands climate varies with latitude, elevation, other topography, and continental location. In rugged mountain areas such as the Andes of South America, climates can vary based on such factors as whether a slope faces north or south and whether it is exposed to winds carrying moisture.

Understanding climate helps you understand about the general weather conditions in an area. In the next section, you will learn about the variety of soils and vegetation on the earth.

Geographic Thinking

Making Comparisons
B How are precipitation amounts in a tundra climate similar to those of a desert climate?

REGION Life is hard during the long, cold, and dark winter in the subarctic. The only places where the temperatures are colder are the icecaps of Greenland and the Antarctic.

SECTION 3 Assessment

1 Places & Terms

Identify and explain where in the region these would be found.

- tundra
- permafrost

2 Taking Notes

REGION Review the notes you took for this section.

World Climates

- What are the five basic climate regions?
- What are the factors that determine climate?

3 Main Ideas

a. How do tropical climates differ from each other?

b. How do desert regions differ from each other?

c. How are Humid subtropical and Mediterranean climates different from each other?

4 Geographic Thinking

Making Generalizations
How are the climates of the Northern Hemisphere different from the climates of the Southern Hemisphere?

Think about:

- sizes and locations of the continents

 See Skillbuilder Handbook, page R6.

GeoActivity

MAKING COMPARISONS Study the descriptions of climates in this chapter. Then either draw pictures or find pictures that illustrate the climates. Using a hanger and string, create a **mobile** displaying world climate regions.

RAND McNALLY | Map and Graph Skills

Interpreting Climographs

How many seasons are in a year where you live? In some parts of the world the climate is the same all year long. Other places have only two seasons—wet and dry. Still others experience changes in temperature and precipitation almost every month. A climograph allows you to quickly determine what the climate is like in a place. If you have two climographs you may compare two different places.

THE LANGUAGE OF GRAPHS A **climograph** shows the average daily temperature and precipitation for each month of the year for a specific location. This information shows what the climate is like over a year. Use the green line on the graph to find the average temperature and the blue bars to find average rainfall.

> **SUNSHINE STATE STANDARDS**
> **Key Standard SS.B.2.4.1.**
> The student understands how social, cultural, economic, and environmental factors contribute to the dynamic nature of regions.
> **FCAT LA.A.2.4.1 Reading:** Identify Main Idea, Details, and Methods

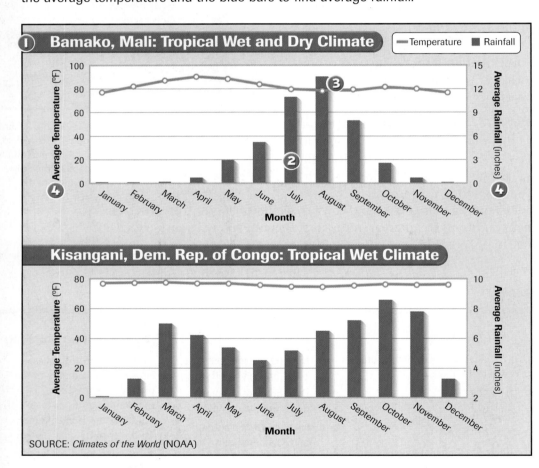

Bamako, Mali: Tropical Wet and Dry Climate — Temperature ■ Rainfall

Kisangani, Dem. Rep. of Congo: Tropical Wet Climate

SOURCE: *Climates of the World* (NOAA)

1 The title indicates the place, sometimes its absolute location, and the type of climate.

2 Each blue bar shows average rainfall for one month of the year. For example, more than 13 inches of rain falls in Bamako in August.

3 The green line shows the average temperature. For example, the July temperature in Bamako is 80°F.

4 Precipitation can be shown in inches (in.) or centimeters (cm.). Temperature can be shown in Fahrenheit (F°) or Celsius (C°) degrees.

Map and Graph Skills Assessment

1. Analyzing Data
What information is shown on each side of the vertical axis?

2. Analyzing Data
What are the rainy months in Bamako? How much rain falls in the rainiest month?

3. Drawing Conclusions
How is the tropical wet and dry climate of Bamako different from the tropical wet climate of Kisangani?

64 CHAPTER 3

Soils and Vegetation

Main Ideas

• Soil and climate help to determine the vegetation of a region.

• Human land use alters the vegetation in both positive and negative ways.

Places & Terms

ecosystem   coniferous

biome   savanna

deciduous   steppe

rain forest

SUNSHINE STATE STANDARDS
Key Standard SS.B.2.4.1 The student understands how social, cultural, economic, and environmental factors contribute to the dynamic nature of regions.
FCAT LA.A.1.4.2 Reading: Strategies

A HUMAN PERSPECTIVE In the 1870s, a settler described prairie land in Tazewell County, Illinois, as having western meadow lilies "as high as a boy's head," rippling waves of wildflowers, and grass so dense that a man on horseback 30 yards away could not be seen. At that time, the land produced crops of grains, such as corn, wheat, and oats. In most places in the world where people have settled, the land continues to be used for agricultural purposes, such as farming, herding, and timber production. Soil and vegetation have a direct impact on which of those activities the people living in a region can perform.

Soil Regions

Soil is a thin layer of weathered rock, humus, air, and water. It shapes human existence in many ways. The world's food supply depends greatly on the top six inches of soil (sometimes called topsoil). Such factors as depth, texture, and humus content of the soil determine the type of vegetation that can be supported in a region. That, in turn, helps to influence which human activities may take place there. As you study the chart below, notice the relationship of climate to the characteristics of the soil. Soil characteristics and climate are major influences in vegetation regions.

Vegetation Regions

Vegetation regions are natural environments that provide the stage for human activities such as farming, raising livestock, and producing timber. Soil, temperature, and moisture influence the type of vegetation that thrives naturally in a region. Vegetation patterns are identified on the basis of the ecosystems they support. An **ecosystem** is an interdependent community of plants and animals. The ecosystem of a region is referred to as a **biome.** Biomes are further divided into forest, grassland, desert, and tundra.

Soil Differences

Soil Characteristic	Wet Climate	Dry Climate	Warm Climate	Cold Climate
Depth	deep	shallow	deep	shallow
Texture	intermediate to fine	coarse	fine	coarse
Weathering	chemical	physical	rapid	slow
Humus Content	variable	low	low	abundant
Acidity	acidic	not acidic	less acidity	higher acidity

SOURCE: *Physical Geography*, Ralph Scott

SKILLBUILDER: Interpreting Charts

❶ **PLACE** What characteristics would soil in a cold, dry climate most likely have?

❷ **REGION** How does the soil in warm and wet climates differ from the soil in cold and dry climates in terms of depth and texture?

Tropical rain forest
Tropical grassland
Desert and dry shrub
Temperate grassland
Mediterranean shrub
Deciduous and mixed forest
Coniferous forest
Tundra
Highland
Icecap

Robinson Projection

SKILLBUILDER: Interpreting Maps

❶ **REGION** Which continent has the greatest area of tropical rain forest?

❷ **REGION** What vegetation regions are found in the continental United States?

FORESTLANDS Forest regions are categorized by the types of trees they support—broadleaf or needleleaf. Broadleaf trees, such as maple, oak, birch, and cottonwood, are also called **deciduous** trees. The **rain forest** is located in the tropical zone and is covered with a heavy concentration of broadleaf trees. In the tropical rain forest region, some broadleaf trees stay green all year. In the deciduous region, trees shed their leaves at least once during the year. This region is located almost exclusively in the Northern Hemisphere. Sometimes deciduous trees are mixed with needleleaf trees, such as pine, fir, and cedar, to form a mixed forest region. Needleleaf trees are also called **coniferous** trees because they are cone bearing. They are found in huge stands in northern regions of North America, Asia, and Europe.

GRASSLANDS Grasslands, mostly flat regions dotted with a few trees, are called by different terms. In the tropical grassland region, the flat, grassy, mostly treeless plains are called **savanna.** In the Northern Hemisphere, the terms **steppe** or prairie are used to identify temperate grasslands. Vast areas of Eurasia are covered with steppe. In the Southern Hemisphere, the temperate grasslands may be referred to as pampas.

DESERT AND TUNDRA The plants that live in these extreme climates are specially adapted to tolerate the dry or cold conditions. In the tundra, plants that hug the ground, such as mosses and lichen, are best adapted to survive the cold dry climate. In the desert, plants that can conserve water and withstand heat, such as cacti, sagebrush, or other shrubs, dot the landscape.

Geographic Thinking

Seeing Patterns
Ⓐ Study the map above. What patterns do you see in the relationship of forestlands to grasslands?

Before

After

Human Impact on the Environment

As you can imagine, the impact of human activities on soil and vegetation is immense. Throughout this book, you will read about the ways that human beings either have adapted to the land or have altered it to meet their needs. Human activities that affect the environment include building dams or irrigation systems, planting food crops, or slashing and burning the vegetation.

The two photographs above show you an example of a human-environment interaction. The photograph to the left shows Glen Canyon on the Colorado River before a dam was built to create a huge lake. The lake—Lake Powell—was created to provide irrigation water, hydroelectric power, and recreational facilities. The photograph on the right shows a part of Lake Powell today. It is 186 miles long, has 1,900 miles of shoreline, and in places is 500 feet deep. As you can see, this human activity has caused changes in the environment.

The next chapter will help you understand the human side of geography and its relationship to the physical world.

HUMAN–ENVIRONMENT INTERACTION Photographs of Glen Canyon show the same site before and after it was filled with the waters of Lake Powell. **How has the landscape changed as the result of the creation of the lake?**

SECTION 4 Assessment

1 Places & Terms

Explain the meaning of each of the following terms.

- ecosystem
- biome
- rain forest
- savanna
- steppe

2 Taking Notes

REGION Review the notes you took for this section.

Soils & Vegetation

- How are soil and vegetation linked?
- What are the four types of biomes?

3 Main Ideas

a. What soil factors influence type of vegetation in a region?

b. What is the difference between coniferous and deciduous trees?

c. What is unique about vegetation in the desert and tundra regions?

4 Geographic Thinking

Making Inferences What impact have humans had on soil and vegetation? **Think about:**

- altering the land to meet needs
- careless use of the land

RESEARCH LINKS CLASSZONE.COM

GeoActivity

EXPLORING LOCAL GEOGRAPHY Use the Internet to find out about the current vegetation of your state and what it was like before becoming populated. Draw two **maps** to show the contrast between the two time periods. Write a sentence summarizing what you learned.

VISUAL SUMMARY
CLIMATE AND VEGETATION

Seasons and Weather

- Seasons occur because of the earth's revolution and tilt.
- Weather is the condition of the atmosphere on a daily basis.
- Weather extremes disrupt normal patterns of living.

Climate

- Climate is the atmospheric condition over a long period of time.
- Climate is affected by wind and ocean currents, latitude, elevation, and topography.
- Global climate changes include El Niño and the greenhouse effect.

World Climate Regions

- There are five basic climate regions: tropical, dry, mid-latitude, high latitude, and highland.
- The two most significant factors in climate are temperature and precipitation.

Soils and Vegetation

- Soil characteristics include texture, depth, and humus content.
- Soil and climate are major influences on vegetation regions.
- Vegetation patterns are based on ecosystems.

Reviewing Places & Terms

A. Briefly explain the importance of each of the following.

1. weather
2. climate
3. precipitaton
4. convection
5. El Niño
6. greenhouse effect
7. ecosystem
8. biome
9. rain forest
10. savanna

B. Answer the questions about vocabulary in complete sentences.

11. In what type of situation would it be more important to know about weather instead of climate?
12. How are climate and weather related?
13. Which of the above terms deal with types of vegetation?
14. What role does convection play in precipitation?
15. Which of the above terms deals with increases in average global temperature?
16. Which of the above terms has to do with dramatic changes in Pacific Ocean water temperature?
17. What is the relative location of rain forests?
18. What does savanna have in common with steppe and prairie?
19. Which of the above terms could be affected by the greenhouse effect?
20. What is the relationship between an ecosystem and a biome?

Main Ideas

Seasons and Weather (pp. 49–53)

1. What causes the changing seasons on earth?
2. What are the major factors that cause weather?
3. What are the different types of precipitation?

Climate (pp. 54–58)

4. What are four factors that influence climate?
5. How do ocean currents affect climate?
6. What might be some causes of global warming?

World Climate Regions (pp. 59–64)

7. What general information about climate is included in a description of a climate region?
8. What are the five basic climate regions?

Soils and Vegetation (pp. 65–67)

9. How does climate affect soil?
10. How are forestlands defined?

Critical Thinking

1. Using Your Notes

Use your completed chart to answer these questions.

Seasons & Weather	
Climate	
World Climates	
Soils & Vegetation	

a. How are seasons, weather, and climate connected to each other?

b. How would knowing about the climate of a region help you determine the vegetation of the region?

2. Geographic Themes

a. **REGION** Why are there few subarctic climate zones in the Southern Hemisphere?

b. **LOCATION** How does location affect climate?

3. Identifying Themes

How might the climate of an area be affected by global warming? Which of the five themes apply to this situation?

4. Drawing Conclusions

What is incorrect about defining a desert by landforms such as sand dunes?

5. Making Inferences

Why is a hurricane such a deadly storm?

Additional Test Practice, pp. S1–S37

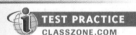 **TEST PRACTICE** CLASSZONE.COM

Geographic Skills: Interpreting Graphs

Temperature Variations

Use the graph to answer the following questions.

1. **MOVEMENT** Which decade (10-year span) had the highest temperatures?

2. **MOVEMENT** In approximately which year did temperatures begin to consistently rise above the average?

3. **HUMAN–ENVIRONMENT INTERACTION** What impact might the greenhouse effect have on the temperature changes?

Using straws, devise a three-dimensional model to show the information on the graph. Be sure to provide time frames and temperature information on your model.

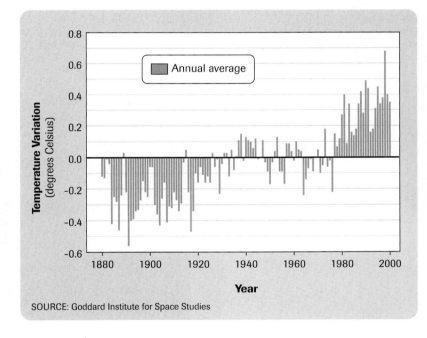

SOURCE: Goddard Institute for Space Studies

 INTERNET ACTIVITY

Use the links at **classzone.com** to do research about global warming. Choose one of the nine regions in this textbook. Focus on determining the effects of global warming on the region, especially on coastal areas.

Creating a Multimedia Presentation Combine charts, maps, or other visual images in an electronic presentation showing how the earth will be affected by global warming.

HUMAN GEOGRAPHY
People and Places

Petroglyphs like this one
from the Fremont culture
(found in Dinosaur
National Monument)
offer evidence of human
life in the desert of the
Colorado Plateau.

GeoFocus

What is human geography about?

Taking Notes Copy the graphic organizer below into your notebook. Use it to record information about human geography.

The Elements of Culture

Main Ideas

- Human beings are members of social groups with shared and unique sets of behaviors and attitudes.
- Language and religion are two very important aspects of culture.

Places & Terms

culture	**cultural hearth**
society	**acculturation**
ethnic group	**dialect**
innovation	**religion**
diffusion	

BASICS

SUNSHINE STATE STANDARDS
Key Standard SS.B.2.4.1 The student understands how social, cultural, economic, and environmental factors contribute to the dynamic nature of regions.

Other Standards SS.B.1.4.4, B.2.4.2

FCAT LA.A.1.4.2 Reading: Strategies

A HUMAN PERSPECTIVE In an article titled "The 100% American," anthropologist Ralph Linton described how a typical American, in eating breakfast, had borrowed from other cultures.

> He has coffee, an Abyssinian plant, with cream and sugar. Both the domestication of cows and the idea of milking them originated in the Near East, while sugar was first made in India. . . . As a side dish he may have the egg of a species of bird domesticated in Indo-China, or thin strips of the flesh of an animal domesticated in Eastern Asia.

Borrowing from other cultures is common around the world, even if we are not aware of it.

Defining Culture

What makes us similar to some people in the world but different from most others? The answer is culture. **Culture** is the total of knowledge, attitudes, and behaviors shared by and passed on by the members of a specific group. Culture acts as a blueprint for how a group of people should behave if they want to fit in with the group. It ties us to one group and separates us from other groups—and helps us to solve the problems that all humans face. Culture involves the following factors:

- food and shelter
- religion
- relationships to family and others
- language
- education
- security/protection
- political and social organization
- creative expression

A group that shares a geographic region, a sense of identity, and a culture is called a **society.** Sometimes you will hear the term **ethnic group** used to refer to a specific group that shares a language, customs, and a common heritage. An ethnic group has an identity as a separate group of people within the region where they live. For example, the San peoples—known as the Bushmen of the Kalahari Desert in Africa—live in a specific territory, speak their own language, and have a social organization distinct from other groups living in the region.

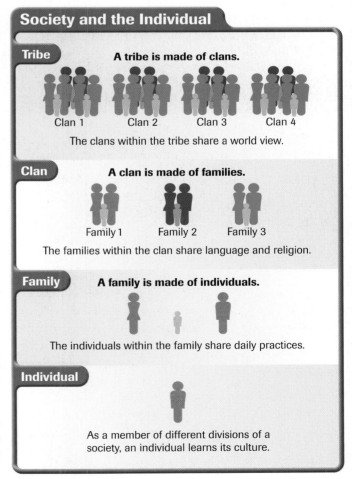

Society and the Individual

Tribe — A tribe is made of clans.

Clan 1   Clan 2   Clan 3   Clan 4

The clans within the tribe share a world view.

Clan — A clan is made of families.

Family 1   Family 2   Family 3

The families within the clan share language and religion.

Family — A family is made of individuals.

The individuals within the family share daily practices.

Individual

As a member of different divisions of a society, an individual learns its culture.

Culture Change and Exchange

Cultures and societies are always in the process of changing. Change comes very slowly to some societies and rapidly to others. It can come about through innovation or the spread of ideas or behaviors from one culture to another.

INNOVATION Taking existing technology and resources and creating something new to meet a need is called **innovation.** For example, to solve the need for storage of goods, some societies invented baskets woven from reeds because reeds were abundant. Other cultures developed clay pots to solve the same problem.

Innovation and invention may happen on purpose or by accident. History is filled with examples of "accidents" that changed the life of a society. For example, the first cooked meat may have happened by accident, but it led to the practice of cooking most food rather than eating it raw.

MOVEMENT A satellite dish brings the outside world to a Mongolian family living in this traditional house called a yurt. **How does this picture show acculturation?**

DIFFUSION Good ideas or inventions are hard to keep secret—they spread when people from different societies, or their ideas and inventions, come into contact with one another. This spread of ideas, inventions, or patterns of behavior is called **diffusion.** In an age of electronic technology, diffusion can happen very quickly. Television and the Internet speed ideas and facilitate the sale of goods around the globe. Almost no group of people can avoid some kind of contact with other societies.

Geographic Thinking

Seeing Patterns
🔺 In which locations would diffusion happen less frequently?

A **cultural hearth** is a site of innovation from which basic ideas, materials, and technology diffuse to many cultures. River civilizations such as those along the Indus River in South Asia, Huang He in East Asia, the Nile River in Africa, and the Tigris and Euphrates in Southwest Asia are the best known cultural hearths.

ACCULTURATION Exposure to an innovation does not guarantee that a society will accept that innovation. Individuals in the society must decide whether the innovation is useful and consistent with its basic principles. **Acculturation** occurs when a society changes because it accepts or adopts an innovation. An example of acculturation might be wearing jeans instead of traditional garments.

Sometimes individuals or a group adopt innovations that radically change the society. The resulting changes may have a positive or a negative effect on the society, depending on how the change came about. If change is forced on a group, it may have negative consequences. On the other hand, if the individuals or a group accept the change, it may lead to a better life for everyone. For example, the lives of thousands of people in Somalia were saved when they were persuaded to be vaccinated for smallpox in the 1970s.

Language

Language is one of the most important aspects of culture because it allows the people within a culture to communicate with each other. Language reflects all aspects of culture, including the physical area occupied by the society. For example, a society that lives in the subarctic or tundra region may have many different words to describe various forms of snow. However, those words would be useless for a culture in a place with no snow.

LANGUAGE AND IDENTITY Language helps establish a cultural identity. It builds a group identity and a sense of unity among those who speak the language. If a language is spoken throughout a political region, a spirit of unity and sometimes nationalism (a strong feeling of pride in one's nation) grows. Language can also divide people. If more than one language is spoken in an area, but one language seems to be favored, then conflict sometimes results. In Canada, for example, where both English and French are spoken, French Canadians pressured the government to recognize both French and English as official languages.

LANGUAGE FAMILIES Geographers estimate that between 3,000 and 6,500 languages are spoken across the world today. The languages are categorized by placing them with other similar languages in language families. (See page 74.) Today's languages evolved from earlier languages. One of the earlier languages, called Nostratic, developed in the area known today as Turkey. Nostratic is believed to be the basis of the Indo-European languages that you see on the chart on page 74. Languages as different as English, Russian, Hindi, and Greek all developed from the Indo-European family.

Versions of a language are called dialects. A **dialect** reflects changes in speech patterns related to class, region, or other cultural changes. For example, in the United States, dialects might include a Southern drawl, a Boston accent, or even street slang.

LANGUAGE DIFFUSION Like other aspects of culture, language can be diffused in many ways. It may follow trade routes or even be invented. For example, Swahili developed as a trade language between Arabic traders and Bantu-speaking tribes on Africa's east coast. Sometimes a blended language develops to aid communication among groups speaking several languages. In Louisiana, the presence of French, African, and North American peoples resulted in a blended language called Louisiana Creole.

A second way diffusion occurs is through migration. As people settle in new locations, the language they carry with them sometimes takes hold in the region. For example, colonists from Europe brought the English, Spanish, French, and Dutch languages to North and South America, Africa, Australia, and parts of Asia.

BACKGROUND
The language spoken by the largest number of native speakers is Mandarin Chinese, with an estimated 885 million speakers.

5 THEMES

BASICS

MOVEMENT

Spanglish

As more and more Spanish-speaking people moved to the United States, a blended language developed—Spanglish. The new language takes some English words and "Spanish-izes" them. In turn, some Spanish words are "English-ized."

Spanglish frequently shows up when a speaker doesn't know the correct terms in one language. Take the phrase, "click the mouse." In Spanglish, click may become "clickea" or mouse might be "el mouse" or "el raton." The final result might be "clickea el raton," or "click el mouse."

This switching back and forth between languages is called code switching and is common with many foreign language speakers.

MEDICAL SPANGLISH
TRUDY ESPINOZA-ABRAMS
How to Examine a Spanish-Speaking Patient Without Knowing a Single Word of Spanish

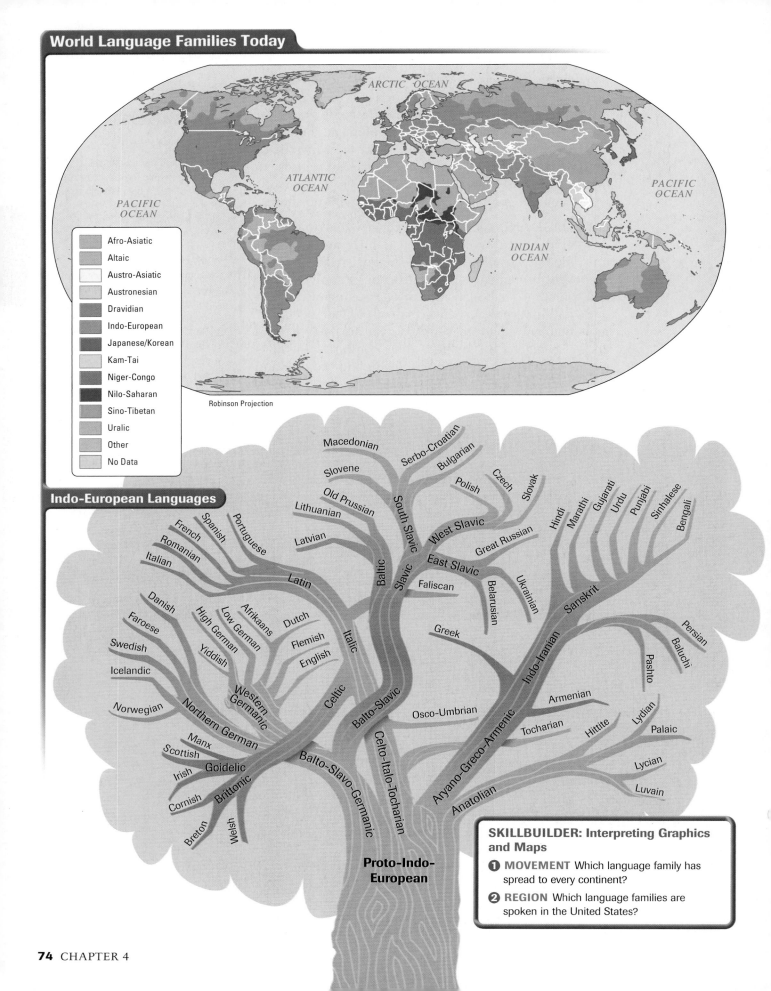

ARCTIC OCEAN

ATLANTIC OCEAN

PACIFIC OCEAN

PACIFIC OCEAN

INDIAN OCEAN

Robinson Projection

- Afro-Asiatic
- Altaic
- Austro-Asiatic
- Austronesian
- Dravidian
- Indo-European
- Japanese/Korean
- Kam-Tai
- Niger-Congo
- Nilo-Saharan
- Sino-Tibetan
- Uralic
- Other
- No Data

Indo-European Languages

Macedonian
Serbo-Croatian
Bulgarian
Slovene
Czech
Slovak
Old Prussian
Polish
Lithuanian
Hindi
Marathi
Gujarati
Urdu
Punjabi
Sinhalese
Bengali
Latvian
South Slavic
West Slavic
Portuguese
Spanish
French
Romanian
Italian
Slavic
Great Russian
Baltic
East Slavic
Latin
Faliscan
Belarusian
Ukrainian
Sanskrit
Danish
Afrikaans
Dutch
Persian
Faroese
High German
Low German
Flemish
Baluchi
Swedish
Yiddish
English
Italic
Greek
Indo-Iranian
Pashto
Icelandic
Western Germanic
Celtic
Armenian
Norwegian
Northern German
Balto-Slavic
Osco-Umbrian
Tocharian
Hittite
Lydian
Palaic
Manx
Scottish
Aryano-Greco-Armenic
Irish
Goidelic
Balto-Slavo-Germanic
Celto-Italo-Tocharian
Lycian
Cornish
Brittonic
Luvain
Breton
Welsh
Anatolian

Proto-Indo-European

SKILLBUILDER: Interpreting Graphics and Maps

❶ MOVEMENT Which language family has spread to every continent?

❷ REGION Which language families are spoken in the United States?

Religion

An aspect of culture that has a great deal of influence on people's lives is religion. **Religion** consists of a belief in a supernatural power or powers that are regarded as the creators and maintainers of the universe. Religions establish beliefs and values that define how people worship the divine being or divine forces and how they behave toward each other. Traditionally, religions have been categorized as one of three types:

- **monotheistic,** with a belief in one god
- **polytheistic,** with a belief in many gods
- **animistic** or traditional, often with a belief in divine forces in nature

SPREAD OF RELIGION Religions spread across the world through diffusion and through converts, people who give up their former beliefs for a new religion. Some religions, such as Christianity, Islam, and Buddhism, actively seek to convert people to their beliefs. Other religions, such as Judaism and Hinduism, do not. Finally, isolated pockets of religions, mostly animist, are found in Japan, Central Africa, Oceania, and among Native Americans of both North and South America. **◁B**

Geographic Thinking

Seeing Patterns
B How does location contribute to the isolation of animist practice?

Major Religions

Three major religions of the world began in Southwest Asia and two in South Asia. The religions of Southwest Asia—Judaism, Christianity, and Islam—are monotheistic and share similar basic beliefs, and some prophets and teachers. Of the South Asian religions, Buddhism represents an adaptation of Hinduism.

JUDAISM The oldest of the Southwest Asian religions, Judaism is concentrated in Israel. Followers, called Jews, live in Israel, the United States, Canada, South America, and many European cities. Established more than 3,200 years ago, Judaism is the oldest monotheistic religion. It is considered an ethnic religion with a long tradition of faith and culture tied tightly together. The basic laws and teachings come from a holy book called the Torah. The religious center of Judaism is the city of Jerusalem in Israel.

CHRISTIANITY Christianity evolved about 2,000 years ago from the teachings of Judaism. It, too, is monotheistic. Christianity is based on the teachings of Jesus Christ, whom Christians believe was the Son of God. The teachings of Jesus are recorded in the New Testament of the Bible. The religion spread from Jerusalem, first through the work of the Apostle Paul and, later, by many missionaries. It is the largest of all the religions with 2 billion followers. Christians live on every continent. Christianity has three major groups: Roman Catholic, Protestant, and Eastern Orthodox.

ISLAM The third religion that originated in Southwest Asia is Islam. It is based on the teachings of the Prophet Muhammad, who began teaching around 613 A.D. Its followers are known as Muslims. Islam is a monotheistic religion in which followers worship God, who is called Allah in Arabic. The religion has close ties to the prophets and teachers of Judaism and Christianity. The holy book of the Muslims is the

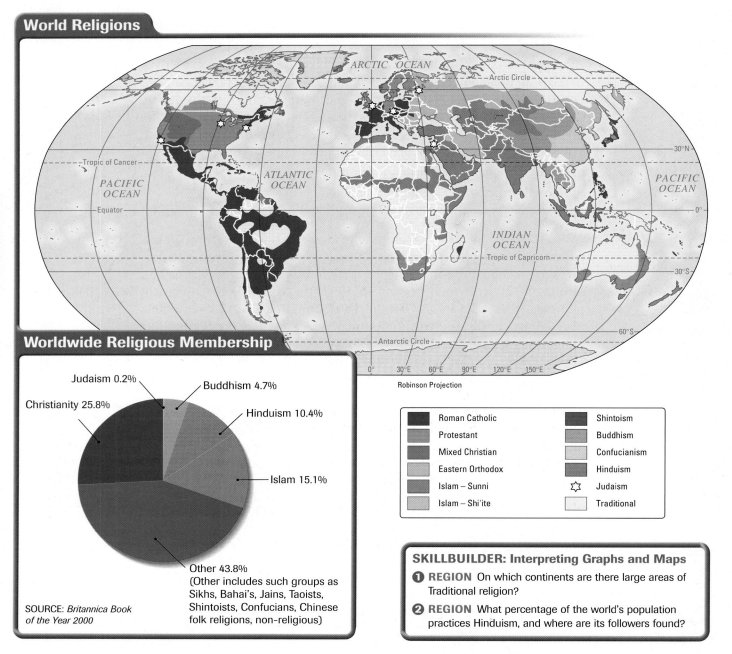

World Religions

ARCTIC OCEAN

Arctic Circle

Tropic of Cancer

PACIFIC
OCEAN

ATLANTIC
OCEAN

Equator

PACIFIC
OCEAN

INDIAN
OCEAN

Tropic of Capricorn

Antarctic Circle

Robinson Projection

Worldwide Religious Membership

- Judaism 0.2%
- Buddhism 4.7%
- Christianity 25.8%
- Hinduism 10.4%
- Islam 15.1%
- Other 43.8%
  (Other includes such groups as Sikhs, Bahai's, Jains, Taoists, Shintoists, Confucians, Chinese folk religions, non-religious)

SOURCE: *Britannica Book of the Year 2000*

Roman Catholic	Shintoism
Protestant	Buddhism
Mixed Christian	Confucianism
Eastern Orthodox	Hinduism
Islam – Sunni	☆ Judaism
Islam – Shi'ite	Traditional

SKILLBUILDER: Interpreting Graphs and Maps

1 REGION On which continents are there large areas of Traditional religion?

2 REGION What percentage of the world's population practices Hinduism, and where are its followers found?

Qur'an. Islam spread from Southwest Asia to Africa, Central, South, and Southeast Asia, and parts of the Balkans in Europe. The two major divisions of Islam are Sunni and Shiíte.

HINDUISM One of the world's oldest religions, Hinduism dates back about 5,000 years. It is an ethnic religion concentrated in India, but has followers elsewhere. Hinduism is usually considered polytheistic because a Hindu may believe in one god or many gods, each of whom represents an aspect of the divine spirit, Brahman. The religious requirements of a caste system—levels of fixed social classes with specific rites and duties—shape many aspects of Hindus' lives and culture.

BUDDHISM An offshoot of Hinduism, Buddhism developed about 563 B.C. in India, near the Nepal border. Its founder, Siddhartha Gautama (also called the Buddha or Enlightened One), rejected the Hindu idea of caste. Buddha's teachings promote the correct way of living in order to reach an enlightened spiritual state called nirvana. Missionaries spread the Buddha's teaching from India to Southeast Asia, China, Japan, and Korea. Buddhism has several branches, the largest of which are Theravada, Mahayana, Lamaism, and Zen.

OTHER ASIAN PRACTICES In parts of East Asia, three belief systems are widely practiced. They are Confucianism, Taoism, and Shinto. Sometimes those belief systems are thought of as religions and sometimes as philosophies of life. All of them have specific ways of life and behaviors associated with them.

Creative Cultural Expressions

All cultures have ways of expressing themselves creatively. The environment and culture in which an artist lives is reflected in the artistic product. Cultures produce performing arts, visual arts, and literature.

Performing arts developed by a culture often include music, dance, theater, and film. Music is a cultural aspect found in all societies. The instruments on which the music is played and the style of music are unique to each group.

Visual arts include architecture, painting, sculpture, and textiles. The style of the visual arts will reflect materials available in the region and cultural themes. ◄

Oral and written literature, such as poems, folk tales, and stories, often illustrate aspects of the culture such as attitudes and behaviors. They can also be a reflection of the environment in which they are produced.

Throughout this book, you will find discussions of creative cultural expressions. As you study them, remind yourself that each culture is unique—as are the artistic expressions that the people from that culture produce.

Geographic Thinking

Seeing Patterns
▷ How might climate affect the visual arts of a region?

HUMAN–ENVIRONMENT INTERACTION This Peruvian bone flute dates back to sometime before 700 A.D. Bone flutes are among the oldest of all musical instruments.
In what way does this instrument show human-environment interaction?

Assessment

❶ Places & Terms

Explain the meaning of each of the following terms.

- culture
- society
- ethnic group
- diffusion
- acculturation
- dialect

❷ Taking Notes

MOVEMENT Review the notes you took for this section.

| Human Geography |
| Cultural |

- In what ways is culture diffused?
- Which religions have spread from the place where they were founded?

❸ Main Ideas

a. What factors make up culture?

b. In what ways is language spread?

c. What are the major religions of the world?

❹ Geographic Thinking

Determining Cause and Effect What role do innovation and diffusion play in changing a culture? **Think about:**

- contact with other groups
- acculturation

RESEARCH LINKS
CLASSZONE.COM

MAKING COMPARISONS Choose one of the factors of culture listed on page 71. Then select three countries. Use the Internet to find information on how each culture solves the problems associated with the factor you selected. Create a **database** showing the results of your research.

Population Geography

Main Ideas

• People are not distributed equally on the earth's surface.

• The world's population continues to grow, but at different rates in different regions.

Places & Terms

birthrate	population pyramid
fertility rate	
mortality rate	push-pull factors
infant mortality rate	population density
rate of natural increase	carrying capacity

SUNSHINE STATE STANDARDS

Key Standard SS.B.1.4.1 The student uses a variety of maps, geographic technologies including geographic information systems (GIS) and satellite produced imagery, and other advanced graphic representations to depict geographic problems.

Other Standards SS.B.2.4.2, B.2.4.5

FCAT LA.A.1.4.2 Reading: Strategies

A HUMAN PERSPECTIVE In 1999, the world's population reached 6 billion people. To get an idea of how many people that is, consider this:

If you had a *million* dollars in thousand dollar bills, the stack would be 6.3 inches high. If you had a *billion* dollars in thousand dollar bills, the stack would be 357 feet high, or about the length of a football field including the end zones. Now multiply by 6. Six billion dollars would be almost 6 football fields high.

At the world's natural growth rate in 1999, that 6 billion population figure was reached by the births of 230,000 people each day.

Worldwide Population Growth

The earth's population hit the one billion mark in the early 1800s. As the world industrialized, people grew more and better food and improved sanitation methods, and the population of the world began to soar. As more and more women reached childbearing age, the number of children added to the population also increased. As you can see in the diagram at the right, by 1930 two billion people lived on the earth. Notice that the number of years between each billion mark gets smaller.

BIRTH AND DEATH RATES A population geographer studies aspects of population such as birth and death rates, distribution, and density. To understand population growth, geographers calculate several different statistics. One is the **birthrate,** which is the number of live births per thousand population. In 2000, the highest birthrate in the world was more than 54 per thousand in Niger, and the lowest rate was about 8 per thousand in Latvia. The world average birthrate is 22 per thousand.

Another way to study population is to look at the fertility rate. The **fertility rate** shows the average number of children a woman of childbearing years would have in her lifetime, if she had children at the current rate for her country. A fertility rate of 2.1 is necessary just to replace current population. Today, the worldwide average fertility rate is about 3.0.

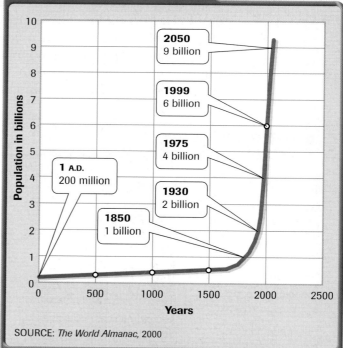

World Population Growth

2050 9 billion

1999 6 billion

1975 4 billion

1930 2 billion

1850 1 billion

1 A.D. 200 million

SOURCE: *The World Almanac,* 2000

SKILLBUILDER: Interpreting Graphs

❶ **ANALYZING DATA** How long did it take for the population to reach one billion?

❷ **MAKING GENERALIZATIONS** How have the intervals between increases changed?

U.S. Population Pyramids, 2000 and 2050

A population pyramid presents a quick picture of a country's population distribution by age and sex. The effects of events in society can also be seen. Notice that in the year 2000 pyramid there is a bulge between ages 35 to 49. This reflects the "baby boom" generation born after World War II.

SKILLBUILDER: Interpreting Graphs

❶ **ANALYZING DATA** How old are the people in the "baby boom" generation in the 2000 pyramid?

❷ **DRAWING CONCLUSIONS** Why will the numbers for the very elderly (85+) increase so much by the year 2050?

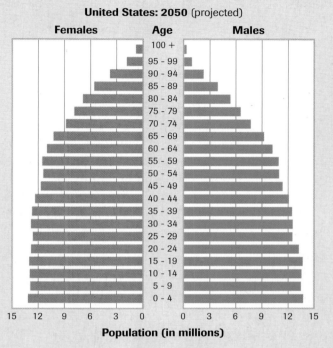

SOURCE: U.S. Census Bureau

BASICS

The **mortality rate**—also called the death rate—is the number of deaths per thousand people. In general, a society is considered healthy if it has a low mortality rate. However, some healthy nations have higher mortality rates because they have large numbers of elderly people.

For this reason, geographers also look at infant mortality rates in measuring how healthy the people of a nation are. The **infant mortality rate** shows the number of deaths among infants under age one per thousand live births. In the 1800s, the worldwide infant mortality rate was about 200 to 300 deaths per thousand live births. At the beginning of the 21st century, improved health care and nutrition led to a much lower rate worldwide. However, some parts of the world still record as many as 110 infant deaths per thousand. To find the rate at which population is growing, subtract the mortality rate from the birthrate. The difference is the **rate of natural increase,** or population growth rate. ◀Ａ

POPULATION PYRAMID Another way to analyze populations is to use a **population pyramid,** a graphic device that shows sex and age distribution of a population. A population pyramid allows geographers to examine how events in society, such as wars, famine, or epidemics, affect the population of a country or region. Study the population pyramids shown above to learn how to interpret these graphics.

🌐 **Geographic Thinking**

Seeing Patterns

Ａ▶ What will the rate of natural increase be like if the birthrate is high and the mortality rate is low?

Population Distribution

The billions of people in the world are not distributed equally across the earth. Some lands are not suitable for human habitation. In fact, almost 90 percent of the world's population lives in the Northern Hemisphere. One in four people in the world lives in East Asia, and one of every two people lives in either East Asia or South Asia. Several factors, including climate, altitude, and access to water, influence where people live.

HABITABLE LANDS Almost two-thirds of the world's population lives in the zone between 20° N and 60°N latitude. Some of the lands in this zone have suitable climate and vegetation for dense human habitation. They are warm enough and wet enough to make agriculture possible. In addition, populations are concentrated along coastal regions and river valleys. The lightly populated areas are in polar regions, heavily mountainous regions, and desert regions. **B**

URBAN–RURAL MIX Currently, more than half of the world's population lives in rural areas, but that number is changing rapidly. More people are moving into cities—particularly cities with populations of more than one million people. Twenty-six giant cities, called megacities, are home to a total of more than 250 million people. The largest of these is Tokyo, with more than 28 million inhabitants. These huge cities struggle with overcrowded conditions and immense demand for water and sanitation. You'll learn more about cities and their populations in the Urban Geography section of this chapter.

Geographic Thinking

Seeing Patterns
B Why are populations concentrated along coastal regions and river valleys?

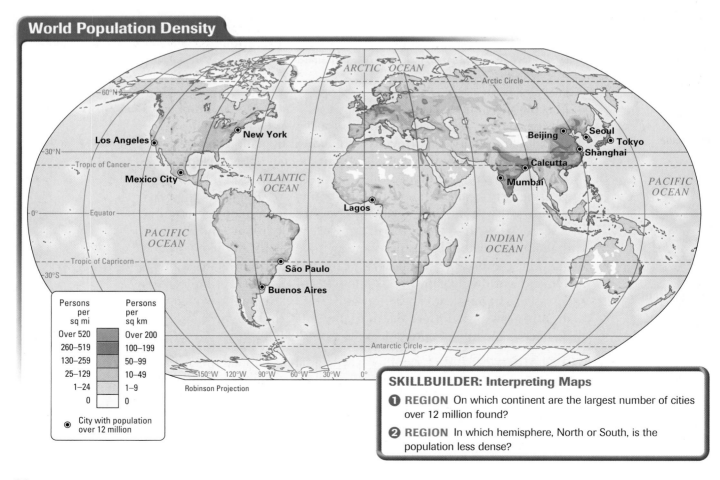

World Population Density

Persons per sq mi / Persons per sq km

Over 520	Over 200
260–519	100–199
130–259	50–99
25–129	10–49
1–24	1–9
0	0

● City with population over 12 million

Robinson Projection

SKILLBUILDER: Interpreting Maps

❶ REGION On which continent are the largest number of cities over 12 million found?

❷ REGION In which hemisphere, North or South, is the population less dense?

PLACE Nanjing Road in Shanghai, China, is considered one of the busiest streets in the world. **What problems do people in overcrowded cities face?**

MIGRATION The large-scale migration of people from one location to another also alters the distribution of population. Reasons for migrating are sometimes referred to as **push-pull factors.** Push factors are those that cause people to leave their homeland and migrate to another region. Environmental conditions, such as drought or other natural disasters, are examples of push factors. Other push factors are political, such as war or the persecution of certain groups of people for ethnic or religious reasons. For example, more than one million Rwandans left their country for other parts of Africa in the wake of a civil war there in 1994. Pull factors draw or attract people to another location. Countries with good economic opportunities and high salaries are the likely destinations for migrants. Favorable climate is another pull factor.

Geographic
Thinking

Making Comparisons
▶ Do you think push factors or pull factors result in larger migrations?

Population Density

To understand how heavily populated an area is, geographers use a figure called **population density.** This figure is the average number of people who live in a measurable area, such as a square mile. The number is reached by dividing the number of inhabitants in an area by the total amount of land they occupy.

Because population is not distributed evenly across the land, the number may be misleading for an entire nation. Certain areas may be densely populated, while others are quite thinly populated. For example, according to the 1990 census, the population density of the United States was 70.3 people per square mile. But as you can see on the population density table on the next page, Alaska—with its huge land area and small population—had a density of one person per square mile. On the other hand, New Jersey, with a small land area and large population, had a very high density at 1,098 people per square mile. Remember, too, that population density may change over time.

Regional Population Density

Region	Highest Density (per square mile)		Lowest Density (per square mile)	
United States and Canada	New Jersey	1,098	Alaska	1.10
			Nunavut	0.01
Latin America	Barbados	1,560	French Guiana	6.00
Europe	Monaco	45,333	Iceland	7.00
Russia and the Republics	Armenia	331	Kazakhstan	14.00
Africa	Rwanda	711	Namibia	6.00
Southwest Asia	Bahrain	2,594	Saudi Arabia	26.00
South Asia	Maldives	2,469	Bhutan	48.00
East Asia	South Korea	1,234	Mongolia	4.00
Southeast Asia, Australia, and Oceania	Singapore	16,714	Australia	6.00

SOURCE: Population Reference Bureau 2000 World Population Data

SKILLBUILDER: Interpreting Charts

❶ **ANALYZING DATA** Which region seems to be the most densely populated?

❷ **MAKING INFERENCES** Why might Korea be more densely populated than China, which is in the same region?

CARRYING CAPACITY Another aspect of population density statistics is the ability of the land to support a population. **Carrying capacity** is the number of organisms a piece of land can support. A region with fertile land may be able to support far more people than one with land of poor quality or with little land available for cultivation.

The level of technology of a group living on the land may affect carrying capacity. Improved farming techniques, such as irrigation, use of fertilizers, and mechanized farm equipment, will generally increase the carrying capacity of land.

In some locations, few if any people make their living by farming. However, other aspects of their economy allow a small area of land to support a large number of people. Notice the density of Singapore shown in the chart at left. A city state located at the tip of Malaysia, Singapore is a center of international finance and shipping. The wealth these activities bring allows people to import food. Thus, Singapore is able to support millions of people even though it has little farmable land. ▶

In the next section, you'll learn how the world's population forms into political units.

Geographic Thinking

Using the Atlas
◀ Use the map on pages A22–A23 to find the location of Singapore. On what bodies of water is Singapore located?

Use the map on pages A22–A23

SECTION 2 Assessment

❶ **Places & Terms**

Explain the meaning of each of the following terms.
• birthrate
• mortality rate
• rate of natural increase
• push-pull factors
• population density

❷ **Taking Notes**

PLACE Review the notes you took for this section.

Human Geography
↓
Population

• How does a population pyramid help you understand population in a place?
• What factors influence where people live?

❸ **Main Ideas**

a. How is the rate of natural increase determined?

b. Why must the population density figures for a country be used with caution?

c. Where does the majority of the world's population live?

❹ **Geographic Thinking**

Making Inferences What role has industrialization played in population growth?

Think about:
• infant mortality rate
• improved living conditions

[S] **See Skillbuilder Handbook, page R4.**

GeoActivity

SEEING PATTERNS Choose one continent to study on the satellite image on page 88. Compare the satellite image with an atlas map of the same area. Write an **explanation** of which landforms or water bodies have played a part in the distribution of population that you see in the satellite image.

Political Geography

Main Ideas
- The world is divided into many political regions.
- Local, national, and regional governments control aspects of life within the boundaries of the unit.

Places & Terms

state	**monarchy**
nation	**dictatorship**
nation-state	**communism**
democracy	**landlocked**

BASICS

SUNSHINE STATE STANDARDS
Key Standard SS.B.2.4.3 The student understands how the allocation of control of the Earth's surface affects interactions between people in different regions.

Other Standards SS.B.1.4.4, C.1.4.1

FCAT LA.A.1.4.2 Reading: Strategies

A HUMAN PERSPECTIVE Abdoulaye Sowe, a Senegalese farmer, chose a spot to build his new house near the Senegalese border guard's shack. He believed the guard shack was in Senegal. But long-time residents of the area told him that, before the shack was built, a guard used to sit near a tree that was considered the border marker. The tree was several hundred feet north of Sowe's house. Technically, Sowe now lived in the country of Gambia, not Senegal. Sowe's dilemma points out the difficulty of pinpointing borders that create political units.

Nations of the World

Governmental units of the world can be described in either political or geographic terms. Generally, we use the political term **state** to describe an independent unit that occupies a specific territory and has full control of its internal and external affairs. Often the term "country" is used to mean state.

Nation refers to a group of people with a common culture living in a territory and having a strong sense of unity. When a nation and a state occupy the same territory, that territory is called a **nation-state.** Many countries of the world are nation-states. However, it is possible for a nation not to have a territory. When that happens, the group without a territory is called a stateless nation. Examples of stateless nations include Palestinians, Kurds, and Basques.

TYPES OF GOVERNMENT All countries must choose a type of government. Generally, the type of government falls into one of these categories:

- **Democracy** Citizens hold political power, either directly or through elected representatives. Example: the United States.

- **Monarchy** A ruling family headed by a king or queen holds political power and may or may not share the power with citizen bodies. Example: the United Kingdom or Saudi Arabia.

- **Dictatorship** An individual or group holds complete political power. Example: North Korea or Afghanistan.

- **Communism** In this government and economic system, nearly all political power and means of production are held by the government in the name of all the people.

Whatever the type of government, it must deal with issues that have to do with the territory and people of the state.

PLACE National flags fly at the United Nations headquarters in New York City.

Political Geography of the Korean Peninsula

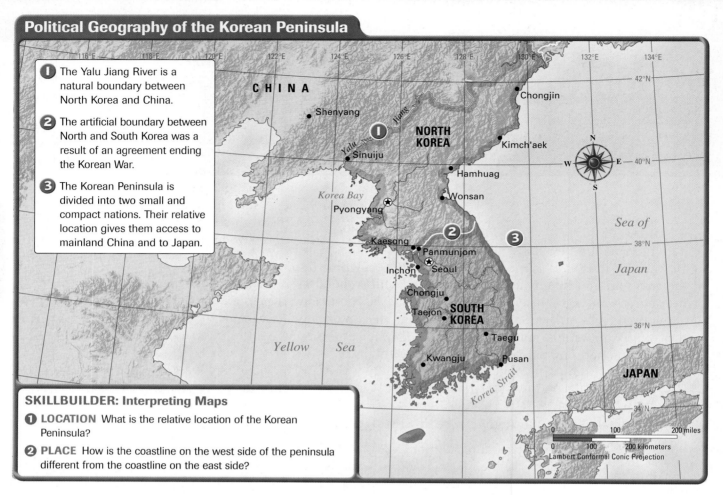

1. The Yalu Jiang River is a natural boundary between North Korea and China.

2. The artificial boundary between North and South Korea was a result of an agreement ending the Korean War.

3. The Korean Peninsula is divided into two small and compact nations. Their relative location gives them access to mainland China and to Japan.

SKILLBUILDER: Interpreting Maps

❶ **LOCATION** What is the relative location of the Korean Peninsula?

❷ **PLACE** How is the coastline on the west side of the peninsula different from the coastline on the east side?

Geographic Characteristics of Nations

Three geographic characteristics are very important in describing a country. These characteristics are: 1) size, 2) shape, and 3) relative location. The combination of these characteristics makes each nation unique. By looking at the map above, you will see how these characteristics helped shape the political geography of the Korean Peninsula.

SIZE You might assume that the physical size of a country has much to do with its wealth and power. However, this is not always true. For example, the political division of the United Kingdom known as England once controlled a significant empire of colonies around the globe. Even so, a larger nation, such as the United States, China, or Russia, has the potential to be more powerful because it has more resources and people on which to build military or economic power.

SHAPE Countries can be compact, such as Germany, or long like Chile. Some countries are fragmented, like Japan, which is made up of many islands. The shape of a country can have an impact on how easily it can be governed, how goods are moved to all areas of the country, and how it relates to neighboring countries. ▶

LOCATION The relative location of a country can be very important. A **landlocked** country—one surrounded by other land and with no direct outlet to the sea—must find ways to build connections to the rest of the world to get goods in and out of the country. Bolivia is an example of a landlocked country. In contrast, the location of the tiny city-state of

🌐**Geographic Thinking**

Making Comparisons
◀ Which of the three shapes describes the United States?

84 CHAPTER 4

Singapore in Southeast Asia gives it access to major shipping lanes between East Asia and South Asia. The resulting trade brings great wealth to the port. A nation surrounded by hostile neighbors must deal with issues of protection and security.

National Boundaries

Boundaries or borders set the limits of the territory controlled by a state. Within its borders, the state can do such things as collect taxes, set up a legal code, and declare an official language. A state may claim all of the resources found within its boundaries. Because so much is at stake, states are very protective of their borders. The two basic types of national boundaries are natural and artificial.

NATURAL BOUNDARIES A natural boundary is based on physical features of the land, such as rivers, lakes, or chains of mountains. The Rio Grande, for example, is a river that forms a natural boundary between part of Mexico and part of the United States. Natural boundaries may seem like an easy way to separate one country from another, but they do present problems. Traditionally, a river or lake boundary is fixed in the middle of the body of water. What if a river shifts its course? Which country gets additional land—or loses it? ◀B▶

ARTIFICIAL BOUNDARIES An artificial boundary is a fixed line generally following latitude or longitude lines. The 49°N latitude line that separates the United States from Canada is an example. These lines are often formally defined in boundary treaties between countries. Sometimes a conquering country imposes boundaries on lands it has taken over. The lines established may not match boundaries previously found in that location, which can lead to internal problems or even war.

Africa is a good example of how boundary lines can divide groups of people or put groups that have long been enemies together in one state. When parts of Africa were divided by European colonial powers in the 1800s, the boundary lines for Nigeria included the traditional lands of the Hausa-Fulani people, the Yoruba people, and the Ibo people. Under British control, the three groups were forced to follow British rules. When

Geographic Thinking◀

Using the Atlas
▶B Use the map on page A10. What physical features make up the natural boundaries between the United States and Canada?

MOVEMENT The Great Wall of China is an example of an artificial boundary. It was built to stop invading armies.
How does the wall also illustrate a type of natural boundary?

NATIONAL

Size Very large units composed of many medium and small units

Effect Little direct contact with the people

Role Deals with issues affecting the entire nation, such as security or international diplomatic relations

Example United States

STATE/REGIONAL

Size Larger units composed of many smaller units

Effect More direct contact with the people than national units

Role Deals with issues that affect all of the smaller units, such as licensing drivers

Example States or regional groups, such as the Tennessee Valley Authority

LOCAL

Size Smaller units of government

Effect Very direct contact with the people

Role Deals with issues that are narrow in scope, such as streets and sanitation

Example A school district or town

Britain left, there was controversy over the control of the lands. One group, the Ibo, attempted to withdraw from Nigeria and form its own nation-state—Biafra. A civil war resulted, and the attempt to split away failed.

Regional Political Systems

Countries often are divided into smaller political units to make governing more efficient. The most common local units of government are cities, towns, and villages. Other types of political units might include school districts.

Smaller political units often combine to form larger regional units, such as counties, provinces, and states. Here, too, there may be districts for providing a service or product to an area that crosses several political units. For example, the Tennessee Valley Authority (TVA) regulates water usage in a seven-state region.

Countries may join with each other to form international political, military, or economic units. Groups of states within a regional area may band together to promote mutual goals. An example is the European Union, which you'll learn more about in Chapter 14.

BACKGROUND
The TVA built dams, hydroelectric plants, and flood control projects on the Tennessee River and its tributaries.

The largest political unit is the United Nations, which has nearly 200 members who work to improve political, cultural, and economic conditions across the globe. In the next section, you'll learn that almost half of the world's population lives in urban areas that include political units called cities.

SECTION 3 Assessment

① Places & Terms

Explain the meaning of each of the following terms.

• state
• nation
• nation-state
• democracy
• monarchy
• dictatorship

② Taking Notes

PLACE Review the notes you took for this section.

Human Geography
↓
Political

• What are three geographic characteristics of countries?
• What are three types of governments?

③ Main Ideas

a. How do the three basic geographic characteristics affect a nation?

b. What is the difference between natural and artificial boundaries?

c. Why do local and regional political systems exist?

④ Geographic Thinking

Making Inferences Which type of boundary would most likely cause the greatest political problems? **Think about:**

• types of natural borders
• artificial boundaries

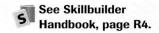
See Skillbuilder Handbook, page R4.

GeoActivity

EXPLORING LOCAL GEOGRAPHY Using a map of the United States, study the boundaries of the 50 states. Create a **database** that shows the names of states with 1) all artificial boundaries, 2) all natural boundaries, 3) mixed boundaries. Write several sentences summarizing your data.

Urban Geography

Main Ideas
- Nearly half the world's population lives in urban areas.
- Cities fulfill economic, residential, and cultural functions in different ways.

Places & Terms
urban geography

city

suburb

metropolitan area

urbanization

central business district (CBD)

SUNSHINE STATE STANDARDS
Key Standard SS.B.2.4.1 The student understands how social, cultural, economic, and environmental factors contribute to the dynamic nature of regions.

Other Standards SS.B.2.4.2, B.2.4.6

FCAT LA.A.1.4.2 Reading: Strategies

A HUMAN PERSPECTIVE Around 4500 B.C. in Sumer, an ancient country in what today is Iraq, the city of Ur was settled. Eventually it grew to be home to as many as 34,000 people. Archaeologists believe that it was one of the first cities in the world. Within the city walls, a broad avenue led up to an immense temple with a roof that loomed 80 feet above the ground. Surrounding the temple were private homes and large open markets with shops on streets resembling those in cities of Southwest Asia today. Some people lived in two-story houses with balconies and even had clay-lined drains for waste disposal. A canal ran through the city from the river to a harbor built on its northern edge. This was not an overgrown village, but a real city.

In the centuries since, cities have grown so important that geographers have developed the field of **urban geography**—the study of how people use space in cities.

Growth of Urban Areas

Today, much of the population of the world lives in cities. **Cities** are not just areas with large populations—they are also centers of business and culture. Cities are often the birthplace of innovation and change in a society. Urban lifestyles are different from those of towns, villages, or rural areas. When geographers study urban areas, they consider location, land use, and functions of the city.

URBAN AREAS An urban area develops around a main city called the central city. The built-up area around the central city may include **suburbs,** which are political units touching the borders of the central city or touching other suburbs that touch the city. These suburbs are within commuting distance of the city. Some suburbs are mostly residential, while others have a whole range of urban activities.

Smaller cities or towns with open land between them and the central city are called exurbs. The city, its suburbs, and exurbs link together economically to form a functional area called a **metropolitan area.** A megalopolis is formed when several metropolitan areas grow together. An example of a megalopolis is the corridor in the northeastern United States including Boston, New York, Philadelphia, Baltimore, and Washington, D.C.

PLACE Both the old city and the new parts of Cairo, Egypt, can be seen in this view.
Why do you think the old parts of the city were not torn down and replaced with new buildings?

BASICS

87

PLACE Urban areas are clearly visible in this satellite view of earth at night. The light blue areas are "reflective" areas with either snow pack or sand.
Which regions of the earth have few urban areas?

URBANIZATION The dramatic rise in the number of cities and the changes in lifestyle that result is called **urbanization.** The trend to live in cities increased rapidly over the last two centuries. As more and more people moved into cities to find work, the cities and their surrounding areas grew. Today, some cities are enormous in physical area and have populations exceeding 10 million residents. As you can see above, cities are found on all continents except Antarctica.

City Locations

Around the world, cities have certain geographic characteristics in common. Many cities are found in places that allow good transportation, such as on a river, lake, or coast. Others are found in places with easy access to natural resources. Sacramento, California, for instance, grew rapidly after gold was discovered in 1848 in north-central California. Because of their geographic advantages, cities serve as economic bases, attracting businesses and people to work in those businesses.

Cities are often places where goods are shifted from one form of transportation to another. For example, the city of Chicago, Illinois, is a transportation hub for goods produced in the upper Great Lakes states. Goods are sent by air, truck, or train to Chicago on Lake Michigan, then to the U.S. east coast and the rest of the world.

Cities may specialize in certain economic activities because of their location. For example, the city of Pittsburgh, Pennsylvania, which is located close to iron ore and coal sources, became a steel-producing center. The same is true for the city of Sheffield in England. Some urban areas may grow or expand because of economic activities located in the city. Brasília, the capital of Brazil, has grown to 1.8 million people since 1960 because of all the government agencies and activities there. Cultural, educational, or military activities may also attract people to a specific location.

Geographic Thinking

Using the Atlas
Ⓐ Use the map of North America on page A10. What waterway leads from the Great Lakes to the Atlantic Ocean?

Land Use Patterns

Urban geographers also study land use, the activities that take place in cities. Basic land use patterns found in all cities are:

- **residential,** including single-family housing and apartment buildings
- **industrial,** areas reserved for manufacturing of goods
- **commercial,** used for private business and the buying and selling of retail products

The core of a city is almost always based on commercial activity. This area of the city is called the **central business district (CBD).** Business offices and stores are found in this part of the city. In some cities, very expensive housing may also be found there. Predictably, the value of the land in the CBD is very high. In fact, the land is so expensive that sky-scrapers are often built to get the most value from the land.

As you move away from the CBD, other functions become more important. For example, residential housing begins to dominate land use. Generally, the farther you get from the CBD, the lower the value of the land. Lower land values may lead to less expensive housing. Tucked into these less expensive areas are industrial activities and retail areas, such as shopping centers, markets, or bazaars. However, the patterns for urban activities vary by culture and geography. Study the models below to learn more about urban land use patterns. ◀ᴮ

⊕Geographic Thinking◀

Seeing Patterns

ᴮ▶ Why do industrial activities take place where land is less expensive?

Urban Area Models

Geographers may use a model to illustrate patterns they find in the use of space. The models below are patterns of land use in urban areas.

Concentric Zone Model

An early model showed the CBD as the "bull's-eye" of the urban area. It is surrounded by other activities.
by E. W. Burgess

Sector Model

Activities are concentrated in wedges or sectors, which may follow transportation lines or natural features such as a river.
by H. Hoyt

Multiple Nuclei Model

Districts, called nuclei, specialize in one urban activity, and are found throughout the urban area.
by C. D. Harris and E. L. Ullman

- Central business district
- Wholesale and light manufacturing
- Low-income housing
- Middle-income housing
- High-income housing
- Low-income and high-income housing
- Middle-income and high-income housing
- Heavy manufacturing
- Outlying business district
- Outer suburban housing
- Outer suburban industry
- High-income commuter zone

SKILLBUILDER: Interpreting Graphics

❶ **MAKING GENERALIZATIONS** Where is low-income housing found in each of the models?

❷ **MAKING COMPARISONS** What has happened to business and industry activities in the multiple nuclei model as compared to the other two models?

Urban Functions: Chicago

Clark   State

State of Illinois Building
RANDOLPH
Daley Center
City Hall/ County Building
CLARK
LASALLE
Lake
Randolph
Washington
Washington
MADISON
Madison

○━━ Elevated train lines and station

○━━ Subway train lines and station

Ⓣ–Ⓣ Walk between stations for free transfer

♿ Disabled Accessible station

🛍 Shopping

🎭 Theaters

SKILLBUILDER: Interpreting Maps

❶ **LOCATION** What other government building is located near the State of Illinois Center?

❷ **PLACE** What urban functions are found in the area shown?

The Functions of Cities

The city is the center of a variety of functions. The map at the left shows a portion of the CBD of Chicago, Illinois. Notice that shopping, entertainment, and government services are located there. Large office buildings occupy much of the rest of the area shown.

Many cities also have educational and cultural activities such as libraries or museums located in the CBD. The Manhattan section of New York City, for example, is home to about 70 museums. Other functions of the city—such as manufacturing, wholesaling, residential, recreation, and a variety of religious and social services—may be located in other parts of the city.

Cities need a great deal of space to accomplish these functions, which makes good transportation absolutely essential. Major cities may have several forms of mass transit, such as bus systems, subways, or commuter trains, to move thousands of people to and from the areas of the city where the various functions take place. In some areas, freeway systems link people in the suburbs to the activities in the city. Geographers often study a city's transportation system to understand how well the city is fulfilling its functions. ▶

In the next section, you'll learn more about economic geography that takes place across the globe.

Geographic Thinking

Making Comparisons
Ⓒ How are city transportation systems different from those of towns or villages?

SECTION 4 Assessment

❶ **Places & Terms**

Explain the meaning of each of the following terms.
- city
- suburb
- metropolitan area
- urbanization
- central business district (CBD)

❷ **Taking Notes**

LOCATION Review the notes you took for this section.

Human Geography
↓
Urban

- What functions or activities are located away from the CBD?
- In what types of relative locations are many cities found?

❸ **Main Ideas**

a. What components make up a metropolitan area?

b. What are some basic land use patterns in cities?

c. What are some functions of an urban area?

❹ **Geographic Thinking**

Making Inferences How does land value influence the activities that take place on a piece of urban land? **Think about:**
- land use patterns
- the CBD

 See Skillbuilder Handbook, page R4.

GeoActivity

EXPLORING LOCAL GEOGRAPHY Survey the CBD of the city you live in or one close to you. Make notes of the urban functions you see there. Create a **sketch map** of your CBD. Be sure to label the areas or buildings, and the urban functions they fill.

Economic Geography

5

A HUMAN PERSPECTIVE One of the most valuable of natural resources—petroleum—wasn't always used as a source of energy. Until the world began to run on gasoline-powered machinery, oil was used for a variety of purposes. Native Americans, for instance, used "rock oil" for medicinal purposes. Egyptians used oil as a dressing for wounds. Ancient Persians wrapped oil-soaked fibers around arrows, lit them, and fired them into the city of Athens in 480 B.C.

Sometimes a resource only becomes valuable after the technology to use it is developed. In today's world, petroleum is vital to providing power for industry, commerce, and transportation. Petroleum plays a powerful role in the economies of nations that supply it and consume it.

Economic Systems

An **economy** consists of the production and exchange of goods and services among a group of people. Economies operate on a local, regional, national, or international level. Geographers study economic geography by looking at how people in a region support themselves and how economic activities are linked across regions.

TYPES OF ECONOMIC SYSTEMS The way people produce and exchange goods and services is called an **economic system.** In the world today, there are four basic types of economic systems:

- **Traditional Economy** Goods and services are traded without exchanging money. Also called "barter."
- **Command Economy** Production of goods and services is determined by a central government, which usually owns the means of production. Production does not necessarily reflect the consumer demand. Also called a planned economy.
- **Market Economy** Production of goods and services is determined by the demand from consumers. Also called a demand economy or capitalism.
- **Mixed Economy** A combination of command and market economies provides goods and services so that all people will benefit.

Economic behaviors and activities to meet human needs take place within these economic systems.

Main Ideas

- Economic activities depend on the resources of the land and how people use them.
- The level of economic development can be measured in different ways.

Places & Terms

economy
economic system
command economy
market economy
natural resources
infrastructure
per capita income
GNP
GDP

BASICS

<u>SUNSHINE STATE STANDARDS</u>
Key Standard SS.D.2.4.5 The student understands basic terms and indicators associated with levels of economic performance and the state of the economy.

Other Standards SS.B.2.4.3, D.2.4.1

FCAT LA.A.1.4.2 Reading: Strategies

PLACE A woman sells goods on a Moscow street. Russia is changing from a command economy to a market economy.
Is the activity in this photograph an example of a command or market economy?

Economic Geography **91**

Economic Activities

People may choose from a variety of methods to meet their basic needs. Some groups simply raise enough food or animals to meet their need to eat, but have little left over to sell to others. This is called subsistence agriculture. In other areas, market-oriented agriculture produces crops or animals that farmers sell to markets.

In some places, industries dominate economic activities. Small industries often involve a family of craftspersons who produce goods to be sold in a local area. Since they often take place in the home, these businesses are referred to as cottage industries. Finally, commercial industries meet the needs of people within a very large area. Economic behaviors are related to the economic activities described below.

LEVELS OF ECONOMIC ACTIVITY No matter how small or large a business is, it operates at one of four economic levels. The four levels of economic activity describe how materials are gathered and processed into goods or how services are delivered to consumers.

Primary Activities involve gathering raw materials such as timber for immediate use or to use in the making of a final product.

Secondary Activities involve adding value to materials by changing their form. Manufacturing automobiles is an example.

Tertiary Activities involve providing business or professional services. Salespeople, teachers, or doctors are examples.

Quaternary Activities provide information, management, and research services by highly-trained persons.

The more developed an economy is, the greater the number and variety of activities you will find.

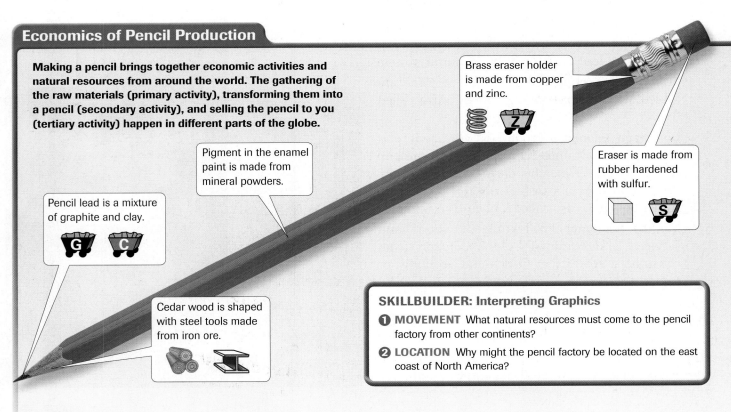

Geographic Thinking

Making Comparisons
Ⓐ Into which level of activity would insurance sales fit?

Economics of Pencil Production

Making a pencil brings together economic activities and natural resources from around the world. The gathering of the raw materials (primary activity), transforming them into a pencil (secondary activity), and selling the pencil to you (tertiary activity) happen in different parts of the globe.

Brass eraser holder is made from copper and zinc.

Eraser is made from rubber hardened with sulfur.

Pigment in the enamel paint is made from mineral powders.

Pencil lead is a mixture of graphite and clay.

Cedar wood is shaped with steel tools made from iron ore.

SKILLBUILDER: Interpreting Graphics

❶ **MOVEMENT** What natural resources must come to the pencil factory from other continents?

❷ **LOCATION** Why might the pencil factory be located on the east coast of North America?

The Economics of Natural Resources

An important part of economic geography is understanding which resources a nation possesses. **<u>Natural resources</u>** are materials on or in the earth—such as trees, fish, or coal—that have economic value. Materials from the earth become resources only when the society has the technology and ability to transform those resources into goods. So, iron ore is useless until people have the technology to produce steel from it.

Natural resources are abundant but are not distributed equally around the world. As a result, when geographers study the economy of a country, they look closely at the location, quality, and quantity of its natural resources. They also divide natural resources into three basic types:

- **Renewable**—These resources can be replaced through natural processes. Examples include trees and seafood.
- **Non-renewable**—These resources cannot be replaced once they have been removed from the ground. Examples include metals, such as gold, silver, and iron, and non-metals, such as gemstones, limestone, or sulfur. Also included are fossil fuels, petroleum, natural gas, and coal. They are the basis of energy production.
- **Inexhaustible energy sources**—These resources, which are used for producing power, are the result of solar or planetary processes and are unlimited in quantity. They include sunlight, geothermal heat, winds, and tides. **◀B**

Natural resources are a major part of world trade. This is especially true of the fossil fuels, since industry relies on them for both power and raw materials in manufacturing. The value of a natural resource depends on the qualities that make it useful. For example, trees can provide lumber for building or pulp for paper. Countries trade for raw materials that they need for energy and to manufacture products.

Geographic Thinking◀

Making Comparisons

B What advantage do inexhaustible energy sources have over fossil fuels?

Legend:
- Petroleum
- Pumice
- Sulfur
- Clay
- Zinc
- Graphite
- Copper
- Cedar logs
- Iron
- Rubber

Pencil factory

Ships

Ship registration

NORTH AMERICA
EUROPE
ASIA
AFRICA
SOUTH AMERICA
AUSTRALIA

Levels of economic development are measured in goods and services available in a country. In this graphic, the possessions of three families reflect economic development levels.

DEVELOPING NATION
Mali (family of 11)

5 ceramic pots
2 water kettles
2 sieves for sifting grain
1 bicycle
1 radio

NATION IN TRANSITION
Cuba (family of 9)

4 bicycles
3 televisions
2 stereos
3 radios
1 VCR

Economic Support Systems

Producing and distributing goods and services requires a series of support systems. The most important of these services is infrastructure.

INFRASTRUCTURE A nation's **infrastructure** consists of the basic support systems needed to keep an economy going, including power, communications, transportation, water, sanitation, and education systems. The more sophisticated the infrastructure, the more developed the country.

One of the most important systems in the infrastructure is transportation. Geographers look at the patterns of roads and highways, ports, and airports to get an idea of how transportation affects economic growth. For example, the country of Honduras has only one major north-south highway. The highway leads to port cities where a major export, bananas, is shipped out of the country. Areas not accessible to the major highway remain undeveloped.

Communications systems give geographers an idea of how a country is linked internally as well as with the outside world. Countries with a strong economy are linked internally and externally by high-speed Internet and satellite communications.

The level of available technology and access to it is also an indicator of the development of a country. A country may have valuable natural resources but be unable to profit from them because its people lack the skills to make use of them. Technology may be available, but a country may lack educated workers to run and maintain sophisticated equipment.

Measuring Economic Development

Geographers use a variety of standards to make comparisons among economies. One is **per capita income,** the average amount of money earned by each person in a political unit. Another way of comparing economies examines levels of development based on economic activities such as industry and commerce. Still others use a standard of living that reflects a society's purchasing power, health, and level of education.

GNP AND GDP A commonly-used statistic to measure the economy of a country is the **gross national product (GNP).** The **GNP** is the total value of all goods and services produced by a country over a year or some other specified period of time.

Because economies have become so interconnected, the GNP may reflect the value of goods or services produced in one country by a com-

DEVELOPED NATION

Japan (family of 4)

3 bicycles   1 microwave oven
3 radios   1 motor vehicle
1 telephone   1 computer
1 television   1 VCR

SOURCE: *Material World: A Global Family Portrait* by Peter Menzel

pany based in another country. For example, the value of sport shoes produced in Thailand by an American company is counted as U.S. production, even though the shoes were not produced in the United States. To adjust for situations like this, a second statistic is used—**GDP, or gross domestic product**—which is the total value of all goods and services produced *within* a country in a given period of time.

DEVELOPMENT LEVELS Countries of the world have different levels of economic development. Developing nations are nations that have a low GDP and limited development on all levels of economic activities. These countries lack an industrial base and struggle to provide their residents with items to meet their basic needs.

Developed nations, on the other hand, are countries with a high per capita income and varied economy, especially with quaternary activities such as computer software development. Western European nations, Japan, Canada, and the United States have highly developed economies.

In this chapter, you've learned that human geography is a complex mix of human activities and the earth's resources. As you study the regions of the world, remember that a geographer views those regions by looking at the space and the interactions that take place there.

BACKGROUND
Developing countries that have greatly improved their GDP are called countries in transition.

SECTION 5 Assessment

1 Places & Terms

Explain the meaning of each of the following terms.

• economy
• natural resources
• infrastructure
• per capita income
• GDP

2 Taking Notes

PLACE Review the notes you took for this section.

• What are the four basic economic systems?
• What are the three types of resources?

3 Main Ideas

a. What are the basic activities in each of the four economic activity levels?

b. What role do natural resources play in the economy of a country?

c. What systems are a part of a country's infrastructure?

4 Geographic Thinking

Drawing Conclusions Fossil fuels are non-renewable resources. What does this suggest about worldwide supplies of this energy?
Think about:
• industrial need for power
• alternative sources of power

MAKING COMPARISONS Study the types of economic systems on page 91. Create a series of **illustrations** showing the differences among the systems. Be sure your illustrations show the role of the consumer and the government in determining what goods or services are produced in each type of economy.

VISUAL SUMMARY
PEOPLE AND PLACES

The Elements of Culture

- All human groups have a culture.
- Language and religion are a part of culture.

Population Geography

- The world's population is expanding rapidly.
- Most of the world's population lives in the Northern Hemisphere.

Political Geography

- Size, shape, and location influence political geography.
- States of the world have a variety of political systems.

Urban Geography

- Urban areas have expanded rapidly and now are home to about one half of the world's population.
- Functions of cities are similar.
- Land use patterns are unique to a place.

Economic Geography

- Resources, available technology, and economic systems shape the economy of a state.
- Economic activities are based on how goods or services are produced and traded.

Reviewing Places & Terms

A. Briefly explain the importance of each of the following.

1. culture
2. diffusion
3. rate of natural increase
4. population density
5. state
6. nation
7. urbanization
8. economy
9. infrastructure
10. GDP

B. Answer the questions about vocabulary in complete sentences.

11. What is the growth in the number of cities called?
12. Which term above refers to the blueprint for the behaviors of a group?
13. How is the birthrate different from the rate of natural increase?
14. How is population density determined?
15. How is a nation different from a state?
16. Which term refers to the spread of ideas, innovations and inventions, and patterns of behavior?
17. How are the economy and the infrastructure related to each other?
18. What does the GDP number tell you about a country's economy?
19. Which terms above are associated with population geography?
20. What are some examples of infrastructure?

Main Ideas

The Elements of Culture (pp. 71–77)

1. What is the purpose of culture?
2. Why is language so important to a culture?

Population Geography (pp. 78–82)

3. What geographic factors influence population distribution?
4. How is population density different from population distribution?

Political Geography (pp. 83–86)

5. What are the geographic characteristics of a state?
6. What is the difference between a country with a democracy and one with a dictatorship?

Urban Geography (pp. 87–90)

7. What are some characteristics of city locations?
8. What are the basic land use patterns in cities?

Economic Geography (pp. 91–95)

9. Why does a country need an infrastructure?
10. How are natural resources related to a country's economy?

Critical Thinking

1. Using Your Notes

Use your completed chart to answer these questions.

Human Geography
- Cultural
- Population
- Political
- Urban
- Economic

a. Which type of human geography focuses on how goods and services are produced and distributed by a country?

b. What do population geographers study?

2. Geographic Themes

a. **MOVEMENT** How might migration affect both population distribution and density?

b. **PLACE** What are some characteristics of an urban area?

3. Identifying Themes

How do landform and climate affect the distribution of population? Which of the five themes apply to this situation?

4. Making Inferences

Why might two groups of people living in the same area develop different cultures?

5. Identifying and Solving Problems

What reasons might countries have to form a regional political unit?

Additional Test Practice, pp. S1–S37

TEST PRACTICE
CLASSZONE.COM

Geographic Skills: Interpreting Maps

Dominant World Cities*

Use the map to answer the following questions.

1. **REGION** Which continent has the most dominant world cities shown?

2. **REGION** Which continents do not have dominant world cities?

3. **MOVEMENT** Into which continent does the most activity appear to flow? Give a reason for your answer.

*Based on number of international banks and transactions

- ◉ Dominant world city
- ○ Major world city
- — Major economic ties

Molleweide Projection

GeoActivity

Using a blank map of the world, mark in the cities shown on this map. Then go to page 80. Add the cities with more than 12 million shown on that map. On the back of your map, write two observations about the cities on your map.

INTERNET ACTIVITY

Use the links at classzone.com to do research about population growth. Focus on the projected growth by 2050. Identify ten places where predicted growth will be the greatest and ten with little predicted growth.

Creating a Database Create a **database** showing your findings about worldwide growth. Create separate databases for the fastest growth and for the slowest growth. Be sure to label your databases.

Unit 2

The United States and Canada

The United States and Canada are two of the world's largest countries with vast lands and abundant resources. They occupy four-fifths of the continent of North America.

MOVEMENT Thousands of cars enter and leave Chicago, Illinois, daily. They use the vast expressway system that links the city to its surrounding suburbs and to interstate highways.

PLACE Cowhands and tourists from around the world gather in the western Canadian city of Calgary, Alberta, each July for the Calgary Stampede—the world's largest rodeo.

GeoData

LOCATION The United States and Canada extend from the Atlantic Ocean to the Pacific Ocean and from the Arctic Ocean to the Gulf of Mexico (only the United States).

REGION The two countries are often referred to as Anglo America, because both were once British colonies and also share a common language—English.

MOVEMENT Both countries were settled by immigrants from all over the world, beginning with their first settlers who migrated from Asia after the last Ice Age.

For more information on the United States and Canada . . .

RESEARCH LINKS
CLASSZONE.COM

LOCATION The majestic falls of the Niagara River are shared by both the United States and Canada. The American Falls, to the left, are in New York state; Horseshoe Falls, to the right, are in Ontario, Canada.

PREVIEW
Unit 2
Today's Issues in the United States and Canada

Today, the United States and Canada face the issues previewed here. As you read Chapters 5, 6, and 7, you will learn helpful background information. You will study the issues themselves in Chapter 8.

In a small group, answer the questions below. Then have a class discussion of your answers.

Exploring the Issues

1. **TERRORISM** Consider news stories that you have heard about terrorist groups in other countries. Make a list of the countries and the type of terrorist activity in each.

2. **URBAN SPRAWL** Why is the ever-expanding spread, or sprawl, of cities and suburbs a problem? What can be done to improve the quality of life in these areas?

3. **DIVERSE SOCIETIES** Search the Internet for information about diversity in the United States or Canada. What strategies or actions are being taken to help these many cultures unify?

For more on these issues in the United States and Canada . . .

CURRENT EVENTS
CLASSZONE.COM

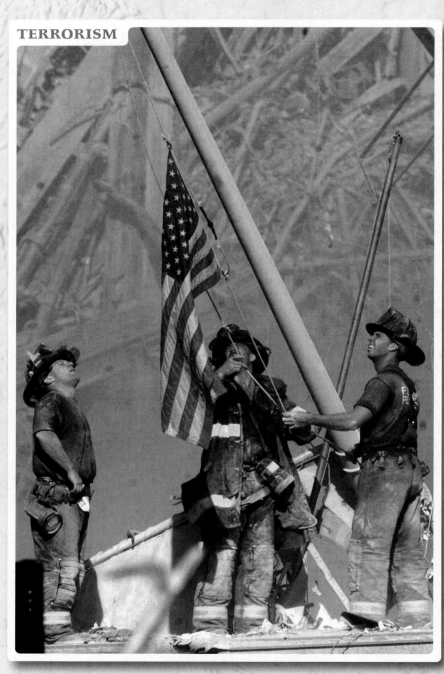

TERRORISM

How can a country protect itself from terrorism?

A surprise attack, such as the one on the World Trade Center in New York City, is just one way terrorists attempt to intimidate governments and civilian populations to further their objectives.

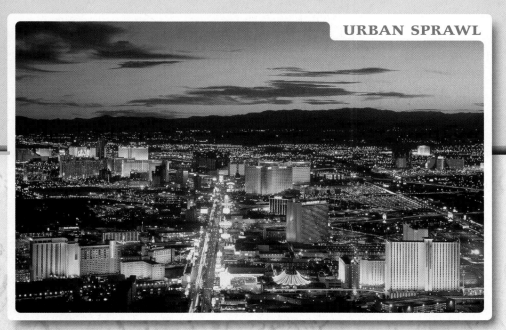

How can urban sprawl be controlled?

Urban communities, such as Las Vegas shown here, are trying to solve problems caused by urban areas spreading farther and farther out.

CASESTUDY

DIVERSE SOCIETIES

How can many cultures form a unified nation?

The diverse population of the United States is reflected in this group of California students. How to bring many cultures together as one nation is a continuing challenge for the United States, and for Canada, as well.

Patterns of Physical Geography

SUNSHINE STATE STANDARDS

Key Standard SS.B.1.4.1 The student uses a variety of maps, geographic technologies including geographic information systems (GIS) and satellite-produced imagery, and other advanced graphic representations to depict geographic problems.

Other Standards SS.B.2.4.1, D.2.4.6

FCAT LA.A.2.2.7 Reading: Recognize Compare and Contrast

Use the Unit Atlas to add to your knowledge of the United States and Canada. As you look at the maps and charts, notice geographic patterns and specific details about the region.

After studying the illustrations, graphs, and physical map on these two pages, jot down answers to the following questions in your notebook.

Making Comparisons

1. Compare the world's longest river, the Nile, to the Mississippi. How much difference is there in the lengths of the two rivers?

2. Compare the landmass and population of the United States to those of Canada. What statement can be made about the two countries?

3. Compare the mountain peaks of the United States to those of Canada. What statement can be made about the height of these mountains?

For updated statistics on the United States and Canada . . .

DATA UPDATE
CLASSZONE.COM

Comparing Data

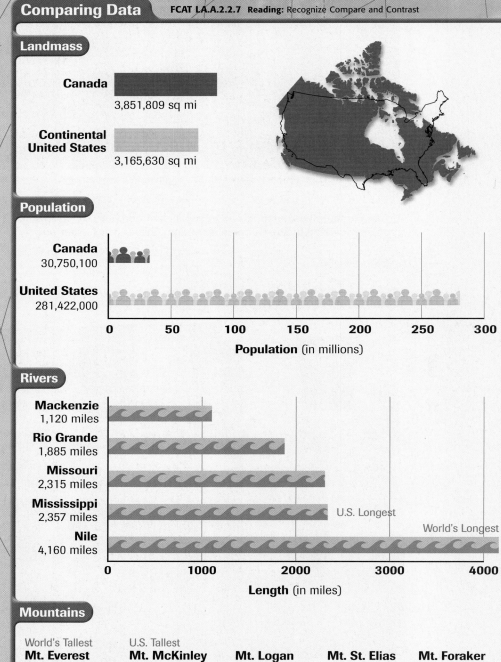

Landmass

Canada
3,851,809 sq mi

Continental United States
3,165,630 sq mi

Population

Canada
30,750,100

United States
281,422,000

Population scale: 0   50   100   150   200   250   300
Population (in millions)

Rivers

Mackenzie 1,120 miles
Rio Grande 1,885 miles
Missouri 2,315 miles
Mississippi 2,357 miles — U.S. Longest
Nile 4,160 miles — World's Longest

Length scale: 0   1000   2000   3000   4000
Length (in miles)

Mountains

World's Tallest	U.S. Tallest			
Mt. Everest	**Mt. McKinley**	**Mt. Logan**	**Mt. St. Elias**	**Mt. Foraker**
Nepal-Tibet	United States	Canada	U.S.-Canada	United States
29,035 feet	20,320 feet	19,524 feet	18,008 feet	17,400 feet

ARCTIC OCEAN

RUSSIA

Greenland Sea

ICELAND

Chukchi Sea

Bering Strait

Bering Sea

Beaufort Sea

BROOKS RANGE

Ellesmere Island

Greenland

Arctic Circle

Denmark Strait

Aleutian Islands

ALASKA RANGE

Mt. McKinley 20,320 ft. (6,194 m)

Yukon R.

Queen Elizabeth Islands

Baffin Bay

Davis Strait

Kodiak Is.

MACKENZIE MTS.

Mackenzie R.

Victoria Island

Baffin Island

Mt. Logan 19,551 ft. (5,959 m)

Gulf of Alaska

Great Bear Lake

COAST MOUNTAINS

Labrador Sea

Queen Charlotte Is.

Great Slave Lake

Hudson Bay

Lake Athabasca

CANADIAN SHIELD

Newfoundland

Vancouver I.

ROCKY MOUNTAINS

CANADA

Lake Winnipeg

James Bay

Gulf of St. Lawrence

0   250   500 miles
0   250   500 kilometers
Azimuthal Equal–Area Projection

PACIFIC OCEAN

COAST RANGES

CASCADES

Columbia R.

GREAT PLAINS

L. Superior

St. Lawrence R.

APPALACHIAN MOUNTAINS

L. Michigan

L. Huron

L. Ontario

L. Erie

SIERRA NEVADA

GREAT BASIN

Missouri R.

Mississippi R.

UNITED STATES

Mt. Whitney 14,494 ft. (4,421 m)

Death Valley –282 ft. (–86 m)

Colorado R.

Ohio R.

Bermuda Is.

Channel Is.

Mississippi R.

COASTAL PLAIN

ATLANTIC OCEAN

Hawaiian Islands

PACIFIC OCEAN

Nihau   Kauai
Oahu
Molokai
Lanai   Maui
HAWAII   Kahoolawe

Hawaii

0   75   150 miles
0   75   150 kilometers

Rio Grande

Gulf of California

Gulf of Mexico

BAHAMAS

Tropic of Cancer

West Indies

CUBA

Hispaniola

Caribbean Sea

Elevation

13,100 ft. (4,000 m.)
6,600 ft. (2,000 m.)
1,600 ft. (500 m.)
650 ft. (200 m.)
0 ft. (0 m.)
Below sea level

▲ Mountain peak
Glacier

MEXICO

BELIZE

GUATEMALA

HONDURAS

NICARAGUA

EL SALVADOR

COSTA RICA

PANAMA

VENEZUELA

COLOMBIA

N   W   E   S

Unit ATLAS

Patterns of Human Geography

After the coming of European settlers in the 17th century, the political map of North America changed quickly and significantly. Study the historical and political maps of the United States and Canada on these two pages. In your notebook, answer these questions.

Making Comparisons

1. What differences do you notice when you compare the map of 1600 with the map of the United States and Canada today?

2. Which names of native peoples are found as geographic names on the map on page 105?

3. Which country was more sparsely settled by native peoples in 1600?

Selected Native Peoples of North America, c. 1600

ARCTIC OCEAN

Inuit · Inuit · Inuit · Inuit · Inuit · Inuit · Inuit · Inuit · Inuit
Aleut · Kutchin · Arctic Circle
Kaska
Haida · Chipewyan · Hudson Bay
Cree
Kwakiutl
Nootka · Micmac
Salish · Blackfeet · Ojibwa
Chinook · Nez Perce · Assiniboin · Ottawa · Algonquin
Crow · Mandan · Huron
Yurok · Cheyenne · Sioux · Iroquois
Pomo · Shoshone · Fox · Erie · Susquehannock
Shoshone · Illinois · Miami
PACIFIC OCEAN · Arapaho · Shawnee
Ute · ATLANTIC OCEAN
Chumash · Hopi · Apache · Chickasaw · Cherokee
Navajo · Pueblo · Kiowa
Papago · Apache · Wichita · Creek
Choctaw · Apalachee
Natchez
Gulf of Mexico
Tropic of Cancer

0   500   1,000 miles
0   500   1,000 kilometers
Azimuthal Equal–Area Projection

60°N   70°N
50°N
40°N
30°N
110°W   100°W   90°W   80°W   70°W

Major food source
- Animals and wild plants
- Cultivated plants
- Fish
- Animals
- Wild plants
- **Crow**   Native peoples

RUSSIA

ARCTIC OCEAN

Greenland Sea

ICELAND

Chukchi Sea

Bering Strait

Bering Sea

Beaufort Sea

Baffin Bay

GREENLAND (Den.)

Denmark Strait

Arctic Circle

ALASKA (U.S.)

Anchorage

Yukon R.

YUKON TERRITORY

NORTHWEST TERRITORIES

Great Bear Lake

NUNAVUT

Davis Strait

Labrador Sea

Gulf of Alaska

Mackenzie R.

Great Slave Lake

Hudson Bay

NEWFOUNDLAND

National capital
Other city

0   250   500 miles
0   250   500 kilometers
Azimuthal Equal-Area Projection

BRITISH COLUMBIA

ALBERTA

Edmonton

SASKATCHEWAN

Lake Athabasca

CANADA

MANITOBA

Lake Winnipeg

ONTARIO

James Bay

QUEBEC

Gulf of St. Lawrence

PRINCE EDWARD ISLAND

Vancouver

Calgary

Winnipeg

St. Lawrence R.

NEW BRUNSWICK

NOVA SCOTIA

Seattle

WASHINGTON

Columbia R.

PACIFIC OCEAN

OREGON

MONTANA

N. DAKOTA

MINN.

L. Superior

WIS.

L. Huron

L. Michigan

Ottawa

Montreal

MAINE

VT.

N.H.

Toronto

Boston

MASS.

IDAHO

WYOMING

S. DAKOTA

Missouri R.

Mississippi R.

Minneapolis

IOWA

Chicago

MICH.

Detroit

L. Erie

L. Ontario

N.Y.

New York

R.I.

CONN.

Salt Lake City

N.J.

San Francisco

NEVADA

UTAH

Colorado R.

COLORADO

NEBRASKA

UNITED STATES

KANSAS

Kansas City

St. Louis

MO.

ILL.

IND.

OHIO

Ohio R.

KENTUCKY

W.VA.

VIRGINIA

Philadelphia

DEL.

MD.

Washington, D.C.

Bermuda (U.K.)

CALIFORNIA

Los Angeles

ARIZONA

NEW MEXICO

Phoenix

San Diego

OKLAHOMA

ARK.

TENNESSEE

N.C.

S.C.

Atlanta

GEORGIA

ATLANTIC OCEAN

Dallas

TEXAS

MISS.

ALA.

LA.

Houston

New Orleans

Rio Grande

Gulf of California

FLORIDA

Miami

BAHAMAS

Tropic of Cancer

MEXICO

Gulf of Mexico

CUBA

HAITI

DOMINICAN REPUBLIC

BELIZE

Caribbean Sea

HONDURAS

GUATEMALA

EL SALVADOR

NICARAGUA

PANAMA

COSTA RICA

COLOMBIA

Hawaiian Islands

PACIFIC OCEAN

Nihau

Kauai

Oahu

Honolulu

Molokai

Lanai

Maui

HAWAII

Kahoolawe

Hawaii

0   75   150 miles
0   75   150 kilometers

N
W   E
S

Unit ATLAS

Regional Patterns

These pages contain three thematic maps and an infographic. The infographic illustrates economic connections between the United States and Canada. The maps show economic activities, population density, and areas affected by natural hazards.

Study these two pages and then answer the questions below in your notebook.

Making Comparisons

1. Where are the areas of greatest population density found in each country? Do settlement patterns have any relationship to the threat of natural hazards?

2. Where are manufacturing and trade concentrated in the United States and Canada? Why might this be so?

Canada-U.S. Connections

CANADA

Immigration

21,751 people (1996)

4,550 people (1998)

Trade

US$174,844 million (1998)

US$156,308 million (1998)

Direct Investment

US$51,000 million (1998)

US$103,908 million (1998)

Tourism

14.1 million travelers (1999)

14.8 million travelers (1998)

UNITED STATES

Source: *The Europa World Year Book 2000*

This graphic shows that the geographic nearness of the United States and Canada has resulted in economic connections.

Economic Activities of the U.S. and Canada

ARCTIC OCEAN

PACIFIC OCEAN

Hudson Bay

CANADA

UNITED STATES

ATLANTIC OCEAN

Gulf of Mexico

- Manufacturing and trade
- Commercial farming
- Livestock raising
- Subsistence farming
- Nomadic herding
- Forestry
- Commercial fishing
- Hunting, fishing, and forestry
- Little or no economic activity

0   500   1,000 miles
0   500   1,000 kilometers
Azimuthal Equal–Area Projection

Natural Hazards of the U.S. and Canada

ARCTIC OCEAN

Beaufort Sea

Baffin Bay

Davis Strait

Arctic Circle

60°N
50°N

PACIFIC OCEAN

Gulf of Alaska

Hudson Bay

40°N

CANADA

ATLANTIC OCEAN

30°N

UNITED STATES

20°N

Earthquakes*
▲ Volcanoes*
Tsunamis
◄•• Tropical storm track
Areas at high risk for tornadoes
Selected rivers subject to flooding
Areas subject to desertification
*20th century

Gulf of Mexico

Tropic of Cancer

10°N

0   500   1,000 miles
0 500 1,000 kilometers
Azimuthal Equal–Area Projection

120°W   110°W   100°W   90°W   80°W   70°W   60°W

US & CANADA

Population Density of the U.S. and Canada

ARCTIC OCEAN

Arctic Circle

50°N

PACIFIC OCEAN

Hudson Bay

40°N

Edmonton
Calgary
CANADA
Vancouver
Seattle
Winnipeg
Quebec
Montreal

Persons per sq mi	Persons per sq km
Over 520	Over 200
260–519	100–199
130–259	50–99
25–129	10–49
1–24	1–9
0	0

◉ Metropolitan area greater than 2 million

Minneapolis
Toronto
Boston
Detroit
New York
Philadelphia
San Francisco
Chicago
Baltimore
Washington, D.C.

UNITED STATES

ATLANTIC OCEAN

30°N

Los Angeles
San Diego
Phoenix
Dallas
Atlanta

Houston

Gulf of Mexico

Tropic of Cancer

Miami

0   500   1,000 miles
0 500 1,000 kilometers
Azimuthal Equal–Area Projection

120°W   110°W   100°W   90°W   80°W   70°W   60°W

107

Regional Data File

Flag	State or Territory/ Capital	Population (2000)	Population Rank (2000)	Infant Mortality (per 1,000 live births) (1998)
	Alabama Montgomery	4,447,100	23	10.2
	Alaska Juneau	626,900	48	5.9
	Arizona Phoenix	5,130,600	20	7.5
	Arkansas Little Rock	2,673,400	33	8.9
	California Sacramento	33,871,600	1	5.8
	Colorado Denver	4,301,300	24	6.7
	Connecticut Hartford	3,405,600	29	7.0
	Delaware Dover	783,600	45	9.6
	District of Columbia*	572,100	—	12.5
	Florida Tallahassee	15,982,400	4	7.2
	Georgia Atlanta	8,186,500	10	8.5
	Hawaii Honolulu	1,211,500	42	6.9
	Idaho Boise	1,294,000	39	7.2
	Illinois Springfield	12,419,300	5	8.4
	Indiana Indianapolis	6,080,500	14	7.6
	Iowa Des Moines	2,926,300	30	6.6
	Kansas Topeka	2,688,400	32	7.0
	Kentucky Frankfort	4,041,800	25	7.5
	Louisiana Baton Rouge	4,469,000	22	9.1

Study the charts on the United States and Canada and their political subdivisions—states, provinces, and territories. In your notebook, answer these questions.

Making Comparisons

1. Which state of the United States and which province or territory of Canada have the most people? Is each also the largest in total area in its country? Locate them on the map. What is significant about their locations?

2. Which state of the United States and which province or territory of Canada have the least people? Is each also the smallest in total area in its country? Locate them on the map.

(continued on page 110)

Notes:
* The federal district of Washington, D.C., is the capital city of the United States.
a In constant 1996 dollars.
b Percentage of the population, 25 years old or older, with high school diploma or higher.
c Includes land and water, when figures are available.

For updated statistics on the United States and Canada . . .

DATA UPDATE
CLASSZONE.COM

Doctors (per 100,000 pop.) (1998–1999)	Population Density (per square mile)	Urban/Rural Population (%) (1990)	Per Capita Income[a] ($US) (1999)	High School Graduates[b] (%) (1998)	Area Rank (2000)	Total Area[c] (square miles)	
198	85.1	60 / 40	21,941	78.8	30	52,237	
167	1.0	68 / 32	27,274	90.6	1	615,230	
202	45.0	88 / 12	24,199	81.9	6	114,006	
190	50.3	54 / 46	21,146	76.8	28	53,182	
247	213.2	93 / 7	28,513	80.1	3	158,869	
238	41.3	82 / 18	30,291	89.6	8	104,100	
354	614.3	79 / 21	37,452	83.7	48	5,544	
234	327.0	73 / 27	29,341	85.2	49	2,396	
737	8,412.6	100 / 00	36,554	83.8	51	68	
238	266.7	85 / 15	26,796	81.9	23	59,928	
211	138.8	63 / 37	26,007	80.0	24	58,977	
265	187.6	89 / 11	26,623	84.6	47	6,459	
154	15.5	57 / 43	22,418	82.7	14	83,574	
260	214.4	85 / 15	29,908	84.2	25	57,918	
195	167.0	65 / 35	24,949	83.5	38	36,420	
173	51.9	61 / 39	24,600	87.7	26	56,276	
203	32.7	69 / 31	25,467	89.2	15	82,282	
209	100.0	52 / 48	22,147	77.9	37	40,411	
246	90.0	68 / 32	21,794	78.6	31	49,651	

Unit ATLAS

Regional Data File

Flag	State or Territory/ Capital	Population (2000)	Population Rank (2000)	Infant Mortality (per 1,000 live births) (1998)
	Maine Augusta	1,274,900	40	6.3
	Maryland Annapolis	5,296,500	19	8.6
	Massachusetts Boston	6,349,100	13	5.1
	Michigan Lansing	9,938,400	8	8.2
	Minnesota St. Paul	4,919,479	21	5.9
	Mississippi Jackson	2,844,700	31	10.1
	Missouri Jefferson City	5,595,200	17	7.7
	Montana Helena	902,200	44	7.4
	Nebraska Lincoln	1,711,300	38	7.3
	Nevada Carson City	1,998,300	35	7.0
	New Hampshire Concord	1,235,800	41	4.4
	New Jersey Trenton	8,414,400	9	6.4
	New Mexico Santa Fe	1,819,00	36	7.2
	New York Albany	18,976,500	3	6.3
	North Carolina Raleigh	8,049,300	11	9.3
	North Dakota Bismarck	642,200	47	8.6
	Ohio Columbus	11,353,100	7	8.0
	Oklahoma Oklahoma City	3,450,700	27	8.5
	Oregon Salem	3,421,400	28	5.4

Making Comparisons
(continued)

3. Which six states of the United States and which three provinces or territories of Canada have the highest per capita income? Locate them on the map. What factors might account for this?

4. Which are the six most highly urbanized states of the United States? In which three provinces or territories of Canada do at least 80 percent of the people live in urban areas? Are these states and provinces or territories the same as those that have the highest per capita incomes?

(continued on page 112)

Notes:
a In constant 1996 dollars.
b Percentage of the population, 25 years old or older, with high school diploma or higher.
c Includes land and water, when figures are available.

Doctors (per 100,000 pop.) (1998–1999)	Population Density (per square mile)	Urban/Rural Population (%) (1990)	Per Capita Income[a] ($US) (1999)	High School Graduates[b] (%) (1998)	Area Rank (2000)	Total Area[c] (square miles)	
223	37.8	45 / 55	23,867	86.7	39	33,741	
374	430.7	81 / 19	30,757	84.7	42	12,297	
412	687.1	84 / 16	34,168	85.6	45	9,241	
224	102.8	71 / 29	26,625	85.4	11	96,705	
249	56.6	70 / 30	29,281	89.4	12	86,943	
163	58.9	47 / 53	19,608	77.3	32	48,286	
230	80.3	69 / 31	25,040	82.9	21	69,709	
190	6.1	53 / 47	21,337	89.1	4	147,046	
218	22.1	66 / 34	26,235	87.7	16	77,358	
173	18.1	88 / 12	29,022	89.1	7	110,567	
237	133.1	51 / 49	29,552	84.0	44	9,283	
295	1,024.3	89 / 11	34,525	86.5	46	8,215	
212	15.0	73 / 37	21,097	79.6	5	121,598	
387	351.5	84 / 16	32,459	81.5	27	53,989	
232	153.0	50 / 50	25,072	81.4	29	52,672	
222	9.1	53 / 47	22,488	84.3	18	70,704	
235	253.3	74 / 26	25,895	86.2	34	44,828	
169	49.4	68 / 32	21,802	84.6	20	69,903	
225	35.2	71 / 29	25,947	85.5	10	97,132	

Unit ATLAS

Regional Data File

Flag	State or Territory/ Capital	Population (2000)	Population Rank (2000)	Infant Mortality (per 1,000 live births) (1998)
	Pennsylvania Harrisburg	12,281,100	6	7.1
	Rhode Island Providence	1,048,300	43	7.0
	South Carolina Columbia	4,012,000	26	9.6
	South Dakota Pierre	754,800	46	9.1
	Tennessee Nashville	5,689,300	16	8.2
	Texas Austin	20,851,800	2	6.4
	Utah Salt Lake City	2,233,200	34	5.6
	Vermont Montpelier	608,800	49	7.0
	Virginia Richmond	7,078,500	12	7.7
	Washington Olympia	5,894,100	15	5.7
	West Virginia Charleston	1,808,300	37	8.0
	Wisconsin Madison	5,363,675	18	7.2
	Wyoming Cheyenne	493,800	50	7.2

U.S. Territories

Flag	State or Territory/ Capital	Population (2000)	Population Rank (2000)	Infant Mortality (per 1,000 live births) (1998)
	American Samoa Pago Pago	65,400	–	11.0 (2000)
	Guam Agana	154,600	–	7.0 (2000)
	Puerto Rico San Juan	3,915,800	–	10.0 (2000)
	U.S. Virgin Islands Charlotte Amalie	120,900	–	10.0 (2000)

Making Comparisons (continued)

5. Which seven states of the United States and which three provinces or territories of Canada have the highest infant mortality rate? the lowest? What relationship do these figures appear to have to the urban/rural population ratio?

6. Which U.S. territory has the largest population and largest area? Which has the smallest population and the smallest area?

(continued on page 114)

Notes:

a In constant 1996 dollars.

b Percentage of the population, 25 years old or older, with high school diploma or higher.

c Includes land and water, when figures are available.

Doctors (per 100,000 pop.) (1998–1999)	Population Density (per square mile)	Urban/Rural Population (%) (1990)	Per Capita Income[a] ($US) (1999)	High School Graduates[b] (%) (1998)	Area Rank (2000)	Total Area[c] (square miles)
291	266.6	69 / 31	27,420	84.1	33	46,058
338	851.6	86 / 14	24,418	80.7	50	1,231
207	128.6	55 /45	22,467	78.6	40	31,189
184	9.8	50 / 50	24,007	86.3	17	77,121
246	135.0	61 / 39	24,461	76.9	36	42,146
203	78.0	80 / 20	25,363	78.3	2	267,277
200	26.3	87 / 13	22,333	89.3	13	84,904
305	63.3	32 / 68	24,758	86.7	43	9,615
241	167.2	69 / 31	28,193	82.6	35	42,326
235	83.4	76 / 24	28,968	92.0	19	70,637
215	74.6	36 / 64	19,973	76.4	41	24,231
227	82.0	66 / 34	26,212	88.0	22	65,499
171	5.0	65 / 35	24,864	90.0	9	97,818
0.3 (1996)	727.2	33 / 67	3,270 (1995)	61.3 (1995)	—	90
0.9 (1995)	712.5	38 / 62	19,000 (1996)	73.1 (1995)	—	217
1.8	1,116.2	72 / 28	9,800 (1995)	49.7 (1989)	—	3,508
1.1 (1989)	707.1	37 / 63	10,942 (1995)	58.6 (1995)	—	171

Unit ATLAS

Regional Data File

Making Comparisons
(continued)

7. Which state and which province or territory is the most densely populated? Which state and which territory is the least densely populated? Are the most densely populated the smallest in area and the least populated the largest in area?

Flag	Province or Territory/ Capital	Population (2000)	Population Rank (2000)	Infant Mortality (per 1,000 live births) (1997)
	Alberta Edmonton	2,997,200	4	4.8
	British Columbia Victoria	4,063,800	3	4.7
	Manitoba Winnipeg	1,147,900	5	7.5
	New Brunswick Fredericton	756,600	8	5.7
	Newfoundland St. John's	538,800	9	5.2
	Northwest Territories Yellowknife	42,100	11	10.9
	Nova Scotia Halifax	941,000	7	4.4
	Nunavut Iqaluit	27,700	13	N/A
	Ontario Toronto	11,669,300	1	5.5
	Prince Edward Island Charlottetown	138,900	10	4.4
	Quebec Quebec City	7,372,400	2	5.6
	Saskatchewan Regina	1,023,600	6	8.9
	Yukon Territory Whitehorse	30,700	12	8.4
	Canada Ottawa, Ontario	30,750,100	—	5.5
	United States Washington, D.C.	281,422,000	—	7.0

Sources:
Bureau of Economic Analysis, U.S. Dept. of Commerce
Canadian Institute for Health Information, online
Census 2000, U.S. Census Bureau, online
Digest of Educational Statistics 2000, online
Europa World Year Book 2000
Merriam-Webster's Geographical Dictionary, 1997
Northwest Territories Bureau of Statistics, online
Pan-American Health Organization, online
Statistical Abstract of the United States, 1999 and 2000
Statistics Canada, online
World Factbook 2000, CIA online
N/A = not available

Notes:
[a] In constant 1996 dollars.
[b] Percentage of the population, 25 years old or older, with high school diploma or higher.
[c] Includes land and water, when figures are available.

Doctors (per 100,000 pop.) (1998)	Population Density (per square mile)	Urban/Rural Population (%) (1996)	Per Capita Income[a] ($US) (1996)	High School Graduates[b] (%) (1998)	Area Rank (2000)	Total Area[c] (square miles)	
162	11.7	80 / 20	30,038	86	6	255,285	
193	11.1	82 / 18	31,592	87	5	366,255	
177	4.6	72 / 28	26,829	79	8	250,934	
153	26.7	49 / 51	26,607	78	11	28,345	
171	12.4	57 / 43	27,692	71	10	43,359	
92	0.08	42 / 58	33,738 (1994)	64 (1996)	3	503,951	
196	44.0	55 / 45	25,712	78	12	21,425	
N/A	0.03	N/A	27,421 (1994)	N/A	1	818,959	
178	28.3	83 / 17	32,537	84	4	412,582	
128	49.4	44 / 56	25,534	74	13	2,814	
211	12.4	78 / 22	28,826	78	2	594,860	
149	4.1	63 / 34	26,463	82	7	251,700	
149	0.2	60 / 40	36,130	67 (1996)	9	186,661	
185	8.0	78 / 22	23,000 (1999)	82	—	3,851,809	
251	74.3	76 / 24	33,900 (1999)	83	—	3,787,319	

Chapter 5

PHYSICAL GEOGRAPHY OF
THE UNITED STATES and CANADA
A Land of Contrasts

SECTION 1
Landforms and
Resources

SECTION 2
Climate and
Vegetation

SECTION 3
Human–Environment
Interaction

The 3,593-foot El Capitan
is one of many cliffs that
soar above the valley
floor in California's
Yosemite National Park.

GeoFocus

What is alike and what is different about the lands of the United States and Canada?

Taking Notes Copy the graphic organizer below into your notebook. Use it to record information from the chapter about the physical geography of the United States and Canada.

Landforms	
Resources	
Climate and Vegetation	
Human-Environment Interaction	

Landforms and Resources

Main Ideas
- The United States and Canada have vast lands and abundant resources.
- These two countries share many of the same landforms.

Places & Terms

Appalachian Mountains

Great Plains

Canadian Shield

Rocky Mountains

Great Lakes

Mackenzie River

CONNECT TO THE ISSUES

URBAN SPRAWL Urban development in the United States is generally determined by the location of landforms and the abundance of natural resources.

SUNSHINE STATE STANDARDS
Key Standard SS.B.2.4.1 The student understands how social, cultural, economic, and environmental factors contribute to the dynamic nature of regions.

Other Standards SS.B.1.4.3, B.2.4.6

FCAT LA.A.1.4.2 Reading: Strategies

A HUMAN PERSPECTIVE The beauty and abundance of the land was a source of wonder to early explorers of North America. One who traveled the Atlantic coast referred to the "amazing extent of uncultivated land, covered with forests, and intermixed with vast lakes and marshes." A 17th–century French expedition described "a beautiful river, large, broad, and deep" (the Mississippi). Still others found "an unbounded prairie" (the Great Plains), "shining mountains" (the Rocky Mountains), and "an infinite number of fish" (along the Pacific coast). To the continent's first settlers, the land was "strong and it was beautiful all around," according to an old Native American song.

Landscape Influenced Development

The United States and Canada occupy the central and northern four-fifths of the continent of North America. Culturally, the region is known as Anglo America because both countries were colonies of Great Britain at one time and because most of the people speak English. (The southern one-fifth of the continent—Mexico—is part of Latin America.) The two countries are bound together not only by physical geography and cultural heritage, but also by strong economic and political ties.

VAST LANDS The United States and Canada extend across North America from the Atlantic Ocean on the east to the Pacific on the west, and from the Arctic Ocean on the north to the Gulf of Mexico on the south (only the United States). In total area, each ranks among the largest countries of the world. Canada ranks second, behind Russia, and the United States is third. Together, they fill one-eighth of the land surface of the earth.

ABUNDANT RESOURCES In addition to their huge landmass, the United States and Canada are rich in natural resources. They have fertile soils, ample supplies of water, vast forests, and large deposits of a variety of minerals. This geographic richness has for centuries attracted immigrants from around the world and has enabled both countries to develop into global economic powers.

LOCATION Pittsburgh, Pennsylvania, is located where the Allegheny and Monongahela rivers meet to form the Ohio River.

Landform Regions of the U.S. and Canada

ARCTIC OCEAN

① East Quoddy Head in New Brunswick

ARCTIC COASTAL PLAIN

INTERMOUNTAIN BASINS AND PLATEAUS

ROCKY MOUNTAINS

PACIFIC MOUNTAINS AND VALLEYS

INTERMOUNTAIN BASINS AND PLATEAUS

Mackenzie R.

Columbia R.

Colorado R.

CANADIAN SHIELD

Hudson Bay

ARCTIC COASTAL PLAIN

INTERIOR

GREAT PLAINS

PLAINS

L. Superior

Mississippi R.

Missouri R.

L. Michigan

Huron

Ontario

Erie

St. Lawrence R.

APPALACHIAN HIGHLANDS

PIEDMONT

②

①

PACIFIC OCEAN

ATLANTIC OCEAN

INTERIOR HIGHLANDS

Ohio R.

Mississippi R.

GULF-ATLANTIC COASTAL PLAIN

③

Rio Grande

Gulf of Mexico

Tropic of Cancer

N E S W

② Great Regina Plain in Saskatchewan

0   250   500 miles
0   250   500 kilometers
Azimuthal Equal-Area Projection

③ Cypress Gardens in Florida

Many and Varied Landforms

All major types of landforms are found in the United States and Canada. If you look at the map on the opposite page, you will see that both countries share many of these landforms. The most prominent are eastern and western mountain chains and enormous interior plains.

THE EASTERN LOWLANDS A flat, coastal plain runs along the Atlantic Ocean and the Gulf of Mexico. One section, called the Atlantic Coastal Plain, begins as narrow lowland in the northeastern United States and widens as it extends southward into Florida. This area features many excellent harbors. A broader section of the plain—the Gulf Coastal Plain—stretches along the Gulf of Mexico from Florida into Texas. The Mississippi River empties into the Gulf from this region.

Between these plains and the nearby Appalachian (A·puh·LAY·chun) Highlands is a low plateau called the Piedmont (PEED·MAHNT). This area of rolling hills contains many fast-flowing rivers and streams.

BACKGROUND
The word *piedmont* comes from *pied*, meaning "foot," and *mont*, for "mountain." A piedmont is found at the foot of a mountain chain.

THE APPALACHIAN HIGHLANDS West of the coastal plain are the Appalachian highlands. The gently sloping **Appalachian Mountains** are in this region. They are one of the two major mountain chains in the United States and Canada. Both chains run north to south. The Appalachian Mountains extend some 1,600 miles from Newfoundland in Canada to Alabama. There are several mountain ranges in the Appalachian system. Among them are the Green and the Catskill mountains in the north and the Blue Ridge and the Great Smoky mountains in the south.

Because the Appalachians are very old—more than 400 million years old—they have been eroded by the elements. Many peaks are only between 1,200 and 2,400 feet high. The Appalachian Trail, a scenic hiking path 2,160 miles long, spans almost the entire length of the chain.

THE INTERIOR LOWLANDS A huge expanse of mainly level land covers the interior of North America. It was flattened by huge glaciers thousands of years ago. The terrain includes lowlands, rolling hills, thousands of lakes and rivers, and some of the world's most fertile soils.

The interior lowlands are divided into three subregions: the Interior Plains, the Great Plains, and the Canadian Shield. The Interior Plains spread out from the Appalachians to about 300 miles west of the Mississippi River. They gradually rise from a few hundred feet above sea level to about 2,000 feet. To the west are the **Great Plains,** a largely treeless area that continues the ascent to about 4,000 feet. The **Canadian Shield** lies farther north. This rocky, mainly flat area covers nearly 2 million square miles around Hudson Bay. It averages 1,500 feet above sea level but reaches over 5,000 feet in Labrador. ◀Ⓐ

Making Comparisons
Ⓐ Which of the interior lowlands has the highest elevation?

THE WESTERN MOUNTAINS, PLATEAUS, AND BASINS West of the plains are the massive, rugged **Rocky Mountains,** the other major mountain system of the

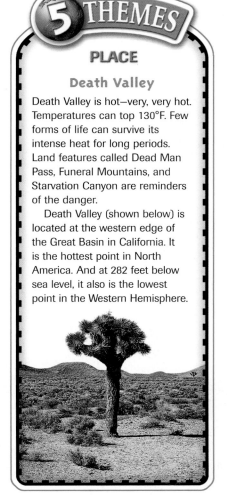

PLACE

Death Valley

Death Valley is hot—very, very hot. Temperatures can top 130°F. Few forms of life can survive its intense heat for long periods. Land features called Dead Man Pass, Funeral Mountains, and Starvation Canyon are reminders of the danger.

Death Valley (shown below) is located at the western edge of the Great Basin in California. It is the hottest point in North America. And at 282 feet below sea level, it also is the lowest point in the Western Hemisphere.

United States and Canada. The Rockies are a series of ranges that extend about 3,000 miles from Alaska south to New Mexico. Because they are relatively young—about 80 million years old—the Rockies have not been eroded like the Appalachians. Many of their jagged, snow-covered peaks are more than 12,000 feet high. The **Continental Divide** is the line of highest points in the Rockies that marks the separation between rivers flowing eastward and westward. B

Between the Rockies and the Pacific Ocean is an area of mixed landforms. A series of ranges, including the Sierra Nevada and the Cascade Range, run parallel to the Pacific coastline from California to Alaska. North America's highest peak—Mt. McKinley (also called by its Native American name, Denali)—is in Alaska, towering 20,320 feet above sea level. Major earthquakes occur near the Pacific ranges. Between these

Geographic Thinking

Making Comparisons
B How do the Rockies differ from the Appalachians?

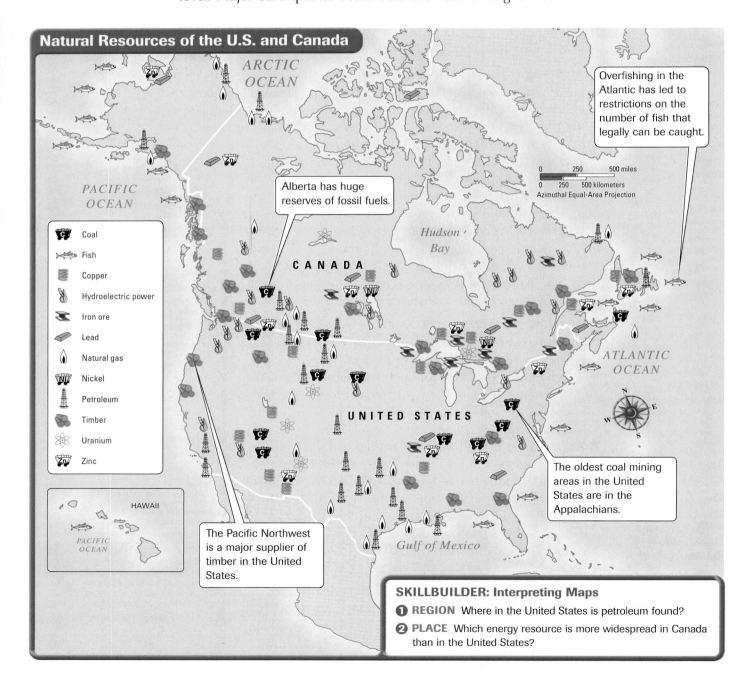

Natural Resources of the U.S. and Canada

Overfishing in the Atlantic has led to restrictions on the number of fish that legally can be caught.

Alberta has huge reserves of fossil fuels.

The oldest coal mining areas in the United States are in the Appalachians.

The Pacific Northwest is a major supplier of timber in the United States.

Coal
Fish
Copper
Hydroelectric power
Iron ore
Lead
Natural gas
Nickel
Petroleum
Timber
Uranium
Zinc

HAWAII
PACIFIC OCEAN

0   250   500 miles
0   250   500 kilometers
Azimuthal Equal-Area Projection

ARCTIC OCEAN
PACIFIC OCEAN
Hudson Bay
CANADA
UNITED STATES
ATLANTIC OCEAN
Gulf of Mexico

SKILLBUILDER: Interpreting Maps
❶ **REGION** Where in the United States is petroleum found?
❷ **PLACE** Which energy resource is more widespread in Canada than in the United States?

ranges and the Rockies are steep cliffs, deep canyons, and lowland desert areas called basins.

THE ISLANDS Canada's northernmost lands are islands riding the icy seas near the Arctic Circle. Three of the islands—Ellesmere, Victoria, and Baffin—are huge. In North America, only Greenland is larger.

Two island chains created by volcanic activity are part of the westernmost United States. The rugged, treeless Aleutian Islands extend in an arc off the coast of Alaska. The lush, tropical Hawaiian Islands, though politically part of the United States, are not geographically part of North America. They lie in the central Pacific, about 2,400 miles to the southwest.

Resources Shape Ways of Life

The landforms of the United States and Canada hold a rich variety and abundance of natural resources. Both countries are leading agricultural and industrial nations because of this wealth of resources.

OCEANS AND WATERWAYS The United States and Canada possess ample water resources. They are bounded by three oceans—Atlantic, Pacific, and Arctic. The United States is also bounded by the Gulf of Mexico. As a result, both countries have important shipping and fishing industries.

Inland, large rivers and lakes serve as sources of transportation, hydroelectric power, irrigation, fresh water, and fisheries. Eight of the world's 15 largest lakes are found in this region. Among these are the **Great Lakes**— Huron, Ontario, Michigan, Erie, and Superior. As you will see on page 129, these lakes and the St. Lawrence River form one of the world's major shipping routes.

The continent's longest and busiest river system is the Mississippi-Missouri-Ohio. The Mississippi River runs almost the north-south length of the United States, from Minnesota to the Gulf of Mexico. (See map at right.) The Mississippi's main tributaries, the Ohio and Missouri rivers, are major rivers in their own right. Canada's longest river is the **Mackenzie River,** which is part of a river system that flows across the Northwest Territories to the Arctic Ocean. ◀

LAND AND FORESTS One of the richest natural resources of the United States and Canada is the land itself. Both countries are large and contain some of the most fertile soils in the world. In fact, the land is so productive that North America is the world's leading food exporter. Much of this agricultural land is found in the plains regions and in river valleys.

Geographic Thinking

Using the Atlas
▶ Use the map on page 103. Find the Mackenzie River. Into which body of water does it empty?

The Mississippi River

The Mississippi begins its 2,357-mile journey southward in Lake Itasca, Minnesota.

About 500 million tons of freight, including grain, are carried on the river each year.

Ocean-going ships can only navigate the Mississippi to Baton Rouge—80 miles north of New Orleans—because of low water.

0   100   200 miles
0   100   200 kilometers
Albers Equal-Area Projection

SKILLBUILDER: Interpreting Maps

❶ **LOCATION** What states have the Mississippi River for at least part of their border?

❷ **MOVEMENT** What rivers empty into the Mississippi?

REGION This West Virginia coal mine is in one of the world's most important coal-producing regions—the Appalachian highlands. **What other region in North America is an important coal producer?**

The United States and Canada also have huge forests. About one-half of Canada is covered by woodlands, as is one-third of the United States. Canada's forests cover more land than those of the United States, but the United States has more kinds of trees because of its more varied climate. Both countries are major producers of lumber and forest products.

MINERALS AND FOSSIL FUELS As you saw on the map on page 120, the United States and Canada have large quantities and varieties of minerals and fossil fuels. These resources gave both countries the means to industrialize rapidly.

Valuable deposits of iron ore, nickel, copper, gold, and uranium are found in the Canadian Shield. Scattered among the western mountains are gold, silver, copper, and uranium. Both countries also have substantial deposits of coal, natural gas, and oil, and well-developed networks for distributing these energy-producing fossil fuels. Important coal-producing areas are the Appalachian highlands and the northern Great Plains. Significant deposits of oil and natural gas are found in the Great Plains, Alaska, and along the Gulf of Mexico. ▶

The United States is the world's biggest consumer of energy resources. Its need for these fuels is so great that it is a major importer. In fact, most of Canada's energy exports go to its neighbor to the south.

In the next section, you will read how some landforms of the United States and Canada have affected climate and vegetation patterns.

Seeing Patterns
◀ Why are oil and natural gas important to highly-industrialized nations?

SECTION 1 ▸ Assessment

1 Places & Terms

Identify and explain where in the region these would be found.

- Appalachian Mountains
- Great Plains
- Canadian Shield
- Rocky Mountains
- Great Lakes

2 Taking Notes

LOCATION Review the notes you took for this section.

Landforms	
Resources	

- What is the relative location of the Great Lakes?
- What is the relative location of most of Canada's islands?

3 Main Ideas

a. What landforms are shared by the United States and Canada?

b. Why are the Great Lakes important to both the United States and Canada?

c. Why do most of Canada's energy exports go to the United States?

4 Geographic Thinking

Making Generalizations What makes the United States and Canada leading industrial nations? **Think about:**

- available resources
- oceans and waterways

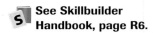
See Skillbuilder Handbook, page R6.

EXPLORING LOCAL GEOGRAPHY Using the maps on pages 103 and 118, identify the landforms located in your state. Then draw a **sketch map** of your state showing the major landforms and water bodies.

Climate and Vegetation

Main Ideas
- Almost every type of climate is found in the 50 United States because they extend over such a large area north to south.
- Canada's cold climate is related to its location in the far northern latitudes.

Places & Terms
permafrost
prevailing westerlies
Everglades

US & CANADA

A HUMAN PERSPECTIVE A little gold and bitter cold—that is what thousands of prospectors found in Alaska and the Yukon Territory during the Klondike gold rushes of the 1890s. Most of these fortune hunters were unprepared for the harsh climate and inhospitable land of the far north. Winters were long and cold, the ground frozen. Ice fogs, blizzards, and avalanches were regular occurrences. You could lose fingers and toes—even your life—in the cold. But hardy souls stuck it out. Legend has it that one miner, Bishop Stringer, kept himself alive by boiling his sealskin and walrus-sole boots and then drinking the broth.

Shared Climates and Vegetation

The United States and Canada have more in common than just frigid winter temperatures where Alaska meets northwestern Canada. Other shared climate and vegetation zones are found along their joint border at the southern end of Canada and the northern end of the United States.

If you look at the map on page 125, you will see that the United States has more climate zones than Canada. This variety, ranging from tundra to tropical, occurs because the country extends over such a large area north to south. Most of the United States is located in the mid-latitudes, where the climates are moderate. Canada is colder because so much of it lies far north in the higher latitudes.

COLDER CLIMATES The Arctic coast of Alaska and Canada have tundra climate and vegetation. Winters are long and bitterly cold, while summers are brief and chilly. Even in July, temperatures are only around 40°F. The land is a huge, treeless plain. Much of the rest of Canada and Alaska have a subarctic climate, with very cold winters and short, mild summers. A vast forest of needle-leafed evergreens covers the area. In some places, there is **permafrost,** or permanently frozen ground.

The Rocky Mountains and the Pacific ranges have highland climate and vegetation. Temperature and vegetation vary with elevation and latitude. Generally, the temperature is colder and the vegetation is more sparse in the higher, more northerly mountains. The mountains also influence the temperature and precipitation of surrounding lower areas. For example, the

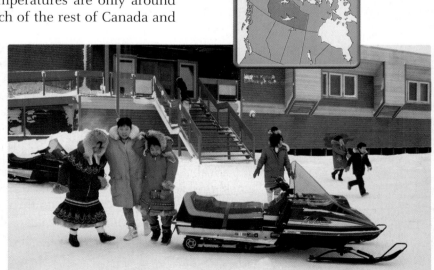

MOVEMENT The snowmobile has replaced the dogsled as transportation in many parts of the Northwest Territories. Here, a mother picks up her children from school.

coastal ranges protect the coast from cold Arctic air from the interior. In the United States, the western mountains trap Pacific moisture. This makes lands west of the mountains rainy and those east very dry.

MODERATE CLIMATES The north central and northeastern United States and southern Canada near the U.S. border have a humid continental climate. Winters are cold and summers warm. Climate and soil make this one of the world's most productive agricultural areas, yielding an abundance of dairy products, grain, and livestock. In the northern part of this climate zone, summers are short. There are mixed forests of deciduous and needle-leafed evergreen trees. Most of the population of Canada is concentrated here. In the southern part of this zone, which is in the United States, summers are longer. For the most part, deciduous forests are found east of the Mississippi River and temperate grasslands are found to the west. Ⓐ

The Pacific coast from northern California to southern Alaska, which includes British Columbia, has a climate described as marine west coast. This climate is affected by Pacific Ocean currents, the coastal mountains, and the **prevailing westerlies**—winds that blow from west to east in the middle of the latitudes. The summers are moderately warm. The winters are long and mild, but rainy and foggy. Vegetation is mixed, including dense forests of broad-leafed deciduous trees, needle-leafed evergreens, and giant California redwoods. The Washington coast even has a cool, wet rain forest.

🌐 **Geographic Thinking**◄

Seeing Patterns
Ⓐ Why is most of Canada's population clustered in the humid continental region?

Differences in Climate and Vegetation

The milder, dry, and tropical climates of North America are found south of 40°N latitude. Much of the United States is located in these climate zones; little of Canada is.

MILDER CLIMATES Most southern states have a humid subtropical climate. This means that summers are hot and muggy, with temperatures ranging from about 75°F to 90°F. Winters are usually mild and cool. Moist air from the Gulf of Mexico brings rain during the winter. The combination of mild temperatures and adequate rainfall provides a long growing season for a variety of crops—from citrus fruits in Florida to peanuts in Georgia. Broad-leafed evergreen trees and needle-leafed evergreen trees are found in this region. The central and southern coasts of California have a Mediterranean climate. Summers are dry, sunny, and warm. Winters are mild and somewhat rainy. Temperatures range from 50°F to 80°F year-round. A long growing season and irrigation make this a rich farming area for fruits and vegetables. Ⓑ

🌐 **Geographic Thinking**◄

Making Comparisons
Ⓑ Why don't central and southern California have a marine west coast climate?

DRY CLIMATES The Great Plains and dry northern parts of the Great Basin have a semiarid climate. This means dry weather—only about 15 inches of rain annually—and vegetation that is mainly short grasses and shrubs. The southwestern states have a desert climate. In these states, the weather is usually hot and dry. Less than 10 inches of rain falls each year. Some cactus plants thrive, but much of the area is barren rock or sand. Large desert areas are the Mojave and the Sonoran.

TROPICAL CLIMATES In the United States, only Hawaii and southern Florida have tropical climates. The islands of Hawaii have a tropical wet climate that supports lush rain forests. Temperatures vary only

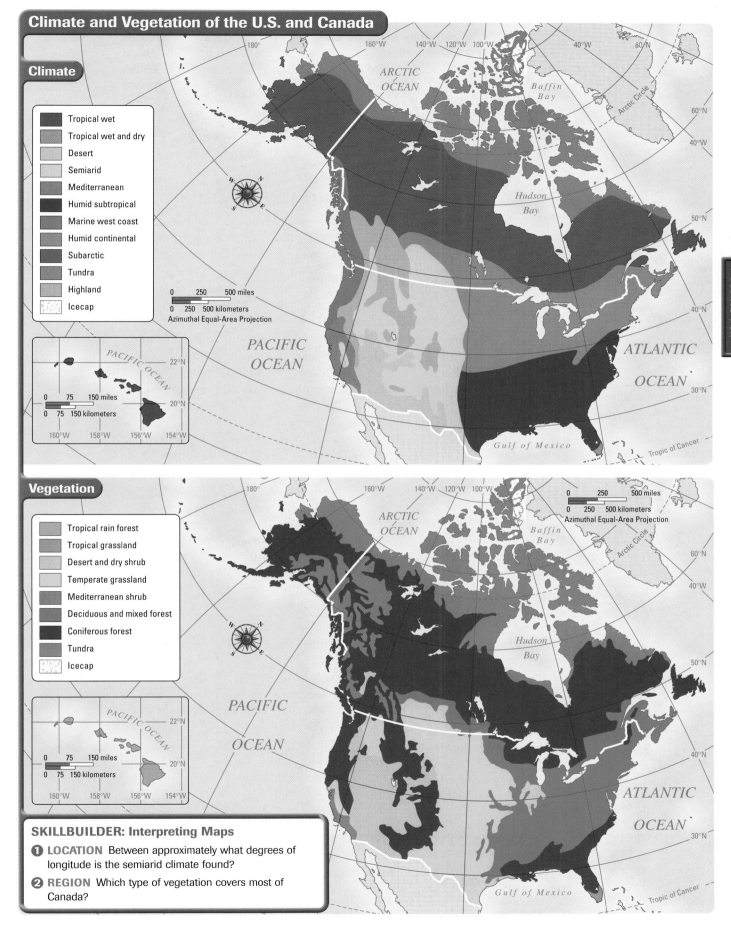

Climate and Vegetation of the U.S. and Canada

Climate

- Tropical wet
- Tropical wet and dry
- Desert
- Semiarid
- Mediterranean
- Humid subtropical
- Marine west coast
- Humid continental
- Subarctic
- Tundra
- Highland
- Icecap

0   250   500 miles
0   250   500 kilometers
Azimuthal Equal-Area Projection

0   75   150 miles
0   75   150 kilometers

ARCTIC OCEAN

Baffin Bay

Hudson Bay

PACIFIC OCEAN

ATLANTIC OCEAN

Gulf of Mexico

Tropic of Cancer

Arctic Circle

PACIFIC OCEAN

Vegetation

- Tropical rain forest
- Tropical grassland
- Desert and dry shrub
- Temperate grassland
- Mediterranean shrub
- Deciduous and mixed forest
- Coniferous forest
- Tundra
- Icecap

0   250   500 miles
0   250   500 kilometers
Azimuthal Equal-Area Projection

0   75   150 miles
0   75   150 kilometers

ARCTIC OCEAN

Baffin Bay

Hudson Bay

PACIFIC OCEAN

ATLANTIC OCEAN

Gulf of Mexico

Tropic of Cancer

Arctic Circle

SKILLBUILDER: Interpreting Maps

❶ **LOCATION** Between approximately what degrees of longitude is the semiarid climate found?

❷ **REGION** Which type of vegetation covers most of Canada?

US & CANADA

REGION Deadly ice storms like this one in Watertown, New York, create chaos each winter, especially in heavily populated areas. **What are some of the hazards of this form of extreme weather?**

a few degrees in the 70s°F. Mount Waialeale (wy•AH•lay•AH•lay) on Kauai island receives about 460 inches of rain annually, and is one of the wettest spots on earth. Southern Florida has a tropical wet and dry climate. It is nearly always warm, but has wet and dry seasons. Vegetation is mainly tall grasses and scattered trees, like those in the **Everglades,** a huge swampland that covers some 4,000 square miles.

Effects of Extreme Weather

Weather in the United States and Canada can be harsh and sometimes deadly. You can see the areas affected by extreme weather and climate conditions by looking at the natural hazards map on page 107.

In both cold and mild climates, severe storms can trigger widespread devastation. Warm air from the Gulf of Mexico and cold Canadian air masses sometimes clash over the plains region to produce violent thunderstorms, tornadoes, and blizzards. As you read in Unit 1, tornadoes strike so often in an area of the Great Plains that it is called "Tornado Alley." In summer and fall, hurricanes that sweep along the Atlantic and Gulf coasts can cause great damage. Winter snowstorms may bring normal life to a temporary halt in many cities, such as the one shown in the photo on this page.

Disasters can also result from too much precipitation in a short time or too little over a long period. Heavy rainfall can cause flooding. Lands along major rivers, such as the Mississippi, are especially at risk. Too little rain or too much heat may bring on droughts and dust storms or spark destructive forest fires.

In this section, you read about the varied climates and vegetation of the United States and Canada. In the next section, you will learn how physical geography has shaped life in these countries.

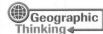

Geographic Thinking

Making Comparisons

How do climate and vegetation differ between Mediterranean and tropical climates?

SECTION 2 Assessment

1 Places & Terms

Identify and explain where in the region these would be found.

• permafrost
• prevailing westerlies
• Everglades

2 Taking Notes

REGION Review the notes you took for this section.

Climate and Vegetation

• What climate regions do the United States and Canada share?
• What climate regions are found in the United States but not in Canada?

3 Main Ideas

a. How do the prevailing westerlies change the climate of parts of the United States and Canada?

b. In which region would you find the dry climates?

c. In which climate type would you find the Everglades?

4 Geographic Thinking

Seeing Patterns Why doesn't all of Alaska have cold, snowy winters? **Think about:**

• location
• prevailing westerlies

RESEARCH LINKS
CLASSZONE.COM

GeoActivity

MAKING COMPARISONS Make a list of five Canadian cities and five U.S. cities. Then use the Internet to find out the average monthly temperature and monthly rainfall for each city. Create a **database** with the information. Then summarize your findings.

Human–Environment Interaction

Main Ideas

- Humans have dramatically changed the face of North America.
- European settlements in the United States and Canada expanded from east to west.

Places & Terms

nomad

Beringia

St. Lawrence Seaway

lock

CONNECT TO THE ISSUES

URBAN SPRAWL The spreading of cities and suburbs over wider areas—urban sprawl—is causing problems.

US & CANADA

SUNSHINE STATE STANDARDS
Key Standard SS.B.2.4.4 The student understands the global impact of human changes in the physical environment.
Other Standards SS.B.2.4.5
FCAT LA.A.1.4.2 Reading: Strategies

A HUMAN PERSPECTIVE The sun-baked American Southwest was a harsh environment for its early inhabitants, the ancestors of today's Pueblo peoples. But these early settlers made good use of available resources. From the land, they took clay and stone building materials. They built multi-room, apartment-like dwellings in cliffs. This gave protection against daytime heat, nighttime cold, and human and animal enemies. From plants and animals, the early settlers got food and clothing. They survived because they adapted to their environment.

Settlement and Agriculture Alter the Land

Before humans came, North American landforms were changed only by natural forces, such as weathering and erosion. That changed when the first settlers—the ancestors of the native peoples of North America—arrived thousands of years ago.

SETTLEMENT The first inhabitants of the area of North America now known as the United States and Canada were **nomads,** people who move from place to place. Most archaeologists believe that they probably migrated from Asia over **Beringia,** a land bridge that once connected Siberia and Alaska. These migrants moved about the land. They hunted game, fished, and gathered edible wild plants. Since water was necessary for survival, these first Americans made temporary settlements along coastlines and near rivers and streams. They adjusted to extremes of temperature and climate. They also adapted to the region's many natural environments, including mountains, forests, plains, and deserts.

AGRICULTURE Many early settlements became permanent after agriculture replaced hunting and gathering as the primary method of food production about 3,000 years ago. When people began to cultivate crops, they changed the landscape to meet their needs. In wooded areas, early farmers cut down trees for lumber to build houses and to burn as fuel. To plant crops, they plowed the rich soil of river valleys and flood plains using hoes of wood, stone, and bone. They dug ditches for irrigation. Vegetables they first cultivated—corn, beans, and squash—are now staples around the world.

Agriculture remains an important economic activity in the United States and Canada. In fact, both countries are leading exporters of agricultural products.

REGION Irrigation has opened land in dry areas to farming. Tracts such as these in New Mexico are watered by a method called center-pivot, which taps underground water.
What are some other ways water can be brought to dry land?

127

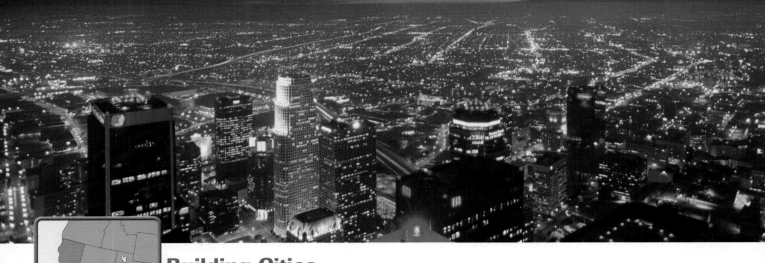

Building Cities

Where a city is built and how it grows depends a great deal on physical setting. As you read, living near water was crucial to early settlers, as it would be to those who followed. Other factors that can affect the suitability of a site are landscape, climate, weather, and the availability of natural resources. Some of these factors played a role in the development of two major cities of the region.

HUMAN–ENVIRONMENT INTERACTION Los Angeles sprawls out almost as far as the eye can see in this photo. **What changes were made to the environment as the city grew?**

Building Cities

Where a city is built and how it grows depends a great deal on physical setting. As you read, living near water was crucial to early settlers, as it would be to those who followed. Other factors that can affect the suitability of a site are landscape, climate, weather, and the availability of natural resources. Some of these factors played a role in the development of two major cities of the region.

MONTREAL—ADAPTING TO THE WEATHER Montreal, Quebec, is Canada's second largest city and a major port—even though its temperature is below freezing more than 100 days each year. Montreal's location on a large island where the St. Lawrence and Ottawa rivers meet made it an appealing site to early French explorers. The French built a permanent settlement there in 1642. The community was founded at the base of Mount Royal and grew by spreading around the mountain. To make the city's severe winters more endurable, people went inside and underground. In fact, large areas of Montreal have been developed underground, including a network of shops and restaurants.

LOS ANGELES—CREATING URBAN SPRAWL Unlike Montreal, Los Angeles, California, has a mild climate year-round. It also has a desirable location on the Pacific coast. Hundreds of thousands of people were pouring into this once small Spanish settlement by the early 1900s. As a result, the city expanded farther and farther into nearby valleys and desert-like foothills. During the 1980s, Los Angeles became the second most populous city in the United States. However, rapid population expansion brought problems. These included air pollution, inadequate water supplies, and construction on earthquake-threatened land. But such problems did not stop the city's growth. Los Angeles itself now covers about 469 square miles. Its metropolitan area spreads over 4,060 square miles.

Building cities was just one way humans interacted with their environment. Another was in the construction of transportation systems to make movement from place to place less difficult.

Geographic Thinking

Making Comparisons
Ⓐ How has climate influenced the development of Los Angeles and Montreal?

Overcoming Distances

The native peoples and the Europeans who followed encountered many obstacles when they moved across the land. They faced huge distances, large bodies of water, formidable landforms, and harsh climates. But they spanned the continent and changed the natural environment forever.

TRAILS AND INLAND WATERWAYS Some of the early peoples who came across the land bridge from Siberia blazed trails eastward. Others followed the Pacific coast south toward warmer climates. Still others remained in the northwest, in what are now Alaska and northern Canada.

When Europeans from England and France crossed the Atlantic to North America, they set up colonies along the coast. Then, they moved inland. As they did, they carved overland trails, including the National and Wilderness roads and the Oregon and Santa Fe trails. They also used inland waterways, such as the Mississippi and Ohio rivers. To connect bodies of water, they built a network of canals. The Erie Canal across upstate New York opened in 1825 and made the first navigable water link between the Atlantic and the Great Lakes. **◀B**

North America's most important deepwater ship route—the **St. Lawrence Seaway**—was completed in the 1950s as a joint project of the United States and Canada. As you can see from the map on this page, the seaway connects the Great Lakes to the Atlantic Ocean by way of the St. Lawrence River. Ships are raised and lowered some 600 feet by a series of **locks,** sections of a waterway with closed gates where water levels are raised or lowered. The seaway enables huge, oceangoing vessels to sail into the industrial and agricultural heartland of North America.

Geographic Thinking ◀

Seeing Patterns
B Why was it important to link waterways?

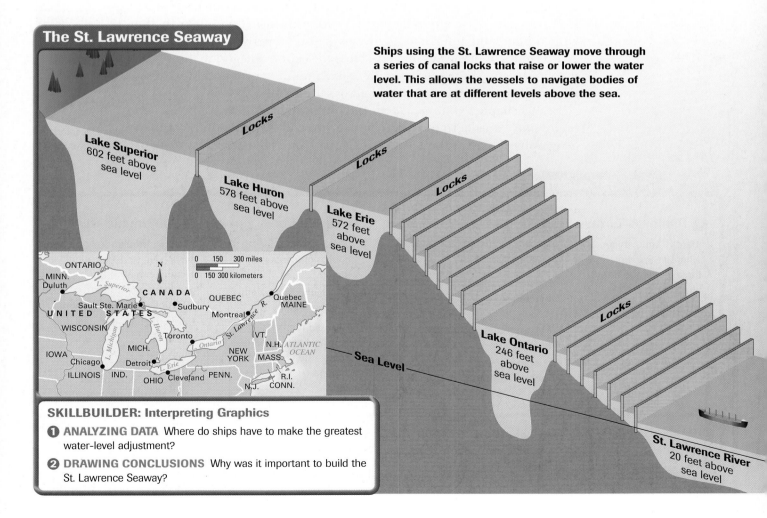

The St. Lawrence Seaway

Ships using the St. Lawrence Seaway move through a series of canal locks that raise or lower the water level. This allows the vessels to navigate bodies of water that are at different levels above the sea.

Lake Superior 602 feet above sea level

Locks

Lake Huron 578 feet above sea level

Locks

Lake Erie 572 feet above sea level

Locks

Sea Level

Lake Ontario 246 feet above sea level

Locks

St. Lawrence River 20 feet above sea level

SKILLBUILDER: Interpreting Graphics

❶ **ANALYZING DATA** Where do ships have to make the greatest water-level adjustment?

❷ **DRAWING CONCLUSIONS** Why was it important to build the St. Lawrence Seaway?

TRANSCONTINENTAL RAILROADS The marriage of the steam locomotive and the railroads made crossing the continent from the Atlantic to the Pacific quicker and easier. Railroad building began in North America in the early 19th century. But many of the physical features shown on the map on page 103 presented natural barriers. To make way, railroad workers had to cut down forests, build bridges over streams, and blast tunnels through mountains.

The first transcontinental railroad was completed across the United States in 1869. A trans-Canada railroad, from Montreal to British Columbia, was completed in 1885. These railroads carried goods and passengers cross-country, promoting economic development and national unity as they went. Today, the United States has the world's largest railway system, and Canada the third largest.

NATIONAL HIGHWAY SYSTEMS Before the railroads came, there were roads that connected towns and cities and provided pathways to the interior. But it was the development of the automobile in the early 20th century that spurred roadbuilding. Today, both the United States and Canada have extensive roadway systems. The United States has about 4 million miles of roads, while Canada has about 560,000 miles.

As you read earlier, much of Canada's population is concentrated in the south. So, Canadians built their major highways east to west in the southern part of the country, connecting principal cities. The Trans-Canada Highway, Canada's primary roadway, stretches about 4,860 miles from St. John's, Newfoundland, to Victoria, British Columbia. In the United States, the interstate highway system is a network of more than 46,000 miles of highways that crisscross the country. Begun in the 1950s, it connects the United States with Canada on the north and Mexico on the south, and also runs east-west across the country.

In this chapter, you read about the physical geography of the United States and Canada. In the next chapter, you will learn about the human geography of one of these countries—the United States.

Making Comparisons
C How is the Trans-Canada Highway similar to and different from the U.S. interstate highway system?

3 Assessment

1 Places & Terms

Identify and explain where in the region these would be found.

• nomad
• Beringia
• lock
• St. Lawrence Seaway

2 Taking Notes

MOVEMENT Review the notes you took for this section.

Human-Environment Interaction

• Why are railroads important to a nation's development?
• In what ways did settlers in Canada and the United States move across the continent?

3 Main Ideas

a. What factors affect the choice of location of a city?

b. Why is the St. Lawrence Seaway important?

c. How did methods of moving people and goods across the continent change over time?

4 Geographic Thinking

Making Inferences In what ways have transportation systems crossing the continent altered the environment? **Think about:**

• construction of canals and railroads
• building cities

S **See Skillbuilder Handbook, page R4.**

ASKING GEOGRAPHIC QUESTIONS Obtain and study a highway map of your state. Then come up with a geographic question about the map, perhaps one considering geographic features that caused the location of a highway. Answer the question and make a **class presentation** using visuals.

Map and Graph Skills

Reading a Highway Map

San Antonio, Texas, is a part of a metropolitan area of more than one million people, located in south central Texas. It has been a crossroads for much of its history—for its earliest Native American settlers, the Spanish who came later, and finally, the Texans who won independence from Mexico not long after the battle of the Alamo. Looking at the map below, you can see that the city remains a meeting point, crisscrossed by interstate, U.S., state, and county highways.

THE LANGUAGE OF MAPS The primary purpose of a **highway map** is to show the location of roadways in an area and the distance between places. But highway maps usually include much other information. For example, they may identify important sites, such as airports, parks, and universities.

SUNSHINE STATE STANDARDS
Key Standard SS.B.1.4.1 The student uses a variety of maps, geographic technologies including geographic information systems (GIS) and satellite-produced imagery, and other advanced graphic representations to depict geographic problems.

FCAT LA.A.2.4.1 Reading: Identify Main Idea, Details, and Methods

San Antonio and Vicinity, 2001

Copyright by Rand McNally & Co.

1 The title identifies the area covered by the map.

2 The key shows the symbols used on the map and explains what they mean. For example, the ✈ symbol shows where airports are located.

3 Points of interest, such as the Alamo (B–2) or Sea World (A–2), are marked by small red squares or by pink ribbons, depending on their size.

Map and Graph Skills Assessment

1. Seeing Patterns
Which interstate highways pass through the center of San Antonio?

2. Making Decisions
Which interstate highway and U.S. highway would you take to the Alamo when coming from the southeast?

3. Analyzing Data
By the most direct route, how far is Live Oak from Leon Valley by highway?

Reading a Highway Map **131**

VISUAL SUMMARY
PHYSICAL GEOGRAPHY OF THE UNITED STATES AND CANADA

Landforms

Major Mountain Ranges:
Rocky Mountains, Appalachian Mountains

Major Waterways:
Mississippi-Missouri-Ohio river system, Great Lakes, Mackenzie River, Columbia River, Rio Grande River, Colorado River

Interior Lowlands:
Great Plains, Canadian Shield, Interior Plains

Resources

• Both the United States and Canada have huge mineral and fossil fuel resources.

• Forest lands cover about one-third of the United States and one-half of Canada.

Climate and Vegetation

• Canada's climates and vegetation are related to its far northern location.

• The United States includes regions that are in almost every climate and vegetation zone.

Human-Environment Interaction

• Movement westward altered the land in both the United States and Canada.

• Transportation networks helped develop the land and economy of the region.

Reviewing Places & Terms

A. Briefly explain the importance of each of the following.

1. Appalachian Mountains
2. Rocky Mountains
3. Great Plains
4. Canadian Shield
5. Great Lakes
6. Mackenzie River
7. prevailing westerlies
8. Everglades
9. lock
10. St. Lawrence Seaway

B. Answer the questions about vocabulary in complete sentences.

11. Which of the places listed above are found both in the United States and Canada?
12. Which of the mountain chains form a boundary with the Canadian Shield?
13. The Great Plains are bounded on one side by which landform listed above?
14. The Hudson Bay is found in which place listed above?
15. Which two waterways are linked?
16. Which place above is a huge swampland?
17. Which of the places are subregions of the Interior Lowlands?
18. What climate region in North America is influenced by the prevailing westerlies?
19. Why are the Great Lakes and the St. Lawrence Seaway important?
20. Why are locks needed on the St. Lawrence Seaway?

Main Ideas

Landforms and Resources (pp. 117–122)

1. How do the Eastern Lowlands differ from the Interior Lowlands?
2. What is the Continental Divide?
3. Why are the United States and Canada leading food producers?
4. What are the most abundant natural resources in the United States and Canada?

Climate and Vegetation (pp. 123–126)

5. In what type of climate would you expect to find permafrost?
6. Which climates are found in the United States and not in Canada?
7. What type of vegetation covers most of Canada?

Human-Environment Interaction (pp. 127–131)

8. How did the earliest inhabitants of the United States and Canada, those who arrived before the Europeans, alter the land?
9. What problems arose in Los Angeles with rapid expansion?
10. How did the settlers of the United States and Canada overcome the distances across the continent?

Critical Thinking

1. Using Your Notes

Use your completed chart to answer these questions.

Landforms	
Resources	

a. How is the location of cities related to landforms and to climate?

b. How is Canada's economy affected by its climate and vegetation?

2. Geographic Themes

a. **MOVEMENT** Write a sentence describing the movement of people and goods across the United States and Canada over the last 200 years.

b. **PLACE** How have the Great Lakes contributed to the development of both the United States and Canada?

3. Identifying Themes

In developing their city, how did the people of Montreal solve the problems of a severe climate? Which of the five themes apply to this situation?

4. Making Inferences

What aspects of physical geography have contributed to the economic success of the United States and Canada?

5. Seeing Patterns

How did the presence of north-to-south flowing rivers in the United States affect its development?

Additional Test Practice, pp. S1–S37

TEST PRACTICE
CLASSZONE.COM

US & CANADA

Geographic Skills: Interpreting Maps

Physical Profile of the United States

Use the map below to answer the following questions.

1. **REGION** What might be said about the land between the Appalachians and the Mississippi?

2. **PLACE** What is the difference in altitude between the Coastal ranges and the Sierra Nevada?

3. **REGION** What happens to the land as you move west of the Mississippi?

GeoActivity

Create a three-dimensional model of the cross section on this page. Use colors to indicate elevations and label the physical features you show. Create a legend for your model.

Profile line

INTERNET ACTIVITY

Use the links at **classzone.com** to conduct research on the landforms of the United States and Canada. Focus on finding pictures of major and well-known landforms and waterways.

Creating a Multimedia Presentation From your research, select a series of pictures to include in a presentation on the theme "A Land of Contrasts." List the Web sites you used in preparing your report.

Chapter

6

SECTION 1
History and
Government of
the United States

SECTION 2
Economy and Culture
of the United States

SECTION 3
Subregions of
the United States

HUMAN GEOGRAPHY OF THE UNITED STATES
Shaping an Abundant Land

Four Subregions of the United States

Northeast
South
Midwest
West

GeoFocus

What factors shaped the development of the United States?

Taking Notes In your notebook, copy a cluster diagram like the one shown. As you read, take notes about the history, economy, culture, and modern life of the United States and its subregions.

History and Government

Economy and Culture

The United States

Subregions

History and Government of the United States

Main Ideas

- The United States is a "nation of immigrants," settled by people from all over the world.
- The United States is the most diverse and highly industrialized and urbanized nation in the world.

Places & Terms

migration

Columbian Exchange

Louisiana Purchase

frontier

suburb

representative democracy

A HUMAN PERSPECTIVE Women were North America's first farmers. In all early cultures except the hunter-gatherer culture of the Southwest, women cultivated the land. They discovered which wild plants could be used as food for the family. They planted the seeds, tended the garden, harvested the crops, and prepared food for meals. Corn, beans, and squash were the first of these foods. Women also learned which leaves, bark, roots, stems, and berries could be used for medicines. Their efforts helped to ensure the survival of human settlement in North America—and the part of the land that became the United States.

Creating a Nation

The United States occupies nearly two-fifths of North America. It is the world's third largest country in both land area and population. It is rich in natural resources and is also fortunate to have a moderate climate, fertile soil, and plentiful water supplies. For thousands of years, this bounty has attracted waves of immigrants who came to find a better life. This continuing immigration is a recurring theme in the country's history; so is the constant **migration,** or movement, of peoples within the United States.

MANY PEOPLES SETTLE THE LAND As you read in Chapter 5, the first inhabitants of North America were believed to be nomads who came from Asia at least 13,000 or more years ago. These people settled the continent, spreading south along the Pacific coast and east to the Atlantic. Over the centuries, they developed separate cultures, as the map on page 104 shows. These native peoples occupied the land undisturbed until the 15th century, when Europeans began to explore what they called the "New World." The Spanish arrived first. They searched the present-day Southeast and Southwest for gold and other treasure. In 1565, they founded St. Augustine, Florida, the oldest permanent European settlement in the United States.

The French and English came later. France was interested in fisheries and the fur trade. In the early 1600s, the French settled along the northern Atlantic Coast and the St. Lawrence River in what is now Canada. The English arrived at about the same time. During the 1600s and 1700s,

US & CANADA

CONNECT TO THE ISSUES

TERRORISM Beginning in the late 20th century, the United States has been subjected to terrorist attacks by individuals and groups opposed to its policies.

SUNSHINE STATE STANDARDS

Key Standard SS.B.2.4.1 The student understands how social, cultural, economic, and environmental factors contribute . . .

Other Standards SS.A.4.4.1, A.5.4.1, A.5.4.6, C.1.4.3

FCAT LA.A.1.4.2 Reading: Strategies

HUMAN-ENVIRONMENT INTERACTION Early Native American settlers in the Southwest often built their dwellings into canyon walls. The dwellings shown are in Mesa Verde National Park in Colorado. **Why did the earliest settlers choose such locations for their dwellings?**

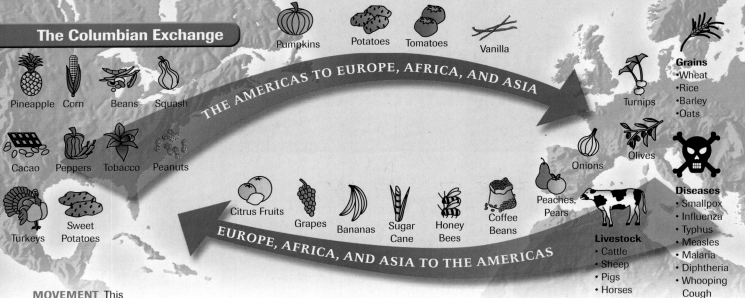

The Columbian Exchange

Pumpkins Potatoes Tomatoes Vanilla

Pineapple Corn Beans Squash

Cacao Peppers Tobacco Peanuts

Turkeys Sweet Potatoes

THE AMERICAS TO EUROPE, AFRICA, AND ASIA

Citrus Fruits Grapes Bananas Sugar Cane Honey Bees Coffee Beans Peaches, Pears

EUROPE, AFRICA, AND ASIA TO THE AMERICAS

Turnips Olives Onions

Grains
•Wheat
•Rice
•Barley
•Oats

Diseases
• Smallpox
• Influenza
• Typhus
• Measles
• Malaria
• Diphtheria
• Whooping Cough

Livestock
• Cattle
• Sheep
• Pigs
• Horses

MOVEMENT This infographic shows how plants, animals, and diseases were transferred between the Eastern and Western hemispheres as trade followed the voyages of Christopher Columbus to the Americas.

they settled to the south—on rivers and bays along the Atlantic coast from present-day Maine to Georgia. The English made their first permanent settlement in Jamestown, Virginia, in 1607.

European colonies often displaced Native Americans. In 1617, the Europeans brought Africans to America to work as slave laborers on cotton and tobacco plantations in the South. The coming of the Europeans also began what historians call the **Columbian Exchange.** The infographic above shows how the arrival of Europeans in the Western Hemisphere affected the lives of both Europeans and the native peoples.

ESTABLISHING AND MAINTAINING THE UNION The French and the English eventually fought in North America over trade and territory. In 1763, Great Britain gained control of all of North America east of the Mississippi River. But its control was short-lived. Britain's 13 American colonies soon began to resent the policies forced on them by a government thousands of miles away across the Atlantic. Their protests led to the American Revolution (1775–1783) and the founding of the United States of America. The new nation grew rapidly, and settlers pushed westward to the Mississippi. In 1803, the United States nearly doubled in size when the government purchased the vast plains region between the Mississippi and the Rocky Mountains from France. This territory became known as the **Louisiana Purchase.**

In the early 1800s, immigrants from Western Europe arrived in great numbers. They settled in cities in the Northeast, where industrialization was beginning. One such city was Lowell, Massachusetts, which had become a booming textile center by the 1840s. The newcomers also moved to rich farmlands in what is now the Midwest.

Meanwhile, sectionalism was growing. People were placing loyalty to their region, or section, above loyalty to the nation. The result was rising political and economic tensions between an agricultural South dependent on slave labor and the more industrialized North. These tensions led to the Civil War (1861–1865). It took four years of bloody fighting and many more years of political conflict to reunite the country.

BACKGROUND About 600,000 Africans were brought to the United States to work as slave laborers from 1617 until the importation of slaves was banned in 1808.

An Industrial and Urban Society

In the second half of the 19th century, millions of Americans were on the move. They settled on newly opened lands west of the Mississippi and in the rapidly industrializing cities of the North and Midwest.

WESTWARD MOVEMENT From departure points such as Independence, Missouri, hundreds of thousands of pioneers left in covered wagons bound for the West. They blazed trails that crossed prairie, plains, desert, and mountains, moving toward the Pacific. A wagon train on the Oregon Trail might have taken up to six months to reach its destination 2,000 miles away. ◀A

To make way for white settlers, the U.S. government removed Native Americans from their lands by treaty, or by force. In Chapter 5, you read that the first transcontinental railroad across the United States was completed in 1869. Railroads brought people to the West, and western cattle and products to markets in the East. By 1890, about 17 million people lived between the Mississippi and the Pacific. The free, open land that had been available and suitable for settlement—the **frontier**—was now fully settled.

INDUSTRIALIZATION AND URBANIZATION As the West was being settled, immigrants—mainly from Western and Eastern Europe—poured into the United States. About 14 million came from 1860 to 1900.

Some joined the movement to the West. Others settled in urban areas undergoing industrialization. Cities such as New York, Boston, Pittsburgh, Cleveland, Detroit, and Chicago expanded rapidly. Both recent immigrants and large numbers of Americans from rural areas came to cities such as these to work in textile, steel, oil, food processing, and other industries. The United States was being transformed from a rural, agricultural nation to an urban, industrialized one.

World Power and Domestic Change

As the 20th century began, the United States was the dominant economic and political power in the Western Hemisphere. By the century's end, it would be the world's sole superpower.

LOOKING BEYOND ITS BORDERS The United States had tried to avoid involvement in foreign affairs during its decades of growth. Because of its ample natural and human resources, it had been almost self-sufficient from its founding. Its farms grew the food necessary for survival, and the nation's factories produced the manufactured goods it needed. It was also protected

Geographic Thinking◀

Using the Atlas

Ⓐ Refer to the map on page 103. What landforms must be crossed by pioneers going from Independence, Missouri, to the Pacific coast?

Development of the West

1803 The United States purchases French territory west of the Mississippi.

1804–1806 **Lewis and Clark** expedition explores the area of the Louisiana Purchase.

1840s **Wagon trains** begin moving pioneers to the West.

1869 A symbolic **"golden spike"** is used to mark the completion of a transcontinental railroad across the United States.

1898 The United States continues its westward expansion, annexing Hawaii.

1890 Land available for settlement on the western frontier has nearly disappeared.

1913
Use of an **assembly line** in Ford auto plants streamlines manufacturing.

1920
Regular radio programming by station KDKA in Pittsburgh begins the era of mass communication.

1947
The first mass television audience watches baseball's World Series.

1959
The development of the **integrated circuit** would make the widespread use of computers possible.

1961
U.S. manned exploration of space starts as Alan B. Shepard, Jr., is launched into suborbit of the Earth.

1969
The U.S. Department of Defense develops a computer network that later leads to the Internet.

2000
Mapping **human genetic material (DNA)** is a breakthrough in biotechnology.

DNA

from foreign conflicts by two vast oceans—the Atlantic and the Pacific. But a global economic depression and two world wars brought significant changes. When World War II ended in 1945, the United States was the only major nation that had escaped physical damage and had a healthy economy.

SOCIAL CHANGE AND TECHNOLOGICAL GROWTH The last half of the 20th century was a time of rapid social change. Americans were on the move. Large numbers of people began migrating from cities to surrounding **suburbs,** the communities outside of a city. Some Americans left the colder climates of the Northeast and Midwest for the warmer South and West. Also, immigrants continued to arrive by the hundreds of thousands. But now they came mainly from the countries of Latin America and Asia. **B**

These years saw much social unrest, especially during the 1960s and 1970s. The civil rights movement fought to gain equal rights for African Americans. The feminist movement sought equality for women. Also, many students and others protested U.S. involvement in a war between Communist and non-Communist forces in Vietnam (1955–75).

During this period, the U.S. economy boomed, despite some periods of economic downturn, or recession. The economy, too, was being transformed. Changes in technology altered the way goods were produced. The use of computers revolutionized the workplace. Providing services and information technology surpassed industrial production in importance. The United States also became the world's greatest economic power. Today, it plays a major role in a global economy that is increasingly competitive.

LIVING IN A GLOBAL SOCIETY Meanwhile, American political influence spread throughout the world after the Second World War. The United States became the leader of the world's non-Communist nations. Their goal was to stop the spread of communism, spearheaded by the Soviet Union (now Russia). A competition for world influence called the Cold War (roughly 1945–1991) followed. When communism in Europe collapsed in 1991, the United States emerged as the world's sole superpower. As such, it has used its diplomatic and military power to try to keep the peace and to further American interests in the international community.

Geographic Thinking

Seeing Patterns
B What kinds of movement were taking place in the United States in the last half of the 20th century?

Government of the United States

EXECUTIVE

President

Carries out laws

Vice-President, Executive Departments, and Administrative Agencies

Assist the president in administering laws

LEGISLATIVE

Congress

Enacts laws

House of Representatives   **Senate**

JUDICIAL

Supreme Court

Reviews decisions of lower courts and interprets laws

Federal, State, and Local Courts

Judge violations of laws and settle disputes

Governing the People

One of the strengths of the United States is the political system created by the U.S. Constitution, drawn up in 1787. The United States is a **representative democracy,** where the people rule through elected representatives. It is also a federal republic, where powers are divided among the federal, or national, government and various state governments.

As you can see on the chart above, there are three separate and equal branches of the federal government. The executive branch, headed by the president, carries out the laws. The president also approves or vetoes proposed laws. The legislative branch makes the laws, and the judicial branch interprets the laws by reviewing decisions of lower courts. The 50 states also have executive, legislative, and judicial branches. They exercise powers not specifically granted to the federal government by the Constitution.

In this section, you read about the history and government of the United States. In the next, you will learn about its economy and culture.

SECTION Assessment

❶ Places & Terms
Explain the meaning of each of the following terms.
- migration
- Columbian Exchange
- Louisiana Purchase
- frontier
- suburb
- representative democracy

❷ Taking Notes
MOVEMENT Review the notes you took for this section.

History and Government

The United States

- Where did people migrate from to populate North America?
- Where did people move after the frontier was fully settled?

❸ Main Ideas
a. Why did the United States attract so many immigrants?

b. How was the United States able to become a world power?

c. How are the powers of government in the United States divided?

❹ Geographic Thinking
Making Inferences How did the physical geography of the United States contribute to its economic growth? **Think about:**
- land and mineral resources
- its relative global location

S See Skillbuilder Handbook, page R4.

GeoActivity

EXPLORING LOCAL GEOGRAPHY Make a list of physical features that would have attracted settlement to your area. Then do research or call your local historical society to find out when your community was founded and what groups settled there. Combine your findings in a **report** about your community.

Economy and Culture of the United States

Main Ideas

- The United States has the world's largest and most diversified economy.
- American products and popular culture are recognized around the world.

Places & Terms

export

free enterprise

service industry

postindustrial economy

multinational

CONNECT TO THE ISSUES
URBAN SPRAWL
Urbanization has helped economic growth, but it has also caused a variety of problems.

SUNSHINE STATE STANDARDS
Key Standard SS.B.2.4.1 The student understands how social, cultural, economic, and environmental factors contribute to the dynamic nature of regions.
Other Standards SS.A.5.4.2
FCAT LA.A.1.4.2 Reading: Strategies

A HUMAN PERSPECTIVE The average American worker in 1790 was a self-employed farmer. The farmer spent each work day, sunrise to sunset, in backbreaking labor in the field. Most of the crops and livestock raised were consumed by the farm family. In the 1890s, the average American worker labored in a manufacturing or service industry, for long hours and low wages, often under unsafe conditions. Laborers in factories, for example, worked 60 hours a week for a total wage of $12; some were as young as 12 years of age.

At the start of the 21st century, the average worker was spending most of the workday in an office in front of a computer, processing information or providing services. The standard workweek was 40 hours; the government regulated workplace safety; and salaries generally covered living expenses, leisure-time activities, and perhaps, even savings.

The World's Greatest Economic Power

The United States has about 7 percent of the world's land area and about 5 percent of the world's population. But it has the world's largest economy—the most powerful, diverse, and technologically advanced in the world. The United States is a world leader in agricultural products, manufactured goods, and global trade. In fact, it accounts for more than 10 percent of the world's **exports,** which are goods sold to another country.

Three factors have contributed to the overall success of the American economy—available natural resources, a skilled labor force, and a stable political system that has allowed the economy to develop. The economy is run largely on **free enterprise.** In this economic system, private individuals own most of the resources, technology, and businesses, and can operate them for profit with little control from the government.

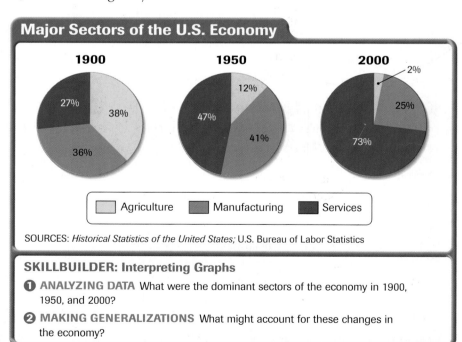

Major Sectors of the U.S. Economy

1900
38%
27%
36%

1950
12%
47%
41%

2000
2%
25%
73%

Agriculture Manufacturing Services

SOURCES: *Historical Statistics of the United States;* U.S. Bureau of Labor Statistics

SKILLBUILDER: Interpreting Graphs

❶ **ANALYZING DATA** What were the dominant sectors of the economy in 1900, 1950, and 2000?

❷ **MAKING GENERALIZATIONS** What might account for these changes in the economy?

Agriculture and Industry of the United States

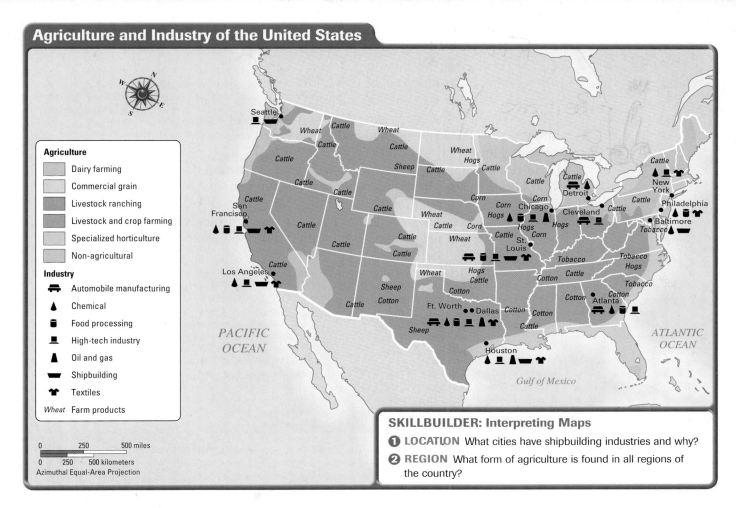

Agriculture
- Dairy farming
- Commercial grain
- Livestock ranching
- Livestock and crop farming
- Specialized horticulture
- Non-agricultural

Industry
- Automobile manufacturing
- Chemical
- Food processing
- High-tech industry
- Oil and gas
- Shipbuilding
- Textiles
- *Wheat* Farm products

0   250   500 miles
0   250   500 kilometers
Azimuthal Equal-Area Projection

SKILLBUILDER: Interpreting Maps

❶ **LOCATION** What cities have shipbuilding industries and why?

❷ **REGION** What form of agriculture is found in all regions of the country?

AN AGRICULTURAL AND INDUSTRIAL GIANT The United States not only feeds itself but also helps to feed the world. American farms and ranches supply about 40 percent of the world's production of corn, 20 percent of its cotton, and about 10 percent of its wheat, cattle, and hogs. Fertile soil, a favorable climate, and the early mechanization of the country's farms are mainly responsible for this bounty. Different areas of the country produce different products, as you can see from the map on this page. The Midwest and South, for example, specialize in crop farming, while livestock ranching is concentrated in the West.

The industrial output of the United States is larger than that of any other country. Advances in technology, especially in electronics and computers, revolutionized industry and led to the creation of new products and methods of production. Leading industries are petroleum, steel, transportation equipment, chemicals, electronics, food processing, telecommunications, consumer goods, lumber, and mining. ◀

Major industrial centers have long been located along the Atlantic Coast and around the Great Lakes. In recent decades, a variety of industries have also started up in urban areas in the South and along the Pacific coast. Over time, some areas have become associated with certain products, such as Detroit (automobiles), Seattle (aircraft), and northern California, in an area called Silicon Valley (computers).

A POSTINDUSTRIAL ECONOMY The graphs on page 140 show the rich farming and manufacturing traditions of the United States. But

Geographic Thinking

Seeing Patterns
Ⓐ Why might industrial centers be located near bodies of water?

they also indicate that the American economy today is driven by service industries. A **service industry** is any kind of economic activity that produces a service rather than a product. Nearly three out of four Americans now work in service-related jobs, such as information processing, finance, medicine, transportation, and education. This economic phase is called a **postindustrial economy,** one where manufacturing no longer plays a dominant role.

The United States is the world's major trading nation, leading the world in the value of its exports and imports. It exports raw materials, agricultural products, and manufactured goods. Automobiles, electronic equipment, machinery, and apparel are some of its principal imports. Its North American neighbors, Canada and Mexico, are two of its most important trading partners. Many American corporations engage in business worldwide and are called **multinationals.**

Geographic Thinking

Seeing Patterns
B Where do some of the natural resources of the United States go?

A Diverse Society

Because the United States is a nation of immigrants, it is a nation of different races and ethnic traditions. The majority of Americans, about 70 percent, trace their ancestry to Europe. Hispanic Americans, mainly

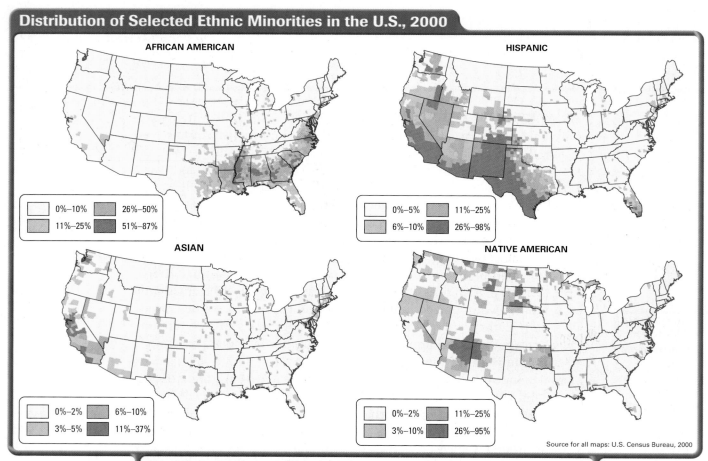

Distribution of Selected Ethnic Minorities in the U.S., 2000

AFRICAN AMERICAN

0%–10% 26%–50%
11%–25% 51%–87%

HISPANIC

0%–5% 11%–25%
6%–10% 26%–98%

ASIAN

0%–2% 6%–10%
3%–5% 11%–37%

NATIVE AMERICAN

0%–2% 11%–25%
3%–10% 26%–95%

Source for all maps: U.S. Census Bureau, 2000

SKILLBUILDER: Interpreting Maps

❶ **REGION** What subregion has significant numbers of most of the ethnic groups shown?

❷ **MOVEMENT** Compare this map with the map on page 104. What has changed about the distribution of Native Americans since 1600?

from Central and South America, make up about 13 percent of the population; African Americans, about 12 percent; Asian Americans, 4 percent; and Native Americans, 1 percent. The largest ethnic groups are English, German, Irish, African, French, Italian, Scottish, Polish, and Mexican. The maps on page 142 show the distribution of some groups.

LANGUAGES AND RELIGION English has been the dominant language of the United States since its founding. Spanish is the second most commonly spoken language. Typically, immigrants have spoken their native language until they learned English.

Religious freedom has been a cornerstone of American society. Today, more than 1,000 different religious groups practice their faiths in the United States. By far, the majority of the American people—85 percent—are Christians. About 56 percent are Protestants and 28 percent Roman Catholics. Jews and Muslims each account for about 2 percent of the religious population.

THE ARTS AND POPULAR CULTURE The United States has a rich artistic heritage, the product of its diverse population. Its first artists were Native Americans, who made pottery, weavings, and carvings. Early European settlers brought with them the artistic traditions of their homelands. Truly American styles developed in painting, music, literature, and architecture in the 19th century. Artists depicted the country's expansive landscape and scenes of American life both on the western frontier and in the cities. One 19th-century American creation, the skyscraper, changed urban architecture all over the world.

Today, motion pictures and popular music are two influential American art forms. Hollywood, California, is the center of the movie industry in the United States. American films provide entertainment for the world. Many ethnic groups contributed to the musical heritage of the United States. For example, jazz, blues, gospel, and rock 'n' roll have African-American origins. Country and bluegrass music developed among Southern whites whose ancestors came from the British Isles.

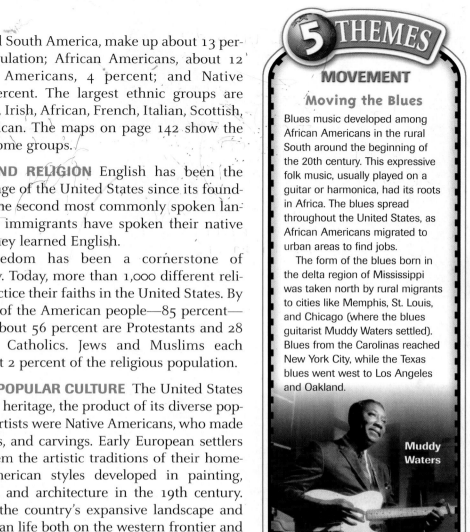

5 THEMES

MOVEMENT
Moving the Blues

Blues music developed among African Americans in the rural South around the beginning of the 20th century. This expressive folk music, usually played on a guitar or harmonica, had its roots in Africa. The blues spread throughout the United States, as African Americans migrated to urban areas to find jobs.

The form of the blues born in the delta region of Mississippi was taken north by rural migrants to cities like Memphis, St. Louis, and Chicago (where the blues guitarist Muddy Waters settled). Blues from the Carolinas reached New York City, while the Texas blues went west to Los Angeles and Oakland.

Muddy Waters

US & CANADA

American Life Today

More than 280 million people live in the United States. The majority enjoy a high standard of living. Despite coming from many ethnic and racial groups, they generally live and work together. They are pursuing what attracted their ancestors to the New World and came to be called "the American dream," a better life for themselves and their children.

WHERE AMERICANS LIVE About 80 percent of Americans live in cities or surrounding suburbs. Americans moved first from rural areas to cities and then from cities to suburbs. The shift to the suburbs was made possible by the widespread ownership of automobiles. There is one auto

HUMAN–ENVIRONMENT INTERACTION Lake Michigan and its shoreline provide Chicago residents with many opportunities for recreation.
What might some of these recreational opportunities be?

for every 1.3 Americans. A highly developed transportation network that includes highways, expressways, railroads, and airlines aids mobility.

HOW AMERICANS LIVE, WORK, AND PLAY Nearly 50 percent of American adults of working age are employed. Almost half of them are women. As you read earlier, about seven out of ten Americans in the workforce hold service industry jobs. Many are highly skilled positions, which require advanced education. Americans have always valued education, seeing it as a means to provide equality and opportunity. As a result, all children from the ages of 6 or 7 to age 16 are required to attend school. Nine out of ten students are in the public school system, where education is free through secondary school. The United States also has more than 2,300 four-year public and private colleges and universities.

Americans have a wide range of choices for leisure-time activities. As either spectators or players, they take part in sports such as baseball, basketball, football, golf, soccer, tennis, and skiing. Most major cities have professional sports teams. Americans of all ages also use their free time to engage in hobbies, visit museums and libraries, and watch television and movies. Another favorite activity is spending time on the computer, surfing the Internet or playing video games.

Unfortunately, not all Americans live well. More than one in ten lives in poverty. It is a continuing challenge for government and society to try to bring these people into the mainstream of American life. In the next section, you will learn about life in the country's subregions.

SECTION **2** **Assessment**

1 Places & Terms

Explain the meaning of each of the following terms.

- export
- free enterprise
- service industry
- postindustrial economy
- multinational

2 Taking Notes

REGION Review the notes you took for this section.

- Where are the industrial centers in the United States?
- Where do the majority of Americans live?

3 Main Ideas

a. What three factors have contributed to the success of the American economy?

b. What are the geographic origins of some American musical styles?

c. What invention made life in the suburbs possible?

4 Geographic Thinking

Making Comparisons How is the economy of the United States today different from its economy 50 years ago?
Think about:
- postindustrial economy
- multinational trade

 See Skillbuilder Handbook, page R3.

EXPLORING LOCAL GEOGRAPHY Study the maps on page 142. Find your state. Create a **sketch map** of your state and show the location of major ethnic groups that live in your state.

Subregions of the United States

Main Ideas

- The United States is divided into four major economic and cultural subregions.
- There are both similarities and differences among the subregions of the United States.

Places & Terms

New England
megalopolis
the Midwest
the South

metropolitan area
the West

CONNECT TO THE ISSUES
DIVERSE SOCIETIES While diversity can be a strength, it has also been the cause of tension and conflict among regions.

SUNSHINE STATE STANDARDS
Key Standard SS.B.2.4.1 The student understands how social, cultural, economic, and environmental factors contribute to the dynamic nature of regions.

FCAT LA.A.1.4.2 Reading: Strategies

A HUMAN PERSPECTIVE America's back roads were the beat of reporter and author Charles Kuralt for more than 20 years. Beginning in the 1960s, he traveled by van through every region of the country. In his "On the Road" series for television, he reported on the uniqueness of the lives of ordinary Americans. He said that he wanted to make these trips off the beaten path because most people traveled across the country on interstate highways without seeing the "real" America. Whether he visited Minnesota's lake country or a small New England town, Kuralt spotlighted America's regional diversity. In fact, one of the key strengths of the United States is the variety of life in its subregions—the Northeast, the Midwest, the South, and the West.

The Northeast

As you can see on the map on page 134, the Northeast covers only 5 percent of the nation's land area. But about 20 percent of the population lives there. The six northern states of the subregion—Maine, Vermont, New Hampshire, Massachusetts, Rhode Island, and Connecticut—are called **New England.** The other three—Pennsylvania, New York, and New Jersey—are sometimes referred to as Middle Atlantic states. (Maryland and Delaware, which are included in the South in this book, are sometimes included in the Middle Atlantic states.)

AMERICA'S GATEWAY Because of its location along the Atlantic coast, the Northeast contains many of the areas first settled by Europeans. The region served as the "gateway" to America for millions of immigrants from all over the world. Many people still engage in fishing and farming,

LOCATION BosWash is the name given to the highly urbanized northeastern seaboard of the United States.

Urbanization in the Northeast

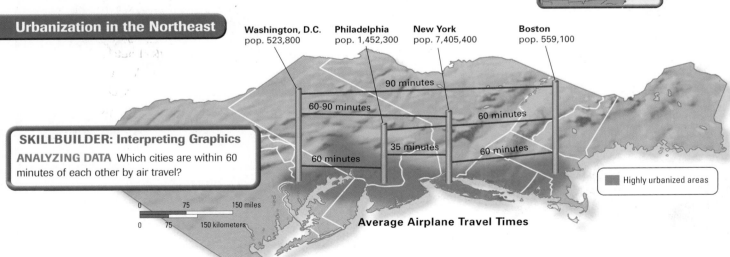

Washington, D.C.
pop. 523,800

Philadelphia
pop. 1,452,300

New York
pop. 7,405,400

Boston
pop. 559,100

90 minutes

60-90 minutes

60 minutes

35 minutes

60 minutes

60 minutes

Highly urbanized areas

SKILLBUILDER: Interpreting Graphics
ANALYZING DATA Which cities are within 60 minutes of each other by air travel?

0   75   150 miles
0   75   150 kilometers

Average Airplane Travel Times

as the Northeast's early settlers did. But the region's coastal and inland waters turned it into the heart of trade, commerce, and industry for the nation. In fact, the Northeast is one of the most heavily industrialized and urbanized areas in the world. The Atlantic seaboard cities of Philadelphia, Boston, and New York City serve as international trade centers.

Coal, iron ore, and oil—found mainly in Pennsylvania—fueled the industrialization of the region. Traditional industries, such as iron and steel, petroleum, and lumber, still play a role in the region's economy. But most Northeasterners are now employed in such manufacturing and service industries as electronics, communications, chemicals, medical research, finance, and tourism. Pennsylvania, New York, and New Jersey have rich farmlands, but much of New England is too hilly or rocky to grow crops easily. Ⓐ

Parts of the Middle Atlantic states are often referred to as the "rust belt" because of their declining and abandoned traditional industries. They share this term with some of the states of the Midwest. In recent times, many "rust belt" industries have moved to the warmer climates of the "sunbelt" in the South and West.

GROWTH OF THE MEGALOPOLIS The nation's first megalopolis developed in the Northeast. A **megalopolis** is a region in which several large cities and surrounding areas grow together. You can see the extent of the "BosWash" megalopolis, as it is called, in the illustration on page 145.

Geographic Thinking

Using the Atlas
Ⓐ Refer to the map on page 106. What economic activities are shown for the Northeast?

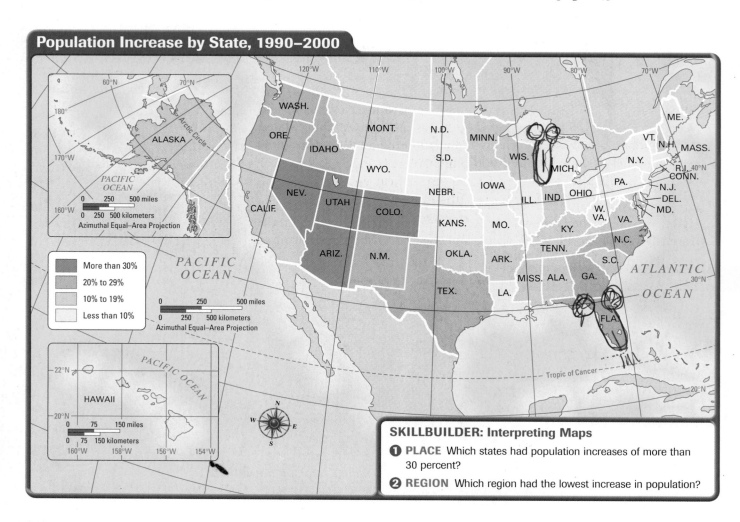

Population Increase by State, 1990–2000

More than 30%
20% to 29%
10% to 19%
Less than 10%

SKILLBUILDER: Interpreting Maps

❶ **PLACE** Which states had population increases of more than 30 percent?

❷ **REGION** Which region had the lowest increase in population?

It stretches through 500 miles of highly urbanized areas from Boston in the north to Washington, D.C., the national capital, in the south. It contains one-sixth of the U.S. population. New York City, the country's cultural and financial center, is located here. Rapid road, rail, and air links have been vital to its economic development and expansion into the South. You will read more about urban growth in Chapter 8.

The Midwest

The subregion that contains the 12 states of the north-central United States is called the **Midwest.** Because of its central location, the Midwest is called the American heartland. It occupies about one-fifth of the nation's land and almost one-fourth of its people live there. Since the Revolutionary War, immigrants from all over the world have made it their destination. Many early settlers came from Britain, Germany, and Scandinavia. Vast, largely flat plains are a distinctive feature of the region. So are numerous waterways, including the Great Lakes and the Mississippi River and its many tributaries.

The Changing Face of U.S. Agriculture

	1950	1990
Farm Population:	25 million	4.6 million
Number of Farms:	5.3 million	2.1 million
Average Farm Size:	216 acres	461 acres

AGRICULTURAL AND INDUSTRIAL HEARTLAND The Midwest is the nation's "breadbasket." Fertile soil, adequate rainfall, and a favorable climate enable Midwesterners to produce more food and feed more people than farmers in any comparable area in the world. Among the main products are corn, wheat, soybeans, meat, and dairy goods. Agriculture also is the foundation for many of the region's industries, including meatpacking, food processing, farm equipment, and grain milling. Other traditional industries are steel and automaking.

Its central location and excellent waterways make the Midwest a trade, transportation, and distribution center. Chicago, Illinois, which is located near the southwestern shores of Lake Michigan, is the cultural, financial, and transportation hub of the Midwest. Most of the region's major cities developed near large bodies of water, which were essential for early transportation. Cleveland, Detroit, Chicago, and Milwaukee grew near the Great Lakes, and Cincinnati, St. Louis, Minneapolis, St. Paul, Kansas City, and Omaha developed along rivers. ◀B

CHANGING FACE OF THE MIDWEST Like other regions, the Midwest is changing. The number of farms is declining. More Midwesterners are now employed in providing services than in traditional industries. The region's metropolitan areas are expanding as urban dwellers and businesses leave the central cities for the suburbs. People and industries are also moving to the warmer South and West.

Geographic Thinking ◀

Making Comparisons
B▶ What do the major cities of the Midwest have in common with those of the Northeast?

Connect to the Issues

URBAN SPRAWL

Traffic Congestion in Atlanta

Atlanta, Georgia, is one of the most traffic-clogged areas in the United States. Urban sprawl is a cause. Like many cities, Atlanta has experienced rapid population growth and suburbanization in recent decades. The Atlanta metropolitan area spreads out over 20 counties and contains nearly 4 million people. This growth brought roadbuilding, and more roads brought more traffic. Residents drive an average of 35 miles a day to reach their destinations—more than anywhere else in the country.

The South

The South is a subregion that covers about one-fourth of the land area of the United States and contains more than one-third of its population. Among its 16 states are 11 that made up the Confederacy during the Civil War. One of these states—Texas—is sometimes included in an area of the West called the Southwest. The South's warm climate, fertile soils, and many natural resources have shaped its development.

THE OLD SOUTH Like the Northeast, the South was also the site of early European settlement. In fact, Virginia was England's first American colony. The South has a mix of cultures that reflects the diversity of its early settlers. In addition to people of British heritage, there are the descendants of Africans brought as slave laborers and Hispanics whose families first migrated from Mexico to Texas. Cajuns of French-Canadian origin and Creoles of French, Spanish, and African descent are found in Louisiana, while Florida is home to many Hispanics who came from Cuba.

Once a rural agricultural area, the South is rapidly changing and its cities growing. Along with the Southwest, it is often referred to as the "sunbelt" because of its climate.

THE NEW SOUTH Agriculture was the South's first economic activity, and cotton, tobacco, fruits, peanuts, and rice are still grown there. Also, livestock production is important in states such as Texas and Arkansas. The South's humid subtropical climate at first hindered industrialization. But the widespread use of air conditioning beginning in the 1950s and the region's vast stores of energy resources—oil, coal, natural gas, and water—gave a boost to industry.

In recent times, the South has attracted many manufacturing and service industries fleeing the harsh weather of the "rust belt." Major industries include petroleum, steel, chemicals, food processing, textiles, and electronics. The South's climate draws millions of tourists and retirees, too. Atlanta, Georgia—a financial, trade, and transportation center—is the hub of the New South. Miami, Tampa-St. Petersburg, New Orleans, Houston, Dallas-Fort Worth, and San Antonio are other rapidly growing **metropolitan areas**—large cities and nearby suburbs and towns.

The West

Look on the map on page 134, and you will see that **the West** is a far-flung subregion consisting of 13 states. It stretches from the Great Plains to the Pacific Ocean and includes Alaska to the north and Hawaii in the Pacific. The West covers about one-half of the land area of the United States but has only about one-fifth of the population. It is a region of dramatic and varied landscapes.

People settle in the West today as they did during its frontier days: wherever landforms and climate are favorable. Some areas, such as its many deserts, are sparsely settled. Nonetheless, California is the

BACKGROUND
Washington, Oregon, and Idaho are often called the Northwest. California, Arizona, New Mexico, Nevada, Colorado, Utah, and Texas are called the Southwest.

country's most populous state because of excellent farmland, good harbors, and a mild climate. The West is the most rapidly growing region in the United States. Los Angeles, the country's second largest city, is the West's cultural and commercial center.

DEVELOPING THE WEST The West's growth in the 20th century was helped by air conditioning and by irrigation. The map on this page, for example, shows how water from the Colorado River in Arizona has been diverted to serve many areas. Water supply aided development of inland cities such as Las Vegas, Tucson, and Phoenix.

The economic activities of the West are as varied as its climate and landscape. Among them are farming, ranching, food processing, logging, fishing, mining, oil refining, tourism, filmmaking, and the production of computers. Many cities with good harbors, including Seattle, Los Angeles, and Long Beach, make foreign trade—especially with Asia—important.

You read about the subregions of the United States in this section. In the next chapter, you will learn about the human geography of Canada.

BACKGROUND
According to the 2000 census, the population of the West grew by 20 percent from 1990.

Colorado River Basin

Volume of water
(millions of acre–feet)
IN   OUT
2+   2+
1–2   1–2
0–1   0–1
● City   ▮ Dam
〰〰〰 Aqueduct

0   100   200 miles
0   100   200 kilometers
Albers Equal-Area Projection

IDAHO
WYOMING
UTAH
COLORADO
Green R.
Colorado R.
Gunnison R.
Dolores R.
San Juan R.
NEVADA
Las Vegas
Lake Mead
Lake Powell
Grand Canyon
Little Colorado R.
CALIFORNIA
Colorado R.
ARIZONA
NEW MEXICO
Los Angeles
Phoenix
San Diego
Tucson
UNITED STATES
MEXICO
PACIFIC OCEAN
Gulf of California

US & CANADA

SKILLBUILDER: Interpreting Maps

❶ **PLACE** What area receives the largest volume of water from the Colorado River?

❷ **MOVEMENT** Which states contribute water to the Colorado River?

SECTION 3 Assessment

❶ Places & Terms

Explain the meaning of each of the following terms.
- New England
- megalopolis
- the Midwest
- the South
- metropolitan area
- the West

❷ Taking Notes

REGION Review the notes you took for this section.

The United States
↓
Subregions

- What are the four subregions of the United States?
- Which subregion is the largest in land area?

❸ Main Ideas

a. Why is the Northeast one of the most heavily industrialized and urbanized areas?

b. How is the economy of the Midwest changing?

c. What helped the economy of the West to grow?

❹ Geographic Thinking

Seeing Patterns How has air conditioning changed the economic activities of the subregions of the United States? **Think about:**

- the South and the West
- the "rust belt" and the "sunbelt"

RESEARCH LINKS
CLASSZONE.COM

GeoActivity

MAKING COMPARISONS Use the Internet to find more information on the economies of the four subregions. Create a **database** comparing the top five industries in each of the four subregions.

Disasters!

🏴 SUNSHINE STATE STANDARDS
Key Standard SS.B.2.4.4 The student understands the global impact of human changes in the physical environment.
FCAT LA.B.1.4.3 Writing: Edit Final Documents

The Dust Bowl

Years of unrelenting drought, misuse of the land, and the miles-high dust storms that resulted (shown here) devastated the Great Plains in the 1930s. Rivers dried up, and heat scorched the earth. As livestock died and crops withered, farms were abandoned. Thousands of families—more than two million people—fled to the West, leaving behind their farms and their former lives. Most of these "Okies," as they were called (referring to Oklahoma, the native state of many), made their way over hundreds of miles to California. There they tried to find work as migrant farm laborers and restart their lives. The drought lasted nearly a decade, and it took years for this productive agricultural region to recover.

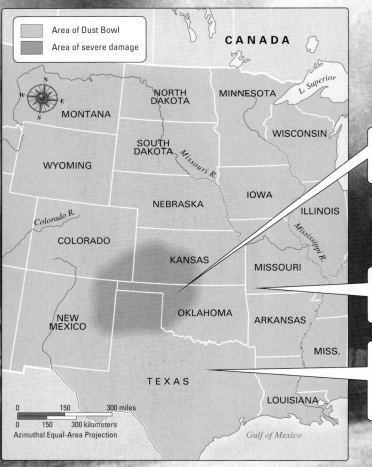

Area of Dust Bowl

Area of severe damage

CANADA

MONTANA

NORTH DAKOTA

MINNESOTA

L. Superior

WISCONSIN

SOUTH DAKOTA

Missouri R.

WYOMING

IOWA

NEBRASKA

ILLINOIS

Colorado R.

Mississippi R.

COLORADO

KANSAS

MISSOURI

NEW MEXICO

OKLAHOMA

ARKANSAS

MISS.

TEXAS

LOUISIANA

Gulf of Mexico

0   150   300 miles
0   150   300 kilometers
Azimuthal Equal-Area Projection

The worst of the devastation was centered in parts of five states—Oklahoma, Kansas, Colorado, New Mexico, and Texas.

Dust from the Great Plains was reported by ships to have blown as far east as 500 miles out into the Atlantic Ocean in 1934.

The most terrible dust storm came on April 14, 1935. A blinding black cloud of swirling dust rolled across the southern plains, blotting out the sun, suffocating animals, and burying machinery.

Thousands of farms like this one in Cimarron County, Oklahoma, were turned into dust-covered wastelands by the drought and dust storms of the 1930s.

Migrants from the Dust Bowl were forced to live any way they could while trying to find jobs picking vegetables or fruit. This mother and her seven children lived in a tent in a California migrant camp, eating vegetables found on the ground and birds they killed.

GeoActivity

REMEMBERING THE VICTIMS

Use the Internet to find personal accounts of Dust Bowl families. Then create a **documentary proposal** about one of them.

- Begin with a brief overview of how the drought affected the family.
- Add a sketch map showing where they lived and copies of any photos available, with captions for each.
- Present your proposal to a panel of student producers.

RESEARCH LINKS
CLASSZONE.COM

GeoData

CAUSES

- Years of poor agricultural practices, such as overplowing and overgrazing, stripped away about 96 million acres of grasslands in the southern plains.
- Seven years of drought, or dry weather, turned the soil to dust.

EFFECTS

- Hundreds of millions of tons of soil were blown away.
- Crops withered and livestock died.
- More than 2 million plains people abandoned their farms.

PREVENTIVE MEASURES

Experts in crop production and soil management proposed the use of scientific farming methods, including

- contour plowing, or plowing across a hill rather than up and down, to stop wind and water erosion
- terracing, or planting crops in stair-stepped rows, to prevent soil erosion
- planting trees to hold the soil in place and to slow the force of the wind

VISUAL SUMMARY
HUMAN GEOGRAPHY OF THE UNITED STATES

History and Government

- The United States was populated by a diverse group of immigrants.
- The United States expanded westward and industrialized.
- The government of the United States is a representative democracy.
- At the start of the 21st century, the United States was the only remaining superpower.

Economy and Culture

- Fertile land, valuable resources, and good location help make the United States an economic leader.
- Much of the U.S. economy is based on service industries.
- Most of the U.S. population lives in urban areas.

Subregions of the United States

- ○ The Northeast region is heavily populated and industrialized.
- ○ The Midwest produces a variety of agricultural and manufactured goods but is shifting to some service industries.
- ● The South is rapidly becoming more industrialized.
- ○ The West is a rapidly growing economic region.

Reviewing Places & Terms

A. Briefly explain the importance of each of the following.

1. migration
2. Columbian Exchange
3. suburb
4. representative democracy
5. free enterprise
6. service industry
7. postindustrial economy
8. multinational
9. megalopolis
10. metropolitan area

B. Answer the questions about vocabulary in complete sentences.

11. What role did migration play in populating the United States?
12. What are some examples of items in the Columbian Exchange?
13. Which of the above terms are associated with urban geography?
14. What type of government does the United States have?
15. What is an advantage of free enterprise?
16. How are the service industry and postindustrial economy related?
17. What is an example of a service industry?
18. What makes a business a multinational corporation?
19. In which region is an example of a megalopolis found?
20. How are the terms suburb and metropolitan area related?

Main Ideas

History and Government of the United States (pp. 135–139)

1. Why is the United States called a "nation of immigrants?"
2. How did the Louisiana Purchase change the United States?
3. What factors led the United States to become a superpower?

Economy and Culture of the United States (pp. 140–144)

4. Why is the United States a leader in agricultural production?
5. What are some examples of the cultural diversity of the United States?
6. In what industry do most Americans work?

Subregions of the United States (pp. 145–151)

7. What changes have taken place in the industrial base of the Northeast?
8. What role did water play in the development of the Midwest?
9. What industries are found in the South today?
10. How did California become the nation's most populous state?

Critical Thinking

1. Using Your Notes

Use your completed chart to answer these questions.

- a. What resources have been important in the development of the United States?
- b. Which subregions make up the "rust belt" and which the "sunbelt"? How are they related?

2. Geographic Themes

- a. **REGION** How has the economy of the South changed?
- b. **MOVEMENT** How has U.S. population shifted since the country began?

3. Identifying Themes

How did air conditioning and irrigation change the population of the West? Which of the five themes apply to this situation?

4. Determining Cause and Effect

What was the effect of the United States becoming industrialized?

5. Making Generalizations

What has been the result of the United States being populated by many different groups of people?

Additional Test Practice, pp. S1–S37

TEST PRACTICE
CLASSZONE.COM

Geographic Skills: Interpreting Maps

U.S. Population and Geographic Centers

Use the map at right to answer the following questions.

1. **MOVEMENT** In which year did the population center cross the Mississippi River?

2. **MOVEMENT** How would you describe the difference between changes in the geographic center and changes in the population center?

3. **REGION** In which region was the population center from 1790 through 1850?

GeoActivity

Create a series of four maps showing movement of the population center of the United States in 50-year periods. Use the map on this page to help you. Start with the period from 1790 to 1840.

INTERNET ACTIVITY

Use the links at **classzone.com** to do research about the expansion of the United States. Look for the dates when territory was added to the United States.

Writing About Geography Write a report about your findings. Include a map showing the territory acquired to help present the information. List the Web sites that were your sources.

HUMAN GEOGRAPHY OF CANADA
Developing a Vast Wilderness

Four Subregions of Canada

Atlantic Provinces
Core Provinces
Prairie Provinces
Pacific Province and Territories

0   150   300 miles
0   150   300 kilometers
Azimuthal Equal-Area Projection

GeoFocus

How was such an immense land developed?

Taking Notes Copy the graphic organizer below into your notebook. Use it to record information about the human geography of Canada.

History and Government

Economy and Culture

Canada

Subregions

History and Government of Canada

A HUMAN PERSPECTIVE Around A.D. 980, a Viking named Erik the Red sailed to Greenland. Soon after, about 3,000 Vikings colonized the region. About A.D. 1000, Erik's son Leif led an expedition that landed off the Atlantic coast of North America on what is now Newfoundland. Leif called the area Vinland, after the wild grapes that grew there. The Vikings built a settlement but later abandoned it. Five centuries would pass before another European, an Italian navigator named Giovanni Caboto, would come to North America. In 1497, exploring for the English, Caboto (John Cabot in English) landed in Newfoundland and claimed the region for England. European exploration and colonization followed.

The First Settlers and Colonial Rivalry

Canada's vast size and its cold climate significantly affected its development. So did the early migrations of people across its land, the bitter territorial rivalry between the two European nations that colonized it—England and France—and their conflict with the First Nations peoples.

EARLY PEOPLES As you read in Chapter 5, one of the greatest migrations in history took place thousands of years ago, after the last Ice Age. Migrants from Asia began moving into North America across an Arctic land bridge that connected the two continents. Some early peoples remained in what are now the Canadian Arctic and Alaska. These were the ancestors of the Inuit (or Eskimos). Others, the ancestors of the North

Main Ideas
- French and British settlement greatly influenced Canada's political development.
- Canada's size and climate affected economic growth and population distribution.

Places & Terms

province

Dominion of Canada

confederation

parliamentary government

parliament

prime minister

CONNECT TO THE ISSUES
DIVERSE SOCIETIES
Conflict between Canadians of French and English ancestry has been a factor throughout much of Canada's history.

SUNSHINE STATE STANDARDS
Key Standard SS.B.1.4.4 The student understands how cultural and technological characteristics can link or divide regions.
Other Standards SS.A.3.4.3. C.1.4.1
FCAT LA.A.1.4.2 Reading: Strategies

LOCATION Quebec City, located on high ground above the St. Lawrence River, was the site of the first permanent French settlement in Canada. **Why was this a desirable location?**

American Indian peoples, gradually moved south, into present-day British Columbia and beyond. When the ice melted, they moved throughout Canada. They settled where they could grow crops.

COLONIZATION BY FRANCE AND BRITAIN During the 16th and 17th centuries, French explorers claimed much of Canada. Their settlements were known as New France. The British, too, were colonizing North America along the Atlantic coast. To both countries, the coastal fisheries and the inland fur trade were important. Soon, the French and British challenged each other's territorial claims. Britain defeated France in the French and Indian War (1754–1763), forcing France to surrender its territory. But French settlers remained.

Steps Toward Unity

By the end of the 18th century, Canada had become a land of two distinct cultures—Roman Catholic French and Protestant English. Conflicts erupted between the two groups, and in 1791, the British government split Canada into two **provinces,** or political units. Upper Canada (later, Ontario), located near the Great Lakes, had an English-speaking majority, while Lower Canada (Quebec), located along the St. Lawrence River, had a French-speaking population. The land to the northwest, called Rupert's Land, was owned by a British fur-trading company.

BACKGROUND
Upper Canada was upriver—on the St. Lawrence—from Lower Canada (Quebec).

ESTABLISHING THE DOMINION OF CANADA Over the next few decades, Quebec City, Montreal, and Toronto developed as major cities in Canada. Population soared as large numbers of immigrants came from Great Britain. Railways and canals were built, and explorers moved across western lands seeking better fur-trading areas.

The conflicts between English-speaking and French-speaking settlers had not ended, however. By the late 1830s, there were serious political and ethnic disputes in both Upper and Lower Canada. The British government decided that major reform was needed. In 1867, it passed the British North America Act creating the **Dominion of Canada.** The Dominion was to be a loose **confederation,** or political union, of Ontario (Upper Canada), Quebec (Lower Canada), and two British colonies on the Atlantic coast—Nova Scotia and New Brunswick. The Dominion

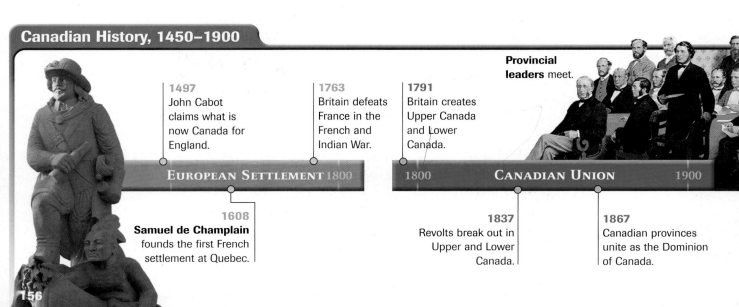

Canadian History, 1450–1900

Provincial leaders meet.

1497
John Cabot claims what is now Canada for England.

1763
Britain defeats France in the French and Indian War.

1791
Britain creates Upper Canada and Lower Canada.

EUROPEAN SETTLEMENT 1800

1608
Samuel de Champlain founds the first French settlement at Quebec.

1800 **CANADIAN UNION** 1900

1837
Revolts break out in Upper and Lower Canada.

1867
Canadian provinces unite as the Dominion of Canada.

Territorial Growth of Canada

1600s

Beaufort Sea
Baffin Bay
Labrador Sea
Hudson Bay
NEWFOUNDLAND
RUPERT'S LAND
NEW FRANCE
ACADIA
LOUISIANA
ATLANTIC OCEAN
13 COLONIES

1867

Beaufort Sea
Baffin Bay
ALASKA (U.S.)
NORTH WEST TERRITORY
Labrador Sea
Hudson Bay
NEWFOUNDLAND
BRITISH COLUMBIA
RUPERT'S LAND
QUEBEC
ONTARIO
NOVA SCOTIA
NEW BRUNSWICK
ATLANTIC OCEAN
UNITED STATES

Today

	French
	British
	Canadian
—	Boundary of present-day Canada

Dates indicate when provinces or territories joined Canada.

ARCTIC OCEAN
Beaufort Sea
ALASKA (U.S.)
YUKON TERRITORY 1898
NORTHWEST TERRITORIES 1869
NUNAVUT 1999
Labrador Sea
NEWFOUNDLAND 1949
BRITISH COLUMBIA 1871
ALBERTA 1905
SASKATCHEWAN 1905
MANITOBA 1870
Hudson Bay
ONTARIO 1867
QUEBEC 1867
PRINCE EDWARD ISLAND 1873
NOVA SCOTIA 1867
NEW BRUNSWICK 1867
Ottawa
UNITED STATES
ATLANTIC OCEAN

0   250   500 miles
0   250   500 kilometers
Azimuthal Equal-Area Projection

SKILLBUILDER: Interpreting Maps

❶ **PLACE** What is the newest political unit in Canada?

❷ **REGION** How did Rupert's Land change politically over time?

had self-government but remained part of the British Empire. Ottawa, in Ontario, became the capital.

As the map above shows, the Dominion grew rapidly. It gained control of Rupert's Land in 1869. By 1871, Canada stretched from the Atlantic to the Pacific, as Manitoba, British Columbia, and Prince Edward Island were added. Soon the Yukon Territory, Alberta, and Saskatchewan followed. Only Newfoundland remained outside the union, not joining until the mid-20th century.

Geographic Thinking

Making Comparisons
Ⓐ How was Canada's westward movement similar to that of the United States?

Continental Expansion and Development

With so much area to settle, Canada set about making its land accessible to pioneers. Successful settlement of the west would depend on good transportation routes: roads, canals, and railroads. Ⓐ

FROM THE ATLANTIC TO THE PACIFIC In 1872, the government began construction of a transcontinental railroad. In 1885, the main line of the railway, from Montreal to Vancouver, was completed. The coasts were now linked by rail. A little more than a decade later, gold was discovered in the Yukon. Fortune-hunters from around the world headed to Canada. Not long after, copper, zinc, and silver deposits also were found in Canada, prompting the building of new railroads and towns. At the same time, immigrants from other parts of Europe besides Britain were coming to Canada's vast open lands. The Dominion was taking on a new character.

PLACE The Ceremonial Guard parades in front of the parliament buildings in Ottawa, Ontario, Canada's capital city.

URBAN AND INDUSTRIAL GROWTH For much of the time after settlement, Canadians lived in rural areas and engaged in farming. But as the population grew and natural resources were developed, Canada became more urban and industrial. Cities and towns first sprang up wherever farming was possible. Later, these same areas became manufacturing and service industry centers, drawing more people to them. Nearly all of this growth took place within 100 miles of the U.S. border. There, the climate was warmer, the land more productive, and transportation linking east and west more widely available. Like its neighbor to the south, Canada developed into a major economic power in the 20th century. **B**

Governing Canada

Canada was recognized as an independent nation by Britain in 1931. Like Great Britain, Canada has a **parliamentary government,** a system in which legislative and executive functions are combined in a legislature called a **parliament.** A central federal government and smaller provincial and territorial governments govern Canada. Although Canada is independent, its symbolic head of state remains the British monarch. Parliament handles all legislative matters. The Parliament consists of an appointed Senate and an elected House of Commons. The majority party's leader in Parliament becomes **prime minister,** or head of the government. Each of Canada's ten provinces has its own legislature and premier (prime minister). The federal government administers the territories.

In this section, you read about the history and government of Canada. In the next section, you will learn about life in Canada today.

Geographic Thinking

Using the Atlas
B Use the atlas on page 105. List the major Canadian cities within 200 miles of the Canadian/U.S. border.

SECTION

Assessment

1 Places & Terms

Identify and explain these terms.

- province
- Dominion of Canada
- confederation
- parliamentary government
- parliament
- prime minister

2 Taking Notes

PLACE Review the notes you took for this section.

- How is Upper Canada different from Lower Canada?
- What mineral discoveries spurred development of Canada?

3 Main Ideas

a. How did the French and Indian War change Canada?

b. Where did nearly all growth in Canada's industry and urban areas take place?

c. How is Canada's federal government different from the federal government of the United States?

4 Geographic Thinking

Drawing Conclusions How did the early settlement of Canada lead to a diverse society? **Think about:**

- New France
- French and Indian War

RESEARCH LINKS
CLASSZONE.COM

SEEING PATTERNS Use the Internet to find the percentage of French-speaking and English-speaking citizens in each of Canada's provinces and territories. Create a **map** of Canada and write in the percentages for each province or territory.

Economy and Culture of Canada

Main Ideas
- Canada is highly industrialized and urbanized, with one of the world's most developed economies.
- Canadians are a diverse people.

Places & Terms

First Nations

métis

reserve

CONNECT TO THE ISSUES

DIVERSE SOCIETIES
Canada is a land of immigrants with many diverse cultures.

SUNSHINE STATE STANDARDS
Key Standard SS.B.2.4.1 The student understands how social, cultural, economic, and environmental factors contribute to the dynamic nature of regions.

FCAT LA.A.1.4.2 Reading: Strategies

US & CANADA

A HUMAN PERSPECTIVE The fur trade was a major economic activity in early Canada. It began in the 16th century, when Canada's Native American peoples, now known as the **First Nations,** started trading with European fishermen along the northern Atlantic coast. A brisk trade soon developed, and trappers and traders poured into Canada. They came first from France and later, from England. As the trade expanded westward, it depended heavily on daring French-Canadian boatmen called *voyageurs*. They moved animal pelts from the wilderness to trading posts, often paddling 16 hours a day. According to one trader, these hardy souls often endured "privation and hardship, not only without complaining, but even with cheerfullness."

An Increasingly Diverse Economy

Canada is one of the world's richest countries. It is highly industrialized and urbanized. As you just read, Canada's early economy was based largely on the trade of its many natural resources. Today, the manufacturing and service industries fuel the nation's economic engines.

CANADA'S PRIMARY INDUSTRIES Farming, logging, mining, and fishing are important Canadian industries. They account for more than 10 percent of the country's gross domestic product (GDP). Only about 5 percent of Canada's land is suitable for farming, and only about 3 percent of the labor force is employed in agriculture. Nevertheless, Canada produces large amounts of food for domestic use and for export. Canada's biggest export trade is in forest products. No other country exports more wood pulp and paper products than Canada.

Mining, too, is a major industry because of Canada's extensive mineral deposits. Uranium, zinc, gold, and silver are just a few of the minerals Canada exports to the world.

Three ocean coastlines—Atlantic, Pacific, and Arctic—give Canadians access to ample fish supplies. Canadian fish consumption per capita is low, so much of Canada's catch is exported. In fact, Canada exports more fish than any other country.

THE MANUFACTURING SECTOR About 15 percent of Canadians earn their living from manufacturing. Their efforts account for nearly one-fifth of the nation's GDP. Automobiles, steel, household appliances, electronics, and high-tech and mining equipment are

Canadian Economy*

1951
- Other Primary Industries 4%
- Agriculture 18%
- Manufacturing 26%
- Services 51%

1995
- Other Primary Industries 2%
- Agriculture 3%
- Manufacturing 15%
- Services 79%

*Based on rounded employment statistics
SOURCE: *Canada Year Book 1994; Canada Year Book 1997*

SKILLBUILDER: Interpreting Graphs

❶ **ANALYZING DATA** Which sector showed the greatest increase in growth from 1951 to 1995? the greatest decrease in growth?

❷ **MAKING GENERALIZATIONS** What might account for these changes in the economy?

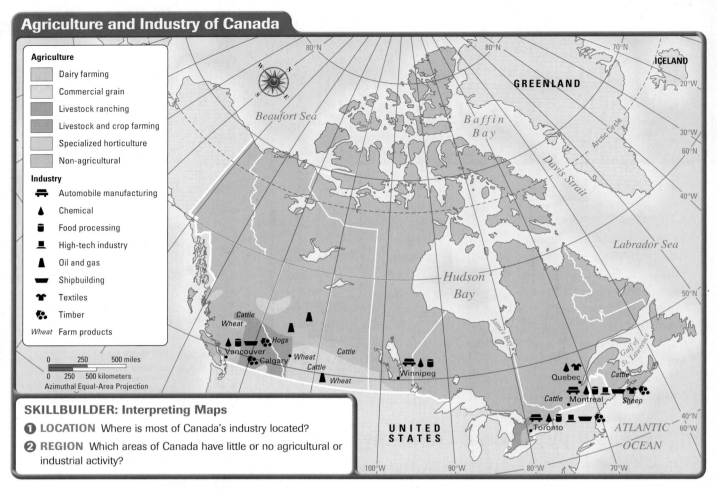

Agriculture and Industry of Canada

Agriculture

- Dairy farming
- Commercial grain
- Livestock ranching
- Livestock and crop farming
- Specialized horticulture
- Non-agricultural

Industry

- Automobile manufacturing
- Chemical
- Food processing
- High-tech industry
- Oil and gas
- Shipbuilding
- Textiles
- Timber
- *Wheat* Farm products

0   250   500 miles
0   250   500 kilometers
Azimuthal Equal-Area Projection

SKILLBUILDER: Interpreting Maps

❶ **LOCATION** Where is most of Canada's industry located?

❷ **REGION** Which areas of Canada have little or no agricultural or industrial activity?

---

just some of the products Canada manufactures. Most of the manufacturing is done in the Canadian heartland, which reaches from Quebec City, Quebec, to Windsor, Ontario. Ⓐ

SERVICE INDUSTRIES DRIVE THE ECONOMY Canada's service industries are the country's real economic powerhouse. In fact, more than 60 percent of the GDP comes from service industries. Those industries employ more Canadians than all other industries combined. Service industries include finance, utilities, trade, transportation, tourism, communications, insurance, and real estate. Canada's spectacular natural beauty has made tourism one of the fastest growing of the service industries. At the end of the 20th century, the Canadian tourism industry employed the same percentage of workers—about 3 percent—as those who were engaged in agriculture.

Historically, Canada's economy has always relied on trade. The fur trade between Canada's native peoples and European fishermen was just the start of what would become a key Canadian industry. The United States is Canada's chief trading partner. This is largely because the two nations share the longest open border in the world and the same language—English. In 1994, Canada and the United States, along with Mexico, signed the North American Free Trade Agreement (NAFTA). This pact made trade between them even easier than before. At the turn of the 21st century, about 85 percent of Canada's exports went to the United States, and about 75 percent of Canada's imports came from its neighbor to the south.

Geographic Thinking

Making Comparisons

Ⓐ How is the Canadian heartland similar to the northeast region of the United States?

A Land of Many Cultures

From its earliest settlement, Canada has been a land of diverse cultures. The first settlers were the Inuit and the First Nations peoples who came after the last Ice Age. Many thousands of years later, the English and French arrived, bringing their languages and traditions with them. Interaction between the French and native peoples gave rise to another culture, the **métis** (may·TEES), people of mixed French and native heritage.

More recent immigrants from Europe and Asia also have made their contributions to the cultural mix. As in the United States, Canada's cultural richness has come from all corners of the world.

BACKGROUND
Official documents and information are printed both in English and in French.

LANGUAGES AND RELIGION Canada is officially a bilingual country. It has an English-speaking majority and a French-speaking minority. (Only in Quebec are French speakers in the majority.) In addition, the languages of First Nation peoples still survive, and the native languages of immigrants can be heard on many city streets.

As the English and the French settled Canada, their different cultures became a source of conflict. The English were largely Protestant, and the French were Roman Catholics. Religious and cultural conflicts between the two groups have continued over the years, as noted in the graphic at the bottom of this page. Today, these two religions continue to dominate Canadian society. But Muslims, Jews, and other religious groups are represented in ever-increasing numbers.

Geographic Thinking

Seeing Patterns
B Which physical factors influence Canada's population distribution?

CANADA'S POPULATION Settlement patterns in Canada have always been influenced by the country's harsh environment and the accessibility of transportation routes. Canada's port cities—especially Montreal, Toronto, and Vancouver—and its rich farmlands make up the country's most densely settled areas. In fact, more than 80 percent of all Canadians live on just 10 percent of the land. This region is mostly along a 100-mile-wide strip of land just north of the U.S. border. B

Clash of Cultures

Problems

English-speaking majority

French-speaking minority

Quebec—home to most French-Canadians

Separatism proposed in Quebec

Four centuries of English-French tension

Solutions
Canadian government promotes cultural diversity.

English and French are made dual official languages.

growing up in...Canada

These boys are playing ice hockey on an outdoor rink in Fergus, Ontario. Hockey is Canada's national pastime. Children learn to play this Canadian-invented sport at an early age. Many boys dream of playing professional hockey in the National Hockey League. On any given day, young people and adults can be found playing or watching a game at neighborhood ice rinks.

If you lived in Canada, you would pass these milestones:
- You could attend a private preschool at age 3 or 4.
- You would begin elementary school at age 5 or 6 and would be required to attend until age 16.
- You would choose to get a job or attend a college or university after high school graduation at age 18.
- You could drive at age 16.
- You could vote at age 18.
- You could get married at age 18 without written consent.

Canada's population has become increasingly urban. At the beginning of the 20th century, about one-third of the people lived in urban areas. By the end of the century, nearly four-fifths were city dwellers. Some Canadian population groups are clustered in certain areas. For example, about 75 percent of all French Canadians reside in Quebec. Many of Canada's native peoples are found on the country's 2,300 **reserves,** public land set aside for them by the government. The territories in the remote Arctic north are home to most of the Inuit. Large numbers of Canadians of Asian ancestry live on the West Coast.

CONNECT TO THE ISSUES
DIVERSITY
Which major cultural groups are found in Canada?

Life in Canada Today

Most Canadians live active personal and professional lives and enjoy a relatively high standard of living. In 1998, Canada's labor force was nearly evenly split between men and women. Men made up about 55 percent of the work force and women, about 45 percent. As the chart on page 159 shows, Canada's service industries employ more than 75 percent of the work force. Manufacturing is a distant second, accounting for approximately 15 percent of Canadian workers. Canada's population is well educated. The oldest university, Laval, was established in Quebec during the period of French settlement. The first English-speaking universities were founded in New Brunswick and Nova Scotia in the 1780s. Today, Canada boasts a 97 percent literacy rate.

SPORTS AND RECREATION Canadians value their leisure time and use it to engage in many recreational activities. Sports such as skating, ice hockey, fishing, skiing, golf, and hunting are popular. Canadians also enjoy their professional sports teams. Canada has its own football league and its professional ice hockey, baseball, and basketball teams compete in U.S. leagues. The Canadian love of sport goes back to its native peoples, who developed the game we know as lacrosse, and to its early European settlers, who developed ice hockey. Two annual events that are favorites nationwide are the Quebec Winter Carnival, held in Quebec City, and the Calgary Stampede, pictured on page 99.

THE ARTS Not surprisingly, Canada's long history and cultural diversity have given the nation a rich artistic heritage. The earliest Canadian literature was born in the oral traditions of the First Nations peoples. Later, the writings of settlers, missionaries, and explorers lent French and English influences to the literature.

The early visual arts included the realistic carvings of the Inuit and the elaborately decorated totem poles of the First Nations peoples of the West Coast. The artistry of the Inuit carvings has been evident since prehistoric times. Inuit carvers used ivory, whalebone, and soapstone to carve figurines of animals and people in scenes from everyday life. A uniquely Canadian style of painting developed among a group of Toronto-based artists called the Group of Seven early in the 20th century. The performing arts—music, dance, and theater—enjoyed spectacular growth during the last half of the century. The Stratford Festival in Ontario, honoring William Shakespeare, is known worldwide.

In this section, you read about life in Canada today. In the next section, you will learn more about Canada's subregions.

HUMAN–ENVIRONMENT INTERACTION This Inuit artist carves a sculpture of two polar bears from gray soapstone.

SECTION 2

Assessment

1 Places & Terms

Identify and explain these terms.

- First Nations
- métis
- reserve

2 Taking Notes

REGION Review the notes you took for this section.

- Which industries drive Canada's economy?
- In which region is the majority of the population located?

3 Main Ideas

a. Why are Canada and the United States close trading partners?

b. How have Canada's urban areas changed?

c. What is Canada's work force like?

4 Geographic Thinking

Drawing Conclusions
How have Canada's physical resources contributed to its economic prosperity? **Think about:**

- its location
- its primary industries

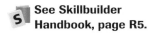 **See Skillbuilder Handbook, page R5.**

MAKING COMPARISONS Study the information in Chapter 6, Section 2, about the U.S. economy. Create a **Venn diagram** with three circles showing the economic activities Canada and the United States have in common and those that are unique to each.

Comparing Cultures

Transportation

As you have read, one of the five themes of geography is movement— how people move themselves and their goods across the Earth's surface. The earliest humans moved by foot from place to place. Later, they used animals, both to ride and as pack animals. Needing to cross streams, ancient people built primitive boats from available materials, such as wood and reeds. Over the centuries, advances in technology from wheeled vehicles to the steam engine to the construction of lighter-than-air craft has enabled people in different regions to meet the challenges posed by their environments.

Canada

Vietnam

Algeria

Peru

SUNSHINE STATE STANDARDS
Key Standard SS.B.1.4.4 The student understands how cultural and technological characteristics can link or divide regions.
FCAT LA.B.1.4.3 Writing: Edit Final Documents

In North African countries like Algeria, camels are often called "ships of the desert" because they can carry freight and people across long distances. The Arabian, or one-humped, camel shown here in the Sahara Desert can cover 40 miles a day for four days carrying 400 pounds.

Flat, smooth roadways crisscrossing Vietnam make it easy for these workers to transport hundreds of fish traps from workshops to customers on the coast by bicycle.

In the northernmost reaches of Canada, roads are scarce. So, vast distances between places are more easily covered by small planes that can touch down on land or water, like this one flying into Cochrane, Ontario.

This crescent-shaped boat on Lake Titicaca in Peru is made from a reedlike plant. Native peoples of the region have made these boats for centuries.

GeoActivity

RESEARCHING TRANSPORTATION

Working with a partner, use the Internet to research transportation around the world. Then prepare a report that shows the design of a **Web page** highlighting some aspect of world transportation.

- Create text to present the information you have found.
- Select suitable images.
- Locate appropriate links for visitors to your Web site.

 RESEARCH LINKS CLASSZONE.COM

GeoData

LAND TRANSPORTATION

- In the United States, there is one car for every two persons; in Somalia, one for every 500.
- One of the world's longest single rail systems, Russia's Trans-Siberian Railway, covers a distance of 5,867 miles from Moscow to the port of Nakhodka.
- Snowmobiles have replaced dogsleds as transport in remote, cold climates of North America.
- China has more bicycles—about 540,000,000—than any other country.
- Animals, including dogs, horses, donkeys, mules, camels, and elephants, still provide transport for many people around the world.

AIR TRANSPORTATION

- Airliners carried 137 million passengers on more than 1 million flights from the United States to other countries from June 1999 to June 2000.

WATER TRANSPORTATION

- Some modern cruise ships and ocean liners are more than 900 feet long and can carry upwards of 2,000 passengers on a voyage.

Subregions of Canada

Main Ideas
- Canada is divided into four subregions—the Atlantic, Core, and Prairie Provinces, and the Pacific Province and the Territories.
- Each subregion possesses unique natural resources, landforms, economic activities, and cultural life.

Places & Terms

Atlantic Provinces	**Prairie Provinces**
Quebec	**British Columbia**
Ontario	**Nunavut**

CONNECT TO THE ISSUES
URBAN SPRAWL Much of Canada's population is in urban areas within 100 miles of the U.S.-Canadian border.

SUNSHINE STATE STANDARDS
Key Standard SS.B.2.4.1 The student understands how social, cultural, economic, and environmental factors contribute to the dynamic nature of regions.

FCAT LA.A.1.4.2 Reading: Strategies

A HUMAN PERSPECTIVE The Grand Banks, a shallow section of the North Atlantic off the coast of Newfoundland, make up one of the earth's richest fishing grounds. In fact, it was the abundance of fish—including cod, haddock, herring, and mackerel—that first attracted Europeans to the region centuries ago. Today, thousands of hardy Canadians make their living fishing in these coastal waters. One, Alex Saunders of Labrador, remarked that "fishing is a disease. Once you start, you keep at it, do whatever's necessary. I jeopardize my home, all my possessions just to keep this boat going and keep fishing." The Grand Banks are part of the Atlantic Provinces, one of Canada's four subregions.

The Atlantic Provinces

Canada is divided into ten provinces and three territories. Each has a unique population, economy, and resources. Eastern Canada is the location of the four **Atlantic Provinces**—Prince Edward Island, New Brunswick, Nova Scotia, and Newfoundland.

HARSH LANDS AND SMALL POPULATIONS As you can see on the chart below, the Atlantic Provinces are home to just 8 percent of Canada's population. Of these people, most live in coastal cities, such as Halifax, Nova Scotia, and St. John, New Brunswick. The small population is due largely to the provinces' rugged terrain and severe weather.

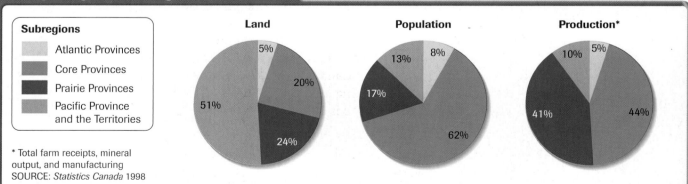

Comparing the Subregions of Canada

Subregions
- Atlantic Provinces
- Core Provinces
- Prairie Provinces
- Pacific Province and the Territories

Land: 5%, 20%, 24%, 51%

Population: 8%, 13%, 17%, 62%

Production*: 5%, 10%, 41%, 44%

* Total farm receipts, mineral output, and manufacturing
SOURCE: *Statistics Canada* 1998

SKILLBUILDER: Interpreting Graphs
❶ **ANALYZING DATA** Which subregion has the highest production?
❷ **MAKING COMPARISONS** How do the Pacific Province and the Territories compare overall to the other three subregions?

Geographic Thinking

Using the Atlas

A Look at the map on page 154. Which bodies of water do the Atlantic Provinces border?

For example, about 85 percent of the land in Nova Scotia cannot be farmed because of rocky hills and poor soil. In New Brunswick, forests cover 90 percent of the land. Newfoundland—made up of the island of Newfoundland, Labrador, and nearby islands—is visited by fierce storms that roar up the Atlantic seaboard. A

ECONOMIC ACTIVITIES Despite the sometimes harsh conditions, the people of the Atlantic Provinces have learned to use what the land and the sea offer them. For example, New Brunswick's dense forests provide the province with its largest industry—logging. This industry produces lumber, wood pulp, and paper products. The Gulf of St. Lawrence and coastal waters supply plentiful stocks of seafood for export. Also, there is mining for zinc, copper, lead, and silver.

Logging and fishing are mainstays of the economy of Nova Scotia, too. This province boasts one of the largest fish-processing plants in North America. In addition, shipbuilding and trade through the port of Halifax provide more employment and revenue. Until the 20th century, fishing was the principal industry in Newfoundland. Today, the province also has healthy mining and logging industries. Moreover, its hydroelectric-power resources are part of a system supplying power to Quebec and parts of the northeastern United States.

5 THEMES

MOVEMENT

Acadians to Cajuns

Colonists from France founded the colony of Acadia on the eastern coast of what is now Canada in 1604. Tensions flared between these settlers and later arrivals from England and Scotland, however.

In 1713, the British gained control of Acadia and renamed it Nova Scotia (New Scotland). They expelled about 4,000 descendants of the original Acadians. Many eventually settled in southern Louisiana. Today, their culture still thrives in the Mississippi Delta area, where the people are called Cajuns (an alteration of Acadian).

The Core Provinces— Quebec and Ontario

In 1608, Samuel de Champlain, a French explorer, built a fort, the first European structure in what is now Canada, at present-day Quebec City. Four centuries later, the lands he colonized are part of the country's most dynamic region—**Quebec** and **Ontario,** Canada's Core Provinces.

THE HEARTLAND OF CANADA Quebec and Ontario are often referred to as Canada's heartland, and with good reason. Three out of five Canadians live there. Ontario is the largest province in terms of population, Quebec in land area. Most of the settlement in these inland provinces is found along the Great Lakes and the St. Lawrence River. Each province is the core of one of Canada's two major cultures. A large number of Canada's English-speaking majority live in Ontario. For most French-speaking Canadians, Quebec is home.

CANADA'S POLITICAL AND ECONOMIC CENTER Ontario and Quebec are at the center of Canada's political and economic life. Ottawa is the capital of the federal government. It is located in southeastern Ontario, right next to the border of Quebec province. Quebec has its own political importance as the heart of French Canadian life.

Ontario and Quebec also power Canada's economy. Together, they account for more than 35 percent of Canadian agricultural production, 45 percent of its mineral output, and 70 percent of its manufacturing. As the map on page 160 shows, they supply a wide variety of products. Toronto, located on the shores of Lake Ontario, is not only the country's most populous city but also its banking and financial hub. Montreal, located on the St. Lawrence River, is Canada's second largest city. It is the center of economic and political activity in Quebec province.

The Prairie Provinces

To the west of the hustle and bustle of Ontario and Quebec lie the **Prairie Provinces**—Manitoba, Saskatchewan, and Alberta.

CANADA'S BREADBASKET Canada's Prairie Provinces are part of the Great Plains of North America. These three provinces are the center of the nation's agricultural yield. They account for 50 percent of Canada's agricultural production. The land of the Prairie Provinces, however, consists of more than just fertile soil. About 60 percent of Canada's mineral output comes from this region of the country. Alberta itself has the nation's largest known deposits of coal and oil and produces 90 percent of Canada's natural gas.

A CULTURAL MIX The people of the Prairie Provinces are a diverse group. Manitoba has large numbers of Scots-Irish, Germans, Scandinavians, Ukrainians, and Poles. The town of St. Boniface boasts the largest French-Canadian population outside Quebec. The population of Saskatchewan also includes immigrants from South and East Asia and is home to the métis. Alberta is perhaps the most diverse of all. In addition to European immigrants, this province also has significant Indian, Japanese, Lebanese, and Vietnamese populations. **B**

Geographic Thinking

Seeing Patterns
B Why might Alberta have attracted such a diverse population?

The Pacific Province and the Territories

The province of British Columbia along with the three territories—Yukon Territory, Northwest Territories, and Nunavut—make up Canada's western and northern lands.

REGION The vast fertile plains of the Prairie Provinces, shown here in Regina, Saskatchewan, provide wheat for Canadians and the world.

BRITISH COLUMBIA Canada's westernmost province is **British Columbia.** Nearly all of it lies within the Rocky Mountain range. As a result, three-fourths of the province is 3,000 feet or more above sea level. More than half of the land is densely forested, and nearly one-third is frozen tundra, snowfields, and glaciers. Most of the population is found in the southwest. This is the location of British Columbia's two largest cities, Victoria and Vancouver. The economy is built on logging, mining, and hydroelectric-power production. Vancouver is Canada's largest port and has a prosperous shipping trade. **C**

Geographic Thinking

Using the Atlas
C Using a world map, locate Vancouver. Where might many of the goods shipped from its port be headed?

THE TERRITORIES Canada's three territories make up 41 percent of the country's land mass. Yet, they are too sparsely populated to be provinces. The Yukon Territory, with a population around 30,000, lies north of British Columbia and is largely an unspoiled wilderness. Directly east is the Northwest Territories, an area that extends into the Arctic. It has a population of about 41,000 people.

Nunavut was carved out of the eastern half of the Northwest Territories in 1999. It is home to many of Canada's Inuit. (See "Geography Today" on this page.) Even though the land is rugged and climatic conditions are severe, economic activities take place in the territories. Mining, fishing, and some logging are the principal industries, and these widely scattered activities explain why the settlements are so dispersed.

In this chapter and the last, you read about the human geography of the United States and Canada. In the next chapter, you will learn about some of the issues that are facing those countries today.

Geography TODAY

Nunavut

Nunavut is large, cold, undeveloped, and sparsely settled. It is also Canada's newest territory—its flag is shown below. In 1999, the Canadian government split off the eastern half of the Northwest Territories and created a territory that would settle the land claims of the Inuit. *Nunavut* means "our land" in the Inuit language. About 30,000 people live in its almost 820,000 square miles—an area more than three times the size of Alberta.

SECTION 3 Assessment

① Places & Terms

Identify and explain where in the region these would be found.

- Atlantic Provinces
- Quebec
- Ontario
- Prairie Provinces
- British Columbia

② Taking Notes

REGION Review the notes you took for this section.

- What is the major economic activity of the Atlantic Provinces?
- Which provinces make up the Prairie Provinces?

③ Main Ideas

a. Why is the population of the Atlantic Provinces so small?

b. Why are Ontario and Quebec called the heartland of Canada?

c. What economic activities take place in British Columbia?

④ Geographic Thinking

Making Inferences Which subregions have the greatest potential for economic growth? **Think about:**

- already developed subregions
- each subregion's natural resources

 See Skillbuilder Handbook, page R4.

GeoActivity

MAKING COMPARISONS Review the differences among the subregions of Canada. Create a **brochure** that illustrates the economic activities, population characteristics, and major cities of the subregions.

VISUAL SUMMARY
HUMAN GEOGRAPHY OF CANADA

History and Government

- French and British settlement of the region had a major effect on its political development.
- The vastness of Canada and its harsh climate have affected the country's population distribution and its economic growth.

Economy and Culture

- Canada is one of the world's most industrialized and urbanized nations.
- Canada has diverse cultures.

Subregions of Canada

- The Atlantic Provinces are the smallest of the subregions.
- The Core Provinces of Canada are Quebec and Ontario.
- The Prairie Provinces are the breadbasket of Canada.
- The Pacific Province and the Territories contain huge tracts of largely undeveloped land.

Reviewing Places & Terms

A. Briefly explain the importance of each of the following.

1. New France
2. Dominion of Canada
3. province
4. prime minister
5. First Nations
6. Atlantic Provinces
7. Quebec
8. Ontario
9. Prairie Provinces
10. British Columbia

B. Answer the questions about vocabulary in complete sentences.

11. Who were the original settlers of Canada?
12. Where was New France located?
13. How is Canada divided politically?
14. What is the title of the leader of Canada?
15. Which provinces made up the original part of the Dominion of Canada?
16. Which provinces make up Canada's core?
17. Which provinces are known as Canada's "breadbasket"?
18. Which province has the majority of Canada's French speakers?
19. Which is Canada's westernmost province?
20. Which provinces are the smallest and least populated?

Main Ideas

History and Government of Canada (pp. 155–158)

1. Why were the French and the British interested in colonizing the area of North America that became the United States and Canada?
2. How did the French and Indian War change the history of Canada?
3. In what ways is the expansion and development of Canada similar to that of the United States?
4. How is Canada's government different from that of the United States?

Economy and Culture of Canada (pp. 159–165)

5. What is Canada's largest export product?
6. Which two languages and religions dominate Canadian culture?
7. Where do most Canadians live?

Subregions of Canada (pp. 166–169)

8. In which provinces would you expect to find a large fishing industry?
9. Which provinces power Canada's economy?
10. Why are the Prairie Provinces so important to the Canadian economy?

Critical Thinking

1. Using Your Notes

Use your completed chart to answer these questions.

a. Which of the subregions has the least developed resources and why?

b. What types of service industry drive the Canadian economy?

2. Geographic Themes

a. **REGION** How has climate affected the distribution of population in Canada?

b. **PLACE** How are the Pacific Province and the Territories different from the rest of the subregions?

3. Identifying Themes

How did immigration shape the culture of Canada? Which of the five themes of geography applies to the development of Canadian culture?

4. Determing Cause and Effect

What impact did French and British settlement have on modern life in Canada?

5. Drawing Conclusions

Why are Quebec and Ontario considered the core of Canada?

Additional Test Practice, pp. S1–S37

TEST PRACTICE
CLASSZONE.COM

Geographic Skills: Interpreting Maps

Major Languages of Canada

Use the map to answer the questions.

1. **LOCATION** What is the relative location of the French speakers?

2. **MOVEMENT** Which native language is spoken over the widest area?

3. **REGION** What is the predominant language spoken in most areas near the U.S. border?

GeoActivity

Choose one of the Native American languages shown on the map. Do some research to find out about the people who speak that language. Write a brief report of your findings and include a sketch map of the location of that language.

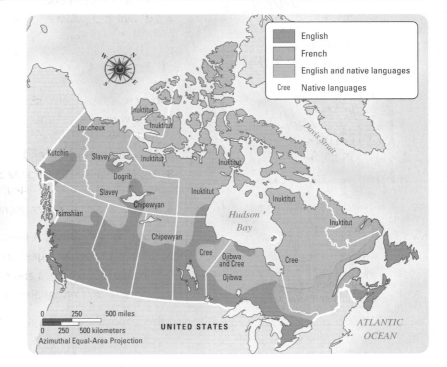

INTERNET ACTIVITY

Use the links at **classzone.com** to do research about the art of the Inuit people. Look for pictures of works that can be copied and background about the art itself.

Creating an Oral Presentation Put together the pictures you have copied and the information about the art for an oral presentation. Be sure to show how geography influenced the art of Canada.

Chapter 8

SECTION 1
The Fight Against Terrorism

SECTION 2
Urban Sprawl

CASESTUDY

DIVERSE SOCIETIES FACE CHANGE

For more on the issues in the United States and Canada . . .

 CURRENT EVENTS
CLASSZONE.COM

New York City firefighters raise the American flag amid the rubble of the World Trade Center after the terrorist attack of September 11, 2001.

TODAY'S ISSUES
The United States and Canada

GeoFocus

How can people cooperate to solve problems?

Taking Notes In your notebook, copy a cause-and-effect chart like the one shown below for each issue. Then take notes on the causes and effects of some aspect of each issue.

	Causes	Effects
Issue 1: Terrorism		
Issue 2: Urban Sprawl		
Case Study: Diverse Societies		

The Fight Against Terrorism

How can a country protect itself from terrorism?

Main Ideas
- Terrorism threatens the safety and security of society.
- The United States launched a war against international terrorism after being attacked on September 11, 2001.

Places & Terms
terrorism

global network

coalition

biological weapon

SUNSHINE STATE STANDARDS
SS.A.3.4.10 The student understands the political, military, and economic events since the 1950s that have had a significant impact on international relations.

Other Standards SS.A.5.4.8

FCAT LA.A.1.4.2 Reading: Strategies

A HUMAN PERSPECTIVE For Karl Co, a 15-year-old sophomore at Stuyvesant High School in New York City, September 11, 2001, began as "such a normal day." From his classroom, Karl had a clear view of the World Trade Center, just four blocks away. On a normal day, about 50,000 people worked in and 70,000 visited the twin towers. When the north tower burst into flames and smoke, Karl first thought, "It's a bomb. I'm going to die." Then the south tower erupted, and, shortly after, both collapsed. The students soon learned terrorists had crashed airliners into the towers, and the school was evacuated.

The September 11 Attacks

The students at Stuyvesant High had witnessed an act of **terrorism.** Terrorism is the unlawful use of, or threatened use of, force or violence against individuals or property for the purpose of intimidating or causing fear for political or social ends. Like many countries, the United States has been subjected to terrorism, both at home and abroad. But the September 11, 2001, attacks were the most destructive acts of terrorism ever committed on American soil.

On that morning, 19 Arab terrorists hijacked four airliners. They crashed two planes into the World Trade Center towers and one into the Pentagon, the U.S. military headquarters near Washington, D.C. The fourth plane crashed in Pennsylvania without striking its intended target, after some passengers overwhelmed the hijackers.

THE DESTRUCTION The hijacked planes were loaded with fuel. They became destructive missiles as they crashed into their targets. Thousands of workers escaped before the damaged skyscrapers collapsed. Fire and raining debris caused nearby buildings to collapse as well. At the Pentagon, the plane tore a 75-foot hole in the building's west side.

About 3,000 people died in the attacks. The dead included 265 plane passengers and 343 New York City firefighters who had entered the towers to rescue those trapped inside. Nine buildings in the city's financial district were completely destroyed or partly collapsed, and six others suffered major damage. The disaster area covered 16 acres.

THE TERRORISTS Immediately after the attacks, investigators worked to identify both the hijackers and those who directed the attacks. The evidence pointed to a **global network,** or worldwide interconnected group, of extremist Islamic terrorists led by Osama bin Laden, a Saudi Arabian millionaire. The group, known as al-Qaeda, was formed to fight the Soviet invasion of Afghanistan in 1979. Al-Qaeda later began to oppose

BACKGROUND
Osama bin Laden offered to help the Saudi Arabian government when Iraq invaded Kuwait in 1990 and threatened Saudi Arabia. He was angered when the Saudis turned to the United States for military help instead.

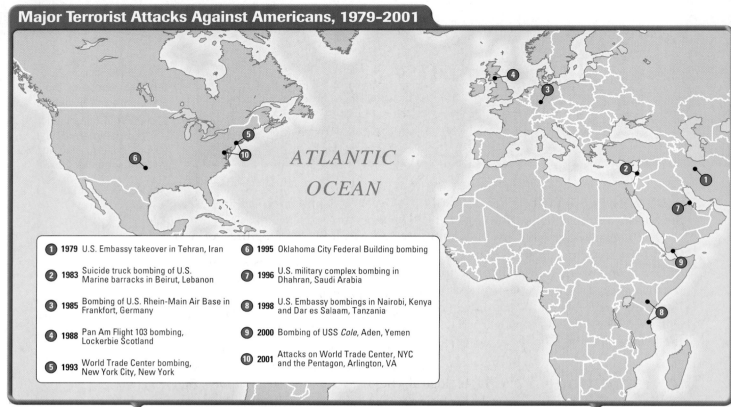

Major Terrorist Attacks Against Americans, 1979–2001

ATLANTIC OCEAN

1. **1979** U.S. Embassy takeover in Tehran, Iran
2. **1983** Suicide truck bombing of U.S. Marine barracks in Beirut, Lebanon
3. **1985** Bombing of U.S. Rhein-Main Air Base in Frankfort, Germany
4. **1988** Pan Am Flight 103 bombing, Lockerbie Scotland
5. **1993** World Trade Center bombing, New York City, New York
6. **1995** Oklahoma City Federal Building bombing
7. **1996** U.S. military complex bombing in Dhahran, Saudi Arabia
8. **1998** U.S. Embassy bombings in Nairobi, Kenya and Dar es Salaam, Tanzania
9. **2000** Bombing of USS *Cole*, Aden, Yemen
10. **2001** Attacks on World Trade Center, NYC and the Pentagon, Arlington, VA

SKILLBUILDER: Interpreting Maps

LOCATION What region was the site of the most attacks on Americans?

American influence in Muslim lands. It started to target Americans and U.S. allies after the Persian Gulf War in 1991. Since its founding, al-Qaeda has carried out numerous terrorist attacks.

Aftermath of the Attacks

The September 11 attacks shocked and distressed not only Americans but people around the world. President George W. Bush declared war on terrorism and called on other nations to join the United States in fighting global terrorism. He also pushed for new security measures at home and authorized a search for suspected terrorists.

INTERNATIONAL WAR ON TERRORISM The United States organized a **coalition,** or an alliance, of nations to fight the war on terrorism. Canada, China, Great Britain, Pakistan, Russia, and many other nations joined the coalition. They pledged to share information, arrest terrorists in their countries, and seize the financial assets of terrorist groups. The coalition also supported military action in Afghanistan, where al-Qaeda was based. As part of Operation Enduring Freedom, the United States began bombing Afghanistan in October 2001, and later sent in ground forces. By mid-March 2002, Afghanistan's extremist Taliban regime had been removed from power and the al-Qaeda network overthrown.

In March 2003, President Bush expanded the war on terrorism by taking military action against Iraq. The President claimed that Iraqi dictator Saddam Hussein posed a threat to national security. Major combat in Iraq ended in May soon after Hussein's regime had been toppled.

Geographic Thinking

Using the Atlas
A Locate Afghanistan on the political map on page A22. What is its location in relation to Saudi Arabia?

HOMELAND SECURITY New airport security measures were enacted after the September 11 attacks. In addition, extra precautions were taken at public places where large numbers of people gather, such as sports stadiums. Other possible targets—nuclear power plants and water supply systems—expanded security. The Department of Homeland Security, led by Secretary Tom Ridge, was established to coordinate antiterrorist efforts.

Facing Terrorist Threats

Terrorism has been a global problem for decades. The prevention of terrorist attacks is one of the most difficult tasks facing the world today.

Geographic Thinking

Making Comparisons

B How does a war on terrorism differ from a conventional war against another country?

TERRORIST OPERATIONS AND WEAPONS Terrorists act in secret and can move from country to country while pursuing their objectives. Some terrorist groups want territory, like Palestinian extremists who use violence trying to gain a homeland in Southwest Asia. Other terrorists, such as the domestic terrorists who bombed the Federal Building in Oklahoma City in 1995, want to attack government policies. **B**

Terrorists can use other weapons besides bombs and fuel-laden planes, including biological, chemical, and nuclear weapons. **Biological weapons** refer to bacteria and viruses that can be used to harm or kill people, animals, or plants. The United States went on an anthrax alert after traces of the anthrax bacteria were found in letters sent to some members of Congress and the news media after the September attacks.

BALANCING SECURITY AND FREEDOM The United States and its allies hope to reduce terrorism by breaking up terrorist groups and by increasing security to make it harder for terrorists to act. But there are many kinds of terrorist threats, and the fight against global terrorism could go on for many years. Democratic countries also have to meet the challenge of providing security for citizens while preserving freedom and individual rights.

SECTION 1 Assessment

1 Places & Terms

Identify and explain the following terms.

- terrorism
- global network
- coalition
- biological weapon

2 Taking Notes

REGION Review the notes you took for this section.

	Causes	Effects
Issue 1		
Terrorism		

- Why are the United States and its allies so concerned about terrorism?
- How has terrorism affected the policies of the United States and its allies?

3 Main Ideas

a. What happened in the terrorist attacks on the United States on September 11, 2001, and who was believed to be responsible?

b. How did the United States respond to the attacks?

4 Geographic Thinking

Drawing Conclusions What might be some difficulties facing the United States and its allies in fighting terrorism?
Think about:

- terrorists moving from country to country
- the variety of weapons available to terrorists

RESEARCH LINKS CLASSZONE.COM

GeoActivities

EXPLORING LOCAL GEOGRAPHY Do research to learn how the fight against terrorism is being waged in your state. Write a **press release** describing one of these antiterrorist measures.

Urban Sprawl

How can urban sprawl be controlled?

Main Ideas
- Many metropolitan areas in the United States and Canada have sprawled, or spread out, farther and farther.
- Cities are focusing on smart-growth solutions to urban sprawl.

Places & Terms

urban sprawl

infrastructure

smart growth

sustainable community

SUNSHINE STATE STANDARDS
SS.B.2.4.2 The student understands past and present trends in human migration and cultural interaction and their impact on physical and human systems.

Other Standards SS.B.2.4.4, B.2.4.7

FCAT LA.A.1.4.2 Reading: Strategies

A HUMAN PERSPECTIVE Richard Baron is a real estate developer who tried to address the related problems of urban sprawl and inadequate low-income housing. In 1996, he began building Murphy Park, an affordable and attractive housing complex in mid-town St. Louis, Missouri. The development has more than 400 units and contains both apartments and townhouses. It has plenty of green space, art and day-care centers, and an elementary school. More than half of Murphy Park's units are reserved for people with low income. Baron's solution—to bring the attractive features of suburban living to the city—is one of many that are being applied to the problem of urban sprawl.

Growth Without a Plan

Those Americans and Canadians who can afford it often choose to work in a city but live in its suburbs. They are usually attracted by new, upscale housing, better public services, and open space. As suburbs become more numerous, metropolitan areas become larger and more difficult to manage. (See chart to the right.)

URBAN SPRAWL Poorly planned development that spreads a city's population over a wider and wider geographical area is called **urban sprawl.** As outlying areas become more populated, the land between them and the city fills in as well.

In the United States and Canada, urban sprawl is becoming a matter of increasing concern. From 1970 to 2000, people who worked in U.S. cities moved farther and farther from urban centers. The population density of cities in the United States decreased by more than 20 percent as people in cities moved to suburbs and outlying areas. About 30,000 square miles of rural lands were gobbled up by housing developments. For example, the population of the city of Chicago decreased during this period from 3.4 million people to 2.8 million. But the Chicago metropolitan area grew from about 7.0 million persons to 7.3 million.

Canada is less populated than the United States but faces similar problems. In the 1990s, more than 75 percent of all Canadians lived in urban areas.

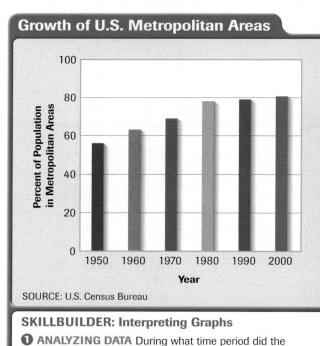

Growth of U.S. Metropolitan Areas

Percent of Population in Metropolitan Areas

(y-axis: 0, 20, 40, 60, 80, 100)

(x-axis: 1950, 1960, 1970, 1980, 1990, 2000)

Year

SOURCE: U.S. Census Bureau

SKILLBUILDER: Interpreting Graphs

❶ **ANALYZING DATA** During what time period did the largest increase in metropolitan growth occur?

❷ **MAKING GENERALIZATIONS** What has happened to metropolitan growth since 1980?

PLACE Las Vegas, Nevada, is a perfect example of urban sprawl. In the 1970s (left), it was a small city. In the 1990s (right), it became the fastest growing city in the country. **What are some of the differences between the photos of Las Vegas above?**

CAUSES OF URBAN SPRAWL Sprawl occurs in metropolitan areas that allow unrestricted growth or that have no plans to contain it. Other factors include the widespread use of automobiles and the building of expressways. Autos and relatively cheap gasoline enable Americans to drive many miles to and from their jobs. Despite clogged highways and long commutes, Americans prefer their cars to mass transit. Expressways provide the means for continued reliance on the automobile.

Yet, despite sprawl, there are many reasons why Americans have moved to suburbs. Some people want open spaces or better schools and housing. Still others want to try to recapture the sense of community they experienced while growing up. They want their children to know their neighbors and have a backyard in which to play. Only recently have urban planners started to design big-city neighborhoods to give a sense of community, hoping to slow the flight to the suburbs.

Urban Sprawl's Negative Impact

Urban sprawl has a negative impact on the quality of life in many ways. As suburbs grow, more commuter traffic strains the infrastructure. **Infrastructure** consists of the basic facilities, services, and machinery needed for a community to function. For example, roads and bridges need maintenance. More cars on the road for more time adds to air pollution, too. Also, sources of water, such as rivers or underground aquifers (layers of water-holding rock or soil), become depleted. ◀

Urban sprawl also has other costs. The cost of providing streets, utilities, and other public facilities to suburban communities is often at least 25 per cent higher than for high-density residences in a city. Urban sprawl also separates classes of people. When those in upper-income brackets choose to live in outlying areas, lower-income residents often become isolated in inner-city areas.

Geographic Thinking

Seeing Patterns
A What problems has the automobile caused?

Solutions to Sprawl

More and more cities are developing plans for **smart growth,** which is the efficient use and conservation of land and other resources. Most often this involves encouraging development close to or inside the limits of existing cities. Good public transportation systems help to make smart growth possible by cutting down on auto traffic.

PORTLAND'S GROWTH BOUNDARY In 1979, the city of Portland, Oregon, drew a line around itself to create an urban growth boundary. Building was allowed inside the boundary. The surrounding green space was off limits to developers. This decision caused controversy but has paid off. Portland has contained urban sprawl.

VANCOUVER'S PLAN FOR SUSTAINABLE COMMUNITIES Since 1961, Vancouver, British Columbia, has seen the population of its metropolitan area double. The growth of outlying suburbs often took place at the expense of forests, farms, and flood plains. In 1995, the Greater Vancouver Regional Board adopted a plan to manage growth. It involved turning suburbs into **sustainable communities,** that is, communities where residents could live and work. The same solution was applied to Vancouver's downtown area, where about 40 percent of its residents now walk to work. This has cut down on commuting.

Geographic Thinking

Making Comparisons
B How were the urban growth actions of Portland and Vancouver similar?

GRASSROOTS OPPOSITION In some metropolitan areas, citizens have banded together to offer their own solutions to urban sprawl. For example, citizens in Durham, North Carolina, opposed additional commercial development along a congested area of a nearby interstate highway. They formed CAUSE—Citizens Against Urban Sprawl Everywhere. The organization is working against sprawl through education and political activism.

In this section, you read about the challenge of urban sprawl. In the Case Study that follows, you will learn about challenges increasingly diverse societies bring to the United States and Canada.

Assessment

❶ Places & Terms

Identify and explain the following places and terms.

- urban sprawl
- infrastructure
- smart growth
- sustainable community

❷ Taking Notes

HUMAN-ENVIRONMENT INTERACTION Review the notes you took for this section.

	Causes	Effects
Issue 2: Urban Sprawl		

- What are some of the causes of urban sprawl?
- What are some of the effects of urban sprawl?

❸ Main Ideas

a. What happens when metropolitan areas spread farther and farther out?

b. What are some of the ways cities are dealing with urban sprawl?

c. What are some of the ways citizens are dealing with urban sprawl?

❹ Geographic Thinking

Drawing Conclusions
What would happen to the environment if urban sprawl were not controlled? **Think about:**

- the negative effects of urban sprawl
- the quality of life in the United States and Canada

EXPLORING LOCAL GEOGRAPHY Pair with another student and choose a metropolitan area in the United States or Canada to research. Then prepare a **report** on the condition of urban sprawl in that area and present your report to the class. Discuss the effects of urban sprawl and what steps, if any, are being taken to control the sprawl.

RAND McNALLY **Map and Graph Skills**

Reading a Bounded-Area Map

Urban growth over time is the theme of this map of the Baltimore, Maryland, and Washington, D.C., areas. Both Baltimore and Washington grew from small cities to important metropolitan areas, spreading outward in all directions. At one time, nearly 30 miles of unsettled area separated them. Today, much of this area has been built up as the Baltimore and Washington metropolitan areas have spread.

THE LANGUAGE OF MAPS **Bounded-area maps** show the distribution of some feature of interest, such as climate, vegetation, precipitation, or, in this case, urban growth in a region. Bounded-area maps use lines, colors, and patterns to communicate information.

SUNSHINE STATE STANDARDS
Key Standard SS.B.1.4.1 The student uses a variety of maps, geographic technologies including geographic information systems (GIS) and satellite-produced imagery, and other advanced graphic representations to depict geographic problems.

FCAT LA.A.2.4.1 **Reading:** Identify Main Idea, Details, and Methods

Urban Growth in Baltimore and Washington ❶

Copyright by Rand McNally & Co.

❶ The title gives you the subject matter of the map.

❷ The key explains the meanings of the colors and symbols.

❸ This map shows the gradual spread of urban areas from two neighboring cities—Baltimore and Washington. The map covers the period of time from 1800 to 1992.

Map and Graph Skills Assessment

1. Seeing Patterns
Like most early settlements, Baltimore and Washington were founded near essential geographic features. What were they?

2. Analyzing Data
During which time period did the greatest expansion take place for the Washington metropolitan area?

3. Drawing Conclusions
At what physical location do the two metropolitan areas seem to have merged?

CASESTUDY

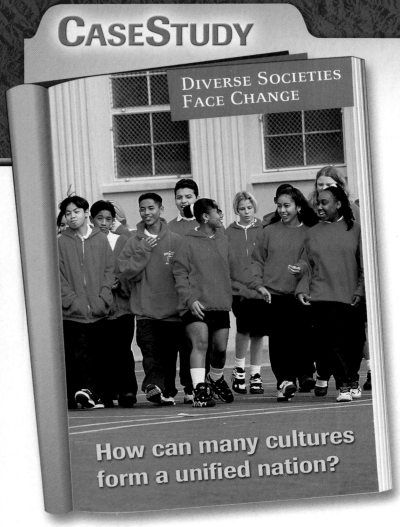

DIVERSE SOCIETIES
FACE CHANGE

How can many cultures form a unified nation?

The diverse heritage
of the United States is
evident in this group of
students in California.

SUNSHINE STATE STANDARDS

Key Standard SS.B.2.4.2 The student
understands past and present trends in
human migration and cultural interaction
and their impact on physical and human
systems.

Other Standards SS.A.1.4.3, A.5.4.2

FCAT LA.A.2.4.8 Reading: Synthesize
and Conclude

As you read earlier in this unit, the first immigrants to North America are believed to have come from Asia. They are thought to have crossed a land bridge that existed in what is now the Bering Strait thousands of years ago. Since that time, millions of people from countries all over the world have immigrated to the United States and Canada. They have come in search of a new life in a new homeland. The challenge for citizens and governments of both the United States and Canada is to make sure that these diverse peoples continue to remain unified.

"Mosaic" or "Melting Pot"

After centuries of immigration, the United States and Canada are culturally diverse. They contain large populations of the world's cultures. Ethnic neighborhoods with populations of Asians, Eastern Europeans, and Latin Americans are found in most large cities of both countries. In New York City alone, immigrant schoolchildren speak more than 100 different languages. The arrival of so many peoples over the years left the United States and Canada with the difficult task of forming a unified society. Each country approached the task of unifying its many cultures differently.

CANADA'S CULTURAL "MOSAIC" Canada's earliest settlers were its native peoples. Its first European settlers came, as you have learned, from two distinct cultural groups—French and English. All of these groups kept their separate identities as the nation developed. Also, Canada encouraged immigration from all over the world. It wanted to fill its vast lands and expand its workforce and its domestic markets. These immigrants also were encouraged to retain their cultural heritage.

As a result, many Canadians have strong ethnic ties. In fact, as you read in Chapter 7, the ethnic identity of French-speaking citizens in Quebec has been so strong that at times they have even considered separating themselves from the Canadian confederation.

The Canadian government has officially recognized the multicultural nature of Canada. In 1988, it enacted the Canadian Multiculturalism Act to protect and promote diversity. Many Canadians believe that this policy ensures equality for people of all origins and enriches their nation. But not all agree. Some Canadians feel that diversity has promoted difference at the expense of "Canadianness."

AMERICA'S "MELTING POT" For many years, people in the United States believed that assimilation was the key. It was thought to be the best way to build one nation from many different peoples. Assimilation occurs when people from a minority culture assume the language, customs, and lifestyles of people from the dominant culture. Native Americans were an example. In the late 19th century, they were encouraged and even forced to learn English, adopt Western dress, and become Christians to assimilate into the dominant white culture.

People expected immigrants to assimilate, too. Those who did not could face prejudice because of their cultural differences. Immigrants soon learned that life would be easier if they adopted the ways of their new country—if they underwent "Americanization." Most of these immigrants had come from Europe. Many wanted to assimilate. They wanted to adopt a common language and culture—to become Americans.

New Immigrants Challenge Old Ways

The immigrants who came to the United States in the late 20th century brought different attitudes. They came mainly from Latin America and Asia. They were culturally or racially unlike earlier immigrant groups, who had come mainly from Europe. These later immigrants were less willing to give up their traditions and beliefs in order to assimilate.

DIVIDED OPINION Some Americans felt that the new immigrants did not understand what made the United States unique. According to this point of view, America's strength has come from blending its diverse cultures to create something new—an American. They also believed that encouraging different languages and customs would promote separation, not unity. In response, they wanted immigration limited and English made the official language.

SEE
PRIMARY SOURCE C

Other Americans, including many educators, held different views. They thought that American society would benefit by stressing multiculturalism, as the Canadians do.

As you can see, bringing many cultures together is a continuing challenge both in the United States and in Canada. So, how can cultural diversity be preserved and national unity forged? The Case Study Project and primary sources that follow will help you explore this question.

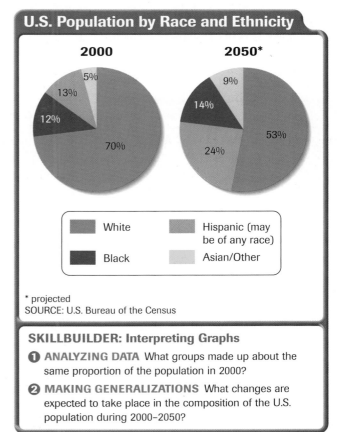

U.S. Population by Race and Ethnicity

2000

5%
13%
12%
70%

2050*

9%
14%
24%
53%

- White
- Black
- Hispanic (may be of any race)
- Asian/Other

* projected
SOURCE: U.S. Bureau of the Census

SKILLBUILDER: Interpreting Graphs

❶ **ANALYZING DATA** What groups made up about the same proportion of the population in 2000?

❷ **MAKING GENERALIZATIONS** What changes are expected to take place in the composition of the U.S. population during 2000–2050?

CASE STUDY

PROJECT

Talk Show Discussion

Primary sources A, B, C, D, and E offer differing opinions about assimilation and maintaining cultural identity. Use them along with your own research from the library or Internet to prepare for a talk show discussion on the issue of today's cultural diversity.

RESEARCH LINKS
CLASSZONE.COM

Suggested Steps

1. With a group totaling five students, prepare a talk show discussion on the topic, "Can Many Cultures Form a Unified Nation?" One member should act as the discussion leader. Each of the other members should select one of the following positions: for assimilation or against assimilation.

2. Think about the following questions as you prepare for your role. "Must a unified nation have a single culture?" "What are the advantages and disadvantages of assimilation, or the advantages and disadvantages of multiculturalism, in unifying a nation?"

3. Use online and print resources to research your topic.

4. Write an opening statement of your position. Prepare visuals, such as charts or graphs, if you need them to support your position.

5. Present your position as a part of the talk show. Discuss with the leader and other group members the focus question given above.

Materials and Supplies

- posterboard
- colored markers
- reference books, newspapers, and magazines
- Internet access

PRIMARY SOURCE A

Newspaper Article *In 1998, the* Washington Post *published a series of articles titled* The Myth of the Melting Pot. *Staff writer* **William Booth** *offered the following comments about immigration and cultural identity in his piece,* "One Nation, Indivisible: Is It History?"

The immigrants of today come not from Europe but overwhelmingly from the still developing world of Asia and Latin America. They are driving a demographic shift so rapid that within the lifetimes of today's teenagers, no one ethnic group—including whites of European descent—will comprise a majority of the nation's population. . . .

[M]any historians argue that there was a greater consensus in the past on what it meant to be an American, a yearning for a common language and culture, and a desire—encouraged, if not coerced [forced] by members of the dominant white Protestant culture—to assimilate. Today, they say, there is more emphasis on preserving one's ethnic identity, of finding ways to highlight and defend one's cultural roots.

PRIMARY SOURCE B

Social Commentary *Michelle Young is a writer and editor. Much of her work has focused on issues of multiculturalism. In the following excerpt from a 1996 article in the online publication* Career Magazine, *Young contrasts assimilation with multiculturalism.*

The melting pot concept spoke of all Americans being part of the enormous "cultural stew" we call America. . . . Many people . . . saw the United States of America as a place where historical hurts from their homelands could be erased. . . .

But America was not the nation they'd been promised, where the streets were paved with gold. Many newcomers knew that from experience because "they" were doing the paving! As a result, people began to realize that the concept of the melting pot just wasn't realistic. . . .

In contrast to the melting pot, multiculturalism encourages us to take pride in our own roots first, in our ingredients we've added to what has become America's multicultural stew. The nation's promise lies in that multicultural stew, and by appreciating our own cultures, we develop an eagerness to learn about others' origins.

Political Commentary *Patrick Buchanan is a politician who was the presidential candidate of the Reform Party in 2000. Buchanan was a strong supporter of immigration reform and assimilation, as is evident in these words posted on his Web site on August 6, 2000.*

> GeoNet
>
> Back | Forward | Reload | Home | Images | Print | Security | Stop
>
> Location:
>
> If America is to survive as "one nation," we must take an immigration "time out" to mend the melting pot. As President, I will: Halt illegal immigration by securing our borders. Stand with the three-in-four Americans who agree that mass legal immigration must be reduced by restoring the 20th century average of 250,000 to 300,000 immigrants per year. Support a national campaign of assimilation to teach newly adopted Americans our culture, history, traditions, and English language.

Government Law *The Canadian Multiculturalism Act was passed by the Canadian parliament in 1988. Its purpose was to make the preservation and enhancement of multiculturalism in Canada the law of the land.*

". . . It is hereby declared to be the policy of the Government of Canada to . . . (b) recognize and promote the understanding that multiculturalism is a fundamental characteristic of the Canadian heritage and identity and that it provides an invaluable resource in the shaping of Canada's future; . . . (c) promote the full and equitable participation of individuals and communities of all origins in the continuing evolution and shaping of all aspects of Canadian society and assist them in the elimination of any barrier to that participation; . . . (f) encourage and assist the social, cultural, economic, and political institutions of Canada to be both respectful and inclusive of Canada's multicultural character; . . . (g) promote the understanding and creativity that arise from the interaction between individuals and communities of different origins."

Government Document *The 2000 census form contained detailed racial and ethnic classifications, showing the diverse peoples that make up the population of the United States.*

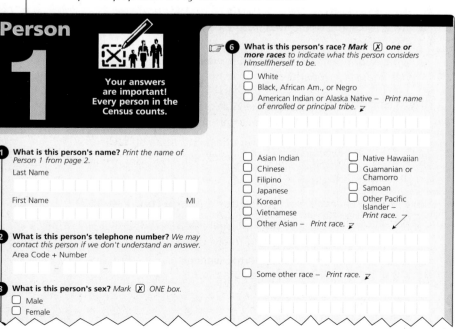

PROJECT **CheckList**

Have I . . .

✔ fully researched my topic?

✔ taken into account both sides of an issue?

✔ created informative visuals that make my presentation clear and interesting?

✔ practiced the delivery of my presentation?

VISUAL SUMMARY
TODAY'S ISSUES IN THE UNITED STATES AND CANADA

Conflict

The Fight Against Terrorism

- Terrorists attack the United States on September 11, 2001.

- The United States increases security at home and searches for suspected terrorists within the country.

- A coalition of nations led by the United States launches a war against global terrorism.

- The war begins in Afghanistan, where those responsible for the September attacks—the al-Qaeda terrorists led by Osama bin Laden—are based.

Economics

Urban Sprawl

- Many metropolitan areas in North America have spread out farther and farther.

- This has caused problems such as traffic congestion, air pollution, strains on infrastructure, rising housing costs, and the separation of the well-off from the poor.

- Some governments and citizens are promoting "smart growth" as an answer to urban sprawl.

Government

Case Study: Diverse Societies Face Change

- Centuries of immigration from all parts of the world have given the United States and Canada diverse populations.

- The United States and Canada have approached unifying their many cultures differently.

- Bringing diverse peoples together is a continuing challenge for both countries.

Reviewing Places & Terms

A. Briefly explain the importance of each of the following.

1. terrorism
2. global network
3. coalition
4. biological weapon
5. urban sprawl
6. infrastructure
7. smart growth
8. sustainable community

B. Answer the questions about vocabulary in complete sentences.

9. What is the objective of terrorism?
10. What are the characteristics of a global network?
11. What is the name for an alliance of nations?
12. Which of the terms above might be used to refer to anthrax?
13. How does urban sprawl contribute to air pollution?
14. What are some of the elements that make up infrastructure?
15. Which term involves encouraging development close to or inside city limits?
16. What did Vancouver try to turn into sustainable communities?
17. What is the relationship between the terms terrorism and global network?
18. What is the objective of employing a biological weapon?
19. How does urban sprawl cause housing costs to rise?
20. What system is an important component of smart growth?

Main Ideas

The Fight Against Terrorism (pp. 173–175)

1. What are some of the actions governments can take when faced with terrorism?
2. What are some of the weapons used by terrorists to further their objectives?
3. What might become a problem for democratic governments waging war against terrorism?

Urban Sprawl (pp. 176–179)

4. What are some of the causes of urban sprawl?
5. What are some of the negative effects of urban sprawl?
6. How are governments and concerned citizens trying to find solutions to urban sprawl?

Case Study: Diverse Societies Face Change (pp. 180–183)

7. Why have the United States and Canada become diverse societies?
8. How have Americans reacted to diversity?
9. How have Canadians reacted to diversity?
10. What are some ways suggested for Americans to meet the challenges of the new immigrants?

Critical Thinking

1. Using Your Notes

Use your completed chart to answer these questions.

	Causes	Effects
Issue 1: Terrorism		
Issue 2: Urban Sprawl		

a. How might a negative effect of urban sprawl be halted?

b. What are some of the positive effects of diverse societies?

2. Geographic Themes

a. **MOVEMENT** How have terrorists been able to form global networks?

b. **HUMAN-ENVIRONMENT INTERACTION** How has the spread of urban sprawl affected the environment?

3. Identifying Themes

If you were a government official, how would you promote smart growth? Which of the five themes are reflected in your answer? Explain.

4. Making Decisions

What factors do democratic governments have to consider when waging a war against an enemy such as global terrorism?

5. Making Comparisons

How do the Canadian and American approaches to a diverse society differ?

Additional Test Practice, pp. S1–S37

TEST PRACTICE
CLASSZONE.COM

US & CANADA

Geographic Skills: Interpreting Graphs

Region of Last Residence of Legal Immigrants to the United States, 1901–1998

Use the graph to answer the following questions.

1. **ANALYZING DATA** What was the percentage of immigrants from Europe during 1901–1910? during 1991–1998?

2. **MAKING COMPARISONS** Which two regions supplied the largest percentage of immigrants to the United States during the last century?

3. **DRAWING CONCLUSIONS** What significant change took place in the pattern of immigration during the 20th century?

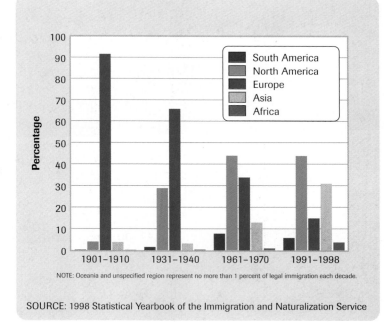

NOTE: Oceania and unspecified region represent no more than 1 percent of legal immigration each decade.

SOURCE: 1998 Statistical Yearbook of the Immigration and Naturalization Service

Do research to create a chart showing the total number of immigrants from each region during the 20th century. Display the figures for each region on an outline map of the world.

INTERNET ACTIVITY

Use the links at **classzone.com** to research immigration to Canada. Focus on changes in the regions from which immigrants came in the 20th century.

Writing About Geography Write a report on your findings. Combine with a chart listing the regions and the percentages.

Unit 30

Latin America

Latin America includes parts of North America, Central America and the Caribbean, and South America. The region covers many latitudes from north to south of the equator.

MOVEMENT Villagers from surrounding areas bring their goods to market in the Aztec city of Tenochtitlán, depicted in this mural by Diego Rivera.

HUMAN–ENVIRONMENT INTERACTION Chacobo Indians make the dugout canoes they use to explore in the Amazon River basin in northern Bolivia.

GeoData

LOCATION Latin America extends from Mexico southward across the equator to nearly reach Antarctica in the Southern Hemisphere.

REGION It is called "Latin America" because the two main languages spoken there—Spanish and Portuguese—developed from Latin.

REGION This region is bordered by two oceans (Atlantic and Pacific), the Gulf of Mexico, and the Caribbean Sea.

For more information on Latin America . . .

RESEARCH LINKS
CLASSZONE.COM

PLACE Sugarloaf Mountain is a famous landmark that looks out over Guanabara Bay in Rio de Janeiro, Brazil. The statue of Christ atop the mountain reflects the importance of the Catholic faith to millions of Latin Americans.

Unit PREVIEW 3

Today's Issues in Latin America

Three of the most important issues that concern Latin America today are resources, democracy, and the income gap between rich and poor.

As you read Chapters 9 and 10, you will learn helpful background information. You will study the issues themselves in Chapter 11.

In a small group, answer the following questions. Then participate in a class discussion of your ideas.

Exploring the Issues

1. **RESOURCES** What are some resources that are becoming increasingly scarce in the world?

2. **DEMOCRACY** What are some threats to democracy in the world today? What conditions might be necessary for democracy to thrive?

3. **INCOME GAP** Why might an income gap exist in a country? How might a growing gap between rich and poor affect a country?

For more on these issues in Latin America . . .

CURRENT EVENTS
CLASSZONE.COM

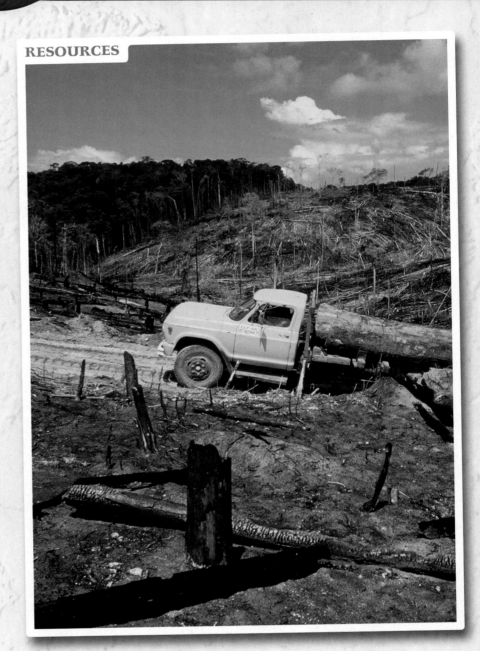

RESOURCES

How can we preserve and develop the rain forest?

Agriculture and timber harvesting in Brazil are reducing the size of the rain forests by destroying thriving ecosystems, but are providing food and export products.

DEMOCRACY

How can Latin Americans gain a voice in government?

Demonstrators in Chile rally in support of putting former dictator General Augusto Pinochet on trial. The signs say, "Judgment for Pinochet—truth and justice for Chile."

CASESTUDY

How can the economic gulf between rich and poor be bridged?

There is a growing gap between rich and poor in Latin America, with all the problems of slums, homeless children, and street crime. Here, a young girl stands above polluted water in a slum in Belém, Brazil.

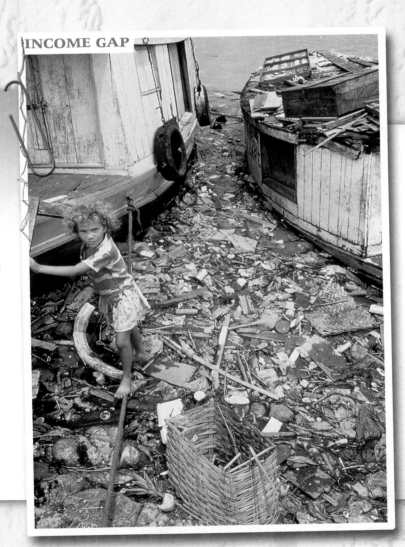

INCOME GAP

189

Patterns of Physical Geography

SUNSHINE STATE STANDARDS
Key Standard SS.B.1.4.1 The student uses a variety of maps, geographic technologies including geographic information systems (GIS) and satellite-produced imagery, and other advanced graphic representations to depict geographic problems.

Other Standards SS.B.2.4.1

FCAT LA.A.2.2.7 Reading: Recognize Compare and Contrast

Use the Unit Atlas to add to your knowledge of Latin America, which stretches from Mexico to the tip of South America. As you look at the maps and graphs, notice geographic patterns and specific details about the region. For example, the graph gives details about two large rivers in the region.

After studying the graphs and physical map on these two pages, jot down answers to the following questions in your notebook.

Making Comparisons

1. Which river systems dominate South America?

2. How are the Andes Mountains of South America similar in location to the Rocky Mountains of the United States?

3. Compare Latin America's landmass and population to those of the United States. Based on that data, how might the overall population densities of the two compare?

For updated statistics on Latin America . . .

DATA UPDATE
CLASSZONE.COM

Comparing Data

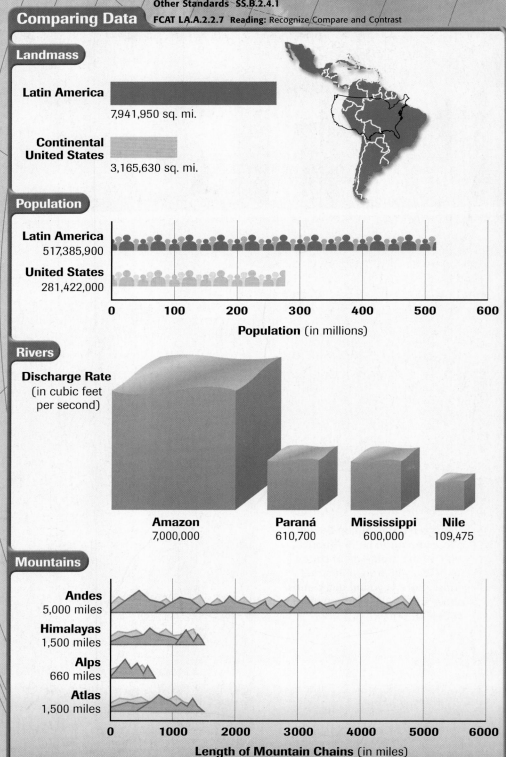

Landmass

Latin America
7,941,950 sq. mi.

Continental United States
3,165,630 sq. mi.

Population

Latin America
517,385,900

United States
281,422,000

0   100   200   300   400   500   600
Population (in millions)

Rivers

Discharge Rate (in cubic feet per second)

Amazon
7,000,000

Paraná
610,700

Mississippi
600,000

Nile
109,475

Mountains

Andes
5,000 miles

Himalayas
1,500 miles

Alps
660 miles

Atlas
1,500 miles

0   1000   2000   3000   4000   5000   6000
Length of Mountain Chains (in miles)

UNITED STATES

ATLANTIC OCEAN

DOMINICAN REPUBLIC

Puerto Rico

Hispaniola I.

ST. KITTS & NEVIS

ANTIGUA & BARBUDA

Caribbean Sea

Guadeloupe

DOMINICA

Martinique

ST. LUCIA

BARBADOS

ST. VINCENT & THE GRENADINES

GRENADA

TRINIDAD & TOBAGO

Gulf of California

Sierra Madre Occidental

Rio Grande

Gulf of Mexico

Tropic of Cancer

MEXICO

Yucatán Peninsula

Sierra Madre Oriental

BAHAMAS

Greater Antilles

WEST

CUBA

HAITI

JAMAICA

INDIES

Baja California

CENTRAL AMERICA

BELIZE

HONDURAS

GUATEMALA

EL SALVADOR

NICARAGUA

Caribbean Sea

Netherlands Antilles

Lesser Antilles

ATLANTIC OCEAN

Panama Canal

COSTA RICA

PANAMA

VENEZUELA

Orinoco R.

Llanos

GUYANA

SURINAME

FRENCH GUIANA

COLOMBIA

Guiana Highlands

Negro R.

Equator

Galápagos Is.

ECUADOR

AMAZON BASIN

Amazon R.

SOUTH AMERICA

PACIFIC OCEAN

PERU

Madeira R.

BRAZIL

ANDES

Lake Titicaca

BOLIVIA

Mato Grosso Plateau

Araguaia R.

BRAZILIAN HIGHLANDS

Gran Chaco

Paraguay R.

Paraná R.

Atacama Desert

Tropic of Capricorn

PARAGUAY

ANDES

Mt. Aconcagua 22,831 ft. (6959 m)

Pampas

URUGUAY

ARGENTINA

Rio de la Plata

CHILE

Patagonia

ATLANTIC OCEAN

N
W   E
S

Elevation

13,100 ft.	(4,000 m.)
6,600 ft.	(2,000 m.)
1,600 ft.	(500 m.)
650 ft.	(200 m.)
0 ft.	(0 m.)

Below sea level

▲ Mountain peak

Tierra del Fuego

Falkland Is.

South Georgia Is.

Cape Horn

Drake Passage

0   500   1,000 miles
0   500   1,000 kilometers
Azimuthal Equal–Area Projection

Unit ATLAS

Patterns of Human Geography

Study the historical and political maps of Latin America on these two pages. In your notebook, answer these questions.

Making Comparisons

1. What differences do you notice when you compare the 1800 map to the map of Latin America today?

2. What are some of the similarities between the 1800 map and the contemporary map of Latin America?

3. What former Portuguese colony in South America is the largest country in the region today?

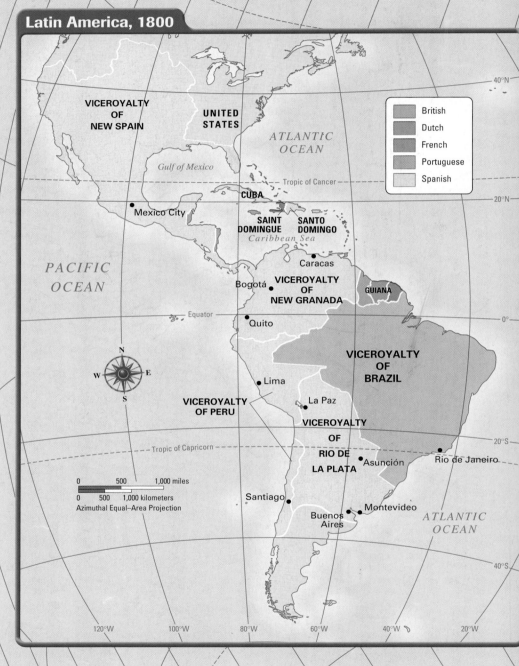

Latin America, 1800

	British
	Dutch
	French
	Portuguese
	Spanish

VICEROYALTY OF NEW SPAIN

UNITED STATES

ATLANTIC OCEAN

Gulf of Mexico

Tropic of Cancer

CUBA

• Mexico City

SAINT DOMINGUE   SANTO DOMINGO

Caribbean Sea

• Caracas

Bogotá •   VICEROYALTY OF NEW GRANADA

GUIANA

PACIFIC OCEAN

Equator

• Quito

VICEROYALTY OF BRAZIL

• Lima

• La Paz

VICEROYALTY OF PERU

VICEROYALTY OF

Tropic of Capricorn

RIO DE LA PLATA

• Asunción

Rio de Janeiro •

• Santiago

Buenos Aires •   • Montevideo

ATLANTIC OCEAN

0   500   1,000 miles
0   500   1,000 kilometers
Azimuthal Equal–Area Projection

40°N
20°N
0°
20°S
40°S

120°W   100°W   80°W   60°W   40°W   20°W

Latin America: Political

UNITED STATES

MEXICO
- Tijuana
- Ciudad Juárez
- Chihuahua
- Monterrey
- Guadalajara
- México City ★
- Córdoba
- Puebla
- Acapulco

Gulf of California
Rio Grande
Gulf of Mexico
Tropic of Cancer

CUBA
- Havana ★

BAHAMAS

West Indies
Greater Antilles
Cayman Is. (U.K.)

BELIZE
- Belmopan ★
GUATEMALA
- Guatemala City ★
HONDURAS
- Tegucigalpa ★
EL SALVADOR
- San Salvador ★
NICARAGUA
- Managua ★
COSTA RICA
- San José ★
PANAMA
- Panamá City ★

JAMAICA
- Kingston

HAITI
- Port-au-Prince ★

Caribbean Sea
Netherlands Antilles (Neth.)
Aruba (Neth.)

Inset box (top right):
- Turks & Caicos (U.K.)
- **DOMINICAN REPUBLIC** — Santo Domingo ★
- Virgin Is. (U.S. & U.K.)
- San Juan
- Puerto Rico (U.S.)
- Anguilla (U.K.)
- **ST. KITTS & NEVIS**
- **ANTIGUA & BARBUDA**
- Guadeloupe (Fr.)
- **MONTSERRAT (U.K.)**
- Martinique (Fr.)
- **DOMINICA**
- **ST. LUCIA**
- **BARBADOS**
- **GRENADA**
- **ST. VINCENT & THE GRENADINES**
- **TRINIDAD & TOBAGO**

ATLANTIC OCEAN
Caribbean Sea
Lesser Antilles

VENEZUELA
- Maracaibo
- Caracas ★
- Mérida

COLOMBIA
- Medellín
- Bogotá ★
- Cali

GUYANA
- Georgetown ★
SURINAME
- Paramaribo ★
- Cayenne
FRENCH GUIANA (Fr.)

Orinoco R.

ECUADOR
- Quito ★
- Guayaquil

Equator
Galápagos Is. (Ec.)

Negro R.
Amazon R.
- Manaus
- Belém
Madeira R.
Araguaia R.

PERU
- Lima ★

BRAZIL
- Fortaleza
- Recife
- Salvador
- Brasília ★
- Goiânia
- Belo Horizonte
- Rio de Janeiro
- São Paulo
- Curitiba
- Pôrto Alegre

BOLIVIA
- La Paz ★
- Santa Cruz
- Sucre ★

PARAGUAY
- Asunción ★

Paraguay R.
Paraná R.

PACIFIC OCEAN

Tropic of Capricorn

CHILE
- Santiago ★
Juan Fernández Is. (Chile)

ARGENTINA
- Rosario
- Buenos Aires ★

URUGUAY
- Montevideo ★

Río de la Plata

ATLANTIC OCEAN

Falkland Is. (U.K.)
South Georgia (U.K.)

Legend
- ★ National capital
- ● Other city

0   500   1,000 miles
0   500   1,000 kilometers
Azimuthal Equal–Area Projection

Unit ATLAS

Regional Patterns

On these pages are several thematic maps and a pie graph. One map shows the climates of Latin America. Another depicts the urbanization of the region. A third map shows the languages of the region. Look at them and see what you can learn about Latin America. Answer these questions in your notebook.

Making Comparisons

1. What is the climate in much of the interior of South America? How does it differ from the climate along much of the coast? How might the climate have affected settlement in the interior?

2. What language do the people speak in Brazil? What language is spoken in most countries in the region?

3. Where is most of the population located in South America? Where is there less population? Why might people have settled in these areas rather than the others?

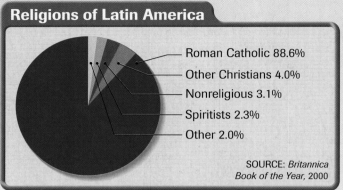

Religions of Latin America

- Roman Catholic 88.6%
- Other Christians 4.0%
- Nonreligious 3.1%
- Spiritists 2.3%
- Other 2.0%

SOURCE: *Britannica Book of the Year*, 2000

Climates of Latin America

ATLANTIC OCEAN

Gulf of Mexico

Tropic of Cancer

20°N

Caribbean Sea

PACIFIC OCEAN

Equator

0°

Tropic of Capricorn

20°S

ATLANTIC OCEAN

40°S

- Tropical wet
- Tropical wet and dry
- Desert
- Semiarid
- Mediterranean
- Humid subtropical
- Marine west coast
- Highland

0   500   1,000 miles
0   500   1,000 kilometers
Azimuthal Equal–Area Projection

120°W   100°W   80°W   60°W   40°W   20°W

Languages of Latin America

Indo-European
Other languages
French Spoken language

Spanish
Gulf of Mexico
English
ATLANTIC OCEAN
Maya
Spanish
Spanish
English
English
Haitian Creole
French
Caribbean Sea
Spanish
Spanish
English
Sranantongo, Dutch
French
Spanish
Quechua
Aymara
Guarani
Portuguese
Spanish
PACIFIC OCEAN
ATLANTIC OCEAN

0   500   1,000 miles
0   500   1,000 kilometers
Azimuthal Equal–Area Projection

Urbanization of Latin America

Guadalajara
Monterrey
Gulf of Mexico
ATLANTIC OCEAN
Mexico City
MEXICO
BAHAMAS
GUATEMALA
BELIZE
CUBA
JAMAICA
Guatemala City
HONDURAS
DOMINICAN REPUBLIC
HAITI
EL SALVADOR
NICARAGUA
Santo Domingo
COSTA RICA
PANAMA
Caribbean Sea
Caracas
Medellín
VENEZUELA
GUYANA
Bogotá
SURINAME
COLOMBIA
FRENCH GUIANA
ECUADOR
Lima
PERU
BRAZIL
Fortaleza
BOLIVIA
Recife
PACIFIC OCEAN
Salvador
PARAGUAY
Belo Horizonte
Santiago
São Paulo
Rio de Janeiro
CHILE
ARGENTINA
Curitiba
Buenos Aires
URUGUAY
Pôrto Alegre
ATLANTIC OCEAN

Percentage of population living in urban areas

More than 75%
50% to 75%
Less than 50%
No data

20
10
0
2000 population (millions)

LATIN AMERICA

195

Regional Data File

Study the charts on the countries of Latin America. In your notebook, answer these questions.

Making Comparisons

1. Which four Latin American countries have the most people? Locate them on the map on page 193. Are they also the largest countries?

2. Which four Latin American countries have the fewest people? Locate them on the map on page 193.

3. Which seven Latin American countries have the highest GDP (gross domestic product)? Which countries have the lowest? What factors might account for this?

(continued on page 198)

Notes:
a A comparison of the prices of the same items in different countries is used to figure these data.

b Includes land and water, where figures are available.

For updated statistics on Latin America . . .

DATA UPDATE
CLASSZONE.COM

Country Flag	Country/ Capital	Population (2000 estimate)	Life Expectancy (years) (1995–2000)	Birthrate (per 1,000 pop.) (2000)	Infant Mortality (per 1,000 live births) (2000)
	Antigua and Barbuda St. John's	68,000	71	22	17.1
	Argentina Buenos Aires	37,048,000	73	19	19.2
	Bahamas Nassau	310,000	74	21	18.4
	Barbados Bridgetown	259,000	76	14	14.2
	Belize Belmopan	254,000	75	32	33.9
	Bolivia La Paz, Sucre	8,281,000	61	30	67.0
	Brazil Brasília	170,115,000	67	21	40.0
	Chile Santiago	15,211,000	75	18	10.5
	Colombia Bogotá	40,037,000	70	26	28.0
	Costa Rica San José	3,589,000	76	22	12.6
	Cuba Havana	11,139,000	76	14	7.2
	Dominica Roseau	76,000	78	16	14.6
	Dominican Republic Santo Domingo	8,443,000	71	28	46.6
	Ecuador Quito	12,646,000	69	27	40.0
	El Salvador San Salvador	6,280,000	69	30	35.0
	Grenada St. George's	98,000	71	29	14.3
	Guatemala Guatemala City	12,670,000	64	37	45.0

Doctors (per 100,000 pop) (1992–1997)	GDP[a] (billions $US) (1998–1999)	Import/Export[a] (billions $US) (1998–1999)	Literacy Rate (percentage) (1998)	Televisions (per 1,000 pop.) (1996–1998)	Passenger Cars (per 1,000 pop.) (1991–1998)	Total Area[b] (square miles)
114	0.5	0.330 / 0.038	95	452	207	171
268	367.0	25 / 23	97	289	136	1,073,514
152	5.6	1.74 / 0.363	95	896	245	5,386
125	2.9	1.01 / 0.211	97	283	167	166
55	0.7	0.320 / 0.150	93	180	10	8,867
130	24.2	1.6 / 1.1	84	115	26	424,162
127	1,057.0	48.7 / 46.9	84	316	84	3,300,154
110	185.1	13.9 / 15.6	95	232	62	292,257
116	245.1	10.0 / 11.5	91	217	31	439,735
141	26.0	6.5 / 6.4	95	387	14	19,730
530	18.6	3.2 / 1.4	96	239	2	42,804
49	0.2	0.120 / 0.061	94	175	104	290
216	43.7	8.2 / 5.1	83	84	14	18,815
170	54.5	2.8 / 4.1	91	293	22	109,483
107	18.1	4.15 / 2.5	78	250	6	8,124
50	0.4	0.200 / 0.027	96	325	94	133
93	47.9	4.5 / 2.4	67	126	9	42,042

Regional Data File

Country Flag	Country/ Capital	Population (2000 estimate)	Life Expectancy (years) (1995–2000)	Birthrate (per 1,000 pop.) (2000)	Infant Mortality (per 1,000 live births) (2000)
	Guyana Georgetown	698,000	64	24	63.0
	Haiti Port-au-Prince	6,423,000	54	33	102.6
	Honduras Tegucigalpa	6,130,000	69	33	41.8
	Jamaica Kingston	2,609,000	75	22	24.4
	Mexico Mexico City	99,639,000	72	24	31.5
	Nicaragua Managua	5,074,000	68	36	40.0
	Panama Panama City	2,857,000	74	22	20.6
	Paraguay Asunción	5,505,000	70	32	27.0
	Peru Lima	27,136,000	68	27	43.0
	St. Kitts and Nevis Basseterre	43,000	67	20	24.0
	St. Lucia Castries	157,000	72	19	16.8
	St. Vincent and the Grenadines Kingstown	112,000	73	19	20.4
	Suriname Paramaribo	434,000	70	26	29.3
	Trinidad and Tobago Port-of-Spain	1,295,000	74	14	18.6
	Uruguay Montevideo	3,313,000	74	16	14.5
	Venezuela Caracas	24,170,000	72	25	21.0
	United States Washington, D.C.	281,422,000	77	15	7.0

Making Comparisons
(continued)

4. Latin America has several countries with populations under 100,000. Which of these has the smallest total area?

5. Use the map on page 193 to identify one country in Central America and another in the Caribbean. For each country, calculate per capita GDP by dividing total GDP by population. Which country has the higher per capita GDP?

Sources:
Europa World Year Book 2000
Human Development Report 2000, United Nations
International Data Base, 2000, U.S. Census Bureau online
Merriam-Webster's Geographical Dictionary, 1997
Statesman's Yearbook 2001
2000 World Population Data Sheet, Population Reference Bureau online
UNESCO *World Education Report 2000*
WHO Estimates of Health Personnel, World Health Organization online
World Almanac and Book of Facts 2001
World Factbook 2000, CIA online

Notes:
[a] A comparison of the prices of the same items in different countries is used to figure these data.
[b] Includes land and water, where figures are available.

Doctors (per 100,000 pop.) (1992–1997)	GDP[a] (billions $US) (1998–1999)	Import/Export[a] (billions $US) (1998–1999)	Literacy Rate (percentage) (1998)	Televisions (per 1,000 pop.) (1996–1998)	Passenger Cars (per 1,000 pop.) (1991–1998)	Total Area[b] (square miles)	
18	1.9	0.620 / 0.574	98	59	34	83,000	
8	9.2	0.762 / 0.322	48	5	5	10,714	
83	14.1	2.7 / 1.6	73	90	14	43,433	
140	8.8	2.7 / 1.4	86	323	17	4,471	
186	865.5	142.1 / 136.8	91	261	87	761,600	
86	12.5	1.5 / 0.573	68	190	16	50,193	
167	21.0	6.4 / 4.7	91	187	54	33,659	
110	19.9	3.2 / 3.1	93	101	14	157,047	
93	116.0	8.4 / 5.9	89	144	20	496,222	
117	0.2	0.160 / 0.042	90	244	130	139	
47	0.7	0.290 / 0.075	82	211	68	238	
88	0.3	0.180 / 0.048	82	162	44	150	
25	1.5	0.461 / 0.406	93	217	111	63,251	
79	9.4	3.0 / 2.4	98	331	107	1,980	
370	28.0	3.4 / 2.1	97	242	147	68,498	
236	182.8	11.8 / 20.9	92	185	68	352,143	
251	9,255.0	820.8 / 663.0	97	847	489	3,787,319	

PHYSICAL GEOGRAPHY OF LATIN AMERICA
From the Andes to the Amazon

Angel Falls in eastern Venezuela is the world's tallest waterfall. Named after James Angel, an American pilot who spotted it from his airplane in 1935, it is 3,212 feet tall.

GeoFocus

What effect has physical geography had on the settling of Latin America?

Taking Notes Copy the graphic organizer below into your notebook. Use it to record information from the chapter about the physical geography of Latin America.

Landforms	
Resources	
Climate and Vegetation	
Human-Environment Interaction	

Landforms and Resources

Main Ideas
- Latin America's landforms include highlands, lowlands, mountains, and plains.
- The Andes Mountains and the Amazon River are the region's most remarkable physical features.

Places & Terms

Andes Mountains

llanos	Orinoco River
cerrado	Amazon River
pampas	Paraná River

CONNECT TO THE ISSUES
RESOURCES People in Latin America have often struggled over the best way to develop and use natural resources.

SUNSHINE STATE STANDARDS
Key Standard SS.B.1.4.3 The student uses mental maps of physical and human features of the world to answer complex geographic questions.

Other Standards SS.B.1.4.1, B.2.4.3

FCAT LA.A.1.4.2 Reading: Strategies

A HUMAN PERSPECTIVE Simón Bolívar was a general who led the South American wars of independence against Spain. In August 1819, Bolívar led approximately 2,500 soldiers on a daring march from Venezuela over the mountains into present-day Colombia. Coming from this direction, over the massive barrier of the Andes Mountains, Bolívar and his troops were able to advance unseen. Bolívar's soldiers surprised the Spanish army and won a great victory. Military leaders such as Bolívar were able to use the geography of the region to help the South American republics win their independence from Spain.

Mountains and Highlands

Latin America has an enormous span from north to south, as you can see from the map on page 191. It reaches from the border between the United States and Mexico down to Tierra del Fuego at the southern-most tip of South America, a distance of about 7,000 miles. It covers part of North America, all of Central and South America, and the Caribbean Islands. Its highlands, lowlands, rain forests, and plains are bounded by the Atlantic and Pacific oceans, the Gulf of Mexico, and the Caribbean Sea. The mountains of Latin America form one of the great ranges of the world.

THE ANDES MOUNTAINS The **Andes Mountains** of the South American continent are part of a chain of mountain ranges that run through the western portion of North, Central, and South America. This range is called the Rockies in the United States, the Sierra Madre in Mexico, and the Andes in South America. There are many active volcanoes throughout the region.

All along the west and south coasts of South America, the Andes Mountains are a barrier to movement into the interior. As a result, more settlement in South America has occurred along the eastern and northern coasts.

Even so, the mountain ranges of Latin America were the home of some of the most important civilizations in the hemisphere, including the Inca in Peru.

MOVEMENT Two sure-footed guanacos climb the foothills of the Andes in Patagonia, a region that includes parts of Argentina and Chile.

HIGHLANDS Other ranges in Latin America include the Guiana Highlands in the northeast section of South America. Highlands are made up of the mountainous or hilly sections of a country. The highlands of Latin America include parts of Venezuela, Guyana, Suriname, French Guiana, and Brazil. The Brazilian Highlands (see the map on page 203) are located along the east coast of Brazil.

Plains for Grain and Livestock

South America has wide plains that offer rich soil for growing crops and grasses for grazing livestock.

LLANOS OF COLOMBIA AND VENEZUELA Colombia and Venezuela contain vast plains called **llanos** (LAH·nohs), which are grassy, treeless areas used for livestock grazing and farming. They are similar to the Great Plains in the United States and the pampas of Argentina.

PLAINS OF AMAZON RIVER BASIN Brazil also contains expansive plains in the interior of the country. These are the **cerrado** (seh·RAH·doh), savannas with flat terrain and moderate rainfall that make them suitable for farming. Much of this land is undeveloped. However, the government of Brazil is encouraging settlers to move into the interior and develop the land.

PAMPAS OF ARGENTINA AND URUGUAY In parts of South America, the plains are known as **pampas** (PAHM·puhs), areas of grasslands and rich soil. Pampas are found in northern Argentina and Uruguay. The main products of the pampas are cattle and wheat grain. A culture of the gaucho has grown up in the region, centered on the horsemen of the pampas. **A**

The Amazon and Other Rivers

The countries of Central America and the Caribbean do not have the extensive river systems that are found in South America. In North America, the Rio Grande, which forms part of the border between the United States and Mexico, is longer than any other river in Mexico, Central America, or the Caribbean. However, these areas are all bordered by water. As a result, they are less dependent on river systems for transportation than is South America.

South America has three major river systems. The Orinoco is the northernmost river system, with the Amazon also in the north, and the Paraná in the south of the continent.

ORINOCO RIVER The **Orinoco River** winds through the northern part of the continent, mainly in Venezuela. It flows more than 1,500 miles, partly along the Colombia-Venezuela border, to the Atlantic. The Orinoco River basin drains the interior lands of both Venezuela and Colombia. Some of the areas drained by the Orinoco are home to the few remaining Native American peoples, such as the Yanomamo.

5 THEMES

HUMAN-ENVIRONMENT INTERACTION

The Gaucho

Gauchos, the cowboys of Argentina and Uruguay, wear ponchos to help protect them from bad weather. They tuck the tops of their baggy trousers into riding boots. Like American cowboys and the *vaqueros* of Mexico, they wear hats with wide brims to help protect them from sun and rain on the pampas.

Their tools include the knife and the bola, a special kind of sling. It is made of stones fastened to the ends of cowhide thongs. The thrower hurls the bola at the legs of an animal, tripping it and throwing it to the ground.

Geographic Thinking

Seeing Patterns
A How are the llanos, cerrado, and pampas of South America similar to the Great Plains of the United States?

AMAZON RIVER Farther south, the **Amazon River** flows about 4,000 miles from west to east, emptying into the Atlantic Ocean. Its branches start in the Andes Mountains of South America, close to the Pacific. Yet it flows eastward across the central lowlands toward the Atlantic. The Amazon River is fed by over 1,000 tributaries, some of which are large rivers in themselves. The Amazon carries more water to the ocean than any other river in the world. In fact, it carries more water to the ocean than the next seven largest rivers of the world combined.

PARANÁ RIVER The **Paraná River** has its origins in the highlands of southern Brazil. It travels about 3,000 miles south and west through Paraguay and Argentina, where it is fed by several rivers, and then turns eastward. The last stretch of the river, where it turns into an estuary of the Paraná and Uruguay rivers between Argentina and Uruguay, is called the Río de la Plata. An estuary is the wide lower course of a river where its current is met by the tides.

Landforms and Rivers of Latin America

SKILLBUILDER: Interpreting Maps

❶ **MOVEMENT** Which rivers empty into the Atlantic Ocean?

❷ **REGION** What mountains run along the western edge of South America?

Major Islands of the Caribbean

The Caribbean Islands consist of three major groups: the Bahamas, the Greater Antilles, and the Lesser Antilles. (See the map on page 191.) These islands together are sometimes called the West Indies and were the first land encountered by Christopher Columbus when he sailed to the Western Hemisphere in 1492. They served as a base of operations for the later conquest of the mainland by the Spanish.

The Bahamas are made up of hundreds of islands off the southern tip of Florida and north of Cuba. They extend southeast into the Atlantic Ocean. Nassau is the capital and largest city in the Bahamas.

THE GREATER ANTILLES The Greater Antilles are made up of the larger islands in the Caribbean. These include Cuba, Jamaica, Hispaniola, and Puerto Rico. The island of Hispaniola is divided between the countries of Haiti and the Dominican Republic.

🌐 **Geographic Thinking** ←

Using the Atlas
B ▶ Use the map on page 191. Which of the Antilles are closer to the coast of South America?

THE LESSER ANTILLES The Lesser Antilles are the smaller islands in the region southeast of Puerto Rico. The Lesser Antilles are divided into the Windward Islands and Leeward Islands. The Windward Islands face winds that blow across them. The Leeward Islands enjoy a more sheltered position from the prevailing northeasterly winds. ◀B

Resources of Latin America

Latin America is a treasure house of natural resources. These include mineral resources, such as gold and silver, as well as energy resources, such as oil and natural gas. In addition, the region is rich in agricultural and forest resources, such as timber. These resources have drawn people to the region for centuries.

MINERAL RESOURCES Gold, silver, iron, copper, bauxite (aluminum ore), tin, lead, and nickel—all these minerals are abundant in Latin America. In addition, mines throughout the region produce precious gems, titanium, and tungsten. In fact, South America is among the world's leaders in the mining of raw materials.

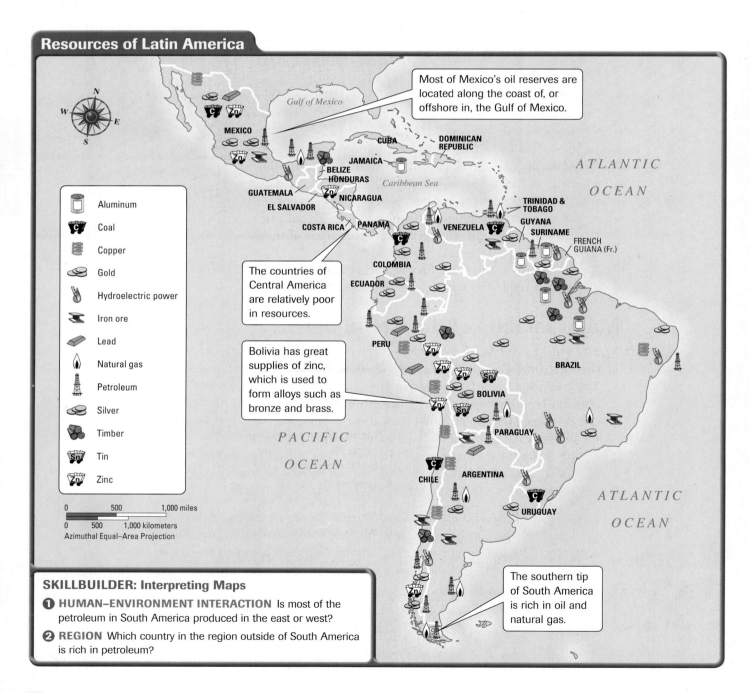

Resources of Latin America

Most of Mexico's oil reserves are located along the coast of, or offshore in, the Gulf of Mexico.

The countries of Central America are relatively poor in resources.

Bolivia has great supplies of zinc, which is used to form alloys such as bronze and brass.

The southern tip of South America is rich in oil and natural gas.

Legend:
- Aluminum
- Coal
- Copper
- Gold
- Hydroelectric power
- Iron ore
- Lead
- Natural gas
- Petroleum
- Silver
- Timber
- Tin
- Zinc

0   500   1,000 miles
0   500   1,000 kilometers
Azimuthal Equal–Area Projection

SKILLBUILDER: Interpreting Maps

❶ **HUMAN–ENVIRONMENT INTERACTION** Is most of the petroleum in South America produced in the east or west?

❷ **REGION** Which country in the region outside of South America is rich in petroleum?

Many of these minerals are mined and then exported to other parts of the world, where they are made into valuable goods. For example, Jamaica was originally a plantation economy that depended on the sale of bananas and sugar for its livelihood. Then it turned to the mining and processing of bauxite (aluminum ore) in an attempt to make the country less dependent on agriculture and tourism. Today, this resource is mainly an export that is shipped elsewhere for industrial use.

ENERGY RESOURCES Oil, coal, natural gas, uranium, and hydroelectric power are all plentiful in Latin America. Venezuela and Mexico have major oil reserves. Brazil is rich in hydroelectric power because of its many rivers (including the mighty Amazon) and waterfalls. It is also rich in oil and gas.

Trinidad has discovered vast reserves of natural gas. New factories have turned Trinidad into a major exporter of methanol and ammonia. Natural gas has also attracted developers to the island.

In Mexico and Venezuela, oil has been a very important resource. Venezuela sits on top of major oil deposits. This resource was developed into a significant oil industry. Mexico has huge oilfields centered along the Gulf coast. Because of its reserves, Mexico is able to export oil to other countries. However, changes in the global price of oil have had a great impact on the economies of these countries. ◀

Latin America has great variety in its climate and vegetation. You will read about each in the next section.

CONNECT TO THE ISSUES
RESOURCES
▶ How do the countries of the region make use of their natural resources?

Connect to THE Issues

RESOURCES

Rain Forest Medicines
Vegetation in the rain forests has yielded many products used to make modern drugs and medicines. These include quinine, which is used to treat malaria, and curare, which is used to relax muscles.

Scientists believe that many of the potential medicines and drugs of the rain forest remain undiscovered. Destroying the rain forests damages the habitats of plants or animals that might even provide a cure for cancer. In the picture below, a man is using a plant to soothe an earache.

LATIN AMERICA

SECTION 1 Assessment

① Places & Terms

Identify and explain where in the region these would be found.

- Andes Mountains
- llanos
- cerrado
- pampas
- Orinoco River
- Amazon River
- Paraná River

② Taking Notes

PLACE Review the notes you took for this section.

Landforms	
Resources	

- What types of landforms are found in Latin America?
- What is their relative location?

③ Main Ideas

a. How did the Andes Mountains affect settlement along the western coast of South America?

b. How are the landforms of the region both an advantage and disadvantage?

c. What effect did natural resources have on the development of the region?

④ Geographic Thinking

Drawing Conclusions How might the Amazon River have affected movement into the interior of South America?

Think about:

- the network of travel offered by a river system

S **See Skillbuilder Handbook, page R5.**

GeoActivities

SEEING PATTERNS Pair with a partner and draw a **sketch map** of Latin America's rivers and mountains. Use arrows to indicate the directions the rivers flow. Why does the Amazon flow all the way east across the continent even though its headwaters begin in the Andes Mountains along the west coast?

Interpreting a Precipitation Map

This map shows differences in annual precipitation throughout South America. Suppose you have been given a chance to live in either Manaus, Brazil, or Buenos Aires, Argentina, for a year. You don't want to live in a city where it rains a lot. Which city would you choose? To help make your decision, find the two cities on the Unit Atlas map on page 193. Then find their locations on this precipitation map.

THE LANGUAGE OF MAPS A **precipitation map** is a type of thematic map. Many precipitation maps show differences in annual precipitation within a given region.

SUNSHINE STATE STANDARDS
Key Standard SS.B.1.4.1 The student uses a variety of maps, geographic technologies including geographic information systems (GIS) and satellite-produced imagery, and other advanced graphic representations to depict geographic problems.

FCAT LA.B.1.4.2 Writing:
Draft and Revise

Precipitation in South America

3 Annual Precipitation 2

- < 10 in. (25 cm)
- 10-20 in. (25-50 cm)
- 20-40 in. (50-100 cm)
- 40-60 in. (100-150 cm)
- 60-80 in. (150-200 cm)
- > 80 in. (200 cm)

0 200 400 600 800 1000 Miles

0 400 800 1200 1600 Kilometers

Copyright by Rand McNally & Co.

Copyright by Rand McNally & Co.

1 The title gives you the subject matter of the map.

2 The amount of annual precipitation is shown both in inches and centimeters.

3 The key shows the colors used on the map and explains their meaning. Each color shows a different range of annual precipitation.

Map and Graph Skills Assessment

1. Making Comparisons
Where are you likely to experience more rain—in Peru or Brazil?

2. Drawing Conclusions
Does Guyana have heavy or light annual precipitation?

3. Making Inferences
Is there heavier annual precipitation in the northern or southern parts of the continent?

Climate and Vegetation

Main Ideas
- Latin America has a variety of climates, from the cold peaks of the Andes to the Amazon rain forest.
- The vegetation of Latin America ranges from grasslands to the largest rain forest in the world.

Places & Terms

rain forest

CONNECT TO THE ISSUES
RESOURCES Latin America's climate and vegetation make up a habitat that is threatened by economic development.

SUNSHINE STATE STANDARDS
Key Standard SS.B.2.4.1 The student understands how social, cultural, economic, and environmental factors contribute to the dynamic nature of regions.
FCAT LA.A.1.4.2 Reading: Strategies

A HUMAN PERSPECTIVE In the 17th century, missionaries and Indians in the area of present-day Paraguay were at times attacked by jaguars, the great cats of Latin America. In 1637, packs of jaguars roamed the countryside, attacking humans. The Indians built barricades for protection from the savage cats. But the jaguars remained a source of fear. The cats were a factor that had to be taken into account in settling and protecting towns and villages. There was no question about it—jaguars and other creatures thrived in the humid climate and thick vegetation of the tropical rain forests.

A Varied Climate and Vegetation

The climate of Latin America ranges from the hot and humid Amazon River basin to the dry and desert-like conditions of northern Mexico and southern Chile. Rain forest, desert, and savanna are all found in the region.

The vegetation varies from rain forests to grasslands and desert scrub. It ranges from the thick trees of the rain forests to mosses of the tundra.

This variety of climate and vegetation is due to several factors. First, Latin America spans a great distance on each side of the equator. Second, there are big changes in elevation because of the massive mountains in the region. Third, the warm currents of the Atlantic Ocean and the cold currents of the Pacific Ocean affect the climate.

Tropical Climate Zones

The tropical climate zones of the region produce both rain forests and the tree-dotted grasslands known as savannas. Rain forests are abundant in Central America, the Caribbean, and South America. Savannas are found in South America.

TROPICAL WET <u>Rain forests</u> are dense forests made up of different species of trees. They form a unique ecosystem—a community of plants and animals living in balance. The climate in these areas is hot and rainy year round. The largest forest is the

Vegetation of Latin America

[Map of Latin America showing vegetation zones with coordinates 110°W, 90°W, 70°W, 50°W and latitudes 20°N, 0°, 20°S, 40°S. Features labeled: Gulf of Mexico, Caribbean Sea, PACIFIC OCEAN, ATLANTIC OCEAN, Equator.]

Scale: 0 — 500 — 1,000 miles
0 — 500 — 1,000 kilometers
Azimuthal Equal–Area Projection

Legend:
- Tropical rain forest
- Tropical grassland
- Desert and dry shrub
- Temperate grassland
- Mediterranean shrub
- Deciduous and mixed forest
- Highland

SKILLBUILDER: Interpreting Maps
❶ **REGION** In what part of the region is the largest rain forest?
❷ **REGION** What form of vegetation covers most of the southeastern part of South America?

Amazon rain forest, which covers more than two million square miles of South America. Much of this rain forest is located in Brazil.

Rain forests contain many exotic plants and creatures. Scientists have counted more than 2,500 varieties of trees in the Amazon rain forest. These include the Brazil nut tree, which grows 150 feet high. Animals include the anaconda, among the largest snakes in the world, the jaguar, and the piranha, a sharp-toothed, meat-eating fish.

TROPICAL WET AND DRY Wet and dry climates, found primarily in South America, support savannas, which are grasslands dotted with trees common in tropical and subtropical regions. These areas have hot climates with seasonal rain. Savannas are found in Brazil, Colombia, and Argentina.

BACKGROUND
The anaconda lives in and near the rivers of tropical South America. It may grow as long as 25 feet.

Dry Climate Zones

Dry climate zones are found in Mexico on the North American continent and in various countries of South America. Neither Central America nor the Caribbean, though, has dry climate zones.

SEMIARID A semiarid climate is generally dry, with some rain. Vast, semiarid, grass-covered plains are often found in such climates. Desert shrubs also grow in semiarid regions. Such regions are found in Mexico, Brazil, Uruguay, and Argentina.

Vertical Climate Zones in Latin America

Climate and vegetation vary widely, depending on the elevation. The diagram below shows the main climate zones as defined by elevation, with the different plants and animals found in each zone.

SKILLBUILDER: Interpreting Graphics
❶ **HUMAN–ENVIRONMENT INTERACTION** Which zones are the most productive for growing crops?
❷ **HUMAN–ENVIRONMENT INTERACTION** What impact might vertical climate zones have on migration and settlement?

TIERRA HELADA
About 15,000 feet

SNOW LINE
The lower boundary of a snow-covered area

MOUNTAIN TUNDRA

Llamas
Sheep

TIERRA FRIA
10,000–12,000 feet

TREE LINE
Elevation above which trees tend not to grow

CLOUD FOREST
Forest near mountain peaks with constant cloud cover

Barley
Potatoes
Apples
Wheat

TIERRA TEMPLADA
6,000–6,500 feet

WET FOREST

Cotton   Coffee
Corn   Beans
Wheat   Citrus Fruit

TIERRA CALIENTE
2,500–3,000 feet

DRY FOREST

SWAMP

Cacao   Pineapple
Rice   Sugar Cane
Bananas

DESERT Parts of northern Mexico are classified as desert, as is much of the coast of Peru. The Atacama Desert is in northern Chile. Likewise, Argentina's southern zone, Patagonia, contains a desert. The deserts of the region are made up of shrubs growing in gravel or sand.

Mid-Latitude Climate Zones

The mid-latitude, moderate climate zones in the region are located south of the equator, from approximately Rio de Janeiro in Brazil southward.

HUMID SUBTROPICAL Humid subtropical areas have rainy winters and hot, humid summers. Parts of Paraguay, Uruguay, southern Brazil, southern Bolivia, and northern Argentina (including Buenos Aires) are located in humid, subtropical climates. The vegetation is varied.

MEDITERRANEAN Mediterranean climate zones experience hot, dry summers and cool, moist winters. Part of Chile along the west coast is in this zone. You have experienced a similar climate if you have ever been to California. The vegetation in this climate is mainly chaparral.

MARINE WEST COAST Marine west coast climate zones are characterized by cool, rainy winters and mild, rainy summers. One such climate region runs along the coast of southwestern South America. Parts of southern Chile and Argentina have this climate. If you have spent time in Oregon or Washington, you have experienced this type of climate. Forests are the typical vegetation.

Geographic Thinking

Seeing Patterns
A Where are most of the highland climate zones located?

HIGHLANDS Highland climate zones vary from moderate to cold, depending on elevation. Other factors influence highland climates, such as wind, sunlight, and landscape. Highland climates are found in the mountains of Mexico and South America. **A**

In the next section, you will read about how human-environment interaction affects the quality of life in Latin America.

Assessment

1 Places & Terms

Identify and explain where in the region this would be found.

• rain forest

2 Taking Notes

PLACE Review the notes you took for this section.

Climate and Vegetation

• What vegetation characterizes the Amazon River basin?
• What types of climate zones are found in Latin America?

3 Main Ideas

a. What are two reasons for the variety of climate and vegetation found in Latin America?

b. What effect might elevation have on growing crops and grazing livestock in the region?

c. What are the three main types of moderate climate zones in the region?

4 Geographic Thinking

Making Inferences How might the climate and vegetation of Latin America have affected migration, settlement, and ways of life?
Think about:

• the impact of deserts and rain forests on settlement

RESEARCH LINKS
CLASSZONE.COM

GeoActivity

ASKING GEOGRAPHIC QUESTIONS Research on the Internet the climate and vegetation in your state. Devise three geographic questions, such as "What is the dominant climate zone in my state?" Choose one of your questions and then write a **paragraph** explaining your findings. Be sure to list your sources.

Human–Environment Interaction

Main Ideas

• The people of Latin America have altered the land through agriculture and urbanization.

• Tourism is having a growing impact on the environment of Latin America.

Places & Terms

slash-and-burn

terraced farming

push factors

pull factors

infrastructure

CONNECT TO THE ISSUES

INCOME GAP The income gap can be seen in the landless poor, the cities, and the tourist industry.

SUNSHINE STATE STANDARDS
Key Standard SS.B.2.4.2 The student understands past and present trends in human migration and cultural interaction and their impact on physical and human systems.

Other Standards SS.B.2.4.4

FCAT LA.A.1.4.2 Reading: Strategies

A HUMAN PERSPECTIVE High in the Andes Mountains, in what is present-day Peru, the ancient Inca needed fields in which to grow crops. By the 1200s, in the highlands around their capital of Cuzco and elsewhere, the Inca carved terraces out of the steep sides of the Andes Mountains. They built irrigation channels to bring water to the terraces. Because of their activity, they were able to grow crops for thousands of people on the slopes of previously barren hillsides. In this way, the Inca altered their environment to meet their needs.

Agriculture Reshapes the Environment

Native peoples were the first in the Western Hemisphere to change their environment to grow food. They burned the forest to clear land for planting and diverted streams to irrigate crops. They built raised fields in swampy areas and carved terraces out of hillsides.

SLASH–AND–BURN To clear fields, native peoples used the **slash-and-burn** technique—they cut trees, brush, and grasses and burned the debris to clear the field. This method was particularly effective in humid and tropical areas.

Today, farmers practice the same method as they move into the Amazon River basin in Brazil and clear land for farming in the rain forest. But the non-landowning poor who are clearing and then settling the

Slash-and-Burn Farming

❶ Farmers cut trees, brush, and grasses to clear a field.

❷ They then burn the debris and use the ashes to fertilize the soil.

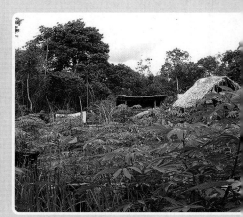

❸ Farmers plant crops for a year or two, which exhausts the soil.

land sometimes use destructive farming practices. After a few years, they find that the soil is exhausted—all the nutrients have been drained from the land. Then they move on and clear a new patch to farm. This is one of the reasons for the steady shrinking of the rain forests. (For more about the rain forest, see Chapter 11, Section 1, page 245.) ◀A

TERRACED FARMING **Terraced farming** is an ancient technique for growing crops on hillsides or mountain slopes. It is an especially important technique in the mountainous areas of the region. Farmers and workers cut step-like horizontal fields into hillsides and slopes, which allow steep land to be cultivated for crops. The technique reduces soil erosion. As you read earlier, the Inca practiced terraced farming hundreds of years ago in Peru. The Aztecs of Mexico also used terraced farming.

Urbanization: The Move to the Cities

Throughout Latin America, people are moving from rural areas into the cities. They leave farms and villages in search of jobs and a better life. Cities have grown at such a rapid pace in Latin America that today the region is as urban as Europe or North America.

FROM COUNTRY TO CITY Argentina, Chile, and Uruguay are the most highly urbanized countries in South America. In these countries, more than 85 percent of the people live in cities. In Brazil, too, most people live in cities and towns.

People move to the cities in the hope of improving their lives. Many people in rural areas struggle to make a living and feed their families by subsistence farming. With a great deal of effort, they grow barely enough food to keep themselves and their families alive.

Both push and pull factors are at work in moving peasants and farmers off the land and drawing them to the cities. **Push factors** are factors that "push" people to leave rural areas. They include poor medical care, poor education, low-paying jobs, and ownership of the land by a few rich people. **Pull factors** are factors that "pull" people toward cities. They include higher-paying jobs, better schools, and better medical care. ◀B

RAPIDLY GROWING CITIES Six cities in South America rank among the region's largest in population. These include São Paulo and Rio de Janeiro in Brazil, Buenos Aires in Argentina, Lima in Peru, Bogotá in Colombia, and Santiago in Chile. But the most populous city in all of Latin America is Mexico City. Estimates of its population vary from approximately 18 to 20 million people for the city alone to about 30 million for the entire greater metropolitan area.

Similar problems afflict cities throughout the region. Slums spread over larger and larger urban areas. Often unemployment and crime increase. In addition to social problems, there are many environmental problems. These include high levels of air

CONNECT TO THE ISSUES
RESOURCES
▶A What is the impact of slash-and-burn on the rain forest?

CONNECT TO THE ISSUES
INCOME GAP
▶B How might push and pull factors affect the gap between rich and poor?

4 Fields often remain barren or are reclaimed by brush, grass, trees, and scrub.

Growth of Cities, 1968–2000

People in Millions

20

15

10

5

0

Buenos Aires   Lima   Mexico City   Rio de Janeiro   Santiago   São Paulo

■ 1968   ■ 2000

SOURCE: *The Times Atlas of the World*

SKILLBUILDER: Interpreting Graphs

❶ **MAKING COMPARISONS** Which city had the largest population in 1968? In 2000?

❷ **MAKING COMPARISONS** Which two cities showed the biggest increase in population between 1968 and 2000?

PLACE Pedestrians crowd a street during a festival in Buenos Aires, Argentina.

pollution from cars and factories. Some cities have shortages of drinkable water as local supplies are used up and underwater supplies are drained.

To make matters worse, local governments cannot afford facilities to handle the population increase. This **infrastructure** includes such things as sewers, transportation, electricity, and housing.

Tourism: Positive and Negative Impacts

Tourism is a growth industry throughout Latin America. It is especially important in Mexico and the Caribbean. But despite the money it brings in to the economies of the region, tourism is a mixed blessing.

ADVANTAGES OF TOURISM Every year millions of tourists visit the resorts of Latin America, spending money and helping to create jobs. New hotels, restaurants, boutiques, and other businesses have sprung up on the islands of the Caribbean and in Mexico to serve the tourist trade. Luxurious cruise ships anchor in the ports of the region. They carry travelers who spend money on souvenirs and trips around the islands. Lavish restaurants serve expensive meals to these tourists. Staffing those ships, hotels, and restaurants are local people who profit from the visitors in their midst.

Resorts offer many activities that provide jobs for local residents. For example, local guides conduct tours of the natural wonders and beautiful scenery. Local companies may offer guided rafting trips down rivers. Sailing and snorkeling expeditions into the waters of the Caribbean and Pacific reveal exotic marine life. All of these activities bring money into the region and employ local people.

In this way, tourism can play a part in reducing the income gap between rich and poor. Jobs in hotels, restaurants, and resorts raise incomes and give the local people a stake in their society.

DISADVANTAGES OF TOURISM Despite the income and jobs that tourism brings to various places in Latin America, it causes problems as well. As resorts are built in previously unspoiled settings, congestion occurs and pollution increases.

The tourism industry often puts a great strain on the local communities where it builds its resorts. Further, there is an obvious gap between rich tourists and less well-off local residents. This has produced resentment and hostility in places such as Jamaica in the Caribbean and Rio de Janeiro in Brazil.

More important, local governments can run up large public debts by borrowing money to build tourist facilities. Airports and harbors must be constructed. Hotels and resorts must be built. Sewage systems and shopping areas must be expanded.

Often the owners of these hotels and airlines do not live in the tourist country. Typically, they send their profits back home. Further, these absentee owners often make decisions that are not in the tourist country's best interest. The owners may be able to influence local elections and business decisions. ◀ⓒ

In the next chapter, you will read about the human geography of Latin America, including its history, culture, economics, and daily life.

CONNECT TO THE ISSUES
DEMOCRACY
ⓒ▶ How might absentee ownership of tourist facilities undermine democracy in a tourist country?

HUMAN–ENVIRONMENT INTERACTION
A luxury cruise ship is docked in the beautiful harbor of Charlotte Amalie, St. Thomas in the Virgin Islands.
What might be the impact of tourists on the local economy?

LATIN AMERICA

SECTION 3 Assessment

① Places & Terms

Identify and explain the significance of each in the region.

- slash-and-burn
- terraced farming
- push factors
- pull factors
- infrastructure

② Taking Notes

HUMAN-ENVIRONMENT INTERACTION Review the notes you took for this section.

Human-Environment Interaction

- What are the steps in slash-and-burn farming?
- What are some of the problems of cities in the region?

③ Main Ideas

a. How have humans changed the environment in Latin America to make it more suitable for agriculture?

b. What factors have drawn people from the countryside into the cities of the region?

c. What are some of the advantages of tourism to the Caribbean?

④ Geographic Thinking

Making Inferences How might the cities of Latin America deal with the increasing demands placed on them by their expanding populations? **Think about:**

- water, sewage, and electricity
- transportation and housing

Ⓢ **See Skillbuilder Handbook, page R4.**

SEEING PATTERNS Pair with a partner and create a **travel poster** about a place in the region that you would like to visit. Show various activities and sports available at the place you choose.

Chapter 9 Assessment

VISUAL SUMMARY
PHYSICAL GEOGRAPHY OF LATIN AMERICA

Landforms

Major Mountain Ranges: Andes, Sierra Madres

Major Rivers: Orinoco, Amazon, Paraná

Major Plains: pampas of Argentina and Uruguay, llanos of Colombia and Venezuela, cerrado of Brazil

Resources

• Latin America has important mineral and energy resources.

• Venezuela and Mexico have major oil reserves.

Climate and Vegetation

• The variety of climate and vegetation in Latin America is caused by the great distance from north to south, variations in elevation, and ocean currents.

• Latin America has many rain forests.

Human-Environment Interaction

• Two techniques that farmers have used in the region are slash-and-burn and terraced farming.

• Cities in Latin America have grown at a rapid pace, and the region is now highly urbanized.

• Tourism has both advantages and disadvantages for the region.

Reviewing Places & Terms

A. Briefly explain the importance of each of the following.

1. Andes Mountains
2. llanos
3. pampas
4. Orinoco River
5. Amazon River
6. rain forest
7. slash-and-burn
8. terraced farming
9. push factors
10. infrastructure

B. Answer the questions about vocabulary in complete sentences.

11. What two countries does the Orinoco River drain?
12. Where are the Andes Mountains located?
13. What agricultural technique involves using ashes to fertilize the soil?
14. What characteristics do the pampas and llanos have in common?
15. What are some of the problems that afflict cities throughout the region?
16. Which river drains the largest rain forest in the region?
17. What are some factors that are pushing farmers off the land and into the cities?
18. Which is the northernmost of the great rivers of South America?
19. What farming technique is especially useful in mountainous regions?
20. What are the main products of the pampas?

Main Ideas

Landforms and Resources (pp. 201–206)

1. How have the Andes Mountains affected settlement in South America?
2. What are the two main purposes for which the plains and grasslands of the region are used?
3. What are the three major island groups of the Caribbean?
4. What Caribbean island is rich in natural gas, and what impact has this had on the economy?

Climate and Vegetation (pp. 207–209)

5. In what part of the region are savannas most common?
6. How do the vertical climate zones of Latin America affect agriculture?
7. What is the dominant vegetation of the Amazon river basin?

Human-Environment Interaction (pp. 210–213)

8. What is the main disadvantage of the slash-and-burn method of growing crops?
9. What factors tend to pull people into the cities from their farms?
10. What are some of the disadvantages of tourism in the region?

Critical Thinking

1. Using Your Notes

Use your completed chart to answer these questions.

Landforms	
Resources	

   a. Where are most of the mountains of South America located?

   b. What are some examples of mineral and energy resources found in abundance in Latin America?

2. Geographic Themes

   a. **LOCATION** Where are some of the largest plains found in Latin America?

   b. **REGION** What are the settlement patterns of South America in terms of the interior and the coast?

3. Identifying Themes

Based on landforms and climate, which areas of Latin America would be the least agriculturally productive? Which of the five themes are reflected in your answer?

4. Drawing Conclusions

What factors must people in the region consider when they are deciding whether to move from the country to the city?

5. Making Comparisons

What are some of the advantages and disadvantages of tourism to a community?

Additional Test Practice, pp. S1–S37

TEST PRACTICE
CLASSZONE.COM

Geographic Skills: Interpreting Maps

The Tributaries of the Amazon

Use the map to answer the following questions.

1. **MOVEMENT** In what general direction do the Amazon and its tributaries flow?

2. **PLACE** Into which ocean does the Amazon empty?

3. **REGION** What countries are drained by the Amazon and its tributaries?

Create your own sketch map of the physical geography of Latin America. Combine the information from this map with the information from the landforms map on page 203.

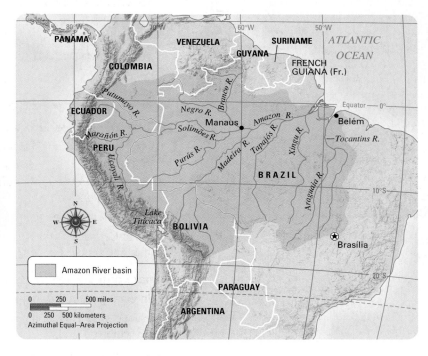

INTERNET ACTIVITY

Use the links at **classzone.com** to do research on the most rapidly growing cities in Latin America. Focus on the impact that rapid growth has on the residents of a city.

Writing About Geography Write a report of your findings. Include a map that shows the fastest growing cities. Combine it with a chart that lists common problems of rapid growth.

HUMAN GEOGRAPHY OF LATIN AMERICA
A Blending of Cultures

Four Subregions of Latin America

Legend:
- Mexico
- Central America and the Caribbean
- Spanish-Speaking South America
- Brazil

GeoFocus

Which different cultures have blended in Latin America?

Taking Notes In your notebook, copy a cluster diagram like the one below. For each subregion of Latin America, take notes about its history, economics, culture, and modern life.

Mexico — Latin America — Central America and the Caribbean — Spanish-Speaking South America — Brazil

Mexico

Main Ideas
• Native and Spanish influences have shaped Mexico.
• Mexico's economy may expand because of democracy and trade.

Places & Terms
Spanish conquest
Tenochtitlán
Institutional Revolutionary Party (PRI)
mestizo
maquiladoras
NAFTA

CONNECT TO THE ISSUES
DEMOCRACY Economic development is helping to shape the increasingly democratic culture of Mexico.

SUNSHINE STATE STANDARDS
Key Standard SS.B.2.4.2 The student understands past and present trends in . . .

Other Standards SS.A.3.4.3

FCAT LA.A.1.4.2 Reading: Strategies
PLACE Independence Monument stands at a busy intersection of the Paseo de la Reforma in Mexico City.

A HUMAN PERSPECTIVE Quetzalcoatl (keht·SAHL·koh·AHT·l) was a god worshiped by the Toltec and Aztec peoples of Mexico and Central America. According to Native American legend, Quetzalcoatl traveled east across the sea. It was said that he would return some day, bringing peace. One day, messengers brought Montezuma, the Aztec emperor, news that strangers had arrived from across the sea. Montezuma thought that these strangers might be Quetzalcoatl and his servants. Instead, it was Hernando Cortés and his soldiers, who would claim the land for Spain. When the Spanish landed, the cultures of two widely separated regions came into contact, which forever changed the Aztec and Spanish worlds—and made Mexico what it is today.

Colonialism and Independence

The history of Mexico is the story of the conflict between native peoples and settlers from Spain and the Spanish conquest of the region. The result was a blending of Indian and Spanish cultures that has greatly affected Mexico's development.

NATIVE AMERICANS AND THE SPANISH CONQUEST The territory of present-day Mexico was originally occupied by many different native peoples. These people included the residents of Teotihuacán, an early city-state, the Toltecs, the Maya (in the Yucatán Peninsula), and the Aztecs, as well as a number of other smaller groups or tribes.

The rich fabric of native life in Mexico was torn apart by the **Spanish conquest.** In 1519, Hernando Cortés landed on the coast of Mexico. Cortés and his men marched into the interior of the country until they reached the Aztec city of **Tenochtitlán** (teh·NOH·tee·TLAHN), the site today of Mexico City. By 1521, Cortés and his soldiers had conquered the Aztecs.

COLONY AND COUNTRY For centuries afterward, Mexico was a part of the Spanish empire. Mexico's abundant resources, such as gold and silver, made it a great prize. In 1821, Mexico achieved independence from Spain under Agustín de Iturbide, who proclaimed himself emperor in 1822. Then,

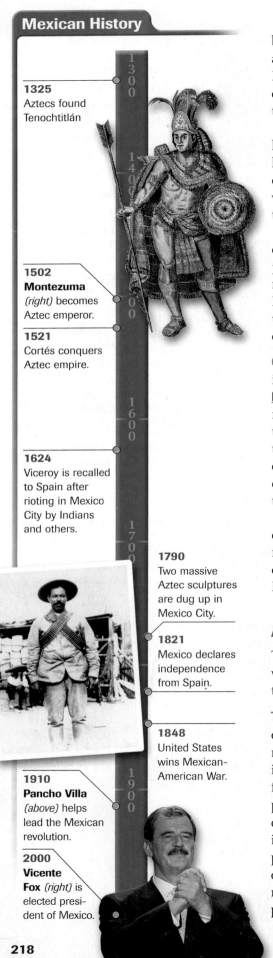

1325
Aztecs found
Tenochtitlán

1502
Montezuma
(right) becomes
Aztec emperor.

1521
Cortés conquers
Aztec empire.

1624
Viceroy is recalled
to Spain after
rioting in Mexico
City by Indians
and others.

1790
Two massive
Aztec sculptures
are dug up in
Mexico City.

1821
Mexico declares
independence
from Spain.

1848
United States
wins Mexican-
American War.

1910
Pancho Villa
(above) helps
lead the Mexican
revolution.

2000
**Vicente
Fox** *(right)* is
elected presi-
dent of Mexico.

beginning in the mid-19th century, Benito Juárez led a reform movement and became president of Mexico. He worked for separation of church and state, better educational opportunities, and a more even distribution of the land.

Under Spanish rule, and even after independence, land had been unequally distributed. A few rich landowners owned haciendas (estates or ranches) that covered most of Mexico's farmland. Landless peasants worked on these haciendas. Juárez tried to remedy this problem by giving some land to the peasants.

Juárez was eventually succeeded by Porfirio Díaz, a dishonest politician who ruled Mexico for more than 30 years. His harsh and corrupt rule brought about a revolution and civil war, led by Francisco Madero, Pancho Villa, and Emiliano Zapata. A new constitution was adopted in 1917. It redistributed nearly half of Mexico's farmland to peasants.

ONE-PARTY RULE In 1929, a new political party arose in Mexico. This was the **Institutional Revolutionary Party (PRI).** It helped to introduce democracy and maintain political stability for much of the 20th century. It continued the policy of redistributing land to the peasants. However, because it did not tolerate opposition, fraud and corruption undermined the democratic process. In 1997, two parties opposed to the PRI won a large number of seats in the congress.

In 2000, Vicente Fox, the National Action Party candidate, was elected president of Mexico. For the first time in 71 years, the PRI did not control Mexico's congress or presidency. This election showed that Mexico was gradually becoming more democratic. Ⓐ

A Meeting of Cultures

The culture of Mexico is a blend of Spanish influences with original native cultures. Mexico's native population has helped to shape the country's self-image.

THE AZTECS AND THE SPANISH Before the arrival of the Spanish, Mexico was a place of many advanced native cultures. For example, the Aztec empire arose in the Valley of Mexico, a mountain basin about 7,500 feet above sea level. According to legend, the Aztec people arrived there around A.D. 1200 from the deserts of northern Mexico. Then they built their capital of Tenochtitlán, a city of beautiful temples, palaces, gardens, and lakes. Canals linked parts of the city. People grew food on islands in Lake Texcoco surrounding the city. Tenochtitlán was where the Aztecs practiced human sacrifice in their temples.

CONNECT TO THE ISSUES
DEMOCRACY
Ⓐ How did the PRI both help and hinder democracy?

218

When Cortés and the Spanish conquered the Aztec empire, they destroyed most of the capital and built Mexico City on top of the ruins of Tenochtitlán. Today, though, ancient Aztec ruins and relics keep turning up as modern projects in Mexico City are built. Like the ruins, the past is still very much present in Mexico. ◄ⓑ

● **Geographic Thinking** ◄

Seeing Patterns

ⓑ What does Mexico City's site on top of the Aztec city suggest about the location?

The Spanish brought their language and Catholic religion, both of which dominate modern Mexico. In spite of Spanish cultural diffusion, though, Mexico's Indian heritage remains very strong. In fact, the name of the country comes from *Mexica,* an older name for the Aztecs. Mexico has a large **mestizo** population—people of mixed Spanish and Native American heritage.

MEXICAN PAINTERS Mexico has a long heritage of architecture and art. In the 20th century, Mexico's tradition of painting took the form of public art. Many important painters portrayed the history of Mexico on the walls of its public buildings. Among the important Mexican mural painters of the 20th century were José Orozco, Diego Rivera, David Siqueiros, and Juan O'Gorman. (See the Diego Rivera mural showing the city of Tenochtitlán on page 186.) Frida Kahlo was an important Mexican painter known for her self-portraits. Most of the important Mexican painters blended European and Native American influences.

AN ARCHITECTURAL HERITAGE The Native Americans constructed beautiful temples and public buildings, often in the shape of pyramids. At Teotihuacán, for example, the people built a city of pyramids, many of which were topped with temples. The Aztec city of Tenochtitlán was filled with temples and palaces before it was demolished by the Spanish. The Spanish buildings included beautiful missions that were scattered throughout the territory they conquered. Later the Spanish built huge cathedrals, such as the Metropolitan Cathedral in Mexico City. This cathedral is located on the main square, or zocalo, of the city.

HUMAN–ENVIRONMENT INTERACTION
This painting by Juan O'Gorman (1905-1982) portrays Father Miguel Hidalgo, a Mexican priest and a leader of the revolt against Spanish rule in 1810. **What does the painting suggest about Hidalgo's support among the people?**

Economics: Cities and Factories

Mexico continues to struggle with two main economic challenges. First, it is attempting to close a long-standing gap between rich and poor people. Second, it is attempting to develop a modern industrial economy. Mexico had traditionally been an agricultural society, but it started to industrialize in the middle of the 20th century.

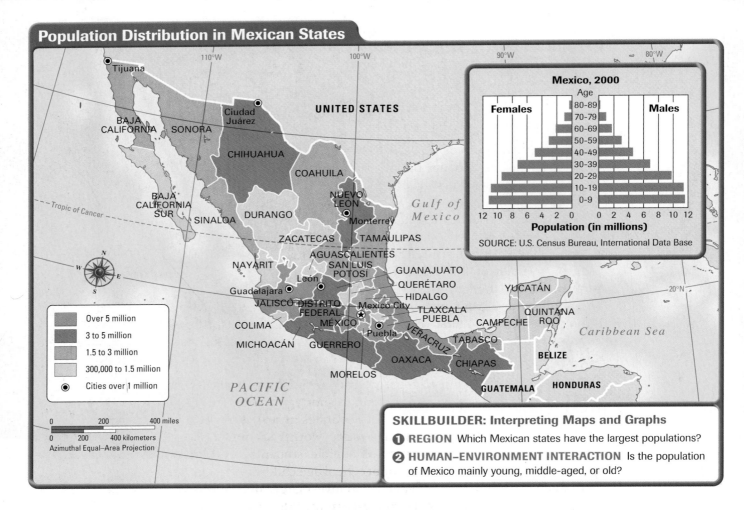

Population Distribution in Mexican States

Mexico, 2000

Age
80–89
70–79
60–69
50–59
40–49
30–39
20–29
10–19
0–9

Females | Males

Population (in millions)

SOURCE: U.S. Census Bureau, International Data Base

Over 5 million
3 to 5 million
1.5 to 3 million
300,000 to 1.5 million
Cities over 1 million

Azimuthal Equal–Area Projection

SKILLBUILDER: Interpreting Maps and Graphs

❶ REGION Which Mexican states have the largest populations?

❷ HUMAN–ENVIRONMENT INTERACTION Is the population of Mexico mainly young, middle-aged, or old?

POPULATION AND THE CITIES Mexicans are moving to cities because they see economic opportunities there. Jobs in cities provide a way to narrow the gap between rich and poor because such jobs pay more than those in rural areas. Mexico's population of about 52 million in 1970 almost doubled by the year 2000. Its population is largely very young.

OIL AND MANUFACTURING Mexico's economy includes a large industry based on its oil reserves in and along the coast of the Gulf of Mexico. Mexico has emphasized its oil industry as an important part of developing an industrial economy. The profits from oil have helped to finance development, especially in manufacturing industries.

Manufacturing is the most important part of Mexico's recent economic development. Many of the new factories are located in the north of the country, along the border with the United States. **Maquiladoras** are factories in Mexico that assemble imported materials into finished products that are then exported, mostly to the United States. These products include electronic equipment, clothing, and furniture.

Mexico is a vital member, along with the United States and Canada, of **NAFTA** (North American Free Trade Agreement). This important trade agreement has created a huge zone of cooperation on trade and economic issues. Trade is expected to contribute to the economic prosperity of the member nations, creating jobs for millions of people. Under NAFTA, import tariffs on manufactured goods are being slowly reduced and eventually will disappear.

Mexican Life Today

The people of Mexico face big challenges in today's world. Jobs, emigration, and education are foremost among their concerns. Many of these issues relate to the income gap between rich and poor.

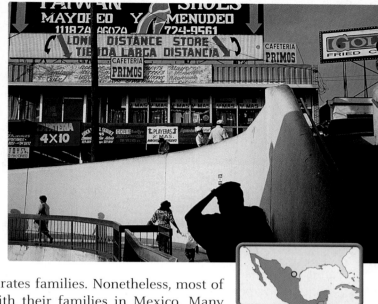

EMIGRATION Emigration has had an impact on family life in Mexico. Mexico shares a 2,000-mile border with the United States. Many workers leave Mexico and travel to the United States in search of work. This separates families. Nonetheless, most of these workers remain in touch with their families in Mexico. Many send money back to their native villages. Often, after a year or two working in the United States, they return to Mexico with savings to help improve living conditions for their extended families.

MOVEMENT
Pedestrians use a walkway in crossing from Nuevo Laredo, Mexico, into Laredo, Texas. Shop signs are in English and Spanish.

WORK AND SCHOOL The rapidly growing population and various government policies have contributed to a shortage of jobs. This has led many Mexicans to migrate to the United States in search of work.

Without education and training, young workers cannot find good jobs. In recent years, attendance of eligible students at school has improved. Today, about 85 percent of school-age children attend school. In the coming years, Mexico will have to invest large sums in education to provide a better life for its young citizens. Education will become even more important as Mexico becomes more industrialized. ◀ⓒ

CONNECT TO THE ISSUES
INCOME GAP
▶ How might the income gap be narrowed in Mexico?

In the next section, you will read about Central America and the Caribbean. This subregion links North America and South America.

SECTION 1 Assessment

❶ Places & Terms

Identify and explain the following terms.

- Spanish conquest
- Tenochtitlán
- Institutional Revolutionary Party (PRI)
- mestizo
- maquiladoras
- NAFTA

❷ Taking Notes

REGION Review the notes you took for this section.

- Which two main cultures blended to form modern Mexico?
- Where do most of Mexico's people live today?

❸ Main Ideas

a. How might democratic reforms and improved trade agreements contribute to a stronger economy in Mexico?

b. What effect might Mexico's young population have on its development?

c. In what ways have Native American and Spanish influences shaped Mexico?

❹ Geographic Thinking

Making Generalizations
How might a shortage of jobs in Mexico affect the movement of its people?
Think about:

- why one might travel to the United States in search of work
- what factors in Mexico might lead people to move

GeoActivity

MAKING COMPARISONS Pair with a partner and make a **chart** of the ten most heavily populated states of Mexico arranged in order from most to least heavily populated. Then compare your chart with a map, and mark those states that are closest to the U.S. border.

Central America and the Caribbean

A HUMAN PERSPECTIVE Central America forms an isthmus, a land bridge between North and South America. It also divides two oceans. This geographic fact has made the region attractive to the United States and other major world powers and has helped to keep the area fragmented and politically unstable. For example, in the early 20th century, the United States wanted to build a canal across Panama that would connect the Atlantic and Pacific oceans. In 1903, Panama was still a province of Colombia, which did not like the idea. The United States encouraged a revolution in Panama, and when it won its independence, Panama granted the United States a ten-mile-wide zone in which to build a canal. Central America had become a crossroads of world trade.

Native and Colonial Central America

Central America is a cultural hearth as well as a crossroads. A **cultural hearth** is a place from which important ideas spread. Usually, it is the heartland or place of origin of a major culture. The Mayan people built a great civilization in the area that spread throughout the region. The homeland of the Maya stretched from southern Mexico into northern Central America. During the 800s, the Maya began to abandon many of their cities. Why they did so remains a mystery to be solved by archaeologists.

Wooden snake carved by a Taino artist

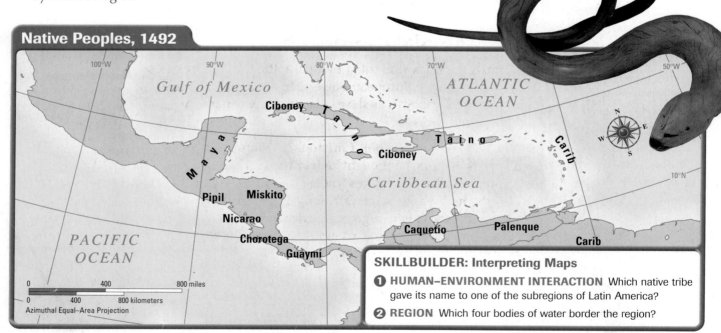

Native Peoples, 1492

Gulf of Mexico

Maya

Ciboney

Taino

Ciboney

Taino

ATLANTIC OCEAN

Carib

Caribbean Sea

Pipil

Miskito

Nicarao

Chorotega

Guaymi

PACIFIC OCEAN

Caquetío

Palenque

Carib

SKILLBUILDER: Interpreting Maps

❶ **HUMAN–ENVIRONMENT INTERACTION** Which native tribe gave its name to one of the subregions of Latin America?

❷ **REGION** Which four bodies of water border the region?

0   400   800 miles
0   400   800 kilometers
Azimuthal Equal–Area Projection

MAYAN INFLUENCE The Maya built many cities with temples and palaces in present-day Belize, Guatemala, El Salvador, and Honduras. Each city was an independent state ruled by a god-king and served as a center for religious ceremony and trade. One of their most spectacular cities was Tikal, located in the dense, steamy jungle of northern Guatemala, considered the center of Mayan civilization. The pyramids at Tikal were among the tallest structures in the Americas until the 20th century. The influence of the Maya spread over a region from Mexico to El Salvador. The Mayan culture was carried to other regions through military alliances and trade.

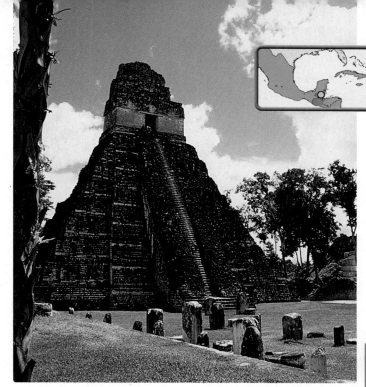

HUMAN–ENVIRONMENT INTERACTION This pyramid at Tikal towers over the great plaza of the ancient city. A temple sits on top of the pyramid. **What might this and similar buildings at Tikal suggest about Mayan civilization?**

THE SPANISH IN CENTRAL AMERICA The Spanish conquest of the Aztecs in Mexico opened the door to Spanish control of Central America. Spain ruled Central America until the 19th century. Mexico declared its independence from Spain in 1821. Up to that point, Central America had been governed from Mexico. In 1823, however, the whole region declared its independence from Mexico and took the name of the **United Provinces of Central America.**

By the late 1830s, the United Provinces had split into separate nations. These became El Salvador, Nicaragua, Costa Rica, Guatemala, and Honduras. Later, Panama broke off from Colombia and became an independent country in Central America. Belize, a former British colony, broke away from British Honduras.

Native and Colonial Caribbean

Geographic Thinking

Using the Atlas
A Use the maps on pages 216 and 222. Why might the Caribbean have been settled by more European powers than was Central America?

Although Central America was ruled by Spain, the Caribbean was settled and claimed by many European powers. In addition, Africans who were brought to the Caribbean as slaves played an important role in the settling of the Caribbean. **A**

CARIBBEAN INFLUENCES When Christopher Columbus reached the Caribbean islands in 1492, he thought he had reached the East Indies in Asia. Therefore, he called the natives "Indians." The inhabitants of these islands called themselves the Taino (TY·noh). The Spanish settled some of the islands and established sugar plantations, which were well suited to the climate and soil of the islands. They attempted to use the Taino as forced labor, but many of the natives died from disease and mistreatment.

To replace the Taino, European slave traders brought Africans to the Caribbean by force and put them to work on plantations. As a result, Africans have had a lasting influence on Caribbean life and culture.

Caribbean Colonies

Country	Colony	Major Cultural Influences
Spain	Cuba, Dominican Republic, Puerto Rico	Spanish language Catholic religion
France	Haiti, Guadeloupe, Martinique	French language Catholic religion
Great Britain	Jamaica, Barbados, St. Lucia, St. Vincent, Grenada, Trinidad and Tobago, British Virgin Islands	English language Protestant and Catholic religions
Netherlands	Netherlands Antilles	Dutch language Protestant religion
Denmark	Danish West Indies [1]	Danish language [2] Protestant religion

[1] Became U.S. Virgin Islands in 1917. [2] English is now the official language.

SKILLBUILDER: Interpreting Charts

1 REGION Which European country had the most colonies in the Caribbean?

2 PLACE In the colonies of which European countries was the Catholic religion dominant?

A COLONIAL MOSAIC By the 19th century, the Spanish, French, British, Dutch, and Danish all claimed islands in the Caribbean. Most of the European powers were there to profit from the sugar trade. This trade depended on the forced labor of workers brought in chains from Africa.

CARIBBEAN INDEPENDENCE The first independence movement in Latin America began as a slave revolt in the Caribbean on the island of Haiti. In the 18th century, Haiti was a French colony with an important sugar industry. Africans brought to the island by force worked on the sugar plantations and other plantations. In the 1790s, Toussaint L'Ouverture (too·SAN·loo·vehr·TOOR) led a slave rebellion in Haiti and took over the government of the island. By 1804, Haiti had achieved independence from France. Cuba achieved independence from Spain in 1898 as a result of the Spanish-American War. After an occupation by United States forces, the island became self-governing in 1902. Jamaica and Trinidad and Tobago did not achieve full independence from Great Britain until 1962.

Cultural Blends

Central America and the Caribbean are close to each other geographically, and their cultures show a blending of influences. This mixture affects everything from religion to language.

CULTURE OF CENTRAL AMERICA As you've read, the culture of Central America blends two major elements: Native American influences with those of Spanish settlers. The Spanish were the dominant group of European settlers in Central America—their language remains dominant in the area today. Catholicism is the major religion, although Protestant missionaries are active in the region.

The Spanish took land away from the natives of the region. The conquerors cut down forests, opened up land for grazing livestock, and introduced new crops, such as wheat. They created large farms and ranches, built towns, and moved the native peoples off the land and into the towns. All this altered the way of life in the region.

CULTURE OF THE CARIBBEAN A greater variety of influences was at work in the Caribbean. The Spanish, French, British, Danish, and Dutch existed side by side with the African and Native American. Residents of the islands are of European, African, or mixed ancestry. B

African influences were especially important. Most of the people are descendants of the African slaves brought to the islands to work on the

Geographic Thinking

Making Comparisons
B How does the culture of the Caribbean differ from the culture of Central America?

growing up in...Cuba

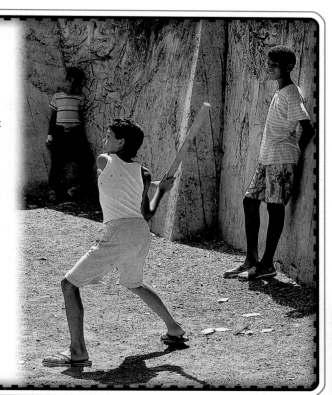

This boy is playing baseball, a sport as popular in Cuba as it is in the United States. Baseball traveled from the United States to Cuba in the late 1800s. Baseball is considered the island's national pastime, just as it is in the United States.

Young people in Cuba receive many benefits from the Communist government, including free education and health care. The education system extends from preschool programs through college to graduate programs. However, young people, like all Cubans, live in a police state that limits their economic and political freedoms.

If you lived in Cuba, here are some rights you would enjoy and restrictions you would face:

- You would receive a free education.
- You would receive free medical care.
- You would attend school from age 6 to somewhere between ages 11 and 15.
- You could attend free concerts, ballets, and plays.
- Your freedom of speech and writing would be restricted.
- Your economic opportunities would be very limited.

sugar plantations. They left a lasting mark on all aspects of culture in the islands, including village life, markets, and choice of crops.

The religions of the Caribbean include Catholic and Protestant, as well as Santeria, which combines certain African practices and rituals with Catholic elements. Voodoo is practiced on the island of Haiti. Rastafarianism is a religious and political movement based in Jamaica.

Spanish is spoken on the most populous islands in the Caribbean: Cuba, with a population of about 11 million, and the Dominican Republic, with a population of about 8.5 million. There are also many French speakers (Haiti alone has a population of more than 6 million). English dominates in Jamaica, with a population of almost 3 million. There is a smattering of Dutch and Danish also spoken in the region.

Economics: Jobs and People

In general, most of the people in the countries of the region are poor. This is, in part, a legacy of colonialism. The early success of the sugar crop benefited colonial planters, not the native or African laborers. Also, the region faced competition in the sugar market, and eventually the sugar trade declined. Further, the fact that natural resources were exported and not used locally left the region economically weakened.

FARMING AND TRADE Sugar cane plantations in the Caribbean provide the region's largest export crop. Other important export crops are bananas, citrus fruits, coffee, and spices. All these crops are well adapted to the climate and soil of the region. Many people work on the plantations that grow crops for export. But the pay is poor, and as a result, average per-capita income in the Caribbean is very low.

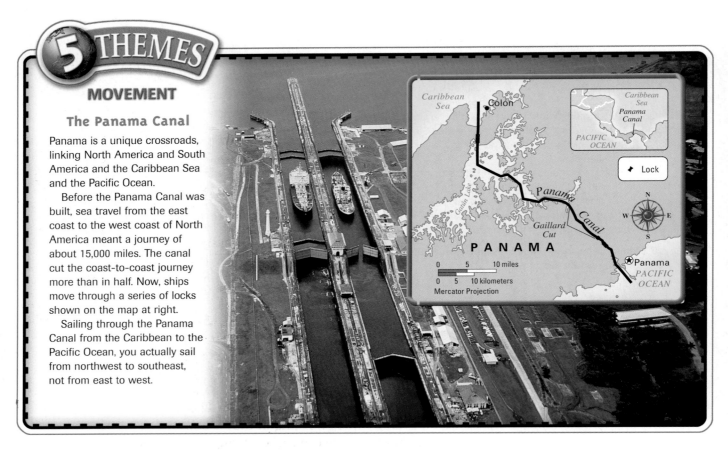

MOVEMENT

The Panama Canal

Panama is a unique crossroads, linking North America and South America and the Caribbean Sea and the Pacific Ocean.

Before the Panama Canal was built, sea travel from the east coast to the west coast of North America meant a journey of about 15,000 miles. The canal cut the coast-to-coast journey more than in half. Now, ships move through a series of locks shown on the map at right.

Sailing through the Panama Canal from the Caribbean to the Pacific Ocean, you actually sail from northwest to southeast, not from east to west.

In Central America, too, the main source of income is the commercial farming practiced on large plantations. These farms produce 10 percent of the world's coffee and 10 percent of the world's bananas. Central America's mines and forests also provide resources for export. ▶

Trade is important because of the **Panama Canal,** which cuts through the land bridge and connects the Atlantic and Pacific oceans. Ships from both hemispheres use the canal, making Panama a crossroads of world trade. The canal made possible the exchange of both goods and ideas.

WHERE PEOPLE LIVE AND WHY Population patterns in Central America and the Caribbean are directly related to their economies. Both Central America and the Caribbean have populations of between 30 and 40 million people. But in Central America, most of the people make their living on farms and, as a result, live in rural areas.

Many of the islands in the Caribbean are densely populated. More than 11 million people live on Cuba, the largest of the islands. Most people live in urban areas, where they hope to find jobs in tourism. The cities attract people who are seeking a better way of life. Unfortunately, many end up living in slums. The region is working to find a way to channel more of the profits from tourism and farming to benefit local communities.

Popular Culture, Tourism, and Jobs

Education and jobs are a major concern to the people of Central America and the Caribbean. Music, heavily influenced and shaped by the African heritage in the region, is an important part of the popular culture of Central America and the Caribbean.

CONNECT TO THE ISSUES
RESOURCES
◀ What resources are exported from Central America and the Caribbean?

MUSIC OF THE CARIBBEAN Both reggae and calypso music started in the Caribbean. **Calypso** music began in Trinidad. Calypso combines musical elements from Africa, Spain, and the Caribbean. Calypso songs are accompanied by steel drums and guitars, and they have improvised lyrics.

Reggae developed in Jamaica in the 1960s. Many reggae songs deal with social problems and religion. African music, Caribbean music, and American music all fed into the roots of reggae. Bob Marley of Jamaica was a pioneer of reggae. The music of the Caribbean is one of the elements that lures tourists to the region, creating jobs for local residents.

BACKGROUND
Bob Marley's son, David "Ziggy" Marley, is carrying on his father's musical legacy.

TOURISM AND THE INFORMAL ECONOMY Rapid population growth in the Caribbean is contributing to high unemployment, especially among the young. Many people flee rural areas and move to the cities in search of jobs. Too often, however, they lack job skills. There are schools to help prepare students for jobs in agriculture and tourism.

Tourism is, in fact, an increasingly important industry. Local residents of the islands are able to find jobs working in the hotels, resorts, and restaurants there. In addition, people can make a living working as guides and assistants on fishing excursions, sailing trips, snorkeling adventures, hiking expeditions, and other activities for tourists.

People also find jobs in the **informal economy,** which takes place outside official channels, without benefits or protection for workers. These include jobs such as street vending, shining shoes, and a variety of other activities and services that provide people with a small income.

In Section 3, you will read about Spanish-speaking South America.

HUMAN-ENVIRONMENT INTERACTION Many of Bob Marley's songs reflect his faith and political beliefs. **How might popular culture express important ideas and political beliefs?**

SECTION 2 Assessment

1 Places & Terms

Identify and explain the following places and terms.

- cultural hearth
- United Provinces of Central America
- Panama Canal
- calypso
- reggae
- informal economy

2 Taking Notes

REGION Review the notes you took for this section.

Central America and the Caribbean

Latin America

- What European countries had colonies in the Caribbean?
- Which European country settled most of Central America?

3 Main Ideas

a. What are the major groups that blended to form the culture of this region?

b. What are some major sources of income in the economies of Central America and the Caribbean?

c. What forms of music have evolved in the region?

4 Geographic Thinking

Drawing Conclusions How did the establishment of sugar plantations by Europeans affect the settlement of the Caribbean? **Think about:**

- the people brought in to work on the plantations

RESEARCH LINKS
CLASSZONE.COM

GeoActivity

MAKING COMPARISONS Pair with a partner and make a **poster** about the Panama Canal. Do research on the Internet and illustrate your poster with maps and diagrams of the locks in the canal. Provide statistical data about the canal that compares it with other canals, such as the Suez Canal.

Disasters!

SUNSHINE STATE STANDARDS
Key Standard SS.B.2.4.1 The student understands how social, cultural, economic, and environmental factors contribute to the dynamic nature of regions.
FCAT LA.A.2.4.4 Reading: Research

Volcano on Montserrat

Montserrat is an island in the Caribbean. One of the outstanding features of the island is its large volcano located in the Soufrière Hills. The volcano had been dormant for approximately five centuries when it began to erupt in 1995. The eruptions continued through 1996 and became particularly severe in 1997. The large map of the island (below) shows the area affected by the eruptions. The dates on the map show the expanding "zones of exclusion." A zone of exclusion is an area too dangerous for people to enter. Two-thirds of the island is now uninhabitable.

Soufrière Hills

October '96

June '97

February '97

Sept '97

July '97

Plymouth

ATLANTIC OCEAN

Montserrat
Caribbean Sea

SOUTH AMERICA

Plymouth, the capital and largest city on the island of Montserrat, lies downwind of Soufrière Hills volcano. As a result, it has been covered with a gray shroud of ash.

Fiery eruptions illuminated the nighttime sky as lava and ashes poured out of the volcano's cone.

GeoData

OTHER FAMOUS VOLCANOES

 A.D. 79
Mount Vesuvius erupted, and thousands of people died when they were buried under ash and mud or breathed the poisonous fumes.

 1707
Mount Fuji erupted. It is the highest and most sacred mountain in Japan.

 1943
Paricutin was a volcano that formed in the middle of a cornfield in Mexico. It last erupted in 1943.

 1980
Mt. St. Helens in Washington State erupted with tremendous force. The eruption lasted nine hours and killed 60 people.

 2000
Popocatépetl in Mexico erupted in its biggest explosion in a thousand years.

Spanish-Speaking South America

Main Ideas
• Native peoples and settlers from Spain have shaped the culture of South America.
• Regional economic cooperation will help raise people's standards of living.

Places & Terms
Inca   Mercosur
Quechua

CONNECT TO THE ISSUES
INCOME GAP The countries of South America are trying to find ways to narrow the gap between rich and poor.

SUNSHINE STATE STANDARDS
Key Standard SS.B.2.4.1 The student understands how social, cultural, economic, and environmental factors contribute to the dynamic nature of regions.

Other Standards SS.A.3.4.3, B.1.4.4

FCAT LA.A.1.4.2 Reading: Strategies

A HUMAN PERSPECTIVE In the early 1500s, the Inca empire was at the height of its glory. Then Spanish soldiers under the command of Francisco Pizarro invaded the South American empire. The Spanish attacked the Inca army, killed many of its warriors, and took the emperor prisoner. The Spaniards held him for ransom. Although the Inca filled a room with silver and gold to win his release, the Spanish executed the emperor. This broke the spirit of the Inca nation, already weakened by civil war, and the Spanish conquered the rest of the empire. As in Mexico, Central America, and the Caribbean, the Spanish conquest would have a deep effect on the history and culture of South America.

Conquest and the End of Spanish Rule

South America is divided into two main regions, based in part on whether the people speak Spanish or Portuguese. In this section, you will learn about Spanish-speaking South America. This region is composed of Argentina, Bolivia, Chile, Colombia, Ecuador, Guyana, Paraguay, Peru, Uruguay, and Venezuela. Suriname is a Dutch-speaking country. French Guiana is a part of France.

THE INCA One of the great civilizations of the Americas arose in the rugged Andes Mountains of Peru. This civilization was created by the **Inca**—descendants of people who came across a land bridge from Siberia to Alaska and eventually crossed the Isthmus of Panama into South America. When they reached the west coast of South America,

South America after the Spanish Conquest

1532–1533
Francisco Pizarro invades and conquers the Inca empire in Peru.

1608
Jesuit state of Paraguay is established.

1739
Spanish establish viceroyalty of New Granada, encompassing all territory between Orinoco and Amazon rivers.

1600

1700

1550
This **ceremonial goblet** from Cuzco shows a jaguar, sacred to the Inca.

1647
Santiago, Chile, is destroyed by an earthquake.

they found the Andes Mountains, which rise to heights of more than 20,000 feet in some places. In spite of the harsh terrain, the Inca were able to build an advanced civilization.

They built their empire on the foundation of earlier cultures. From their capital at Cuzco in Peru, the Inca extended their power. They brought other tribes under their control and built a great empire.

By 1500, the Inca empire extended 2,500 miles along the west coast of South America. It ran from present-day Ecuador in the north to Argentina in the south. A road system that was about 20,000 miles long crossed mountains and deserts to link the empire. ◀**A**

THE SPANISH CONQUEST As you read earlier, Pizarro and his soldiers invaded and conquered the Inca empire. The Spanish were primarily interested in claiming the gold and silver of the Inca.

The Spanish settlers forced the natives to work in mines and on farms and ranches. The Spanish landlords received the rights to the labor of the natives from officials in Spain, who passed laws to protect the Indians. But in spite of the laws, many of the settlers abused the natives or worked them to death.

The presence of the Spanish had an important geographic effect on the Inca, who were forced to move from their villages to large plantations. This disrupted and destroyed Inca families and communities, and made the region difficult to govern even into the 20th century. ◀**B**

The Spanish forced their own language and religion on the conquered peoples. The **Quechua** (KEHCH•wuh) language of the Inca was overshadowed by Spanish as the settlers became the dominant culture. Likewise, the Inca religion of the native peoples was replaced by the Catholic religion of the conquerors as the official religion. Spanish rule in the region continued for almost 300 years. But one lasting legacy of the Inca is that millions of native peoples still speak Quechua.

INDEPENDENCE MOVEMENTS Inspired by the American Revolution (1776) and the French Revolution (1789), the countries of South America sought their independence from Spain in the first half of the 19th century. Two great leaders of independence movements in the region in the first half of the 19th century were Simón Bolívar and José

Geographic Thinking
Seeing Patterns
A How might a road system have helped to hold the Inca empire together?

CONNECT TO THE ISSUES
DEMOCRACY
B What effect might the disruption of Inca life have had on the development of democracy in the region?

LATIN AMERICA

1777
Spain and Portugal resolve disputes about colonies in South America.

1820s
Simón Bolívar leads many countries of South America in their fight for independence from Spain.

1946
Juan Perón is elected president of Argentina.

1800

1900

1780
Peruvian Indians rebel against Spain.

1873
Peace treaty fixes frontier between Argentina and Chile along the ridge of the Andes.

2000
Alberto Fujimori resigns as president of Peru.

231

de San Martín. Bolívar helped to liberate the countries of Colombia, Venezuela, Ecuador, and Bolivia. José de San Martín helped to free the countries of Argentina, Chile, and Peru from Spanish rule.

Argentina and Chile were the first to achieve independence because they were the farthest from Lima, the center of Spanish control. However, once independence was achieved, geography contributed to the failure of various countries to unify or work together for common goals. The continent has tended to be populated around its edges, with mountains and rain forests limiting interaction. This has contributed to underdevelopment and political instability.

GOVERNMENT BY THE FEW Oligarchy (government by the few) and military rule have characterized the governments of many of the countries of South America since they won their independence from Spain. In fact, before his death in 1830, Simón Bolívar had become discouraged about the future of democracy in Latin America.

Throughout South America, authoritarian rule—which stresses obedience to authority over individual freedom—delayed the development of democracy. Although many South American nations gained freedom in the 1800s, hundreds of years of colonialism had their effects. Strong militaries, underdeveloped economies, and social class divisions still exist in the region today.

CONNECT TO THE ISSUES

DEMOCRACY

How might better interaction and communication affect the development of democracy?

A Cultural Mosaic

South America is one of the most culturally complex regions in the world, due in part to the region's isolation after independence. These countries form a cultural mosaic—a number of societies with different cultures living near each other but not mixing.

LITERATURE Spanish-speaking South America has a strong literary heritage. Particularly in the last quarter of the 20th century, South American writers claimed the world's attention with their extraordinary novels. Perhaps the most famous of these writers is Gabriel García Márquez of Colombia, who won the Nobel Prize for literature in 1982. Among his best-known novels are *One Hundred Years of Solitude* (1967) and *The General in His Labyrinth* (1989), a novel about Simón Bolívar.

MUSIC Popular music and folk music are important artistic traditions in South America. You can hear street music everywhere throughout the region. Musicians play drums, guitars, marimbas, maracas, and flutes, among other instruments. This music combines Indian, African, and European elements to make a thick cultural brew, as can be heard in the tango of Argentina. Classical music is also important in the region. Many cities in South America have symphony orchestras and opera companies.

ARTS AND CRAFTS Beautiful craftwork and handmade items can be found throughout Latin America. Pottery, textiles, glasswork, and metalwork all manage to combine beauty and usefulness. Many handmade

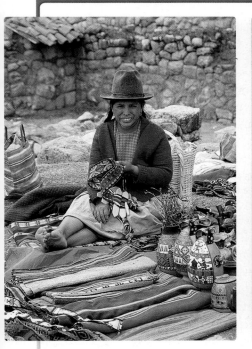

A native woman displays a variety of goods for sale at a crafts market in Chinchero, Peru. Her wares include blankets, pottery, and items of clothing.

Handmade furniture is still found throughout the region. This carpenter shows a chair that he has made in his workshop in Sicuani, Peru.

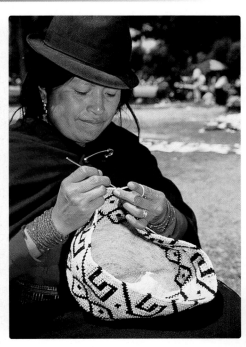

A Cotopaxi native woman weaves a basket at an open market in Alameda Park in Quito, Ecuador.

items are decorated with folk art or Indian religious symbols. Beautiful examples of handmade items can be found in tools and other household items throughout the region. Indian weavers, for example, make ponchos from the wool of the animals of the region, such as llamas and alpacas.

Economics: Resources and Trade

Most economies in South American countries are based upon agriculture and the mining and extraction of resources such as oil and minerals. However, the income gap between rich and poor reflects the region's poverty and failure to develop economically after independence. Economic development of the entire region holds out the hope of improving the lives of millions of people.

ECONOMIES OF THE REGION One of the advantages in the region is that it produces a wide variety of products. This is because of its unique combination of resources, landforms, climate, and vegetation. In the north, Guyana, Suriname, and French Guiana grow crops for export on large farms. Colombia and Venezuela both have huge oil reserves that are probably their greatest economic asset.

In the west, Peru has an important fishing industry. Ecuador exports huge quantities of shrimp. Bolivia has deposits of tin, zinc, and copper.

In the south, Argentina produces great quantities of grain and livestock on its vast pampas. Uruguay is a prosperous agricultural country that has major farming and grazing areas in its portion of the pampas. Paraguay exports products such as soybeans, cotton, and animal hides.

Caribbean Sea

VENEZUELA
GUYANA
SURINAME
FRENCH GUIANA
COLOMBIA
ECUADOR
PERU
B R A Z I L
PACIFIC OCEAN
BOLIVIA
ATLANTIC OCEAN
PARAGUAY
ARGENTINA
URUGUAY
CHILE

N W E S

Member
Associate member
Non-member

0   500   1,000 miles
0   500   1,000 kilometers
Azimuthal Equal–Area Projection

Geographic Cooperation: A Common Market

- **Mercosur** is an economic common market that began operating in the southern cone of South America in 1995.

- Goals of a free-trade zone among member nations:

  1. to make member economies more stable;

  2. to increase trade within region and thereby decrease dependency on unstable global markets;

  3. to channel some of the profits of improving economies to those people and groups that most need help.

- The name Mercosur is formed from the Spanish phrase Mercado Común del Sur, which means Southern Common Market.

- There are more than 220 million consumers in this market.

- The combined Gross Domestic Product of the member nations is more than one trillion dollars a year.

SKILLBUILDER: Interpreting Maps

❶ **REGION** How many countries in South America are not full members of Mercosur?

❷ **LOCATION** What characteristics do the members of Mercosur share in terms of location?

CHILE'S SUCCESS STORY Chile is South America's greatest economic success story. It has been able to participate in the global economy by trading the products of its mines and fields with nations as far away as Japan. The export of fruit and vegetables to North American markets is an important part of Chile's economy because its harvest comes during the Northern Hemisphere's winter. Chile also has huge deposits of copper, which remains its largest export. However, Chile has recently begun to focus on its own hemisphere. It has been a leader in working for economic cooperation in the region, where it is an associate member of Mercosur. (See the chart and map above.) Associate members (Chile and Bolivia) are countries with free-trade agreements with Mercosur.

Education and the Future

The people of Spanish-speaking South America face a number of challenges. Education is a critical issue as young people move to the cities in search of jobs.

LITERACY IN SOUTH AMERICA The countries of Spanish-speaking South America have higher literacy rates than do the countries of Central America and the Caribbean, or Mexico and Brazil. In Argentina, Chile, and Uruguay, for example, literacy rates are higher than 90 percent. Moreover, the literacy rates for women are about the same as for men in those three countries; in fact, in Uruguay, the rate is slightly higher for women. Most of the countries of South America support colleges, universities, and technical schools that train students for careers. As measured by the number of students in school and copies of daily newspapers and books published per capita, most of the countries of the region show high rates of education and literacy.

THE CASE OF CHILE Chile's literacy rate for the total adult population is around 95 percent. For young people between the ages of 15 and 19, it is even higher—close to 98 percent. The number of books and daily newspapers sold and read is very high—approximately 46 copies of daily newspapers are sold for every 100 people.

Education is very important in Chile. When they are between the ages of 6 and 13, all children must attend school, and public education is free. Higher education has suffered because of political unrest. The universities had been independent and of high quality. Then a military coup led by General Augusto Pinochet overthrew Salvador Allende's government in 1973. Afterwards, the military introduced reforms that undermined higher education. Nonetheless, since Pinochet's departure from power in 1990, universities have regained some of their independence and standards. Today, there are many business schools in Chile that have contributed to the country's economic success.

In the next section you will read about Brazil. This Portuguese-speaking country is the giant of South America, both in terms of population and land area.

REGION The writer Isabel Allende, niece of Salvador Allende, is an important novelist in Latin America. Her most famous book may be *The House of the Spirits* (1982).

Assessment

① Places & Terms

Identify and explain the importance of each of the following.

- Inca
- Quechua
- Mercosur

② Taking Notes

PLACE Review the notes you took for this section.

Latin America

Spanish-Speaking South America

- Which countries besides Spain sent settlers to South America?
- Which countries in South America have the highest literacy rates?

③ Main Ideas

a. What have been some obstacles to democratic government in South America?

b. What was the extent of the Inca empire in South America?

c. What are some of the arts and crafts of the region?

④ Geographic Thinking

Drawing Conclusions Why might the southern cone of South America have decided to form a trade group?

Think about:

- the geography of the region
- the region's economies

S See Skillbuilder Handbook, page R5.

SEEING PATTERNS Pair with a partner and draw a **sketch map** of South America. Fill in the map with the names of the various countries and the dominant language spoken in each.

Brazil

Main Ideas

• Native peoples, Portuguese, and Africans have shaped Brazil.

• Brazil has the largest territory and the largest population of any country in Latin America.

Places & Terms

Treaty of Tordesillas

Carnival

samba

capoeira

CONNECT TO THE ISSUES

RESOURCES Brazil is a giant country rich in natural resources that must be developed and used wisely.

A HUMAN PERSPECTIVE In 1807, Napoleon's armies invaded Portugal. As the French army approached the capital of Lisbon, the Portuguese royal family boarded ships to escape capture. They sailed to Brazil, Portugal's largest colony, taking their court and royal treasury with them. For the next 14 years, Brazil was the heart of the Portuguese empire. During that time Brazilians developed a sense of their own independence. As you will read, a member of the Portuguese royal family was to play a decisive role in gaining Brazil's freedom from Portugal.

History: A Divided Continent

Geography played an important role in the colonization of South America by Spain and Portugal. The two European powers reached an agreement to divide South America. In the resulting **Treaty of Tordesillas** (1494), Portugal gained control over the land that became present-day Brazil. In this section, you will look at Portuguese-speaking Brazil, the largest country in South America.

SUNSHINE STATE STANDARDS
Key Standard SS.B.2.4.2 The student understands past and present trends in human migration and cultural interaction and their impact on physical and human systems.

Other Standards SS.B.1.4.4, B.2.4.6

FCAT LA.A.1.4.2 Reading: Strategies

NATIVE PEOPLES AND PORTUGUESE CONQUEST

The territory of Brazil was originally home to native peoples divided into hundreds of tribes and language groups. Various estimates place the number of native peoples between one million and five million when the first colonists arrived in the early 1500s.

The first Portuguese colonists hoped to find gold or silver but were disappointed when they could find neither. Then they cleared out huge areas of forest where they created sugar plantations. Brazil soon became a source of wealth for Portugal because the demand for sugar was so great.

The patterns of settlement were along the coast, where cities such as Rio de Janeiro were established, rather than in the interior where rain forests made farming difficult. Eventually, the colonists cleared more land in the west for sugar plantations. In the process, the Portuguese conquered the native tribes and put them to work on the plantations. When natives died from diseases brought by the colonists, the Portuguese brought African slaves to Brazil by force to replace them. Today millions of Brazilians are of mixed European, African, and native ancestry.

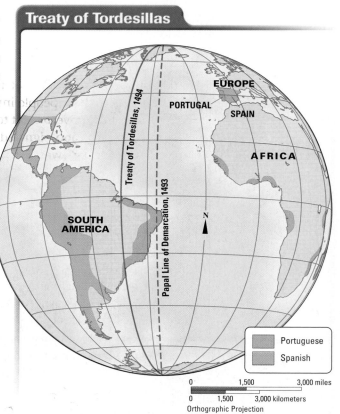

Treaty of Tordesillas

EUROPE
PORTUGAL
SPAIN
AFRICA
SOUTH AMERICA
Treaty of Tordesillas, 1494
Papal Line of Demarcation, 1493
N

Portuguese
Spanish

0   1,500   3,000 miles
0   1,500   3,000 kilometers
Orthographic Projection

INDEPENDENCE FOR BRAZIL Brazil remained a Portuguese colony from 1500 to 1822. After Napoleon's defeat in 1815, many people in Brazil demanded independence from Portugal. However, the Portuguese government wanted Brazil to remain a colony. But the Brazilians kept pushing for independence. Finally, thousands of them signed petitions asking Dom Pedro, the son of Portugal's king, to rule Brazil as an independent country. He agreed, and in September of 1822, he declared Brazil's independence from Portugal.

A National Culture

The culture of Brazil includes Portuguese influences, Native American elements, and African influences. But unlike other South American countries, Brazil has had more success in blending its ethnic groups.

THE PEOPLE OF BRAZIL When the first Europeans arrived in 1500, millions of native people lived in what is now Brazil. But today, only about 200,000 live in the depths of the Amazon rain forest. Thousands of the native peoples died from diseases brought by the European colonists.

Brazil has become home to many immigrants from other nations. Large numbers of people from Portugal, Germany, Italy, and Spain have settled there, as have immigrants from Lebanon and Syria. Brazil also has the largest Japanese population outside Japan. **A**

LANGUAGE AND RELIGION The Portuguese brought their language and their Catholic religion with them to Brazil. Today, Brazil has the largest Catholic population in the world. In addition, Protestants make up almost 20 percent of the population. Many other Brazilians, mainly those of African or mixed ancestry, practice religions that combine African beliefs with Catholicism.

ARCHITECTURE OF BRASÍLIA The architect Oscar Niemeyer designed the buildings for the new capital of Brasília, which was built in the interior of Brazil beginning in 1957. Part of the reason for locating the capital 600 miles inland was to draw people into the interior. The move of the government to the new capital city in 1960 signaled the opening of the country's west.

Geographic Thinking

Making Comparisons

A How does the population of Brazil resemble that of the United States?

LATIN AMERICA

HUMAN-ENVIRONMENT INTERACTION Oscar Niemeyer designed these government offices for Brasília. The Senate meets in the domed building, and the Chamber of Deputies meets in the bowl-like building.

An Economic Giant Awakens

Brazil is a growing economic power. Much of this power is based on its vast area, its abundance of natural resources, and its people. Its economy is the tenth largest in the world. Its diverse population of about 170 million people contributes to its economic strength.

AN INDUSTRIAL POWER Natural resources have helped make Brazil an industrial power. It has deposits of iron and bauxite, as well as other minerals used in manufacturing. In addition, tin and manganese reserves are abundant. It also has supplies of gold, silver, titanium, chromite, tungsten, and quartz.

More than a thousand rivers, including the Amazon, flow through Brazil. Power plants located along these rivers produce electricity. In addition, Brazil's large reserves of oil and natural gas contribute to its industrial might.

Brazil is one of the most industrialized of South American countries, with one of the largest steel plants in the region. It is a leading maker of automobiles. Over half of its cars use ethanol, a fuel that comes from sugar cane and is less expensive than imported oil. **B**

CONNECT TO THE ISSUES
RESOURCES
B How do Brazil's natural resources contribute to its industrial success?

MIGRATION TO THE CITIES Despite its economic successes, Brazil remains a country with a vast gap between the rich and the poor. Increasing urbanization is one result of attempts by many Brazilians to improve their lives by seeking jobs in the cities.

The movement of people in Brazil from country to city reflects changes in agriculture that pushed people off the land. It also reflects the growth in manufacturing that pulled people to the cities. In 1960, about 22 percent of the population lived in the cities. By 1995, more than 75 percent of the people lived in cities.

MIGRATION TO THE INTERIOR There has also been a move into the interior. About 80 percent of the people live within 200 miles of the sea. But the government is encouraging settlement of the interior to develop its many resources. Commercial agriculture is an important part of the economy in the western interior. That is because of the *cerrado*—the fertile grasslands, similar to the Great Plains in the United States, that provide rich farmland. Many Brazilians are willing to move to the interior to improve their economic situation.

Natural Resources of Brazil

Legend:
- Aluminum
- Gold
- Hydroelectric power
- Iron ore
- Manganese
- Natural gas
- Nickel
- Petroleum
- Timber
- Tin

0   500   1,000 miles
0   500   1,000 kilometers
Azimuthal Equal–Area Projection

SKILLBUILDER: Interpreting Maps

1 LOCATION In what part of Brazil are most of its timber resources located?

2 LOCATION Is most of Brazil's tin located along the coasts or in the interior of the country?

Brazilian Life Today

Brazil is a country of great variety in its city life, music, and holidays.

FROM CARNIVAL TO MARTIAL ARTS The most colorful feast day in Brazil is **Carnival.** In Rio de Janeiro, people in costumes ride on floats through the streets. Carnival takes place to the music of the **samba,** a Brazilian dance with African influences.

Capoeira is a martial art and dance that developed in Brazil from African origins. Angolans who were taken to Brazil by the Portuguese brought this martial art and dance with them.

PLACE Young men demonstrate the martial art of *capoeira*.

CITY LIFE IN RIO DE JANEIRO Brasília is the political capital of Brazil, and São Paulo is its economic heart and largest city, but Rio de Janeiro is the cultural center. The residents of Rio are among the country's leaders in important cultural activities and institutions.

Rio has one of the most spectacular natural settings in the world. Sugarloaf Mountain, Guanabara Bay, and Copacabana Beach are just a few of the breathtaking sights.

There is a darker side to life in Rio, and that is caused by the widening gap between rich and poor. Desperately poor slums, called *favelas,* dot the hillsides. Crime waves and drug abuse are two results of the poverty. Recently, however, government officials have launched programs to bring in electrical power, paved streets, and sewers. ◄**c**

In the next chapter, you will read about three important issues that affect Latin America—resources, democracy, and the income gap.

CONNECT TO THE ISSUES

INCOME GAP

▶ What might be the impact of poverty and the income gap on democratic government?

Assessment

① Places & Terms

Identify and explain the importance of each of the following.
- Treaty of Tordesillas
- Carnival
- samba
- capoeira

② Taking Notes

PLACE Review the notes you took for this section.

- Which European country sent the most settlers to Brazil?
- Who lived in Brazil before the European settlers arrived?

③ Main Ideas

a. What crop did settlers first grow in Brazil and what effect did it have on the makeup of the population?

b. How do Brazil's rivers contribute to its wealth?

c. What are some aspects of Brazilian culture that show an African influence?

④ Geographic Thinking

Drawing Conclusions What is the relationship between coast and interior in the settling of Brazil? **Think about:**
- the patterns of settlement along the coast
- the resources of the interior

EXPLORING LOCAL GEOGRAPHY Rio de Janeiro is almost two different cities—one rich and one poor. Pair with a partner and draw a **map** that divides your city, town, or neighborhood in two. Decide which parts are better off than others. What resources and features distinguish one part from another?

Comparing Cultures

Festivals and Holidays

Different cultures around the world have their own festivals and holidays—occasions for celebration. Often these special days have a religious significance. Carnival, for example, is a period of merrymaking that is celebrated in many Christian countries just before Lent, a season of fasting and penitence. On these two pages, you will learn about this and other festivals around the world. Three of the festivals—those in Brazil, Venice, and India—have their roots in religion. One of the holidays—that in Hong Kong—celebrates the beginning of a new year.

Italy

China

Brazil

India

Samba dancers in Rio de Janeiro, Brazil, celebrate Carnival by dancing in the streets. Carnival is the period of merrymaking just before Lent.

In Venice, Italy, masks are used to celebrate Carnival, a revel that features elaborate costumes.

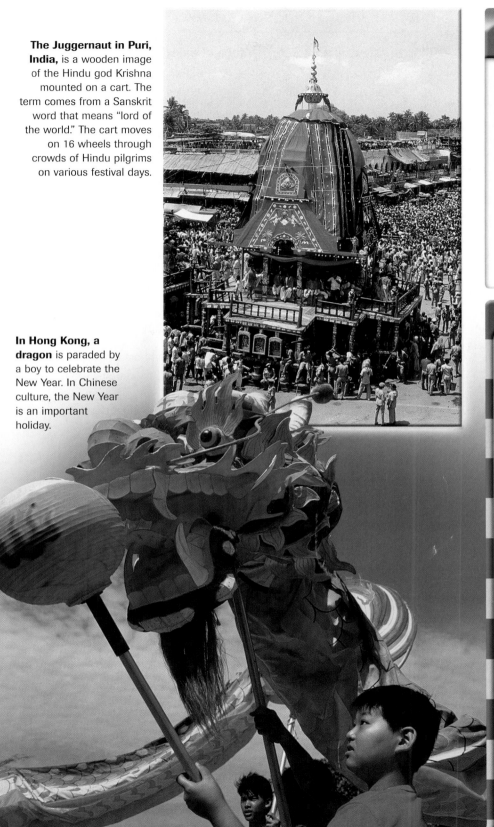

The Juggernaut in Puri, India, is a wooden image of the Hindu god Krishna mounted on a cart. The term comes from a Sanskrit word that means "lord of the world." The cart moves on 16 wheels through crowds of Hindu pilgrims on various festival days.

In Hong Kong, a dragon is paraded by a boy to celebrate the New Year. In Chinese culture, the New Year is an important holiday.

GeoActivity

CREATING A POSTER

Working with a partner, use the Internet to research one of the festivals or holidays listed below. Then create a **poster** about the holiday.

- Use visuals and captions to describe the festival or holiday you have chosen.

- Research a different festival and make a second poster to compare festivals from different countries.

RESEARCH LINKS
CLASSZONE.COM

GeoData

FESTIVALS AND HOLIDAYS AROUND THE WORLD

RELIGIOUS

Christianity
Christmas
Easter

Judaism
Rosh Hashanah
Passover

Islam
Feast of Sacrifice
Festival of Breaking Fast
Ashura

Hinduism
Holi
Diwali

OTHER
Independence Day
New Year's Day
Cinco de Mayo
Bastille Day
May Day
Kwanzaa
Thanksgiving

VISUAL SUMMARY
HUMAN GEOGRAPHY OF LATIN AMERICA

Subregions of Latin America

○ **Mexico**
- Native peoples and Spanish settlers have shaped the history and culture of Mexico.
- Economic expansion and an increasingly democratic government have developed together.

● **Central America and the Caribbean**
- Native peoples, settlers from many European countries, and Africans have shaped Central America and the Caribbean.
- The economies of the region rely primarily on agriculture and tourism.

○ **Spanish-Speaking South America**
- The countries of South America are developing strategies to improve their economies.
- Among these strategies are wide-ranging trade agreements, including Mercosur.

● **Brazil**
- Brazil is the giant of Latin America.
- Settled originally by the Portuguese, Brazil has welcomed immigrants from all over the world.
- Its economy is among the ten largest in the world.

Reviewing Places & Terms

A. Briefly explain the importance of each of the following.

1. Tenochtitlán
2. Institutional Revolutionary Party (PRI)
3. NAFTA
4. cultural hearth
5. United Provinces of Central America
6. Panama Canal
7. Inca
8. Mercosur
9. Treaty of Tordesillas
10. Carnival

B. Answer the questions about vocabulary in complete sentences.

11. What body of water surrounded Tenochtitlán?
12. Whose election signaled the end of one-party rule in Mexico?
13. Why is the Panama Canal important to world trade?
14. Which two European powers signed the Treaty of Tordesillas?
15. Which countries are associate members of Mercosur?
16. In what city of Brazil is Carnival celebrated in a particularly colorful way?
17. Which countries besides Mexico are members of NAFTA?
18. Why are Central America and the Andes Mountains around Cuzco cultural hearths?
19. Which countries made up the United Provinces of Central America?
20. What language did the Inca speak?

Main Ideas

Mexico (pp. 217–221)

1. What was the Spanish attitude toward Aztec culture?
2. What are the maquiladoras?

Central America and the Caribbean (pp. 222–229)

3. In terms of who settled there, how is the Caribbean different from Mexico and Central America?
4. Which two parts of the economy provide most of the income in Central America and the Caribbean?
5. What are some of the most important export crops in the region?

Spanish-Speaking South America (pp. 230–235)

6. Which countries are full members of Mercosur?
7. Which countries have literacy rates higher than 90 percent?
8. What happened to the Inca language after the Spanish conquest?

Brazil (pp. 236-241)

9. What is the ethnic makeup of Brazil?
10. What are some of the darker aspects of life in Brazil today?

Critical Thinking

1. Using Your Notes

Use your completed chart to answer these questions.

a. Which two European countries colonized the most territory in Latin America?

b. What are some of the ways in which Latin America is developing economically in recent years?

2. Geographic Themes

a. **HUMAN–ENVIRONMENT INTERACTION** How has the Amazon River been used and developed?

b. **MOVEMENT** What has restricted the movement of people from the coast of South America into the interior?

3. Identifying Themes

Interaction between European powers and native peoples occurred throughout the region. What are some of the consequences of this interaction? Which of the five themes are reflected in your answer?

4. Identifying and Solving Problems

What are some of the ways that individual citizens of Latin America are working to improve their economic situation?

5. Making Comparisons

How are Spanish-speaking and Portuguese-speaking South America alike and different?

Additional Test Practice, pp. S1–S37

TEST PRACTICE
CLASSZONE.COM

Geographic Skills: Interpreting Maps

City of Tenochtitlán

Use the map to answer the questions.

1. **PLACE** This is a Spanish map of the Aztec city of Tenochtitlán. Why did the city require roadway connections to the mainland?

2. **MOVEMENT** Why might this site have been a good location for a city?

3. **HUMAN–ENVIRONMENT INTERACTION** What purpose might the canals within the city have served?

GeoActivity

Create a map of a fortress city of your design. Your map should make use of the natural advantages afforded by the site you have chosen.

INTERNET ACTIVITY

Use the links at **classzone.com** to do research on economic growth in Latin America. Focus on the impact of free-market reforms on the income gap.

Creating Graphs and Charts Present a report of your findings. Include a chart that shows which countries have introduced free-market reforms and what impact these reforms have had on closing the income gap.

For more on these issues in Latin America . . .

 CURRENT EVENTS
CLASSZONE.COM

TODAY'S ISSUES
Latin America

Timber harvesting (as shown here in Bahia, Brazil) and agriculture have had a devastating effect on the Latin American rain forest.

GeoFocus

How can citizen participation help solve problems?

Taking Notes In your notebook, copy a cause-and-effect chart like the one below. Then take notes on causes and effects of some aspect of each issue.

	Causes	Effects
Issue 1: Resources		
Issue 2: Democracy		
Case Study: Income Gap		

Rain Forest Resources

How can we preserve and develop the rain forest?

Main Ideas

- Special-interest groups make competing demands on the resources of the rain forest.
- As the rain forests are destroyed, the quality of life on Earth is threatened.

Places & Terms

biodiversity

deforestation

global warming

debt–for–nature swap

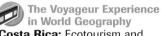

The Voyageur Experience in World Geography
Costa Rica: Ecotourism and Economic Development

SUNSHINE STATE STANDARDS
Key Standard SS.B.2.4.4 The student understands the global impact of human changes in the physical environment.

FCAT LA.A.2.4.5 Reading: Identify Persuasion and Appeal

A HUMAN PERSPECTIVE In 1997, biologist Marc van Roosmalen made an incredible discovery. An Amazonian Indian had brought the biologist a tiny monkey huddled inside a tin can. Van Roosmalen realized that the monkey was a kind of pygmy marmoset never before seen by scientists. Over the next three years, Van Roosmalen and his colleagues located the native region of this creature and along the way observed plants and animals unknown to science. These scientists had confirmed the richness of plant and animal life in the Amazon rain forest of Brazil. But for other people, the forest (once cleared) holds the promise of something more—land for farming and timber for sale.

Rain Forest Land Uses

The rain forest is an important global resource. Its vegetation helps to clean the earth's atmosphere, regulate the climate, and shelter several million species of plants, insects, and other wildlife. Scientists have just begun to investigate and understand the rain forest's **biodiversity**—its wide range of plant and animal species. And yet, this variety of life is being destroyed at a rapid rate. At the end of the 20th century, nearly 50 million acres of rain forest worldwide were being destroyed every year.

CLEARING THE RAIN FORESTS
The world's demand for timber is great. The Amazon rain forest contains tropical hardwoods, such as mahogany and cedar, that are harvested for export by the timber industry.

Native peoples, living in poverty, travel into the rain forest in search of land on which they can grow crops. They clear the forest,

Major Rain Forests of Latin America

110°W · Gulf of Mexico · 70°W · 50°W · 30°W · 20°N · Caribbean Sea · ATLANTIC OCEAN · Equator · 0° · PACIFIC OCEAN · N · W E · S · 20°S · 40°S

0   500   1,000 miles
0 500 1,000 kilometers
Azimuthal Equal-Area Projection

☐ Original rain forest
▦ Rain forest, 2000

SKILLBUILDER: Interpreting Maps

❶ **HUMAN–ENVIRONMENT INTERACTION** Has the rain forest contracted or expanded in recent years? Why might this be so?

❷ **REGION** Around what latitude is most of the rain forest clustered? Why might this be?

not realizing that the soil is not very fertile. Also, cutting down the trees exposes the land to erosion. After a few years, this new farmland becomes less productive, resulting in the need for more timber clearing.

Livestock, too, have been introduced into the rain forest. Ranchers need land on which to graze their cattle, and by clearing the forests for pasture, they can produce a steady supply of beef for the export market.

POPULATION PRESSURES More than half of the Amazon rain forest is located in Brazil. That country's growing population is contributing to the rain forest's decline. The estimated population of Brazil in 2000 was about 173 million people. With an annual growth rate between half a percent and 1 percent, Brazil's population is expected to reach 200 million by 2020. With that many people to shelter, some developers want to build homes on land now covered by the rain forest. **A▶**

Geographic Thinking◀

Using the Atlas
◀A Use the map on page 191. In what other countries besides Brazil is the Amazon rain forest located?

The Price of Destruction

There is a cost to pay for **deforestation**—cutting down and clearing away of trees—in the rain forest. The short-term benefits are offset by the high price Latin America and the world are paying in damage to the environment.

ENVIRONMENTAL CONCERNS Rain forests help to regulate the earth's climate. They do this by absorbing carbon dioxide and producing oxygen. As the forests disappear, however, much less carbon dioxide is absorbed. The carbon dioxide that is not absorbed builds up in the atmosphere. This buildup prevents heat from escaping into space. The temperature of the atmosphere begins to rise, and weather patterns start to change. By the beginning of the 21st century, evidence of this **global warming** appeared around the world, causing scientific concern. A common method for clearing the rain forest, known as slash-and-burn (see pages 210–211), produces carbon dioxide and other harmful gases.

PLANTS AND ANIMALS IN DANGER Although the world's rain forests cover about 6 percent of the earth's surface, they are home to an estimated 50 percent of the world's plant and animal species. Medical researchers are developing the processes needed to make use of the many plants that rain-forest dwellers have harvested for thousands of years. The forest dwellers have used these plants to make medicines that heal wounds and cure disease. What is lost as the rain forests disappear is more than biodiversity and a stable environment. The rain forests also hold secrets of nature that might improve and extend the quality of people's lives.

HUMAN–ENVIRONMENT INTERACTION A naturalist and a biologist attach a radio transmitter to a bird to track its movements in the rain forest.
Why might scientists wish to track birds?

BACKGROUND These gases are referred to as greenhouse gases because they help keep heat in the atmosphere.

Moving Toward Solutions

Saving the rain forests of Latin America is an issue that affects people around the world. Creative solutions will be required to make sure that the forests are not sacrificed to economic development.

A JUGGLING ACT A central problem facing many Latin American countries is how to balance competing interests. Some countries in the region are attempting to restrict economic development until they can find the right balance between economic growth and the preservation of the rain forests.

For example, grassroots organizations are closely observing development projects in the rain forests. Their mission is to educate people about the value of the rain forests and, when necessary, to organize protests against plans that would damage the environment.

Geographic Thinking

Seeing Patterns
B How might the income gap affect the use of the rain forest?

FIGHTING ECONOMICS WITH ECONOMICS Some people think that since economic gain is at the heart of rain forest destruction, the affected governments should be paid to preserve the forests. One such plan is known as a **debt-for-nature swap.** **B**

Many Latin American nations are burdened by tremendous debt. They've borrowed money to improve living conditions, and now they are struggling to pay it back. In a debt–for–nature swap, an environmental organization agrees to pay off a certain amount of government debt. In return, the government agrees to protect a certain portion of the rain forest. Governments get debt relief; environmentalists get rain forest preservation. This approach was successful in Bolivia. There, an international environmental group paid off some government debt in exchange for the protection of an area of forest and grassland.

The movement to preserve the rain forests has many supporters in the region, as well as around the world. The battle to preserve the rain forests may be one in which everybody wins.

LATIN AMERICA

SECTION Assessment

① Places & Terms

Identify and explain the following places and terms.

- biodiversity
- deforestation
- global warming
- debt-for-nature swap

② Taking Notes

HUMAN–ENVIRONMENT INTERACTION Review the notes you took for this section.

	Causes	Effects
Issue 1: Resources		

- Why are the rain forests being destroyed?
- What effect might the destruction of the rain forest have on climate?

③ Main Ideas

a. What are some of the important resources of the rain forest?

b. What are some of the costs of the destruction of the rain forest?

c. What are some factors that might slow destruction of the rain forest?

④ Geographic Thinking

Making Inferences What might happen to the rain forest in the future? **Think about:**

- economic pressures to destroy the rain forest
- reasons to preserve the rain forest

S **See Skillbuilder Handbook, page R4.**

GeoActivity

MAKING COMPARISONS Pair with a partner and make a **chart** of the largest rain forests in the world. Then make a copy of a map of the world and color in on the map the rain forests on your chart.

Interpreting Satellite Images

Satellites are orbiting "eyes in the skies." They can give us detailed views of landforms, vegetation, and bodies of water. The satellite image below shows part of the rain forest in the state of Rondônia in Brazil.

THE LANGUAGE OF MAPS A **satellite image** is a visible-light, radar, or infrared picture of land or water taken from space. Depending on the equipment used, satellite images can show land features such as those shown below—ground vegetation and a lake as well as a river that shows some flooding (in the loop below the center of the image). **Landsat satellites** are orbiting satellites that measure reflected light to show features on the earth's surface, including vegetation. A landsat satellite image shows changes in vegetation over time by using a series of images.

SUNSHINE STATE STANDARDS
Key Standard SS.B.1.4.1
The student uses a variety of maps, geographic technologies including geographic information systems (GIS) and satellite-produced imagery, and other advanced graphic representations to depict geographic problems.

FCAT LA.A.2.4.8 Reading: Synthesize and Conclude

A Satellite View of the Rain Forest ❶

Landsat Image

Sketch Map

KEY:
- ∼ WATER (RIVER, LAKE, RESERVOIR)
- — ROAD
- ▨ FLOODED AREA, SWAMP
- ∩ DAM
- ● TOWN

Madeira River

Pôrto Velho

Jamari River

❶ Satellite images are useful in constructing maps, updating maps, and making them more explicit.

❷ In Landsat images, shallow water appears light blue. Thick vegetation appears red. Sparse vegetation appears white.

❸ A researcher made a sketch of the Landsat image, adding names of towns and rivers.

Map and Graph Skills Assessment

1. Making Inferences
The town of Pôrto Velho is near the intersection of what two means of transportation?

2. Making Decisions
In what direction would you travel in going from Pôrto Velho to the Jamari River?

3. Drawing Conclusions
What sort of vegetation predominates in the Landsat image? How can you tell?

Giving Citizens a Voice

How can Latin Americans gain a voice in government?

Main Ideas
• Despite obstacles, democracy is beginning to succeed in Latin America.
• The success of Latin American democracies depends on political, economic, and social reforms.

Places & Terms
oligarchy   caudillo

junta   land reform

SUNSHINE STATE STANDARDS
Key Standard SS.C.1.4.4 The student understands the role of special interest groups, political parties, the media, public opinion, and majority/minority conflicts on the development of public policy and the political process.

Other Standards SS.A.3.4.3

FCAT LA.A.1.4.2 Reading: Strategies

A HUMAN PERSPECTIVE From the late 1970s through the early 1980s, the Argentine military waged a campaign of terror against those who supported political reform. As many as 30,000 people mysteriously disappeared. People accused of being terrorists and revolutionaries were kidnapped and questioned. Some were tortured, and then killed or "disappeared"—their bodies were never found. In an effort to learn the truth about their loved ones, a group of women, calling themselves the Mothers of Plaza de Mayo, staged weekly protests in the plaza in Buenos Aires. Their protests were part of the larger attempt by citizens of the region to gain a voice in how their governments were being run.

A Struggle to Be Heard

Latin Americans today seek more democratic governments. Democracy depends on free and fair elections, citizen participation, majority rule with minority rights, and guaranteed freedoms. However, Latin America has shown little support for democratic rule until recently.

THE LEGACY OF COLONIALISM After the Spanish conquest of the region in the 16th century, Native Americans in Central and South America were ruled by governors who took their orders from the king and queen of Spain. Even when Latin American countries won their independence during the 1800s, they continued to be governed mainly by small groups of Spanish colonists.

This government by the few, known as **oligarchy** (AHL·ih·GAHR·kee), was not democratic. The government censored the press, limited free speech, and punished dissent. It also discriminated against all who were not part of the Spanish ruling class. Elections were held, but there was never any doubt who was in charge. If the government was unable to control the people, the military would step in, seize power, and form a new, harsher government known as a **junta** (HOON·tah), which was run by the generals.

THE RULE OF THE *CAUDILLO* Throughout the 20th century, many Latin American countries were ruled by a **caudillo** (kow·DEE·yoh), a military dictator or political boss, such as Juan Perón in Argentina. The caudillo's

"My goodness, if I'd known how badly you wanted democracy I'd have given it to you ages ago."

support came from the military and the wealthy. Surprisingly, the caudillo was sometimes elected directly by the people.

For example, from the 1920s until the end of the 20th century, Mexico was governed by caudillos who were members of the *Partido Revolucionario Institucional* (PRI), or the Institutional Revolutionary Party. For 71 years the PRI dominated Mexican politics.

Opposition parties were legal, but the PRI used fraud and corruption to win elections. Opposition parties made big gains in the 1997 congressional elections. In 2000, Vicente Fox became the first non-PRI president since the adoption of Mexico's constitution in 1917. Finally, it seemed Mexico was ready to fully accept democracy.

BACKGROUND
Caudillo is a Spanish word that means "leader" or "chief."

Establishing Stable Democracies

Creating democracies in Latin America requires political, economic, and land reforms.

THE GOALS OF REFORM One goal of political reform is to establish constitutional government. A freely elected government that respects the law is the basis of democracy. Participation of citizens in political affairs is also critical. This requires that people be well educated and provided with economic security.

Political and economic stability are two sides of the same coin. A lack of prosperity is usually accompanied by social and political unrest.

Argentina in the 1980s was one example of how economic problems damaged a developing democracy. In 1983, Raúl Alfonsín was elected president of Argentina in that nation's first free election in many years. He was faced with a ruined economy after years of military rule.

Argentina suffered from inflation—a rise in the prices of goods and services. To fight inflation, the newly-elected president froze all wages and prices. He issued a new currency to replace the peso. (Later, the peso was brought back.) At first these measures seemed successful, but by 1989, inflation was severe again. In 1989, Argentina elected a new president, Carlos Menem. He introduced a number of capitalist reforms. These included reducing government spending and selling off state-controlled industries and utilities.

Another goal of reform is to recognize and increase the role of women in politics. Throughout the region, women are running for office and taking an active role in government. For example, Marta Suplicy was elected mayor of São Paulo, Brazil, in 2000.

LAND REFORM Latin American countries had been ruled by a wealthy elite. Economic power, as well as land, was in the hands of the few. To spread the wealth more fairly, some governments set up a program of **land reform,** the process of breaking up large landholdings and giving portions of the land to land-poor peasant farmers.

Geographic Thinking

Seeing Patterns
A What effect might the income gap have on political stability in a democracy?

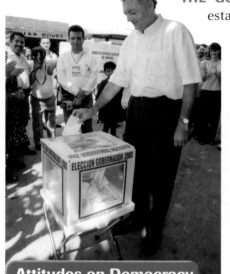

Attitudes on Democracy

Latinobarometro, a Chilean organization, conducts polls asking Latin Americans from a number of countries what they think about different political issues. Recently, the organization asked residents of various countries the following question:

Is democracy the best system of government?

Brazil	50% agree
Central America	49%
Ecuador	41%
Mexico	45%
Paraguay	44%
Peru	21%
Uruguay	86%

SOURCE: *Latinobarometro,* 1998

In Mexico, for example, the process of land reform began with Benito Juarez. He was a Zapotec Indian from a small farm who was elected Mexico's president in 1858. One of his main reform goals was to redistribute the land so that rich landowners could not keep other Mexicans in a cycle of poverty. After the Mexican Revolution in the early part of the 20th century, there was another attempt at land reform. This gave people a better chance at economic equality.

All of these reforms have been aimed at creating stability. With a sound foundation, democracy has a better chance of taking root.

REGION Marta Suplicy holds a press conference after being elected mayor of São Paulo, Brazil, in 2000. **What does her election suggest about the role of women in politics in Brazil?**

Assessment

① Places & Terms

Identify and explain the following places and terms.

- oligarchy
- junta
- caudillo
- land reform

② Taking Notes

HUMAN–ENVIRONMENT INTERACTION Review your notes.

	Causes	Effects
Issue 2: Democracy		

- What problems has democracy faced in Latin America?
- What are some of the effects of political reform in the region?

③ Main Ideas

a. How did colonialism affect the development of democracy?

b. What are some of the goals of political reform in the region?

c. Why was land reform necessary, and what was its purpose?

RESEARCH LINKS
CLASSZONE.COM

④ Geographic Thinking

Drawing Conclusions
What are the prospects of democracy in the region?
Think about:

- political reforms
- economic reforms

SEEING PATTERNS Pair with a partner and choose a country in Latin America to research on the Internet. Then prepare a **report** on the condition of democracy in that country and present your report to the class. Discuss what kind of government the country has, the number and names of political parties, and the nature of its legislative and executive functions.

CASESTUDY

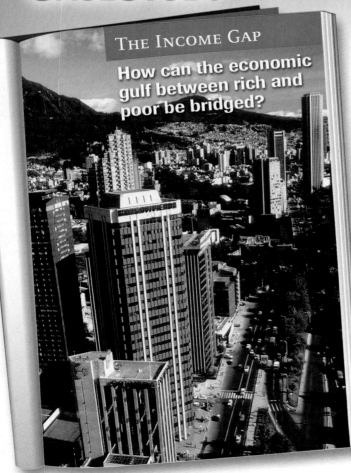

THE INCOME GAP

How can the economic gulf between rich and poor be bridged?

Bogotá, Colombia's glittering financial district

SUNSHINE STATE STANDARDS
Key Standard SS.D.2.4.1 The student understands how wages and prices are determined in market, command, tradition-based, and mixed economic systems and how economic systems can be evaluated by their ability to achieve broad social goals such as freedom, efficiency, equity, security, and growth.

Other Standards SS.A.1.4.3, C.1.4.1, C.2.4.5

FCAT LA.A.2.4.8 Reading: Synthesize and Conclude

Along the oceanfront in Rio de Janeiro, Brazil, gleaming office buildings and hotels share the boulevards with trendy restaurants and exclusive shops.

Behind all this glitter and glamour, however, is another world, hidden from sight—the *favelas*, or slums, of Rio. Here, the poor live among swamps and garbage dumps, and on barren hillsides.

These contrasting conditions are evidence of what economists call an income gap. This is the difference between the quality of life enjoyed by the rich and the poor. In many Latin American countries, the gap is widening. Some solutions have been proposed for this problem.

The Nature of the Problem

As you've learned in this unit, the income gap in Latin America has many causes, some of which reflect the impact of colonialism in the region. There are three angles to exploring the income gap: it is a moral issue, an economic dilemma, and a political problem.

A MORAL ISSUE Some people argue that Latin America's income gap raises important ethical questions. How can any caring society, they ask, justify vast wealth in the hands of a few while most people live in poverty from which they will likely never escape? The Catholic Church and other religious faiths in Latin America have argued that narrowing the gap between rich and poor is more than just an economic necessity; it is a matter of social justice.

AN ECONOMIC DILEMMA Most Latin American countries now have free-market economies with a minimum of government rules. A free-market economy offers many people the freedom and rewards they need to create wealth. However, in Latin America the poor often lack the basic skills that would make taking part in the economy possible.

Often, the poor have little education. Many cannot read. Most cannot find jobs. Those who find work may end up sweeping streets or shining shoes. Conditions in the slums breed disease and encourage crime. In fact, the life spans of slum dwellers are shorter than those of the middle and upper classes. To the poor of Latin America, the doors to economic equality appear shut.

A POLITICAL PROBLEM Poverty can make people desperate. Those who think they have nothing to lose are sometimes willing to take great risks.

SEE
PRIMARY SOURCE C

Throughout history, battles have been waged and governments have been overthrown by citizens protesting what they regard as an unjust society in which a few have too much while the many have too little.

Argentina, Bolivia, Brazil, Colombia, El Salvador, and Guatemala have all seen bloody rebellions put down by harsh military measures. In the process, human rights and human dignity have been violated. The story is usually the same. The rebels seek economic justice, and the military protects the wealthy. Clearly, attitudes will have to change before the poor in Latin America will be able to participate fully in their nations' economies. Some attitudes are already changing as, for example, more money is going to education.

Possible Solutions

SEE
PRIMARY SOURCE A

The income gap in Latin America varies from one country to another. For example, according to a recent report issued by the United Nations' Development Program, nearly 45 percent of all Brazilians live in poverty, existing on less than two dollars a day. In Ecuador, Paraguay, and Uruguay, on the other hand, the income gap is much narrower than it is in Brazil.

EDUCATION, POLITICS, AND ECONOMICS Many of the countries of the region have put in place free-market economies that they hope will eventually help to narrow the gap by providing economic opportunity and stability for all citizens.

Along with market economies, democracy is now seen by many countries as an essential part of the equation needed to achieve widespread prosperity. Democracy provides an outlet for protest and opposition so that policies can be adjusted to reflect the will of the majority of the people.

Finally, education is an important part of the mix. A literate, well-educated population will be needed to fill the jobs that will become available in an increasingly complex economy. A case study project on the income gap follows on the next two pages.

REGION A girl plays amid garbage and polluted water in Belém, Brazil. **What do the photographs on these pages suggest about the distribution of money in the region?**

The Income Gap **253**

CASE STUDY

PROJECT

Multimedia Report

Primary sources A, B, C, and D offer information about the income gap in Latin America. Use these resources along with your own research to prepare a multimedia report. The report should define the income gap, personalize it with accounts from the very poor, and identifiy possible solutions.

RESEARCH LINKS
CLASSZONE.COM

Suggested Steps

1. Research possible solutions or initiatives to deal with the income gap in Latin America.

2. Use video, audio, online, and print resources to research your topic.

3. Think about the following questions during your research:

   • What are the roots of the income gap?

   • How does the income gap hinder the participation of the poor in national economies?

   • What are some possible solutions to the problem?

4. Create charts and graphs and use videotapes, audio CDs, and other electronic media to make your report clear and convincing.

5. Prepare a brief talk to introduce and explain your topic.

Materials and Supplies

   • Reference books, newspapers, and magazines
   • Computer with Internet access
   • Printer
   • VCR and television
   • CD player

PRIMARY SOURCE A

Graph *This pie graph shows income distribution in Latin America. The gap was wider at the end of the 1990s than at the end of the 1970s.*

Income Distribution in Latin America

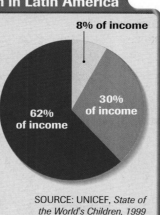

■ **Poorest 40%**
Poorest 40 percent of the population has only 8 percent of the income.

■ **Wealthiest 20%**
The wealthiest 20 percent controls 62 percent of the income.

■ **Middle 40%**
The middle 40 percent of the population has 30 percent of the income.

8% of income

62% of income

30% of income

SOURCE: UNICEF, *State of the World's Children, 1999*

PRIMARY SOURCE B

Cable News Story *For the homeless children of Rio de Janeiro, the income gap is more than just an economic hardship. It is a matter of life and death, as detailed in this report filed by CNN correspondent Marina Marabella.*

April 29, 1996—Four men, including three police officers, went on trial in Rio Monday for the 1993 slaying of eight street children. The murder, the worst massacre of children on record in Brazil, took place outside Candelaria Cathedral in the city center. . . .

Of all the dangers faced by Rio's homeless children, the one they fear the most is being murdered by death squads while they sleep. "When we can, we sleep during the day," said Ricardo, 13. "It's too risky at night". . .

Yvonne Bezerra de Mello has spent years helping Brazil's estimated 2,000 to 3,000 street children. "Until now, no policemen were ever convicted for killing street kids. This is a very good step for Brazilian justice," she said.

She and other human rights activists say the death squads that murder Brazil's homeless children are hired by shopkeepers and others to get rid of those suspected of stealing. . . .

[O]fficial police estimates say about 500 of Rio's homeless children are murdered each year.

Newspaper Report *On September 5, 2000, Steven Gutkin filed this story from Caracas, Venezuela, to* The Times of India Online. *It shows clearly that the consequences of the income gap can be found throughout Latin America.*

Caracas—The Sambil shopping mall in eastern Caracas is Latin America's largest. It boasts 450 stores, two movie theatres, an amusement park, a 30,000-gallon aquarium—and a McDonald's where Big Macs cost a half day's pay for the average Venezuelan worker.

A slum just a few miles to the west has open sewers running alongside tin shacks perched on unstable hillsides, flies buzzing in uncollected garbage and idle young men nursing bullet wounds. Blanca Vera, 65, lifts her baby granddaughter's blouse to reveal blotches on her tiny stomach. "This is from the pollution," she says.

[I]nequality of wealth and opportunity is a huge obstacle to development in Latin America. The existence of so many have-nots threatens to undermine the success of the region's two great experiments of recent years: democracy and free markets.

In Chile, the highest-paid 6 percent of workers get 30 percent of salaries, while 75 percent of workers get just 4 percent, according to the United Nations' Economic Commission for Latin America and the Caribbean.

Some blame the growing inequality on globalization. . . . Yet most economists say the real culprit is not globalization but misguided state policies that deprive the poor of a decent education, fail to collect taxes, and encourage corruption.

There's another factor that's harder to define but likely is just as real: a culture of elitism that regards poor people as unworthy. "You can't operate in a globalized economy with a narrow, tiny elite sector that has absolutely no connection or appreciation of the vast majority of people in society," says Michael Shifter, a Latin America specialist at the Washington-based Inter-American Dialogue.

Magazine Article *There are some initiatives to deal with the consequences of poverty. A reporter for the British magazine,* The Economist, *wrote about a program in Pôrto Alegre, Brazil, to help street children.*

"Is it true that in your country parents can be jailed for beating their children?" 16-year-old Jose asks your correspondent. Clearly there is no need to ask what made him run away from home, to become, briefly, one of Brazil's "street children." Luckily for him, the city on whose streets he ended up sleeping is Pôrto Alegre. Its municipal council this year, for the second year running, won an award given by the Abrinq Foundation, a Brazilian children's rights charity, to the local authority with the best social services for children. After only a short while on the streets, Jose now sleeps in a council-run dormitory and spends most of his days in the city's "Open School," which allows current and former street children to come and go as they please, aiming gradually to draw them back to something like a normal life and perhaps to an education. . . .

Pôrto Alegre is one of a handful of cities . . . that are trying. The services they offer are modest: a shelter where the children can sleep, eat, and wash; a day center staffed with a few teachers, drug counsellors, and so on; and some staff to patrol the streets at night looking for children in need.

PROJECT CheckList

Have I . . .

✓ fully researched my topic?

✓ searched for a mix of media sources from which to build my report?

✓ created informative visuals that make my report clear and convincing?

✓ practiced the delivery of my presentation?

✓ made sure that I am familiar with the video and audio equipment I plan to use?

VISUAL SUMMARY
TODAY'S ISSUES IN LATIN AMERICA

Environment

Rain Forest Resources
- There are a number of competing demands on the resources of the rain forest.
- Farmers, ranchers, environmentalists, the timber industry, and pharmaceutical companies all have their own interests in the rain forests of the region.
- Intelligent management and development of the rain forests depend on careful balancing of these competing interests.

Government

Giving Citizens a Voice
- After a long struggle to overcome the legacy of colonialism, most countries in Latin America are struggling toward more democratic forms of government.
- Political stability and economic progress often go hand in hand.

Economics

Case Study: The Income Gap
- The gap between rich and poor in Latin America presents a challenging problem.
- It is likely that a widening income gap will undermine political stability in the region.
- For this reason, government, businesses, and education must all work together to try to narrow the gap.

Reviewing Places & Terms

A. Briefly explain the importance of each of the following.

1. biodiversity
2. deforestation
3. global warming
4. debt-for-nature swap
5. oligarchy
6. junta
7. caudillo
8. land reform

B. Answer the questions about vocabulary in complete sentences.

9. Why is the biodiversity of the rain forest important?
10. What are some examples of the kinds of trees being harvested in the rain forest?
11. What is one byproduct of slash-and-burn clearing of the rain forest that is harming the atmosphere?
12. Why is it in the interest of governments to participate in debt-for-nature swaps?
13. Why is an oligarchy undemocratic?
14. Why is a junta undemocratic?
15. From where does the caudillo gain support?
16. Who benefits from land reform?
17. Is the biodiversity of the region increasing or decreasing?
18. In a debt-for-nature swap, what does the government agree to do?
19. Who loses in a program of land reform?
20. Which of the eight terms listed above represent the negative impact of colonialism on the politics of the region?

Main Ideas

Rain Forest Resources (pp. 245–248)

1. Why is the rain forest an important global resource?
2. What are some of the reasons the rain forest is being cleared?
3. What is one mission of the grassroots organizations in the rain forest?

Giving Citizens a Voice (pp. 249–251)

4. Who are some democratically elected leaders in the region?
5. What are some of the elements upon which democracy depends?
6. What sorts of reforms are essential to stable democracy in the region?

Case Study: The Income Gap (pp. 252–255)

7. Which groups have argued that the income gap presents a moral issue?
8. What is the basic economic dilemma confronted by poor people in Latin America?
9. Why is the income gap a political issue?
10. Do all countries of Latin America have a similar income gap? Explain.

Critical Thinking

1. Using Your Notes

Use your completed chart to answer these questions.

	Causes	Effects
Issue 1: Resources		
Issue 2: Democracy		

a. How might the income gap undermine democracy?

b. What effect might the exploitation of rain forest resources have upon the income gap in the region?

2. Geographic Themes

a. **MOVEMENT** What effect has the movement of people had on the rain forest?

b. **REGION** What are some of the major historical facts that have hindered the development of democracy in Latin America?

3. Identifying Themes

How might the use and development of the region's resources be connected to the gap between rich and poor? Which of the five themes apply to this situation?

4. Making Decisions

If you were a government official in the region, how might you try to balance competing demands on rain forest resources?

5. Drawing Conclusions

How might democratic government in the region promote economic prosperity?

Additional Test Practice, pp. S1–S37

TEST PRACTICE
CLASSZONE.COM

Geographic Skills: Interpreting Graphs

Poverty in Latin America

Use the graph to answer the following questions.

1. **REGION** In which three countries of Latin America is the percentage of people living in poverty the lowest?

2. **REGION** In which three countries is the poverty rate highest?

3. **PLACE** Brazil is the largest country in the region, in terms of both area and population. What is its poverty rate?

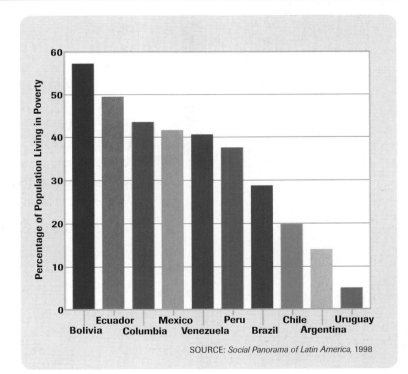
SOURCE: *Social Panorama of Latin America, 1998*

GeoActivity

Create a poster showing the effects of poverty and the income gap in one or more countries in the region. Include a map, as well as photographs and diagrams.

INTERNET ACTIVITY

Use the links at **classzone.com** to do research about the Amazon rain forest. Focus on solutions and strategies to slow the dwindling of the rain forest.

Creating Multimedia Presentations Combine charts, maps, or other visual images in an electronic presentation showing strategies for preserving the rain forest.

Unit 4

Europe

Europe is the world's second smallest continent. Located in the Northern Hemisphere, Europe has great diversity of landforms and cultures.

LOCATION The dazzling White Cliffs of Dover in England face the English Channel. The cliffs are made of soft chalk and are slowly eroding.

258

GeoData

REGION Many people view the Ural Mountains as the eastern border of Europe, but for historic and cultural reasons, Russia and other former republics of the Soviet Union are in Unit 5.

PLACE Europe's coastline is longer than that of Africa, the world's second largest continent.

HUMAN-ENVIRONMENT INTERACTION Historically, Europeans used the oceans and seas to make voyages for exploration and trade. Their culture spread around the world.

For more information on Europe . . .

RESEARCH LINKS
CLASSZONE.COM

PLACE The Eiffel Tower stands 984 feet above the Paris skyline. It was completed in 1889 for an International Exposition celebrating the French Revolution.

MOVEMENT Europeans are wildly enthusiastic about soccer. Teams and fans travel to matches held all over the world. In this game, held during the 1998 World Cup matches, Germany played Italy.

Unit PREVIEW 4

Today's Issues in Europe

Today, Europe faces the issues previewed here. As you read Chapters 12 and 13, you will learn helpful background information. You will study the issues themselves in Chapter 14.

In a small group, answer the questions below. Then participate in a class discussion of your answers.

Exploring the Issues

1. **CONFLICT** Search a print or online newspaper for articles about ethnic or religious conflicts in Europe today. What do these conflicts have in common? How are they different?

2. **POLLUTION** Make a list of possible pollution problems faced by Europe and those faced by the United States. How are these problems similar? Different?

3. **UNIFICATION** To help you understand the issues involved in unifying Europe, compare Europe to the United States. Imagine what might occur if each U.S. state were its own country. List five problems that might result.

For more on these issues in Europe . . .

CURRENT EVENTS
CLASSZONE.COM

CONFLICT

How can people resolve their differences?

In central Bosnia, a child stands near the ruins of a Muslim mosque. Bosnian Croats destroyed the mosque during an "ethnic cleansing" campaign to drive out Muslims during the 1992-1995 Bosnian war.

POLLUTION

How can Europeans clean up their environment?

On February 13, 2000, cyanide-polluted water from a Romanian mine reached Hungary. The cyanide killed thousands of fish, some of which are shown here washed up on the banks of the Tisza River.

CASESTUDY

Will there be a United States of Europe?

Over the centuries, wars and conflicts have ravaged Europe, but since 1950, Europe's nations have begun working together. As the new century begins, economics may be the key to uniting Europe.

UNIFICATION

THIS MUST BE THE STEERING COMMITTEE

EURO

Patterns of Physical Geography

SUNSHINE STATE STANDARDS

Key Standard SS.B.1.4.1 The student uses a variety of maps, geographic technologies including geographic information systems (GIS) and satellite-produced imagery, and other advanced graphic representations to depict geographic problems.

Other Standards SS.A.3.4.9, B.2.4.1

FCAT LA.A.2.2.7 Reading: Recognize Compare and Contrast

Use the Unit Atlas to add to your knowledge of Europe. As you look at the maps and charts, notice geographic patterns and specific details about the region. For example, the chart gives details about the rivers and mountains of Europe.

After studying the graphs and physical map on these two pages, jot down answers to the questions below in your notebook.

Making Comparisons

1. Compare Europe's size and population to that of the United States. Based on that data, how might the population densities of the two compare?

2. Compare Europe's longest river, the Danube, to the Mississippi. How much difference is there in the lengths?

3. Which countries have many mountains? How might those mountains affect human life there?

Comparing Data

Landmass

Europe
1,888,688 sq mi

Continental United States
3,165,630 sq mi

Population

Europe
510,898,860

United States
281,422,000

| 0 | 100 | 200 | 300 | 400 | 500 | 600 |

Population (in millions)

Rivers

Elbe
724 miles

Rhine
820 miles

Danube
1,776 miles

Mississippi
2,357 miles — U.S. Longest

Nile
4,160 miles — World's Longest

| 0 | 1000 | 2000 | 3000 | 4000 |

Length (in miles)

Mountains

World's Tallest **Mt. Everest**	U.S. Tallest **Mt. McKinley**	**Mont Blanc**	**Monte Rosa**	**Dom**
Nepal-Tibet	United States	France-Italy	Switzerland-Italy	Switzerland
29,035 feet	20,320 feet	15,771 feet	15,203 feet	14,913 feet

For updated statistics on Europe . . .

DATA UPDATE
CLASSZONE.COM

ICELAND

Norwegian Sea

Faroe Is.

Shetland Is.

Orkney Is.

Hebrides

HIGHLANDS

NORWAY

SWEDEN

FINLAND

Gulf of Bothnia

IRELAND

North Sea

BRITISH ISLES

UNITED KINGDOM

Jutland

DENMARK

Gotland

Öland I.

ESTONIA

RUSSIA

LATVIA

LITHUANIA

Land's End

English Channel

Channel Is.

NETHERLANDS

IJSSELMEER

Elbe R.

RUSSIA

BELARUS

ATLANTIC OCEAN

BELGIUM

Rhine R.

LUXEMBOURG

GERMANY

NORTHERN EUROPEAN PLAIN

Vistula R.

Oder R.

POLAND

Loire R.

Seine R.

BLACK FOREST

CZECH REPUBLIC

UKRAINE

Danube R.

SLOVAKIA

CARPATHIAN MTS.

MOLDOVA

Cape Finisterre

Bay of Biscay

MASSIF CENTRAL

FRANCE

SWITZERLAND

LIECHTENSTEIN

AUSTRIA

HUNGARY

SLOVENIA

ROMANIA

PORTUGAL

Ebro R.

PYRENEES

ANDORRA

Rhône R.

Mt. Blanc 15,771 ft. (4,807 m.)

ALPS

Po R.

MONACO

APENNINES

SAN MARINO

CROATIA

BOSNIA & HERZEGOVINA

Danube R.

BALKAN MTS.

Tagus R.

MESETA

Corsica

Elba

VATICAN CITY

ITALY

Adriatic Sea

YUGOSLAVIA

BULGARIA

Black Sea

SPAIN

Majorca

Minorca

Balearic Is.

Sardinia

Tyrrhenian Sea

MACEDONIA

ALBANIA

Cape St. Vincent

Strait of Gibraltar

Mediterranean

Mt. Etna 10,902 ft. (3,323 m.)

Sicily

Sea

GREECE

Aegean Sea

TURKEY

PELOPONNESUS

Cyclades

Rhodes

ALGERIA

TUNISIA

MALTA

Crete

Elevation

13,100 ft. (4,000 m.)
6,600 ft. (2,000 m.)
1,600 ft. (500 m.)
650 ft. (200 m.)
0 ft. (0 m.)
Below sea level

▲ Mountain peak
Glacier

250 / 500 miles
250 / 500 kilometers
Azimuthal Equidistant Projection

LIBYA

EGYPT

263

EUROPE

Unit ATLAS

Patterns of Human Geography

After World War I (1914–1918), the political map of Europe changed radically. Empires disappeared, and new countries were born. Study the political maps of Europe in 1914 and Europe today to see what changes took place in the 20th century. Then answer these questions in your notebook.

Making Comparisons

1. Which nations appear on the map of Europe today but don't appear on the 1914 map?

2. Which nations existed in 1914 but no longer exist today?

3. Which nations are larger now than they were in 1914?

4. Which nations are smaller than they were in 1914?

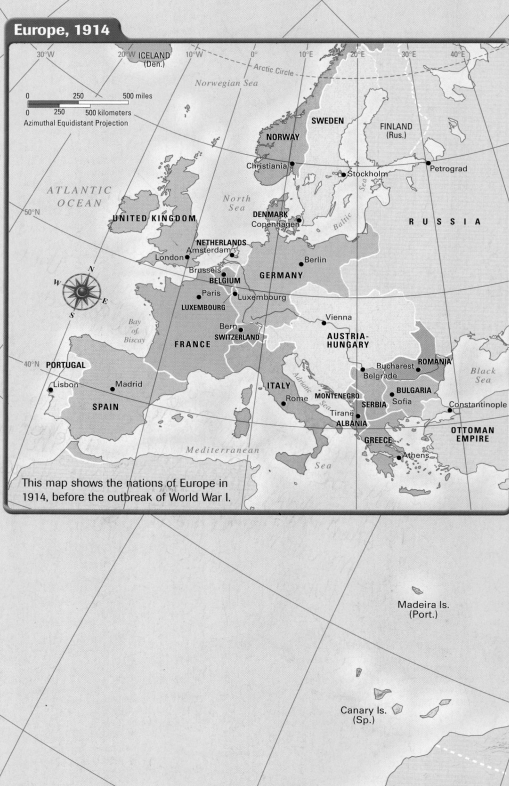

Europe, 1914

Azimuthal Equidistant Projection

0 250 500 miles
0 250 500 kilometers

This map shows the nations of Europe in 1914, before the outbreak of World War I.

Reykjavík

ICELAND

20°W   10°W   0°   10°E   20°E

Arctic Circle

Norwegian Sea

Faroe
Islands
(Den.)

Shetland Is.
(Br.)

Trondheim

NORWAY

SWEDEN

*Gulf of
Bothnia*

FINLAND

Tampere

60°N

Bergen

Oslo

Helsinki

Glasgow

Stockholm

*North
Sea*

Göteborg

*Baltic
Sea*

ESTONIA

RUSSIA

Belfast

Edinburgh

LATVIA

Dublin

Cork

IRELAND

**UNITED
KINGDOM**

DENMARK

Copenhagen

LITHUANIA

RUSSIA

BELARUS

EUROPE

Portsmouth

London

English Channel

NETHERLANDS

Amsterdam

Brussels

Hamburg

Berlin

POLAND

Poznań

Warsaw

**ATLANTIC

OCEAN**

BELGIUM

LUXEMBOURG

Luxembourg

GERMANY

Frankfurt

Prague

CZECH REPUBLIC

50°N

UKRAINE

Nantes

Paris

SLOVAKIA

Bratislava

*Bay
of
Biscay*

FRANCE

Bern

SWITZERLAND

LIECHTENSTEIN

AUSTRIA

Vienna

Graz

Budapest

MOLDOVA

Bordeaux

Milan

Venice

SLOVENIA

Ljubljana

Zagreb

HUNGARY

ROMANIA

PORTUGAL

ITALY

CROATIA

San
Marino

Belgrade

Bucharest

*Black
Sea*

Lisbon

Madrid

ANDORRA

Marseille

MONACO

Corsica
(Fr.)

SPAIN

Barcelona

*Tyrrhenian
Sea*

**BOSNIA &
HERZEGOVINA**

Sarajevo

YUGOSLAVIA

BULGARIA

Sofia

Skopje

40°N

Seville

Balearic Islands
(Sp.)

Sardinia
(It.)

**VATICAN
CITY**

Rome

Naples

*Adriatic
Sea*

Tiranë

MACEDONIA

ALBANIA

GREECE

*Aegean
Sea*

TURKEY

M e d i t e r r a n e a n

Athens

MOROCCO

ALGERIA

Sicily
(It.)

MALTA

Valletta

S e a

N

W   E

S

Crete
(Gr.)

National capital

Other city

0   250   500 miles

0   250   500 kilometers

Azimuthal Equidisant Projection

TUNISIA

10°E

20°E

LIBYA

EGYPT

265

Regional Patterns

These two pages contain a pie graph and three thematic maps. The pie graph shows the religions of Europe. The maps show other important features of Europe: its generally mild climate, its diversity of languages, and its high population density. After studying these two pages, answer the questions below in your notebook.

Making Comparisons

1. Where are the coldest climates to be found in Europe? Is the population density high or low in those areas? Give possible reasons for that pattern.

2. What do you notice about the number of languages in Europe? Do they belong to one language group or several? Explain whether the pattern of languages would be more likely to increase or decrease conflict in the region.

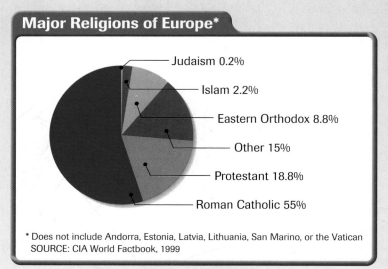

Major Religions of Europe*

Judaism 0.2%
Islam 2.2%
Eastern Orthodox 8.8%
Other 15%
Protestant 18.8%
Roman Catholic 55%

* Does not include Andorra, Estonia, Latvia, Lithuania, San Marino, or the Vatican
SOURCE: CIA World Factbook, 1999

Climates of Europe

Semiarid
Mediterranean
Marine west coast
Humid subtropical
Humid continental
Subarctic
Tundra
Highland

0   250   500 miles
0   250   500 kilometers
Azimuthal Equidistant Projection

Languages of Europe

Major Indo-European Branches
- Germanic
- Romance
- Slavic

Other Indo-European Branches
- Celtic
- Hellenic
- Illyrian

Uralic Language Family
- Finno-Ugric

Other Languages
- Basque
- Areas with significant concentrations of other languages (usually adjacent national languages)

French Spoken language

0   250   500 miles
0   250   500 kilometers
Azimuthal Equidistant Projection

Icelandic
Sami
Norwegian Sea
Faeroese
Finnish
Scots Gaelic
English
Norwegian
Swedish
North Sea
Baltic Sea
Irish Gaelic
English
Danish
Welsh
Frisian
English
Dutch
German
Polish
ATLANTIC OCEAN
Breton
Alsatian
Czech
Slovak
Bay of Biscay
French
Romanian
Galician
Hungarian
Black Sea
Basque
Slovene
Spanish
Provençal
Serbo-Croatian
Bulgarian
Portuguese
Italian
Adriatic Sea
Macedonian
Catalan
Albanian
Greek
Mediterranean Sea

EUROPE

Population Density of Europe

Persons per sq mi
- Over 520
- 260–519
- 130–259
- 25–129
- 1–24
- 0

Persons per sq km
- Over 200
- 100–199
- 50–99
- 10–49
- 1–9
- 0

0   250   500 miles
0   250   500 kilometers
Azimuthal Equidistant Projection

Reykjavík
Arctic Circle
Norwegian Sea
60°N
Helsinki
Oslo
Stockholm
North Sea
Baltic Sea
Dublin
Copenhagen
50°N
London
Amsterdam
Berlin
Brussels
Warsaw
Luxembourg
Paris
Prague
Bay of Biscay
Vienna
Bratislava
Bern
Budapest
Ljubljana
Zagreb
Bucharest
Sarajevo
Belgrade
Black Sea
Lisbon
Madrid
Sofia
Rome
Skopje
Adriatic Sea
Tiranë
40°N
Mediterranean Sea
Athens
Valletta
ATLANTIC OCEAN

20°W   10°W   0°   10°E   20°E   30°E

267

Unit ATLAS

Regional Data File

Country Flag	Country/ Capital	Population (2000)	Life Expectancy (years) (2000)	Birthrate (per 1,000 pop.) (2000)	Infant Mortality (per 1,000 live births) (2000)
	Albania Tiranë	3,431,000	71	19	41.3
	Andorra Andorra la Vella	67,000	83	11	6.4
	Austria Vienna	8,094,000	78	10	4.9
	Belgium Brussels	10,246,000	78	11	5.6
	Bosnia & Herzegovina Sarajevo	3,809,000	73	13	25.2
	Bulgaria Sofia	8,152,000	71	8	14.9
	Croatia Zagreb	4,600,000	73	11	8.2
	Czech Republic Prague	10,275,000	75	9	4.6
	Denmark Copenhagen	5,330,000	77	12	4.7
	Finland Helsinki	5,177,000	78	11	4.2
	France Paris	59,353,000	79	13	4.8
	Germany Berlin	82,141,000	77	9	4.7
	Greece Athens	10,596,000	78	10	6.7
	Hungary Budapest	10,020,000	71	9	8.9
	Iceland Reykjavík	281,000	80	15	4.0
	Ireland Dublin	3,795,000	76	15	6.2
	Italy Rome	57,820,000	78	9	5.5
	Liechtenstein Vaduz	33,000	73	14	5.1
	Luxembourg Luxembourg	438,000	77	13	5.0

Study the charts on the countries of Europe. In your notebook, answer these questions.

Making Comparisons

1. Make a list of the top five European countries in GDP. Where are each of these countries located, relative to the rest of Europe? What pattern do you notice?

2. Look at Albania's life expectancy, infant mortality, and number of doctors. Judging from these statistics, does Albania have good health care?

3. Use the map on page 265 to choose a country in Eastern Europe. How many televisions and cars does it have per 1,000 people? How does that compare to the United States?

(continued on page 270)

Notes:
[a] A comparison of the prices of the same items in different countries is used to figure these data.
[b] Includes water, when figures are available.

For updated statistics on Europe . . .

DATA UPDATE
CLASSZONE.COM

Doctors (per 100,000 pop.) (1990–1998)	GDP[a] (billions $US) (1999)	Import/Export[a] (billions $US) (1996–1999)	Literacy Rate (percentage) (1991–1998)	Televisions (per 1,000 pop.) (1996–1998)	Passenger Cars (per 1,000 pop.) (1996–1997)	Total Area[b] (square miles)	
129	5.6	0.9 / 0.2	83	161	10 (1990)	11,100	
253	1.2 (1996)	1.0 / 0.6	100	315	552	174	
302	190.6	69.9 / 62.9	100	516	468	32,378	
395	243.4	172.8 / 187.3	99	510	434	11,787	
143	6.2	3.0 / 0.5	86	94	23	19,741	
345	34.9	5.3 / 3.8	98	366	202	42,822	
229	23.9	7.6 / 4.5	98	267	160	21,830	
303	120.8	29.0 / 26.9	99	447	428	30,448	
290	127.7	43.9 / 49.5	100	585	339	16,637	
299	108.6	30.7 / 43.0	100	640	378	130,560	
303	1,373.0	280.8 / 304.7	99	601	437	212,934	
350	1,864.0	587.0 / 610.0	100	580	504	137,830	
392	149.2	24.9 / 12.4	97	466	223	50,950	
357	79.4	25.1 / 22.6	99	437	222	35,919	
326	6.4	2.4 / 1.9	100	356	489	39,768	
219	73.7	39.6 / 66.0	100	456	292	27,135	
554	1,212.0	206.9 / 242.6	98	486	540	116,320	
100	0.730	0.9 / 2.5	100	371	592 (1993)	62	
272	14.7	8.6 / 7.5	100	619	515	999	

Regional Data File

Country Flag	Country/ Capital	Population (2000)	Life Expectancy (years) (2000)	Birthrate (per 1,000 pop.) (2000)	Infant Mortality (per 1,000 live births) (2000)
	Macedonia Skopje	2,033,000	73	15	16.3
	Malta Valletta	390,000	77	12	5.3
	Monaco Monaco	34,000	79	20	5.9
	Netherlands Amsterdam	15,921,000	78	13	5.0
	Norway Oslo	4,487,000	79	13	4.0
	Poland Warsaw	38,648,000	74	10	8.9
	Portugal Lisbon	10,013,000	76	11	6.0
	Romania Bucharest	22,432,000	70	11	20.5
	San Marino San Marino	27,000	80	11	8.8
	Slovakia Bratislava	5,401,000	73	11	8.8
	Slovenia Ljubljana	1,968,000	75	9	5.2
	Spain Madrid	39,466,000	78	9	5.7
	Sweden Stockholm	8,866,000	80	10	3.5
	Switzerland Bern	7,142,000	80	11	4.8
	United Kingdom London	59,750,000	77	12	5.7
	Vatican City Vatican City	860 (1999)	N/A	N/A	N/A
	Yugoslavia Belgrade	10,662,000	73	11	10.4
	United States Washington, D.C.	281,422,000	77	15	7.0

Making Comparisons (continued)

4. Europe has several countries with populations under 100,000 people. Which of these has the smallest total area?

5. Use the map on page 265 to identify the two countries on the Scandinavian Peninsula. For each of those countries, calculate per capita GDP by dividing total GDP by population. Which country has the higher per capita GDP?

Sources:
Europa World Year Book 2000
Human Development Report 2000, United Nations
International Data Base, 2000, U.S. Census Bureau online
Merriam-Webster's Geographical Dictionary, 1997
Stateman's Yearbook 2001
2000 World Population Data Sheet, Population Reference Bureau online
WHO Estimates of Health Personnel, World Health Organization online
World Almanac and Book of Facts 2000
World Factbook 2000, CIA online
N/A = not available

Notes:
a A comparison of the prices of the same items in different countries is used to figure these data.
b Includes land and water, when figures are available.

Doctors (per 100,000 pop.) (1990-1998)	GDP[a] (billions $US) (1999)	Import/Export[a] (billions $US) (1999)	Literacy Rate (percentage) (1991-1998)	Televisions (per 1,000 pop.) (1996-1998)	Passenger Cars (per 1,000 pop.) (1996-1997)	Total Area[b] (square miles)	
204	7.6	1.6 / 1.2	89	250	132	9,927	
261	5.3	2.7 / 1.8	91	518	321	124	
664	0.9	Included in figures for France	100	690	548	0.6	
251	365.1	152.0 / 169.0	100	543	372	16,033	
413	111.3	38.6 / 47.3	100	579	399	125,050	
236	276.5	40.8 / 27.8	99	413	195	124,807	
312	151.4	34.9 / 25.0	91	542	295	35,514	
184	87.4	9.6 / 8.4	98	226	106	92,042	
252	0.5 (1997)	Included in figures for Italy	99	346	955	23	
353	45.9	11.2 / 10.1	100	402	185	18,923	
228	21.4	9.7 / 8.4	99	356	343	7,819	
424	677.5	137.5 / 112.3	97	506	384	195,363	
311	184.0	67.9 / 85.7	100	531	417	173,730	
323	197.0	99.0 / 98.5	100	535	460	15,942	
164	1,290.0	305.9 / 271.0	100	645	434	94,548	
N/A	N/A	N/A	100	N/A	N/A	0.17	
203	20.6	3.3 / 1.5	98	27	173	39,448	
251	9,255.0	820.8 / 663.0	97	847	489	3,787,319	

PHYSICAL GEOGRAPHY OF EUROPE
The Peninsula of Peninsulas

Sognafjord, north of the city of Bergen, Norway, has only about five and a half hours of light per day in mid-December.

GeoFocus

What effect does physical geography have on the lives of Europeans?

Taking Notes Copy the graphic organizer below into your notebook. Use it to record information from the chapter about the physical geography of Europe.

Landforms	
Resources	
Climate and Vegetation	
Human–Environment Interaction	

Landforms and Resources

Main Ideas

• Europe is composed of many peninsulas and islands.

• Europe's landforms also include large plains and mountain ranges.

Places & Terms

fjord	*Massif Central*
uplands	peat
Meseta	

CONNECT TO THE ISSUES

UNIFICATION Resources helped Western Europe develop industry before other regions. The European Union began in Western Europe.

SUNSHINE STATE STANDARDS

Key Standard SS.B.1.4.3 The student uses mental maps of physical and human features of the world to answer complex geographic questions.

Other Standards SS.B.1.4.1, B.2.4.3

FCAT LA.A.1.4.2 Reading: Strategies

A HUMAN PERSPECTIVE Elephants in Europe? In 218 B.C., Hannibal, a general from Carthage in North Africa, attacked the Roman Empire, which was at war with Carthage. He moved 38 war elephants and an estimated 60,000 troops across the Mediterranean Sea to Spain. To reach Italy, his armies had to cross the Pyrenees Mountains, the Rhone River, and the Alps. Hannibal used rafts to float the elephants across the Rhone. In the Alps, steep paths and slick ice caused men and animals to fall to their deaths. Despite this, Hannibal arrived in Italy with 26,000 men and a few elephants, and he defeated Rome in many battles. His crossing of the Alps was a triumph over geographic barriers.

Peninsulas and Islands

On a map you will see that Europe is a large peninsula stretching to the west of Asia. Europe itself has many smaller peninsulas, so it is sometimes called a "peninsula of peninsulas." Because of these peninsulas, most locations in Europe are no more than 300 miles from an ocean or sea. As you can imagine, the European way of life involves using these bodies of water for both business and pleasure.

NORTHERN PENINSULAS In northern Europe is the Scandinavian Peninsula. Occupied by the nations of Norway and Sweden, it is bounded by the Norwegian Sea, the North Sea, and the Baltic Sea. More than almost any other place in Europe, this peninsula shows the results of the movement of glaciers during the Ice Age. The glaciers scoured away the rich topsoil and left only thin, rocky soil that is hard to farm.

In Norway, glaciers also carved out **fjords** (fyawrdz), which are steep U-shaped valleys that connect to the sea and that filled with seawater after the glaciers melted. Fjords provide excellent harbors for fishing boats. The fjords are often separated by narrow peninsulas.

The Jutland Peninsula is directly across the North Sea from Scandinavia. Jutland forms the largest part of Denmark and a small part of Germany. This peninsula is an extension of a broad

Major European Peninsulas

0   250   500 miles
0   250   500 kilometers
Azimuthal Equidistant Projection

Norwegian Sea

SCANDINAVIAN PENINSULA

ATLANTIC OCEAN

North Sea

JUTLAND PENINSULA

Baltic Sea

Bay of Biscay

PYRENEES

ALPS

Adriatic Sea

IBERIAN PENINSULA

ITALIAN PENINSULA

BALKAN PENINSULA

Black Sea

Mediterranean Sea

SKILLBUILDER: Interpreting Maps

❶ **LOCATION** Where are Europe's major peninsulas located in relation to each other?

❷ **REGION** Why might each peninsula be considered a region?

EUROPE

plain that reaches across northern Europe. Its gently rolling hills and swampy low-lying areas are very different from the rocky land of the Scandinavian Peninsula.

SOUTHERN PENINSULAS The southern part of Europe contains three major peninsulas:

- The Iberian Peninsula is home to Spain and Portugal. The Pyrenees Mountains block off this peninsula from the rest of Europe.
- The Italian Peninsula is home to Italy. It is shaped like a boot, extends into the Mediterranean Sea, and has 4,700 miles of coastline.
- The Balkan Peninsula is bordered by the Adriatic, Mediterranean, and Aegean Seas. It is mountainous, so transportation is difficult.

ISLANDS Another striking feature of Europe is its islands. The larger islands are Great Britain, Ireland, Iceland, and Greenland, all located in the North Atlantic. Although far from mainland Europe, Iceland and Greenland were settled by Scandinavians and have maintained cultural ties with the mainland. Over the centuries, many different groups have occupied the smaller Mediterranean Sea islands of Corsica, Sardinia, Sicily, and Crete. All of Europe's islands have depended upon trade. ▶

Geographic Thinking

Seeing Patterns
◀ What geographic advantages do islands have that help to promote trade?

Mountains and Uplands

The mountains and uplands of Europe may be viewed as walls because they separate groups of people. They make it difficult for people, goods, and ideas to move easily from one place to another. These landforms also affect climate. For example, the chilly north winds rarely blow over the Alps into Italy, which has a mild climate as a result.

MOUNTAIN CHAINS The most famous mountain chain in Europe is the Alps. On a map you can see that the Alps arc across France, Italy, Germany, Switzerland, Austria, and the northern Balkan Peninsula. They cut Italy off from the rest of Europe. Similarly, the Pyrenees restrict movement from France to Spain and Portugal. Both ranges provide opportunities for skiing, hiking, and other outdoor activities.

Running like a spine down Italy, the Apennine Mountains divide the Italian Peninsula between east and west. The Balkan Mountains block

HUMAN-ENVIRONMENT INTERACTION
The Wetterhorn in the Swiss Alps stands 12,142 feet above the city in the valley below. **How do the mountains affect the lives of the people in the valley?**

off the Balkan Peninsula from the rest of Europe. Historically, they also have isolated the peninsula's various ethnic groups from each other.

UPLANDS Mountains and uplands differ from each other in their elevation. **Uplands** are hills or very low mountains that may also contain mesas and high plateaus. Some uplands of Europe are eroded remains of ancient mountain ranges. Examples of uplands include the Kjølen (CHUR·luhn) Mountains of Scandinavia, the Scottish highlands, the low mountain areas of Brittany in France, and the central plateau of Spain called the **Meseta** (meh·SEH·tah). Other uplands border mountainous areas, such as the Central Uplands of Germany, which are at the base of the Alps. About one-sixth of French lands are located in the uplands called the **Massif Central** (ma·SEEF sahn·TRAHL).

BACKGROUND
Brittany is a region located on a peninsula in northwest France.

Rivers: Europe's Links

Traversing Europe is a network of rivers that bring people and goods together. These rivers are used to transport goods between coastal harbors and the inland region, aiding economic growth. Historically, the rivers also have aided the movement of ideas.

Two major castle-lined rivers—the Danube and the Rhine—have served as watery highways for centuries. The Rhine flows 820 miles from the interior of Europe north to the North Sea. The Danube cuts through the heart of Europe from west to east. Touching 9 countries over its 1,771-mile length, the Danube River links Europeans to the Black Sea.

Many other European rivers flow from the interior to the sea and are large enough for ships to traverse. Through history, these rivers helped connect Europeans to the rest of the world, encouraging both trade and travel. Europeans have explored and migrated to many other world regions. **B**

Rivers of Europe

SKILLBUILDER: Interpreting Maps
❶ MOVEMENT Which rivers empty into the North Sea? Into the Mediterranean Sea?
❷ PLACE What port is at the mouth of the Rhine?

Geographic Thinking

Seeing Patterns
B How does the direction in which European rivers flow aid in linking Europeans to the world?

Fertile Plains: Europe's Bounty

One of the most fertile agricultural regions of the world is the Northern European Plain (see the map on page 263), stretching in a huge curve across parts of France, Belgium, the Netherlands, Denmark, Germany, and Poland. Relatively flat, this plain is very desirable agricultural land that has produced vast quantities of food over the centuries. However, the plain's flatness has also allowed armies and groups of invaders to use it as an open route into Europe. Smaller fertile plains used for farming also exist in Sweden, Hungary, and Lombardy in northern Italy.

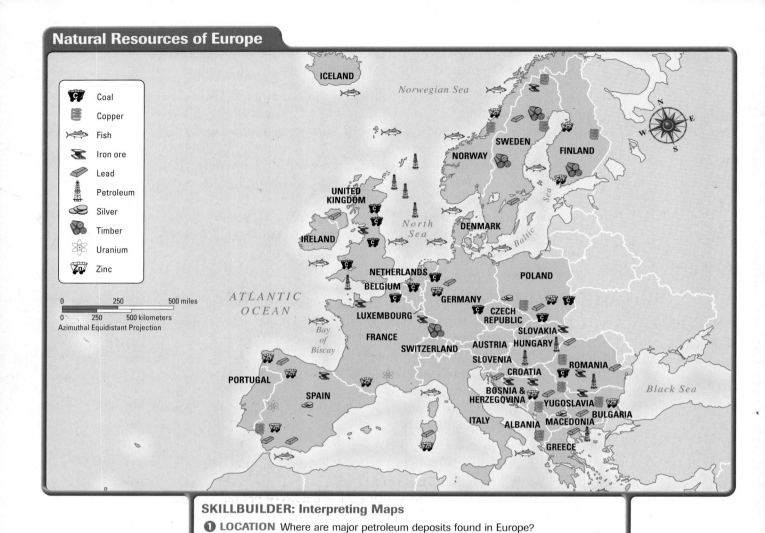

Natural Resources of Europe

Legend:
- C — Coal
- Copper
- Fish
- Iron ore
- Lead
- Petroleum
- Silver
- Timber
- Uranium
- Zn — Zinc

0   250   500 miles
0   250   500 kilometers
Azimuthal Equidistant Projection

SKILLBUILDER: Interpreting Maps

① **LOCATION** Where are major petroleum deposits found in Europe?

② **REGION** Which countries in Europe have relatively few natural resources?

Resources Shape Europe's Economy

Europe has abundant supplies of two natural resources—coal and iron ore—needed for an industrialized economy. The map above shows a band of coal deposits stretching from the United Kingdom across to Belgium and the Netherlands and from there to France, Germany, and Poland. Near many of these coal deposits are iron ore deposits. Having both of these resources makes it possible to produce steel. The Ruhr (roor) Valley in Germany, the Alsace-Lorraine region of France, and parts of the United Kingdom are heavily industrialized because these minerals are found there and good transportation exists. But as a result, these regions have suffered from industrial pollution. (See Chapter 14 for more on pollution.) ◖

ENERGY Oil and natural gas were found beneath the North Sea floor in 1959. Energy companies began to tap gas fields between the United Kingdom and the Netherlands. In 1971, new technologies made it possible to construct offshore oil rigs in the North Sea despite its deep, stormy waters. Norway, the Netherlands, the United Kingdom, and Denmark now pump oil from rigs as far as 400 miles out in the ocean. The North Sea oil fields are major sources of petroleum for the world.

CONNECT TO THE ISSUES
POLLUTION
◖ What types of pollution might industry create?

AGRICULTURAL LAND About 33 percent of Europe's land is suitable for agriculture. The world average is 11 percent, so Europe is especially well off. The land produces a variety of crops: grains, grapes, olives, and even cork. Timber is cut from vast forests on the Scandinavian Peninsula and in the Alps.

BACKGROUND
Cork is the outer bark of the cork oak tree.

Resources Shape Life

As is true of every region, the resources available in Europe help shape the lives of its people. Resources directly affect the foods people eat, the jobs they hold, the houses in which they live, and even their culture. For example, traditional European folk tales often take place in deep, dark forests that were a major part of the European landscape centuries ago.

The distribution of resources also creates regional differences within Europe. For instance, because Ireland lacks energy sources, the Irish cut peat from large beds and burn it as fuel. **Peat** is partially decayed plant matter found in bogs. In contrast, coal is plentiful in other parts of Europe and has been mined for centuries. For example, generations of Polish miners have worked the mines that modern-day Poles work.

Just as landforms and resources influence the lives of people, so does climate. In Section 2, you will learn that the climates of Europe are mild near the Atlantic Ocean and grow harsher inland. You will also learn about the climates of the Mediterranean and the Arctic regions.

PLACE Harvesting peat is common in Ireland because other fuel sources are scarce. **Why is it cut in blocks?**

Assessment

① Places & Terms

Identify and explain where in the region these would be found.

- fjord
- uplands
- *Meseta*
- *Massif Central*
- peat

② Taking Notes

PLACE Review the notes you took for this section.

Landforms	
Resources	

- What types of landforms are found in Europe?
- What resources help with farming?

③ Main Ideas

a. Why is Europe called a "peninsula of peninsulas"?

b. How are the landforms of Europe both an advantage and a disadvantage to life in Europe?

c. How did natural resources help Europe to become industrialized?

④ Geographic Thinking

Drawing Conclusions
What role did the waterways of Europe play in the development of its economy?
Think about:

- the nearness to seas and oceans
- the network of rivers

RESEARCH LINKS
CLASSZONE.COM

GeoActivity

EXPLORING LOCAL GEOGRAPHY Do research to learn the top three natural resources in your state. Then study the map on page 276 to determine which European country has the most resources in common with your state. Create a **Venn Diagram** showing the resources your state has in common with that country and the resources that are different.

Climate and Vegetation

Main Ideas
- Much of Europe has a relatively mild climate because of ocean currents and warm winds.
- Eastern Europe has a harsher climate because it is farther from the Atlantic Ocean.

Places & Terms
North Atlantic Drift

sirocco

mistral

CONNECT TO THE ISSUES
POLLUTION Industrial air pollution leads to acid rain, which kills trees and other vegetation.

SUNSHINE STATE STANDARDS
Key Standard SS.B.2.4.1 The student understands how social, cultural, economic, and environmental factors contribute to the dynamic nature of regions.

Other Standards SS.B.1.4.2

FCAT LA.A.1.4.2 Reading: Strategies

A HUMAN PERSPECTIVE Because of Greece's mild climate, the ancient Greeks spent much time outdoors. Greek men liked to talk with their friends in the marketplace. They also enjoyed sports. Large crowds gathered for athletic contests that were held during religious festivals. The most important of these was a footrace held every four years in the town of Olympia, a contest called the Olympic Games. In time, these games came to include other sports such as wrestling. In this form, they were the model for our modern Olympics. If ancient Greece had had a cold climate, we might not have Olympic Games today.

Westerly Winds Warm Europe

A marine west coast climate exists in much of Europe—from northern Spain across most of France and Germany to western Poland. It also exists in the British Isles and some coastal areas of Scandinavia. With warm summers and cool winters, the region enjoys a milder climate than do most regions at such a northern latitude.

The nearby ocean and the dominant winds create this mild climate. The **North Atlantic Drift,** a current of warm water from the tropics, flows near Europe's west coast. The prevailing westerlies, which blow west to east, pick up warmth from this current and carry it over Europe. No large mountain ranges block the winds, so they are felt far inland. They also carry moisture, giving the region adequate rainfall.

Climographs: Fargo and Paris

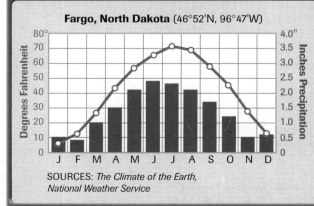

Fargo, North Dakota (46°52'N, 96°47'W)

SOURCES: *The Climate of the Earth,* National Weather Service

Paris, France (48°58'N, 2°27'E)

SOURCES: *Weather America, World Weather Guide*

Average Temperature

Average Precipitation

Fargo, North Dakota — Paris, France

SKILLBUILDER: Interpreting Graphs

MAKING COMPARISONS Which of these two locations is farther north? Which has the milder climate? Explain how you determined which was milder.

Geographic Thinking←

Making Comparisons
A▷ Would you expect the high Alps to be more or less densely populated than the surrounding region? Why?

The Alps create a band of harsher conditions next to this climate zone. Because of their high elevation, the Alps have a much colder climate. Above 5,000 feet, snow can reach a depth of 33 feet in winter. ◀A

FORESTS TO FARMS Originally, mixed forests covered much of the marine west coast climate region. Over the centuries, people cleared away most of the forest so they could settle and farm the land. Today, farmers in the region grow grains, sugar beets, livestock feed, and root crops such as potatoes.

Harsher Conditions Inland

People who live far from the Atlantic Ocean do not benefit from the moderating influence of the westerlies. As a result, much of Sweden and Finland and the eastern parts of Poland, Slovakia, and Hungary have a humid continental climate, as does all of Romania. These places have cold, snowy winters and either warm or hot summers (depending upon their latitude). In general, the region receives adequate rainfall, which helps agriculture.

Like most of Europe, the region has suffered much deforestation, but the forests that do survive tend to be coniferous. The region also has broad fertile plains that were originally covered with grasses. Today, farmers grow grains such as wheat, rye, and barley on these plains. Other major crops include potatoes and sugar beets.

The Sunny Mediterranean

A mild climate lures people to live and vacation in the region bordering the Mediterranean Sea. This Mediterranean climate extends from southern Spain and France through Italy to Greece and other parts of the Balkan Peninsula. Summers are hot and dry with clear, sunny skies, while winters are moderate and wet. One reason for the climate is that mountain ranges block cold north winds from reaching the Iberian, Italian, and Balkan peninsulas.

SPECIAL WINDS An exception to this pattern is the Mediterranean coast of France, which is not protected by high mountains. In winter, this coast receives the **mistral** (MIHS·truhl), a cold, dry wind from the north. ◀B

Most Mediterranean countries experience a wind called the sirocco. The **sirocco** (suh·RAHK·oh) is a hot, steady south wind that blows from North Africa across the Mediterranean Sea into southern Europe. Some siroccos pick up moisture from the sea and produce rain; others carry dust from the desert.

EUROPE

REGION In some Mediterranean fields, such as this one in southern France, olive trees and grape vines are grown side by side. **Why might farmers choose to plant a field with two crops instead of one?**

Geographic Thinking←

Using the Atlas
B▷ Locate southern France on the map on page 263. What type of landform borders the Mediterranean Sea there?

PLACE In the village of Jukkasjärvi, Sweden, the Ice Hotel is built every winter out of 10,000 tons of ice and 30,000 tons of snow. **How does climate make this possible?**

THE CLIMATE ATTRACTS TOURISTS

The Mediterranean region has primarily evergreen shrubs and short trees that grow in climates with hot, dry summers. The region's major crops are citrus fruits, olives, grapes, and wheat. The sunny Mediterranean beaches also attract thousands of people, making tourism a major industry in the region.

Land of the Midnight Sun

In far northern Scandinavia, along the Arctic Circle, lies a band of tundra climate. As explained in Chapter 3, the land in such a climate is often in a state of permafrost, in which the subsoil remains frozen year-round. No trees grow there—only mosses and lichens. To the south of this lies the subarctic climate, which is cool most of the time with very cold, harsh winters. Little grows there but stunted trees. Because of the climate, agriculture is limited to southern Scandinavia.

This far northern region witnesses sharp variations in the amount of sunlight received throughout the year. Winter nights are extremely long, as are summer days. North of the Arctic Circle, there are winter days when the sun never rises and summer days when the sun never sets. The region is often called the Land of the Midnight Sun.

In the next section, you will read about ways in which Europeans have altered their environment—both positively and negatively.

BACKGROUND
A lichen is an organism made of a fungus and an alga growing together.

SECTION 2 Assessment

❶ Places & Terms

Identify these terms and explain how they affect climate.

- North Atlantic Drift
- mistral
- sirocco

❷ Taking Notes

REGION Review the notes you took for this section.

Climate and Vegetation	

- Which regions of Europe have the harshest, coldest climates?
- Which climate zones produce the richest variety of vegetation?

❸ Main Ideas

a. How do the North Atlantic Drift and the prevailing westerlies affect Europe's climate?

b. How are a mistral and a sirocco different?

c. Why is northern Scandinavia sometimes called the Land of the Midnight Sun?

❹ Geographic Thinking

Making Decisions If you wanted to attract tourists to far northern Scandinavia, how would you advertise the region? **Think about:**

- recreational activities suitable for such a climate

RESEARCH LINKS
CLASSZONE.COM

MAKING COMPARISONS Choose a place in Europe, and then find a place in North America at about the same latitude. Do Internet research to learn about the climate and vegetation of the two places. Create a **chart** comparing the two.

Map and Graph Skills

Interpreting a Bar Graph

How much rain and snow does your area receive in a year? Average yearly precipitation varies widely throughout the United States, with extremes ranging from a low of less than 2 inches a year in Death Valley, California, to as much as 151.25 inches a year in Yakutat, Alaska. The figures for average yearly precipitation don't reveal how much rain or snow falls in a given month, but they can provide a general indication of a place's suitability for agriculture or other activities.

THE LANGUAGE OF GRAPHS A **bar graph** is a visual way of showing quantities. On a bar graph, it is easy to see how different examples in a category compare; the longer the bar, the greater the quantity. Depending on the subject, the quantities are expressed using measurements such as inches, dollars, or tons. The categories vary from graph to graph. Time periods and places are common categories. Below, a bar graph shows annual precipitation for several European cities.

SUNSHINE STATE STANDARDS
Key Standard SS.B.1.4.1
The student uses a variety of maps, geographic technologies including geographic information systems (GIS) and satellite-produced imagery, and other advanced graphic representations to depict geographic problems.
FCAT LA.B.1.4.2 Writing: Draft and Revise

Average Annual Precipitation in Europe

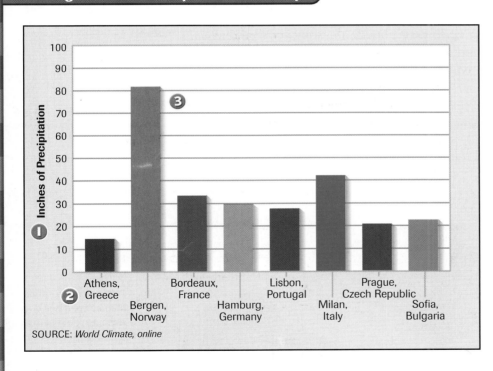

SOURCE: *World Climate, online*

1 The vertical axis tells you that on this graph, the precipitation is expressed in inches.

2 The horizontal axis tells you that the category is selected cities of Europe.

3 A quick glance at this bar graph tells you which cities have high and low amounts of precipitation. By examining the bars more carefully and measuring their heights against the horizontal lines, you can estimate actual amounts of precipitation.

Map and Graph Skills Assessment

1. Analyzing Data
Which cities on this graph have the lowest and highest amounts of annual precipitation?

2. Drawing Conclusions
To which city would you move if your doctor advised you to live in a dry climate?

3. Analyzing Data
What is the average annual precipitation for these eight cities?

Human–Environment Interaction

Main Ideas
- The Dutch and the Venetians altered lands to fit their needs by constructing polders and canals.
- Uncontrolled logging and acid rain destroy forests.

Places & Terms
dike	terpen
polder	Zuider Zee
seaworks	Ijsselmeer

CONNECT TO THE ISSUES
POLLUTION Water pollution is creating conditions that kill the fish in Venice's lagoon.

SUNSHINE STATE STANDARDS
Key Standard SS.B.2.4.5 The student knows how humans overcome "limits to growth" imposed by physical systems.

Other Standards SS.B.2.4.4

FCAT LA.A.1.4.2 Reading: Strategies

A HUMAN PERSPECTIVE "1800 DIE IN WIND-WHIPPED FLOOD WATERS!" February 1, 1953, witnessed a disaster in the Netherlands. Winds estimated at 110 to 115 miles per hour piled up gigantic waves that ripped through **dikes**—earthen banks—holding back the North Sea. When the storm was over, 4.5 percent of the Netherlands was flooded, and thousands of buildings were destroyed. The Netherlands is prone to floods because much of its land is below sea level.

Polders: Land from the Sea

An old saying declares, "God created the world, but the Dutch created Holland." (Holland is another name for the Netherlands.) Because the Dutch needed more land for their growing population, they reclaimed land from the sea. At least 40 percent of the Netherlands was once under the sea. Land that is reclaimed by diking and draining is called a **polder.**

Making a Polder

❶ Earthen dikes are built around a shallow area of water.

❷ The water is gradually pumped away and drained off the land.

❸ Seawater leaves salt in the soil. Rain gradually washes the salt away.

❹ Alfalfa is often the first crop sown. It has deep roots, which break up soil; alfalfa is also used for livestock feed.

❺ In time, the land can be used to grow many crops—such as Dutch tulips.

Windmills once supplied the power used to pump water from polder land. Today electric pumps are used to drain the land.

SKILLBUILDER: Interpreting Graphics
❶ HUMAN–ENVIRONMENT INTERACTION Why does it take time for polder land to be ready for farming?
❷ PLACE How would the process be different if a polder were made in a place where there is freshwater, not saltwater?

SEAWORKS The Dutch erected **seaworks,** structures that are used to control the sea's destructive impact on human life. Those seaworks include dikes and high earthen platforms called **terpen.** The dikes hold back the sea, while the terpen provide places to go for safety during floods and high tides.

Over the centuries, the Dutch found ways to reinforce the dikes and to control water in the low-lying areas the dikes protected. In the 1400s, the Dutch began using their windmills to power pumps that drained the land. When the French conqueror Napoleon viewed a site with 860 windmills pumping an area dry, he reportedly said, "Without equal." Today the pumps use electric motors instead of windmills. ◀A

TRANSFORMING THE SEA Another remarkable Dutch alteration of their environment was the transformation of the **Zuider Zee** (ZEYE·duhr ZAY). It was an arm of the North Sea and is now a fresh-water lake. The idea was originally proposed in 1667. But it was not until the late 1800s and early 1900s that the Dutch perfected a plan to build dikes all the way across the entrance to the Zuider Zee. Since no saltwater flowed into that body of water, it eventually became a fresh-water lake. It is now called **Ijsselmeer** (EYE·suhl·MAIR). The land around the lake was drained, creating several polders that added hundreds of square miles of land to the Netherlands.

Waterways for Commerce: Venice's Canals

Like the Netherlands, Venice, Italy, is a place where humans created a unique environment. About 120 islands and part of the mainland make up the city of Venice. Two of the largest islands are San Marco and Rialto. A broad waterway called the Grand Canal flows between them.

Moving people or goods in Venice depends upon using the more than 150 canals that snake around and through the islands. Consequently, to get from one place to another in Venice, you generally have two choices: take a boat or walk. Almost anything that is moved on wheels elsewhere is moved by water in Venice.

AN ISLAND CITY GROWS Venice began when people escaping invaders took shelter on inhospitable islands in a lagoon. They remained there and established a settlement that eventually became Venice. The city is located at the north end of the Adriatic Sea, a good site for a port. As a result, trade helped Venice grow.

BUILDING ON THE ISLANDS Building Venice required construction techniques that took into account the swampy land on the islands. Builders sunk wooden pilings into the ground to help support the structures above. So many pilings were required that oak forests in the northern Italian countryside and in Slovenia were leveled to supply the wood. The weight of the buildings is so great that it has compressed the underlying ground. This is one of the reasons that Venice is gradually sinking. Other reasons include rising sea levels and the removal of too much groundwater by pumping.

PROBLEMS TODAY Severe water pollution threatens historic Venice. Industrial waste, sewage, and saltwater are combining to eat away the

Geographic Thinking ◀

Making Comparisons
Ⓐ▶ What are possible dis-advantages of windmills and of electric pumps?

BACKGROUND
A land link to Venice was built in 1846. A railway bridge connected Venice to the mainland.

EUROPE

Human–Environment Interaction **283**

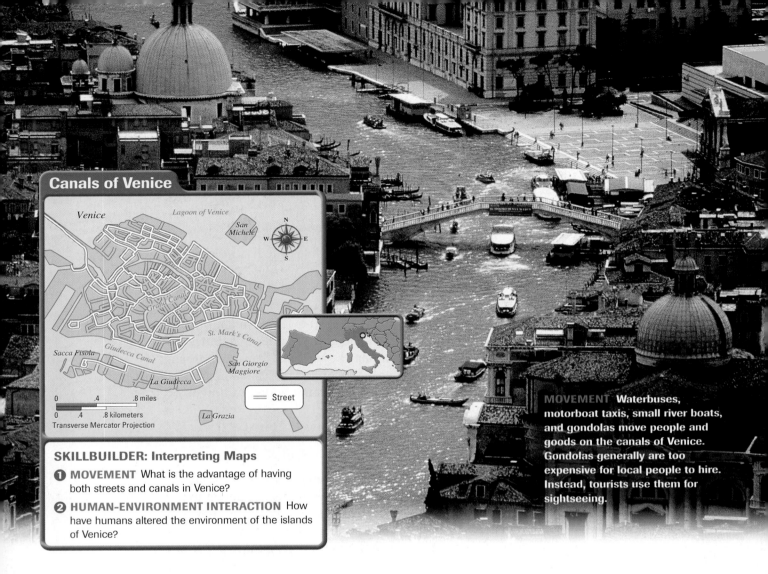

Canals of Venice

Venice

Lagoon of Venice

San Michele

Grand Canal

St. Mark's Canal

Sacca Fisola

Giudecca Canal

La Giudecca

San Giorgio Maggiore

La Grazia

0   .4   .8 miles
0   .4   .8 kilometers
Transverse Mercator Projection

═══ Street

SKILLBUILDER: Interpreting Maps

❶ **MOVEMENT** What is the advantage of having both streets and canals in Venice?

❷ **HUMAN-ENVIRONMENT INTERACTION** How have humans altered the environment of the islands of Venice?

MOVEMENT Waterbuses, motorboat taxis, small river boats, and gondolas move people and goods on the canals of Venice. Gondolas generally are too expensive for local people to hire. Instead, tourists use them for sightseeing.

foundations of buildings and damage the buildings themselves. Erosion has allowed increased amounts of seawater into the lagoon. Because of this, floods also endanger the city. In November 1966, six feet of flood-water engulfed the city and ruined many of its buildings and the art-work that they housed. Agricultural runoff flowing into Venice's harbor creates conditions that promote algae growth, sometimes called "killer algae." These algae grow rapidly and, after they die, decay. The decaying process uses up oxygen in the water, so that fish also die. Dead fish attract insects and create a stench, especially in warm weather.

A Centuries-Old Problem: Deforestation

Throughout history, humans have damaged and destroyed Europe's forests. The term deforestation means the clearing of forests from an area. Often when we think of deforestation, we think of losing the great rain forests of the world, such as those in South America, which you learned about in Unit 3. But people have also been clearing the forests of Europe since ancient times. Forests provided wood to burn for fuel and to use as building material for ships and houses. When Europeans began to develop industry in the 1700s and 1800s, they needed even

HUMAN–ENVIRONMENT INTERACTION A forest in Bohemia in the Czech Republic is dying from the effects of acid rain.
Why would restoring the forest be a slow process?

EUROPE

more wood to make charcoal for blast furnaces. Eventually, they used coal as a fuel in place of wood, but not before huge areas of Europe had lost their native forests.

ACID RAIN STRIPS FORESTS In the 1960s, people noticed that many trees of the Black Forest in Germany were discolored, losing needles and leaves, and dying. In time, scientists identified one cause of the tree deaths as acid rain. Europe's factories produce high amounts of sulfur dioxide and nitrogen oxide emissions. These combine with water vapor and oxygen to form acid rain or snow. Winds carry the emissions to other parts of Europe, affecting an estimated one-fourth of all European forests. This problem has hit Scandinavia particularly hard, since the prevailing winds blow in that direction. As mentioned earlier, the Black Forest in Germany also has suffered extreme damage. To save the remaining forests, nations must work together to reduce air pollution. You can read more about this in Chapter 14. **B**

As you will read in Chapter 13, the ways people live upon the land and interact with each other make up the human geography of Europe.

CONNECT TO THE ISSUES
UNIFICATION
B How might a union of nations affect the clean-up effort?

Assessment

1 Places & Terms

Identify and explain where in the region these would be found.
• dike
• polder
• seaworks
• terpen
• Zuider Zee
• Ijsselmeer

2 Taking Notes

HUMAN-ENVIRONMENT INTERACTION Review your notes for this section.

Human-Environment Interaction	

• What are examples of human adaptation to the environment?
• What are examples of an environment changed by humans?

3 Main Ideas

a. How have the people of the Netherlands been able to create more land for their country?

b. How has pollution affected the city of Venice?

c. How has industrialization hurt the forests of Europe?

4 Geographic Thinking

Making Comparisons
What is similar about the ways that the people of the Netherlands and the people of Venice interact with their environments? **Think about:**
• seaworks in the Netherlands
• canals in Venice

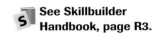
See Skillbuilder Handbook, page R3.

SEEING PATTERNS Pollution has affected both Venice and the forests of Scandinavia. Create two **cause-and-effect charts** outlining the causes and effects of pollution in each place. Then write a sentence or two summarizing the similarities.

Chapter 12 Assessment

VISUAL SUMMARY
PHYSICAL GEOGRAPHY OF EUROPE

Landforms

Major Peninsulas:
Scandinavian, Jutland, Iberian, Italian, Balkan

Major Mountain Ranges:
Alps, Pyrenees, Carpathians, Apennines, Balkans

Major Rivers: Danube, Rhine, Seine, Loire, Elbe, Oder

Resources

- Oil from North Sea oil rigs is an important energy source for Europe.
- Coal and iron ore are found in abundance, making heavy industry possible.

Climate and Vegetation

- The North Atlantic Drift and the prevailing westerlies moderate much of Europe's climate.
- Lands bordering the Mediterranean Sea have a climate that encourages large-scale commercial agriculture.

Human-Environment Interaction

- Polders are an example of how Europeans have altered their environment.
- The canals of Venice demonstrate how Europeans have adapted to their environment.
- Deforestation of the land is a long-standing environmental problem in Europe.

Reviewing Places & Terms

A. Briefly explain the importance of each of the following.

1. fjord
2. uplands
3. *Meseta*
4. *Massif Central*
5. peat
6. mistral
7. polder
8. seaworks
9. terpen
10. Zuider Zee

B. Answer the questions about vocabulary in complete sentences.

11. What are fjords and where are they found?
12. Which of the above terms are examples of uplands?
13. What is France's highland area called?
14. How does the North Atlantic Drift influence climate?
15. In what part of Europe would you find the mistral?
16. How is peat used?
17. Which of the above terms is a type of seaworks?
18. How did the Zuider Zee become Ijsselmeer?
19. What are polders and where are they found?
20. Which of the above terms are associated with human-environment interaction?

Main Ideas

Landforms and Resources (pp. 273-277)

1. How do the mountain ranges of Europe impact the lives of the people who live near them?
2. Why are the rivers of Europe an important aspect of its geography?
3. Where are the most important oil fields of Europe located, and which countries pump oil from them?

Climate and Vegetation (pp. 278-281)

4. How do the prevailing westerlies affect the climate of Europe? Explain which part of Europe is most affected.
5. In which climate area of Europe would you find citrus fruits growing? Explain why.
6. What types of vegetation are found on the Scandinavian Peninsula?

Human-Environment Interaction (pp. 282-285)

7. Why did the Dutch build seaworks?
8. In what ways have the people of the Netherlands changed the physical geography of their land?
9. What kinds of pollutants are found in the Venice canals?
10. Why were forests chopped down in Europe?

Critical Thinking

1. Using Your Notes

Use your completed chart to answer these questions.

Landforms	
Resources	

a. Which of the human-environment interactions try to make the best use of landforms?

b. Which interactions focus on problems with resources?

2. Geographic Themes

a. **PLACE** In what ways has the physical geography of the Balkan Peninsula affected the people who live there?

b. **LOCATION** How would you describe Europe's location relative to bodies of water and to other regions?

3. Identifying Themes

Considering the climate and landforms, evaluate which areas of Europe would be the most agriculturally productive. Which of the five themes apply to this situation?

4. Identifying and Solving Problems

What factors must the people of Venice consider when dealing with the water pollution in their city?

5. Making Comparisons

How are the Scandinavian Peninsula and the Italian Peninsula alike and how are they different? Discuss landforms, resources, and climates.

Additional Test Practice, pp. S1–S37

TEST PRACTICE
CLASSZONE.COM

Geographic Skills: Interpreting Maps

Mountain Ranges of Europe

Use the map to answer the following questions.

1. **MOVEMENT** Which mountains hinder travel between Spain and France?

2. **REGION** Which mountain ranges are in Eastern Europe?

3. **LOCATION** What is the relative location of the Alps?

GeoActivity

Create your own sketch map of the physical geography of Europe. Combine the information from this map with the information from the rivers map on page 275 and the peninsulas map on page 273.

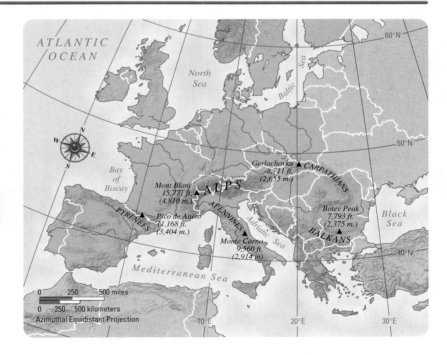

INTERNET ACTIVITY

Use the links at **classzone.com** to do research about acid rain in Europe. Focus on one aspect of acid rain, such as how the European Union is fighting acid rain or how European students learn about acid rain.

Writing About Geography Write a report of your findings. Include a map or a chart that visually presents information on acid rain. List the Web sites that you used in preparing your report.

Chapter 13

SECTION 1
Mediterranean Europe

SECTION 2
Western Europe

SECTION 3
Northern Europe

SECTION 4
Eastern Europe

HUMAN GEOGRAPHY OF EUROPE
Diversity, Conflict, Union

Four Subregions of Europe

ICELAND

Arctic Circle

Norwegian Sea

NORWAY

SWEDEN

FINLAND

North Sea

IRELAND

UNITED KINGDOM

NETHERLANDS

DENMARK

Baltic Sea

BELGIUM

LUXEMBOURG

GERMANY

POLAND

CZECH REPUBLIC

SLOVAKIA

ATLANTIC OCEAN

Bay of Biscay

FRANCE

SWITZERLAND

LIECHTENSTEIN

AUSTRIA

HUNGARY

ROMANIA

SLOVENIA

CROATIA

PORTUGAL

ANDORRA

SPAIN

SAN MARINO

MONACO

VATICAN CITY

ITALY

BOSNIA & HERZEGOVINA

Adriatic Sea

YUGOSLAVIA

BULGARIA

MACEDONIA

ALBANIA

GREECE

Mediterranean Sea

MALTA

Legend:
- Mediterranean
- Western
- Northern
- Eastern

0   250   500 miles
0   250   500 kilometers
Azimuthal Equidistant Projection

GeoFocus

How have cultural differences in Europe caused conflict?

Taking Notes In your notebook, copy a cluster diagram like the one shown below. As you read, take notes about the history, economics, culture, and modern life of each subregion of Europe.

Northern — Europe — Eastern
Western — Europe — Mediterranean

Mediterranean Europe

Main Ideas
- The ancient Greek and Roman civilizations and the Renaissance all began in Mediterranean Europe.
- In the 20th century, the region has seen economic growth and political turmoil.

Places & Terms

city-state   Renaissance

republic   aqueduct

Crusades

CONNECT TO THE ISSUES

UNIFICATION Membership in the European Union has helped the economies of the Mediterranean nations.

The Voyageur Experience in World Geography
Italy: Natural Hazards and Disasters

SUNSHINE STATE STANDARDS
Key Standard SS.B.2.4.2 The student understands past and present trends in human migration and cultural interaction and their impact on physical and human systems.

Other Standards SS.A.2.4.4, A.2.4.5, A.2.4.7, A.3.4.10

FCAT LA.A.1.4.2 Reading: Strategies

PLACE In Athens, ancient ruins such as the Parthenon, shown here, stand near modern buildings.

A HUMAN PERSPECTIVE Have you ever heard the saying, "All roads lead to Rome"? The Mediterranean region was home to the two great civilizations of ancient Europe—ancient Greece and ancient Rome. The city of Rome was founded in about 753 B.C., and Rome conquered a huge empire by about A.D. 100. To aid communication and make it possible for the army to march quickly to distant locations, Rome built a large network of well-paved roads. In ancient Europe, most roads did indeed lead to Rome, enabling that city to control a vast region.

A History of Ancient Glory

Two geographic advantages helped the Mediterranean to become the region where European civilization was born. First, the mild climate made survival there easier than in other areas. So societies had time to develop complex institutions such as government. Second, the nearby Mediterranean Sea encouraged overseas trade. When different societies trade with each other, they also exchange ideas. The spread of ideas often leads to advances in knowledge.

GREECE: BIRTHPLACE OF DEMOCRACY Beginning about 2000 B.C., people from the north moved onto the Balkan Peninsula. They built villages there. The region is mountainous, so those villages were isolated from each other and developed into separate city-states. A **city-state** is a political unit made up of a city and its surrounding lands.

Ancient Greece left a lasting legacy to modern civilization. The city-state of Athens developed the first democracy, a government in which the people rule. In Athens, all free adult males were citizens who had the right to serve in the law-making assembly. Athenian democracy helped inspire the U.S. system of government. And Greek science, philosophy, drama, and art helped shape modern culture.

In the 400s B.C., conflict weakened Greece. Several city-states fought a costly series of wars with Persia, an empire in southwest Asia. Then Athens fought a ruinous

EUROPE

Christian areas around A.D. 500
Romance language spoken, present-day
Boundary of Roman Empire A.D. 395

North Sea
ATLANTIC OCEAN
40°N
Rhine R.
Rome
Danube R.
Black Sea
30°N
Mediterranean Sea
20°N

0   500   1,000 miles
0   500   1,000 kilometers
Azimuthal Equidistant Projection

10°W   0°   10°E   20°E   30°E   40°E   50°E

SKILLBUILDER: Interpreting Maps

❶ **REGION** Which waterways formed part of the northern boundary of the Roman Empire?

❷ **MOVEMENT** Which Roman cultural influence was more widespread, Christianity or Romance languages?

war with Sparta, a rival Greek city-state. Finally, in 338 B.C., Macedonia (a kingdom to the north) conquered Greece. Beginning in 336 B.C., the Macedonian general Alexander the Great conquered Persia and part of India. His empire spread Greek culture but broke apart after his death.

THE ROMAN EMPIRE As Greece lost power, a state to the west was rising. That state, Rome, ruled most of the Italian Peninsula by 275 B.C. At the time, Rome was a **republic,** a government in which citizens elect representatives to rule in their name.

The Roman Empire grew by conquering territory overseas, including the Iberian and Balkan peninsulas. At home in Italy, unrest over inequalities led to decades of turmoil that caused Romans to seek strong leaders. Rome began to be ruled by an emperor, ending the republic.

One of Rome's overseas territories was Palestine, the place where Jesus was born. Christianity spread from there across the empire, and by the late 300s, Christianity was Rome's official religion.

By A.D. 395, the empire was too big for a single government, so it split into a western and an eastern half. The Western Roman Empire grew weak, in part because of German invaders from the north, and fell in A.D. 476. The Eastern Roman Empire lasted nearly 1,000 years longer.

BACKGROUND
The Roman republic was a model for modern governments such as those of France and the United States.

Moving Toward Modern Times

After 476, the three Mediterranean peninsulas had very different histories. The Balkan Peninsula stayed part of the Eastern Roman Empire (also called the Byzantine Empire) for nearly 1,000 years. Beginning in the 1300s, Italy saw the birth of the Renaissance, and in the 1400s, Portugal and Spain launched the Age of Exploration.

ITALIAN CITY-STATES The invaders who overran the Italian Peninsula had no tradition of strong central government. Italy eventually became divided into many small states and remained so for centuries.

In 1096, European Christians launched the **Crusades,** a series of wars to take Palestine from the Muslims. Italians earned large profits by supplying the ships that carried Crusaders to the Middle East. Italian cities such as Florence and Venice became rich from banking and foreign trade. This wealth helped them grow into powerful city-states.

The **Renaissance,** which began in the Italian city-states, was a time of renewed interest in learning and the arts that lasted from the 14th through 16th centuries. It was inspired by classical art and writings. Renaissance ideas spread north to the rest of Europe.

But the wealth of Italy did not protect it from disease. In 1347, the bubonic plague reached Italy from Asia and in time killed millions of Europeans. (See pages 294–295.)

SPAIN'S EMPIRE In the 700s, Muslims from North Africa conquered the Iberian Peninsula. Muslims controlled parts of the Iberian Peninsula for more than 700 years. Spain's Catholic rulers, Ferdinand and Isabella, retook Spain from the Muslims in 1492.

Also in 1492, Queen Isabella paid for Christopher Columbus's first voyage. Portugal had already sent out many voyages of exploration. Both Spain and Portugal established colonies in the Americas and elsewhere. Their empires spread Catholicism and the Spanish and Portuguese languages throughout the world.

REGION Italian Renaissance paintings often show the Virgin Mary and baby Jesus. Muslim art, like the Spanish wall design below (*bottom*), often uses calligraphy to praise God.

BACKGROUND
The Renaissance shaped modern life by stressing classical culture, material comfort, and the value of individuals.

The Virgin and Child Surrounded by Five Angels, Sandro Botticelli

A Rich Cultural Legacy

Mediterranean Europe's history shaped its culture by determining where languages are spoken and where religions are practiced today. And the people of the region take pride in the artistic legacy of the past.

ROME'S CULTURAL LEGACY Unlike many areas of Europe that Rome conquered, Greece retained its own language. Greek was, in fact, the official language of the Byzantine Empire. In contrast, Portuguese, Spanish, and Italian are Romance languages that evolved from Latin, the language of Rome.

The two halves of the Roman Empire also developed different forms of Christianity. The majority religion in Greece today is Eastern Orthodox Christianity. Roman Catholicism is strong in Italy, Spain, and Portugal. ◀

CENTURIES OF ART This region shows many signs of its past civilizations. Greece and Italy have ancient ruins, such as the Parthenon, that reveal what classical

Geographic Thinking

Making Comparisons
A What is similar about the cultural legacies left by the Roman and Spanish empires?

Alhambra Palace, Granada, Spain

architecture was like. Spain has Roman **aqueducts,** structures that carried water for long distances, and Muslim mosques, places of worship.

The region also has a long artistic legacy, which includes classical statues, Renaissance painting and sculpture, and modern art produced by such artists as Pablo Picasso of Spain. The pictures on page 291 contrast Renaissance Italian art with Muslim Spanish art.

Economic Change

Because of the Mediterranean region's sunny climate and historic sites, tourism has long been a large part of its economy. In other ways, the economy has been changing rapidly since World War II.

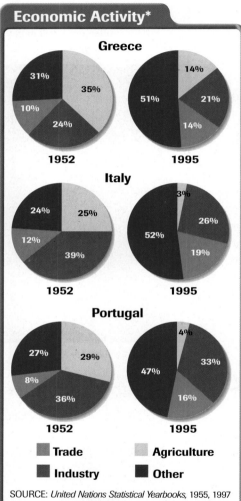

Economic Activity*

Greece

31% | 35% | 10% | 24% | 1952

14% | 21% | 14% | 51% | 1995

Italy

24% | 25% | 12% | 39% | 1952

3% | 26% | 19% | 52% | 1995

Portugal

27% | 29% | 8% | 36% | 1952

4% | 33% | 16% | 47% | 1995

- Trade
- Industry
- Agriculture
- Other

SOURCE: *United Nations Statistical Yearbooks,* 1955, 1997

NOTES: *Industry* includes mining and construction; *other* includes government, utilities, transportation, and service industries.

* as percentage of GDP

SKILLBUILDER: Interpreting Graphs

❶ **SEEING PATTERNS** From 1952 to 1995, which economic activities increased and which decreased?

❷ **MAKING INFERENCES** Why do you think the category "other" changed so significantly? Give possible reasons.

AGRICULTURE TO INDUSTRY In general, the Mediterranean nations are less industrial than those of Northern and Western Europe. For centuries, the region's economy was based on fishing and agriculture. Fishing remains important, and olives, grapes, citrus, and wheat are still major agricultural crops.

But in the late 20th century, the region's economy grew and changed. Today, manufacturing is increasing. The making of textiles is Portugal's biggest industry. Spain is a leading maker of automobiles, and Italy is a major producer of clothing and shoes. Service industries, such as banking, also make up a much larger part of the economy than before.

In the 1980s, Greece, Portugal, and Spain joined the European Union (EU). This aided growth by promoting trade with other EU nations and by making financial aid from the EU available.

ECONOMIC PROBLEMS The region still faces economic challenges. For example, Italy's northern region is much more developed than its southern half. The reasons for this include the following:

- The north is closer to other industrial countries of Europe, such as Germany and France.
- The south has poorer transportation systems.
- The government tried to promote growth in the south but made bad choices. It started industries that did not benefit the local people.

Another problem is that the entire Mediterranean region is poor in energy resources and relies heavily on imported petroleum. This makes the region vulnerable because trade problems or wars could halt oil supplies and prevent industries from functioning.

BACKGROUND
The EU is an economic and political alliance of 15 nations. Italy was one of the founding members.

Modern Mediterranean Life

Mediterranean Europe saw political turmoil in the 20th century. Two dictators, Benito Mussolini in Italy and Francisco Franco in Spain, ruled for long periods. After Franco died in 1975, Spain set up a constitutional government. After World War II, Italy became a republic but has had dozens of governments since then. Greece has also experienced political instability.

THE BASQUES Spain has had an ongoing conflict with a minority group. The Basque people live in the western foothills of the Pyrenees. Their language is the only pre-Roman language still spoken in southwestern Europe. In the late 1970s, Spain granted the Basque region self-rule. But some Basques want complete independence and have used violence to fight for it. The conflict remains unresolved.

CITY GROWTH The transition from agriculture to manufacturing and service industries has encouraged people to move from the country to the city. Urban growth has created housing shortages, pollution, and traffic jams. The people of Mediterranean Europe want to preserve their historic cities, so they are trying to solve these problems. For example, Athens is expanding its subway system to reduce traffic and pollution.

Despite their problems, Mediterranean cities give intriguing insight into the past. In Rome and Athens, classical ruins stand near modern buildings. Florence has glorious works of Renaissance art. Granada, Spain, has Catholic cathedrals and a Muslim palace. In Section 2, you will read about Western Europe, a region that also has a rich history.

Geographic Thinking

Using the Atlas
B Locate the Basque language on the map on page 267. What other country besides Spain has Basque speakers?

PLACE Pamplona, Spain, holds a festival in which young men run through the streets before a herd of stampeding bulls.
What might this activity show about Spanish culture?

EUROPE

Assessment

1 Places & Terms

Identify these terms and explain their importance in the region's history or culture.

- city-state
- republic
- Crusades
- Renaissance
- aqueduct

2 Taking Notes

REGION Review the notes you took for this section.

- What are the two ancient civilizations of this region?
- What type of movement is the result of recent economic change?

3 Main Ideas

a. How was the Renaissance an example of the movement of ideas?

b. What is Rome's cultural legacy in Mediterranean Europe today?

c. How has Mediterranean Europe's economy changed since World War II?

4 Geographic Thinking

Identifying and Solving Problems What might help preserve the historic cities of Mediterranean Europe?
Think about:

- how to provide housing and reduce both pollution and traffic

RESEARCH LINKS
CLASSZONE.COM

GeoActivity

ASKING GEOGRAPHIC QUESTIONS Review the paragraph about the Crusades on page 291. Write three to five geographic questions about the Crusades, such as "Why did many Crusaders purchase supplies for their ships in Italy?" Do research to answer as many of your questions as possible. Then create a set of **quiz show questions and answers.**

Disasters!

SUNSHINE STATE STANDARDS
Key Standard SS.B.2.4.2 The student understands past and present trends in human migration and cultural interaction and their impacton on physical and human systems.
FCAT LA.A.2.4.4 Reading: Research

Bubonic Plague

By the 1300s, Italian merchants were growing rich from the trade in luxury goods from Asia. Then in October 1347, trading ships sailed into the port of Messina, Sicily, carrying a terrifying cargo—the disease we now call bubonic plague. Over the next four years, the plague spread along trade routes throughout Europe. An estimated 25 million Europeans died, about one-fourth to one-third of the population. In terms of its death toll, the plague (also called the Black Death) was the worst disaster Europe ever suffered.

Spread of the Bubonic Plague

Extent of bubonic plague in:
- 1347
- 1348
- 1349
- 1350
- 1351
- Relatively unaffected
- ○ City that was relatively unaffected
- ● City with repeated outbreaks

0   150   300 miles
0   150   300 kilometers
Azimuthal Equidistant Projection

ATLANTIC OCEAN

North Sea

Baltic Sea

Oxford
London
Bremen
Lübek
Amiens
Liège
FLANDERS
Paris
BOHEMIA
POLAND
Nuremberg
Vienna

Milan
Venice
Avignon
Genoa
Pisa
Florence
Siena
Barcelona
Corsica
Rome
Majorca
Sardinia
Black Sea
Constantinople
Mediterranean Sea
Messina
Sicily
Crete
Cyprus

As the plague spread through Europe, the city of Milan and areas of Poland and Bohemia remained relatively untouched. No one knows exactly why those regions were spared.

ATLANTIC OCEAN
EUROPE
ASIA
MONGOLIA
CHINA
INDIA
AFRICA
PACIFIC OCEAN
INDIAN OCEAN
→ Spread of bubonic plague

The plague originated in Asia. It moved west to Europe with rats traveling in caravans of trade goods and on trading ships.

Transmission of the Plague

1 The bacterium that causes bubonic plague, *Yersinia pestis,* lives in the guts of fleas. The fleas bite rats and feed on their blood, infecting them with the disease.

2 Sometimes, an infected rat comes into contact with humans. Because the rat is dying, the fleas jump onto the humans to feed off them.

3 People catch bubonic plague from flea bites. In some, the plague enters their lungs, becoming pneumonic plague. These victims cough, sneeze, and spit up infected blood and saliva—spreading the disease more quickly.

GeoData

PREVENTIVE MEASURES

In the 1300s, most doctors recommended these methods of purifying the air to prevent plague:

- Burn richly scented incense.
- Fill the house with flowers.
- Sprinkle the floors with vinegar.
- Have doctors wear a bird mask with perfume in the beak.

OTHER DISASTROUS EPIDEMICS

1507–1518
Smallpox killed one-third to one-half of the people of Cuba, Haiti, and Puerto Rico.

1918–1919
About 30 million people died from an influenza outbreak that spread around the world.

2000
A UN report said that AIDS had killed 19 million people worldwide. Seven African countries had 20 percent of their population infected.

2
Western Europe

Main Ideas
- France and the Germanic countries developed very different cultures.
- These cultural differences led to conflicts that shaped the history of Western Europe.

Places & Terms

Benelux	**nationalism**
Reformation	**Holocaust**
feudalism	**Berlin Wall**

CONNECT TO THE ISSUES
UNIFICATION France and Germany have resolved their past conflicts and now cooperate in the European Union.

SUNSHINE STATE STANDARDS
Key Standard SS.B.2.4.1 The student understands how social, cultural, economic, and environmental factors contribute to the dynamic nature of regions.

Other Standards SS.A.3.4.2, A.3.4.6, D.2.4.6

FCAT LA.A.1.4.2 Reading: Strategies

A HUMAN PERSPECTIVE Today, the French call Émile Durkheim the father of French sociology (the study of society). But he wasn't always honored. During World War I, some French patriots considered him a disloyal foreigner. Why? Perhaps it was because he had a German last name and came from Lorraine, a region that had switched between French and German rule many times. France and Germany have long had a deep rivalry, based in part on cultural differences.

A History of Cultural Divisions

France and Germany are the dominant countries in Western Europe. They are the two largest countries, and their access to resources, ports, and trade routes helped them to build productive economies.

French culture is strong in France and Monaco; German culture is strong in Germany, Austria, and Liechtenstein. Switzerland and the **Benelux** countries of Belgium, the Netherlands, and Luxembourg have their own cultures—but also have been influenced by Germany and France. Western Europe's cultural divisions have historic roots.

ROME TO CHARLEMAGNE One cultural division, language, dates from ancient times. By 50 B.C., the Roman Empire had conquered the Celtic tribes in what is now France. French is one of the Romance languages that evolved from Latin (Rome's language). But Rome never fully conquered the Germanic tribes that migrated into the lands east of France. Germanic languages are still spoken there. (See the chart on page 297.)

Western European History, 800–2000

800
Charlemagne unites much of Europe.

1347
Bubonic plague starts to sweep through Europe.

1455
First printing of Gutenberg Bible

1516
Leonardo da Vinci moves to France, bringing Renaissance ideas.

MIDDLE AGES

RENAISSANCE AND REFORMATION

1099
Crusaders from Europe capture Jerusalem from Muslims.

1517
Martin Luther criticizes the Catholic Church. The Reformation begins.

In the late 700s, a Germanic king, Charlemagne, conquered most of the region. However, his empire began to fall apart soon after his death. Western Europe remained a region of small, competing kingdoms.

THE REFORMATION A religious movement created new differences. During the Renaissance (see Section 1), scholars questioned authority. Some people even began to question the Catholic Church. In 1517, Martin Luther published 95 statements that criticized church practices that he believed were wrong. That began the **Reformation**, a period when many Christians broke away from the Catholic Church and started Protestant churches. Mutual hostility led Catholics and Protestants to fight religious wars that tore Europe apart.

Today, France is mostly Catholic. The Netherlands, Switzerland, and Germany contain both Protestants and Catholics. In Germany, Protestants live mainly in the north and Catholics in the south of the country. ◀️Ⓐ

CONNECT TO THE ISSUES

CONFLICT

Ⓐ Why might conflict result if neighboring countries adopt different religions?

The Rise of Nation-States

The period between the fall of Rome and the Renaissance is called the Middle Ages. During this time, Europeans gradually developed the nation-state, an independent nation of people with a common culture.

NATIONALISM During the centuries after Rome fell, **feudalism** gradually developed in Europe. This was a political system in which powerful lords owned most of the land. They gave some land to nobles in exchange for military service by those nobles. Over time, strong kings gained power over feudal lords, and nationalism evolved. **Nationalism** is the belief that people should be loyal to their nation, the people with whom they share land, culture, and history.

Nationalism often causes groups to want their own countries, so it contributed to the rise of modern nation-states. France was one of the

5 THEMES

REGION

Diversity of Languages

Nation	Languages Spoken
Austria	German
Belgium	Flemish, French, German
Germany	German
France	French
Liechtenstein	German, Alemannic dialect
Luxembourg	Luxembourgian, German, French
Monaco	French, English, Italian, Monegasque dialect
Netherlands	Dutch
Switzerland	German, French, Italian, Romansch

SOURCE: *The National Geographic Desk Reference, World Book*

EUROPE

NATIONALISM

1765 James Watt improves the steam engine.

1789 French Revolution begins.

1812 **Napoleon** controls much of Europe.

1871 **Otto von Bismarck** unifies Germany.

1914–1918 World War I

20TH CENTURY

1939–1945 World War II. In the **Holocaust**, 6 million Jews are murdered.

1945–1991 Cold War

Western Europe **297**

first nation-states. By the late 1600s, French kings held absolute power, which they often used to benefit themselves, not their people. In 1789, the people began a rebellion—the French Revolution. They deposed the king and formed a republic. But in a few years, an army officer named Napoleon Bonaparte seized power. In 1804, he made himself emperor. Napoleon tried to conquer all of Europe but was defeated.

The nation-states of Europe became strong rivals. From the 1600s to 1945, wars repeatedly broke out between France and Austria or between France and the German states (later Germany). Germany did not unify as a nation until 1871. It was one of many European countries affected by a new wave of nationalism in the 1800s.

Western Europe also experienced industrial growth in the 1800s. Industrialism caused European nations to set up colonies in other lands in order to gain raw materials and markets. Many European nations saw each other as rivals in the race to gain colonies. You will learn more about the effects of colonialism as you read this book. **B**

Geographic Thinking

Seeing Patterns
B Why might industrialism cause a country to want colonies?

MODERN CONFLICTS The nationalistic rivalry and competition for colonies among European nations helped cause World War I. The Allied Powers (including France) fought the Central Powers (Germany, Austria-Hungary, and their allies). The Allied Powers won and imposed harsh terms on Germany. German resentment over those terms helped cause World War II, in which Germany, led by Adolf Hitler and the Nazis, tried to conquer Europe. The Nazis also carried out the **Holocaust**, a program of mass murder of European Jews and other minorities. In 1945, the Allies defeated Germany.

After the war, Germany was split into two nations. West Germany was allied with non-Communist Europe and the United States. East Germany was allied with the Communist Soviet Union. The capital city of Berlin, located in East Germany, was also divided, cut in two by the **Berlin Wall**. In 1989, anti-Communist reforms swept Europe, and in response to protests, East Germany opened the Berlin Wall.

In 1990, the two Germanys reunited under a democratic government. In recent years, France and Germany have tried to end the rivalry that so often led to war. These two nations were leaders in the movement toward establishing the European Union. (See the Case Study on pages 326–329.)

BACKGROUND
The Nazis were a political party that created a government that controlled all aspects of German life. They held many racist beliefs.

Economics: Diversity and Luxury

Since the Middle Ages, Western Europe has been rich in agriculture, and in the 1800s, it was one of the first regions to industrialize. The region's economy remains strong because it includes agriculture and manufacturing, plus high-tech and service industries.

REGION Picturesque old castles, such as the Castle Reichenstein in Germany, were built for defense purposes. Now they are tourist attractions.
Why do you think this castle was built on a hillside?

Major Industries of France and Germany

France

Lille
Paris
Strasbourg
Nantes
Lyon
Grenoble
Bordeaux
Toulouse
Nice
Marseille

Germany

Kiel
Hamburg
Bremen
Hannover
Berlin
Mülheim an der Ruhr
Dortmund
Düsseldorf
Cologne
Leipzig
Dresden
Frankfurt
Nürnberg
Stuttgart
Munich

Legend		
⊛ National capital	🛬 Aerospace	☂ Optics	〰 Textiles
• Other city	🧪 Chemicals	⚗ Research & development	🚗 Vehicle assembly
⬤ Major business center	🔲 Electronics	⚓ Shipbuilding	🍇 Wine
══ Major highway	☼ Engineering		
── Other road			

0   100   200 miles
0   100   200 kilometers
Lambert Conformal Conic Projection

SKILLBUILDER: Interpreting Maps

❶ **LOCATION** What is the relative location of business centers? Give possible reasons.

❷ **MOVEMENT** Use the Unit Atlas to find the border between France and Germany. Which French and German cities might make good international trading partners?

AGRICULTURE TO HIGH-TECH Dairy farming and livestock provide most of the agricultural income in Belgium, France, the Netherlands, and Switzerland. These countries produce and export dairy products. In addition, France is the largest producer of agricultural products in Western Europe. Its major crops include wheat, grapes, and vegetables.

Western Europe was a leader in developing industry because it was rich in coal and iron ore. Today, the region has three of Europe's top manufacturing nations: France, Germany, and the Netherlands. The maps above show the major industries of France and Germany.

High-tech and service industries are also very important. Electronics is a major product of the Netherlands. Germany also produces electronics, as well as scientific instruments. France has one of the world's fastest passenger trains, the TGV (*train à grande vitesse*, or high-speed train), and a space program. France also relies heavily on nuclear energy. Nuclear plants produce nearly 75 percent of its electricity. ◀**C**

Switzerland specializes in the service industry of banking. One reason for this is that Switzerland refuses to fight in wars, so people believe that money is safer there.

TOURISM AND LUXURY Because of its varied scenery, mild climate, and historic sites, Western Europe is popular with tourists. Tourism is a major part of the French, Swiss, and Austrian economies.

Western Europe exports luxury goods to the world. For example, some German cars and Swiss watches are considered status symbols.

Geographic Thinking

Making Comparisons

▶ Which high-tech industry do Germany and the Netherlands have in common?

growing up in...The Netherlands

This girl is doing *wadlopen*, or mud walking. As many as 25,000 people a year take part in this popular Dutch pastime. When the tide goes out on the Waddenzee (part of the North Sea), it leaves mud flats. Mud walking can be extremely strenuous exercise; at times, the mud can reach up to a person's thighs! The activity can also be risky. If the mud walkers don't leave the flats before the tide returns, they are in danger of being drowned.

Another popular activity for young people in the Netherlands is ice skating. The Netherlands has an extensive network of canals that link its major rivers. During the Middle Ages, the Dutch began to skate on these frozen canals in the winter. The sport of speed skating originated in the Netherlands.

If you grew up in the Netherlands, you would pass these milestones:
- You would go to school from age 5 to age 18.
- In primary school, you would learn to swim, usually by age 9.
- You could drive at 18.
- You could vote at 18.
- You could marry at 18.

France is famous for its high-fashion clothing and gourmet foods. The Netherlands exports high-quality flower bulbs, such as colorful tulips.

ECONOMIC PROBLEMS One nation in the region, Germany, has had economic problems recently. When Germany reunified, the new nation faced difficulties because the West had a much higher standard of living. East Germany's factories were outdated compared with those in the West, and many shut down. Germany has been working steadily to foster growth in the former East Germany, but progress will take time. By 1998, the East produced only six percent of the nation's exports.

Great Music and Art

Each Western European country has a distinct identity, shaped in part by language and religion. Even with these differences, one thing is true of the region as a whole—it has a strong artistic legacy.

MUSIC Germany and Austria are famous for music. Johann Sebastian Bach, who wrote music for church services, was German. So was Ludwig van Beethoven, who composed symphonies and other works. He wrote music even after going deaf. Austrian composers include Wolfgang Amadeus Mozart, who was a child genius.

PAINTING France and the Netherlands have had many important painters. Jan Van Eyck was a painter from Flanders (a region now divided among France, the Netherlands, and Belgium) who perfected techniques for using oil paints. Jan Vermeer and Rembrandt were Dutch artists who painted with great realism. Major French painters include the impressionist Claude Monet and postimpressionists Paul Cézanne and Paul Gauguin, who paved the way for modern art.

BACKGROUND Many landscape paintings of the Netherlands show its flat, low terrain. The sea is also a frequent subject.

Modern Life

Because of their strong economies, Western Europeans enjoy a high standard of living and generally can afford to buy material goods such as cars and computers. Most Western Europeans live in cities.

CITY LIFE In general, Western European cities are interesting and pleasant places to live. Most have good public transportation systems. They offer many cultural attractions: movies, concerts, art galleries, and museums. Crime rates are lower than in the United States.

Geographic Thinking

Using the Atlas

▶ Refer to the climate map on page 266. What role does climate play in Western Europeans' enjoyment of the outdoors?

As a rule, Europeans live in smaller homes than Americans do. Because of this, they often socialize in public places. Friends might meet in cafes, sitting at outdoor tables if the weather is nice. Also, most cities have many lovely parks that their citizens regularly enjoy. ◀

One difference between Western Europe and the United States is that Europeans receive more paid vacation time. For example, Germans have about 30 vacation days a year. Vacationing Europeans often leave the city to engage in outdoor activities like biking, hiking, or skiing.

RECENT CONFLICTS In recent decades, immigration has been a source of conflict here. In the 1980s, increasing numbers of "guest workers" from Yugoslavia and Turkey came to West Germany for jobs. When the German economy declined, some angry Germans committed discrimination and even violence against immigrants. In response, millions of other Germans protested racism.

Austria has also faced tensions. Political leader Joerg Haider made controversial remarks that defended former Nazis and that immigrants found insulting. Many feared a rebirth of racist politics, so in 2000 Haider had to resign as party head—yet he remained a force in Austrian public life.

In Section 3, you will read about Northern Europe, a region that includes the Nordic countries, the United Kingdom, and Ireland.

SECTION 2 Assessment

① Places & Terms

Identify these terms and explain their importance in the region's history or culture.

- Benelux
- Reformation
- feudalism
- nationalism
- Holocaust
- Berlin Wall

② Taking Notes

REGION Review the notes you took for this section.

- What are major aspects of Western Europe's artistic legacy?
- What are some characteristics of modern life in Western Europe?

③ Main Ideas

a. How do language and religion reflect the cultural division in Western Europe?

b. Which Western European leaders tried to unify Europe through conquest?

c. In what way does Western Europe have a diverse economy?

④ Geographic Thinking

Making Generalizations
How does the economic strength of a nation affect its willingness to welcome immigrants? **Think about:**

- whether immigrants are more welcome when jobs are scarce or plentiful
- the experience of Germany since the 1980s

GeoActivity

MAKING COMPARISONS Study the two maps on page 299. Create a **Venn Diagram** showing the businesses that France and Germany have in common and those that each have separately.

Northern Europe

Main Ideas
- The United Kingdom and the Nordic countries have seafaring histories that often led to conquest.
- The region played a role in developing representative government and industry.

Places & Terms

Nordic countries   **Silicon Glen**

parliament   **euro**

CONNECT TO THE ISSUES
UNIFICATION Some nations in Northern Europe have held back from full participation in the European Union.

SUNSHINE STATE STANDARDS
Key Standard SS.B.2.4.1 The student understands social, cultural, economic, and environmental factors contribute to the dynamic nature of regions.

Other Standards SS.A.2.4.7, A.2.4.8, B.2.4.2, D.2

FCAT LA.A.1.4.2 Reading: Strategies

MOVEMENT This helmet is from Sutton Hoo, a burial site in England that included a ship. Some scholars think that site shows Viking influence.

A HUMAN PERSPECTIVE In World War II, Germany perfected a new military tactic, the blitzkrieg. Using a massive force of dive-bombers, tanks, and artillery, the German army rapidly surprised, attacked, and defeated a foe before it could mount a defense. Germany used blitzkriegs to invade Poland, Belgium, the Netherlands, and France. But Germany couldn't launch a swift land attack against the United Kingdom on the island of Great Britain. Germany tried to destroy Britain by first bombing it from the air, but such a campaign took time, so Britain was able to fight back. In time, Britain and its allies won the war. Throughout its history, Britain's status as an island has been a geographic advantage.

A History of Seafaring Conquerors

Today, Northern Europe consists of the United Kingdom, Ireland, and the Nordic countries. The **Nordic countries** are Denmark, Finland, Iceland, Norway, and Sweden. The history of this region has been a history of using the sea and of conquest.

EARLY CONQUERORS In ancient times, waves of migrating people settled Northern Europe. Each new group tended to push the previous residents out of its way. As a result, the earlier groups ended up living at the tips or along the coasts of Northern Europe's peninsulas and islands. For example, the Sami, descendants of one of the earliest migrating groups, now live in far northern Scandinavia and Finland.

The ancient inhabitants of Great Britain were Celtic. Roman armies conquered southern Britain by about A.D. 80. In the 400s, Germanic tribes invaded, driving out the Romans and gradually pushing the Celts north and west.

Beginning about 795, a group of seafaring warriors from Denmark, Norway, and Sweden terrorized Europe. These Norsemen, or Vikings, sailed in long ships to coastal towns and conducted hit-and-run raids. They conquered parts of Britain and sailed to Iceland, Greenland, and even North America. They also had a settlement in Normandy (a part of France named for the Norsemen) and moved into Russia.

In 1066, William the Conqueror of Normandy conquered England (the largest kingdom in Britain) and began to rule it. The Normans spoke French, and over time the English language acquired many words of French origin.

DREAMS OF EMPIRE Denmark, Sweden, and Norway each became a kingdom during the 900s. Sweden was a strong power in the 1600s, but no Nordic country ever became a major empire.

In contrast, Great Britain built an empire that strongly affected the rest of the world. First, the English set out to control the British Isles. Over time, England won control of its neighbors, Wales, Ireland, and Scotland. In 1801, the nation became known as the United Kingdom of Great Britain and Ireland.

Britain drew on its geographic advantages to grow in strength. As you read earlier, Britain's status as an island helped protect it. After 1066, no outside power ever successfully invaded Britain. In addition, the British people had much experience as sailors. This helped them to build a strong navy and to develop overseas trade.

Drawing on its economic and naval strength, Great Britain built a global empire. By the 1800s, it had colonies in the Americas, Asia, Africa, and Oceania. A popular saying declared, "The sun never sets on the British Empire." One consequence of the empire is that the English language and British culture spread worldwide. ◀A

Geographic Thinking◀

Seeing Patterns
A▶ Why would a strong navy be helpful in building an empire?

Moving into the Modern Age

Great Britain played a role in shaping our modern world in two ways. It helped to develop representative government. Also, the industrial revolution started in Britain and spread to other countries.

REPRESENTATIVE GOVERNMENT Britain's government is a monarchy that also has a parliament. A **parliament** is a representative lawmaking body whose members are elected or appointed. (In some cases, they inherit the position.) Over the centuries, English rulers lost power to the English Parliament, so a more representative government evolved. For example, in 1215 nobles forced the king to sign the Magna Carta. That

Advances in Representative Government

Parliament	Magna Carta	English Bill of Rights	Female Representation
930	**1215**	**1689**	Late **1990s**
Iceland established the *Althing,* called the world's oldest parliament. The English Parliament began in the late 1200s.	The Magna Carta granted English nobles certain rights. Over time, it inspired other people to demand their rights.	The Bill of Rights established free elections and gave the English Parliament power over the monarchy.	The Nordic countries had a high percentage of women in their parliaments, ranging from 25 to 43 percent.

EUROPE

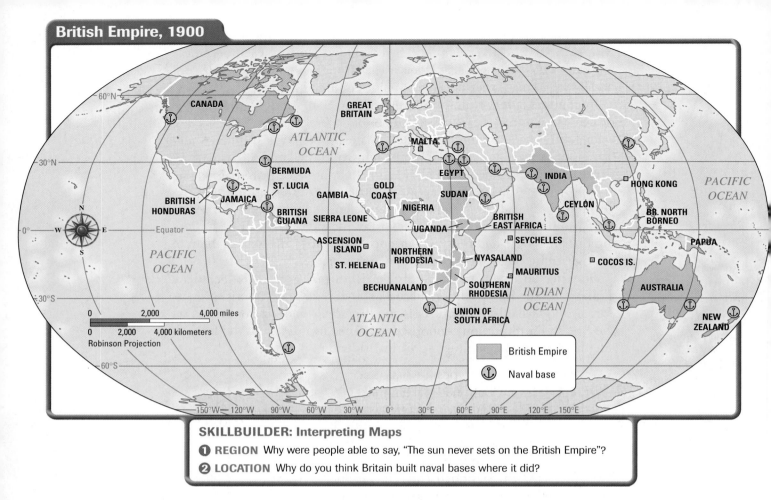

CANADA

GREAT
BRITAIN

ATLANTIC
OCEAN

MALTA

EGYPT

INDIA

HONG KONG

PACIFIC
OCEAN

BERMUDA

ST. LUCIA

GAMBIA

GOLD
COAST

SUDAN

CEYLON

BR. NORTH
BORNEO

BRITISH
HONDURAS

JAMAICA

BRITISH
GUIANA

NIGERIA

BRITISH
EAST AFRICA

PAPUA

SIERRA LEONE

UGANDA

SEYCHELLES

COCOS IS.

ASCENSION
ISLAND

NORTHERN
RHODESIA

NYASALAND

PACIFIC
OCEAN

ST. HELENA

MAURITIUS

AUSTRALIA

BECHUANALAND

SOUTHERN
RHODESIA

INDIAN
OCEAN

ATLANTIC
OCEAN

UNION OF
SOUTH AFRICA

NEW
ZEALAND

Equator

0   2,000   4,000 miles

0   2,000   4,000 kilometers

Robinson Projection

British Empire

Naval base

SKILLBUILDER: Interpreting Maps

❶ **REGION** Why were people able to say, "The sun never sets on the British Empire"?

❷ **LOCATION** Why do you think Britain built naval bases where it did?

document inspired such political ideas as trial by jury and no taxation without representation. Those ideas later spread to the United States, Canada, and various British colonies.

The Nordic countries also developed representative government. Iceland's parliament, which has been meeting since 930, is the oldest parliament in the world.

INDUSTRIAL REVOLUTION As you read in Chapter 12, deposits of iron ore and coal helped Britain to be the first nation to industrialize. Industry used coal as fuel and iron to make machinery. The growth of industry motivated Britain's empire building. Britain imported raw materials from its colonies and sold finished goods to those colonies.

In the 1800s, the industrial revolution spread from Britain to other countries, especially Belgium, France, Germany, and the United States. Of the Nordic countries, Sweden developed the most industry.

SINCE 1900 In the 20th century, the Nordic countries did not heavily involve themselves in other nations' affairs. But Great Britain played a major role in both world wars, fighting as one of the victorious Allies.

After World War II, the British Empire underwent major change as nearly all of its colonies gained independence. Since then, some former colonies, such as Nigeria, have had ethnic conflicts. Many of the conflicts arose because the British had set the boundaries of their colonies without regard to where rival ethnic groups lived. (See the Case Study in Unit 6, on pages 468–471.)

BACKGROUND
As you learned in Chapter 12, France, Belgium, and Germany also had coal deposits. That promoted industrial growth.

THE IRISH QUESTION The British still face a problem that has roots in the past. Protestant English rulers strengthened their hold on Catholic Ireland by seizing Irish land and giving it to Scottish and English Protestants. That left many Irish in poverty. In the 1840s, potato crops failed and caused famine. Over a million Irish fled to other lands.

Many Irish called for independence, and in 1921, Britain divided Ireland into two states. The Republic of Ireland gained independence in 1921. Northern Ireland, which had a Protestant majority, remained part of the United Kingdom. Since then, religious conflict and anti-British violence have plagued Northern Ireland. ◄B

Geographic Thinking

Seeing Patterns

B How have politics, economics, and religion all contributed to the conflict in Northern Ireland?

Economics: Diversity and Change

Today, Northern Europe has a highly developed and varied economy. Manufacturing and traditional economic activities such as fishing and forestry remain important. As is true in all developed countries, the service and information economies are growing.

INDUSTRY AND RESOURCES Sweden and the United Kingdom have many types of manufacturing in common. For example, both nations have strong motor vehicle and aerospace industries. Both also produce paper products, food products, and pharmaceuticals.

Northern Europe's economy benefits from its many natural resources. Sweden exports timber. Iceland relies heavily on its fishing industry and the production of fish products. Norway earns a large portion of its income from North Sea oil.

HIGH-TECH Technology is swiftly changing the economy of Northern Europe. For example, the production of computer software and hardware has been a major part of Ireland's economy since the 1970s. The section of Scotland between Glasgow and Edinburgh is called **Silicon Glen** because it has so many high-tech companies (which use silicon computer chips). Silicon Glen produces 32 percent of Europe's personal computers and 51 percent of Europe's notebook computers.

BACKGROUND
The word *glen* is from the Scottish term for valley.

UNION OR INDEPENDENCE? Most nations of this region joined the European Union (EU), but Norway has chosen not to do so. Even in nations belonging to the European Union, people have mixed feelings about the EU policy that they should adopt a common currency called the **euro.** In September 2000, Denmark voted against adopting the euro. Economics professor Jesper Jespersen agreed with that decision. He said, "I believe Denmark should retain its own currency . . . [because] our economy is in many ways independent of the eurozone [the region using the euro]." (See the Case Study on pages 326–329 for more about the EU.)

Connect TO THE Issues

UNIFICATION

Norway Rejects the EU

In 1994, Norwegians voted 52 percent to 48 percent against joining the European Union. Norway did not become a separate nation until 1905, so many Norwegians feared losing their independence and national identity.

Another reason for the vote against joining is that the economy was booming. This prosperity was due to Norway's status as the world's second-largest exporter of crude oil. Some Norwegians feared that Norway would lose control over its valuable oil resources if it joined the EU.

Cultural Similarities and Modern Art

Throughout most of history, Northern Europe has not been culturally diverse. Even today, the Nordic nations have populations that consist mostly of one ethnic group. In recent years, however, the United Kingdom, particularly its capital London, has grown more diverse. That is partially due to immigration from former colonies, such as India. Researchers estimate that by the year 2006, about 1.9 million of London's 7 million residents will belong to an ethnic minority.

MOVEMENT
Portobello Road in London has antique shops and stalls. As shown here, immigration has given London a diverse population.
What might draw people to a city like London?

SIMILAR LANGUAGES AND RELIGIONS The language map on page 267 shows the effect of historic migrations into this region. Most people of Northern Europe speak a Germanic language. When Germanic tribes migrated to the Scandinavian Peninsula and the British Isles, they pushed the previous inhabitants north and west. Today, the Sami language is spoken in the far north. Celtic languages such as Welsh, Irish Gaelic, and Scottish Gaelic survive on the northern and western edges of the British Isles. ◐

The Reformation, which began in nearby Germany in the 1500s, swept through Northern Europe. Several different Protestant churches took root there. Most of the region is still Protestant. Only Ireland kept Catholicism as its main faith.

MODERN CULTURE AND LITERATURE The Nordic countries have influenced many modern cultures. The Norwegian playwright Henrik Ibsen is sometimes called the father of modern drama. Ingmar Bergman, a Swedish director, influenced movies with his intensely personal films. Both men raised psychological issues in their work that remain important in modern life.

Great Britain and Ireland have had their strongest artistic influence on world literature. Many people consider William Shakespeare the greatest playwright of all time. Nearly 400 years after his death, his works are still performed on stage and also adapted for movies. The English poet William Wordsworth popularized the use of everyday speech in poetry. English novelists of the 1800s, such as Charlotte Brontë, influenced later novels. The Irish novelist James Joyce shaped modern fiction by exploring techniques to portray human thought.

Geographic Thinking

Using the Atlas
◐ Refer to the language map on page 267. Which Germanic languages are spoken in Northern Europe?

Life in Northern Europe

In Northern Europe, most people live in cities and have a high standard of living. One aspect that distinguishes Northern Europe from most other regions is that its women have made great strides toward political equality. In the late 1990s, women made up 25 percent of the parliament in Iceland, 36 percent in Norway, 37 percent in Finland and Denmark, and 43 percent in Sweden.

SOCIAL WELFARE Overall, the governments of Northern Europe take great responsibility for the welfare of their people. This is especially true of the Nordic countries, which provide many welfare services for their citizens. For example, Finland, Norway, and Sweden give families a yearly allowance to help raise their children. The Nordic governments help fund national health insurance programs. Britain also has a national health insurance program. To pay for the programs, the people in those countries have very high taxes.

DISTINCTIVE CUSTOMS Some social customs of Northern Europe have gained worldwide fame. For example, the British are known for afternoon tea, a small meal of sandwiches, breads, cakes, and tea. Swedes developed the smorgasbord. It is a large assortment of hot and cold dishes served buffet style. Finns are famous for their sauna, in which people sit in a hot room to work up a sweat that cleans the skin's pores. Afterward, they plunge into a cold bath or icy lake.

LEISURE Even though the Nordic countries have some of the coldest climates in Europe, outdoor sports remain popular there. Some of the sports in the winter Olympics developed in Norway and the other Nordic countries. They include cross-country skiing and ski jumping.

Many British enjoy horseback riding, horse jumping, and fox hunting. These traditionally were pastimes for the wealthy upper classes on their large country estates. In addition, the British developed two sports that are unique. Rugby is a form of football, and cricket is played with a ball, a bat, and wickets. Spread by British colonialism, cricket is played around the world.

In Section 4, you will read about Eastern Europe, a region that continues to be torn apart by ethnic conflicts.

5 THEMES

MOVEMENT

Tea Time

Nothing seems more English than tea, but it is really an import from Asia. Dutch traders introduced tea to Europe, and it was sold for the first time in England in 1657. Tea soon became Britain's national beverage.

Perhaps one reason for its popularity is that clean water was scarce; boiling water for tea purified it. Tea also had caffeine, giving tea drinkers energy during the long stretch between the midday meal and supper. The custom of taking food with afternoon tea began in the 1800s.

SECTION 3 Assessment

1 Places & Terms

Identify these terms and explain their importance in the region's history, culture, or economy.

- Nordic countries
- parliament
- Silicon Glen
- euro

2 Taking Notes

REGION Review the notes you took for this section.

- Where did the Industrial Revolution begin and to where did it spread?
- What are some characteristics of governments in Northern Europe?

3 Main Ideas

a. How did conquest influence the languages spoken in Northern Europe?

b. How did the Industrial Revolution spur the growth of Britain's empire?

c. How did the Reformation affect Northern Europe?

4 Geographic Thinking

Determining Cause and Effect Why is there conflict in Northern Ireland? **Think about:**

- the history of Britain's relationship with Ireland
- religious differences
- arguments for and against a union of the Republic of Ireland and Northern Ireland

SEEING PATTERNS Compare the map on page 304 with the world map on pages A4 and A5 to learn the present names of former British colonies. Then do research to learn which former colonies still use English as an official language. Present this information on a **chart.**

Comparing Cultures

Geographic Sports Challenges

Over time, humans have found ways to enjoy even the most forbidding climates and terrains. Some popular sports evolved from activities that people used to overcome geographic challenges, such as mountains or snowy climates. Other sports were created to take advantage of special geographic features, such as recurring winds or waves. On these two pages, you will learn about geographically inspired sports from around the world.

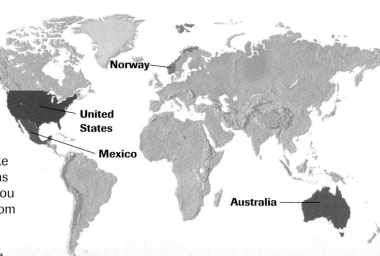

Norway

United States

Mexico

Australia

Surfing, shown here off the coast of Australia, dates back to prehistoric times. It may have originated when Polynesian sailors of the Pacific Islands needed to reach land from large canoes floating offshore.

Skiing originated as a means of travel in northern Europe, and ski jumping probably evolved in hilly Norway. In 1924, ski jumping became an Olympic sport. Competitors are judged not only on how far they jump but also on the technique they use.

SUNSHINE STATE STANDARDS
Key Standard SS.B.1.4.3
The student uses mental maps of physical and human features of the world to answer complex geographic questions.

FCAT LA.A.2.2.7 Reading: Recognize Compare and Contrast

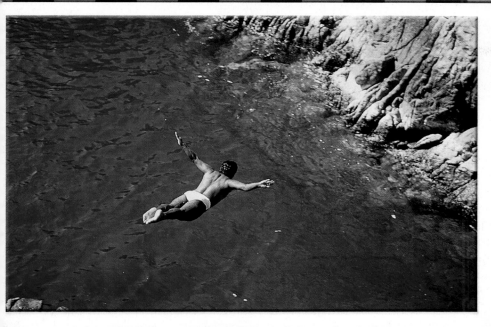

Acapulco, Mexico, is famous for its cliff diving. This dangerous sport often involves diving from heights nearly three times higher than those used in Olympic platform diving. Cliff divers have been killed by hitting their heads on rocks.

The Iditarod Sled Dog Race is held in Alaska. Susan Butcher, shown here, was the first person to have won it three years in a row. The Inuit people first used sled dogs to travel across snow-covered terrain; racing evolved later.

GeoActivity

EXPLORING MOUNTAIN CLIMBING

Working with a small group, use the Internet to research mountain climbing, another geographic sports challenge. Then create a **presentation** about the sport.

- Draw a world map, label popular mountains to climb, and give their altitudes.
- Make a chart listing the dangers of mountain climbing.

RESEARCH LINKS
CLASSZONE.COM

GeoData

Skiing
- Skis that are more than 4,000 years old have been found in Scandinavian bogs.
- Skiing was once a military skill. Norwegian troops skied in the Battle of Oslo in 1200.

Surfing
- The explorer James Cook first reported seeing surfing in 1778.
- European missionaries banned surfing in 1821. It was revived in 1920 by a Hawaiian, Duke Kahanamoku.

Cliff Diving
- Women did not compete at Acapulco until 1996.
- Divers enter the water at speeds of up to 65 mph.

Sled Dog Racing
- The Iditarod honors a 1925 emergency mission to deliver medicine to Nome, Alaska.
- During the 1985 race, a moose charged across Susan Butcher's path. The collision that resulted killed 2 dogs and wounded 13 other dogs.

Eastern Europe

Main Ideas
- Eastern Europe has great cultural diversity because many ethnic groups have settled there.
- Many empires have controlled parts of the region, leaving it with little experience of self-rule.

Places & Terms
cultural crossroads

balkanization

satellite nation

market economy

folk art

anti-Semitism

CONNECT TO THE ISSUES
CONFLICT Nationalism and ethnic differences have fueled conflicts that have torn apart the Balkans in recent times.

SUNSHINE STATE STANDARDS
Key Standard SS.B.2.4.1 The student understands how social, cultural, economic, and environmental factors contribute to the dynamic nature of regions.

Other Standards SS.A.2.4.7, A.3.4.9, A.3.4.10

FCAT LA.A.1.4.2 Reading: Strategies

A HUMAN PERSPECTIVE Eastern Europe has many plains that allow invaders to move from east to west and vice versa. In World War II, Germany invaded the Communist Soviet Union, killing millions. After the war, the Soviet Union decided to protect itself from invasion by setting up a political barrier. So it established Communist governments in the nations of Eastern Europe, which lay between the Soviet Union and its enemies to the west. Soviet dictator Joseph Stalin wanted Eastern Europe to "have governments whose relations to the Soviet Union are loyal." For decades, the Soviet Union crushed political reform and free trade in Eastern Europe. The region is still recovering.

History of a Cultural Crossroads

Eastern Europe's location between Asia and the rest of Europe shaped its history. Many groups migrated into the region, creating great diversity. Strong empires ruled parts of Eastern Europe, delaying the rise of independent nation-states there. Today the region includes Albania, Bosnia and Herzegovina, Bulgaria, Croatia, the Czech Republic, Hungary, Macedonia, Poland, Romania, Slovakia, Slovenia, and Yugoslavia.

CULTURES MEET Eastern Europe is a **cultural crossroads**, or a place where various cultures cross paths. Since ancient times, people moving between Europe and Asia—traders, nomads, migrants, and armies—have passed through this region. Because the region is an important crossroads, many world powers have tried to control it.

Eastern European History, 1389–2000

1389
The Ottoman Empire defeats the Serbs at the Battle of Kosovo.

1566
Suleiman I, the Ottoman ruler, dies during a siege in Hungary.

1686
The Austrians drive the Ottomans out of Hungary.

1867
Hungary demands equal status with Austria. The empire becomes Austria-Hungary.

CONFLICT AMONG EMPIRES

1618
Bohemia (now the Czech Republic) revolts against its Austrian ruler, starting the Thirty Years' War.

1795
The Russian ruler **Catherine the Great** divides Poland among Russia, Prussia, and Austria.

EMPIRES AND KINGDOMS By about A.D. 100, ancient Rome held the Balkan Peninsula, Bulgaria, Romania, and parts of Hungary. After the Roman Empire was split, the Byzantine Empire held onto those lands for centuries. In the 1300s and 1400s, the Ottoman Empire of Turkey (see Unit 7) gradually took over the southern part of Eastern Europe.

Various Slavic groups moved into Eastern Europe from the 400s through the 600s. Several kingdoms, such as Poland in the north and Serbia on the Balkan Peninsula, formed. In the late 800s, a non-Slavic group called the Magyars swept into what is now Hungary and in time established a kingdom. The Ottomans later conquered it.

Beginning in the 1400s, the nation of Austria became a great power. Austria drove the Ottomans out of Hungary and took control of that state. In the late 1700s, Austria, Prussia (a German state), and Russia divided up Poland among themselves. Poland ceased to exist.

BACKGROUND
Romania means "land of the Romans."

Turmoil in the 20th Century

Responding to centuries of foreign rule, most ethnic groups in Eastern Europe fiercely guarded their identities. Many wanted their own nation-states, even though few had a history of self-rule. These characteristics sparked many conflicts in Eastern Europe during the 20th century. (A)

CONNECT TO THE ISSUES
CONFLICT
(A) What might happen if two different ethnic groups wanted to establish a nation on the same land?

WAR AFTER WAR By 1908, the Balkan nations of Bulgaria, Greece, Montenegro, Romania, and Serbia had broken free from the Ottoman Empire. In 1912, Greece, Bulgaria, and Serbia went to war against the Ottomans, who lost most of their remaining European territory. In 1913, the Balkan countries fought over who should own that territory. Their actions led to a new word, **balkanization.** The term refers to the process of a region breaking up into small, mutually hostile units.

The Slavic nation of Serbia also wanted to free the Slavs in Austria-Hungary. In 1914, a Serb assassinated an Austrian noble, sparking World War I. Austria-Hungary and Serbia each pulled their allies into the conflict until most of Europe was involved. After the war, Austria and Hungary split apart. Albania, Bulgaria, Czechoslovakia, Poland, and Yugoslavia gained independence. The Ottoman Empire ended and was replaced by the nation of Turkey.

1914
A Serb kills Austrian **Archduke Francis Ferdinand.** World War I erupts.

1939
Germany overruns Poland. World War II starts.

1946–1948
Communist governments are set up in Eastern Europe.

1989
Czechoslovakia, Hungary, Romania, and Poland end Communist rule.

TWO WORLD WARS

COMMUNISM AND DEMOCRACY

1918
The Kingdom of Serbs, Croats, and Slovenes (now Yugoslavia) is created.

1945
Josip Broz Tito becomes dictator of Yugoslavia.

2000
Yugoslavia elects a reform leader, Vojislav Kostunica, as president.

311

In 1939, Germany seized Poland, starting World War II. Near the end of that war, the Soviet Union advanced through Eastern Europe as part of an Allied strategy to crush Germany from two sides. The Soviet Union later refused to withdraw from Eastern Europe until it had set up Communist governments there. Eastern Europe became a region of **satellite nations**—nations dominated by another country.

RECENT CHANGES The Soviet Union controlled Eastern Europe for four decades. But by the late 1980s, the Soviet Union had severe economic problems, and a new leader, Mikhail Gorbachev, was making reforms. As one reform, he gave Eastern Europe more freedom.

The impact was dramatic. Eastern Europeans demanded political and economic reforms. In 1989, Czechoslovakia, Hungary, Poland, and Romania ended Communist control of their governments and held free elections. In 1990, Bulgaria and Yugoslavia followed suit.

Instability followed. The old governments had taught people to be loyal only to the Communist Party. After those governments fell, people

MOVEMENT In 1989, the desire for democracy swept Eastern Europe. Country after country saw demonstrations like this one in Budapest, Hungary.

Communist and Non-Communist Europe, 1949 and 2000

SKILLBUILDER: Interpreting Maps

❶ **LOCATION** In 1949, near what country were the Communist nations of Europe located?

❷ **REGION** How would you describe the political change that happened in the region?

returned to ethnic loyalties. That was especially true in Yugoslavia, a nation consisting of six republics. In the early 1990s, four of the six Yugoslav republics voted to become separate states. Serbia objected, leading to civil war. (See Chapter 14 for details.) In contrast, Czechoslovakia peacefully split into the Czech Republic and Slovakia.

Developing the Economy

Because of its fertile plains, Eastern Europe has traditionally been a farming region. After 1948, the Soviet Union promoted industry there.

INDUSTRY Under communism, the government owned all factories and told them what to produce. This system was inefficient because industries had little motive to please customers or to cut costs. Often, there were shortages of goods. Eastern European nations traded with the Soviet Union and each other, so they didn't keep up with the technology of other nations. As a result, they had difficulty selling goods to nations outside Eastern Europe. And their outdated factories created heavy pollution.

After 1989, most of Eastern Europe began to move toward a **market economy**, in which industries make the goods consumers want to buy. Many factories in Eastern Europe became privately owned instead of state owned. The changes caused problems, such as inflation, the closing of factories, and unemployment. Since then, however, many factories have cut their costs and improved production. As a result, the Czech Republic, Hungary, and Poland have all grown economically. ◀B

Per Capita GDP in Eastern Europe

(graph: vertical axis "in U.S. Dollars (adjusted to 1990 prices)" with values $0, $1000, $2000, $3000, $4000, $5000; horizontal axis "Years" with 1990, 1992, 1994, 1996; lines for Hungary, Poland, Bulgaria, Albania)

SOURCE: *United Nations Statistical Yearbook, 1996*

SKILLBUILDER: Interpreting Graphs

❶ **SEEING PATTERNS** Which of these four countries have seen economic improvement since 1990? Explain.

❷ **DRAWING CONCLUSIONS** In terms of per capita GDP, which country has the best standard of living? Explain.

LINGERING PROBLEMS Some Eastern European nations have had trouble making economic progress—for many different reasons.

- Albania's economic growth is slowed by old equipment, a lack of raw materials, and a shortage of educated workers.
- Few of Romania's citizens have money to invest in business. In addition, the Romanian government still owns some industries. Foreigners don't want to invest their money in those industries.
- The civil wars of the 1990s damaged Yugoslavia and its former republics of Bosnia and Herzegovina and Croatia. Equipment and buildings were destroyed; workers were killed or left the country.

In general, it will take years for Eastern Europe to overcome the damage caused, in part, by decades of Communist control.

CONNECT TO THE ISSUES
UNIFICATION
B▷ Do you think the nations of Eastern Europe will want to join the European Union? Why or why not?

A Patchwork Culture

Because Eastern Europe contains a variety of ethnic groups, the region as a whole is a patchwork of different languages and religions.

CULTURAL DIVERSITY The map on page 267 shows the languages of Eastern Europe. The number of languages makes it difficult to unify the region. In some places, the national language is most closely related to a language spoken in a different region. For example, Hungarian is related to Finnish, and Romanian is related to Italian, French, and Spanish. Neither are related to the Slavic languages of the countries around them. This pattern was created by long-ago migrations.

Similarly, many different religions can be found in Eastern Europe. The Roman Empire introduced Catholicism, and after Rome fell, the Byzantine Empire spread Eastern Orthodox Christianity. Some countries also have a Protestant minority. And under the Ottoman Empire, some Eastern Europeans converted to Islam.

The region also has a small Jewish minority. Jews once made up a much higher percentage of Eastern Europeans, but in the Holocaust, Nazi Germany killed 6 million Jews. About half of them were from Poland. After World War II, many surviving Jews migrated to Israel.

FOLK ART Religious belief, rural customs, and Byzantine art have all influenced Eastern European folk art. In general, **folk art** is produced by rural people with traditional lifestyles instead of by professional artists. Eastern European folk artists create items such as pottery, woodcarving, and embroidered traditional costumes.

Many Eastern European ethnic groups also have their own folk music. This music influenced the region's classical musicians. Frédéric Chopin based some of his piano music on Polish dances. Anton Dvořák wove Czech folk music into his compositions.

Geographic Thinking

Seeing Patterns

C Why do you think folk art has remained important in Eastern Europe?

Moving Toward Modern Life

Since their Communist governments fell, many Eastern Europeans have expressed a longing for more economic growth and political freedom. These goals provide the region with some major challenges.

LESS URBAN DEVELOPMENT Eastern Europe has several large cities, such as Prague in the Czech Republic. More than 1,000 years old, Prague is one of Europe's most interesting cities, with quaint buildings, a rich history of music and culture, and thriving industries.

In general, though, Eastern Europe is much less urban than the rest of Europe. For example, the percentage of city dwellers is only 40 percent in Bosnia and Herzegovina and only 37 percent in Albania.

As Eastern Europe develops more industry, its cities will grow. That will have both positive and negative effects. Cities are often places of culture, learning, and modern technology. But urban growth creates problems such as pollution, traffic jams, and housing shortages.

CONFLICT As you read earlier, many Eastern Europeans have fierce loyalties to their own ethnic groups. One result of that has been conflict. For example, many Serbs hate Croats (KROH•ATS) because they believe the Croats betrayed them in World War II by working with the Nazis.

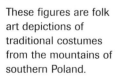

These figures are folk art depictions of traditional costumes from the mountains of southern Poland.

PLACE Crossing the Vltava River in Prague is the famous 650-year-old Charles Bridge. The bridge is now reserved for pedestrians. **Why do you think cars are banned from this bridge?**

EUROPE

Eastern European minority groups have often faced discrimination. Throughout history, Jews have suffered from **anti-Semitism**, which is discrimination against Jewish people. Another minority that experiences prejudice is the Romany, or Gypsy, people who are scattered across Eastern Europe. Traditionally, the Romany have moved from place to place. Because of this, other groups often look down on them.

DEMOCRACY To obtain true democracy, Eastern Europeans need to overcome old hatreds and work together. They also need to accept democratic ideals such as the rule of law—which means that government officials must obey the law. The dictators that ruled Eastern Europe in the past did not do so. But in recent years, Eastern Europeans have often held their leaders accountable. For example, in 2000, the Yugoslav people forced a dictator to accept election results that turned him out of office. You will read about this event in Chapter 14, along with other major issues of European life today.

Assessment

① Places & Terms

Identify these terms and explain their importance in the region.

- cultural crossroads
- balkanization
- satellite nation
- market economy
- folk art
- anti-Semitism

② Taking Notes

REGION Review the notes you took for this section.

- What country dominated Eastern Europe after World War II?
- What problems did the move toward a market economy cause?

③ Main Ideas

a. Why is Eastern Europe considered a cultural crossroads?

b. What role did the Soviet Union play in the rise and fall of communism in Eastern Europe?

c. What are some important ways that Eastern Europe is different from Western Europe?

④ Geographic Thinking

Making Inferences The Balkan region has been called the "powder keg of Europe." Why do you think it earned that name? **Think about:**

- the wars in 1912 and 1913
- World War I

 See Skillbuilder Handbook, page R4.

EXPLORING LOCAL GEOGRAPHY Like Eastern Europe, most places in the United States have been controlled by various cultural groups or nations over time. Research the history of your area and create a **time line,** like the one on pages 310-311, listing changes in control.

VISUAL SUMMARY
HUMAN GEOGRAPHY OF EUROPE

Subregions of Europe

● **Mediterranean Europe**

- The influence of ancient Greece, ancient Rome, and Renaissance Italy on art, philosophy, religion, and language shaped modern life.

- In the late 1900s, Mediterranean Europe began to have more manufacturing and service industries.

○ **Western Europe**

- Germany and France developed very different cultures, and throughout history, conflicts between them involved much of Europe.

- Western Europe has a highly developed economy. It is a leader in the economic and political alliance known as the European Union.

● **Northern Europe**

- This region was a leader in the Industrial Revolution and the rise of representative government.

- The region has a history of seafaring conquerors. Great Britain established an empire that spread British culture and the English language worldwide.

● **Eastern Europe**

- Because it is a cultural crossroads, Eastern Europe has a diverse culture with many ethnic groups.

- Domination by outside powers, most recently the Soviet Union, has characterized the region's history.

Reviewing Places & Terms

A. Briefly explain the importance of each of the following.

1. city-state
2. republic
3. Benelux
4. nationalism
5. Berlin Wall
6. Nordic countries
7. euro
8. cultural crossroads
9. balkanization
10. satellite nation

B. Answer the questions about vocabulary in complete sentences.

11. Which of the terms above are the names of regions?
12. Would a supporter of nationalism want to adopt the euro? Explain.
13. Which of the terms above have to do with conflict?
14. In which part of Europe did the countries become satellite nations of the Soviet Union?
15. How does the geographic theme of movement relate to a cultural crossroads?
16. Which ancient civilization was organized into city-states and which was a republic?
17. In what part of Europe is Benelux found?
18. What is the origin of the term *balkanization*?
19. Which of the terms above can also be applied to the United States? Explain.
20. Which two major peninsulas are found in the Nordic countries?

Main Ideas

Mediterranean Europe (pp. 289–295)

1. What legacy did ancient Athens leave for modern governments?
2. What effect did the empires of Spain and Portugal have on the rest of the world?
3. Why does Spain have a conflict with the Basque people?

Western Europe (pp. 296–301)

4. How did the Reformation create new cultural divisions?
5. How did nationalism lead to conflicts?
6. For what artistic legacy are Germany and Austria famous?

Northern Europe (pp. 302–309)

7. Who were the Vikings, and what did they do?
8. What geographic advantages helped Great Britain build its empire?

Eastern Europe (pp. 310–315)

9. Why did independent nation-states develop later in Eastern Europe than in Western Europe?
10. What problems existed in the Eastern European economy under Communist rule?

Critical Thinking

1. Using Your Notes

Use your completed chart to answer these questions.

a. What similarities exist between the ways the Roman Empire and the British Empire influenced other regions of the world?

b. In what ways are Eastern Europe and Northern Europe different?

2. Geographic Themes

a. **LOCATION** Do you think the location of France and Germany relative to the rest of Europe is a geographic advantage or disadvantage? Explain.

b. **MOVEMENT** What geographic reason might account for the fact that Spain and Great Britain colonized much of the Americas?

3. Identifying Themes

Explain which countries were the first to develop industry and which developed industry later. If you identify those countries on a map, what spatial patterns do you see? Which geographic themes relate to your answer?

4. Seeing Patterns

How did ancient migrations affect the pattern of where certain languages are spoken in Europe today? Give examples.

5. Making Inferences

Millions of Europeans have migrated to other parts of the world. What are some geographic factors that you think might have encouraged this?

Additional Test Practice, pp. S1–S37

TEST PRACTICE
CLASSZONE.COM

EUROPE

Geographic Skills: Interpreting Maps

A Divided Germany

Use the map to answer the following questions.

1. **PLACE** How did the size of West Germany compare with that of East Germany?

2. **LOCATION** In which of the two countries was the city of Berlin located?

3. **LOCATION** Which of the two Germanys was closer to the Soviet Union?

GeoActivity

West Germany was divided into several zones after World War II. Use a history book or historical atlas to learn which three countries controlled those zones. Create a historical map showing the zones.

INTERNET ACTIVITY

Use the links at **classzone.com** to do research about the population of a single society in Europe. Look for such information as age distribution, religions, ethnic or minority groups, and literacy rates.

Constructing a Population Pyramid Use the information you have gathered to construct a population pyramid describing the population characteristics of the European society you have chosen.

SECTION 1
Turmoil in the Balkans

SECTION 2
Cleaning Up Europe

CASESTUDY
THE EUROPEAN UNION

For more on these issues in Europe . . .

CURRENT EVENTS
CLASSZONE.COM

TODAY'S ISSUES
Europe

Throughout the 1990s, ethnic conflict tore apart the Balkan region.

GeoFocus

How can international cooperation resolve issues?

Taking Notes In your notebook, copy a cause-and-effect chart like the one shown below. Then take notes on the causes and effects of the issues.

	Causes	Effects
Issue 1: Conflict		
Issue 2: Pollution		
Case Study: Unification		

Turmoil in the Balkans

How can people resolve their differences?

Main Ideas

- Yugoslavia was a nation of many ethnic groups distributed among six republics.
- When Serbia tried to dominate Yugoslavia, other republics broke away. This sparked conflict.

Places & Terms

Slobodan Milošević

South Slavs

ethnic cleansing

KLA

Vojislav Kostunica

SUNSHINE STATE STANDARDS

Key Standard SS.A.3.4.10 The student understands the political, military, and economic events since the 1950s that have had a significant impact on international relations.

Other Standards SS.A.2.4.6

FCAT LA.A.1.4.2 Reading: Strategies

EUROPE

A HUMAN PERSPECTIVE The Serbian leader **Slobodan Milošević** (SLOH·buh·DAHN muh·LOH·suh·VIHCH) tried to increase Serbia's power over the rest of Yugoslavia. As a result, in 1991 and 1992, four republics left Yugoslavia. Serbia went to war against them but lost. In 1999, an international court accused Milošević (who was the Yugoslav president by then) and Serbian troops of war crimes in those conflicts. Many nations ended trade with Yugoslavia in protest, and the country grew poorer.

In 2000, Yugoslavia voted Milošević out of office. When he refused to accept the election results, thousands of people protested until he admitted defeat. In doing so, the Yugoslav people showed that they wanted peace and a normal relationship with the world. This may have been a turning point in the long history of conflict in the Balkans.

Roots of the Balkan Conflict

One conflict in the Balkans is that different groups want control of the same land. The causes of this conflict go back centuries. In the 500s, Slavic people migrated from Poland and Russia and settled in the Balkan Peninsula. They were called the **South Slavs.** Each group of South Slavs (the Croats, the Slovenes, and the Serbs) formed its own kingdom.

FOREIGN RULERS In the 1300s, the Muslim Ottoman Empire tried to conquer the Balkan Peninsula. In 1389, the Ottomans defeated the Serbian Empire at the Battle of Kosovo Polje. The Ottomans also ruled Bosnia and Herzegovina. Elsewhere in the Balkans, Austria ruled Slovenia, and Hungary ruled Croatia. Over time, foreign rule created differences among the South Slavs. For instance, under Muslim rule, the Serbs clung to Christianity, while many Bosnians converted to Islam.

Both Serbs and Albanians had lived in Kosovo, a part of the Serbian Empire. When the Muslims seized power, many Serbs fled Kosovo, so the region became more Albanian in culture.

YUGOSLAVIA IS FORMED In 1878, Serbia broke free of the Ottoman Empire. Many Serbs wanted all the South Slavs to be free of foreign rule and to unite in one nation. That desire helped to spark World War I.

In 1918, the Kingdom of the Serbs, Croats, and Slovenes was formed. In 1929, the king renamed it Yugoslavia (which means "Land of the South Slavs") to help end ethnic divisions.

PLACE This painting, *The Kosovo Maiden* (1917) by Uros Predic, shows a woman giving water to a wounded Serb after the Battle of Kosovo Polje. The painting has become a symbol of national pride for many Serbs.

June 1991
Croatia and Slovenia declare independence. Yugoslavia fights them.

March 1992
Bosnia declares independence. Serbia fights it.

March 1999
NATO begins bombing Serbia.

1990

1995

2000

January 1992
The UN negotiates a cease-fire in Croatia.

February 1998
Serbia attacks Kosovo.

June 1999
Serbian troops withdraw from Kosovo.

The conflicts of the 1990s caused millions of refugees to leave their homes. These refugees are from Kosovo.

COMMUNIST RULE During World War II, Germany and Italy invaded Yugoslavia. The Croats cooperated with the Nazis, and the Croat leader ordered the massacre of Jews and Serbs. Many other Yugoslavs joined the Chetniks or the Partisans, two rival groups fighting the Nazis.

One Partisan leader was Josip Broz Tito, head of the Communist Party. After the war, Tito became the dictator of Yugoslavia. He encouraged the Serbs, Croats, and other groups to think of themselves as Yugoslavs.

In 1946, a new constitution organized Yugoslavia into a nation of six republics: Bosnia and Herzegovina, Croatia, Macedonia, Montenegro, Serbia, and Slovenia. Serbia had two self-governing provinces, Kosovo and Vojvodina. The map on page 322 shows that Croatia and Bosnia were ethnically mixed and contained many Serbs. **A**

Ethnic Tension Boils Over

In 1980, Tito died, and the presidency began to rotate among leaders from the many republics and provinces. No single person ran the country.

FEAR OF SERBIA Slobodan Milošević began to propose the creation of a Greater Serbia. Serbia would expand its borders to include other territories with Serbian populations. This plan alarmed Croats and Bosnians. Then in 1991, Serbia blocked a Croat from becoming president.

In response, Slovenia and Croatia declared their independence. In June 1991, the Serbian-led Yugoslav army invaded both republics. The Slovenes quickly achieved freedom. But Croatia had a large Serbian minority, and past Serb-Croat hatreds exploded in all-out war. The fighting claimed thousands of lives before the United Nations arranged a cease-fire in January 1992. Slovenia and Croatia remained free.

WAR IN BOSNIA In March 1992, Bosnia and Herzegovina declared independence. Bosnia's Muslims and Croats backed the move, but its Serbs (and Serbia) launched a war to stop it. The Serbs used murder and violence to get rid of Bosnia's Muslims and Croats. The policy of trying to eliminate an ethnic group through violence is called **ethnic cleansing.** More than 200,000 people died, while over 2 million people fled their homes.

In 1995, the United States sponsored peace negotiations, and in December, a peace treaty was signed. Bosnia remained independent.

Geographic Thinking

Seeing Patterns
A How might having a mixed population affect the stability of Croatia and Bosnia?

BACKGROUND
By 1992, only Serbia and Montenegro remained part of Yugoslavia.

WAR IN KOSOVO The Serbs had never forgotten their long-ago defeat at Kosovo Polje. They saw the province as a sacred part of Serbia's heritage. But in the 1990s, Kosovo was inhabited mostly by Albanians, who spoke a non-Slavic language and whose religion was Islam.

Serbia, led by Milošević, tried to assert control over Kosovo and to wipe out its Albanian culture. In response, Kosovo demanded independence. In the 1990s, a group called the Kosovo Liberation Army (**KLA**) began to carry out attacks against Serbian officials. The Serbian government responded by bombing villages and began a campaign of ethnic cleansing against Albanians. **B**

In March 1999, NATO started bombing Serbia to force it to stop the violence. In June, Milošević withdrew his troops from Kosovo. After they pulled out, international officials found horrifying evidence of Serbian atrocities.

AN UNCERTAIN FUTURE In 2000, the Yugoslav people elected a reform leader named **Vojislav Kostunica** (VAW·yee·SLAHV kahsh·TOO·neet·sah) as president.

Even as Kostunica took office, the outlook for peace was unclear. Ethnic loyalties still created tension. The decade of wars had created millions of refugees. And the wars' destruction had created widespread poverty.

Another cause of tension was that many people in Kosovo and the republic of Montenegro wanted independence. In 2002, the leaders of Serbia and Montenegro signed an agreement pledging cooperation between the two former Yugoslav regions. They formed a new unit called Serbia-Montenegro. Section 2 discusses an issue that affects not only the Balkans but all of Europe—pollution.

Geographic Thinking

Making Comparisons
B How were Serbia's actions in Kosovo similar to its actions in Bosnia and Herzegovina?

Geography TODAY

Land Mines

All over the world, land mines remain after war and cause countless injuries and deaths. Bosnia alone has an estimated 750,000 active mines.

Scientists are trying to find ways to detect buried mines, so they can be removed. Some are using bees. Bees gathering pollen sometimes carry chemical traces from land mines to their hives. Sensors can be put in the hives to detect those chemicals. But scientists have to find a way to track the bees back to the mine fields.

Other scientists, such as the one below, are working to develop machines to detect buried mines.

EUROPE

SECTION 1 Assessment

1 Places & Terms

Identify these terms and explain their relationship to the issue.
- Slobodan Milošević
- South Slavs
- ethnic cleansing
- KLA
- Vojislav Kostunica

2 Taking Notes

PLACE Review the notes you took for this section.

	Causes	Effects
Issue 1: Conflict		

- Where was the historic battle in which the Ottomans defeated the Serbs?
- Which two republics suffered brutal wars after independence?

3 Main Ideas

a. How did Tito try to overcome the differences among ethnic groups in Yugoslavia?

b. What was the plan to create Greater Serbia?

c. How did the rest of the world get involved in the Balkan conflicts?

4 Geographic Thinking

Drawing Conclusions
Was Milošević's effort to make Serbia stronger successful? Give examples.

Think about:
- the reaction of other Yugoslav republics to Serbia's actions
- the reaction of the international community

GeoActivity

MAKING COMPARISONS Working from a history book, historical atlas, or other resource, make a sequence of **maps** showing changes in the political boundaries of the Balkans over the last 100 years. Possible dates for maps include 1912, 1919, 1946, and 1995.

Interpreting a Thematic Map

This map shows the republics and provinces that made up the former country of Yugoslavia. It also shows the major ethnic and religious groups throughout the region. In the 1990s, civil wars raged throughout this part of Europe. These wars were rooted in centuries-old ethnic and religious conflicts. This map shows the ethnic distribution that contributed to those conflicts.

THE LANGUAGE OF MAPS A **thematic map** illustrates a specific feature, or features, of a region. As this map shows, thematic maps may use color to convey information.

SUNSHINE STATE STANDARDS
Key Standard SS.B.2.4.1 The student understands how social, cultural, economic, and environmental factors contribute to the dynamic nature of regions.
FCAT LA.A.1.4.2 Reading: Strategies

Ethnic Groups in the Former Yugoslavia

Key

Albanian
Croat
Hungarian
Macedonian
Montenegrin
Muslim
Serb
Slovene
No majority present

—— Former Yugoslavia
——— Republic boundaries
– – – Provincial boundaries

0   50   100 Mi.
0 50 100 150 Km.

Source: CIA Reference Map Series, 1993
Copyright by Rand McNally & Co.

❶ The key illustrates the colors used and what they represent. It also shows symbols for boundaries.

❷ The different colored areas on the map indicate the majority ethnic group in each area. The colors do not imply that no one from a different group lives in the area.

❸ This map shows three types of political boundaries: the boundary of the former Yugoslavia, boundaries of the republics that were part of it, and boundaries of provinces that belonged to the republic of Serbia.

Copyright by Rand McNally & Co.

Map and Graph Skills Assessment

1. Analyzing Data
Which republics had Serbs as part of their populations?

2. Drawing Conclusions
What republic had the most diverse population?

3. Making Inferences
How did the ethnic composition of the most diverse republic relate to its relative location?

Cleaning Up Europe

How can Europeans clean up their environment?

Main Ideas
- Pollution has many complex causes and results. It often spreads across borders, contaminating a region.
- The nations of Europe are cooperating to try to clean up their environment.

Places & Terms

cyanide

European Environmental Agency

particulates

smog

ozone

The Voyageur Experience in World Geography
Greece: Urbanization and the Environment

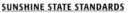
SUNSHINE STATE STANDARDS
Key Standard SS.B.2.4.4 The student understands the global impact of human changes in the physical environment.
FCAT LA.A.1.4.2 Reading: Strategies

EUROPE

A HUMAN PERSPECTIVE In January 2000, a gold mine in Romania released cyanide into local streams. The **cyanide,** a deadly poison, flowed into the Tisza River in Hungary. Before the accident, the river held some of Europe's rarest fish. The poison killed an estimated 80 percent of the fish in the Tisza. Balazs Meszaros, whose family has commercially fished the Tisza for generations, said, "Now I don't know how I am going to live." Even worse than the loss of jobs was the threat to health. Experts feared that the poison would seep into wells and contaminate crops and livestock. The damage will take years to undo.

Pollution is a complex example of human-environment interaction. People damage the environment, which in turn affects human lives. For instance, pollution is thought to cause 1 out of every 17 deaths in Hungary. Because cleaning up pollution is time-consuming, difficult, and costly, it remains a serious issue in Europe—and around the world.

Saving Europe's Water

As the story of the Tisza demonstrates, pollution rarely remains at its point of origin but often spreads to neighboring regions. As a result, water pollution is a problem that concerns almost all of Europe.

CAUSES OF WATER POLLUTION Mines and factories create much of Europe's water pollution. Industries often discharge chemicals into streams and rivers. Factories sometimes bury solid waste. Poisons from this waste seep into ground water and contaminate wells and rivers. And, as you read in Chapter 12, the burning of coal and other fuels causes acid rain. Acid rain changes the chemistry of lakes and rivers, often killing fish.

The link between industry and pollution creates a dilemma. Most countries want to develop industry, and some accept environmental damage as the price they must pay for progress. Other nations force industry to use pollution controls, but these are usually expensive.

HUMAN-ENVIRONMENT INTERACTION A cyanide spill poisoned Eastern Europe's streams and rivers. These dead fish are from the Tisza River in Hungary.

Industry is not the only source of water pollution. Other sources include the following:

- **Sewage** Ideally, cities should have treatment plants that remove harmful substances from sewage before it is released into bodies of water. But in Poland, for example, from 1988 to 1990, 44 percent of the cities had no sewage treatment plants. The water in most of Poland's rivers is unsafe to drink. It has also contaminated the soil so that some crops are toxic.

- **Chemical fertilizers** Rain washes fertilizers from fields into bodies of water, where they cause algae and plants to grow faster than fish can eat them. The plants and algae die and decay, a process that uses up oxygen. The lack of oxygen kills fish—which then decay, using more oxygen. In time, these bodies of water can no longer support life.

- **Oil spills** For example, in December 1999, a tanker sank off the west coast of France and spilled 10,000 tons of oil that spread along 250 miles of coastline. The oil killed tens of thousands of shorebirds.

CLEANING UP THE WATER Because water pollution spreads so easily, nations must cooperate to solve the problem. For example, pollution levels in the Rhine River rose sharply in the mid-1900s. To correct this, representatives from France, Germany, Luxembourg, the Netherlands, and Switzerland formed the International Commission for the Protection of the Rhine. Since it began meeting in 1950, the commission has recommended programs such as the treatment of sewage before it enters the Rhine. As a result, pollution of the Rhine has decreased.

In addition, the European Union has passed environmental laws that its member nations must obey. The EU also set up the **European Environmental Agency,** which provides the EU with reliable information about the environment.

Improving Europe's Air Quality

Although they are often considered separately, the different types of pollution are connected. For example, water pollution can be caused by air pollution—because rain washes chemicals out of dirty air and into bodies of water.

CAUSES OF AIR POLLUTION Air pollution is made up of harmful gases and **particulates,** very small particles of liquid or solid matter. Many human activities create air pollution by expelling these gases and particulates into the atmosphere.

- **Using fossil fuels** The burning of petroleum, gas, and coal causes much air pollution. It contributes

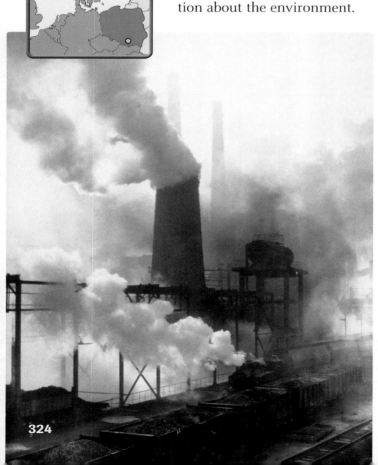

HUMAN–ENVIRONMENT INTERACTION This mill in Nowa Huta, Poland, is making coke—a byproduct of coal. The smokestacks cause heavy air pollution.
What else besides the smokestacks might be causing air pollution?

BACKGROUND
The word *smog* was formed by combining the words *smoke* and *fog*.

to the formation of **smog**—a brown haze that occurs when the gases released by burning fossil fuels react with sunlight to create hundreds of harmful chemicals. One such chemical is **ozone,** a form of oxygen that causes health problems.

- **Fires** Forest fires caused by careless human behavior and the burning of garbage release smoke and particulates into the atmosphere.
- **Chemical use** Dry cleaning, refrigeration, air conditioning, and the spraying of pesticides are among the human activities that release harmful chemicals into the air.
- **Industry** Factories discharge chemicals such as sulfur into the air. The factories of former Communist countries have been especially heavy polluters. Because of this, air pollution levels are much higher in the former East Germany than in the United States.

RESULTING PROBLEMS Breathing polluted air can contribute to respiratory diseases such as asthma, bronchitis, and emphysema. Air pollution is also suspected to be one of the causes of lung cancer. In addition, air pollution harms livestock and stunts plant growth. It also causes acid rain, which kills forests and damages buildings, such as the famous Parthenon in Athens, Greece.

CLEANING UP THE AIR Individual European countries are passing laws to make their air safer to breathe. France, for example, now requires improved thermal insulation of new buildings. This reduces the need to burn fossil fuels for heat. Other European governments are also passing laws to protect the air.

Nations are also cooperating to clean the air. For example, in 1998, the members of the European Union agreed that, starting in 2000, they would require reduced emissions from cars and vans. As that example indicates, a leader in the effort to restore Europe's environment will be the European Union—which is discussed in the following Case Study.

Geographic Thinking

Seeing Patterns
A You learned in Chapter 13 that Eastern Europe used old technology. How might this relate to pollution?

SECTION 2 Assessment

1 Places & Terms

Identify these terms and explain their relationship to the issue.

- cyanide
- European Environmental Agency
- particulates
- smog
- ozone

2 Taking Notes

HUMAN-ENVIRONMENT INTERACTION Review the notes you took for this section.

	Causes	Effects
Issue 2: Pollution		

- What river has an international group been trying to save?
- What diseases are linked to air pollution?

3 Main Ideas

a. What dilemma is faced by countries that are developing industry?

b. What is a harmful result of burning fossil fuels?

c. Why is the European Union a leader in the fight against pollution?

4 Geographic Thinking

Seeing Patterns How are the different types of pollution interrelated?
Think about:
- how air pollution, water pollution, and buried waste cause other types of pollution

 See Skillbuilder Handbook, page R8.

EXPLORING LOCAL GEOGRAPHY Find out how your community deals with pollution. Learn about laws passed by your local government, environmental safeguards used by industry, or water treatment facilities. Then write a **news article** on the subject.

CaseStudy

UNIFICATION: THE EUROPEAN UNION

Will there be a United States of EUROPE?

EU headquarters in Brussels, Belgium

SUNSHINE STATE STANDARDS
Key Standard SS.A.3.4.10 The student understands the political, military, and economic events since the 1950s that have had a significant impact on international relations.

Other Standards SS.A.1.4.3, B.2.4.3

FCAT LA.A.2.4.8 Reading: Synthesize and Conclude

Europe's long history of conflict reached a crisis in World War II (1939-1945). In the wake of that destructive war, two goals emerged: to rebuild the nations' shattered economies and to prevent new conflict. Some people believed the best way to achieve both goals was to unify Europe. As you read the Case Study, consider the pros and cons of that idea.

Steps Toward Unity

In 1951, France and West Germany began the process of unification by signing a treaty that gave control of their coal and steel resources to a multinational group, the European Coal and Steel Community (ECSC). Italy and the Benelux countries also joined the ECSC. The six countries' leaders thought this alliance would have many positive results. Because the nations would depend on each other for industrial resources, their economies would suffer if they fought again. No country could prepare for war secretly because each knew what the others were manufacturing. In addition, the ECSC would set a tone of cooperation that would help Europe rebuild its economy.

The next step toward unity came in 1957 with the formation of the European Economic Community (EEC), also called the Common Market. This alliance removed trade barriers, set common economic goals, and allowed people to live and work in any member country. Between 1958 and 1968, trade among the EEC nations quadrupled.

In 1967, the EEC merged with the ECSC and another European alliance to become the European Community (EC). In 1973, the EC began to admit other European nations. (See the map on page 327.)

The Road to European Unity

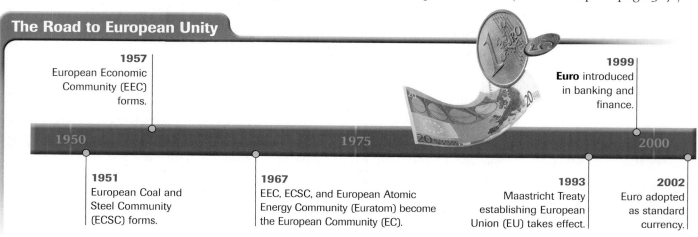

1951 European Coal and Steel Community (ECSC) forms.

1957 European Economic Community (EEC) forms.

1967 EEC, ECSC, and European Atomic Energy Community (Euratom) become the European Community (EC).

1993 Maastricht Treaty establishing European Union (EU) takes effect.

1999 **Euro** introduced in banking and finance.

2002 Euro adopted as standard currency.

1950   1975   2000

The European Union Today

In 1993, the Maastricht Treaty took effect, and the European Union (EU) replaced the EC. With 15 member nations, the EU faces many issues. They include settling political and economic differences, replacing national currencies with the euro, and expanding EU membership.

ECONOMICS AND POLITICS EU members wonder how the union will affect their national economies. For example, workers may move to areas with higher wages, creating shifts in national populations.

SEE PRIMARY SOURCE Ⓐ

Further, some countries believe that switching to the euro will mean losing control of economic factors such as interest rates. Others don't want to give up the national identities associated with having their own currencies. But many people believe the euro has benefits. These include greater business efficiency and increased international trade. In 1999, financial institutions began to calculate transactions in euros. Euros will begin to be used in everyday life in 2002.

SEE PRIMARY SOURCE Ⓑ

The EU also affects politics. For example, on February 4, 2000, Joerg Haider and his Freedom Party became part of a coalition government in Austria. (In a coalition government, several parties share power.) In the past, Haider had made statements that were sympathetic to Nazi Germany, so EU nations criticized Austria for its support of Haider. Haider did step down, but some observers fear that a controversial leader like Haider could some day tear the EU apart.

EXPANDING THE EU One of the complex issues facing the EU is growth. In time, it might expand to 28 countries that presently have about 475 million people. Running such a huge alliance could be difficult. Many of the proposed members were once Communist nations. In general, they are less prosperous and have little experience of democracy. Such differences may create tensions that the EU will have to resolve.

SEE PRIMARY SOURCE Ⓒ

On the following pages, you will find primary sources about the EU. Use them to form your own opinion.

EUROPE

The European Union, 2000

Legend:
- Original European alliance
- Later European Union members
- European Union candidates
- Non-member countries
- 1973 Year of joining European alliance

ICELAND
SWEDEN 1995
FINLAND 1995
NORWAY
ATLANTIC OCEAN
ESTONIA
LATVIA
LITHUANIA
North Sea
Baltic Sea
IRELAND 1973
UNITED KINGDOM 1973
DENMARK 1973
NETHERLANDS 1951
BELGIUM 1951
(1990) (WEST) GERMANY 1951
POLAND
CZECH REPUBLIC
LUXEMBOURG
SLOVAKIA
Bay of Biscay
SWITZERLAND
AUSTRIA 1995
HUNGARY
FRANCE 1951
SLOVENIA
CROATIA
ROMANIA
PORTUGAL 1986
SPAIN 1986
BOSNIA-HERZEGOVINA
YUGOSLAVIA
Black Sea
BULGARIA
ALBANIA
MACEDONIA
Mediterranean Sea
ITALY 1951
GREECE 1981
TURKEY
MALTA
CYPRUS

0 250 500 miles
0 250 500 kilometers
Azimuthal Equidistant Projection

SKILLBUILDER: Interpreting Maps

❶ **MOVEMENT** In what years did the largest expansion of the European alliance occur? What countries joined?

❷ **REGION** Which region of Europe is not part of the EU? Why?

CASESTUDY

PROJECT — *Panel Discussion*

Primary sources A to E on these two pages present differing opinions on expansion of the EU. Use these sources and your own research to prepare for a panel discussion on EU expansion. You might use the Internet and the library for research.

RESEARCH LINKS
CLASSZONE.COM

Suggested Steps

1. Choose a European (EU or non-EU) country to represent.
2. Research your country's position on EU expansion. Use encyclopedias, books, or the Internet to help you find the right information.
3. Consider the following questions during your research.
   - Why do certain countries want to join the EU?
   - What do current EU members have to gain and lose in expansion?
   - Why do certain countries want to remain independent?
4. Create a visual to be shown during the panel discussion.
5. Give a 2–3 minute speech that introduces your country's position.

Materials and Supplies

- Writing paper
- Posterboard
- Felt-tip markers
- Encyclopedias and reference books
- Computer
- Internet access

PRIMARY SOURCE Ⓐ

Political Commentary *Global Britain, a conservative group in the United Kingdom, gave this view of the euro on January 25, 1999. Although the United Kingdom belongs to the EU, it is reluctant to adopt the euro, a central issue for EU expansion.*

The Single Currency is a political project designed to hasten the creation of a Single European State in which nation-states like Britain would be provinces. . . . In joining the Single Currency, a nation hands over control of its interest rate, exchange rate and gold and currency reserves, as well as control over tax and spending, to [the EU]. All of this is set out in the Maastricht Treaty which Britain signed in 1992. . . . There are 43 nation-states in Europe, of which only 11 have joined the "single" European currency. Those 11 countries, unlike Britain, are in varying degrees economic satellites of Germany and France. . . . A single currency eliminates the interest rate and exchange rate safety valves, which allow changing national economies to adjust to each other. . . .
Preparations for the "single" currency have already helped to cause mass unemployment in Germany, France, and Italy, where real jobless rates are at least three times as high as in Britain.

PRIMARY SOURCE Ⓑ

Speech *Günter Verheugen of Germany, the European Commissioner for Enlargement, expressed his views on EU expansion in speeches in the United States on April 4–6, 2000. Germany is an original member of the EU and its predecessors.*

Enlargement is the biggest challenge the Union is facing at the dawn of the new millennium. . . . We are committed to this historical mission: to integrate the Central and East European countries which can and want to participate in our common achievements. . . . Our objective is to promote political and economic stability—and make this process irreversible. . . . What are the political benefits? First and foremost, the enlargement process is vital for securing political stability, democracy and respect of human rights on the European continent as a whole. . . . Political stability and freedom will be increased throughout Europe. Against the background of many years of crisis . . . the only way to achieve lasting stability in Europe is further integration.

Data *Eurobarometer is a company that surveys public opinion. It asked people living in the 15 EU countries how they felt about various countries joining the EU. This chart lists the various countries and the support for them.*

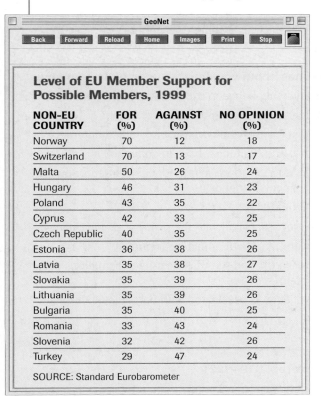

GeoNet

Back | Forward | Reload | Home | Images | Print | Stop

Level of EU Member Support for Possible Members, 1999

NON-EU COUNTRY	FOR (%)	AGAINST (%)	NO OPINION (%)
Norway	70	12	18
Switzerland	70	13	17
Malta	50	26	24
Hungary	46	31	23
Poland	43	35	22
Cyprus	42	33	25
Czech Republic	40	35	25
Estonia	36	38	26
Latvia	35	38	27
Slovakia	35	39	26
Lithuania	35	39	26
Bulgaria	35	40	25
Romania	33	43	24
Slovenia	32	42	26
Turkey	29	47	24

SOURCE: Standard Eurobarometer

Political Analysis *Edmund L. Andrews published this article in the* New York Times *on June 21, 1999. He examined some of the problems and issues of EU expansion into Central Europe.*

By becoming [EU] members, the Central European nations would eventually gain full access to European markets. Their citizens would be free to live and work throughout Western Europe. . . .

As more detailed negotiations loom . . . between the European Union and the Poles, Czechs, and Hungarians . . . both sides face the need for painful change. . . .

Central Europeans have the added burden of history. Many of them remain suspicious of Germany, the European Union's largest power and Central Europe's neighbor. And most adults, reared under Communism, are still adjusting to . . . the Western way of doing things.

As for the European Union, the prospect of a flood of labor from the East raises irrational fears among Westerners already grumbling about too many immigrants. . . . Another big fear [in Central Europe] is that foreigners—by which most people mean Germans—will buy up their land, which is another basic right accorded to anybody living within the European Union.

Political Cartoon *Pat Oliphant, a political cartoonist, shows the leaders of the EU trying to navigate stormy seas on a euro.*

PROJECT CheckList

Have I . . .

✓ researched my country's perspective?

✓ answered all relevant questions?

✓ created an interesting, colorful visual for the discussion?

✓ practiced my speech?

VISUAL SUMMARY
TODAY'S ISSUES IN EUROPE

Conflict

Turmoil in the Balkans
- Yugoslavia was a nation of many ethnic groups distributed among six republics.
- Serbia tried to dominate Yugoslavia, causing several republics to declare independence. Brutal wars followed. The UN and the United States negotiated peace.
- Seeking to re-establish control over Kosovo, Serbia tried to drive Albanians from Kosovo. NATO intervened to stop the violence.

Environment

Cleaning Up Europe
- Industry, sewage, agriculture, and other activities have caused water and air pollution in Europe.
- Pollution has caused disease, damaged buildings, and harmed livestock.
- Both national and international efforts are being made to clean up Europe.

Economics

The European Union
- After the destruction of World War II, France, Germany, Italy, and the Benelux countries joined in an economic alliance to foster cooperation.
- In time, this alliance began to admit other nations and to pursue more general goals.
- The alliance became the European Union (EU) in 1993. The EU faced the issues of adopting a common currency, settling political and economic differences, and expanding EU membership.

Reviewing Places & Terms

A. Briefly explain the importance of each of the following.

1. Slobodan Milošević
2. South Slavs
3. ethnic cleansing
4. KLA
5. Vojislav Kostunica
6. cyanide
7. European Environmental Agency
8. particulates
9. smog
10. ozone

B. Answer the questions about vocabulary in complete sentences.

11. What is the relationship between ozone and smog?
12. What effect did cyanide have on the rivers of Europe?
13. How are Slobodan Milošević and Vojislav Kostunica different?
14. What do Milošević and Kostunica have in common?
15. Which of the terms listed above might appear in a report by the European Environmental Agency?
16. Who were the South Slavs?
17. Who was the leader associated with the policy of ethnic cleansing?
18. Which groups were targets of ethnic cleansing?
19. Can Slobodan Milošević and the KLA best be described as allies or enemies? Explain.
20. Which type of pollution is associated with particulates? Explain.

Main Ideas

Turmoil in the Balkans (pp. 319–322)

1. How did historic events contribute to the conflict over Kosovo?
2. How did the diversity of Bosnia and Herzegovina's population contribute to the conflict there?
3. What did international officials discover after Serbian forces withdrew from Kosovo?
4. What are possible sources of future conflict in the Balkans?

Cleaning Up Europe (pp. 323–325)

5. What are the effects of acid rain?
6. Which region became heavily polluted under Communist rule?
7. Why is pollution such a difficult issue to resolve?

The European Union (pp. 326–329)

8. What organizations were forerunners of the European Union?
9. Why did European leaders believe that an economic alliance would help prevent war?
10. What are some possible problems associated with admitting formerly Communist countries to the EU?

Critical Thinking

1. Using Your Notes

Use your completed chart to answer these questions.

	Causes	Effects
Issue 1: Conflict		
Issue 2: Pollution		

a. Which of these issues has caused physical damage to Europe? Explain.

b. Do you think the issues are linked? Explain.

2. Geographic Themes

a. **REGION** In what way is the European Union creating a new region?

b. **MOVEMENT** What natural processes spread pollution from its point of origin?

3. Identifying Themes

Reread the story about the Tisza River on page 323. How do the five themes of geography relate to that story?

4. Making Inferences

What factors do you think led the Yugoslav people to vote Slobodan Milošević out of office?

5. Drawing Conclusions

How important is international cooperation in solving Europe's problems? Explain using specific examples.

Additional Test Practice, pp. S1–S37

TEST PRACTICE
CLASSZONE.COM

Geographic Skills: Interpreting Graphs

Trade with EU, 1995
(as percentage of total trade)

Use the graph to answer the following questions.

1. **PLACE** Which country does the highest percentage of its trade within the EU?

2. **PLACE** Which two countries do the lowest percentage of trade with the EU?

3. **MOVEMENT** Judging by the countries shown here, is there more trade within the EU or between the EU and non-member countries? Explain.

Research trade statistics for the eight EU countries not shown here. Create an expanded graph showing data for all 15 EU members.

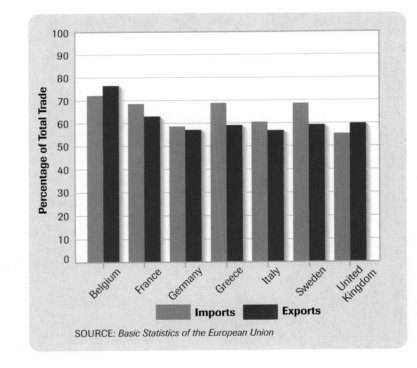

SOURCE: *Basic Statistics of the European Union*

EUROPE

INTERNET ACTIVITY

Use the links at **classzone.com** to do research about pollution in Europe. Learn about the "Green" political parties and their views on what should be done.

Writing About Geography Write a summary of your findings. Include a chart listing the programs proposed by the "Green" political parties. List the Web sites that were your sources.

Unit 5

Russia and the Republics

Between 1922 and 1991, Russia and most of the Republics were part of the Union of Soviet Socialist Republics (USSR), also known as the Soviet Union.

LOCATION Shoppers stroll around Russia's famous State Department Store. The mall, which opened in 1893, is located in Moscow, the capital of Russia.

GeoData

REGION Russia and the Republics cross over 11 time zones and cover nearly one-sixth of the earth's land surface.

LOCATION Most of the region is hundreds of miles from the open sea.

HUMAN-ENVIRONMENT INTERACTION Freezing temperatures can continue so long that people use frozen rivers as roadways.

For more information on Russia and the Republics . . .

RESEARCH LINKS
CLASSZONE.COM

RUSSIA & REP.

PLACE The Caucasus Mountains stretch between the Black and Caspian seas. A great variety of peoples have settled in the region surrounding the mountains.

MOVEMENT Invaders from Arabia brought Islam to the southern areas of the region by the 8th century. Beautiful mosques adorn many of the region's cities.

333

Unit PREVIEW 5

Today's Issues in Russia and the Republics

Today, Russia and the Republics face the issues previewed here. As you read Chapters 15 and 16, you will learn helpful background information. You will study the issues themselves in Chapter 17.

In a small group, answer the questions below. Then participate in a class discussion of your answers.

Exploring the Issues

1. **CONFLICT** Search a newspaper for articles about conflicts in Russia and the Republics today. What do these conflicts have in common? How are they different?

2. **ECONOMIC CHANGE** Think about the different economic systems you learned about in Chapter 4. How might changing from a command economy to a market economy be difficult?

3. **NUCLEAR LEGACY** What impact could Soviet nuclear programs have on the region's economy?

For more on these issues in Russia and the Republics . . .

CURRENT EVENTS
CLASSZONE.COM

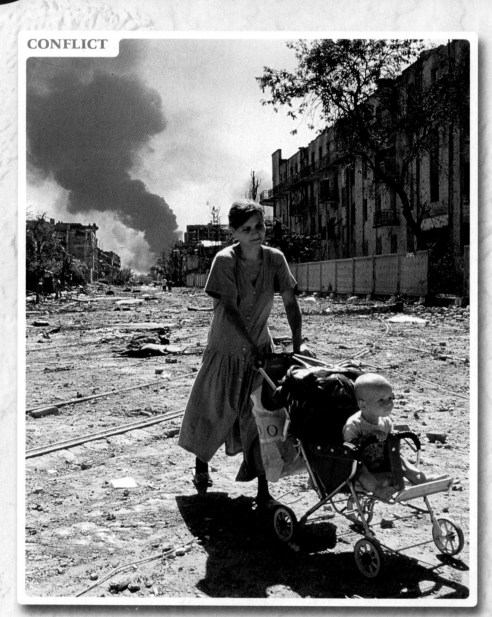

CONFLICT

How do new nations establish law and order?

After the collapse of the Soviet Union in 1991, groups in different parts of the region took up arms to fight for independence. This photo shows a woman and child from a region of Russia called Chechnya. Russia invaded Chechnya twice in the 1990s to end an independence movement in the region.

ECONOMIC CHANGE

How does a nation change its economic system?

For more than 70 years, the Soviet government made all the important economic decisions in the region. This cartoon illustrates a major economic challenge faced by the region's new leaders, as demonstrated here by former Russian president Boris Yeltsin. The leaders are trying to move their nations from a command economy to a market economy.

CASESTUDY

How have Soviet decisions affected new leaders?

In 1965, Soviet officials exploded a nuclear bomb to create this lake in Kazakhstan. The blast exposed nearby residents to harmful radiation. The region's new leaders inherited many problems caused by Soviet nuclear programs.

NUCLEAR LEGACY

Unit ATLAS

Patterns of Physical Geography

Russia and the Republics span two continents. The part of the region that lies to the west of the Ural Mountains is part of Europe. The part of the region that lies to the east of the Urals is part of Asia.

Use the Unit Atlas to add to your knowledge of Russia and the Republics. As you study the maps and charts, notice geographic patterns and specific details about the region.

Jot down answers to the following questions in your notebook.

Making Comparisons

1. What ocean lies to the north of Russia and the Republics? How might this ocean affect the region's climate?

2. How much deeper is Lake Baikal than the deepest lake in the United States?

3. Based on these maps and charts, which region do you think has the higher population density: Russia and the Republics or the United States? Why?

For updated statistics on Russia and the Republics . . .

DATA UPDATE
CLASSZONE.COM

Comparing Data

Lakes

	World's Deepest	U.S. Deepest		
	Lake Baikal Asia (Russia) 5,715 feet	**Crater Lake** North America 1,932 feet	**Caspian Sea** Europe-Asia 3,363 feet	**Lake Issyk-Kul** Asia (Kyrgyzstan) 2,303 feet

Depth (feet): 0, 1,000, 2,000, 3,000, 4,000, 5,000, 6,000

SUNSHINE STATE STANDARDS

Key Standard SS.B.1.4.1 The student uses a variety of maps, geographic technologies including geographic information systems (GIS) and satellite-produced imagery, and other advanced graphic representations to depict geographic problems.

Other Standards SS.B.1.4.2, B.2.4.1

FCAT LA.A.2.2.7 Reading: Recognize Compare and Contrast

ARCTIC

+ North Pole

Wrangel Island

Chukchi Peninsula

Chukchi Sea

East Siberian

New Siberian Islands

Laptev Sea

CHERSKIY RANGE

KOLYMA MTS.

KORYAK MTS.

Indigirka R.

Kolyma R.

Lena R.

VERKHOYANSK RANGE

RUSSIA

RUSSIAN FAR EAST

Kamchatka Peninsula

CENTRAL SIBERIA

SIBERIAN PLATEAU

Lower Tunguska R.

Lena R.

Sea of Okhotsk

Sakhalin Island

Kuril Islands

Yenisey R.

Angara R.

STANOVOY RANGE

YABLONOVY RANGE

Amur R.

Ussuri R.

Lake Baikal

SAYAN MTS.

MONGOLIA

CHINA

Sea of Japan

JAPAN

PACIFIC OCEAN

RUSSIA & REP.

Elevation

13,100 ft.	(4,000 m.)
6,600 ft.	(2,000 m.)
1,600 ft.	(500 m.)
650 ft.	(200 m.)
0 ft.	(0 m.)

Below sea level

▲ Mountain peak

0   250   500 miles
0   250   500 kilometers
Two–Point Equidistant Projection

Comparing Data

Landmass

Russia and the Republics
8,600,340 sq mi

Continental United States
3,165,630 sq mi

Population

Russia and the Republics
289,730,000

United States
281,422,000

0   50   100   150   200   250   300

Population (in millions)

337

Unit ATLAS

Patterns of Human Geography

In 1991, the political geography of Russia and the Republics changed dramatically. For decades, the region's 15 republics had been part of the Soviet Union. Each of the republics became independent after 1991, when the Soviet Union collapsed.

Study the map of the former Soviet Union and the map of Russia and the Republics today. Then answer these questions in your notebook.

Making Comparisons

1. Where are most of the region's smaller republics located?

2. What was the largest republic in the Soviet Union? What is the largest republic in the region today?

3. To which of the Soviet Socialist Republics did Kaliningrad belong?

ARCTIC OCEAN

Svalbard (Nor.)

Franz Josef Land

North Sea

NORWAY

SWEDEN

Barents Sea

Novaya Zemlya

Kara Sea

Murmansk

Baltic Sea

FINLAND

White Sea

Tallinn

ESTONIA

Lake Ladoga

Riga

RUSSIA

LITHUANIA LATVIA

St. Petersburg

Arkhangelsk

POLAND

Vilnius

Lake Onega

N. Dvina R.

Gulf of

Minsk

BELARUS

Moscow

Yaroslavl

Ob R.

L'viv

Homel'

UKRAINE

Kiev

Chernobyl

R U S S I A

Ob R.

MOLDOVA

Dnieper R.

Nizhniy Novgorod

Volga R.

Kazan

Kama R.

Chişinău

Kharkiv

Voronezh

Izhevsk

Perm

Odessa

Simbirsk

Yekaterinburg

Dnipropetrovs'k

Saratov

Togliatti

Irtysh R.

Zaporizhzhya

Donets'k

Samara

Ufa

Tobol R.

Black Sea

Rostov

Volgograd

Chelyabinsk

Sea of Azov

Novosibirsk

Krasnodar

Omsk

Astrakhan

Astana

GEORGIA

Grozny

Semey

TURKEY

Tbilisi

Caspian Sea

KAZAKHSTAN

Zaysan Lake

ARMENIA

Yerevan

Aral Sea

Lake Balkhash

AZER.

AZERBAIJAN

Baku

Syr Darya R.

IRAQ

Anu Darya R.

UZBEKISTAN

Almaty

TURKMENISTAN

Tashkent

Bishkek

Ashgabat

Bukhoro

Samarqand

IRAN

Dushanbe

TAJIKISTAN

KYRGYZSTAN

AFGHANISTAN

Tropic of Cancer

PAKISTAN

INDIA

NEPAL

Russia and the Republics: Political

ARCTIC OCEAN

+North Pole

East Siberian Sea

Wrangel Island

Chukchi Sea

Bering Sea

Severnaya Zemlya

New Siberian Islands

Laptev Sea

Indigirka R.

Kolyma R.

Lena R.

• Oymyakon

RUSSIA

Norilsk •

Lower Tunguska R.

Yakutsk •

Lena R.

Yenisey R.

Angara R.

Lake Baikal

Krasnoyarsk •

Irkutsk •

Amur R.

Khabarovsk •

Vladivostok •

CHINA

MONGOLIA

NORTH KOREA

Petropavlovsk-Kamchatski •

Sea of Okhotsk

Sakhalin Island

Kuril Islands

Sea of Japan

JAPAN

PACIFIC OCEAN

★ National capital
• Other city

| 0 | 250 | 500 miles |
| 0 | 250 | 500 kilometers |

Two–Point Equidistant Projection

80°N   70°N   60°N   180°   170°E   160°E   40°N

RUSSIA & REP.

Former Soviet Union, 1989

| 0 | 500 | 1,000 miles |
| 0 | 500 | 1,000 kilometers |

Two-Point Equidistant Projection

ARCTIC OCEAN

Arctic Circle

Bering Sea

KALININGRAD (R.S.F.S.R.)

FINLAND

Baltic Sea

LITHUANIAN S.S.R.

ESTONIAN S.S.R.

POLAND

LATVIAN S.S.R.

SLOV.

BELORUSSIAN S.S.R.

ROMANIA

UKRAINIAN S.S.R.

RUSSIAN SOVIET FEDERATED SOCIALIST REPUBLIC (R.S.F.S.R.)

MOLDAVIAN S.S.R.

Black Sea

TURKEY

GEORGIAN S.S.R.

Aral Sea

KAZAKH S.S.R.

Lake Baikal

ARMENIAN S.S.R.

Caspian Sea

Lake Balkhash

AZERBAIJAN S.S.R.

TURKMEN S.S.R.

UZBEK S.S.R.

KIRGHIZ S.S.R.

MONGOLIA

Sea of Okhotsk

Sea of Japan

N. KOREA

JAPAN

S. KOREA

PACIFIC OCEAN

IRAN

TADZHIK S.S.R.

CHINA

NOTE: S.S.R. is the abbreviation for Soviet Socialist Republic

60°N   80°N   80°N   60°N   40°N

20°E   40°E   60°E   100°E   120°E

Unit ATLAS

Regional Patterns

These two pages contain a pie graph and three thematic maps. The pie graph shows the religions of Russia and the Republics. The maps show other important features of the region: its different climates, numerous ethnic groups, and population density. After studying these two pages, answer the questions below in your notebook.

Making Comparisons

1. Where is the population of Russia and the Republics most dense? Which climate do those areas have? How might climate affect population density?

2. How would you describe the ethnic and religious populations of Russia and the Republics? Which is the most wide-spread ethnic group in the region?

Religions of Russia and the Republics

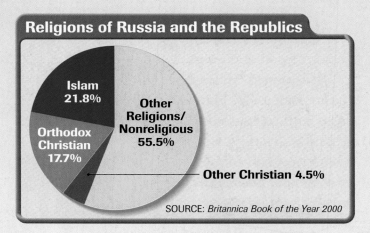

Islam 21.8%

Other Religions/ Nonreligious 55.5%

Orthodox Christian 17.7%

Other Christian 4.5%

SOURCE: *Britannica Book of the Year 2000*

Climates of Russia and the Republics

Desert
Semiarid
Mediterranean
Humid subtropical
Humid continental
Subarctic
Tundra
Highland

ARCTIC OCEAN

Bering Sea

Baltic Sea

Arctic Circle

50°N

Sea of Okhotsk

Black Sea

Aral Sea

Caspian Sea

Lake Balkhash

Lake Baikal

40°N

Sea of Japan

0   500   1,000 miles
0   500   1,000 kilometers
Two-Point Equidistant Projection

50°E   60°E   70°E   80°E   90°E   100°E   110°E

Ethnic Groups

ALTAIC
Turkish
- Azerbaijani
- Kazakh
- Kyrgyz
- Turkish
- Uzbek
- Yakut
- Other Turkic

URALIC
Finish
- Estonian
- Karelian
- Other Finnish

OTHER
- Caucasian
- Mongolian
- Sparsely populated

INDOEUROPEAN
Slavic
- Belarusian
- Russian
- Ukrainian

Baltic
- Latvian
- Lithuanian

INDOEUROPEAN (con't.)
Other
- Armenian
- Moldovan
- Tajik

ARCTIC OCEAN
Bering Sea
Sea of Okhotsk
Arctic Circle
Baltic Sea
RUSSIA
ESTONIA
LITHUANIA LATVIA
BELARUS
MOLDOVA UKRAINE
Black Sea
R U S S I A
GEORGIA
ARMENIA
AZERBAIJAN
Caspian Sea
TURKMENISTAN
UZBEKISTAN
KAZAKHSTAN
KYRGYZSTAN
TAJIKISTAN

0   500   1,000 miles
0   500   1,000 kilometers
Two–Point Equidistant Projection

80°N
60°N
180°
160°E
40°N
140°E
120°E
100°E
80°E
60°E

Population Density

Persons per sq mi	Persons per sq km
Over 520	Over 200
260–519	100–199
130–259	50–99
25–129	10–49
1–24	1–9
0	0

ARCTIC OCEAN
Bering Sea
Sea of Okhotsk
Arctic Circle
Baltic Sea
Murmansk
Tallinn
Riga
Vilnius
St. Petersburg
Minsk
Moscow
Kiev
Nizhniy Novgorod
Chişinău
Kharkiv
Kazan   Perm
Donets'k
Samara   Ufa
Yekaterinburg
Rostov
Chelyabinsk
Black Sea
Omsk
Krasnoyarsk
Novosibirsk
Irkutsk
Tbilisi
Astana
Yerevan
Caspian Sea
Baku
Aral Sea
Vladivostok
Sea of Japan
Tashkent
Almaty
Ashgabat
Bishkek
Dushanbe

0   500   1,000 miles
0   500   1,000 kilometers
Two–Point Equidistant Projection

80°N
60°N
180°
160°E
40°N
140°E
120°
100°E
80°E
60°E

341

Unit ATLAS

Regional Data File

Study the charts on the countries of Russia and the Republics. In your notebook, answer these questions.

Making Comparisons

1. Which five republics have the highest infant mortality rates? Do you notice any pattern?

2. Examine the literacy rates for the region. What do the figures tell you about the value placed on education in the region?

Sources:
CIA World Factbook 2000 online
Europa World Year Book 2000
Human Development Report 2000,
   United Nations
International Data Base (IDB), 2000
   updates, U.S. Census Bureau online
*Merriam-Webster's Geographical
   Dictionary,* 3d ed., 1998
Statesman's Yearbook 2001
WHO Estimates of Health Personnel,
   1998, World Health Organization
   online
World Almanac and Book of Facts 2001
World Education Report 2000,
   UNESCO online
2000 World Population Data Sheet,
   Population Reference Bureau online

Notes:
[a] Life expectancy figures for Russia and several other republics in the former USSR declined significantly in the 1990s.
[b] A comparison of the prices of the same items in different countries is used to figure these data.
[c] Includes land and water, when figures are available.

**For updated statistics on
Russia and the Republics . . .**

DATA UPDATE
CLASSZONE.COM

Country Flag	Country/ Capital	Population (2000 estimate)	Life Expectancy[a] (years) (2000)	Birthrate (per 1,000 pop.) (2000)	Infant Mortality (per 1,000 live births) (2000)
	Armenia Yerevan	3,809,000	75	11	41
	Azerbaijan Baku	7,734,000	72	18	83
	Belarus Minsk	10,004,000	68	9	15
	Estonia Tallinn	1,433,000	70	8	13
	Georgia Tbilisi	5,454,000	73	11	53
	Kazakhstan Astana	14,865,000	65	17	59
	Kyrgyzstan Bishkek	4,929,000	67	26	77
	Latvia Riga	2,416,000	70	8	16
	Lithuania Vilnius	3,697,000	72	10	15
	Moldova Chişinău	4,276,000	67	13	43
	Russia Moscow	145,231,000	67	9	20
	Tajikistan Dushanbe	6,374,000	68	34	117
	Turkmenistan Ashgabat	5,239,000	66	29	73
	Ukraine Kiev	49,509,000	68	9	22
	Uzbekistan Tashkent	24,760,000	69	26	72
	United States Washington, D.C.	281,422,000	77	15	7

Doctors (per 100,000 pop.) (1998)	GDP[b] (billions $US) (1999 est.)	Import/Export[b] (billions $US) (1999)	Literacy Rate (percentage) (1998)	Televisions (per 1,000 pop.) (1996–1998)	Passenger Cars (per 1,000 pop.) (1996–1997)	Total Area[c] (square miles)	
316	9.9	0.782 / 0.24	98	217	2	11,506	
360	14.0	1.46 / .885	99	254	36	33,436	
443	55.2	5.76 / 6.0	99	314	111	80,154	
297	7.9	3.4 / 2.5	99	480	294	17,413	
436	11.7	0.84 / 0.33	99	472	80	26,911	
353	54.5	4.8 / 5.2	99	234	61	1,048,300	
301	10.3	0.59 / 0.515	97	44	32	76,641	
282	9.8	2.8 / 1.9	99	593	174	24,595	
395	17.3	4.5 / 3.3	99	376	242	25,174	
400 (1995)	9.7	0.56 / 0.47	98	297	46	13,012	
421	620.3	48.2 / 75.4	99	420	120	6,592,812	
201	6.2	0.77 / 0.634	99	285	31	55,251	
300 (1997)	7.7	1.25 / 1.1	98	201	N/A	188,455	
299	109.5	11.8 / 11.6	99	490	97	233,089	
309	59.3	3.1 / 2.9	88	273	37	173,591	
251	9,255.0	820.8 / 663.0	97	847	489	3,787,319	

SECTION 1
Landforms and Resources

SECTION 2
Climate and Vegetation

SECTION 3
Human–Environment Interaction

PHYSICAL GEOGRAPHY OF RUSSIA AND THE REPUBLICS
A Land of Extremes

Russia's Lake Baikal is the world's deepest lake and holds over 20 percent of the earth's fresh water. Russians treasure Lake Baikal as much as Americans treasure the Grand Canyon.

GeoFocus

How do the extremes of physical geography in Russia and the Republics affect the lives of the region's people?

Taking Notes Copy the graphic organizer below into your notebook. Use it to record information from the chapter about the physical geography of Russia and the Republics.

Landforms	
Resources	
Climate and Vegetation	
Human-Environment Interaction	

Landforms and Resources

A HUMAN PERSPECTIVE Russia and the Republics occupy a tremendous expanse of territory—approximately three times the land area of the United States. The region sprawls across the continents of both Europe and Asia and crosses 11 time zones. When laborers in the western city of Kaliningrad are leaving their jobs after a day's work, herders on the region's Pacific coast are just beginning to awaken their animals for the next day's grazing.

Northern Landforms

The geography of Russia and the Republics is the geography of nearly one-sixth of the earth's land surface—over eight and a half million square miles. In spite of this huge size, the region's landforms follow a simple overall pattern. You can divide the northern two-thirds of the region into four different areas. Moving from west to east, they are the Northern European Plain, the West Siberian Plain, the Central Siberian Plateau, and the Russian Far East. (See the physical map on pages 336–337 of the Unit Atlas.)

THE NORTHERN EUROPEAN PLAIN The Northern European Plain is an extensive lowland area. It stretches for over 1,000 miles from the western border of Russia and the Republics to the Ural Mountains.

One of the world's most fertile soils—**chernozem,** or black earth—is abundant on this plain. It sometimes occurs in layers three feet deep or more. Because of the high quality of its soil, many of the region's agricultural areas are located on this plain.

Nearly 75 percent of the region's 290 million people live on this plain. Three of the region's largest cities are located there: Moscow, Russia's capital; St. Petersburg; and Kiev, the capital of Ukraine.

Main Ideas

- Flat plains stretch across the western and central areas of the region. In the south and east, the terrain is more mountainous.
- Many resources in Russia and the Republics are in hard-to-reach regions with brutal climates.

Places & Terms

chernozem

Ural Mountains

Eurasia

Transcaucasia

Central Asia

Siberia

CONNECT TO THE ISSUES

ECONOMIC CHANGE Leaders must strike a balance between environmental protection and economic growth.

SUNSHINE STATE STANDARDS
Key Standard SS.B.1.4.3 The student uses mental maps of physical and human features of the world to answer complex geographic questions.

Other Standards SS.B.1.4.1, B.2.4.3
FCAT LA.A.1.4.2 Reading: Strategies

PLACE Ukraine, which lies on the Northern European Plain, has been called the region's breadbasket because of the enormous grain crops produced on its farms.

RUSSIA & REP.

WEST SIBERIAN PLAIN The **Ural Mountains** separate the Northern European and West Siberian plains. Some geographers recognize the Urals as a dividing line between Europe and Asia. Others consider Europe and Asia to be a single continent, which they call **Eurasia.**

The West Siberian Plain lies between the Urals and the Yenisey River and between the shores of the Arctic Ocean and the foothills of the Altay Mountains. Because the plain tilts northward, its rivers flow toward the Arctic Ocean.

CENTRAL SIBERIAN PLATEAU AND RUSSIAN FAR EAST Although extensive plains lie east of the Yenisey River, uplands and mountains are the dominant landforms. High plateaus—with average heights of 1,000 to 2,000 feet—make up the Central Siberian Plateau, which lies between the Yenisey and Lena rivers.

East of the Lena River lies the Russian Far East and its complex system of volcanic ranges. The Kamchatka Peninsula alone contains 120 volcanoes, 20 of which are still active. The Sakhalin and Kuril islands lie south of the peninsula. Russia seized the islands from Japan after World War II. Japan still claims ownership of the Kuril Islands.

BACKGROUND
Russia and Japan never signed a formal peace treaty after World War II ended in 1945. Technically, they are still at war.

Southern Landforms

The southern areas of Russia and the Republics feature towering mountains, barren uplands, and semiarid grasslands.

THE CAUCASUS AND OTHER MOUNTAINS The Caucasus Mountains stretch across the land that separates the Black and Caspian seas. The mountains form the border between Russia and **Transcaucasia**—a region that consists of the republics of Armenia, Azerbaijan, and Georgia. Farther east, along the southern border of Russia and the Republics, rises a colossal wall of mountains, including the Tian Shan, shown below.

Some of these mountains are located along the southeastern border of **Central Asia**—a region that includes the republics of Kazakhstan,

LOCATION The Tian Shan, which is Chinese for "Heavenly Mountains," stretch for nearly 1,500 miles, mainly between China and Kyrgyzstan. **Why might a river be flowing at the base of these mountains?**

Transcaucasia and Central Asia

RUSSIA

URAL MTS.

Irtysh R.

Ural R.

SKILLBUILDER: Interpreting Maps

❶ **LOCATION** Which country in Transcaucasia borders the Caspian Sea?

❷ **MOVEMENT** Which rivers flow into the Aral Sea?

0   250   500 miles
0   250   500 kilometers
Two-Point Equidistant Projection

Zaysan Lake

Kirghiz Steppe **KAZAKHSTAN** *Kazakh Uplands*

Caucasus Mountains

Caspian Depression

Lake Balkhash

Lake Issyk Kul

Mt. Elbrus 18,510 ft. (5,642 m.)

Kyzyl Kum Desert

Syr Darya R.

Black Sea

Aral Sea

Turan Plain

TIAN SHAN

CAUCASUS MTS.

GEORGIA

Caspian Sea

UZBEKISTAN

KYRGYZSTAN

ARMENIA

AZERBAIJAN

Kara Kum Desert

Amu Darya R.

Communism Peak 24,590 ft. (7,495 m.)

TURKEY

AZER.

TURKMENISTAN

TAJIKISTAN *PAMIRS*

IRAN

Kara Kum Desert

RUSSIA & REP.

Kyrgyzstan, Tajikistan, Turkmenistan, and Uzbekistan. These ranges are so high that they prevent moist air from entering the region from the south, contributing to the arid climate of Central Asia. ◀A

THE TURAN PLAIN An extensive lowland called the Turan Plain lies between the Caspian Sea and the mountains and uplands of Central Asia. Although two major rivers, the Syr Darya and Amu Darya, cross the plain, much of the lowland is very dry. Two large deserts stretch across the plain—the Kara Kum and the Kyzyl Kum.

Rivers and Lakes

Some of the world's longest rivers flow through the vast plains of Russia and the Republics. The region also boasts some of the largest and deepest lakes in the world.

DRAINAGE BASINS AND RIVERS The region's rivers flow through a number of large drainage basins. You may recall from Chapter 2 that a drainage basin is an area drained by a major river and its tributaries. The main drainage basins in Russia and the Republics are the Arctic Ocean, Caspian Sea, Pacific Ocean, Baltic Sea, Black Sea, and Aral Sea basins.

The Arctic basin is the region's largest. The basin's three powerful rivers—the Ob, the Yenisey, and the Lena—drain an area of more than

Geographic Thinking

Using the Atlas
Ⓐ Examine the climate map on page 340. What is the relationship between landforms and climate zones in Central Asia?

Landforms and Resources **347**

three million square miles. These rivers deliver water to the Arctic Ocean at a combined rate of nearly 1,750,000 cubic feet per second. ▶B

The Volga River, the longest river on the European continent, drains the Caspian Sea basin. The Volga begins near Moscow and flows southward for about 2,300 miles until it arrives at the Caspian. This important waterway carries about 60 percent of Russia's river traffic.

LAKES In addition to some of the world's longest rivers, Russia and the Republics also boast some of the largest lakes on our planet. Two of them, the Caspian and Aral seas, are located in Central Asia.

The Caspian Sea, which is actually a saltwater lake, stretches for nearly 750 miles from north to south, making it the largest inland sea in the world. The Aral Sea, which lies east of the Caspian, is also a saltwater lake. Since the 1960s, the Aral has lost about 80 percent of its water volume. This enormous loss is the result of extensive irrigation projects that have diverted water away from the rivers that feed the lake. Unless drastic action is taken, the Aral Sea could vanish within 20 to 30 years.

LAKE BAIKAL The crown jewel among the region's lakes is Lake Baikal—the deepest lake in the world. At its deepest point, Baikal is more than a mile from the surface to the bottom. From north to south, the lake stretches for nearly 400 miles. It holds 20 percent of the world's fresh water.

Though it has some pollution, most of Lake Baikal is remarkably clean. Thousands of species of plants and animals live in the lake. Twelve hundred species, including the world's only freshwater seal, are unique to Lake Baikal.

Regional Resources

Russia and the Republics have a great wealth of natural resources. Regional leaders have found it difficult to properly manage these resources. One challenge has been how to transport resources from harsh and distant regions. Another has been how to use the resources without damaging the environment in the process.

Geographic Thinking

Seeing Patterns
B Examine the map on pages 336–337. Why might many of the region's rivers flow toward the north?

Fossil Fuels

Natural Gas Reserves (1997)
World Total: 140,074,431,000 cubic meters

- Russia 34.4%
- Other 34.7%
- Iran 15.0%
- Europe 4.7%
- Other Asia 11.2%

Petroleum Reserves (1994–96)
World Total: 157,769,452,000 metric tons

- Saudi Arabia 22.6%
- Other 46.0%
- Russia 13.5%
- Iraq 9.7%
- Kuwait 8.2%

SOURCE: *Goode's World Atlas, 20th Edition*

SKILLBUILDER: Interpreting Graphs

❶ **ANALYZING DATA** What country had the largest reserves of natural gas in 1997?

❷ **ANALYZING DATA** About how many cubic meters of natural gas did Russia have in 1997?

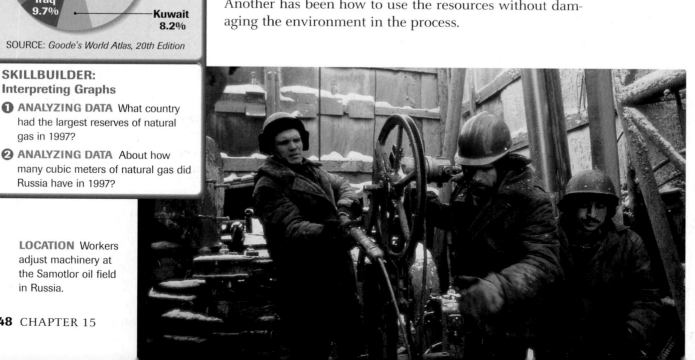

LOCATION Workers adjust machinery at the Samotlor oil field in Russia.

ABUNDANT RESOURCES Russia and the Republics boast huge reserves of coal, deposits of iron ore, and other metals. The region is also a leading producer of oil and natural gas. Petroleum deposits around the Caspian Sea are among the world's largest.

Russia's vast forests hold one-fifth of the world's timber resources. And the region's powerful rivers make it one of the world's largest producers of hydroelectric power.

RESOURCE MANAGEMENT Harsh climates, rugged terrain, and vast distances make it difficult for Russia and the Republics to remove resources from the ground and transport them to markets. Many of these resources are located in the frigid arctic and subarctic region of **Siberia**—the part of Russia that lies on the continent of Asia. Businesses find it difficult to attract workers to this severe region. **C**

When businesses have been able to exploit regional resources successfully, they have often done so at great cost to the environment. Mining operations have caused significant damage, as has the production of oil and gas. Russia's hydroelectric plants have also caused substantial damage. Dams and the plants' discharge of unusually hot water—known as thermal pollution—have caused significant damage to surrounding plant and animal habitats.

Dramatic political and economic change in recent years will continue to make resource management difficult. Leaders will have to balance the need for economic growth with their responsibility to protect the environment.

Geographic Thinking
Seeing Patterns
▶ Why might workers be unwilling to take jobs in Siberia?

Connect to THE Issues
ECONOMIC CHANGE
Change in Norilsk

In the photo below, a plane arrives in the remote nickel-mining town of Norilsk, which is not accessible by road. Until the 1990s, the government provided money for people willing to work in this remote region.

But the demand for Norilsk's nickel has faded, and unemployment and poverty there have increased. Now the Russian government is paying to move people out of the area. Leaders must act quickly, though. In the brutal Siberian winter, poverty is deadly.

RUSSIA & REP.

Assessment
SECTION 1

❶ Places & Terms
Explain the importance of each of the following terms and places.
- chernozem
- Ural Mountains
- Eurasia
- Transcaucasia
- Central Asia
- Siberia

❷ Taking Notes
REGION Review the notes you took for this section.

Landforms	
Resources	

- What is the name of the region's westernmost lowland?
- What mountain range separates Russia from Transcaucasia?

❸ Main Ideas
a. Why might a large part of the region's population live on the Northern European Plain?

b. What factor contributes to the dry conditions on the Turan Plain?

c. Why is the Volga one of the region's most important rivers?

❹ Geographic Thinking
Making Generalizations
Why has resource management been a problem for leaders in Russia and the Republics? **Think about:**
- where resources are located
- how resources are extracted or used

GeoActivity

EXPLORING LOCAL GEOGRAPHY Do more research on Lake Baikal and on the deepest lake in the state in which you live. Make a **poster** that visually compares the size and depth of the two lakes. Provide other information on your poster, including the volume of water in each of the lakes.

Climate and Vegetation

Main Ideas
• Much of Russia and the Republics lies in subarctic and tundra climate zones.
• In the region's southern areas, semiarid and desert climates feature warmer winters and hot summers.

Places & Terms
continentality

taiga

CONNECT TO THE ISSUES
CONFLICT Ethnic conflict has disrupted the flow of tourist dollars into some areas of the region.

SUNSHINE STATE STANDARDS
Key Standard SS.B.2.4.1 The student understands how social, cultural, economic, and environmental factors contribute to the dynamic nature of regions.
Other Standards SS.B.1.4.2
FCAT LA.A.1.4.2 Reading: Strategies

A HUMAN PERSPECTIVE Large areas of Russia and the Republics are extremely cold during much of the year. For example, the Siberian town of Oymyakon has reportedly had temperatures as low as −95°F. At such temperatures, the cold can crack steel and cause tires to explode. When you exhale, your breath freezes into crystals that fall to the ground and make a noise that Siberians call "the whispering of the stars." Some of the region's native peoples believe that, in the coldest weather, words themselves freeze, and that, when warmer weather arrives and thaws the crystals, the words come to life and begin to speak. "Suddenly the air fills with out-of-date gossip, unheard jokes, and cries of forgotten pain."

A Climate of Extremes

As you can see on the climate map on page 340, Russia and the Republics have some very cold climates. But the region also features warmer climates, such as the subtropical areas of Transcaucasia, and the semiarid and desert zones of Central Asia.

MAJOR CLIMATE REGIONS Humid continental and subarctic climates dominate much of Russia and the Republics. These climates reflect the influence of the region's high latitude and the impact of the wall of mountains in the southeast. The region's enormous size also has a major effect on its climates. Much of the region is hundreds of miles from the moderating influence of the sea. The effect of this distance on climate is called **continentality.**

Distance from the sea affects the amount of precipitation the region gets, as well as its temperatures. Most of the region's moisture comes from the Atlantic Ocean. But the air coming from the ocean loses its moisture as it travels farther and farther inland. Distance from the seas also results in extreme temperatures. In Siberia, average monthly temperatures rarely exceed 50°F and sometimes drop below -90°F.

The long stretches of cold weather in the region have a unique impact on daily life. Siberians, for example, use frozen rivers and lakes as roads for part of the year. Temperatures are so consistently low that the region is covered by a layer of permanently frozen subsoil called permafrost. This layer can reach depths of 1,500 feet.

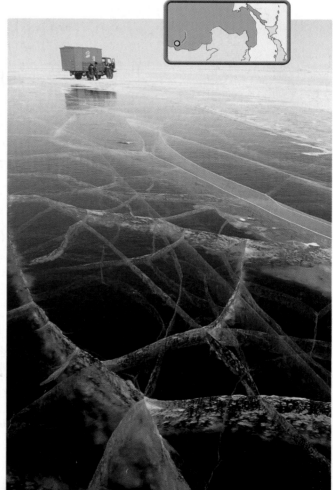

MOVEMENT The crew driving this truck is using the frozen surface of Lake Baikal to transport cargo.

While humid continental and subarctic climates dominate the northern and eastern areas of the region, Russia and the Republics also have warmer climates. A wall of mountains in the southeastern areas of the region blocks moist air traveling northward from the Indian and Pacific oceans. The mountains contribute to the semiarid and desert climates of Central Asia.

In Transcaucasia, moist air from the Mediterranean Sea contributes to a subtropical climate zone. The region's health resorts were a favorite destination of tourists until ethnic conflict made traveling there dangerous. ◀🅐

⊕ **Geographic Thinking**◀

Using the Atlas

🅐 Examine the map on page 340. In which climate region do you think the layer of permafrost will be deepest?

Vegetation Regions

Russia and the Republics have four major vegetation regions. These regions run east to west in wide strips. Moving from north to south, they are the tundra, forest, temperate grassland, and desert.

TUNDRA The tundra region of Russia and the Republics falls mostly in the Arctic climate zone. Only specific types of vegetation—such as mosses, lichens, small herbs, and low shrubs—are able to survive in the tundra's polar conditions.

FOREST South of the tundra lies the largest forest on earth—the **taiga**. The taiga contains primarily coniferous trees. Many fur-bearing animals,

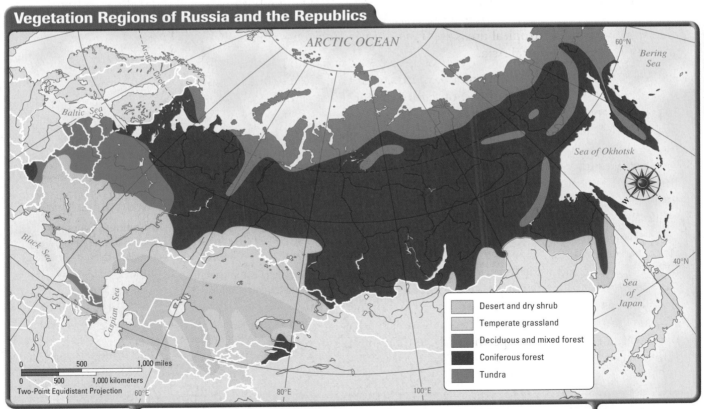

Vegetation Regions of Russia and the Republics

ARCTIC OCEAN

Bering Sea

Baltic Sea

Sea of Okhotsk

Black Sea

Caspian Sea

Sea of Japan

60°N

40°N

60°E   80°E   100°E

0   500   1,000 miles
0   500   1,000 kilometers
Two-Point Equidistant Projection

Legend:
- Desert and dry shrub
- Temperate grassland
- Deciduous and mixed forest
- Coniferous forest
- Tundra

RUSSIA & REP.

SKILLBUILDER: Interpreting Maps

❶ **REGION** What kind of vegetation is most common to the east of the Caspian Sea?

❷ **LOCATION** At what latitudes does the tundra give way to coniferous forests?

such as sable, fox, and ermine, live in the taiga. Elk, bear, and wolves also make their homes in the forest.

South of the taiga, deciduous trees begin to mix with coniferous species. In lower latitudes, the deciduous trees become dominant.

STEPPE The steppe is the name of the temperate grassland that extends from southern Ukraine through northern Kazakhstan to the Altay Mountains. The highly fertile chernozem soil is found in the steppe and helps to make the grassland a major source of grain for Russia and the Republics.

DESERT Deserts and semiarid lands occupy the wide plains in the west and central areas of Central Asia. The two main deserts are the Kara Kum, which covers most of the republic of Turkmenistan, and the Kyzyl Kum, which is located in western Uzbekistan. Together, the two deserts occupy an area of about 230,000 square miles. In the following section, you will learn how efforts to irrigate these regions resulted in one of the world's greatest environmental catastrophes.

SECTION 2 Assessment

1 Places & Terms

Explain the importance of each of the following terms and places.

- continentality
- taiga

2 Taking Notes

REGION Review the notes you took for this section.

Climate and Vegetation

- How can climate affect transportation?
- To what depths can permafrost extend in Russia and the Republics?

3 Main Ideas

a. How does distance from the sea affect the region's climate?

b. In what way is the climate of Transcaucasia unique?

c. What are the major vegetation regions in Russia and the Republics?

4 Geographic Thinking

Determining Cause and Effect How are climate and vegetation related? **Think about:**

- average temperatures
- precipitation

S **See Skillbuilder Handbook, page R9.**

SEEING PATTERNS Choose a city in Russia and the Republics. Collect data on the average monthly temperatures and precipitation in the city. Then create a **climograph** that illustrates the results of your research.

Human-Environment Interaction

3

A HUMAN PERSPECTIVE Since the 1960s, irrigation policies in Central Asia have had a dramatic impact on the Aral Sea. A recent visitor to an old Aral fishing village described the change: "I stood on what had once been a seaside bluff . . . but I could see no water. The sea was twenty-five miles away." The dried-up seabed had become a graveyard for abandoned ships. The powerful winds were covering local populations with polluted dust picked up from the seabed. Thousands of people have left the region, and those who remain risk illness, or even death. In this section, you will read more about the complex relationship between the environment and the people of Russia and the Republics.

The Shrinking Aral Sea

Between 1960 and the present, the Aral Sea lost about 80 percent of its water. Central Asian leaders now face one of the earth's greatest environmental tragedies.

A DISAPPEARING LAKE The Aral Sea receives most of its water from two rivers, the Amu Darya and the Syr Darya. Before the 1960s, these rivers delivered nearly 13 cubic miles of water to the Aral Sea every year. But in the 1950s, officials began to take large amounts of water from the rivers to irrigate Central Asia's cotton fields. Large-scale irrigation projects, such as the 850-mile-long Kara Kum canal, took so much water from the rivers that the flow of water into the Aral slowed to a trickle. The sea began to evaporate.

EFFECTS OF AGRICULTURE Agricultural practices in Central Asia caused other problems for the Aral Sea. Cotton growers used pesticides and fertilizers. These chemicals were being picked up by **runoff**—rainfall not absorbed by the soil that runs into streams and rivers. The runoff carried the chemicals into the rivers that feed the Aral, with devastating effects. Of the 24 native species of fish once found in the sea, none are left today.

Main Ideas

- The region's harsh climate has been both an obstacle and an advantage to its inhabitants.
- Attempts to overcome the region's geographic limits have sometimes had negative consequences.

Places & Terms

runoff

Trans-Siberian Railroad

CONNECT TO THE ISSUES
ECONOMIC CHANGE New regional leaders must solve economic problems caused by the former Soviet Union.

SUNSHINE STATE STANDARDS
Key Standard SS.B.2.4.4 The student understands the global impact of human changes in the physical environment.

Other Standards SS.A.1.4.1, B.2.4.6

FCAT LA.A.1.4.2 Reading: Strategies

HUMAN-ENVIRONMENT INTERACTION These two images, taken in 1976 and 1997, show what happened after agricultural officials began diverting water from the rivers that feed the Aral Sea.

RUSSIA & REP.

PLACE Camels walk by the rusting hulks of abandoned ships on what was once the floor of the Aral Sea. **Why might the ships have been abandoned?**

Soon the damage spread beyond the lake. The retreating waters of the Aral exposed fertilizers and pesticides, as well as salt. Windstorms began to pick up these substances and dump them on nearby populations.

This pollution has caused a sharp increase in diseases. The incidence of throat cancer and respiratory diseases has risen dramatically. Dysentery, typhoid, and hepatitis have also become more common. Child mortality rates in Central Asia are among the highest in the world.

SAVING THE ARAL Scientists estimate that even to keep the lake at its present levels, you would have to remove 9 of the 18 million acres that are now used for farming. This would create terrible hardship for the farmers who depend on those fields for their livelihood. But many argue that only such drastic measures can save the Aral.

The Russian Winter

The frigid landscapes of Siberia lie far from Central Asia. But the rugged inhabitants of Siberia are also familiar with hardship.

COPING IN SIBERIA More than 32 million people make their homes in Siberia. The climate presents unique challenges to its inhabitants, especially during winter.

Scientists have recorded the most variable temperatures on earth in Siberia. In the city of Verkhoyansk, temperatures have ranged from –90°F in the winter to 94°F in the summer—a span of 184 degrees. But most of the time it is cold. Temperatures drop so low that basic human activities become painful. A worker in the Siberian mining center at Norilsk explained how he and fellow workers turned up their collars and turned down the ear flaps of their fur caps so that only their eyes were visible. "Even then," he reported, "your eyes would be so cold that you'd close one until the one you were looking with froze, and then swap over."

The change of seasons brings little relief. Warmer weather melts ice and snow and leaves pools of water that become breeding grounds for mosquitoes and black flies. The problem becomes severe in the spring.

Geographic Thinking

Using the Atlas
Ⓐ Examine the maps on pages 340–341. What relationship do you see between population density and climate?

Swamps form when northward flowing rivers, swollen by spring rains, run into still-frozen water further north. Soon, enormous black clouds of insects are attacking Siberia's residents.

The climate also affects construction in Siberia. Permafrost makes the ground in Siberia iron-hard. However, a heated building will thaw the permafrost. As the ground thaws, buildings sink, tilt, and eventually topple over. To prevent such problems, builders raise their structures a few feet off the ground on concrete pillars.

WAR AND "GENERAL WINTER" Russia's harsh climate has caused difficulties for its inhabitants, but it has also, at times, come to their aid.

In the early 1800s, the armies of the French leader Napoleon Bonaparte were taking control of Europe. In the spring of 1812, Napoleon decided to extend his control over Russia. He gathered his army together in Poland and from there began the march on Moscow.

But as his troops advanced, so did the seasons. When Napoleon arrived in Moscow in September, the Russian winter was not far behind. Moreover, the citizens of Moscow had set fire to their city before fleeing, so there was no shelter for Napoleon's troops.

Napoleon had no choice but to retreat during the bitter Russian winter. He left Moscow with 100,000 troops. But by the time his army arrived back in Poland, the cruel Russian winter had helped to kill more than 90,000 of his soldiers. Some historians believe that Russia's "General Winter" succeeded in defeating Napoleon where the armies of Europe had failed. **◄B**

Geographic Thinking◄

Seeing Patterns
B Besides climate, what other geographic factors might an army invading Russia have to consider?

Crossing the "Wild East"

At the end of the 19th century, Siberia was similar to the "Wild West" of the United States. Travel through the region was dangerous and slow. For these reasons, Russia's emperor ordered work to start on a **Trans-Siberian Railroad** that would eventually link Moscow to the Pacific port of Vladivostok.

RUSSIA & REP.

Rail Routes Across Russia

Rail Routes
— Trans-Siberian Railroad
— Trans-Manchurian Railroad
— Baikal-Amur Mainline
+1 hr. Time difference from Moscow
200 Miles between cities
★ Capital
• City

SKILLBUILDER: Interpreting Maps

❶ LOCATION As a train moves eastward after passing over the Ural Mountains, what is the first major stop?

❷ MOVEMENT What railroad route would you take if you wanted to pass north of Lake Baikal?

355

MOVEMENT A train from Ukraine travels on Trans-Siberian tracks on its journey toward Vladivostok. **What impact do railroads have on commerce?**

AN ENORMOUS PROJECT The project was a massive undertaking. The distance to be covered was more than 5,700 miles, and the tracks had to cross seven time zones. Between 1891 and 1903, approximately 70,000 workers moved 77 million cubic feet of earth, cleared more than 100,000 acres of forest, and built bridges over several major rivers.

RESOURCE WEALTH IN SIBERIA Russian officials did not undertake this massive project simply to speed up travel. They also wanted to populate Siberia in order to profit from its many resources.

Ten years after the completion of the line in 1904, nearly five million settlers, mainly peasant farmers, had taken the railway from European Russia to settle in Siberia.

As migrants streamed into Siberia, resources, such as coal and iron ore, poured out. Siberia, one author wrote, began to yield riches that "she has under guard of eternal snow and ice, so long held in trust for future centuries." In the years that followed, the railroad would aid the political and economic development of Russia and the Republics, which you will read about in the next chapter.

SECTION 3 Assessment

① Places & Terms

Explain the importance of the following terms.

- runoff
- Trans-Siberian Railroad

② Taking Notes

REGION Review the notes you took for this section.

| Human-Environment Interaction |

- What precautions must builders take in Siberia? Why?
- How did the construction of the Trans-Siberian Railroad affect the region's landscape?

③ Main Ideas

a. Why is the Aral Sea shrinking?

b. How has the region's harsh climate helped its inhabitants?

c. What were the main reasons for the construction of the Trans-Siberian Railroad?

④ Geographic Thinking

Making Decisions If you were a regional leader, what steps would you take to end the Aral Sea disaster? **Think about:**

- how your solutions will affect people in the region

RESEARCH LINKS CLASSZONE.COM

MAKING COMPARISONS Do more research on the Trans-Siberian Railroad. Then do research on the construction of the transcontinental railroad in the United States. Use a **Venn diagram** to compare and contrast the two projects.

Understanding Time Zones

In 1884, international officials agreed to divide the map of the earth's surface into 24 time zones, one for each hour of the day. Because the earth rotates 360° each day, each zone was to represent 15° longitude (360° ÷ 24 hours = 15°). Officials used the prime meridian (0°) as the starting point for the time zones. They named this base time Greenwich Mean Time (GMT). The International Date Line was set at 180° longitude. To the east of this line, the calendar date is one day earlier than to the west.

THE LANGUAGE OF MAPS A **time zone map** shows the time zones that are in use around the world today. Officials have adjusted the boundaries of many time zones to keep political units, such as countries, within a single time zone.

SUNSHINE STATE STANDARDS
Key Standard SS.B.1.4.1 The student uses a variety of maps, geographic technologies including geographic information systems (GIS) and satellite-produced imagery, and other advanced graphic representations to depict geographic problems.
FCAT LA.A.1.4.2 Reading: Strategies

Time Zones of the World

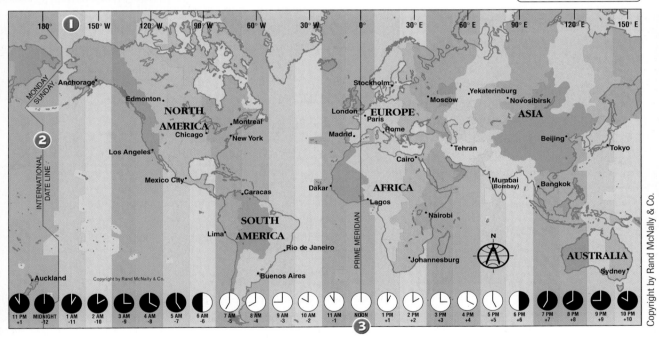

Non-standard time zones
Time varies from the standard time zone by less than an hour.

Copyright by Rand McNally & Co.

1 Each band of color represents one time zone.

2 Officials set the International Date Line at 180°, but the line moves east or west of it in places to avoid dividing countries.

3 Positive and negative numbers show the difference between local time and Greenwich Mean Time.

Map and Graph Skills Assessment

1. Drawing Conclusions
How many time zones are there in the continental United States?

2. Making Comparisons
What is the current time in the time zone in which you live? What is the current time in Greenwich, England?

3. Drawing Conclusions
If it is 6:00 Sunday morning in New York, what are the day and time in Auckland, New Zealand?

Chapter 15 Assessment

VISUAL SUMMARY
PHYSICAL GEOGRAPHY OF RUSSIA AND THE REPUBLICS

Landforms

Major Geographical Areas: Northern European Plain, West Siberian Plain, Central Siberian Plateau, Russian Far East, Turan Plain

Important Mountain Ranges: Urals, Caucasus, Tian Shan

Important Rivers and Lakes: Caspian and Aral seas, Lake Baikal, Volga, Ob, Yenisey, and Lena rivers

Resources

- Regional resources include huge coal reserves and deposits of iron ore and other metals.
- The Caspian Sea region has enormous reserves of oil and gas.

Climate and Vegetation

- Continentality and a wall of high southeastern mountains have a major impact on the climate of Russia and the Republics.

Human-Environment Interaction

- The shrinking of the Aral Sea is an example of the dramatic impact that agricultural policies can have on the environment.
- The hardships faced by Napoleon's army show how Russia's environment influenced human events.
- The construction of the Trans-Siberian Railway changed the population distribution and economic geography of the region.

Reviewing Places & Terms

A. Briefly explain the importance of each of the following.

1. chernozem
2. Ural Mountains
3. Eurasia
4. Transcaucasia
5. Central Asia
6. Siberia
7. continentality
8. taiga
9. runoff
10. Trans-Siberian Railroad

B. Answer the questions about vocabulary in complete sentences.

11. What is the name of the region crossed by the Trans-Siberian Railroad?
12. Which region is located south of the Caucasus Mountains?
13. What is chernozem and where is it found?
14. How can runoff affect the environment?
15. What are the five republics located in Central Asia?
16. Why are the Ural Mountains important for geographers?
17. What is the name of the non-European part of Russia?
18. Which vegetation region allows Russia to boast one-fifth of the world's timber resources?
19. Why do Russia and the Republics receive limited precipitation?
20. Which landmass is named after the continents of Asia and Europe?

Main Ideas

Landforms and Resources (pp. 345–349)

1. What facts could you provide to give an idea of the enormous size of Russia and the Republics?
2. How does the tilt of the West Siberian Plain affect the region's physical geography?
3. How is the region's use of its resources affected by climate?

Climate and Vegetation (pp. 350–352)

4. What are major influences on the region's climate?
5. How does latitude affect the type of vegetation found in Russia's forests?
6. Where is the steppe located in Russia and the Republics?

Human-Environment Interaction (pp. 353–357)

7. What effect have irrigation projects had on the Aral Sea?
8. How has the shrinking of the Aral Sea affected public health in the surrounding region?
9. What factors contribute to the formation of swamps in Siberia, and how do the swamps affect people living in the region?
10. How long did it take to complete the main line of the Trans-Siberian Railway?

Critical Thinking

1. Using Your Notes

Use your completed chart to answer these questions.

Landforms	
Resources	

a. Which region contains a large number of volcanoes?

b. Who was "General Winter"?

2. Geographic Themes

a. **HUMAN-ENVIRONMENT INTERACTION** How has Siberia's climate affected transportation in the region?

b. **MOVEMENT** What impact did the Trans-Siberian Railway have on Russia's population?

3. Identifying Themes

What factor might explain why Russia and the Republics receive relatively little precipitation and frequently experience extreme temperatures? Which of the five themes applies to this situation?

4. Determining Cause and Effect

What is a major factor contributing to the large subtropical climate zone in Transcaucasia?

5. Drawing Conclusions

Given what you have read about the dependency of Central Asian farmers on the water from the Amu Darya and Syr Darya rivers, how likely do you think it is that the Aral Sea will eventually recover?

Additional Test Practice, pp. S1–S37

TEST PRACTICE CLASSZONE.COM

Geographic Skills: Interpreting Maps

Mineral Resources and Pollution

Use the map to answer the following questions.

1. **REGION** This map shows how close mining sites are to polluted areas. Why might the two be related?

2. **MOVEMENT** How might locating a mining site near a river affect the spread of pollution?

3. **PLACE** Why might the areas around Moscow and St. Petersburg be polluted even though there seem to be few mining sites nearby?

GeoActivity

Do more research on mining pollution's impact on public health in one area of the region. Use presentation software to share your results.

INTERNET ACTIVITY

Use the links at classzone.com to do research on Siberia. Focus on how people cope with the region's low temperatures. For example, investigate the kinds of clothing people wear or how they move about in the winter.

Writing About Geography Write a report of your findings. Include photos or illustrations that visually present information about life in the region. List the Web sites that you used in preparing your report.

Chapter 16

SECTION 1
Russia and the
Western Republics

SECTION 2
Transcaucasia

SECTION 3
Central Asia

HUMAN GEOGRAPHY OF
RUSSIA AND THE REPUBLICS
A Diverse Heritage

Three Subregions of Russia and the Republics

Legend:
- Russia and the Western Republics
- Transcaucasia
- Central Asia

0   500   1,000 miles
0 500 1,000 kilometers
Two-Point Equidistant Projection

GeoFocus

How did Russia's expansion affect the region's geography?

Taking Notes In your notebook, copy a cluster diagram like the one shown. As you read, take notes about the history, economics, culture, and modern life of each subregion of Russia and the Republics.

Russia and the Western Republics

Main Ideas

- From modest beginnings, Russia expanded to become the largest country in the world.
- The rise and fall of the Soviet Union affected the world's political geography.

Places & Terms

Baltic Republics

czar

Russian Revolution

USSR

Cold War

command economy

collective farm

CONNECT TO THE ISSUES

ECONOMIC CHANGE The region is struggling to move from a command economy to a market economy.

A HUMAN PERSPECTIVE Early in the 1500s, the Russian leader Ivan the Great put an end to two centuries of foreign rule in his homeland. Russia then entered a period of explosive growth. From its center in Moscow, Russia expanded at a rate of about 55 square miles a day for the next four centuries. During the expansion, Russians made so much progress toward the east that they swallowed up a future U.S. state, Alaska. Russia had taken control of the territory by the late 18th century but did not sell it to the United States until 1867.

A History of Expansion

Russia's growth had lasting effects on nearby lands and peoples. You can see these effects even today in the republics to its west: Belarus, Moldova, Ukraine and the **Baltic Republics** of Estonia, Latvia and Lithuania. But Russian expansion not only affected its neighbors. It also had an impact on the entire world's political geography.

BIRTH OF AN EMPIRE The Russian state began in the region between the Baltic and Black seas. In the ninth century, Vikings from Scandinavia came to the region to take advantage of the river trade between the two seas. They established a settlement near what is now Kiev, a city near the Dnieper River. In time, the Vikings adopted the customs of the local Slavic population. Soon the settlement began to expand.

Expansion was halted in the 13th century with the arrival of invaders from Mongolia, called Tatars. The ferocity of those Mongol warriors is legendary. It is said that "like molten lava, they destroyed everything in their path." The Tatars sacked Kiev between 1237 and 1240.

The Mongols controlled the region until the 1500s, when Ivan the Great, the powerful prince of Moscow, put an end to their rule. Russia continued once again to expand to the east. By the end of the 17th century, it had built an empire that extended to the Pacific Ocean. As the leaders of Russia added more territory to their empire, they also added more people. Many of these people belonged to different ethnic groups, spoke different languages, and practiced different religions.

SUNSHINE STATE STANDARDS
Key Standard SS.B.2.4.1 The student understands how social, cultural, economic, and environmental factors contribute to the dynamic nature of regions.

Other Standards SS.B.2.4.6, C.1.4.1

FCAT LA.A.1.4.2 Reading: Strategies

MOVEMENT This Mongol armor from the 14th or 15th century includes a case for bow and arrows. Mongol warriors were skilled archers, even on horseback.

Russian and Soviet Expansion

Legend:
- Russian territory, 1462
- 1463 to 1598
- 1599 to 1689
- 1690 to 1795
- 1796 to 1947
- Boundary of Soviet Union in 1947
- Boundary of Russia today

0   500   1,000 miles
0   500   1,000 kilometers
Two-Point Equidistant Projection

ARCTIC OCEAN

St. Petersburg
Kiev
Moscow
SIBERIA
Sea of Okhotsk
URAL MOUNTAINS
Ob R.
Yenisey R.
Lena R.
Amur R.
L. Baikal
Volga R.
Dnieper R.
Black Sea
Caspian Sea
Aral Sea
Sea of Japan

SKILLBUILDER: Interpreting Maps

❶ MOVEMENT When did the Russian Empire expand beyond the Ural Mountains?

❷ REGION When did the Russian Empire absorb most of Siberia?

RUSSIA LAGS BEHIND WESTERN EUROPE Russia's territorial growth was rapid, but its progress in other ways was less impressive. Russian science and technology lagged behind that of its European rivals. Peter the Great, who was <u>**czar**</u>—or emperor—of Russia from 1682 to 1725, tried to change this. For example, he moved Russia's capital from Moscow to a city on the Baltic Sea. The new capital, named St. Petersburg, provided direct access by sea to Western Europe. Russians called St. Petersburg their "window to the West."

Peter the Great made impressive strides toward modernizing Russia, but the empire continued to trail behind the West. While the Industrial Revolution swept over many Western European countries in the first half of the 1800s, Russia did not even begin to industrialize until the end of the century. When industry did come to Russia, it resulted in harsh working conditions, low wages, and other hardships. These problems contributed to the people's anger at the czars who ruled Russia.

BACKGROUND
The word *czar* comes from the Latin for *Caesar*, the title of address for Roman emperors.

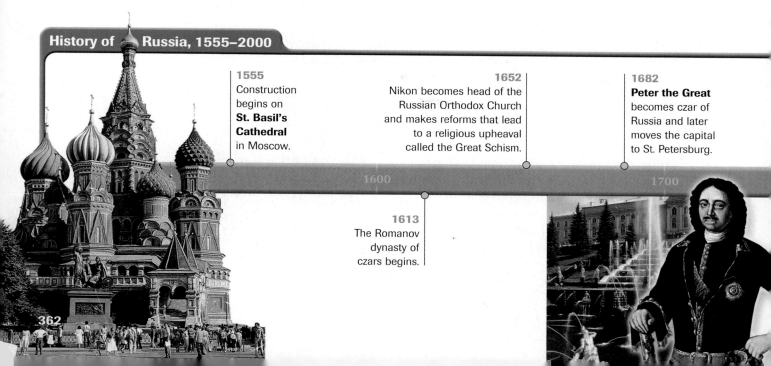

History of Russia, 1555–2000

1555
Construction begins on **St. Basil's Cathedral** in Moscow.

1652
Nikon becomes head of the Russian Orthodox Church and makes reforms that lead to a religious upheaval called the Great Schism.

1682
Peter the Great becomes czar of Russia and later moves the capital to St. Petersburg.

1600

1700

1613
The Romanov dynasty of czars begins.

362

THE RISE AND FALL OF THE SOVIET UNION During World War I (1914–1918), the Russian people's anger exploded into revolt. In 1917, the **Russian Revolution** occurred, ending the rule of the czars. The Russian Communist Party, led by V. I. Lenin, took control of the government. The Party also took charge of the region's economy and gave Communist leaders control over all important economic decisions.

By 1922, the Communist Party had organized the different peoples absorbed during the centuries of Russia's imperial expansion. This new nation was called the Union of Soviet Socialist Republics (**USSR**), or the Soviet Union for short. The leaders of the Soviet Union ruled the nation from its new capital in Moscow.

By the time World War II broke out in 1939, Joseph Stalin had taken over the leadership of the USSR. In 1941, he led the Soviet Union in the fight against Nazi Germany. However, as the war dragged on, relations between the Soviet Union and its allies—including the United States— began to worsen.

After the war, Stalin installed pro-Soviet governments in the Eastern European countries that his armies had liberated from Germany. U.S. leaders feared that a new stage of Russian expansion was beginning and that Stalin would spread communism all over the globe. By the late 1940s, tensions between the United States and the Soviet Union led to conflict. Diplomats called this conflict the **Cold War** because it never grew into open warfare between the two nations. **A**

The rivalry between the two superpowers continued into the mid-1980s. At that time, Soviet leader Mikhail Gorbachev started to give more economic and political freedom to the Soviet people. This began a process that led to the collapse of the Communist government and the Soviet Union in 1991—and the end of the Cold War.

After the fall of the Soviet Union, the region was divided into 15 independent republics. Of these, Russia, formally known as the Russian Federation, is the largest and most powerful. Today, Russia has a popularly elected president. Its legislature, the Federal Assembly, is divided into two chambers—the Federation Council and the State Duma.

Geographic Thinking

Using the Atlas
A Examine the map on page 339. Why do you think the Soviet Union had so much power over Eastern Europe?

1812
The French general, **Napoleon** (below), retreats during winter after a failed attack on Russia.

1861
Czar Alexander II issues an order freeing all Russian serfs, that is, peasants held in servitude.

1991
The Soviet Union falls, and Russia becomes independent.

2000
The Russians elect **Vladimir Putin** president.

1800

1900

1917
The Russian Revolution occurs. **Lenin** (above left), then **Stalin** (above right), take power.

1922
Russia becomes part of the Soviet Union.

REGION The Soviet government's control over the economy was often inefficient. Citizens had to wait in line for hours, even to buy basic consumer goods, such as a handbag.

Building a Command Economy

The communists who overthrew czarist Russia in 1917 had strong ideas about the future. When they put their ideas into practice, they drastically transformed the economic geography of the region.

AN ECONOMIC DREAM The communists had been inspired by the work of Karl Marx, a German philosopher who had examined the history of economic systems. Marx believed that the capitalist system was doomed because it concentrated wealth in the hands of a few and left everyone else in poverty. He predicted that a communist system would replace capitalism. In a communist society, he argued, citizens would own property together, and everyone would share the wealth.

A HARSH REALITY To move their society toward communism, Soviet leaders adopted a **command economy**—one in which the central government makes all important economic decisions. The government took control of the major sources of the state's wealth, including land, mines, factories, banks, and transportation systems. Government planners decided what products factories would manufacture, what crops farms would grow, and even what prices merchants would charge for their goods.

Rapid industrialization became a major goal of Soviet planning. Even farming became an industry under Stalin. The Soviet government created enormous **collective farms** on which large teams of laborers were gathered to work together. People were moved to the farms by the thousands. By 1939, nearly nine out of ten farms were collectives. The Soviets had firmly established their power over the countryside.

Although industrial and agricultural production increased, the region's people had to make great sacrifices for this rapid transformation. Millions of citizens starved to death in famines caused, in part, by the creation of collective farms. Those who survived soon realized that only a small number of individuals had benefited from the economic changes.

Many people tried to do something about this betrayal, but at great risk. Under Stalin's rule, the police swiftly punished any form of protest. Some historians estimate that Stalin was responsible for the deaths of more than 14 million people.

Since the fall of the Soviet Union in 1991, leaders in Russia and the Republics have tried to reduce the state's monopoly on economic power and return some control to private individuals and businesses. You will learn more about these changes in Chapter 17. **B**

CONNECT TO THE ISSUES
ECONOMIC CHANGE
B Considering how long the Soviet command economy lasted, why might the change to a market economy be hard for the region's citizens?

A Rich Culture

Russia and the Western Republics faced hard times under the czars and the communists. But these leaders could not destroy the cultural and spiritual traditions of the region's people.

ETHNICITY AND RELIGION The region has a rich variety of ethnic groups because of the many peoples absorbed during the centuries of Russian expansion. Russia has the greatest ethnic diversity of the region's republics. Russians make up the largest ethnic group there, with about 80 percent of the total. But nearly 70 other peoples live in Russia, including Finnish, Turkic, and Mongolian peoples. (See the map on page 341 of the Unit Atlas.)

Russia and the Western Republics are home to a great number of religions. Most Russians follow Orthodox Christianity, a religion Russia adopted in the 10th century. But the region is home to many other religions, including Buddhism and Islam. Judaism is also an important religion in the region. However, persecution has led large numbers of Jews to emigrate, especially to Israel and the United States. **C**

ARTISTIC GENIUS Religion and art are closely related in Russia and the Western Republics. The art and architecture of Orthodox Christian churches, for example, are among the region's earliest artistic achievements. Even today, citizens adore the beautiful onion-shaped domes and the icons—images of sacred Christians—that ornament the churches.

Regional culture went through great change after Peter the Great began to promote communication with Western Europe. As Russian artists combined artistic ideas from the West with their own experiences, a truly golden age of culture began.

Geographic Thinking

Seeing Patterns
How did the expansion of the Russian Empire affect the ethnic and religious makeup of the region?

HUMAN-ENVIRONMENT INTERACTION The two churches in this photo are on Kizhi Island, in Karelia, Russia. The churches' onion domes help to prevent the accumulation of snow during the winter.
How can architecture reflect the influence of geography?

365

REGION The Communist Party recruited artists to help promote Soviet industry. The poster above, from 1947, and the one below, from 1931, promise punishment for laziness and rewards for hard work.

In the 18th and 19th centuries, audiences around the world marveled at the work of writers such as Aleksandr Pushkin and Feodor Dostoyevsky. Their dramatic scenes and colorful psychological studies give an important portrait of Czarist Russia.

Great composers such as Peter Tchaikovsky and Igor Stravinsky also earned worldwide attention, as did the Russian ballet. Russian ballet companies, such as the Kirov and Bolshoi, are famous for producing magnificent dancers and creative choreographers, such as Mikhail Baryshnikov.

Art underwent another major change after the Communist Party began to outlaw artists who did not work in the official style. This style, called socialist realism, promoted Soviet ideals by optimistically showing citizens working to create a socialist society. In spite of the censorship, many artists took great risks to continue producing original work. Since the collapse of the Soviet Union, artistic expression has begun to gain strength.

Tradition and Change in Russian Life

Since the collapse of the Soviet Union, the region is more open to the influence of other countries—especially those in the West. At the same time, the region's people continue to honor their traditions and work hard to preserve them.

A MORE OPEN SOCIETY The region's people—especially in larger cities—have begun to enjoy more social and cultural opportunities. Large cities, such as Moscow and St. Petersburg, now resemble major cities in the West. City dwellers can read books, magazines, and newspapers from all over the world. They are able to keep up with new movies, music, and clothing trends. They can also experience a wide variety of foods and cuisines.

Although the variety of social and cultural opportunities has increased, native traditions have survived. For example, in spite of the many cuisines now available in Russian cities, many Russians still favor their traditional foods. Many of the foods, such as rye bread,

Geographic
Thinking

Seeing Patterns
D How do
Russian foods
reflect regional
geography?

reflect the large crops of grain produced on the region's steppes. Kasha is another popular food made from grain. It is cooked and eaten with butter. Even Russia's national drink, vodka, is made from rye or wheat grains. D

DACHAS* AND *BANYAS Only a quarter of Russia's population lives in rural areas. Even so, many Russians cherish the nation's countryside. Nearly 30 percent of the population own homes in the country, where they spend weekends and vacations. These homes, called *dachas,* are usually small, plain houses and often have gardens in which to grow vegetables.

One of the customs that Russians enjoy both in the countryside and the cities is visiting a *banya.* A *banya* is a bathhouse in which Russians perform a cleaning ritual that combines a dry sauna, steam bath, and often a plunge into ice-cold water.

Russians begin the ritual by warming up in a sauna heated to around 200°F. They then move into a steam room, where they use birch twigs to ease the muscles and perfume the body. After spending time in the steam room, many bathers plunge into an icy-cold pool—which might be a hole cut in the ice of a river or a lake. The ice bath is followed by hot tea, and the process is repeated. A visit to the *banya* can sometimes last for two to three hours.

The preservation of such customs and traditions by the Russian people has played an important role since the fall of the Soviet Union. It has helped to make the change from the isolated Soviet past to the more open society of the present less difficult.

PLACE A man enjoys an ice-cold dip during his trip to the *banya.*

RUSSIA & REP.

Assessment

1 Places & Terms

Explain the importance of each of the following terms and places.

- Baltic Republics
- czar
- Russian Revolution
- USSR
- Cold War
- command economy
- collective farm

2 Taking Notes

REGION Review the notes you took for this section.

Russia and the Western Republics

Russia and the Republics

- How did the Russian Empire lag behind its European rivals?
- How did the Communist Party control artistic expression?

3 Main Ideas

a. What was the extent of the Russian Empire's expansion between the 9th century and the end of the 17th century?

b. What were the origins of the Soviet Union?

c. How did the Soviet Union come to an end?

4 Geographic Thinking

Making Inferences How did the economic policies of the Soviet Union affect its human geography? **Think about:**

- industrialization
- collective farms

S See Skillbuilder Handbook, page R4.

EXPLORING LOCAL GEOGRAPHY You read in this section how Russia's traditional food is related to its geography. Do research on the traditional foods where you live, and try to determine how they might be related to the physical or human geography of your region. Explain the connections that you find in an **oral report.**

Disasters!

SUNSHINE STATE STANDARDS
Key Standard SS.B.2.4.4 The student understands the global impact of human changes in the physical environment.
FCAT LA.B.1.4.1 Writing: Strategies

Nuclear Explosion at Chernobyl

On April 28, 1986, engineer Cliff Robinson arrived at Sweden's Forsmark nuclear power plant. He was startled when a radiation detector went off as he entered his office. When he checked the radiation levels on his clothing, he could not believe his eyes. "My first thought," said Robinson, "was that a war had broken out and that somebody had blown up a nuclear bomb." What Forsmark had detected was a radioactive cloud from the city of Chernobyl—site of a Soviet nuclear power plant nearly 800 miles away.

One of Chernobyl's nuclear reactors had exploded, spewing radioactive dust across the region. It took two days for Soviet officials to admit that the explosion had occurred. The blast killed 31 people. No one is certain what toll accident-related diseases will take on the region's population in the future.

The Spread of Radiation from Chernobyl

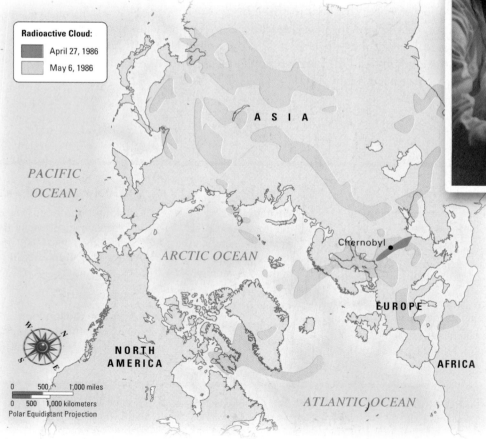

Radioactive Cloud:
- April 27, 1986
- May 6, 1986

ASIA

PACIFIC OCEAN

ARCTIC OCEAN

Chernobyl

EUROPE

NORTH AMERICA

AFRICA

ATLANTIC OCEAN

0   500   1,000 miles
0   500   1,000 kilometers
Polar Equidistant Projection

Workers test radiation levels from a helicopter. After the explosion, hundreds of thousands of workers helped in cleanup operations. Many were exposed to radiation and required emergency medical treatment.

The radioactive cloud from Chernobyl eventually spread over the entire Northern Hemisphere.

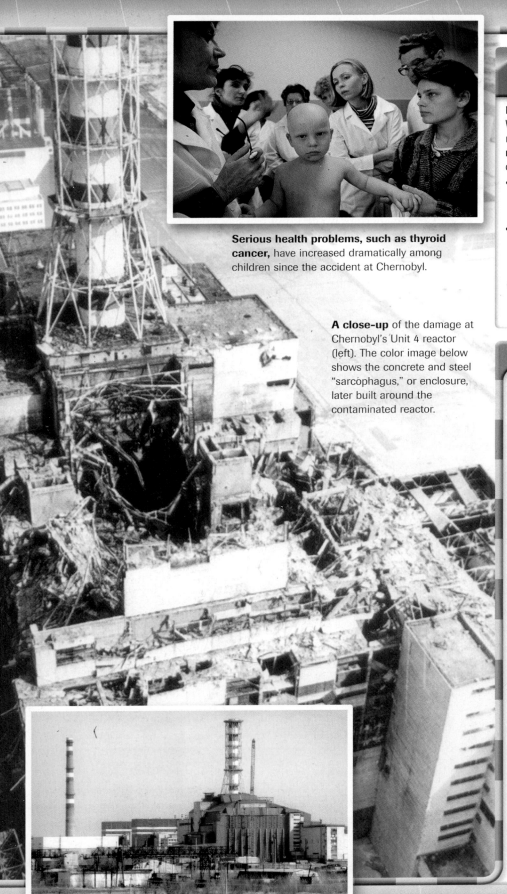

Serious health problems, such as thyroid cancer, have increased dramatically among children since the accident at Chernobyl.

A close-up of the damage at Chernobyl's Unit 4 reactor (left). The color image below shows the concrete and steel "sarcophagus," or enclosure, later built around the contaminated reactor.

GeoActivity

PLANNING A PRESENTATION
With a partner, use the Internet to research Chernobyl today. Plan a **multimedia presentation** about the disaster's legacy.

- Design charts, graphs, and maps that show the disaster's impact on public health and the environment.
- Include personal stories from individuals whose lives have been affected by the explosion.

RESEARCH LINKS
CLASSZONE.COM

GeoData

DAMAGE REPORT

- The Chernobyl plant is located about 80 miles north of Kiev, Ukraine's capital.
- The plant once employed nearly 9,200 people.
- On April 26, 1986, a poorly planned safety experiment led to the explosion at Chernobyl, which was made worse by a faulty reactor design.
- The reactor explosion was the world's worst civilian nuclear accident.
- The explosion contaminated around 100,000 square miles of land in Ukraine, Russia, and Belarus.
- Officials evacuated and resettled approximately 250,000 people from different towns around Chernobyl.
- Chernobyl continued to produce electricity until December 15, 2000, when officials finally shut down its last operating reactor.
- Costs related to the disaster have been estimated at over $300 billion.

Transcaucasia

A HUMAN PERSPECTIVE Throughout history, human beings have migrated through Transcaucasia, which today consists of the republics of Armenia, Azerbaijan, and Georgia. Recent discoveries have shown just how early such migrations began. In the summer of 1999, a team of scientists discovered two 1.7-million-year-old human skulls in the Transcaucasian republic of Georgia. They were the oldest human fossils found outside Africa. Reports suggest that the skulls could belong to the first people to have migrated from Africa.

A Gateway of Migration

People have long used Transcaucasia as a migration route, especially as a gateway between Europe and Asia. Trade routes near the Black Sea led to the thriving commercial regions of Mediterranean Europe. And trade routes leading to the Far East began on the shores of the Caspian Sea.

A VARIETY OF CULTURES Because of the presence of so many trade routes, Transcaucasia has been affected by many different peoples and cultures. Today, more than 50 different peoples live in the region.

Migrants brought a great variety of languages to the region. Arab geographers called the region *Jabal Al-Alsun,* or the "Mountain of Language." The Indo-European, Caucasian, and Altaic language families are the region's most common.

MIGRATION BRINGS RELIGIONS The people of Transcaucasia follow a number of different religions. However, most of the region's people belong to either the Christian or the Islamic faith.

Main Ideas
- Transcaucasia has been a gateway between Europe and Asia.
- The Caspian Sea's oil and gas reserves have given the region great economic potential.

Places & Terms
Red Army

supra

CONNECT TO THE ISSUES
CONFLICT Ethnic tensions in Transcaucasia erupted in conflict after the fall of the Soviet Union.

SUNSHINE STATE STANDARDS
Key Standard SS.B.2.4.1 The student understands how social, cultural, economic, and environmental factors contribute to the dynamic nature of regions.

Other Standards SS.B.2.4.2, B.2.4.3, D.2.4.6

FCAT LA.A.1.4.2 Reading: Strategies

Languages Around the Caucasus

INDO-EUROPEAN
- **Armenian** Armenian
- **Iranian** Kurdish, Ossetic
- **Slavic** Russian

CAUCASIAN
- **Abkhazo-Adyghian** Abkhaz, Adyghian
- **Kartvelian** Georgian, Mingrelian/Laz
- **Nakho-Dagestanian** Avar, Chechen, Dargin, Lak, Lezgi, Tabasaran

ALTAIC
- **Turkic** Azerbaijani, Karachay, Kumyk

OTHER LANGUAGES

- - - Transcaucasia

0   100   200 miles
0 100   200 kilometers
Lambert Azimuthal Equal-Area Projection

SKILLBUILDER: Interpreting Maps

❶ **REGION** Which is the most common language group in Azerbaijan?

❷ **PLACE** Which language is spoken in the Nagorno-Karabakh region of Azerbaijan?

These faiths arrived in the region at an early date, because Transcaucasia is close to the areas in Southwest Asia where the two religions began. Armenia and Georgia, for example, are among the oldest Christian states in the world. Armenia's King Tiridates III converted to Christianity in A.D. 300. A year later, he made his state the first in the world to adopt Christianity.

Not long after the 7th-century beginnings of Islam in Southwest Asia, Muslim invaders stormed into the southern Caucasus and converted many Transcaucasians to Islam. Today, the great majority of Azerbaijan's people are Muslim.

CONFLICT The region's diverse population has not always lived together in harmony. Tensions seldom erupted into open hostility under the rigid rule of the Soviets. However, after the collapse of the USSR in 1991, tensions among different groups have resulted in violence. Civil war broke out in Georgia, and Armenia fought a bitter war with Azerbaijan over a disputed territory called Nagorno-Karabakh.

The story of conflict is not new to Transcaucasia. Its history of conflict, as you will read below, can be explained, in part, by its location.

CONNECT TO THE ISSUES

CONFLICT

A Why did ethnic tensions seldom erupt into violence during the Soviet era?

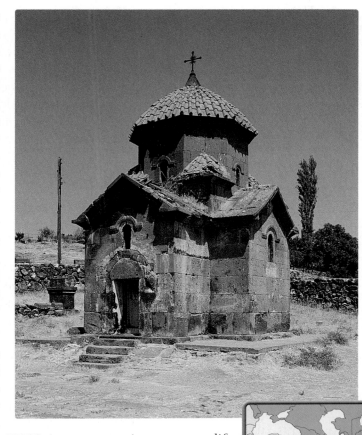

PLACE The beautiful Karmravor Church is located in the Armenian village of Ashtarak. It dates from the 7th century. **How long after Armenia adopted Christianity was the church built?**

A History of Outside Control

Over the centuries, Transcaucasia has been a place where the borders of rival empires have come together. Imperial armies have repeatedly invaded the region to protect and extend those borders.

CZARIST AND SOVIET RULE In the 18th century, the troops of the Russian Empire joined the list of invaders. Russia's southward expansion had begun as early as the 1500s, but it was only in the 1700s that the czar's army began making progress south of the Caucasus Mountains.

The inhabitants of the region resisted the Russians, but the czar's troops prevailed. By 1723, Peter the Great's generals had taken control of Baku, the capital of Azerbaijan. In 1801, Russia annexed Georgia. In 1828, Russian armies took control of a large stretch of Armenian territory, including the plain of Yerevan. By the late 1870s, the czar's troops had added Transcaucasia to the Russian Empire.

After the Russian Revolution in 1917, the Transcaucasian republics enjoyed a brief period of independence. By the early 1920s, however, the **Red Army**—the name of the Soviet military—had taken control of the region.

In the decades following the Soviet takeover, the people of Transcaucasia experienced the same painful economic and political changes as the rest of the Soviet Union. Many people lost their lives in famines triggered by the shift to collective farming or were killed because of their political beliefs. The republics of Transcaucasia regained their political independence in 1991 after the fall of the Soviet Union. Since then, the region's leaders have struggled to rebuild their nations' economies.

BACKGROUND
Stalin was especially harsh on Transcaucasia, even though he was from the Georgian town of Gori.

Economic Potential

Today, economic activity in the Transcaucasian republics ranges from the tourism and wine industries of subtropical Georgia to large-scale oil production in Azerbaijan.

AGRICULTURE AND INDUSTRY Although much of Transcaucasia's terrain is mountainous, each of the republics has a significant agricultural output. Transcaucasians have taken advantage of the region's climate and the potential of the limited amount of land fit for farming.

The humid subtropical lowlands and foothills of the region are ideal for valuable crops such as tea and fruits. Grapes are one of the most important fruit crops. Georgians use the grapes cultivated along their Black Sea coast to produce their famous wines. Georgia's mild climate also once fueled a profitable tourist industry.

There was little industry in Transcaucasia before the Soviet Union took control of the region. Soviet planners transformed Transcaucasia from a largely agricultural area into an industrial and urban region.

PLACE

Trouble in Georgia

In the late 1980s, more than 3.6 million tourists visited Georgia each year. But tourism slowed to a trickle after ethnic conflict broke out in the region in the early 1990s.

One conflict took place in Abkhazia—a resort area that stretches for more than 100 miles along Georgia's Black Sea coast. Ethnic Abkhazians sought independence and rebelled against Georgia, which sent troops to prevent the uprising. The conflict remained unresolved at the beginning of 2001.

In this photo, from 1993, soldiers help a boy flee from street fighting in Sokhumi, the capital of Abkhazia.

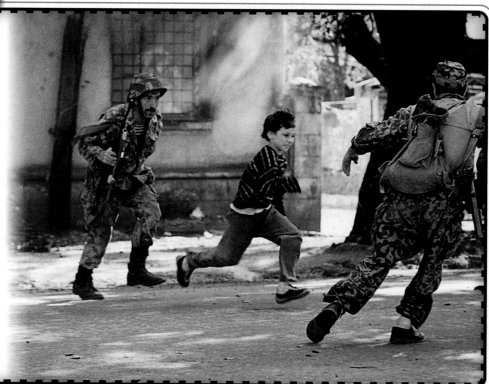

A number of industrial centers built by the Soviets continue to produce iron, steel, chemicals, and consumer goods for the region's economy. But today, the oil industry is most important. The oil industry has an impact not only on oil-rich republics, such as Azerbaijan. It also affects Armenia and Georgia because oil producers want to build pipelines across their territory to bring the oil to market.

LAND OF FLAMES The significance of oil in the region has a long history. In fact, the name Azerbaijan means "land of flames." The republic's founders chose the name because of the fires that erupted seemingly by magic from both the rocks and the waters of the Caspian Sea. The fires were the result of underground oil and gas deposits.

DIVIDING THE CASPIAN SEA Since the breakup of the Soviet Union, Azerbaijan and the other four countries bordering the Caspian Sea have argued about whether the Caspian is an inland sea or a lake. The resolution of this argument will decide how resources are divided among the five countries.

If the Caspian is a sea, then each country has legal rights to the resources on its own part of the sea bed. If it is a lake, the law says that most of the resource wealth must be shared equally among each of the countries. Azerbaijan, with large reserves off its coast, says the Caspian is an inland sea. Russia, with few off-shore reserves, insists that the Caspian is a lake. ◀ B

The oil industry has given the region's people hope for a better life. But oil revenue has benefited few Transcaucasians. Many continue to live in poverty.

🌐 **Geographic Thinking** ◀

Seeing Patterns

B ▶ How can the geographic definition of a body of water affect economic relationships?

Dividing the Caspian

As Lake

RUSSIA — KAZAKHSTAN — GEORGIA — Caspian Sea — Joint area — UZBEKISTAN — AZERBAIJAN — Baku — TURKMENISTAN — AZER. — ARMENIA — IRAN

As Inland Sea

RUSSIA — KAZAKHSTAN — GEORGIA — Caspian Sea — UZBEKISTAN — AZERBAIJAN — Baku — TURKMENISTAN — AZER. — ARMENIA — IRAN

SKILLBUILDER: Interpreting Maps

REGION Which are the five countries that border the Caspian Sea?

RUSSIA & REP.

Modern Life in Transcaucasia

Although times are tough for many, the region has much to offer, including a well-educated population and a reputation for hospitality.

AN EDUCATED PEOPLE The educational programs of the Soviet Union had a largely positive impact on its people. At the time of the Russian Revolution, only a small percentage of Transcaucasia's population was literate. Communist leaders decided to train a new generation of skilled workers who would be prepared to undertake the tasks of industrial development and modernization. They succeeded, as literacy rates in Transcaucasia rose to nearly 99 percent, among the highest in the world. Today, high quality educational systems remain a priority for Transcaucasians.

HOSPITALITY In their quest for a modern system of education, Transcaucasians have not forgotten the value of their traditions. Among the most important are the region's mealtime celebrations.

PLACE At a dinner party held in the Georgian town of Kutol, a woman raises her glass to deliver a toast. **How do the foods you see in the image reflect what you have read about Georgia's climate?**

The Georgian **supra,** or dinner party, is one of the best examples of such gatherings. The word *supra* means tablecloth but also refers to any occasion at which people gather to eat and drink.

A *supra* involves breathtaking quantities of food and drink. Meals begin at a table spread with a great number of cold dishes. Two or three hot courses and fruit and desserts follow those. Georgians add locally grown foods, such as grated walnuts, garlic, and an array of herbs and spices to their recipes. And they are able to serve meals with remarkable freshness, thanks to the region's mild climate.

In addition to food and drink, a *supra* is accompanied by a great number of toasts, short speeches given before taking a drink. Georgians take the toasts very seriously because they show a respect for tradition, eloquence, and the value of bringing people together—a goal of great importance for the future of the region.

SECTION 2 Assessment

❶ Places & Terms

Explain the importance of each of the following terms.

- Red Army
- *supra*

❷ Taking Notes

REGION Review the notes you took for this section.

- How do Transcaucasia's republics differ in terms of religion?
- What sorts of activities take place during a Georgian *supra*?

❸ Main Ideas

a. How would you describe the ethnic and linguistic makeup of Transcaucasia?

b. What roles did Russia and the Soviet Union play in Transcaucasia?

c. How has the oil industry affected the people of Transcaucasia?

❹ Geographic Thinking

Determining Cause and Effect How did the economic goals of the Soviet Union affect educational values in Transcaucasia? **Think about:**

- Transcaucasia's economy before the 1920s
- the impact of economic changes on the region's workers

MAKING COMPARISONS Carry out more research on the religions of Transcaucasia. Then write a **script** for a five minute documentary that compares the architectural styles used in two different houses of worship.

Central Asia

Main Ideas
- Soviet officials drew borders in Central Asia that are making it difficult for the region's new leaders to establish stability.
- Central Asians have preserved many cultural traditions despite decades of colonization.

Places & Terms

Silk Road	nomad
Great Game	yurt

CONNECT TO THE ISSUES
NUCLEAR LEGACY Soviet nuclear testing will have a long-term impact on the region.

SUNSHINE STATE STANDARDS
Key Standard SS.B.2.4.3 The student understands how the allocation of control of the Earth's surface affects interactions between people in different regions.

Other Standards SS.B.2.4.2

FCAT LA.A.1.4.2 Reading: Strategies

A HUMAN PERSPECTIVE Central Asia has inspired the dreams of many adventurers—and presented them with many dangers. In the 19th century, agents of the mighty British Empire found that even they were not safe there. In 1842, two British officers were captured in the Central Asian city of Bukhoro. For months, the city's ruler kept the men in an underground bug-pit that swarmed with ticks, rats, and scaly vermin. In June of that year, he forced the two officers to dig their own graves and then beheaded them. In spite of the dangers, people have journeyed across Central Asia throughout history.

A Historical Crossroads

Today, Central Asia consists of five independent republics: Kazakhstan, Kyrgyzstan, Tajikistan, Turkmenistan, and Uzbekistan. Travelers first began to make their way across the region in large numbers around 100 B.C. Many of them joined caravans making the 4,000-mile journey between China and the Mediterranean Sea.

THE SILK ROAD Traders called this route the **Silk Road,** after the costly silk they bought in China. In addition to silk, traders carried many other goods on their horses and camels. These included gold, silver, ivory, jade, wine, spices, amber, linen, porcelain, grapes, perfumes—even

The Silk Road

SKILLBUILDER: Interpreting Maps

❶ **LOCATION** Which river is the city of Tashkent close to?

❷ **MOVEMENT** Which body of water did the Silk Road's westbound traffic move toward?

RUSSIA & REP.

Silk Production

① Silk moths lay eggs that hatch into caterpillars called silkworms.

② The worms feed on mulberry leaves and grow up to 70 times their original size.

③ When full grown, the worms produce a thread, which they use to spin a cocoon.

④ This Kyrgyz woman is dipping cocoons in hot water to loosen the threads that she will then wind onto a reel.

⑤ A single cocoon yields about 3,000–5,000 feet of thread. It takes about 3,000 cocoons to make just one pound of raw silk.

⑥ Silk garments are popular items at a market.

ostriches and acrobats. The Silk Road also became a route for spreading ideas, technology, and religion.

Traffic on the Silk Road slowed in the 14th century, giving way to less expensive sea routes. Even so, you can still experience the legacy of the Silk Road in the magnificent cities—such as Samarqand and Bukhoro—built to take advantage of the trade.

THE GREAT GAME Interest in Central Asia exploded again in the 19th century when Great Britain and the Russian Empire began to struggle for control of the region. Russian troops were moving southward, and British leaders wanted to stop the advance before the troops could threaten Britain's possessions in India.

Both sides recruited daring young officers who made journeys through the region in disguise. These officers worked to create maps of Central Asia and to win local leaders to their side. Arthur Connoly—one of the British officers executed in Bukhoro—called this struggle between the two empires the **Great Game.**

By the end of the 19th century, the Russian Empire had won control of Central Asia. In the 1920s, the Soviet Union took control and governed the region until 1991. Since the collapse of the Soviet Union, the Central Asian republics have been independent.

BACKGROUND Bukhoro and Samarqand marked halfway points where travelers could meet and take advantage of the cities' markets and services.

An Uncertain Economic Future

In Chapter 15, you read about the problems caused by Soviet irrigation programs in Central Asia. Other Soviet programs have also caused problems in the region.

NUCLEAR TESTING Until the late 1980s, the Soviet nuclear industry was the economic mainstay of Semey (renamed Semipalatinsk), a city in northeastern Kazakhstan. Between 1949 and 1989, scientists exploded 470 nuclear devices in "the Polygon," a vast nuclear test site southwest of Semey.

The nuclear tests were so close to Semey that citizens could see the mushroom clouds of the above-ground explosions. Later, underground explosions cracked walls in towns 50 miles away. The testing caused widespread health problems. Winds spread nuclear fallout over a 180,000-square-mile area, exposing over a million people to dangerous levels of radiation. Exposure caused dramatic increases in the rates of leukemia, thyroid cancer, birth defects, and mental illness. Although testing at the site ended in 1989, the harmful effects of radiation will continue for years to come. **◀A**

⊕ **Geographic Thinking**◀

Seeing Patterns
A What are the harmful effects of nuclear testing?

PETROLEUM AND PROSPERITY More hopeful is the potential for oil to bring wealth to Central Asia. Regional leaders see great promise in the oil and gas reserves of the Caspian Sea. In addition, engineers have recently discovered oil fields in Kazakhstan and Turkmenistan. These discoveries have triggered what many are calling the new "Great Game," as nations all over the world begin to compete for profits from the region's resources.

For Central Asia's resources to benefit its people, however, leaders must first establish stable political and legal institutions. The cultural geography of Central Asia, though, will make this goal especially difficult to achieve.

Cultures Divided and Conquered

Central Asia has a large number of ethnic groups, as the chart to the right shows. Before the Russian Revolution, each group lived in a particular region where it could follow its own way of life.

SOVIETS FORM NATIONS When the Soviets took control of Central Asia, they used the differences among the ethnic groups to establish their own authority in the region.

Soviet planners carved the region into five new nations that corresponded to the largest ethnic groups—Kazakh, Kyrgyz, Tajik, Turkmen, and Uzbek. However, when they drew the borders of these nations, they deliberately left large numbers of one ethnic group as minorities in the neighboring republics of other ethnic groups.

That explains why Uzbeks form about 24 percent of the population of Tajikistan and why two of the major

Ethnic Groups

Central Asia (1999)

Group	Percent
Uzbek	41%
Russian	15%
Kazakh	15%
Tajik	9%
Turkmen	6%
Kyrgyz	4%
Ukrainian	2%
German	1%
Karakalpak	1%
Tatar	1%
Other	5%

SOURCE: *CIA World Factbook 1999*

SKILLBUILDER:
Interpreting Charts

REGION What is the second largest ethnic group in Central Asia?

growing up in...Kyrgyzstan

Like children in the other former Soviet republics, the young people of Kyrgyzstan face a future filled with challenges. But most of the country's young people are prepared to meet those challenges. Children in Kyrgyzstan go to school from the ages of 6 to 15, and the nation's literacy rate stands at more than 97 percent.

The children in this photo are celebrating a birthday with their family. They are in a yurt set up for the occasion. Among the dishes on the table are *manti* (sheep dumplings), *irkat* (a salad made of noodles and grated carrots), and *kymys* (a drink made from fermented horse milk).

If you lived in Kyrgyzstan, here is what you might experience:

- Since 75 percent of Kyrgyz practice Islam, you might be Muslim.

- You might become a farmer, since nearly half of Kyrgyzstan's people earn their living that way.

- You might find it hard to keep in touch with friends since just 8 out of 100 people own phones.

- Watching TV would also be difficult. Only 2 out of 10 people own a TV.

- You would earn the right to vote and become eligible for military service at the age of 18.

cities inside Uzbekistan, Samarqand and Bukhoro, are populated by ethnic Tajiks. Ethnic Uzbeks also make up 9 percent of Turkmenistan's and nearly 14 percent of Kyrgyzstan's populations. Soviet leaders tried to prevent opposition to their rule by using the tensions that existed among these different groups. **B**

LANGUAGE AND RELIGION Although the peoples of Central Asia are divided by a number of ethnic and political loyalties, there are unifying forces in the region as well. Islam, which was brought by Muslim warriors from Southwest Asia in the 8th and 9th centuries, is one of the strongest. Also, most Central Asians speak languages related to Turkish. Many people also speak Russian, once the region's official language.

The Survival of Tradition

Central Asia endured decades of upheaval under Russian and Soviet rule. Even so, many of the region's traditions have survived.

NOMADIC HERITAGE The expansive grasslands of Central Asia are ideal for nomadic peoples. **Nomads** are people who have no permanent home. As seasons change, they move from place to place with their animals in search of food, water, and grazing land.

During the years of Soviet control, the number of nomads in Central Asia decreased dramatically as officials forced people onto collective farms. Even so, you can still find nomads in the region. In central Kyrgyzstan, for example, herders set up their tents near Lake Song-Köl during the summer months. They bring their animals there to graze on the lush pastures of the valley.

Geographic Thinking

Using the Atlas
B Look at the maps on pages 338–339 and 341. Compare the political and ethnic borders in Central Asia. In which regions do you see a potential for conflict?

Because they are always on the move and must carry what they own, nomads have few possessions. They usually carry what is most useful. Even so, many of the possessions of Central Asia's nomads are both useful and beautiful.

YURTS Among the most valuable of the nomads' possessions are their tents—called **yurts.** Yurts are light and portable. They usually consist of several layers of felt stretched around a wooden frame, often made of willow. The outermost layer of felt is coated with the waterproof fat of sheep.

As the photo on page 378 shows, the inside of a yurt can be stunningly beautiful. To block the wind, nomads hang reed mats, intricately woven with the grasses of the steppe. For storage, they suspend woven bags on their tent walls. The inlaid wooden saddles of their horses and their carved daggers also ornament the yurt.

Perhaps the most beautiful and useful of all the yurt's furnishings are the handwoven carpets. Their elaborate designs, colored with natural plant and beetle dyes, have made the carpets famous. Nomads use them for sleeping, or as floor coverings, wall linings, and insulation.

PRESERVING TRADITIONS The nomadic lifestyle of the peoples of Central Asia is not nearly as widespread as it once was. But many people are working hard to preserve the tradition. One group has organized a network of shepherds' families in Kyrgyzstan who are willing to take in guests. In this way, tourists can experience the daily life of the shepherds, who, in turn, receive a source of income for their families. Central Asians will benefit greatly from such imaginative and productive uses of their traditions.

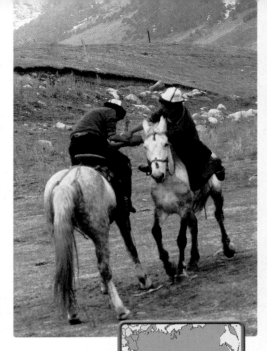

HUMAN-ENVIRONMENT INTERACTION Two Kyrgyz men wrestle on horseback. This sport, in which contestants try to unseat their opponents, requires strength, skill, and good horsemanship.

RUSSIA & REP.

SECTION 3 Assessment

1 Places & Terms

Explain the importance of each of the following terms.
- Silk Road
- Great Game
- nomad
- yurt

2 Taking Notes

REGION Review the notes you took for this section.

Russia and the Republics   Central Asia

- What were some of the objects traded or transported over the Silk Road?
- Why have some people suggested that a new Great Game is beginning in Central Asia?

3 Main Ideas

a. What was the cause of the Great Game?

b. What impact has Soviet nuclear testing had in Central Asia?

c. What are two important unifying forces in Central Asia?

4 Geographic Thinking

Drawing Conclusions How did the Soviet Union use the human geography of Central Asia to establish control of the region? **Think about:**
- ethnic groups in the region
- how Soviet planners drew borders

RESEARCH LINKS
CLASSZONE.COM

GeoActivity

SEEING PATTERNS Carry out more research on the lives of nomads in Central Asia. Focus on the period before the Soviet Union took control of the region. Then make up a **diary entry** that describes the daily activity of a typical nomadic family.

Comparing Cultures

Homes and Shelters

The geography of the region in which people live influences the nature of their homes and shelters. People who live in forested areas, for example, might build log cabins. People living in grasslands, on the other hand, may use thatch—plant stalks and leaves—to build their homes. On these two pages, you will learn how homes in different parts of the world reflect local geographic possibilities and limitations.

Greenland

Kyrgyzstan

Spain

Indonesia

Arctic peoples in Canada and Greenland take advantage of their environment by using blocks of snow to build dome-shaped winter shelters called igloos. They sometimes add windows made with sheets of ice or seal intestines.

The portable yurts of Kyrgyz herders are suited to their nomadic lifestyle.

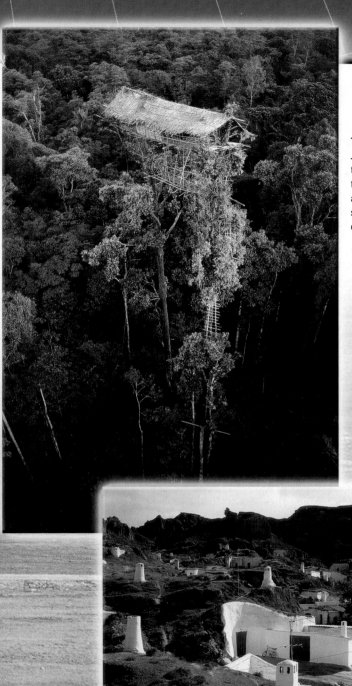

The Korowai of Irian Jaya, Indonesia, live in tree houses that protect them from rival tribes, as well as the insects, scorpions, and snakes of the rain forest.

People in the Spanish town of Guadix have turned underground caves into homes to protect against the region's extreme temperatures.

GeoActivity

CREATING AN EXHIBIT

Working with a partner, use the Internet to do research on homes in a region other than those shown on these two pages. Create an **exhibit** that shows the relationship between the region and its homes.

- Construct a model of the homes you are researching.
- Add a world map to the exhibit that shows where the homes are located.

RESEARCH LINKS
CLASSZONE.COM

GeoData

Igloos
- The blocks of snow in an igloo are about 2 feet high, 4 feet long, and 8 inches thick.
- An experienced builder can finish an igloo in one to two hours.

Caves
- About 50 percent of Guadix's inhabitants live underground.
- Some of Guadix's caves are quite luxurious, with marble floors, modern kitchens, fax machines, and Internet connections.

Tree Houses
- The Korowai people build tree houses as high as 150 feet above ground.
- Korowai tree houses have separate areas for men and women, each with its own entrance.

Yurts
- A nomadic family can set up their yurt in approximately a half-hour.
- Felt—the material used to cover yurts—is a fabric of compressed animal fibers, such as wool or fur.

VISUAL SUMMARY
HUMAN GEOGRAPHY OF RUSSIA AND THE REPUBLICS

Subregions of Russia and the Republics

● **Russia and the Western Republics**
- The explosive growth of the Russian Empire and the following decades of Soviet rule have had a lasting impact on both the physical and human geography of the region.
- The dramatic economic changes that accompanied the rise and fall of the Soviet Union affected both Russia and the Republics and the world.

○ **Transcaucasia**
- Migrating peoples have created a mosaic of languages and ethnicities in Transcaucasia.
- Today, leaders in Transcaucasia are struggling to maintain harmony among the region's different cultural groups and bring stability to the region's three newly-independent republics.

● **Central Asia**
- Central Asia's fractured cultural geography still reflects the political goals of the old Soviet government.
- Powerful unifying forces, such as Islam, may help the region's new republics as they continue to rebuild their social and economic systems.

Reviewing Places & Terms

A. Briefly explain the importance of each of the following.

1. Baltic Republics
2. czar
3. Russian Revolution
4. USSR
5. Cold War
6. command economy
7. collective farm
8. Red Army
9. Silk Road
10. yurt

B. Answer the questions about vocabulary in complete sentences.

11. What were the emperors of the Russian Empire called?
12. What are the names of the three former Soviet republics located on the Baltic Sea?
13. What event ended the Russian Empire and the rule of the czars?
14. What is another name for the Soviet Union?
15. What was the name of the 20th-century conflict between the United States and the Soviet Union?
16. In what type of system are all major economic decisions made by the central government?
17. How did the Soviet Union turn agriculture into an industry?
18. What was the name of the Soviet military?
19. What caravan route contributed to the growth of magnificent trading cities such as Samarqand?
20. What is the name for the felt-covered dwellings of Central Asia's nomads?

Main Ideas

Russia and the Western Republics (pp. 361–369)

1. What former Soviet republics are located west of Russia?
2. What event delayed the growth of Russia before the 16th century?
3. What were the origins of the Cold War?
4. What is the largest religious group in Russia and the Western Republics?

Transcaucasia (pp. 370–374)

5. Of what republics does Transcaucasia consist?
6. Transcaucasia's location between which two seas made it an ideal migration route?
7. What factors may have contributed to instability in Transcaucasia?

Central Asia (pp. 375–381)

8. Of what republics does Central Asia consist?
9. Why did the Silk Road cross over Central Asia?
10. How did Islam become a major religion in Central Asia?

Critical Thinking

1. Using Your Notes

Use your completed chart to answer these questions.

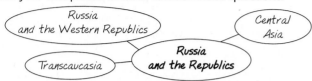

a. What percentage of the Russian population lives in rural areas?

b. What are the main religions in Transcaucasia?

2. Geographic Themes

a. **PLACE** Why did Azerbaijan's founders call it the "land of flames"?

b. **LOCATION** Where was the Soviet nuclear test site called "the Polygon" located?

3. Identifying Themes

Which country in Russia and the Western Republics has the greatest ethnic diversity, and what is its largest ethnic group? Which of the five themes applies to this situation?

4. Making Comparisons

How did the rise of the Soviet Union affect Transcaucasia and Central Asia?

5. Making Generalizations

How can the type of government that a country has affect the kind of work the country's artists create?

Additional Test Practice, pp. S1–S37

TEST PRACTICE
CLASSZONE.COM

Geographic Skills: Interpreting Maps

Central Moscow

Use the map to answer the following questions.

1. **LOCATION** On what river does Russia's capital lie?

2. **MOVEMENT** Which of the ring roads would you take to visit Gorky Park?

3. **MOVEMENT** In which direction would you walk to get from Lenin's tomb to the State Department Store?

1. The Kremlin
2. State Department Store
3. Bolshoi Theatre
4. Lenin's Tomb
5. St. Basil's Cathedral
6. Duma (Russian Parliament)
7. Red Square
8. Gorky Park

GeoActivity

Choose one of the buildings shown on this map, and carry out further research on that building. Create a poster that includes a sketch of the site's floor plan and a paragraph about the history of the building.

INTERNET ACTIVITY

Use the links at **classzone.com** to do research on two of the former Soviet republics to the west of Russia. Focus on the characteristics of the republics' geography and people.

Creating Charts and Graphs Use your research to create charts and graphs that compare the two republics that you have chosen. List the Web sites that you used in preparing your report.

RUSSIA & REP.

SECTION 1
Regional Conflict

SECTION 2
The Struggle for
Economic Reform

CASE STUDY
THE SOVIET UNION'S
NUCLEAR LEGACY

For more on these issues in
Russia and the Republics . . .

 CURRENT EVENTS
CLASSZONE.COM

This woman and child are
from the Russian Republic
of Chechnya. Russia
invaded Chechnya twice
in the 1990s to prevent
the republic from
becoming independent.

TODAY'S ISSUES
Russia and the Republics

GeoFocus

What impact has the fall of the Soviet Union had on the region?

Taking Notes In your notebook, copy a cause-and-effect chart like the one below. Then take notes on causes and effects of some aspect of each issue.

	Causes	Effects
Issue 1: Conflict		
Issue 2: Economy		
Case Study: Nuclear Legacy		

Regional Conflict

How do new nations establish law and order?

Main Ideas

- Regional tensions, once under Soviet control, have flared up in Russia and the Republics.
- Some of the most violent conflicts have occurred in the Caucasus region.

Places & Terms

Caucasus

Chechnya

Nagorno-Karabakh

SUNSHINE STATE STANDARDS

Key Standard SS.B.2.4.3 The student understands how the allocation of control of the Earth's surface affects interactions between people in different regions.

FCAT LA.A.2.4.1 Reading: Identify Main Idea, Details, and Methods

A HUMAN PERSPECTIVE The powerful central government of the Soviet Union once maintained tight control over Russia and the Republics. But when the Soviet Union collapsed in 1991, central authority weakened. Crime, conflict, and other signs of instability increased. As one former Soviet citizen put it, "We're floating in a zone of half-lawlessness, half-law. . . . We destroyed the old system but replaced it with nothing. There is a vacuum."

A number of ethnic and religious groups have taken advantage of this vacuum to seek control over their own affairs. In several regions, their demands have resulted in conflict. Leaders in these regions have tried to gain control over the conflicts and bring them to an end. The test for many leaders has been how to preserve law and order without returning to the undemocratic rule of the Soviet era.

A Troubled Caucasus

Among the different subregions of the former Soviet Union, the Caucasus has experienced some of the most violent conflicts. The **Caucasus,** or Caucasia, is a region that straddles the Caucasus Mountains, which stretch between the Black and Caspian seas. To the north of the mountains lie republics that are part of Russia—including Chechnya, Dagestan, Ingushetia, and North Ossetia. To the south are the republics of Transcaucasia, which were once part of the Soviet Union but are now independent countries: Armenia, Azerbaijan, and Georgia.

The Caucasus is a land of great complexity. Inhabitants of the region, which is about the size of the state of California, speak dozens of distinct languages and belong to approximately 50 different ethnic groups.

The Caucasus

International boundary

Administrative boundary

SKILLBUILDER: Interpreting Maps

❶ **LOCATION** On what seacoast is Abkhazia situated?

❷ **LOCATION** In what countries do North and South Ossetia lie?

As the Soviet Union began to break up in the late 1980s, several of these ethnic groups began to take up arms to win their own independent territories. In the following decade, hundreds of thousands of people died in the conflicts that resulted.

CHECHNYA Among the republics that remained part of Russia after the collapse of the Soviet Union, <u>**Chechnya**</u> has experienced the worst vio-

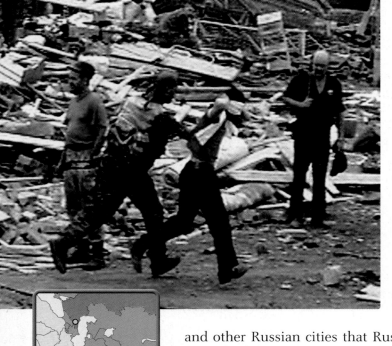

lence. In response to Chechnya's demand for independence, Russia invaded Chechnya twice in the 1990s, causing over 100,000 casualties.

Russia first invaded Chechnya in 1994. By the spring of 1995, Russian troops were in control of more than two-thirds of the republic's territory, and they had captured the capital, Grozny, and other major towns. But Chechen rebels continued to fight from hideouts in the surrounding mountains. Unable to defeat the rebels, Russia reluctantly entered into a peace agreement with Chechnya, ending the first phase of the war in August 1996.

Russia invaded Chechnya again in October 1999. The invasion began after a series of bombings in Moscow and other Russian cities that Russian leaders blamed on Chechen terrorists. The invasion continued into 2001. As of that time, no one was certain when the conflict would end.

PLACE This television image shows the results of a bomb attack in August 2000 in the Chechen town of Argun. A Russian soldier leads away a captured prisoner. **Why might the Russian army have trouble defeating the Chechen rebels?**

GEORGIA Russia is not the only former Soviet republic that has experienced instability. The Ossetian people living in the central Georgian region of South Ossetia fought against Georgian troops off and on from 1989 to 1992. They wanted to unite South Ossetia with North Ossetia, located in Russia. This violent struggle resulted in 2,000 deaths and over 40,000 refugees before a truce put an end to the conflict in June 1992.

Following the truce in South Ossetia, another violent conflict erupted in Abkhazia, a once-popular resort region in northwestern Georgia. Abkhazians declared independence in July 1992. In the following months, they forced Abkhazia's Georgian population—over 250,000 people—to leave the region. Many died while crossing snow-covered mountains to safer areas. By September 1993, the Abkhazians had driven Georgian troops from the region. In spite of their success, Abkhazia still lay in ruins in 2001. And the fate of the Georgian refugees remained to be settled.

Geographic Thinking

Seeing Patterns
A How are the two conflicts in Georgia that you read about similar?

ARMENIA AND AZERBAIJAN Conflict has also plagued the region south of Georgia, where Armenia and Azerbaijan fought over a mountainous area of Azerbaijan called <u>**Nagorno–Karabakh.**</u> Leaders in Azerbaijan say that the region's history proves that Nagorno-Karabakh belongs to them. Armenia claims Nagorno-Karabakh because over three-quarters of its population is ethnic Armenian.

The dispute began long ago and was raging in the early 1920s, when the Soviet army took control of the region. Soviet authorities kept the dispute under control until the late 1980s, when Armenians and Azerbaijanis began to fight for control over the region.

The fighting continued on and off for nearly six years. Eventually Armenia won control of the territory. A cease-fire was declared in 1994, but by then, tens of thousands of people had died. Nearly a million had become refugees.

Hope on the Horizon?

In spite of all this conflict in the region, many believe that there is some hope for the future. In April 2001, U.S. Secretary of State Colin Powell hosted the latest round of direct talks between the presidents of Armenia and Azerbaijan. The talks, which were held in Florida, were aimed at reaching a lasting peace settlement between the two nations. In Georgia, the government of President Edvard Shevardnadze has been a stabilizing force.

Fighting has continued in Chechnya, and the human costs of the war have continued to mount. In February 2001, Russian officials reported that more than 15,000 soldiers (2,700 Russians and 13,000 Chechen guerrillas) had died since the second war began. Public support for the war, which was high when it began in October 1999, is now declining. The economic costs of the war have also become a burden. These factors may help to bring an end to the conflict. In the next section, you will read more about the economic challenges faced by Russian leaders since the fall of the Soviet Union.

Geography TODAY

Exclaves

Armenians claim that Nagorno-Karabakh is an "exclave" of Armenia. Geographers define an exclave as part of a country that is isolated from the main part and is surrounded by foreign territory. (See map below.)

Like other exclaves, Nagorno-Karabakh has presented regional leaders with difficult challenges, such as how to accommodate the wishes of a region's minority population when they differ from those of the region's majority. These challenges have severely tested the stability of Azerbaijan—the country that surrounds Nagorno-Karabakh.

Assessment

1 Places & Terms

Explain the importance of each of the following places.

- Caucasus
- Chechnya
- Nagorno-Karabakh

2 Taking Notes

REGION Review the notes you took for this section.

	Causes	Effects
Issue 1: Conflict		

- Why might Abkhazia's tourist industry have declined in the 1990s?

3 Main Ideas

a. Why did ethnic tensions in Russia and the Republics seldom result in armed conflict before the 1990s?

b. Why did Russian troops invade Chechnya in 1994 and 1999?

c. What led to the conflict between Armenia and Azerbaijan?

4 Geographic Thinking

Making Comparisons Why might ethnic differences cause problems in one region or society but not in another?

Think about:

- the type of government in the region

RESEARCH LINKS
CLASSZONE.COM

GeoActivity

ASKING GEOGRAPHIC QUESTIONS Search for articles on a conflict in Caucasia. Create **flash cards** that raise geographic questions about the conflict, such as "How did geography help keep Russian troops from defeating Chechen rebels?" The back of the card might read "Rebels hid in the region's mountainous terrain." Consider features of both physical and human geography.

The Struggle for Economic Reform

How does a nation change its economic system?

Main Ideas
- Russia has struggled to move from a command economy to a market economy.
- Russia's enormous size and widespread criminal activity have made economic reform difficult.

Places & Terms

privatization

distance decay

The Voyageur Experience in World Geography
Russia: Rebuilding a Nation

A HUMAN PERSPECTIVE Russians have faced many hardships since the breakup of the Soviet Union. But few have been as difficult to overcome as the collapse of the Soviet command economy. After the Soviet Union collapsed in 1991, the region's people began to participate in a capitalist system. One Russian bitterly summed up the sudden transition in this way: "You developed your capitalist markets in the West over hundreds of years, and our government wants our people to go to sleep one night in a Communist world and wake up the next morning in a capitalist one." One of the toughest problems facing Russia's leaders is how to carry out economic reforms without causing too much turmoil for the nation's citizens.

Steps Toward Capitalism

After the Soviet collapse, Russia tried to move quickly toward a capitalist system. This meant ending the tight control that the central government held over economic activity.

PRIVATIZATION In January 1992, Russia removed the price controls that had been set by the Soviet government on goods sold within the country. The effect was dramatic. Almost immediately, the prices of many goods increased by 250 percent.

In the same year, Russia began to sell government-owned businesses to individuals and private companies. This process was called **privatization.** But few Russians had enough money to buy large businesses. So, leaders offered vouchers to the public. The vouchers were like loans that could be used to purchase businesses. The purchasers promised to repay the government with future profits.

But the policy had mixed success. Many of the new businesses were not profitable, and their owners were unable to repay their vouchers. The failures contributed to an economic crash in Russia in 1998. In spite of this shaky start, though, over 60 percent of the country's workforce worked in the private sector by the end of the 20th century.

THE HIGH COST OF ECONOMIC CHANGE Since the 1998 crash, Russia's economy has moved slowly toward recovery. But the movement toward a market economy has yet to benefit most Russians. By the end of the 1990s, nearly 40 percent of the Russian population lived

PLACE The many Western fast-food chains popping up in Moscow are symbols of economic change.
Why might fast-food chains have been rare in Russia before 1991?

SUNSHINE STATE STANDARDS
Key Standard SS.D.2.4.1 The student understands how wages and prices are determined in market, command, tradition-based, and mixed economic systems and how economic systems can be evaluated by their ability to achieve broad social goals such as freedom, efficiency, equity, security, and growth.

FCAT LA.A.2.4.1 Reading: Identify Main Idea, Details, and Methods far below the poverty line. Some people even wondered whether things had been better under the Soviet Union.

Obstacles to Economic Reform

Russians have made slow, if painful, strides toward capitalism. Even so, many obstacles remain. Russia's enormous size and the rise of organized crime are among the most important.

DISTANCE DECAY A major obstacle facing economic reformers is **distance decay.** This means that long distances between places make communication and transportation difficult. Russia is an enormous nation, stretching across 11 time zones. Spread over this vast area are 89 different regional governments. The interaction and cooperation of these regional leaders with Moscow is crucial if the government's economic reforms are to be successful. But because the central government in Moscow has been weak, officials far from the capital sometimes refuse to carry out the government's reform programs.

In the spring of 2000, Russian President Vladimir Putin created seven large federal districts to gain more control over regional leaders. Each has its own governor-general. Putin hopes that the heads of the new federal districts will force regional officials to carry out the economic reforms that Moscow wants. ◢

Geographic Thinking ◄

Seeing Patterns

Ⓐ Some Russians have objected to the creation of new federal districts. Why might there be disagreement over the districts?

Federal Districts of Russia

Central
Far Eastern
Northwest
Siberian
Southern
Urals
Volga
★ District Capital

St. Petersburg
Moscow
Nizhniy Novgorod
Yekaterinburg
Rostov
Novosibirsk
Khabarovsk

0   500   1,000 miles
0   500   1,000 kilometers
Two-Point Equidistant Projection

White lines indicate Russia's 89 regional governments.

SKILLBUILDER: Interpreting Maps

❶ **PLACE** What is the capital of the Northwest Federal District?

❷ **LOCATION** Approximately how many miles separate Moscow and Khabarovsk?

ORGANIZED CRIME As the government tries to improve the economy, it must also face a powerful enemy—organized crime. The "Russian mafia," as criminal organizations in the republic are sometimes labeled, grew rapidly during the 1990s.

By the end of the decade, the mafia had created its own economy. In 1998, the government estimated that organized criminals controlled 40 percent of private companies and 60 percent of state-owned enterprises. Russian criminal activity also expanded outside of Russia. The mafia even tried to sell a Russian submarine to drug barons in Colombia.

PLACE Officers from a special police force in Moscow arrest a suspected mafia car thief in August 1997. **Why might organized crime present a special problem for the Russian government?**

The growth of organized crime has slowed economic reform by rewarding illegal activity over honest business. And because illegal activities often go undetected, the government cannot collect taxes on them. Russian officials have taken initiatives to combat organized crime, including the addition of more officers to a special tax police.

FUTURE PROSPECTS In February 2001, Russia's prime minister reported increases in tax and customs revenues. Government officials said the increases are a sign that the Russian economy is on track. If the growth in revenues continues, Russia will be better able to come to terms with the legacy of the Soviet Union and will be able to improve the living standards of its population.

In addition to the economic problems inherited from the Soviet Union, this legacy includes the problems created by Soviet nuclear programs, which you will read about in the next section.

SECTION 2 Assessment

❶ Places & Terms
Explain the importance of each of the following terms.
- privatization
- distance decay

❷ Taking Notes
REGION Review the notes you took for this section.

	Causes	Effects
Issue 2: Economy		

- Why did the Russian government issue vouchers in 1992?
- What impact might organized crime have on government revenue?

❸ Main Ideas
a. What is one of the toughest issues facing Russia's economic reformers?

b. How has Russia moved toward a capitalist system?

c. What are some of the obstacles to economic reform?

❹ Geographic Thinking
Drawing Conclusions Why did President Putin establish seven new federal districts in Russia? **Think about:**
- the number of its regional governments
- Russia's size

S **See Skillbuilder Handbook, page R5.**

SEEING PATTERNS Do research on a U.S. company doing business in Russia. Create a set of **guidelines** that the company might follow in conducting business in Russia.

SUNSHINE STATE STANDARDS
Key Standard SS.D.2.4.5 The student understands basic terms and indicators associated with levels of economic performance and the stateof the economy.
FCAT LA.A.1.4.2 Reading: Strategies

Reading Line and Pie Graphs

Russia's economy has changed dramatically since the fall of the Soviet Union. To keep track of these changes and plan for the future, economists gather statistics. Presenting statistical data visually in graph form makes the data easier to read.

THE LANGUAGE OF GRAPHS **Line graphs** show the relation between two variables. The line graph below shows changes in Russia's unemployment rate. The vertical axis lists rates of unemployment. The horizontal axis shows the passage of time.

Pie graphs use percentages to show the relationship of parts to a whole. The pie represents the whole, and each slice of the pie represents a part. The pie graph below shows the distribution of income in Russia.

Economic Conditions in Russia

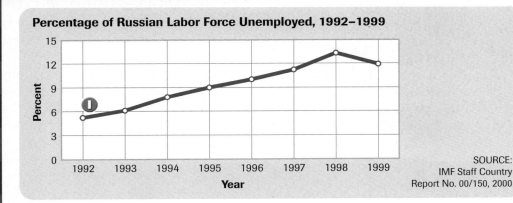

Percentage of Russian Labor Force Unemployed, 1992–1999

SOURCE: IMF Staff Country Report No. 00/150, 2000

❶ After the Soviet Union and its command economy collapsed in 1991, Russia became a separate republic. As it struggled to reform its economy, the rate of unemployment began to rise.

❷ In 1999, only 18.5 percent of Russia's population earned more than $981.

❸ The color key shows the income ranges that correspond to the different slices of the pie graph.

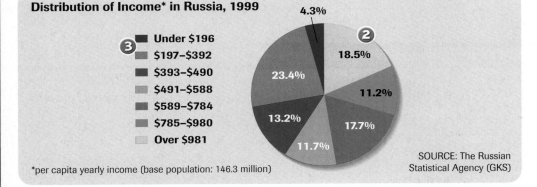

Distribution of Income* in Russia, 1999

❸
- Under $196
- $197–$392
- $393–$490
- $491–$588
- $589–$784
- $785–$980
- Over $981

*per capita yearly income (base population: 146.3 million)

SOURCE: The Russian Statistical Agency (GKS)

Map and Graph Skills Assessment

1. Seeing Patterns
What was the trend in Russia's unemployment rate after 1992? When did it begin to change?

2. Analyzing Data
What was Russia's unemployment rate in 1998?

3. Analyzing Data
What percentage of Russians earned less than $491 in 1999?

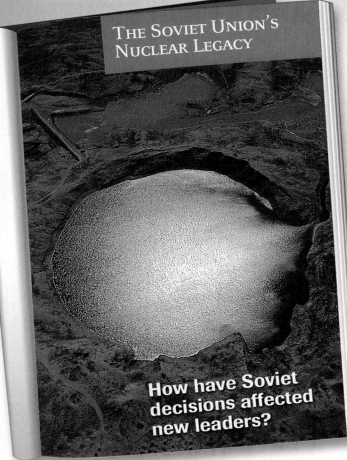

THE SOVIET UNION'S NUCLEAR LEGACY

How have Soviet decisions affected new leaders?

In 1965, Soviet officials used a nuclear bomb to create this reservoir in Semey, Kazakhstan.

A s you have read, the breakup of the Soviet Union sparked regional conflicts and economic hardship. Equally serious were the problems caused by the Soviet Union's nuclear programs. These included nuclear warheads atop ballistic missiles, poorly constructed and maintained nuclear power stations, and decaying nuclear waste dumps. All threatened the region's people and environment.

An Unwelcome Legacy

When the USSR fell apart in the early 1990s, leaders around the world had serious concerns about the fate of the region's nuclear weapons. The Soviet Union, which had once controlled those weapons, was now separated into 15 independent republics. World leaders wanted to know who was in control of the weapons, where they were located, and how well they were protected. They also wondered what would become of the nuclear scientists who had worked on the weapons systems.

The weapons industry was just part of the problem. As the 1986 disaster at Chernobyl had so clearly shown, many of the region's nuclear reactors were badly built and poorly managed. Many reactors of the same design as the one that exploded at Chernobyl still exist. Observers fear another disaster may occur in the region.

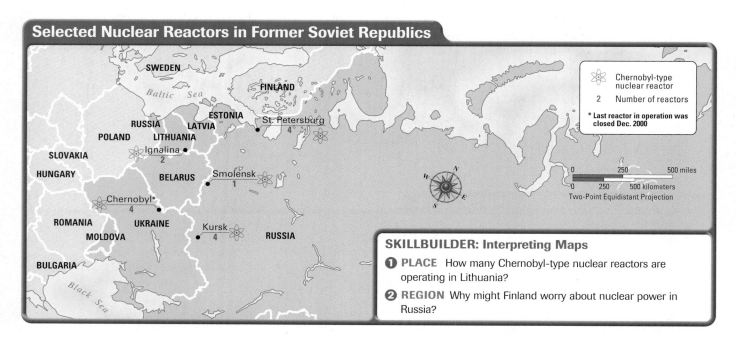

Selected Nuclear Reactors in Former Soviet Republics

Chernobyl-type nuclear reactor

2   Number of reactors

* Last reactor in operation was closed Dec. 2000

0   250   500 miles
0   250   500 kilometers
Two-Point Equidistant Projection

SKILLBUILDER: Interpreting Maps

❶ **PLACE** How many Chernobyl-type nuclear reactors are operating in Lithuania?

❷ **REGION** Why might Finland worry about nuclear power in Russia?

The Consequences of Collapse

The nuclear legacy of the USSR has had serious political, economic, and environmental consequences.

POLITICAL TENSIONS When the communist government could no longer keep the USSR together, the security of the region's nuclear materials became uncertain. This has caused political tension between the region's leaders and other nations, especially the United States.

SEE
PRIMARY SOURCE Ⓐ

In January 2000, a task force of former U.S. officials issued a report that suggested just how important the issue is. The report said that the possibility of Russian nuclear materials being stolen or misused is "the most urgent unmet national security threat" facing the United States. The task force recommended a $30 billion program to help ensure the safety of Russia's nuclear weapons.

ECONOMIC HEALTH The Soviet Union's nuclear legacy also affects the economic health of Russia and the former Soviet Republics. For example, many regional leaders have been reluctant to shut down aging Soviet reactors because of the expense of building new plants that run on other kinds of fuel, such as natural gas.

Some republics have taken questionable steps to revive their economies. For instance, Russian lawmakers recently approved plans to make their country the world's nuclear dump. In January 2001, the Duma, or legislature, gave preliminary approval to a plan to import, store, and treat nuclear waste from other countries. Officials hope the project will earn Russia as much as $21 billion over the next ten years.

ENVIRONMENTAL PROSPECTS Plans for the disposal of other nations' nuclear waste angered Russian environmentalists. But other developments have given some hope that the region's environmental prospects might improve. In December 2000, the government of Ukraine finally shut down the last active reactor at Chernobyl. Officials there pledged to spend millions of dollars on a new protective dome for the site.

Help has also come from overseas. In October 2000, a U.S.-funded treatment plant opened near the White Sea. The 17-million-dollar facility will treat radioactive waste from Russia's fleet of nuclear submarines—waste that used to be dumped in the sea.

SEE
PRIMARY SOURCE Ⓓ

You will learn more about these developments as you examine the primary sources and complete the Case Study Project on the following pages.

PLACE A Ukrainian official examines a nuclear missile just before it is to be dismantled as part of a U.S.-sponsored program. **Why would the United States sponsor this program in Ukraine?**

The Soviet Union's Nuclear Legacy **393**

CASESTUDY

Damage Assessment Report

Primary sources A to D on these two pages offer different views of the Soviet Union's nuclear legacy. Use these resources and your own research to prepare a damage assessment report of the region's nuclear situation today.

RESEARCH LINKS
CLASSZONE.COM

Suggested Steps

1. Choose a nuclear threat to investigate and examine its political, economic, and environmental consequences.

2. Use online and print resources to research your topic.

3. Be sure your damage assessment includes both causes and effects. Also, explain the steps being taken by regional officials to address the problems.

4. Search for interesting statistics, compelling stories, and first-person accounts to enliven your assessment.

5. Provide maps, charts, graphs, and photos to add visual interest to the assessment.

6. Prepare a brief oral introduction that introduces and explains your topic.

Materials and Supplies

- posterboard
- colored markers
- computer with Internet access
- reference books, newspapers, and magazines
- printer

PRIMARY SOURCE A

Political Cartoon *This cartoon by* **Nick Anderson** *illustrates the frightening prospect of a collapsing nuclear superpower.*

Copyright © 2000 Nick Anderson, The Washington Post Writers Group. Reprinted with permission.

Editorial Commentary *On January 21, 1999, the* New York Times *offered its comments on Russia's nuclear legacy.*

There is no longer any threat of Russia's deliberately attacking the United States. But Moscow's still-formidable stocks of nuclear bombs, nuclear ingredients, and biological and chemical warfare agents pose a different kind of danger. Much of this material is inadequately secured, and the workers guarding it are paid poorly or not at all. That creates an unacceptably high risk that some material could be sold to potential aggressors like Iraq, Libya, North Korea, or Serbia. Many Russian weapons scientists are also unemployed or unpaid and vulnerable to foreign recruitment.

During the Cold War, the United States spent trillions of dollars to deter Russia from using its nuclear, biological, and chemical weapons. It would not take much more than $10 billion to eliminate most of the risks from those weapons today.

News Report *In his dispatch of September 30, 1997,* London Daily Telegraph *reporter Christopher Lockwood relates yet another terrible tale from Russia's nuclear legacy of an environmental disaster waiting to happen.*

Nothing on the outside indicates what lies within the retired Russian supply ship *Lepse* except the presence of a Kalashnikov-armed guard and the fact that the vessel is moored at the farthest possible point of the Atomplot shipyard in Murmansk.

In fact, *Lepse* may well be the most terrifying vessel on Earth, loaded with a deadly cargo of warped nuclear-reactor parts and spent fuel rods that would be sufficient to poison the world's population. . . .

For the past six years, Norway and Finland have been negotiating with Russia in an attempt to clear up the mess left by Russia's Northern Fleet, which had its headquarters in Severomorsk, near Murmansk. About 200 disused nuclear reactors and tens of thousands of fuel rods are haphazardly stored at its bases around Murmansk, in the Kola Peninsula.

"If there is a catastrophe in the Kola Peninsula, it can affect the whole of Europe's climate, perhaps for hundreds of years," said Norwegian Defense Minister Joergen Kosmo.

News Report *On December 15, 2000, 14 years and 7 months after the reactor explosion at Chernobyl, Ukraine's president ordered the plant closed. The excerpt below, written by* New York Times *reporter Michael Wines, outlines the economic impact that the shutdown will have.*

The closing of Unit 3 [the plant's last working reactor] will cut off 5 percent of the electricity supply in a nation already deeply in [debt] to Russia for natural gas and dogged by shortages in its shoddily run power grid.

The closing will also gradually eliminate jobs of thousands of Ukrainians whose work depends, directly or indirectly, on Chernobyl's continued operation as a power plant. Beyond the layoffs at the plant itself, thousands of Ukrainians provide goods or services to Chernobyl workers.

Ukraine also faces immense costs in the future— $750 million to cover the disaster site with a new [protective dome], hundreds of additional millions of dollars to remove 180 tons of lethal melted fuel and steel from the damaged core of Unit 4 and to store it safely, millions to build a new heating system and other necessities for the crews that will permanently care for the idle reactor site and millions for solid and liquid waste-processing plants to handle the fuel from the closing of Unit 3.

PROJECT **CheckList**

Have I . . .

✓ fully researched my topic?

✓ balanced my report by discussing both sides of the issue?

✓ created informative visuals that make my report clear and interesting?

✓ practiced explaining my report?

✓ anticipated questions others might ask and prepared answers?

VISUAL SUMMARY
TODAY'S ISSUES IN RUSSIA AND THE REPUBLICS

Conflict

Regional Conflict

- Since the fall of the Soviet Union in 1991, a number of ethnic and religious groups have sought more control over their own affairs. Their demands have frequently led to conflict.

- Regional leaders who are trying to end these conflicts face a dilemma. How can they maintain order without resorting to the undemocratic rule of the past?

Economics

The Struggle for Economic Reform

- Another dilemma facing leaders in Russia and the former Soviet republics is how to move away from the old Soviet command economy toward a market economy.

- Leaders are struggling to make reforms without causing too much turmoil for citizens.

Government

The Soviet Union's Nuclear Legacy

- The impact of Soviet nuclear programs did not end with the fall of the Soviet Union in 1991. Russia and the Republics inherited the former state's nuclear weapons, power plants, and waste.

- This legacy has had serious political, economic, and environmental consequences.

Reviewing Places & Terms

A. Briefly explain the importance of each of the following.

1. Caucasus
2. Chechnya
3. Nagorno-Karabakh
4. privatization
5. distance decay

B. Answer the questions about vocabulary in complete sentences.

6. In which nation is Chechnya located?
7. Which region is the subject of a dispute between Armenia and Azerbaijan?
8. How might a nation move from a command economy to a market economy?
9. What is another name for Caucasia?
10. What is the name for the decreasing interaction between places as the distance between them increases?

Main Ideas

Regional Conflict (pp. 385–387)

1. What is the connection between the fall of the Soviet Union and the outbreak of ethnic conflicts in Russia and the Republics?
2. Why might ethnic tensions in the Caucasus be stronger than in other regions?
3. In the Russian part of Caucasia, where has the most serious conflict taken place?

The Struggle for Economic Reform (pp. 388–391)

4. Over the past decade, what has been one of the major goals of Russian economic reformers?
5. How have reformers moved Russia toward a market economy?
6. What are some of the problems faced by economic reformers?

Case Study: The Soviet Union's Nuclear Legacy (pp. 392–395)

7. Why were world leaders concerned about the security of nuclear weapons in Russia and the Republics after 1991?
8. What other aspect of the Soviet nuclear legacy concerned observers?
9. How has the United States assisted Russia in dealing with the nuclear legacy of the Soviet Union?
10. How are the nuclear policies of Russia related to its economic problems?

Critical Thinking

1. Using Your Notes

Use your completed chart to answer these questions.

	Causes	Effects
Issue 1: Conflict		
Issue 2: Economy		

a. What caused several ethnic groups in the Caucasus to believe they might successfully demand independence in the 1990s?

b. What is the intended effect of Russia's new federal districts?

2. Geographic Themes

REGION Why did the division of the USSR into 15 independent republics concern observers of the region's nuclear programs?

3. Identifying Themes

Why did the United States fund a nuclear waste treatment plant near the White Sea? Which of the five themes applies to this situation?

4. Making Inferences

Why might Russian economic reformers worry about causing too much hardship for citizens?

5. Drawing Conclusions

Why do you think Russian legislators want to import, store, and treat nuclear waste from other countries in spite of the environmental risks involved?

Additional Test Practice, pp. S1–S37

TEST PRACTICE
CLASSZONE.COM

Geographic Skills: Interpreting Graphs

Global Male Life Expectancy

Use the graph to answer the following questions.

1. **PLACE** How does male life expectancy in Russia differ from world trends?

2. **PLACE** What was the life expectancy of Russian men in 1990? In 2000?

3. **PLACE** What might account for the dip in life expectancy for Russian men?

Create another line graph that shows how the population of Russia changed during the same period of time.

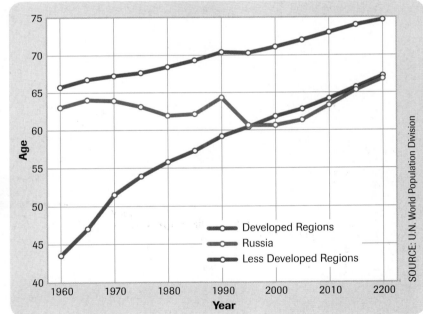

SOURCE: U.N. World Population Division

- Developed Regions
- Russia
- Less Developed Regions

INTERNET ACTIVITY

Use the links at **classzone.com** to do research on current economic conditions in Russia. Compare the statistics you find on the Russian economy, such as inflation and poverty rates, with statistics on the U.S. economy.

Creating a Multimedia Presentation Create a multimedia presentation of your findings. Include maps and graphs that visually present the information that you discovered.

Unit 6

Africa

Africa is the world's second largest continent. Its unique location—almost centered over the equator—affects its vegetation, climate, and population patterns.

LOCATION
A man prays in front of the pyramids at Giza in Egypt.

MOVEMENT
People travel to a market outside of Mali's Great Mosque in Djenné. The mosque is one of the world's largest mud-brick buildings.

REGION Around 650 million of Africa's 800 million people live south of the Sahara. They are divided into more than 800 ethnic groups, each with its own language, religion, and culture.

HUMAN-ENVIRONMENT INTERACTION Roughly two-thirds of all Africans live in rural areas or small villages and earn a living as farmers.

PLACE The ancient Romans called the continent Africa, possibly from the Latin *aprica,* meaning "sunny," or the Greek *aphrike,* meaning "without cold."

For more information on Africa . . .

RESEARCH LINKS
CLASSZONE.COM

PLACE Africa's tallest mountain, Mount Kilimanjaro, towers above northeastern Tanzania as a giraffe roams the grassy plain below.

399

Unit PREVIEW 6

Today's Issues in Africa

Africa faces the issues previewed here. As you read Chapters 18 and 19, you will learn background information. You will study the issues themselves in Chapter 20. In a small group, answer the questions below. Then have a class discussion of your answers.

Exploring the Issues

1. **ECONOMIC DEVELOPMENT** Make a list of some of the pros and cons of economic development. How would economic development benefit people living in Africa?

2. **HEALTH CARE** Search the Internet for information about how African nations are trying to slow the spread of various diseases. What strategies and actions are being employed by these countries?

3. **EFFECTS OF COLONIALISM** Find one news story about political or ethnic violence. How might colonialism be a cause or have contributed to the problem?

For more on these issues in Africa . . .

CURRENT EVENTS
CLASSZONE.COM

ECONOMIC DEVELOPMENT

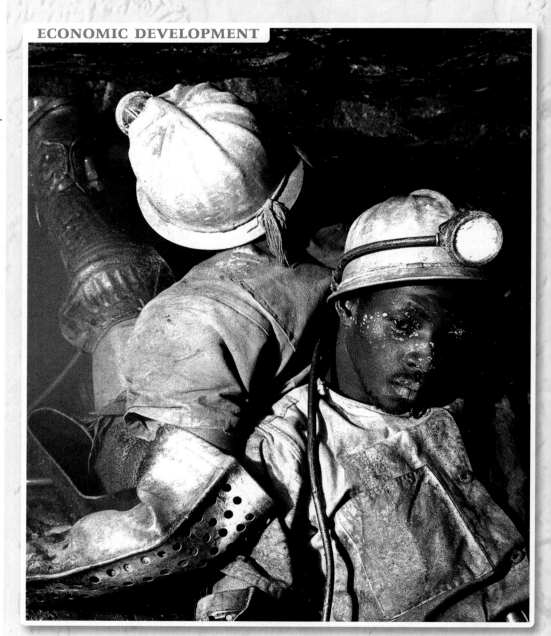

How can African nations develop their economies?

African nations rely too much on the exportation of natural resources. These miners in Johannesburg, South Africa, mine gold, one of the country's main exports.

HEALTH CARE

How can African countries eliminate the diseases that threaten their people and cultures?

A health clinic in Nairobi, Kenya, attempts to slow the spread of AIDS through various education programs.

← CLINIC

CASESTUDY

How can African nations bring peace and stability to their people?

Many African countries are still suffering from the effects of colonialism. Africa's problems after colonialism are shown in this cartoon about the Democratic Republic of the Congo (formerly known as Zaire). This cartoon shows that there are no easy solutions.

EFFECTS OF COLONIALISM

APATHY

NEGLECT

ZAIRE

AMBIVALENCE

INTERNATIONAL COMMUNITY

INTERVENTION

DESTINATION UNKNOWN...

KING
30·10·96
THE CITIZEN

Patterns of Physical Geography

SUNSHINE STATE STANDARDS
Key Standard SS.B.1.4.1 The student uses uses a variety of maps, geographic technologies including geographic information systems (GIS) and satellite-produced imagery, and other advanced graphic representations to depict geographic problems.

Other Standards SS.B.2.4.1, B.2.4.3

Use the Unit Atlas to add to your knowledge of Africa. As you look at the maps and charts, notice geographic patterns and specific details about the region. After studying the graphs and physical map on these two pages, jot down in your notebook the answers to the questions below.

Making Comparisons

1. Compare Africa's size and population to that of the United States. How much larger in terms of population and size is Africa compared to the United States?

2. Compare Africa's longest river, the Nile, to the Mississippi. How much difference is there in the lengths?

3. How much bigger is the Sahara than the largest desert in the United States? What is the difference in size between the Sahara and the continental United States?

For updated statistics on Africa . . .

DATA UPDATE
CLASSZONE.COM

Comparing Data

FCAT LA.A.2.2.7 Reading: Recognize Compare and Contrast

Landmass

Africa
11,677,240 sq mi

Continental United States
3,165,630 sq mi

Population

Africa 800,245,000
United States 281,422,000

| 0 | 100 | 200 | 300 | 400 | 500 | 600 | 700 | 800 | 900 |

Population (in millions)

Rivers

Niger 2,600 miles
Congo 2,900 miles
U.S. Longest
Mississippi 2,357 miles
World's Longest
Nile 4,160 miles

| 0 | 1000 | 2000 | 3000 | 4000 | 5000 |

Length (in miles)

Deserts

World's Largest
Sahara
Africa
3,500,000 sq. miles

U.S. Largest
Mojave
United States
25,000
square miles

Namib
Africa
102,248
square miles

Kalahari
Africa
about 100,000
square miles

Africa: Physical

UNITED KINGDOM
GERMANY
FRANCE
SWITZ.
HUNGARY
CROATIA
ROMANIA
YUGO.
ITALY
BULGARIA
SPAIN
ALB.
PORTUGAL
GREECE
TURKEY
Strait of Gibraltar
ATLAS MOUNTAINS
Mediterranean Sea
CYPRUS
LEBANON
SYRIA
IRAN
Madeira Is. (Port.)
MOROCCO
TUNISIA
Gulf of Sidra
Suez Canal
ISRAEL
IRAQ
Canary Islands
JORDAN
KUWAIT
WESTERN SAHARA (MOROCCO)
ALGERIA
LIBYA
EGYPT
SAUDI ARABIA
QATAR
AHAGGAR MOUNTAINS
Nile R.
U.A.E.
Cape Verde
Tropic of Cancer
L. Nasser
S A H A R A
Nubian Desert
Red Sea
MAURITANIA
Tibesti Mountains
Senegal R.
MALI
NIGER
CAPE VERDE
S A H E L
CHAD
ERITREA
YEMEN
SENEGAL
Niger R.
Blue Nile
Gulf of Aden
GAMBIA
BURKINA FASO
SUDAN
DJIBOUTI
GUINEA-BISSAU
L. Chad
White Nile
L. Tana
GUINEA
NIGERIA
ETHIOPIAN PLATEAU
HORN OF AFRICA
SIERRA LEONE
CÔTE D'IVOIRE
GHANA
TOGO
BENIN
Benue R.
ETHIOPIA
LIBERIA
Mt. Cameroon 13,451 ft. (4,100 m)
CENTRAL AFRICAN REPUBLIC
Gulf of Guinea
CAMEROON
SOMALIA
EQUATORIAL GUINEA
SÃO TOMÉ AND PRÍNCIPE
Ubangi R.
Congo R.
UGANDA
KENYA
Mt. Kenya 17,058 ft. (5,199 m)
Equator
GABON
REP. OF CONGO
C O N G O B A S I N
L. Turkana
ATLANTIC OCEAN
DEMOCRATIC REPUBLIC OF CONGO
RWANDA
BURUNDI
Lake Victoria
Mt. Kilimanjaro 19,341 ft. (5,895 m)
SEYCHELLES
ANGOLA
TANZANIA
Pemba Is.
Zanzibar Is.
L. Tanganyika
Katanga Plateau
COMOROS
St. Helena
ANGOLA
ZAMBIA
MALAWI
L. Nyasa
Victoria Falls
Zambezi R.
MOZAMBIQUE
MAURITIUS
NAMIBIA
ZIMBABWE
Mozambique Channel
MADAGASCAR
Réunion
Tropic of Capricorn
NAMIB DESERT
BOTSWANA
Limpopo R.
K A L A H A R I D E S E R T
Orange R.
LESOTHO
SWAZILAND
SOUTH AFRICA
Karroo
Drakensberg
INDIAN OCEAN
Cape of Good Hope

AFRICA

Elevation
13,100 ft. (4,000 m.)
6,600 ft. (2,000 m.)
1,600 ft. (500 m.)
650 ft. (200 m.)
0 ft. (0 m.)
Below sea level
▲ Mountain peak

0 400 800 miles
0 400 800 kilometers
Lambert Azimuthal Equal-Area Projection

403

Unit ATLAS

Patterns of Human Geography

Colonialism in Africa, 1913

In the years preceding World War I (1914–1918), the political map of Africa changed dramatically. European colonial powers had replaced traditional African states and empires. Study the political maps of Africa in 1913 and Africa today to see how the continent changed by the end of the 20th century. Then answer these questions in your notebook.

Making Comparisons

1. What independent nations appear on the map of Africa in 1913 and also appear on the map of Africa today?

2. Which two European powers controlled the most land in Africa in 1913? Which country controlled the least amount?

3. Which countries in Africa today formed French West Africa in 1913?

4. Which three African countries emerged from colonialism with the most territory?

UNITED KINGDOM

FRANCE SWITZ. GERMANY
CROATIA HUNGARY ROMANIA
PORTUGAL SPAIN ITALY YUGO. BULGARIA
ALB. GREECE TURKEY
MADEIRA IS. (Port.)
Strait of Gibraltar
Algiers Tunis
Oran Mediterranean Sea
Rabat TUNISIA Tripoli
Casablanca MOROCCO Gulf of Sidra
CANARY ISLANDS (Spain)
CYPRUS SYRIA
LEBANON
ISRAEL
Suez Canal
Alexandria JORDAN
Cairo
Giza
IRAQ
IRAN
KUWAIT
SAUDI ARABIA
QATAR
U.A.E.

WESTERN SAHARA (MOROCCO)
ALGERIA
LIBYA
EGYPT
Nile R.
L. Nasser
Red Sea
Tropic of Cancer

CAPE VERDE
Praia
MAURITANIA
Nouakchott
MALI
Senegal R.
Dakar SENEGAL
Banjul GAMBIA
Bissau
GUINEA-BISSAU
Bamako
Niger R.
BURKINA FASO
Niamey
NIGER
CHAD
N'Djamena
L. Chad
Omdurman
Khartoum
SUDAN
White Nile
Blue Nile
ERITREA
Asmara
DJIBOUTI Gulf of Aden
Djibouti
L. Tana

Conakry GUINEA
Freetown SIERRA LEONE
Monrovia LIBERIA
Yamoussoukro
CÔTE D'IVOIRE
Ouagadougou
GHANA
Abidjan Accra
Lomé
TOGO
BENIN
Porto-Novo
Ibadan
Lagos
NIGERIA
Abuja
Benue R.
CAMEROON
Douala
Yaoundé
Malabo
EQUATORIAL GUINEA
SÃO TOMÉ AND PRÍNCIPE
Gulf of Guinea
CENTRAL AFRICAN REPUBLIC
Bangui
Ubangi R.
Congo R.
ETHIOPIA
Addis Ababa
SOMALIA
Mogadishu

Libreville
São Tomé
GABON
REPUBLIC OF CONGO
Brazzaville
Kinshasa
DEMOCRATIC REPUBLIC OF CONGO
RWANDA
Kigali
BURUNDI
Bujumbura
UGANDA
Kampala
Lake Victoria
KENYA
Nairobi
TANZANIA
Pemba
Zanzibar
Dar es Salaam
SEYCHELLES
Victoria
Equator

ATLANTIC OCEAN
Luanda
ANGOLA
Lubumbashi
L. Tanganyika
L. Nyasa
ZAMBIA
MALAWI
Lilongwe
COMOROS
Moroni

ST. HELENA (U.K.)
Lusaka
Victoria Falls
Zambezi R.
Harare
ZIMBABWE
MOZAMBIQUE
Mozambique Channel
MADAGASCAR
Antananarivo
MAURITIUS
Port Louis
RÉUNION (Fr.)

NAMIBIA
BOTSWANA
Limpopo R.
Windhoek
Tropic of Capricorn
Gaborone
Pretoria
Maputo
Johannesburg
Mbabane
SWAZILAND
Orange R.
Bloemfontein
Maseru
LESOTHO
Durban
SOUTH AFRICA
Cape Town
INDIAN OCEAN

N W E S

★ National capital
● Other city

0 400 800 miles
0 400 800 kilometers
Lambert Azimuthal Equal-Area Projection

AFRICA

Unit ATLAS

Regional Patterns

These two pages contain a graph and two thematic maps. The graph shows the religions of Africa. The maps show other important features of Africa: its diversity of languages and its population distribution. After studying these two pages, jot down in your notebook the answers to the questions below.

Making Comparisons

1. Where are most of the people in Africa living? In what areas of Africa are the fewest people living?

2. What geographic factors may account for these population patterns?

3. What do you notice about the number of languages in Africa? Do they belong to one language group or several?

Religions of Africa

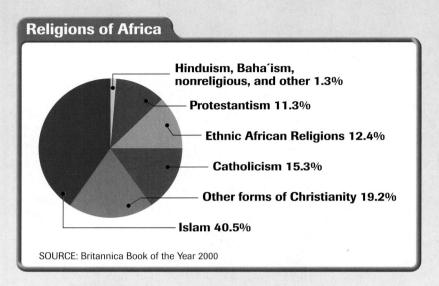

Hinduism, Baha'ism, nonreligious, and other 1.3%

Protestantism 11.3%

Ethnic African Religions 12.4%

Catholicism 15.3%

Other forms of Christianity 19.2%

Islam 40.5%

SOURCE: Britannica Book of the Year 2000

Population Distribution of Africa

Metropolitan Areas
- One dot represents 100,000 people
- ◉ Greater than 10 million
- • 2 to 6 million

0   400   800 miles
0   400   800 kilometers
Lambert Azimuthal Equal-Area Projection

Languages of Africa

Strait of Gibraltar

Mediterranean Sea

Arabic

Arabic

Red Sea

Tuareg

Teda

Arabic

Beja

Gulf of Aden

Fulani

Wolof

Malinke

Bambara

Songhai

More

Hausa

Kanuri

Fulani

Nuer

Amharic

Mende

Akan

Yoruba

Fulani

Oromo

Igbo

Sango

Dinka

Somali

Gulf of Guinea

Lingala

Ganda

Kikuyu

Kinyarwanda

ATLANTIC

OCEAN

Kongo

Kirundi

Masai

N

W — E

S

Luba

Swahili

Bemba

Mbundu

Makua

Shona

Mozambique Channel

Malagasy

!Kung

Nama

Sotho

Zulu

INDIAN

OCEAN

Afrikaans

Xhosa

English

Legend

	Afro-Asiatic
	Austronesian
	Indo-European
	Khoisan
	Niger-Congo
	Nilo-Saharan
Luba	Language spoken

0   400   800 miles

0   400   800 kilometers

Lambert Azimuthal Equal-Area Projection

AFRICA

Regional Data File

Unit ATLAS

Country Flag	Country/ Capital	Population (2000)	Life Expectancy[a] (years) (2000)	Birthrate (per 1,000 pop.) (2000)	Infant Mortality (per 1,000 live births) (2000)
	Algeria Algiers	31,471,000	69	29	44.0
	Angola Luanda	12,878,000	47	48	125.0
	Benin Porto-Novo	6,396,000	50	45	93.9
	Botswana Gaborone	1,576,000	44	32	57.2
	Burkina Faso Ouagadougou	11,946,000	47	47	105.3
	Burundi Bujumbura	6,054,000	47	42	74.8
	Cameroon Yaoundé	15,422,000	55	37	77.0
	Cape Verde Praia	401,000	68	37	76.9
	Central African Republic, Bangui	3,513,000	45	38	96.7
	Chad N'Djamena	7,977,000	48	50	109.8
	Comoros Moroni	578,000	59	38	77.3
	Congo, Democratic Republic of, Kinshasa	51,965,000	49	48	108.6
	Congo, Republic of, Brazzaville	2,831,000	48	40	108.6
	Côte d'Ivoire Yamoussoukro	15,980,000	47	38	112.2
	Djibouti Djibouti	638,000	48	39	115.0
	Egypt Cairo	68,344,000	65	26	52.3
	Equatorial Guinea Malabo	453,000	50	41	108.0
	Eritrea Asmara	4,142,000	55	43	81.8

Study the charts on the countries of Africa. In your notebook, answer these questions.

Making Comparisons

1. Which three African countries have the most people? Locate them on the map. Are they also the largest countries in terms of total area?

2. Which three African countries have the fewest people? Locate them on the map. Are they the smallest countries in terms of total area?

3. Look at Angola's life expectancy, infant mortality, and number of doctors. Judging from these statistics, does Angola have good health care?

(continued on page 410)

Notes:
[a] Life expectancy figures for many African countries are declining significantly, mainly due to poverty, politics, and the spread of AIDS.
[b] Doctors are defined as graduates of a school of medicine in any medical field.
[c] A comparison of the prices of the same items in different countries is used to figure these data.
[d] Includes land and water, when figures are available.

For updated statistics on Africa . . .

DATA UPDATE
CLASSZONE.COM

Doctors[b] (per 100,000 pop.) (1992–1998)	GDP[c] (billions $US) (1999)	Import/Export[c] (billions $US) (1997–1999)	Literacy Rate (percentage) (1998–1999)	Televisions (per 1,000 pop.) (1996–1998)	Passenger Cars (per 1,000 pop.) (1996–1997)	Total Area[d] (square miles)	
85	147.6	9.3 / 13.7	66	68	17	919,590	
8	11.6	3.0 / 5.0	42	124	21	481,351	
6	8.1	0.566 / 0.396	38	91	6	43,483	
24	5.7	2.05 / 2.36	76	27	53	231,804	
3	12.4	0.572 / 0.311	22	6	3	105,869	
6	4.2	0.108 / 0.056	46	10	2	10,759	
7	31.5	1.5 / 2.0	74	81	7	183,591	
17	0.618	0.225 / 0.038	73	45	29	1,557	
4	5.8	0.17 / 0.195	44	5	3	240,534	
3	7.6	0.359 / 0.288	39	2	1	495,752	
7	0.41 (1998)	0.05 / 0.009	59	4	18	719	
7	35.7	0.46 / 0.53	59	43	7	905,365	
25	4.15	0.77 / 1.7	78	8	10	132, 047	
9	25.7	2.6 / 3.9	45	70	11	124,503	
14	0.55	0.44 / 0.26	62	73	31	8,958	
202	200.0	15.8 / 4.6	54	127	20	386,900	
25	0.96	0.3 / 0.555	81	162	9	10,830	
3	2.9	0.44 / 0.053	52	14	2	47,320	

Unit ATLAS

Regional Data File

Making Comparisons
(continued)

4. Use the map on page 405 to choose a country in East Africa. How many televisions and cars does it have per 1,000 people? How does that compare to the United States?

5. Make a list of the top three African countries in GDP. Where are these countries located? Do you notice any pattern?

6. Use the map on page 405 to identify two countries in Southern Africa. For each of those countries, calculate per capita GDP by dividing total GDP by population. Which country has the higher per capita GDP?

(continued on page 412)

Country Flag	Country/ Capital	Population (2000)	Life Expectancy[a] (years) (2000)	Birthrate (per 1,000 pop.) (2000)	Infant Mortality (per 1,000 live births) (2000)
	Ethiopia Addis Ababa	64,117,000	46	45	116.0
	Gabon Libreville	1,226,000	52	38	87.0
	Gambia Banjul	1,305,000	45	43	130.0
	Ghana Accra	19,534,000	58	34	56.2
	Guinea Conakry	7,466,000	45	42	98.0
	Guinea-Bissau Bissau	1,213,000	45	42	130.0
	Kenya Nairobi	30,340,000	49	35	73.7
	Lesotho Maseru	2,143,000	53	33	84.5
	Liberia Monrovia	3,164,000	50	50	139.1
	Libya Tripoli	5,114,000	75	28	33.3
	Madagascar Antananarivo	14,858,000	52	44	96.3
	Malawi Lilongwe	10,385,000	39	41	126.8
	Mali Bamako	11,234,000	53	47	122.5
	Mauritania Nouakchott	2,670,000	54	41	92.0
	Mauritius Port Louis	1,189,000	70	17	19.4
	Morocco Rabat	28,778,000	69	23	37.0
	Mozambique Maputo	19,105,000	40	41	133.9
	Namibia Windhoek	1,771,000	46	36	68.3

Notes:

[a] Life expectancy figures for many African countries are declining significantly, mainly due to poverty, politics, and the spread of AIDS.

[b] Doctors are defined as graduates of a school of medicine in any medical field.

[c] A comparison of the prices of the same items in different countries is used to figure these data.

[d] Includes land and water, when figures are available.

Doctors[b] (per 100,000 pop.) (1992–1998)	GDP[c] (billions $US) (1999)	Import/Export[c] (billions $US) (1997–1999)	Literacy Rate (percentage) (1998–1999)	Televisions (per 1,000 pop.) (1996–1998)	Passenger Cars (per 1,000 pop.) (1996–1997)	Total Area[d] (square miles)	
4	33.3	1.25 / 0.42	36	5	0.8	471,776	
19	7.9	1.2 / 2.4	63	136	21	103,346	
4	1.4	0.201 / 0.132	35	4	7	4,127	
6	35.5	2.5 / 1.7	69	115	5	92,100	
13	9.2	0.56 / 0.695	36	41	2	94,925	
17	1.1	0.023 / 0.027	37	N/A	3	13,948	
13	45.1	3.3 / 2.2	81	21	10	224,960	
5	4.7 (1998 est.)	0.7 / 0.235	82	24	3	11,720	
2	2.85	0.142 / 0.039	38	27	9	43,000	
128	39.3	7.0 / 6.6	78	143	126	679,358	
11	11.5	0.793 / 0.6	65	46	4	226,658	
2	9.4	0.512 / 0.51	58	2	3	47,747	
5	8.5	0.65 / 0.64	38	11	3	478,764	
14	4.9	0.444 / 0.425	41	91	7	397,955	
85	12.3	2.1 / 1.7	84	228	61	790	
46	108.0	9.5 / 7.1	47	160	39	172,413	
4	18.7	1.44 / 0.3	42	4	4	302,328	
30	7.1	1.5 / 1.4	81	32	38	318,000	

Unit ATLAS

Regional Data File

Making Comparisons
(continued)

7. Calculate the GDP per capita for Sierra Leone, Zambia, and Eritrea by dividing GDP by population. Where do those countries rank in life expectancy? What might be the relationship between a country's GDP and its life expectancy?

Country Flag	Country/ Capital	Population (2000)	Life Expectancy[a] (years) (2000)	Birthrate (per 1,000 pop.) (2000)	Infant Mortality (per 1,000 live births) (2000)
	Niger Niamey	10,076,000	41	54	123.1
	Nigeria Abuja	123,338,000	52	42	77.2
	Rwanda Kigali	7,229,000	39	43	120.9
	São Tomé and Príncipe São Tomé	160,000	64	43	50.8
	Senegal Dakar	9,481,000	52	41	67.7
	Seychelles Victoria	82,000	71	18	8.5
	Sierra Leone Freetown	5,233,000	45	47	157.1
	Somalia Mogadishu	7,253,000	46	47	125.8
	South Africa, Pretoria/ Cape Town/Bloemfontein	43,421,000	55	25	45.4
	Sudan Khartoum	29,490,000	51	33	69.5
	Swaziland Mbabane	1,004,000	38	41	107.7
	Tanzania Dodoma	35,306,000	53	42	98.8
	Togo Lomé	5,019,000	49	42	79.7
	Tunisia Tunis	9,619,000	69	22	35.0
	Uganda Kampala	23,318,000	42	48	81.3
	Zambia Lusaka	9,582,000	37	42	109.0
	Zimbabwe Harare	11,343,000	40	30	80.0
	United States Washington, D.C.	281,422,000	77	15	7.0

Sources:
ABC-CLIO
CIA World Factbook 2000 online
Columbia Gazetteer
Population Reference Bureau 2000 online
Statesman's Yearbook 2001
UN Human Development Report 2000
U.S. Census Bureau online
World Almanac 2000
World Health Organization online
N/A = not available

Notes:

[a] Life expectancy figures for many African countries are declining significantly, mainly due to poverty, politics, and the spread of AIDS.

[b] Doctors are defined as graduates of a school of medicine in any medical field.

[c] A comparison of the prices of the same items in different countries is used to figure these data.

[d] Includes land and water, when figures are available.

412 UNIT 6

Doctors[b] (per 100,000 pop.) (1992–1998)	GDP[c] (billions $US) (1999)	Import/Export[c] (billions $US) (1997–1999)	Literacy Rate (percentage) (1998–1999)	Televisions (per 1,000 pop.) (1996–1998)	Passenger Cars (per 1,000 pop.) (1996–1997)	Total Area[d] (square miles)	
4	9.6	0.266 / 0.269	15	26	4	489,189	
19	110.5	10.0 / 13.1	61	67	5	356,669	
4	5.9	0.242 / 0.071	64	N/A	2	10,169	
47	.169	0.02 / 0.005	73	227	30	372	
8	16.6	1.2 / 0.925	36	41	12	76,124	
132	.59	0.363 / 0.091	84	190	85	178	
7	2.5	0.166 / 0.041	31	26	4	27,699	
4	4.3	0.327 / 0.187	24	13	2	246,200	
56	296.1	26.0 / 28.0	85	125	102	471,445	
9	32.6	1.26 / 0.58	56	141	1	967,494	
15	4.2	1.05 / 0.825	78	107	29	6,705	
5	23.3	1.44 / 0.828	74	21	2	364,898	
8	8.6	0.45 / 0.4	55	20	17	21,853	
70	52.6	7.47 / 5.8	69	198	28	63,378	
4	24.2	1.1 / 0.471	65	26	1	91,134	
7	8.5	1.15 / 0.9	76	137	16	290,585	
14	26.5	2.0 / 2.0	87	29	3	150,820	
251	9,255.0	820.8 / 663.0	97	847	489	3,787,319	

SECTION 1
Landforms and Resources

SECTION 2
Climate and Vegetation

SECTION 3
Human–Environment Interaction

PHYSICAL GEOGRAPHY OF AFRICA
The Plateau Continent

The Zambezi River plunges over Victoria Falls on the border between Zambia and Zimbabwe.

GeoFocus

What effect does physical geography have on the lives of Africans?

Taking Notes Copy the graphic organizer below into your notebook. Use it to record information about the physical geography of Africa.

Landforms	
Resources	
Climate and Vegetation	
Human–Environment Interaction	

Landforms and Resources

Main Ideas

- A large plateau covers most of Africa.
- Africa's natural resources made it appealing to European colonizers.

Places & Terms

basin
Nile River
rift valley
Mount Kilimanjaro
escarpment

CONNECT TO THE ISSUES
COLONIALISM Africa's valuable resources still attract the world's industrialized countries.

SUNSHINE STATE STANDARDS
Key Standard SS.B.2.4.3 The student understands how the allocation of control of the Earth's surface affects interactions between people in different regions.

Other Standards SS.B.1.4.1, B.1.4.3

FCAT LA.A.1.4.2 Reading: Strategies

A HUMAN PERSPECTIVE Angola's rebel leader Jonas Savimbi kept his forces fighting by bargaining with arms dealers and haggling with international diamond traders. Diamonds—one of the world's most precious and valuable gems—have enriched some of Africa's countries, including Botswana and South Africa. However, in other diamond-rich countries such as Angola, people use diamonds to fund costly and bloody civil wars. Rebel groups in Angola and the Angolan government sold diamonds on the world market and then used the money from the sale to buy weapons. The sale of diamonds funded a war that killed more than 500,000 Angolans and left more than 4 million homeless. A country's or continent's resources are used for a variety of purposes.

A Vast Plateau

Africa's shape and landforms are the result of its location in the southern part of the ancient supercontinent of *Pangaea,* which you read about in Chapter 2. About 200 million years ago, *Pangaea* began to break up. Over thousands of years, North and South America, Antarctica, Australia, and India drifted into their current positions. Present-day Africa, however, moved very little.

AFRICA'S PLATEAU A huge plateau covers most of Africa. It rises inland from narrow lowlands along the coast. Except for the coasts of Mozambique and Somalia, much of the continent lies at least 1,000 feet above sea level. This plateau is Africa's most prominent physical feature. As a result, geographers sometimes refer to Africa—the world's second largest continent—as the "plateau continent."

BASINS AND RIVERS Throughout this plateau lie several huge **basins,** or depressions, which you'll notice on the map on the right. Each basin spans more than 625 miles across and is as much as 5,000 feet deep. Water collects in the Chad Basin, and rivers flow through the Sudan, Congo, and Djouf basins.

Basins of Africa

Map legend:
- Basins
- Plateaus and mountains
- Rift valleys

0 400 800 miles
0 400 800 kilometers
Lambert Azimuthal Equal-Area Projection

Labels on map: ATLAS MOUNTAINS, Mediterranean Sea, AHAGGAR MOUNTAINS, SAHARA, Tibesti Mountains, Senegal R., DJOUF BASIN, Niger R., SAHEL, CHAD BASIN, SUDAN BASIN, Nile R., Red Sea, Tropic of Cancer, White Nile, Blue Nile, ETHIOPIAN PLATEAU, Benue R., ATLANTIC OCEAN, Gulf of Guinea, Ubangi R., Congo R., Equator, CONGO BASIN, L. Victoria, GREAT RIFT VALLEY, Mt. Kenya 17,058 ft. (5,199 m), Mt. Kilimanjaro 19,341 ft. (5,895 m), L. Tanganyika, L. Nyasa, Zambezi R., KALAHARI BASIN, Limpopo R., Mozambique Channel, Madagascar, Tropic of Capricorn, Orange R., Drakensberg, Karroo, INDIAN OCEAN

SKILLBUILDER: Interpreting Maps

❶ **REGION** Which basin contains the most complex river system?

❷ **LOCATION** Which basin lies completely south of the equator?

The world's longest river, the **Nile River,** flows more than 4,000 miles through Uganda and Sudan and into Egypt. Its waters have provided irrigation for the region for thousands of years. More than 95 percent of Egyptians depend on the Nile for their water. In fact, the average population density along the Nile is more than 3,320 people per square mile. Compare that to the average population density of 177 people per square mile in all of Egypt.

Africa's rivers contain many waterfalls, rapids, and gorges. These features make the rivers less useful for transportation than shorter rivers on other continents. The 2,900-mile-long Congo River forms the continent's largest network of waterways. But a series of 32 cataracts, or waterfalls, makes large portions of that river impassable.

Furthermore, meandering courses also make Africa's rivers difficult to use for transportation. For example, the Niger River begins in West Africa and flows north toward the Sahara, where it forms an interior delta and turns to the southeast. It then cuts through Nigeria and forms another huge delta as it empties into the Gulf of Guinea. Ⓐ

Geographic Thinking

Using the Atlas
Ⓐ Use the physical map on page 403 to find out what other rivers in Africa follow winding courses.

Distinctive African Landforms

Africa does not have a long chain of mountains, such as the Rocky Mountains in North America or the Himalayas in Asia. However, Africa's valleys and lakes add to the continent's varied landscape.

RIFT VALLEYS AND LAKES The continent's most distinctive landforms are in East Africa. As the continental plates pulled apart over millions of years, huge cracks appeared in the earth. The land then sank to form long, thin valleys—called **rift valleys.** The rift valleys, which you can see on the map on page 415, show that the eastern part of Africa is pulling away from the rest of Africa. These rift valleys stretch over 4,000 miles from Jordan in Southwest Asia to Mozambique in Southern Africa.

PLACE Masai tribespeople climb the walls of the Great Rift Valley in Tanzania.
How were the rift valleys formed?

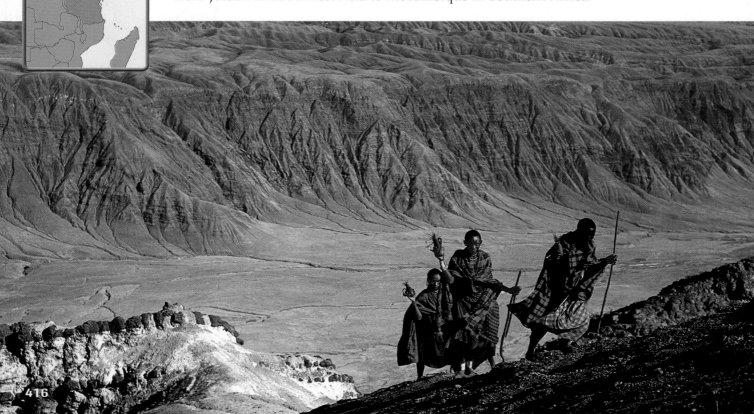

A cluster of lakes formed at the bottoms of some of these rift valleys. These African lakes are unusually long and deep. Lake Tanganyika, the longest freshwater lake in the world, stretches about 420 miles and reaches a depth of more than 4,700 feet.

However, Africa's largest lake, Lake Victoria, sits in a shallow basin between two rift valleys. It is the world's second largest freshwater lake but is only 270 feet deep. **◄B**

Geographic Thinking

Making Comparisons
B How is Lake Victoria different from Lake Tanganyika?

MOUNTAINS Africa contains mainly volcanic mountains. Mount Kenya and **Mount Kilimanjaro,** Africa's highest mountain, are both volcanoes. Volcanic activity also produced the Ethiopian Highlands, the Tibesti Mountains in the Sahara, and Mount Cameroon in West Africa. In addition, volcanic rock covers the Great Escarpment in Southern Africa. An **escarpment** is a steep slope with a nearly flat plateau on top. The Great Escarpment marks the edge of the continent's plateau in Southern Africa.

Africa's Wealth of Resources

The story of Africa's natural resources is at once a story of plenty and one of scarcity. Africa has a huge amount of the world's minerals. But many African countries lack the industrial base and money to develop them.

A WEALTH OF MINERALS Africa's minerals make it one of the world's richest continents. African nations contain large amounts of gold, platinum, chromium, cobalt, copper, phosphates, diamonds, and many other minerals. For example, South Africa is the world's largest producer of chromium. Chromium is an element used in manufacturing stainless steel.

South Africa also produces nearly 80 percent of the world's platinum and nearly 30 percent of the world's gold. Another important resource, cobalt, is used in high-grade steel for aircraft and industrial engines. African nations produce about 42 percent of the world's cobalt, mostly from the Democratic Republic of the Congo and Zambia. Ores and minerals account for more than half of the total value of Africa's exports.

Africa's great mineral wealth, however, has not meant economic prosperity for most of its population. In the 19th and 20th centuries, European colonial rulers developed Africa's natural resources for export to Europe to manufacture goods there. As a result, many African nations have been slow to develop the infrastructure and industries that could turn these resources into valuable products. **◄C**

CONNECT TO THE ISSUES
ECONOMIC DEVELOPMENT
C Why hasn't Africa's mineral wealth translated into wealth for most of its citizens?

OIL RESOURCES Libya, Nigeria, and Algeria are among the world's leading petroleum producers. Other countries, such as Angola and Gabon, have huge untapped oil reserves. Libya, Nigeria, Algeria, and Angola combine to produce over seven percent of the world's oil.

Angola illustrates why valuable resources don't always benefit most Africans. Recently discovered offshore oil deposits will likely enable

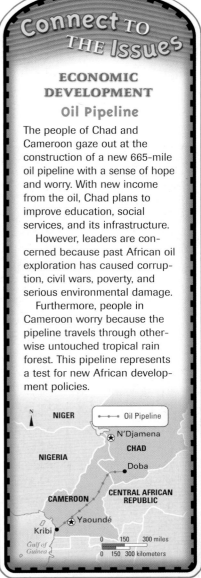

Connect to THE Issues

ECONOMIC DEVELOPMENT
Oil Pipeline

The people of Chad and Cameroon gaze out at the construction of a new 665-mile oil pipeline with a sense of hope and worry. With new income from the oil, Chad plans to improve education, social services, and its infrastructure.

However, leaders are concerned because past African oil exploration has caused corruption, civil wars, poverty, and serious environmental damage.

Furthermore, people in Cameroon worry because the pipeline travels through otherwise untouched tropical rain forest. This pipeline represents a test for new African development policies.

AFRICA

Angola to surpass Nigeria as Africa's most oil-rich country. American oil companies pay Angola a fee for drilling rights and the oil. However, the Angolan government spends the money on an ongoing civil war. This war is caused in part by ethnic divisions resulting from years of colonialism. Angola invests little money in schools, hospitals, or other public infrastructure.

Geographic Thinking

Seeing Patterns
How does Angola make money from its resources?

Diversity of Resources

From rain forests to roaring rivers, Africa possesses an incredible diversity of resources.

MAJOR COMMODITIES After oil, coffee is the most profitable commodity in Africa. Even though few Africans drink coffee, the continent grows 20 percent of the world's supply.

Lumber is another important commodity. Nigeria leads African nations in lumber exports and ranks eighth worldwide in that area. However, logging is depleting Africa's forests. Every year loggers clear an area of land in Africa about twice the size of New Jersey. Other major commodities include sugar, palm oil, and cocoa. Côte d'Ivoire is the world's largest exporter of cocoa beans, the main ingredient in chocolate.

Agriculture is the single most important economic activity in Africa. About 66 percent of Africans earn their living from farming. In addition, farm products account for nearly one-third of the continent's exports. Farmers benefit from Africa's climate, which you will read about in the next section.

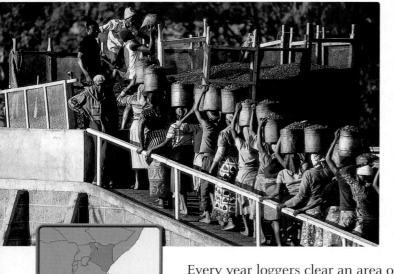

MOVEMENT Kenyan workers carry coffee berries to a pulping machine.

SECTION 1 Assessment

1 Places & Terms

Identify and explain where in the region these would be found.

• basin
• Nile River
• rift valley
• Mount Kilimanjaro
• escarpment

2 Taking Notes

PLACE Review the notes you took for this section.

Landforms	
Resources	

• What types of landforms are found in Africa?
• What kinds of resources does Africa possess?

3 Main Ideas

a. Why is Africa called the "plateau continent"?

b. What are some of Africa's distinctive landforms?

c. Why do you think Africa's abundance of natural resources has not translated into economic wealth for most of its population?

4 Geographic Thinking

Seeing Patterns How has Africa's physical geography affected its ability to use its resources for economic development? **Think about:**

• its use of rivers for transportation

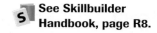
See Skillbuilder Handbook, page R8.

EXPLORING LOCAL GEOGRAPHY Examine a physical map of your state or region. Then study the map on page 403 to determine which African country has the most similar physical geography to your region or state. Create a **Venn diagram** identifying which physical features your state or region has in common with that country and the features that are different.

Map and Graph Skills

Reading an Economic Activity Map

Subsistence farming and nomadic herding are the primary economic activities in large sections of Africa. Even though African nations have a wealth of natural resources, mining and drilling for these resources are not evenly distributed throughout the continent. The thematic map below shows a wide variety of economic activities in Africa.

THE LANGUAGE OF MAPS An **economic activity map** is a thematic map that shows the location of economic activities over a large area such as a continent.

SUNSHINE STATE STANDARDS
Key Standard SS.B.1.4.1 The student uses a variety of maps, geographic technologies including geographic information systems (GIS) and satellite-produced imagery, and other advanced graphic representations to depict geographic problems.

FCAT LA.A.1.4.2 Reading: Strategies

Economic Activities in Africa

Copyright by Rand McNally & Co.

1. Each color represents the economic activity in which the majority of people are engaged.

2. The black symbols represent major drilling and mining for natural resources.

3. The symbols and colors show the combination of economic activities and natural resources in a particular location. For example, this map shows that Southern Africa contains livestock raising, mining, commercial fishing, and commercial farming.

Map and Graph Skills Assessment

1. Making Generalizations
In what region of Africa does most of the livestock raising take place?

2. Making Inferences
Why do you think so many manufacturing and trade centers are located near rivers or on the coasts?

3. Drawing Conclusions
What is the most common type of farming done in Africa?

Climate and Vegetation

Main Ideas
- Africa contains dry and hot deserts, warm tropics, and permanently snow-capped mountains.
- Africa's vegetation includes thick rain forests, tall grasslands, and desert areas.

Places & Terms

Sahara   Serengeti Plain

aquifer   canopy

oasis

CONNECT TO THE ISSUES
ECONOMIC DEVELOPMENT
Africa's tropical rain forests are being cut down for farmland and valuable timber.

A HUMAN PERSPECTIVE In 1352, 48-year-old Ibn Battuta, a great traveler from Morocco, set out for the empire of Mali in West Africa. His most challenging obstacle was the Sahara, a desert nearly the same size as the continental United States. Battuta and his caravan set out in February. They traveled only in early morning and early evening to avoid the midday heat. Even so, they still battled temperatures of nearly 100 degrees during the day and freezing temperatures at night. Reaching Mali around April, Batutta covered more than 1,000 miles, all on foot. The Sahara today remains just as hazardous—fewer than 2 million of Africa's approximately 800 million people live in it.

SUNSHINE STATE STANDARDS
Key Standard SS.B.2.4.1 The student understands how social, cultural, economic, and environmental factors contribute to the dynamic nature of regions.

Other Standards SS.B.1.4.1, B.2.4.4

FCAT LA.A.1.4.2 Reading: Strategies

A Warm Continent

You can see from the map on page 421 that Africa lies almost entirely between the tropic of Cancer and the tropic of Capricorn. This location gives most of Africa warm, tropical temperatures.

THE DESERTS The **Sahara** is the largest desert in the world. Sahara actually means "desert" in Arabic. It stretches about 3,000 miles across the continent, from the Atlantic Ocean to the Red Sea, and also runs 1,200 miles from north to south. Temperatures can rise as high as 136.4°F in the summer, hot enough to fry an egg on the sand. But temperatures can also fall below freezing at night in winter.

Only about 20 percent of the Sahara consists of sand. Towering mountains, rock formations, and gravelly plains make up the rest. For instance, the Tibesti Mountains, located mostly in northwestern Chad, rise to heights of more than 11,000 feet. Other African deserts include the Kalahari and the Namib.

Travel in the Sahara is risky because of the extreme conditions. Many travelers rely on the camel as desert transportation. A camel can go for

PLACE Rolling sand dunes are only a small part of the Sahara's varied landscape.
How might an expanding desert affect the lives of the people living near it?

up to 17 days without water. In addition, wind-blown sand has little effect on a camel. It closes its nostrils and just keeps walking.

Ironically, as much as 6,000 feet under this hottest and driest of places lie huge stores of underground water called **aquifers.** In some places, this water has come to the surface. Such a place is called an **oasis.** It supports vegetation and wildlife and is a critical resource for people living in the desert.

THE TROPICS Africa has a large tropical area—the largest of any continent. In fact, nearly 90 percent of the continent lies within the tropics of Cancer and Capricorn, as you can see on the map to the right. Temperatures run high most of the year. The hottest places are in the parts of the Sahara that lie in the nation of Somalia. July temperatures average between 110°F and 115°F almost every day. Differences in temperature between winter and summer in the Tropics are barely noticeable. Differences in temperature between night and day actually tend to be greater than any difference between seasons. A saying in Africa says that nighttime is the "winter" of the tropics. ◀A

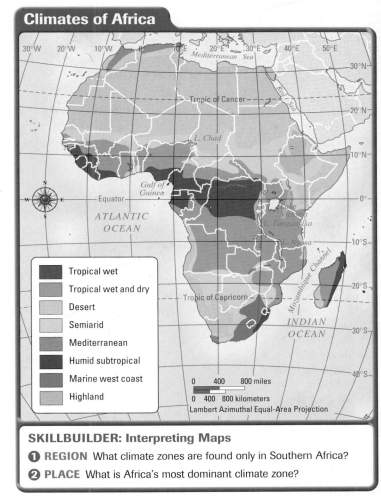

Climates of Africa

Tropical wet
Tropical wet and dry
Desert
Semiarid
Mediterranean
Humid subtropical
Marine west coast
Highland

0   400   800 miles
0   400   800 kilometers
Lambert Azimuthal Equal-Area Projection

SKILLBUILDER: Interpreting Maps
❶ **REGION** What climate zones are found only in Southern Africa?
❷ **PLACE** What is Africa's most dominant climate zone?

Geographic Thinking
Using the Atlas
Ⓐ Which climate regions of Africa do the tropics of Cancer and Capricorn pass through?

Sunshine and Rainfall

Rainfall in Africa is often a matter of extremes. Some parts get too much rain, while other parts receive too little. The amount of rainfall can also vary greatly from year to year as well as season to season. These variations have had a tremendous impact on East Africa, which endured several droughts in the 1980s and 1990s.

RAINFALL PATTERNS The rain forest in Central Africa receives the most precipitation, as rain falls throughout the year. Most of the rest of Africa, however, has one or two rainy seasons. Africa's tropical savanna stretches through the middle of the continent. It covers nearly half the total surface area of Africa. Rainy seasons in this area can last up to six months. The closer an area is to the equator, the longer the rainy season. The closer an area is to the desert, the longer the dry season.

Africa's west coast also receives a great deal of rain. The region around Monrovia, Liberia, experiences an average annual rainfall of more than 120 inches. In contrast, many parts of Africa barely get 20 inches of rain over the course of a year. In the Sahara and other deserts, rain may not fall for years. Children living in those areas may not see rain until they are five or six years old!

AFRICA'S MODERATE AREAS A Mediterranean climate exists on the northern and southern tips of the continent. Clear, blue skies in these places are normal. Rain falls usually only in the winter—December and January in North Africa and June and July in Southern Africa. Summer temperatures in Johannesburg, South Africa, average around 68°F.

A Grassy Continent

Africa's vegetation—like its climate—is almost mirrored north and south of the equator. Africa's vegetation consists of grasslands, rain forests, and a wide variety of other plant life.

BACKGROUND
Serengeti means "endless plains" in the Masai language.

TROPICAL GRASSLAND Tropical grassland covers most of the continent. One example of this grassland is the **Serengeti Plain** in northern Tanzania. Its dry climate and hard soil prevent the growth of trees and many crops, but these conditions are perfect for growing grass. Serengeti National Park, located within the Serengeti Plain, contains some of the best grasslands in the world. Some of these grasses can grow taller than the average person. The abundance of grass makes Serengeti National Park an ideal place for grazing animals. Huge herds of wildebeests, gazelles, and zebras roam there. It is the place where the largest numbers of land mammals still make annual migrations.

PLACE These wilde- beests live in Serengeti National Park, which was founded in 1951. **How might the park help conservation efforts in Africa?**

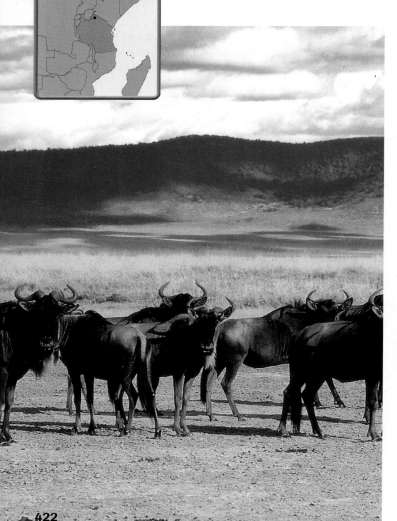

Africa's Extremes

An enormous tropical rain forest stretches across Central Africa.

RAIN FOREST The major rain forests of Africa sit on the equator in the area of the Congo Basin. One square acre of rain forest can contain almost 100 different kinds of trees. It may also be home to hundreds of species of birds. The massive number of plants, leaves, and trees block out much of the sunlight that would otherwise hit the floor of the rain forest. Beneath this umbrella of vegetation, the air is hot and filled with moisture. As a result, plants and other vegetation quickly decompose, or decay. For example, a fallen leaf in Europe decomposes in about a year. A leaf on the jungle floor in Africa decomposes in about six weeks. B

Most animals in a rain forest live in the canopy. The **canopy** refers to the uppermost layer of branches, about

Geographic Thinking

Seeing Patterns
B How do rain forests maintain such a high level of moisture?

422

150 feet above the ground. Birds, monkeys, and flying foxes move from tree to tree and enjoy the bounty of the rain forest. A large number of snakes live in these rain forests, too. The Gaboon viper, the largest African viper, can weigh as much as 18 pounds and have fangs more than two inches long. Another snake, the black-necked cobra, can shoot its venom more than eight feet through the air.

BACKGROUND
The National Cancer Institute estimates that 70 percent of the plants found useful for cancer treatment are found only in rain forests.

However, farmers using slash-and-burn agricultural methods are endangering the existence of the rain forest. As you read in Chapter 9, slash-and-burn farming is a method in which people clear fields by cutting and burning trees and other vegetation, the ashes of which fertilize the soil. After farmers have exhausted the soil, they burn another patch of forest. Slash-and-burn farming is responsible for the nearly complete destruction of Madagascar's rain forest. Experts estimate that over half of Africa's original rain forest has been destroyed.

VARIETIES OF PLANTLIFE All of Africa's regions contain a variety of vegetation. North Africa contains sizable oak and pine forests in the upper reaches of the Atlas Mountains. The mangrove tree of West Africa sprouts up along river banks in swamps and river deltas. Mangrove tree roots are breeding grounds for fish. They also help to build up dry land by holding silt. In the next section, you will read about different ways that people in Africa have interacted with their environment.

MOVEMENT
Animals, such as this chimpanzee, move about the Ituri rain forest in the Democratic Republic of the Congo.

AFRICA

SECTION 2 Assessment

① Places & Terms

Explain the meaning of each of the following terms.

• Sahara
• aquifer
• oasis
• Serengeti Plain
• canopy

② Taking Notes

PLACE Review the notes you took for this section.

Climate and Vegetation	

• What are the different climates found in Africa?
• How does climate affect the vegetation of Africa?

③ Main Ideas

a. What is the largest climatic feature in Africa?

b. Why does most of Africa have high temperatures?

c. What are the different kinds of vegetation growing in Africa?

④ Geographic Thinking

Making Comparisons What are the similarities between the climates of Africa north and south of the equator?
Think about:

• the Sahara
• where the equator cuts across Africa

RESEARCH LINKS
CLASSZONE.COM

MAKING COMPARISONS Choose a place in Africa and a place in the United States at about the same latitude. Use encyclopedias or the Internet to compare the climate and vegetation of the two places. Create a **chart** comparing the two locations.

Human–Environment Interaction

Main Ideas
- The Sahara's expansion is causing problems for Africa's farmers.
- The Nigerian oil industry has caused serious environmental damage in the Niger delta.

Places & Terms
Niger delta
Sahel
desertification
Aswan High Dam
silt

CONNECT TO THE ISSUES
COLONIALISM European colonialism has caused political, economic, and environmental problems in Africa today.

A HUMAN PERSPECTIVE Akierou Awe lives in a mud-brick house in Nigeria's **Niger delta,** a region that contains most of Nigeria's oil. On the morning of July 10, 2000, Awe's four sons had been collecting fuel from a leaking pipeline to help scrape out a living in this poverty-stricken region. They hoped to resell the fuel for more than the going rate of 21 cents a quart. Suddenly, an explosion shook the area, and a fire spread along a mile-long stretch of the pipeline. The blast killed more than 300 people, including three of Awe's sons. This accident is one of many in the recent past that have claimed the lives of hundreds of Nigerians. Nigeria has become one of the top oil producers in the world, but at the cost of thousands of lives and major environmental ruin in the region.

Desertification of the Sahel

Sahel means "shore of the desert" in Arabic. You can see from the physical map on page 403 that the Sahel is a narrow band of dry grassland that runs east to west along the southern edge of the Sahara. People use the Sahel for farming and herding. Since the 1960s, the desert has spread into the Sahel. This shift of the desert is called desertification. **Desertification** is an expansion of dry conditions into moist areas that are next to deserts. Normally, it results from nature's long-term cycle, but as you can see in the illustration below, human activity is speeding up the process.

HUMAN CAUSES OF DESERTIFICATION Geographers and other scientists have identified several human activities that increase the pace of desertification. For example, allowing overgrazing of vegetation by

SUNSHINE STATE STANDARDS
Key Standard SS.B.2.4.4 The student understands the global impact of human changes in the physical environment.
FCAT LA.A.1.4.2 Reading: Strategies

The Process of Desertification

1 The Sahel receives little rainfall. The vegetation lives in a fragile state, having barely enough water and food to survive.

2 Farming, overgrazing by livestock, and burning wood for fuel all contribute to desertification.

livestock exposes the soil. Animals also trample the soil, making it more vulnerable to erosion.

Farming also increases the pace of desertification. When farmers clear the land to plant crops, they expose the soil to wind, which can cause erosion. In addition, when farmers drill for water to irrigate crops, they put further stress on the Sahel. Widespread drilling and more irrigation increase salt levels in the soil, which prevent the growth of vegetation.

Increasing population levels are an indirect cause of desertification. More people require more food. As a result, farmers continue to clear more land for crops, burn more wood for fuel, and overfarm the land they already have.

RESULTS OF DESERTIFICATION Desertification has affected many parts of Africa. For example, large forests once existed around Khartoum, Sudan. In addition, desertification is slowly destroying a tropical rain forest around Lake Chad in the southern edge of the Sahel. Slowing desertification is difficult. Some African countries have increased tree planting and promoted more efficient use of forests and farmland in hopes of slowing the process. ◀A

Geographic Thinking ◀

Using the Atlas
A▶ Refer to the physical map on page 403. What countries are probably most affected by desertification of the Sahel?

Harming the Environment in Nigeria

Another environmental issue concerns the discovery of oil in Nigeria in 1956. Rich oil deposits in the Niger delta made Nigeria one of Africa's wealthiest countries. However, in drilling for oil, the Nigerian government and foreign oil companies have often damaged the land and harmed the people living in the Niger delta.

A MAJOR OIL PRODUCER Nigeria is the sixth leading oil exporter in the world. Two million barrels are extracted each day, much of it shipped to the United States. Oil accounts for 80 to 90 percent of Nigeria's income.

During the 1970s, high oil prices made Nigeria one of the wealthiest nations in Africa. As a result, the government borrowed heavily against the future sale of its oil. However, oil prices eventually fell, and the Nigerian government owed millions of dollars to other nations, including the United States. Mismanagement, poor planning, corruption, and a decline in oil prices left Nigeria poorer than before the oil boom.

3 During desertification, dry grasses die and are replaced by tougher plants like shrubs. These plants do not cover the soil as well as grass.

4 With less vegetation covering the soil, any rain that falls evaporates quickly. Over the years, the wind then blows the dry soil into a desert-like state.

DESTROYING THE LAND AND PEOPLE The damage caused by oil companies and the Nigerian government has been severe. More than 4,000 oil spills have occurred in the Niger delta over the past four decades. Cleanup operations have been slow and sometimes non-existent. Fires often resulted, causing acid rain and massive deposits of soot, and people in the region contracted respiratory diseases. In addition, between 1998 and 2000, oil pipeline explosions killed more than 2,000 people—including three of Akierou Awe's sons.

Many of these explosions were not accidents but were caused intentionally. Bandits, in cooperation with corrupt government officials and the military, drain fuel from the pipelines and then resell it. In 1999, these bandits damaged about 500 pipelines. Once the bandits finish draining oil, local villagers arrive. They use small cans to collect any spilled oil and then sell it. **B**

A NEW START In May 1999, Olusegun Obasanjo became Nigeria's new president. Although a former Nigerian military leader himself, he has distanced himself from the armed forces. He has started many economic reforms and fired corrupt government officials. Now he faces the task of finding ways for Nigeria to benefit from oil.

Controlling the Nile

Egypt faces environmental challenges caused by another resource—water. Throughout history, the Egyptians have tried to control the floodwaters of the Nile River. Ancient Egyptians built canals and small dams. In spite of these efforts, though, the people still experienced cycles of floods and droughts. To solve these problems, Egyptians completed the first Aswan Dam on the Nile in 1902, which quickly became outmoded.

THE ASWAN HIGH DAM Four miles upriver from the first Aswan Dam, the Egyptians cut a huge channel through the land beside the Nile River. The builders used the rocks from the channel as a base for their new creation—the **Aswan High Dam**—which was completed in 1970. Lake Nasser, which Egypt shares with Sudan, is the artificial lake created behind the dam. It stretches for nearly 300 miles.

Geographic Thinking

Seeing Patterns
B Why did bandits and corrupt government officials drain fuel from the pipelines?

Aswan High Dam

Mediterranean Sea
Alexandria
30°N
Cairo
El Minya
LIBYA
EGYPT
SINAI PEN.
Asyut
Nile R.
ARABIAN DESERT
Red
N
25°N — W — E
S
Aswan High Dam
Aswan
First Cataract
Sea
Tropic of Cancer
Lake Nasser
25°E
SUDAN
NUBIAN DESERT
35°E
40°E

Flood plain

0   150   300 miles
0   150   300 kilometers
Lambert Azimuthal
Equal-Area Projection

HUMAN– ENVIRONMENT INTERACTION The Aswan High Dam has helped Egypt control the flooding of the Nile River.

What are some of the benefits of the Aswan High Dam?

The dam gives farmers a regular supply of water. It holds the Nile's floodwaters, releasing them as needed so that farmers can use the water effectively for irrigation. As a result of the dam, farmers can now have two or three harvests per year rather than one. Irrigation canals even keep some fields in continuous production through the use of artificial fertilizers. The dam has increased Egypt's farmable land by 50 percent. The dam has also helped Egypt avoid droughts and floods.

BACKGROUND
The channel next to the Aswan High Dam produces about 40 percent of Egypt's electricity, and Lake Nasser supports commercial fishing.

PROBLEMS WITH THE DAM Though the dam has provided Egypt with many benefits, it has also created some problems. During the dam's construction, many people had to be relocated, including thousands of Nubians, whose way of life was permanently changed. In addition, one of ancient Egypt's treasures, the temples at Abu Simbel, had to be moved. Other smaller ancient treasures could not be saved and now lie at the bottom of Lake Nasser.

The dam also decreased the fertility of the soil around the Nile. First, the river no longer deposits its rich **silt**, or sediment, on the farmland. Farmers must now rely on expensive artificial fertilizers to enrich the soil. Second, this year-round irrigation has resulted in a rising water table in Egypt. As a result, salts from deep in the earth have decreased the fertility of the soil. Before the dam was built, floodwaters flushed out the salt. Now expensive field drains have to be installed. ◀C

Geographic Thinking ◀

Seeing Patterns
▶ How do farmers fertilize their land now that the dam traps all the silt?

Rates of malaria and other diseases have increased due to greater numbers of mosquitos, which thrive in the still waters of Lake Nasser and the irrigation canals. Furthermore, because Lake Nasser holds the floodwaters, Egyptians lose millions of gallons of fresh water every year to evaporation. Measuring the success of the Aswan High Dam is difficult. For all the ways it has helped Egyptians, it has also created new problems.

SECTION 3 ▶ Assessment

1 Places & Terms

Explain the meaning or identify the location of each of the following terms.

- Niger delta
- Sahel
- desertification
- Aswan High Dam
- silt

2 Taking Notes

HUMAN–ENVIRONMENT INTERACTION Review the notes you took for this section.

Human-Environment Interaction	

- Which activities illustrate human control of the environment?
- Which examples illustrate an environment changed by humans?

3 Main Ideas

a. What are some of the causes of desertification?

b. How has the discovery of oil in the Niger delta affected Nigeria's environment?

c. What were some of the reasons that the Egyptian government built the Aswan High Dam?

4 Geographic Thinking

Drawing Conclusions Do you think that the benefits of the Aswan High Dam have outweighed its problems?

Think about:

- the dam's effect on Egypt's food supply and farmers

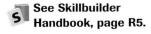 **See Skillbuilder Handbook, page R5.**

ASKING GEOGRAPHIC QUESTIONS Study the map of the Aswan High Dam on page 426. Write three geographic questions about the map, such as one concerning the location of the dam. Write a **report** answering one of your three questions. Then present your findings to the class.

VISUAL SUMMARY
PHYSICAL GEOGRAPHY OF AFRICA

Landforms and Resources

- A large plateau covers most of Africa.
- Long, thin valleys, called rift valleys, stretch along East Africa.
- Africa contains many valuable resources including oil, diamonds, and gold.

Climate and Vegetation

- The Sahara, the largest desert in the world, stretches across northern Africa.
- Nearly 90 percent of Africa lies within the Tropics.
- A large, grassy area called the Serengeti Plain provides an ideal natural habitat for Africa's wild animals.

Human-Environment Interaction

- Desertification results from nature's cycle, farming, overgrazing, and clearing too much land for crops.
- People and the environment in Nigeria have suffered as a result of the country's poor management and corruption of the oil industry.
- The Aswan High Dam helped to increase Egypt's food supply but has also caused environmental problems.

Reviewing Places & Terms

A. Briefly explain the importance of each of the following.

1. Nile River
2. rift valley
3. escarpment
4. Sahara
5. oasis
6. Serengeti Plain
7. Sahel
8. desertification
9. Aswan High Dam
10. silt

B. Answer the questions about vocabulary in complete sentences.

11. What is sediment that is deposited on farmland by rivers and also acts as a fertilizer?
12. What is the longest river in the world?
13. What does the pulling apart of continental plates create?
14. What is the largest desert in the world?
15. What is the process in which dry conditions spread into areas that are moist?
16. Where do Africa's large mammal migrations take place?
17. What supports vegetation and is a critical resource for people living in the desert?
18. What is a narrow region of grassland on the southern edge of the Sahara?
19. What marks the edge of Africa's plateau in Southern Africa?
20. Which of the terms above is an example of how humans have adapted to the environment?

Main Ideas

Landforms and Resources (pp. 415–419)

1. In what ways does the Nile River support life?
2. What are some of the abundant resources in Africa?
3. Why does oil in Angola not always benefit Angolans?

Climate and Vegetation (pp. 420–423)

4. What is the physical geography of the Sahara?
5. What is the general pattern of rainfall in Africa?
6. How does the Serengeti Plain help support much of Africa's wildlife?
7. What are some of the benefits of rain forests?

Human-Environment Interaction (pp. 424–427)

8. How might desertification affect people's lives in the Sahel?
9. What are some problems created by the Nigerian oil industry?
10. What are some of the problems created by the Aswan High Dam?

Critical Thinking

1. Using Your Notes

Use your completed chart to answer these questions.

Landforms	
Resources	

  a. Why has Africa not been able to take advantage of its abundant resources?

  b. What are some of the problems facing Africa's rain forests?

2. Geographic Themes

  a. **REGION** What are some of the aspects of Africa's physical geography that make interior transportation difficult?

  b. **LOCATION** In what way does Africa's location impact its climate?

3. Identifying Themes

How does desertification alter Africa's surrounding environment? Which of the five themes of geography apply to this situation?

4. Making Generalizations

How has the Aswan High Dam affected the lives of Egyptians?

5. Seeing Patterns

Has the Nigerian oil industry and the Aswan High Dam had positive or negative effects on the surrounding environment? Explain.

Additional Test Practice, pp. S1–S37

TEST PRACTICE
CLASSZONE.COM

Geographic Skills: Interpreting Maps

Profile of Africa

Use the profile to answer the following questions.

1. **PLACE** What is the tallest landform on the map?

2. **MOVEMENT** How many feet would a person have to climb to reach the peak of the Ahaggar Mountains from the lowest point at this latitude?

3. **REGION** How does this profile illustrate Africa's nickname as the plateau continent?

GeoActivity

Sketch your own profile of Africa. Use this profile as a model for your own map. Examine the physical map on page 403 and choose a latitude from which to draw your profile.

AFRICA

INTERNET ACTIVITY

Use the links at classzone.com to do research about desertification. Focus on determining the long-term effects of desertification in the Sahel.

Creating a Multimedia Presentation Combine charts, maps, or other visual images in an electronic presentation showing how the Sahel will be affected by desertification.

HUMAN GEOGRAPHY OF AFRICA
From Human Beginnings to New Nations

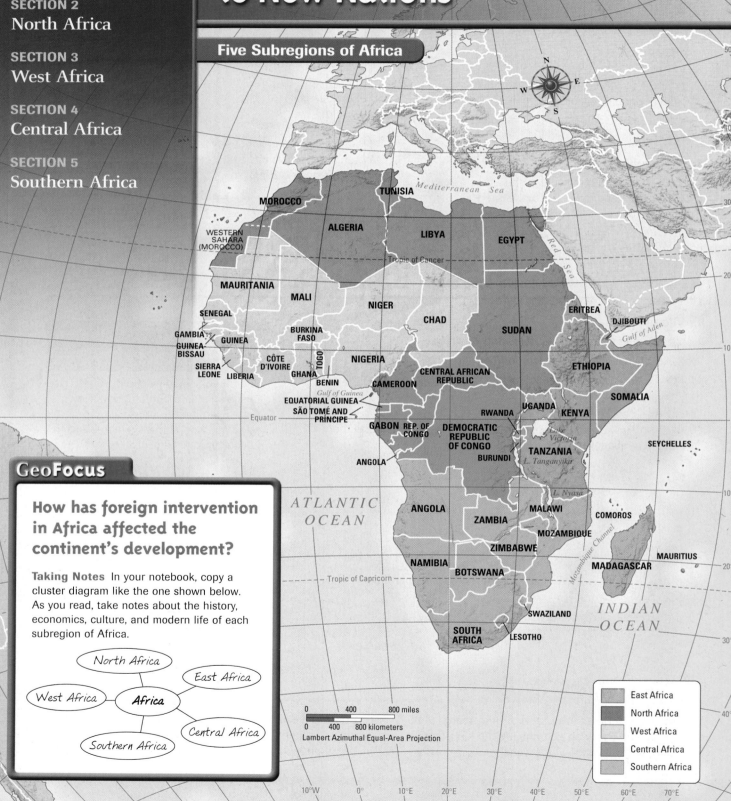

Five Subregions of Africa

	East Africa
	North Africa
	West Africa
	Central Africa
	Southern Africa

0   400   800 miles
0   400   800 kilometers
Lambert Azimuthal Equal-Area Projection

GeoFocus

How has foreign intervention in Africa affected the continent's development?

Taking Notes In your notebook, copy a cluster diagram like the one shown below. As you read, take notes about the history, economics, culture, and modern life of each subregion of Africa.

North Africa
East Africa
West Africa — Africa — Central Africa
Southern Africa

East Africa

Main Ideas

- East Africa is known as the "cradle of humanity."
- East Africa's location has made it a trading center.

Places & Terms

Olduvai Gorge

Aksum

Berlin Conference

cash crop

Masai

pandemic

CONNECT TO THE ISSUES
ECONOMIC DEVELOPMENT
East Africa's political conflicts have limited its economic development.

SUNSHINE STATE STANDARDS
Key Standard SS.B.2.4.1 The student understands how social, cultural, economic, and environmental factors contribute to the dynamic nature of regions.

Other Standards SS.A.1.4.2, B.2.4.6

FCAT LA.A.1.4.2 Reading: Strategies

A HUMAN PERSPECTIVE East Africa is called the "cradle of humanity" because of the large number of prehistoric human remains found in the region. In 1931, Louis Leakey, an English archaeologist, began doing research in **Olduvai Gorge,** located in northern Tanzania. Olduvai Gorge has contained the most continuous known record of humanity. The gorge has yielded fossils from 65 individual hominids, or humans that walk upright. In 1959, Leakey and his wife, Mary Leakey, discovered a fossil there of a species called *Homo habilis,* the first human creatures to make stone tools. They lived about two million years ago. Throughout history, East Africa has been a crossroads of humanity because of its geographic position near seas and oceans.

Continental Crossroads

Bounded on the east by the Red Sea and Indian Ocean, East Africa includes Burundi, Djibouti, Eritrea, Ethiopia, Kenya, Rwanda, Seychelles, Somalia, Tanzania, and Uganda. Scientists believe that the world's first humans lived there.

A TRADING COAST East Africa was also a place where early civilizations developed. An important civilization was **Aksum,** which emerged in present-day Ethiopia in the A.D. 100s. Its location on the Red Sea and the Indian Ocean made it an important trading center and contributed to its expansion and power. People from Aksum regularly traded with the people of Egypt and the eastern Roman Empire.

During the sixth century, however, Aksum lost many trading partners, and several geographic factors weakened the empire. Traders on routes between the eastern Mediterranean region and Asia began passing through the Persian Gulf rather than

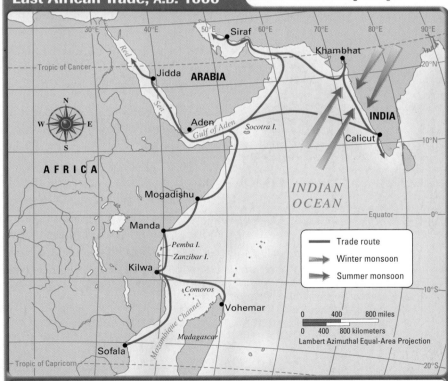

East African Trade, A.D. 1000

Trade route
Winter monsoon
Summer monsoon

0 400 800 miles
0 400 800 kilometers
Lambert Azimuthal Equal-Area Projection

SKILLBUILDER: Interpreting Maps

❶ **MOVEMENT** How far would a trader have to travel to go from Calicut to Sofala?

❷ **HUMAN–ENVIRONMENT INTERACTION** Which monsoon would a trader rely on to sail from Africa to India?

East Africa **431**

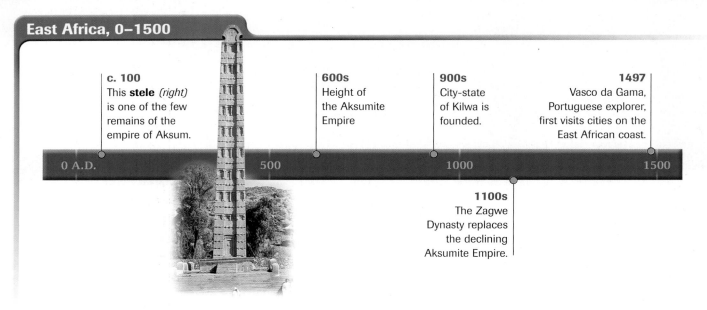

c. 100
This **stele** (right) is one of the few remains of the empire of Aksum.

600s
Height of the Aksumite Empire

900s
City-state of Kilwa is founded.

1497
Vasco da Gama, Portuguese explorer, first visits cities on the East African coast.

0 A.D.   500   1000   1500

1100s
The Zagwe Dynasty replaces the declining Aksumite Empire.

the Red Sea. In addition, the cutting down of forests and overuse of the soil led to a population decline, which reduced the empire's power.

Around the seventh century, Arab, Persian, and Indian traders once again made East Africa an international trading center. By 1300, many trading cities dotted the eastern coast of Africa. The trading city of Kilwa emerged as one of the most important cities of the time. Kilwa flourished on the southern coast of what is now Tanzania. All this movement of goods, ideas, and people made East Africa a cultural crossroads.

Colonization Disrupts Africa

In the 19th century, Europe's industrialized nations became interested in Africa's raw materials. Those European nations wanted to colonize and control parts of Africa to obtain those resources.

SCRAMBLE FOR AFRICA Europeans did not want to fight over Africa. To prevent European wars over Africa, 14 European nations convened the **Berlin Conference** in 1884–1885 to lay down rules for dividing Africa. No African ruler was invited to attend this conference, even though it concerned Africa's land and people. By 1914, only Liberia and Ethiopia remained free of European control.

Nations that attended the Berlin Conference decided that any European country could claim land in Africa by telling other nations of their claims and by showing they could control the area. The European nations divided Africa without regard to where African ethnic or linguistic groups lived. They set boundaries that combined peoples who were traditional enemies and divided others who were not. Europe's division of Africa is often cited as one of the root causes of the political violence and ethnic conflicts in Africa in the 20th century.

ETHIOPIA AVOIDS COLONIZATION Ethiopia is one country that escaped European colonization. Ethiopia's emperor, Menelik II, skillfully protected his country from the Italian invasion with weapons from France and Russia. In addition, the Ethiopian army had a greater knowledge of the area's geography than did the Italians. As a result, Ethiopia defeated Italy in 1896.

Geographic Thinking

Seeing Patterns
A Which group of nations participated in the Berlin Conference? Which group did not?

BACKGROUND
The Ethiopian victory was the first time native Africans successfully defended themselves against a colonial power.

East Africa, 1750–2000

1855
Kassa Hailu consolidates his rule over present-day Ethiopia.

1978
Jomo Kenyatta *(right)*, Kenya's first prime minister and an important African leader, dies.

1952
The Mau Mau rebellion against the British begins in Kenya.

1750   1875   2000

1873
East Africa's busiest slave market, Zanzibar, closes.

1896
Ethiopian forces under **Menelik II** *(far left)* defeat Italians.

1994
Hundreds of thousands die in battles between the Hutu and the Tutsi ethnic groups in Rwanda.

CONFLICT IN EAST AFRICA By the 1970s, most of East Africa had regained its independence from Europe. However, internal disputes and civil wars became a serious problem. For example, colonialism inflamed the peoples of Rwanda and helped to cause a bloody conflict in the 1990s.

One cause of those problems was that European colonial powers had not prepared East African nations for independence. Furthermore, the ethnic boundaries created by the Europeans forced cultural divisions that had not existed before colonialism. Those cultural divisions often caused internal conflicts among native groups. Colonialism also greatly affected the economy of East Africa, which today centers around tourism and farming.

Farming and Tourism Economies

Agriculture forms the economic foundation of East Africa. In addition, East Africa's world-famous wildlife parks generate millions of dollars of revenue.

FARMING IN EAST AFRICA East Africa is more than 70 percent rural. Since European colonization in the 19th century, countries have relied more on **cash crops** such as coffee, tea, and sugar, which are grown for direct sale. They bring in much-needed revenue but reduce the amount of farmland that otherwise could be devoted to growing food for use in the region. Relying on cash crops for revenue can be risky because the price of crops varies according to the world market. **B**

East Africa's agricultural balance is changing, however, because people are leaving farms for greater economic opportunities in cities. For example, Addis Ababa, the capital of Ethiopia, has grown by more

Geographic Thinking

Seeing Patterns
B How does growing cash crops both help a country's economy and hurt the people living in the country?

5 THEMES

REGION

Ethiopia-Eritrea War

In 1993, Eritrea gained its independence from Ethiopia after a violent and bloody war. But in 1998, the two countries became embroiled in a border conflict over the town of Badme.

Ethiopia occupied the town because it included an Ethiopian ethnic group. Eritrea responded by blocking Ethiopia's access to the Red Sea. This blockade cut off Ethiopia from its only port, making it a landlocked country.

In 1999, the fighting became full-scale conventional warfare. More than 100,000 people were killed on both sides. The conflict had a devastating impact on the people and the economies of the two countries.

AFRICA

East Africa **433**

growing up in...Kenya

The Masai are members of an ethnic group that live in Kenya. All Masai children address adults as either "mother" or "father."

A typical Masai girl *(pictured at the right)* takes on responsibilities that include:

- household chores
- child care
- the processing and distribution of milk

Each boy is assigned to a group called an age-set. Boys at the bottom of the age-set do the following:

- herd young animals
- learn to protect the herd from predatory animals

Between the ages of 14 and 18, boys receive a new name in a ceremony marking their transition from youth to manhood.

Around eight years of age, boys and girls have the upper part of their ears pierced. Two years later, the lower lobes are pierced. Wooden plugs are inserted into the holes to increase their size. Masai consider large ear lobes to be beautiful.

than one million people since 1991. However, such rapid population growth can put a strain on a city's resources and a country's agricultural production.

TOURISM CREATES WEALTH AND PROBLEMS One of the main economic activities in East Africa is tourism. The region's vast wildlife parks in Kenya, Uganda, and Tanzania are world famous. In 1938, Europeans created the game reserves because they were killing animals for sport at a high rate. Most African peoples did not need the parks because they hunted only for survival. However, the wild animal parks, which are no longer used for hunting, have now become important sources of income for Africans, generating millions of dollars each year from tourists.

Competing demands for the parkland exist, though. For example, Kenya's increasing population requires more food. As a result, some groups want to eliminate or reduce the size of the wildlife reserves to create more farmland. Some desperate farmers have even begun to plow the land around the parks.

BACKGROUND
Serengeti National Park in Tanzania covers nearly 6,000 square miles and contains 35 species of plains animals and 350 species of birds.

Maintaining Traditional Cultures

East Africa's position as a major trading region has given it a diverse culture. It is a melting pot of more than 160 different ethnic groups.

CULTURES OF EAST AFRICA Two major ethnic groups in East Africa are the **Masai** and the Kikuyu. The Masai, whom you read about above, are an East African ethnic group that lives on the grasslands of the rift valleys in Kenya and Tanzania. Most of the Masai herd livestock and farm the land.

Typical Masai dress includes clothes made from calfskin or buffalo hide. Women wear long skirt-like robes, while men wear a shorter version of the robe. They often grease their clothes with cow fat to protect themselves from the sun and rain. The Masai are also known for making intricate beadwork and jewelry.

The Kikuyu are the largest ethnic group in Kenya, numbering around 6.6 million. Their homeland is centered around Mount Kenya. Like the Masai, the Kikuyu traditionally were herders. However, today the Kikuyu live throughout the country and work in a variety of jobs. During British colonial rule, the Kikuyu organized a society called the Mau Mau, which fought against the British. The British killed around 11,000 Africans—mostly Kikuyu—during the Mau Mau rebellion between 1952 and 1960. ◀

Geographic Thinking◀

Seeing Patterns
▶ How have the lives of the Kikuyu changed during the last century?

Health Care in Modern Africa

The people of East Africa face many health care problems. The most critical is acquired immune deficiency syndrome (AIDS), which spread throughout Africa in the 1980s and 1990s.

HEALTH CARE IN AFRICA AIDS has become a pandemic and is having a devastating effect on the continent. A **pandemic** is an uncontrollable outbreak of a disease affecting a large population over a wide geographic area.

AIDS is caused by the human immunodeficiency virus (HIV). People infected with HIV do not necessarily have AIDS and can carry HIV for years without knowing it. As a result, AIDS statistics can be misleading. The number of people who have AIDS lags behind the number of those infected with HIV. Though AIDS education is increasing, some governments hide the scope of the disease. Many doctors in Africa say that more AIDS cases exist than are reported.

Some medical geographers predict that the populations of Africa's worst affected countries could decline by 10 to 20 percent.

You will read more about AIDS and other major health issues in Chapter 20. In the next section , you will learn about North Africa.

SECTION 1

Assessment

1 Places & Terms

Identify these terms and explain their importance in the region's history or culture.

- Olduvai Gorge
- Aksum
- Berlin Conference
- cash crop
- Masai
- pandemic

2 Taking Notes

PLACE Review the notes you took for this section.

- How did Aksum's location help the empire grow?
- What are some of the problems created by tourism?

3 Main Ideas

a. Why did East Africa become an international trading center early in its history?

b. How did the Berlin Conference change Africa?

c. How is AIDS affecting the population of Africa?

4 Geographic Thinking

Making Generalizations In what way has colonialism affected East Africa? **Think about:**

- the Berlin Conference
- problems in the 20th century

S **See Skillbuilder Handbook, page R6.**

GeoActivity

SEEING PATTERNS Do research to learn about two ethnic groups other than the Masai and the Kikuyu in East Africa. Create a **time line** tracing the origins of those ethnic groups to the present day. Examine the groups' history, movement patterns, and evolution of their lifestyles.

Disasters!

SUNSHINE STATE STANDARDS
Key Standard SS.B.2.4.4 The student understands the global impact of human changes in the physical environment.
FCAT LA.A.2.4.4 Reading: Research

Famine in Somalia

Famine—an extreme and long-term shortage of food—causes widespread hunger and sometimes death to millions of people. Natural causes, such as weather, plant diseases, and massive insect infestations, can cause famine. Drought is the most common natural cause. In addition, human beings can cause famine. Wars and political violence often destroy crops and prevent the adequate distribution of food. The worst famines usually involve a combination of both human and natural causes. The Horn of Africa, which includes Ethiopia and Somalia, has been the site of recent famines in the 1980s and 1990s.

Natural Causes

A lack of rain in successive seasons resulted in drought. Drought prevented the growth of enough food to feed the country's population.

Human Causes

Somali gunmen often looted relief shipments and then extracted payment for protecting relief workers. Other political causes, such as disagreements between warring factions, also prevented the delivery of food supplies.

Results

Thirsty Somalis plead for water delivered by the International Red Cross in Baidoa, Somalia, in 1992. Aid agencies estimated that famine killed between 25 and 50 people a day in this town in 1992.

GeoActivity

UNDERSTANDING FAMINE
Working with a partner, use the Internet to research different international aid organizations. Then write a **news report** about those organizations.

- Create a visual aid comparing the various groups.
- Include information about how the groups are funded.

RESEARCH LINKS
CLASSZONE.COM

GeoData

FAMINE IN SOMALIA
In the early 1990s, more than 300,000 Somalis died of famine, and another 30,000 died in a related civil war.

- Principal causes included drought, desertification, and civil war.
- Underlying causes, such as increased growth of cash crops and reliance on livestock, stemmed from a history of foreign intervention dating back to Italian and British colonization in the 19th century.

OTHER FAMINES

1876–1878 India
Drought caused famine that killed about five million people.

1932–1934 Soviet Union
Between six and eight million peasants died because of actions by the government.

1958–1960 China
Around 20 million people died during government reforms.

North Africa

A HUMAN PERSPECTIVE According to legend, around 814 B.C. a Phoenician queen founded **Carthage,** one of the great cities of ancient Africa. She located it on a peninsula on the Gulf of Tunis. The location was ideal. The Lake of Tunis protected the rear of the peninsula from invasion. In addition, because Carthage was on the coast of the Mediterranean Sea, it had access to trading routes. Consequently, it became a trading and commercial force in the ancient world for hundreds of years. Carthage's history shows that a city's or a civilization's geographic position always plays an important part in its ability to thrive and grow.

Roots of Civilization in North Africa

North Africa includes Algeria, Egypt, Libya, Morocco, Sudan, and Tunisia. Egypt and the Nile River valley formed a cultural hearth, a place where ideas and innovations come together to change a region. Those ideas and innovations reached other regions through cultural diffusion.

EGYPT BLOSSOMS ALONG THE NILE The Nile River made possible the existence of the great civilization of ancient Egypt. The river flooded at roughly the same time every year, providing the people with water and rich soil for their crops. The ancient Greek historian Herodotus remarked in the fifth century B.C. that Egypt was the "gift of the Nile."

Egyptians had been living in farming villages around the Nile River since 3300 B.C. Each village followed its own customs and rituals. Around 3100 B.C., a strong king united all of Egypt and established the first Egyptian dynasty. The history of ancient Egypt would span 2,600 years and around 30 dynasties. During the Middle Kingdom, Egyptian god-kings, called Pharaohs, ruled Egypt. Egyptians believed that those kings ruled even after death, and they built pyramids to house the Pharaohs' remains.

Movement influenced ancient Egypt and the Nile valley. Egyptian ideas about farming, the building of their cities, and their system of

HUMAN-ENVIRONMENT INTERACTION An irrigation ditch from the Nile River nourishes the fields outside Al Fayyam, Egypt.
Why has Egypt been called the "gift of the Nile"?

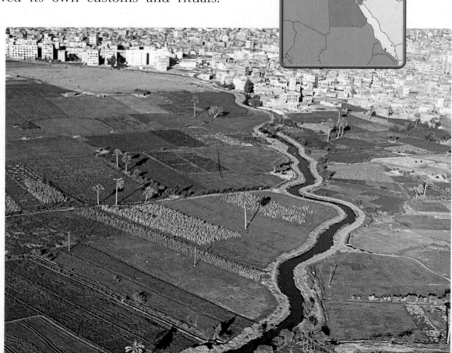

writing may have come from the Mesopotamians, who lived in what is now Southwest Asia. Egyptians pioneered the use of geometry in farming to set boundaries after the Nile's annual flood. Furthermore, Egyptian medicine was famous throughout the ancient world. Egyptians could make splints for broken bones and effectively treat wounds and fevers. Trade and travel on the Nile River, the Mediterranean and Red seas, and overland trade routes helped spread those practices.

ISLAM IN NORTH AFRICA North Africa lies close to Southwest Asia and across the Mediterranean Sea from Europe. As a result, it has been invaded and occupied by many people and empires from outside Africa. Greeks and Romans from Europe and Phoenicians and Ottoman Turks from Southwest Asia all invaded North Africa.

Islam, however, remains the major cultural and religious influence in North Africa. Islam, a monotheistic religion, is based on the teachings of the prophet Muhammad, whom you will read about in Chapter 22. Muslim invaders from Southwest Asia brought their language, culture, and religion to North Africa. Beginning in A.D. 632, the successors of Muhammad began to spread Islam through conquest and through trade. Around 634, Muslim armies swept into lower Egypt, which was then part of the Byzantine Empire. By 750, Muslims controlled most of North Africa. Muslims bound their territory together with a network of sea-linked trading zones. They used the Mediterranean Sea and the Indian Ocean to connect North Africa and Europe with Southwest Asia. ◀

Using the Atlas
A Using the map on this page and the unit atlas on page 405, identify the first Islamic countries in Africa.

Expansion of Islam, 750–1500

Marrakesh · Tunis · Mahdia · Tripoli · Alexandria · Constantinople · Cairo · Medina · Mecca · Timbuktu · Tadmekka · Mogadishu · Mombasa · Zanzibar · Kilwa

Mediterranean Sea · *Tropic of Cancer* · *Red Sea* · Lake Chad · Lake Victoria · Lake Tanganyika · Lake Nyasa · *Mozambique Channel* · *Equator* · *ATLANTIC OCEAN* · *Tropic of Capricorn* · *Madagascar* · *INDIAN OCEAN*

Extent of Islam 750
Extent of Islam 900
Extent of Islam 1100
Extent of Islam 1500

0   400   800 miles
0   400   800 kilometers
Lambert Azimuthal Equal-Area Projection

SKILLBUILDER: Interpreting Maps

❶ **PLACE** On which continent did Islam begin?

❷ **MOVEMENT** Between which years did Islam achieve its greatest growth in Africa?

Economics of Oil

North Africa began with an economy b... course of its history, it evolved int... cash crops and mining. Today... covery of oil in the region.

BLACK GOLD Oil has... African countries, includ... surpassed farm produ... Furthermore, oil make... Algeria supply the...

Although oil has helped the economies of those countries, it has also caused some problems. For example, Libya's labor force cannot meet the demands of the oil industry because of a lack of training and education. Oil companies therefore are forced to give many high-paying jobs to foreign workers. Despite the oil industry, overall unemployment is still a problem. As a result, large numbers of North Africans have migrated to Europe in search of jobs.

A Culture of Markets and Music

North African culture is a combination of Arabic influences and traditional African ethnic groups.

NORTH AFRICAN *SOUKS* *Souks,* or marketplaces, are common features of life in North Africa. A country *souk* opens early in the morning. Tents are erected, and storytellers, musicians, and fortunetellers entertain the crowds. A typical city *souk* is located in the *medina,* or old section, of a North African town or city. A *medina* has narrow, winding streets. Some of the best *souks* in North Africa can be found in Marrakesh, Morocco. The markets are known for high-pressure sales, and shoppers must be prepared to bargain fiercely for the lowest price. B

In both the city and the country, people fill the *souks* throughout the day. All kinds of bartering and haggling take place for a range of products, including brightly colored clothes, spices, and a variety of foods. The aroma of lamb, spices, and animals fills the air. It is also a place where one can eat traditional foods such as couscous, a kind of steamed grain.

PROTEST MUSIC Algeria is home to **_rai,_** a kind of music developed in the 1920s by poor urban children. *Rai* was at first carefree and centered around topics for youths. The music is fast paced and contains elements of popular Western music.

Before Algerian independence in 1962, however, performers began using *rai* to communicate Algerian resentment toward their French

Geographic Thinking

Making Comparisons
◀ How are country and city *souks* alike? Different?

MOVEMENT
Moroccans flood this typical market in Marrakesh.
What role do markets play in the movements of goods and people?

colonizers. After independence, the Algerian government tried to ban *rai*. In the 1990s, Islamic fundamentalists have criticized *rai* for its Western-style qualities. *Rai* is now used as a form of rebellion against Islamic fundamentalists, especially by women.

Changing Roles of Women

Modern life in North Africa is in a constant state of change. The role of women, especially, has shifted during the past several years.

WOMEN AND THE FAMILY North African households tend to be centered around males. Men go out to work in offices or on farms. Few women hold jobs after they marry. Men and women also generally eat and pray separately.

Women's roles, however, are changing, especially in Tunisia, where having more than one wife at a time has been abolished. It has also increased the penalty for spousal abuse. Moreover, either spouse can now seek a divorce. In addition, Tunisia no longer permits preteen girls in arranged marriages and requires equal pay for equal jobs.

Women in North Africa have also made gains outside the home, particularly in cities. Growing numbers of them, for instance, have professional jobs. Women hold seven percent of Tunisia's parliamentary seats and manage nearly nine percent of the businesses in Tunis, the capital of Tunisia.

In the next section, you will read about how trade formed the foundation of ancient civilizations in West Africa.

MOVEMENT Two women in Western-style clothing pause outside a popular marketplace in Marrakesh, Morocco.

AFRICA

Assessment

① Places & Terms

Identify these terms and explain their importance in the region's history or culture.

- Carthage
- Islam
- *rai*

② Taking Notes

PLACE Review the notes you took for this section.

- What is the single biggest cultural influence in North Africa?
- Which commodity supports some of North Africa's economies?

③ Main Ideas

a. How did the Nile help support the growth of ancient Egypt?

b. Where did Islam spread after its beginnings in Southwest Asia?

c. In which ways have women's roles changed in North Africa?

④ Geographic Thinking

Drawing Conclusions
How has Islam influenced life in North Africa? **Think about:**

- its impact on women
- the religion that people practice

RESEARCH LINKS
CLASSZONE.COM

GeoActivity

SEEING PATTERNS Use the Internet or encyclopedias to learn about all the economic and recreational activities supported by the Nile River. Then create an **illustration** of the Nile River with those activities taking place.

West Africa

A HUMAN PERSPECTIVE A visit to **Gorée Island,** off the coast of Senegal, can be a moving experience. This island served as one of the busiest points for exporting slaves during the slave trade. From the mid-1500s to the mid-1800s, Europeans transported about 20 million Africans through Gorée Island. The island has a slave house, a dark, damp building that housed captive Africans. Europeans packed these captives onto slave ships bound for plantations in the Americas. Approximately 20 percent of all Africans died on the transatlantic voyage—and the rest never saw their West African homes or families again. Slavery had a profound effect on West Africa that is still being felt there today.

A History of Rich Trading Empires

West Africa includes Benin, Burkina Faso, Cape Verde, Chad, Côte d'Ivoire, Gambia, Ghana, Guinea, Guinea-Bissau, Liberia, Mali, Mauritania, Niger, Nigeria, Senegal, Sierra Leone, and Togo. West Africa is a cultural hearth, and its ideas and practices spread to North America and Europe.

Main Ideas
- Wealth from the gold and salt trades supported a series of West African empires.
- West Africa has a rich cultural tradition that has influenced many parts of the world.

Places & Terms
Gorée Island

stateless society

Ashanti

CONNECT TO THE ISSUES
COLONIALISM European nations took raw materials from West Africa. Today many West African countries rely on exports to support their economies.

SUNSHINE STATE STANDARDS
Key Standard SS.B.2.4.1 The student understands how social, cultural, economic, and environmental factors contribute to the dynamic nature of regions.

Other Standards SS.A.2.4.8, B.2.4.6

FCAT LA.A.1.4.2 Reading: Strategies

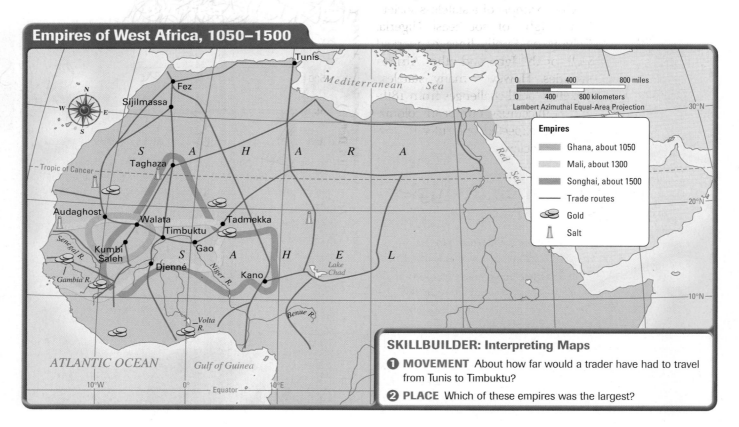

Empires of West Africa, 1050–1500

Empires
- Ghana, about 1050
- Mali, about 1300
- Songhai, about 1500
- Trade routes
- Gold
- Salt

SKILLBUILDER: Interpreting Maps

❶ MOVEMENT About how far would a trader have had to travel from Tunis to Timbuktu?

❷ PLACE Which of these empires was the largest?

THREE TRADING EMPIRES The empires of Ghana, Mali, and Songhai thrived in West Africa because of their location on trade routes across the Sahara. Gold and salt were the main products traded. By A.D. 200, trade across the Sahara had existed for many years.

Many of the trade routes crossed an area farmed by the Sonike people. They called their leader *ghana,* or war chief. Traders began to refer to this area as Ghana, which grew rich from taxing the traders who passed through its territory. Traders exchanged mostly gold and salt. Ghana became an empire around A.D. 800 but began to decline in power by the end of the 11th century. ◀

By 1235, the kingdom of Mali emerged. Mali's first great leader, Sundiata, conquered Ghana. He promoted agriculture and reestablished the gold and salt trade. Some experts estimate that until 1350, about two-thirds of the world's gold came from West Africa. Around 1400, Mali declined because of a lack of leadership and the discovery of new gold fields farther east.

Around 1400, the empire of Songhai replaced Mali. Sunni Ali ruled for 28 years, beginning in 1464. In 1591, a Moroccan army invaded Songhai and defeated it, destroying the empire.

STATELESS SOCIETIES West Africa is filled with many different cultures and peoples. Before colonialism, some of these people lived in what are called stateless societies.

A **stateless society** is one in which people rely on family lineages to govern themselves, rather than an elected government or a monarch. A lineage is a family or group that has descended from a common ancestor. Members of a stateless society work through their differences to cooperate and share power.

One example of a stateless society is the Igbo of southeast Nigeria. Relying on family lineages worked well for the Igbo and other African societies. However, many stateless societies faced challenges from 18th- and 19th-century European colonizers, who expected one ruler to govern the society.

West Africa Struggles Economically

Trade is as important to West Africa today as it was in the past. The economic well-being of West Africa is based on the sale of its products to industrialized countries in Europe, North America, and Asia. The economies of West Africa range in strength from the relatively solid economy of Ghana to the weak economy of Sierra Leone.

Geographic Thinking

Seeing Patterns
◀ Why did three empires prosper and grow in this area of West Africa?

BACKGROUND
One stateless society, the Nuer of southern Sudan, organized thousands of people without an official ruler.

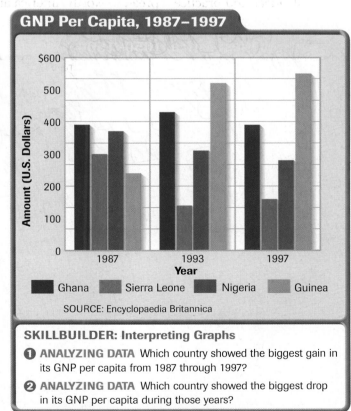

GNP Per Capita, 1987–1997

Amount (U.S. Dollars)

Year: 1987, 1993, 1997

■ Ghana   ■ Sierra Leone   ■ Nigeria   ■ Guinea

SOURCE: Encyclopaedia Britannica

SKILLBUILDER: Interpreting Graphs

❶ **ANALYZING DATA** Which country showed the biggest gain in its GNP per capita from 1987 through 1997?

❷ **ANALYZING DATA** Which country showed the biggest drop in its GNP per capita during those years?

AFRICA

GHANA'S STABILITY Ghana's economy relies primarily on the export of gold, diamonds, magnesium, and bauxite to the industrialized world. Ghana has a per capita income of $1,900, the second highest in West Africa. However, its per capita income is low compared to the industrialized world.

Ghana's transition from colonialism to democracy has had setbacks, including military rule and civil war. However, in 1992, 1996, and 2000, Ghana held free and fair elections. As a result of this new political stability, the economy is growing at a healthy rate. But other West African countries have not been as fortunate. **B**

Geographic Thinking

Seeing Patterns
B How is the economy of Ghana similar to those of the ancient West African kingdoms?

PROBLEMS IN SIERRA LEONE The worst economic conditions in West Africa exist in Sierra Leone, which once produced some of the world's highest-quality diamonds. However, years of political instability and civil wars have left the economy in shambles. In addition, a relatively uneducated population—with a 31 percent literacy rate—leaves a shortage of skilled workers. Finally, the road and transportation system contains few highways and only 800 miles of roads. In contrast, Benin, another West African country close to Sierra Leone in size, has about 5,000 miles of roads.

HUMAN-ENVIRONMENT INTERACTION A West African weaver makes *kente* cloth. **What are some skills that a weaver might need?**

Cultural Symbols of West Africa

West African cultures, such as the Ashanti and Benin, have produced elaborate craftwork and colorful textiles.

ASHANTI CRAFTS The **Ashanti,** who live in what is now Ghana, are known for their work in weaving colorful *asasia*—what Westerners usually call *kente* cloth. The designs of *kente* cloth contain colorful woven geometric figures with specific meanings. Only royalty were allowed to wear *kente* cloth.

Other crafts include making masks and carving wooden stools. An Ashanti stool symbolizes the unity between ancestral spirits and the living members of a family. Fathers often give their sons a stool as their first gift. In the case of kings, the stool represents the unity of the state with its people.

BENIN ART The kingdom of Benin, which has no direct connection with the current country of Benin, arose in what is now Nigeria in the 1200s. Benin artists made beautiful objects of metal and terra cotta. However, their most important works were fashioned from brass and are called Benin "bronzes." They include statues, masks, and jewelry. A common subject of Benin "bronzes" was that of the queen mother.

Music in Daily Life

Music is a large part of life in West Africa. West African music has become an important influence on world music.

WEST AFRICAN MUSIC West African popular music involves a blend of traditional African music with American forms of jazz, blues, and reggae—which also had their origins in West Africa because of the slave trade and the contact between the two regions. Over the years, West African musicians used French and English lyrics to attract an international audience. West African music is played on a wide variety of drums and other instruments such as the kora, a cross between a harp and a lute. The kora originated in what is now Guinea-Bissau.

King Sunny Adé, also known as the "minister of enjoyment," is a popular musician from Nigeria. King Sunny and his band, the African Beats, play an informal type of music characterized by tight vocals, complex guitar work, traditional talking drums, percussion instruments, and the pedal steel guitar and accordion.

In Section 4, you can read more about culture and life in Central Africa.

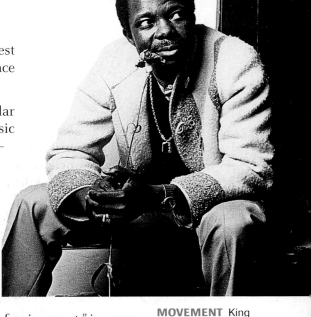

MOVEMENT King Sunny Adé's music blends sounds from North America and West Africa. **How do you think music moved from West Africa to North America?**

Assessment

1 Places & Terms

Identify these terms and explain their importance in the region's history or culture.

- Gorée Island
- stateless society
- Ashanti

2 Taking Notes

HUMAN-ENVIRONMENT INTERACTION Review the notes you took for this section.

- How did natural resources affect the ancient empires in West Africa?
- How do stateless societies differ from those with a centralized government?

3 Main Ideas

a. What three empires flourished because of trade in West Africa?

b. What are some of the roadblocks to economic development in West Africa?

c. What is the significance of the stool in Ashanti society?

4 Geographic Thinking

Making Comparisons How do the economics of Sierra Leone and Ghana differ?
Think about:

- Ghana's political stability
- the state of infrastructure in Sierra Leone

RESEARCH LINKS
CLASSZONE.COM

MAKING COMPARISONS Review the information about the West African economies on pages 443–444. Using the Internet or encyclopedias, find the per capita income of four other West African countries during the last ten years. Then create a **chart** comparing their growth or decline during that time.

Comparing Cultures

Feasts

All over the world, people celebrate certain events by holding a ritual feast. The autumn harvest, when the season's crops are gathered, is an important time in most cultures. As a result, many people have a special meal to celebrate the earth's bounty. Most harvest feasts are accompanied by a legend or story that tells of the feast's origins. For example, the American harvest feast began in 1621 when Pilgrims invited Native Americans to join them in a three-day celebration marking the harvest.

SUNSHINE STATE STANDARDS

Key Standard SS.B.2.4.1 The student understands how social, cultural, economic, and environmental factors contribute to the dynamic nature of regions.

FCAT LA.A.2.2.7 Reading: Recognize Compare and Contrast

People in India celebrate *Sankranti* by eating on traditional banana leaf plates. *Sankranti* celebrates the end of the year's harvest. Rice is a staple of this meal.

Chinese celebrate the moon festival in Hong Kong. Throughout history, the Chinese have planted and harvested according to the moon. The Chinese eat moon-shaped pastries filled with red bean and lotus seed paste.

Americans gather for their Thanksgiving feast. Roast turkey, potatoes, and pumpkin pie are traditional dishes for this meal.

GeoActivity

EXPLORING TRADITIONAL FEASTS
Working with a small group, use the Internet to research another feast from another culture. Then create a **presentation** about this feast.

• Write a short paragraph about the origin of the feast.

• Gather pictures of the traditional foods eaten at the feast.

• Identify other rituals besides eating that are part of this celebration.

RESEARCH LINKS
CLASSZONE.COM

A Ga chief in Ghana shares ceremonial food and drink during the Homowo harvest feast. The meal includes palm oil fish stew consisting of steamed corn dough, bream (fish), and okra.

GeoData

Homowo harvest feast

• According to traditional beliefs, any Ga person failing to celebrate Homowo will incur the wrath of deceased ancestors and die.

• Some Homowo events include opening the fishing season and house purification.

Thanksgiving

• Abraham Lincoln officially proclaimed Thanksgiving a national holiday in 1863. Canada first adopted Thanksgiving as a national holiday in 1879.

Sankranti

• A general housecleaning and the burning of unwanted possessions symbolizes the destruction of evil. Children also fill the sky wih kites in a kite-flying spectacle.

Moon Festival

• During the Tang Dynasty (A.D. 618–906), the moon festival was made an official holiday.

• During the Yuan Dynasty (1279–1368), Mongolians had taken over China. So the Chinese hid messages inside moon cakes to communicate with each other about their plans for rebellion.

Central Africa

Main Ideas
- The Bantu migrations helped to populate the African continent.
- European nations divided Africa without regard to ethnic groups or language.

Places & Terms
Bantu migrations
King Leopold II
Mobutu Sese Seko
Fang sculpture

CONNECT TO THE ISSUES
COLONIALISM European colonial policies so divided Africans that the region suffers from ethnic conflict today.

SUNSHINE STATE STANDARDS
Key Standard SS.B.2.4.1 The student understands how social, cultural, economic, and environmental . . .
Other Standards SS.A.3.4.3, D.2.4.1
FCAT LA.A.1.4.2 Reading: Strategies

A HUMAN PERSPECTIVE A Congo riverboat ride from Kinshasa to Kisangani in the Democratic Republic of the Congo is a journey all visitors should take. The riverboat is essentially a floating village. Each barge shakes with music and dancing. In addition, the Congolese fill the riverboat with market stalls stocked with all types of food. The smell of smoked fish and a variety of live animals, including monkeys, tortoises, and crocodiles, fills the air. Farmers slaughter pigs and goats on board, and merchants bargain with each other for a range of products. The journey can present a valuable snapshot of life in Central Africa.

Bantu Migrations and Colonial Exploitation

Central Africa includes Cameroon, Central African Republic, Democratic Republic of the Congo, Republic of the Congo, Equatorial Guinea, Gabon, and São Tomé and Princípe. Europeans first began their African colonization in Central Africa.

BANTU MIGRATIONS The Bantu are a group of peoples and cultures who speak one of the Bantu languages. Beginning around 2000 B.C. in what is now southeastern Nigeria, the Bantu people moved southward throughout Africa. On the way they spread their languages and their cultures. This mass migration is called the **Bantu migrations.**

The Bantu may have begun this journey because of a land shortage. The Bantu migrations are a key event in Africa's history. They produced a great diversity of cultures but also helped link various areas of the continent. Today, around 120 million Africans speak one of the hundreds of Bantu languages.

Bantu Migrations, 2000 B.C.–A.D. 1000

Overset
- Desert and dry shrub
- Tropical rain forest
- → Migration route

Original Bantu Area
2000 B.C.
Congo River
CENTRAL AFRICAN RAINFOREST
Equator
Lake Victoria
Lake Tanganyika
Lake Nyasa
INDIAN OCEAN
A.D. 1–500
Zambezi R.
NAMIB DESERT
A.D. 500–1000
KALAHARI DESERT
Orange R.
Limpopo R.
ATLANTIC OCEAN
Tropic of Capricorn

0   500   1,000 miles
0   500   1,000 kilometers
Azimuthal Equal-Area Projection

SKILLBUILDER: Interpreting Maps
❶ **MOVEMENT** About how many years did it take the Bantu to reach Southern Africa?
❷ **HUMAN–ENVIRONMENT INTERACTION** What physical obstacles did the Bantu have to overcome on their journey south?

THE SLAVE TRADE Europeans wanted slaves for their plantations in the Americas. In the 15th century, the Portuguese established the island of São Tomé off the coast of what is now Gabon as the initial base for trade in African captives. European traders traveled to Africa and waited on the coast. African merchants then brought potential slaves to them. The merchants traded for guns and other goods. ◀A

Many African rulers took part in the slave trade. They already had been selling slaves to other African rulers and Arabs. So, they saw no difference in selling them to Europeans. Some Africans, however, objected. One African ruler protested to the king of Portugal. Nevertheless, by the end of the slave trade in 1870, Europeans had transported millions of slaves to the Americas and Europe.

START OF COLONIALISM In the mid-1800s, Central Africa consisted of hundreds of different ethnic groups, which followed traditional religions and spoke hundreds of different languages. Politically, they ranged from large empires to small villages. Europeans had been in Africa since the mid-15th century but had stayed mainly on the coast. The rugged interior geography of Africa prevented further movement.

But that changed when **King Leopold II** of Belgium developed an interest in the Congo after it had been explored in the 1870s. He wanted to open the African interior to European trade along the Congo River. By 1884, Leopold controlled this area and paved the way for the Berlin Conference, which you read about in Section 1. The Berlin Conference established this area as the Congo Free State. Leopold used forced labor to gather rubber, palm oil, ivory, and other resources. ◀B

EFFECTS OF COLONIALISM During the 19th and 20th centuries, primarily the Belgians and French colonized Central Africa. Most Central African countries gained their independence in the 1960s, but the borders imposed on the Africans during colonialism posed problems. Those borders disrupted long-standing systems of government in Africa, did not consider ethnic regions, and grouped traditional enemies together.

Before colonization, a village, a tribal chief, or a group of elders would consult with various leaders within a village to make decisions that affected only that village. This type of organization is a stateless society, which you read about on page 443 in Section 3. During colonization, Europeans installed more centralized governments that destroyed the organizing principle of stateless societies. After colonization ended, new African governments in the 1960s were then forced to govern a diverse population. Inexperienced leaders were often corrupt and abused their power.

Geographic Thinking

Seeing Patterns
A▶ How did European traders obtain slaves from Africa's interior?

CONNECT TO THE ISSUES
COLONIALISM
B▶ Why did Africa become such a prized place for European powers?

IN THE RUBBER COILS.

MOVEMENT King Leopold II of Belgium takes control of Central Africa.
Why is King Leopold shown as a serpent?

AFRICA

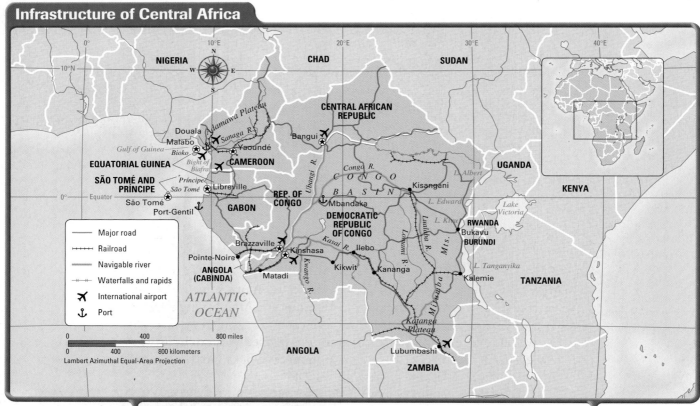

Infrastructure of Central Africa

Legend:
— Major road
+++ Railroad
— Navigable river
+++ Waterfalls and rapids
✈ International airport
⚓ Port

0   400   800 miles
0   400   800 kilometers
Lambert Azimuthal Equal-Area Projection

SKILLBUILDER: Interpreting Maps

❶ **MOVEMENT** Why do you think most of the transport routes begin in the middle of the continent and end on the coast?

❷ **MOVEMENT** What different modes of transport would you use to take goods from Kisangani in the Democratic Republic of the Congo to the coast?

The Economic Legacy of Colonialism

The economic geography of Central Africa is similar to that of the other regions of Africa. Many of the countries suffer from a lack of infrastructure and rely too much on the export of raw materials.

ECONOMIC EFFECTS Central Africa's economy is still recovering from the effects of colonialism: the loss of resources, the disruption of its political systems, and the cultural and ethnic oppression of its people. European colonizers invested little in Central Africa. The only economic infrastructure they developed was to aid the removal of raw materials. They left little money to develop roads, railroads, airports, or a productive education system for the people of those countries. ▶

CONGO'S ECONOMIC CHAOS A good example of economic problems caused by colonization can be seen in the Democratic Republic of the Congo. The country possesses huge amounts of natural resources such as gold, copper, and diamonds. However, European colonization and a personal desire for power and riches by postcolonial leaders left the country in a state of disarray.

In the Democratic Republic of the Congo, for example, **Mobutu Sese Seko,** the country's leader from 1967 until 1997, brought the country's businesses under national control. He then began to take kickbacks in order to profit from this reorganization. The country's economy, educational system, and social structure began a rapid decline thereafter.

CONNECT TO THE ISSUES
ECONOMIC DEVELOPMENT
◀ Why are many African countries still having difficulty developing their economies?

Mobutu used the army to maintain his own power. His regime finally gave way in 1997 to that of Laurent Kabila. But Kabila's leadership only led to more violence in Central Africa. By 1999, Angola, Namibia, Zimbabwe, Chad, Rwanda, and Uganda all had troops in the Democratic Republic of the Congo and were competing for its territory and resources. In 2001, Kabila was assassinated, and his son Joseph succeeded him. The Democratic Republic of the Congo is still struggling to establish a stable political system.

The Influence of Central African Art

Central African art shares common ideas and themes with art in other parts of Africa, including expressions of traditional African cultures and the struggle against colonialism.

CENTRAL AFRICAN ART For much of the 20th century, some of Central Africa's art has reflected attitudes toward colonialism. After having attained independence in the 1960s, however, these countries wanted to establish their own identities. As a result, many countries banned Western influences in their art. For example, in the 1970s, Mobutu Sese Seko launched a program to promote African—in particular, Congolese—culture above that of the West. Artists who participated wanted to recover the personality of African art by using materials they considered African in origin. ◀)

CONNECT TO THE ISSUES
COLONIALISM
▶ How might Mobutu's arts program have been a reaction against colonialism?

Today, artists from a new generation who did not experience colonialism are coming of age. They are focusing on issues of political instability, urban life, social justice, and crime.

FANG SCULPTURE Prior to the 20th century, few people in Europe knew much about African art. However, in 1907 the famous Spanish artist Pablo Picasso saw a display of African **Fang sculpture** in Paris, and it captivated him. After that, Picasso began using African themes in his work.

The Fang, who live in Gabon, southern Cameroon, and Equatorial Guinea, are famous for their carvings. They carve wooden masks, which are painted white with facial features outlined in black. They also carve boxes that contain the skulls and bones of deceased ancestors. These boxes are decorated with figures to protect their contents.

In this painting, *When There is Work, the Village Expands*, the houses in the background represent the village. The people moving in front are cooperating to make the village grow.

Improving Education

In recovering from the effects of colonialism, Central African countries are placing their hopes on education. Improved education should produce more skilled workers and citizens who are better able to participate in democratic governments.

EDUCATION FACES BARRIERS Adequate schooling for many of Africa's young people is in short supply. In 2001, experts estimate that less than half of sub-Saharan Africa's 16- to 20-year-olds attend school. Education problems in Central Africa include a shortage of trained teachers, a high dropout rate, and a shortage of secondary schools.

Central Africa's more than 700 languages also pose barriers. The language used in school is often different from the one used at home. For example, in Gabon—a former colony of France—French is the only language of instruction, though most people speak one of the Bantu languages outside the classroom.

LEARNING IN CENTRAL AFRICA Students' education varies in Central Africa. In Cameroon, most children leave school at around the age of 12. In the Central African Republic, children between the ages of 6 and 14 are required to go to school.

Many Central African countries are improving their educational systems, however. In 1991, Cameroon created two new universities. In addition, Libreville University in Gabon, founded in the 1970s, now has more than 4,000 students.

The Republic of the Congo offers vocational, agricultural, and teacher training courses. In addition, many countries are starting programs to educate young people about health care issues such as the spread of disease. Those countries hope that better education will slow the spread of AIDS, the Ebola virus, cholera, and other diseases.

You will read in Section 5 about how ancient trade networks and gold formed the economic foundation of Southern Africa.

SECTION 4 Assessment

❶ Places & Terms

Identify these terms and explain their importance in the region's history or culture.

- Bantu migrations
- King Leopold II
- Mobutu Sese Seko
- Fang sculpture

❷ Taking Notes

MOVEMENT Review the notes you took for this section.

- How did the Bantu migrations affect Africa's population?
- Who were the first Europeans to establish the African slave trade?

❸ Main Ideas

a. How did colonialism in Central Africa begin?

b. What are the subjects of the works of today's artists in Central Africa?

c. What problems does education face in Central Africa?

❹ Geographic Thinking

Seeing Patterns How did colonialism affect most African countries? **Think about:**

- their natural resources
- 20th century conflicts

See Skillbuilder Handbook, page R8.

EXPLORING LOCAL GEOGRAPHY Review the information about the Central African infrastructure on page 450. Create a **sketch map** showing all the major roads, highways, and railroads in your own neighborhood.

Southern Africa

Main Ideas

- Great Zimbabwe and the Mutapa Empire thrived on the gold trade.
- The wealth of Southern Africa is tied to the land, and conflicts over land and resources often result.

Places & Terms

Great Zimbabwe

Mutapa Empire

apartheid

Nelson Mandela

CONNECT TO THE ISSUES
HEALTH CARE AIDS threatens Southern Africa's youth and could significantly reduce the region's population.

SUNSHINE STATE STANDARDS
Key Standard SS.B.2.4.1 The student understands how social, cultural, economic, and environmental factors contribute to the dynamic nature of regions.

Other Standards SS.A.2.4.8

FCAT LA.A.1.4.2 Reading: Strategies

A HUMAN PERSPECTIVE In April 2000 in Zimbabwe, armed men attacked the farmhouse of a white farmer whose family has lived in Zimbabwe for generations. A political crisis that goes back to Britain's colonial rule caught white farmers in a violent crossfire. British colonial rule ended in 1980, but more than 4,000 white farmers in Zimbabwe still own one-third of the best land in a country of about 10 million blacks. The British and the white farmers have made attempts to equalize land ownership, but Zimbabwe's leaders have not taken advantage of these opportunities. Instead, they have targeted individual white farmers who own that land. This conflict illustrates a critical issue in all of Southern Africa—that blacks far outnumber whites but still own little of the land.

Gold Trade Builds Empires

Southern Africa includes Angola, Botswana, Comoros, Lesotho, Madagascar, Malawi, Mauritius, Mozambique, Namibia, South Africa, Swaziland, Zambia, and Zimbabwe. The history of Southern Africa involves a blending of colonialism with African cultures and the development of gold-trading empires.

GOLD TRADE SPAWNS GREAT ZIMBABWE The majority of the people in Southern Africa are Bantu-speaking peoples, including the Shona people. Around 1000, the Shona established a city called **Great Zimbabwe** in what is now the country of Zimbabwe.

From the 1200s to the 1400s, Great Zimbabwe became the capital of a thriving gold-trading area. But for unknown reasons, around 1450 the Shona abandoned Great Zimbabwe. One theory is that cattle grazing had exhausted the nearby grasslands, and overfarming had ruined the soil.

MUTAPA EMPIRE According to local legend, a man named Mutota left Great Zimbabwe around 1440 and settled in a fertile valley to the north. He founded a new state to replace Great Zimbabwe. By the time Mutota died, the **Mutapa Empire** extended throughout all of present-day Zimbabwe except the eastern part.

PLACE Pictured below are the walls of Great Zimbabwe.
What do the materials used to build the walls reveal about the local physical geography?

453

The Mutapa Empire thrived on the gold trade. In the 1500s, however, the Portuguese arrived and began interfering with the politics there. Soon, the Mutapa Empire began to decline. This event showed the increasing role Europeans would play in Southern Africa.

ETHNIC CLASH FOR SOUTHERN AFRICA As Europeans migrated to Southern Africa in the 1700s and 1800s, their presence led to conflicts with Africans. As the map below shows, many different ethnic groups were already living in Southern Africa. They competed with each other and with the Europeans for control of the land. In the early 19th century, the Zulu controlled a large area in Southern Africa. However, the British defeated the Zulu and by the late 19th century had taken over their land.

In the 1890s, the British battled the Dutch farmers, or Boers, in the Boer War for control of the region. The Boers had arrived in Southern Africa in the mid-1600s. The British won the war and formed the Union of South Africa in 1902. South Africa is currently a country in the region of Southern Africa.

THE POLICY OF APARTHEID IN SOUTH AFRICA In 1948, the white minority government of South Africa instituted a policy of **apartheid,** or complete separation of the races. It banned social contact between blacks and whites and established segregated schools, hospitals, and neighborhoods. Although blacks made up 75 percent of the population, they received only a small percentage of the land. The government kept the best land for whites.

In 1912, blacks had founded the African National Congress (ANC) to fight for their rights. In 1949, **Nelson Mandela** emerged as one of the

Geographic Thinking

Seeing Patterns
A What led to the conflicts between Europeans and groups of people already living in Southern Africa?

BACKGROUND
Segregation is the separation of people on the basis of race or ethnicity.

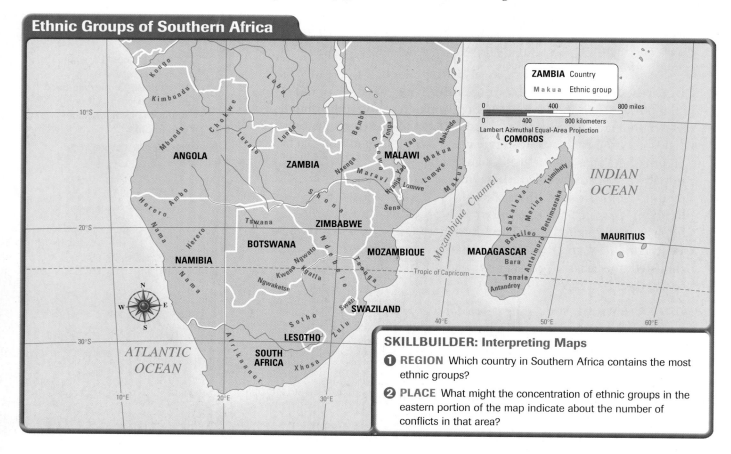

Ethnic Groups of Southern Africa

ZAMBIA Country
Makua Ethnic group

0   400   800 miles
0   400   800 kilometers
Lambert Azimuthal Equal-Area Projection

SKILLBUILDER: Interpreting Maps

❶ **REGION** Which country in Southern Africa contains the most ethnic groups?

❷ **PLACE** What might the concentration of ethnic groups in the eastern portion of the map indicate about the number of conflicts in that area?

leaders of the ANC, and he led a long struggle to end apartheid that resulted in his being imprisoned. By the 1980s, nations around the world—including the United States—pressured South Africa to end apartheid. In 1989, F. W. de Klerk became the president, and he wanted to change South Africa.

As a result, South Africa experienced a peaceful revolution, and the government ended its apartheid laws. An election that involved members of all races in South Africa took place in 1994. Mandela, having been released from prison, won the election and became president. In 1996, the government passed a new, democratic constitution that guarantees the rights of all citizens.

Southern Africa Grows Economically

The economies of Southern African countries are some of the most advanced in Africa. However, many countries are struggling to raise the standard of living for blacks, who get the worst jobs, own the least productive land, and attend the worst schools.

SOUTH AFRICA The policy of apartheid has hurt the economy of South Africa. Because of apartheid, foreign nations imposed economic sanctions that prevented their countries from conducting business with or investing in South Africa. In addition, the policy led to poor education of blacks, creating an uneducated mass of young people. As a result, two economies exist in South Africa.

One segment of South Africa has an upper-middle-income economy like that of the United States. South Africa possesses great cities with huge industrial complexes, such as Johannesburg and Cape Town. It also has modern, mechanized farms and large ranches. In contrast, though, South Africa also has poverty-stricken rural areas. Black townships and shantytowns also fill portions of the cities. Furthermore, the government currently faces problems arising from unequal land distribution and a severe housing shortage. **B**

Geographic Thinking

Making Comparisons
B What are the two segments of South Africa's economy?

SUCCESS AT A COST Botswana illustrates a problem that exists in many African countries today. It made a great deal of money from valuable resources but has serious agricultural problems and an unequal distribution of wealth. Botswana gained its independence from Britain in 1966 and subsequently experienced long-term economic growth. In 1966, its per capita income stood at $69. In 1997, that figure had risen to $3,900 per capita.

Southern Africa, 1800–2000

1819
The **Zulu** (left) establish their supremacy in Southern Africa.

1836
Boers (right) come into conflict with native groups in Southern Africa.

1891
DeBeers gained 90 percent of African diamond industry.

1905
The world's largest diamond, called the **"Star of Africa,"** (above) is cut in South Africa.

1912
The African National Congress is formed.

1948
Apartheid begins in South Africa.

1973
Swaziland bans political parties, and its king assumes absolute power.

1994
Nelson Mandela and **F. W. de Klerk** (below) shake hands after Mandela wins South Africa's first multiracial election.

Botswana's wealth is based on minerals. People discovered diamonds there shortly after the country's independence from Britain. By 1995, Botswana had become the world's third largest diamond producer. Diamonds account for more than 63 percent of government revenue. A problem, however, is the uneven distribution of the profits—an issue in many African countries.

CONNECT TO THE ISSUES
ECONOMIC DEVELOPMENT
How has Botswana increased its wealth?

Approximately 80 percent of the people work as farmers and never benefit from the diamond revenue. The other 20 percent grow wealthy from diamond money. One problem developing from this unequal distribution is that wealthy people are purchasing large tracts of land for cattle ranching from poor farm owners. As a result, poor farmers often move to less productive land. Meat production then increases, but overall food production actually decreases. The country winds up producing only 50 percent of the food needed to feed its population. The rest must be imported or come from international aid.

AIDS AFFECTS SOUTHERN AFRICA By 1999, the most severe AIDS-affected countries were in Southern Africa. In Zimbabwe and Botswana, for example, more than 25 percent of all adults were infected with HIV, the virus that causes AIDS. In Botswana, the life expectancy was 60 years old in 1994 but had declined to 39 years of age in 1999. The disease also has far-ranging implications for any country's economic well-being. In Botswana, many highly trained diamond sorters have died from the disease.

REGION Colorfully painted Ndebele houses, like the one shown below, are common in South Africa. **Why might the Ndebele have painted their houses in this way?**

Celebrations of Southern Africa

Southern Africa is a rich mosaic of cultures and traditions. More than any other region, it is a mix of African and European cultures.

A VARIETY OF DANCES Celebrations and festivals are a large part of life in Southern Africa. The Chewa people perform a dance called the *gule wa mkulu,* which reflects their traditional religious beliefs. Dancers dress in ragged costumes of cloth and animal skins. They wear masks and sometimes walk on stilts.

The Tumbuka people in northern Malawi perform the *vimbuza,* a dance performed by healers who wish to cure people of sickness. Other dances include the *benji* dance of the Yao people in southern Malawi. This dance, performed by Yao warriors, pokes fun at what these warriors saw as the desire of the European militaries to march and have parades.

In Madagascar, during the *hira gasy* festival, costumed groups of 25 or more people play music, perform dances, and act out stories. The themes are upbeat and praise the virtues of honesty and respect for elders.

Living in Southern Africa

Johannesburg, South Africa, is one of Southern Africa's largest cities and offers its residents a variety of opportunities and experiences.

Geographic Thinking

Seeing Patterns

D What resource fueled the growth of both Johannesburg and Great Zimbabwe?

JOHANNESBURG About 100 years ago, Johannesburg began as a small mining town and grew because of nearby gold reserves. Today, greater Johannesburg is a city of more than six million people with many different ethnicities and lifestyles. The center of Johannesburg looks like most modern big cities, with a cluster of skyscrapers dotting the skyline. However, as a result of apartheid, greater Johannesburg developed into two different cities. To the north lie the spacious suburbs that were once exclusively white. To the south are poor black townships. ◁D

MODERN AND TRADITIONAL LIFESTYLES Some Southern Africans live a modern lifestyle as doctors, lawyers, and businesspeople. These people live in tree-lined suburbs that look no different from those found in the United States. Many blacks, on the other hand, because of apartheid's legacy, still work in menial and unskilled jobs. They still live in the former black-only homelands and shantytowns.

Some ethnic groups of Southern Africa follow more traditional patterns as farmers, traders, or herders. For example, the Zulu either work in menial jobs, such as mining, or cling to their traditional roles as farmers and metalworkers. The Zulu have a long tradition of making hoes, spears, axes, and other tools and weapons.

In the next chapter you will read more about major issues facing Africa today, including economic development, health care, and the effects of colonialism.

AFRICA

SECTION 5 ▶ Assessment

❶ Places & Terms

Identify these terms and explain their importance in the region's history or culture.

- Great Zimbabwe
- Mutapa Empire
- apartheid
- Nelson Mandela

❷ Taking Notes

PLACE Review the notes you took for this section.

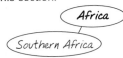

Africa

Southern Africa

- What was the basis for the growth of Great Zimbabwe?
- How would you describe the occupations of the people who live in Southern Africa?

❸ Main Ideas

a. Who ended the system of apartheid in South Africa?

b. How is AIDS affecting Botswana's economy?

c. What are some of the major traditional cultural activities in Southern Africa?

❹ Geographic Thinking

Identifying and Solving Problems How did apartheid affect the economy of South Africa? **Think about:**

- how blacks were treated
- international economic sanctions

RESEARCH LINKS
CLASSZONE.COM

GeoActivity

MAKING COMPARISONS Review the information about Botswana's economy on pages 455–456. Using the Internet or encyclopedias, find out where the major natural resources are located in each country of the region. Then create a **resources map** of Southern Africa.

VISUAL SUMMARY
HUMAN GEOGRAPHY OF AFRICA

Subregions of Africa

● East Africa
- East Africa's location on the Red Sea and Indian Ocean has made it a major trading center throughout history.
- AIDS has become a major health problem in East Africa.

● North Africa
- The Nile River supported the growth of ancient Egypt.
- Islam is the major cultural and religious influence in North Africa.

○ West Africa
- Gold and salt provided the basis for three great empires in West Africa.
- Many of West Africa's economies rely too much on exporting raw materials.

● Central Africa
- The Bantu migrations helped to populate the African continent.
- Colonialism caused long-term damage to the economies and cultures of African nations.

● Southern Africa
- Gold provided the basis for great empires in Southern Africa.
- Apartheid hurt the economies of Southern Africa because of international economic sanctions and inadequate education of blacks.

Reviewing Places & Terms

A. Briefly explain the importance of each of the following.

1. Berlin Conference
2. pandemic
3. Islam
4. stateless society
5. Ashanti
6. Bantu migrations
7. Fang sculpture
8. Great Zimbabwe
9. apartheid
10. Nelson Mandela

B. Answer the questions about vocabulary in complete sentences.

11. Which term is used to describe the policy used to separate blacks and whites in South Africa?
12. What type of art influenced some of Pablo Picasso's work?
13. What meeting by European nations set the rules and conditions for the takeover of Africa?
14. Which African people place a high value on wooden stools?
15. What is the system called that uses family lineages to govern people?
16. Who led the ANC in the second half of the 20th century and helped to end apartheid in South Africa?
17. What is the largest cultural and religious influence in North Africa?
18. Which empire thrived on the gold trade in Southern Africa?
19. What term describes a disease outbreak affecting a large population in a wide geographic area?
20. What movement of people helped to bring a sense of unity of language to much of Africa?

Main Ideas

East Africa (pp. 431–437)

1. How did East Africa's location help it to become a major international trading center?
2. What impact did the Berlin Conference have on Africa?

North Africa (pp. 438–441)

3. How did Islam become the biggest influence in North Africa?
4. How have women's roles in North Africa changed over the years?

West Africa (pp. 442–447)

5. What are the similarities and differences among the three West African kingdoms of Ghana, Mali, and Songhai?
6. What are some of the problems faced by West African economies?

Central Africa (pp. 448–452)

7. Why were the Bantu migrations important in African history?
8. What are some of the problems facing education in Central Africa?

Southern Africa (pp. 453–457)

9. How have natural resources affected the economy of Southern Africa?
10. How was apartheid brought to an end?

Critical Thinking

1. Using Your Notes

Use your completed chart to answer these questions.

a. How were the precolonial kingdoms of West Africa similar to or different from the precolonial kingdoms of Southern Africa?

b. How did colonialism change Africa and its people?

2. Geographic Themes

a. **MOVEMENT** How did the movement of Islam from Southwest Asia to North Africa affect the African continent?

b. **HUMAN-ENVIRONMENT INTERACTION** What role did natural resources play in the colonization of Africa?

3. Identifying Themes

How did natural resources affect the formation of ancient African kingdoms and empires? Which of the five themes apply to this situation?

4. Making Comparisons

How did stateless societies in Africa differ from centralized governments?

5. Determining Cause and Effect

What prompted the Berlin Conference, and what effects did it have on Africa's culture and economy?

Additional Test Practice, pp. S1–S37

TEST PRACTICE
CLASSZONE.COM

Geographic Skills: Interpreting Graphs

Languages of Nigeria

Use the graph below to answer the following questions.

1. **ANALYZING DATA** What percentage of Nigerians speak English?

2. **MAKING GENERALIZATIONS** Which language group is the most commonly spoken?

3. **MAKING INFERENCES** How might the number of languages in Nigeria affect a newly formed democratic government?

GeoActivity

Choose another country in Africa. Then using the library, encyclopedias, or other reference books, create your own language pie chart.

SOURCE: Ethnologue.com

INTERNET ACTIVITY

Use the links at **classzone.com** to do research on the people of one African country. Look for such information as age range, religions, ethnic groups, literacy rates, and per capita income.

Constructing a Population Pyramid Using the information you have gathered, construct a population pyramid describing the population characteristics of the society you have chosen.

Chapter 20

TODAY'S ISSUES
Africa

SECTION 1
Economic Development

SECTION 2
Health Care

CASE STUDY
EFFECTS OF COLONIALISM

For more on these issues in Africa . . .

 CURRENT EVENTS
CLASSZONE.COM

Miners in Johannesburg,
South Africa, dig for gold.

GeoFocus

How are African nations trying to resolve the issues facing their countries?

Taking Notes In your notebook, copy a cause-and-effect chart like the one shown below for each issue. Then take notes on the causes and effects of the issues.

	Causes	Effects
Issue 1: Economic Development		
Issue 2: Health Care		
Case Study: Effects of Colonialism		

Economic Development

How can African nations develop their economies?

Main Ideas

- Africa's history of colonization has had long-term effects on its economy.
- Barriers to African economic development include illiteracy, foreign debt, and a lack of manufacturing industries.

Places & Terms

"one-commodity" country

commodity

diversify

A HUMAN PERSPECTIVE Mauwa Funidi wonders about the future of her country, the Democratic Republic of the Congo, as she looks around the rundown university library where she works. She has not been paid her salary of 12 dollars per month in many months. Classes at the university have been suspended because of a lack of funds. Funidi survives only by selling little bags of charcoal on the streets of Kisangani. Funidi, like many other Africans, is trying to scrape out a living on a continent where people's standard of living has gotten worse over the last 30 years. Nevertheless, many African countries have vowed to change their fortunes with better government, better relations with neighbors, more investment in education, and a diverse economy.

SUNSHINE STATE STANDARDS
Key Standard SS.B.2.4.7 The student understands the concept of sustainable development.

Other Standards SS.B.2.4.5, B.2.4.2

FCAT LA.A.1.4.2 Reading: Strategies

Africa's Economy Today

Most African nations have little manufacturing of their own. Their economies are based on providing raw materials—oil, minerals, or agricultural products—to the world's industrialized countries.

A HISTORY OF PROBLEMS As you learned in the previous chapter, European colonizers exploited Africa's resources and people during the past few centuries. Millions of Africans were sold into slavery, and countless others have died in Africa from harsh working conditions while obtaining raw materials for foreign interests. In addition, the land has been mined and drilled with little regard for the environment. This history of exploitation has limited Africa's economic growth and fostered political instability. Without political stability, consistent economic growth is difficult.

HUMAN-ENVIRONMENT INTERACTION Much of Africa's infrastructure is undeveloped. With few paved roads, trucks get bogged down on muddy roads, such as this one in the Democratic Republic of the Congo.

AFRICA'S ECONOMIC STATUS Today, most African countries are worse off economically than they were in the 1960s, just after many of them gained independence from European colonizers. In the last 30 years, average incomes in Africa have decreased, while they have increased in most of the rest of the world. Africa accounts for only 1 percent of total world GNP and 1.5 percent of total dollar value of world exports—both

461

small numbers compared to Africa's population and natural resources. The whole of Africa's economy is about as large as that of Argentina's.

Furthermore, the economic infrastructure needed for substantial growth is not in place. Roads, airports, railroads, and ports are not adequate to help African nations further their economic growth. **A**

In addition, most Africans don't have access to computers or other aspects of high technology. High technology has fueled economic growth in other parts of the world such as North America, Europe, and Asia.

Geographic Thinking

Seeing Patterns
A Why do you think good roads are important to the functioning of an economy?

On the Road to Development

Despite this legacy of exploitation, African nations are struggling to build economies based on the careful use of natural and human resources.

REDUCING DEBT AND INCREASING COOPERATION When the colonial nations pulled out of Africa, they often left the newly independent nations without money for transportation, education, and businesses. To build their economies, African countries borrowed heavily. By 1997, total public debt of sub-Saharan African governments—about 227 billion dollars—was strangling them. As a result, many Western leaders have urged their countries to forgive Africa's debts so that it has more money to build its economies.

Another way that Africa seeks to improve its economy is through regional cooperation. The Economic Community of West African States (ECOWAS) and the Southern African Development Community (SADC) are both striving to promote trade. For example, ECOWAS is working toward removing duties and creating a common currency. Efforts of SADC include working to improve the transportation and communication infrastructures.

BACKGROUND
In 1998, over 57 percent of Africa's total GNP went to repaying its debts.

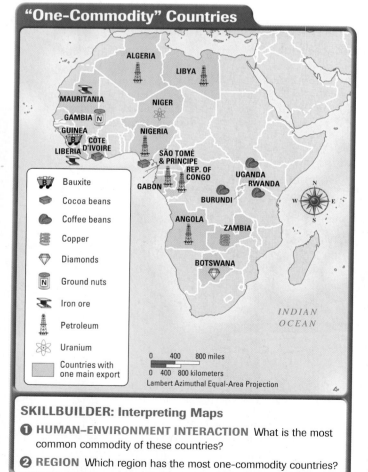

"One-Commodity" Countries

ALGERIA
LIBYA
MAURITANIA
NIGER
GAMBIA N
GUINEA
NIGERIA
CÔTE
LIBERIA D'IVOIRE
SÃO TOMÉ
& PRINCIPE
REP. OF
CONGO
UGANDA
RWANDA
GABON
BURUNDI
ANGOLA
ZAMBIA
BOTSWANA

INDIAN
OCEAN

B Bauxite
    Cocoa beans
    Coffee beans
    Copper
    Diamonds
N Ground nuts
    Iron ore
    Petroleum
    Uranium
    Countries with
    one main export

0   400   800 miles
0 400 800 kilometers
Lambert Azimuthal Equal-Area Projection

SKILLBUILDER: Interpreting Maps

❶ HUMAN–ENVIRONMENT INTERACTION What is the most common commodity of these countries?

❷ REGION Which region has the most one-commodity countries?

BUILDING INDUSTRIES The economy of many African nations is based on the export of raw materials. Furthermore, several of Africa's countries rely on just one or two principal commodities for much of their earnings. These are called **"one-commodity" countries.** A **commodity** is an agricultural or mining product that can be sold. The value of a commodity varies from day to day based on worldwide supply and demand. That makes the economies of the producing nations—especially "one-commodity" countries—unstable. Economists believe African nations must **diversify,** or create variety in, their economies and promote manufacturing to achieve economic growth and stability.

BACKGROUND
The Highland's Water Project of Lesotho will eventually allow the country to generate its own electricity, instead of having to buy it from South Africa.

Geographic Thinking

Seeing Patterns
B Why do you think education is important to Africa's economy?

Some African nations are making strides toward that goal. In East Africa, Djibouti is using its location on the Gulf of Aden to establish a major international shipping center.

Educating Workers

A key to developing Africa's economies is improving its education system to provide people with a high level of skills. African nations must also find ways to prevent their educated citizens from leaving the continent.

IMPROVING EDUCATION A large barrier to economic development in Africa is an unschooled population. For example, the average length of school attendance for African women has increased only by 1.2 years in the last 40 years. In some countries, such as Angola and Somalia, civil wars have all but destroyed the school systems. **B**

Some African countries, however, are making progress. For example, in Algeria, 94 percent of the country's school-age population receive a formal education. Mauritius has also made huge gains. Currently, 83 percent of Mauritians over the age of 15 are literate.

REVERSING THE BRAIN DRAIN Another priority is slowing the departure of African professionals to Western countries. In 1983, the International Organization for Migration began a campaign to encourage these professionals to return home.

As Africa moves into the 21st century, efforts to improve education, invest in industry, and create stable governments provide hope for the future.

Geography TODAY

Hi-Tech Tracking

As the scorching sun of the Kalahari Desert beats down on Karel Kleinman, he puts information into a palm-sized computer. Kleinman tracks animals in the same desert as his !Koi grandfather did. But now Kleinman uses high technology to follow the animals.

Louis Liebenberg of South Africa developed this application to collect information about animals more efficiently. For example, some of the data will help protect certain species from drought. Liebenberg's idea both protects Africa's resources and shows how well-educated people can solve problems.

AFRICA

SECTION
Assessment

❶ Places & Terms

Explain the meaning of each of the following terms.

- "one-commodity" country
- commodity
- diversify

❷ Taking Notes

PLACE Review the notes you took for this section.

	Causes	Effects
Issue 1		

- What are some of the causes of economic problems of African countries?
- What impact is Africa's debt having on its ability to build its economy?

❸ Main Ideas

a. What has happened to people's incomes over the last half-century?

b. What is one problem for "one-commodity" countries?

c. Why is improving education important to Africa's economy?

❹ Geographic Thinking

Making Generalizations
What actions should African nations take to form a solid economic foundation? **Think about:**

- economic cooperation
- education

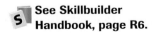
S **See Skillbuilder Handbook, page R6.**

GeoActivity

EXPLORING LOCAL GEOGRAPHY Find out how your city or state promotes economic development. Learn about laws passed to promote growth or tax breaks given to certain industries. Then write a **news article** on the topic.

SUNSHINE STATE STANDARDS
Key Standard SS.B.1.4.1
The student uses a variety of maps, geographic technologies including geographic information systems (GIS) and satellite-produced imagery, and other advanced graphic representations to depict geographic problems.

FCAT LA.A.1.4.2 Reading: Strategies

Reading a City Map

Johannesburg, South Africa, is one of the youngest major cities in the world. It grew rapidly following the discovery of gold in 1886. Today, it is South Africa's largest city and the country's financial and industrial center. Looking at the city map below, you can see that the streets of the city center are laid out in a grid. A grid is something resembling a framework of crisscrossing parallel bars.

THE LANGUAGE OF MAPS A **city map** is essentially another kind of road map. However, it is usually set at a larger scale than a state road map in order to show greater detail to guide both visitors and residents. Many city maps show the names of streets, major tourist attractions, bus and train stations, and other useful buildings.

Johannesburg

▨	Parks
▨	Principal buildings
▨	Rail/Bus stations
▬	Major highways
—	Streets and roads
┼┼┼	Railways

0   0.1   0.2 Mi.
0   0.1   0.2   0.3 Km.

Johannesburg, South Africa

Copyright by Rand McNally & Co.

❶ Points of interest are shown to help tourists plan their visit.

❷ Labeling major streets is necessary to guide people around the city.

❸ Letters at the top and bottom and numbers on the sides identify the grid sections created by the black lines. The grid sections help readers find places on the map. Most city maps have an index listing places on the map and the grid sections where they appear.

Map and Graph Skills Assessment

1. Making Generalizations
If you took the train into Johannesburg, how would you get to the railway museum by foot and about how long would it take?

2. Drawing Conclusions
Where is the most likely place for a picnic in this part of the city? What are the place's index coordinates?

3. Making Inferences
If you spent a weekend in Johannesburg, what are at least five activities available to you in the city?

Health Care

How can African countries eliminate the diseases that threaten their people and cultures?

Main Ideas
- Epidemic diseases are killing Africa's people in huge numbers.
- African nations and countries around the world are using a variety of methods, including education, to eradicate disease.

Places & Terms
AIDS
cholera
malaria
tuberculosis
UNAIDS

SUNSHINE STATE STANDARDS
Key Standard SS.D.2.4.3 The student understands how government taxes, policies, and programs affect individuals, groups, businesses, and regions.

Other Standards SS.B.2.4.1

FCAT LA.A.1.4.2 Reading: Strategies

A HUMAN PERSPECTIVE On June 1, 2001, Nkosi Johnson died from the human immunodeficiency virus (HIV)—the virus that causes **acquired immune deficiency syndrome (AIDS).** He was the longest living South African child born with HIV. In February, he celebrated his 12th birthday—but weighed just 27 pounds. Living with a foster mother, the child had become a symbol of hope in a nation suffering from AIDS. He frankly discussed the problems of the disease and received cheers at the world's largest AIDS conference in Durban, South Africa, in July 2000. His plight was typical of many on the continent, as African nations struggle to deal with this and other diseases.

Disease and Despair

Controlling AIDS and other diseases is essential if Africans are to improve their quality of life and live a normal lifespan.

SERIOUS DISEASES African nations are threatened by a variety of diseases. Inadequate sanitation and lack of a clean water supply can lead to **cholera,** an infection that is often fatal if not treated. In 2000–2001, widespread flooding caused some cases of cholera in Mozambique, but international relief efforts prevented a widespread outbreak.

Diseases in Africa, 1900 and 2000

Leading Diseases 1900

Malaria
First reference in Greece around 400 B.C.

Sleeping Sickness
First described around A.D. 1300 in present-day Mali.

Smallpox
First evidence c. 1156 B.C. in Egypt. Eradicated A.D. 1977.

Leading Diseases 2000

Malaria
Ninety percent of world's estimated 250 million malaria cases occur in Africa.

Sleeping Sickness
Affects 60 million people annually in Africa.

AIDS
Origins of HIV traced to Central Africa in 1959.

SKILLBUILDER: Interpreting Charts
❶ **MAKING COMPARISONS** What was a leading disease in Africa in 1900 but not in 2000?
❷ **DRAWING CONCLUSIONS** What disease occurs in Africa in 2000 but not in 1900?

Mosquitos carrying **malaria**—an infectious disease marked by chills and fevers that is often fatal—are common in African countries. The disease has become resistant to standard drugs because of overuse of those drugs in treating the disease during the past several decades. AIDS and HIV, however, create the most severe problems. Seventy percent of the world's adult AIDS cases and 80 percent of the world's children with AIDS are in African nations. AIDS is often accompanied by **tuberculosis,** a respiratory infection spread between humans.

AIDS Stalks the Continent

In 2000, AIDS took the lives of three million people worldwide. Of these, 2.4 million lived in sub-Saharan Africa. In Swaziland, three of every four deaths were attributed to AIDS. The AIDS epidemic in Swaziland has caused life expectancy there to drop from 58 years to 39 years. In 2000, nearly 26 million people in Africa were living with either HIV or AIDS.

A HIGH PRICE TO PAY Widespread disease has economic consequences. People who are sick work less or not at all, earn less, and thus are pushed further into poverty. Economists project that by 2010, the GDP of South Africa will be 17 percent lower than it would have been if not for AIDS. Furthermore, AIDS patients' medical care is also expensive. **UNAIDS,** the UN program that studies the world's AIDS epidemic, estimates that $4.63 billion will be needed to fight AIDS in Africa.

Nations Respond

Response to these epidemics comes both from African nations and from countries around the world.

A VARIETY OF ANSWERS To fight malaria and other insect-borne diseases, African nations have used spraying programs since the 1930s to reduce the number of insects. In 2000, the Global Fund for Children's Vaccines pledged more than $250 million for use over the next five years for immunization programs in Africa, Asia, Latin America, and Europe.

Some African countries are fighting disease by improving their health care systems. Gabon, for example, has used oil revenues to improve its health care system substantially. In addition, the African Development Fund approved a loan of nearly 12.3 million dollars to enable Mozambique to upgrade its public health facilities.

BACKGROUND
According to the U.S. Agency for International Development, by 2010, nearly 30 million children will have lost at least one parent to AIDS.

Geographic Thinking

Using the Atlas
Ⓐ Using the atlas and the map on the left, which other countries could rely on revenues from oil to improve their health care systems?

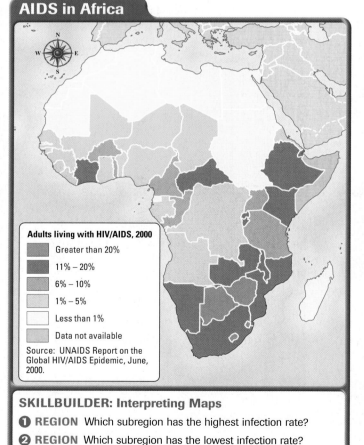

AIDS in Africa

Adults living with HIV/AIDS, 2000
- Greater than 20%
- 11% – 20%
- 6% – 10%
- 1% – 5%
- Less than 1%
- Data not available

Source: UNAIDS Report on the Global HIV/AIDS Epidemic, June, 2000.

SKILLBUILDER: Interpreting Maps
❶ **REGION** Which subregion has the highest infection rate?
❷ **REGION** Which subregion has the lowest infection rate?

STRATEGIES AGAINST AIDS

Fighting and preventing AIDS is being done on many levels. In December 2000, South Africa and Brazil reached an agreement to work together on AIDS prevention and care. Brazil's public health policies to combat AIDS and other diseases are considered a model for developing countries.

SUCCESS STORIES Two countries, Uganda and Senegal, have had success in reducing the spread of HIV. Uganda's government has spearheaded efforts to combat AIDS. For example, in 1997, Uganda began to offer same-day HIV tests and education programs. Infection rates among 15 to 24 year olds have dropped by 50 percent. On the other hand, Senegal has controlled the spread of the disease from the outset through an intensive education program. Infection rates have remained below two percent since the mid-1980s. **B**

UNAIDS says that HIV infection rates in 2000 in sub-Saharan Africa dropped by 200,000 cases from 1999. However, UNAIDS cautions that the drop in HIV infection rates could mean that almost as many people are dying of AIDS as are being infected with HIV. Nevertheless, many African nations are taking action. With these efforts, African countries can build an effective health care system and make progress against the epidemics that threaten its peoples and cultures.

Geographic Thinking

Making Comparisons

B What are the differences in the ways that Uganda and Senegal have tried to slow the spread of AIDS?

PLACE Kenyans gather outside a health clinic near Nairobi to learn about the dangers of AIDS.

AFRICA

SECTION 2 Assessment

1 Places & Terms

Explain the meaning of each of the following terms.

- AIDS
- cholera
- malaria
- tuberculosis
- UNAIDS

2 Taking Notes

PLACE Review the notes you took for this section.

	Causes	Effects
Issue 2		

- What are some of the serious diseases affecting African countries?
- How has AIDS affected Swaziland?

3 Main Ideas

a. What are some of the causes of cholera and malaria?

b. How is AIDS affecting the population of Africa's countries?

c. Why might the drop in HIV infection rates not indicate progress in slowing AIDS?

4 Geographic Thinking

Identifying and Solving Problems How have African nations slowed the spread of the continent's diseases?

Think about:

- the different programs
- international cooperation

RESEARCH LINKS
CLASSZONE.COM

MAKING COMPARISONS Using encyclopedias or the Internet, find out what the leading diseases are in the United States and identify their primary causes. Compare your findings to the leading diseases in Africa in a **chart** on the topic.

EFFECTS OF
COLONIALISM

How can African nations bring peace and stability to their people?

OUR FREE NATION - NA-MIBIA

Young people celebrate Namibia's independence from South Africa in 1990.

The Voyageur Experience in World Geography
Kenya: National Identity and Unity

SUNSHINE STATE STANDARDS
Key Standard SS.B.2.4.6 The student understands the relationships between resources and the exploration, colonization, and settlement of different regions of the world.

Other Standards SS.A.1.4.3, A.3.4.3

FCAT LA.A.2.4.8 Reading: Synthesize and Conclude

Africa, at the beginning of the 19th century, was home to great empires and rich cultures such as the Zulu, the Ashanti, and the Hausa. At the end of the 19th century, Africa was a place of European colonial power and oppression. European governments and financial agents based in such places as French West Africa, Belgian Congo, and British East Africa controlled much of the continent. Africa has not been the same since. Much of the poverty and violence of the 20th century is the direct result of colonialism. As you read the Case Study, consider how Africa might overcome the legacy of European colonialism.

Colonizing Africa

During the 15th century, Portuguese ships, looking for trade routes to Asia, landed in Africa. Soon other European countries established coastal trading stations there.

EUROPEANS IN AFRICA By the mid-1800s, Europeans knew of Africa's rich natural resources. They wanted these raw materials to fuel their own industrial economies and to establish markets to sell and trade their goods. In 1884–1885, the Berlin Conference, which you read about in Chapter 19, set down rules for dividing up Africa. European colonial control of Africa began to end in the early 20th century, but most African countries gained their independence in the 1960s. The Europeans did long-term damage to Africa, affecting its cultural and ethnic boundaries, and ruining its economy.

Challenges of Independence

When the European colonial powers were forced to leave Africa, the newly independent African countries did not have stable governments in place. For the next 40 years, many of the newly established African nations and their peoples suffered through dictatorships and civil wars. Many of these conflicts had lasting consequences for the continent's economy and the people's well-being.

COLONIAL TRANSITION European governments did not understand the incredible ethnic diversity in Africa. Certain African ethnic groups are living together today only because European colonizers established national borders that grouped them together. Examine the map on page 469 and you will see the ethnic and cultural complexity in

SEE
PRIMARY SOURCE **B**

Africa. Each area marked by a red line is an ethnic group. Many of these groups now reside together in the present-day countries created by Europeans. Many groups living in the same country are historical enemies. For example, German and Belgian colonial governments aggravated historically tense relations between the Hutu and Tutsi ethnic groups in present-day Rwanda and Burundi. In the early 1990s, the ethnic violence between these two groups resulted in a war that led to the deaths of hundreds of thousands of people.

Because of the way these colonial borders were drawn, many African governments had difficulty getting different ethnic groups to cooperate in building stable democracies. Dictators, such as Mobutu Sese Seko of what is now the Democratic Republic of the Congo, became common. In addition, many Africans had no experience living in democratic governments.

Traditional Ethnic Boundaries of Africa

—— Ethnic group

0   400   800 miles
0 400 800 kilometers
Lambert Azimuthal Equal-Area Projection

SKILLBUILDER: Interpreting Maps

❶ **PLACE** Which modern-day country probably contains the most traditional ethnic groups?

❷ **REGION** Which subregion of Africa was probably the least affected by the postcolonial reconstruction of Africa's boundaries?

CAUSE FOR HOPE Establishing a democratic tradition is a primary goal for many African nations. Only through political stability can a nation bring peace and prosperity to its people. In the past decade, some African nations have been making progress. In 1994, the white minority government in South Africa finally yielded power to the black majority, ending decades of government-sanctioned racial discrimination and social injustice.

SEE
PRIMARY SOURCE **D**

Furthermore, in 2001, Ghana swore in a new president in a peaceful transfer of power, unlike the coups and assassinations that had occurred during previous changes of government. These events are promising in a continent that is hoping for radical progress in the 21st century. Complete the Case Study Project on the following two pages to learn more about how Africa is dealing with the effects of colonialism.

MOVEMENT Voters line up during elections in South Africa.
How will elections help improve the lives of people in Africa?

469

CaseStudy

News Report

Primary sources A, B, C, D, and E on these two pages are about colonial and postcolonial Africa. Use these resources along with your own research to prepare a news report on postcolonial Africa.

Suggested Steps

1. Select one African country to study.
2. Use online and print resources to research your country's precolonial, colonial, and postcolonial history.
3. Highlight its people, resources, colonizers, and postcolonial activity.
4. Prepare a news report on the current status of your country, covering such topics as conflicts, the health and welfare of its people, the economy, and prospects for the future.
5. Practice your news report in front of a small audience. Ask them for ways to improve it.
6. Use a tape recorder or video recorder to tape your broadcast.

Materials and Supplies

- computer with Internet access
- reference books, newspapers, magazines, and encyclopedias
- tape recorder or video recorder

RESEARCH LINKS
CLASSZONE.COM

PRIMARY SOURCE A

Eyewitness Account *In his desire for more and more rubber from the Congo, Belgian King Leopold II adopted terrorism as his preferred method of persuasion. In 1899, the British vice consul offered this eyewitness account.*

An example of what is done was told me up the Ubangi [River]. This officer's method was to arrive in canoes at a village, the inhabitants of which invariably bolted on their arrival; the soldiers were then landed, and commenced looting, taking all the chickens, grain, etc. out of the houses; after this, they attacked the natives until able to seize their women; these women were kept as hostages until the chief of the district brought in the required number of kilograms of rubber. The rubber having been brought, the women were sold back to their owners for a couple of goats apiece, and so he continued from village to village until the requisite amount of rubber had been collected.

PRIMARY SOURCE B

Statement of Principle *Kwame Nkrumah was the leader of postcolonial Ghana until he was overthrown in 1966. In his book, I Speak of Freedom, published in 1961, he wrote about his hopes for postcolonial Africa.*

For centuries, Europeans dominated the African continent. The white man [claimed] the right to rule and to be obeyed by the non-white; his mission, he claimed, was to "civilize" Africa. Under this cloak, the Europeans robbed the continent of vast riches and inflicted unimaginable suffering on the African people.

All this makes a sad story, but now we must be prepared to bury the past with its unpleasant memories and look to the future. All we ask of the former colonial powers is their goodwill and cooperation to remedy past mistakes and injustices and to grant independence to the colonies in Africa.

It is clear that we must find an African solution to our problems, and that this can only be found in African unity. Divided we are weak; united, Africa could become one of the greatest forces for good in the world.

News Analysis *Ron Daniels, writing in the magazine* Black World Today, *offered this analysis of the Trade and Development Act of 2000. This law recognizes the need to promote economic growth and reduce poverty in Africa, but the law only helps a small number of countries.*

How ironic, tragic even, that as we prepare to enter a new century and millennium, Africa, the motherland, is so afflicted by poverty, underdevelopment, hunger, disease, corruption, and debt that African leaders, out of desperation . . . , are in effect begging to be recolonized. How ironic that the continent whose historical underdevelopment under slavery and colonialism, whose vast human and material resources contributed mightily to the enrichment and development of Europe and America must now turn to the former slave-masters and colonizers for a "bail-out."

Political Cartoon *Cartoonist Alan King drew this cartoon in 1996. The cartoon appeared in the* Ottawa Citizen *in Ottawa, Canada. King shows the unending cycle of indecisive attitudes on the part of the international community. The Democratic Republic of the Congo, which was formerly known as Zaire, suffers from these indecisive attitudes.*

Editorial Commentary *On January 8, 2001, the* New York Times *editorial page included this essay on the changes that have taken place in Ghana. The editorial was titled "An African Success Story."*

In its first two decades of independence, the West African nation of Ghana was an archetypal political disaster, brought low by successive coups and dictatorships, corruption and near total economic collapse. Today, Ghana is a welcome African example of legitimate democracy and successful economic reform. In an unusually peaceful transfer of power, a civilian government that grew out of a military regime has accepted an election defeat and surrendered power to the opposition.

John Kufuor, an Oxford-trained lawyer and businessman, and the leader of Ghana's opposition New Patriotic Party, was sworn in as president yesterday. He defeated John Atta Mills, the incumbent vice president, in an election widely viewed as free and fair. President Jerry Rawlings, the charismatic former flight lieutenant who has dominated Ghana for nearly 20 years, stepped down after reaching a constitutional two-term limit as elected president.

PROJECT *CheckList*

Have I . . .

✓ fully researched the country I chose to investigate?

✓ included information about the current status of the country?

✓ taped my broadcast in the form of an actual news report?

VISUAL SUMMARY
TODAY'S ISSUES IN AFRICA

Economics

Economic Development
- Africa's economy suffered because many European nations exploited Africa for its resources.
- African nations are concentrating on economic cooperation and economic diversification to build their economies.
- Many African nations are improving their educational systems to produce skilled workers.

Environment

Health Care
- Diseases are killing millions in Africa. They include cholera, malaria, tuberculosis, and AIDS.
- AIDS is threatening the continent's population and reducing life expectancies in many countries.
- Many African nations are improving efforts to educate citizens about AIDS.

Government

Effects of Colonialism
- European nations began colonizing Africa once exploration revealed a vast amount of valuable natural resources.
- Colonialism caused much political and ethnic violence because it disrupted many long-standing political and ethnic boundaries.

Reviewing Places & Terms

A. Briefly explain the importance of each of the following.

1. "one-commodity" country
2. commodity
3. diversify
4. AIDS
5. cholera
6. malaria
7. tuberculosis
8. UNAIDS

B. Answer the questions about vocabulary in complete sentences.

9. What is a nation called when it relies on one product for its economic well-being?
10. What is the name of the disease that is carried by a mosquito and was also a leading disease in both 1900 and 2000?
11. What is the name of the respiratory disease that often accompanies AIDS?
12. What is the process whereby countries employ many different ways to help their economies grow?
13. What disease is spread by poor sanitation and a polluted water supply?
14. What is a product called that is bought and sold and has value in a worldwide market?
15. Which organization tracks the world's AIDS problem?

Main Ideas

Economic Development (pp. 461–464)

1. How has Africa's economic status changed during the past 40 years?
2. What is one of the main problems preventing Africa from spending money on economic development?
3. What is a danger with a country's having only one valuable product that it relies on for its economic well-being?

Health Care (pp. 465–467)

4. How are African nations fighting some of the diseases afflicting their continent?
5. What are some of the economic implications of disease in Africa?
6. What do Uganda's and Senegal's AIDS programs have in common?
7. Why might the drop in HIV infection rates be misleading?

Effects of Colonialism (pp. 468–471)

8. What are some of the empires and peoples that controlled areas of Africa at the beginning of the 19th century?
9. What was one of the main reasons that European countries wanted to control Africa?
10. Why did colonization cause so much political and ethnic violence in the 20th century?

Critical Thinking

1. Using Your Notes

Use your completed chart to answer these questions.

	Causes	Effects
Issue 1: Economic Development		
Issue 2: Health Care		

a. What is the primary foundation for most African nations' economies?

b. How might disease and economic development be related?

2. Geographic Themes

a. **MOVEMENT** How are diseases such as malaria and cholera spread?

b. **REGION** In what way is the modern map of Africa not a true reflection of the continent's people?

3. Identifying Themes

How would you relate one of the five themes of geography to the primary way in which African nations support their economies?

4. Making Inferences

How do you think Africa's economic health affects the spread of diseases such as cholera and AIDS?

5. Drawing Conclusions

How important do you think regional cooperation is in building Africa's economy? Why?

Additional Test Practice, pp. S1–S37

TEST PRACTICE
CLASSZONE.COM

Geographic Skills: Interpreting Maps

Dates of African Independence

Use the map at right to answer the following questions.

1. **PLACE** Which two countries remained free of European control?

2. **PLACE** Which country most recently gained its independence?

3. **REGION** Which decade saw the most countries gain independence?

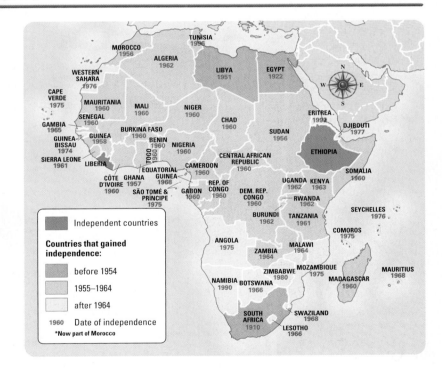

MOROCCO 1956
TUNISIA 1956
ALGERIA 1962
LIBYA 1951
EGYPT 1922
WESTERN SAHARA* 1976
CAPE VERDE 1975
MAURITANIA 1960
MALI 1960
NIGER 1960
CHAD 1960
ERITREA 1993
DJIBOUTI 1977
GAMBIA 1965
SENEGAL 1960
BURKINA FASO 1960
SUDAN 1956
GUINEA-BISSAU 1974
GUINEA 1958
BENIN 1960
NIGERIA 1960
CENTRAL AFRICAN REPUBLIC 1960
ETHIOPIA
SIERRA LEONE 1961
LIBERIA
TOGO 1960
CAMEROON 1960
SOMALIA 1960
CÔTE D'IVOIRE 1960
GHANA 1957
EQUATORIAL GUINEA 1968
REP. OF CONGO 1960
UGANDA 1962
KENYA 1963
SÃO TOMÉ & PRÍNCIPE 1975
GABON 1960
DEM. REP. CONGO 1960
RWANDA 1962
SEYCHELLES 1976
BURUNDI 1962
TANZANIA 1961
COMOROS 1975
ANGOLA 1975
ZAMBIA 1964
MALAWI 1964
ZIMBABWE 1980
MOZAMBIQUE 1975
MAURITIUS 1968
NAMIBIA 1990
BOTSWANA 1966
MADAGASCAR 1960
SOUTH AFRICA 1910
SWAZILAND 1968
LESOTHO 1966

Independent countries

Countries that gained independence:
before 1954
1955–1964
after 1964
1960 Date of independence
*Now part of Morocco

GeoActivity

Choose one country in West Africa that was once controlled by France. Then using the library, encyclopedias, or other reference books, research how France's influence is still felt today in that country's economy, government, schools, and language.

INTERNET ACTIVITY

Use the links at **classzone.com** to do research on the postcolonial economy of one African country. Look for attempts to diversify the economy, education programs, growth in per capita income, and amount of manufacturing.

Writing About Geography Write a report of your findings. Include charts, pie graphs, and other visuals to help present the information. List the Web sites that you used as sources.

Unit 7

Southwest Asia

Southwest Asia, sometimes called a cradle of civilization, is the home of oil rich lands, vast deserts, and difficult political problems.

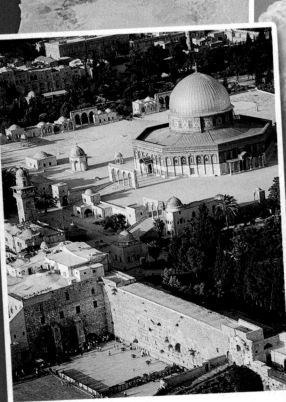

PLACE Two holy places in Jerusalem, Israel, can be seen in this photograph: a shrine known as the Dome of the Rock, which is sacred to Muslims, and the Western Wall, a spot sacred to Jews.

HUMAN-ENVIRONMENT INTERACTION
Flares of burning natural gas are common sights at oil wells in the Al-Ghawar oil field in Saudi Arabia.

GeoData

REGION More than half of the world's oil reserves are found in this region.

HUMAN-ENVIRONMENT INTERACTION Some experts believe that the freshwater supplies of the Arabian peninsula will be exhausted in the next 25 to 30 years.

LOCATION Southwest Asia connects three continents: Europe, Asia, and Africa.

For more information on Southwest Asia . . .

RESEARCH LINKS
CLASSZONE.COM

MOVEMENT Crossing the desert areas of Southwest Asia by land would be almost impossible without oases to provide water and a resting place. This oasis was on the caravan route from Yemen to Palestine.

SW ASIA

Today's Issues in Southwest Asia

Today, Southwest Asia faces the issues previewed here. As you read Chapters 21 and 22, you will learn helpful background information. You will study the issues themselves in Chapter 23.

In a small group, answer the questions below. Then participate in a class discussion of your answers.

Exploring the Issues

1. POPULATION RELOCATION Think about why a group of people may leave a place they call home. What problems might relocation cause for the group? Then make a list of the reasons people relocate and the problems that are caused by moving.

2. ECONOMIC DEVELOPMENT Make a list of major rivers found in the region and a list of major rivers found in the United States. How do the lists compare? What does this suggest about scarce resources in the region?

3. RELIGIOUS CONFLICT Study the cartoon on page 477. Who are the figures in the cartoon?

For more on these issues in Southwest Asia . . .

CURRENT EVENTS
CLASSZONE.COM

POPULATION RELOCATION

What kind of population movement is taking place in Southwest Asia?

This nomadic Kurdish family rests in the hills of eastern Turkey. The Kurds claim a homeland that crosses the boundaries of five countries: Turkey, Iraq, Iran, Syria, and Armenia.

ECONOMIC DEVELOPMENT

How can oil wealth help develop the region's economies?

Wealth from oil wells, like this one located at Al Ghawar in Saudi Arabia, may be used to develop economic activities that do not depend on oil.

CaseStudy

Who should control Jerusalem?

In this cartoon, the dove symbolizes peace between Arabs and Israelis in Southwest Asia. Jerusalem plays a vital role in the peace process.

RELIGIOUS CONFLICT

www.markfiore.com

Patterns of Physical Geography

SUNSHINE STATE STANDARDS
Key Standard SS.B.1.4.1 The student uses a variety of maps, geographic technolo including geographic information systems (GIS) and satellite-produced imagery, and other advanced graphic representations to depict geographic problems.

Other Standards SS.B.1.4.2, B.2.4.1, B.2.4.3

FCAT LA.A.2.2.7 Reading: Recognize Compare and Contrast

Use the Unit Atlas to add to your knowledge of Southwest Asia. As you look at the maps and charts, notice geographic patterns and specific details about the region. For example, the chart gives details about the mountains and deserts of Southwest Asia.

After studying the graphics and physical map on these two pages, jot down answers to the following questions in your notebook.

Making Comparisons

1. Which of Southwest Asia's deserts is about the same size as the Mojave Desert of the United States?

2. How do the tallest mountains of Southwest Asia compare to the tallest U.S. mountain?

3. Which mountain chains cut off Turkey and Iran from the rest of the region? How might isolation affect the way a country develops economically?

For updated statistics on Southwest Asia . . .

DATA UPDATE
CLASSZONE.COM

Comparing Data

Landmass

Southwest Asia
2,673,262 sq mi

Continental United States
3,165,630 sq mi

Population

Southwest Asia
262,678,000

United States
281,422,000

| 0 | 100 | 200 | 300 |

Population (in millions)

Deserts

World's Largest
Sahara
Africa
3,500,000
square miles

U.S. Largest
Mojave
United States
25,000
square miles

Rub al-Khali
Arabian
Peninsula
250,000
square miles

An-Nafud
Arabian
Peninsula
25,000
square miles

Negev
Israel
4,700
square miles

Mountains

World's Tallest	U.S. Tallest			
Mt. Everest	**Mt. McKinley**	**Damavand**	**Mt. Ararat**	**Mt. Hermon**
Nepal-Tibet	United States	Iran	Turkey	Lebanon-Syria
29,035 feet	20,320 feet	18,606 feet	16,945 feet	9,232 feet

UKRAINE
MOLDOVA
ROMANIA
BULGARIA
RUSSIA
KAZAKHSTAN
KYRGYZSTAN
UZBEKISTAN
TAJIKISTAN

Black Sea
Sea of Marmara
Bosporus
GEORGIA
ARMENIA
AZERBAIJAN
Caspian Sea
Pontic Mountains
Anatolia
Dardanelles
TURKEY
TURKMENISTAN
Mt. Ararat
16,945 ft. (5,165 m.) AZER.
Lake Van
Lake Urmia
Elburz Mountains
▲ Mt. Damavand
18,934 ft. (5,771 m.)
Amu Darya
Hindu Kush
Khyber Pass
3,518 ft. (1,072 m.)
Taurus Mountains
Aegean Sea
Crete (Gr.)
N. CYPRUS
CYPRUS
Mediterranean Sea
LEBANON
SYRIA
Euphrates River
Tigris River
Diyala R.
Dasht-e-Kavir
Plateau Of Iran
AFGHANISTAN
▲ Mt. Hermon
9,232 ft. (2,814 m.)
ISRAEL
Dead Sea
-1,312 ft. (-400 m.)
Syrian Desert
IRAQ
ZAGROS MOUNTAINS
IRAN
Dasht-e-Lut
JORDAN
KUWAIT
An-Nafud
Najd
Persian Gulf
PAKISTAN
EGYPT
Red Sea
Hejaz
BAHRAIN
QATAR
Strait of Hormuz
OMAN
Gulf Of Oman
Tropic of Cancer
SAUDI ARABIA
UNITED ARAB EMIRATES
Arabian Sea
ARABIAN PENINSULA
OMAN
Rub Al-Khali
SUDAN
Mediterranean Sea
ISRAEL
Golan Heights
LEBANON
West Bank
Gaza Strip
Sinai Peninsula
EGYPT
JORDAN
SAUDI ARABIA
YEMEN
INDIAN OCEAN
Suez Canal
Gulf of Suez
Negev
Socotra (Yemen)
ETHIOPIA
DJIBOUTI
Gulf Of Aden
SOMALIA
Equator

0 25 50 miles
0 25 50 kilometers

Elevation
13,100 ft. (4,000 m.)
6,600 ft. (2,000 m.)
1,600 ft. (500 m.)
650 ft. (200 m.)
0 ft. (0 m.)
Below sea level
▲ Mountain peak

0 250 500 miles
0 250 500 kilometers
Lambert Conformal Conic Projection

SW ASIA

479

Patterns of Human Geography

After World War II (1939-1945), the nation of Israel was created in 1948. Since that time, the peoples and nations of the region have been in conflict with one another.

Study the political map of Southwest Asia and the Israel maps at the right to see how possession of the lands changed. Then write the answers to these questions in your notebook.

Making Comparisons

1. Which areas did Israel occupy in 1967?

2. Study both maps of Israel and the political map and write a sentence describing the changes in land possession from 1948 to the present.

3. What nation is in possession of the Sinai Peninsula today?

4. Which four nations surround the Golan Heights? Who controls the area?

Israel, 1948 and 1967

1948

LEBANON
SYRIA
Mediterranean Sea
WEST BANK
Jerusalem
Dead Sea
ISRAEL
TRANSJORDAN
EGYPT
Red Sea

Proposed by UN, 1947
- Jewish state
- Arab state
- International zone

0 25 50 miles
0 25 50 kilometers
Lambert Conformal Conic Projection

1967

CYPRUS
LEBANON
SYRIA
GOLAN HEIGHTS
Mediterranean Sea
WEST BANK
Jerusalem
Dead Sea
GAZA STRIP
ISRAEL
JORDAN
Suez Canal
SINAI PENINSULA
Gulf of Suez
Gulf of Aqaba
EGYPT
SAUDI ARABIA
Red Sea

- Israel before 1967 war
- Territory occupied by Israel, June 1967

0 50 100 miles
0 50 100 kilometers
Lambert Conformal Conic Projection

MOLDOVA

ROMANIA

BULGARIA

UKRAINE

RUSSIA

KAZAKHSTAN

KYRGYZSTAN

UZBEKISTAN

Black Sea

Sea of Marmara

Bosporus

Istanbul

Samsun

GEORGIA

ARMENIA   AZERBAIJAN

TAJIKISTAN

Ankara

Dardanelles

Erzurum

AZER.

TURKMENISTAN

Izmir

T U R K E Y

Lake Van

Tabriz

Mashhad

Kabul

Aegean Sea

Lake Urmia

Adana

Crete (Gr.)

Aleppo

N. CYPRUS

Nicosia

CYPRUS

Euphrates River

Mosul

Arbil

Tigris River

Tehran

Qom

A F G H A N I S T A N

Mediterranean Sea

LEBANON

Beirut

SYRIA

Damascus

I R A N

ISRAEL

Jerusalem

Amman

Baghdad

I R A Q

Esfahan

30°N

JORDAN

Basra

Shiraz

PAKISTAN

EGYPT

KUWAIT

Kuwait

Persian Gulf

Manama

Strait of Hormuz

OMAN

Gulf Of Oman

BAHRAIN

Doha

Abu Dhabi

Muscat

Tropic of Cancer

Red Sea

Medina

Riyadh

QATAR

UNITED ARAB EMIRATES

Arabian Sea

70°E

20°N

Jiddah

Mecca

S A U D I   A R A B I A

OMAN

0 25 50 miles

0 25 50 kilometers

LEBANON

Mediterranean Sea

Golan Heights

SUDAN

Haifa

ISRAEL

Jordan R.

Tel Aviv-Yafo

West Bank

Jerusalem

*Gaza Strip

Dead Sea

Y E M E N

Sanaa

INDIAN OCEAN

Port Said

Suez Canal

Amman

Socotra (Yemen)

Suez

Gulf of Suez

EGYPT

JORDAN

Aden

Gulf of Aden

SW ASIA

SAUDI ARABIA

DJIBOUTI

10°N

* The status of the West Bank and Gaza Strip is under negotiation

ETHIOPIA

⭐ National capital

● Other city

SOMALIA

0   250   500 miles

0   250   500 kilometers

Lambert Conformal Conic Projection

Dashed border indicates disputed boundary

Regional Patterns

These two pages contain a graph and three thematic maps. The graph and two of the maps show the ethnic and religious diversity of Southwest Asia. The third map shows you how people in the region earn a living. After studying these two pages, answer the questions below in your notebook.

Making Comparisons

1. What percentage of the population is Kurdish and where are Kurds found in the region?

2. What area has holy places for three major religions? Why might the location of these places be a problem?

3. What energy sources are found in the region?

4. What is the main economic activity in the region? What does that suggest about the land and the population on it?

Ethnic Groups of Southwest Asia*

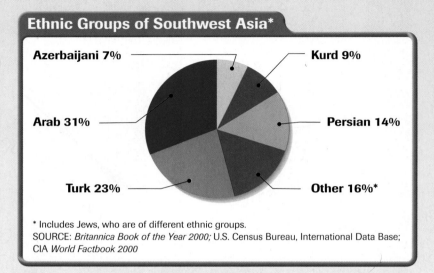

Azerbaijani 7%
Kurd 9%
Arab 31%
Persian 14%
Turk 23%
Other 16%*

* Includes Jews, who are of different ethnic groups.
SOURCE: *Britannica Book of the Year 2000;* U.S. Census Bureau, International Data Base; CIA *World Factbook 2000*

Ethnic Regions of Southwest Asia

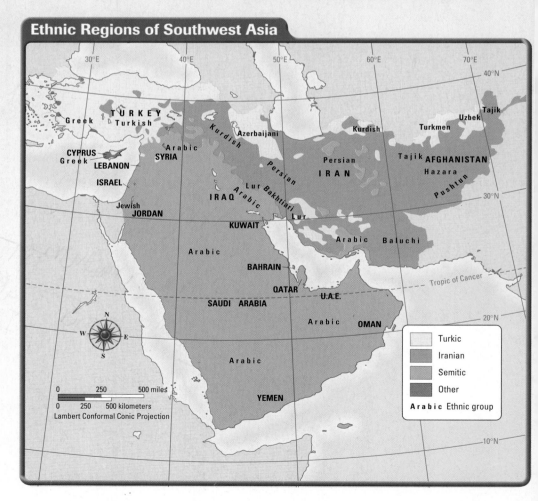

☐	Turkic
☐	Iranian
☐	Semitic
☐	Other
A r a b i c	Ethnic group

0   250   500 miles
0   250   500 kilometers
Lambert Conformal Conic Projection

Religious Groups of Southwest Asia

N W E S

★ Ankara
✝ Ephesus
T U R K E Y

Nicosia
CYPRUS
Mashhad ☾
Kabul ★

SYRIA
LEBANON
Beirut ★
✝ Damascus
Tehran ★
Qom ☾
I R A N
AFGHANISTAN

ISRAEL
Jerusalem ★
★ Amman
JORDAN
Baghdad ★ ☾
Karbala ☾
An Najaf ☾
I R A Q

KUWAIT
Kuwait ★ ☾

Tropic of Cancer
Medina ☾ ☾
Riyadh ★
BAHRAIN
Manama ☾
Doha
QATAR
Abu Dhabi ★
U.A.E.
Muscat ★
OMAN

Mecca ☾
SAUDI ARABIA

Sanaa ★
YEMEN

Inset map

LEBANON
Zefat ☆
SYRIA
GOLAN HEIGHTS
Mt. Carmel ☆✝
Sea of Galilee
☆ Tiberias ✝
Nazareth ✝

ISRAEL
WEST BANK
JORDAN
Jordan R.

GAZA STRIP
Jerusalem ✝ ☾
Bethlehem ✝
Hebron ☾ ☾

0   25   50 miles
0   25   50 kilometers

0   250   500 miles
0   250   500 kilometers
Lambert Conformal Conic Projection

Religious group
- Christian
- Druze
- Jewish
- Sunni Muslim
- Shi'ite Muslim

Holy place
- ✝ Christian
- ☆ Jewish
- ☾ Sunni Muslim
- ☾ Shi'ite Muslim

Economic Activities of Southwest Asia

Black Sea
Caspian Sea
Mediterranean Sea
Gulf of Suez
Red Sea
Persian Gulf
Gulf of Oman
Arabian Sea
INDIAN OCEAN
Gulf of Aden

SW ASIA

Activities
- Commercial farming
- Commercial fishing
- Forestry
- Nomadic herding
- Subsistence farming
- Little or no economic activity

Resources
- Cr Chromium
- C Coal
- Copper
- Hydroelectric power
- Iron ore
- Lead
- Natural gas
- Petroleum
- Phosphate

0   250   500 miles
0   250   500 kilometers
Lambert Conformal Conic Projection

N W E S

483

Unit ATLAS

Regional Data File

Study the information on the countries of Southwest Asia. In your notebook, answer these questions.

Making Comparisons

1. Which nations have more doctors per 100,000 population than the United States?

2. Study the information to determine which nation after Afghanistan is the poorest. On which categories did you base your judgment?

3. Using the map on page 479, make a list of the nations that border the Persian Gulf. How many of those nations have more exports than imports?

Sources:
Human Development Report 2000, UN
International Data Base, U.S. Census Bureau online
Merriam-Webster's Geographical Dictionary, 3d ed., 1997
World Education Report 2000, UNESCO online
World Population Data Sheet 2000, Population Reference Bureau online
WHO Estimates of Health Personnel, online
World Almanac and Book of Facts 2001
World Factbook 2000, CIA online

Notes:
ᵃ A comparison of the prices of the same items in different countries is used to figure these data.
ᵇ Includes land and water, when figures are available.

For updated statistics on Southwest Asia . . .

DATA UPDATE
CLASSZONE.COM

Country Flag	Country/ Capital	Population (2000 estimate)	Life Expectancy (years) (2000)	Birthrate (per 1,000 pop.) (2000)	Infant Mortality (per 1,000 live births) (2000)
	Afghanistan Kabul	26,668,000	46	43	149.8
	Bahrain Manama	691,000	69	22	8.1
	Cyprus Nicosia	882,000	77	14	7.8
	Iran Tehran	67,411,000	69	21	30.8
	Iraq Baghdad	23,115,000	59	38	127.0
	Israel Jerusalem	6,227,000	78	22	6.0
	Jordan Amman	5,083,000	69	33	34.0
	Kuwait Kuwait	2,190,000	72	24	12.5
	Lebanon Beirut	4,202,000	70	23	34.5
	Oman Muscat	2,353,000	71	44	25.0
	Qatar Doha	591,000	72	20	20.0
	Saudi Arabia Riyadh	21,607,000	70	35	46.4
	Syria Damascus	16,482,000	67	33	34.6
	Turkey Ankara	65,311,000	69	22	37.9
	United Arab Emirates Abu Dhabi	2,835,000	74	24	16.0
	Yemen Sanaa	17,030,000	59	39	75.3
	United States Washington, D.C.	281,422,000	77	15	7.0

Doctors (per 100,000 pop.) (1996–1998)	GDP[a] (billions $US) (1998–1999)	Import/Export[a] (billions $US) (1998–1999)	Literacy Rate (percentage) (1998–1999)	Televisions (per 1,000 pop.) (1998)	Passenger Cars (per 1,000 pop.) (1996–1997)	Total Area[b] (square miles)	
11	21.0	0.2 / 0.1 1996	32	10	2	250,775	
100	8.6	3.5 / 3.3	87	467	242	255	
255	Greek Cypriot 9.0 Turkish Cypriot 0.8	GrkCyp 3.5 / 1.1 TrkCyp 0.4 / 0.1	97	322	316	3,572	
85	347.6	13.8 / 12.2	75	63	26	635,932	
55	59.9	8.9 / 12.7	54	80	32	168,927	
385	105.4	30.6 / 23.5	96	290	224	7,992	
166	16.0	3.0 / 1.8	89	80	40	34,575	
189	44.8	8.1 / 13.5	81	370	318	6,880	
210	16.2	5.7 / 0.9	85	366	325	3,949	
133	19.6	5.4 / 7.2	69	657	108	82,000	
126	12.3	4.2 / 6.7	80	401	151	4,400	
166	191.0	28.0 / 48.0	75	257	89	865,000	
144	42.2	3.2 / 3.3	73	67	9	71,498	
121	409.4	36.0 / 26.0	84	189	53	301,380	
181	41.5	27.5 / 34.0	75	104	144	32,278	
23	12.7	2.3 / 2.0	44	28	15	203,849	
251	9,255.0	820.8 / 663.0	97	847	489	3,787,319	

SECTION 1
Landforms and Resources

SECTION 2
Climate and Vegetation

SECTION 3
Human–Environment Interaction

PHYSICAL GEOGRAPHY OF SOUTHWEST ASIA
Harsh and Arid Lands

Wind-shaped sand dunes in Arabia's An-Nafud Desert sometimes reach a height of 600 feet.

GeoFocus

Why does the physical geography make this a vital region?

Taking Notes Copy the graphic organizer below into your notebook. Use it to record information from the chapter about the physical geography of Southwest Asia.

Landforms	
Resources	
Climate and Vegetation	
Human-Environment Interaction	

Landforms and Resources

A HUMAN PERSPECTIVE Artillery shells and sniper fire rained down on the lands below a small plateau in southwestern Syria. Airplanes bombed the military positions on the plateau itself. Families in nearby villages huddled in their homes, hoping for the shelling to stop. Israeli Army engineers struggled to build a road to enable tanks to reach the top. Thousands died in the 1967 war when Syria and Israel fought for control of the **Golan Heights,** also called Al Jawlan, a hilly plateau overlooking the Jordan River and the Sea of Galilee. This landform's strategic location has made it the site of conflict in Southwest Asia for decades. It is one of many landforms that divide the region.

Landforms Divide the Region

People sometimes picture Southwest Asia as a region of rippling sand dunes and parched land occasionally interrupted with an oasis. But the lands of Southwest Asia actually range from green coastal plains to snow-peaked mountains. Southwest Asia forms a land bridge connecting Asia, Africa, and Europe. As you can see on the map on page 37, the region is situated at the edge of a huge tectonic plate. Parts of the Arabian Peninsula are pulling away from Africa, and parts of the Anatolian Peninsula are sliding past parts of Asia. Still other plates are pushing up mountains in other areas of the Asian continent.

PENINSULAS AND WATERWAYS The most distinctive landform in Southwest Asia is the Arabian Peninsula, which is separated from the continent of Africa by the Red Sea on the southwest and from the rest of Asia by the Persian Gulf on the east. The Red Sea covers a rift valley created by the movement of the Arabian plate. The Zagros, Elburz, and Taurus mountains at the north side of the plate cut off part of the region from the south. Another important landform in the region is the Anatolian Peninsula, which is occupied by the country of Turkey. It marks the beginning of the Asian continent. (See the map on page 479.)

Both peninsulas border on strategic waterways. On the southwest side of the Arabian Peninsula are the Red Sea and a strategic opening to the Mediterranean Sea—the Suez Canal. Goods from Asia flow through this canal to ports in Europe and North Africa.

Main Ideas

- The Southwest Asian landforms have had a major impact on movement in the region.
- The most valuable resources in Southwest Asia are oil and water.

Places & Terms

Golan Heights

wadi

Tigris River

Euphrates River

Jordan River

Dead Sea

CONNECT TO THE ISSUES

RESOURCES Enormous oil reserves have brought changes to the economic and political standing of this region.

SUNSHINE STATE STANDARDS
Key Standard SS.B.1.4.3 The student uses mental maps of physical and human features of the world to answer complex geographic questions.
Other Standards SS.B.2.4.3
FCAT LA.A.1.4.2 Reading: Strategies

PLACE The Golan Heights are a strategic location near the source of water in the region. **How will control of this area affect those who live on lands below the top of the plateau?**

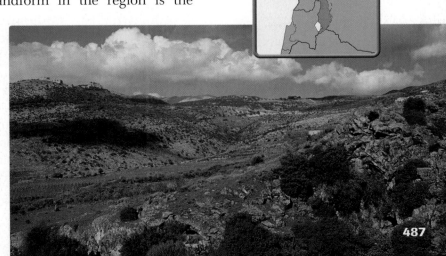

SW ASIA

487

The Anatolian Peninsula is located between the Black Sea and the Mediterranean Sea. Two narrow waterways, the Bosporus Strait and the Dardenelles Strait, are situated at the west end of the peninsula. Both straits have always been highly desirable locations for controlling trade and transportation to Russia and the interior of Asia.

Farther south is a narrow passageway leading from the Arabian Sea to the Persian Gulf called the Straits of Hormuz. These straits are the only waterway to the huge oilfields of Kuwait, Saudi Arabia, and Iraq. Because access to oil is essential to the world-wide economy, this waterway is very important.

BACKGROUND
The Persian Gulf is also called the Arabian Gulf.

PLAINS AND HIGHLANDS Much of the Arabian Peninsula is covered by plains. Because of the dry, sandy, and windy conditions, few activities using the land take place here. Most of the land is barren with some low hills, ridges, and **wadis,** which are riverbeds that remain dry except during the rainy seasons. On the southwestern corner of the peninsula, a range of mountains—the Hejaz Mountains—pokes out of the land. People living on the Arabian Peninsula have adapted to the harsh conditions by living nomadic lives in search of water.

The heart of Iran is a plateau surrounded by mountains. Isolated and very high, the land is a stony, salty, and sandy desert. The foothills surrounding the plateau are able to produce some crops. Much of the Anatolian Peninsula is also a plateau. Some areas are productive for agriculture, while other areas support flocks of grazing animals such as sheep and goats. The Northern Plain of Afghanistan, a well-watered agricultural area, is surrounded by high mountains that isolate it from other parts of the region. Ⓐ

MOUNTAINS Rugged mountains divide the land and countries. As you study the map on page 479, you will see that the Hindu Kush Mountains of Afghanistan are linked with other ranges of mountains that frame southern Asia. Afghanistan is landlocked and mountainous, so contact with the outside world is difficult.

The Zagros Mountains on the western side of Iran help isolate that country from the rest of Southwest Asia. The Elburz Mountains south of the Caspian Sea cut off easy access to that body of water by Iran. Finally, the Taurus Mountains separate Turkey from the rest of Southwest Asia. In spite of these physical barriers, people, goods, and ideas move through the entire region. One of the ways they move is by water.

Geographic Thinking

Making Comparisons
Ⓐ How are the plateaus of Iran and Anatolia different?

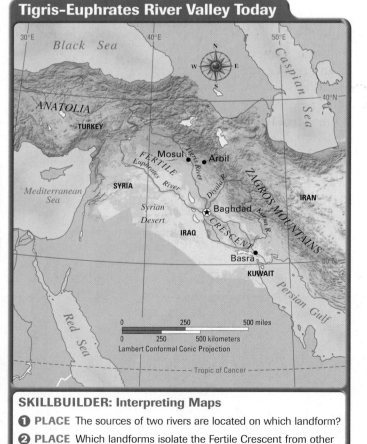

Tigris-Euphrates River Valley Today

Black Sea

ANATOLIA
TURKEY

Mosul • Arbil

FERTILE
Euphrates River
Tigris River

SYRIA

Mediterranean Sea

Cyprus

Syrian Desert

Baghdad

IRAN

ZAGROS MOUNTAINS

Diyala R.

Karun R.

IRAQ

CRESCENT

Basra •

KUWAIT

Caspian Sea

Persian Gulf

Red Sea

0   250   500 miles
0   250   500 kilometers
Lambert Conformal Conic Projection

- - - Tropic of Cancer - - -

SKILLBUILDER: Interpreting Maps
❶ **PLACE** The sources of two rivers are located on which landform?
❷ **PLACE** Which landforms isolate the Fertile Crescent from other parts of the region?

PLACE

The Dead Sea

The Dead Sea is a landlocked salt lake, so salty that almost nothing can live in the water. It has been described as the world's largest spa. (A spa is a place with healing waters.) For thousands of years, people have come to the edges of the landlocked sea to bathe in its mineral waters and soak in its black mineral mud.

Imagine floating in water so salty that you cannot sink. Salt concentration in the Dead Sea water is 31.5 percent, nine times higher than in the world's oceans. The evaporation rate of the water is about 55 inches per year, keeping the water very salty despite the flow of fresh water from the Jordan River.

WATER BODIES Southwest Asia is almost completely surrounded by bodies of water. They provide vital avenues for trade and access to other parts of the region and to the rest of the world. However, because much of the region is arid, there are few rivers that flow the entire year. As you can see on the map on page 488, two of the most important rivers—the **Tigris** and the **Euphrates**—supported several ancient river valley civilizations in an area called the Fertile Crescent. They included Sumerians, Assyrians, Babylonians, and Chaldeans.

Today, the Tigris and Euphrates flow through parts of Turkey, Syria, and Iraq. The valleys are fertile, well watered, and good for agriculture. The two rivers flow almost parallel to each other for hundreds of miles before joining at a place called Shatt al Arab. They spread out into slow moving water and swamps, finally emptying into the Persian Gulf. ◀B

Tumbling down from the mountains of Lebanon near Mt. Hermon, the **Jordan River** provides one of the most precious resources in the entire region—water. Farther south, the river serves as a natural boundary between Israel and Jordan. The Jordan River flows into the salty waters of the **Dead Sea,** a landlocked salt lake. The Dead Sea is so salty that only bacteria can live in the waters. Thousands of years ago the earth was heaved up on the south end of the area now controlled by Israel. The outlet to the sea was blocked, creating the salt lake. The Dead Sea is 1,349 feet below sea level—the lowest place on the exposed crust of the earth. (See The Dead Sea, above.)

CONNECT TO THE ISSUES

B▶ **RESOURCES**
Why is control of water resources important in this region?

Resources for a Modern World

It is almost impossible to think about resources in Southwest Asia without including oil. It is the region's most abundant resource. Major oil

HUMAN–ENVIRONMENT INTERACTION Men work at an oil drilling compound in the Rub al-Khali desert.
How will oil drilling change this area?

fields are located in the Arabian Peninsula, Iran, and Iraq, with natural gas fields close by. Since these fossil fuels run cars and trucks, factories, and power plants all over the world, they provide the major portion of income for nations with petroleum reserves.

AN OIL-RICH REGION Today, about one-half of the world's oil reserves are found in Southwest Asia, along the coast of the Persian Gulf, and at offshore drilling sites in the Gulf itself. The presence of these large reserves has made the region important because so many countries, including the United States, depend on its oil.

OTHER RESOURCES The most valuable resource in parts of Southwest Asia is water. In mountainous lands such as Turkey, Iran, Lebanon, and Afghanistan, water is plentiful compared to the rest of the region. It can be harnessed for hydroelectric power. However, elsewhere, water is a scarce resource that must constantly be guarded and carefully used. Efforts to conserve water have been a part of the culture of the people living in the region for thousands of years. **C**

Southwest Asia has deposits of other resources such as coal, metallic minerals such as copper, and non-metallic minerals such as potash and phosphates. However, the deposits are scattered and not very large. Iran and Turkey have good-sized deposits of coal. Around the Dead Sea are significant reserves of salts such as calcium chloride. However, these salt deposits, which are used in manufacturing and chemical processes, have not been heavily developed.

The harsh land and the desert climate that you will learn about in the next section make life in this region a challenge.

Geographic Thinking

Making Comparisons
C Why might hydroelectric power be better to use than oil?

Assessment

1 Places & Terms

Identify and explain where in the region these would be found.

- Golan Heights
- wadi
- Tigris River
- Euphrates River
- Jordan River
- Dead Sea

2 Taking Notes

LOCATION Review the notes you took for this section.

Landforms	
Resources	

- Which waterways are considered important for trade?
- In which area of the region are the greatest deposits of oil found?

3 Main Ideas

a. In what ways do landforms divide the region?

b. Why are the Red Sea and Suez Canal of strategic value in the region?

c. How did the presence of oil in the region change the region's importance in the global economy?

4 Geographic Thinking

Drawing Conclusions Which resource do you believe is more important in Southwest Asia—water or oil?
Think about:

- the scarcity of water
- the economic value of oil

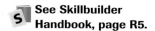 **See Skillbuilder Handbook, page R5.**

MAKING COMPARISONS Study the map on page 483, focusing on energy sources in the region. Create a **map** that shows the location of these energy sources. Label each country that has such sources.

Climate and Vegetation

2

A HUMAN PERSPECTIVE In the spring of 1999, three Canadian explorers retraced the steps of Sir Wilfred Thesiger's 1946 epic journey across the Rub al-Khali on the Arabian Peninsula. It is one of the most extreme deserts in the world. Like Sir Wilfred, they crossed using camels, not four-wheel drive vehicles. But unlike Sir Wilfred, the Canadians were equipped with late 20th-century explorers' tools—personal location beacons, a satellite phone for communications, and laptop computers for recording details of the journey. Crossing this great arid expanse was physically challenging and took 40 days to complete. But for many of the region's inhabitants, survival in the lands of this region is a challenge every day.

Variety in Arid Lands

Southwest Asia is extremely arid. Most areas receive less than 18 inches of precipitation a year. A huge portion of its land area is covered with rough, dry terrain that varies from huge tracts of sand dunes to great salt flats. Study the Map Skills on page 494 to learn more about desert vegetation. Because the region is so dry, its rivers do not flow year round. The vegetation and animals living in the desert can survive on little water and in extreme temperatures. In many areas of Southwest Asia, irrigation has transformed the deserts into productive farmland.

In other parts of the region, a Mediterranean climate prevails, making the land green and lush for at least part of each year. The land in Southwest Asia is broken up by ranges of mountains and plateaus. As a result, highland climates are found in many parts of the region.

Deserts Limit Movement

Spread across the region, the deserts effectively reduce travel and limit almost all human-environment interaction. The surfaces of the desert may be covered with sand, salt, or rocks.

SANDY DESERTS The most famous desert in the region is the **Rub al-Khali,** also known as the Empty Quarter. A local name for the desert is the "place where no one comes out." It is a vast desert

Main Ideas
- Most of Southwest Asia has a very arid climate.
- Irrigation is critical to growing crops in this very dry region.

Places & Terms
Rub al-Khali

oasis

salt flat

CONNECT TO THE ISSUES
POPULATION RELOCATION
The climate of Southwest Asia limits interaction between countries in the region.

SUNSHINE STATE STANDARDS
Key Standard SS.B.2.4.1 The student understands how social, cultural, economic, and environmental factors contribute to the dynamic nature of regions.

Other Standards SS.B.2.4.3

FCAT LA.A.1.4.2 Reading: Strategies

MOVEMENT A Bedouin caravan crosses a dry, rocky desert in Judea, a part of Israel.
How do conditions in the desert restrict movement?

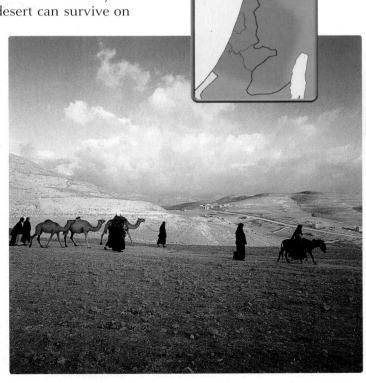

SW ASIA

Climate and Vegetation **491**

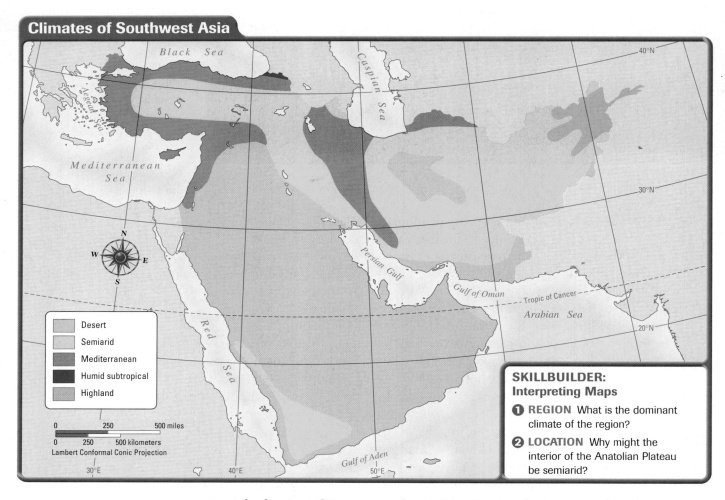

Climates of Southwest Asia

SKILLBUILDER:
Interpreting Maps

❶ **REGION** What is the dominant climate of the region?

❷ **LOCATION** Why might the interior of the Anatolian Plateau be semiarid?

Legend:
- Desert
- Semiarid
- Mediterranean
- Humid subtropical
- Highland

0   250   500 miles
0   250   500 kilometers
Lambert Conformal Conic Projection

---

approximately the size of Texas—on the Arabian Peninsula. It is one of the largest sandy deserts in the world, covering about 250,000 square miles with sand ridges and dunes that reach as high as 800 feet. During the summer, the temperature on the surface of the sand often exceeds 150°F. As many as 10 years may pass without rainfall.

Next to the Rub al-Khali is the An-Nafud Desert. An occasional oasis interrupts its reddish dunes. An **oasis** is an area in the desert where vegetation is found because water is available, usually from underground springs. Severe sandstorms and brutal heat make this desert a barrier to travel across the Arabian Peninsula.

Extending north from the An-Nafud is the Syrian Desert. It separates the coastal regions of Lebanon, Israel, and Syria from the Tigris and Euphrates valleys. (See the map on page 479.) Finally, the desert area that occupies parts of Israel is the Negev Desert. Unlike some deserts, this one produces crops through extensive irrigation. ◢A

SALT DESERTS As you learned in Chapter 3, lands in the rain shadow of a mountain range are usually arid or semiarid. Lands in Iran are good examples of this effect. In Iran, the high mountains block rain, and dry winds increase evaporation. So when winds evaporate the moisture in the soil, chemical salts remain, creating a **salt flat.** In Iran there are two salt flat deserts—the Dasht-e Kavir in central Iran and the Dasht-e Lut in eastern Iran. The lands here are salt-crusted, surrounded by quicksand-like salt marshes, and extremely hot. These rugged lands are almost uninhabited and are barriers to easy movement across Iran.

Geographic Thinking

Seeing Patterns
Ⓐ How is it possible for crops to be produced in desert areas?

492 CHAPTER 21

Semiarid Lands

On the fringes of the deserts are regions with a semiarid climate. These semiarid areas have warm to hot summers with enough rainfall to support grass and some low-growing shrubs. Both cotton and wheat can be grown in this climate. The lands offer good pasture for animals. In Turkey, large herds of mohair goats graze on these lands. Their hair, and fabrics made from it, are among Turkey's exports.

Well-Watered Coast Lands

Although much of Southwest Asia is arid or semiarid, it does have some areas with adequate rainfall. Along the Mediterranean coast and across most of Turkey, hot summers and rainy winters like those in southern California create a good climate for growing citrus fruits, olives, and vegetables. Because of mild winter temperatures in winter and heavy irrigation in the dry summer, farmers can grow crops year round. The Mediterranean climate is a comfortable one in which to live, so these areas are heavily populated. **B**

For thousands of years, the valleys of the Tigris and Euphrates have been the site of intensive farming. Both Turkey and Iraq have constructed dams on the rivers to provide irrigation water all year long.

Climate, vegetation, and landforms have had a major impact on human-environment interaction in Southwest Asia. In the next section, you will see how oil and water have shaped life in this region.

Geographic Thinking

Making Comparisons
B How are Turkey and southern California similar?

PLACE Workers pick cotton in a field in Turkey.
Which of Turkey's climates would be good for cotton production?

SECTION 2 **Assessment**

① Places & Terms

Identify and explain where in the region these would be found.

• Rub al-Khali
• oasis
• salt flat

② Taking Notes

PLACE Review the notes you took for this section.

Climate and Vegetation

• What are the two types of deserts in this region?
• Why are the coast lands heavily populated?

③ Main Ideas

a. How do deserts affect movement in the region?

b. In what ways are the semiarid lands different from the desert?

c. What agricultural products are raised in the coastal areas?

④ Geographic Thinking

Making Comparisons How do the two types of deserts in the region differ from each other? **Think about:**
• characteristics of deserts
• location of deserts

RESEARCH LINKS CLASSZONE.COM

SW ASIA

GeoActivity

MAKING COMPARISONS Do some research on the deserts identified in this section. Create a **database** showing information about those deserts. Consider including such information as type, location, and size.

Reading a Vegetation Map

Southwest Asia is a region with large areas of vegetation specially adapted for dry conditions. The natural vegetation of a region depends on many factors, including soil type, location, elevation, and climate type.

THE LANGUAGE OF MAPS A **vegetation map** shows the location of major types of plants in a region. It includes the natural vegetation found in the area and usually does not include plants introduced as agricultural crops. The map uses colors to indicate the vegetation types. Unlike the map boundaries, the boundaries on earth for the areas are not rigid but gradually blend into each other.

SUNSHINE STATE STANDARDS
Key Standard SS.B.1.4.1 The student uses a variety of maps, geographic technologies including geographic information systems (GIS) and satellite-produced imagery, and other advanced graphic representations to depict geographic problems.

FCAT LA.A.1.4.2 Reading: Strategies

Vegetation of Southwest Asia

Copyright by Rand McNally & Co.

Key:
- Desert and dry shrub
- Mediterranean shrub
- Temperate grassland
- Deciduous and mixed forest
- Little or no vegetation

1 The key illustrates the types of vegetation found in the region. Each color on the map represents the major vegetation in that area.

2 This area has little or no vegetation, and probably is a desert.

3 Areas along the coasts of large bodies of water often have different vegetation from the kinds found inland.

4 Look for patterns that might give you clues about landforms in the region. Here, the mixed forest may indicate a mountainous area.

Map and Graph Skills Assessment

1. Making Generalizations
What type of vegetation is found in the lands bordering the Persian Gulf?

2. Making Comparisons
Along which bodies of water is the vegetation region different from regions farther inland?

3. Drawing Conclusions
In general, how would you describe the vegetation of this region?

Human–Environment Interaction

3

A HUMAN PERSPECTIVE Icebergs for fresh water? As you have seen, fresh water is in short supply in Southwest Asia. In 1977, a Saudi prince, Muhammad ibn Faisal, formed a company to investigate the possibility of towing icebergs from Antarctica to the port of Jidda on the Red Sea. The icebergs would then be melted to release huge quantities of fresh water. It cost one million dollars to find out that no ship was powerful enough to tow an enormous iceberg, and there was no way to keep the iceberg from breaking up on the way. In 1981, the iceberg project was suspended. This story illustrates just how precious fresh water is in Southwest Asia. For centuries, people living in the region have struggled to find fresh water for themselves and for crops.

Providing Precious Water

Water has been a valuable resource since life began on earth. Even though oil brings a great deal of money into Southwest Asia, the most critical resource in this dry region is water. Fresh water supplies are available only in small amounts and not consistently. Ancient civilizations constantly faced the problem of finding and storing water in order to survive and prosper. Today, the same challenge exists for modern nations. To find reliable water supplies, nations today use both ancient and modern practices. The pictures on page 496 include examples of both ancient and modern techniques for providing water.

DAMS AND IRRIGATION SYSTEMS Ancient practices for providing water work well for small fields but are not efficient for large-scale farming. To meet the needs of large farms and for growing populations, countries must construct dams and irrigation systems. Turkey is building a series of dams and a man-made lake on the upper Euphrates River. The dams and lake will provide water and hydroelectricity for parts of the country. But the project is controversial—countries downstream from the dam will lose the use of the water for irrigation or hydroelectricity.

The National Water Carrier project in Israel carries water from the northern part of the country to sites in the nation's center and south. The water comes from mountain areas, including the Golan Heights, the Jordan River, and Lake Kinneret (Sea of Galilee). Some of the water is used in agricultural projects in the Negev Desert, and some for drinking

Main Ideas
- Water is critical to regional physical survival and economic development.
- Discovery of oil increased the global economic importance of Southwest Asia.

Places & Terms

drip irrigation	crude oil
desalinization	refinery
fossil water	

CONNECT TO THE ISSUES
RESOURCES Southwest Asian nations face the challenge of how to use the income from oil resources to develop their economies.

SUNSHINE STATE STANDARDS
Key Standard SS.B.2.4.4 The student understands the global impact of human changes in the physical environment.
Other Standards SS.B.1.4.3
FCAT LA.A.1.4.2 Reading: Strategies

PLACE Date palms thrive in this oasis in the arid country of Oman. **Where does the water for an oasis come from?**

SW ASIA

Water Systems

1. **Drip irrigation** places water just at the root zone, reducing evaporation of precious water. This system is located in the Negev Desert in Israel.

2. A bag of water is collected by using this pump. It is a part of a **qanat**—a system of underground brick-lined tunnels and wells that collect runoff water from the mountains.

3. This **irrigation canal** in Oman has delivered water for over a thousand years. The canals are carefully maintained to provide water for agriculture.

4. A **noria**—or waterwheel run by the flow of water or by animal power—is used to lift water from the river to the fields. These two are located in Syria on the Orontes River.

water. Because the water sources flow through several countries and access to the water is restricted, the National Water Carrier Project is a source of international conflict. **A▶**

MODERN WATER TECHNOLOGY Several countries in the region use **drip irrigation.** This is the practice of using small pipes that slowly drip water just above ground to conserve water used for crops. Other nations are developing ways to use ocean water. **Desalinization,** the removal of salt from ocean water, is done at technically sophisticated water treatment plants. However, the desalinated water may be too salty to use for irrigation so it is used in sewage systems. Desalinization plants are very expensive and cannot provide adequate quantities of water to meet all the needs of people in Southwest Asia. Another alternative source of water, especially for agriculture, is the treatment of wastewater. Wastewater treatment plants constructed in the region fail to generate enough water to meet all the needs.

Water pumped from underground aquifers is called **fossil water,** because it has been in the aquifer for very long periods of time. Fossil water has very little chance of being replaced because this region has too little rainfall to recharge the aquifers. It is estimated that at the current rate water is being pumped, only about 25 to 30 years of water usage remain. Finding ways to conserve or even reuse water must be a top priority for the nations of this region.

Geographic Thinking◀

Making Comparisons
A How are the water projects of Turkey and Israel different?

Oil From the Sand

The oil fields discovered in the sands of Southwest Asia have been a bonanza for the region. These fields contain about one-half of all of the petroleum reserves in the world. Petroleum is the source of gasoline for automobiles, heating oil, and the basis of many chemicals used to make everything from fertilizers to plastics. Thus, petroleum products are an important part of the world economy. Having huge oil resources makes Southwest Asia a very important region economically.

FORMING PETROLEUM Oil and natural gas deposits were formed millions of years ago when an ancient sea covered the area of Southwest Asia. Microscopic plants and animals lived and died in the waters. Their remains sank and became mingled with the sand and mud on the bottom of the sea. Over time, pressure and heat transformed the material into hydrocarbons, which form the chemical basis of oil and natural gas.

Oil and natural gas do not exist in large pools beneath the ground, but are trapped inside rocks. You could hold a rock containing oil in your hand and not be able to see the oil because it is trapped in the microscopic pores of the rock. The more porous the rock, the more oil can be stored. A barrier of nonporous rock above the petroleum deposit prevents the gas or oil from moving out of the rock and to the surface.

Engineers use sophisticated equipment to extract, or remove, the oil. It also takes technical skill and special equipment to find deposits of oil. For this reason, oil was not discovered in some parts of the region until the 1920s and 1930s.

EARLY EXPLORATION Industrialization and the increasing popularity of automobiles made petroleum a highly desired resource. Beginning in the late 1800s, oil companies searched all over the world for oil resources. The first Southwest Asia oil discovery was in 1908 in Persia, now known as Iran. In 1938, oil companies found more oil fields in the Arabian Peninsula and Persian Gulf. Then, World War II interrupted further exploring. In 1948, oil companies discovered portions of what would become one of the world's largest oil fields at *al-Ghawar,* just on the eastern edge of the Rub al-Khali. This field contains more than one-quarter of all Saudi Arabia's reserves of oil. ◀B

TRANSPORTING OIL Petroleum that has not been processed is called **crude oil.** Crude oil pumped from the ground must be moved to a **refinery.** The job of a refinery is to convert the crude oil into useful products. Pipelines transport the crude oil either to refineries or to ports where the oil is picked up by tankers and moved to other places for processing. Study the diagram on page 498 to learn how oil is processed and moved.

Geography TODAY

Ruins vs. Water

In 2000, archaeologists in southeastern Turkey unearthed parts of the ancient city of Zeugma, revealing magnificent Roman mosaics—only to realize that a man-made lake would soon submerge the new find.

Located about half a mile away from an historic treasure, Birecik Dam is part of a chain of dams located on the Euphrates River. It was built to provide water for irrigation and hydroelectric power for the region.

Archaeologists had only a few months to save outstanding examples of Roman art, such as the mosaic you see below. The rising waters covered the art before all of it could be rescued.

Geographic Thinking◀

Seeing Patterns
B▶ Why did oil companies continue to search for oil deposits in Southwest Asia?

Processing Petroleum

Oil Field

Storage

Oil Refinery

Pumping Station

1. Drilling rigs cut through nonporous rock above the trapped crude oil and natural gas and pump it to storage tanks.

2. Natural gas, water, and sediments are removed from the crude oil. Oil is sent to the pumping station.

3. The crude oil is pumped to tankers or sent to a refinery to be processed. Some pipelines carry as much as a million barrels a day.

4. At the oil refinery, the crude oil is converted into useful products like gasoline.

5. The products are transported to markets all over the world. Ocean-going tankers carry more than a million barrels; railroad tank cars carry about 1,500 barrels; tank trucks hold about 300 barrels.

Oil Pipelines in Southwest Asia

RUSSIA

Black Sea

GEORGIA

ARMENIA   AZERBAIJAN
Baku

Caspian Sea

40°N

TURKEY

Dörtyol

CYPRUS   Tartus

LEBANON

SYRIA   Sidon

Haifa

Mediterranean Sea

ISRAEL

IRAQ

AFGHANISTAN

IRAN

Suez Canal

JORDAN

30°N

Abadan

Basra
Kuwait   Khark Is.

Strait of Tiran

KUWAIT

Bandar-e Abbas

Al Ahmadi

Lavan Is.

Strait of Hormuz

EGYPT

Ras Tanura   Manama

Doha

Persian Gulf

Gulf of Oman

Matrah   Tropic of Cancer

Yanbu
al Bahr

BAHRAIN

Umm Said

QATAR

U.A.E.

Arabian Sea

20°N

SAUDI ARABIA

OMAN

Red Sea

Salif

YEMEN

0   250   500 miles

0   250   500 kilometers

Lambert Conformal Conic Projection

Bab el Mandeb

Gulf of Aden

50°E

60°E

10°N

N W E S

Legend:
- Oil field
- Gas field
- ▲ Major oil port
- •—• Pipeline

Oil Production

Millions of barrels per day

9

8

7

6

5

1990 1991 1993 1995 1997 1999

■ Saudi Arabia   ■ United States

SOURCE: U.S. Department of Energy

SKILLBUILDER: Interpreting Maps

❶ **REGION** Where are the largest number of oil and gas fields located?

❷ **MOVEMENT** In what direction is much of the oil moved?

Geographic Thinking

Using the Atlas
▶ Use the maps on pages 481 and 498. What countries would likely receive oil shipments from ports located on the Mediterranean Sea?

Placement of pipelines depends on the location of existing ports or access to worldwide markets. Study the map on page 498. Notice that in this region, the pipelines move the crude oil to ports on the Persian Gulf, the Red Sea, and the Mediterranean Sea. From these locations, oil tankers carry the petroleum to markets in the rest of the world. ◀

In some places, refineries process the crude oil near ports. Tanks to hold the oil products are located at port facilities. Many Southwest Asian nations have updated and outfitted their ports to service the very large ocean-going tankers.

RISKS OF TRANSPORTING OIL Moving oil from one location to another always involves the risk of oil spills. The largest oil spill ever recorded occurred in January 1991, during the Persian Gulf War. A series of tankers and oil storage terminals in Kuwait and on islands off its coast were blown up. More than 240 million gallons of crude oil were spilled into the water and on land.

Buried pipelines in Southwest Asia help reduce the danger of above-ground accidents. However, oil spills on land do happen. Because oil is such a valuable commodity, the pipelines are carefully monitored for any drop in pressure that might signal a leak in the line. Any leaks are quickly repaired.

On the other hand, ocean-going tankers transporting oil are at a much higher risk for causing pollution. Many tankers operate in shallow and narrow waterways such as the Red Sea, the Suez Canal, the Persian Gulf, and the Straits of Hormuz. Here, there is danger of oil spills due to collisions or running aground. Most modern tankers have double hulls so that minor accidents will not result in oil spills. In addition, oil-producing nations in Southwest Asia have taken legal steps to protect their environments.

In the next chapter, you will learn more about the people and cultures of the subregions of Southwest Asia.

SECTION 3 ▶ Assessment

❶ Places & Terms

Identify and explain where in the region these would be found.

- drip irrigation
- desalinization
- fossil water
- crude oil
- refinery

❷ Taking Notes

HUMAN–ENVIRONMENT INTERACTION Review the notes you took for this section.

Human–Environment Interaction	

- What are some ways water is supplied in this region?
- In what ways is oil moved from the source to the market place?

❸ Main Ideas

a. Why must both ancient and modern water supply methods be used in the region?

b. Why might water projects in Southwest Asia cause controversy?

c. What are some of the risks in transporting oil?

❹ Geographic Thinking

Making Inferences What impact has technology had on the supply of oil and water in the region? **Think about:**

- finding large reserves of oil or water
- environmental hazards

RESEARCH LINKS
CLASSZONE.COM

ASKING GEOGRAPHIC QUESTIONS Study the map of oil pipelines on page 498. Devise three geographic questions about the map, such as "What problems might there be in choosing locations for these pipelines?" Choose one of your questions and write several **paragraphs** answering the question. Present your findings to the class. Be sure to identify your data sources.

Chapter 21 Assessment

VISUAL SUMMARY

PHYSICAL GEOGRAPHY OF SOUTHWEST ASIA

Landforms

Peninsulas: Anatolian, Arabian

Mountain Ranges: Hindu Kush, Elburz, Zagros, Taurus

Major Waterways: Tigris, Euphrates, Jordan, Red Sea-Suez Canal, Bosporus Strait, Straits of Hormuz

Resources

- Water is a scarce resource.
- Oil is an abundant resource that shapes the region's economy.

Climate and Vegetation

Deserts:
- Rub al-Khali, An-Nafud, Syrian, and Negev are mostly sandy.
- Dasht-e Kavir and Dasht-e Lut are salt flat deserts.

Human-Environment Interaction

- Water is provided through both old and new technologies.
- Oil is pumped from the ground, processed, and transported out of Southwest Asia.

Reviewing Places & Terms

A. Briefly explain the importance of each of the following.

1. Golan Heights
2. wadi
3. Tigris River
4. Euphrates River
5. oasis
6. salt flat
7. drip irrigation
8. desalinization
9. crude oil
10. refinery

B. Answer the questions about vocabulary in complete sentences.

11. Where would you most likely find a wadi?
12. The Golan Heights are an example of which type of landform?
13. Where were several ancient river valley civilizations located?
14. Which terms above deal with water usage?
15. Why are refineries needed?
16. Where might you find a refinery?
17. Why is drip irrigation used?
18. Where would you find a salt flat desert in Southwest Asia?
19. What is the source of water for an oasis?
20. What are drawbacks to using water from a desalinization plant?

Main Ideas

Landforms and Resources (pp. 487–490)

1. How do the landforms of the region restrict movement?
2. What are the most valuable resources in the region and why are they valuable?
3. How large are the oil reserves in the region?

Climate and Vegetation (pp. 491–494)

4. What types of deserts are found in the region?
5. Why is extensive irrigation needed in the region?
6. Where in the region are well-watered lands found?

Human-Environment Interaction (pp. 495–499)

7. What are some examples of the ways in which water is provided in the region?
8. In what ways do major water projects cause political problems?
9. Where are the major oil fields in the region located?
10. What are some dangers in transporting oil?

Critical Thinking

1. Using Your Notes

Use your completed chart to answer these questions.

Landforms	
Resources	

a. How are landforms and desert climate connected?

b. How is oil production related to the economy of the region?

2. Geographic Themes

a. **LOCATION** Why is the relative location of Southwest Asia important to world trade of oil?

b. **PLACE** Why is the Persian Gulf considered a strategic location?

3. Identifying Themes

Why are the Tigris and Euphrates rivers so important to Southwest Asia? Which of the five themes applies to this situation?

4. Making Generalizations

In what ways do oil and water shape the lives of the people of Southwest Asia?

5. Making Inferences

How does climate affect the distribution of population in the region?

Additional Test Practice, pp. S1–S37

 TEST PRACTICE CLASSZONE.COM

Geographic Skills: Interpreting a Cartogram

Estimated Worldwide Oil Reserves

Use the cartogram at the right to answer the following questions. (See page 22 or page 733 for more on cartograms.)

1. **PLACE** Which nations have the greatest oil reserves?

2. **PLACE** What is the approximate amount of reserves for the United States?

3. **REGION** How does this cartogram help to explain the importance of the region?

GeoActivity

Create a three-dimensional model to show the information on the cartogram. Be sure to label each of the countries and give an approximate total amount of oil reserves.

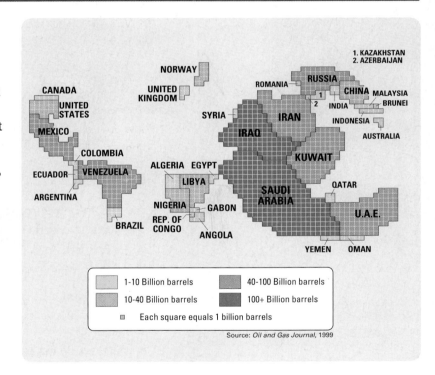

Source: *Oil and Gas Journal*, 1999

 INTERNET ACTIVITY

Use the links at **classzone.com** to do research about oil production. Find out what products are made from crude oil.

Creating Graphs and Charts Create an illustrated chart showing the types of products that are produced from petroleum. List the Web sites that you used in preparing your report.

SECTION 1
The Arabian
Peninsula

SECTION 2
The Eastern
Mediterranean

SECTION 3
The Northeast

HUMAN GEOGRAPHY OF SOUTHWEST ASIA
Religion, Politics, and Oil

Three Subregions of Southwest Asia

Black Sea

Caspian Sea

60°E   70°E

TURKEY

CYPRUS

Mediterranean Sea

SYRIA

LEBANON

ISRAEL

JORDAN

IRAQ

IRAN

AFGHANISTAN

KUWAIT

Persian Gulf

BAHRAIN

QATAR

OMAN

Gulf of Oman

Tropic of Cancer

SAUDI ARABIA

U.A.E.

Arabian Sea

OMAN

Red Sea

YEMEN

Gulf of Aden

INDIAN OCEAN

Equator

Arabian Peninsula
Eastern Mediterranean
Northeast

0   250   500 miles
0   250   500 kilometers
Lambert Conformal Conic Projection

N
W   E
S

GeoFocus

What impact have religion and oil had on Southwest Asia?

Taking Notes In your notebook, copy a cluster diagram like the one below. As you read, take notes about the history, culture, and modern life of each subregion of Southwest Asia.

Northeast

Southwest Asia

Arabian Peninsula

Eastern Mediterranean

The Arabian Peninsula

Main Ideas

- The Arabian Peninsula is heavily influenced by the religious principles of Islam.
- Oil production dominates the economy of the region.

Places & Terms

Mecca	**mosque**
Islam	**theocratic**
Muhammad	**OPEC**

CONNECT TO THE ISSUES
RELIGIOUS CONFLICT
Muslim claims to land in the region laid the foundation for future conflict.

SUNSHINE STATE STANDARDS
Key Standard SS.B.2.4.1 The student understands how social, cultural, economic, and environmental factors contribute to the dynamic nature of regions.

Other Standards SS.A.2.4.6, B.2.4.6, D.2.4.1

FCAT LA.A.1.4.2 Reading: Strategies

A HUMAN PERSPECTIVE Two million people pour into the Saudi Arabian city of Mecca for a few weeks each year. They come from all over the world. In the past, the trip to Mecca involved a difficult journey across oceans and over miles of desert. Today, pilgrims arrive on airplanes. These people are fulfilling the Islamic religious duty of hajj, which is a pilgrimage to the holiest city of Islam—**Mecca.** For five or more days, all are dressed in simple white garments and all perform special activities, rituals, and ceremonies. It is a powerful example of spiritual devotion by the followers of one of the three major religions that claim a home in Southwest Asia.

Islam Changes Desert Culture

The modern nations in this subregion are Bahrain, Kuwait, Oman, Saudi Arabia, Qatar, United Arab Emirates, and Yemen. They are located at the intersection of three continents: Africa, Asia, and Europe. Because of this location, there were many opportunities for trade, and exchange of culture and religion.

TOWN AND DESERT In the past, some towns in the subregion served as trade centers for caravans moving across the deserts. Other cities were ports where goods were exchanged from the Silk Roads in East Asia, Indian Ocean trade from South Asia, and Mediterranean Sea trade from Europe. Still other towns were near oases and fertile lands along major rivers.

Nomadic desert dwellers called Bedouins moved across the peninsula from oasis to oasis. They adapted to the harsh conditions of the desert and built a culture based on strong family ties. They often fought against other families and clans for pasturelands for their livestock. Their fighting skills would eventually help to spread a new religion that developed in the region—Islam.

Islam is a monotheistic religion based on the teachings of its founder, the Prophet **Muhammad.** Muhammad lived part of his life in the city of Mecca.

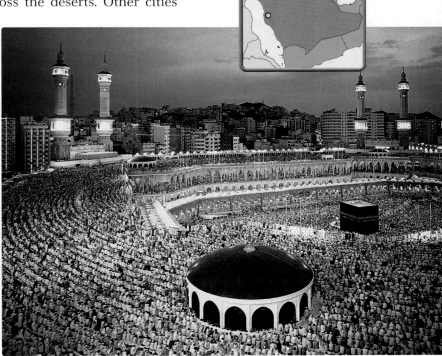

PLACE Thousands of Muslim pilgrims gather at the holy site of the Ka'aba in Mecca. The Ka'aba is the black box at the right in the picture.

ISLAM BRINGS A NEW CULTURE The new religion united the people of the Arabian Peninsula in a way that had not been done previously. Islam requires certain religious duties of all who follow its teachings. The basic duties are called the Five Pillars. By performing these religious duties, all converts to Islam, called Muslims, practiced a similar culture. The Five Pillars are:

- **Faith** All believers must testify to the following statement of faith: "There is no God but Allah, and Muhammad is the Messenger of Allah."
- **Prayer** Five times a day, Muslims face toward the holy city of Mecca to pray. They may do this at a place of worship called a **mosque** or wherever they find themselves at the prayer times.
- **Charity** Muslims believe they have a responsibility to support the less fortunate by giving money for that purpose.
- **Fasting** During the Islamic holy month of Ramadan, Muslims do not eat or drink anything between sunrise and sunset. This action reminds Muslims that there are things in life more important than eating. It is also a sign of self-control and humility.
- **Pilgrimage** All able Muslims are expected to make a pilgrimage (hajj) to Mecca at least once during their lifetime.

BACKGROUND
Ramadan is the ninth month of the 12-month lunar year calendar used by Muslims. It does not match the calendar used by most Americans.

THE SPREAD OF ISLAM As more and more people on the Arabian Peninsula began to convert to Islam, they spread its teachings. Armies of Bedouin fighters moved across the desert, conquered lands, and put Muslim leaders in control. Arabic language and Islamic teachings and culture spread across Southwest Asia. Muslim armies spread across three continents—Asia, Africa, and Europe. By the Middle Ages, a large area of the world was controlled by Muslim empires.

Governments Change Hands

The governments of lands controlled by Muslims were **theocratic.** This means religious leaders control the government. Rulers relied on religious law and consulted with religious scholars on running the country.

Arabian Peninsula History

The gold-capped domes of **Al-Khadhimain Mosque** in Baghdad, Iraq, were constructed early in the 16th century.

1936
Oil discovered in Saudi Arabia.

750
Muslim Empires at their peak

1839
British seize part of Arabian Peninsula.

500 A.D.   750   1000   1500   1750   2000

613
Muhammad begins preaching.

632
The Prophet Muhammad dies.

1566
Ottoman Empire at its peak

1960
OPEC established.

In some of the modern nations of this region—Iran, for example—religious leaders are in control of the government.

COLONIAL POWERS TAKE CONTROL Toward the end of the 1600s, the leaders of Muslim nations were weak. At the same time, countries like Britain and France were growing in power and establishing empires throughout the world. Much of Southwest Asia fell under the control of those two nations, especially after World War I and the breakup of the Muslim-held Ottoman Empire. The region was valuable to colonial powers for two reasons: because of the Suez Canal, a vital link between colonial holdings in the rest of Asia and European ports, and because oil was discovered there after 1932.

However, only a part of the region was colonized. On the Arabian Peninsula, a new power was rising. It was Abdul al-Aziz Ibn Saud. A daring leader, Abdul al-Aziz consolidated power over large areas of the Arabian Peninsula in the name of the Saud family. By the end of the 1920s, only small countries on the Arabian Gulf and parts of Yemen remained free of his control. The whole area became known as Saudi Arabia in 1932. Descendants of Abdul al-Aziz still rule Saudi Arabia today. ◀**A**

Geographic Thinking◀

Using the Atlas

A Using the map on page 479, make a list of the countries that were not under the control of Abdul al-Aziz.

Oil Dominates the Economy

The principal resource in the economy of the Arabian Peninsula is oil. The region grew in global importance as oil became more important to the economies of all nations. Arabian Peninsula nations make almost all of their export money and a large share of GDP from oil, so oil prices are very important to them. Large increases in oil prices allow the oil-producing nations to funnel money into development of other parts of their economies, especially water development projects.

In 1960, a group of oil-producing nations, including Saudi Arabia and Kuwait, established an organization to coordinate policies on selling petroleum products. The group is the Organization of Petroleum Exporting Countries, also known as **OPEC.** The purpose of OPEC is to help members control worldwide oil prices by adjusting oil prices and production quotas. OPEC is a powerful force in international trade. Other Southwest Asian members include Qatar, the United Arab Emirates, Iran, and Iraq.

BACKGROUND Other members of OPEC include Algeria, Gabon, Indonesia, Libya, Nigeria, and Venezuela.

Modern Arabic Life

Changes in the nations of the Arabian Peninsula during the 20th century were dramatic. The region is developing quickly with an emphasis on modernizing. Use of Western technology and machines undermined traditional ways of life. Camels, which used to be the mainstay of life in

Connect to THE Issues

RESOURCES

Oil and the Economy

Many of the oil-producing countries are heavily dependent on oil as a major source of business. Kuwait, which is almost floating on oil because its resources are so great, generates about one-half of its GDP from petroleum. Notice in the chart below that the nations in this subregion are dependent on oil for at least 30 percent of their GDP.

Because oil is a non-renewable resource, it will eventually run out. These nations must work to find other sources of income to replace oil revenues when they are depleted.

Oil Income Percentage of GDP*

*Oman and Yemen not available
SOURCE: *CIA World Factbook 2000*

SW ASIA

the Arabian Peninsula, are no longer used as extensively as they once were. Pick-up trucks, automobiles, and motorcycles have replaced them.

Gone, too, are some of the traditional marketplaces called bazaars or souks (sooks). These open-air markets brought together buyers and sellers with a great variety of merchandise, food, and entertainment. The market was a place to meet neighbors or friends, or to conduct business. Today, Western-style supermarkets or malls may be the shopping location of choice instead of the traditional bazaar.

THE CHANGE TO URBAN LIFE Cities were always a part of life in Southwest Asia. However, because of changes in the economy, the entire area is much more urbanized. Millions of people abandoned their lives as villagers, farmers, and nomads and moved into cities. In 1960, the region was about 25 percent urbanized. By the 1990s, this number had risen to about 58 percent. According to estimates, 70 percent of the population will live in cities by 2015. Saudi Arabia has an urban population of 83 percent. About 4 million people jam the capital, Riyadh. 🅑

As the economy switched to providing petroleum and petroleum products, the types of jobs available in cities changed as well. Workers who could read and write and had technical skills were in great demand. Arabic nations on the peninsula scrambled to upgrade educational systems to meet the needs of the technological age. When those needs could not be fully met, foreign workers were brought in to work at jobs the native population could not fill. As a result, a large number of foreign workers now live in peninsula countries. In some cases, such as Qatar, only one in five workers is a native of the land.

RELIGIOUS DUTIES SHAPE LIVES Despite its rapid modernization, some aspects of Muslim culture have remained the same for centuries. If you traveled to Southwest Asia, one of the first things you would likely notice is that women cover their heads, hair, and sometimes faces with a scarf or veil. This is in keeping with the belief that covering those parts of the body is pleasing to God. Women's roles have gradually expanded during the 20th century. More Arabic women are becoming educated and are able to pursue careers in other nations. Because

Geographic Thinking

Making Comparisons
🅑 How does the percentage of people living in cities of the Arabian Peninsula compare to that of the United States?

PLACE Camels are transported to pasture land by truck.
How does this photograph illustrate the change oil production has made in the region?

506

family is viewed as very important, many women stay at home to manage household affairs. ◄C

As you read earlier in this section, all Muslims are expected to perform certain activities. One of the duties, prayer, is performed at prescribed times—dawn, noon, mid-afternoon, sunset, and before bed. Faithful Muslims stop the activities they are engaged in to carry out this responsibility. In some countries, traffic stops during prayer time. If a person is not near a place of worship, he or she may unroll a small prayer rug on which to kneel to pray. On Fridays, the day for congregational prayer, Muslims assemble for prayers at a mosque.

PLACE The female doctor above shows a blend of traditional and modern lifestyles. **How does this photograph illustrate changes in the roles of women in the region?**

Fasting in the month of Ramadan is another duty that shapes the lives of Muslims. During this month, adult Muslims do not eat or drink from before dawn until sunset. Fasting is a way of reminding Muslims of the spiritual part of their lives. After sunset, Muslims may eat a light meal of lentil or bean soup, a few dates, yogurt, and milky tea. A festival, 'Id al-Fitr, marks the end of Ramadan. New clothes, gifts, and elaborate dinners, along with acts of charity, are part of the celebration.

Since the Muslim culture is found throughout Southwest Asia, many of the same activities of modern life on the Arabian peninsula take place in other areas of Southwest Asia as well. However, as you will learn in the next section, other groups with different religions and lifestyles also live in the region.

Assessment

1 Places & Terms

Explain the meaning of each of the following terms.

- Mecca
- Islam
- Muhammad
- mosque
- theocratic
- OPEC

2 Taking Notes

REGION Review the notes you took for this section.

- How have Islamic beliefs affected this region?
- Why did this region grow in economic importance?

3 Main Ideas

a. What are the Five Pillars of Islam?

b. Why was the region of Southwest Asia important to colonial powers?

c. What is the purpose of OPEC?

4 Geographic Thinking

Drawing Conclusions
How has the presence of large deposits of oil changed the lives of the people of the Arabian peninsula? **Think about:**

- where people live
- the types of jobs available

 RESEARCH LINKS
CLASSZONE.COM

GeoActivity

MAKING COMPARISONS Use the Internet to find more information on the increase in oil production over the last 25 years for the nations shown in the graph on page 505. Create a **line graph** showing the increases in oil production for the five nations.

SW ASIA

Comparing Cultures

Religious Architecture

Throughout the world and across time, people have created spaces in their communities for the worship of God. Sometimes the space is reserved for only a special few, such as priests. Other times the space is designed to bring many worshippers together to create a sense of community. Religious requirements, available building materials, and artistic expression come together in the "houses of god."

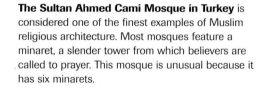

SUNSHINE STATE STANDARDS

Key Standard SS.A.3.4.4 The student knows the significant ideas and texts of Buddhism, Christianity, Hinduism, Islam, and Judaism, their spheres of influence in the age of expansion, and their reforms in the 19th century.

FCAT LA.A.2.2.7 Reading: Recognize Compare and Contrast

A Buddhist temple, such as this one located in Chufu, China, is sometimes called a pagoda. The temple itself usually is a wooden hall with several tiled roofs that curve up on the edges.

The Sultan Ahmed Cami Mosque in Turkey is considered one of the finest examples of Muslim religious architecture. Most mosques feature a minaret, a slender tower from which believers are called to prayer. This mosque is unusual because it has six minarets.

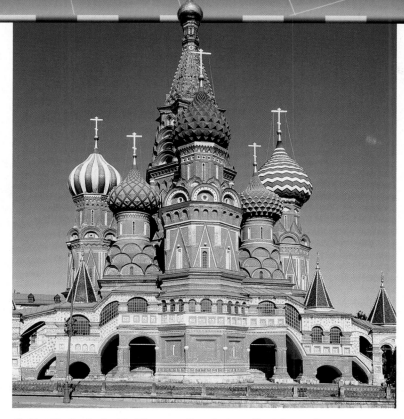

St. Basil's Cathedral in Moscow, Russia, is really eight smaller churches around a main one. The basic plan of the church forms a cross. The exterior was originally white. The colorful domes are covered with roof tiles that were added in the 17th century.

The Pyramid of the Sun in Mexico is the largest Meso-American religious structure. Its size was designed to inspire awe in the worshipper. A small temple on the top was usually visited only by priests.

GeoActivity

CREATING A MODEL

Choose one of the major religions of the world. With a small group, use the Internet to research more about the religious architecture of that religion.

- Create a model of a worship space showing the unique aspects of that religion's architecture.

- Create a brochure explaining your model.

RESEARCH LINKS
CLASSZONE.COM

GeoData

PLACES OF WORSHIP

THE MOSQUE

- Muslims are instructed to face toward Mecca when they pray. Inside the mosque, a special recess in the wall—*mihrab*—marks the direction of Mecca.

- The Sultan Ahmed Cami Mosque is also called the Blue Mosque because of the bluish haze given to the interior by 21,043 blue-glazed tiles on the walls.

THE PYRAMID

- Standing 216 feet high and 720 by 760 feet at the base, the Pyramid of the Sun is one of the largest structures of its type in the Western Hemisphere.

ST. BASIL'S CATHEDRAL

- St. Basil's was built by Ivan IV, also called Ivan the Terrible, as an offering to God for military victories over Tatar armies.

- Legend has it that the architect of St. Basil's was blinded so that he could never create anything similar to St. Basil's.

The Eastern Mediterranean

Main Ideas
- The holy places of three religions are found in this subregion.
- There is a great deal of political tension among nations in this subregion.

Places & Terms
Western Wall
Dome of the Rock
Zionism
Palestine Liberation Organization (PLO)

CONNECT TO THE ISSUES
RELIGIOUS CONFLICT Creation of the nation of Israel led to conflict in the region.

SUNSHINE STATE STANDARDS
Key Standard SS.B.2.4.1 The student understands how social, cultural, economic, and environmental factors contribute to the dynamic nature of regions.

Other Standards SS.A.3.4.4, B.2.4.6

FCAT LA.A.1.4.2 Reading: Strategies

PLACE Christian pilgrims walk on the road to the Mount of Olives on a holy day—Palm Sunday.

A HUMAN PERSPECTIVE On September 28, 2000, riots broke out in the city of Jerusalem. The cause was a visit by an Israeli political leader to a Jewish holy place at a location on the Temple Mount. Muslims also have a holy place on the Temple Mount. They viewed the visit by the Israeli leader as disrespectful to Muslims. Hundreds of people died in the civil unrest that followed.

To understand why a simple visit to a holy place would cause such problems, it is necessary to understand the deep-seated hostility Arabs and Jews feel for each other. They have an enormous disagreement over the control of the city of Jerusalem and of the land called the Occupied Territories. (See the map on page 480.) In fact, the relations between Arabs and Jews affect the entire region of the Eastern Mediterranean.

Religious Holy Places

Three major monotheistic religions—Judaism, Christianity, and Islam—were founded in Southwest Asia. All three claim Jerusalem as a holy city. The City of Jerusalem, which covers 42 square miles, has Jewish, Christian, Armenian Christian, and Muslim sections. Followers of all three religions come to the Old City to visit locations with strong spiritual meaning.

JEWISH PRESENCE For Jews, Jerusalem, the capital of Israel, is the center of their modern and ancient homeland. Located in the old part of the city, the Temple Mount once housed the religion's earliest temples. There, King Solomon built the First Temple. The Second Temple was constructed after the Jews returned to their homeland in 538 B.C. Modern Jews come to pray at the holiest site in Jerusalem, a portion of the Second Temple known as the **Western Wall**—also called the Wailing Wall. It is the only remaining piece of the Second Temple, which was destroyed in A.D. 70 by the Romans.

CHRISTIAN HERITAGE For Christians, Jerusalem is the sacred location of the final suffering and crucifixion of Jesus. Towns and villages important in the life of Jesus are found near Jerusalem. Every year, Christians visit places like the Mount of Olives and the Church of the Holy Sepulchre by the thousands. When Jerusalem was under Muslim control, Christians launched the Crusades to regain the lands and place them under the

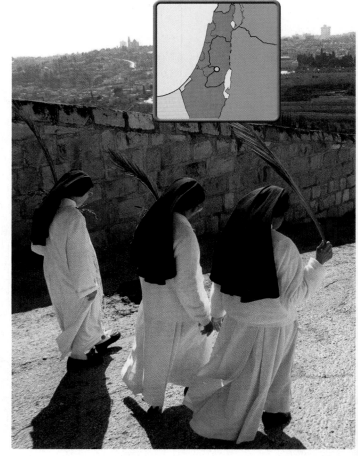

control of Christians. Eventually, the lands returned to the control of Muslims and remained that way until the nation of Israel was established in May of 1948.

ISLAMIC SACRED SITES After Mecca and Medina, Jerusalem is considered the third most holy city to Muslims. A shrine there, called **Dome of the Rock,** houses the spot where Muslims believe the Prophet Muhammad rose into heaven. Jews believe it is the site where Abraham, a Jewish fore-father, prepared to sacrifice his son Isaac to God. The Dome of the Rock and a nearby mosque, Al-Aqsa, are located on the Temple Mount next to the Western Wall. Because these most holy sites are so close together, they have been the site of clashes between Jews and Muslims. ◁A

CONNECT TO THE ISSUES
RELIGIOUS CONFLICT
▶A What problems might emerge when three different religious groups claim the same area as a holy place?

PLACE Muslim visitors gather at the Dome of the Rock, a holy site in the city of Jerusalem. **How did control of Jerusalem change over many centuries?**

A History of Unrest

The nations of the Eastern Mediterranean have been plagued with a history of political tension and unrest. The Ottoman Empire, a Muslim government based in Turkey, ruled the Eastern Mediterranean lands from 1520 to 1922. But the Ottoman Empire grew weaker and less able to solve problems with groups seeking independence. By the beginning of the 20th century, its collapse was not far away. The Ottoman Empire sided with Germany during World War I. At the end of the war, the Ottoman Empire fell apart. Britain and France received the lands in the Eastern Mediterranean as part of the war settlement.

BACKGROUND
The League of Nations gave the Ottoman lands to France and Britain.

THE LEGACY OF COLONIALISM After World War I, Britain and France divided the Ottoman lands in the Eastern Mediterranean region. France took the northern portion, including the present-day countries of Lebanon and Syria. Britain controlled the southern section, which included the present-day nations of Jordan and Israel. Britain and France were supposed to rule these lands until they were ready for independence. During the time of their control, the French frequently played different religious groups against each other. Those tensions remain in the region today. The Syrians hated the French and in the 1920s and 1930s rebelled against them. Lebanon became independent in 1943, and Syria gained independence in 1946.

BRITISH CONTROL PALESTINE The land controlled by Britain was known as Palestine. In the 19th century, a movement called **Zionism** began. Its goal was to create and support a Jewish homeland in Palestine. Jewish settlers started buying land and settling there. By 1914, just before World War I, about 12 percent of the population in Palestine was Jewish. After the war, the British took command of the region and continued to allow Jewish immigration to Palestine. Early

SW ASIA

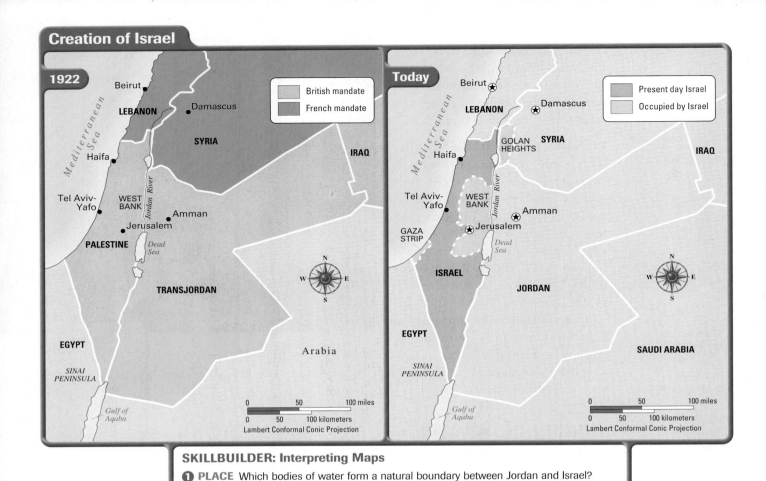

Creation of Israel

1922

British mandate
French mandate

Mediterranean Sea
Beirut
LEBANON
Damascus
SYRIA
Haifa
IRAQ
Tel Aviv-Yafo
WEST BANK
Jordan River
Amman
Jerusalem
PALESTINE
Dead Sea
TRANSJORDAN
EGYPT
Arabia
SINAI PENINSULA
Gulf of Aqaba

0   50   100 miles
0   50   100 kilometers
Lambert Conformal Conic Projection

Today

Present day Israel
Occupied by Israel

Mediterranean Sea
Beirut
LEBANON
Damascus
GOLAN HEIGHTS
SYRIA
Haifa
IRAQ
Tel Aviv-Yafo
WEST BANK
Jordan River
Amman
Jerusalem
GAZA STRIP
Dead Sea
ISRAEL
JORDAN
EGYPT
SINAI PENINSULA
SAUDI ARABIA
Gulf of Aqaba

0   50   100 miles
0   50   100 kilometers
Lambert Conformal Conic Projection

SKILLBUILDER: Interpreting Maps

❶ **PLACE** Which bodies of water form a natural boundary between Jordan and Israel?

❷ **PLACE** Which three areas are occupied by Israel?

on, Arabs and Jews in the region cooperated. But as more and more Jews poured into Palestine to escape persecution in Germany, the Arabs resisted the establishment of a Jewish state. In 1939, to reduce tensions the British halted Jewish immigration to Palestine.

As you study the map on this page, you will see that the area controlled by the British was divided into two sections—Transjordan and Palestine. The land was divided to relieve tensions between Arabs and Jews. An Arab government jointly ruled Transjordan with the British. Britain controlled Palestine, along with local governments that included both Jews and Arabs.

CREATING THE STATE OF ISRAEL At the end of World War II, thousands of Jewish survivors of the Holocaust wanted to settle in Palestine. Palestine was considered the Jewish homeland. World opinion supported the establishment of a Jewish nation-state. Britain eventually referred the question of a Jewish homeland to the United Nations. In 1947, the United Nations developed a plan to divide Palestine into two states—one for Arabs and one for Jews.

Arabs in the region did not agree with the division. However, the nation of Israel was established on May 14, 1948. Immediately, the surrounding Arab nations of Egypt, Syria, Lebanon, Jordan, Iraq, Saudi Arabia, and Yemen invaded Israel to prevent the establishment of the state. Jewish troops fought back. By the 1950s, Israel was a firmly established nation. The 1948 war was the beginning of hostilities that continue to this day.

Geographic Thinking

Using the Atlas
🅱 Use the Atlas on page 480. How was the land Israel occupied in 1967 different from the land it held in 1948?

Caught in the middle of this turmoil were Palestinian Arabs and Christians. Many of these people had roots in Palestine that went back for centuries. They either fled their homes or were forced into UN-sponsored refugee camps just outside Israel's borders. The land designated for the Palestinians on the West Bank and Gaza Strip is under Israeli control. In the 1960s, the **Palestine Liberation Organization (PLO)** was formed to regain the land for Palestinian Arabs. Over the years, the PLO has pursued political and military means to take possession of Arab land in Israel and allow refugees to return to their homes.

In 2003, the PLO named Mahmoud Abbas (also known as Abu Mazen) as the first Palestinian prime minister. Abu Mazen agreed to support a peace plan for the Middle East called the "road map." The goals of this step-by-step plan included establishing a Palestinian state and resolving the rights of the Palestinian refugees.

Modernizing Economies

The nations in the Eastern Mediterranean subregion are young. Most became independent shortly after World War II. Cyprus received its independence from Britain in 1960. Political divisions, refugees, and a weak infrastructure make it difficult to develop healthy economies.

REFUGEES AND CIVIL WARS The creation of Israel produced a large number of Palestinian refugees. Today, those refugees and their descendants total almost 3.6 million people. They are scattered across many of the countries in the region. Some still live in UN-sponsored camps.

Many of the refugees have struggled to find food, shelter, and employment. Providing education and other services for them is difficult for nations such as Jordan, one of the poorest in the region—and the one with the largest Palestinian refugee population.

Civil wars in Lebanon and Cyprus have also caused huge economic problems. Lebanon, a more developed nation, was hard hit by a civil war that lasted from 1975 to 1976. The conflict widened to include other nations, and in 1982 Israel invaded Lebanon. Some Israeli troops remained in Lebanon until 2000.

MODERN INFRASTRUCTURE All of the nations of the Eastern Mediterranean subregion have great potential for developing agriculture, tourism, and trade. What many of them lack, however, is an infrastructure that would support a growing economy. Roads in war-torn areas, for example, must be rebuilt. Especially needed are irrigation systems to make the area bloom. Better communication systems and power sources are needed for developing high-tech industries in the region. Israel has been able to build sophisticated industries such as computer software development.

Connect TO THE Issues

POPULATION

Palestinian Refugee Camps

In 1949, the UN authorized the creation of 53 Palestinian refugee camps. The camps were supposed to be used only for a short time until the Palestinians were resettled. That was over 50 years ago. Today, most of the Palestinians living in the camps were actually born there and have never been to the lands designated for the Palestinian state.

The camps house upwards of 35,000 people and some as many as 50,000 people. The UN and other nations provide money for education and health care needs. Since the Israeli government restricts all travel for work, economic opportunities are very limited.

SW ASIA

growing up in...Israel

This young woman is a member of the Israel Defense Forces.
Unmarried Jewish young women are required to serve for two years. They serve in various parts of the armed forces, in jobs such as tank instructors, helicopter pilots, military police, rescue workers, and office workers. They are not permitted to serve in active combat units. Service in the armed forces helps build unity and identity for Israelis.

If you lived in Israel, you would pass these milestones:

- You would go to school from age 5 to age 15.
- At age 14, you would choose between going to a technical school or a more academic school.
- You could begin working at age 15.

- You could drive at age 17.
- You could get married at age 17.
- You would enter the armed forces at age 18: men for 3 years, women for 2 years.

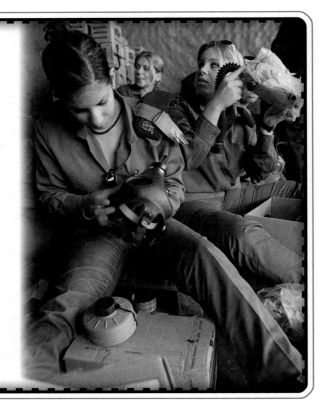

Modern Life

Modern life in the Eastern Mediterranean is a curious blend of old and new. Strong cultural traditions exist but they are combined with changes that were brought about by modern innovations. Cell phones, computers, and Internet access are increasingly common. One aspect of life here that remains quite traditional, however, is the dining experience.

EATING OUT, EATING IN Eating in restaurants in Eastern Mediterranean countries is not as common as in the United States. Some restaurants have separate sections for men and women. Cafes serving coffee and tea are generally for men only. Most meals are eaten in the home. Families and sometimes friends gather to have meals. The last meal of the day is usually served between 8 and 11 P.M.

Typically, a meal begins with small portions of hummus, ground chickpeas mixed with lemon juice and parsley, and baba ganouzh, an eggplant dip served with pita, a flat bread with a pocket. A salad called tabbouleh, made of bulgur (cracked wheat), parsley, onions, mint, tomatoes, and lemon juice, is common. Chicken or lamb is more likely to be served as a main course than beef. Many meals are finished with fresh fruit or sweets such as kolaicha, a sweet cake made of barley flour, sugar, oil, and cardamom seed. Thick coffee or tea is also served. The host of a dinner may not eat with the guests so that he can attend to all their needs during the meal.

A VARIETY OF CULTURES Muslim Arabs make up the majority of people who live in the countries of the Eastern Mediterranean. However, in several nations, especially Lebanon and Israel, there is a variety of cultures.

🌐 Geographic Thinking◄

Making Comparisons
◄ In what ways is the dining experience in this region different from that of the United States?

Since the seventh century, Lebanon has been a refuge for both Muslims and Christians. Many of the Muslims there are Shi'ites, as compared to the Sunni majorities in many of the other nations in this region. A small group of Druze also live in Lebanon. This tightly knit group is very secretive about its religious practices. The members live in the mountainous areas of Lebanon and also in Israel and Syria. Christians of the Maronite tradition (Roman Catholics following Eastern Orthodox practices) and the Eastern Orthodox tradition make up a large minority in Lebanon. Together, these groups present a wide variety of cultures and religious practices. The variety makes it difficult to build unity in the country.

Israel is a land with a tremendous variety of immigrants. The majority of immigrants are Jewish, and they arrive from all over the globe. They come from the United States, Eastern Europe, the Mediterranean region, Russia, and Ethiopia. The focus of Jewish culture helps to draw most of this diverse group together.

In addition, Israel is home to Arab Muslims of several different groups. Bedouins live in the Negev Desert. Druze, Sunni, and a group called Circassians come from the Caucasus Mountains area. Also living in Israel is a small number of Christians and people following the Baha'i faith. The combination of all these groups brings a variety of languages and lifestyles to Israel.

In the next section, you will learn about countries in this region with ethnic backgrounds that are Turkish or Persian.

PLACE A woman walks along the beachfront of Beirut, Lebanon. **How does Lebanon's relative location make it a refuge for Muslims and Christians?**

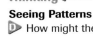
Seeing Patterns
D How might the small size of Israel and Lebanon affect the way groups of people living there relate to each other?

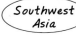

Assessment

1 Places & Terms

Explain the meaning of each of the following terms.

- Western Wall
- Dome of the Rock
- Zionism
- Palestine Liberation Organization

2 Taking Notes

PLACE Review the notes you took for this section.

Southwest Asia — Eastern Mediterranean

- What are some religious holy places found in this subregion?
- What factors have made it difficult to develop this subregion economically?

3 Main Ideas

a. How did colonial rule set up tension in the subregion?

b. What impact have refugees and civil wars had on modernizing the economies of this subregion?

c. In addition to Muslims, what other groups live in the Eastern Mediterranean nations?

4 Geographic Thinking

Determining Cause and Effect How did the creation of the nation of Israel increase tension in the subregion? **Think about:**

- religious differences
- division of Palestine

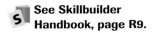 **See Skillbuilder Handbook, page R9.**

MAKING COMPARISONS Review the maps on page 480 and page 512. Create a series of four **sketch maps** that show how the state of Israel changed between 1922 and 1976. Write a caption on each map describing the change from the previous map.

SW ASIA

The Northeast

Main Ideas

• The nations in this subregion are Muslim but most are not part of the Arab culture.

• The nations in the Northeast range from developed to very poorly developed.

Places & Terms

Kurds   Shi'ite

Mesopotamia   Taliban

Sunni

CONNECT TO THE ISSUES

POPULATION RELOCATION The Kurds' movement across this subregion has caused conflict.

SUNSHINE STATE STANDARDS

Key Standard SS.B.2.4.1 The student understands how social, cultural, economic, and environmental factors contribute to the dynamic nature of regions.

Other Standards SS.A.2.4.2, B.2.4.3

FCAT LA.A.1.4.2 Reading: Strategies

A HUMAN PERSPECTIVE On March 16, 1988, Iraqi Air Force planes released poisonous gases over the Kurdish town of Halabja, Iraq. An estimated 5,000 **Kurds,** an ethnic group in Southwestern Asia, died from the chemical weapons attack. The Kurdish people have occupied the lands they call Kurdistan for thousands of years. In the modern world, those lands are located in Turkey, Iraq, and Iran. For most of the 20th century, these three nations disagreed with the Kurds over control of these lands. In fact, clashes over land have been the focus of much unrest in the northeastern part of Southwest Asia.

A Blend of Cultures

The nations in this subregion include Turkey, Iran, Iraq, and Afghanistan. They are mostly Muslim in religion, but only Iraq is Arabic in cultural life. All these nations were influenced by early civilizations and empires in the region.

EARLY CIVILIZATIONS Part of the cultural hearth known as the Fertile Crescent is located here. Some of the earliest civilizations in the world developed in Iraq along the Tigris and Euphrates rivers. Sumer, Babylonia, Assyria, and Chaldea all built empires in **Mesopotamia,** the "land between the rivers."

The Hittites, whose empire stretched across what is Turkey today, brought innovations such as the use of iron weapons. Persia, which developed in the region occupied by Iran today, introduced innovations in government organization.

ETHNIC AND RELIGIOUS VARIETY Living in this subregion are members of many ethnic groups, including Turks, Kurds, Persians, and Assyrians. The map on page 482 shows where these groups live. They speak languages such as Turkish and Farsi, which are different from the Arabic that is spoken in the rest of the region.

Though the different ethnic groups all follow Islam, tensions exist. After the death of the Prophet Muhammad, Muslims divided into two main branches—the **Sunni** and the **Shi'ite.** About 83 percent of all Muslims are Sunni. Most Iranians are Shi'ite.

Northeast Ethnic Areas

| | Kurdish area |
| | Shi'ite area of Iraq |

RUSSIA • Black Sea • GEORGIA • ARMENIA • AZERBAIJAN • TURKEY • AZER. • Caspian Sea • SYRIA • IRAQ • IRAN • SAUDI ARABIA • KUWAIT • Persian Gulf

40°E — 40°N — 30°N — 0

0   150   300 miles

0   150   300 kilometers

Lambert Conformal Conic Projection

SKILLBUILDER: Interpreting Maps

❶ **REGION** Which country has the largest area inhabited by Kurds?

❷ **REGION** What is the approximate size of the area inhabited by the Kurds?

Clashes Over Land

Clashes over land in this region increased after World War I. Some were disagreements over homelands claimed by ethnic groups whose demands for land were ignored. Other disputes were over control of valuable oil fields.

HOMELANDS AND REFUGEES The Kurds have been called a stateless nation. At the end of World War I, they were promised a homeland but never received it. Clashes between the Kurds and the governments of Turkey, Iran, and Iraq have prevented the Kurds from becoming a nation-state.

CONNECT TO THE ISSUES
POPULATION RELOCATION
 How might land claims and refugee status affect movement across the region?

Because of its location, Iran has become home to refugees fleeing oppressive governments in both Afghanistan and Iraq. In fact, Iran has the largest refugee population of any nation in the world. Iraqi Shi'ites persecuted by their government have sought refuge with fellow Shi'ites in Iran. Decades of war drove many Afghan refugees to Iran, although some began to return in 2002. ◄A

CONTROL OF OIL FIELDS Access to the oil-rich regions on the Persian Gulf is strategically important for all nations that import oil. Between 1980 and 1990, Iran and Iraq fought a war over control of oil fields. Then, in 1990–1991, Iraq invaded Kuwait, starting the Persian Gulf War. The United States and 32 other nations fought to drive the Iraqis out of Kuwait and keep oil fields open.

Clashes Over Leadership

The war on terrorism declared by President George W. Bush led to clashes over leadership in the Northeast subregion. Within a month of the attacks against the United States on September 11, 2001, the United States and the coalition forces fought in Afghanistan, where the terrorists responsible for the attacks were being harbored. In 2003, fear for national security prompted the United States to declare war on Iraq and its leader, Saddam Hussein.

OVERTHROW OF THE TALIBAN A fundamentalist Muslim political group called the **Taliban** was protecting Osama bin Laden and his al-Qaeda terrorist network in Afghanistan. On October 7, 2001, U.S.-led coalition forces launched Operation Enduring Freedom to seize the terrorists' financial assets and destroy their infrastructure. By March 2002, the Taliban had been removed from power. A transitional government, headed by Hamid Karzai, replaced the repressive regime. However, some Taliban and al-Qaeda leaders, including Osama bin Laden, managed to escape the coalition forces.

PLACE In Afghanistan, coalition forces prepare explosives to blow up caves that shelter Taliban forces. **What difficulties did the coalition forces face fighting in the mountainous terrain of Afghanistan?**

OVERTHROW OF SADDAM HUSSEIN After the Persian Gulf War ended in 1991, the United Nations ordered Saddam Hussein to destroy his biological and chemical weapons. President George W. Bush, however, believed that the Iraqi dictator was continuing to develop and expand a weapons of mass destruction program. As a result, American and British forces launched Operation Iraqi Freedom in March 2003 to stamp out Hussein's ability to wage mass war or aid terrorists. Major combat ended on May 1, and the long process of working toward a democratic government in Iraq began. Although Saddam Hussein was overthrown, he and other top members of his government had avoided capture as of July 2003.

Reforming Economies

The nations in this subregion face a variety of economic challenges. All of them have limited agricultural land. Production must become more efficient in order to produce surplus crops to sell elsewhere. Most of these nations have oil or natural gas resources that can generate revenue. This money is needed to update and expand transportation systems, communication systems, power generation plants, and water and sanitation systems.

PLACE This monument located in Tehran is dedicated to the Iranian Revolution. **Why might the government have built such a monument?**

MAKING PROGRESS Turkey and Iran are making progress in modernizing their economies. Turkey is developing its water resources and hydroelectric plants to supply energy and to boost production of cotton and other agricultural products. It is the only nation in this subregion that produces significant amounts of steel. Turkey straddles two continents—Europe and Asia—which makes it ideally located for trade. B

Changes in Iran's government have had a major impact on its economic progress. Government attitudes have swung between strong support for economic growth to no plans for change. The current government is supporting growth. Oil money fuels most of the plans for developing a diversified economy. But Iran is still recovering from a war with Iraq (1980–1990) that severely harmed its economy.

PROGRESS INTERRUPTED For many years, war and political problems in Iraq and Afghanistan prevented these countries from improving their economies. After Iraq invaded Kuwait in 1990, economic restrictions were imposed, limiting much of Iraq's foreign trade. As a result, the Iraqi people have lacked basic goods such as food and medicine and other medical supplies.

Afghanistan is one of the poorest nations in the world. Most of its people are engaged in agriculture

Geographic Thinking

Seeing Patterns
B Why might Turkey's location increase its desire to develop international trade?

and animal herding. Afghanistan has great mineral resources, but civil war and turmoil during the U.S.-led war against the Taliban in 2001 and 2002 interrupted any attempts at progress in the area. After the Taliban regime was removed from power, however, the transitional government began taking steps toward rebuilding Afghanistan's economy.

Modern and Traditional Life

As the nations of this subregion move into the new century, they face internal struggles. In each country, a division exists between those who want to adopt a modern lifestyle and those who want to preserve more traditional ways.

Nowhere was this division more apparent than in Afghanistan. There, the Taliban imposed strict rules on people's behavior. After the regime was toppled in 2002, however, newly installed president Hamid Karzai began restoring civil liberties and improving education.

In Turkey, Iran, and Iraq, groups similar to the Taliban exist but have not been able to gain control of the governments there. These fundamentalist Muslim groups have very different ideas from each other about the way people should behave. It has led to conflicts within the societies that have sometimes flared into serious political problems.

In the next chapter, you will study more about issues that affect the countries of Southwest Asia.

PLACE An Iranian woman works on a wool rug. The high quality hand-woven rugs are a valuable trade item.
How does the photograph demonstrate a traditional lifestyle?

Assessment

① Places & Terms

Explain the meaning of each of the following terms.

• Kurds
• Mesopotamia
• Sunni
• Shi'ite
• Taliban

② Taking Notes

REGION Review the notes you took for this section.

• What role has oil played in clashes over land in this subregion?

• Why are there so many refugees in this subregion?

③ Main Ideas

a. How are the people who live in the Northeast different from those who live in other parts of Southwest Asia?

b. What do the nations in this subregion need to do to develop their economies?

c. Why did the United States overthrow some of the leaders in the subregion?

④ Geographic Thinking

Making Inferences What impact do political problems have on economic progress?
Think about:

• the economies of Turkey and Iran

• the economies of Iraq and Afghanistan

RESEARCH LINKS
CLASSZONE.COM

SEEING PATTERNS Review the information on ethnic and religious variety, and national economies of the countries in this section. Also visit the Internet for more information on the topics. Then create a **database** showing your information.

SW ASIA

Disasters!

🌴 **SUNSHINE STATE STANDARDS**
Key Standard SS.B.1.4.3 The student uses mental maps of physical and human features of the world to answer complex geographic questions.
FCAT LA.B.1.4.1 Writing: Strategies

Earthquake in Turkey

As the Arabian Plate pushes northward, it squeezes the Anatolian Plate into the Eurasian Plate. Caught like a slippery seed squeezed between two fingers, the Anatolian Plate slips westward. This movement causes the earth to quake. At 3 A.M. on August 17, 1999, residents of Gölcük, a city near Izmit, Turkey, were thrown from their beds by 45 seconds of earth-shaking terror. When it was over, the quake—which measured 7.4 on the Richter Scale—had taken the lives of 17,000 people and caused billions of dollars of damage.

Izmit, Turkey, was at the epicenter of the quake. It is located on one of the world's most active fault lines—the North Anatolian Fault. Since 1939, 11 major quakes have hit along the Anatolian Fault Line.

The quake destroyed 85,000 buildings. Many of the buildings were poorly constructed with inferior building materials. Floors of buildings "pancaked" and crushed the residents.

About 40,000 families were made homeless by the quake. Survivors were housed in 168 tent cities. Unfortunately, few were winterized, and thousands of people shivered through Turkey's winter.

GeoActivity

MAKING A DEMONSTRATION
Working with a small group, use the Internet to research the causes and effects of earthquakes. Then create a **demonstration** about earthquakes.

* Build a model or create a diagram showing how an earthquake occurs.
* Create a chart showing the type of damage caused by earthquakes.
* Add a world map showing the major fault lines.

RESEARCH LINKS
CLASSZONE.COM

GeoData

THE MERCALLI INTENSITY SCALE
* The Mercalli Intensity Scale measures an earthquake's effect on people and buildings.
* Mercalli ranges from I to XII. Here are some examples.

I.	No damage
VI.	Pictures fall off the wall
VII.	Slight damage to structures
X.	Most masonry structures destroyed; landslides; ground cracked
XII.	Total damage

RICHTER SCALE
* The Richter Scale measures the magnitude of energy released during an earthquake.
* Here are some examples of Richter Scale measurements:

2	Just felt
4.5	Damage newsworthy
7	A major quake
8	Great damage
8.9	Largest quake ever recorded

VISUAL SUMMARY
HUMAN GEOGRAPHY OF SOUTHWEST ASIA

Subregions of Southwest Asia

⬤ **The Arabian Peninsula**
- The teachings of Islam shape the lives of the people of the region.
- Oil forms the basis of the economy of the region.
- The subregion has experienced rapid modernization.

⬤ **The Eastern Mediterranean**
- The region has holy places of three religions: Judaism, Christianity, and Islam.
- The Jewish nation-state of Israel was created in 1948.
- Political unrest in the region has disrupted life and created problems with refugees and the economy.

⬤ **The Northeast**
- The region has a variety of ethnic groups, most of whom practice Islam.
- The region has economies that range from developed to one of the poorest nations in the world—Afghanistan.
- There are divisions among the people of this region over modern and traditional lifestyles.

Reviewing Places & Terms

A. Briefly explain the importance of each of the following.

1. Mecca
2. Islam
3. OPEC
4. Western Wall
5. Dome of the Rock
6. Zionism
7. Palestine Liberation Organization
8. Sunni
9. Shi'ite
10. Taliban

B. Answer the questions about vocabulary in complete sentences.

11. Why is Mecca an important site to Muslims?
12. How are Islam, Sunni, and Shi'ite related to each other?
13. Which branch of Islam has the largest number of followers?
14. Where are the Western Wall and the Dome of the Rock located?
15. With which religion is the Dome of the Rock associated?
16. Why is the Western Wall important to Jews?
17. Which of the terms above is associated with international oil trade?
18. What is the goal of the Palestine Liberation Organization?
19. How is Zionism connected to the formation of the state of Israel?
20. In which country were members of the Taliban harboring terrorists?

Main Ideas

The Arabian Peninsula (pp. 503–509)

1. How did the teachings of Islam unite the people of the Arabian Peninsula?
2. Why is oil so important to the economies of the Arabian Peninsula?
3. How has modern Arabic life changed in the past 50 years?

The Eastern Mediterranean (pp. 510–515)

4. For which religions is Jerusalem a holy city?
5. Why was the state of Israel created?
6. What factors have made it difficult to build healthy economies in the Eastern Mediterranean countries?
7. How are populations of Lebanon and Israel different from other countries in the region?

The Northeast (pp. 516–521)

8. How are language, ethnic groups, and religion in the Northeast region different from other parts of Southwest Asia?
9. What steps need to be taken to improve the economies of the Northeast region?
10. Why are there internal struggles in some of the nations of the Northeast region?

Critical Thinking

1. Using Your Notes

Use your completed chart to answer these questions.

a. How is Israel different from the other nations in the region?

b. How must infrastructure be changed in the region?

2. Geographic Themes

a. **HUMAN-ENVIRONMENT INTERACTION** What impact does the presence of oil in the region have on the economies of the countries in Southwest Asia?

b. **LOCATION** How would Israel's relative location be described?

3. Identifying Themes

Which nations are dealing with large numbers of refugees or immigrants? Which of the five themes applies to this situation?

4. Making Inferences

How has the presence of many different ethnic groups in this region caused political unrest?

5. Making Generalizations

In what ways has oil production changed life in Southwest Asia?

Additional Test Practice, pp. S1–S37

TEST PRACTICE
CLASSZONE.COM

Geographic Skills: Interpreting Maps

Ottoman Empire, 1683

Use the map at the right to answer the following questions.

1. **LOCATION** What is the relative location of the Ottoman Empire?

2. **PLACE** On which continents was the Ottoman Empire located?

3. **PLACE** Which large bodies of water are within the Ottoman Empire?

GeoActivity

On a current map showing the same area as in the map at the right, outline the Ottoman Empire. Make a list of the modern countries that were once a part of the Ottoman Empire.

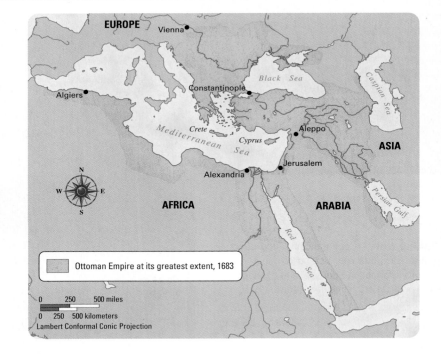

Ottoman Empire at its greatest extent, 1683

0   250   500 miles
0   250   500 kilometers
Lambert Conformal Conic Projection

INTERNET ACTIVITY

Use the links at **classzone.com** to do research about OPEC. Make a list of the current members of the organization. Focus on the impact on the price of oil as a result of actions taken by the group.

Analyzing Data Study the data you collected on oil prices and the actions of OPEC. Create charts or graphs to illustrate the information. Then write a generalization about the information you found.

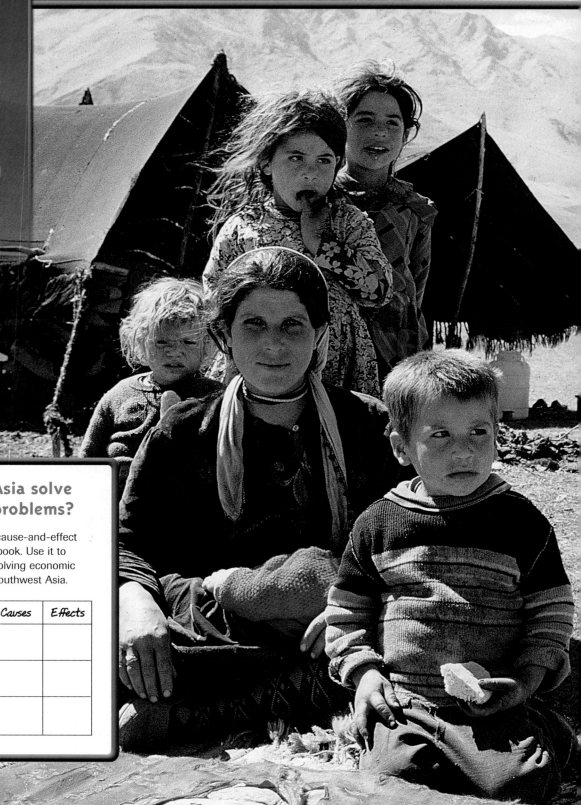

Chapter 23

SECTION 1
Population Relocation

SECTION 2
Oil Wealth Fuels Change

CASESTUDY

RELIGIOUS CONFLICT OVER LAND

For more on these issues in Southwest Asia . . .

CURRENT EVENTS
CLASSZONE.COM

TODAY'S ISSUES
Southwest Asia

A Kurdish family rests at its camp in eastern Turkey. Many Kurds are nomadic and move across lands in several countries.

GeoFocus

Can Southwest Asia solve long-standing problems?

Taking Notes Copy the cause-and-effect chart below into your notebook. Use it to record information about solving economic and political problems in Southwest Asia.

	Causes	Effects
Issue 1: Population Relocation		
Issue 2: Economic Development		
Case Study: Religious Conflict		

524

Population Relocation

What kind of population movement is taking place in Southwest Asia?

Main Ideas
- Economic growth brings foreign workers to the region.
- Political factors have shifted the region's population.

Places & Terms
guest workers

stateless nation

Palestinians

West Bank

Gaza Strip

SUNSHINE STATE STANDARDS
Key Standard SS.B.2.4.2 The student understands past and present trends in human migration and cultural interaction and their impact on physical and human systems.

FCAT LA.A.1.4.2 Reading: Strategies

A HUMAN PERSPECTIVE In the 1980s, Kurds living in Turkey were attacked by the Turkish military. The parents of 10-year-old Garbi Yildirim feared for their son's safety. Reluctantly they sent him from Turkey to live with relatives in Germany. When Garbi reached his 18th birthday, he was notified by the German government that he would have to return to Turkey. Upon his return, he knew that he would have to serve in the Turkish military. This meant he would have to use weapons against his own people—the Kurds. He refused to return to Turkey and was placed in a deportation prison to await the recommendation of a German court on the case. Garbi's case is an example of the problems some ethnic groups face in Southwest Asia.

New Industry Requires More Workers

Life in Southwest Asia in 1900 seemed only slightly different from life there in 1100. Some people lived in villages or cities while others moved livestock from one source of water to another.

Then, in the early years of the 20th century, everything changed. Geologists discovered huge deposits of petroleum and natural gas under the sands and seas of Southwest Asia. Western oil companies quickly leased land in the region and supplied the technology and the workers to pump the fuel from the ground.

Many countries in Southwest Asia grew enormously wealthy from oil profits. The oil boom set off decades of rapid urbanization. Extensive road construction made cities and towns more accessible. Many thousands of people migrated to the cities in search of jobs and a chance to share in the region's newfound riches. So many jobs were available that some were left unfilled.

FOREIGN WORKERS To fill the job openings, companies recruited people, mostly from South and East Asia. These **"guest workers"** are largely unskilled laborers. They fill jobs that the region's native peoples find culturally or economically unacceptable. In parts of the Arabian Peninsula, the immigrant workers actually outnumber the native workers. For example, in 1999, nearly 90 percent of the United Arab Emirates (UAE) work force was made up of immigrants.

PLACE Great wealth makes this United Arab Emirates golf club possible. In the middle of the desert, it features green fairways, a pool, and a freshwater lake. Guest workers fill jobs at sites like this.

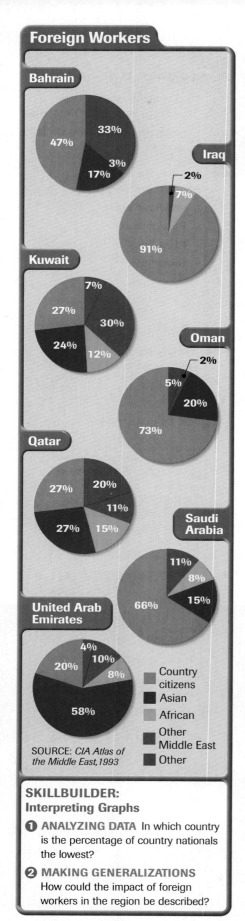

Foreign Workers

Bahrain

33%
3%
17%
47%

Iraq

2%
7%
91%

Kuwait

7%
30%
12%
24%
27%

Oman

2%
5%
20%
73%

Qatar

20%
11%
15%
27%
27%

Saudi Arabia

11%
8%
15%
66%

United Arab Emirates

4%
10%
8%
20%
58%

- Country citizens
- Asian
- African
- Other Middle East
- Other

SOURCE: *CIA Atlas of the Middle East, 1993*

SKILLBUILDER: Interpreting Graphs

❶ **ANALYZING DATA** In which country is the percentage of country nationals the lowest?

❷ **MAKING GENERALIZATIONS** How could the impact of foreign workers in the region be described?

PROBLEMS OF GUEST WORKERS The presence of so many guest workers has led to problems. Cultural differences often exist between the guest workers and their employers. Misunderstandings over certain customs can result in severe penalties. For example, a Filipino man was given six months in jail and expelled from the UAE for brushing past a woman on a bus. Arabs viewed his behavior as insulting to the woman.

Sometimes the workers must live in special districts apart from the Arab population. Some workers have been abandoned. Others receive no wages for months at a time. Many immigrants find themselves unemployed and without money to get back home.

The large number of guest workers is a concern to the governments of Southwest Asia. Some government officials worry that depending on these workers will prevent their nation's own workers from developing their skills. Others worry about the intolerance and even violence that these workers face. And, finally, some fear the immigrants could weaken their country's sense of national identity. Solving the cultural and economic issues over guest workers will be a challenge to the governments of the region. Ⓐ

Political Refugees Face Challenges

Rapidly changing economic conditions have caused population shifts in Southwest Asia. Political conflict in the region has also caused relocation.

STATELESS NATION One of the longest conflicts has been over the ethnic group known as the Kurds. After World War I, the Allies recommended creating a national state for the group. Instead, the land intended for the Kurds became part of Turkey, Iraq, and Syria. The Kurds became a **stateless nation**—a nation of people without a land to legally occupy. Turkey, Iraq, Iran, and Syria tried to absorb the Kurds into their populations but were not successful. The Kurds resisted control in each of the countries. Governments forcibly moved thousands of Kurds in an attempt to control them.

In Iraq, this forced migration ruined Kurdish homes, settlements, and farms. As you read in Chapter 22, the Iraqi government used deadly chemical weapons on settlements of Kurds to kill them or force them to leave the area. In the year 2000, as many as 70,000 Kurds had been displaced from areas they called home. Many of the Kurds have been forced to live in crowded relocation camps.

Geographic Thinking

Seeing Patterns
Ⓐ How did changes in the economy of the region change the make-up of the population?

PALESTINIAN REFUGEES Another group of people who have been displaced in the region are the **Palestinians.** They are the Arabs and their descendants who lived or still live in the area formerly called Palestine and now called Israel. Palestinians live in relocation camps in Israel, in other parts of the region, and throughout the world. This group of people, like the Kurds, consider themselves a stateless nation.

As you read in Chapter 22, war immediately followed the creation of Israel in 1948. Arabs in Palestine were promised a homeland. (See map on page 512.) However, Israel occupied some of those lands during the 1948-49 war. Between 520,000 and 1,000,000 persons fled Israel. Fifty-two refugee camps for Arab Palestinians were established in Lebanon, Jordan, Syria, the West Bank, and the Gaza Strip. The **West Bank** is a strip of land on the west side of the Jordan River. Jordan originally controlled the land, but it lost control of the land in a war with Israel in 1967. The **Gaza Strip** is a territory along the Mediterranean Sea just northeast of the Sinai Peninsula. Israel occupied it in the same 1967 war. B

The refugees have not been able to return to the areas of Israel that they claim are theirs. The number of Palestinians living in the refugee camps or in other parts of Southwest Asia has now swelled to an estimated 3.6 million persons. By 2005 there will be an estimated 8.2 million worldwide. Thousands have lived and died in refugee camps without ever being able to return to lands they claim as their homeland. Their presence and their demand to return to Palestine are at the heart of many conflicts in the region.

PLACE Palestinian and Israeli teens discuss concerns they share about their future in the region. **How could land claims in Israel affect these students' future?**

⊕ **Geographic Thinking**

Making Comparisons

B In what ways are the reasons for the Kurds' or Palestinians' land claims different?

Assessment

❶ Places & Terms

Identify and explain where in the region these would be found.

- guest workers
- stateless nation
- Palestinians
- West Bank
- Gaza Strip

❷ Taking Notes

MOVEMENT Review the notes you took for this section.

	Causes	Effects
Issue 1: Population Relocation		

- What are the causes of population movement in the region?
- What are "stateless nations"?

❸ Main Ideas

a. Why is there a need for guest workers in this region?

b. What makes the Kurds a stateless nation?

c. In which areas are Palestinian refugee camps found?

❹ Geographic Thinking

Identifying and Solving Problems What problems are created by the presence of guest workers in the region, and how might the problems be solved? **Think about:**

- cultural differences
- national identity

S **See Skillbuilder Handbook, page R10.**

MAKING COMPARISONS Do some additional research to find out more about the land claims of the Kurds and the Palestinians. Then create a **Venn diagram** showing the ways in which the Kurds' and the Palestinians' land claims are similar to and different from each other.

Interpreting a Population Density Map

How crowded is the area in which you live? Are there cities near you that have very large populations? Population density maps help geographers learn the distribution as well as the density of the population. Notice how the map below shows that Southwest Asia has areas of very dense population and other areas where almost no one lives.

THE LANGUAGE OF MAPS A **population density map** shows where people live and how crowded the conditions are. Population density is measured by dividing the total population in an area by the total number of square miles or square kilometers. The results are stated as numbers of persons per square mile or square kilometer. The density is indicated by colors. Population maps also use symbols to show cities with large populations.

SUNSHINE STATE STANDARDS

Key Standard SS.B.1.4.1
The student uses a variety of maps, geographic technologies including geographic information systems (GIS) and satellite-produced imagery, and other advanced graphic representations to depict geographic problems.

FCAT LA.A.2.2.7 Reading: Recognize Compare and Contrast

Population Density of Southwest Asia

Copyright by Rand McNally & Co.

1. The key uses colors to show ranges of population density and symbols to show cities of different sizes.

2. Notice that densities are greater near large cities.

3. Population density patterns show heavier populations in some areas near water.

4. Uninhabited areas usually are regions with inhospitable climates or landforms.

Map and Graph Skills Assessment

1. Drawing Conclusions
In which parts of the region are the largest number of cities found?

2. Making Comparisons
Which of the two cities, Aleppo or Beirut, is more densely populated?

3. Making Generalizations
Use the atlas map on page 481. Which country has the largest areas of uninhabited land?

Oil Wealth Fuels Change

How can oil wealth help develop the region's economies?

Main Ideas
- Oil wealth brings political and economic changes to the region.
- To achieve a diversified economy, countries need to improve infrastructure and resource use.

Places & Terms

strategic commodity

human resources

The Voyageur Experience in World Geography
United Arab Emirates:
Oil and Water Resources

A HUMAN PERSPECTIVE On October 2, 1995, Queen Noor of the Kingdom of Jordan gave a speech on the role of women in Southwest Asian economies. In her speech, she identified an important change in the economies of Southwest Asia:

> The changing environment in our region holds the promise of new opportunity for businessmen and women. Middle Eastern women are overcoming discriminatory socio-cultural constraints [limitations] that once denied them equal access to services and hindered [slowed] their participation in the economy.

Queen Noor described one of the ways in which countries in the region are using the skills of their people to change the economy. Today, money earned from the region's most important export—oil—is helping to build a more diverse economy.

Meeting the Global Demand

At the start of the 21st century, oil fueled the world's industries and transportation—and its economies. This "black gold" was so vital that oil became a **strategic commodity,** a resource so important that nations will go to war to ensure its steady supply.

Southwest Asia contains much of the oil supply. As you learned in Chapter 21, about 64 percent of the world's proven oil deposits and 34 percent of its reserves of natural gas are found in this region. By the year 2020, exports from Southwest Asia will probably provide about 44.5 million barrels of oil per day, or about 50 percent of world demand.

These oil reserves haven't always been of great benefit. One problem is that the world's oil prices rise and fall unpredictably. As a result, Southwest Asian countries cannot always plan how much revenue oil will bring in. Unpredictable oil prices have also made it difficult for the region's nations to have steady economic growth. For instance, when oil prices were low in 1996 and 1997, Southwest Asia's economies grew slowly. Because of that experience, the nations of that region realized that they could not continue to base their economies only on oil.

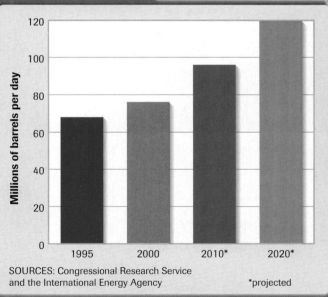

World Oil Demand

(bar graph, Millions of barrels per day)

| Year | 1995 | 2000 | 2010* | 2020* |

SOURCES: Congressional Research Service and the International Energy Agency   *projected

SKILLBUILDER: Interpreting Graphs

❶ **MAKING GENERALIZATIONS** By about how much will oil demand increase by the year 2020?

❷ **ANALYZING DATA** During which decade is demand projected to increase most sharply?

SW ASIA

Using Oil Wealth to Diversify

To promote more economic growth, the oil-rich nations of Southwest Asia face three challenges in the way that they use oil profits. First, each has to modernize its infrastructure. Second, each has to develop its agricultural, mineral, and water resources. Finally, the people of each nation have to gain access to higher education and job training.

MODERNIZING THE INFRASTRUCTURE The region has improved its infrastructure. Saudi Arabia, for example, has built new roads in rural areas, irrigation networks, and facilities to store agricultural products. It has also built desalinization plants that remove the salt from seawater and provide water for cities and industrial use.

Other nations have constructed airports, shopping malls, and port facilities. These efforts are not always well coordinated, though. Some years ago, the UAE built four international airports to serve an area about the size of the state of Maine. Needless to say, these airports are greatly underused.

Toward the end of the 20th century, nations in the region began putting together information technology systems to serve businesses. Dubai launched a plan in 2000 called Internet City. The plan made it possible for its government to conduct business on-line.

DEVELOPING RESOURCES To create a diversified economy, nations of the area have to develop resources besides oil. One of the greatest needs is to develop agriculture. The region's arid conditions mean that the area is not able to produce great quantities of food. To trap much-needed water for agricultural production, governments have built dams. They have also dug deep wells to tap the water trapped in huge underground reservoirs.

Saudi Arabia can boast several economic success stories. By 1985, improvements in agriculture allowed the Saudis to completely meet the nation's demand for dairy products, red meat, poultry, and eggs. The biggest Saudi success story, however, was wheat production. The Saudis were determined to reduce their dependence on imported wheat. They improved water supplies so that grain production could be expanded. By 1992, they were producing more than four million tons of grain per year. This was enough to actually meet their needs and to have wheat to export. This diversification of the Saudi economy would not have happened without significant investment in infrastructure. That investment, in turn, was made possible by oil profits.

HUMAN–ENVIRONMENT INTERACTION Using overhead sprinkler systems to bring water to desert areas will make them green. Compare the watered fields to the rest of the Negev Desert shown in the lower picture.

BACKGROUND Water produced by desalinization is not always pure enough for drinking purposes but can be used in sanitation.

Geographic Thinking

Seeing Patterns
How are the expansion of water production and increased agricultural output connected?

Geographic Thinking

Making Comparisons
B How is the diversification of Oman's economy different from that of Saudi Arabia?

Other nations are making efforts to develop other mineral resources. Oman revived its copper industry and chromium mines. Chromium is used in steel production for jet aircraft. Expanding these industries allowed the Omani economy to reduce its dependence on oil profits. ◀B

HUMAN RESOURCES People are a valuable resource in any nation. Southwest Asian nations are developing their **human resources**—the skills and talents of their people. Many of those nations also realize that they must invest in all their people, including women. Providing education and technology training is critical. Nations are expanding the opportunities for their citizens to gain an education. For example, Kuwait has established free education for all children through the university level. For students who wish to study outside the country, the government pays the fees and provides money to cover living expenses.

Many societies in Southwest Asia have strict rules concerning women's roles in society. Often it is difficult for women to get an education and find employment. However, the shortage of workers in the region has opened economic opportunities for women. Important economic and political changes are taking place in Southwest Asia. As the nations work to develop their physical and human resources, opportunities for all who live there will expand. A successful economy is built on the efforts of all its people working together toward the goal of diversification.

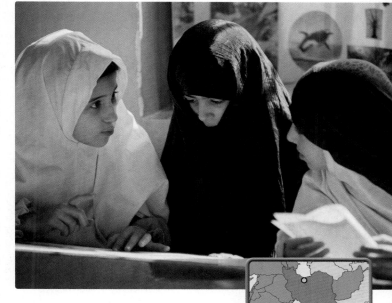

PLACE Muslim girls in Tehran, Iran, discuss a lesson.
Why is it important for all citizens to be educated?

SECTION 2 Assessment

1 Places & Terms
Identify and explain the meaning of these terms.

- strategic commodity
- human resources

2 Taking Notes
REGION Review the notes you took for this section.

	Causes	Effects
Issue 2: Economic Development		

- Why are this region's resources so valuable?
- What changes need to be made to the region's infrastructure?

3 Main Ideas
a. What effect have unpredictable oil prices had on the economy of the region?

b. What steps have nations in the region taken to diversify their economic base?

c. Why must the human resources of the region be developed?

4 Geographic Thinking
Determining Cause and Effect How has oil wealth changed the economy of the region? **Think about:**

- the cost of modernizing the infrastructure
- the need for a diverse economy

S **See Skillbuilder Handbook, page R9.**

GeoActivity

MAKING COMPARISONS Do some research to find information about the projected freshwater supplies for the nations in the region. Create a set of symbols to represent the projected water supply figures. Then draw a **map** of the region, and place the appropriate water supply symbol on each nation.

SW ASIA

Religious Conflict Over Land

Who should control Jerusalem?

Jerusalem checkpoints deepen Palestinian resentment.

C onflict between Jews and Arabs over land and statehood in Southwest Asia disrupts life in the region. One aspect of this conflict centers around Jerusalem. The city is sacred to Jews, Christians, and Muslims. Control of Jerusalem is a deeply emotional issue that affects the region's politics and population.

Control of Jerusalem

After World War II, the UN recommended that the city of Jerusalem become an international city. It would be under the control of an international body rather than an Arab or a Jewish government. But by the end of the Arab-Israeli war in 1948, Jerusalem was divided between Arabs and Israelis. Arabs took the Old City and East Jerusalem located in the West Bank sector. The Israelis took control of West Jerusalem. During the Six-Day War of 1967, the Israelis captured the rest of Jerusalem.

Control of the holy sites within the Old City also became an issue. Although the Israelis captured the city, the Muslims retained control of their holy site, *Haram ash-Sharif*, called the Temple Mount by the Jews.

As the Israelis gained control of the entire city of Jerusalem, they began adding Arab lands to the city. They placed Jewish settlements on those lands. Palestinian Arabs fled or were forced to leave the settlement lands. The Palestinians in Jerusalem and elsewhere have maintained they should have the "right of return" to the lands in Israel. Their claims are supported by United Nations Resolution 194, which states that Palestinians have the "right of return" to former homelands.

1978
Camp David Accords set up Palestinian self-rule in West Bank.

| 1940 | Arab-Israeli Conflict | 1960 | 1970 | 1980 | 1990 | 2000 | 2010 |

1948
The **State of Israel** is created; war with Arabs follows immediately.

1967
Israel takes control of Jerusalem, West Bank, and Gaza Strip at the end of the Six-Day War.

1993
Oslo Accords allow Palestinians to establish self-rule in West Bank and Gaza Strip.

2003
A "road map" for peace is launched, calling for the establishment of a Palestinian state and security guarantees for Israel.

West Bank

Israel

West Bank

Israel

West Jerusalem

OLD CITY

East Jerusalem

Muslim Quarter

Christian Quarter

DOME OF THE ROCK (Muslim)

Jewish Quarter

Western Wall (Jewish)

DAVID'S TOWER

Armenian Quarter

Al-Aqsa Mosque (Muslim)

Temple Mount or Haram ash-Sharif

SUNSHINE STATE STANDARDS
Key Standard SS.B.2.4.3 The student understands how the allocation of control of the Earth's surface affects interactions between people in different regions.

Other Standards SS.A.1.4.3, B.1.4.5

FCAT LA.A.2.4.8 Reading: Synthesize and Conclude

Proposed Solutions to the Conflict

SEE
PRIMARY SOURCE D

The emotional and political issue of who should control Jerusalem makes it a very difficult diplomatic problem to solve. Because both the Israelis and the Palestinians claim Jerusalem as the capital of their nation, neither is willing to give it up to the other group. The following solutions have been proposed for control of Jerusalem:

- Palestinians retain control of certain parts of East Jerusalem while Israel annexes several Jewish settlements near Jerusalem. This would enlarge Israeli territory in the area.

- Israel retains control of West Jerusalem and the Jewish Quarter of the Old City, but the Palestinians control the Old City and East Jerusalem. This is basically how the city is controlled today.

SEE
PRIMARY SOURCE C

- Palestinians control the Temple Mount but give up the right of return to Israel. The Israeli government fears that the sheer numbers of returning Palestinians would overwhelm Israel.

- An international agency has control of all holy sites.

On the following pages, you will find primary sources that present different views on the control of the city of Jerusalem. Use them to help you form an opinion about the best way to solve the problem.

CASE STUDY

PROJECT

A Peace Conference

Primary sources A, B, C, D, and E on these two pages offer differing views about control of Jerusalem. Use these resources along with your own research to prepare a peace conference that presents both Israeli and Arab solutions for control of Jerusalem.

RESEARCH LINKS
CLASSZONE.COM

Suggested Steps

1. Choose one of the proposed solutions to the control of Jerusalem to investigate.

2. Use online and print resources to research the positions of Israelis, Palestinians, and Americans.

3. Create visuals—maps, charts, graphs—to make the conference discussion clearer.

4. Select two or three representatives from each group to take part in the conference. The rest of the class should act as journalists, take notes on the presentation, and be prepared to ask questions of the representatives.

Materials and Supplies

• Posterboard
• Markers
• Reference books, newspapers, and magazines
• Video monitor with VCR or DVD capability
• Computer with Internet access/printer

PRIMARY SOURCE A

United Nations Resolution *UN Resolution 181, adopted on November 29, 1947, declared that Jerusalem would become an international city with both Jewish and Muslim inhabitants.*

Part III City of Jerusalem

A. The City of Jerusalem shall be established as a *corpus separatum* [separate body] under a special international regime and shall be administered by the United Nations. The Trusteeship Council shall be designated to discharge the responsibilities of the Administering Authority on behalf of the United Nations.

*　　*　　*

C. 1(a) To protect and to preserve the unique spiritual and religious interests located in the city of the three great monotheistic faiths throughout the world, Christian, Jewish, and Moslem; to this end to ensure that order and peace, and especially religious peace, reign in Jerusalem.

(b) To foster co-operation among all the inhabitants of the city in their own interests as well as in order to encourage and support the peaceful development of the mutual relations between the two Palestinian peoples throughout the Holy Land.

PRIMARY SOURCE B

Official Statement *This statement was made December 31, 2000, by the Palestinian cabinet, which opposed President Clinton's plan for resolving the issue of "right of return" and control of the holy sites in Jerusalem.*

The Palestinian leadership confirms its commitment to the full right of refugees to return to their lands and homes in accordance with Resolution 194, the cabinet said, referring to the United Nations resolution adopted in December 1948.

Our people will never, under any circumstances, concede one inch from our Jerusalem and our Islamic and Christian holy sites.

Personal Observation *Yossi Sarid, head of the Meretz party in Israel, is a leading advocate of peace in the region. On December 31, 2000, he expressed his opinion on the central issue of the Palestinian right of return.*

There is only one issue that could, God forbid, make this [Clinton peace proposal] fail, and that is the right of return. It is important for the Palestinians to understand and internalize this. Realization of the right of return means—how should I put it?—the suicide of Israel.

If we open the gates to hundreds of thousands of refugees, that means the state of Israel as created by the Zionist dream will be bankrupt.

Editorial Commentary *Kenneth L. Woodward, religion editor for* Newsweek *magazine, expresses an opinion about why any solution for the Jerusalem question is one that is important not just to Jews and Arabs but to millions of others.*

Thus, for billions of believers who may never see it, Jerusalem remains a city central to their sacred geography. This is why the future of the city is not just another Middle Eastern conflict between Arabs and Jews. . . . Both Israel and the Palestinians have real roots in the Holy Land, and both want to claim Jerusalem as their capital. The United Nations, supported by the Vatican, would have the city internationalized under its jurisdiction. The issue, however, is not merely one of geopolitics. There will be no enduring solution to the question of Jerusalem that does not respect the attachments to the city formed by each faith. Whoever controls Jerusalem will always be constrained by the meaning the city has acquired over three millenniums of wars, conquest and prophetic utterance.

Political Cartoon *Mark Fiore drew this cartoon about the situation in Jerusalem. What message is the cartoonist sending about prospects for peace between Israelis and Palestinians?*

PROJECT **CheckList**

Have I . . .

✓ looked at all sides of the issue?

✓ identified the key players and their points of view?

✓ created informative visuals that make my presentation clear and interesting?

✓ practiced the delivery of my presentation?

VISUAL SUMMARY
TODAY'S ISSUES IN SOUTHWEST ASIA

Population

Population Relocation
- Urban areas in the region have grown significantly since the 1960s.
- Thousands of foreign workers fill jobs in the region.
- Kurds claim homelands in four countries: Turkey, Iraq, Iran, and Syria.
- Arab Palestinians claim lands in Israel.

Economics

Oil Wealth Fuels Change
- Huge oil resources shape the region's economy.
- The infrastructure needs to be updated.
- The region's economy must be diversified.
- Human resources need to be developed.

Conflict

Religious Conflict Over Land
- Jerusalem is holy to three major religions: Judaism, Christianity, and Islam.
- Israel controls Jerusalem.
- Control of holy sites in Jerusalem is one aspect of the conflict.
- Arab Palestinians claim the "right of return" to Jerusalem, after leaving it as the result of wars.

Reviewing Places & Terms

A. Briefly explain the importance of each of the following.

1. guest workers
2. stateless nation
3. Palestinians
4. West Bank
5. Gaza Strip
6. strategic commodity
7. human resources

B. Answer the questions about vocabulary in complete sentences.

8. Why is it necessary to have guest workers in Southwest Asia?
9. Which terms above refer to land areas in Israel?
10. Which of the above terms includes the location of Jerusalem?
11. Why might Palestinians and Kurds be considered stateless nations?
12. Which group claims the right of return to the Gaza Strip?
13. Why is oil considered a strategic commodity?
14. In what way could water be considered a strategic commodity?
15. What groups make up human resources?

Main Ideas

Population Relocation (pp. 525–528)

1. What concerns have been raised about foreign workers in the region?
2. Why don't the Kurds have a homeland?
3. Which lands are claimed by Arab Palestinians?
4. Where do a large majority of Palestinians live?

Oil Wealth Fuels Change (pp. 529–531)

5. Why must nations stop depending solely on oil wealth?
6. Which areas of the region's economy need to be developed and diversified?
7. Why is providing education and technology training an important aspect of developing human resources?

Religious Conflict Over Land (pp. 532–535)

8. How did the Israelis gain control of Jerusalem?
9. What is the "right of return"?
10. What are some proposed solutions to the issue of control of Jerusalem?

Critical Thinking

1. Using Your Notes

Use your completed chart to answer these questions.

	Causes	Effects
Issue 1: Population Relocation		
Issue 2: Economic Development		

  a. How did the Kurds become a stateless nation?

  b. What effect has an expanding economy had on population relocation in the region?

2. Geographic Themes

  a. **MOVEMENT** How are Palestinian refugee camps and the "right to return" related?

  b. **REGION** Why is this region considered to be a strategic location?

3. Identifying Themes

Why is the control of Jerusalem such a difficult issue to resolve? Which of the five themes applies to this situation?

4. Making Inferences

Why must some oil wealth be used to develop water resources in the region?

5. Making Decisions

Which of the proposed solutions for the control of Jerusalem do you favor and why?

Additional Test Practice, pp. S1–S37

TEST PRACTICE
CLASSZONE.COM

Geographic Skills: Interpreting Graphs

Availability of Water Resources*

Use the graph at the right to answer the following questions.

1. **MAKING COMPARISONS** Which country is projected to have the greatest available water supplies by 2050? Which country will have the least?

2. **MAKING INFERENCES** What are some reasons why the availability of water resources will decrease?

GeoActivity

Use the Regional Data File to create a chart showing the population of the nations listed in the Water Stress Index. Create a second bar graph showing water stress by placing the countries in order by population.

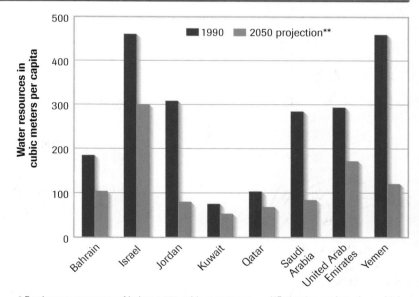

* Freshwater resources of below 1,000 cubic meters per year per capita will likely cause chronic water shortages.

**Estimates are based on a high projection of population increase.

SOURCE: Adapted from Robert Engelman and Pamela LeRoy, *Sustaining Water: An Update*, Population Action International, Washington D.C. 1995

 INTERNET ACTIVITY

Use the links at classzone.com to do research on water scarcity in the region and proposed solutions to the problem. Focus on finding a solution that would be environmentally friendly.

Identifying and Solving Problems Using the information you gathered, propose a solution to the need for fresh water in Southwest Asia. Support your proposal with charts or graphs illustrating both the need for water and the sources of fresh water.

SW ASIA

Unit 8 · South Asia

South Asia includes the Indian subcontinent and its nearby islands. It is a region of ancient cultures, spectacular landforms, and rapidly growing populations.

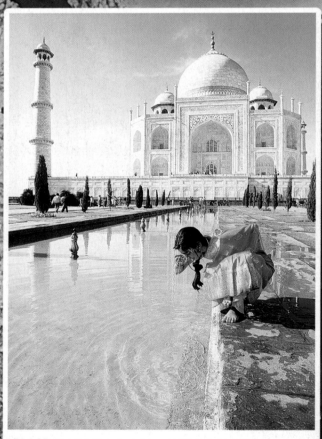

PLACE The Taj Mahal, at Agra, India, is said to be one of the world's most beautiful buildings. Constructed of marble, it was built in the 17th century by Emperor Shah Jahan as a tomb for his wife.

SOUTH ASIA

LOCATION Elephants wearing richly decorated cloth coverings are central figures in the 14-night Esala Perahera festival in Kandy, Sri Lanka. It is one of many religious festivals held in South Asia.

REGION The world's highest mountains, the majestic snow-capped Himalayas, form the northern border of the Indian subcontinent. Mt. Everest, to the left, is the world's tallest peak at 29,035 feet.

Today's Issues in South Asia

Today, South Asia faces the issues previewed here. As you read Chapters 24 and 25, you will learn helpful background information. You will study the issues themselves in Chapter 26.

In a small group, answer the questions below. Then have a class discussion of your answers.

Exploring the Issues

1. **POPULATION** What might be some of the effects of rapid population growth on both humans and the environment?

2. **EXTREME WEATHER** Consider news stories that you have heard or read about that refer to extreme weather in various parts of South Asia. Make a list of the types of extreme weather that affect South Asians.

3. **TERRITORIAL DISPUTE** Search the Internet for the latest information about the dispute over Kashmir. What position does each side hold?

For more on these issues in South Asia . . .

CURRENT EVENTS
CLASSZONE.COM

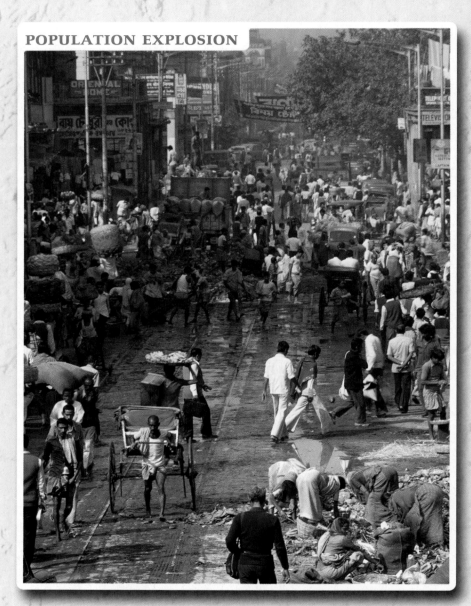

POPULATION EXPLOSION

How can South Asia's population growth be managed?

Many problems come with rapid population growth, including crowded cities. Kolkata, pictured here, had a population of more than 4 million in the 1990s, and a population density of more than 61,900 persons per square mile.

EXTREME WEATHER

How do people cope with extreme weather?

People find a way to continue with their lives despite the severe flooding that plagues South Asia during the summer monsoons. Residents of Dhaka, Bangladesh, shown here, navigate flooded streets as best they can.

CASESTUDY

How can India and Pakistan resolve their dispute over Kashmir?

India and Pakistan have spent millions of dollars to develop nuclear weapons in their continuing dispute over Kashmir. This has left less money to spend on improving the lives of their citizens.

TERRITORIAL DISPUTE

CARLSON ©1998
MILWAUKEE JOURNAL SENTINEL

INDIA'S POOR

PAKISTAN'S POOR

Patterns of Physical Geography

SUNSHINE STATE STANDARDS
Key Standard SS.B.1.4.1 The student uses a variety of maps, geographic technolog
including geographic information systems (GIS) and satellite-produced imagery, and o
advanced graphic representations to depict geographic problems.

Other Standards SS.A.2.4.2, B.1.4.3, B.2.4.1

FCAT LA.A.2.2.7 Reading: Recognize Compare and Contrast

Use the Unit Atlas to add to your knowledge of South Asia. As you look at the maps and charts, notice geographic patterns and specific details about the region. For example, the chart to the right gives details about the rivers and mountains of South Asia.

After studying the illustrations, graphs, and physical map on these two pages, jot down in your notebook the answers to the following questions.

Making Comparisons

1. How much longer is the Nile than each of the three major rivers of South Asia?

2. Compare the size and population of South Asia to that of the United States. Which is larger in terms of size? Which is larger in terms of population?

3. How do the tallest mountains of South Asia compare to the tallest U.S. mountain?

For updated statistics on
South Asia . . .

DATA UPDATE
CLASSZONE.COM

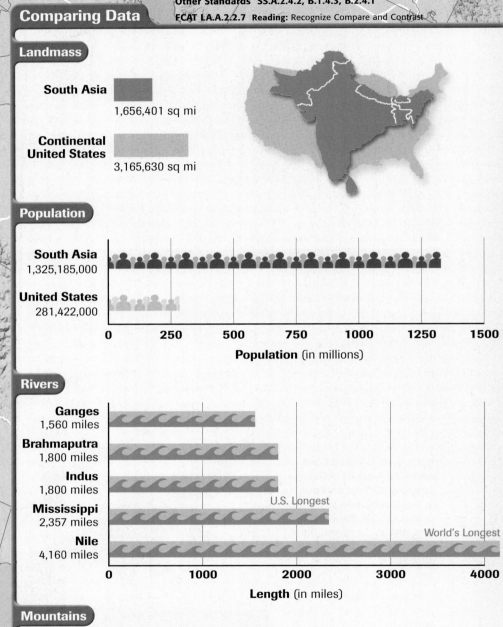

Comparing Data

Landmass

South Asia
1,656,401 sq mi

Continental United States
3,165,630 sq mi

Population

South Asia
1,325,185,000

United States
281,422,000

0   250   500   750   1000   1250   1500

Population (in millions)

Rivers

Ganges
1,560 miles

Brahmaputra
1,800 miles

Indus
1,800 miles

Mississippi
2,357 miles   *U.S. Longest*

Nile
4,160 miles   *World's Longest*

0   1000   2000   3000   4000

Length (in miles)

Mountains

World's Tallest	U.S. Tallest			
Mt. Everest	**Mt. McKinley**	**K2**	**Kanchenjunga**	**Makalu**
Nepal-China	United States	Pakistan	India-Nepal	Nepal-China
29,035 feet	20,320 feet	28,250 feet	28,208 feet	27, 824 feet

AFGHANISTAN

HINDU KUSH

Khyber Pass

Sulaiman Range

Indus R.

PAKISTAN

Indus R.

Thar Desert

Rann of Kutch

Gulf of Khambhat

K2 28,250 ft. (8,611 m.)

Karakoram

Ravi R.

HIMALAYA MTS.

CHINA

Mt. Everest 29,035 ft. (8,850 m.)

NEPAL

BHUTAN

Brahmaputra R.

INDO-GANGETIC PLAIN

Ganges R.

BANGLADESH

Ganges Delta

MYANMAR

INDIA

Vindhya Range

Narmada R.

Chota Nagpur Plateau

Arabian Sea

Godavari R.

DECCAN

Krishna R.

PLATEAU

WESTERN GHATS

EASTERN GHATS

Bay of Bengal

Andaman Is.

Andaman Sea

Laccadive Sea

Laccadive Is.

Tropic of Cancer

MALDIVES

Palk Str.

Gulf of Mannar

SRI LANKA

Nicobar Is.

Equator

INDIAN OCEAN

| 0 | 250 | 500 miles |
| 0 | 250 | 500 kilometers |

Two-Point Equidistant Projection

Elevation

13,100 ft.	(4,000 m.)
6,600 ft.	(2,000 m.)
1,600 ft.	(500 m.)
650 ft.	(200 m.)
0 ft.	(0 m.)
Below sea level	

▲ Mountain peak

Unit ATLAS

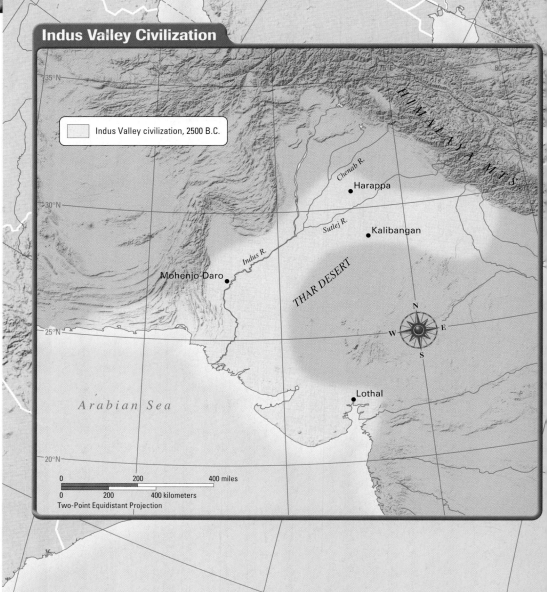

Patterns of Human Geography

The first great civilization of South Asia developed along the banks of the Indus River more than 4,000 years ago. Study the historical map of the Indus Valley civilization and the political map of South Asia on these two pages. In your notebook, jot down the answers to these questions.

Making Comparisons

1. In which countries of modern South Asia was the Indus Valley civilization located? Which of these countries is the larger country?

2. What might have been some of the reasons for a civilization developing at that location?

3. What modern city or cities are closest to the locations of ancient Mohenjo-Daro, Harappa, Kalibangan, and Lothal? (In some cases, more than one city will be an acceptable answer.)

Indus Valley Civilization

Indus Valley civilization, 2500 B.C.

HIMALAYA MTS.

Chenab R.

● Harappa

Sutlej R.

● Kalibangan

Indus R.

Mohenjo-Daro ●

THAR DESERT

Arabian Sea

● Lothal

0   200   400 miles
0   200   400 kilometers
Two-Point Equidistant Projection

AFGHANISTAN

CHINA

Controlled by China,
also claimed by India

Kashmir

Islamabad
Rawalpindi

Indus R.

Faisalabad   Lahore

Punjab

Baluchistan

Indus R.

Makran   **PAKISTAN**

Hyderabad

Karachi

Tropic of Cancer

Delhi
New Delhi

Jaipur

Kanpur   Lucknow

NEPAL   Kathmandu

Thimphu
BHUTAN

Brahmaputra R.

INDIA

Ganges R.

Varanasi

BANGLADESH

Dhaka

*Arabian
Sea*

Ahmadabad

Narmada R.

Surat

*Gulf of
Khambhat*

INDIA

Nagpur

Kolkata
(Calcutta)

Chittagong

MYANMAR

Mumbai
(Bombay)

Pune

Krishna R.

Hyderabad

Godavari R.

Vijayawada

*Bay of
Bengal*

*Laccadive
Sea*

Bangalore

Chennai
(Madras)

Lakshadweep
(Ind.)

Andaman Is.
(Ind.)

*Andaman
Sea*

MALDIVES

*Gulf of
Mannar*

Colombo   **SRI LANKA**

Nicobar Is.
(Ind.)

Male

INDIAN OCEAN

Equator

★ National capital

● Other city

| 0 | 250 | 500 miles |
| 0 | 250 | 500 kilometers |

Two-Point Equidistant Projection

SOUTH ASIA

545

Unit ATLAS

Regional Patterns

These two pages contain a graph and three thematic maps. The graph shows the religions of South Asia. The maps show other important information about religion, population density, and economics. Study these two pages and then jot down in your notebook the answers to the questions below.

Making Comparisons

1. What percentage of the population of Sri Lanka is Hindu, and where are most of the Hindus located? Why might Hindus have settled in Sri Lanka rather than in other areas?

2. Which is the most densely populated country of South Asia?

3. What is the main economic activity in much of South Asia?

South Asia: Religions by Country

Percent (%) of the Population

Bangladesh, Bhutan, India, Maldives, Nepal, Pakistan, Sri Lanka

Christian   Islam   Buddhism   Sikhism   Hinduism   Traditional

SOURCE: The World Factbook 2000

Religions of South Asia

Legend:
- Mixed Christian
- Islam – Sunni
- Buddhism
- Sikhism
- Hinduism
- Traditional

PAKISTAN, NEPAL, BHUTAN, BANGLADESH, INDIA, SRI LANKA, MALDIVES

Arabian Sea, Bay of Bengal, INDIAN OCEAN

Tropic of Cancer

0   150   300 miles
0   150   300 kilometers
Two-Point Equidistant Projection

Population Density of South Asia

30°N

Rawalpindi • • Islamabad
Faisalabad • • Lahore
Karachi ⊙
Arabian Sea
20°N
Delhi ⊙
Jaipur •
Kanpur •
Lucknow •
Kathmandu • Thimphu •
Ahmadabad •
Surat •
Nagpur •
Kolkata ⊙
Dhaka ⊙
Chittagong •
Mumbai ⊙
Pune •
Hyderabad •
Bay of Bengal
Tropic of Cancer
10°N
Bangalore •
Chennai •
Colombo •
INDIAN OCEAN
Male •
70°E
80°E
90°E
100°E

0   250   500 miles
0   250   500 kilometers
Two-Point Equidistant Projection

Persons per sq mi	Persons per sq km
Over 520	Over 200
260–519	100–199
130–259	50–99
25–129	10–49
1–24	1–9
0	0

⊙ Metropolitan area greater than 10 million

Economic Activity of South Asia

PAKISTAN
Arabian Sea
NEPAL
BHUTAN
INDIA
BANGLADESH
Bay of Bengal
MALDIVES
SRI LANKA
INDIAN OCEAN

0   250   500 miles
0   250   500 kilometers
Two-Point Equidistant Projection

- Manufacturing and trade
- Commercial farming
- Subsistence farming
- Nomadic herding
- Forestry
- Commercial fishing
- Little or no economic activity

Unit ATLAS

Regional Data File

Country Flag	Country/ Capital	Population (2000 estimate)	Life Expectancy (years) (2000 estimate)	Birthrate (per 1,000 pop.) (2000)	Infant Mortality (per 1,000 live births) (2000)
	Bangladesh Dhaka	128,133,000	59	27	82.2
	Bhutan Thimphu	877,000ᶜ	66	40	70.7
	India New Delhi	1,002,142,000	61	27	72.0
	Maldives Male	286,000	71	35	27.0
	Nepal Kathmandu	23,930,000	57	36	78.5
	Pakistan Islamabad	150,648,000	58	39	91.0
	Sri Lanka Colombo	19,169,000	72	18	17.3
	United States Washington, D.C.	281,422,000	77	15	7.0

Study the information on the countries of South Asia. In your notebook, jot down the answers to these questions.

Making Comparisons

1. Which two South Asian countries have the fewest people? Are they the smallest in area? Locate them on the map.

2. Which South Asian country has the most people? Is it the largest in area? Locate it on the map.

3. Which nation do you think is the poorest? Which factors did you consider in making your choice?

Sources:
Europa World Year Book 2000
Human Development Report 2000,
  United Nations
International Data Base, 2000, U.S.
  Census Bureau online
Merriam-Webster's Geographical
  Dictionary, 1997
Statesman's Yearbook 2001
2000 World Population Data Sheet,
  Population Reference Bureau
  online
UNESCO World Education Report
  2000
WHO Estimates of Health Personnel,
  World Health Organization online
World Almanac and Book of Facts
  2001
World Factbook 2000, CIA online
N/A = not available

Notes:
ᵃ A comparison of the prices of the same items in different countries is used to figure these data.
ᵇ Includes land and water, when figures are available.
ᶜ Due to census disagreements, the population has been reported as high as 2 million.

For updated statistics on South Asia . . .

DATA UPDATE
CLASSZONE.COM

Profile of South Asia

Indus River   *Punjab*   *Delhi*

8,000 m
7,000 m
6,000 m
5,000 m
4,000 m
3,000 m
2,000 m
1,000 m
0 m
                                                                    2,400

Doctors (per 100,000 pop.) (1992–1999)	GDPa (billions $US) (1999 estimate)	Import/Exporta (billions $US) (1998–1999)	Literacy Rate (percentage) (1998)	Televisions (per 1,000 pop.) (1996–1998)	Passenger Cars (per 1,000 pop.) (1996–1999)	Total Areab (square miles)	
20	187	8.01 / 5.1	40	7	1	55,126	
16	2.1	0.122 / 0.111	42 (1995)	19	1	16,000	
48	1,805	50.2 / 36.3	56	69	4	1,195,063	
40	0.54	0.312 / 0.098	96	39	3	115	
4	27.4	1.2 / 0.485	39	4	N/A	54,362	
57	282	9.8 / 8.4	44	88	8	310,403	
37	50.5	5.3 / 4.7	91	92	12	25,332	
251	9,255	820.8 / 663.0	97	847	489	3,787,319	

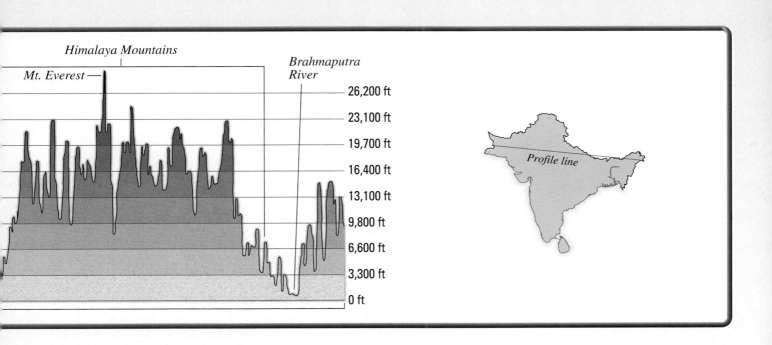

Himalaya Mountains

Mt. Everest —

Brahmaputra River

26,200 ft
23,100 ft
19,700 ft
16,400 ft
13,100 ft
9,800 ft
6,600 ft
3,300 ft
0 ft

Profile line

PHYSICAL GEOGRAPHY OF SOUTH ASIA
The Land Where Continents Collided

Spectacular mountain peaks tower above a valley floor in northern Pakistan.

GeoFocus

How do mountains and rivers affect the lives of the people of South Asia?

Taking Notes Copy the graphic organizer below into your notebook. Use it to record information from the chapter about the physical geography of South Asia.

Landforms	
Resources	
Climate and Vegetation	
Human-Environment Interaction	

Landforms and Resources

Main Ideas
- South Asia is a subcontinent of peninsulas bordered by mountains and oceans.
- A wide variety of natural resources helps sustain life in the region.

Places & Terms
Himalaya Mountains

subcontinent

alluvial plain

archipelago

atoll

CONNECT TO THE ISSUES
TERRITORIAL DISPUTE
Kashmir is an area in the western Himalayas on the border of India and Pakistan. It has been a source of dispute between the two countries.

SUNSHINE STATE STANDARDS
Key Standard SS.B.1.4.3 The student uses mental maps of physical and human features of the world to answer complex geographic questions.

Other Standards SS.B.2.4.3

FCAT LA.A.1.4.2 Reading: Strategies

A HUMAN PERSPECTIVE Thousands of years ago, the Hindus of what is now north India imagined a gigantic mountain reaching more than 80,000 miles into the sky. They believed that this enormous peak, called Mt. Meru, was the center of the physical and spiritual world. In their writings, they described "rivers of sweet water" flowing down the sides of the mountain. While Mt. Meru exists only in myth, it did have a real-life inspiration—Mt. Everest, the world's tallest mountain peak at 29,035 feet above sea level. Mt. Everest and the other towering peaks of the **Himalaya Mountains** have been a lure to mountain climbers around the world. Many climbers had died on Everest's icy slopes before Sir Edmund Hillary and Tenzing Norgay, his Sherpa guide, became the first people to reach its summit in 1953.

Mountains and Plateaus

The Himalayas are part of South Asia, a region that includes seven countries—India, Pakistan, Bangladesh, Bhutan, Nepal, Sri Lanka, and the Maldives. South Asia is sometimes called a **subcontinent,** a large landmass that is smaller than a continent. In fact, it is often referred to as the Indian subcontinent because India dominates the region. Although South Asia is about half the size of the continental United States, it has more than one billion inhabitants—one-fifth of the world's population.

Formation of the Himalayas

The land now called the Indian subcontinent was once separated from Asia by an ocean. About 180 million years ago, this land began drifting north toward Asia. About 50 million years ago, the two land masses collided. The land in the collision zone was forced upward to form the Himalayas.

As you saw on the map on page 543, natural barriers help to separate the South Asian subcontinent from the rest of Asia. The Himalayas and other mountain ranges form the northern border, while water surrounds the rest of the region. The South Asian peninsula, which extends south into the Indian Ocean, is bordered by the Arabian Sea to the west and the Bay of Bengal to the east.

NORTHERN MOUNTAINS Millions of years ago, the land that is now South Asia was actually part of East Africa. About 50 million years ago, it split off and drifted northward. As the illustration on page 551 shows, it collided with Central Asia. The gradual collision of these two large tectonic plates forced the land upward into enormous mountain ranges. These mountains, which are still rising, now form the northern edge of the South Asian subcontinent.

The magnificent Himalayas are a system of parallel mountain ranges. They contain the world's highest mountains, with nearly two dozen peaks rising to 24,000 feet or above. The Himalayas stretch for 1,500 miles and form a giant barrier between the Indian subcontinent and China. Mt. Everest, the world's tallest peak, sits at the heart of the Himalayas. Nestled high up within these mountains are the remote, landlocked kingdoms of Nepal and Bhutan. Ⓐ

The Hindu Kush are mountains that lie at the west end of the Himalayas. They form a rugged barrier separating Pakistan from Afghanistan to the north. For centuries, the Hindu Kush stood in the way of Central Asian tribes trying to invade India. Bloody battles have been fought over control of major land routes through these mountains, including the Khyber Pass. The mighty Karakoram Mountains rise in the northeastern portion of the chain. They are the home of the world's second highest peak, K2.

SOUTHERN PLATEAUS The collision of tectonic plates that pushed up the Himalayas also created several smaller mountain ranges in central India, including the Vindhya (VIHN•dyuh) Range. To the south lies the Deccan Plateau. This large tableland tilts east, toward the Bay of Bengal, and covers much of southern India. Two mountain ranges, the Western Ghats and the Eastern Ghats, flank the plateau, separating it from the coast. These mountains also block most moist winds and keep rain from reaching the interior. As a result, the Deccan is a largely arid region.

Rivers, Deltas, and Plains

The Northern Indian Plain, or Indo-Gangetic Plain, lies between the Deccan Plateau and the northern mountain ranges. This large lowland region stretches across northern India and into Bangladesh. It is formed by three great river systems: the Indus, the Ganges, and the Brahmaputra.

GREAT RIVERS The three great rivers of South Asia have their origins among the snowcapped peaks of the high

Connect to THE Issues

EXTREME WEATHER

THE GANGES DELTA

Water, water, and more water! Three major rivers meet in Bangladesh to form the Ganges Delta at the Bay of Bengal, shown in the satellite photo below. They are the Brahmaputra, the Ganges, and the Meghna.

These rivers bring rich alluvial soil to the delta, a region covering 65,500 square miles. But above all, these rivers bring water. Every summer, melting snow and monsoon-driven rains force the rivers to burst their banks. In fact, so much water comes that central Bangladesh is turned into an inland sea before the land dries.

🌐 **Geographic Thinking**◄

Seeing Patterns
◄Ⓐ What role have the Himalayas played in the development of Nepal and Bhutan?

BACKGROUND
The name *Himalayas* is Sanskrit for "abode of snow."

Himalayas. The Indus flows west and then south through Pakistan to the Arabian Sea. The Ganges drops down from the central Himalayas and flows eastward across northern India. The Brahmaputra winds its way east, then west and south through Bangladesh. The Ganges and Brahmaputra eventually meet to form one huge river delta before entering the Bay of Bengal.

FERTILE PLAINS These rivers play a key role in supporting life in South Asia. Their waters provide crucial irrigation for agricultural lands. They also carry rich soil, called alluvial soil, on their journey down from the mountains. When the rivers overflow their banks, they deposit this soil on **alluvial plains,** lands that are rich farmlands. As a result, the Indo-Gangetic Plain is one of the most fertile farming regions in the world.

The Indo-Gangetic Plain is also the most heavily populated part of South Asia. In fact, the area contains about three-fifths of India's population. Many of the subcontinent's largest cities, including New Delhi and Kolkata in India, and Dakha in Bangladesh, are located there. Population densities at the eastern end of the plain, particularly in the Ganges-Brahmaputra delta, are especially high, as you can see on the map on page 547. To the west, in the area between the Indus and Ganges rivers, the plain becomes drier and requires more irrigation. To the south lies one of the world's most arid regions—the Thar, or Great Indian Desert. ◀B

Offshore Islands

Two island groups are also countries of South Asia—Sri Lanka and the Maldives. Sri Lanka is located in the Indian Ocean just off India's southeastern tip. The Maldives island group is situated farther off the Indian coast to the southwest.

SRI LANKA: THE SUBCONTINENT'S "TEAR DROP" Sri Lanka (sree LAHNG·kuh) is a large, tear-shaped island country. It is a lush tropical land of great natural beauty. Dominating the center of the island is a range of high, rugged mountains that reach more than 8,000 feet in elevation. Many small rivers cascade from these mountains to the lowlands below. The northern side of the island consists of low hills and gently rolling farmland. Circling the island is a coastal plain that includes long, palm-fringed beaches.

THE MALDIVES ARCHIPELAGO The Maldives comprise an **archipelago,** or island group, of more than 1,200 small islands. These islands stretch north to south for almost 500 miles off the Indian coast near the equator. The islands (shown at right) are the low-lying tops of submerged volcanoes, surrounded by coral reefs and shallow lagoons. This type of island is called an **atoll.** The total land area of the Maldives is 115 square miles (roughly twice the size of Washington, D.C.). Only about 200 of the islands are inhabited.

Geographic Thinking◀

Using the Atlas
B▶ Use the map on page 543. Locate the Thar Desert. What two countries share its land?

PLACE Not one of the more than 1,200 small coral islands that make up the Maldives rises more than six feet above the Indian Ocean.
How might global warming affect these islands?

Landforms and Resources **553**

Natural Resources of South Asia

Pakistan's major resources are all energy sources—coal, gas, oil, and uranium.

PAKISTAN

NEPAL

BHUTAN

BANGLADESH

INDIA

Arabian Sea

Gemstones from Sri Lanka

India has a large share of the world's known reserves of iron ore.

Bay of Bengal

Sri Lanka supplies the world with a variety of gemstones.

SRI LANKA

MALDIVES

INDIAN OCEAN

	Aluminum
	Chromium
	Coal
	Copper
	Gemstones
	Graphite
	Iron ore
	Manganese
	Mica
	Natural gas
	Petroleum
	Titanium
	Uranium

0   250   500 miles
0   250   500 kilometers
Two–Point Equidistant Projection

SKILLBUILDER: Interpreting Maps

❶ **LOCATION** How would you describe the distribution of petroleum resources in South Asia?

❷ **REGION** Why might terrain be a reason no major mineral resources are shown in Nepal?

Natural Resources

The natural beauty of the southern islands is just one of the many physical assets of South Asia. In fact, the subcontinent boasts a wide variety of natural resources that support human life. At the same time, South Asia's rapidly growing population puts great pressure on its land and resources.

WATER AND SOIL South Asia relies heavily on its soil and water resources to provide food through farming and fishing. The great river systems that bring alluvial soil down from the mountains help enrich the land. They also bring the water necessary for crops to grow. Both small- and large-scale irrigation projects divert the water to the farmlands that need it. Many types of fish are also found in South Asian rivers and coastal waters, including mackerel, sardines, carp, and catfish.

South Asian waters also provide a means of transportation and power. Boats travel the rivers and coastlines, carrying goods and people from town to town. Governments also are working to harness hydroelectric energy from the waters. For example, India and Pakistan have a number of hydroelectric and irrigation projects underway.

FORESTS Timber and other forest products are another important resource in South Asia. Rain forests in India produce hardwoods like sal and teak, along with bamboo and the fragrant sandalwood. Highland forests in Bhutan and Nepal have thick stands of pine, fir, and other softwood trees. Deforestation is a severe problem, however. It causes

BACKGROUND
Only one-tenth of India's original forest cover remains uncut.

soil erosion, flooding, landslides, and loss of wildlife habitats. Over-cutting has devastated formerly dense forests in India, Bangladesh, and Sri Lanka.

MINERALS Much of South Asia's energy is still generated from mineral resources. For example, India ranks fourth in the world in coal production and has enough petroleum to supply about half its oil needs. India, Pakistan, and Bangladesh also have important natural gas resources. Uranium deposits in India provide fuel for nuclear energy.

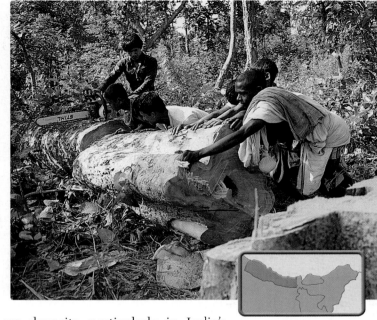

South Asia also has large iron-ore deposits, particularly in India's Deccan Plateau. India is one of the world's leading exporters of iron ore, which is also used in that country's large steel industry. Other South Asian minerals include manganese, gypsum, chromium, bauxite, and copper.

India supplies most of the world's mica, a key component in electrical equipment. This is one of the reasons that India has a growing computer industry. Mica is also found in Nepal. India and Sri Lanka both have substantial gemstone deposits. India is traditionally known for its diamonds, while Sri Lanka produces dozens of types of precious and semi-precious stones. The island is most famous for its beautiful sapphires and rubies.

In this section, you read about the landforms and resources of South Asia. In the next section, you will learn about climate and vegetation.

HUMAN-ENVIRONMENT INTERACTION
These Nepalese are harvesting timber from depleted forests in southern Nepal.
What are some ways deforestation might affect the lives of South Asians?

SOUTH ASIA

Assessment

1 Places & Terms

Identify and explain where in the region these would be found.

• Himalaya Mountains

• subcontinent

• alluvial plain

• archipelago

• atoll

2 Taking Notes

PLACE Review the notes you took for this section.

Landforms	
Resources	

• What mountain ranges separate the subcontinent from the rest of Asia?

• Why might South Asia have a large steel industry?

3 Main Ideas

a. When and how was South Asia formed?

b. What are South Asia's three largest rivers, and what is their source?

c. How do the island countries that lie off the subcontinent's coast differ from one another?

4 Geographic Thinking

Seeing Patterns How do the Himalayas contribute to South Asia's resource wealth? **Think about:**

• river systems

• agriculture

S **See Skillbuilder Handbook, page R8.**

MAKING COMPARISONS Do research on one of the mountain climbing expeditions to the peak of Mt. Everest. Write a **news article** about the expedition and present it to the class. Use standard sentence structure, spelling, grammar, and punctuation.

Climate and Vegetation

Main Ideas

- Climate conditions in South Asia range from frigid cold in the high mountains to intense heat in the deserts.
- Seasonal winds affect both the climate and vegetation of South Asia.

Places & Terms

monsoon

cyclone

CONNECT TO THE ISSUES

EXTREME WEATHER Seasonal droughts and flooding take a heavy toll in lives and property in South Asia each year.

A HUMAN PERSPECTIVE Every April and May, much of South Asia bakes in the heat. People endure temperatures that regularly top 100°F. Dust fills the air, and streams dry up. People walk for miles looking for water. Then—when it seems that no one can survive another day—the clouds roll in. The skies open up, and the rains come. People celebrate when the land turns green.

But their celebration is short-lived, as the downpour continues. Soon, the ground can hold no more water. Rivers overflow their banks. Families are forced from their homes as towns and cities are flooded. Thousands may die before the waters eventually recede, and the land dries out. South Asians see this cycle repeat itself each year.

SUNSHINE STATE STANDARDS

Key Standard SS.B.2.4.1 The student understands how social, cultural, economic, and environmental factors contribute to the dynamic nature of regions.

FCAT LA.A.1.4.2 Reading: Strategies

Climate—Wet and Dry, Hot and Cold

Half of the climate zones that exist on Earth can be found in South Asia. This means that South Asians must adapt to widely varying conditions.

CLIMATE ZONES South Asia has six main climate zones, as you can see on the map on page 557. The highland zone has the coldest climate. This is the area of the Himalayas and other northern mountains, where snow exists year-round. The lower elevations, which include the lush foothills and valleys of Nepal, Bhutan, and northern India, are much warmer. They are in the humid subtropical zone that stretches across South Asia. The Indo-Gangetic Plain also occupies much of this region.

The semiarid zone—a region of high temperatures and light rainfall—is found at the western end of the Plain and in parts of the Deccan Plateau. The desert zone covers much of the lower Indus Valley, in the borderlands of western India and southern Pakistan. The driest part of

MOVEMENT Camels, who can go days without water, are used to move goods and people across the sands of the Thar Desert, which straddles northwest India and southeast Pakistan.

What does this photo show about the climate and vegetation of the Thar Desert?

Climate and Vegetation of South Asia

Climate

0 250 500 miles
0 250 500 kilometers
Two-Point Equidistant Projection

Tropic of Cancer
Arabian Sea
Bay of Bengal
INDIAN OCEAN
Equator

- Tropical wet
- Tropical wet and dry
- Desert
- Semiarid
- Humid subtropical
- Highland

Vegetation

0 250 500 miles
0 250 500 kilometers
Two-Point Equidistant Projection

Tropic of Cancer
Arabian Sea
Bay of Bengal
INDIAN OCEAN
Equator

- Tropical rain forest
- Tropical grassland
- Desert and dry shrub
- Temperate grassland
- Deciduous and mixed forest
- Highland

SKILLBUILDER: Interpreting Maps

❶ **LOCATION** Which countries have only one type of vegetation?

❷ **REGION** Which areas of South Asia receive the most rainfall?

this area, the Thar Desert, gets very little rain—averaging 10 inches a year. The tropical wet zone is found along the western and eastern coasts of India and in Bangladesh. Temperatures are high, and rainfall is heavy. In fact, Cherrapunji in northeastern India holds the world's record for rainfall in a month—366 inches. Southern Sri Lanka also has a tropical wet climate, while the north is tropical wet and dry.

MONSOONS AND CYCLONES Although climate varies in South Asia, the region as a whole is greatly affected by **monsoons,** or seasonal winds. Each year, from October through February, dry winds blow across South Asia from the northeast. From June through September, the winds blow in from the southwest, bringing moist ocean air. Heavy rains fall, especially in the southwestern and Ganges Delta portions of South Asia. The illustration on page 598 shows how the monsoons blow across the region.

This rainfall is crucial to life on the subcontinent. Yet, the monsoons can cause severe hardship for millions, especially those living in the lowlands of India and Bangladesh. The monsoons also are highly unpredictable. Some areas may get too little rain, while others get too much. The monsoons are a sometimes beneficial, sometimes difficult feature of life in South Asia. ◀A

The most extreme weather pattern of South Asia is the **cyclone,** a violent storm with fierce winds and heavy rain. Cyclones are most destructive in Bangladesh, a low-lying coastal region where high waves can swamp large parts of the country. A severe cyclone can cause

Geographic Thinking ◀

Seeing Patterns
Ⓐ How are the monsoons both beneficial and destructive to South Asia?

SOUTH ASIA

Saving the Tigers

The Indian subcontinent's magnificent Bengal Tiger was nearing extinction in the early 1970s. Hunters killed them for sport and skins and as a source of traditional medicine. Only about 1,800 remained.

Today, through the efforts of conservationists and governments, the Bengal Tiger is a protected species. Its numbers are on the rise. An estimated 3,250 to 4,700 Bengal Tigers now roam in protected jungle and grassland areas mainly in India and Bangladesh, but also in parts of Nepal, Bhutan, and Myanmar. Several hundred are found in zoos around the world.

widespread damage and kill thousands of people. In the Disasters! feature on pages 578–579, you will read about a cyclone that killed more than 300,000 in 1970.

Vegetation: Desert to Rain Forest

Plant life in South Asia varies according to climate and altitude. As you can see on the map on page 557, vegetation ranges from desert shrub and temperate grasslands to dense forests in the wettest areas.

VEGETATION ZONES The most forested parts of South Asia lie within the tropical wet zone, particularly the western coast of India and southern Bangladesh. Lush rain forests of teak, ebony, and bamboo are found there, along with mangroves in the delta areas. In the highland zone, which includes northern India, Nepal, and Bhutan, there are forests of pine, fir, and other evergreens. The river valleys and foothills of the humid subtropical zone have forests of sal, oak, chestnut, and various palms. But deforestation is a problem everywhere. For example, less than one-fifth of India's original forests remain. Cutting down forests has caused soil erosion, flooding, climate changes, and lost wildlife habitats.

In the semiarid areas of South Asia, such as the Deccan Plateau and the Pakistan-India border, there is less vegetation. The main plant life is desert shrubs and grasses. The driest areas, like the Thar Desert, have little plant life, and as a result, few people live there. The tropical wet and dry climate of northern Sri Lanka produces both grasses and trees. How South Asians interact with their environment will be discussed in the next section.

Geographic Thinking

Using the Atlas
B Use the atlas on pages 543 and 547. What is the average population density in the Thar Desert?

2 Assessment

1 Places & Terms

Explain the importance of each of the following places and terms.

- monsoon
- cyclone

2 Taking Notes

PLACE Review the notes you took for this section.

Climate and Vegetation	

- How many different climate zones does South Asia have?
- What percentage of India's original forest remains today?

3 Main Ideas

a. In what part of South Asia is there a desert climate?

b. What are monsoons, and when do they affect South Asia?

c. Where are South Asia's tropical rain forests located?

4 Geographic Thinking

Making Inferences What might be some of the long-term effects of deforestation on life in South Asia? **Think about:**

- soil erosion and flooding
- climate changes
- lost wildlife habitats

RESEARCH LINKS
CLASSZONE.COM

GeoActivity

SEEING PATTERNS Do more research on the different trees that grow in South Asia, such as teak, ebony, and bamboo. Create a **sketch map** of the region that shows where these various trees grow.

Map and Graph Skills

SUNSHINE STATE STANDARDS
Key Standard SS.B.1.4.1 The student uses a variety of maps, geographic technologies including geographic information systems (GIS) and satellite-produced imagery, and other advanced graphic representations to depict geographic problems.
FCAT LA.A.2.2.7 Reading: Recognize Compare and Contrast

Reading a Weather Map

Suppose you have decided to take a trip to South Asia and want to know what the weather in the area you are going to visit will be like. To see what the weather is predicted to be for the next several days, you would look at a weather map. Most daily newspapers and news broadcasts show weather maps for a region or a country every day.

THE LANGUAGE OF MAPS A **weather map** shows weather conditions and patterns for a specific area at a point in time. Weather maps show temperatures, precipitation, weather fronts (rapid changes in weather), and air pressure. The weather map below shows weather conditions in South Asia on a typical day during the winter monsoon season—February 21, 2001.

Weather Map of South Asia

1 The key shows colors and patterns that are used to indicate temperatures and precipitation. The temperatures are shown in both Fahrenheit and Celsius.

2 Letter symbols on the map represent high and low pressure systems. Air pressure is the force of the air pressing down on the earth's surface.

3 These symbols show weather fronts. In addition to showing whether a warm front or a cold front is approaching an area, the symbols show in which direction the front is moving.

Copyright by Rand McNally & Co.

Map and Graph Skills Assessment

1. Drawing Conclusions
Which South Asian cities are having temperatures over 70°F?

2. Making Comparisons
Which area of South Asia would have the most pleasant weather conditions for a visitor at the time?

3. Making Inferences
Judging from the map, will the weather in northwestern India stay the same or change?

Human–Environment Interaction

A HUMAN PERSPECTIVE <u>Hinduism</u> is the religion of most Indians. During one Hindu religious festival, millions of Indians gather near the city of Allahabad, where the Ganges and Yamuna rivers meet. A temporary tent city goes up, complete with markets, temples, and teahouses. People visit the market stalls and pray at the temples. They also watch plays based on Hindu myths and legends.

Mainly, though, the Hindus wait for the appointed moment when they will wade into the Ganges and wash their sins away in its holy waters. To Hindus, the <u>Ganges River</u> is not only an important water resource, but it is also a sacred river. It is the earthly home of the Hindu goddess Ganga.

Living Along the Ganges

The Ganges is the most well-known of all the South Asian rivers. It flows more than 1,500 miles from its source in a Himalayan glacier to the Bay of Bengal. Along the way, it drains a huge area nearly three times the size of France. This area is home to about 350 million people. Although it is shorter than both the Indus and Brahmaputra rivers, the impact of the Ganges on human life in the region is enormous.

A SACRED RIVER The Ganges is extremely important for the livelihood of Indians. It provides water for drinking, farming, and transportation. Just as important, though, is the spiritual significance of the river. The Ganges is known in India as *Gangamai,* which means "Mother Ganges." In Bangladesh, where the Ganges joins the Brahmaputra, the river is called the Padma. According to Hindu beliefs, the Ganges is a sacred river that brings life to its people. As you read above, the Hindus worship the river as a goddess, and they believe its waters have healing powers.

Many temples and sacred sites line the banks of the Ganges. In some places, wide stone steps lead down to the water. Pilgrims come from all parts of the world to drink and bathe in its waters. They also come to scatter the ashes of deceased family members on the river.

At Varanasi (shown at right), one of the most sacred sites on the Ganges, thousands of people gather every day. As the sun rises, Hindu pilgrims enter the water for purification and prayer. They float baskets of flowers and burning candles on the water, as bells ring and trumpeters blow on conch shells. It is a daily celebration of their faith in the Ganges and its sacred waters.

> ## Main Ideas
> - Rivers play a central role in the lives of South Asians.
> - Water pollution and flooding pose great challenges to South Asian countries.
>
> ## Places & Terms
> | | |
> |---|---|
> | **Hinduism** | **storm surge** |
> | **Ganges River** | **estuary** |

> **CONNECT TO THE ISSUES**
> **POPULATION** The large population of South Asia is in danger of using up the region's water resources.

SUNSHINE STATE STANDARDS
Key Standard SS.B.2.4.4 The student understands the global impact of human changes in the physical environment.
Other Standards SS.B.2.4.5
FCAT LA.A.1.4.2 Reading: Strategies

A POLLUTED RIVER Unfortunately for the people of India, the Ganges is in trouble. After centuries of intense human use, it has become one of the most polluted rivers in the world. Millions of gallons of raw sewage and industrial waste flow into the river every day. The bodies of dead animals float on the water. Even human corpses are thrown into the river. As a result, the water is poisoned with toxic chemicals and deadly bacteria. Thousands of people who bathe in the river or drink the water become ill with stomach or intestinal diseases. Some develop life-threatening illnesses, such as hepatitis, typhoid, or cholera.

Since 1986, the Indian government has tried to restore the health of the river. Plans have called for a network of sewage treatment plants to clean up the water and for tougher regulations on industrial polluters. So far, however, progress has been slow. Few of the proposed treatment plants are in operation, and factories and cities are still dumping waste into the river.

Pollution in the Ganges remains an enormous problem. It will take a great deal of time, effort, and money to clean up the river. It will also require a change in the way people view the river. According to many Hindu believers, the Ganges is too holy to be harmed by pollution. If there is a problem with the water, they believe that "Mother Ganges" will fix it.

MOVEMENT Each year, millions of Hindu pilgrims come to the city of Varanasi, in northern India, to bathe in the waters of the Ganges—the sacred river of their religion.

The Ganges River

Length	1,560 miles
Source	Gangotri glacier, western Himalayas, 10,302 feet above sea level
Mouth	Bay of Bengal
Delta Area	65,500 square miles in India and Bangladesh
Name, in Hindi	Gangamai, or Ganga

SKILLBUILDER: Interpreting Maps

REGION Which countries are part of the Ganges river basin?

**HUMAN-
ENVIRONMENT
INTERACTION**
Bangladeshi workers
carry hundred-pound
bags of clay across the
Feni River bottom at
low tide. The bags were
used in the construc-
tion of the dam pictured
on the next page.

**What might be a
reason for using
people rather than
trucks for this job?**

Controlling the Feni River

Just as the Ganges is the lifeblood of India, the rivers of Bangladesh are crucial to that country's survival. Many rivers emerge from the Chittagong Hills in the southeast. One of these rivers is the Feni, which flows into the Bay of Bengal just east of the huge delta that makes up most of the southern part of the country. The Feni begins as a small hill stream, but it becomes a wide, slow-moving river by the time it enters the bay. **A**

A RIVER OVERFLOWS The Feni flows through a low-lying coastal plain that borders the Bay of Bengal before it reaches the sea. This flat, marshy area is subject to flooding during the wet season. At that time, monsoon rains swell the river and may cause it to overflow its banks. Also a problem are the cyclones that sweep across the Bay of Bengal. They bring high waters—called **storm surges**—that swamp low-lying areas. You saw a photo of this area on page 552.

Over the years, storm surges at the mouth of the Feni River have caused tremendous hardship. Sea water surges up the river and onto the coastal flatlands. Villages and fields are flooded, causing great destruction. On smaller streams, villagers sometimes build earthen dikes to block the water and protect their farmlands. But such structures are not effective against the flooding of large rivers.

In the 1980s, engineers in Bangladesh proposed building an earthen dam for the Feni. Closing the Feni to build the dam would be very difficult, though. The mouth of the river is nearly a mile wide, posing major problems for dam construction. The cost of building such a dam would also be enormous. A poor country like Bangladesh has limited financial and technological resources.

USING PEOPLE POWER Bangladesh did have one key asset for such a project—abundant human resources. With its large population, the country had plenty of unskilled workers available for construction work. To help plan the job, Bangladesh hired engineers from the Netherlands. As you read in Unit 4, the Dutch have had great experience in flood control.

**Geographic
Thinking**

Using the Atlas
A Use the map on page 543. Find the highest elevated area in Bangladesh—the Chittagong Hills. What is their elevation?

From the beginning in 1984, the project emphasized the use of cheap materials and low-tech procedures. The first step was to lay down heavy mats made of bamboo, and reeds weighted with boulders. This was done to prevent erosion of the river bottom. Workers piled more boulders on top and then covered them with clay-filled bags. After six months' work, they had built a partial closure across the mouth of the Feni River.

At that point, gaps in the wall still allowed water to flow in and out. Engineers had chosen February 28, 1985—the day of lowest tides—as the day to close the river. When the tide went out, 15,000 workers rushed to fill in the gaps with clay bags. In a seven-hour period, they laid down 600,000 bags. When the tide came back, the dam was closed.

COMPLETING THE DAM After that, dump trucks and earthmovers added more clay to raise the dam to a height of 30 feet. Then, workers placed concrete and brick over the sides of the dam and built a road on top. Bangladesh now had the largest **estuary** (an arm of the sea at the lower end of a river) dam in South Asia. But a crucial question remained—would the dam hold against a major storm?

The test came three months later, when a cyclone roared into the Bay of Bengal. A storm surge hit the dam, but the dam held. The lands and villages behind the dam were spared the worst effects of the storm. The success of the Feni River closure offers hope for similar solutions in other low-lying areas of Bangladesh and South Asia. ◄ⓑ

In this chapter, you read about the physical geography of South Asia. In the next chapter, you will learn about the human geography of the region—its history, government, economy, and culture.

CONNECT TO THE ISSUES

EXTREME WEATHER

ⓑ Why might dams such as the one on the Feni River help to prevent the effects of extreme weather?

SECTION 3 ▸ Assessment

❶ Places & Terms

Identify and explain the significance of each in the region.

- Hinduism
- Ganges River
- storm surge
- estuary

❷ Taking Notes

PLACE Review the notes you took for this section.

Human-Environment Interaction	

- What do the people of India call the Ganges River?
- Why do pilgrims visit the Ganges?

❸ Main Ideas

a. What is the spiritual significance of the Ganges for India's Hindus?

b. Why are rituals performed in the Ganges dangerous?

c. How have Bangladeshis sought to prevent storm surges from flooding coastal lowlands?

❹ Geographic Thinking

Making Inferences Why might pilgrims continue to bathe in and drink water from the Ganges River even though it is polluted? **Think about:**

- how much pilgrims know about the river
- the religious importance of the river

SOUTH ASIA

EXPLORING LOCAL GEOGRAPHY Learn more about common religious beliefs where you live. Are there places in your community that believers hold to be sacred? Create a **report** that describes your findings.

VISUAL SUMMARY
PHYSICAL GEOGRAPHY OF SOUTH ASIA

Landforms

Mountains and Plateaus: Himalayas, Hindu Kush, Karakoram Mountains, Eastern and Western Ghats, and Vindhya Range; Deccan and Karnataka plateaus

Rivers, Deserts, and Plains: Indus, Ganges, and Brahmaputra rivers; Thar Desert; Indo-Gangetic Plain

Islands: Sri Lanka, Maldives Archipelago

Resources

- South Asia counts heavily on its soil and water resources for farming, fishing, transportation, and power.
- Coal, petroleum, uranium, and natural gas are plentiful in South Asia. The region also boasts large deposits of iron ore and other minerals, as well as substantial but dwindling timber resources.

Climate and Vegetation

- South Asia's climate ranges from frigid cold in the mountainous north to intense heat in the desert regions to the south.
- Seasonal winds, called monsoons, have an enormous impact on the region's vegetation.

Human-Environment Interaction

- The people of South Asia have strong economic and spiritual ties to their great rivers, especially the Ganges.
- Even so, the region's unpredictable storms and severe problems with water pollution have complicated these ties.

Reviewing Places & Terms

A. Briefly explain the importance of each of the following.

1. Himalaya Mountains
2. subcontinent
3. archipelago
4. atoll
5. monsoon
6. cyclone
7. Hinduism
8. Ganges River
9. storm surge
10. estuary

B. Answer the questions about vocabulary in complete sentences.

11. What geographic term above can be used to describe the Maldives?
12. What is the religion of most of India's people?
13. Where is the world's tallest mountain peak?
14. Which river is home to the Hindu goddess Gangamai?
15. What is the most extreme weather pattern in South Asia?
16. What is another name for South Asia's landmass?
17. What is the name of the broad seaward end of a river mouth?
18. What is caused by the cyclones that sweep across the Bay of Bengal?
19. What seasonal winds play a large role in South Asia?
20. What island type is the top of a submerged volcano surrounded by coral reefs?

Main Ideas

Landforms and Resources (pp. 551–555)

1. Which mountain ranges resulted from the collision of what is now the Indian subcontinent with Asia?
2. What two tectonic plates were involved in this collision?
3. In which directions do the three major rivers originating in the Himalayas flow?
4. Why is India's supply of mica important?

Climate and Vegetation (pp. 556–559)

5. When are South Asia's monsoon seasons?
6. What are the advantages and disadvantages of the southwest monsoons?
7. Why are the people in Bangladesh vulnerable to cyclones?

Human-Environment Interaction (pp. 560–563)

8. Why is the Ganges River so polluted?
9. Why do Hindu pilgrims bring the ashes of deceased family members to the river?
10. How long did it take the Bangladeshi people to build a dam across the Feni River?

Critical Thinking

1. Using Your Notes

Use your completed chart to answer these questions.

Landforms	
Resources	

a. Where is the Deccan Plateau?

b. What is the most heavily populated plain in South Asia?

2. Geographic Themes

a. **LOCATION** Which bay is located south of Bangladesh?

b. **PLACE** Which island's center is dominated by a range of high rugged mountains?

3. Identifying Themes

How can you explain the enormous wall of mountain ranges that separate South Asia from the rest of Asia? Which of the five themes applies to this situation?

4. Making Inferences

Why might the Khyber Pass be considered of crucial military importance?

5. Making Generalizations

How does weather cause suffering in South Asia?

Additional Test Practice, pp. S1–S37

TEST PRACTICE
CLASSZONE.COM

Geographic Skills: Interpreting Maps

Precipitation in South Asia

Use the maps at right to answer the following questions.

1. **REGION** In which season does South Asia get most of its precipitation?

2. **REGION** How much precipitation does central India receive during the winter?

3. **PLACE** How much rainfall does Bangladesh receive in the summer?

GeoActivity

Do more research on precipitation in South Asia. Focus on the drought that struck the region in 2000—what some observers have called the worst drought in 100 years. Use presentation software to share your results.

Winter Precipitation

Summer Precipitation

- 40+ in. (100+ cm)
- 20–40 in. (50–100 cm)
- 10–20 in. (25–50 cm)
- 5–10 in. (12.5–25 cm)
- Under 5 in. (Under 12.5 cm)

0   250   500 miles
0   250 500 kilometers
Two-Point Equidistant Projection

INTERNET ACTIVITY

Use the links at **classzone.com** to do research on the different kinds of wildlife that are found in South Asia. Try to identify specific areas in the region where these different animals live.

Creating a Sketch Map Use your research to create a sketch map that shows the locations of different animal habitats. Add pictures and captions to your map. Use the captions to explain why the locations are suited to specific animals.

SOUTH ASIA

Four Subregions of South Asia

India
Pakistan and Bangladesh
Nepal and Bhutan
Sri Lanka and the Maldives

PAKISTAN

NEPAL

BHUTAN

BANGLADESH

Tropic of Cancer

Arabian
Sea

I N D I A

Bay of
Bengal

SRI LANKA

MALDIVES

Equator

INDIAN OCEAN

0   250   500 miles
0   250   500 kilometers
Two-Point Equidistant Projection

GeoFocus

How have the different cultures of South Asia developed?

Taking Notes In your notebook, copy a cluster diagram like the one below. For each subregion of South Asia, take notes about its history, economics, culture, and modern life.

India

Pakistan and
Bangladesh

South Asia

Nepal and Bhutan

Sri Lanka and
the Maldives

India

Main Ideas

• India is the largest country in South Asia and has the most developed economy.

• Indian culture is deeply influenced by religion.

Places & Terms

Mughal Empire

raj

nonviolent resistance

land reform

Green Revolution

caste system

CONNECT TO THE ISSUES

POPULATION India's huge and diverse population presents many social, economic, and political challenges.

SUNSHINE STATE STANDARDS
Key Standard SS.B.2.4.1 The student understands how social, cultural, economic, and environmental . . .
Other Standards SS.A.2.4.8, C.1.4.1, D.2.4.1
FCAT LA.A.1.4.2 Reading: Strategies

A HUMAN PERSPECTIVE At midnight on August 14, 1997, India celebrated the 50th anniversary of its independence from Great Britain. Thousands of people flooded the streets of the capital, New Delhi, and waved the orange, white, and green flag of India. Fifty years before, Prime Minister Jawaharlal Nehru had spoken to the nation. "A moment comes," he said, "when we step out from the old to the new, . . . and when the soul of a nation, long suppressed, finds utterance [expression]." Since then, India has emerged as a modern and powerful country. But it has also preserved its links to the past.

Invasions, Empires, and Independence

India is an ancient land. Its culture and history date back more than 4,000 years. For centuries, foreign invaders came to conquer India but were absorbed into Indian life. As a result, Indian culture is a blend of many different customs and traditions.

EARLY HISTORY Indian civilization began in the Indus Valley (now in Pakistan) around 2500 B.C. A thousand years later, invaders crossed the mountains of the Hindu Kush and spread across northern India. They were Aryans, a light-skinned people from the plains north of Iran. Aryan culture played a key role in the development of Indian civilization.

The Aryans established small kingdoms on the Ganges Plain. They pushed darker-skinned, native Indians, called Dravidians, toward the south. Later, Persian and Greek invaders occupied the Indus Valley. But they did not conquer the Aryan kingdoms of the Ganges.

Two great Indian empires eventually emerged on the lower Ganges. Beginning in 321 B.C., the Mauryan Empire united most of India. The great Mauryan leader Asoka helped spread Buddhism throughout Asia. Several centuries later, the Gupta Empire came to power. It ruled over northern India during an age of peace and prosperity.

New waves of invaders from Central Asia and, later, Southwest Asia began entering India in the A.D. fifth century. Muslims conquered the Indus

Ancient Empires of India

60°E   70°E   80°E   90°E

0   250   500 miles
0   250   500 kilometers
Two-Point Equidistant Projection

Hindu Kush

Indus R.

30°N

HIMALAYA MTS.

Tropic of Cancer

Ganges R.

20°N

Arabian Sea

Bay of Bengal

10°N

0° Equator

INDIAN OCEAN

	Mauryan Empire, 250 B.C.
	Gupta Empire, A.D. 400
	Mughal Empire, A.D. 1700

SKILLBUILDER: Interpreting Maps

❶ **LOCATION** What is the farthest north-south and east-west extent of the Gupta Empire?

❷ **MOVEMENT** Which empire moved farthest south?

SOUTH ASIA

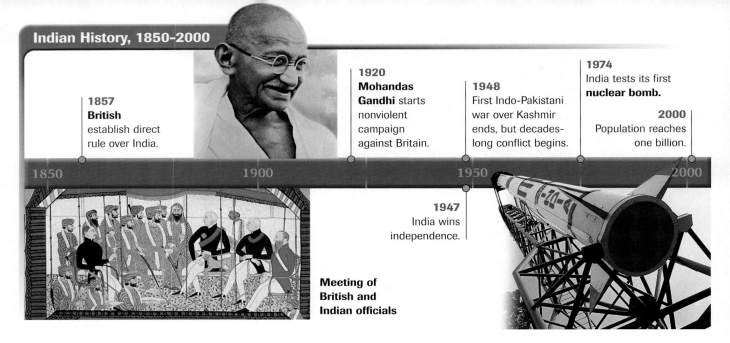

Indian History, 1850–2000

1857
British establish direct rule over India.

1920
Mohandas Gandhi starts nonviolent campaign against Britain.

1948
First Indo-Pakistani war over Kashmir ends, but decades-long conflict begins.

1974
India tests its first **nuclear bomb.**

2000
Population reaches one billion.

1850   1900   1950   2000

1947
India wins independence.

Meeting of British and Indian officials

Valley and then occupied the Ganges Plain. By the early 1500s, they had established the **Mughal Empire** throughout much of India. Muslim rule brought new customs that sometimes conflicted with those of the native Hindus.

EUROPEANS ARRIVE Also in the 1500s, European traders came to India, looking for spices, cloth, and other goods not available in Europe. They soon established trade relations with India's rulers. French, Dutch, and Portuguese traders set up trading colonies in India—but it was the British who finally won out.

Through its trading arm, the British East India Company, Britain gained control over India's trade with Europe in 1757. In 1857, the British government put down a revolt and established direct rule over India. The period of direct British control, called the **raj,** lasted for nearly 90 years.

British rule brought some benefits to India, but most Indians did not like colonialism. The great Indian leader Mohandas Gandhi began an opposition movement based on **nonviolent resistance**—a protest movement that does not use violence to achieve its goals. Eventually, Britain gave in and granted India its freedom. At midnight on August 14, 1947, India became independent.

Independence also brought the division of India. The Muslims of West and East Pakistan (now Pakistan and Bangladesh, respectively) chose to separate from India, which was strongly Hindu, and form a separate country. This division caused violence to break out between Hindus and Muslims. Mass migrations across the new borders caused great hardship and suffering. ▶ A

Governing the World's Largest Democracy

India's first prime minister, Jawaharlal Nehru, was an associate of Gandhi. Under Nehru's leadership, India adopted a constitution and became a democratic republic in 1950. With a population of more than one billion, India is presently the world's largest democracy.

Geographic Thinking

Using the Atlas
A Use the atlas on page 545. Locate India, West Pakistan (now Pakistan), and East Pakistan (now Bangladesh). Which country does not share a border with China?

Indian democracy reflects elements of both the American and the British systems. Like the United States, India is a federation of states held together by a strong central government. However, like Britain, it is a parliamentary democracy. The leader of the majority party in parliament becomes prime minister and head of the government.

Many different ethnic, cultural, and religious factors influence Indian politics. One major factor is relations between Hindus and Muslims. India is strongly Hindu, but its Muslim minority numbers around 150 million people. So, Indian leaders must take Muslim interests into account. Two other minorities, Sikhs and Tamils, also play a key role in Indian politics. In 1984, Sikhs who were angered by Indian policies assassinated Prime Minister Indira Gandhi, the daughter of Nehru. Seven years later, Tamil extremists assassinated Indira Gandhi's son, Prime Minister Rajiv Gandhi. Despite such violence, India manages to resolve most of its political conflicts peacefully. In a challenging postcolonial world, Indian democracy has survived.

BACKGROUND
Mohandas Gandhi, the founder of modern India, was also assassinated. A Hindu extremist who opposed Gandhi's attempts to resolve the Hindu-Muslim conflict killed him.

Economic Challenges

Another challenge for India is to promote economic growth and raise standards of living. The government has adopted a variety of policies to achieve these goals. But progress has been slow. India has one of the world's largest economies, but per capita income remains low. About half of India's people live in poverty.

DEPENDENCE ON FARMING
About two-thirds of India's people rely on farming for their livelihood. The majority of farms, however, are very small, and crop yields are low. Most farm families struggle to survive on what they can grow for themselves.

One solution being considered for this problem is **land reform**—a more balanced distribution of land among farmers than now exists. In the late 1990s, 5 percent of India's farm families owned nearly 25 percent of India's farmland. Because the large landowners have great political influence, land-reform proposals have never made much progress. ◄B

One change has made a major difference, though. After a series of famines in the 1960s, agricultural scientists introduced new

Geographic Thinking

Seeing Patterns
B⊳ What changes might come about through land reform?

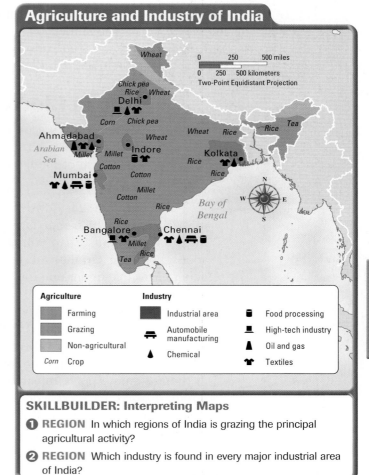

Agriculture and Industry of India

0   250   500 miles
0 250 500 kilometers
Two-Point Equidistant Projection

Agriculture
Farming
Grazing
Non-agricultural
Corn Crop

Industry
Industrial area
Automobile manufacturing
Chemical

Food processing
High-tech industry
Oil and gas
Textiles

SKILLBUILDER: Interpreting Maps

❶ **REGION** In which regions of India is grazing the principal agricultural activity?

❷ **REGION** Which industry is found in every major industrial area of India?

SOUTH ASIA

India **569**

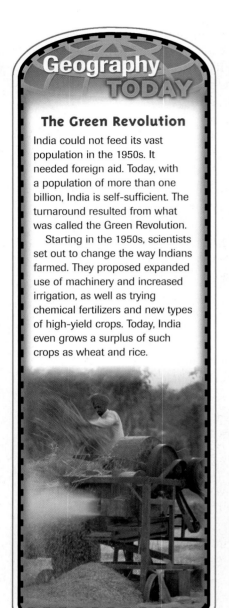

Geography TODAY

The Green Revolution

India could not feed its vast population in the 1950s. It needed foreign aid. Today, with a population of more than one billion, India is self-sufficient. The turnaround resulted from what was called the Green Revolution.

Starting in the 1950s, scientists set out to change the way Indians farmed. They proposed expanded use of machinery and increased irrigation, as well as trying chemical fertilizers and new types of high-yield crops. Today, India even grows a surplus of such crops as wheat and rice.

farming techniques and higher-yielding grain varieties to improve production. This program, later called the **Green Revolution,** increased crop yields. The increases were especially dramatic for wheat, but rice production also expanded. Still, many peasant farmers lack the land and money to take advantage of these technological improvements.

GROWING INDUSTRY Although agriculture is the main economic activity in India, industry is also an important element. Cotton textiles have long been a major product of India. Beginning in the late 1940s, however, other industries began to develop. As the map on page 569 shows, India is now a major producer of iron and steel, chemicals, machinery, and food products. The main industrial regions are centered around Kolkata (Calcutta) in the east, Mumbai (Bombay) and Ahmadabad in the west, Chennai (Madras) in the south, and Delhi in the north. **C**

The western industrial zone has led the way in the modernization of Indian industry. Today, Mumbai is India's most prosperous city and leading commercial center. Its industries include metals, chemicals, and electronics. Other areas are now following Mumbai's lead. The southern city of Bangalore has become India's high-tech center. It is home to hundreds of computer software companies that are taking advantage of India's low wages and highly skilled workers. To some observers, Bangalore represents the future of the modern Indian economy.

Geographic Thinking

Making Comparisons
C How has economic development changed India?

Life in Modern India

While India's economy is modernizing, many Indians still live and work in traditional ways. This blend of old and new is typical of modern life in India.

DAILY LIFE Marriage and family remain at the center of Indian life. Most Indians follow the custom of arranged marriages—in which marriage partners are chosen by their families. But more affluent urban young people increasingly choose their own spouses. Indian families are large. Often many relatives from several generations live under one roof. Marriages are usually male-dominated, and divorce is rare.

Most Indians eat a largely vegetarian diet based on rice, legumes, and flatbreads called *chapati* or *roti*. Some Indians eat meat, fish, and chicken, often in spicy dishes called curry. But meat consumption is limited by both Muslim and Hindu religious practices.

Indians enjoy sports, music, and movies. Some of the country's most popular sports are soccer, field hockey, and cricket—a sport similar to baseball adopted from the British. Classical Indian music, featuring traditional instruments such as the sitar and the tabla, still has a large audience. But modern pop music is finding favor with India's youth. They also flock to movie theaters, where foreign films compete with local productions. The Indian film industry is based in Mumbai.

These young women from the state of Rajasthan dress in traditional clothing to attend a fair. Festivals of all kinds are part of life for people of all ages in India. The traditional clothing worn by females in India includes embroidered skirts, head shawls, and lots of jewelry. In many places, however, Western-style clothing has replaced the traditional, especially for young people. Even though changes are taking place, females in India are treated differently from males both inside and outside the home. Females, for example, have more family responsibilities and less access to higher education and professional jobs.

If you lived in India, you would pass these milestones:

- You would receive some schooling, as Indian law provides free education from age 6 through age 14. In some areas, though, you could be working even before the age of 10.
- In school, you would study history, geography, science, math, and moral education.
- You might be married at age 16 if you were a female living in a rural area and at age 17 if you were a female in an urban area.
- You could enter the military at age 17 if you were a male.
- You could vote at age 18.

EDUCATION Most Indians still work on farms or in small craft industries. As the economy changes, though, more people are finding work in factories and offices. Education is a key factor in this change. In towns and cities, most middle-class children attend school. Literacy—the ability to read and write—has risen steadily since the 1950s. In city slums and rural areas, however, school attendance is irregular and literacy rates are low. The government has placed a high priority on improving public education to better prepare its citizens for the future.

Indian Culture

The culture of India is a rich blend of the different linguistic, ethnic, and religious groups.

MANY LANGUAGES The Indian constitution recognizes 18 major language groups, but more than 1,000 languages and dialects are spoken in India. Hindi is the official language. English, too, is widely spoken as a common language, especially by those working in government and business. Southern India is a distinct subregion, dating back to the Aryan conquest of northern India. The language and ethnicity of this region is Dravidian rather than Indo-European. Southern India has four major languages: Telugu, Tamil, Kannada, and Malayalam.

HINDUISM India is a land of great variety, but the dominant force in the lives of most Indians is Hinduism. Hinduism is a complex religion with roots in Aryan culture. Hindus, who make up around 80 percent of the population, believe in many gods. They also believe in reincarnation—the rebirth of souls after death. The moral consequences of a person's actions, known as karma, help determine how a person is reincarnated.

BACKGROUND Hinduism is not based on the teachings of one person or deity like many other religions. It has been shaped by many ethnic, religious, and cultural groups.

SOUTH ASIA

REGION Shiva is one of the major gods of Hinduism. As in this 18th-century painting, Shiva is often represented in the character of a many-headed, many-armed destroyer or restorer.

The **caste system** was the Aryan system of social classes. Today, it remains one of the cornerstones of Hinduism. Four basic castes made up the original system: the Brahmans (priests and scholars), the Kshatriyas (rulers and warriors), the Vaisyas (farmers and merchants), and the Sudras (artisans and laborers).

Over time, these castes were further divided into smaller groupings. Outside the system altogether were the *dalits*, or untouchables, who had the lowest status in Indian society. (This class was officially eliminated in the Indian constitution.)

According to Hindu belief, each person is born into a caste and has a certain moral duty, known as dharma, that is specific to that caste. A person can move into a different caste only through reincarnation. While the system brought social order, it also caused discrimination and limited people's ability to improve their lot in life.

OTHER RELIGIONS Other faiths also play a key role in Indian life. These include Jainism, Christianity, Sikhism, and Buddhism—which originated in northern India. Islam also exerts a strong cultural influence in certain parts of the country. But millions of Muslims left the country after India won independence in 1947. They chose to move to the new Muslim states founded in the northwestern and northeastern parts of the subcontinent. You will read about those states—now called Pakistan and Bangladesh—in the next section.

Assessment

❶ Places & Terms

Identify these terms and explain their importance in the region.

- Mughal Empire
- raj
- nonviolent resistance
- land reform
- Green Revolution
- caste system

❷ Taking Notes

PLACE Review the notes you took for this section.

- Before Europeans arrived, which groups of people contributed to India's history?
- What are some of the major influences on Indian politics today?

❸ Main Ideas

a. What happened after the Europeans arrived in India?

b. What is the traditional Indian custom regarding marriage?

c. What are the central beliefs of the Hindu religion?

❹ Geographic Thinking

Making Inferences What might be some of the problems caused by the Hindu caste system? **Think about:**

- being born into a caste
- being able to move into a different caste only through reincarnation

RESEARCH LINKS
CLASSZONE.COM

GeoActivity

SEEING PATTERNS Review the information about the arrival of Europeans in India on page 568. Then use the Internet or encyclopedias to learn more about British policies and actions during their rule. Create a **political cartoon** that illustrates British policies, actions, or attitudes during that time.

Pakistan and Bangladesh

A HUMAN PERSPECTIVE Some workers in the port of Chittagong, Bangladesh, have an unusual job. They are ship breakers. When ocean-going ships reach the end of their useful life, they take their last voyage to Chittagong. There, ship breakers wait on the beach with sledgehammers, crowbars, torches, and wrenches. They attack each ship, tearing it apart piece by piece. Within weeks, they can dismantle a ship. Then, they sell its scrap metal for recycling purposes. The job doesn't pay very well, but it is necessary work for the shipping industry, the workers, and the Bangladeshi economy.

New Countries, Ancient Lands

Like India, Pakistan and Bangladesh are young countries with an ancient history and with rapidly growing populations. They, too, are striving to make their way in the modern world.

EARLY HISTORY The largest of the world's first civilizations arose in what is now Pakistan. The **Indus Valley civilization** began around 2500 B.C. It featured well-planned cities like Harappa and Mohenjo-Daro, which had brick buildings (shown below) and sophisticated sanitation systems. The map on page 544 depicts the extent of the civilization at the height of its power. It fell around 1500 B.C., and the Aryans invaded soon after. Later on, the Mauryan, Gupta, and Mughal empires ruled the territory that included modern Pakistan and Bangladesh. The British were the next to take control of the region.

The Indian Subcontinent

1947

KASHMIR

WEST PAKISTAN

INDIA

EAST PAKISTAN

CEYLON

0   250   500 miles
0   250   500 kilometers
Two-Point Equidistant Projection

Disputed by India and Pakistan

1972

KASHMIR

PAKISTAN

CHINA

NEPAL   BHUTAN

INDIA   BANGLADESH

SRI LANKA

0   250   500 miles
0   250   500 kilometers
Two-Point Equidistant Projection

Disputed by India and Pakistan

Disputed by India and China

Cease-fire line

SKILLBUILDER: Interpreting Maps

❶ **PLACE** What had happened to the territory of Kashmir by 1972?

❷ **REGION** What other changes had taken place in South Asia from 1947 to 1972?

PARTITION AND WAR The end of British rule in 1947 brought the **partition,** or division, of British India. Two new countries were created—India (predominantly Hindu) and mainly Muslim Pakistan (separated into West Pakistan and East Pakistan). Partition led to much violence between Muslims and Hindus. About one million people died in the conflict. Another 10 million fled across national borders. Muslims in India moved to Pakistan, while Hindus in Pakistan crossed into India.

West Pakistan and East Pakistan shared a religious bond, but ethnic differences and their 1,100-mile separation eventually drove them apart. The people of East Pakistan began to call for their own state. But the government in West Pakistan opposed such a move. Civil war broke out in 1971. That year, with help from India, East Pakistan won its independence as Bangladesh.

MILITARY RULE Both Pakistan and Bangladesh have had political struggles since independence. Short periods of elected government have alternated with long periods of military rule. Political corruption has plagued both countries. Pakistan also has fought several destructive wars with India over the territory of **Kashmir.** These wars are discussed in the Case Study in Chapter 26. In the 1990s, both Bangladesh and Pakistan had women prime ministers, a rarity in the Muslim world.

BACKGROUND
Bangladesh means "land of the Bangla (or Bengal)-speaking people."

Struggling Economies

Pakistan and Bangladesh have large, rapidly growing populations. In fact, Bangladesh is the eighth most populous country in the world. Both have economies that depend primarily on agriculture. As in India, per capita incomes are low, and much of the population lives in poverty. Bangladesh is one of the poorest countries in the world.

SUBSISTENCE FARMING Most farmers in Pakistan and Bangladesh work small plots of land and struggle to grow enough crops to feed their families. The government has tried to help modernize farming methods, but many farmers continue to follow less productive traditional ways. Climate also hinders crop yields. Large areas of Pakistan are arid, while Bangladesh is severely affected by seasonal monsoons and cyclones.

The most productive farming areas of Pakistan are the irrigated portions of the Indus Valley. Here, farmers grow enough cotton and rice to allow for export. The farmers also produce substantial amounts of wheat for domestic consumption. The moist delta lands of Bangladesh are ideal for the cultivation of rice, the country's principal food crop. The main export crop is jute (a plant used in the production of rope, carpets, and industrial-quality sacks). Fishing, mainly for freshwater fish, is also vital to the economy of Bangladesh.

SMALL INDUSTRY Neither Pakistan nor Bangladesh is highly industrialized. Most factories are relatively small and lack the capital, resources, and markets required for expansion. Even so, both countries are trying to increase their industrial base. They have growing textile industries that provide an important source of revenue and employment. Both countries export cotton garments, and Pakistan also exports wool carpets and leather goods. **A**

Geographic Thinking

Making Comparisons
A How do the economies of Pakistan and Bangladesh compare with each other?

An important economic development has been the introduction of **microcredit.** This policy makes small loans available to poor **entrepreneurs,** people who start and build a business. Businesses that are too small to get loans from banks can often join forces to apply for these microloans. They then accept joint responsibility for repaying the loan. This program, begun in Bangladesh, has helped small businesses grow in South Asia and has raised living standards for many producers, especially women.

Economic Activity in Pakistan and Bangladesh

Textiles in Pakistan

Pakistan*
- 25%
- 48%
- 27%

Bangladesh**
- 30%
- 53%
- 17%

■ Agriculture ■ Industry □ Services

*1999 Estimate, **1998 Estimate
SOURCE: *World Fact Book 2000*

Fishing in Bangladesh

SOUTH ASIA

SKILLBUILDER: Interpreting Graphs
❶ **MAKING COMPARISONS** Which of the two countries is more industrialized?
❷ **ANALYZING DATA** In both Pakistan and Bangladesh, which economic sector employs the most people?

One Religion, Many Peoples

Most of the people of Pakistan and Bangladesh are Muslims. In both countries, Islam is an important unifying force. At the same time, ethnic differences promote cultural diversity, particularly in Pakistan.

ISLAMIC CULTURE Islam has long played an important role in Pakistan and Bangladesh. Both lands were key parts of the Muslim Mughal Empire that ruled the Indian subcontinent for centuries, and their cultures bear the stamp of Islam. The faithful observe Islamic customs. These include daily prayer and participation in **Ramadan,** a month-long period of fasting from sunrise to sunset. Mosques in both countries are often large and impressive structures.

The two countries differ somewhat in their Islamic practices, however. In general, Pakistan is stricter in imposing Islamic law on its citizens. For example, many Pakistanis follow the custom of *purdah,* the seclusion of women. This custom prevents women from having contact with men who are not relatives. When women appear in public, they must wear veils. In Bangladesh, purdah is much less common and religious practices are less strict.

REGION Most Pakistanis are Sunni Muslims. Here, men attend a Muslim prayer service in a mosque in Karachi.

ETHNIC DIVERSITY Pakistan is also more ethnically diverse than Bangladesh. Pakistan has five main ethnic groups—Punjabis, Sindhis, Pathans, Muhajirs, and Balochs. Each group has its own language. The Punjabis make up more than half of the population. Each group has its own regional origins within the country except for the Muhajirs, who migrated from India as a result of the partition in 1947. To avoid favoring one region or group over another, the government chose Urdu—the language of the Muhajirs—as the national language. Today, most Pakistanis understand Urdu, even though they may use another language as their primary language.

In contrast, the people of Bangladesh are mainly Bengalis. Bengal is the historic region that includes Bangladesh (once known as East Bengal) and the Indian state of West Bengal. Bengalis speak a language based on Sanskrit, the ancient Indo-Aryan language. Bangladesh also has a small population of Urdu-speaking Muslims and various non-Muslim tribal groups. About 10 percent of the population are Hindus.

BACKGROUND Punjabi is the principal spoken language of Pakistan because the majority of Pakistanis are Punjabis. Arabic is a secondary language for Muslim Pakistanis.

Modern Life and Culture

As in India, life in Pakistan and Bangladesh revolves around the family. Arranged marriages are common, and families tend to be large. Most people live in small villages, in simple homes made of such materials as sun-baked mud, bamboo, or wood. The large cities are busy places, crowded with traffic and pedestrians. People in both countries enjoy sports such as soccer and cricket, and also enjoy going to see movies.

A LOVE OF POETRY Poetry is a special interest in both Pakistan and Bangladesh, where the tradition of oral literature is strong. Many Pakistanis memorize long poems and can recite them by heart. Poets are popular figures, and poetry readings—called *mushairas*—can draw thousands of people, much like a rock concert does in some countries.

The greatest literary figure in Bangladesh is the poet Rabindranath Tagore, who won the Nobel Prize for Literature in 1913. Although Tagore was born in Calcutta (now Kolkata), India, he wrote about the Ganges and his Bengal homeland. Bangladesh adopted his song, "My Golden Bengal," as its national anthem.

MUSIC AND DANCE Music and dance are also important forms of expression in Bangladesh and Pakistan. Both countries share music traditions similar to those of India. Folk music of various types is popular in cities and in rural areas. *Qawwali*—a form of devotional singing performed by Muslims known as Sufis—is famous not only in South Asia but also in parts of Europe and the United States. Bangladesh also has a long tradition of folk dances, in which elaborately costumed dancers act out Bengali myths, legends, and stories.

You have been reading about Pakistan and Bangladesh, India's western and eastern neighbors. Next, you will learn about India's northern neighbors, Nepal and Bhutan.

Seeing Patterns
B What roles do music and dance play in the lives of the people of Pakistan and Bangladesh?

POPULATION

Millions of Bangladeshis

Bangladesh is the eighth most populous country in the world. About 130 million people live there. This population, half that of the United States, lives on a land area smaller than Wisconsin. Almost 40 percent of the people are under 15—and the population continues to grow.

The population explosion has brought many problems, including malnutrition and disease. Bangladesh's neighbors—India (one billion people) and Pakistan (about 150 million)—also have rapidly expanding populations.

SECTION 2 Assessment

1 Places & Terms
Identify each of the following places and terms.
- Indus Valley civilization
- partition
- Kashmir
- microcredit
- entrepreneur
- Ramadan

2 Taking Notes
PLACE Review the notes you took for this section.

- How were the countries of Pakistan and Bangladesh formed?
- What role does farming play in the economies of Pakistan and Bangladesh?

3 Main Ideas
a. What have been some of the problems for Pakistan and Bangladesh since they were formed?

b. What role does Islam play in Pakistan and Bangladesh?

c. How would you describe Pakistan's ethnic makeup?

4 Geographic Thinking
Making Comparisons How do Pakistan and Bangladesh differ in their Islamic practices? **Think about:**
- the treatment of women
- how much of Pakistan follows strict Islamic law

RESEARCH LINKS
CLASSZONE.COM

GeoActivities

MAKING COMPARISONS Review the information about Islam on page 576. Then use the Internet or an encyclopedia to compare Islam in Pakistan or Bangladesh with a Muslim country in either Africa or Southwest Asia. Create a **chart** comparing the two countries using such topics as treatment of women, eating practices, and how strictly a country enforces Islamic law.

SOUTH ASIA

Disasters!

SUNSHINE STATE STANDARDS
Key Standard SS.B.1.4.1 The student uses a variety of maps, geographic technologies including geographic information systems (GIS) and satellite-produced imagery, and other advanced graphic representations to depict geographic problems.
FCAT LA.B.1.4.3 Writing: Edit Final Documents

The Cyclone of 1970

On November 13, 1970, a violent tropical storm struck Bangladesh, bringing death and destruction in its wake. Hundreds of thousands of people and their homes, crops, and animals were swept away in the fury of the 20th century's worst tropical storm. The cyclone's winds, rains, and floods claimed an estimated 300,000 to 500,000 lives. Also, approximately one million were left homeless, roughly 80 percent of the rice crop was lost, and about 70 percent of the country's fishing boats were wrecked. More than any other South Asian country, Bangladesh—with its low-lying coastal plain—suffers from these frequently occurring storms.

Eye of the storm

Bands of rain

Direction of wind rotation

The damage inflicted on this village in Bangladesh in 1991 is typical of the destructive force of a cyclone's winds and the torrential rains and floods that are a part of this weather system.

Concrete shelters constructed on stilts, as shown here, and reinforced school buildings are refuges from high floodwaters and winds that can knock down all but the strongest buildings.

GeoActivity

ANNOUNCING THE DAMAGE

Use the Internet to research the cyclone of November 1970. Read accounts of its destructive force. Gather data on the storm itself and the damage that it caused. Then prepare a **press release** about the storm.

- Begin with an overview of the storm.
- Provide a map and statistics.
- Present your press release to a group of student reporters.

 RESEARCH LINKS
CLASSZONE.COM

GeoData

TROPICAL STORMS

Violent tropical storms are called cyclones in the Indian Ocean, typhoons in the northwestern Pacific Ocean, and hurricanes in the Atlantic Ocean. These storms:

- develop over tropical waters in the late summer and fall when ocean temperatures are warmest
- usually begin as a cluster of thunderstorms that start to spiral and then form a single violent storm
- may be as wide as 675 miles
- have winds that range from 75 to 150 miles per hour
- generally last a week but some may take two or three weeks to die out
- produce heavy flooding that is the cause of most of the destruction and deaths
- inflict most of their damage along coastlines

OTHER BANGLADESHI STORMS

- May 28–29, 1963—22,000 deaths
- May 11–12, 1965—17,000 deaths
- June 1–12, 1965—30,000 deaths
- April 30, 1991—139,000 deaths

Nepal and Bhutan

3

Main Ideas
- Nepal and Bhutan are land-locked Himalayan kingdoms.
- Rugged terrain and an isolated location have had a great impact on life in Nepal and Bhutan.

Places & Terms
constitutional monarchy

Sherpa

Siddhartha Gautama

mandala

CONNECT TO THE ISSUES
ECONOMIC DEVELOPMENT Decades of isolation and difficult topography have limited economic growth in Nepal and Bhutan.

SUNSHINE STATE STANDARDS
Key Standard SS.B.2.4.1 The student understands how social, cultural, economic, and environmental factors contribute to the dynamic nature of regions.

Other Standards SS.D.2.4.1

FCAT LA.A.1.4.2 Reading: Strategies

A HUMAN PERSPECTIVE In the novel *Lost Horizon,* James Hilton described an imaginary mountain valley called Shangri-La, hidden high in the Himalayas. He wrote, "The floor of the valley, hazily distant, welcomed the eye with greenness; sheltered from winds . . . completely isolated by the lofty and sheerly unscalable ranges on the further side." Shangri-La was an earthly paradise: a land of peace, harmony, and beauty, where hunger, disease, and war did not exist. Hilton located this mythical land somewhere in Tibet, but it could just as easily have been in Nepal or Bhutan. Although neither of these countries is a paradise, both are remote lands of great beauty and peace.

Mountain Kingdoms

Nepal and Bhutan share a number of important characteristics. Both are located in the Himalayas, a factor that has had a great impact on their history and economic development. Both also are kingdoms with strong religious traditions.

GEOGRAPHIC ISOLATION The main geographic feature of Nepal and Bhutan is their mountainous landscape. Each country consists of a central upland of ridges and valleys leading up to the high mountains, with a small lowland area along the Indian border. The towering, snow-capped Himalayas run along the northern border with China. They are craggy and forbidding and have steep mountain passes and year-round ice fields. The world's tallest mountain peak, Mt. Everest, is located there.

The rugged landscape of Nepal and Bhutan has isolated the two countries throughout their histories. Their mountainous terrain and landlocked location—neither country has access to the sea—made them hard to reach and difficult to conquer and settle. China controlled Bhutan briefly in the 18th century. In the 19th century, Great Britain had influence over both countries because of its control of neighboring India. But Nepal and Bhutan generally remained independent and isolated. In fact, until the past few decades, foreigners rarely entered either country.

EVOLVING MONARCHIES For much of their history, Nepal and Bhutan were split into small religious kingdoms or ruling states. Hindu kings ruled in Nepal, while Buddhist priests controlled Bhutan. In time, unified kingdoms emerged in both countries, led by hereditary monarchs who passed the throne on to their heirs.

Today, the governments of both Nepal and Bhutan are **constitutional monarchies**—kingdoms in which the ruler's powers are limited by a

REGION Richly decorated cloths that display Buddhist religious symbols, such as the cloth shown below, have covered the thrones of Bhutanese rulers. **Why might there be religious symbols on a throne cloth used by secular rulers?**

PLACE A blend of the old and the new is evident in the architecture of this square in Kathmandu, Nepal's capital city. **Why might this rich cultural tradition make Kathmandu attractive to tourists?**

constitution. In Bhutan, the king is still the supreme ruler, while in Nepal the king shares power with an elected parliament. Both governments face difficult political challenges, including the need to balance the interests of their two powerful neighbors, China and India. Both countries also face difficult economic challenges.

Developing Economies

Decades of isolation and difficult topography have limited economic development in Nepal and Bhutan. Now each country is trying to find effective ways to promote economic growth.

LIMITED RESOURCES Nepal and Bhutan are poor countries with economies based mainly on agriculture. Because of the mountainous terrain, neither country has much land suitable for cultivation. Most farm plots are small, soils are poor, and erosion is a problem. Farmers create terraces on the mountainsides to increase the amount of farmland and limit soil loss, a process you read about in Chapter 9. Common farm products include rice, corn, potatoes, and wheat. Common livestock are cattle, sheep, and yaks—longhaired animals related to the ox. In Bhutan, the government has promoted the growing of fruit for export and has tried to improve farming practices.

The timber industry is very important to both countries, although deforestation is a problem. The forests of Nepal are being cut down at a rate of about 1 percent a year. But some valuable timberlands remain. Around 70 percent of Bhutan is still forested. A growing manufacturing sector of the economy includes wood products, food processing, and cement production. Most trade for both countries is with India. ◀

INCREASING TOURISM One of the fastest growing industries in Nepal is tourism. Tourists come from around the world to visit the valley of Kathmandu, the capital, and to climb the Himalayas. Hotels and restaurants, transportation, and other services have grown to meet the needs of the tourist industry. But tourism is a mixed blessing. It has

Making Comparisons
A▶ What activities are important to the economies of Nepal and Bhutan?

SOUTH ASIA

Nepal and Bhutan **581**

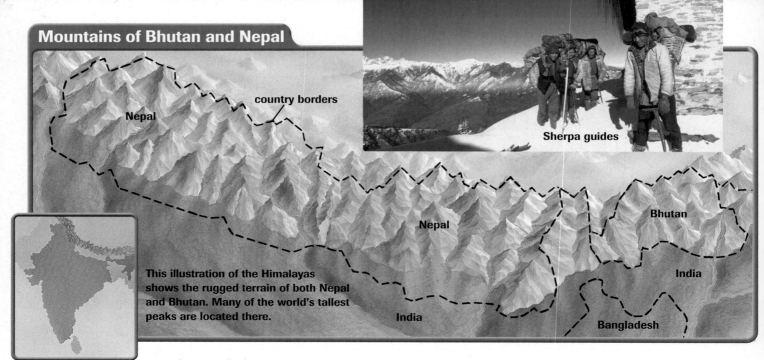

Mountains of Bhutan and Nepal

Nepal

country borders

Sherpa guides

Nepal

Bhutan

India

India

Bangladesh

This illustration of the Himalayas shows the rugged terrain of both Nepal and Bhutan. Many of the world's tallest peaks are located there.

HUMAN-ENVIRONMENT INTERACTION The Sherpa are known for their mountaineering skills and their ability to carry heavy loads at high altitudes.

Why might mountain climbers seek out the Sherpas as guides and porters?

damaged the environment, particularly on mountain slopes, where increased trash and pollution have been most noticeable.

Bhutan, which offers many of the same natural attractions as Nepal, has taken a different approach to tourism. Concerned about the impact of tourists on national life, Bhutan regulates the tourist industry. It allows only limited numbers of visitors and keeps some areas of the country off-limits. Even so, tourism is providing increasing revenues to Bhutan and offers significant economic potential for the future.

Rich Cultural Traditions

Visitors to Nepal and Bhutan come not only for the spectacular mountain scenery but also for a glimpse of the rich cultural traditions of the Himalayan people.

A MIX OF PEOPLES Various ethnic groups inhabit the Himalayan region. In Nepal, the majority of the people are Indo-Nepalese Hindus whose ancestors came from India many centuries ago. These groups speak Nepali, a variation of Sanskrit, an ancient Indo-Aryan language. Nepal also has a number of groups of Tibetan ancestry. Among them are the **Sherpas.** These people from the high Himalayas are the traditional mountain guides of the Everest region.

The main ethnic group in Bhutan is the Bhote, who also trace their origins to Tibet. Most Bhotes live in two-story houses made of wood and stone. The families live on the second floor, while the first floor is reserved for livestock. Bhutan also has a sizable Nepalese minority in the southern lowlands. The Nepalese have preserved their language and customs, even though the government of Bhutan has tried to assimilate them into national life.

RELIGIOUS CUSTOMS Religion is a powerful force in both Nepal and Bhutan. Although the great majority of Nepalese are Hindus, Buddhism also has deep roots in Nepal. The founder of Buddhism, **Siddhartha Gautama,** known as the Buddha, was born on the borders of present-day

BACKGROUND Another Nepalese people, the Gurkhas from the valleys west of Kathmandu, are known as fierce fighters. They have been recruited since the mid-19th century to serve in the British and Indian armies.

Nepal and India in the sixth century B.C. Buddhist teachings initially took hold in Nepal but were later replaced by Hinduism when Hindu rulers came to power. Today, Hindu practices still show traces of Buddhist influence.

Buddhism is the official religion of Bhutan. The people practice a Tibetan style of Buddhism, which includes the use of **mandalas**—geometric designs that are symbols of the universe and aid in meditation. Early communities in Bhutan were organized around large fortress-monasteries, which are still found in many parts of the country. Also scattered around the countryside are small shrines that were built to house sacred relics and are excellent examples of Buddhist architecture.

REGION Masked dancers perform a traditional Tibetan ceremony during a religious festival in Bhutan.

THE ARTS AND RECREATION Folk art and festivals are an important feature of Himalayan culture. Artisans make beautiful metal bells, swords, and jewelry, and carve intricate wooden sculptures. They also weave colorful textiles from silk, cotton, and wool. During festivals in Nepal and Bhutan, musicians play traditional songs on flutes, drums, and long brass horns. At the same time, people in elaborate costumes perform dances based on religious stories. Bhutan is also famous for its archery competitions. This tradition goes back to ancient times, when Bhutanese warriors were known as the finest archers in the Himalayas. **B**

In this section, you read about life in South Asia's mountainous north. Next, you will learn about life in the southern islands.

Seeing Patterns
B Why might archery have been a particularly useful military option in Bhutan?

SECTION 3 Assessment

① Places & Terms

Identify these terms and explain their importance in the region.

• constitutional monarchy
• Sherpa
• Siddhartha Gautama
• mandala

② Taking Notes

REGION Review the notes you took for this section.

Nepal and Bhutan — South Asia

• What effect does the mountainous terrain have on the economies of Nepal and Bhutan?
• What religions are practiced in Nepal and Bhutan?

③ Main Ideas

a. What kind of government do Nepal and Bhutan have today?

b. How is tourism affecting the economies of these two countries?

c. What are some of the important features of Himalayan culture?

④ Geographic Thinking

Drawing Conclusions How has the physical geography of Nepal and Bhutan affected their development? **Think about:**

• the mountainous landscape
• their landlocked location

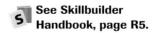
See Skillbuilder Handbook, page R5.

EXPLORING LOCAL GEOGRAPHY Review the information about arts and recreation on this page. Then do research about a festival, athletic competition, or craft that is unique to your city, state, or region. Write a **letter** to a friend in another city, state, or country describing the event or product.

SOUTH ASIA

Sri Lanka and the Maldives

Main Ideas
• Sri Lanka and the Maldives are island countries with strong connections to the South Asian subcontinent.
• Sri Lanka and the Maldives face difficult challenges that affect their political and economic development.

Places & Terms
Sinhalese

Tamils

sultan

CONNECT TO THE ISSUES
TERRITORIAL DISPUTE Tamil rebels in Sri Lanka are fighting to establish an independent state.

A HUMAN PERSPECTIVE For centuries, Sri Lanka and the Maldives have been ports of call for ships from around the world. The Greeks, Romans, Persians, Chinese, and Arabs all knew about these islands. Arab traders referred to Sri Lanka as Serendib, and they called the Maldives the "Money Isles" for their abundance of cowrie shells—seashells first used in ancient times as currency. Later, European traders came for spices, ivory, pearls, and other goods. Throughout history, visitors have been drawn to these islands in the Indian Ocean. The explorer Marco Polo referred to the Maldives as "one of the wonders of the world."

History of the Islands

Because the islands are close to India, Sri Lanka and the Maldives have strong ties to the Indian subcontinent. Even so, each country has its own distinct history.

SETTLEMENT OF SRI LANKA In the sixth century B.C., people from the northern plains of India crossed the narrow strait separating the subcontinent from Sri Lanka. They came to be known as the **Sinhalese.** They absorbed the island's native inhabitants and created an advanced civilization on Sri Lanka. They adopted Buddhism and built sophisticated irrigation systems that allowed farming on land that was dry. In the fourth century A.D., another group of Indians began to arrive. These were the **Tamils**—Dravidian Hindus from southern India. The Tamils brought a different culture and language to Sri Lanka. They settled the northern end of the island, while the Sinhalese moved farther south.

Europeans began to colonize Sri Lanka in the 16th century. First came the Portuguese, followed by the Dutch. The British took control of the island—which they called Ceylon—in 1796 and ruled until its independence in 1948. In 1972, Ceylon changed its name to Sri Lanka and became a republic.

After independence, tensions grew between the Sinhalese and Tamil populations. The minority Tamils (about 18 percent of the population) claimed discrimination at the hands of the Sinhalese majority (about 74 percent). They began to call for an independent state to be called *Tamil Eelam* (Precious Land of the Tamils). In the 1980s, civil war broke out between the government and the rebels, who were called the Tamil Tigers. Violence has claimed many lives since then and continues to disrupt Sri Lankan life.

A MUSLIM STATE IN THE MALDIVES The Maldives were settled by Buddhists and Hindus from Sri Lanka and India some time around

SUNSHINE STATE STANDARDS
Key Standard SS.B.2.4.1 The student understands how social, cultural, economic, and environmental factors contribute to the dynamic nature of regions.

Other Standards SS.A.3.4.3

FCAT LA.A.1.4.2 Reading: Strategies

PLACE The Tamil Tigers are anti-government rebels in Sri Lanka. This is their emblem. **Why might a tiger have been chosen for this militant group's name?**

the sixth century B.C. Later, Arab traders made frequent visits. By the 12th century, the population had converted to Islam. Six dynasties of Muslim rulers, or **sultans,** governed the Maldives after that, despite periods of foreign intervention. In 1968, the Maldives declared itself a republic, headed by an elected president. With its 1,200 islands comprising a land area of just 115 square miles and its population of only about 300,000 people, the Maldives is one of the world's smallest independent countries.

Life in the Islands

As in the rest of South Asia, religion and ethnicity are key factors in the social and cultural life of Sri Lanka and the Maldives.

ETHNIC MOSAIC OF THE ISLANDS Sri Lanka is a diverse mix of ethnic and religious groups. Sinhalese Buddhists make up nearly 75 percent of the population, while Tamil Hindus make up about 18 percent. Around 7 percent of the people are Muslims, who are descended from the early Arab traders. There is also a small community of Christians of mixed European descent, known as Burghers. ◀️🅐

Most Sinhalese live in the southern, western, and central parts of the country. The Tamils are concentrated in the northern Jaffna Peninsula, where much of the fighting has taken place. Another group of Tamils lives in the central highlands. These people are the descendants of Indian migrants who came to work on British plantations in the 19th century. Muslims live mainly in the eastern lowlands. The capital city, Colombo, is a busy urban center. But most Sri Lankans continue to live in smaller towns and villages scattered across the country.

The population of the Maldives is also multi-ethnic. Most of the people are descended from the early Sinhalese and Dravidian inhabitants, who mixed with Arab, Southeast Asian, and Chinese traders over the centuries. The official language is Divehi, a language unique to the Maldives. Arabic, Hindi, and English are also commonly spoken.

CULTURAL LIFE IN SRI LANKA Religion plays a key role in the culture of Sri Lanka. Buddhist and Hindu temples, Muslim mosques, and Christian churches dot the landscape.

🌐 **Geographic Thinking** ←

Using the Atlas

🅐 ▶ Using the atlas on page 543, locate Sri Lanka and the continents of Africa and Asia. Why might this island have been visited by Arab traders during its history?

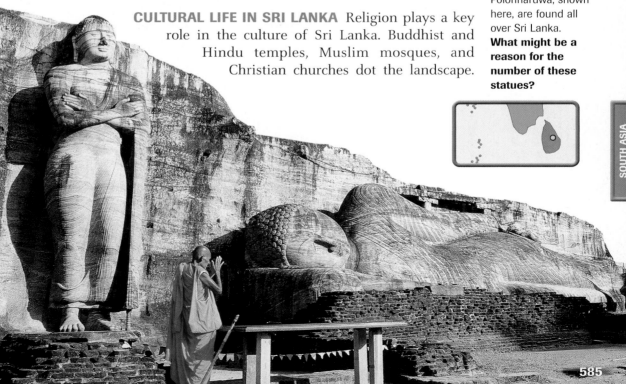

PLACE Large statues of Buddha, such as the 46-foot Sleeping Buddha of Polonnaruwa, shown here, are found all over Sri Lanka. **What might be a reason for the number of these statues?**

SOUTH ASIA

585

Art and literature are strongly influenced by those religious traditions. Folk dancing is a notable cultural tradition. The most famous style is *Kandyan* dancing, the national dance. The dances tell the stories of local kings and heroes and are performed at Buddhist festivals. During the yearly *Perahera* festival, dancers dressed in glittering silver headpieces and jewelry leap and spin in complex, acrobatic movements.

CULTURAL LIFE IN THE MALDIVES Muslim customs have a strong influence on the culture of the Maldives. Islam is the state religion, and no other religions are allowed. One of the highlights of Maldivian culture is *bodu beru* ("big drum") music and dance based on drumming. In a *bodu beru* performance, dancers sway to the drumbeat with increasing intensity. This musical tradition has strong African influences.

Economic Activity in the Islands

Like small countries everywhere, the Maldives and Sri Lanka face tough economic challenges. Yet, each country has made good use of its resources to promote economic growth. Today, Sri Lanka has the highest per capita income in South Asia, and the Maldives is not far behind. **B**

ECONOMIC STRENGTHS Like most of South Asia's economies, the economy of Sri Lanka is based on agriculture—mainly rice farming. But unlike most other countries of the region, Sri Lanka has large areas devoted to plantation agriculture. These large farms produce crops such as tea, rubber, and coconuts for export. While this type of agriculture is

REGION Workers pick tea leaves on a plantation in Sri Lanka.

Geographic Thinking

Making Comparisons

B What might be some of the economic challenges facing small developing countries such as Sri Lanka and the Maldives?

World Tea Production

SOURCE: *Goode's World Atlas, 2000*

(Bar chart showing percentages with y-axis from 0% to 30% for: India, China, Sri Lanka, Kenya, Indonesia, Turkey, Japan, Iran, Other Asia, Other Africa, South America)

declining, Sri Lanka is still one of the world's leading tea-producing countries. Although manufacturing is increasing, other sectors of the Sri Lankan economy are less important. Overcutting has damaged the timber industry, and the fishing and mining industries are relatively small. One exception is gem mining. Sri Lanka is famous for its gemstones—including sapphires, rubies, and topaz.

The economy of the Maldives is different from the economies of the rest of South Asia. Farming is limited by a lack of land, and most food has to be imported. Fishing—for tuna, marlin, and sharks—was long the main economic activity. It still provides one-fourth of the jobs and a large share of the country's export earnings. But it has been replaced in importance by tourism. The islands' beautiful beaches, coral reefs, and impressive marine life draw visitors from around the world.

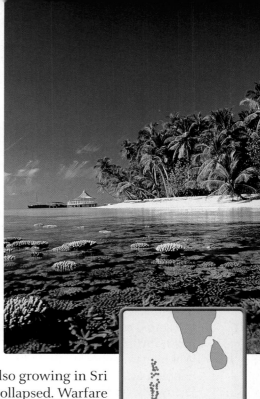

TOUGH CHALLENGES Until the 1980s, tourism was also growing in Sri Lanka. Then civil war began, and the tourist industry collapsed. Warfare has also disrupted other economic activities and damaged the country's infrastructure—its roads, bridges, power systems, and other services. Until peace returns to Sri Lanka, the economy is likely to struggle. While the Maldives is at peace, it faces a challenge of a different kind: global warming. The islands lie very low in the water, and any rise in sea level—caused by melting of the polar icecaps—could flood them completely. Scientists say this could happen by the end of the 21st century.

In this chapter, you read about modern life in South Asia. In the next chapter, you will read about issues facing South Asians.

LOCATION Tourist resorts in the Maldives are built only on previously uninhabited islands.
What might be a reason for locating the resorts on such islands?

Assessment

① Places & Terms
Identify these terms and explain their importance in the region.

- Sinhalese
- Tamils
- sultan

② Taking Notes
MOVEMENT Review the notes you took for this section.

- How were the islands of the Maldives settled?
- Where do the different ethnic groups in Sri Lanka live?

③ Main Ideas
a. What happened between the Sinhalese and the Tamils after Sri Lanka gained independence?

b. What are some of the aspects of cultural life in the Maldives?

c. What are some of the economic strengths of Sri Lanka and the Maldives?

④ Geographic Thinking
Seeing Patterns How do the Maldives's 1,200 islands affect its economy? **Think about:**

- fishing for food or sport
- the number of beaches

See Skillbuilder Handbook, page R8.

SOUTH ASIA

SEEING PATTERNS Review the information about tourism in the Maldives on this page. Do research on different activities for tourists and different places to visit in the country. Then create a **travel poster** advertising the Maldives as an ideal tourist destination.

Comparing Cultures

Musical Instruments

No one is exactly certain when or where music began to be made or what the first musical instrument was. But scholars believe that music has been part of all cultures, possibly even from earliest times. The first musical instrument may have been the human voice, which may have been used to mimic the sound of birds. Next, the human body was used to make rhythms, by clapping hands or stomping feet. When instruments began to be made, early musicians adapted available materials, such as wood and animal skins. Eventually, four basic types of instruments were developed: percussion, wind, string, and keyboard. Today, thousands of different instruments are played worldwide.

United Kingdom

India

Tanzania

Australia

SUNSHINE STATE STANDARDS
Key Standard SS.B.2.4.1 The student understands how social, cultural, economic, and environmental factors contribute to the dynamic nature of regions.
FCAT LA.A.2.2.7 Reading: Recognize Compare and Contrast

The bagpipe is a wind instrument that is associated with Scotland, although it is played in other countries. It consists of an animal skin or rubberized cloth bag fitted with one or more pipes that produce a continuous flow of sound when blown.

The drum is a percussion instrument from Africa that probably was made first from wood or stone. It is played by striking with hands or other objects. These drums are made of skins stretched over a frame. Also shown is another percussion instrument—the xylophone.

The didgeridoo is a wind instrument played by aboriginal people in Australia. Made of bamboo or a hollow sapling, it can be as long as five feet. It is generally painted and used in ritual ceremonies.

GeoActivity

FORMING A BAND

With a small group, research other musical instruments. Plan a band that includes at least one of each of the four types of instruments. Then create **a multimedia presentation.**

• Provide visuals of each instrument.

• Write a description of each instrument's sound.

• Make an audiotape that has the sound of each instrument and play it in class.

 RESEARCH LINKS CLASSZONE.COM

The sitar is a stringed instrument from India. It has a wooden body and is used mainly to play classical music. Anoushka Shankar, shown here with her sitar, is the daughter of famed sitarist Ravi Shankar, who brought the instrument to the world's attention with his playing in the 1960s.

GeoData

OTHER INSTRUMENTS

ASIA

• Empty conch shells with broken tips give off a loud sound when blown and have been used in ceremonies for centuries in many regions, including the islands of Polynesia.

EUROPE

• The organ is the oldest keyboard instrument and was found in ancient Greece more than 2,000 years ago. It gave birth to other keyboard instruments such as the harpsichord, clavichord, and piano.

THE AMERICAS

• Native American cultures have strongly emphasized the voice in making music.

AFRICA

• Wall paintings in 4,000-year-old tombs in Egypt show musicians playing lutes.

• Some African cultures still use a stone gong—a hanging stone that gives off a sound when struck.

Chapter 25 Assessment

VISUAL SUMMARY
HUMAN GEOGRAPHY OF SOUTH ASIA

Subregions of South Asia

○ India
- India is the largest country in South Asia and dominates the region.
- India is the world's largest democracy; Hinduism is its principal religion.

● Pakistan and Bangladesh
- Pakistan and Bangladesh were both eventually formed after the partition of India.
- Farming is the main source of people's livelihoods.
- Islam is the primary cultural force in those countries.

○ Nepal and Bhutan
- Nepal and Bhutan developed in relative isolation because of the Himalaya Mountains.
- Nepal has a religious mix of both Hindus and Buddhists, while Bhutan is a predominantly Buddhist country.

● Sri Lanka and the Maldives
- Sri Lanka contains a variety of ethnic and religious groups, including Sinhalese Buddhists, Tamil Hindus, and Muslims.
- Sri Lanka's economy is based on farming and gem mining, while the Maldives relies on fishing and tourism.

Reviewing Places & Terms

A. Briefly explain the importance of each of the following.

1. Mughal Empire
2. nonviolent resistance
3. caste system
4. partition
5. Kashmir
6. microcredit
7. Sherpa
8. mandala
9. Sinhalese
10. Tamils

B. Answer the questions about vocabulary in complete sentences.

11. How did the great Indian leader Mohandas Gandhi protest British control of India?
12. Over which territory have India and Pakistan fought several wars?
13. What financial aid do poor South Asian entrepreneurs seek?
14. How was the country of West and East Pakistan formed after Indian independence?
15. What did the Muslims establish in India during the 16th century?
16. What people arrived in Sri Lanka from southern India and occupied the northern portion of the island?
17. Who created an advanced civilization in Sri Lanka and built sophisticated irrigation systems?
18. Who guides mountain climbers in the Everest region?
19. What are geometric designs that are symbols of the universe and aid in meditation?
20. What is a Hindu system of social classes?

Main Ideas

India (pp. 567–572)

1. How did Britain gain control of India?
2. What are the major economic activities in India?
3. What are the major languages of India?

Pakistan and Bangladesh (pp. 573–579)

4. What are some of the characteristics of the Indus Valley civilization?
5. What manufactured products are produced in Pakistan and Bangladesh?
6. What type of literature is important in Pakistan and Bangladesh?

Nepal and Bhutan (pp. 580–583)

7. What are some of the groups of people that live in Nepal?
8. What are some important religious customs in Bhutan?

Sri Lanka and the Maldives (pp. 584–589)

9. What are the two major ethnic groups in Sri Lanka and where did they come from?
10. What are some of the challenges facing the economies of Sri Lanka and the Maldives?

Critical Thinking

1. Using Your Notes

Use your completed chart to answer these questions.

a. What role does agriculture play in the economies of the South Asian countries?

b. What are the major religions practiced in the region?

2. Geographic Themes

a. **HUMAN-ENVIRONMENT INTERACTION** How did the mountainous terrain and the landlocked location of Nepal and Bhutan affect their development?

b. **LOCATION** How do the landforms and location of the Maldives ensure that its economy is different from other South Asian countries?

3. Identifying Themes

What groups of people first populated the Indian subcontinent and eventually helped to populate all of South Asia? Which of the five themes apply to this situation?

4. Making Comparisons

How do Pakistan and Bangladesh differ in their practice of Islam?

5. Determining Cause and Effect

What are some of the reasons for the ongoing violence between the Tamils and the Sinhalese in Sri Lanka?

Additional Test Practice, pp. S1–S37

TEST PRACTICE
CLASSZONE.COM

Geographic Skills: Interpreting Maps

Languages of South Asia

Use the map at right to answer the following questions.

1. **LOCATION** How many major languages are spoken in South Asia?

2. **REGION** Which language group is the most commonly spoken?

3. **MOVEMENT** How might the number of languages in South Asia affect its developing economies?

GeoActivity

Choose a country in South Asia in which more than one language is spoken, and prepare a chart showing the number of people speaking each language. Use library references or the Internet for your research.

 INTERNET ACTIVITY

Use the links at **classzone.com** to do research on the people of one South Asian country. Look for such information as life expectancy, religions, ethnic groups, literacy rates, and per capita income.

Writing About Geography Write a report about your findings. Use standard grammar, spelling, sentence structure, and punctuation in your report. List the Web sites that you used as sources.

TODAY'S ISSUES
South Asia

SECTION 1
Population Explosion

SECTION 2
Living with Extreme Weather

CASESTUDY

TERRITORIAL DISPUTE

For more on these issues in South Asia . . .

 CURRENT EVENTS
CLASSZONE.COM

Kolkata is one of India's most densely populated cities.

GeoFocus

How can people and governments work together to solve problems?

Taking Notes In your notebook, copy a cause-effect chart like the one shown below for each issue. Then take notes on the causes and effects of some aspect of each issue.

	Causes	Effects
Issue 1: Population		
Issue 2: Extreme Weather		
Case Study: Territorial Dispute		

Population Explosion

How can South Asia's population growth be managed?

Main Ideas

- Explosive population growth in South Asia has contributed to social and economic ills in the region.
- Education is key to controlling population growth and improving the quality of life in South Asia.

Places & Terms

basic necessities

illiteracy

The Voyageur Experience in World Geography
India: Population and Resources

SUNSHINE STATE STANDARDS
Key Standard SS.B.2.4.5 The student knows how humans overcome "limits to growth" imposed by physical systems.

Other Standards SS.B.1.4.3

FCAT LA.A.1.4.2 Reading: Strategies

A HUMAN PERSPECTIVE On May 11, 2000, at 5:05 A.M., a baby girl was born in a New Delhi hospital. Her parents named her Astha, which means "faith" in the Hindi language. Ordinarily, Astha's birth would not have made news. After all, an estimated 42,000 babies are born in India every day—15,330,000 each year. Astha, however, was special. With this child's birth, the population of India officially hit 1 billion. It was the second country to reach a billion in population; China was the first.

Growing Pains

India's milestone was a mixed blessing. Its population at the beginning of the 21st century is growing so quickly that many of its citizens lack life's **basic necessities**—food, clothing, and shelter. The question for India, and for South Asia as a whole, is how to manage population growth so that economic development can continue.

POPULATION GROWS When India gained its independence from Britain in 1947, the population stood at 300 million. By 2000, the population had more than tripled. India's population is so large that even an annual growth rate of less than 2 percent is producing a population explosion. Unless that growth slows down, in 2045, India will be home to more than 1.5 billion people—all living in a land about one-third the size of the United States. India will be the most populous country in the world, surpassing China.

India is not alone in its skyrocketing population. In fact, of the 10 most populous countries in the world in 1998, three were located in South Asia: India, Pakistan, and Bangladesh. South Asia is home to 22 percent of the world's population. But these people live on less than 3 percent of the world's land area.

INADEQUATE RESOURCES As South Asia's population has increased, regional governments have found it more and more difficult to meet the needs of their people. Widespread poverty and **illiteracy,** the inability to read or

REGION The homeless poor are a common sight in many of India's large cities, such as Mumbai, pictured below. **What might be some ways in which the homeless can be helped?**

SOUTH ASIA

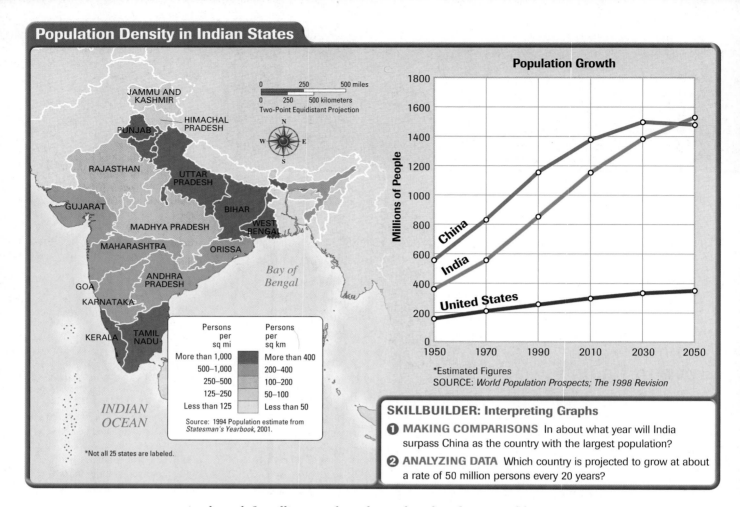

Population Density in Indian States

JAMMU AND KASHMIR
HIMACHAL PRADESH
PUNJAB
RAJASTHAN
UTTAR PRADESH
GUJARAT
BIHAR
MADHYA PRADESH
WEST BENGAL
MAHARASHTRA
ORISSA
GOA
ANDHRA PRADESH
KARNATAKA
KERALA
TAMIL NADU

Bay of Bengal

INDIAN OCEAN

0   250   500 miles
0   250   500 kilometers
Two-Point Equidistant Projection

Persons per sq mi	Persons per sq km
More than 1,000	More than 400
500–1,000	200–400
250–500	100–200
125–250	50–100
Less than 125	Less than 50

Source: 1994 Population estimate from *Statesman's Yearbook*, 2001.

*Not all 25 states are labeled.

Population Growth

China
India
United States

Millions of People: 0, 200, 400, 600, 800, 1000, 1200, 1400, 1600, 1800
Years: 1950, 1970, 1990, 2010, 2030, 2050

*Estimated Figures
SOURCE: *World Population Prospects; The 1998 Revision*

SKILLBUILDER: Interpreting Graphs

❶ MAKING COMPARISONS In about what year will India surpass China as the country with the largest population?

❷ ANALYZING DATA Which country is projected to grow at about a rate of 50 million persons every 20 years?

write, have left millions without hope that their lives would improve. Poor sanitation and the lack of health education have led to outbreaks of disease, which have overwhelmed the region's limited health care systems.

Officials estimate that in order to keep pace with population growth, India will have to do the following *every year:* build 127,000 new village schools, hire nearly 400,000 new teachers, construct 2.5 million new homes, create 4 million new jobs, and produce an additional 6 million tons of food.

Managing Population Growth

South Asia has struggled for decades to find solutions to its population explosion. But efforts have met with only limited success.

SMALLER FAMILIES Today, India spends much of its nearly $1 billion annual health-care budget encouraging Indians to have smaller families. "Let's have small families for a stronger India" is one of the slogans of the campaign. For many reasons, however, these programs have had only limited success. Indian women usually marry before age 18 and start having babies early. Also, for the very poor, children are a source of income. They can beg for money in the streets as early as their third birthday and can work the fields not too many years later. Ⓐ

For many Indians, children represent security in old age. The more children a family has, the more likely someone will be around to take care of the parents when they are elderly. Also, the infant mortality rate

Geographic Thinking

Seeing Patterns
Ⓐ How might smaller families affect India's economic development?

is very high in South Asia—around 75 per 1,000 live births compared to 7 per 1,000 in the United States. As a result, parents try to have many children to ensure that at least some will reach adulthood.

EDUCATION IS A KEY Many factors that affect population growth can be changed through education. However, South Asia's governments have a difficult task ahead of them because education funds are limited. For example, India spends less than $6 per pupil annually on primary and secondary education. (Only a small fraction of this sum is spent on girls.) By contrast, annual per pupil spending on education in the United States is $6,320—more than 1,000 times as much.

BACKGROUND
Statistics for 1997-1998 showed that about 85 percent of Indian boys aged 6 to 12 are in school, compared to about 70 percent of girls.

HUMAN-ENVIRONMENT INTERACTION The rural poor build settlements on unused land in many cities, such as these in Ahmadabad, India.
Why might the rural poor be attracted to urban areas?

Education is essential to break the cycle of poverty and provide South Asians with the means to raise their standard of living. It also helps to improve the status of females by giving them job opportunities outside the home. Better health education also can reduce the need for large families by ensuring that more babies reach adulthood. The future development of South Asia depends on the success of such efforts to control population growth.

In the next section, you will learn how the people of South Asia are coping with another problem—the region's extreme weather.

SECTION Assessment

1 Places & Terms

Explain the importance of each of the following terms and places.

- basic necessities
- illiteracy

2 Taking Notes

PLACE Review the notes you took for this section.

	Causes	Effects
Issue 1: Population		

- How much did India's population grow in the second half of the 20th century?
- If this growth rate continues, what will India's population be in 2045?

3 Main Ideas

a. Why is the size of India's population a problem?

b. How has the government of India addressed population issues?

c. Why have government programs had mixed success?

4 Geographic Thinking

Making Inferences How does the population density in India compare to that in the United States? **Think about:**

- population size
- territorial size

RESEARCH LINKS
CLASSZONE.COM

MAKING COMPARISONS Carry out further research focused on comparing 20th-century population growth in a city in India and one in the United States. Use the data that you gather to create a **line graph** that compares population growth in these two cities.

SOUTH ASIA

Reading a Population Pyramid

Every nation has a certain distribution of population by age group. India, for instance, has a young population; the majority of people are under the age of 30. To show how the population of a country is distributed by age, a population pyramid is a very useful tool.

THE LANGUAGE OF GRAPHS A **population pyramid** is a type of bar graph. It shows the number or percentage of people that fall into specific age groups. It may also compare the distribution of age groups by sex, ethnic group, or some other category. The population pyramid below shows the distribution of age groups by sex in India.

SUNSHINE STATE STANDARDS
Key Standard SS.B.1.4.1 The student uses a variety of maps, geographic technologies including geographic information systems (GIS) and satellite-produced imagery, and other advanced graphic representations to depict geographic problems.

FCAT LA.A.2.2.7 Reading: Recognize Compare and Contrast

Population of India, 2000

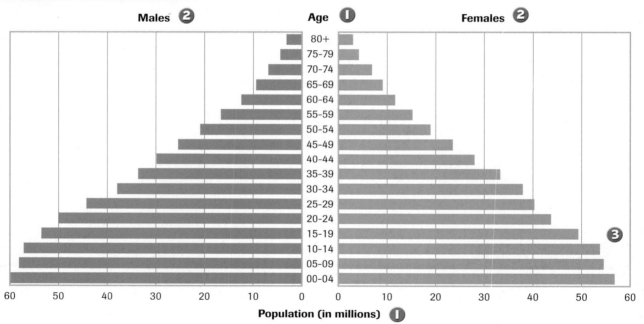

SOURCE: U.S. Census Bureau, International Data Base

❶ The horizontal axis shows population in millions. The vertical axis lists age groups.

❷ The left side of the pyramid shows the population distribution of males in India. The right side shows females.

❸ Notice that there is a steady drop in population as Indians reach their late teens. This indicates that the life expectancy of Indians is relatively short.

Map and Graph Skills Assessment

1. Analyzing Data
Find the bar on the pyramid that would be your age and sex. How many millions of persons fall into that group in India?

2. Making Comparisons
What age group is the largest? What is the largest age group by sex?

3. Making Inferences
What might be said about the male/female composition of the population of India?

Living with Extreme Weather

How do people cope with extreme weather?

Main Ideas
- South Asia experiences a yearly cycle of floods, often followed by drought.
- The extreme weather in South Asia leads to serious physical, economic, and political consequences.

Places & Terms

summer monsoon

winter monsoon

A HUMAN PERSPECTIVE In May 1996, a fierce tornado tore through northern Bangladesh, leaving more than 700 people dead and 30,000 injured. Winds reached speeds of 125 mph. Within 30 minutes, nearly 80 villages had been destroyed. In the town of Rampur, Reazuddin Ahmed and his family sought shelter behind a concrete wall. All the while, houses were tossed into the air around them. Babul Ahmed, Reazuddin's 10-year-old son, described his family's terror: "It was dust and wind everywhere. We prayed to God: 'Save us.'" The tornado that terrorized the family was not unusual. It was just one of many types of extreme weather that plague South Asia and make life both difficult and dangerous.

SUNSHINE STATE STANDARDS
Key Standard SS.B.2.4.1 The student understands how social, cultural, economic, and environmental factors contribute to the dynamic nature of regions.

Other Standards SS.B.1.4.1

FCAT LA.A.1.4.2 Reading: Strategies

The Monsoon Seasons

South Asia is home to an annual cycle of powerful, destructive weather, including the monsoon. The monsoon is a wind system, not a rainstorm. There are two monsoon seasons—the moist summer monsoon and the dry, cool winter monsoon. (The illustrations on the next page show the monsoon pattern in winter and summer.)

The **summer monsoon** is a wind system that blows from the southwest across the Indian Ocean toward South Asia from June through September. These winds stir up powerful storms that release vast amounts of rain and cause severe flooding.

The **winter monsoon** is a wind system that blows from the northeast across the Himalayas toward the sea from October through February. Unlike the summer monsoon, the winter winds carry little moisture. A drought can result if the summer monsoon has failed to bring normal levels of moisture. From March through May, there are no strong prevailing wind patterns.

Impact of the Monsoons

The monsoon winds shape the rhythms of life for South Asia's people and also affect relations between its countries.

PHYSICAL IMPACT The rains that accompany the summer monsoons are critical to the agriculture of

Farming Calendar in India

December · January · February · March · April · May · June · July · August · September · October · November

Harvesting

Cool Season (Winter Monsoon)

Hot Season

Wet Season (Summer Monsoon)

Planting

Inactive

Weeding

Inactive

SOURCE: India-Country Studies

SKILLBUILDER: Interpreting Graphics

❶ **ANALYZING DATA** During what season is there no agricultural activity?

❷ **MAKING INFERENCES** Which season is the most productive?

SOUTH ASIA

Summer and Winter Monsoons

Summer

Himalayas

heavy rain

wet winds from
the southwest

Indian
Ocean

Winter

Himalayas

little moisture

dry winds from
the northeast

Indian
Ocean

SKILLBUILDER: Interpreting Maps

❶ **MOVEMENT** What direction do the summer monsoon winds follow?

❷ **MOVEMENT** What direction do the winter monsoon winds follow?

South Asia, as the farming calendar on page 597 shows. They help nourish the rain forests, irrigate crops, and produce the floodwaters that deposit layers of rich sediment to replenish the soil. However, heavy flooding can also damage crops.

At the same time, the summer monsoon can cause tremendous devastation. Cyclones are common and deadly companions to the summer monsoon. (These storms are called hurricanes in North America.) Cyclones destroy farmland, wipe out villages, and cause massive flooding. Their fury is legendary. As you read in the Disasters! feature on pages 578–579, the 1970 cyclone that struck the southern coast of Bangladesh killed more than 300,000 people. It left hundreds of thousands homeless and destitute. In fact, because of the monsoons, Bangladesh was the site of some of the worst natural disasters of the 20th century.

The droughts that come with the dry winter monsoon bring their own problems. Lush landscapes can become arid wastelands almost overnight. These droughts—along with storms and floods—cause havoc for the people and economies of South Asia. ◭

ECONOMIC IMPACT The climate of South Asia makes agriculture difficult. Crops often disappear under summer floodwaters or wither in drought-parched soil. With so many mouths to feed, the countries of South Asia must buy what they cannot grow, and the threat of famine is ever present. But the people suffer from more than just crop failures. They may also lose their homes and families to weather-related catastrophes. Most people are too poor to rebuild their homes and lives, and

Geographic Thinking

Using the Atlas
◭ Use the maps on page 545 and this page. What country of South Asia seems least affected by the summer and winter monsoons?

governments often lack the necessary resources to provide significant help. However, the people of South Asia have taken some steps to prevent or lessen damage. These include building houses on stilts, erecting concrete cyclone shelters, and building dams to control floodwaters.

The region also receives international aid. Other governments and international agencies have lent billions of dollars to South Asian nations. But often this aid does not go far because of the frequency of disasters. Also, the aid burdens these countries with heavy debts. **B**

Geographic Thinking

Seeing Patterns

B How might the governments of South Asia use foreign aid?

POLITICAL TENSIONS Conditions caused by the weather patterns in South Asia have also caused political disputes. For instance, to bring water to the city of Kolkata, India constructed the Farakka dam across the Ganges at a point just before it enters Bangladesh. (See map on page 545.) Because India and Bangladesh share the Ganges, the dam left little water for drinking and irrigation in southern Bangladesh. Many Bangladeshi farmers lost farmland, and some illegally fled to India.

The two countries finally settled the dispute in 1997, when they signed a treaty giving each country specific water rights to the Ganges. Still, the dispute provided a graphic example of the role weather plays in both the politics and economics of South Asia. In the Case Study that follows, you will read about another political conflict—a territorial dispute between India and Pakistan.

REGION Dams on the Ganges divert water to irrigate Indian farms. But the dams decrease water downstream in Bangladesh. **Why might such a result cause conflict between India and Bangladesh?**

SECTION 2 Assessment

1 Places & Terms

Explain the importance of each of the following terms and places.

• summer monsoon

• winter monsoon

2 Taking Notes

PLACE Review the notes you took for this section.

	Causes	Effects
Issue 2: Extreme Weather		

• What are cyclones called in the United States?

• What kind of devastation can cyclones cause?

3 Main Ideas

a. Why do some people mistake monsoons, which are actually wind systems, for rainstorms?

b. What problems are associated with the winter monsoon?

c. What are some of the economic effects of monsoons?

4 Geographic Thinking

Identifying and Solving Problems How have attempts to address the challenges of South Asian weather patterns sometimes resulted in political disputes? How might disputes be avoided in the future?

Think about:

• the importance of water to the region

• who owns rivers

GeoActivity

ASKING GEOGRAPHIC QUESTIONS Do research on the issue of water distribution in one South Asian country. Then, come up with a geographic question about the issue, perhaps one considering how geography can be used to improve the situation. Answer the question and write a **newspaper article** about the issue.

SOUTH ASIA

CASE STUDY

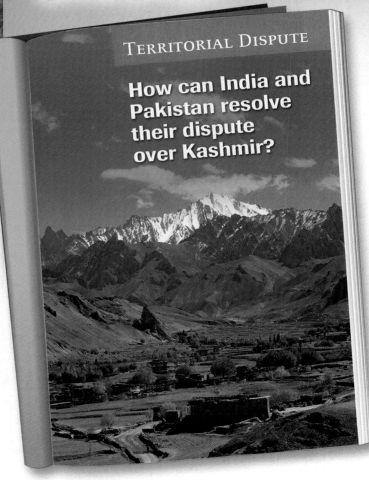

TERRITORIAL DISPUTE

How can India and Pakistan resolve their dispute over Kashmir?

Snowcapped mountains tower over a village in the valley of the Suru River in the disputed territory of Kashmir.

SUNSHINE STATE STANDARDS
Key Standard SS.B.2.4.3 The student understands how the allocation of control of the Earth's surface affects interactions between people in different regions.

Other Standards SS.A.1.4.3, B.1.4.5

FCAT LA.A.2.4.8 Reading: Synthesize and Conclude

Kashmir is a territory of towering mountains, dense forests, and fertile river valleys. It is strategically located at the foot of the Himalayas and is surrounded by India, Pakistan, and China. Since 1947, India and Pakistan have fought to control this territory of 12 million people. The territorial dispute has caused three Indo-Pakistani wars and, in just the last decade alone, cost up to 75,000 lives. It poses a threat to the political stability of South Asia and the economic well-being of the countries involved. And, because both India and Pakistan have nuclear weapons, the Kashmir conflict has the potential to lead to nuclear war.

A Controversy Over Territory

In 1947, the British government formally ended its colonial rule over the Indian subcontinent after 90 years. It partitioned, or divided, the subcontinent into two independent countries. India had a predominantly Hindu population. Pakistan was mostly Muslim. Britain gave each Indian state the choice of joining either country or remaining independent. Muslim states joined with Pakistan, while Hindu states remained part of India. Kashmir, however, had a unique problem.

POLITICS AND RELIGION Kashmir was mainly Muslim, but its leader, the Maharajah of Kashmir, was a Hindu. Faced with a difficult decision, the maharajah tried to keep Kashmir independent. But the plan failed. The maharajah then ceded Kashmir to India in 1947, but Pakistani soldiers invaded Kashmir. After a year's fighting, India still controlled much of the territory. Since then, India and Pakistan have fought two

1999
Indian and Pakistani military clash at cease-fire line.

1972
Cease-fire agreement signed by India and Pakistan.

1974
India explodes its first nuclear device.

1998
Pakistan begins nuclear testing.

1940 KASHMIR CONFLICT 1960 1970 1980 1990 2000

1947
India and Pakistan gain independence.

1948
Year-long **Indo-Pakistani war** over Kashmir ends.

1965
Second Indo-Pakistani war is fought.

1971
India and Pakistan fight again over Kashmir.

600 CHAPTER 26

more wars, in 1965 and in 1971. Although a cease-fire was signed in 1972, the situation remains unresolved. As you can see on the map below, India and Pakistan each control part of the disputed territory. Even China controls a portion, having seized a remote northern mountain area in 1962.

A QUESTION OF ECONOMICS There's more to this conflict than just politics and religion. The Indus River flows through Kashmir, and many of its tributaries originate in the territory. The Indus is a critical source of drinking and irrigation water for all of Pakistan. As a result, the Pakistanis are unwilling to let India control such a vital resource. Kashmir has become a strategic prize that neither country is willing to give up.

A Nuclear Nightmare

SEE
PRIMARY SOURCE B

In 1998, India and Pakistan each tested nuclear weapons. The rest of the world was horrified by the thought that the 50-year-old dispute over Kashmir might finally end with vast areas of South Asia destroyed by nuclear bombs. After the tests, both nations vowed to seek a political solution to the conflict. But the possibility of a nuclear war has made the dispute even more dangerous. Despite frequent cease-fires, the border clashes have continued. Also, Pakistan is supporting Muslims in Kashmir who have been fighting Indian rule since the late 1980s.

SEE
PRIMARY SOURCE A

A QUESTION OF PRIORITIES Both India and Pakistan have large populations and widespread poverty. The money that they have spent on troops, arms, and nuclear programs might have been used to educate millions of children and to address many social problems.

SEE
PRIMARY SOURCE E

Resolving the status of Kashmir would offer the people of India, Pakistan, and Kashmir the peace they need to begin improving the quality of their lives. It would also reduce political tensions in the region. The Case Study Project and primary sources that follow will help you to explore the Kashmir question.

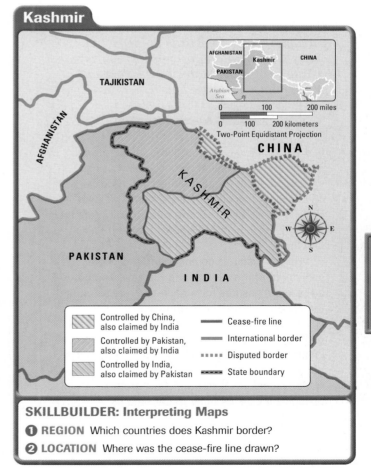

Kashmir

Legend:
- Controlled by China, also claimed by India
- Controlled by Pakistan, also claimed by India
- Controlled by India, also claimed by Pakistan
- Cease-fire line
- International border
- Disputed border
- State boundary

0   100   200 miles
0   100   200 kilometers
Two-Point Equidistant Projection

SKILLBUILDER: Interpreting Maps

❶ **REGION** Which countries does Kashmir border?

❷ **LOCATION** Where was the cease-fire line drawn?

SOUTH ASIA

CASESTUDY

PROJECT

A Newspaper Feature

Primary sources A, B, C, D, and E offer different views of the dispute over Kashmir. Use these resources along with your own research to write a newspaper feature on how the people of Kashmir, India, and Pakistan have suffered in this conflict. Include their own words.

RESEARCH LINKS
CLASSZONE.COM

Suggested Steps

1. Divide into small groups representing ordinary Kashmiris (such as women, farmers, and rebel soldiers), as well as Indian and Pakistani officials or soldiers. Then begin gathering personal accounts about the conflict from newspapers, magazines, and Internet sites.

2. Search for visuals—illustrations, maps, photographs, political cartoons, charts, and graphs—that help illustrate the points you are making.

3. When everyone in the class has collected enough material, work together to plan the feature story.

4. When you have finished planning, prepare the feature.

5. Share your project with other groups at your school or in your community.

Materials and Supplies

- Reference books, newspapers, and magazines
- Computer with Internet access and printer

Government Document *The Ministry of Foreign Affairs of Pakistan published this policy statement on Kashmir in 1999, after a visit to the United States by the* **Pakistani prime minister, Nawaz Sharif.**

In order to find an early and just solution to the 50-year old . . . Kashmir dispute, Pakistan has welcomed offers of good offices and third-party mediation. It has encouraged the international community to play an active role and facilitate the peaceful settlement of disputes between Pakistan and India.

While Pakistan is committed to a peaceful settlement of the Jammu and Kashmir dispute, adequate measures have been taken to safeguard the country's territorial integrity and national sovereignty. Pakistan will continue to extend full political, diplomatic and moral support to the legitimate Kashmiri struggle for their right to self-determination as enshrined in the relevant United Nations resolutions. In the context of the bilateral dialogue, it calls on India to translate its commitments into reality.

PRIMARY SOURCE B

Government Policy Declaration *At a state dinner in India for President Bill Clinton in March 2000,* **Indian President Kocheril Raman Narayanan** *warned that India would fight to protect its interests in Kashmir.*

It has been suggested that the Indian subcontinent is the most dangerous place in the world today, and Kashmir is a nuclear flashpoint. These alarmist descriptions will only encourage those who want to break the peace and indulge in terrorism and violence. The danger is not from us who have declared solemnly that we will not be the first to use nuclear weapons, but rather it is from those who refuse to make any such commitment.

We are publicly committed to the abolition of nuclear weapons together with other nuclear powers who possess them in awesome stockpiles capable of destroying the world many times over. India does not threaten any other country and will not engage in an arms race, but India will maintain a minimum credible nuclear deterrent—no more, no less—for her own security.

Political Speech *Mehbooba Mufti is a leader of the Jammu and Kashmir People's Democratic Party, a political party in Kashmir. In 1999, she spoke about the conflict and her hope that the dispute will be peacefully resolved.*

Everything has changed, mostly for the worse. Take just the physical destruction of whatever we had, the schools, the colleges, the roads, the bridges, the buildings, everything we had for the last 50 years, that has been more or less destroyed. We used to have a very good education system, with very good teachers, but now that has gone. . . .

I think Kashmir finally has to become a bridge between India and Pakistan. Finally. Maybe not today, maybe not tomorrow, but after some years, it is finally going to become a bridge. Have an open relationship. It's a dream!

Personal Story *Kashmiri native Mohammed Aziz lives in Kargil, a city on the border between the Pakistani- and Indian-controlled regions of Kashmir. In 1999, he described how the conflict had affected his hometown.*

We never know when the shell will come. . . . For the last three years, no one sleeps well there. Whoever flees leaves everything there. He takes nothing with him. The cattle are left on their own. Nobody cares for them, so we don't know what happens to them. . . .

Before, tourism was OK. Before the shelling there used to be 25 hotels, but now I don't think any hotel is open. We can't calculate the damage. . . .

The children's education is stopped, and whoever is ill dies because there is no medication nor anyone to care for them. Whoever resides in Kargil, does so at his own risk.

Political Cartoon *This 1998 political cartoon shows how the development of nuclear weapons by India and Pakistan has caused economic suffering among the people of both countries.*

PROJECT CheckList

Have I . . .

✓ fully researched my topic?

✓ located primary source quotations to tell my story?

✓ taken into account both sides of the issue?

✓ arranged the quotations so that they tell a coherent, interesting story?

✓ created informative visuals that make my story clear and interesting?

VISUAL SUMMARY
TODAY'S ISSUES IN SOUTH ASIA

Economics

Population Explosion
- Though only about one-third the size of the United States, India has over three times as many people.
- India's government has taken steps to control population growth but has had only mixed success.
- Many parents continue to have large numbers of children because of India's high infant mortality rates, the extra income brought in by children, and the need for caregivers as parents age.

Environment

Living with Extreme Weather
- The physical damage caused by extreme weather patterns in South Asia, such as cyclones, can be devastating to the region's people.
- The impact of extreme weather is not limited to physical damage. These forces can also disrupt the economy and cause serious political tensions.

Government

Case Study: Territorial Dispute
- Kashmir is a strategically located territory, surrounded by Pakistan, India, and China.
- India and Pakistan have fought three wars over this territory since 1947.
- Money spent by India and Pakistan for armaments, including nuclear weapons, has not been available to help improve the lives of the people of these countries.

Reviewing Places & Terms

A. Briefly explain the importance of each of the following.

1. basic necessities
2. illiteracy
3. summer monsoon
4. winter monsoon

B. Answer the questions about vocabulary in complete sentences.

5. Which winds stir up powerful storms in South Asia that release vast amounts of rain and cause severe flooding?
6. Which winds blow from the southwest across the Indian Ocean toward South Asia from June through September?
7. Food, shelter, and clothing are all examples of what?
8. Which winds blow from the northeast across the Himalayas from October through February?
9. What is the term for the inability to read or write?
10. What was the Indian government finding difficult to provide for its people?

Main Ideas

Population Growth (pp. 593–596)

1. Currently, about how many babies are born in India every day? Annually?
2. Why might the lack of basic necessities in a region concern demographers—people who study population?
3. Why might a high rate of infant mortality affect the size of families?
4. What percentage of the world's population is found in South Asia?
5. How would education play an important role in slowing population growth?

Living with Extreme Weather (pp. 597–599)

6. What are South Asia's two monsoon seasons? How do they differ?
7. When do these wind seasons occur?
8. What are some of the precautions that people in South Asia have taken to lessen the damage caused by cyclones?
9. What type of international aid have the countries of South Asia received?
10. What political tensions have resulted from the effects of extreme weather?

Case Study: Territorial Dispute over Kashmir (pp. 600–603)

11. Where is Kashmir located?
12. What countries have fought three wars over control of Kashmir?
13. When and why did the dispute over Kashmir begin?
14. Why are world leaders particularly concerned about the dispute?
15. What might happen if the dispute were resolved?

Critical Thinking

1. Using Your Notes

Use your completed chart to answer these questions.

	Causes	Effects
Issue 1: Population		
Issue 2: Extreme Weather		

a. Why might parents in India want a large family?

b. Why is Kashmir economically important to Pakistan?

2. Geographic Thinking

a. **REGION** How is the religious make-up of Kashmir related to conflict over the territory?

b. **MOVEMENT** Why might people in India and the other heavily populated countries in South Asia move to other parts of the world?

3. Identifying Themes

Why is Bangladesh especially vulnerable to the cyclones that occasionally devastate the region? Which of the five themes applies to this situation?

4. Making Comparisons

Why might India and Bangladesh fear the weather that can arrive during the summer?

5. Determining Cause and Effect

How might the dispute over Kashmir affect the social and educational programs in the region?

Additional Test Practice, pp. S1–S37

TEST PRACTICE
CLASSZONE.COM

Geographic Skills: Interpreting Graphs

Ethnic Indian Population Outside of India

Use the graph at right to answer the following questions.

1. **PLACE** On what continent outside of South Asia do most Indians live?

2. **PLACE** About how many Indians live in South America?

3. **LOCATION** Why do you think most ethnic Indians living outside of India live in South Asian countries?

GeoActivity

Carry out research on people from India who live in the United States. Create a table of the five cities with the largest populations of people from India.

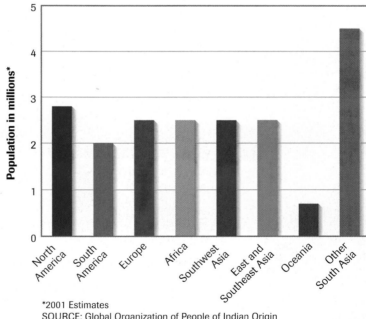

*2001 Estimates
SOURCE: Global Organization of People of Indian Origin

INTERNET ACTIVITY

Use the links at **classzone.com** to continue research on population growth in India. Focus on how the limited availability of basic necessities has affected the daily life of the country's people.

Creating a Multimedia Presentation Use your research to create an electronic presentation. Combine charts, maps, images, objects, and written accounts to provide your audience with a picture of daily life in India.

Unit 9

East Asia

East Asia is made up of a vast mainland area and a number of important islands off the eastern coast.

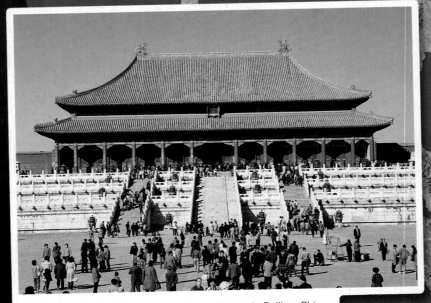

PLACE The Forbidden City is a walled enclosure in Beijing, China. Inside is a complex of palaces where 24 emperors ruled. Once closed to the public, it is now a museum and tourist attraction.

PLACE East Asia includes huge mountains and large deserts.

LOCATION The region is called "East Asia" because it is on the eastern edge of the Asian continent, bordered by the Pacific Ocean to the east, Russia to the north, and the countries of south and southeast Asia to the south.

REGION This area is bordered by a number of bodies of water, including the Pacific Ocean, the Sea of Japan, the East China Sea, and the South China Sea.

For more information on East Asia . . .

RESEARCH LINKS
CLASSZONE.COM

LOCATION Mount Fuji, the highest peak in Japan at 12,388 feet, is a volcano that last erupted in 1707. It is considered a sacred mountain.

HUMAN–ENVIRONMENT INTERACTION
The traditional pagoda, or temple, sits amidst the bustle of economic activity in the city center of Seoul, South Korea.

EAST ASIA

607

Unit PREVIEW 9

Today's Issues in East Asia

Today, East Asia faces the issues previewed here. As you read Chapters 27 and 28, you will learn helpful background information. You will study the issues themselves in Chapter 29.

In a small group, answer the questions below. Then participate in a class discussion of your answers.

Exploring the Issues

1. **PHYSICAL FORCES** What might be some of the effects of earthquakes and volcanoes on daily life in the region? How might the effects be similar or different in an urban and a rural area?

2. **TRADE** What are some items you or your family have bought that were made in East Asia?

3. **POPULATION** Parts of East Asia are very crowded. What might be some of the advantages and challenges of living around so many people?

For more on these issues in East Asia . . .

CURRENT EVENTS
CLASSZONE.COM

PHYSICAL FORCES

How might people in East Asia prepare for earthquakes and volcanoes?

A bus teeters on the edge of a highway torn apart by an earthquake in Kobe, Japan, in 1995.

What are some benefits of global trade?

Hong Kong is a thriving center of trade and economic activity. Once a colony of Britain, it is now a part of China. Its wealth and trading expertise are helping China compete with leading industrial nations.

CASESTUDY

What pressures does population put on the environment?

Subway attendants in Tokyo push people into crowded subway trains. Japan has a large number of people living on a small amount of land.

POPULATION

EAST ASIA

Patterns of Physical Geography

Use the Unit Atlas to add to your knowledge of East Asia. As you look at the maps and charts, notice geographic patterns and specific details about the region. For example, the charts on pages 610–611 give details about the rivers and mountains of East Asia.

After studying the pictures, graphs, and physical map on these two pages, jot down in your notebook the answers to the following questions.

Making Comparisons

1. What three main river systems run from west to east in China?

2. Which of the bodies of water surrounding Japan is the largest?

3. Compare East Asia's size and population to those of the United States. Based on that data, how might the population densities of the two compare?

For updated statistics on East Asia . . .

DATA UPDATE
CLASSZONE.COM

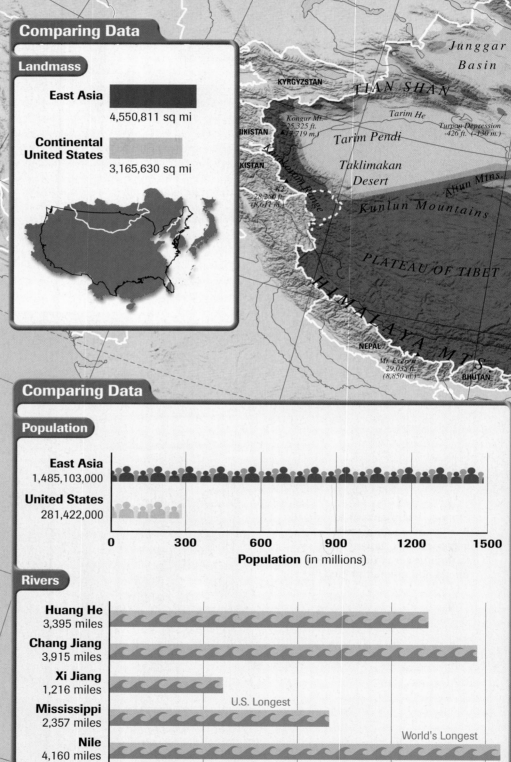

KAZAKHSTAN

Junggar Basin

KYRGYZSTAN

TIAN SHAN

Kongur Mt.
25,325 ft.
(7,719 m.)

Tarim He

Turpan Depression
-426 ft. (-130 m.)

IKISTAN

Tarim Pendi

KISTAN

Taklimakan Desert

Altun Mtns.

Karakoram Range

K2
28,250 ft.
(8,611 m.)

Kunlun Mountains

PLATEAU OF TIBET

HIMALAYA MTS.

NEPAL

Mt. Everest
29,035 ft.
(8,850 m.)

BHUTAN

Comparing Data

Landmass

East Asia
4,550,811 sq mi

Continental United States
3,165,630 sq mi

Comparing Data

Population

East Asia
1,485,103,000

United States
281,422,000

| 0 | 300 | 600 | 900 | 1200 | 1500 |

Population (in millions)

Rivers

Huang He
3,395 miles

Chang Jiang
3,915 miles

Xi Jiang
1,216 miles

Mississippi
2,357 miles
U.S. Longest

Nile
4,160 miles
World's Longest

| 0 | 1000 | 2000 | 3000 | 4000 |

Length (in miles)

SUNSHINE STATE STANDARDS
Key Standard SS.B.1.4.1 The student uses a variety of maps, geographic technologies including geographic information systems (GIS) and satellite-produced imagery, and other advanced graphic representations to depict geographic problems.
Other Standards SS.A.2.4.8, B.1.4.4, B.2.4.1
FCAT LA.A.2.2.7 Reading: Recognize Compare and Contrast

RUSSIA

Sakhalin I.

Hokkaido

MONGOLIA

ALTAI MTS.

MONGOLIAN PLATEAU

G O B I

Great Khingan Mountains

Amur R.

Songhua R.

Liao He

Manchurian Plain

Sea of Japan

Honshu

Mt. Fuji
12,388 ft.
(3,776 m.)

JAPAN

Huang He (Yellow R.)

Mu Us Desert

Yalu Jiang

NORTH KOREA

Korea Bay

Bo Hai

SOUTH KOREA

Cheju I.

Korea Strait

Shikoku

Kyushu

Wei He

Qinling Shandi

CHINA

Huang He (Yellow R.)

Grand Canal

North China Plain

Yellow Sea

PACIFIC OCEAN

Chang Jiang (Yangtze R.)

Gongga Shan
24,790 ft.
(7,556 m.)

East China Sea

Dongting Hu

Poyang Hu

Ryukyu Islands

Mekong R.

Salween R.

Xi Jiang (West R.)

Taiwan Strait

TAIWAN

MYANMAR

VIETNAM

LAOS

THAILAND

Gulf of Tonkin

Hainan

South China Sea

Luzon Strait

PHILIPPINES

Elevation	
13,100 ft.	(4,000 m.)
6,600 ft.	(2,000 m.)
1,600 ft.	(500 m.)
650 ft.	(200 m.)
0 ft.	(0 m.)
Below sea level	
▲ Mountain peak	

0   250   500 miles
0   250   500 kilometers
Two–Point Equidistant Projection

EAST ASIA

Comparing Data

Mountains

World's Tallest **Mount Everest**	U.S. Tallest **Mount McKinley**	**Mount Kongur**	**Mount Paektu**	**Mount Fuji**
Nepal-Tibet	United States	China	Korea	Japan
29,035 feet	20,320 feet	25,325 feet	9,022 feet	12,388 feet

Patterns of Human Geography

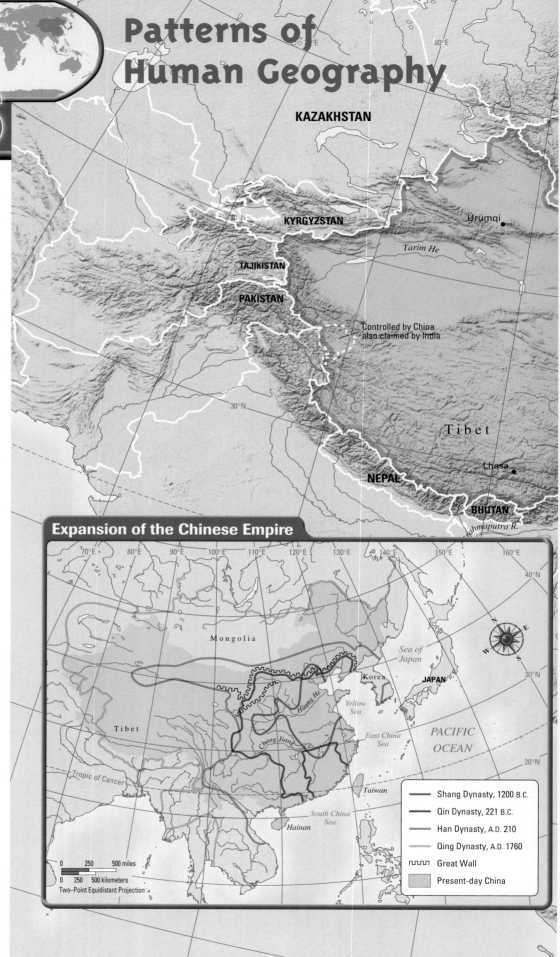

KAZAKHSTAN

KYRGYZSTAN

TAJIKISTAN

PAKISTAN

Ürümqi

Tarim He

Controlled by China also claimed by India

70°N

40°N

30°N

T i b e t

Lhasa

NEPAL

BHUTAN

Brahmaputra R.

80°E

Over the course of centuries, the political map of East Asia has changed. The Chinese empire expanded over thousands of years, absorbing much of the region. Study the historical and political maps of East Asia on these two pages. In your notebook, answer these questions.

Making Comparisons

1. What differences do you notice when you compare the historical map of the Chinese empire to the map of East Asia today?

2. What are some of the similarities between the historical map and the contemporary map of East Asia?

3. What countries in the region used to be a part of the Chinese empire but are now independent? Which country in the region was never a part of the empire?

Expansion of the Chinese Empire

70°E 80°E 90°E 100°E 110°E 120°E 130°E 140°E 150°E 160°E

40°N

30°N

20°N

Mongolia

Sea of Japan

Korea

JAPAN

Huang He

Yellow Sea

East China Sea

PACIFIC OCEAN

Tibet

Chang Jiang

Tropic of Cancer

Taiwan

South China Sea

Hainan

0   250   500 miles
0   250   500 kilometers
Two–Point Equidistant Projection

	Shang Dynasty, 1200 B.C.
	Qin Dynasty, 221 B.C.
	Han Dynasty, A.D. 210
	Qing Dynasty, A.D. 1760
⊓⊓⊓⊓	Great Wall
	Present-day China

Sakhalin I.

RUSSIA

Amur R.

M a n c h u r i a

Songhua R.

Ulaanbaatar ⊛

MONGOLIA

Harbin

Changchun

Liao He

Shenyang

Yalu Jiang

Hokkaido

• Sapporo

Sea of Japan

Honshu

JAPAN

Tokyo ⊛

Nagoya • • Yokoha

NORTH
KOREA

⊛ Pyongyang

Huang He (Yellow R.)   Great Wall

⊛ Beijing

Tianjin

Bo Hai

Korea
Bay

⊛ Seoul
SOUTH
KOREA
Pusan

Kyoto •
• Osaka
Hiroshima •

Fukuoka •

Great Wall

Huang He (Yellow R.)

Grand Canal

Yellow
Sea

Cheju I.

Korea Strait

Shikoku

Kyushu

*Qinghai
Hu*

• Lanzhou

Wei He

Xi'an •

CHINA

Chengdu •

Chang Jiang (Yangtze R.)

Chongqing •

Three
Gorges
Dam

*Dongting
Hu*

Nanjing •

Wuhan •

Hangzhou •

Shanghai •

*Poyang
Hu*

Wenzhou •

East China
Sea

PACIFIC
OCEAN

N

W   E

S

Ryukyu Islands

Kunming •

Xi Jiang (West R.)

Guangzhou •
Hong Kong •
Macao •

Mekong R.

Salween R.

VIETNAM

MYANMAR

THAILAND   LAOS

Gulf of
Tonkin

Hainan

South China
Sea

Taipei •
⊛
TAIWAN

Taiwan Strait

*Luzon
Strait*

Philippine Sea

PHILIPPINES

⊛ National capital
• Other city
···· Great Wall

0   250   500 miles
0   250   500 kilometers
Two-Point Equidistant Projection

EAST ASIA

Unit ATLAS

Regional Patterns

These two pages contain a graph and three thematic maps. The graph shows the religions of East Asia. The maps show other important features of East Asia: its vegetation, languages, and population density. After studying these two pages, answer the questions below in your notebook.

Making Comparisons

1. Where is most of the population located in China? Why might people have settled in these areas rather than in other areas?

2. Which is the smallest country in East Asia?

3. What is the vegetation in much of southern China, Taiwan, southern Korea, and southern Japan? How does it differ from the vegetation in Mongolia?

Religions of East Asia

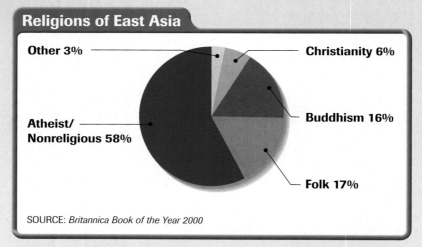

Other 3%

Christianity 6%

Atheist/ Nonreligious 58%

Buddhism 16%

Folk 17%

SOURCE: *Britannica Book of the Year 2000*

Vegetation of East Asia

Tropical rain forest
Tropical grassland
Desert and dry shrub
Temperate grassland
Deciduous and mixed forest
Coniferous forest
Highland

Languages of East Asia

Mongolian

Kazakh

Northern Mandarin Chinese

Uigur

Sea of Japan

Tajik

Mongolian

Mongolian

Mongolian

Yellow Sea

Turkic

Tibetan

PACIFIC OCEAN

Tibetan

Tibetan

Northern Mandarin Chinese

Wu Chinese

East China Sea

Southern Mandarin Chinese

Miao-Yao

Xiang Chinese

Gan Chinese

Min Chinese

Thai

Hakka Chinese

Min Chinese

Yue Chinese

South China Sea

	Altaic
	Austro-Asiatic
	Indo-European
	Japanese
	Korean
	Sino-Tibetan
	Tai-Kadai
Tajik	Spoken language

0   250   500 miles
0   250   500 kilometers
Two-Point Equidistant Projection

N E W S

Population Density of East Asia

Ulaanbaatar

Harbin

Ürümqi

Shenyang

Sea of Japan

Tokyo

Yokohama

Pyongyang

Osaka

Beijing

Seoul

Tianjin

Yellow Sea

PACIFIC OCEAN

Shanghai

Chengdu

Wuhan

East China Sea

Lhasa

Taipei

Guangzhou

Hong Kong

South China Sea

0   250   500 miles
0   250   500 kilometers
Two-Point Equidistant Projection

N E W S

Persons per sq mi	Persons per sq km
Over 520	Over 200
260–519	100–199
130–259	50–99
25–129	10–49
1–24	1–9
0	0

⊙ Metropolitan area greater than 10 million

EAST ASIA

Unit ATLAS

Regional Data File

Country Flag	Country/ Capital	Population (2000)	Life Expectancy (years) (2000)	Birthrate (per 1,000 pop.) (2000)	Infant Mortality (per 1,000 live births) (2000)
	China* Beijing	1,264,536,000	71	15	31.4
	Japan Tokyo	126,876,000	80	9	3.5
	Mongolia Ulaanbaatar	2,472,000	63	20	34.1
	North Korea Pyongyang	21,688,000	70	21	26.0
	South Korea Seoul	47,275,000	74	14	11.0
	Taiwan Taipei	22,256,000	75	13	6.6
	United States Washington, D.C.	281,422,000	77	15	7.0

Study the charts on the countries of East Asia. In your notebook, answer these questions.

Making Comparisons

1. Which countries have the most people? Locate them on the map. Are they also the largest countries in terms of total area?

2. In which part of the region are the highest elevations located? What might this suggest about settlement patterns in the region?

Sources:
Europa World Year Book 2000
Human Development Report 2000, United Nations
International Data Base, 2000, U.S. Census Bureau online
Merriam-Webster's Geographical Dictionary, 1997
Statesman's Yearbook 2001
2000 World Population Data Sheet, Population Reference Bureau online
U.S. Census Bureau, 2000 Census
WHO Estimates of Health Personnel, World Health Organization online
World Almanac and Book of Facts 2001
World Education Report 2000, UNESCO online
World Factbook 2000, CIA online
N/A = not available

Notes:
* Figures do not include Hong Kong or Macao, both Special Administrative Regions.
[a] A comparison of the prices of the same items in different countries is used to figure these data.
[b] Includes land and water, when figures are available.

For updated statistics on East Asia . . .

DATA UPDATE
CLASSZONE.COM

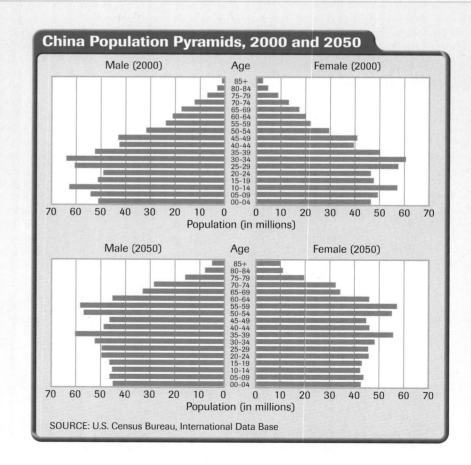

China Population Pyramids, 2000 and 2050

SOURCE: U.S. Census Bureau, International Data Base

616 UNIT 9

Doctors (per 100,000 pop.) (1995–1998)	GDP[a] (billions $US) (1998–1999)	Import/Export[a] (billions $US) (1998–1999)	Literacy Rate (percentage) (1998)	Televisions (per 1,000 pop.) (1998)	Passenger Cars (per 1,000 pop.) (1996–1997)	Total Area[b] (square miles)	
162	4,800.0	165.8 / 194.9	82	205	4	3,704,427	
193	2,950.0	275.4 / 413.0	99	684	367	143,619	
243	6.1	0.472 / 0.317	83	45	8	604,247	
N/A	22.6	0.859 / 0.680	99	48	N/A	46,609	
127	625.7	104.4 / 144.0	98	334	165	38,022	
N/A	357.0	91.5 / 121.6	94	395	198	13,887	
251	9,255.0	820.8 / 663.0	97	847	489	3,787,319	

Profile of East Asia

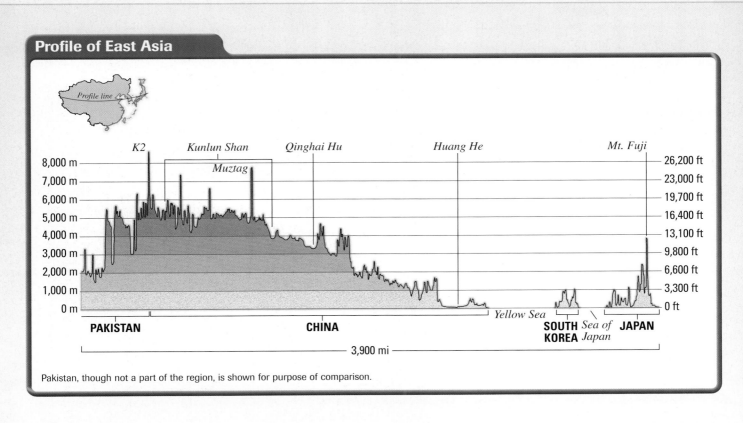

Pakistan, though not a part of the region, is shown for purpose of comparison.

PHYSICAL GEOGRAPHY OF EAST ASIA
A Rugged Terrain

The Great Wall is an ancient line of fortifications across northern China. Its oldest sections were built in the third century B.C. by hundreds of thousands of laborers. Over the years, it proved ineffective against invaders.

GeoFocus

How does physical geography influence the lives of East Asians?

Taking Notes Copy the graphic organizer below into your notebook. Use it to record information about the physical geography of East Asia.

Landforms	
Resources	
Climate and Vegetation	
Human-Environment Interaction	

Landforms and Resources

Main Ideas
- East Asia has a huge mainland area that includes rugged terrain.
- East Asia has a number of important islands off its eastern coast.

Places & Terms
Kunlun Mountains

Qinling Shandi Mountains

Huang He

Chang Jiang

Xi Jiang

CONNECT TO THE ISSUES
PHYSICAL FORCES East Asia's rough terrain and unevenly distributed resources have influenced settlement and ways of life in the region.

SUNSHINE STATE STANDARDS
Key Standard SS.B.1.4.3 The student uses mental maps of physical and human features of the world to answer complex geographic questions.

Other Standards SS.B.1.4.1, B.2.4.3

FCAT LA.A.1.4.2 Reading: Strategies

A HUMAN PERSPECTIVE Time and again in its early history, China was attacked by invaders from the steppes of Central Asia. The Chinese built and extended the Great Wall over many centuries in an attempt to keep out such invaders from Mongolia. From the Yellow Sea to the Gobi Desert, the wall twisted for thousands of miles across China. The wall was built by hundreds of thousands of peasant workers. Many died from the backbreaking labor or the severe weather. The Great Wall remains one of the largest building feats in history—partly because it had to cross mile after mile of China's difficult terrain.

Landforms: Mountains and Plateaus

East Asia stretches from the western provinces of China to the eastern coast of Japan. Mongolia, Taiwan, North Korea, and South Korea are the other countries in the region. East Asia includes high mountains, vast deserts, cold climates, and Pacific waters. The mostly rugged terrain was formed by the collision of tectonic plates. One result of these natural barriers was to limit people's movement and increase their isolation.

MOUNTAIN RANGES OF THE REGION High mountains in the region limited contact between people living in China and in other parts of Asia. The world's highest mountains are located on the western edge of East Asia in southwestern and northwestern China and western Mongolia. The **Kunlun Mountains,** which are located in the west of China, are the source of two of China's great rivers, the Huang He (Yellow) and the Chang Jiang (Yangtze). In southeastern and east central China, the **Qinling Shandi Mountains** divide the northern part of China from the south.

PLATEAUS AND PLAINS The landscape of East Asia is among the roughest in the world. The mountain areas in the western part of the region restricted movement and were underpopulated. Although few flat surfaces exist, the region has some low basins and barren deserts. These include the Plateau of Tibet (also known as the Xizang Plateau), the Tarim Pendi Basin in western China, and the Taklimakan Desert in western China. All these areas are sparsely populated.

PLACE The Potala Palace in Lhasa, Tibet, has many floors and more than 1,000 rooms. It was once the residence of the Dalai Lama and other monks and is now a major pilgrimage site.

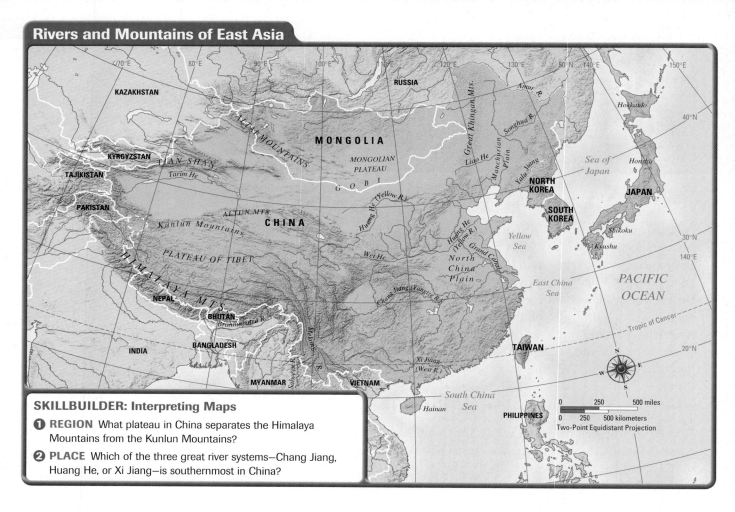

Rivers and Mountains of East Asia

SKILLBUILDER: Interpreting Maps

❶ **REGION** What plateau in China separates the Himalaya Mountains from the Kunlun Mountains?

❷ **PLACE** Which of the three great river systems—Chang Jiang, Huang He, or Xi Jiang—is southernmost in China?

One of the largest deserts in the world—the Gobi—stretches from northwest China into Mongolia. It covers more than 500,000 square miles, which is larger than Texas and California combined. The Mongolian Plateau reaches into northeastern China. Northern China encompasses the Manchurian Plain and the North China Plain.

Peninsulas and Islands

East Asia includes a number of important peninsulas. Most of these form a part of China, although one peninsula contains independent nations. In addition, a number of islands off the coast of China include possessions of China as well as independent nations.

THE COAST OF CHINA The eastern coast of China features several peninsulas. These include the Shandong Peninsula, the Leizhou Peninsula, and the Macao Peninsula. Macao was owned by Portugal until 1999, when it returned to Chinese control. Because of its peninsulas, China has a long coastline that has allowed several major port cities, such as Shanghai, to develop. Bordering China on the east is the Korean Peninsula, which contains the two independent nations of North Korea and South Korea.

THE ISLANDS OF EAST ASIA An important feature of East Asia is the continental shelf—the submerged border of the continent— that extends east from China. A number of islands stand above this continental shelf. The isolation of the islands has permitted them to develop in greater security and peace than parts of the mainland. Further, many of these islands have developed trading economies.

The islands off China include Hainan and part of Hong Kong. Long one of the major harbors in the world, Hong Kong (while originally a part of China) used to be a British colony. In 1997, Hong Kong once again came under the authority of mainland China.

The smaller nations of East Asia are located on islands and peninsulas. For example, Japan is an island nation with enormous economic power. Taiwan is a separate island that at one time belonged to mainland China—and is still claimed by China.

River Systems

China has three great rivers, which have been critical to the development of China's civilization. The rivers have helped to feed hundreds of millions of people because of the fields and crops they irrigate.

THE HUANG HE The **Huang He** (or Yellow River) of northern China starts in the Kunlun Mountains in the west. It winds east for about 3,000 miles before emptying into the Yellow Sea. Both the sea and the river get their names from the yellow silt, or particles of soil, that the river carries to its delta. Another name for the river is "China's Sorrow" because of the terrible floods that it has caused.

THE CHANG JIANG The **Chang Jiang** (or Yangtze River) is the longest river in all of Asia. The name Chang Jiang means "long river." It flows about 3,900 miles from Xizang (Tibet) to the East China Sea. The river has been a major trade route since ancient times. Even today, the Chang Jiang carries most of the goods shipped on China's waterways. But this river, too, floods frequently, causing a great deal of damage to nearby villages, as well as to the surrounding countryside. ◄A

CONNECT TO THE ISSUES
A► How might rivers facilitate trade?

THE XI JIANG The **Xi Jiang** (or West River) runs its course in the south of China. It flows eastward through southeast China and joins up with

MOVEMENT
Workers pull a boat ashore along the Huang He (Yellow River).
What are some of the uses that people might make of a river?

EAST ASIA

621

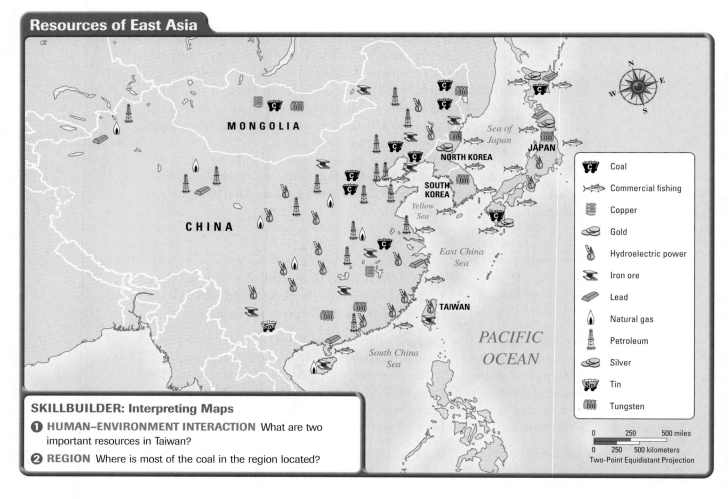

Resources of East Asia

Coal	
Commercial fishing	
Copper	
Gold	
Hydroelectric power	
Iron ore	
Lead	
Natural gas	
Petroleum	
Silver	
Tin	
Tungsten	

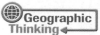

0   250   500 miles
0   250   500 kilometers
Two-Point Equidistant Projection

SKILLBUILDER: Interpreting Maps

❶ **HUMAN–ENVIRONMENT INTERACTION** What are two important resources in Taiwan?

❷ **REGION** Where is most of the coal in the region located?

the Pearl River (Zhu Jiang) to flow into the South China Sea. The Xi Jiang joins with three other rivers to form an estuary (where the river's current meets the ocean's tides) between Hong Kong and Macao. Important mineral resources are located in this river's valley.

OTHER RIVERS OF THE REGION The Yalu Jiang is another important river of the region. The Yalu, which is about 500 miles long, forms the border between North Korea and China. It is important historically because in 1950, Chinese troops entered the Korean War by crossing the river and attacking United Nations forces.

Resources of East Asia

Natural and mineral resources are unevenly distributed throughout East Asia. China, for example, is rich in natural resources. Mongolia and North Korea also have substantial mineral resources. However, Japan, South Korea, and Taiwan have limited natural resources. Even so, these latter three nations have grown into major economic powers. **B**

LAND AND FORESTS The number of mountains in East Asia means that the amount of land available for agriculture is limited. For this reason, China's population is concentrated in the east, where river basins are located. The land in these valleys is highly productive, allowing the Chinese to grow rice and many other crops. In contrast, the mountainous western regions of China are more sparsely populated.

Geographic Thinking

Seeing Patterns
B What are the three nations of the region that have grown into major economic powers, and what do they have in common?

Forests are also abundant in the region. China, Japan, Taiwan, and both North Korea and South Korea all have forest resources. Japan has been able to keep most of its forests in reserve by buying timber and other forest products from other regions of the world.

MINERAL AND ENERGY RESOURCES China has large energy reserves of petroleum, coal, and natural gas, and Korea has coal reserves. Japan also has deposits of coal. China's resources have enabled it to be self-sufficient for much of its history. In contrast, Japan's shortage of resources has forced it to trade for what it needs.

China's mineral resources include iron ore, tungsten, manganese, molybdenum, magnesite, lead, zinc, and copper. North and South Korea possess important tungsten, gold, and silver reserves. Japan has reserves of lead, silver, and coal.

WATER RESOURCES China's long river systems are important to the country's economy. They provide crop irrigation, hydroelectric power, and transportation. To control flooding on the Chang Jiang and produce more electricity, China is building the Three Gorges Dam. (See pages 628–630.) The Huang He and Xi Jiang also provide hydroelectric power and a means of transportation.

People in East Asia look to the sea for food. In fact, Japan has developed one of the largest fishing industries in the world. Japanese factory ships process huge amounts of seafood for human consumption throughout the world, as well as in Japan.

You will read about East Asia's climate zones in the next section. You will also read about its vegetation.

Seeing Patterns

In what ways might river systems be important to an economy?

Geography TODAY

The Japanese Fishing Industry

There is great competition among the world's nations to harvest the resources of the sea. Sophisticated and mechanized factory ships process the catch while still at sea.

Japan's fishing industry is larger than that of the United States or any country in Western Europe. Fleets of Japanese fishing vessels, such as the sea bass fishing boat shown below, trawl the oceans far from Japan to bring fish back to the home islands. Tuna, mackerel, salmon, and cod are eaten by the Japanese.

SECTION 1 Assessment

1 Places & Terms

Identify each of the following places and terms.

- Kunlun Mountains
- Qinling Shandi Mountains
- Huang He
- Chang Jiang
- Xi Jiang

2 Taking Notes

PLACE Review the notes you took for this section.

Landforms	
Resources	

- What types of landforms are found in East Asia?
- What are their relative locations?

3 Main Ideas

a. How might the river basins of China have affected settlement patterns?

b. How are the landforms of East Asia an advantage to life in the region?

c. What effect might natural resources have had on the development of East Asia?

4 Geographic Thinking

Drawing Conclusions How might China's three large river systems have affected the development of agriculture and trade in the area? **Think about:**

- the obstacles that mountains and deserts present to agriculture
- the network of travel and communication offered by a river system

SEEING PATTERNS Pair with a partner and draw a **map** of East Asia's rivers and mountains. Use arrows to indicate the directions the rivers flow. Why do the three main rivers of China flow all the way east across the continent even though their headwaters begin in the mountains of the west?

EAST ASIA

Interpreting a Contour Map

Suppose that you are vacationing on the Japanese island of Hokkaido. As part of your trip, you will be climbing Mount Asahi, the highest point on the island. The members of your group decide to study a contour map to understand the challenge that faces you. You can use a contour map to get a better idea of elevation and the steepness of the mountain.

THE LANGUAGE OF MAPS A **contour map** shows elevations and surface configuration by means of contour lines. Contour lines are lines on a map that show points of equal elevation. These lines are also called isolines. Numbers on the contour lines show the elevation in meters.

SUNSHINE STATE STANDARDS
Key Standard SS.B.1.4.1 The student uses a variety of maps, geographic technologies including geographic information systems (GIS) and satellite-produced imagery, and other advanced graphic representations to depict geographic problems.

FCAT LA.A.2.4.1 Reading: Identify Main Idea, Details, and Methods

Elevation on Hokkaido

1 Sapporo, the largest city on the island, is situated at a low elevation.

2 Mount Asahi is the highest point on the island.

3 The key shows that Mount Asahi is a peak. The key shows that the red lines are contour lines. If you were to follow one contour line around its entire perimeter, you would remain at the same elevation throughout your walk.

Copyright by Rand McNally & Co.

Map and Graph Skills Assessment

1. Seeing Patterns
How high, in meters, is Mount Asahi? What is the elevation of the last contour line on the map before the peak?

2. Making Decisions
From what direction of the compass would you approach Mount Asahi if you wanted to make the steepest climb?

3. Drawing Conclusions
Where on the island do the isolines converge most densely to show a very dramatic increase in elevation?

Climate and Vegetation

Main Ideas
- East Asia has a dry highland climate in the west.
- The region has a humid climate in the east.

Places & Terms

typhoon

Taklimakan Desert

Gobi Desert

CONNECT TO THE ISSUES
POPULATION To feed its population, East Asian countries have had to farm in highly productive ways.

SUNSHINE STATE STANDARDS
Key Standard SS.B.2.4.1 The student understands how social, cultural, economic, and environmental factors contribute to the dynamic nature of regions.

Other Standards SS.B.2.4.4

FCAT LA.A.1.4.2 Reading: Strategies

A HUMAN PERSPECTIVE Kublai Khan was the ruler of the Mongol Empire (which included China) in the 13th century. In 1281, the Great Khan sent a huge fleet against Japan. A **typhoon**—a tropical storm that occurs in the western Pacific—swept across the Sea of Japan and sank the Mongol ships or dashed them against the rocky Japanese shore. The typhoon had changed the course of history. Typhoons occur in parts of East Asia, but in other ways the weather is similar to that of the United States. Both are at the same latitude, and both have similar climate zones.

High Latitude Climate Zones

The climates in the highest latitudes present a serious challenge to all but the most hardy nomads and herders. These zones generally have severely cold climates. In addition, they tend to be very dry.

SUBARCTIC Subarctic climate zones occur in a small sliver along Mongolia's and China's northern borders with Russia. The summers in these areas range from cool to cold. The winters are brutally cold, testing the survival skills of the inhabitants. The climate is generally dry.

The typical vegetation of this region is the northern evergreen forest. Varieties of mosses and lichens also grow on rocks and tree trunks throughout subarctic zones.

HIGHLAND Highland climates are found mostly in western China. The temperature in highland zones varies with latitude and elevation. In general, the farther north the latitude and the higher the elevation, the colder the climate. The severe climate and topography of the western highlands are two of the reasons that the area is sparsely populated.

The vegetation in the highlands also varies with elevation. Forests and alpine tundra are the typical vegetation. Vast tundras reach as far as the eye can see. Tundras have no trees, and the soil a few feet below the surface is permanently frozen. In this environment, only mosses, lichens, and shrubs can grow. Because of the cold and the difficulty of growing crops, few people scratch out a living here.

HUMAN-ENVIRONMENT INTERACTION A 78-year-old woman tends sheep from the back of a camel in a semiarid zone typical of Mongolia.
What does the occupation of sheepherding and livestock grazing suggest about the vegetation in Mongolia?

625

Climate Comparison, East Asia and North America

Legend — Labels indicate similar climates in North America:
- Tropical wet
- Desert
- Semiarid
- Humid subtropical
- Humid continental
- Subarctic
- Highland

SKILLBUILDER: Interpreting Maps

❶ **REGION** The southern coast of China is comparable in climate to which area of the United States?

❷ **REGION** Which country in the region has a climate similar to the state of Georgia in the United States?

Mid-latitude Zones

Mid-latitude zones are much more comfortable to live in because of their moderate climates. The land is productive, and the rainfall is sufficient for agriculture. An important resource of these zones is their forests.

HUMID CONTINENTAL Northeastern China, North Korea, northern South Korea, and northern Japan all have humid continental climates. The forests of the region are mainly coniferous in the humid continental zone. Temperate grasslands ideal for grazing are also found in these areas. However, over the years agriculture has transformed the landscape and replaced many of the forests.

HUMID SUBTROPICAL Southeastern China, southern South Korea, southern Japan, and northern Taiwan are in a humid subtropical zone. The forests in such zones are both deciduous and coniferous. The broad-leafed, deciduous trees are usually found in the north. The coniferous forests are especially typical of areas with sandy soils in the south. However, loggers and farmers have greatly reduced the forests in the southeast. Ⓐ

Dry Zones

Dry zones of the region include both steppes and deserts. There is relatively little vegetation. These zones are not well suited to agriculture

CONNECT TO THE ISSUES
POPULATION
Ⓐ Why might most of East Asia's population be centered in the mid-latitude zones?

and so have not been much settled by people. Instead, nomads have used the semiarid areas to graze livestock.

SEMIARID Parts of the Mongolian Plateau make up the semiarid zones of the region. The vegetation of semiarid zones consists mainly of short grasses, which provide food for grazing animals and livestock.

DESERT Most of the deserts in the region are found in the west central area of the mainland. The **Taklimakan Desert** is located in western China between the Tian Shan and Kunlun Mountains. The **Gobi Desert** is located in northern China and southeast Mongolia. The Gobi is a prime area for finding dinosaur fossils, since thousands of these animals roamed through the region millions of years ago. B

Geographic Thinking

Making Comparisons
B Why might the dry zones of the region be less densely populated?

Tropical Zones

The tropical zones of East Asia contain mainly wet climates. The most common vegetation is the rain forest.

TROPICAL WET The tropical climate zone in East Asia is fairly small. It includes a small strip of land along China's southeastern coast, the island of Hainan, and the southern tip of Taiwan. These areas have high temperatures, heavy rainfall, and high humidity every month of the year. The tropical rain forest in these places is made up of tall dense forests of broadleaf trees.

In the next section, you will read how human-environment interactions affect the quality of life in rural China and urban Japan.

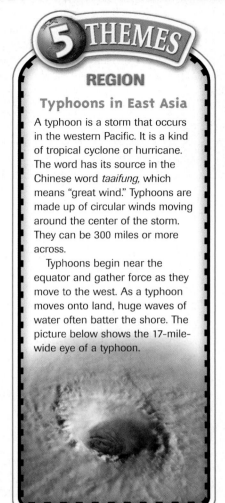

5 THEMES

REGION

Typhoons in East Asia

A typhoon is a storm that occurs in the western Pacific. It is a kind of tropical cyclone or hurricane. The word has its source in the Chinese word *taaifung*, which means "great wind." Typhoons are made up of circular winds moving around the center of the storm. They can be 300 miles or more across.

Typhoons begin near the equator and gather force as they move to the west. As a typhoon moves onto land, huge waves of water often batter the shore. The picture below shows the 17-mile-wide eye of a typhoon.

SECTION 2 Assessment

1 Places & Terms

Identify each of the following places and terms.

- typhoon
- Taklimakan Desert
- Gobi Desert

2 Taking Notes

PLACE Review the notes you took for this section.

Climate	
Vegetation	

- What types of climate are found in East Asia?
- What vegetation characterizes the western reaches of China?

3 Main Ideas

a. In what ways are the climates of the United States and China similar?

b. What effect might severe weather (such as typhoons) have on crops?

c. What has been the human impact on mid-latitude climate zones in the region?

4 Geographic Thinking

Making Inferences How might the climate and vegetation of East Asia have affected patterns of settlement in the region? **Think about:**

- the impact of deserts, steppes, and tundra on patterns of settlement

 See Skillbuilder Handbook, page R4.

GeoActivity

EXPLORING LOCAL GEOGRAPHY East Asia has many kinds of climate. Pair with a partner and make a **poster** that shows the climate of East Asia in which you would most want to live. Include photographs, postcards, maps, and charts. Is there any location in the United States that is similar to your preferred climate?

EAST ASIA

Human–Environment Interaction

Main Ideas
- The Chinese are building the Three Gorges Dam to control flooding.
- The Japanese have developed creative ways to use their limited amounts of land.

Places & Terms
Three Gorges Dam
PCBs
landfill

CONNECT TO THE ISSUES
PHYSICAL FORCES One reason why the Three Gorges Dam is being built is to control flooding of the Chang Jiang.

SUNSHINE STATE STANDARDS
Key Standard SS.B.2.4.4 The student understands the global impact of human changes in the physical environment.

Other Standards SS.B.2.4.2

FCAT LA.A.2.4.1 Reading: Identify Main Idea, Details, and Methods

A HUMAN PERSPECTIVE Hundreds of thousands of Chinese died in floods in the 20th century. Most of these deaths were caused by the flooding of the Chang Jiang and the Huang He rivers. These vast river floodplains are home to, and help feed, hundreds of millions of people, and this makes people vulnerable to the rivers' wrath. In addition to the many deaths, the flooding has also forced millions of people to abandon their homes. You will read more about one such flood in Chapter 28 (pages 640–641). But since the early 1990s, the Chinese have been building an enormous new dam on the Chang Jiang that will help to control flooding. This is one example of how East Asians have shaped their environment.

The Three Gorges Dam

The **Three Gorges Dam** is being built on the Chang Jiang in China. The dam will, in part, help to control flooding along the great river, the third longest in the world after the Nile and the Amazon. But the dam is also expected to generate power and to allow ships to sail farther into China.

Building the Three Gorges Dam

The picture at right, below, shows the city of Fengdu and its suspension bridge. The picture at far right, enhanced by computer imaging, shows how the rising water created by the Three Gorges Dam will cover all of Fengdu except for a few hilltops. The city's population of 65,000 will be moved to a new location.

AN ENGINEERING FEAT The Three Gorges Dam is China's largest construction project and will be the world's biggest dam. When completed, the dam will tower more than 600 feet high and will span a valley more than one mile wide. This dam will create a reservoir nearly 400 miles long. At least 1,000 towns and villages will disappear under the waters of the reservoir when the dam is completed.

POSITIVE EFFECTS The building of the Three Gorges Dam is a complicated issue because it will have both positive and negative effects. Experts disagree about whether the dam should be built. But the Chinese government, which began construction of the dam in 1993, argues that the dam will have three positive effects.

First, the dam will help control the frequent flooding of the Chang Jiang, which causes great damage and loss of life. This is critical because the Chang Jiang irrigates about half of China's crops. Also, the river drains about one-fifth of China's total land area.

Second, the dam will generate huge amounts of electrical power. Giant turbines will produce electricity that will be hooked up to electrical grids in central and eastern China. This will improve the reliability of electricity throughout China. By some estimates, the dam's turbines will produce about 10 percent of China's electrical power. (See the bar chart below for a comparison of the projected generating capacity of the Three Gorges Dam with other large dams.)

Finally, the dam will make it easier for ships to reach China's interior. A series of locks along the river will raise ocean-going ships up from the river to the reservoir. The Chang Jiang carries more than half of the goods moving on China's interior waterways. The dam and the locks will increase shipping capacity and decrease shipping costs. ◀

Geographic Thinking ◀

Seeing Patterns
A ▶ What are three benefits of building the dam?

Facts and Figures

- Length of river: 3,964 miles
- Length of reservoir: 370 miles
- Height of dam: 610 feet
- Width of dam: 1.3 miles
- Number of turbines: 26, generating 18,200 megawatts of electricity
- Lives lost to flooding: about one million deaths in 20th century
- Location of dam: about 1,500 miles from the ocean
- Many hundreds of miles from headwaters in western mountains of China

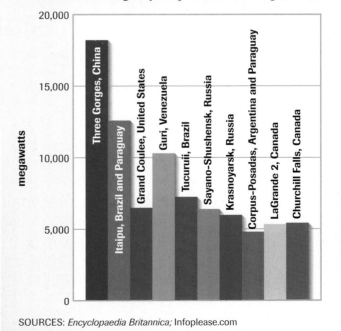

Electric Generating Capacity of World's Largest Dams

SOURCES: *Encyclopaedia Britannica;* Infoplease.com

HUMAN–ENVIRONMENT INTERACTION The river dolphin, the white crane, and the alligator are just three of the species endangered by the construction of the Three Gorges Dam. **Why might the dam be a threat to various species?**

NEGATIVE EFFECTS Most observers agree that the Three Gorges Dam will also have negative effects. The central issue is whether the negative impact on the environment will be greater than the positive benefits.

First, the human costs of the dam will be enormous. Huge numbers of people will have to be moved—somewhere between one million and two million people. Also, hundreds of historical sites and scenic spots will be submerged.

Second, the dam is likely to cost more money than originally anticipated. The Chinese government first estimated the cost at approximately $11 billion dollars. However, other estimates now place the cost closer to $75 billion. A number of banks and other financial institutions have chosen not to participate in the financing of the dam because of their concerns about the cost.

Third, environmental concerns about the dam trouble many observers. The giant reservoir created by the dam will put hundreds of square miles of land under water. This will reduce the habitat of many animals. It is feared that abandoned factories submerged under the reservoir may leak contaminating chemicals into the water. The huge reservoir will affect the climate and temperature of the region as well as the plant and animal life. Such species as the alligator, leopard, sturgeon, white crane, and river dolphin may not survive.

The Three Gorges Dam is scheduled to be completed in 2009. However, the Chinese government has not been careful in protecting the environment from the consequences of building the dam. Some international groups are reluctant to invest in the project because of environmental concerns, and this might delay its completion.

Use of Space in Urban Japan

Throughout history, the geographic challenges facing Japan have been different from those facing China. One of the most important challenges is that Japan is made up of a series of mountainous islands. Most of the cities are on the coasts of these islands. But because of nearby mountains, many of the cities cannot expand to absorb any more of the Japanese population, which is about 127 million people. Tokyo is a good example. One of the world's largest cities, it holds more than 25 million people. There is, however, no more land for the city to grow.

CROWDED LIVING AND WORKING SPACES More than 60 percent of the Japanese people live on only about three percent of the land. The population is clustered along the narrow flat coastal plains.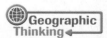

These plains are among the most densely populated areas in the world. The largest cities in Japan are Tokyo, Yokohama, Osaka, Nagoya, and Sapporo. Close to 80 percent of the people in Japan live in cities.

Partly because of their large populations, some Japanese cities have become very polluted. For example, in the 1950s and 1960s, a number

Geographic Thinking

Seeing Patterns
B What might be some negative effects of the dam?

Geographic Thinking

Using the Atlas
C Use the map on page 615. Why might the Japanese people live on such a small percentage of coastal land?

of Japanese cities experienced poisoning from mercury and **PCBs**—industrial pollutants that build up in animal tissue and can cause disease and birth defects. PCBs were banned in 1977. However, cars and factories still cause massive levels of air and noise pollution.

ADAPTING TO LIMITED SPACE
The Japanese have shown great ingenuity in adapting to limited space. Because of the cost of land, houses are small by American standards. The rooms are separated by sliding screens and are sparsely furnished. People sleep on thin mattresses called futons that can be rolled up and stored during the day.

Many people, especially in the biggest cities, live in apartments. It is not uncommon for a family of four to live in a one-bedroom apartment. Some Japanese attempt to escape the overcrowding by moving away from the city to distant suburbs, but they must commute for two or even three hours a day to and from work.

One of the solutions to the shortage of space is landfill. **Landfill** is a method of solid waste disposal in which refuse is buried between layers of dirt to fill in or reclaim low-lying ground. The Japanese have used landfill to reclaim land for most of the major cities along the coast. Tokyo, for example, has built factories and refineries on landfill sites. One result of the use of landfill sites has been to enlarge some of Japan's ports. These reclaimed areas are designed to handle the great number of ships that sail in and out of the port.

You will explore more about how East Asians live in the next chapter, on human geography.

HUMAN–ENVIRONMENT INTERACTION
Capsule hotels in Japan provide tiny rooms for overnight guests.

Assessment

① Places & Terms
Identify and explain the significance of each in the region.
- Three Gorges Dam
- PCBs
- landfill

② Taking Notes
HUMAN–ENVIRONMENT INTERACTION Review the notes you took for this section.

Human-Environment Interaction	

- Which of the examples in this chapter illustrate human adaptation to the environment?
- Which examples illustrate an environment changed by humans?

③ Main Ideas
a. What might be a positive effect of the Three Gorges Dam?

b. What might be a negative effect of the Three Gorges Dam?

c. Why are most of Japan's large cities located along its coast?

④ Geographic Thinking
Determining Cause and Effect What were some of the reasons that led to the building of the Three Gorges Dam? **Think about:**
- the effects of living near an unpredictable river

RESEARCH LINKS
CLASSZONE.COM

GeoActivity

ASKING GEOGRAPHIC QUESTIONS Pair with a partner and research a dam in the United States to compare with the Three Gorges Dam. Devise three geographic questions about the dams, such as "How much concrete was used in the construction of the dams?" Then make a **chart** or **graph** in which you provide data to answer the questions. Be sure to identify your sources.

EAST ASIA

VISUAL SUMMARY
PHYSICAL GEOGRAPHY OF EAST ASIA

Landforms

Major Mountain Ranges: Himalayas, Kunlun, Altun, Altay, Qinling Shandi

Major Rivers: Huang He, Chang Jiang, Xi Jiang

Major Deserts: Taklimakan, Gobi

Major Plateaus and Plains: Plateau of Tibet, Tarim Pendi Basin, Mongolian Plateau, Manchurian Plain, North China Plain

Resources

- China, Mongolia, and North Korea have significant natural resources.
- Japan, South Korea, and Taiwan have limited natural resources.

Climate and Vegetation

- East Asia has a dry continental climate in the west and a humid climate in the east.
- Its mid-latitude zones, both humid continental and humid subtropical, are the most densely populated areas.

Human-Environment Interaction

- The Three Gorges Dam is being built along the Chang Jiang to control flooding.
- Urban Japan is very crowded, and people must adapt to space limitations.

Reviewing Places & Terms

A. Briefly explain the importance of each of the following.

1. Kunlun Mountains
2. Huang He
3. Chang Jiang
4. Xi Jiang
5. typhoon
6. Taklimakan Desert
7. Gobi Desert
8. Three Gorges Dam
9. PCBs
10. landfill

B. Answer the questions about vocabulary in complete sentences.

11. On which river will the Three Gorges Dam attempt to control flooding?
12. What is another name for a tropical cyclone or hurricane?
13. What is the source of two of China's great rivers?
14. Which river joins with others to form an estuary between Hong Kong and Macao?
15. How have landfill sites been used in Tokyo?
16. Where in the region is there a rich supply of dinosaur fossils?
17. What has contributed to the poisoning and pollution of the environment in Japanese cities?
18. Which desert is located in western China near the Kunlun Mountains?
19. Which river is known as "China's Sorrow"?
20. What project is supposed to contain flooding?

Main Ideas

Landforms and Resources (pp. 619–624)

1. Why are the Kunlun Mountains especially important to China?
2. What is the approximate size of the Gobi Desert?
3. What are some of the important islands off the coast of China?
4. Why are China's three river systems so important to the country?

Climate and Vegetation (pp. 625–627)

5. In which latitude and climate zones is most of China's productive agricultural land located?
6. What landforms make up the dry zones of the region?
7. What two factors affect vegetation and temperature in the highland climate?

Human-Environment Interaction (pp. 628–631)

8. What will be some benefits of the Three Gorges Dam?
9. What will be some drawbacks of the dam?
10. What are some of the ways in which the Japanese have adapted to living in a crowded space?

Critical Thinking

1. Using Your Notes

Use your completed chart to answer these questions.

Landforms	
Resources	

a. Where are the highest mountains in China located?

b. What are some energy resources found in abundance in China and Korea?

2. Geographic Themes

a. **LOCATION** Where is the largest desert found in East Asia?

b. **REGION** Write a sentence or two describing the settlement patterns of East Asia in terms of its mountains and coasts.

3. Identifying Themes

Based on landforms and climate, which areas of East Asia would be the least agriculturally productive? Which of the five themes are reflected in your answer?

4. Making Decisions

What factors must people in China consider when they are trying to decide what to do about flooding along one of their great rivers?

5. Drawing Conclusions

How does a typhoon create so much damage?

Additional Test Practice, pp. S1–S37

TEST PRACTICE
CLASSZONE.COM

Geographic Skills: Interpreting Maps

Precipitation in East Asia

Use the map at right to answer the following questions.

1. **REGION** Which parts of the region have the least precipitation?

2. **REGION** Which parts of the region have the most precipitation?

3. **MOVEMENT** How might precipitation patterns have affected settlement in the region?

GeoActivity

Create a way to display the map information in graph form. Be sure to list the six countries of the region by name in your graph.

120+ in. (300+ cm)
80–120 in. (200–300 cm)
40–80 in. (100–200 cm)
20–40 in. (50–100 cm)
10–20 in. (25–50 cm)
Under 10 in. (Under 25 cm)

0   400   800 miles
0   400   800 kilometers
Two-Point Equidistant Projection

INTERNET ACTIVITY

Use the links at **classzone.com** to do research on the most productive agricultural regions of East Asia. You might focus on the impact that precipitation has had on settlement patterns and crop growth.

Creating Multimedia Presentations Combine charts, maps, or other visual images in an electronic presentation that shows the most productive farming areas and the most common crops in the region.

Chapter
28

SECTION 1
China

SECTION 2
Mongolia
and Taiwan

SECTION 3
The Koreas:
North and South

SECTION 4
Japan

HUMAN GEOGRAPHY OF EAST ASIA
Shared Cultural Traditions

Four Subregions of East Asia

China
Mongolia and Taiwan
North Korea and South Korea
Japan

MONGOLIA

NORTH
KOREA

Sea of
Japan

JAPAN

SOUTH
KOREA

Bo Hai

Korea
Bay

Korea Strait

Yellow
Sea

CHINA

East China
Sea

PACIFIC
OCEAN

Tropic of Cancer

80°E

Taiwan Strait

TAIWAN

Luzon
Strait

Philippine Sea

Bay of
Bengal

Gulf of
Tonkin

South China
Sea

Equator

0   250   500 miles
0   250   500 kilometers
Two-Point Equidistant Projection

50°N

40°N

30°N

20°N

10°N

0°

10°S

100°E   110°E   120°E   130°E

GeoFocus

How has China influenced the cultures of East Asia?

Taking Notes In your notebook, copy a cluster diagram like the one below. For each subregion of East Asia, take notes about its history, economics, culture, and modern life.

China

Mongolia
and Taiwan

East
Asia

The Koreas: North
and South

Japan

China

Main Ideas

- China is the world's most populous country.
- China has been the dominant culture of East Asia since ancient times.

Places & Terms

dynasty

spheres of influence

Boxer Rebellion

Mao Zedong

Confucianism

Taoism

Buddhism

CONNECT TO THE ISSUES
POPULATION China's huge population puts a great strain on the environment.

SUNSHINE STATE STANDARDS
Key Standard SS.B.2.4.1 The student understands how social, cultural, economic, and environmental factors contribute to the dynamic nature of regions.
Other Standards SS.A.2.4.3, A.3.4.4, A.3.4.9, D.2.4.1
FCAT LA.A.1.4.2 Reading: Strategies

PLACE Thousands of life-sized terra cotta (clay) soldiers have been unearthed by archaeologists near the tomb of the emperor Shi Huangdi near Xian, China.

A HUMAN PERSPECTIVE In ancient times, China had been open to attack from nomadic horsemen who roamed the plains of northern China and Mongolia. Around 220 B.C., the emperor Shi Huangdi decided to build the Great Wall of China by closing the gaps between smaller walls built by earlier rulers. Hundreds of thousands of peasants were used as forced labor to build the Great Wall. The workers hauled and dumped millions of tons of rubble to fill the core of the wall. From the Yellow Sea in the east to the Gobi desert in the west, the Great Wall twisted and turned for thousands of miles, protecting and isolating China from the barbarian warriors beyond its borders.

China's Early History

China is the world's oldest continuous civilization. The beginnings of that civilization extend back into the mists of prehistory. Because of China's geography—the long distances that separated it from Europe and other continents—it followed its own direction.

EARLY CIVILIZATION AND THE DYNASTIES China has been a settled society for more than 4,000 years. In its earliest days, China was made up of a number of Stone Age cultures. Then it was ruled by dynasties. A **dynasty** is a series of rulers from the same family. The first Chinese dynasty was the Shang. This dynasty arose during the 1700s B.C. It ruled a central area in China for about 600 years until it was overthrown by the Zhou Dynasty, which ruled part of northern China.

The next important dynasty, the Qin (chihn), gave its name to China. In 221 B.C., the Qin Dynasty united a number of smaller states under a strong central government and established an empire. The first Qin emperor was Shi Huangdi, the builder of the Great Wall. The Chinese empire, ruled by different dynasties, lasted for more than 2,000 years.

Another important Chinese dynasty was that of the Han. These rulers pushed the empire into central Asia, home to many nomadic tribes. Many other dynasties followed over the centuries.

In 1644, the Manchu people of Manchuria invaded China and established the Qing (chihng) Dynasty. In 1911, the Manchus were overthrown by revolutionaries, and this ended the dynasties and the Chinese empire.

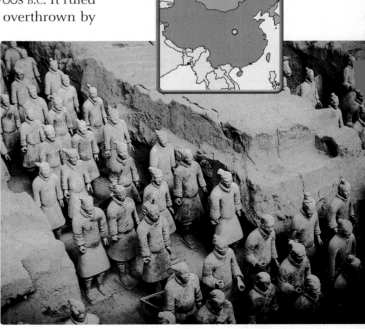

China Opens Up to the World

Even though China remained isolated from other regions for centuries, that started to change in the 13th century. At that time, European travelers began to visit China. Marco Polo, for example, traveled from Venice, Italy, to China in the 13th century and wrote a book about his adventures, *The Travels of Marco Polo.*

China and Europe had few contacts until the 19th century, when European powers sought access to Chinese markets. At that point, China had a weak military and an ineffective government. Europeans took advantage of China and forced it to sign a series of treaties that granted special privileges to the Europeans. Consequently, China was carved up into **spheres of influence** controlled by Britain, France, Germany, Russia, and Japan. This outside control angered China, which burst forth in the **Boxer Rebellion** of 1900. Chinese militants attacked and killed Europeans and Chinese Christians in China. A multinational force of about 20,000 soldiers finally defeated the Boxers.

BACKGROUND
The Boxers were a secret society whose Chinese name meant "fists of righteous unity."

REVOLUTION AND CHANGE After the Boxer Rebellion, the Qing Dynasty, founded by the Manchus, attempted to reform the Chinese government, but it was too late. Many individuals and groups wanted to form a republic, which would give the people a voice in their government. In 1912, Sun Yat-sen and others founded the *Kuomintang,* or Nationalist Party. However, the republic, led by Sun Yat-sen, was undermined by civil war throughout China.

When Sun Yat-sen died in 1925, a general named Chiang Kai-shek took over the Nationalist Party. Chiang's troops fought against the warlords of China and united most of the country in the 1920s. However, throughout the 1920s and 1930s, the Chinese Communist Party became an increasingly powerful force in China.

The Nationalists and the Communists fought for control of China. In 1949, the Communists, under the leadership of **Mao Zedong,** finally defeated the Nationalists. Mao and the Communists ruled mainland China (now called The People's Republic of China) from Beijing. Chiang Kai-shek and the Nationalists fled to the island of Taiwan.

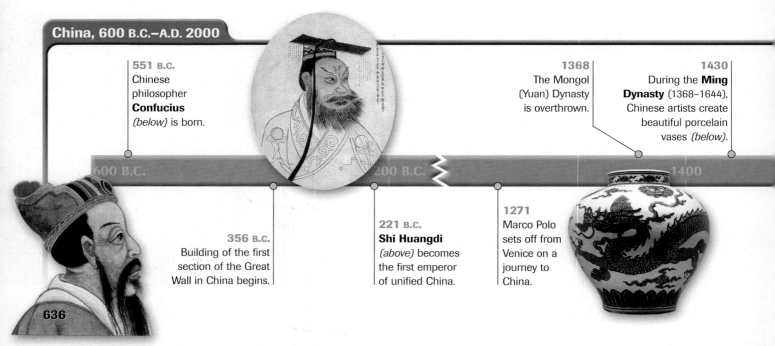

China, 600 B.C.–A.D. 2000

551 B.C.
Chinese philosopher **Confucius** *(below)* is born.

356 B.C.
Building of the first section of the Great Wall in China begins.

221 B.C.
Shi Huangdi *(above)* becomes the first emperor of unified China.

1271
Marco Polo sets off from Venice on a journey to China.

1368
The Mongol (Yuan) Dynasty is overthrown.

1430
During the **Ming Dynasty** (1368–1644), Chinese artists create beautiful porcelain vases *(below)*.

600 B.C.   200 B.C.   1400

After Mao died in 1976, Deng Xiaoping, a moderate, became China's most powerful leader through the 1980s. In 1993, Jiang Zemin became president and Zhu Rongji became premier in 1998. Both focused their attention on developing China's economy.

Rural and Industrial Economies

When the Communist Party came to power in China in 1949, its leaders promised to modernize China by encouraging the growth of industry. From the 1950s through the 1970s, the central government tried to do this by planning all economic activities. That approach led to more failures than successes. Since the 1980s, though, China has allowed the marketplace and the consumer to play a role in the economy. As a result, China now has one of the fastest growing economies in the world.

THE RURAL ECONOMY In spite of this economic growth, China remains a largely rural society, self-sufficient in agriculture. Its great river valleys provide rich soil for crops such as rice to feed the vast population. Most of China's workers—about 60 percent—work on farms.

Farming is possible only on about 13 percent of China's land because so much of western China is made up of mountains and deserts. Even so, China manages to grow enough food to feed its people. Much of the population is concentrated in the areas where food can be grown.

The eastern river basins of China produce crops such as rice, maize, wheat, and sweet potatoes. This productivity is aided by the long growing season in southern China. Farmers there can grow two or more crops on the same land during each year. ◄ⓐ

THE INDUSTRIAL ECONOMY The industrial heartland of China is in the northeast. Here are abundant resources important to manufacturing, such as coal, iron ore, and oil. (See map, page 622.) In addition, the northeast has better transportation systems than the rest of the country.

Shanghai leads China as a center of manufacturing and is one of the great industrial centers in the world. Other Chinese cities with many factories and industries include Beijing and Tianjin. Southeastern China

CONNECT TO THE ISSUES
POPULATION
ⓐ▶ Why is so much of China's population in the east and so little in the west?

1557
Portuguese found colony of Macao on peninsula in China.

1627
Manchu armies overrun northern Korea.

1720
China takes control of Tibet.

1949
Mao Zedong (left) and the Communists gain power in China.

1600

1800

2000

EAST ASIA

1661
Shunzhi *(left),* Qing emperor who came to the throne as a child, dies of smallpox.

1839
War breaks out between Britain and China.

1989
Chinese troops fire on student demonstrators in Tiananmen Square in Beijing.

has industrial centers in Guangzhou, Hangzhou, Suzhou, Wuhan, and Wuxi.

China has developed heavy industries, such as steel and machinery. It also produces consumer goods. For example, the country has a huge textile (cloth) industry that produces goods for the home market and export. Many textiles are exported to the United States.

A Rich and Complex Culture

As the world's oldest civilization, China has one of the world's richest cultures. The country has highly developed art, architecture, literature, painting, sculpture, pottery, printing, music, and theater. In all these areas, the Chinese have made influential contributions to the cultures of Korea, Japan, and other countries in the region.

FROM POTTERY TO PAINTING Some of the earliest Chinese works of art have been found in burial sites. Pottery, bronze vessels, and jade disks have been discovered in the excavation of old tombs. In addition, paintings have been found on tiles decorating the walls of tombs. Chinese artists created beautiful works using different materials, such as clay, bronze, jade, ivory, and lacquer.

CHINESE INVENTIONS The Chinese introduced many inventions to the world, such as paper, printing, and gunpowder. Other Chinese inventions include the compass, porcelain, and silk cloth.

RELIGIOUS AND ETHICAL TRADITIONS China has three major religions or ethical traditions. The beliefs of most people include elements of all three. Those traditions have influenced beliefs throughout the region.

Confucius was a Chinese philosopher who lived from 551 to 479 B.C. He believed in respect for the past and for one's ancestors. He thought that in an orderly society, children should obey their parents and parents should obey the government and emperor. He stressed the importance of education in a well-run society. His thinking about the importance of order, education, and hierarchy in a well-ordered society is called **Confucianism.**

Taoism gets its name from a book called the *Tao-te Ching,* based on the teaching of Lao-tzu, who lived in the sixth century B.C. He believed in the importance of preserving and restoring harmony in the individual and in the universe. He also thought the government should leave the people alone and do as little as possible. Another of his major beliefs was that the individual should seek harmony with nature.

Buddhism came to China from India and grew into an important religion in China by the 300s A.D. Confucianism and Taoism influenced Buddhism as it developed in China. Among ideas important in Buddhism are rebirth and the end of the rebirth cycle.

CONNECT TO THE ISSUES
TRADE
B Why might trade between the United States and China be important to both countries?

BACKGROUND
Other important Chinese art forms include calligraphy and brush painting.

Chinese Artifacts

An ancient Chinese coin *(above left)* is from about 450 B.C. The jade pendant *(above right)* is from about 250 B.C.

This printed book *(above)* from about A.D. 1000 contains a Buddhist prayer. This navigational compass *(left)* dates from the 18th century.

The Most Populous Country

One out of every five people in the world lives in China. This makes it the most populous country in the world.

POPULATION PATTERNS China's estimated population in the year 2000 was about 1.3 billion. Somewhere between 30 and 40 Chinese cities have populations of more than one million people. Many of China's 22 provinces have more people than entire countries. In the year 2000, Henan province was estimated to have a population of about 93 million people—more than the population of Great Britain. **C**

Seventy percent of the people live in 12 provinces located in the east. (See map, page 615.) About 6 percent of the people live in the west on 55 percent of the land.

HEALTH CARE One of the great achievements of China since 1950 has been to provide health care for its enormous and far-flung population. The country has pursued a dual strategy in developing its health-care system.

On the one hand, people make use of traditional Chinese medicines, including herbal remedies. Acupuncture is another important part of Chinese medicine.

On the other hand, China's doctors also use Western medicine to treat disease. Western drugs and surgery have their place in the treatment of illness. Most Chinese cities have hospitals, and the villages have clinics staffed by trained medical workers called "barefoot doctors."

In the next section, you will read about two of China's neighbors, Mongolia and Taiwan. China has greatly influenced both places.

Geographic Thinking

Seeing Patterns
▶ What does the immense size of China suggest about its future?

Connect to THE Issues

POPULATION
One-Child Policy

Because of concerns about a rapidly expanding population, China in 1979 adopted a policy of one child per family. In addition, the country has age restrictions for marriage. A man must be 22 and a woman 20 before they can marry. Those policies have reduced China's birthrate dramatically.

However, the government policy of one child per family has run into opposition. Rural families, in particular, feel the need for more than one child to help work on their farms. Because of these problems, the government has relaxed the one-child policy.

SECTION 1 Assessment

1 Places & Terms

Identify each of the following places and terms.

- dynasty
- spheres of influence
- Boxer Rebellion
- Mao Zedong
- Confucianism
- Taoism
- Buddhism

2 Taking Notes

REGION Use your notes to answer the questions below.

- What are aspects of China's cultural legacy?
- What are some Chinese dynasties?

3 Main Ideas

a. Why is China's rural economy still so important?

b. What are some of China's most important religious ideas?

c. Why is population such an important issue in China?

4 Geographic Thinking

Making Generalizations
How has China's rugged terrain affected its relations with other countries and civilizations? **Think about:**

- the mountains and deserts to the west
- the ocean to the east

S **See Skillbuilder Handbook, page R6.**

GeoActivity

SEEING PATTERNS Pair with a partner and investigate an invention of the Chinese, such as printing or the compass. Then present your findings to the class in a brief **oral report** accompanied by an illustration of the invention.

EAST ASIA

Disasters!

SUNSHINE STATE STANDARDS
Key Standard SS.B.2.4.5 The student knows how humans overcome "limits to growth" imposed by physical systems.
FCAT LA.B.1.4.2 Writing: Draft and Revise

Chang Jiang (Yangtze River) Flood of 1931

Throughout Chinese history, the flooding of the Chang Jiang has cost millions of lives. On average, the Chang Jiang has caused a major flood about every 50 years, although in the past century or so the floods have been more frequent. The floods of 1931 and 1954 were particularly devastating. The 1931 flood resulted from monsoon rains. In May and June of that year, six enormous waves poured down the river, demolishing dams and dikes. More than 35,000 square miles of land were flooded and many thousands of people died. Floods along the Chang Jiang continue to the present day. Bad floods occurred in both 1996 and 1998.

Nanjing was one of the cities in China that remained underwater for weeks because of the 1931 flood.

CHINA

Nanjing

Wuhan

Chang Jiang (Yangtze R.)

Wuchang, Hanyang, and Hankou are three cities that make up one huge urban complex called Wuhan. Much of **Wuhan** remained underwater for more than four months in 1931. The water ranged from 6 feet to 20 feet in depth.

The Three Gorges Dam is currently under construction to control the flooding of the Chang Jiang.

In the city of Hankou during the flood, wealthy people traveled in boats while poor tradespeople waded up to their necks through the water.

This panoramic aerial view of one of the Chinese cities flooded in 1931 was taken by Charles Lindbergh. He was the American aviator who had made the first solo flight across the Atlantic Ocean in 1927.

Along the Chang Jiang, human labor is still essential for flood control. These laborers work with shovels and other tools to fortify the banks of the river with dirt to prevent flooding.

GeoActivity

UNDERSTANDING FLOODS
Working with a partner, use the Internet to research one of the floods listed below. Then create a **presentation** about it.

- Create a diagram showing the extent of the flood, the damage caused by it, and the number of lives lost.
- Add a map of the affected region.
- Write a paragraph explaining how the flood affected the people and life of the region.

RESEARCH LINKS
CLASSZONE.COM

GeoData

OTHER DEADLY RIVER FLOODS

1887
Huang He in northeastern China; possibly more than 1,000,000 people killed

1889
Johnstown, Pennsylvania, on May 31; about 2,200 deaths (more than any other river flood in U.S. history)

1911
Chang Jiang in China; 100,000 killed

1937
Mississippi and Ohio rivers; about 250 killed

1988
Three major rivers in Bangladesh; about 1,600 deaths

1993
Mississippi River; millions of acres flooded; about 50 dead

1998
Chang Jiang in China during July and August; about 4,000 dead

Mongolia and Taiwan

Main Ideas
- Taiwan and Mongolia have developed in the shadow of their giant neighbor—China.
- The countries of the region include both capitalist and socialist economies.

Places & Terms
economic tiger

Pacific Rim

CONNECT TO THE ISSUES
TRADE Trade has helped Taiwan achieve prosperity, while Mongolia has not been as economically successful.

SUNSHINE STATE STANDARDS
Key Standard SS.B.2.4.1 The student understands how social, cultural, economic, and environmental factors contribute to the dynamic nature of regions.

Other Standards SS.A.2.4.11, D.2.4.1

FCAT LA.A.2.2.7 Reading: Recognize Compare and Contrast

A HUMAN PERSPECTIVE The Mongols of the Asian steppe lived their lives on horseback. In 1206, a great leader named Temujin (later called Genghis Khan) united the Mongol clans and led them in conquering much of Asia. He is reported to have said, "Man's greatest good fortune is to chase and defeat his enemy, seize his total possessions, leave his married women weeping and wailing, and ride his horse." The Mongols eventually created the largest unified land empire in history, extending from the Pacific coast of China westward into Europe.

A History of Nomads and Traders

The histories of Mongolia and Taiwan have been closely connected to that of China.

THE MONGOLIAN EMPIRE The Mongols were nomadic herders for thousands of years. Mongol history was changed forever by Genghis Khan, a title that means "supreme conqueror." Genghis Khan died in 1227, having conquered all of Central Asia and begun the conquest of

A Mongol Army on the Move

A Mongol army was like a moving city. The cavalry of 10,000 was accompanied by an even greater number of family members and by tens of thousands of horses and livestock.

A cavalry warrior's weapons included leather armor, a lance, a dagger, a bow and arrows, and his stout, sturdy horse.

Mongol soldiers were superb horsemen, having spent all their lives in the saddle. Hunting and other activities gave young men a chance to practice skills they would use in battle.

Teams of oxen pulled the mobile yurts of the khan and other leaders.

China. He was succeeded by his son Ogadai, who continued his policies of conquest and expansion. Mongol armies commanded by other sons and grandsons of Genghis Khan moved east, west, and south out of Mongolia.

The Mongol empire broke up in the 1300s. Eventually the Chinese gained control of Mongolia in the 17th century. The Chinese ruled Mongolia for hundreds of years. Only in 1911 were the Mongolians finally able to push the Chinese out and achieve their independence.

Under the influence of its powerful neighbor Russia, Mongolia became the Mongolian People's Republic in 1924. For about 72 years, the Communists ruled Mongolia. However, after the fall of the Soviet Union in 1989, the Communist Party in Mongolia lost its power. The country began moving toward political democracy and a free-enterprise economy. Ⓐ

Moscow

Khanate of the Golden Horde

Khanate of the Great Khan

KOREA

JAPAN

GOBI DESERT

Chagatai Khanate

Ilkhanate

Beijing

CHINA

HIMALAYA MTS.

Tropic of Cancer

Black Sea

Caspian Sea

Arctic Circle

Sea of Japan

East China Sea

PACIFIC OCEAN

South China Sea

0   500   1,000 miles

0   500   1,000 kilometers

Two-Point Equidistant Projection

ᒫᒫᒫ Great Wall

—— Border of Mongol Empire

SKILLBUILDER: Interpreting Maps

❶ **REGION** Which khanate controlled Mongolia and China?

❷ **MOVEMENT** What object may have restricted movement between the Gobi desert and the heartland of China?

Ⓖ **Geographic Thinking**

Seeing Patterns

Ⓐ What are some of the countries that have controlled or been controlled by Mongolia over the centuries?

TAIWAN'S LINK TO CHINA The island of Taiwan experienced many prehistoric migrations from southern China and southeast Asia. Malay and Polynesian peoples also settled there. Over the centuries, other settlers and groups of people from China settled on the island. In the sixth century, for example, some Han Chinese arrived. Later, when famine struck Fujian province in the 17th century, a large number of Chinese migrated from the mainland. That contributed to the large Chinese settlements on the island. The Manchu Dynasty conquered Taiwan in 1683. (See Unit Atlas, page 613.)

The Japanese seized Taiwan (then called Formosa) after winning a war with China in 1895. Japan kept the island until its defeat in World War II. Then Chinese Nationalists took control of the island as part of their fight with the Communists for control of mainland China. When the Nationalists lost to the Communists in 1949, they moved their government to Taiwan. There they established the Republic of China. However, the People's Republic of China has never recognized Taiwan as a separate country and considers it a province.

Cultures of Mongolia and Taiwan

China is a cultural hearth that has influenced its neighbors. It has been the source for many of the important ideas and inventions that have shaped Mongolia and Taiwan and the rest of the region.

MONGOLIA Mongolia has both ruled and been ruled by China. Kublai Khan was the Mongol emperor of China when Marco Polo visited in the 13th century. In the mid-14th century, the Chinese rose up against their

EAST ASIA

Mongol rulers and drove them out of China. In the 17th century, the Chinese under the Manchus conquered Mongolia, which they ruled for hundreds of years. This interaction produced a profound cultural influence as the Mongols adopted many aspects of Chinese culture.

The most important festival in Mongolia is the annual Naadam festival of the Three Games of Men. The festival, which dates back 2,300 years, begins each year on July 11. The three games are wrestling, archery, and horse racing. The competitors are highly skilled, and winners receive titles proclaiming their abilities. All of these contests have their roots in the ancient way of life of the Mongolian people.

TAIWAN Unlike Mongolia, Taiwan has a population that is almost exclusively Chinese. Thus, the culture of the island is Chinese. The capital city of Taipei includes Buddhist temples as well as museums of Chinese art. The island has many universities and about 30 daily newspapers. The population is well-educated, and most of the people speak the official language of Northern Chinese (also called Mandarin).

The people of Taiwan combine a number of religious and ethical beliefs. More than 90 percent practice a blend of Buddhism, Confucianism, and Taoism. A small number are Christian and an even smaller percentage practice other religions.

Two Very Different Economies

The economies of Mongolia and Taiwan have roots in the past. Raising livestock, a part of the nomadic life, is at the core of the Mongolian economy. Because Taiwan is an island, trade is key to its economy.

HUMAN-ENVIRONMENT INTERACTION A Mongolian mother and daughter use red paint to mark the horns of their goats.
What purpose might marking goats serve?

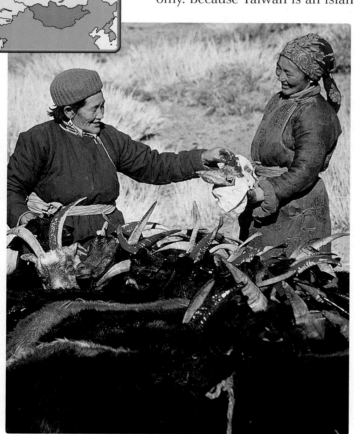

ECONOMIC PROSPECTS FOR MONGOLIA A large part of the population of Mongolia still engages in herding and managing livestock. For centuries, the economy was based on the nomadic herding of sheep, goats, camels, horses, and cattle. More goats are being raised to meet the demands of the cashmere industry, which uses soft wool from goats of the region. Of the millions of animals kept in herds in the country, nearly a third are sheep. Animals and animal products are used for domestic consumption as well as for export.

Although livestock remains the basis of the economy, Mongolia is now committed to the development of other industries. Under the Communist government, the state owned and operated most of the factories in the country. The Soviets guided Mongolia's economy for about 70 years. When the Soviet Union fell apart, Mongolia was one of the first Communist countries to attempt to shift to a market economy. The transition has been difficult as the country has turned increasingly from a Soviet-style managed economy to a free-market economy.

Mongolia has large deposits of fuels such as coal and petroleum. It also has rich deposits of metals such as copper, gold, and iron. Those resources are used in both manufacturing and construction, industries which are of growing importance to the economy.

TAIWAN'S ECONOMIC SUCCESS Taiwan has one of the world's most successful economies. It has succeeded despite the fact that it has few natural resources. However, it has a highly trained and motivated work force.

Taiwan's prosperity is based on its strong manufacturing industries and its trade with other nations. Among the most successful products of its factories are radios, televisions, calculators, and computers. Taiwanese companies sell their products around the world.

Taiwan is considered one of the economic tigers of Asia, along with Singapore and South Korea. An **economic tiger** is a nation that has rapid economic growth due to cheap labor, high technology, and aggressive exports. It is one of the very prosperous economies of the western Pacific. These economies are highly industrialized and trade with nations around the world. They are part of the **Pacific Rim**—the countries surrounding the Pacific Ocean. The Pacific Rim is an economic and social region. It includes the countries of East Asia, Southeast Asia, Australia, New Zealand, Chile, and the west coast of the United States. **B**

Geographic Thinking

Making Comparisons
B What are some differences between the economies of Mongolia and Taiwan?

Daily Life in Mongolia and Taiwan

The daily life of people in Mongolia and Taiwan shows traditional influences as well as modern influences. This blending of old and new can be seen in both work and play.

HERDING IN MONGOLIA As you learned earlier in this section, the people of Mongolia were nomads who guided their animals from grassland to grassland. The land through which they traveled has an unpredictable, hostile environment. The climate is extreme. Long, cold winters lasting six months alternate with short, hot summers of only two months. Severe winter weather makes it difficult for livestock to survive. Bad weather can kill animals from intense cold and starvation.

Nomads live in tents called yurts that are made of felt covered with leather. This is the traditional form of shelter in Mongolia. Yurts can even be found in the capital of Ulaanbaatar.

Today, many of the people of Mongolia still spend their days raising sheep, cattle, and goats. Some still follow the nomadic way of life, but most people care for livestock on farms and ranches. Often these farms have small villages in the center, with shops, offices, and houses.

MOVEMENT
Taiwan's team celebrates winning the Little League World Series in Williamsport, Pennsylvania, in 1996.

WESTERN INFLUENCES IN TAIWAN Although Mongolia remains relatively isolated from the West, Taiwan has opened itself to many Western influences.

For example, baseball has become popular in Taiwan and in other parts of Asia, particularly Japan. As a part of this general interest in the sport, Little League baseball has also become popular in parts of Asia.

Little League became popular after World War II. In 1974, the United States banned teams from foreign countries from the Little League World Series. In part, that was a response to the success of Taiwan's teams which, throughout the 1970s, dominated the World Series. However, they were restored to competition in 1976. By the 1980s, there were leagues in the United States and 30 other countries.

In the next section, you will read about two countries that share one peninsula: North Korea and South Korea.

Assessment

① Places & Terms

Identify each of the following places and terms.

- economic tiger
- Pacific Rim

② Taking Notes

REGION Use your notes to answer the questions below.

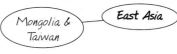

- How are the economies of Mongolia and Taiwan different from one another?
- What effect did Genghis Khan have on the history of the region?

③ Main Ideas

a. In which ways has China influenced its neighbors?

b. What are some of the characteristics of an economic tiger?

c. In what ways does the modern life of Mongolia and Taiwan show a blending of ancient and modern traditions?

④ Geographic Thinking

Drawing Conclusions
How might the locations of Mongolia and Taiwan have made them open to the influence of China? **Think about:**

- the relative locations of Taiwan and Mongolia

RESEARCH LINKS
CLASSZONE.COM

SEEING PATTERNS Pair with a partner and do Internet research on Little League baseball in Taiwan or some other country in East Asia. Create a **poster** showing various teams in the region. You might include photographs and charts in your poster, listing the names of teams, their win-loss records, and any other information your research turns up.

The Koreas: North and South

3

A HUMAN PERSPECTIVE Korea is surrounded by water on three sides and by mountains on its northern border. In the 17th and 18th centuries, Korea chose self-protected isolation and became known as "the hermit kingdom." This isolation has continued in North Korea, which has little contact with other nations even today. However, that may be changing.

A Divided Peninsula

Korea is a peninsula. To the east lies the Sea of Japan. To the west lies the Yellow Sea. To the south lies the Korea Strait. To the north lie China and Russian Siberia. Korea's location has shaped its history.

ANCIENT KOREA AND FOREIGN INFLUENCES The ancestors of today's Koreans probably migrated into the peninsula from Manchuria and North China many thousands of years ago. Over the course of the centuries, different clans or groups controlled different parts of the country. About 2000 B.C., the first state, called Chosen, arose in Korea.

Around 100 B.C., China conquered the northern half of the peninsula. This began the history of invasions by China and Japan. Because of its location, Korea has been a buffer between the two countries.

After being partially conquered by China, the Koreans gradually won back their territory. By the late 300s, the **Three Kingdoms** had formed in the peninsula. These were Koguryo in the northeast, Paekche in the southwest, and Silla in the southeast. In the 660s, Silla conquered the other two kingdoms and controlled the peninsula for hundreds of years.

Main Ideas

- The Korean peninsula is divided into two separate countries.
- North Korea is a Communist country, and South Korea is a republic.

Places & Terms

Three Kingdoms

Seoul

Pyongyang

CONNECT TO THE ISSUES

TRADE South Korea is one of the economic tigers of the region, and much of its prosperity depends upon industry and trade.

SUNSHINE STATE STANDARDS
Key Standard SS.B.2.4.1 The student understands how social, cultural, economic, and environmental factors contribute to the dynamic nature of regions.

Other Standards SS.A.3.4.10, B.1.4.4, D.2.4.1

FCAT LA.A.2.2.7 Reading: Recognize Compare and Contrast

PLACE Kyungbok Palace is located in Seoul, South Korea. **What does the setting of the palace amidst the bustle of Seoul suggest about the culture?**

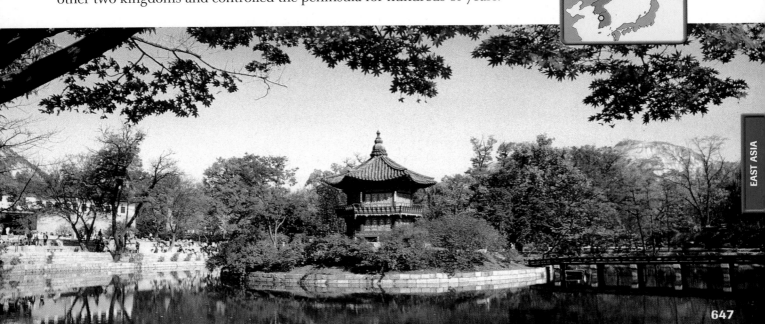

EAST ASIA

647

The Korean War, 1950–1953

1 North Korea Invasion, 1950

2 UN Offensive, 1950

3 Chinese Offensive, 1950

4 Stalemate and Armistice, 1953

Area occupied by Communist forces

Area occupied by UN forces

Movement of Communist forces

Movement of UN forces

0   100   200 miles
0   100   200 kilometers   Lambert Conformal Conic Projection

SKILLBUILDER: Interpreting Maps

1 MOVEMENT Which forces moved south almost to Pusan?

2 REGION Compare maps 1 and 4 above. Did either side gain more territory?

In 1392, a general named Yi Songgye became ruler of Korea. He founded a dynasty that lasted for hundreds of years. But the dynasty ended in 1910, when Japan took control of the entire peninsula. The Japanese ruled Korea until they were defeated in World War II in 1945.

TWO KOREAS: NORTH AND SOUTH After Japan's defeat in the war, the northern part of Korea was controlled by the Soviet Union, and the southern half was supported by the United States. In 1950, Korean troops from the North invaded South Korea, starting the Korean War. The war ended in 1953 with a treaty that divided the peninsula between the Communist state of North Korea and the democratic country of South Korea. The two nations remained hostile toward each other, but in the year 2000, they began discussions on reuniting.

Influences on Korean Culture

The shadow cast by China has fallen across the Korean peninsula. Korean culture, including language, art, and religion, shows this influence. More recently, western economic influences have been very important.

THE CHINESE INFLUENCE In philosophy and religion, Korea has adapted many ideas from China. Confucianism (see Section 1) is a system of teachings based on the beliefs of the Chinese scholar Confucius. His ideas stressing social order have influenced many Koreans. Buddhism, which came to Korea by way of China, has also influenced many Koreans.

OTHER CULTURAL INFLUENCES Since World War II, two major influences have had a profound effect on Korea. First, Communism has molded the culture of North Korea. Non-Communist South Korea, on the other hand, has been greatly influenced by Western culture.

In North Korea, the government only allows art that glorifies Communism or the folk tradition. In South Korea, artists have more freedom of expression. They work with themes drawn from their own history and culture, as well as themes drawn from Western art.

Moving Toward Unity

The most important recent development in North Korea and South Korea is the movement toward unification. However, the communist North and democratic South must overcome years of mutual hostility.

AN ARMED SOCIETY After World War II, both North Korea and South Korea built up huge armies. The armed forces of South Korea number more than 600,000 soldiers and sailors. The armed forces of North Korea are even larger, numbering well over one million.

Both countries have existed with large armies and the threat of another war for many years. Only recently has there been an attempt to defuse the situation to prevent an outbreak of war. War has been a real possibility along the border between North Korea and South Korea, which is guarded by nearly 2 million troops on both sides. ◄A

A SINGLE FLAG There are signs of hope, however. In June 2000, the leaders of both Koreas held a summit meeting at which they declared their intention to reunite the two countries. Shortly after, the defense

Geographic Thinking

Seeing Patterns
A▷ What have been the main differences dividing North Korea and South Korea?

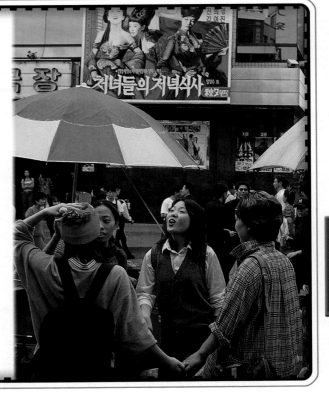

growing up in...South Korea

Young people, like most other South Koreans, follow at least some of the teachings of Confucius. For example, education is highly valued. The state requires by law that students obtain a primary education, and this schooling is free. The majority of children attend secondary schools. More than one million students attend college-level schools in South Korea.

However, in addition to traditional ideas and ways of life, there is a strong western influence in South Korea. This can be seen in the Western clothes worn by these students as they enjoy an outing in the Nampodong shopping district in Pusan, South Korea.

If you lived in South Korea, you would pass these milestones:

- You would be required by law to attend school through 6th grade.
- You would next attend middle school—grades 7 through 9.
- You would then probably attend high school—grades 10 through 12.
- You would be able to vote at age 20.
- The average age for a first marriage is 29 for men and 26 for women.
- The average age of women at the birth of their first child is 27.

The Koreas: North and South **649**

chiefs of the two Koreas met and agreed to reduce tensions along their border. They agreed to discuss clearing land mines so they could rebuild a rail link between the two countries. Perhaps most importantly, families in North Korea and South Korea were allowed to visit each other.

At the summer Olympics held in Sydney, Australia, in 2000, there was another sign of a thaw. The two Koreas marched into the Olympic Stadium under a new flag designed for a single, unified Korea.

Economic and Human Resources

Before the Korean War, the economies of North Korea and South Korea were agricultural. After the war, industry gained in importance in both countries. In many ways, the resources of each country balance one another.

ECONOMIC PATTERNS If North Korea and South Korea reunite, they will form an economic powerhouse. North Korea will be able to provide natural resources and raw materials for South Korea's industries.

South Korea, like Taiwan, is one of the economic tigers of Asia. It is a highly successful and competitive economy. It has the world's largest shipbuilding industry, as well as large automobile, steel, and chemical industries. South Korea is today one of the world's top trading nations.

POPULATION PATTERNS Most of the people in Korea live on plains along the coast or in river valleys among the mountains of the peninsula. South Korea has 45 percent of the Korean peninsula's land area but about 66 percent of its people. **Seoul** is by far the largest city in South Korea, with a population of more than 10 million. The largest city in North Korea is **Pyongyang,** with more than 2.5 million people.

In the next section, you will read about the history, culture, economics, and daily life in Japan.

Assessment

❶ Places & Terms
Identify and explain the significance of each of the following in the region.
- Three Kingdoms
- Seoul
- Pyongyang

❷ Taking Notes
REGION Use your notes to answer the questions below.

- In which ways has China influenced the culture of Korea?
- Which countries in the region have invaded Korea?

❸ Main Ideas
a. What impact has the border between North Korea and South Korea had upon life in both countries?

b. How is the economy of South Korea different from that of North Korea?

c. Which two major influences have shaped North Korea and South Korea since World War II?

❹ Geographic Thinking
Drawing Conclusions How has Korea's physical location affected its history? **Think about:**
- the definition of a peninsula
- the location of Korea's neighbors

S **See Skillbuilder Handbook, page R5.**

SEEING PATTERNS Both Taiwan and South Korea are considered economic tigers of East Asia. What are some characteristics that they share? Make a **Venn diagram** showing the similarities and differences between the two.

Japan

Main Ideas

- Japan has an ancient culture and traditions.
- Japan is the economic giant of East Asia.

Places & Terms

samurai

shogun

CONNECT TO THE ISSUES

PHYSICAL FORCES Japan is vulnerable to devastating earthquakes and huge ocean waves because of its location.

SUNSHINE STATE STANDARDS

Key Standard SS.B.2.4.1 The student understands how social, cultural, economic, and environmental factors contribute to the dynamic nature of regions.

Other Standards SS.A.3.4.9, D.2.4.1

FCAT LA.A.1.4.2 Reading: Strategies

PLACE Takeda Shingen was one of the greatest samurai leaders in 16th century Japan.

What does this painting seem to suggest are some of the qualities of the samurai warrior?

A HUMAN PERSPECTIVE The Japanese flag shows a red sun against a white background. The red sun symbolizes Amaterasu, the sun goddess. According to myth, the Japanese emperor and his family are descended from the goddess. The Japanese call their country *Nippon,* which means "source of the sun." The name *Japan* may have come from a Chinese phrase meaning "origin of the sun," or it may have come from *Chipangu,* a name for the country recorded by Marco Polo.

Samurai and Shogun

Japan lies east of China—toward the rising sun. In their earliest history, the Japanese were close enough to China to feel its civilizing effects, but they were far enough away to be protected from invasion.

ANCIENT JAPAN The original inhabitants of Japan may have come to the islands from the mainland of Asia and from the South Pacific. There is some evidence to suggest that the ancestors of today's Japanese came eastward through Siberia and Korea and entered Japan. By about 1,500 years ago, most of Japan was actively growing food, such as rice. Weapons and tools made of bronze and iron were introduced, along with textiles.

Until the A.D. 300s, Japan was not a unified country. It was made up of hundreds of clans ruling separate territories. Then, by the fifth century, the Yamato clan had become the ruling clan. It claimed descent from the sun goddess, and by the seventh century, its leaders called themselves emperors of Japan.

In 794, the rulers moved the capital to the city of Heian (modern Kyoto). The era from 794 to 1185 is called the Heian period. During this time, Japan's central government was strong, but eventually the great landowners and clan chiefs began to act as independent rulers.

Professional soldiers called **samurai** served the interests of the landowners and clan chiefs. The samurai (the word means "one who guards") served as a bodyguard of warriors loyal to the leader of a clan.

THE SHOGUNS In 1192, after a struggle between two powerful clans, the Japanese emperor created the position of shogun. The **shogun** was the general of the emperor's army with the powers of a military dictator.

EAST ASIA

Japan **651**

All officials, judges, and armies were under his authority. The shoguns appointed governors, called *daimyo,* to each province. They were responsible for maintaining order.

Rule by the shoguns lasted for about 700 years. During those years, the Japanese fought off Mongol invasions and saw the arrival of Portuguese traders, who brought Christianity and firearms to Japan in the 1500s. In 1853, Commodore Matthew Perry's arrival to Japan from the United States ended Japan's isolation. In 1868, the last shogun resigned, and the emperor became head of the government.

EMERGING WORLD POWER During the late 19th century, Japan's government began bringing Japan into the modern age. By the early 20th century, Japan had become a major power.

During the early years of the 20th century, Japan expanded its empire. (See map on next page.) Its interests and those of the United States came into conflict in the Pacific region. On December 7, 1941, the Japanese launched a surprise attack on the U.S. naval base at Pearl Harbor in Hawaii. The attack brought the United States into World War II, which ended with Japan's defeat and surrender in 1945. A

After World War II, the United States headed the occupation of Japan and introduced political and economic reforms. Eventually Japan became a democracy—a constitutional monarchy with an emperor and an elected parliament.

Geographic Thinking

Seeing Patterns
A How might Japan's 20th century empire have reflected its history?

An Economic Powerhouse

After its defeat in World War II, Japan transformed itself into one of the world's most powerful economies. It experienced an economic boom, even though it has few natural resources. Japan is second only to the United States in the size of its economy.

PEOPLE AND PRODUCTS The population of Japan is more than 126 million. About 75 percent of Japan's people live in cities. Sixty percent of the people live on 2.7 percent of the land. Japan has few minorities, and those few are often discriminated against.

Japanese History, 1500–2000

1571
Japan opens port of Nagasaki to overseas trade.

1603
Tokugawa Ieyasu *(below)* becomes shogun of Japan.

1716
Yoshimune becomes shogun of Japan.

1796
The great Japanese printmaker Utamaro (1753–1806) was known for his **portraits of women,** such as the one shown below.

1500   1600   1700   1800

1680
Tsunayoshi becomes shogun of Japan.

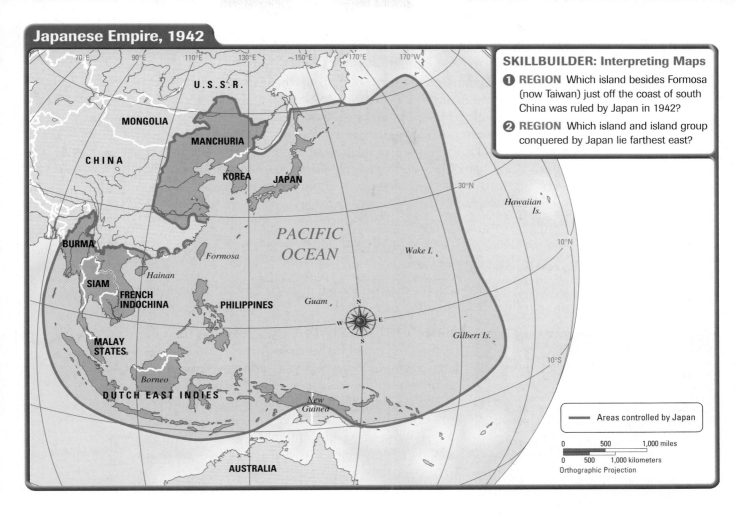

Japanese Empire, 1942

U.S.S.R.

MONGOLIA

MANCHURIA

CHINA

KOREA

JAPAN

BURMA

Formosa

Hainan

SIAM

FRENCH
INDOCHINA

PHILIPPINES

MALAY
STATES

Borneo

DUTCH EAST INDIES

New
Guinea

AUSTRALIA

PACIFIC
OCEAN

Guam

Gilbert Is.

Wake I.

Hawaiian
Is.

30°N

10°N

10°S

70°E 90°E 110°E 130°E 150°E 170°E 170°W

N
W   E
S

Areas controlled by Japan

0   500   1,000 miles
0   500 1,000 kilometers
Orthographic Projection

SKILLBUILDER: Interpreting Maps

❶ **REGION** Which island besides Formosa (now Taiwan) just off the coast of south China was ruled by Japan in 1942?

❷ **REGION** Which island and island group conquered by Japan lie farthest east?

Most of Japan's population and most of its industry and manufacturing are located in a corridor hundreds of miles long along the east coast of the main island of Honshu, with Tokyo as its anchor. The people who live in this corridor form the work force that produces goods sold around the world.

Manufacturing and trade are at the heart of Japan's economy. Japan imports most of the natural resources for its industrial needs. Among the resources it imports are coal and petroleum. Then it uses those resources and others to manufacture products for export to the global market. Among the most important of those products are cars, trucks, and electronic equipment such as televisions and computers.

A strong alliance between business and government has been one of the reasons for Japan's economic success during the second half of the 20th century. After the war, the United States gave economic assistance to Japan. Financial support from the government helped Japanese businesses develop products to market abroad.

1945
The **mushroom cloud** (below) is from an atomic bomb dropped on Nagasaki on August 9, 1945.

1900

2000

1853
A Japanese woodcut shows **Commodore Perry** (above) upon his arrival in Japan.

EAST ASIA

ECONOMIC SLOWDOWN After four decades of rapid growth, Japan's economy began to slow down in the 1990s. As the economic growth rate declined, many companies scaled back their operations, and some went bankrupt. A number of reasons accounted for this slowdown.

Other economies in East Asia, such as those of Taiwan, South Korea, and Hong Kong, provided competition. Then, when the economies of Southeast Asia encountered problems, Japanese investments there lost value. Many banks proved vulnerable. The Japanese stock market suffered big losses. Also, the Japanese people tended to save rather than spend. As a result, the economy became even more dependent on exports, which declined because of competition from other countries. **B**

CONNECT TO THE ISSUES
TRADE
B How are the economies of the region connected?

Japanese Culture

Japanese culture reflects the influences of both East and West. From these influences, Japan has developed its own unique culture.

PLACE Toyozo Arakawa, one of Japan's leading potters, was named a "Living National Treasure" in 1955.
What does the naming of a person as a national treasure say about a culture?

A TRADITIONAL PEOPLE In developing their early culture, the Japanese borrowed from China. Japanese language, religion, art, music, and government were all influenced by the Chinese.

The city of Kyoto is a monument to Japanese culture. The city contains Buddhist temples and Shinto shrines built of wood in the old style. The entire city is a living testament to Japanese ideas of beauty. Gardens, palaces, and temples all reflect a very spare, elegant, and refined style. In Kyoto and throughout Japan, great emphasis is placed on achieving harmony between a building and its natural surroundings.

Traditional drama is still performed in Japan. Noh plays developed during the 14th century. They deal with subjects drawn from history and legend and are performed by actors wearing masks. In the 17th century, Kabuki plays developed. They have colorful scenery, an exaggerated acting style, and vivid costumes.

Japanese painting was influenced by Chinese techniques and themes. Many early Japanese paintings show Buddhist themes that often came to Japan by way of China. Some examples of Japanese artistic works include long picture scrolls, ink paintings, and wood-block prints.

WESTERN INFLUENCES Since the day in 1853 when Commodore Perry sailed his fleet into Tokyo Bay, Japan has been open to Western influences. Those influences are visible in modern-day Japan.

Sports like baseball, golf, sumo wrestling, soccer, and tennis are popular in Japan. The clothes worn by most people are Western in style, although traditional clothing is worn on special occasions.

Western music is also popular in Japan. Rock music is popular among younger Japanese. They listen to Western groups and form rock bands of their own. Many cities in Japan have symphony orchestras that play Western classical music. Jazz is also popular.

Japan has been successful at balancing its traditional styles in art, theater, music, and architecture with influences from the West.

BACKGROUND
A tradition of print-making native to Japan is called *ukiyo-e*, which means "pictures of the floating world," the Japanese term for scenes from everyday life.

Life in Today's Japan

The people of Japan are educated and disciplined. This work force has enabled Japan to achieve prosperity.

EDUCATION Japan's educational system is highly structured. Students often attend school six days a week. They have a shorter summer vacation than American students—just six weeks in late July and August. Students attend six years of elementary school and three years of junior high school. Education is free during those years. Then they spend three years in high school. At the same time, many students attend classes at private schools called *juku* to help get them into good colleges.

Competition among students is high to gain admission to the best universities. Japan has more than 1,000 universities and technical colleges. Universities that rank at the top of the educational system include the University of Tokyo, Kyoto University, Keio University, and Waseda University.

CHANGES IN SOCIETY The Japanese are making some changes in the way their society is run. People are now increasingly demanding an end to pollution and over-crowding. Furthermore, workers at all skill levels are asking for shorter workdays and more vacation time.

In the next chapter, you will read about three important issues in East Asia. These include trade, the pressures of a large population, and the dangers posed by volcanoes around the Pacific Ocean.

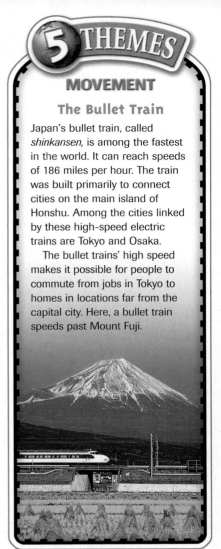

5 THEMES

MOVEMENT

The Bullet Train

Japan's bullet train, called *shinkansen*, is among the fastest in the world. It can reach speeds of 186 miles per hour. The train was built primarily to connect cities on the main island of Honshu. Among the cities linked by these high-speed electric trains are Tokyo and Osaka.

The bullet trains' high speed makes it possible for people to commute from jobs in Tokyo to homes in locations far from the capital city. Here, a bullet train speeds past Mount Fuji.

Assessment

1 Places & Terms

Identify and explain the significance of each of the following in the region.

- samurai
- shogun

2 Taking Notes

REGION Use your notes to answer the questions below.

Japan — East Asia

- What happened to Japan in World War II?
- What is the importance of education in Japan today?

3 Main Ideas

a. What is the basis of Japan's economic prosperity?

b. What are some examples of traditional Japanese culture?

c. How did the Western world influence Japan beginning in the 19th century?

4 Geographic Thinking

Making Inferences How might Japan's isolation and its uniform population have both helped and hindered it in its attempts to achieve prosperity? **Think about:**

- the advantages of uniformity
- the importance of creativity

EAST ASIA

GeoActivity

SEEING PATTERNS Japan has some very distinctive cultural forms, such as Kabuki theater and sumo wrestling. Present a brief **report** to the class on some aspect of Japanese culture, illustrated by visuals that you have found in your research.

Comparing Cultures

Masks

Masks are coverings that disguise the face. Most cultures use masks for a variety of purposes. Followers sometimes wear ceremonial masks during religious celebrations. Actors wear theatrical masks during performances such as those in the classical drama of ancient Greece, China, and Japan. Mourners sometimes placed burial masks over the faces of the dead before they were buried. In ancient Egypt, they placed the mask directly on the mummy or else on the mummy case. Participants sometimes wear festival masks during celebrations such as Mardi Gras in New Orleans or Carnival in Rio de Janeiro.

United States

Japan

Angola

Indonesia

SUNSHINE STATE STANDARDS
Key Standard SS.A.2.4.1 The student understands the early physical and cultural development of humans.

FCAT LA.A.2.2.7 Reading: Recognize Compare and Contrast

A masked dancer in Bali, Indonesia, performs a ritual dance. Balinese dancers move to the music of gongs and flutes. In their dances, each movement and gesture helps to tell the story.

This mask from Angola represents a female ancestor with an elaborate headdress. A member of the Chokwe culture in Africa created this mask out of wood and fibers in the 20th century.

Native American ceremonial masks were used to calm angry spirits. This mask is a product of the Iroquois culture of the northeast woodlands and was used in healing ceremonies.

Japanese masks and costumes are worn by a performer in a Noh drama, the classical drama of Japan. Masked performers create music and dance in a highly stylized manner.

GeoActivity

MAKING MASKS

Use the Internet to research how to make different kinds of masks. Choose materials that are easy to obtain. Then make a **mask** that you will show to the class.

- Use a technique about which you have found information.
- Write a description of the procedure you followed to make the mask.
- Display your mask in an area set aside in the classroom.

RESEARCH LINKS
CLASSZONE.COM

GeoData

ODD FACTS ABOUT MASKS

- In Europe, masks have been discovered that date back as early as 30,000 years ago to Paleolithic times.
- The solid gold death mask of the pharaoh Tutankhamen, which covered the head of his mummy, weighs 22.5 pounds.
- Masks were worn by the performers of tragedies and comedies in ancient Greece.
- The Senesi people of New Guinea use masks that include skirts that cover much of the body.
- The Aleuts of Alaska cover the faces of their dead with wooden masks.
- Death masks made of plaster are sometimes put on the face of the dead to preserve their features for posterity. Death masks exist for Napoleon Bonaparte and Ludwig van Beethoven.
- The mask worn by actor Clayton Moore in the television show *The Lone Ranger* was sold at auction for $33,000.

VISUAL SUMMARY
HUMAN GEOGRAPHY OF EAST ASIA

Subregions of East Asia

● **China**
- China has more people than any other country in the world.
- It is about the same size as the United States in area.
- It has been the dominant culture in the region since ancient times.

○ **Mongolia and Taiwan**
- The histories of Mongolia and Taiwan have been closely linked with that of China.
- They have pursued separate paths of development—Mongolia has had a managed economy, while Taiwan has a capitalist economy based on manufacturing and trade.

● **The Koreas: North and South**
- The Korean peninsula is divided into two separate countries: Communist North Korea and capitalist South Korea.
- Recently, the two countries have begun discussing the possibility of becoming one country.

○ **Japan**
- Japan is a great industrial power.
- It has managed to achieve economic prosperity despite its small land area and limited resources.

Reviewing Places & Terms

A. Briefly explain the importance of each of the following.

1. dynasty
2. Boxer Rebellion
3. Mao Zedong
4. Confucianism
5. Pacific Rim
6. Three Kingdoms
7. Seoul
8. Pyongyang
9. samurai
10. shogun

B. Answer the questions about vocabulary in complete sentences.

11. Which area extends from New Zealand in the western Pacific to Chile in the eastern Pacific?
12. What term means "one who guards"?
13. What is the largest city in North Korea?
14. Which city in the Koreas has about 10 million residents?
15. What event did it take a multinational force of 20,000 soldiers to end?
16. Which term describes a leader with the powers of a military dictator?
17. In which system of thought was there respect for the past and one's ancestors?
18. Who ruled the People's Republic of China from 1949 to 1976?
19. The Shang and the Han are examples of what?
20. Koguryo, Paekche, and Silla made up what?

Main Ideas

China (pp. 635–641)

1. In what ways has China influenced other cultures in the region?
2. How is China able to feed its enormous population?
3. What are some of the basic beliefs of Confucianism?

Mongolia and Taiwan (pp. 642–646)

4. What kind of economy does Mongolia have, and what activity is at its core?
5. What kind of economy does Taiwan have?

The Koreas: North and South (pp. 647–650)

6. Why did North Korea become a communist state and South Korea a democracy?
7. Why is South Korea considered an economic tiger?

Japan (pp. 651–657)

8. Why did Japan emerge onto the world scene in the 19th century?
9. Why is the city of Kyoto in Japan important?
10. Where does Japan get its resources, and how does it use them in its industries?

Critical Thinking

1. Using Your Notes

Use your completed chart to answer these questions.

a. What are some of the ways in which China has influenced the culture of East Asia?

b. What seems to be the general direction of economic development in the region?

2. Geographic Themes

a. **HUMAN-ENVIRONMENT INTERACTION** How have the river basins of eastern China supported a high population density?

b. **REGION** What are some of the natural barriers that have provided isolation or security to the different countries of the region?

3. Identifying Themes

Interaction between cultures occurred throughout the region. What are some of the consequences of this interaction? Which of the five themes are reflected in your answer?

4. Making Inferences

What might be the effect of innovations of modern life, such as computers and the Internet, on the development of democracy and free-market economies in the region?

5. Making Comparisons

How would you compare the economic prosperity and success of managed and capitalist economies in the region?

Additional Test Practice, pp. S1–S37

TEST PRACTICE
CLASSZONE.COM

Geographic Skills: Interpreting Graphs

Stock Market in South Korea

Use the graph at right to answer the following questions.

1. **ANALYZING DATA** When did the stock market in South Korea reach its lowest level?

2. **MAKING COMPARISONS** What was its highest level before its plunge?

3. **DRAWING CONCLUSIONS** What level did it reach by the year 2000? What does this suggest about the economy of South Korea?

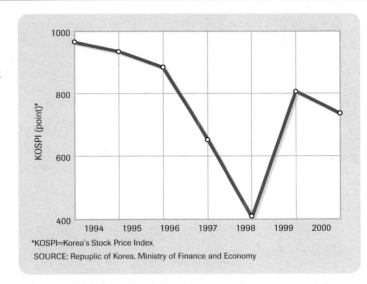

*KOSPI=Korea's Stock Price Index
SOURCE: Republic of Korea, Ministry of Finance and Economy

The stock market in South Korea has seen dramatic ups and downs corresponding to the economic crises in the region in recent years.

GeoActivity

Research stock market activity in one or more of the other countries in the region. Show your findings in a graph tracking stock market activity for the late 1990s.

 INTERNET ACTIVITY

Use the links at **classzone.com** to do research on the Mongol conquests. Focus on the reasons for the success of their conquests and whether the results of their conquests were mainly negative or positive.

Analyzing Data Present the results of your research in a chart that shows the positive and negative effects of the Mongol conquests.

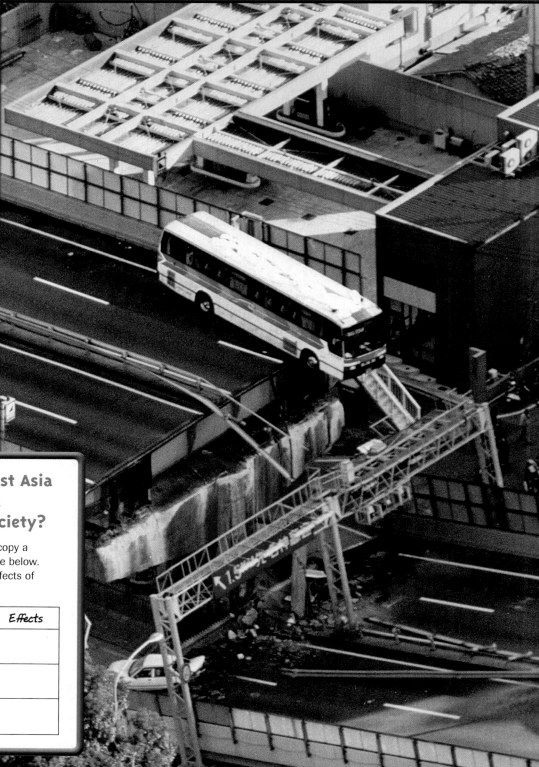

Chapter 29

TODAY'S ISSUES
East Asia

SECTION 1
The Ring of Fire

SECTION 2
Trade and Prosperity

CASESTUDY
POPULATION AND THE QUALITY OF LIFE

For more on these issues in East Asia . . .

CURRENT EVENTS
CLASSZONE.COM

A bus teeters on the edge of a highway torn apart by an earthquake in Kobe, Japan, in 1995.

GeoFocus

How do people in East Asia deal with issues of a rapidly changing society?

Taking Notes In your notebook, copy a cause-and-effect chart like the one below. Then take notes on causes and effects of some aspect of each issue.

	Causes	Effects
Issue 1: Ring of Fire		
Issue 2: Trade		
Case Study: Population		

The Ring of Fire

How might people in East Asia prepare for earthquakes and volcanoes?

Main Ideas
• The islands of Japan form part of a geologically active area called the Ring of Fire.
• Because of its location, Japan has faced disastrous earthquakes, volcanic eruptions, and tsunamis.

Places & Terms
Ring of Fire
Great Kanto earthquake
tsunami

SUNSHINE STATE STANDARDS
Key Standard SS.B.1.4.3 The student uses mental maps of physical and human features of the world to answer complex geographic questions.
Other Standards SS.B.2.4.5
FCAT LA.A.1.4.2 Reading: Strategies

A HUMAN PERSPECTIVE On January 17, 1995, at 5:46 A.M., a severe earthquake rocked Kobe, Japan's sixth largest city. When the dust settled and the last of the fires burned out, about 6,000 people lay dead, and more than 40,000 suffered injuries. The government quickly began rebuilding the port city, but psychologists warned that reviving the spirit of Kobe's people would take time. Many lost family members. Entire neighborhoods vanished. A year after the quake, nearly 50,000 people were still living in temporary shelters, and anger grew against the government. Clearly, much more than glass, steel, bricks, and mortar would be needed to bring Kobe fully back to life.

Physical Forces in the Ring of Fire

Like Kobe, many Japanese cities are threatened by earthquakes. This is because Japan is part of the **Ring of Fire**—a chain of volcanoes that line the Pacific Rim. (See the map on the next page.)

SHIFTING PLATES As you learned in Unit 1, the outer crust of the earth is made up of a number of shifting tectonic plates that continually bump and slide into each other. When a dense oceanic plate meets a less dense continental plate, the oceanic plate slides under the continental plate in a process called subduction. The area where the oceanic crust is subducted is called a trench.

In East Asia, the Pacific oceanic plate encounters the Eurasian continental plate. When the oceanic plate moves under the continental plate, it crumples the continental crust, building mountains and volcanoes such as those that form the Ring of Fire.

At the same time, tremendous stress builds up along the edges of the plates. The stress keeps building until eventually the plates move suddenly and violently. The result is an earthquake.

HUMAN-ENVIRONMENT INTERACTION An elderly woman is carried from a collapsing building during the earthquake in Kobe, Japan, in 1995.
What damage is apparent in the photograph?

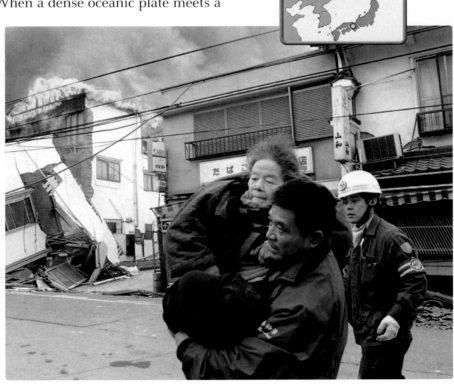

EAST ASIA

The Geology of Japan

The Japanese islands exist because of subduction. The islands were formed by volcanoes created as the Pacific plate slid under the Eurasian plate. But the same forces that build islands can also destroy them.

VOLCANOES Living along the Ring of Fire means living with volcanic activity. From the time historical records were first kept, at least 60 volcanoes have been active on the islands of Japan. In fact, the best-known landform in Japan, Mt. Fuji, is a volcano.

EARTHQUAKES AND TSUNAMIS Earthquakes like the one that destroyed Kobe are common in Japan. An average of 1,000 quakes occur there each year. Most are too mild to affect people's lives. Some, however, cause many deaths and massive destruction. In 1923, the **Great Kanto earthquake** and the fires it caused killed an estimated 140,000 people and left the city of Tokyo in ruins. The quake partially or completely destroyed nearly 700,000 homes. Ⓐ

Another geological threat to Japan comes from the sea. When an earthquake occurs under the ocean floor, part of the floor moves. If the quake is strong enough, this shift may produce a **tsunami,** a huge wave of great destructive power. Underwater volcanic eruptions and coastal landslides can also cause tsunamis. Some waves have reached heights of over 100 feet.

🌐 **Geographic Thinking**◄

Making Comparisons
Ⓐ How many lives were lost in the Great Kanto earthquake compared to the Kobe earthquake?

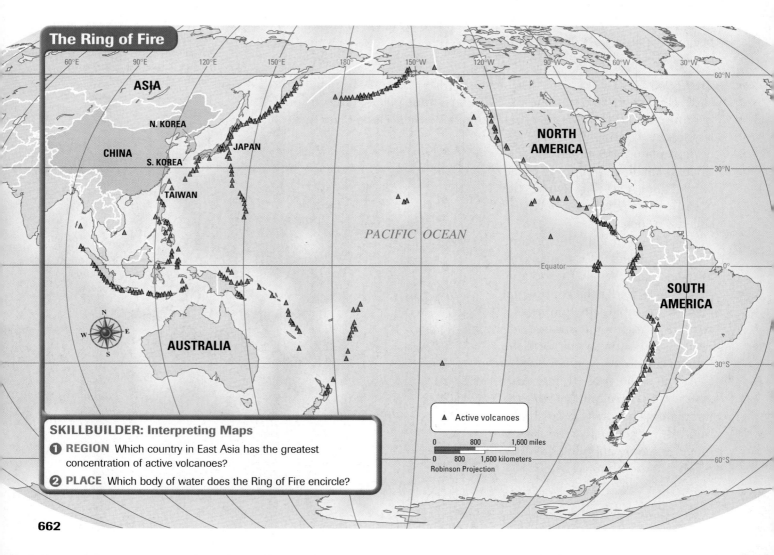

The Ring of Fire

▲ Active volcanoes

0   800   1,600 miles
0   800   1,600 kilometers
Robinson Projection

SKILLBUILDER: Interpreting Maps

❶ **REGION** Which country in East Asia has the greatest concentration of active volcanoes?

❷ **PLACE** Which body of water does the Ring of Fire encircle?

Preparing for Disasters

For thousands of years, people have tried to predict when natural disasters will occur. At the dawn of the 21st century, they are still trying. Vulnerable nations like Japan are working to improve their defenses against the destructive power of geological forces.

PROBLEMS Many older buildings in Japan are not as likely to withstand earthquakes as newer buildings. In addition, some buildings have been constructed on ground or landfill that is not very stable. Underground gas lines are likely to rupture in the event of an earthquake, and leaking gas can catch fire. Crowded blocks and narrow streets spread the fires and hinder rescue operations.

SOLUTIONS Japan has established a strict building code. Whenever a quake rocks some area of the nation, engineers are quick to study how different types of buildings withstood the heaving ground beneath them. The results of their studies affect building codes governing construction materials and techniques. This has made newer buildings safer than older ones.

Because of the dangers, the Japanese people understand the importance of being prepared for disasters. Schoolchildren participate in yearly disaster drills with local fire-fighters. Organizations like the Japanese Red Cross Society and the Asia Pacific Disaster Management Center offer courses on disaster preparedness and management.

Japan and the other countries along the Ring of Fire cannot change the geology that shapes their land. They can, however, learn more about it and prepare to deal with disaster when it strikes next.

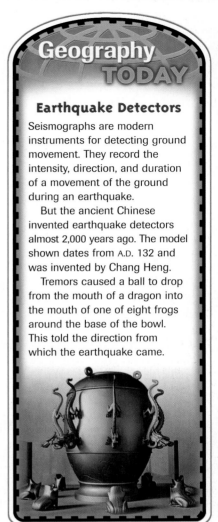

Geography TODAY

Earthquake Detectors

Seismographs are modern instruments for detecting ground movement. They record the intensity, direction, and duration of a movement of the ground during an earthquake.

But the ancient Chinese invented earthquake detectors almost 2,000 years ago. The model shown dates from A.D. 132 and was invented by Chang Heng.

Tremors caused a ball to drop from the mouth of a dragon into the mouth of one of eight frogs around the base of the bowl. This told the direction from which the earthquake came.

Assessment

❶ Places & Terms

Identify and explain the following places and terms.

- Ring of Fire
- Great Kanto earthquake
- tsunami

❷ Taking Notes

HUMAN-ENVIRONMENT INTERACTION Review the notes you took for this section.

	Causes	Effects
Issue 1: Ring of Fire		

- What was the effect of subduction on Japan?
- What causes tsunamis?

❸ Main Ideas

a. What are some of the natural disasters that can strike around the Ring of Fire?

b. What role do shifting plates play in earthquakes?

c. What organizations help the Japanese prepare for natural disasters?

❹ Geographic Thinking

Making Inferences How will Japan respond in the future to natural disasters such as earthquakes? **Think about:**

- how it has responded so far
- its location and the frequency of earthquakes there

See Skillbuilder Handbook, page R4.

GeoActivity

EXPLORING LOCAL GEOGRAPHY Pair with a partner and research the natural disasters that might possibly occur where you live—flood, tornado, hurricane, earthquake, and so forth. Then develop an **Emergency Procedures brochure** that lists the steps you would take to deal with such an emergency.

EAST ASIA

RAND McNALLY — Map and Graph Skills

SUNSHINE STATE STANDARDS
Key Standard SS.B.1.4.1
The student uses a variety of maps, geographic technologies including geographic information systems (GIS) and satellite-produced imagery, and other advanced graphic representations to depict geographic problems.

FCAT LA.A.2.2.7 Reading: Recognize Compare and Contrast

Interpreting a Proportional Circle Map

The earthquake that devastated Kobe, Japan, in 1995 measured 6.8 on the Richter scale, which is a scale for measuring the magnitude of earthquakes. About 6,000 people died and many thousands more were injured. Although the Kobe quake was the most destructive in recent years, there have been many others in Japan in the 1990s. Some of these were more powerful than the Kobe quake but they did not do as much damage.

THE LANGUAGE OF MAPS A **proportional circle map** shows the relative sizes of objects or events, such as earthquakes. This map shows major earthquakes in Japan during a ten-year period beginning in 1991. The larger the circle on the map, the greater the magnitude of the earthquake as measured by the scale.

Major Earthquakes in Japan, 1991–2000

Copyright by Rand McNally & Co.

1 A cluster of circles indicates that an area is prone to frequent quakes.

2 The key explains that the bigger and darker a circle is on the map, the greater the size and intensity of the quake.

3 Values on an earthquake magnitude scale are typically between 1 and 9. This map shows earthquakes with a magnitude of 6 and higher. Each increase of .5 represents an increase in released energy. Scales for measuring earthquakes include the Richter, the moment magnitude, and others.

Map and Graph Skills Assessment

1. Analyzing Data
What was the intensity of the earthquake that struck Kobe?

2. Making Comparisons
On which islands did the most powerful quake occur in this period? In what range did it fall, as measured by the scale?

3. Making Inferences
Why do you think the quake you identified in question 2 was not as destructive as the Kobe quake?

Trade and Prosperity

What are some benefits of global trade?

Main Ideas
- East Asian economies became global powerhouses in the 1970s and 1980s.
- The decline of Asian economies in the 1990s created a crisis that spread around the globe.

Places & Terms

UNICEF

global economy

Jakota Triangle

recession

sweatshop

SUNSHINE STATE STANDARDS
Key Standard SS.D.2.4.6 The student understands factors that have led to increased international interdependence and basic concepts associated with trade between nations.

FCAT LA.A.1.4.2 Reading: Strategies

A HUMAN PERSPECTIVE At the beginning of the 1990s, the economies of East Asia were growing very rapidly. Unfortunately, there was a dark side to this prosperity. In 1995, **UNICEF (the United Nations Children's Fund)** reported that more than half a million children in East Asia were working in factories or begging on the streets. UNICEF regional director Daniel Brooks noted that, due to fast-paced economic growth, "We are seeing the erosion of family values and that includes the exploitation of children." This is one of the important issues facing the region.

Opening Doors

The process by which East Asia became an economic powerhouse took centuries. Until the 1500s, the nations of East Asia had been isolated from the rest of the world. As Western demand for Asian products grew, European traders used a variety of means—including force—to end East Asia's isolation.

Eventually, the economies of the region were to emerge as major players in the global economy. However, foreign intervention and world war lay ahead before East Asian nations achieved widespread prosperity.

OPENING TO THE WEST By the 1800s, the nations of Europe had signed treaties that gave them distinct spheres of influence in the East. These were areas where they could control trade without interference from other Western nations. In 1853, Commodore Matthew Perry set sail from the United States to Japan to persuade the Japanese to establish trade and diplomatic relations with the United States. The naval warships that accompanied Perry intimidated Japan into opening its doors to the United States and the West.

MOVEMENT Japan exports about 4½ million vehicles each year. Here, cars are about to be loaded onto a boat in the port of Nagoya.

EAST ASIA

INDUSTRIALIZATION AND GLOBALIZATION After World War II, the nations of East Asia began industrializing, using cheap labor to produce goods for trade. Trade between East and West steadily increased. The labels "Made in China" and "Made in Japan" on goods became very common in the United States and Europe.

At the same time, regional economies, which had evolved from national economies, began to merge. Eventually, a **global economy** developed, in which nations became dependent on each other for goods and services. For example, Japan imported many natural resources from around the world and then transformed those resources into manufactured goods that it sold around the globe. The nations of East Asia used their supplies of cheap labor to become manufacturing powerhouses. The World Bank described this boom as an "economic miracle."

Powerful Economies of East Asia

During the 1980s and early 1990s, many Asian economies did very well. The most powerful of the Pacific Rim nations of East Asia—Japan, Taiwan, and South Korea—enjoyed record prosperity. These three countries formed a part of a zone of prosperity referred to by some as the **Jakota Triangle**—**Ja**pan, **Ko**rea (South), and **Ta**iwan. By the mid-1990s, however, these economies were experiencing problems.

Exports from Jakota Triangle Countries

Japan's Total Exports: $413 billion (1999)
- Hong Kong 5.2%
- S. Korea 5.4%
- China 5.5%
- Taiwan 7%
- Other 45.9%
- U.S. 31%

Each pie graph shows the exporting country's most important trading partners. In each case, the United States is the biggest customer; however, "Other" (countries not mentioned by name in the graph) is the largest segment of each pie. The icons show some important industries in each country.

South Korea's Total Exports: $144 billion (1999)
- Taiwan 7%
- China 9%
- Other 58%
- U.S. 17%
- Japan 9%

Taiwan's Total Exports: $121.6 billion (1999)
- Singapore 3%
- Japan 10%
- Hong Kong 21%
- Other 40%
- U.S. 26%

JAPAN

Tokyo
Yokohama
Nagoya
Osaka

SOUTH KOREA

Seoul

TAIWAN

Taipei

Industry
- Automobile manufacturing
- Chemicals
- Electronic products
- Plastics
- Shipbuilding
- Steel and metals
- Textiles
- Commercial fishing
- Office machinery
- Machinery and equipment

ECONOMIC PROBLEMS ARISE Although some East Asian economies appeared healthy, they were burdened by debt and mismanagement. The Asian economic miracle had been based in part on efficiency and innovation. It also had been built partly on the sacrifices of very poor and very young workers, who were paid low wages.

In the mid-1990s, a series of banks and other companies went bankrupt (could not pay their debts). This sparked panic among foreign investors, who began selling their Asian stocks and currency. In some countries, riots broke out. In Japan and South Korea, ruling politicians had to resign. Japan's economy entered a **recession**—an extended decline in general business activity. The Asian economic miracle had come to an end. South Korea and Taiwan also experienced recessions.

Geographic Thinking

Seeing Patterns
A▶ What were some of the factors that led to recession in the region?

A GLOBAL RIPPLE EFFECT Because the economies of many nations are interconnected, the crisis in Asia spread throughout the world. Uncertainty led to concern at the New York Stock Exchange and other national exchanges. To prevent a global economic downturn, the World Bank and the International Monetary Fund stepped in, lending money to East Asian countries that promised reform. This began to reverse the downslide, but the world had learned an important lesson—a global economy could threaten prosperity as well as improve it.

THE PROMISE OF REFORM The economic crisis led to an awareness in East Asia that serious reform was necessary. Reform would have to include increased wages for adult workers, as well as a ban on child-labor and forced-labor practices. It would also mean an end to **sweatshops.** These are workplaces where people work long hours for pennies under poor conditions. At the dawn of the 21st century, reforms had begun, and Asian economies were showing new signs of life.

In the next section, you will read about the expanding population of East Asia. The growth in population has had an impact on the quality of life in the region.

SECTION 2 Assessment

❶ Places & Terms

Identify and explain the following places and terms.

- UNICEF
- global economy
- Jakota Triangle
- recession
- sweatshop

❷ Taking Notes

HUMAN-ENVIRONMENT INTERACTION Review the notes you took for this section.

	Causes	Effects
Issue 2: Trade		

- Why is trade important to the economies of the region?
- How did the people of East Asia make possible the "economic miracle"?

❸ Main Ideas

a. How was the prosperity of East Asia linked to the wider world?

b. What were some of the consequences of economic development in the region?

c. What were some of the causes of economic decline in the region?

❹ Geographic Thinking

Making Inferences Why might changes in the global economy have a greater effect on South Korea and Taiwan than on China and Mongolia? **Think about:**

- the global economy
- agriculture and industry

RESEARCH LINKS
CLASSZONE.COM

GeoActivity

SEEING PATTERNS Pair with a partner and choose one country in the region that is heavily dependent on trade—for example, Japan, South Korea, or Taiwan. Then use the Internet to find out how that country's economy did in the year 2000. Give a **class report** on whether the economy is improving.

EAST ASIA

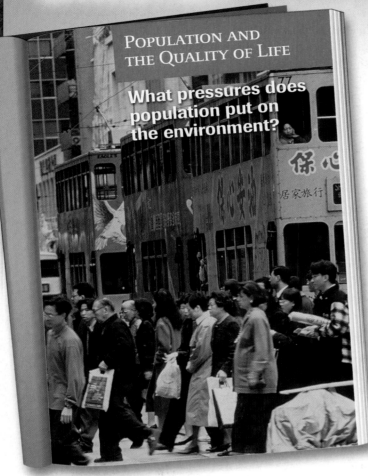

POPULATION AND THE QUALITY OF LIFE

What pressures does population put on the environment?

Trams, buses, and people crowd the streets of Hong Kong.

The Voyageur Experience in World Geography
China: Food for a Billion Plus

SUNSHINE STATE STANDARDS
Key Standard SS.B.2.4.7 The student understands the concept of sustainable development.

Other Standards SS.B.2.4.1, B.2.4.5

FCAT LA.A.2.2.7 Reading: Recognize Compare and Contrast

Because East Asia has changed so much, it's hard to imagine how different the region looked 50 years ago. Today, some of the countries and cities of the region are among the most prosperous in the world. In Japan, South Korea, and Taiwan, the statistics on per capita income, length of life, and literacy are all high. Despite recent problems, the economies are generally prosperous, as can be seen in the glittering shopping districts and luxurious residential neighborhoods of Tokyo, Seoul, and Taipei. But it wasn't always that way. If the big problem of the past was industrializing, today it is managing population.

Patterns of Population

Many of the countries of East Asia have been so successful in dealing with the basic problems of feeding their people and industrializing that they now face other problems. Several of these problems are caused by the expanding populations in the region.

THE SITUATION AT MID-CENTURY At the middle of the 20th century, the nations of East Asia ranked among the least developed in the world. In fact, statistics on health, literacy, fertility, and economics in East Asia mirrored those of the poorest region of the world—sub-Saharan Africa. Widespread poverty was the norm. Life expectancy was short. Fertility rates were high, as were infant and maternal death rates. In 1950, East Asian women often married young and gave birth to six children on average during their lifetimes. Most economies remained rural.

Addressing Population Problems

Policy makers in the region understood that population control was key to solving a wide range of social and economic woes. Among the successful programs were those that stressed education and family planning.

ENVIRONMENTAL STRESS Unrestricted population growth put tremendous strain on the quality of life in the region and on the environment. Food production on existing farmland was barely adequate. The absence of basic sanitation fouled the region's water supplies. In some countries, such as China, the water tables were drained to dangerously low levels. Fortunately, the governments of East Asia recognized this catastrophe-in-the-making. They moved quickly to reverse course.

PROBLEMS AND POLICIES Aggressive family planning programs were begun in the region. Birth rates began leveling off and then dropping. By the year 2000, women were marrying much later and giving birth to an average of 2.5 children. In China alone, the birth rate dropped from 6.22 children per woman in 1950–1955 to just 1.82 in the year 2000.

IMPRESSIVE RESULTS This drop in birth rates, combined with industrialization, led to fast economic growth. By the 1990s, the economies of East Asia were booming, transforming social and economic conditions. In just over a generation, the region's quality of life has improved to the point where life expectancy and literacy rates are among the highest in the world.

The Quality of Life

Although these changes in East Asia have been dramatic, they have not solved all of the region's problems. Some countries in the region, such as China and Japan, are among the most populous in the world. Furthermore, life expectancy in East Asia has increased from 41 years in the period 1950–1955 to 69 years in the year 2000.

SOME ONGOING PROBLEMS The huge populations of the region continue to put pressure on the environment. Even if China were to maintain a modest growth rate of one percent a year, it would still add 13 million people to its population annually.

The growing populations are concentrated in the cities of the region, where they must be provided with housing, sanitation, and transportation. Pollution, overcrowding, and flooding are all problems that are made worse by an expanding population.

However, not all family planning programs were well received. Some citizens criticized China's one-child-per-family policy as harsh and an assault on their rights. In the face of such criticism, the region's family planning efforts were expanded.

Despite these difficulties, East Asia has shown the world that rapid social and economic progress are possible. This requires that people and their leaders join hands with the world community to make difficult decisions and put in place sound policies.

A case study project on population follows on the next two pages.

SEE
PRIMARY SOURCE A

SEE
PRIMARY SOURCE D

Population

Some Major Cities of East Asia, 1995–1999

City	Population (in millions)
Shanghai, China	13.58
Beijing, China	11.30
Seoul, South Korea	10.29
Tianjin, China	9.42
Tokyo, Japan	7.85
Hong Kong, China	6.84
Shenyang, China	5.12
Guangzhou, China	4.49
Wuhan, China	4.25
Pusan, South Korea	3.87
Chongqing, China	3.47
Xian, China	2.97
Nanjing, China	2.96
Taipei, Taiwan	2.60
Osaka, Japan	2.48

SOURCE: The Statesman's Yearbook (2001)

SKILLBUILDER:
Interpreting Charts

❶ **HUMAN-ENVIRONMENT INTERACTION** What are the two largest cities in South Korea?

❷ **REGION** Which country on the chart has most of the largest cities?

PROJECT

A Visual Presentation

Primary sources A, B, C, D, and E offer assessments of East Asia's population challenges. Use these resources along with your own research to prepare maps, graphs, and charts that tell a story about population and quality of life in one nation of East Asia.

RESEARCH LINKS
CLASSZONE.COM

Suggested Steps

1. Choose one East Asian nation to study. Search for information that can be presented visually in charts and graphs. The visuals you create should explain some aspect of the nation's population and quality of life.

2. Use online and print resources to research your topic.

3. Look for information that shows relationships between population and quality of life. For example, one chart might illustrate declining birth rates while another shows rising literacy rates.

4. Include several different types of visuals: pie graphs, line and bar graphs, pictograms, population distribution maps, and so on.

5. Try to make your visuals as colorful as possible. Use color to make the information easier to understand.

6. Prepare a brief oral explanation of your visuals and the story they tell.

Materials and Supplies

- posterboard
- color markers
- computer with Internet access
- books, newspapers, and magazines
- printer

PRIMARY SOURCE A

Bar Graph *This bar graph, prepared from U.S. Census Bureau statistics, shows where and by how much population is expected to grow from 2000 to 2050.*

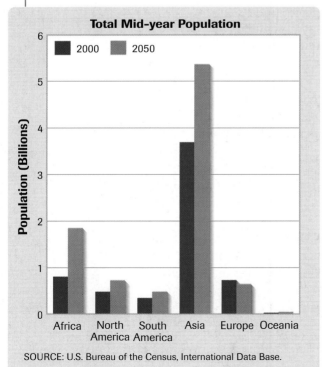

Total Mid-year Population

■ 2000 ■ 2050

Y-axis: Population (Billions), 0 to 6

X-axis: Africa, North America, South America, Asia, Europe, Oceania

SOURCE: U.S. Bureau of the Census, International Data Base.

PRIMARY SOURCE B

Policy Statement *On a trip to Hong Kong in 1998, U.S. President Bill Clinton discussed the issue of pollution in China. He noted that overcrowding and industrialization had led to serious environmental problems that would only get worse if not addressed. The following CNN news story quotes some of Clinton's remarks.*

Clinton addressed a contentious [controversial] issue separating the two countries—global warming. He also announced a series of clean air and water measures to help China, which has five of the most polluted cities in the world, according to environmentalists. . . .

"You know better than I that polluted air and water are threatening your remarkable progress," Clinton said. "Smog has caused entire Chinese cities to disappear from satellite photographs, and respiratory illness is China's number one health problem."

PRIMARY SOURCE C

News Analysis *In this article from Asiaweek.com, the author addresses an interesting problem posed by population growth in Asia.*

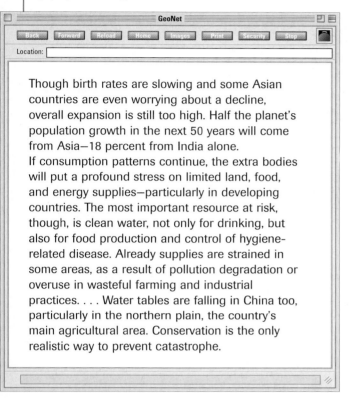

GeoNet

Back | Forward | Reload | Home | Images | Print | Security | Stop

Location:

Though birth rates are slowing and some Asian countries are even worrying about a decline, overall expansion is still too high. Half the planet's population growth in the next 50 years will come from Asia—18 percent from India alone.
If consumption patterns continue, the extra bodies will put a profound stress on limited land, food, and energy supplies—particularly in developing countries. The most important resource at risk, though, is clean water, not only for drinking, but also for food production and control of hygiene-related disease. Already supplies are strained in some areas, as a result of pollution degradation or overuse in wasteful farming and industrial practices. . . . Water tables are falling in China too, particularly in the northern plain, the country's main agricultural area. Conservation is the only realistic way to prevent catastrophe.

PRIMARY SOURCE D

Fact Sheet *In 1997, Population Action International produced a fact sheet that helped explain the relationship between population control and development in East Asia.*

- **A shift to smaller families produced three important demographic changes: slower growth in the number of school-age children, a lower ratio of dependents to working-age adults, and a reduced rate of labor-force growth.** These alone were not enough to create the educated work force, high wages and savings rates, and the capital-intensive industries that now characterize the [region]. But linked to an enterprising business sector, wise public investment, and an equitable education system, demographic change soon became economic opportunity. . . .

- **With fewer children, households placed more of their earnings in savings, and governments reduced public expenditures.** In 1960, there were only 1.3 working-age adults for each child in . . . South Korea, Taiwan, Singapore, and Hong Kong. Because families chose to have fewer children, by 1995 there were 3.1 working-age adults for each child, dramatically reducing the dependency burden and allowing families to save more of their incomes.

PRIMARY SOURCE E

Political Cartoon *This cartoon was created by Nick Anderson in 1999. It shows one cartoonist's viewpoint of the effect of a rapidly expanding population on the natural environment.*

WORLD POPULATION TOPS 6 BILLION

"THERE GOES THE NEIGHBORHOOD..."

PROJECT **CheckList**

Have I . . .

✓ fully researched my topic?

✓ created informative, colorful visuals that make my report clear and interesting?

✓ used charts and graphs to tell a story about population issues in East Asia?

✓ practiced explaining my report?

✓ anticipated questions others might ask and prepared answers?

VISUAL SUMMARY
TODAY'S ISSUES IN EAST ASIA

Environment

The Ring of Fire
- Parts of East Asia are located along the northwestern edge of the Pacific Ocean's Ring of Fire.
- The heavily populated areas of East Asia (especially Japan) are endangered by the earthquakes, volcanic eruptions, and tsunamis along the Ring of Fire.

Economics

Trade and Prosperity
- Most of the nations of East Asia have prospered from trade with each other and with other parts of the world.
- In the second half of the 20th century, many countries in East Asia developed powerful economies.
- In the 1990s, there was a decline in the economies of the region but they have begun to recover.

Population

Case Study: Population and the Quality of Life
- East Asia has a huge population.
- Despite a reduced birth rate, the population in the region will continue to grow well into the 21st century.
- A growing population affects the quality of life in a nation.

Reviewing Places & Terms

A. Briefly explain the importance of each of the following.

1. Ring of Fire
2. Great Kanto earthquake
3. tsunami
4. UNICEF
5. global economy
6. Jakota Triangle
7. recession
8. sweatshop

B. Answer the questions about vocabulary in complete sentences.

9. How many people were killed and how many homes destroyed in the Great Kanto earthquake?
10. What is the basic cause of the physical events that characterize the Ring of Fire?
11. Upon what is the prosperity of the Jakota Triangle primarily based?
12. Why are sweatshops profitable?
13. What sorts of natural disasters occur around the Ring of Fire?
14. How does Japan participate in the global economy?
15. How might economic reform in East Asia affect sweatshops?
16. What besides earthquake damage made the Great Kanto earthquake so destructive?
17. What are three causes of tsunamis?
18. Which countries in the region experienced a recession?
19. What sorts of economies make up the Jakota Triangle?
20. With what issues does UNICEF concern itself?

Main Ideas

The Ring of Fire (pp. 661–664)

1. What causes an earthquake?
2. Why are the Japanese islands so unstable?
3. What are some Japanese organizations that help prepare for disasters?

Trade and Prosperity (pp. 665–667)

4. What effect did Western nations have on economic development in East Asia?
5. What is the connection between industrialization and globalization?
6. What are some of the things that went wrong in the economies of the region?

Case Study: Population and the Quality of Life (pp. 668–671)

7. What are some examples of the stress that population growth puts on the environment?
8. What are some effective ways to manage population growth?
9. How developed was East Asia in the middle of the 20th century?
10. How had East Asia changed by the beginning of the 21st century?

Critical Thinking

1. Using Your Notes

Use your completed chart to answer these questions.

	Causes	Effects
Issue 1: Ring of Fire		
Issue 2: Trade		

a. What are some of the effects of the Ring of Fire?

b. What role did labor play in the booming economies of East Asia after World War II?

2. Geographic Themes

a. **REGION** What are some of the ways that people respond to the dangers of living in the Ring of Fire?

b. **HUMAN-ENVIRONMENT INTERACTION** How does a rising population put a strain on the environment?

3. Identifying Themes

What might be some of the advantages of reducing population growth in the region? Which of the five themes apply to this situation?

4. Determining Cause and Effect

What might be the connection between population and trade in some of the economies of the region?

5. Making Inferences

Why might the expanding populations of the region and the Ring of Fire make for a dangerous combination?

Additional Test Practice, pp. S1–S37

TEST PRACTICE
CLASSZONE.COM

Geographic Skills: Interpreting Graphs

World Population and Growth

Use the graph to answer the questions.

1. **ANALYZING DATA** What was the population of the world in the year 1?

2. **MAKING COMPARISONS** How long did it take for the world's population to double from the year 1?

3. **MAKING COMPARISONS** How many years might it take for the world's population to double after 1974? What is the total expected to be in 2028?

GeoActivity

Do research to create a bar graph showing population growth and doubling time in one country in the region. Compare it with a bar graph showing the same information for the United States. Display the two bar graphs side by side.

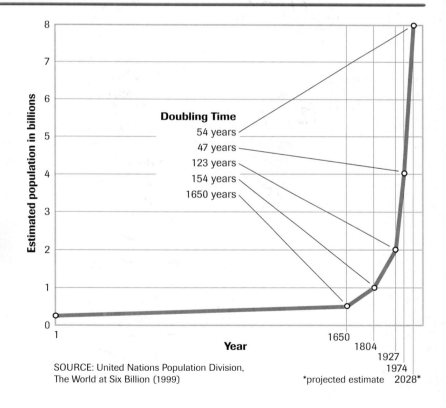

Doubling Time
54 years
47 years
123 years
154 years
1650 years

Estimated population in billions

Year
1650
1804
1927
1974
2028*

SOURCE: United Nations Population Division, The World at Six Billion (1999)

*projected estimate

INTERNET ACTIVITY

Use the links at **classzone.com** to do research about the Ring of Fire. Focus on major eruptions, earthquakes, and tsunamis in the region.

Creating Multimedia Presentations Combine charts, maps, or other visual images in a presentation showing strategies to prepare for natural disasters along the Ring of Fire.

Southeast Asia, Oceania, and Antarctica

Ranging from flat plateaus to volcanic peaks, this region has diverse landforms. The vast Pacific Ocean links the scattered parts of this region together.

REGION Towering cliffs covered with snow and ice are a distinctive characteristic of the landscape of Antarctica.

MOVEMENT Traders travel the rivers of Thailand to sell produce and other goods in that country's famous floating markets.

GeoData

REGION Oceania includes the Pacific Islands not considered to be part of Southeast Asia. Some people include New Zealand and Australia, even though Australia is a continent, not an island.

LOCATION Australia is known as the "Land Down Under." It is the only inhabited continent to lie completely in the Southern Hemisphere.

HUMAN–ENVIRONMENT INTERACTION Farmers have adapted to the region's varied environments. They use terraced fields on steep Southeast Asian slopes and irrigate arid parts of Australia.

For more information on Southeast Asia, Oceania, and Antarctica . . .

RESEARCH LINKS
CLASSZONE.COM

SE ASIA & OCEANIA

Unit PREVIEW

Today's Issues in Southeast Asia, Oceania, and Antarctica

Today, Southeast Asia, Oceania, and Antarctica face the issues previewed here. As you read Chapters 30 and 31, you will learn helpful background information. You will study the issues themselves in Chapter 32.

In a small group, answer the questions below. Then participate in a class discussion of your answers.

Exploring the Issues

1. LAND CLAIMS Search the Internet for information about Aboriginal land claims in Australia. What are the different sides in the conflict?

2. INDUSTRIALISM Make a list of the possible results of industrial growth, both positive and negative. How might a country reduce the negative effects?

3. ENVIRONMENTAL CHANGE Consider news stories that you've heard about global warming and the ozone hole. What are some of the predicted effects? Make a list of all the effects you can remember.

For more on these issues in Southeast Asia, Oceania, and Antarctica . . .

CURRENT EVENTS
CLASSZONE.COM

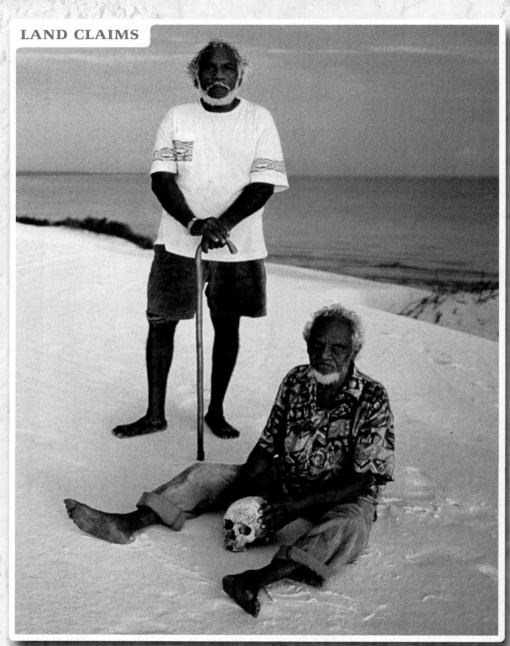

LAND CLAIMS

Should native people be given back their ancestors' land?

These two Aboriginal men are elders of the Wuthathi people. They have come to bury the skull of an ancestor in their homeland. Aboriginal people feel a strong spiritual connection to their land and do not want to be separated from it even in death.

INDUSTRIALISM

How does industrialization affect cities?

This slum in Jakarta, Indonesia, shows how difficult it is to provide adequate housing for the thousands of people who move to cities seeking factory jobs.

CASESTUDY

How have people changed the atmosphere?

The green and blue areas in these satellite images show where the ozone layer over Antarctica is thinnest. Ozone in the stratosphere, a layer of the atmosphere, protects the living things of earth from harmful ultraviolet radiation.

ENVIRONMENTAL CHANGE

OCT 1980   OCT 1981   OCT 1982   OCT 1983   OCT 1984

OCT 1985   OCT 1986   OCT 1987   OCT 1988   OCT 1989

OCT 1990   OCT 1991   OCT 1992   OCT 1993   OCT 1994

OCT 1995   OCT 1996   OCT 1997   OCT 1998   OCT 1999

100 115 130 145 160 175 190 205 220 235 250 265 280 295 310 325 340 355 370 385 400 415 430 445

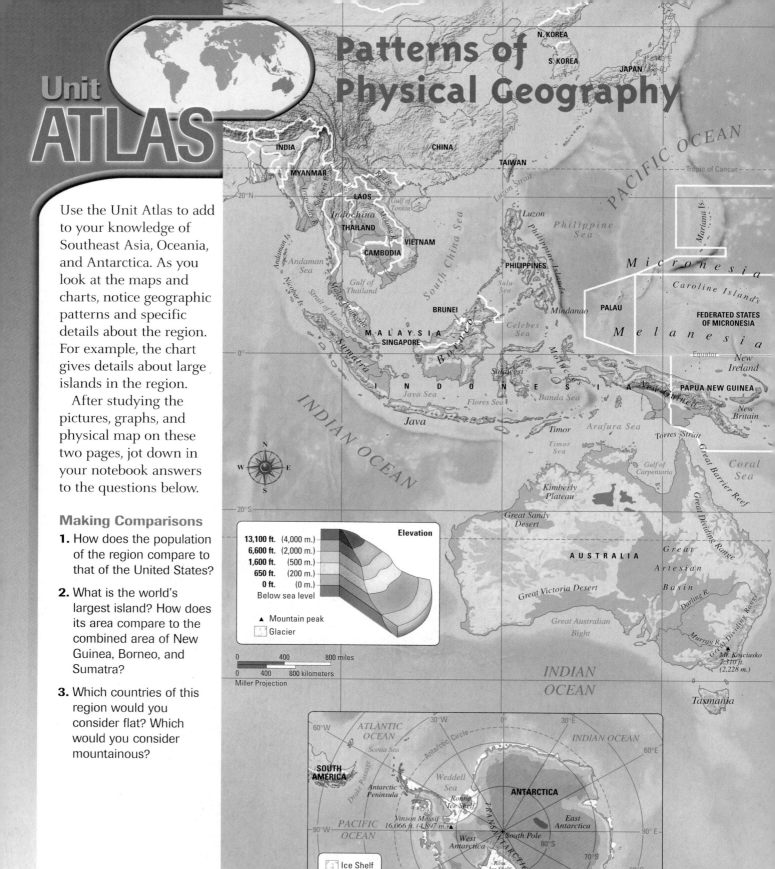

Unit ATLAS

Patterns of Physical Geography

Use the Unit Atlas to add to your knowledge of Southeast Asia, Oceania, and Antarctica. As you look at the maps and charts, notice geographic patterns and specific details about the region. For example, the chart gives details about large islands in the region.

After studying the pictures, graphs, and physical map on these two pages, jot down in your notebook answers to the questions below.

Making Comparisons

1. How does the population of the region compare to that of the United States?

2. What is the world's largest island? How does its area compare to the combined area of New Guinea, Borneo, and Sumatra?

3. Which countries of this region would you consider flat? Which would you consider mountainous?

For updated statistics on Southeast Asia, Oceania, and Antarctica . . .

DATA UPDATE
CLASSZONE.COM

Elevation

13,100 ft. (4,000 m.)
6,600 ft. (2,000 m.)
1,600 ft. (500 m.)
650 ft. (200 m.)
0 ft. (0 m.)
Below sea level

▲ Mountain peak
Glacier

0   400   800 miles
0   400   800 kilometers
Miller Projection

Azimuthal Equidistant Projection

Ice Shelf

0   500   1,000 miles
0   500   1,000 kilometers

Southeast Asia, Oceania, and Antarctica: Physical

Comparing Data

Landmass

Southeast Asia and Oceania 5,065,224.45 sq mi

Continental United States 3,165,630 sq mi

Midway Is.

Wake I.

MARSHALL ISLANDS

Marshall Islands

INTERNATIONAL DATE LINE

Polynesia

Micronesia

Gilbert Is.

KIRIBATI

Line Islands

NAURU

Phoenix Is.

SOLOMON ISLANDS

Melanesia

TUVALU

Santa Cruz Is.

SAMOA

Cook Islands

Society Is.

Tuamotu Archipelago

VANUATU

TONGA

Tahiti

New Caledonia

FIJI

Tropic of Capricorn

Tasman Sea

North Island

NEW ZEALAND

INTERNATIONAL DATE LINE

South Island

PACIFIC OCEAN

Comparing Data

*Antarctica is not included because it has no permanent population.

Population

Southeast Asia and Oceania* 558,475,000

United States 281,422,000

| 0 | 100 | 200 | 300 | 400 | 500 | 600 |

Population (in millions)

Islands

| World's Largest **Greenland** 839,999 sq mi | U.S. Largest **Hawaii** 4,021 sq mi | **New Guinea** 341,631 sq mi | **Borneo** 290,320 sq mi | **Sumatra** 182,542 sq mi |

SE ASIA & OCEANIA

679

Unit
ATLAS

Patterns of Human Geography

Study the map on page 681 to learn about ancient kingdoms and empires of Southeast Asia and the map on both pages to learn about the present-day nations of the region. Then write in your notebook the answers to these questions.

Making Comparisons

1. Which ancient kingdoms or empires have names similar to present-day countries in Southeast Asia? How do their locations compare?

2. Which are the largest countries in the region?

3. Which country includes part of the Asian mainland and part of a large island?

CHINA

N. KOREA

S. KOREA

JAPAN

INDIA

TAIWAN

Tropic of Cancer

MYANMAR

Hanoi

LAOS

Vientiane

Gulf of Tonkin

Yangon

THAILAND

Bangkok

VIETNAM

CAMBODIA

Phnom Penh

Ho Chi Minh City

Andaman Sea

Gulf of Thailand

South China Sea

Luzon Strait

Luzon

Philippine Sea

Quezon City

Manila

PHILIPPINES

Sulu Sea

Davao

Mindanao

NORTHERN MARIANA IS. (U.S.)

GUAM (U.S.)

Micronesia

Palikir

FEDERATED STATES OF MICRONESIA

BRUNEI

Bandar Seri Begawan

Kuala Lumpur

MALAYSIA

Medan

SINGAPORE

Singapore

Celebes Sea

Koror

PALAU

Melanesia

Equator

0°

Sumatra

Palembang

INDONESIA

Jakarta

Bandung

Semarang

Surabaya

Java

Java Sea

Flores Sea

Borneo

Sulawesi

Banda Sea

PAPUA NEW GUINEA

Port Moresby

Strait of Malacca

INDIAN OCEAN

PACIFIC OCEAN

E. Timor (UN Admin.)

Timor Sea

Arafura Sea

Darwin

Gulf of Carpentaria

Coral Sea

20°S

Tropic of Capricorn

AUSTRALIA

Brisbane

Perth

Great Australian Bight

Adelaide

Sydney

Canberra

Melbourne

40°S

N
W   E
S

Tasmania

⭐ National capital

● Other city

INDIAN OCEAN

0   400   800 miles
0   400   800 kilometers
Miller Projection

100°E   120°E   140°E

680 UNIT 10

Southeast Asia, 1200

Champa
Dai Viet
Empire of Pagan
Khmer Empire
Srivijaya Kingdom

EMPIRE OF PAGAN
Pagan
DAI VIET
Hainan
KHMER EMPIRE
Angkor
CHAMPA
Andaman Is.
Andaman Sea
Gulf of Thailand
South China Sea
Strait of Malacca
Sumatra
Malacca
Borneo
Celebes Sea
SRIVIJAYA KINGDOM
Palembang
Java Sea
Strait of Sunda
Java

N W E S

0   400   800 miles
0   400   800 kilometers
Miller Projection
100°E   110°E   120°E

PACIFIC OCEAN

MIDWAY I. (U.S.)

WAKE I. (U.S.)

HAWAII (U.S.)

JOHNSTON ATOLL (U.S.)

MARSHALL ISLANDS
Majuro

Micronesia

Tarawa

NAURU
SOLOMON ISLANDS
Fongafale

KIRIBATI

Polynesia

TOKELAU (N.Z.)

TUVALU
Melanesia
Honiara
WALLIS AND FUTUNA (Fr.)
SAMOA
Apia
AMERICAN SAMOA (U.S.)

COOK ISLANDS (N.Z.)

FRENCH POLYNESIA (Fr.)

VANUATU
Port-Vila
Suva
TONGA

Tahiti
Papeete

NEW CALEDONIA (Fr.)
Nouméa
FIJI
Nuku'alofa
NIUE (N.Z.)

PITCAIRN IS. (U.K.)

Tropic of Capricorn

NORFOLK I. (Aus.)

INTERNATIONAL DATE LINE

Tasman Sea

North Island
Auckland
NEW ZEALAND
Wellington
Christchurch
South Island

PACIFIC OCEAN

(Antarctica inset)

ATLANTIC OCEAN
Scotia Sea
Antarctic Circle
INDIAN OCEAN
SOUTH AMERICA
Weddell Sea
Queen Maud Land
Enderby Land
Drake Passage
Antarctic Peninsula
Palmer Land
Ronne Ice Shelf
ANTARCTICA
PACIFIC OCEAN
South Pole
Marie Byrd Land
Ross Ice Shelf
Wilkes Land
Ross Sea
Victoria Land

Ice shelf

0   500   1,000 miles
0   500   1,000 kilometers
Azimuthal Equidistant Projection

681

SE ASIA & OCEANIA

Regional Patterns

These two pages contain graphs and thematic maps. The graphs show the percentage of ethnic Chinese in Southeast Asian populations and the number of active volcanoes in the region. One map shows the climates of the region. The other shows the major religions of the region. After studying the graphs and maps, jot down in your notebook the answers to the questions below.

Making Comparisons

1. Which Southeast Asian nation has the highest proportion of Chinese in its population?

2. What percentage of the region's active volcanoes are found in Southeast Asia?

3. Where are the coldest climates to be found in the region?

4. Would you describe this as a region of religious diversity? Why or why not?

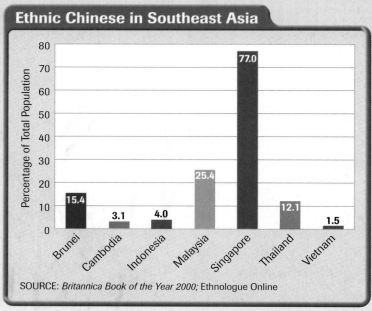

Ethnic Chinese in Southeast Asia

Percentage of Total Population

- Brunei: 15.4
- Cambodia: 3.1
- Indonesia: 4.0
- Malaysia: 25.4
- Singapore: 77.0
- Thailand: 12.1
- Vietnam: 1.5

SOURCE: *Britannica Book of the Year 2000;* Ethnologue Online

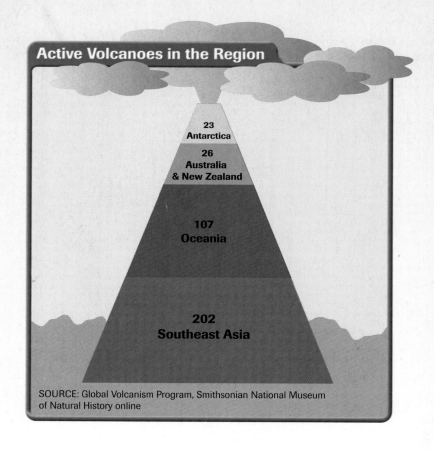

Active Volcanoes in the Region

- 23 Antarctica
- 26 Australia & New Zealand
- 107 Oceania
- 202 Southeast Asia

SOURCE: Global Volcanism Program, Smithsonian National Museum of Natural History online

Climates of the Region

PACIFIC OCEAN

Tropic of Cancer

20°N

Equator

0°

INDIAN OCEAN

20°S

Tropic of Capricorn

40°S

INDIAN OCEAN

ATLANTIC OCEAN

PACIFIC OCEAN

INDIAN OCEAN

Antarctic Circle

80°S

70°S

Azimuthal Equidistant Projection

0   500   1,000 miles
0   500   1,000 kilometers

N
W   E
S

0   500   1,000 miles
0   500   1,000 kilometers
Miller Projection

140°E   160°E   180°

Tropical wet	Humid subtropical
Tropical wet and dry	Marine west coast
Desert	Tundra
Semiarid	Highland
Mediterranean	Icecap

Major Religions of the Region

100°E   120°E   140°E   160°E   180°   160°W   140°W

PACIFIC OCEAN

Tropic of Cancer

20°N

INDIAN OCEAN

Equator   0°

20°S

Tropic of Capricorn

PACIFIC OCEAN

40°S

| Confucianism |
| Protestant |
| Roman Catholic |
| Buddhism |
| Sunni Muslim |
| Traditional |

N
W   E
S

0   500   1,000 miles
0   500   1,000 kilometers
Miller Projection

Regional Data File

Study the charts on the countries of this region.

Making Comparisons

1. Compare the population and total area of Australia to that of the United States. What conclusions can you draw?

2. Make a list of the top three countries in population. What is the difference in population between the top two countries?

3. Make a list of the top three countries in total area. How does this list compare to your list of the most populous countries?

(continued on page 686)

Notes:
ᵃ A comparison of the prices of the same items is used to figure these data.
ᵇ Includes land and water, when figures are available.
* East Timor became an independent country on May 20, 2002.

For updated statistics on Southeast Asia, Oceania, and Antarctica . . .

DATA UPDATE
CLASSZONE.COM

Country Flag	Country/ Capital	Population (2000)	Life Expectancy (years) (2000)	Birthrate (per 1,000, pop.) (2000 estimate)	Infant Mortality (per 1,000 live births) (2000)
	Australia Canberra	19,200,000	79	13	5.3
	Brunei Bandar Seri Begawan	331,000	71	25	24.0
	Cambodia Phnom Penh	12,127,000	56	38	80.8
	East Timor* Dili	737,000	50	25	120.9
	Fiji Suva	811,000	67	22	12.9
	Indonesia Jakarta	212,207,000	64	24	45.7
	Kiribati Tarawa	92,000	62	33	62.0
	Laos Vientiane	5,218,000	51	41	104.0
	Malaysia Kuala Lumpur	23,253,000	73	25	7.9
	Marshall Islands Majuro	68,000	65	26	30.5
	Fed. States of Micronesia Palikir	119,000	66	33	46.0
	Myanmar Yangon	48,852,000	54	30	82.5
	Nauru (no capital)	12,000	61	19	25.0
	New Zealand Wellington	3,836,000	77	15	5.5
	Palau Koror	19,000	67	18	19.2
	Papua New Guinea Port Moresby	4,810,000	56	34	77.0
	Philippines Manila	80,298,000	67	29	35.3
	Samoa Apia	176,000	68	31	25.0
	Singapore Singapore City	4,001,000	78	13	3.2
	Solomon Islands Honiara	434,000	71	37	25.3

Doctors (per 100,000 pop.) (1994–1999)	GDP[a] (billions $US) (1998–1999)	Import/Export[a] (billions $US) (1998–1999)	Literacy Rate (percentage) (1996–1998)	Televisions (per 1,000 pop.) (1998)	Passenger Cars (per 1,000 pop.) (1996–1997)	Total Area[b] (square miles)	
240	416.2	67.0 / 58.0	100	495	474	2,967,909	
85	5.6	1.24 / 2.04	88	239	477	2,226	
30	8.2	1.2 / 0.821	65 (1993)	9	1.2	69,898	
N.A.	0.415 (2001 est.)	0.237 / .008 (2001 est.)	48	79	23	5,641	
48	5.9	0.612 / 0.393	92	18	38	7,055	
16	610.0	21.6 / 48.0	84	66	12	779,675	
30	0.074	0.033 / 0.006	90	N/A	N/A	277	
24	7.0	0.497 / 0.271	57	9	1.7	91,428	
66	229.1	61.5 / 83.5	84	164	143	128,727	
42	0.105 (1997)	0.058 / 0.028 (1997)	93 (1994)	N/A	N/A	70	
57	0.240 (1997)	0.151 / 0.073 (1996)	90 (1991)	N/A	N/A	1,055	
30	121.0 (1996)	1.829 / 0.886 (1996)	83	5	0.7	261,789	
157	0.100 (1993)	0.019 / 0.025 (1991)	99	N/A	N/A	8.2	
217	63.8	11.2 / 12.2	100	514	391	103,736	
110	0.160 (1997)	0.072 / 0.014 (1996)	98 (1990)	N/A	N/A	191	
7	11.6	1.0 / 1.9	72	4	5	178,260	
123	282.0	30.7 / 34.8	95	49	9	115,651	
34	0.485	0.097 / 0.021	98	41	7	1,209	
163	98.0	111.0 / 114.0	91	361	95	225	
14	1.21	0.144 / 0.142	54	6	N/A	11,500	

Regional Data File

Country Flag	Country/ Capital	Population (2000)	Life Expectancy (years) (2000)	Birthrate (per 1,000, pop.) (2000 estimate)	Infant Mortality (per 1,000 live births) (2000)
	Thailand Bangkok	62,043,000	73	16	22.4
	Tonga Nuku'alofa	108,000	71	27	19.0
	Tuvalu Fongafale	10,838	64	22	24.8
	Vanuatu Port-Vila	195,000	65	35	39.0
	Vietnam Hanoi	78,697,000	66	20	36.7
	United States Washington, D.C.	281,422,000	77	15	7.0

Making Comparisons
(continued)

4. Which countries have a literacy rate below 60 percent?

5. For the countries you identified in question 4, look at their ratio of doctors to population. Is it high or low compared to other countries? What might be the relationship between literacy rate and number of doctors?

Territories and Possessions in Oceania

Name	Status
American Samoa	U.S. territory*
Cook Islands	Self-governing area in free association with New Zealand
French Polynesia	French overseas territory
Guam	U.S. territory*
Irian Jaya	Indonesian province
Midway Islands	U.S. possession*
New Caledonia	French overseas territory
Niue	Self-governing area in free association with New Zealand
Norfolk Island	Australian territory
Northern Mariana Islands	U.S. commonwealth*
Pitcairn Islands	British overseas territory
Tokelau	New Zealand territory
Wake Island	U.S. possession*
Wallis and Futuna	French overseas territory

* A commonwealth is a self-governing political unit in voluntary association with the United States; a U.S. territory is not a state but has a governor and a legislature; the U.S. possessions in the Pacific are administered by the Navy.

SOURCE: *World Book Encyclopedia 2000*

Sources:
ASEAN statistics online
Europa World Year Book 2000
Human Development Report 2000, United Nations
International Data Base, 2000, U.S. Census Bureau online
Merriam-Webster's Geographical Dictionary, 1997
Statesman's Yearbook 2001
2000 World Population Data Sheet, Population Reference Bureau online
WHO Estimates of Health Personnel, World Health Organization online
World Almanac and Book of Facts 2001
World Factbook 2000, CIA online
N/A = not available

Notes:
[a] A comparison of the prices of the same items is used to figure these data.
[b] Includes land and water, when figures are available.

686 UNIT 10

Doctors (per 100,000 pop.) (1994–1999)	GDP[a] (billions $US) (1998–1999)	Import/Export[a] (billions $US) (1998–1999)	Literacy Rate (percentage) (1996–1998)	Televisions (per 1,000 pop.) (1998)	Passenger Cars (per 1,000 pop.) (1996–1997)	Total Area[b] (square miles)
24	388.7	45.0 / 58.5	94	189	25	198,455
44	0.238	0.069 / 0.008	93 (1992)	16	31	270
30	0.008 (1995)	0.004 / 0.0002 (1989)	95	N/A	N/A	9
12	0.245	0.076 / 0.034	36	13	21	5,700
48	143.1	11.6 / 11.5	94	43	1	130,468
251	9,255.0	820.8 / 663.0	97	847	489	3,787,319

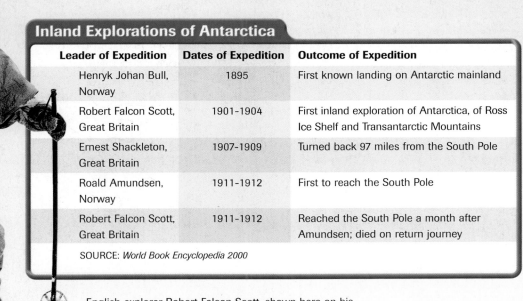

Inland Explorations of Antarctica

Leader of Expedition	Dates of Expedition	Outcome of Expedition
Henryk Johan Bull, Norway	1895	First known landing on Antarctic mainland
Robert Falcon Scott, Great Britain	1901–1904	First inland exploration of Antarctica, of Ross Ice Shelf and Transantarctic Mountains
Ernest Shackleton, Great Britain	1907–1909	Turned back 97 miles from the South Pole
Roald Amundsen, Norway	1911–1912	First to reach the South Pole
Robert Falcon Scott, Great Britain	1911–1912	Reached the South Pole a month after Amundsen; died on return journey

SOURCE: *World Book Encyclopedia 2000*

English explorer Robert Falcon Scott, shown here on his journey to the South Pole in 1912, died on this expedition.

SECTION 1
Landforms and Resources

SECTION 2
Climate and Vegetation

SECTION 3
Human–Environment Interaction

Scuba divers in Australia's Great Barrier Reef can observe some of its more than 1,500 species of fish and approximately 400 species of coral.

PHYSICAL GEOGRAPHY OF SOUTHEAST ASIA, OCEANIA, AND ANTARCTICA
A Region of Extremes

GeoFocus

How does physical geography vary throughout this vast region?

Taking Notes Copy the graphic organizer below into your notebook. Use it to record facts about Southeast Asia, Oceania, and Antarctica.

Landforms	
Resources	
Climate and Vegetation	
Human-Environment Interaction	

Landforms and Resources

Main Ideas

• This region includes two peninsulas of Asia, two continents, and more than 20,000 islands.

• Its landforms include mountains, plateaus, and major river systems.

Places & Terms

archipelago   low island

Oceania   Great Barrier

high island   Reef

CONNECT TO THE ISSUES
INDUSTRIALIZATION
Some countries of this region have used their resources to develop industry, with mixed results.

SUNSHINE STATE STANDARDS
Key Standard SS.B.1.4.2 The student understands the advantages and disadvantages of using maps from different sources and different points of view.
Other Standards SS.B.1.4.1
FCAT LA.A.1.4.2 Reading: Strategies

A HUMAN PERSPECTIVE The Aeta (EE·duh) people of the Philippines lived on the volcano Mount Pinatubo for generations. They knew this volcano so well that they timed the planting and harvesting of their crops by the amount of steam rising from a vent on its slope. In 1991, the Aeta noticed changes in the mountain and concluded that it was about to erupt. Tens of thousands of Aeta fled their homes as did countless other Filipinos. Pinatubo did erupt for the first time in 600 years, spewing ash for miles. Since then, many of the Aeta have formed new communities, but they still miss their homeland. As their story shows, the geologic processes that destroy landforms also disrupt human lives.

Southeast Asia: Mainland and Islands

Southeast Asia has two distinct subregions: the southeastern corner of the Asian mainland and a great number of islands. Both the mainland and the islands have many high mountains.

PENINSULAS AND ISLANDS The most noticeable feature of mainland Southeast Asia is that it lies on two peninsulas. The Indochinese Peninsula, located south of China, has a rectangular shape. In contrast, the Malay Peninsula is a narrow strip of land about 700 miles long, stretching south from the mainland and then curving southeast. It serves as a bridge between the mainland and islands.

Most of the islands of Southeast Asia are found in archipelagoes. An **archipelago** is a set of closely grouped islands, which sometimes form a curved arc. The Philippines and the islands of Indonesia are part of the Malay Archipelago. (See the map on page 680.) A few Southeast Asian islands, such as Borneo, are actually the high points of a submerged section of the Eurasian plate.

MOUNTAINS AND VOLCANOES On the map at right, you can see that the mainland has several mountain ranges, such as the Annamese Cordillera, running roughly north and south. These ranges fan out from a mountainous area to the north.

Southeast Asian Mountains and Rivers

Arakan Yoma
Irrawaddy R.
Salween R.
Red R.
Annamese Cordillera
Gulf of Tonkin
Andaman Sea
Bilauktaung Range
Chao Phraya
Mekong R.
Indochinese
Peninsula
15°N
Gulf of Thailand
Malay Peninsula
South China Sea
10°N
100°E
105°E
N W E S

SKILLBUILDER: Interpreting Maps

❶ **PLACE** Which mountain chain lies east of the Mekong River?

❷ **LOCATION** How would you describe the relative location of the Chao Phraya?

SE ASIA & OCEANIA

Island Formation in the Pacific

High (volcanic) Islands

1. Magma sometimes erupts through cracks in the ocean floor.

2. Over time, layers of lava can build up to form a volcanic cone.

3. Some volcanic cones rise above sea level and become islands.

Low (coral) Islands

1. Some corals form reefs on the sides of volcanic islands.

2. As the island erodes, the reef continues to grow upward.

3. In time, only the low islands of the reef remain.

On the islands, most of the mountains are of volcanic origin. Southeast Asia is part of the Pacific Ring of Fire that you read about in Chapter 29. Volcanic eruptions and earthquakes are natural disasters that frequently occur in this region. (See pages 710–711.)

RIVERS AND COASTLINES The mainland has several large rivers that run from the north through the valleys between the mountain ranges. Near the coast these rivers spread out into fertile deltas. For example, the Mekong (MAY·KAWNG) River begins in China and crosses several Southeast Asian nations before becoming a wide delta on Vietnam's coast. Millions of people rely on the Mekong for farming and fishing.

Southeast Asia's peninsulas and islands give it a long, irregular coastline with many ports. As you can imagine, this has encouraged a great deal of seagoing travel and trade.

RESOURCES Fertile soil is a valuable resource in Southeast Asia. Volcanic activity and flooding rivers both add nutrients back to the soil and keep it rich. Southeast Asians also have access to large numbers of fish in the rivers and nearby seas. Parts of the region have mineral resources, such as petroleum, tin, and gems, which industry can use.

Lands of the Pacific and Antarctica

No one knows how many islands exist in the Pacific Ocean, but some geographers estimate that there are more than 20,000. As a group, the Pacific Islands are called **Oceania.** (The Philippines, Indonesia, and other islands near the mainland are not considered part of Oceania because their people have cultural ties to Asia.) In the southwestern

BACKGROUND
The Mekong River forms part of the boundary between Myanmar and Laos and between Laos and Thailand.

BACKGROUND
Oceania's islands are also called the South Sea Islands.

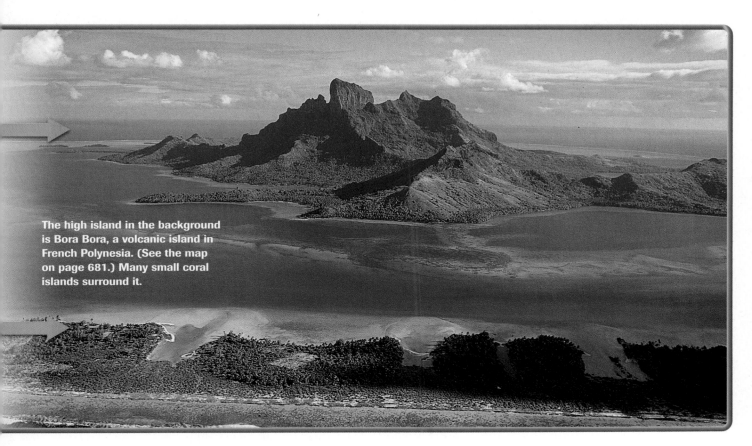

The high island in the background is Bora Bora, a volcanic island in French Polynesia. (See the map on page 681.) Many small coral islands surround it.

Pacific lie New Zealand and Australia, which are often considered part of Oceania, even though Australia is a continent, not an island.

OCEANIA'S MANY ISLANDS One reason geographers don't know the number of islands in Oceania is that it changes. Erosion causes some islands to vanish, while other forces create new islands. Most Pacific islands fall into two categories: **high islands** are created by volcanoes, and **low islands** are made of coral reefs. Although a few of Oceania's islands are large, most are small. If you added the land area of all the islands together, the total would be smaller than the area of Alaska.

Oceania is not rich in resources. The low islands have poor soil, and most of the islands lack minerals. But New Caledonia has nickel, chromium, and iron; New Guinea has copper, gold, and oil; Nauru has phosphate; and both Fiji and the Solomon Islands have gold. The general scarcity of resources has made it difficult to develop industry.

MAJESTIC NEW ZEALAND New Zealand has two main islands, North Island and South Island. Running down the center of South Island is a 300-mile-long mountain range, the Southern Alps. This range has 16 peaks over 10,000 feet high and more than 360 glaciers. Several rivers flow down the eastern slopes to the ocean.

North Island has hilly ranges and a volcanic plateau, but it is much less mountainous than South Island. North Island has fertile farmland and forest that support the lumber industry. In addition, its coastline has natural harbors that are used for seaports. Like South Island, North Island has many rivers running from the mountains to the sea. ◀A

New Zealand has few mineral resources. However, its swift-flowing rivers have allowed its people to build dams that generate electricity.

Geographic Thinking

Seeing Patterns
Ⓐ Judging from the information in this paragraph, what products do you think New Zealand exports?

Also, North Island has a volcanic area with underground steam. Engineers have found ways to use this steam to power generators.

FLAT AUSTRALIA The land mass known as Australia is the smallest continent on earth. It is also the flattest. Near the eastern coast, running roughly parallel to it, is a chain of highlands called the Great Dividing Range. Unlike New Zealand's mountains, few of these peaks rise higher than 5,000 feet. To the west of this range stretches a vast expanse of plains and plateaus, broken by only a few mountains.

Many other differences exist between Australia and New Zealand. For example, Australia has very few rivers. The largest is the Murray River, which flows into the Southern Ocean. Forestry is not a major industry in Australia, but the country is rich in minerals. It is the world's leading supplier of bauxite, diamonds, opals, lead, and coal.

Along Australia's northeast coast lies one of the wonders of nature. The **Great Barrier Reef** is often called the world's largest coral reef, although it is really a 1,250-mile chain of more than 2,500 reefs and islands. Some 400 species of coral are found there.

ICY ANTARCTICA Antarctica is the fifth largest continent. Generally circular in shape, it is centered on the South Pole. Its topography is hidden by a thick ice sheet, but under the ice lies a varied landscape. The Transantarctic Mountains divide the continent in two. East Antarctica is a plateau surrounded by mountains and valleys. West Antarctica is a group of separate islands linked only by the ice that covers them. ▶

Antarctica's ice sheet is the largest supply of fresh water in the world. Geologists believe that resources such as coal, minerals, and perhaps even petroleum may lie beneath the ice. But in 1991, 26 nations agreed not to mine Antarctica for 50 years. In the next section, you will read about Antarctica's harsh climate as well as the climates of Southeast Asia, Oceania, Australia, and New Zealand.

BACKGROUND
People in Australia and New Zealand call the waters around Antarctica the Southern Ocean.

Geographic Thinking◀

Making Comparisons
Ⓑ What are similarities and differences between the physical geographies of Australia and Antarctica?

Assessment

❶ Places & Terms

Identify these terms and explain their importance in the region's physical geography.

- archipelago
- Oceania
- high island
- low island
- Great Barrier Reef

❷ Taking Notes

PLACE Review the notes you took for this section.

Landforms	
Resources	

- What river begins in China and flows to the Vietnamese coast?
- What are the two main islands of New Zealand?

❸ Main Ideas

a. What are the main resources of Southeast Asia?

b. What different resources do Australia and New Zealand have?

c. What landform divides the continent of Antarctica?

❹ Geographic Thinking

Seeing Patterns By what processes do low islands replace high islands? **Think about:**

- the process that causes some islands to disappear
- the diagrams on page 690

RESEARCH LINKS
CLASSZONE.COM

GeoActivity

SEEING PATTERNS Do research to learn about the ways that humans have damaged the Great Barrier Reef. Write the script for a **public service announcement,** telling visitors to Australia what behaviors to avoid. You might also include visuals of the Great Barrier Reef. Use standard grammar, spelling, punctuation, and sentence structure in your script.

Interpreting a Relief Map

Two activities that are popular in New Zealand are mountain climbing and skiing. The relief map below shows mountainous areas, which are suitable to those activities. The mountains also provide some regions of New Zealand with spectacular scenery—especially in the Southern Alps of South Island.

THE LANGUAGE OF MAPS A **relief map** illustrates the differences in elevation that are found in a region. It does this with a combination of colors and shading. The lowest elevations are shown in green, and various shades of brown represent progressively higher elevations. The gray shading shows the locations of mountainous landforms.

SUNSHINE STATE STANDARDS
Key Standard SS.B.1.4.1 The student uses a variety of maps, geographic technologies including geographic information systems (GIS) and satellite-produced imagery, and other advanced graphic representations to depict geographic problems.

FCAT LA.A.2.2.7 Reading: Recognize Compare and Contrast

New Zealand: Physical

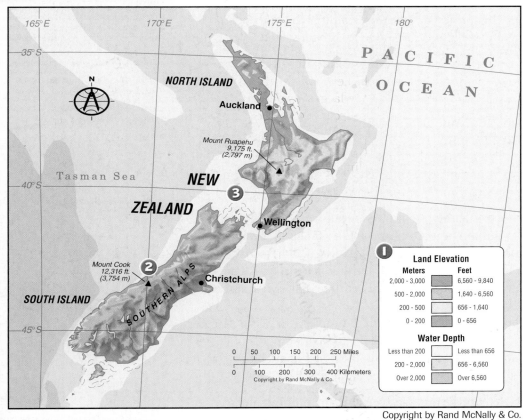

Copyright by Rand McNally & Co.

❶ The key illustrates the colors used on the map and the range of elevation that each color represents.

❷ The symbol for peak is ▲. The map also shows the peaks' names and elevations.

❸ This map clearly shows the difference between the physical geographies of North Island and South Island.

Map and Graph Skills Assessment

1. Seeing Patterns
Which of New Zealand's two large islands is more mountainous?

2. Drawing Conclusions
How high is Mount Cook?

3. Making Inferences
Which island is better suited to farming? Why?

Climate and Vegetation

A HUMAN PERSPECTIVE During the Vietnam War, American troops were sent to fight in unfamiliar Southeast Asia. Among the hardships they endured was the tropical climate. Few had ever lived in a place that had a monsoon season with constant rain. One soldier wrote to his wife, "We live in mud and rain. I'm so sick of rain that it is sometimes unbearable. At night the mosquitoes plague me. . . . The rain drips on me until I go to sleep from exhaustion."

Another soldier wrote to a friend about the vegetation: "Try to imagine grass 8 to 15 feet high so thick as to cut visibility to one yard, possessing razor-sharp edges. Then try to imagine walking through it." As these letters make clear, climate and vegetation can create serious obstacles to military operations—or other activities.

Widespread Tropics

Although the conditions that American soldiers encountered seemed unusual to them, they really aren't rare. Vietnam is just one of many countries in this region with a tropical climate. In fact, tropical climates cover most of Southeast Asia and Oceania. Tropical climates fall into two categories, depending on when it rains during the year.

YEAR-ROUND RAINS A tropical wet climate is found in coastal parts of Myanmar, Thailand, Vietnam, and Oceania, and in most of Malaysia, Indonesia, and the Philippines. Temperatures are high. For example, most of Southeast Asia has an average annual temperature of 80°F. Parts of Southeast Asia receive over 100 inches of rain a year, with some places receiving more than 200 inches.

Although the climate is fairly consistent, variations do exist within the region. Elevation, ocean breezes, and other factors can create cooler temperatures. For example, Indonesia has some locations at such a high elevation that they have glaciers. (See the infographic on page 56.)

WET AND DRY SEASONS Bordering the wet climate is the tropical wet and dry climate, in which monsoons shape the weather. As you read in Unit 8, monsoons are winds that cause wet and dry seasons. This climate is found in parts of Myanmar, Thailand, Laos, Cambodia, and Vietnam—generally to the north or inland of the wet climate. Parts of Oceania and northern Australia also have this climate.

Although temperatures are consistently hot, rainfall varies greatly within the climate zone. Local conditions and

Main Ideas
- This region's climates range from tropical to desert to polar icecap.
- There is a great diversity of plant and animal life, including some species found nowhere else in the world.

Places & Terms
outback

CONNECT TO THE ISSUES
ENVIRONMENTAL CHANGE The hole in the ozone layer, located over Antarctica, has affected the climate of this region.

SUNSHINE STATE STANDARDS
Key Standard SS.B.1.4.3 The student uses mental maps of physical and human features of the world to answer complex geographic questions.
FCAT LA.A.1.4.2 Reading: Strategies

PLACE The Rafflesia, which is native to Indonesia, is the world's largest flower. It is almost three feet across.

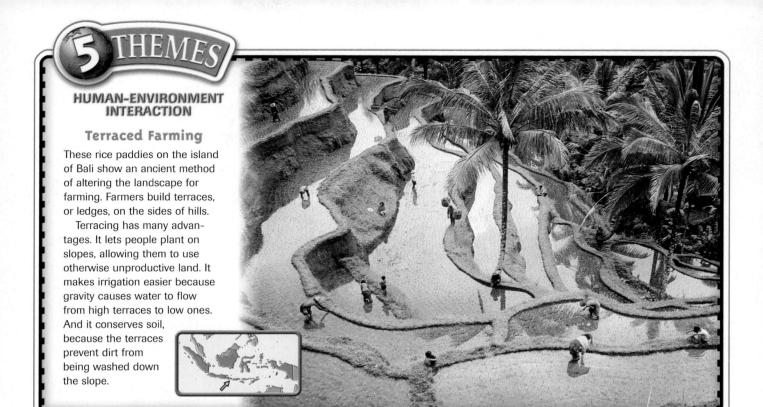

5 THEMES

HUMAN-ENVIRONMENT INTERACTION

Terraced Farming

These rice paddies on the island of Bali show an ancient method of altering the landscape for farming. Farmers build terraces, or ledges, on the sides of hills.

Terracing has many advantages. It lets people plant on slopes, allowing them to use otherwise unproductive land. It makes irrigation easier because gravity causes water to flow from high terraces to low ones. And it conserves soil, because the terraces prevent dirt from being washed down the slope.

landforms can affect precipitation amounts. For example, mountains create rain shadows.

Areas with monsoons often experience disastrous weather. During the wet season, typhoons can occur in Southeast Asia and Oceania.

TROPICAL PLANTS Southeast Asia has one of the greatest diversities of vegetation of any region. For example, it has a remarkable number of tree species. Near the equator are tropical evergreen forests, while deciduous forests are more common in the wet and dry climate zone. Teak, a valuable tree that Asians harvest commercially, comes from these deciduous forests. Southeast Asia also has many types of plants.

In general, Oceania does not have diverse vegetation. The low islands have poor soil and small amounts of rain, so plants don't grow well. Some high islands have rich, volcanic soil and plentiful rain. These islands have abundant flowers and trees, such as the coconut palm.

BACKGROUND
The tropical rain forests of the Philippines alone have more than 3,000 species of trees and 8,000 species of wild plants.

Bands of Moderate Climate

Australia is the only inhabited continent that lies completely in the Southern Hemisphere. New Zealand is even farther south. Australia and New Zealand have generally moderate climates.

Geographic Thinking

Using the Atlas
Ⓐ Find this mountain range on the map on page 678. What is it called?

HOT SUMMERS, MILD WINTERS As Section 1 explained, a mountain chain runs parallel to the east coast of Australia. The strip between the mountains and ocean is divided mostly into two climate zones. The northern part of this strip has a humid subtropical climate, with hot summers, mild winters, and heavy rainfall. It is one of Australia's wettest regions, receiving an average of 126 inches of rain a year. This climate also exists in northern Vietnam, Laos, Thailand, and Myanmar. Ⓐ

SE ASIA & OCEANIA

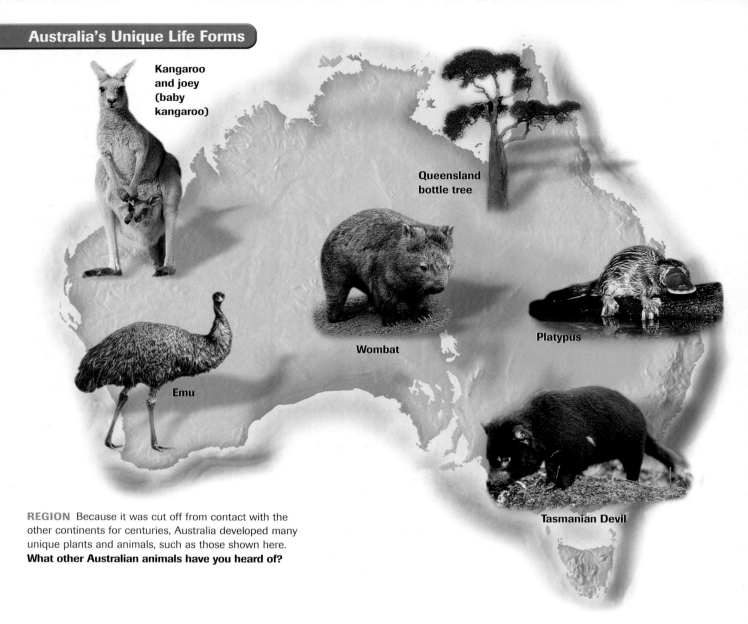

Kangaroo and joey (baby kangaroo)

Queensland bottle tree

Wombat

Platypus

Emu

Tasmanian Devil

REGION Because it was cut off from contact with the other continents for centuries, Australia developed many unique plants and animals, such as those shown here.
What other Australian animals have you heard of?

MILD SUMMERS, COOL WINTERS New Zealand and the southern part of Australia's east coast share a marine west coast climate. The seasons have mild temperatures because ocean breezes warm the land in the winter and cool it in the summer. New Zealand's forests consist primarily of evergreens and tree ferns, which thrive in such a climate.

New Zealand receives rainfall year-round, although the amount varies dramatically from one part of the country to another. For example, the mountains of South Island cause rain to fall on their western slopes, so the eastern part of the island is dryer. Mountains change the climate in another way. The mountainous inland areas of New Zealand are cooler than the coastal areas. Temperatures drop about three-and-a-half degrees for every 1,000-foot rise in elevation.

Mountains influence Australia's climates, too. The Great Dividing Range forces moisture-bearing winds to rise and shed their rain before moving inland. For that reason, the marine west coast and humid subtropical climates exist only on the east coast. That coast is Australia's most heavily populated region. The moist coasts are also the only parts of Australia with enough rain for trees that grow taller than 300 feet.

BACKGROUND
This rate of temperature reduction is true in almost all mountain ranges.

Hot and Cold Deserts

As you learned earlier in this book, there are many types of desert. For example, two very different deserts exist in Australia and Antarctica.

ARID AUSTRALIA One-third of Australia is desert, lying in an oval in the center of the continent. This region receives less than 10 inches of rain a year and is too dry for agriculture or for grazing. Encircling the desert is a band of semiarid climate that receives no more than 20 inches of rain a year. Crops can only be grown there by using irrigation. Several factors cause Australia's dryness. Because it lies in the tropics and subtropics, Australia is very hot, so rain evaporates easily. And as you read earlier, mountains and uplands force the winds from the ocean to rise and shed their rain on the coasts instead of the interior.

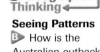
Geographic Thinking

Seeing Patterns
B How is the Australian outback similar to far northern Canada, which you studied in Unit 2?

Very few people live in the dry interior. Australians call the unpopulated inland region the **outback.** The few people who live in the outback receive medical care from the Royal Flying Doctor Service. **B**

THE WHITE DESERT With its lands located around the South Pole, Antarctica is earth's coldest, driest continent. It has an icecap climate. In the winter, inland temperatures can fall to 70°F below zero or colder. Cold air doesn't hold moisture well, so Antarctica's air has only one-tenth the water vapor found in the atmosphere of temperate regions. As a result, Antarctica receives little precipitation and is often called a polar desert. But it has heavy snow and ice cover because the snow that does fall rarely melts.

Antarctica's only plants are those, such as lichens and mosses, that can survive severe cold and long periods of darkness. Its animals are mostly sea life and birds, including several types of penguins.

In Section 3, you will learn about examples of human-environment interaction in this region.

SECTION 2 Assessment

① Places & Terms
Identify this term and explain its importance in the region's physical geography.

• outback

② Taking Notes
PLACE Review the notes you took for this section.

Climate	
Vegetation	

• What types of climates cover most of Southeast Asia and Oceania?

• Where are deserts found?

③ Main Ideas
a. What region has one of the greatest diversities of vegetation of any world region?

b. Why don't low islands generally have diverse vegetation?

c. What effect does elevation have on temperature in the mountains of New Zealand?

④ Geographic Thinking
Making Inferences What aspects of life in the Australian outback might be difficult? **Think about:**

• the need to fly in medical care

• activities that require water

S See Skillbuilder Handbook, page R4.

GeoActivity

EXPLORING LOCAL GEOGRAPHY Learn about the plants and animals that are native to your state. Create an **illustrated map,** like the one on page 696, showing five or six of your state's native life forms. (The examples do not have to be unique to your state, only natives of it.)

SE ASIA & OCEANIA

Human–Environment Interaction

Main Ideas
• Pacific Islanders developed technology that enabled them to travel the Pacific Ocean.
• This region has been damaged by nuclear testing and the introduction of European animals.

Places & Terms
voyaging canoe

outrigger canoe

atoll

Bikini Atoll

CONNECT TO THE ISSUES
LAND CLAIMS The Bikini Islanders lost their homeland when the United States used it for atomic tests.

SUNSHINE STATE STANDARDS
Key Standard SS.B.2.4.4 The student understands the global impact of human changes in the physical environment.

Other Standards SS.B.2.4.2

FCAT LA.A.1.4.2 Reading: Strategies

A HUMAN PERSPECTIVE In May 2000, the Smithsonian Institution honored Mau Piailug for preserving traditional navigation skills. Mau was born in Micronesia. When he was four years old, he began to sail with his grandfather, who taught the boy how to navigate without using instruments. Those methods of navigation were similar to those used by ancient Polynesians. In 1976, Mau was the navigator during an experimental voyage in which a group used a Polynesian-style canoe to travel from Hawaii to Tahiti and back. Since then, Mau has taught many people in the Pacific Islands how to navigate using traditional skills. In doing so, he passed on important knowledge of how ancient people adapted to their environment.

Traveling the Pacific

In ancient times, people around the world found ways to travel great distances in spite of geographic challenges. For example, the people of Arabia discovered that the camel was the perfect pack animal to take across the desert. Similarly, the people who settled the islands of the Pacific developed ways to travel that vast and dangerous ocean.

NAVIGATION CHARTS Most scholars believe that the people who settled the Pacific Islands came from Southeast Asia. They first used land bridges and small rafts and canoes to reach the islands closest to the mainland. In time, they ventured farther out into the Pacific, which required more sophisticated navigation methods.

Pacific Islanders not only relied on stars for navigation, but they also used charts made of sticks and shells. The sticks showed the patterns of waves commonly found in a region. The shells gave the positions of islands. Pacific Islanders closely guarded the secret of how to use these charts until the late 1800s. About that time, they began to use European methods of navigation.

HUMAN-ENVIRONMENT INTERACTION Pacific Islanders used charts like this to record patterns of waves and ocean swells. The shells mark islands.
How might these charts help sailors plan a journey?

forward sail

aft (rear) sail

navigator's seat

deck

splashguard

starboard
(right) hull

port
(left) hull

steering paddle

crossbeams joining the two hulls

SPECIAL CANOES To sail the vast ocean, Pacific Islanders developed huge **voyaging canoes** with double hulls, shown above. Having two hulls made the craft stable and gave it the ability to carry lots of weight. The canoes also had sails to take advantage of the winds. Cabins were sometimes built on the platform atop the hulls to shelter the voyagers and their supplies. Those supplies usually included plants that the travelers hoped to grow in their new homeland.

The large voyaging canoes were awkward to use in the lagoons of the islands where Pacific Islanders settled. In those places, they used the **outrigger canoe.** An outrigger canoe has a frame, with an attached float, extending from one side. The float helps balance the canoe. Ⓐ

Geographic Thinking

Making Comparisons

Ⓐ How was balance achieved in the voyaging canoes and the outrigger canoes?

Invasion of the Rabbits

Just as the people who settled the Pacific Islands carried familiar plants with them, so did the Europeans who colonized Australia. They also brought European animals, such as the rabbit. The impact was disastrous. Although the rabbit is a small, timid animal, it proved to be a force strong enough to nearly ruin the Australian landscape.

THE RABBIT PROBLEM In Europe, many people raise or hunt rabbits for food. In 1859, Thomas Austin released 24 rabbits into Australia so he could hunt them. It was like infecting the continent with a cancer; the rabbit population grew faster than anyone could control it. A single pair of rabbits can have up to 184 descendants in 18 months. Plus, rabbits have few natural enemies—such as foxes—among Australia's wildlife. By 1900, Australia had more than a billion rabbits.

Australia's arid climate produces sparse vegetation. Rabbits graze close to the ground, so they kill or weaken the plants that do grow. Rabbits wiped out native plants and destroyed crops. They ruined pastures, reducing the land's ability to feed herds of sheep. Areas stripped of vegetation suffered erosion. And some of Australia's native animals became endangered because of competition for food. B▷

Geographic Thinking

Making Comparisons
◁B Why are rabbits better suited to Europe than Australia?

REGION When Australia's rabbit population gets out of control, they swarm over the landscape. **How would this affect the region's ability to grow crops?**

CONTROL MEASURES Australians have made efforts to control the number of rabbits. They imported foxes to prey on rabbits, but the growing fox population endangered Australian wildlife just as rabbits had. In the early 1900s, the government built a 2,000-mile fence to keep rabbits from spreading to the southwest. This fence succeeded only temporarily before rabbits broke through to the new region.

In the 1950s, the government infected wild rabbits with a disease called myxomatosis. More than 90 percent of the total rabbit population died. As rabbit numbers decreased, Australian ranches could support nearly twice as many sheep. But rabbits became immune to the disease, and their numbers boomed again—to 300 million by the 1990s.

Now Australians are trying a combination of methods to reduce rabbit numbers: using poison, introducing new diseases, erecting fences, and destroying the warrens and burrows where rabbits live. No one knows if this new program will provide a permanent solution.

Nuclear Testing

Australia is not the only land in this region to be scarred by the consequences of human action. Beginning in the 1940s, the United States and the Soviet Union waged an arms race in which they competed to develop more powerful nuclear weapons. As part of its weapons development program, the United States wanted to test nuclear bombs without endangering American citizens. In the 1940s and 1950s, the United States conducted 66 tests in the Pacific.

TESTS IN BIKINI ATOLL In the Marshall Islands of the central Pacific lies Bikini Atoll. An **atoll** is a ringlike coral island or string of small islands surrounding a lagoon. **Bikini Atoll** was the site of U.S. atomic-weapons tests. (Similar tests were also held on Enewetak Atoll.) C▷

Geographic Thinking

Using the Atlas
◁C Locate the Marshall Islands on the map on page 681. What are the nearest nations to them?

The U.S. government chose Bikini for testing because it lay far away from regular shipping and air travel routes. In 1946, the government moved the 167 Bikini Islanders to another atoll and conducted two atomic-weapons tests.

From 1951 to 1958, the U.S. government held about 60 more tests there. The most dramatic of these was the explosion of a hydrogen bomb that was code-named Bravo. That blast vaporized several islands

BACKGROUND
The two-piece bikini bathing suit was named after the Bikini test because designers claimed the suit was "explosive."

of the Bikini Atoll and contaminated the entire area with high levels of radiation. Many islanders were injured or became ill.

LONG-TERM EFFECTS In the meantime, the Bikini Islanders remained exiled from their homeland. The first atoll to which they were moved proved to be unable to support inhabitants, so in 1948, they were moved to the island of Kili. But they soon grew unhappy because conditions there made it impossible to grow enough food or to engage in fishing.

In the late 1960s, the United States government declared Bikini Atoll safe for humans, and some islanders returned home. Then, in 1978, doctors discovered dangerous levels of radiation in the islanders' bodies. The affected islanders had to leave again. A cleanup began in 1988, but no one knows when Bikini Atoll will again be suitable for human life.

In Chapter 31, you will read more about the history and culture of Oceania, Southeast Asia, Australia, and New Zealand.

Assessment

① Places & Terms

Identify these terms and explain their importance in the region's physical geography.

• voyaging canoe

• outrigger canoe

• atoll

• Bikini Atoll

② Taking Notes

HUMAN-ENVIRONMENT INTERACTION Review the notes you took for this section.

> Human-Environment
> Interaction

• What is an example of humans adapting to the environment?

• What are examples of humans altering the environment?

③ Main Ideas

a. How did Pacific Islanders navigate the ocean in ancient times?

b. How have Australians tried to control the rabbit problem?

c. Why have the Bikini Islanders been unable to return home?

④ Geographic Thinking

Determining Cause and Effect What do the atomic tests on Bikini reveal about the long-term effects of using atomic weapons?

Think about:

• how the blasts affect people and the environment

RESEARCH LINKS
CLASSZONE.COM

MAKING COMPARISONS Do research to learn about French atomic tests in the Pacific. Create a **chart** comparing the French tests to the U.S. tests. You might use such categories as location, impact on people, and current policy about the tests.

SE ASIA & OCEANIA

Chapter 30 Assessment

VISUAL SUMMARY
PHYSICAL GEOGRAPHY OF SOUTHEAST ASIA, OCEANIA, AND ANTARCTICA

Landforms

Southeast Asia: Indochinese Peninsula; Malay Peninsula; Malay Archipelago; mountain ranges and rivers

Oceania: high islands; low islands; New Zealand—South Island and North Island; Australia—Great Dividing Range, Murray River

Antarctica: Transantarctic Mountains; East Antarctica and West Antarctica

Resources

• Southeast Asia has fish, fertile soil, and mineral resources.

• Oceania is generally poor in resources. Some islands have minerals.

• New Zealand has fertile farmland, forests, and rivers. Australia is rich in minerals.

Climate and Vegetation

• Southeast Asia and Oceania have tropical or subtropical climates. Southeast Asia has a great diversity of vegetation.

• Australia has moderate climates on its coasts and arid climates inland. New Zealand has a marine west coast climate.

• Antarctica is a polar desert.

Human-Environment Interaction

• The people who settled the Pacific Islands navigated using traditional methods and doubled-hulled canoes.

• Imported rabbits severely damaged the vegetation of Australia.

• U.S. atomic tests contaminated the Bikini Atoll with radiation.

Reviewing Places & Terms

A. Briefly explain the importance of each of the following.

1. archipelago
2. Oceania
3. high island
4. low island
5. Great Barrier Reef
6. outback
7. voyaging canoe
8. outrigger canoe
9. atoll
10. Bikini Atoll

B. Answer the questions about vocabulary in complete sentences.

11. Which of the terms above are related to Australia?
12. Are atolls high islands or low islands? Explain.
13. Is the Great Barrier Reef most closely related to high islands or low islands? Explain.
14. Which would a tourist be more likely to visit, the outback or the Great Barrier Reef? Why?
15. Which of the subregions contain archipelagoes?
16. Where in Oceania are outrigger canoes used?
17. What are the important features of voyaging canoes?
18. Which of the terms above is associated with human damage to the environment?
19. Are high islands or low islands more likely to have prosperous economies? Why?
20. Which term or terms name a place in Oceania?

Main Ideas

Landforms and Resources (pp. 689–693)

1. What are the two distinct subregions of Southeast Asia?
2. What is the physical pattern formed by the mountain ranges and rivers of mainland Southeast Asia?
3. For what purpose do engineers use the underground steam found in the volcanic area of New Zealand?
4. What is one of the many differences between the physical geographies of Australia and New Zealand?

Climate and Vegetation (pp. 694–697)

5. Where is the tropical wet and dry climate found?
6. How does the Great Dividing Range influence Australia's climate?
7. What are the main plants and animals of Antarctica?

Human-Environment Interaction (pp. 698–701)

8. On the navigation charts of Pacific Islanders, what did the shells represent?
9. Why did the rabbit population grow so quickly in Australia?
10. Why have the Bikini Islanders been unhappy with the places where the U.S. government resettled them?

Critical Thinking

1. Using Your Notes
Use your completed chart to answer these questions.

Landforms	
Resources	

a. What subregion has a large diversity of both landforms and vegetation?

b. How did the type of vegetation found in Australia make it an unsuitable place for the introduction of rabbits?

2. Geographic Themes

a. **LOCATION** Where are the tropical climates of this region located relative to the equator?

b. **MOVEMENT** How does the physical geography of Southeast Asia encourage movement?

3. Identifying Themes
Consider the way that Pacific Islanders used shell maps (see page 698). How does the use of such maps demonstrate all five themes of geography?

4. Determining Cause and Effect
What are some of the negative and positive effects of volcanic activity in Southeast Asia?

5. Identifying and Solving Problems
In general, Oceania has few resources. What problem does this create for Pacific Islanders, and how might they solve it?

Additional Test Practice, pp. S1–S37

TEST PRACTICE
CLASSZONE.COM

Geographic Skills: Interpreting Maps

Bikini Atoll
Use the map to answer the following questions.

1. **PLACE** Which channel leads to the lagoon inside the Bikini Atoll?

2. **LOCATION** What is the absolute location of the Bravo test site?

3. **MOVEMENT** How far did radiation travel from the Bravo test site in order to contaminate Bikini Island?

In addition to Bikini Atoll, other atolls and islands were contaminated with radiation from the U.S. atomic-weapons tests. Do research to learn the names and locations of these islands and atolls. Then create a map showing the full area of radiation contamination.

 INTERNET ACTIVITY

Use the links at **classzone.com** to do research about active volcanoes in Southeast Asia. Look for such information as location and recent eruptions.

Writing About Geography Write a report of your findings. Include a map of the volcanoes and a chart listing recent eruptions. List the Web sites that were your sources.

Chapter 31

SECTION 1
Southeast Asia

SECTION 2
Oceania

SECTION 3
Australia, New Zealand, and Antarctica

HUMAN GEOGRAPHY OF SOUTHEAST ASIA, OCEANIA, AND ANTARCTICA
Migration and Conquest

Three Subregions

Legend:
- Southeast Asia
- Islands of Oceania
- Australia, New Zealand, and Antarctica

Lambert Equal-Area Projection

GeoFocus

How have conquest and colonialism affected this region?

Taking Notes In your notebook, copy a cluster diagram like the one shown. As you read, take notes about the history, economics, culture, and modern life of each subregion.

- Southeast Asia
- Oceania
- The Region
- Australia and New Zealand

Southeast Asia

- Influenced by China and India, Southeast Asia developed many vibrant, complex cultures.
- European colonialism left a legacy that continues to affect the region's politics and economics.

Places & Terms
mandala
Khmer Empire
Indochina
Vietnam War
ASEAN

CONNECT TO THE ISSUES
INDUSTRIALIZATION
Since 1960, many Southeast Asian nations industrialized, while others lagged behind.

SUNSHINE STATE STANDARDS
Key Standard SS.B.2.4.1 The student understands how social, cultural, economic, and environmental factors contribute to the dynamic nature of regions.

Other Standards SS.A.2.4.8, A.3.4.3, D.2.4.1
FCAT LA.A.1.4.2 Reading: Strategies

A HUMAN PERSPECTIVE Much of Southeast Asia is haunted by its colonial past. One example is the divided island of Timor. The Netherlands ruled Western Timor, later part of Indonesia. Portugal ruled East Timor. In 1975, East Timor declared itself an independent state (even though some people living there wanted to join Indonesia). In response, Indonesia invaded the new nation and ruled it for 24 years.

In 1999, Indonesia let East Timor vote on the choice of limited self-rule within Indonesia or independence. When most voters chose independence, pro-Indonesia militias reacted with violence. The United Nations stepped in and helped East Timor prepare for nationhood. In May 2002, the country gained its independence.

The new nation is also one of the poorest. However, the development of a natural gas field in the Timor Sea should help solve East Timor's economic challenges. In fact, the revenue from the sale of the gas is expected to guarantee the new nation a steady income until 2020.

A Long History of Diversity

Since ancient times, many cultures have influenced Southeast Asia, yet it has retained its own character. Today the region includes the nations of Brunei, Cambodia, Indonesia, Laos, Malaysia, Myanmar, the Philippines, Singapore, Thailand, and Vietnam.

EARLY HISTORY China and India influenced ancient Southeast Asia. China ruled northern Vietnam from 111 B.C. to A.D. 939. Chinese art, technology, political ideas, and ethical beliefs shaped Vietnam's culture. Hinduism and Buddhism spread from India and influenced religion and art in much of Southeast Asia. Yet, Southeast Asia kept some of its own traditions, such as more equal roles for women.

Early Southeast Asian states didn't have set borders. Instead, they were **mandalas,** states organized as rings of power around a central court. Those regions of power changed in size over time. A *mandala's* region might overlap that of a neighbor, so rulers had to make alliances for a state to survive. The **Khmer Empire** was a powerful *mandala* that lasted roughly from the 9th to the 15th centuries in what is now Cambodia.

MOVEMENT The temple complex of Angkor Wat in Cambodia was built in the 1100s and dedicated to the Hindu god Vishnu.
How does this temple illustrate the movement of ideas?

POWERFUL STATES The years 1300 through 1800 were important to Southeast Asia's development. Five powerful states existed where Myanmar, Vietnam, Thailand, Java, and the Malay Peninsula are now. Those states were similar to *mandalas* but were larger and more complex. Trade within the region was important to their economies.

During that period, the Burmese, the Vietnamese, the Thai, and the Javanese each began to define their national identities. Urbanization, or the growth of large cities, also took place. For instance, Malacca, on the Malay Peninsula, grew to have about 100,000 people in the early 1500s.

BACKGROUND
The Burmese are the people of Myanmar, which used to be called Burma; the Javanese live in Indonesia.

Colonialism and Its Aftermath

Southeast Asian states not only traded with each other but also with merchants from Arabia and India, who brought Islam to Southeast Asia. Islam attracted many followers, especially in the islands.

EUROPEAN CONTROL Large numbers of Europeans began to arrive in Southeast Asia in 1509. At that time, Europeans had little interest in setting up colonies there, except for the Spanish, who took over the Philippines. Instead, the goal of most Europeans was to obtain wealth.

Europeans used various business methods to take over much of Southeast Asia's trade. As the region's wealth flowed to Europe, local control in Southeast Asian states declined. By the 20th century, Europeans had made all of Southeast Asia except Siam (now Thailand) into colonies. Ⓐ

Colonialism changed Southeast Asia. First, colonial rulers set up centralized, bureaucratic governments with set routines and regulations. Second, Europeans forced the colonies to produce commodities that would help Europe's economy. They included rubber, sugar, rice, tea, and coffee. Third, colonialism had the unintended effect of sparking nationalism. Groups that never had been allies united against European rule. And Southeast Asians who gained Western education learned about political ideas such as self-rule.

Geographic Thinking

Seeing Patterns
Ⓐ Why would a loss of wealth cause local control to weaken?

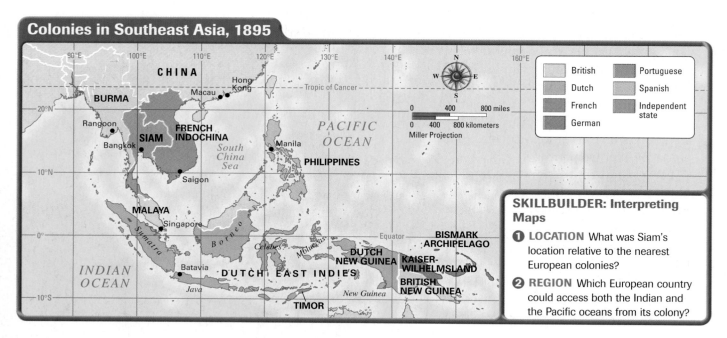

Colonies in Southeast Asia, 1895

Legend:
- British
- Dutch
- French
- German
- Portuguese
- Spanish
- Independent state

SKILLBUILDER: Interpreting Maps

❶ **LOCATION** What was Siam's location relative to the nearest European colonies?

❷ **REGION** Which European country could access both the Indian and the Pacific oceans from its colony?

INDEPENDENCE Claiming to take back "Asia for Asians," Japan occupied Southeast Asia during World War II. Southeast Asians soon realized that Japan was exploiting the region for its own benefit just as Europe had. But unlike the Europeans, the Japanese put Southeast Asians in leadership roles, which gave them valuable experience.

After the war ended, Southeast Asian leaders sought independence. Several Southeast Asian nations gained their freedom peacefully. Indonesia had to fight from 1945 to 1949 to gain independence from the Dutch.

Indochina, a French colony made up of Cambodia, Laos, and Vietnam, suffered decades of turmoil. The Vietnamese defeated the French in 1954, winning independence for Cambodia, Laos, North Vietnam, and South Vietnam. The United States became involved in South Vietnam to prevent its takeover by Communist North Vietnam. The resulting conflict was the **Vietnam War** (1957-1975). In 1973, the United States withdrew. In 1975, South Vietnam surrendered, and Vietnam became one country, ruled by Communists. Also in that year, Communists took over both Cambodia and Laos.

BACKGROUND The name *Indochina* refers to the Indian and Chinese influences on the region. The colony took up only part of the Indochinese Peninsula.

An Uneven Economy

Agriculture is the main source of livelihood in Southeast Asia. Several nations began to industrialize in the 1960s, but industry is unevenly distributed across the region.

TRADITIONAL ECONOMIES The people of Cambodia, Myanmar, Laos, and Vietnam depend mostly on agriculture for income. Rice is the chief food crop in those countries, as it is in almost every Southeast Asian nation. Myanmar is heavily forested and produces much of the world's teak, a yellowish-brown wood valued for its durability.

The lack of industry has many causes. The Vietnam War destroyed factories and roads. Thousands of refugees fled Vietnam, Laos, and Cambodia after the war, reducing the work force. Political turmoil, especially in Cambodia and Myanmar, has continued to block growth.

But some economic growth has occurred. For example, Vietnam has built industry and sought foreign investment and trade.

INDUSTRY AND FINANCE In general, Brunei, Indonesia, Malaysia, the Philippines, Singapore, and Thailand have more highly developed economies than others in the region. Those countries have long been members of **ASEAN,** the Association of Southeast Asian Nations, an alliance that promotes economic growth and peace in the region. (The other four Southeast Asian countries did not join ASEAN until 1995 or later.)

Although these countries didn't begin to industrialize extensively until the 1960s, manufacturing has grown quickly. The processing of agricultural products is the chief industry. Other industries include the production of textiles, clothing, and electronic products. Service industries are also important. For example, Singapore is a center of finance. ◀B

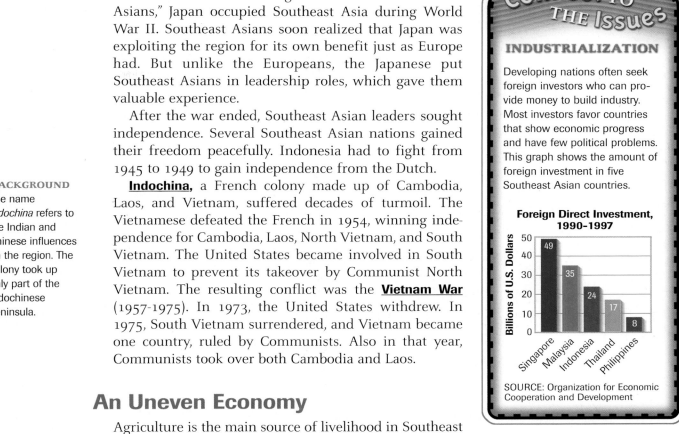

Connect to THE Issues

INDUSTRIALIZATION

Developing nations often seek foreign investors who can provide money to build industry. Most investors favor countries that show economic progress and have few political problems. This graph shows the amount of foreign investment in five Southeast Asian countries.

Foreign Direct Investment, 1990-1997

Billions of U.S. Dollars

Singapore: 49
Malaysia: 35
Indonesia: 24
Thailand: 17
Philippines: 8

SOURCE: Organization for Economic Cooperation and Development

CONNECT TO THE ISSUES
INDUSTRIALIZATION
B ▶ What further effects do you think industrialization will have on Southeast Asia?

SE ASIA & OCEANIA

Energy sources and mining are significant. Brunei receives most of its wealth from petroleum and natural gas reserves, but they are expected to run out in the early 2000s. Southeast Asia's mineral resources include tin, which is found mostly in Indonesia, Malaysia, and Thailand.

A Rich Mosaic of Culture

Although Southeast Asia has absorbed many influences from other regions, it has used them to create a culture that is distinctly its own.

RELIGIOUS DIVERSITY Southeast Asia has much religious diversity. Buddhism is widespread in the region, while the Philippines is mostly Catholic (as a result of Spanish rule), and Indonesia and Brunei are mostly Muslim. In addition, some Southeast Asians practice Hinduism, and others follow traditional local beliefs. ▶

RICH ARTISTIC LEGACY Buddhism and Hinduism have influenced the region's sculpture and architecture. Perhaps the most famous example is the ancient temple complex of Angkor Wat in what is now Cambodia. (See page 705.) Thailand's Buddhist temples are modern examples of religious architecture.

Southeast Asia is also famous for its performing arts and literature. For example, Thailand and Indonesia have traditional forms of dance, in which richly costumed dancers act out stories. In Vietnam, poetry is highly respected. Nearly all Vietnamese know at least part of the 3,253-line poem "Kim van Kieu," which is about love and sacrifice.

● **Geographic Thinking◀**

Using the Atlas
◀ Use the map on page 683 to learn about the major religions in Southeast Asia. What do you notice about the places where Catholicism and Islam are practiced?

growing up in...Thailand

About 95 percent of the people who live in Thailand are Buddhists and follow an ancient tradition of Buddhism that stresses the importance of being a monk. This has led to a unique custom. During their late teens or early twenties, many Thai men become monks for a short time.

The new monks go to live in a monastery where they meditate and study Buddhist teachings. They also shave their heads, wear saffron (orange-yellow) robes, and give up their worldly possessions. Some Thai men remain monks their whole lives, but most leave the monastery after a short period, usually a few weeks or months. After his time as a monk, a young man is considered ready for adult life.

If you grew up in Thailand, you would pass the following milestones:

- At your birth, your parents might ask a Buddhist monk to help them choose your name.
- You would have to attend school for 6 years, between ages 7 and 14. Although higher education is available, very few people can afford it.
- You could vote at age 18.
- If you were a man 18 years of age, you might be drafted to serve in the army.

Changing Lifestyles

Most Southeast Asians live in rural villages and follow traditional ways. However, a growing number of people are moving to cities and leading more modern lives—a trend taking place all around the world.

THE VILLAGES In many Southeast Asian villages, people live in wood houses built on stilts for protection against floods. Roofs are usually made of thatch, although wealthy families may have a tin roof. In Laos, Myanmar, and Thailand, most villages have a Buddhist temple that serves as the center of social life. In Indonesia, most villages have a group of leaders who govern by a system that stresses cooperation.

Some Southeast Asian villagers still wear traditional clothing, such as the *longyi*—a long, tightly wrapped skirt—of Myanmar. Yet modern conveniences are slowly beginning to change village life. For instance, listening to the radio is common in Indonesia and Thailand.

THE CITIES Kuala Lumpur, Malaysia, and Singapore are examples of bustling cities with towering skyscrapers and modern business districts. In Southeast Asian cities, most people live in apartments.

But there is a shortage of housing for the large numbers of people migrating to cities for jobs. Many of them live in makeshift shacks in slums. The dangers of doing that were shown by a disaster in Manila, Philippines. Hundreds of people had built shanties at a city dump. In July 2000, after a typhoon weakened a tower of garbage, it crashed onto those shacks and burst into flames. More than 100 people died.

Another region facing the changes caused by rural-to-urban migration is Oceania. You will read about that region in Section 2.

PLACE People waiting at a bus stop in Kuala Lumpur, Malaysia, wear Western clothes and traditional Muslim attire.
What does this scene show about diversity in Malaysia?

Geographic Thinking
Using the Atlas
 Use the map on page 680 to locate Kuala Lumpur and Singapore. How far apart are these two major cities?

SECTION 1 Assessment

1 Places & Terms

Identify these terms and explain their importance in the region's history or culture.

- *mandala*
- Khmer Empire
- Indochina
- Vietnam War
- ASEAN

2 Taking Notes

PLACE Review the notes you took for this section.

Southeast Asia → The Region

- Where did powerful states exist during the period 1300 to 1800?
- What is the only country in the region that wasn't a colony?

3 Main Ideas

a. How did China and India influence Southeast Asia?

b. How did the Vietnam War affect the economy?

c. What is village life like in Southeast Asia?

4 Geographic Thinking

Drawing Conclusions How has ASEAN helped to create a region within a region?
Think about:

- the goals of ASEAN
- differences between longtime and more recent ASEAN members

 See Skillbuilder Handbook, page R5.

GeoActivity

MAKING COMPARISONS Choose two Southeast Asian nations and research their similarities and differences. Create a **chart** comparing the two countries by using such categories as languages, religions, main economic activities, and types of government.

SE ASIA & OCEANIA

Disasters!

Krakatoa

SUNSHINE STATE STANDARDS
Key Standard SS.B.1.4.1 The student uses a variety of maps, geographic technologies including geographic information systems (GIS) and satellite-produced imagery, and other advanced graphic representations to depict geographic problems.
FCAT LA.E.2.2.1 Literature: Recognize Cause and Effect

Imagine an explosion so destructive that it sends volcanic ash 50 miles into the air and so loud that people hear it about 3,000 miles away. In 1883, the Indonesian volcano Krakatoa (also spelled *Krakatau*) erupted in an explosion that created those effects. But the blast was only the beginning of the disaster. The eruption caused the volcano to collapse into the sea and triggered a series of deadly tsunamis, or giant waves. The greatest of those towered 120 feet high. The tsunami swept the coasts of Java and Sumatra, killing more than 36,000 people.

Krakatoa: The Eruption and the Tsunami

① Krakatoa was a main island consisting of three overlapping volcano cones, plus two small islands.

② After a few months of minor volcanic activity, Krakatoa blew up violently on August 27, 1883.

In the Sunda Strait, in 1927, lava began to flow through a crack in the sea floor beneath the site of the old island. By 1928, a new island was born and named Anak Krakatoa, which means "child of Krakatoa." The island is still volcanically active, but it is not considered dangerous.

GeoData

DUST IN THE WIND

- Krakatoa threw so much ash and dust into the air that temperatures dropped by about 0.9°F around the world.
- The dust filtered light and caused spectacular sunsets around the world for about a year.
- The dust in the atmosphere also made the moon look shades of green and blue.

FIVE DEADLIEST VOLCANOES SINCE 1500

1792
Unzen, Japan:
15,000 dead

1815
Tambora, Indonesia:
92,000 dead

1883
Krakatoa, Indonesia:
36,000 dead

1902
Mount Pelée, Martinique:
30,000 dead

1985
Nevado del Ruiz, Colombia:
25,000 dead

③ All three cones disappeared, leaving only a small island. Massive amounts of sea water were displaced. The disturbance of the ocean created giant tsunamis. The tsunamis destroyed about 163 villages.

Disasters! **711**

Oceania

Main Ideas

• Settled in ancient times by migrating Southeast Asians, Oceania developed three cultural regions.

• Contact with Europeans and Americans disrupted the islanders' traditional ways of life.

Places & Terms

Micronesia

Melanesia

Polynesia

subsistence activities

copra

taro

CONNECT TO THE ISSUES
ENVIRONMENTAL CHANGE A possible rise in sea level from global warming threatens some islands.

SUNSHINE STATE STANDARDS
Key Standard SS.B.2.4.1 The student understands how social, cultural, economic, and environmental factors contribute to the dynamic nature of regions.

Other Standards SS.B.2.4.2, D.2.4.1

FCAT LA.A.1.4.2 Reading: Strategies

A HUMAN PERSPECTIVE Noah Idechong has fought to protect the sea life of Palau, an archipelago east of the Philippines. Palauans have always earned their living by fishing, but in the 1980s, many species of fish were in danger of extinction because they were such popular menu items in Asian restaurants. Idechong began to study the problem in 1988.

His efforts paid off. In 1994, the year Palau became independent, it banned the export of certain species, and fish populations grew again. However, in 2000, the government planned building projects that would help the economy but strain the environment. Idechong kept working to save wildlife. He said, "Palau right now needs . . . people who can say what they want Palau to look like 50 years from now." In other words, Palauans need to decide what to preserve in the face of change.

A History of the Islands

Like Palau, all the nations of Oceania except Nauru are island groups. They are Fiji, Kiribati, Marshall Islands, Federated States of Micronesia, Palau, Papua New Guinea, Samoa, Solomon Islands, Tonga, Tuvalu, and Vanuatu. (Some geographers consider Australia and New Zealand part of Oceania, but those nations are covered in Section 3.)

FIRST ISLANDERS Prehistoric people journeyed from mainland Southeast Asia to nearby Pacific islands using small rafts or canoes and land bridges that have since disappeared. In time, they developed large

PLACE These stone heads are on an altar on Vao, a small island of Vanuatu. They were used in rituals for controlling the weather. **How has time affected the stone heads?**

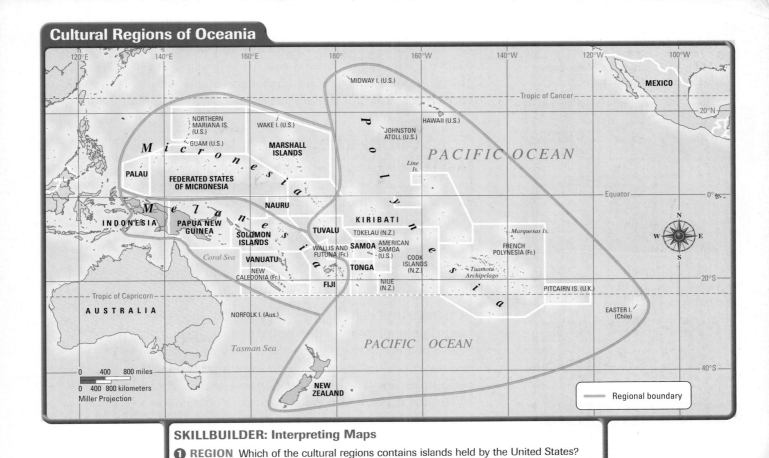

SKILLBUILDER: Interpreting Maps

❶ **REGION** Which of the cultural regions contains islands held by the United States?

❷ **MOVEMENT** Consider what you have learned about ancient migrations of people in the Pacific Ocean. Which cultural region was the last to be settled?

voyaging canoes (see page 699) that enabled them to sail longer distances. For thousands of years, their descendants continued to migrate as far east as Hawaii, as far south as New Zealand, and as far west as Madagascar.

For centuries, the people of Oceania had little contact with the rest of the world, so they developed their own ways of life. Geographers divide Oceania into three regions, defined both by physical geography and culture. The regions are **Micronesia,** meaning "tiny islands," **Melanesia,** meaning "black islands," and **Polynesia,** meaning "many islands."

CONTACT WITH THE WEST Beginning in the 1500s, many Europeans explored the Pacific. Perhaps the most famous was the British captain James Cook, the first European to visit many of the islands.

In the 1800s, European missionaries arrived and tried to convert the islanders to Christianity. Traders came for products such as coconut oil, and sailors hunted whales. Settlers started plantations on which they could grow coconuts, coffee, pineapples, or sugar.

As a result, island societies began to decline. Many islanders died of diseases brought by the Europeans. Western ways often replaced traditional customs. And Europe and the United States took control of the islands and turned them into territories and possessions.

RECENT HISTORY Oceania experienced turmoil in the 20th century. During World War II, the Allies and the Japanese fought fierce battles there to gain control of the Pacific. Afterward, some islands were used as nuclear test sites, not only by the United States (see Chapter 30) but

BACKGROUND
James Cook was also one of the first Europeans to explore Australia and New Zealand. See page 718 for his portrait.

SE ASIA & OCEANIA

Oceania **713**

Many residents of Oceania make a living from traditional activities.

This resident of Fiji is husking coconuts to make copra, or the dried meat of coconuts.

Traditional dances are often performed for tourists. These dancers are from French Polynesia.

Many people of Oceania, such as these Cook Islanders, earn their living from fishing.

also by other countries. Gradually, inhabitants of many of the islands moved toward self-rule. Since 1962, 12 different nations have gained independence. Foreigners still rule the other islands.

A Traditional Economy

Most of Oceania has an economy in which people work not for wages but at **subsistence activities.** These are activities in which a family produces only the food, clothing, and shelter they themselves need. The tiny island of Nauru is an exception. It has a prosperous economy based on the mining of phosphates, used in fertilizer. But Nauru's phosphate deposits are expected to give out early in the 21st century.

AGRICULTURE As Chapter 30 explained, most low islands do not have plentiful or fertile soil. In spite of this, agriculture is the region's main economic activity because many high islands do have soil that supports agriculture. The chief crops are bananas, sugar, cocoa, coffee, and **copra,** which is the dried meat of coconuts. Fishing also provides a significant source of income.

OTHER ECONOMIC ACTIVITIES Since the invention of jet travel, tourism has become very important to the economy of Oceania. This has been a mixed blessing. Although tourists spend money in the islands, they also require hotels, stores, roads, and vehicles. These threaten the islands' environment and traditional ways of life.

A few islands besides Nauru have mining industries. For example, Papua New Guinea is developing a large copper mine with the help of foreign investment. Some industry also exists. Some of the larger towns have factories that produce goods such as coconut oil and soap. As in Southeast Asia, an increasing number of people in the Pacific Islands are moving to cities to find jobs. Ⓐ▶

Culture of the Islands

Oceania has a culture that blends traditional ways with the cultures of Europe and the United States.

LANGUAGE AND RELIGION Oceania is one of the most linguistically diverse regions in the world. Some 1,100 of the world's languages are spoken there. The people of Papua New Guinea alone speak 823 languages. In addition, many Pacific Islanders speak European languages. English is the most common.

Because of missionaries' work and colonialism, Christianity is the most widely spread religion. Even so, some Pacific Islanders still practice their traditional religions.

Geographic Thinking◀

Seeing Patterns
◀ Ⓐ Which characteristics of Oceania might account for its high levels of migration to cities?

THE ARTS Many Pacific Islanders produce arts and crafts, such as baskets and mats woven from the leaves of palm trees or carved wooden masks. Some islanders make a living selling such items to tourists.

Island Life

As in Southeast Asia, two distinct ways of life exist on the islands: traditional village life and more modern city life.

TRADITIONAL LIFE Ways of life varied throughout the islands. In Polynesia, most people lived in villages, ranging from small clusters of houses to large walled settlements. The houses were usually wooden with thatched roofs. Generally, a chief led each village. The villages' economies centered on fishing and farming. One major crop was **taro,** a plant with a starchy root. Taro can be eaten boiled, or it can be made into breads, puddings, or a paste called poi.

Many Polynesian societies were warlike and had frequent conflicts. In contrast, Micronesians tended to exist peacefully with their neighbors. Most Micronesians lived in extended family groups. As in Polynesia, they made a living by fishing and farming, with taro being a main crop.

In Melanesia, villages usually existed by the coast where people could fish. Inland, many people practiced shifting cultivation, moving often to let fields regain fertility. Other Melanesians were hunter-gatherers.

Geographic Thinking

Making Comparisons
B What other regions of the world that you have studied are experiencing these same problems in their growing cities?

RECENT CHANGE Oceania has few cities, but they have been growing as many people move to them for education or jobs. Rapid urban growth has led to sprawling shantytowns and inadequate sanitation facilities. In addition, city dwellers are giving up their traditional ways of life. **B**

But change is also helping Oceania. Modern communications systems can unify countries consisting of scattered island groups and also can link Oceania to the rest of the world. Section 3 will describe the two most westernized nations in the region: Australia and New Zealand.

SECTION 2 Assessment

1 Places & Terms
Identify these terms and explain their importance in the region.
- Micronesia
- Melanesia
- Polynesia
- subsistence activities
- copra
- taro

2 Taking Notes
MOVEMENT Review the notes you took for this section.

- How were the Pacific Islands first settled?
- What type of migration is happening within Oceania today?

3 Main Ideas
a. How did contact with Europeans and Americans affect the societies of the Pacific Islands?

b. What are the chief crops of Oceania?

c. What is distinctive about Oceania in terms of its languages?

4 Geographic Thinking
Determining Cause and Effect How has modern technology both helped and harmed Oceania? **Think about:**
- jet travel
- modern communications

RESEARCH LINKS
CLASSZONE.COM

GeoActivities

SEEING PATTERNS Use the Internet to research several nations and territories in Oceania. Then choose the one that you think would make the best vacation spot. Create a **tourist brochure** that will persuade travelers to visit that place. Check your brochure for correct grammar, spelling, sentence structure, and punctuation.

SE ASIA & OCEANIA

Comparing Cultures

Regional Costumes

Blue jeans have spread around the globe and become a popular item of clothing symbolizing U.S. culture. But traditional items of clothing remain important in many regions of the world. Regional costumes are unique not only because of their styles but also because of the materials from which they are made.

Japan

Fiji

India

Peru

SUNSHINE STATE STANDARDS
Key Standard SS.B.2.4.1 The student understands how social, cultural, economic, and environmental factors contribute to the dynamic nature of regions.

FCAT LA.A.2.2.7 Reading: Recognize Compare and Contrast

In India, the traditional garment of women for centuries has been the sari— five to seven yards of unstitched cloth wrapped around the body. The most valuable saris are made of silk, but saris of cotton and synthetic fabrics are also common.

In Fiji, traditional outfits are made from tapa cloth, a nonwoven fabric made from the inner bark of trees. This woman is wearing a skirt of tapa cloth. Fijians often decorate the cloth with geometric designs painted in brown, black, or reddish bark dyes.

Although colorful silk kimonos symbolize Japan, neither the fabric nor the robe itself originated there. Silk was first developed in China, and kimonos are patterned after a wide-sleeved Chinese robe, the *p'ao*.

These Indians of Peru wear traditional wool clothing woven from llama hair; llamas are native to South America. Each village has it own set of traditional patterns that are woven into its cloth. Some of the designs indicate local landscapes; others depict animals or historical events.

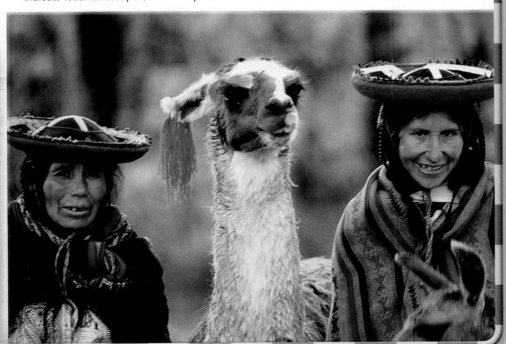

GeoActivity

CREATING A DISPLAY
Working with a partner, use the Internet to research the linen clothing of ancient Egypt or the feather cloaks of Hawaiian chiefs. Create a **display** about this clothing.

• Draw or photocopy an illustration of the clothing. Write a caption giving interesting details about how it was made.

• Create a map showing the country where the clothing originated.

RESEARCH LINKS
CLASSZONE.COM

GeoData

Tapa Cloth
• Tapa cloth is also made in other Melanesian islands, New Guinea, and northern Australia.
• The most popular material for tapa is the inner bark of the mulberry.

Silk
• The Chinese began to produce silk in about 2700 B.C. and kept their methods a secret until about 140 B.C.
• The wide silk or satin sash worn with a kimono is called an obi. It is about 12 feet long.

Cotton
• South Asia was one of the first regions of the world where cotton was cultivated—starting in about 3000 B.C.
• Indian men also wear a type of wrapped garment called a dhoti. Mohandas Gandhi wore a dhoti to show his allegiance to the common Indian man.

Wool
• Wool is the fiber forming the coats of such hairy mammals as sheep, goats, camels, and llamas.
• Intricate textiles have been produced in Peru since about 1000 B.C.

Australia, New Zealand, and Antarctica

Main Ideas

- Both Australia and New Zealand were colonized by Europeans and still have a strong European heritage.
- Because of its harsh climate, Antarctica has no permanent settlements.

Places & Terms

penal colony

Aboriginal people

Maori

Treaty of Waitangi

pakeha

CONNECT TO THE ISSUES

LAND CLAIMS The Aboriginal people of Australia are trying to reclaim ancestral lands.

SUNSHINE STATE STANDARDS
Key Standard SS.B.2.4.1 The student understands how social, cultural, economic, and environmental factors contribute to the dynamic nature of regions.

Other Standards SS.B.2.4.6, D.2.4.1

FCAT LA.A.1.4.2 Reading: Strategies

A HUMAN PERSPECTIVE In 1788, Great Britain founded Sydney, Australia, as a **penal colony**—that is, a place to send prisoners. By the end of the 20th century, Sydney had overcome its origins and earned a reputation as a fun and fascinating international city. That has been due, in part, to a unique combination of physical and cultural geographic assets.

Sydney is located on a deep, beautiful harbor that not only allows the city to function as a port but also provides an arena for sailing and swimming. The mild climate there encourages such outdoor activities. In addition, Sydney has an increasingly diverse population. People who visit the city can view art and dine on food from many cultures.

In 2000, Sydney hosted the Olympic Games. With a physical environment that favors sports and a culture shaped by immigrants, the city seemed a perfect site for an international athletic event.

History: Distant European Outposts

Australia, New Zealand, and Antarctica made up the last region to be explored by Europeans. Australia and New Zealand became British colonies, even though they were already inhabited by people with ancient cultures of their own.

THE ORIGINAL INHABITANTS The **Aboriginal people** migrated to Australia from Asia at least 40,000 years ago. When Europeans arrived in Australia, there were an estimated 500 Aboriginal groups, speaking perhaps 200 different languages. The Aboriginal people had complex

Australia and New Zealand, Prehistory to Today

40,000 B.C.
Australia is gradually settled by Aboriginal people. Their art includes rock paintings like this one in **Kakadu National Park.**

1788
Great Britain starts a penal colony in Australia.

40,000 B.C.   1750 A.D.   1800   1850

1769–1770
Captain James Cook *(right)* explores New Zealand and Australia.

1851
Gold is discovered in **New South Wales,** Australia.

religious beliefs and social structures but a simple economy; they lived by hunting and gathering.

New Zealand was settled first by the **Maori,** who had migrated there from Polynesia more than 1,000 years ago. The Maori lived by fishing, hunting, and farming.

EARLY EXPLORERS During the 1600s and 1700s, several European explorers sailed in the coastal waters of New Zealand and Australia. Captain James Cook of Britain was the first to explore those two lands—New Zealand in 1769 and Australia's east coast in 1770. Antarctica was first discovered in 1820.

BACKGROUND
The name *Australia* comes from the Latin phrase *Terra Australis Incognita,* which means unknown southern land.

EUROPEAN SETTLEMENT In 1788 Britain began to colonize Australia (called New South Wales until 1820) as a place to send prisoners. Having a colony in Australia also gave Britain more Pacific naval bases. New Zealand was colonized by hunters and whalers from Europe, America, and Australia. No permanent settlements were established in Antarctica because of its cold climate.

In Australia, the British colonists had violent conflicts with the Aboriginal people, many of whom were killed. Even greater numbers of native people died from diseases brought by Europeans.

In New Zealand in 1840, the British and several Maori tribes signed the **Treaty of Waitangi,** giving Britain control over New Zealand. But the English and the Maori translations of the treaty differed. The English version gave Great Britain complete control; the Maori version gave Britain "governorship." Disagreement over who owned the land helped cause the Land Wars that lasted from 1845 to 1847 and from 1860 to 1872. In addition, tens of thousands of Maoris died from diseases.

Gold was discovered in Australia in 1851 and in New Zealand in 1861. Hundreds of thousands of people who dreamed of wealth flocked to the two countries, but few miners grew rich. Most, however, stayed there.

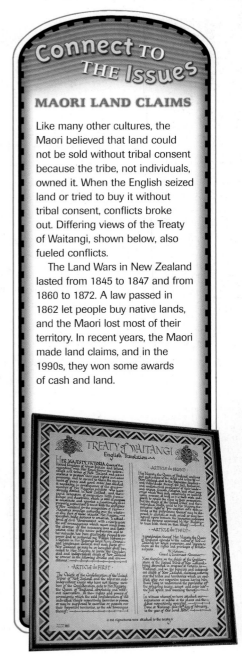

Connect to THE Issues

MAORI LAND CLAIMS

Like many other cultures, the Maori believed that land could not be sold without tribal consent because the tribe, not individuals, owned it. When the English seized land or tried to buy it without tribal consent, conflicts broke out. Differing views of the Treaty of Waitangi, shown below, also fueled conflicts.

The Land Wars in New Zealand lasted from 1845 to 1847 and from 1860 to 1872. A law passed in 1862 let people buy native lands, and the Maori lost most of their territory. In recent years, the Maori made land claims, and in the 1990s, they won some awards of cash and land.

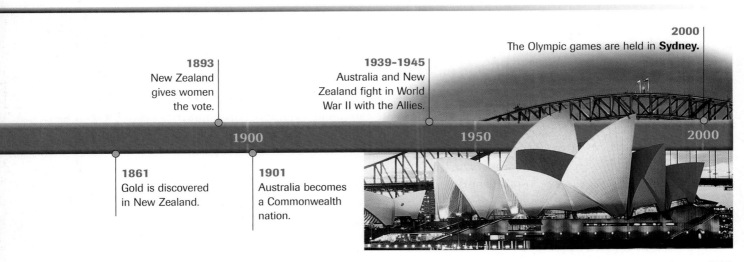

1861
Gold is discovered in New Zealand.

1893
New Zealand gives women the vote.

1900

1901
Australia becomes a Commonwealth nation.

1939-1945
Australia and New Zealand fight in World War II with the Allies.

1950

2000
The Olympic games are held in **Sydney.**

2000

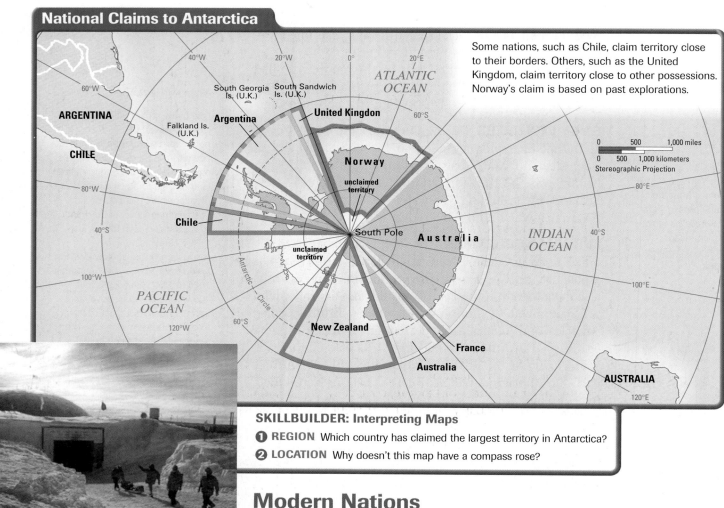

National Claims to Antarctica

Some nations, such as Chile, claim territory close to their borders. Others, such as the United Kingdom, claim territory close to other possessions. Norway's claim is based on past explorations.

REGION Eighteen nations have scientific research stations in Antarctica. This one is run by U.S. scientists.

SKILLBUILDER: Interpreting Maps

❶ REGION Which country has claimed the largest territory in Antarctica?

❷ LOCATION Why doesn't this map have a compass rose?

Modern Nations

Originally, several colonies existed in Australia, but in 1901, they joined into a single, independent nation. New Zealand became self-governing in 1907. Both Australia and New Zealand remained in the British Commonwealth, which is a free association of Great Britain and several of its former colonies.

RIGHTS AND LAND CLAIMS New Zealanders have a long tradition of concern for equal rights and the welfare of its citizens. In 1893, New Zealand became the first country to grant women the vote. It was also one of the first nations to provide pensions for its senior citizens.

In both Australia and New Zealand, native people generally have less education and higher rates of poverty than other citizens. Attempting to improve their lives, the Aboriginal people and the Maori have made claims for the return of their former lands. (See Chapter 32.) A▷

ISSUES A recent issue in Australia was a movement to withdraw from the Commonwealth. In 1999, Australia held a referendum on becoming an independent republic, but voters defeated the proposal, because Australians could not agree on how to choose a head of state.

Antarctica remains unsettled. In 1959, 12 countries drafted a treaty preserving the continent for research. By 2000, 18 countries had scientific research stations there. Seven countries have claimed territory in Antarctica, but many other countries do not recognize those claims.

CONNECT TO THE ISSUES

LAND CLAIMS

◀A How might land ownership improve Aboriginal and Maori lives?

Economy: Meat, Wool, and Butter

As Commonwealth members, Australia and New Zealand prospered by exporting food products and wool to the United Kingdom. So neither country developed much industry. But, since 1950, their exports to the United Kingdom have declined. To continue to prosper, Australia and New Zealand must either develop industry or find other trading partners, such as the nations of nearby Asia.

AGRICULTURE Australia and New Zealand are major exporters of farm products. New Zealand earns much of its income by selling butter, cheese, meat, and wool to other countries. Ranching is so widespread in New Zealand that in 1998 the number of farm animals (including 47.6 million sheep and 8.8 million cattle) was 15 times greater than the number of people! Crops include vegetables and fruits. For example, New Zealand is the world's largest producer of kiwi fruit.

Sheep ranching is also important in Australia, which is the largest exporter of wool in the world. Because so much of Australia is arid, less than ten percent of the land is used to grow crops.

MINING Australia earns a large part of its income from mining. It is the world's top producer of diamonds, lead, zinc, and opals. In addition, it is a major producer of bauxite, coal, copper, gold, and iron ore.

The mining industry faces one difficulty. Many deposits lie in the outback, far from cities. As a result, it is expensive to build the roads and buildings necessary for the mines to operate. Because of the high costs of mining and because Australia has historically lacked capital (money or property invested in business), Australian companies have had to rely on foreign investment. Foreign investors control about half the mining industry, so not all the profits stay within Australia. **B**

⊕ **Geographic Thinking**◄

Seeing Patterns
B What are the pros and cons of foreign investment in industry?

MANUFACTURING AND SERVICE Unlike most developed countries, Australia does not rely heavily on manufacturing. One of the major industries in both Australia and New Zealand is the processing of food products. Because of its forests, New Zealand also produces wood and paper products.

PLACE Sheep ranches dot the New Zealand landscape—here by Mount Egmont.
Why are more ranches than farms found in mountainous areas?

As in all developed countries, service industries have been growing. For example, nearly 65 percent of Australia's jobs are in service industries such as government, communications, and tourism.

THE ECONOMIC FUTURE Both Australia and New Zealand want to develop a more diversified economy that is not so dependent on agriculture. But it will be difficult to develop manufacturing plants that can compete with those in nearby Asia, where the cost of labor is generally lower. Finding a way to maintain prosperity in the face of global economic change is a major issue for these two nations.

Distinctive Cultures

The British colonial past has shaped the cultures of Australia and New Zealand, but they also have developed in distinctive ways.

AUSTRALIA'S CULTURE Most Australians are of British descent, but that proportion is changing because of high rates of immigration from places like Greece, Italy, and Southeast Asia. More than 20 percent of Australians are foreign born. Only about one percent are of Aboriginal descent.

Like the British, Australians drive on the left side of the road, and many enjoy drinking tea. Christianity is the major religion. Australians speak English but also have many colorful terms that are all their own. For example, they call ranches "stations" and wild horses "brumbies."

Australia's environment and history have influenced the arts, too.

REGION The traditional facial markings of the Maori, shown here, are called *moko.*

The Aboriginal people have an ancient tradition of painting human and animal figures. Some of those works can be seen on rock walls around the country. Many Australian painters of European descent have portrayed the landscape. For example, Russell Drysdale is known for his pictures of the outback. Several Australian novelists have written adventure stories about life in the bush country.

NEW ZEALAND'S CULTURE The majority of New Zealanders are of European, mostly British, descent. They are called **pakehas,** a Maori term for white people. The Maori of New Zealand fared somewhat better than the Aboriginal people of Australia; about 15 percent of New Zealand's people are descended from the Maori.

New Zealand's culture blends British and Maori ways. For example, both English and Maori are official languages. Christianity is the main religion, but some churches combine biblical and Maori teachings. ▶

Both cultures have shaped New Zealand's art. Maori art, including intricate woodcarvings and poetic legends, still survives. Western art also thrives. Well-known New Zealand authors have included the novelist Janet Frame and the mystery writer Ngaio Marsh. New Zealand filmmakers Jane Campion and Peter Jackson have made movies that were popular in many countries. And the opera singer Kiri Te Kanawa is admired internationally.

Geographic Thinking

Making Comparisons
◀ How are the experiences of the Aboriginal people and the Maori similar and different?

Modern Life

Australians and New Zealanders have similar lifestyles. For example, about 70 percent of Australians and 70 percent of New Zealanders own their own homes—usually single-family homes with enough land to grow a small garden.

CITY AND COUNTRY Australia and New Zealand are two of the most urbanized countries in the world; about 85 percent of their people live in cities and towns. Australia's large cities have the usual problems of pollution and traffic jams. In contrast, New Zealand's cities are relatively quiet, uncrowded, and pollution-free because of its small population and lack of industry.

In both Australia and New Zealand, many ranchers live far away from settlements. New Zealand has a good system of roads, even in rural areas, which aids travel. In Australia, many wealthy ranchers own private airplanes to help them cross the vast distances in the country. Some of the largest ranches in Australia can have a total land area of thousands of square miles.

RECREATION Both countries have climates that allow people to spend a great deal of time outdoors. As a result, aquatic sports, tennis, and team sports, such as rugby, cricket, and soccer, are very popular. Australia has developed its own form of football, called Australian rules football. Because New Zealand is mountainous, skiing and mountain climbing are common there.

In Chapter 32, you will read about Aboriginal land claims in Australia, industrialization in Southeast Asia, and global environmental change.

Geography TODAY

A "Green" Olympics

For the 2000 Olympics, Sydney used the latest technology to try to build facilities that would harm the environment as little as possible. For example, the Olympic Stadium, shown below, was built with very few harmful PVC plastics. In addition, its playing field was designed to be watered only with rainwater collected on the roof.

Assessment

❶ Places & Terms

Identify these terms and explain their importance in the region's history or culture.

- penal colony
- Aboriginal people
- Maori
- Treaty of Waitangi
- pakeha

❷ Taking Notes

MOVEMENT Review the notes you took for this section.

The Region

Australia and New Zealand

- What mineral lured colonists to Australia and New Zealand?
- To which country did Australia and New Zealand export wool?

❸ Main Ideas

a. How did the Treaty of Waitangi cause a misunderstanding over land ownership in New Zealand?

b. Who owns Antarctica?

c. What are some of the British cultural influences in Australia?

❹ Geographic Thinking

Identifying and Solving Problems How do you think Australia and New Zealand can solve their economic problems? **Think about:**

- their need for new markets
- Asia's large population and its relative closeness
- the Asian nations that have thriving industries

EXPLORING LOCAL GEOGRAPHY Do research to learn which farm animals and minerals (if any) are major products of your state. Create a **Venn Diagram** showing those farm animals and minerals that your state has in common with Australia and those that are unique to each.

VISUAL SUMMARY
HUMAN GEOGRAPHY OF SOUTHEAST ASIA, OCEANIA, AND ANTARCTICA

Subregions of Southeast Asia

○ **Southeast Asia**
- Southeast Asia was influenced by ancient China and India and later by European colonists.
- After World War II, the nations of Southeast Asia became independent.
- Industrialization and urbanization are taking place in many countries.

● **Oceania**
- After being isolated for centuries, the islands of Oceania came under the control of European countries and the United States.
- Since 1962, 12 nations have gained independence.
- Their economies are generally based on agriculture, tourism, and a small amount of industry.

◐ **Australia, New Zealand, and Antarctica**
- The Aboriginal people of Australia and the Maori of New Zealand lost land when European colonists arrived.
- Both Australia and New Zealand are former British colonies that are now Commonwealth nations.
- They both want to diversify their economies.

Reviewing Places & Terms

A. Briefly explain the importance of each of the following.

1. Indochina
2. Vietnam War
3. ASEAN
4. Micronesia
5. Melanesia
6. Polynesia
7. subsistence activities
8. penal colony
9. Aboriginal people
10. Maori

B. Answer the questions about vocabulary in complete sentences.

11. Which of the above terms was a French colony in Southeast Asia?
12. What are the goals of ASEAN?
13. During the Vietnam War, the United States tried to protect South Vietnam from takeover by what group?
14. What are the three cultural regions of Oceania?
15. Which European nation used Australia as a penal colony?
16. Which of the above terms is the region from which the Maori migrated?
17. What is the name of the place to which the Maori migrated?
18. Which of the above terms name regions where you are likely to find subsistence activities?
19. What are some of the subsistence activities found there?
20. How long have Aboriginal people been living in Australia?

Main Ideas

Southeast Asia (pp. 705–711)

1. What were the distinctive characteristics of the states known as *mandalas*?
2. What effect did colonialism have on Southeast Asia?
3. What are some of the major changes that Southeast Asia has undergone since 1960?
4. What are some of the arts for which Southeast Asia is known?

Oceania (pp. 712–717)

5. How far east, south, and west did Pacific Islanders migrate?
6. What caused many island societies to decline starting in the 1800s?
7. What are the major economic activities in Oceania?

Australia, New Zealand, and Antarctica (pp. 718–723)

8. What prevents Australia from benefiting completely from its mining industry?
9. What historic actions demonstrated New Zealanders' concern for equal rights and social welfare?
10. What is the major activity conducted in Antarctica?

Critical Thinking

1. Using Your Notes

Use your completed chart to answer these questions.

a. How does agriculture differ in the three subregions?

b. When and how did various nations of the region gain independence from European control?

2. Geographic Themes

a. **HUMAN-ENVIRONMENT INTERACTION** In what ways has the Pacific Ocean helped to shape the various cultures in this region?

b. **MOVEMENT** What role did migration play in the settling of this region?

3. Identifying Themes

Drawing on what you know about this region, what are general differences between village life and city life? What geographic themes are included in your answer?

4. Seeing Patterns

How did the arrival of Europeans affect Southeast Asia, Oceania, Australia, and New Zealand?

5. Analyzing Data

Use the Regional Data File (pages 684-687) to calculate per capita GDP (total GDP divided by population) for Indonesia, Malaysia, Philippines, Singapore, and Thailand. Rank the countries from highest to lowest. Compare your list to the graph on page 707. What pattern do you notice?

Additional Test Practice, pp. S1–S37

TEST PRACTICE
CLASSZONE.COM

Geographic Skills: Interpreting Maps

Population Distribution of Australia

Use the map at the right to answer the following questions.

1. **REGION** How would you describe the population distribution of Australia?

2. **PLACE** Identify the two most heavily populated cities of Australia. What do you notice about their surrounding regions?

3. **PLACE** Judging from this map, would you characterize Australia as a heavily populated or lightly populated country? Explain.

Copy this map on your own paper. Use the map on page 683 to make a climate map of Australia. Display the maps side by side with a caption explaining the link between climate and population distribution.

 INTERNET ACTIVITY

Use the links at **classzone.com** to do research about two countries from different subregions in this unit. Look for information about government, economic activities, culture, and modern life.

Writing About Geography Write a report comparing the two countries. Include maps, charts, and graphs to help present the information. List the Web sites that were your sources.

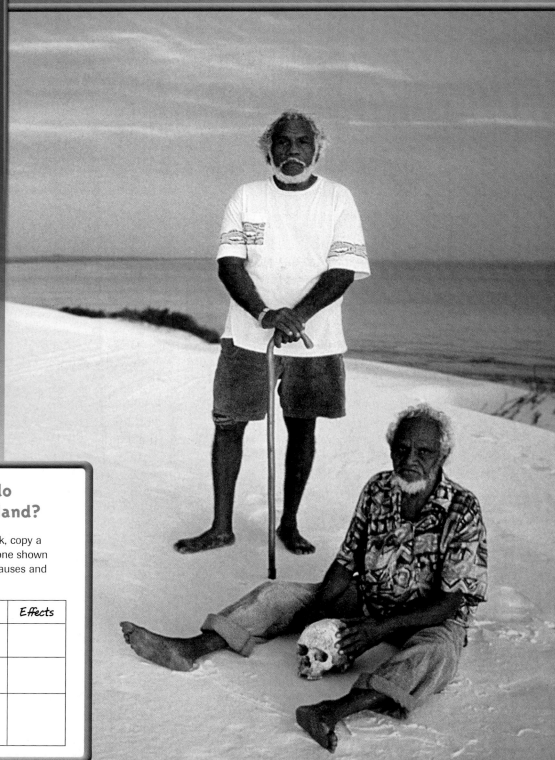

Chapter 32

SECTION 1
Aboriginal Land Claims

SECTION 2
Industrialization Sparks Change

CASESTUDY

GLOBAL ENVIRONMENTAL CHANGE

For more on these issues in Southeast Asia, Oceania, and Antarctica . . .

 CURRENT EVENTS
CLASSZONE.COM

TODAY'S ISSUES
Southeast Asia, Oceania, and Antarctica

Gordon and Alick Pablo, elders of the Wuthathi Aboriginal people, bring a 200-year-old skull of an ancestor to be buried in their homeland.

GeoFocus

What relationship do humans have with land?

Taking Notes In your notebook, copy a cause-and-effect chart like the one shown below. Then take notes on the causes and effects of each issue.

	Causes	Effects
Issue 1: Land Claims		
Issue 2: Industrialization		
Case Study: Environmental Change		

Aboriginal Land Claims

Should native people be given back their ancestors' land?

Main Ideas
• The Aboriginal people of Australia lost their ancestral lands to European colonists.
• Recently they have regained some of that land through court cases.

Places & Terms
assimilation
Stolen Generation
Land Rights Act of 1976
Mabo Case
pastoral leases
Wik Case

SUNSHINE STATE STANDARDS
Key Standard SS.B.2.4.6 The student understands the relationships between resources and the exploration, colonization, and settlement of different regions of the world.
FCAT LA.A.1.4.2 Reading: Strategies

A HUMAN PERSPECTIVE In 1972, the Australian government denied the claims of some Aboriginal people trying to regain ancestral lands. In response, Aboriginal protesters erected a tent on the lawn of Old Parliament House in Canberra and named it the Aboriginal Tent Embassy. They called it an embassy to symbolize their treatment as foreigners in their own country. They chose a temporary shelter instead of a building to symbolize that they had no permanent title to land.

Over the years, the Australian government tried to get rid of the tent embassy by force, by legal action, and by ignoring it in the hope that it would disappear. But in the year 2000, the embassy still stood. Protesters also set up a second tent embassy in Sydney during the Olympics to inform the world of their ongoing struggle to regain land.

Aboriginal People Lose Land

Traditionally, the Aboriginal people had a complex relationship with land. They didn't farm or herd animals but lived by hunting and gathering whatever was available for food. Because of this, they depended completely on nature and saw many places as sacred.

BRITISH POLICY Because Aboriginal people did not use the land in the way that Westerners did—by farming it, mining it, and building on it— British colonists believed that they had no ties to the land. British authorities declared Australia to be *Terra Nullius,* a Latin term that means empty land. Therefore, the British government decided it had the right to take land without making treaties with Aboriginal leaders.

STOLEN LAND When Europeans began to settle Australia in 1788, they chose the most fertile regions. Aboriginal people tried to fight what

Aboriginal Fight for Land, 1960-2000

1967
Aboriginal people become Australian citizens.

1976
Land Rights Act allows Aboriginal people to claim land in Northern Territory.

1992
The ruling in the lawsuit brought by **Eddie Mabo** overturns doctrine of *Terra Nullius.*

1960

1980

2000

1972
Protesters erect the Aboriginal Tent Embassy.

1996
The *Wik* case allows Aboriginal people to claim land leased by farmers and ranchers.

SE ASIA & OCEANIA

they saw as an invasion of their land, but they were defeated because the Europeans had superior weapons. Some Aboriginal people were forced to live on reserves, that is, tracts of less productive land set aside for them. Others lived on the edges of settlements and adopted some European ways, such as working on ranches.

STOLEN CHILDREN The Aboriginal people lost something even more precious than land. Between 1909 and 1969, the Australian government took about 100,000 mixed-race children and gave them to white families to promote assimilation. **Assimilation** occurs when a minority group gives up its culture and adopts the majority group's culture.

Today, Aboriginal people call those children the **Stolen Generation** and feel great anger over their loss. Many Aboriginal people are fighting assimilation by passing their culture on to their children. And one reason they are seeking to regain land is to preserve their way of life.

Geographic Thinking

Seeing Patterns
Ⓐ If a group assimilates, is it more or less likely to seek the return of traditional lands? Explain.

Land Claims

In recent decades, the Aboriginal people have made some progress in winning their rights and regaining ownership of some of their land.

HARD-WON VICTORIES The Aboriginal people were not recognized as full citizens of Australia until 1967. In that year, 91 percent of the Australian people voted to allow the federal government to pass special laws about Aboriginal rights.

The **Land Rights Act of 1976** gave Aboriginal people the right to claim land in the Northern Territory. As a result, Aboriginal people gained ownership of the reserves where they were living and some unoccupied land that the government had owned.

THE *MABO* CASE In 1992, the High Court of Australia handed down a decision that had a tremendous effect on land claims. The case involved Eddie Mabo, a Torres Strait Islander. Mabo had been shocked to learn that under Australian law, his family did not own their traditional lands in the Murray Islands. But because the Mabos had worked the land for generations, the High Court upheld Eddie Mabo's claim. By reaching that decision in the **_Mabo_ Case,** the Court recognized that Aboriginal people had owned land before the British arrived. So the *Mabo* case overturned the doctrine of *Terra Nullius,* by which Britain originally took the land.

Aboriginal Land Claims

Native land determined by statute, consent, or litigation to exist

Extent of native claimant applications as of June 1, 2001

Other

Native title rights can exist and can be exercised alongside the rights of other people as coexistence.

INDIAN OCEAN

Torres Strait

Gulf of Carpentaria

Coral Sea

10°S

20°S

Tropic of Capricorn

NORTHERN TERRITORY

QUEENSLAND

WESTERN AUSTRALIA

SOUTH AUSTRALIA

30°S

Great Australian Bight

NEW SOUTH WALES

0   500   1,000 miles
0   500   1,000 kilometers
Miller Projection

VICTORIA

Tasman Sea

40°S

TASMANIA

120°E   130°E   140°E   150°E

SKILLBUILDER: Interpreting Maps

❶ **LOCATION** Some claims have been made by Torres Strait Islanders. Where is the Torres Strait?

❷ **REGION** If the Aboriginal people were to receive all their land claims, roughly what percentage of Australia would they own?

Geographic Thinking

Making Comparisons
Ⓑ How does the *Mabo* decision compare with Britain's original view of Aboriginal land ownership?

THE *WIK* CASE In 1996, the High Court decided another important case. The Wik people, an Aboriginal group, claimed land that some ranchers and mining companies were using. The case involved two issues that are unique to landholding in Australia.

BACKGROUND
About 42 percent of Australia is subject to pastoral leases.

• The government still owns huge chunks of Australia. Ranchers take out **pastoral leases,** in effect renting the land from the government.

• In earlier cases, Aboriginal people had to prove their traditional relationship to a piece of land in order to claim it.

Aboriginal people could not use land that was taken up by farming or ranching, so it was hard to prove they had a tie to such land. And before 1996, white Australians assumed that pastoral leases wiped out any native land claims. But in the **Wik Case,** the court ruled that Aboriginal people could claim land held under a pastoral lease.

As a result, many white Australians feared having to pay Aboriginal people for land use or even losing access to some land altogether. So the national government amended the *Wik* decision to wipe out many Aboriginal land claims. In response, Aboriginal groups threatened lawsuits. No one knows how the issue will be resolved. In Section 2, you will read about industrialization, another issue related to land use.

SECTION 1 Assessment

① Places & Terms

Identify these terms and explain their relationship to the issue of land claims.

• assimilation
• Stolen Generation
• Land Rights Act of 1976
• *Mabo* Case
• pastoral leases
• *Wik* Case

② Taking Notes

HUMAN-ENVIRONMENT INTERACTION Review the notes you took for this section.

	Causes	Effects
Issue 1: Land Claims		

• Why did the British believe they could take Aboriginal land?
• How did Eddie Mabo prove his family's land ownership?

③ Main Ideas

a. What was the doctrine of *Terra Nullius* and how did it affect land ownership?

b. What were reserves?

c. Why did the national government amend the *Wik* decision?

④ Geographic Thinking

Distinguishing Fact from Opinion When Britain declared Australia to be *Terra Nullius,* was that a fact or an opinion? **Think about:**

• the meaning of that term
• the Aboriginal relationship to land

⑤ See Skillbuilder Handbook, page R11.

MAKING COMPARISONS Research the Nunavut territory in Canada. Write a **proposal** for a documentary that would compare the issue of Aboriginal land claims in Australia with Inuit land claims in Canada. In the proposal, indicate the point of view the documentary would express and the type of photographs and film footage it would use.

SE ASIA & OCEANIA

Industrialization Sparks Change

How does industrialization affect cities?

A HUMAN PERSPECTIVE Some of the largest employers in Southeast Asia are makers of athletic shoes. They provide much-needed jobs for Southeast Asians, but many observers have accused the companies of abusing workers. For example, in 1995, Lap Nguyen began working at a shoe factory in Vietnam. In February 1996, she was promoted to team leader. A month later, she claimed that a manager who was upset about production hit her. Nguyen told a U.S. reporter about the incident.

In 1998, Nguyen talked to the press again, this time about low wages. Her managers were upset about the interview, and she eventually lost her job. The company said that she was a bad worker, but labor groups believe Nguyen lost her job for talking to reporters. As her story shows, growing industries create jobs but sometimes under harsh conditions.

Moving to Find Jobs

For many people struggling to escape poverty, any job—even one with long hours, low pay, and abusive managers—is better than none. For example, Deth Chrib of Cambodia works in a garment factory 16 hours a day, 7 days a week. She is glad she can support her family without resorting to illegal activities. Although her day is long, Deth Chrib says the job is "pretty easy, compared to working on a farm." Across Southeast Asia, people are moving from farms to cities to find work.

Because of this, **industrialization,** or the growth of industry, and the growth of cities are closely linked. It is impossible to study industrialization without studying urban growth. People move to cities because of **push-pull factors.** Push factors are forces that push people out of their homelands, while pull factors pull them to a new place.

PUSH FACTORS Many forces drive rural people off their land. Push factors in Southeast Asia include the following:

- **Lost Resources** Rural areas are suffering soil erosion, deforestation, and water overuse. For example, Thailand has a water shortage in farming areas because of overpumping. Scarce resources make it hard to earn a living.

Main Ideas

- The growth of industry in Southeast Asia has produced positive results such as new jobs and higher wages.
- The growth of industry also produced negative results such as overcrowded cities and pollution.

Places & Terms

industrialization

push-pull factors

The Voyageur Experience in World Geography
Singapore: Industrialization and Migration

SUNSHINE STATE STANDARDS
Key Standard SS.B.2.4.2 The student understands past and present trends in human migration and cultural interaction and their impact on physical and human systems.

Other Standards SS.B.2.4.4

FCAT LA.A.1.4.2 Reading: Strategies

PLACE These Cambodian women work in a factory that makes blue jeans for export to the United States and Europe.
Why do you suppose this industry hires so many women?

- **Scarcity of Land** In the Philippines, for example, 3 percent of the country's landowners hold 25 percent of the land. Sixty percent of rural families don't have enough land to earn a living by farming.
- **Population Growth** As populations grow, land shortages become worse. Farmers who do own land often divide it among many heirs. As a result, the plots become too small to support a family.

PULL FACTORS Equally powerful forces attract people to cities. In Southeast Asia, pull factors include the following:

- **Industry** The opportunity to find a factory job is the biggest pull factor. Many people move to the city temporarily to earn money to send to relatives in rural areas. In 1993, workers in the Philippines sent $2.2 billion home, while Thai workers sent $983 million home.
- **Other Benefits** People move to cities seeking other benefits besides jobs, such as education and government services. However, the desire for education is usually related to a desire for jobs.

IMPACT ON CITIES As is true of cities all over the world, the cities of Southeast Asia are having difficulty dealing with such large numbers of immigrants. The availability of housing has not kept pace with the growing city population. As a result, many new arrivals live in slums.

A larger population generates more pollution. Traffic has increased because greater numbers of workers drive to jobs and greater numbers of trucks transport goods. This causes more air pollution; high levels of particulates are the most serious concern. In Bangkok, Thailand, an estimated 5,000 people a year die from breathing polluted air.

Another problem is the disposal of human waste. Most Southeast Asian cities do not have facilities to treat all their sewage. Untreated sewage, in turn, contaminates water supplies.

Other Results of Industrialization

The growth of industry in Southeast Asia has done more than create rapidly growing cities. It has also affected the economy and the environment.

MOVEMENT Many rapidly growing Southeast Asian cities are overcrowded. That is one of several factors creating slums, such as this one in Jakarta, Indonesia. **Why would high rates of migration to cities cause overcrowding?**

BACKGROUND As you learned in Chapter 14, particulates are very small particles of liquids or solids.

SE ASIA & OCEANIA

ECONOMIC EFFECTS Several Southeast Asian countries have had rapid industrial growth since the 1960s. (See Chapter 31.) One result of this has been an increase in trade and exports.

As industry has grown, the region has seen higher incomes for some citizens. In many Southeast Asian countries, the middle class is expanding. But the income gap between rich and poor remains high. This has the potential to cause social unrest because crime rates often rise in societies in which a few people have wealth while high numbers of people live in poverty. You learned about income gaps in Unit 3.

ENVIRONMENTAL EFFECTS Population growth is not the only cause of increased air and water pollution. Industry can also damage the environment. Factories can pollute the air by burning fossil fuels, and the water and soil by carelessly disposing of toxic materials.

The nature of industry in Southeast Asia makes it hard to control such pollution. A single city may contain thousands of factories and shops. Many of these industries are very small, but together they create a great deal of waste. For example, 30,000 factories in Jakarta, Indonesia, discharge pollutants into the waterways. **A**

Industry has also harmed the environment by using up valuable resources such as water and trees. For instance, textile companies in Bandung, Indonesia, have built illegal wells that deplete water supplies. As a result, some neighborhoods in that city have no water.

In the future, Southeast Asia must reduce the negative effects of industrialization while promoting the positive effects. Cities need to find ways to provide housing and services for all residents. Southeast Asian nations must continue to grow economically, so their citizens will have increased opportunities. The region as a whole must preserve its environment, or industries may abandon the region once its resources are gone. In the Case Study that follows, you will read about environmental changes such as global warming and the hole in the ozone layer.

Geographic Thinking

Making Comparisons
A Would it be harder to monitor the pollution created by a few large factories or many small factories? Why?

Section 2 Assessment

1 Places & Terms

Identify these terms and explain their relationship to recent events in Southeast Asia.

• industrialization

• push-pull factors

2 Taking Notes

MOVEMENT Review the notes you took for this section.

	Causes	Effects
Issue 2: Industrialization		

• Why does industrialization often lead to urbanization?

• What factors push people out of rural areas?

3 Main Ideas

a. What are good and bad aspects of factory work?

b. What are the environmental effects of industrialization?

c. What are the economic effects of industrialization?

4 Geographic Thinking

Drawing Conclusions If industries in Southeast Asia continue to use up the region's resources, how might that affect urban growth? **Think about:**

• the push factors that drive people out of rural areas

RESEARCH LINKS
CLASSZONE.COM

GeoActivities

ASKING GEOGRAPHIC QUESTIONS Study the cartogram of industrial output on page 733. Write three geographic questions about it, such as "What geographic factors enable Thailand to have more industrial output than its neighbors?" Choose one of your questions, do research to find the answer, and write a **report** about what you learn.

Interpreting a Cartogram

SUNSHINE STATE STANDARDS
Key Standard SS.B.1.4.1 The student uses a variety of maps, geographic technologies including geographic information systems (GIS) and satellite-produced imagery, and other advanced graphic representations to depict geographic problems.

FCAT LA.A.2.2.7 Reading: Recognize Compare and Contrast

Even though Southeast Asia has been experiencing industrial growth as a region, not all Southeast Asian nations have prospered equally. A table listing the value of industrial output for the ten countries would give this information in numerical form. A cartogram shows the information visually.

THE LANGUAGE OF MAPS A **cartogram** is a special type of map that conveys a set of data, such as population or GDP. The sizes of the nations on the map are adjusted to reflect the amounts of data each one has. The cartogram below shows the value of industrial output for the nations of Southeast Asia.

Industrial Output of Southeast Asia

0-10
10-100
100-200
200+
Each square equals 2 billion $US

Copyright by Rand McNally & Co.

① The key of this cartogram helps you to intrepret the value of industrial output in two ways. It tells you that each small square equals 2 billion U.S. dollars. It also identifies the colors that the cartogram uses to identify ranges of output.

② Cartograms adjust the sizes of countries to convey relative quantities. The countries' shapes are altered because a cartogram uses squares or straight lines.

③ Comparing a cartogram to a conventional map can show which countries have more or less of the data under study than you would expect from looking at their size alone.

Map and Graph Skills Assessment

1. Analyzing Data
According to the cartogram, how much industrial output does Thailand have?

2. Drawing Conclusions
Which country or countries seem to have a small industrial output compared to their actual size?

3. Drawing Conclusions
Which country or countries seem to have a large industrial output compared to their actual size?

CASE STUDY

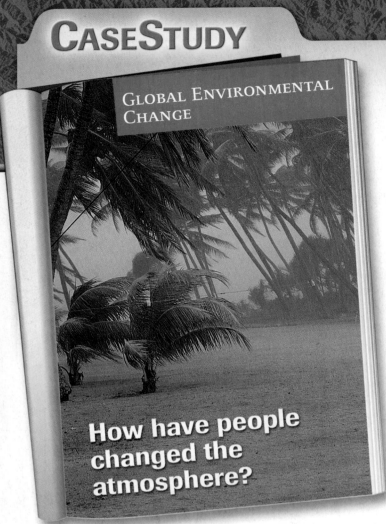

GLOBAL ENVIRONMENTAL CHANGE

How have people changed the atmosphere?

Some people fear that global warming might cause an increase in violent weather.

SUNSHINE STATE STANDARDS
Key Standard SS.B.2.4.4 The student understands the global impact of human changes in the physical environment.

Other Standards SS.A.1.4.3

FCAT LA.A.2.4.8 Reading: Synthesize and Conclude

As you have read in other units, many human activities harm the environment. Among these are the burning of fossil fuels and the use of chemicals such as chlorofluorocarbons (CFCs) in aerosol cans. Many scientists fear these activities are changing the environment in ways that affect the whole world.

Damage to the Environment

Scientists believe that the use of fossil fuels has begun to heat the climate, and the use of chemicals has damaged the ozone layer.

GLOBAL WARMING The burning of fossil fuels releases carbon dioxide (CO_2) into the atmosphere. Carbon dioxide is one of the greenhouse gases—gases that trap the sun's heat. Greenhouse gases serve the useful function of preventing the escape of all the sun's energy into space. Without them, the earth would be cold and lifeless.

Some scientists fear that the atmosphere now has too many greenhouse gases. CO_2 emissions have increased 50 percent since the 1970s. Scientists believe that the increase in CO_2 levels causes the atmosphere to trap too much heat, so temperatures have been gradually rising.

Many people disagree with the theory of global warming. Some say the temperature rise may be due to natural processes. Others say that temperatures have not gone up, that they fall within a normal range.

OZONE HOLE Another change is damage to the ozone layer, which exists high in the atmosphere. It absorbs most of the sun's damaging ultraviolet rays. In the 1970s, scientists discovered a thinning of the ozone layer over Antarctica, often called a hole in the ozone layer. Chemicals such as the chlorine found in CFCs react with ozone and destroy it. Many governments have restricted the use of such chemicals, but others have delayed passing such laws because they are costly for industry.

Looking Toward the Future

Scientists fear that many problems may result from these changes to the environment. Because of that, many people and nations around the world are trying to halt the damage before it is too late.

LONG-TERM EFFECTS One fear about global warming is that even small temperature increases could melt the world's ice caps. This would cause a rise in sea levels that might swamp coastal cities and islands. For example, the low islands of Oceania might disappear.

Some people predict that global warming might change patterns of evaporation and precipitation. This could make violent storms such as typhoons and droughts more common. The location of climate zones and agricultural regions might shift, upsetting the world's economy.

People worry about the ozone layer hole because more ultraviolet rays will reach earth. Ultraviolet rays are linked to such problems as skin cancer, eye damage, and crop damage. Because it lies close to Antarctica, New Zealand may be at higher risk than other regions.

TAKING ACTION In 1992, the UN held the Earth Summit, a conference to discuss ways to pursue economic development while protecting the environment. Representatives of 178 nations attended.

In 1997, the UN held a convention in Kyoto, Japan, to discuss climate change. The conference wrote the Kyoto Protocol, guidelines for developed countries to reduce greenhouse gas emissions. In time, 165 nations signed the treaty. The United States signed the treaty, but the Senate didn't ratify it—fearing that the guidelines might harm U.S. businesses.

On the next two pages are primary sources expressing different views about environmental problems. Use them to form your own opinion.

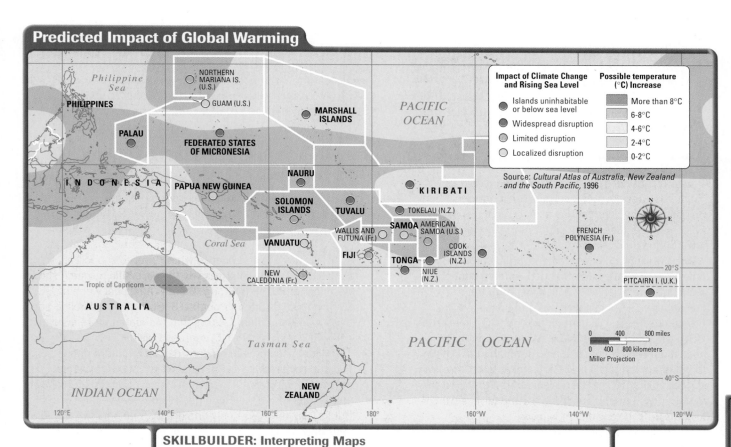

Predicted Impact of Global Warming

Impact of Climate Change and Rising Sea Level
- Islands uninhabitable or below sea level
- Widespread disruption
- Limited disruption
- Localized disruption

Possible temperature (°C) Increase
- More than 8°C
- 6-8°C
- 4-6°C
- 2-4°C
- 0-2°C

Source: *Cultural Atlas of Australia, New Zealand and the South Pacific, 1996*

Miller Projection

SKILLBUILDER: Interpreting Maps

❶ **PLACE** Where are the greatest temperature increases expected to occur?

❷ **PLACE** What places in Oceania are expected to experience the least disruption?

CASESTUDY

PROJECT Political Cartoon

Primary sources A to E on these two pages present differing opinions on global environmental change. Use these sources and your own research to create a political cartoon expressing your opinion. You might use the Internet and the library for research.

RESEARCH LINKS
CLASSZONE.COM

Suggested Steps

1. Use the sources here and your own research to decide if you believe that global warming and the ozone hole are problems.

2. Draw a pencil sketch of a cartoon expressing your opinion about global environmental change. As you decide what to draw, consider the following questions.

   • Do you think that the theories about environmental change are wrong? If so, why are people so concerned about the issue?

   • Do you think environmental change poses a threat to the world's climate? If so, what should be done?

3. Show the sketch to a friend to see if you have conveyed your point. Use your friend's feedback to make your cartoon more effective.

4. Create your final cartoon. You may wish to draw it lightly in pencil and then ink over the pencil marks. Post the cartoon in class.

Materials and Supplies

- Samples of political cartoons
- Drawing paper
- Pencils and erasers
- Felt-tip markers
- Computer
- Internet access

PRIMARY SOURCE A

***Educational Pamphlet** In 1994, the United Nations Environment Programme and the World Meteorological Organization published a pamphlet called* Beginners Guide to the Convention *to help people understand the Kyoto Protocol and the reasons for it.*

Human beings seem to be changing the global climate. The results are uncertain, but if current predictions prove correct, the climatic changes over the coming century will be larger than any since the dawn of human civilization.

The principal change to date is in the earth's atmosphere. . . . We have changed, and are continuing to change, the balance of gases that form the atmosphere. This is especially true of such key "greenhouse gases" as carbon dioxide (CO_2), methane (CH_4), and nitrous oxide (N_2O). (Water vapour is the most important greenhouse gas, but human activities do not affect it directly.) . . . Greenhouse gases are vital because they act like a blanket around the earth. Without this natural blanket the earth's surface would be some 30°C colder than it is today.

The problem is that human activity is making the blanket "thicker." . . . The most direct result, says the scientific consensus, is likely to be a "global warming" of 1.5 to 4.5°C over the next 100 years.

PRIMARY SOURCE B

***Political Commentary** The American Policy Center is a conservative group that wants to promote free enterprise and reduce government regulations. It opposed the Kyoto Protocol and published the article "There is No Global Warming."*

There is no global warming. Period.

You can't find a real scientist anywhere in the world who can look you in the eye and, without hesitation, . . . say "yes, global warming is with us."

There is no evidence whatsoever to support such claims. Anyone who tells you that scientific research shows warming trends . . . is wrong. There is no global warming.

Scientific research through U.S. Government satellite and balloon measurements shows that the temperature is actually cooling—very slightly—.037 degrees Celsius.

A little research into modern-day temperature trends bears this out. For example, in 1936 the Midwest of the United States experienced 49 consecutive days of temperatures over 90 degrees. There were another 49 consecutive days in 1955. But in 1992 there was only one day over 90 degrees and in 1997 only 5 days.

Data *The National Climatic Data Center collects data on temperature and precipitation. In the graph below, the line at zero represents the average annual world temperature for the period* *1880 to 2000. The bars show how much the average temperatures for individual years were higher or lower than the average. Scientists use this graph to spot climate trends.*

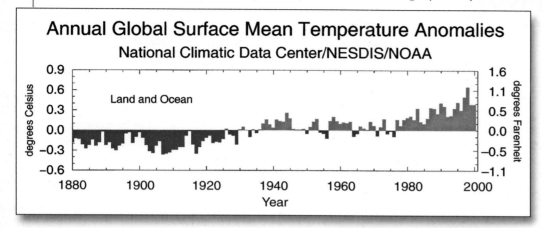

Annual Global Surface Mean Temperature Anomalies
National Climatic Data Center/NESDIS/NOAA

News Article *On October 10, 2000, the* New York Times *published the article "Record Ozone Hole Refuels Debate on Climate" by Andrew C. Revkin. The article appeared in the science section of the paper.*

The hole that opens in the ozone layer over Antarctica each southern spring formed earlier and grew bigger this year than at any time since satellites have been monitoring the polar atmosphere, scientists have reported.

The finding renewed suspicions among atmospheric scientists that global warming could be indirectly abetting the chemical reactions that destroy ozone, but many still say the growth of the hole could also be the result of natural . . . variations in Antarctic weather and other conditions. . . .

The hole is closely watched because the stratosphere's . . . layer of ozone . . . absorbs ultraviolet rays, which could contribute to skin cancers and cataracts and threaten agriculture and ecosystems if they reached the surface.

Satellite Images *Satellites took these images of ozone over Antarctica. The color blue represents areas with an extremely low concentration of ozone, while red shows a high concentration.*

PROJECT CheckList

Have I . . .

✓ researched opinions on global environmental change?

✓ formed my own opinion based on evidence about the issue?

✓ created an interesting cartoon that clearly expresses that opinion?

✓ created a cartoon that is neat enough to print in a newspaper?

VISUAL SUMMARY
TODAY'S ISSUES IN SOUTHEAST ASIA, OCEANIA, AND ANTARCTICA

Government

Aboriginal Land Claims
- When the British first arrived in Australia, British authorities declared the continent to be empty. They decided they had the right to take the land without making treaties.
- Aboriginal people lost much of their land and had to live on reserves.
- Recent court cases have provided the grounds for Aboriginal people to make land claims. However, the Australian government took steps to limit those land claims.

Economics

Industrialization Sparks Change
- The growth of industry often leads to rapid urban growth. People move to cities because of push-pull factors.
- Industrialization creates higher incomes for many, but in Southeast Asia the income gap remains high. This has the potential to cause social unrest.
- Because of the use of fossil fuels and careless waste disposal, industrialization often causes pollution.

Environment

Global Environmental Change
- Many scientists believe that increases in carbon dioxide emission have caused global temperatures to rise; it is feared that global warming might lead to flooding and an increase in droughts and violent weather.
- The use of chemicals such as CFCs has been linked to a thinning of the protective ozone layer. The hole in the ozone layer may let more ultraviolet rays reach the earth and cause cancer, eye damage, and crop damage.

Reviewing Places & Terms

A. Briefly explain the importance of each of the following.

1. assimilation
2. Stolen Generation
3. Land Rights Act of 1976
4. *Mabo* Case
5. pastoral leases
6. *Wik* Case
7. industrialization
8. push-pull factors

B. Answer the questions about vocabulary in complete sentences.

9. What is the relationship between the terms *assimilation* and *Stolen Generation*?
10. Who owned the Australian lands that were held by pastoral leases?
11. Which of the above terms is a pull factor leading to urban growth?
12. To which Australian territory did the Land Rights Act of 1976 apply?
13. What was the main decision in the *Mabo* Case?
14. What was the main decision in the *Wik* Case?
15. How would you apply the term *push factors* to the experience of the Aboriginal people in Australia?

Main Ideas

Aboriginal Land Claims (pp. 727-729)

1. What does the Aboriginal Tent Embassy symbolize?
2. When the Aboriginal people fought European settlement, what enabled the Europeans to win?
3. How did Eddie Mabo prove his family's land ownership?
4. Why did white Australians fear the *Wik* decision?

Industrialization Sparks Change (pp. 730-733)

5. Why do many people in Southeast Asia move temporarily to cities?
6. How has industrialization affected cities?
7. What effect has industrial growth had on trade and exports?

Global Environmental Change (pp. 734-737)

8. What are greenhouse gases?
9. What are the arguments against the theory of global warming?
10. What health problems may increase because of the hole in the ozone layer?

Critical Thinking

1. Using Your Notes

Use your completed chart to answer these questions.

	Causes	Effects
Issue 1: Land Claims		
Issue 2: Industrialization		

a. What caused the hole in the ozone layer?

b. In what way are some of these issues linked? Explain.

2. Geographic Themes

a. **HUMAN-ENVIRONMENT INTERACTION** How has industrialization affected Southeast Asia's water supplies?

b. **MOVEMENT** What impact might global warming have upon the movement of people?

3. Identifying Themes

Consider what you have learned about Aboriginal land claims, industrialization, and global environmental change. Which of the five geographic themes relate to all three issues? Explain.

4. Determining Cause and Effect

How did the Australian government's policy of taking mixed-race children from their families affect the desire of the Aboriginal people to reclaim lands? Explain.

5. Drawing Conclusions

Overall, do you think industrialization is a positive or negative development for Southeast Asia? Explain.

Additional Test Practice, pp. S1–S37

TEST PRACTICE
CLASSZONE.COM

Geographic Skills: Interpreting Graphs

Annual Industrial Production Growth Rate

Use the graph to answer the following questions.

1. **PLACE** For which country were statistics for the year 2000 not available?

2. **PLACE** How would you describe the pattern of industrial growth in Thailand?

3. **REGION** In which year did Southeast Asia as a whole experience economic problems? How can you tell?

GeoActivity

Research the industrial production growth rate for another Southeast Asian country. Copy this graph on your own paper and add the information for the country you researched.

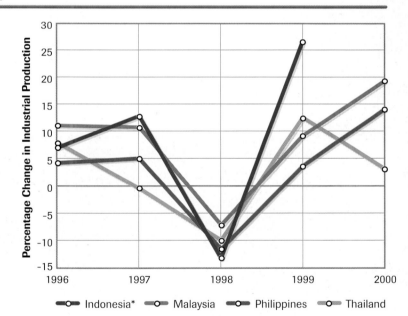

Indonesia* ━ Malaysia ━ Philippines ━ Thailand

*2000 data for Indonesia were unavailable.
SOURCE: Asia Recovery Information Center online, 2001

INTERNET ACTIVITY

Use the links at **classzone.com** to do research about global warming. Look for additional evidence that either supports or refutes the theory.

Creating a Database Compile statistics that either support or refute the theory of global warming. Present these statistics in tables, charts, or graphs.

World Geography

Contents

ı.ı Analyzing Data

Defining the Skill

Analyzing data means studying quantitative information—numbers, proportions, and similar statistics. Data are often presented graphically, in graphs, charts, and maps. When you analyze data, you find patterns, make generalizations and comparisons, and locate facts.

Applying the Skill

The following line graph is titled "World Population Growth." Use the listed strategies to analyze the data presented.

How to Analyze Data

Strategy ❶ Rephrase the title given for the graphic as a question that can lead you to its main idea. For example: "How has world population growth changed over time?"

Strategy ❷ To understand how data are displayed, choose one point on the graph. Identify what piece of data is shown at that point. For example, in the line graph, the point on the line that is right above the horizontal number 1000 represents how many billions of people lived in the world in the year 1000—just under one-half billion.

Strategy ❸ Make a comparison between two points or other parts on the graph. For example, compare the rate of world population growth between 1000 and 1500 with the rate over the following 500 years. You can see that the population barely grew at all between 1000 and 1500, but increased significantly between 1500 and 2000.

Strategy ❹ Answer the question you posed in Strategy 1 in order to summarize data and note a general pattern.

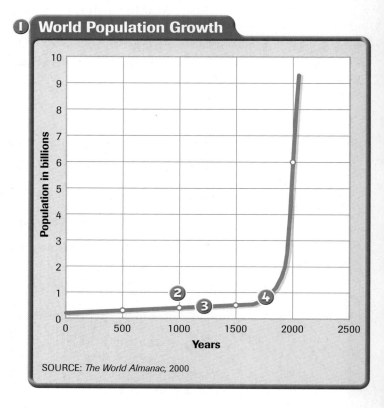

❶ **World Population Growth**

SOURCE: *The World Almanac,* 2000

Write a Summary

Summarize the most important idea in your analysis of the data shown. This summary statement might, for example, answer the question suggested by the graph title.

❹ *The world's population did not even reach the 1-billion mark until the 1800s, but skyrocketed after that and is on its way to 10 billion.*

Practicing the Skill

Turn to Chapter 31, Section 1, "Southeast Asia." Find the feature on page 707 titled "Industrialization." Analyze the data in the bar graph shown. Write a summary of your analysis.

1.2 Making Comparisons

Defining the Skill

Making comparisons means thinking about similarities and differences. Two or more concepts are grouped together because of shared features, but they are distinguished from one another by other features.

Applying the Skill

The following passage tells about economic development. Use the listed strategies to compare two categories of nations.

How to Make Comparisons

Strategy ① Note the concepts being compared. In this passage, categories of economic development are described.

Strategy ② Look for words that signal similarities such as *both, same, similar,* and *like.* Look for words that signal differences or contrasts such as *different, in contrast, however,* and *on the other hand.*

Strategy ③ Sum up what you have learned by telling yourself (a) what concepts are being compared; (b) why they are grouped together; and (c) what their main differences are.

> **LEVELS OF ECONOMIC DEVELOPMENT**
>
> ① Countries of the world have two different levels of economic development. Developing nations have a low GDP per capita. (GDP is Gross Domestic Product, the value of goods and services produced within a country over a year or other period of time.) Developing nations also have limited development on all levels of economic activities. These countries lack an industrial base and struggle to provide for their citizens' basic needs. Many young countries and former colonies are found in this category.
>
> Developed nations, ② on the other hand, are countries with a high per capita income and varied economy. Western European nations, Canada, and the United States are highly developed economies.

Make a Chart

One way to sum up the main points of comparison is with a chart that lists features. The chart below is based on the example passage.

③	Developing nations	Developed nations
GDP per capita	low	high
Variety of economic activities	limited development; lack of industrial base	varied economy
Examples	young countries, former colonies	Western European nations, Canada, U.S.

Practicing the Skill

Turn to Chapter 5, Section 3, "Human-Environment Interaction." Read "Building Cities" on page 128. Identify the main similarities and differences described, and show them in a chart.

1.3 Making Inferences

Defining the Skill

Making inferences involves using information that is directly stated in the text in order to think of, or infer, ideas that are not directly stated. You use logic and your own experience and knowledge to make inferences.

Applying the Skill

The passage below tells about a feature of the climate of South Asia. Use the listed strategies to make inferences about monsoons.

How to Make Inferences

Strategy ❶ Find statements of fact and other stated ideas, such as opinions and generalizations.

Strategy ❷ Ask yourself questions about the stated facts and ideas. Think of likely answers that are not directly stated. For example, the passage states that dry winds blow between October and May, and moist winds blow between June and September. Ask, "What else can I understand from that information?"

Strategy ❸ Make inferences from the facts and ideas. For example, you might infer that the region has two main seasons—a long dry one and a shorter wet one.

MONSOONS

❶ Although climate varies throughout South Asia, the region as a whole is greatly affected by monsoons, or seasonal winds. ❷ Between October and May, dry winds blow across South Asia from the northeast. ❷ Between June and September, the winds reverse and blow in from the southwest, bringing moist air from the ocean. ❶ Heavy rains fall, especially in the southern and eastern portions of South Asia.

❶ Rainfall is crucial to life on the subcontinent. Yet the monsoons can cause severe hardship for millions of South Asians, especially those living in the lowlands of India and Bangladesh. The monsoons are also highly unpredictable. Some areas may get too little rain, while others get too much. The monsoons are an essential but difficult feature of life in South Asia.

Make a Chart

A chart can show the inferences made from stated facts and ideas. The chart below is based on the passage you just read.

❶ Stated Facts and Ideas	❷ Questions	❸ Inferences
The direction of the winds shifts seasonally, from the northeast to the southwest.	What causes the wind patterns to change?	Wind patterns change as Earth changes its position relative to the sun.
Heavy rains follow from winds coming from the ocean.	How do ocean winds carry water?	Water evaporates from the ocean, is carried by the air, and condenses over land.
The monsoons can cause severe hardship, especially in the lowlands.	What problems do the monsoons cause in the lowlands?	Damaging floods can result from monsoon rains.

Practicing the Skill

Turn to Chapter 25, Section 2, "India's Neighbors: Pakistan and Bangladesh." Read the subsection "New Countries, Ancient Lands," on pages 573–574. Use the facts and ideas to infer other ideas. Show your inferences in a chart.

1.4 Drawing Conclusions

Defining the Skill

Drawing conclusions means combining factual information with your own reasoning to formulate a statement that is likely to be true. To draw conclusions, look at the facts and think about what they mean.

Applying the Skill

The following passage offers facts about two of the world's largest lakes. Use the listed strategies to draw conclusions about the information.

How to Draw Conclusions

Strategy ❶ Read carefully to identify and understand the statements of fact, the items of information that can be proved true.

Strategy ❷ Think about which facts fit together and how they fit. List the facts in a diagram and use your own experiences to understand how the facts relate to each other.

Strategy ❸ Come up with a statement, different from one given in the text, that draws a conclusion about the factual information.

> **TWO LARGE LAKES OF CENTRAL ASIA**
>
> ❶ The Caspian Sea, which is actually a saltwater lake, stretches for nearly 750 miles from north to south, making it the largest inland sea in the world. ❶ Recently, the Caspian's water levels have been rising, and have flooded many surrounding villages and towns. ❶ The sea now stands over two yards higher than it did in 1978. Nobody is certain what is causing the change. But scientists say possible causes might include climate change or more water flowing off deforested land.
>
> ❶ The Aral Sea, another of the world's largest lakes, lies east of the Caspian. ❶ Unlike the Caspian, the Aral Sea is shrinking. ❶ Extensive irrigation projects have diverted water away from the lake. ❶ Since 1960, the Aral has lost about 80 percent of its water volume.

Make a Diagram

A diagram can highlight the facts that fit together to point to a conclusion. The diagram below shows a conclusion that can be drawn from the passage above.

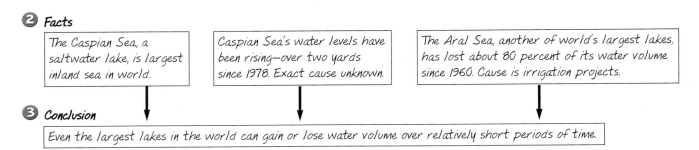

❷ *Facts*

| The Caspian Sea, a saltwater lake, is largest inland sea in world. | Caspian Sea's water levels have been rising—over two yards since 1978. Exact cause unknown. | The Aral Sea, another of world's largest lakes, has lost about 80 percent of its water volume since 1960. Cause is irrigation projects. |

❸ *Conclusion*

Even the largest lakes in the world can gain or lose water volume over relatively short periods of time.

Practicing the Skill

Turn to Chapter 10, Section 1. Read the subsection "Native Americans and the Spanish Conquest" on page 216. Make a diagram to show selected facts and the conclusion you drew from them.

1.5 Making Generalizations

Defining the Skill

Making a generalization means making a broad statement that applies to a number of examples. Generalizations can be made from examples given in one passage, in several sources, or from graphic aids.

Applying the Skill

The following two passages present examples on the same topic. Use the listed strategies to make a generalization based on the examples.

How to Make Generalizations

Strategy ❶ Note the examples given on the same topic.

Strategy ❷ Use a term such as *generally* or *usually* as you decide what the examples have in common.

Strategy ❸ Formulate a logical, general statement that applies to all examples.

OCEANS AND MOUNTAINS

❶ The Canadian coastal ranges prevent the warming of Canada's interior by blocking warm Pacific air. ❶ In the United States, the western mountains trap Pacific moisture. This makes the climate in the lands to the west of the mountains rainy and those to the east very dry.

The North Atlantic Drift, a current of warm water from the tropics, flows near Europe's west coast. The prevailing westerlies, which blow west to east, pick up warmth from this current and carry it over Europe. ❶ No large mountain ranges block the winds, so the influence of the westerlies extends far inland.

Make a Diagram

A diagram can show how examples add up to a generalization. The diagram below is based on the passages you just read.

❶ *Example: Canadian coastal ranges block warm Pacific air from reaching Canada's interior.*

+

❶ *Example: Western mountains of the United States trap Pacific moisture, making the lands on the Pacific side moist and the eastern side dry.*

+

❶ *Example: Atlantic Ocean warmth is carried over Europe because no large mountain ranges block the winds.*

=

❷❸ *Generalization: Mountains generally prevent ocean air from traveling farther inland.*

Practicing the Skill

Find passages about the humid continental climate of the United States and Canada (page 124), of Europe (page 279), and of East Asia (page 626). Make a diagram to show examples and a generalization.

1.6 Making Decisions

Defining the Skill

Making decisions means choosing between two or more courses of action. When you analyze the decisions people have made, you think about the needs they were trying to meet and the consequences of each choice.

Applying the Skill

The following passage describes the problem of rapid population growth facing the Chinese government. Use the listed strategies to analyze the decisions made.

How to Make Decisions

Strategy ❶ Look for a statement of the difficulty. Think about the choices facing the group.

Strategy ❷ Consider possible consequences of each choice.

Strategy ❸ Identify the decisions that were made.

Strategy ❹ Identify actual consequences.

Make a Flow Chart

The process of decision-making can be shown in a flow chart. The flow chart below summarizes the decisions described in the passage you just read.

CONTROLLING CHINA'S POPULATION

One out of every five people in the world lives in China. China's estimated population in the year 2000 was about 1.3 billion. ❶ Because of concerns about a rapidly expanding population, ❸ China in 1979 adopted a policy of one child per family. In addition, the country has age restrictions for marriage—a man must be 22 and a woman 20 before they can marry. ❹ These policies have reduced China's birthrate dramatically.

❹ However, the government policy of one child per family has run into opposition. Rural families, in particular, feel the need for more than one child to help work on their farms. ❹ As a result, the government has relaxed the one-child policy.

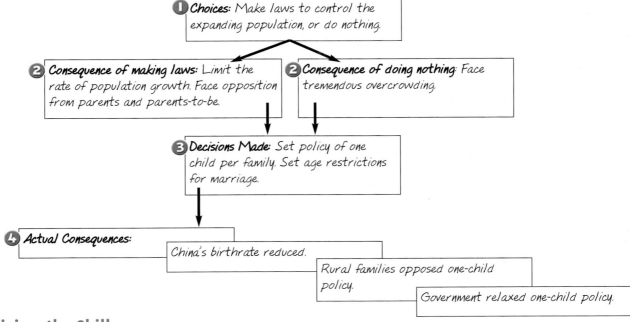

❶ **Choices:** Make laws to control the expanding population, or do nothing.

❷ **Consequence of making laws:** Limit the rate of population growth. Face opposition from parents and parents-to-be.

❷ **Consequence of doing nothing:** Face tremendous overcrowding.

❸ **Decisions Made:** Set policy of one child per family. Set age restrictions for marriage.

❹ **Actual Consequences:**

China's birthrate reduced.

Rural families opposed one-child policy.

Government relaxed one-child policy.

Practicing the Skill

Turn to Chapter 23, Section 1. Read "New Industry Requires More Workers," on pages 525–526. Make a flow chart to show the choices faced by the nations' governments and the consequences of the decisions made.

1.7 Seeing Patterns

Defining the Skill

Seeing patterns involves seeing the overall shape, organization, or trend of geographic characteristics. It often means noting variations or contrasts, and thinking about the "rules" that describe them and could apply to similar situations. Seasonal weather cycles are one example of a pattern; economic changes are another. Graphs, maps, charts, and text passages are all sources of information that help you see patterns.

Applying the Skill

The passage below tells about the economics of oil in North Africa. Use the listed strategies to think about the pattern described.

How to See Patterns

Strategy ① Note any directly stated main ideas about details of geographic characteristics, or changes and contrasts. (If none is directly stated, try to make your own statement of comparison, based on the details in the passage.)

Strategy ② Notice examples that support the ideas.

Strategy ③ Use the word *pattern* in a question about the information. For this passage, you could ask, "What economic pattern is seen in the oil-producing nations of North Africa?" Your answer will sum up the pattern you see. (The chart below has a possible answer.)

Make a Chart

Make a chart to sum up the pattern. The chart below organizes information from the passage you have just read.

AN OIL-BASED ECONOMY

① Oil has transformed the economies of some North African countries, including Libya, Algeria, and Tunisia. ② In Algeria, oil has surpassed farm products as the major export and source of revenue. Furthermore, oil makes up about 99 percent of Libya's exports.

① Although oil has helped the economies of these countries, it has also caused some problems. ② Libya, Algeria, and Tunisia face shortages of skilled labor to carry out this work. For example, Libya's labor force cannot meet the demands of the oil industry because of a lack of training and education. Oil companies are forced to give many high-paying jobs to foreign workers. Even within the oil industry, overall unemployment is still a problem. As a result, large numbers of North Africans have migrated to Europe in search of jobs.

① Main Ideas About Contrasts and Changes	② Examples	③ Summary Statement of Pattern
The oil industry has transformed the economies of some North African countries.	Algeria—oil major export and revenue source. Libya—oil about 99 percent of exports.	A single industry can power the economy of a nation, but an unskilled labor force may not benefit.
Oil helps the economy but also causes problems.	Libya, Algeria, Tunisia face shortages of skilled workers. Libya—labor force lacks training and education. Foreign skilled workers get high-paying jobs. Unemployment, emigration.	

Practicing the Skill

Turn to Chapter 19, Section 5, "Southern Africa." Read the subsection "Success at a Cost" on pages 455–456. Use the information in it to sum up the pattern you see. Use standard grammar, sentence structure, and punctuation in your summary.

1.8 Determining Cause and Effect

Defining the Skill

A **cause** is why something happens. An **effect** is what happens. A single cause can lead to one effect or multiple effects. One effect can have multiple causes. Cause-effect chains are also common, in which a cause leads to an effect that becomes the cause of another effect, and so on.

Applying the Skill

The following paragraphs sum up major events in the recent European past. Use the listed strategies to analyze the cause-effect relationships.

How to Determine Cause and Effect

Strategy ① Use the word *why* to formulate questions about the topic of the passage. Example: *Why was there conflict in Europe?* The answers you find will be the causes.

Strategy ② Look for words such as *because, cause, in order to,* and *reason,* which signal causes. Look for words such as *so, consequence,* and *result,* which signal effects.

Strategy ③ Restate the cause-effect connections in your own words or in a diagram.

① CONFLICT IN EUROPE

Western Europe experienced industrial growth in the 1800s. ② Industrialism caused European nations to set up colonies in other lands in order to gain raw materials and markets. Many European nations saw each other as rivals in the race to gain colonies.

② The nationalistic rivalry and competition for colonies among European nations helped cause World War I. The Allied Powers (including France) fought the Central Powers (Germany, Austria-Hungary, and their allies). The Allies won and imposed harsh terms on Germany. ② German resentment over those terms helped cause World War II, in which Germany, led by Adolf Hitler and the Nazis, tried to conquer Europe.

Make a Diagram

A diagram can show how causes and effects are connected. Because the example passage tells how one event led to another, a cause-effect chain is a useful way to diagram its major ideas.

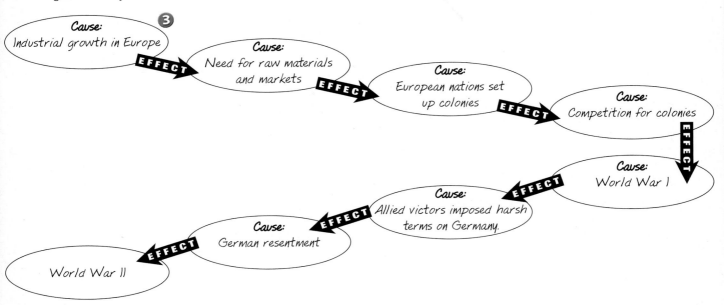

Practicing the Skill

Turn to Chapter 10, Section 4. Read the subsection "Native Peoples and Portuguese Conquest" on page 236. Make a diagram to show major cause-effect connections.

1.9 Identifying and Solving Problems

Defining the Skill

Identifying and solving problems means analyzing the difficulties that are faced by individuals and groups. You determine why the difficulties exist, how people try to overcome them, and what solutions, if any, are achieved.

Applying the Skill

The following paragraph describes a general problem related to the issue of national boundaries, and offers a particular African nation as an example. Use the listed strategies to understand the problem-solution connection.

How to Identify Problems and Solutions

Strategy ❶ Look for a statement of the problem. Note words such as *problem, conflict, difficulty,* or *controversy.* Use the details to ask yourself why the problem exists, and why people wish to overcome it.

Strategy ❷ Identify attempts to solve the problem.

Strategy ❸ Think about the outcome. Ask yourself whether the problem is solved, or whether the outcome is likely to lead to more difficulties.

ARTIFICIAL NATIONAL BOUNDARIES

Africa is a good example of how ❶ boundary lines can divide groups of people or put groups that have long been enemies together in one state. When parts of Africa were divided by European colonial powers, ❶ the boundary lines for Nigeria enclosed the traditional lands of the Hausa-Fulani people, the Yoruba people, and the Ibo people. Under British control, the three groups were forced to follow British rules. When Britain left, there was controversy over the control of the lands. ❷ One group, the Ibo, attempted to withdraw from Nigeria and form its own nation-state, Biafra. ❸ A civil war resulted, and the attempt to split away failed.

Make a Chart

A chart can help you take notes and sum up important ideas about problems and solutions. The chart below shows problems and solutions in the passage you just read.

❶ Problem	Solution Attempts ❷	Outcome ❸
Nigerian boundary lines artificially enclose the traditional lands of three groups of people.	One group, the Ibo, attempted to form a separate nation-state.	Civil war. Attempt to split away failed.

Practicing the Skill

Turn to Chapter 8, Section 2, "Urban Sprawl." Read "Urban Sprawl's Negative Impact" and "Solutions to Sprawl." Make a chart to sum up the problem and possible solutions. Write a summary of the information presented in your chart using standard grammar, sentence structure, and punctuation.

1.10 Distinguishing Fact from Opinion

Defining the Skill

Facts are dates, numbers, names, and statements that can be proved true. **Opinions** are statements that express beliefs, values, and feelings. Although opinions cannot be proved true or false, they can be supported with facts and logical reasons. In order to decide whether to agree with stated opinions, readers must first separate opinion from fact.

Applying the Skill

The following paragraph tells how human-environment interaction affects climate and vegetation. Use the strategies listed below to distinguish fact from opinion.

How to Distinguish Fact from Opinion

Strategy ❶ Notice words that reveal the author's beliefs or feelings. In the sample paragraph, *unfortunately* and *careless* show that opinions are being expressed.

Strategy ❷ Look for statements about future events. These statements are opinions because they cannot be proved.

Strategy ❸ Look for facts that are given as supporting reasons for the statements of opinion.

Strategy ❹ Identify ways in which you can check the facts.

> **HUMAN IMPACT ON THE ENVIRONMENT**
>
> ❶ Unfortunately, the damage that humans cause to soil and vegetation is a by-product of human-environment interaction. ❸ Fragile biomes such as the tundra are easily damaged. Oil pipelines crisscross tundra regions and ❷ bring the threat of leakage and spills. . . .
>
> In the United States, millions of people choose to live in the desert southwest, part of a region known as the Sunbelt. ❸ The desert land is easily eroded, and housing sub-divisions destroy vegetation. In other regions of the world, ❶ careless use of the land often leaves it in a condition that ❷ will not support life, even with sophisticated technological intervention.

Make a Chart

The chart below analyzes the facts and opinions from the passage above.

Opinion ❶ ❷	Supporting Facts ❸	❹ How to Check Facts
Human-environment interaction results in unfortunate damage to soil and vegetation.	Fragile biomes such as the tundra are easily damaged. The desert land of the Sunbelt is easily eroded. Housing sub-divisions destroy vegetation.	Research current articles about human-caused damage to tundra. Research current articles about desert erosion in Sunbelt region. Research current articles about effects of development on vegetation in desert southwest.
The tundra is threatened with oil leakage and spills.	Oil pipelines crisscross tundra regions.	Research oil-industry and news sources.
Careless use of the land often leaves it in a condition that will not support life, even with sophisticated technological intervention.	None given	

Practicing the Skill

Turn to Chapter 3, Section 2, and read the passage "Global Warming." Show opinions and supporting facts in a chart.

1.11 Creating a Sketch Map

Defining the Skill

When you are reading about routes, regions, landforms, political boundaries, or any other geographical information, try to visualize what is described. One way to clarify the information is by **creating a sketch map.** To sketch your own map, use one or more published maps as guides.

Applying the Skill

After reading the passage below, a student sketched the map shown. Read the listed strategies to see how the map was created.

> **WESTWARD MOVEMENT**
>
> From departure points such as Independence, Missouri, hundreds of thousands of pioneers left in covered wagons bound for the West. They blazed trails that crossed prairie, plains, desert, and mountains, moving toward the Pacific. A wagon train on the Oregon Trail might take up to six months to reach its destination 2,000 miles away.

How to Create a Sketch Map

Strategy ❶ Choose a title that sums up what you will show in the map.

Strategy ❷ Consider the purpose of the map as you decide which standard features need to be included. Because the main purpose of this sketch map is to show journeys, it includes a scale of distance. Other maps may require lines of latitude and longitude, for example, and a compass rose.

Strategy ❸ Find one or more maps that you can use to guide the placement of elements and labels. For this sketch, the student consulted a historical map and a physical map.

Strategy ❹ Create a legend to explain any symbols or colors used.

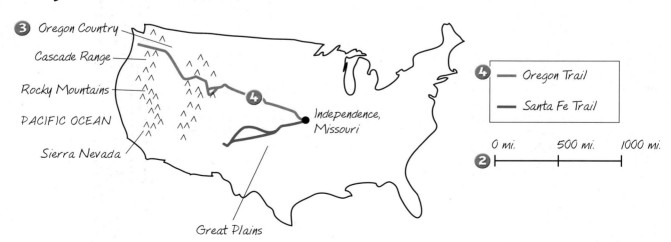

Practicing the Skill

Turn to Chapter 12, Section 1. Read the introductory paragraph "A Human Perspective" on page 273. Create a sketch map of the route of Hannibal's troops. Include the map elements needed to show why Hannibal's achievement was so remarkable.

1.12 Creating Graphs and Charts

Defining the Skill

Whenever your research provides you with information involving numbers and quantities, you can **create graphs and charts** to show patterns in your data. Software programs tend to use the terms *graphs* and *charts* interchangeably. Kinds of graphs and charts include bar graphs, line graphs, pictographs, and pie graphs, which are also called pie charts. The kind you choose depends on your data.

Applying the Skill

The three visuals below are a pie chart, a bar graph, and a line graph. Use the listed strategies to think about their purposes and parts.

How to Create Graphs and Charts

Strategy ① Organize your numerical data. Make a table with rows and columns, or use the grid layout of a spreadsheet. The headings in your table or spreadsheet will correspond to labels in your graph.

Strategy ② Choose the type of graph to create. Are you showing changes over time? A line graph might be best. Are you making a series of comparisons? Consider a bar graph. Do you want to show how parts make the whole? A pie chart shows percentages.

Strategy ③ In line and bar graphs, plot the data along the axes. The X-axis is horizontal; the Y-axis is vertical. Make sure that both axes are labeled with words or numbers.

Strategy ④ Include a legend to indicate what each bar, line, or section represents.

Strategy ⑤ Add a title.

Practicing the Skill

Turn to Chapter 6, Section 3. Look at the data listed on page 147, accompanying the subsection "The Midwest." Show the data in two clearly labeled pie charts. Use graphing software if possible. Write a generalization about the information in each chart using standard grammar, sentence structure, and punctuation.

② Pie Chart

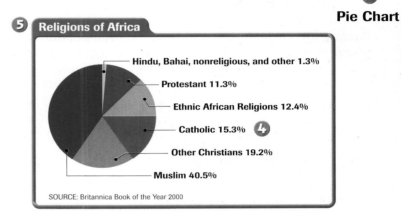

⑤ Religions of Africa

- Hindu, Bahai, nonreligious, and other 1.3%
- Protestant 11.3%
- Ethnic African Religions 12.4%
- Catholic 15.3% ④
- Other Christians 19.2%
- Muslim 40.5%

SOURCE: Britannica Book of the Year 2000

② Bar Graph

⑤ GNP Per Capita, 1987–1997

Amount (U.S. Dollars) — $600, 500, 400, 300, 200, 100, 0

Year: 1987 ... 1997

④ Ghana   Sierra Leone   Nigeria   Guinea

SOURCE: Encyclopaedia Britannica

② Line Graph

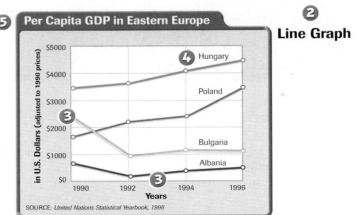

⑤ Per Capita GDP in Eastern Europe

in U.S. Dollars (adjusted to 1990 prices) — $5000, $4000, $3000, $2000, $1000, $0

④ Hungary

Poland

Bulgaria

Albania

Years: 1990, 1992, 1994, 1996

SOURCE: United Nations Statistical Yearbook, 1996

2.1 Creating a Multimedia Presentation

Defining the Skill

Print is a medium of communication. Video and audio recordings, Web pages, and photographic slides are other examples of media. To **create a multimedia presentation,** you collect and display information so that your audience watches, listens, and learns.

Applying the Skill

A multimedia presentation can incorporate high-tech electronics, but it does not have to. A photo essay with audio background, for example, is also an effective multimedia presentation. Use the listed strategies to create your own multimedia presentation.

How to Create a Multimedia Presentation

Strategy ① Choose a topic that lends itself to multimedia. Consider using still or moving images, a script for one or more speakers, sound effects, and music. You might create a travelogue, for example, in which you show your audience a place, and develop a narrative to go with the visual images.

Strategy ② Research the topic to get a general overview. Then narrow the topic to one of manageable size. Make an outline to show the steps you will take to develop your presentation.

Strategy ③ Collect information. Then select the text, images, and audio you plan to use. Show your plan graphically, using a storyboard format, for example.

Strategy ④ Put your presentation together.

Practicing the Skill

Turn to Chapter 4 and read Section 4, "Urban Geography." Choose a topic that you think will work well for a multimedia presentation. Do research, narrow the topic, and make an outline for a future presentation.

2.2 Creating and Using a Database

Defining the Skill

A **database** is any listing system in which related information is organized so that particular items can be retrieved. An electronic library catalog is an example of a database; new information can be added based on the categories, and users input search terms in order to pull out specific listings. Specialized software programs are used to create large, complex databases. Spreadsheet programs are frequently used to create less complex databases.

Applying the Skill

The table below is part of a database for statistics about the countries of Latin America. Use the listed strategies to understand the organization of a database.

How to Create or Use a Database

Strategy ❶ Identify or name the topic of the database table.

Strategy ❷ Define or identify the categories of data. In a computer database, these categories are called fields, and correspond to column headings. A field can specify names, dates or other numbers, or text.

Strategy ❸ The data in each row of a database table form a record. The records are sorted by a particular field—usually alphabetically, or numerically in ascending or descending order. In the table shown, the records are sorted alphabetically by country name.

Strategy ❹ To find a particular piece of data in an existing database, choose a search criterion. The table shown could lead to a list of all countries in which life expectancy is 70 or lower, for example.

❶ Regional Statistics: Latin America (year 2000 estimates)				
Country/Capital ❷	Population ❷	❷ Life Expectancy in years (1995–2000)	❷ Birthrate per 1,000 pop.	Infant Mortality ❷ per 1,000 live births
❸ Antigua and Barbuda/St. John's	68,000	71	22	17.1
❸ Argentina/Buenos Aires	37,048,000	73	19	19.2
❸ Bahamas/Nassau	310,000	74	21	18.4
Barbados/Bridgetown	259,000	76	14	14.2
Belize/Belmopan	254,000	75	32	33.9
Bolivia/La Paz, Sucre	8,281,000	❹ 61	30	67.0
Brazil/Brasilia	170,115,000	❹ 67	21	40.0
Chile/Santiago	15,211,000	75	18	10.5
Colombia/Bogota	40,037,000	❹ 70	26	28.0
Costa Rica/San José	3,589,000	76	22	12.6

Practicing the Skill

Use spreadsheet or database software to input the following fields from the "Regional Data File" for the 50 U.S. states, shown on pages 110–112: Name of State, Population, Population Density, Total Area (square miles). Sort the data (a) alphabetically by name of state and (b) by population, in descending order.

GLOSSARY

A

Aboriginal people *n.* people who migrated to Australia from Asia at least 40,000 years ago; the original settlers of the land. (p. 718)

absolute location *n.* the exact place on earth where a geographic feature is found. (p. 6)

acculturation *n.* the cultural change that occurs when individuals in a society accept or adopt an innovation. (p. 72)

acquired immune deficiency syndrome (AIDS) *n.* a disease caused by the human immunodeficiency virus, or HIV. (p. 465)

Aksum *n.* an important trading capital from the first to the eighth centuries A.D. in what is now Ethiopia; it flourished due to its location near the Red Sea and the Indian Ocean. (p. 431)

alluvial plain *n.* land that is rich farmland, composed of clay, silt, sand, or gravel deposited by running water. (p. 553)

Amazon River *n.* the second longest river in the world, and one of South America's three major river systems, running about 4,000 miles from west to east, and emptying into the Atlantic Ocean. (p. 203)

Andes Mountains *n.* a large system of mountain ranges located along the Pacific coast of Central and South America. (p. 201)

anti-Semitism *n.* discrimination against Jewish people. (p. 315)

apartheid (uh•PAHRT•HYT) *n.* a policy of complete separation of the races, instituted by the white minority government of South Africa in 1948. (p. 454)

Appalachian Mountains *n.* one of two major mountain chains in the eastern United States and Canada, extending 1,600 miles from Newfoundland south to Alabama. (p. 119)

aqueduct *n.* a structure that carries water over long distances. (p. 292)

aquifer *n.* an underground layer of rock that stores water. (p. 421)

archipelago *n.* a set of closely grouped islands. (pp. 553, 689)

ASEAN *n.* the Association of Southeast Asian Nations, an alliance that promotes economic growth and peace in the region. (p. 707)

Ashanti *n.* a people who live in what is now Ghana, in West Africa, and who are known for their artful weaving of colorful *asasia,* or *kente* cloth. (p. 444)

assimilation *n.* a process whereby a minority group gradually gives up its own culture and adopts the culture of a majority group. (p. 728)

Aswan High Dam *n.* a dam on the Nile River in Egypt, completed in 1970, which increased Egypt's farmable land by 50 percent and protected it from droughts and floods. (p. 426)

Atlantic Provinces *n.* the provinces in Eastern Canada— Prince Edward Island, New Brunswick, Nova Scotia, and Newfoundland. (p. 166)

atmosphere *n.* the layers of gases immediately surrounding the earth. (p. 28)

atoll *n.* a ringlike coral island or string of small islands surrounding a lagoon. (pp. 553, 700)

B

balkanization *n.* the process of breaking up a region into small, mutually hostile units. (p. 311)

Baltic Republics *n.* the countries of Latvia, Lithuania, and Estonia, located on the eastern coast of the Baltic Sea. (p. 361)

Bantu migration *n.* the movement of the Bantu peoples southward throughout Africa, spreading their language and culture, from around 500 B.C. to around A.D. 1000. (p. 448)

basic necessity *n.* food, clothing, and shelter. (p. 593)

Benelux *n.* the economic union of Belgium, the Netherlands, and Luxembourg. (p. 296)

Beringia *n.* a land bridge thought to have connected what are now Siberia and Alaska. (p. 127)

Berlin Conference *n.* a conference of 14 European nations held in 1884–1885 in Berlin, Germany, to establish rules for political control of Africa. (p. 432)

Berlin Wall *n.* a wall erected by East Germany in 1961 to cut the capital of Berlin in two, and later dismantled in 1989. (p. 298)

Bikini Atoll *n.* the isolated reef, located in the Marshall Islands of the central Pacific, that was the site of U.S. nuclear bomb tests, consequently contaminating the atoll with high levels of radiation and driving its inhabitants away. (p. 700)

biodiversity *n.* the variety of organisms within an ecosystem. (p. 245)

biological weapon *n.* a bacterium or virus that can be used to harm or kill people, animals, or plants. (p. 175)

biome *n.* a regional ecosystem. (p. 65)

biosphere *n.* all the parts of the earth where plants and animals live, including the atmosphere, the lithosphere, and the hydrosphere. (p. 28)

birthrate *n.* the number of live births per total population, often expressed per thousand population. (p. 78)

blizzard *n.* a heavy snowstorm with winds of more than 35 miles per hour and reduced visibility of less than one-quarter mile. (p. 52)

Boxer Rebellion *n.* an uprising in China in 1900, spurred by angry Chinese militants, or Boxers, over foreign control; several hundred Europeans, Christians, and Chinese died. (p. 636)

British Columbia *n.* Canada's westernmost province, located within the Rocky Mountain range. (p. 169)

Buddhism *n.* a religion that originated in India about 500 B.C. and spread to China, where it grew into a major religion by A.D. 400. (p. 638)

C

calypso *n.* a style of music that began in Trinidad and combines musical elements from Africa, Spain, and the Caribbean. (p. 227)

Canadian Shield *n.* a northern part of the interior lowlands that is a rocky, flat region covering nearly two million square miles and encircling Hudson Bay. (p. 119)

canopy *n.* the area encompassing the tops of the trees in a rain forest, about 150 feet above ground. (p. 422)

capoeira *n.* a martial art and dance that developed in Brazil from Angolans who were taken there by the Portuguese from Africa. (p. 239)

Carnival *n.* the most colorful feast day in Brazil. (p. 239)

carrying capacity *n.* the number of organisms a piece of land can support without negative effects. (p. 82)

Carthage *n.* one of the great empires of ancient Africa, situated on a triangular peninsula on the Gulf of Tunis on the coast of the Mediterranean Sea. (p. 438)

cartographer *n.* a mapmaker. (p. 10)

cash crop *n.* a crop grown for direct sale, and not for use in a region, such as coffee, tea, and sugar in Africa. (p. 433)

caste system *n.* the Aryan system of social classes in India and one of the cornerstones of Hinduism in which each person is born into a caste and can only move into a different caste through reincarnation. (p. 571)

Caucasus *n.* a region that straddles the Caucasus Mountains and stretches between the Black and Caspian seas. (p. 385)

caudillo (kow•DEE•yoh) *n.* a military dictator or political boss. (p. 249)

Central Asia *n.* a region that includes the republics of Kazakhstan, Kyrgyzstan, Tajikistan, Turkmenistan, and Uzbekistan. (p. 346)

central business district (CBD) *n.* the core of a city, which is almost always based on commercial activity. (p. 89)

cerrado (seh•RAH•doh) *n.* a savanna that has flat terrain and moderate rainfall, which make it suitable for farming. (p. 202)

Chang Jiang *n.* (or Yangtze River) the longest river in Asia, flowing about 3,900 miles from Xizang (Tibet) to the East China Sea. (p. 621)

chaparral *n.* the term, in some locations, for a biome of drought-resistant trees. (p. 66)

Chechnya *n.* one of the republics that remains a part of Russia after the collapse of the Soviet Union despite independence movements and violent upheaval. (p. 386)

chemical weathering *n.* a process that changes rock into a new substance through interactions among elements in the air or water and the minerals in the rock. (p. 43)

chernozem *n.* black topsoil, one of the world's most fertile soils. (p. 345)

cholera *n.* a treatable infectious disease that can be fatal and is caused by a lack of adequate sanitation and a clean water supply. (p. 465)

city *n.* an area that is the center of business and culture and has a large population. (p. 87)

city-state *n.* an autonomous political unit made up of a city and its surrounding lands. (p. 289)

climate *n.* the typical weather conditions at a particular location as observed over time. (p. 50)

coalition *n.* an alliance. (p. 174)

Cold War *n.* the conflict between the United States and the Soviet Union after World War II, called "cold" because it never escalated into open warfare. (p. 363)

collective farm *n.* an enormous farm in the Soviet Union on which a large team of laborers were gathered to work together during Joseph Stalin's reign. (p. 364)

Columbian Exchange *n.* the movement of plants, animals, and diseases between the Eastern and Western hemispheres during the age of exploration. (p. 136)

command economy *n.* a type of economic system in which production of goods and services is determined by a central government, which usually owns the means of production. Also called a planned economy. (pp. 91, 364)

commodity *n.* an agricultural or mining product that can be sold. (p. 462)

communism *n.* a system in which the government holds nearly all political power and the means of production. (p. 83)

confederation *n.* a political union. (p. 156)

Confucianism *n.* a movement based on the teachings of Confucius, a Chinese philosopher who lived about 500 B.C.; Confucius stressed the importance of education in an ordered society in which one respects one's elders and obeys the government. (p. 638)

coniferous *adj.* another word for needleleaf trees. (p. 66)

constitutional monarchy *n.* a government in which the ruler's powers are limited by a constitution and the laws of a nation. (p. 580)

continent *n.* a landmass above water on the earth. (p. 27)

Continental Divide *n.* the line of the highest points in North America that marks the separation between rivers flowing eastward and westward. (p. 120)

continental drift *n.* the hypothesis that all continents were once joined into a supercontinent that split apart over millions of years. (p. 29)

continentality *n.* a region's distance from the moderating influence of the sea. (p. 350)

continental shelf *n.* the earth's surface from the edge of a continent to the deep part of the ocean. (p. 36)

convection *n.* the transfer of heat in the atmosphere by upward motion of the air. (p. 54)

copra *n.* the dried meat of coconuts. (p. 714)

core *n.* the earth's center, made up of iron and nickel; the inner core is solid, and the outer core is liquid. (p. 28)

crude oil *n.* petroleum that has not been processed. (p. 497)

Crusades *n.* a series of wars launched by European Christians in 1096 to capture the Holy Land (Palestine) from Muslims. (p. 291)

crust *n.* the thin rock layer making up the earth's surface. (p. 28)

cultural crossroad *n.* a place where various cultures cross paths. (p. 310)

cultural hearth *n.* the heartland or place of origin of a major culture; a site of innovation from which basic ideas, materials, and technology diffuse to other cultures. (pp. 72, 222)

culture *n.* the total of knowledge, attitudes, and behaviors shared by and passed on by members of a group. (p. 71)

cyclone *n.* a violent storm with fierce winds and heavy rain; the most extreme weather pattern of South Asia. (p. 558)

czar *n.* the emperor of Russia prior to the Russian Revolution of 1917 and the subsequent creation of the Soviet Union in 1922. (p. 362)

D

Dead Sea *n.* a landlocked salt lake between Israel and Jordan that is so salty that almost nothing can live in its waters; it is 1,349 feet below sea level, making it the lowest place on the exposed crust of the earth. (p. 489)

debt-for-nature swap *n.* a debt-reducing deal wherein an organization agrees to pay off a certain amount of government debt in return for government protection of a certain portion of rain forest. (p. 247)

deciduous *adj.* a named characteristic of broadleaf trees, such as maple, oak, birch, and cottonwood. (p. 66)

deforestation *n.* the cutting down and clearing away of trees and forests. (p. 246)

delta *n.* a fan-like landform made of deposited sediment, left by a river that slows as it enters the ocean. (p. 43)

democracy *n.* a type of government in which citizens hold political power either directly or through elected representatives. (p. 83)

desalinization *n.* the removal of salt from ocean water. (p. 496)

desertification *n.* an expansion of dry conditions to moist areas that are next to deserts. (p. 424)

dialect *n.* a version of a language that reflects changes in speech patterns due to class, region, or cultural changes. (p. 73)

dictatorship *n.* a type of government in which an individual or a group holds complete political power. (p. 83)

diffusion *n.* the spread of ideas, inventions, or patterns of behavior to different societies. (p. 72)

dike *n.* an earthen bank used to direct or prevent the passage of water. (p. 282)

distance decay *n.* a term referring to the concept that increasing distances between places tend to reduce interactions among them. (p. 389)

diversify *v.* to increase the variety of products in a country's economy; to promote manufacturing and other industries in order to achieve growth and stability. (p. 462)

Dome of the Rock *n.* a shrine in Jerusalem, located on the Temple Mount, which houses the spot where Muslims believe Muhammad rose into heaven and where Jews believe Abraham prepared to sacrifice his son Isaac to God. (p. 511)

Dominion of Canada *n.* the loose confederation of Ontario (Upper Canada), Quebec (Lower Canada), Nova Scotia, and New Brunswick, created by the British North America Act in 1867. (p. 156)

drainage basin *n.* an area drained by a major river and its tributaries. (p. 33)

drip irrigation *n.* the practice of using small pipes that slowly drip water just above ground to conserve water to use for crops. (p. 496)

drought *n.* a long period without rain or with very minimal rainfall. (p. 53)

dynasty *n.* a series of rulers from the same family. (p. 635)

E

earthquake *n.* a sometimes violent movement of the earth, produced when tectonic plates grind or slip past each other at a fault. (p. 39)

economic system *n.* the way people produce and exchange goods. (p. 91)

economic tiger *n.* a country with rapid economic growth due to cheap labor, high technology, and aggressive exports. (p. 645)

economy *n.* the production and exchange of goods and services among a group of people. (p. 91)

ecosystem *n.* an interdependent community of plants and animals. (p. 65)

El Niño (el NEEN•YOH) *n.* a weather pattern created by the warming of the waters off the west coast of South America, which pushes warm water and heavy rains toward the Americas and produces drought conditions in Australia and Asia. (p. 57)

entrepreneur *n.* a person who starts and builds a business. (p. 575)

epicenter *n.* the point on the earth's surface that corresponds to the location in the earth where an earthquake begins. (p. 39)

equator *n.* the imaginary line that encircles the globe, dividing the earth into northern and southern halves. (p. 6)

equinox *n.* each of the two days in a year on which day and night are equal in length; marks the beginning of spring and autumn. (p. 49)

erosion *n.* the result of weathering on matter, created by the action of wind, water, ice, or gravity. (p. 43)

escarpment *n.* a steep slope with a nearly flat plateau on top. (p. 417)

estuary *n.* a broadened seaward end of a river, where the river's currents meet the ocean's tides. (p. 563)

ethnic cleansing *n.* the policy of trying to eliminate an ethnic group. (p. 320)

ethnic group *n.* a group of people who share language, customs, and a common heritage. (p. 71)

Euphrates River *n.* a river of Southwest Asia, which supported several ancient civilizations and flows through parts of Turkey, Syria, and Iraq and empties into the Persian Gulf. (p. 489)

Eurasia *n.* the combined continent of Europe and Asia. (p. 346)

euro *n.* a common currency proposed by the European Union for its member nations. (p. 305)

European Environmental Agency *n.* an agency that provides the European Union with reliable information about the environment. (p. 324)

Everglades *n.* a large subtropical swampland in Florida of about 4,000 square miles. (p. 126)

export *n.* a product or good that is sold from one economy to another. (p. 140)

F

Fang sculpture *n.* carved boxes containing the skulls and bones of deceased ancestors, created by the Fang, who live in Gabon, southern Cameroon, and Equatorial Guinea. (p. 451)

fault *n.* a fracture in the earth's crust. (p. 39)

federal republic *n.* a nation whose powers are divided among the federal, or national, government and various state and local governments. (p. 139)

feudalism *n.* a political system prevailing in Europe from about the 9th to about the 15th centuries in which a king allowed nobles the use of his land in exchange for their military service and their protection of the land. (p. 297)

fertility rate *n.* the average number of children a woman of childbearing years would have in her lifetime, if she had children at the current rate for her country. (p. 78)

First Nations *n.* a group of Canada's Native American people. (p. 159)

fjord (fyawrd) *n.* a long, narrow, deep inlet of the sea between steep slopes. (p. 273)

folk art *n.* handmade items, such as pottery, woodcarving, and traditional costumes, produced by rural people with traditional lifestyles, instead of by professional artists. (p. 314)

fossil water *n.* water pumped from underground aquifers. (p. 496)

free enterprise *n.* an economic system in which private individuals own most of the resources, technology, and businesses, and can operate them for profit with little control from the government. (p. 140)

frontier *n.* the free, open land in the American West that was available for settlement. (p. 137)

G

Ganges River *n.* river in South Asia; an important water resource flowing more than 1,500 miles from its source in a Himalayan glacier to the Bay of Bengal. (p. 560)

Gaza Strip *n.* a territory along the Mediterranean Sea just northeast of the Sinai Peninsula; part of the land set aside for Palestinians, which was occupied by Israel in 1967. (p. 527)

Geographic Information System (GIS) *n.* technology that uses digital map information to create a databank; different "data layers" can be combined to produce specialized maps. GIS allows geographers to analyze different aspects of a specific place to solve problems. (p. 13)

geography *n.* the study of the distribution and interaction of physical and human features on the earth. (p. 5)

glaciation *n.* the changing of landforms by slowly moving glaciers. (p. 44)

glacier *n.* a large, long-lasting mass of ice that moves because of gravity. (p. 44)

global economy *n.* the merging of regional economies in which nations become dependent on each other for goods and services. (p. 666)

global network *n.* a worldwide interconnected group. (p. 173)

global warming *n.* the buildup of carbon dioxide in the atmosphere, preventing heat from escaping into space and causing rising temperatures and shifting weather patterns. (p. 246)

globe *n.* a three-dimensional representation of the earth. (p. 10)

Gobi Desert *n.* a desert located in northern China and southeast Mongolia, and a prime area for finding dinosaur fossils. (p. 627)

Golan Heights *n.* a hilly plateau overlooking the Jordan River and the Sea of Galilee; a strategic location that has been the site of conflict in Southwest Asia for decades. (p. 487)

Gorée Island *n.* an island off the coast of Senegal that served as a major departure point for slaves during the slave trade. (p. 442)

Great Barrier Reef *n.* a 1,250-mile chain of more than 2,500 reefs and islands along Australia's northeast coast, containing some 400 species of coral. (p. 692)

Great Game *n.* a struggle between the British Empire and the Russian Empire for control of Central Asia in the 19th century. (p. 376)

Great Kanto Earthquake *n.* an earthquake in 1923 in Japan that killed an estimated 140,000 people and left the city of Tokyo in ruins. (p. 662)

Great Lakes *n.* a group of five freshwater lakes of central North America between the United States and Canada; the lakes are Huron, Ontario, Michigan, Erie, and Superior. (p. 121)

Great Plains *n.* a vast grassland of central North America that is largely treeless and ascends to 4,000 feet above sea level. (p. 119)

Great Zimbabwe *n.* a city established in what is now Zimbabwe by the Shona around 1000; it became the capital of a thriving gold-trading area. (p. 453)

greenhouse effect *n.* the layer of gases released by the burning of coal and petroleum that traps solar energy, causing global temperature to increase. (p. 58)

Green Revolution *n.* an agricultural program launched by scientists in the 1960s to develop higher-yielding grain varieties and improve food production by incorporating new farming techniques. (p. 569)

Gross Domestic Product (GDP) *n.* the value of only goods and services produced within a country in a period of time. (p. 95)

Gross National Product (GNP) *n.* the total value of all goods and services produced by a country in a period of time. (p. 94)

ground water *n.* the water held under the earth's surface, often in and around the pores of rock. (p. 33)

guest worker *n.* a largely unskilled laborer, often an immigrant from South and East Asia, brought in to the oil-booming countries to fill job openings that the region's native peoples find culturally or economically unacceptable. (p. 525)

H

hemisphere *n.* each half of the globe. (p. 6)

high islands *n.* Pacific islands created by volcanoes. (p. 691)

Himalaya Mountains *n.* a mountain range in South Asia that includes Mount Everest, the world's tallest mountain peak. (p. 551)

Hinduism *n.* the dominant religion of India. (p. 560)

Holocaust *n.* the Nazi program of mass murder of European Jews during World War II. (p. 298)

Huang He (hwahng huh) *n.* a river in northern China, also called the Yellow River, that starts in the Kunlun Mountains and winds east for about 3,000 miles, emptying into the Yellow Sea. (p. 621)

human resources *n.* the skills and talents of employed people. (p. 531)

humus *n.* organic material in soil. (p. 45)

hurricane *n.* a storm that forms over warm, tropical ocean waters. (p. 51)

hydrologic cycle *n.* the continuous circulation of water among the atmosphere, the oceans, and the earth. (p. 32)

hydrosphere *n.* the waters comprising the earth's surface, including oceans, seas, rivers, lakes, and vapor in the atmosphere. (p. 28)

I

Ijsselmeer (EYE•suhl•MAIR) *n.* a freshwater lake separated from the North Sea by a dike and bordered by polders. (p. 283)

illiteracy *n.* the inability to read or write. (p. 593)

Inca *n.* a member of the Quechen peoples of South America who built a civilization in the Andes Mountains in the 15th and 16th centuries. (p. 230)

Indochina *n.* a French colony comprised of Cambodia, Laos, and Vietnam; it won independence from France in 1954. (p. 707)

industrialization *n.* the growth of industry in a country or a society. (p. 730)

Indus Valley civilization *n.* the largest of the world's first civilizations in what is now Pakistan; this was a highly developed urban civilization, lasting from 2500 B.C. to about 1500 B.C. (p. 573)

infant mortality rate *n.* the number of deaths among infants under age one as measured per thousand live births. (p. 79)

infrastructure *n.* the basic support systems needed to keep an economy going, including power, communications, transportation, water, sanitation, and education systems. (pp. 94, 177, 212)

innovation *n.* taking existing elements of society and creating something new to meet a need. (p. 72)

Institutional Revolutionary Party (PRI) *n.* the political party introduced in 1929 in Mexico that helped to introduce democracy and maintain political stability for much of the 20th century. (p. 218)

Islam *n.* a monotheistic religion based on the teachings of the prophet Muhammad, and the biggest cultural and religious influence in North Africa. (pp. 439, 503)

J

Jakota Triangle *n.* a zone of prosperity during the 1980s and early 1990s—Japan, South Korea, and Taiwan. (p. 666)

Jordan River *n.* a river that serves as a natural boundary between Israel and Jordan, flowing from the mountains of Lebanon with no outlet to the Mediterranean Sea. (p. 489)

junta (HOON•tah) *n.* a government run by generals after a military takeover. (p. 249)

K

Kashmir *n.* a region of northern India and Pakistan over which several destructive wars have been fought. (p. 574)

Khmer Empire *n.* a powerful empire that lasted roughly from the 9th to the 15th centuries in what is now Cambodia. (p. 706)

King Leopold II *n.* the Belgian king who opened up the African interior to European trade along the Congo River and by 1884 controlled the area known as the Congo Free State. (p. 449)

KLA (Kosovo Liberation Army) *n.* a group that fought against Serbian attempts to control the region of Kosovo in the 1990s. (p. 321)

Kunlun Mountains *n.* mountains located in the west of China that are the source of two of China's great rivers, the Huang He (Yellow) and the Chang Jiang (Yangtze). (p. 619)

Kurds *n.* an ethnic group in Southwestern Asia that has occupied Kurdistan, located in Turkey, Iraq, and Iran, for about a thousand years, and who have been involved in clashes with these three countries over land claims for most of the 20th century. (p. 516)

L

landfill *n.* a method of solid waste disposal in which refuse is buried between layers of dirt in order to fill in or reclaim low-lying ground. (p. 631)

landform *n.* a naturally formed feature on the surface of the earth. (p. 33)

landlocked *adj.* having no outlet to the sea. (p. 84)

land reform *n.* the process of breaking up large landholdings to attain a more balanced land distribution among farmers. (pp. 250, 569)

Land Rights Act of 1976 *n.* a special law passed for Aboriginal rights in Australia giving Aboriginal people the right to claim land in the Northern Territory. (p. 728)

Landsat *n.* a series of satellites that orbit more than 100 miles above the earth. Each satellite picks up data in an area 115 miles wide. (p. 12)

latitude (lines) *n.* a set of imaginary lines that run parallel to the equator, and that are used in locating places north or south. The equator is labeled the zero-degree line for latitude. (p. 6)

lava *n.* magma that has reached the earth's surface. (p. 40)

lithosphere *n.* the solid rock portion of the earth's surface. (p. 28)

llanos (LAH•nohs) *n.* a large, grassy, treeless area in South America, used for grazing and farming. (p. 202)

lock *n.* a section of a waterway with closed gates where water levels are raised or lowered, through which ships pass. (p. 129)

loess (LOH•uhs) *n.* wind-blown silt and clay sediment that produces very fertile soil. (p. 44)

longitude (lines) *n.* a set of imaginary lines that go around the earth over the poles, dividing it east and west. The prime meridian is labeled the zero-degree line for longitude. (p. 6)

Louisiana Purchase *n.* the territory, including the region between the Mississippi River and the Rocky Mountains, that the United States purchased from France in 1803. (p. 136)

low islands *n.* Pacific islands made of coral reefs. (p. 691)

M

Mabo Case *n.* in Australia, the law case that upheld Aboriginal Eddie Mabo's land claim by which the Court recognized that Aboriginal people had owned land before the British arrived. (p. 728)

Mackenzie River *n.* Canada's longest river, which is part of a river system that flows across the Northwest Territories to the Arctic Ocean. (p. 121)

magma *n.* the molten rock material formed when solid rock in the earth's mantle or crust melts. (p. 28)

malaria *n.* an infectious disease of the red blood cells, carried by mosquitoes, that is characterized by chills, fever, and sweating. (p. 466)

mandala *n.* in Tibetan Buddhism, a geometric design that symbolizes the universe and aids in meditation. (p. 583)

mandala *n.* a state organized as a ring of power around a central court, which often changed in size over time, and which was used instead of borders in early Southeast Asian states. (p. 705)

mantle *n.* a rock layer about 1,800 miles thick that is between the earth's crust and the earth's core. (p. 28)

Maori *n.* the first settlers of New Zealand, who had migrated from Polynesia more than 1,000 years ago. (p. 719)

Mao Zedong *n.* the leader of the Communists in China who defeated the Nationalists in 1949; he died in 1976. (p. 636)

map projection *n.* a way of mapping the earth's surface that reduces distortion caused by converting three dimensions into two dimensions. (p. 10)

map *n.* a two-dimensional graphic representation of selected parts of the earth's surface. (p. 10)

maquiladora *n.* a factory in Mexico that assembles imported materials into finished goods for export. (p. 220)

market economy *n.* a type of economic system in which production of goods and services is determined by the demand from consumers. Also called a demand economy or capitalism. (pp. 91, 313)

Massif Central (ma•SEEF sahn•TRAHL) *n.* the uplands of France, which account for about one-sixth of French lands. (p. 275)

Mecca *n.* the holiest city of Islam, located in Saudi Arabia, where people make pilgrimages to fulfill Islamic religious duty. (p. 503)

mechanical weathering *n.* natural processes that break rock into smaller pieces. (p. 42)

megalopolis *n.* a region in which several large cities and surrounding areas grow together. (p. 146)

Melanesia *n.* a region in Oceania meaning "black islands." (p. 713)

Meseta (meh•SEH•tah) *n.* the central plateau of Spain. (p. 275)

Mesopotamia *n.* a region in Southwest Asia between the Tigris and the Euphrates rivers, which was the location of some of the earliest civilizations in the world; part of the cultural hearth known as the Fertile Crescent. (p. 516)

métis (may•TEES) *n.* a person of mixed French-Canadian and Native American ancestry. (p. 161)

metropolitan area *n.* a functional area including a city and its surrounding suburbs and exurbs, linked economically. (pp. 87, 148)

microcredit *n.* a small loan available to poor entrepreneurs, to help small businesses grow and raise living standards. (p. 575)

Micronesia *n.* one of three regions in Oceania, meaning "tiny islands." (p. 713)

Midwest *n.* the region that contains the 12 states of the north-central United States. (p. 147)

migration *n.* the movement of peoples within a country or region. (p. 135)

Mississippi River *n.* a major river that runs north-south almost the length of the United States, from Minnesota to the Gulf of Mexico, and is part of the longest river system on the continent. (p. 121)

mistral (MIHS•truhl) *n.* a cold, dry wind from the north. (p. 279)

Mobutu Sese Seko *n.* the leader of Zaire, which is now the Democratic Republic of the Congo, from its independence in the 1960s until 1997. He brought the country's businesses under national control, profited from the reorganization, and used the army to hold power. (p. 450)

monarchy *n.* a type of government in which a ruling family headed by a king or queen holds political power and may or may not share the power with citizen bodies. (p. 83)

monsoon *n.* a seasonal wind, especially in South Asia. (p. 558)

moraine *n.* a ridge or hill of rock carried and finally deposited by a glacier. (p. 44)

mortality rate *n.* the number of deaths per thousand. (p. 79)

mosque *n.* an Islamic place of worship, where Muslims pray facing toward the holy city of Mecca. (p. 504)

Mount Kilimanjaro *n.* a volcano in Tanzania in Africa, also Africa's highest peak. (p. 417)

Mughal Empire *n.* the Muslim empire established by the early 1500s over much of India, which brought with it new customs that sometimes conflicted with those of native Hindus. (p. 568)

Muhammad *n.* the founder and a prophet of Islam, who lived part of his life in the city of Mecca. (p. 503)

multinational *n.* a corporation that engages in business worldwide. (p. 142)

Mutapa Empire *n.* a state founded in the 15th century by a man named Mutota and that extended throughout all of present-day Zimbabwe except the eastern part. (p. 453)

N

Nagorno-Karabakh *n.* the mountainous area of Azerbaijan, fought over by Armenia and Azerbaijan. (p. 386)

nation *n.* a group of people with a common culture living in a territory and having a strong sense of unity. (p. 83)

nationalism *n.* the belief that people should be loyal to their nation, the people with whom they share land, culture, and history. (p. 297)

nation-state *n.* the name of a territory when a nation and a state occupy the same territory. (p. 83)

natural resource *n.* a material on or in the earth, such as a tree, fish, or coal, that has economic value. (p. 93)

needleleaf *adj.* characteristic of trees like pine, fir, and cedar, found in northern regions of North America. (p. 66)

Nelson Mandela *n.* one of the leaders of the African National Congress who led a struggle to end apartheid and was elected president in 1994 in the first all-race election in South Africa. (p. 454)

New England *n.* the six northern states in the Northeast United States—Maine, Vermont, New Hampshire, Massachusetts, Rhode Island, and Connecticut. (p. 145)

Niger delta *n.* delta of the Niger River and an area of Nigeria with rich oil deposits. (p. 424)

Nile River *n.* the world's longest river, flowing over 4,000 miles through the Sudan Basin into Uganda, Sudan, and Egypt. (p. 416)

nomad *n.* a person with no permanent home who moves according to the seasons from place to place in search of food, water, and grazing land. (pp. 127, 378)

nonviolent resistance *n.* a movement that uses all means of protest except violence. (p. 568)

Nordic countries *n.* countries of northern Europe, including Denmark, Finland, Iceland, Norway, and Sweden. (p. 302)

NAFTA (North American Free Trade Agreement) *n.* an important trade agreement creating a huge zone of cooperation on trade and economic issues in North America. (p. 220)

North Atlantic Drift *n.* a current of warm water from the Tropics. (p. 278)

Nunavut *n.* one of Canada's territories and home to many of Canada's Inuit; it was carved out of the eastern half of the Northwest Territories in 1999. (p. 169)

O

oasis *n.* a place where water from an aquifer has reached the surface; it supports vegetation and wildlife. (pp. 421, 492)

Oceania *n.* the group of islands in the Pacific, including Melanesia, Micronesia, and Polynesia. (p. 690)

Olduvai Gorge *n.* a site of fossil beds in northern Tanzania, containing the most continuous known record of humanity over the past 2 million years, including fossils from 65 hominids. (p. 431)

oligarchy (AHL•ih•GAHR•kee) *n.* a government run by a few persons or a small group. (p. 249)

"one-commodity" country *n.* a country that relies on one principal export for much of its earnings. (p. 462)

Ontario *n.* one of Canada's Core Provinces. (p. 167)

OPEC *n.* the Organization of Petroleum Exporting Countries, a group established in 1960 by some oil-producing nations to coordinate policies on selling petroleum products. (p. 505)

Orinoco River *n.* a river mainly in Venezuela and part of South America's northernmost river system. (p. 202)

outback *n.* the dry, unpopulated inland region of Australia. (p. 697)

outrigger canoe *n.* a small ship used in the lagoons of islands where Pacific Islanders settled. (p. 699)

ozone *n.* a chemical created when burning fossil fuels react with sunlight; a form of oxygen. (p. 325)

P

Pacific Rim *n.* an economic and social region including the countries surrounding the Pacific Ocean, extending clockwise from New Zealand in the western Pacific to Chile in the eastern Pacific and including the west coast of the United States. (p. 645)

pakehas *n.* a Maori term for white people, for the New Zealanders of European descent. (p. 722)

Palestine Liberation Organization (PLO) *n.* a group formed in the 1960s to regain the Arab land in Israel for Palestinian Arabs. (p. 513)

Palestinians *n.* a displaced group of Arabs who lived or still live in the area formerly called Palestine and now called Israel. (p. 527)

pampas (PAHM•puhs) *n.* a vast area of grassland and rich soil in south-central South America. (p. 202)

Panama Canal *n.* a ship canal cut through Panama connecting the Caribbean Sea with the Pacific Ocean. (p. 226)

pandemic *n.* a disease affecting a large population over a wide geographic area. (p. 435)

Paraná River *n.* a river in central South America and one of its three major river systems, originating in the highlands of southern Brazil, travelling about 3,000 miles south and west. (p. 203)

parliament *n.* a representative lawmaking body whose members are elected or appointed and in which legislative and executive functions are combined. (pp. 158, 303)

parliamentary government *n.* a system where legislative and executive functions are combined in a legislature called a parliament. (p. 158)

particulate *n.* a very small particle of liquid or solid matter. (p. 324)

partition *n.* separation; division into two or more territorial units having separate political status. (p. 574)

pastoral lease *n.* in Australia, a huge chunk of land still owned by the government; ranchers take out leases, renting the land from the government. (p. 729)

PCB *n.* an industrial compound that accumulates in animal tissue and can cause harmful effects and birth defects; PCBs were banned in the United States in 1977. (p. 631)

peat *n.* partially decayed plant matter found in bogs. (p. 277)

penal colony *n.* a place to send prisoners. (p. 718)

per capita income *n.* the average amount of money earned by each person in a political unit. (p. 94)

permafrost *n.* permanently frozen ground. (pp. 63, 123)

polder *n.* land that is reclaimed from the sea or other body of water by diking and drainage. (p. 282)

Polynesia *n.* one of three regions in Oceania, meaning "many islands." (p. 713)

population density *n.* the average number of people who live in a measurable area, reached by dividing the number of inhabitants in an area by the amount of land they occupy. (p. 81)

population pyramid *n.* a graphic device that shows gender and age distribution of a population. (p. 79)

postindustrial economy *n.* an economic phase in which manufacturing no longer plays a dominant role. (p. 142)

Prairie Provinces *n.* in Canada, the provinces west of Ontario and Quebec—Manitoba, Saskatchewan, and Alberta. (p. 168)

precipitation *n.* falling water droplets in the form of rain, sleet, snow, or hail. (p. 50)

prevailing westerlies *n.* winds that blow from west to east. (p. 124)

prime meridian *n.* the imaginary line at zero meridian used to measure longitude east to west, and dividing the earth's east and west halves; also called the Greenwich Meridian because it passes through Greenwich, England. (p. 6)

prime minister *n.* the head of a government; the majority party's leader in parliament. (p. 158)

privatization *n.* the selling of government-owned business to private citizens. (p. 388)

province *n.* a political unit. (p. 156)

pull factor *n.* a factor that draws or attracts people to another location. (pp. 81, 211)

push factor *n.* a factor that causes people to leave their homelands and migrate to another region. (pp. 81, 211, 730)

Pyongyang *n.* the largest city in North Korea, with more than 2.5 million people. (p. 650)

Q

Qin Ling Mountains *n.* mountains in southeastern and east-central China; they divide the northern part of China from the southern part. (p. 619)

Quebec *n.* one of Canada's Core Provinces. (p. 167)

Quechua (KEHCH•wuh) *n.* the language of the Inca Empire, now spoken in the Andes highlands. (p. 231)

R

rai *n.* a kind of popular Algerian music developed in the 1920s by poor urban children that is fast-paced with danceable rhythms; was sometimes used as a form of rebellion to expose political unhappiness. (p. 440)

rain forest *n.* a forest region located in the Tropical Zone with a heavy concentration of different species of broadleaf trees. (pp. 66, 207)

rain shadow *n.* the land on the leeward side of hills or mountains that gets little rain from the descending dry air. (p. 51)

raj *n.* the period of British rule in India, which lasted for nearly 200 years, from 1857 to 1947. (p. 568)

Ramadan *n.* an Islamic practice of month-long fasting from sunup to sundown. (p. 576)

rate of natural increase *n.* also called population growth rate—the rate at which population is growing, found by subtracting the mortality rate from the birthrate. (p. 79)

recession *n.* an extended period of decline in general business activity. (p. 667)

Red Army *n.* the name of the Soviet Union's military. (p. 371)

refinery *n.* a place where crude oil is converted into useful products. (p. 497)

Reformation *n.* a movement in Western Europe beginning in 1517, when many Christians broke away from the Catholic Church and started Protestant churches; this led to mutual hostility and religious wars that tore apart Europe. (p. 297)

reggae *n.* a style of music that developed in Jamaica in the 1960s and is rooted in African, Caribbean, and American music, often dealing with social problems and religion. (p. 227)

relative location *n.* describes a place in relation to other places around it. (p. 6)

relief *n.* the difference in elevation of a landform from the lowest point to the highest point. (p. 36)

religion *n.* the belief in a supernatural power or powers that are regarded as the creators and maintainers of the universe, as well as the system of beliefs itself. (p. 75)

Renaissance *n.* a time of renewed interest in learning and the arts that lasted from the 14th through 16th centuries; it began in the Italian city-states and spread north to all of Europe. (p. 291)

representative democracy *n.* a government in which the people rule through elected representatives. (p. 139)

republic *n.* a government in which citizens elect representatives to rule on their behalf. (p. 290)

reserve *n.* public land set aside for native peoples by the government. (p. 162)

Richter scale *n.* a way to measure information collected by seismographs to determine the relative strength of an earthquake. (p. 40)

rift valley *n.* a long, thin valley created by the moving apart of the continental plates, present in East Africa, stretching over 4,000 miles from Jordan in Southwest Asia to Mozambique in Southern Africa. (p. 416)

Ring of Fire *n.* the chain of volcanoes that lines the Pacific Rim. (pp. 41, 661)

Rocky Mountains *n.* a major mountain system of the United States and Canada, extending 3,000 miles from Alaska south to New Mexico. (p. 119)

Rub al Khali *n.* also known as the Empty Quarter; one of the largest sandy deserts in the world, covering about 250,000 square miles; located on the Arabian Peninsula. (p. 491)

Russian Revolution *n.* the revolt of 1917, in which the Russian Communist Party, led by V. I. Lenin, took control of the government from the czars. (p. 363)

runoff *n.* rainfall not absorbed by soil, which can carry pesticides and fertilizers from fields into rivers, endangering the food chain. (p. 353)

S

Sahara *n.* the largest desert in the world, stretching 3,000 miles across the African continent, from the Atlantic Ocean to the Red Sea, and measuring 1,200 miles from north to south. (p. 420)

Sahel *n.* a narrow band of dry grassland, running east to west on the southern edge of the Sahara, that is used for farming and herding. (p. 424)

St. Lawrence Seaway *n.* North America's most important deepwater ship route, connecting the Great Lakes to the Atlantic Ocean by way of the St. Lawrence River. (p. 129)

St. Petersburg *n.* the old capital of Russia, established by Peter the Great, who moved it there from Moscow because St. Petersburg provided direct access by sea to Western Europe. (p. 362)

salt flat *n.* flat land made of chemical salts that remain after winds evaporate the moisture in the soil. (p. 492)

samba *n.* a Brazilian dance with African influences. (p. 239)

samurai *n.* a professional soldier in Japan who served the interests of landowners and clan chiefs. (p. 651)

satellite nation *n.* a nation dominated by another country. (p. 312)

savanna *n.* the term for the flat, grassy, mostly treeless plains in the tropical grassland region. (p. 66)

seawork *n.* a structure used to control the sea's destructive impact on human life. (p. 283)

sectionalism *n.* when people place their loyalty to their region, or section, above loyalty to the nation. (p. 136)

sediment *n.* small pieces of rock produced by weathering processes. (p. 42)

seismograph (SYZ•muh•GRAF) *n.* a device that measures the size of the waves created by an earthquake. (p. 39)

Seoul *n.* the largest city in South Korea, with a population of more than ten million people. (p. 650)

Serengeti *n.* an area of East Africa, containing some of the best grasslands in the world and many grazing animals. (p. 422)

service industry *n.* any kind of economic activity that produces a service rather than a product. (p. 142)

Sherpa *n.* a person of Tibetan ancestry in Nepal, who serves as the traditional mountain guide of the Mount Everest region. (p. 582)

Shi'ite *n.* one of the two main branches of Islam including most Iranians and some populations of Iraq and Afghanistan. (p. 516)

shogun *n.* the general of the emperor's army with the powers of a military dictator, a position created by the Japanese emperor in 1192 after a struggle between two powerful clans. (p. 651)

Siberia *n.* a region of central and eastern Russia, stretching from the Ural Mountains to the Pacific Ocean, known for its mineral resources and for being a place of political exile. (p. 349)

Siddhartha Gautama *n.* the founder of Buddhism and known as the Buddha, born in southern Nepal in the sixth century B.C. (p. 582)

Silicon Glen *n.* the section of Scotland between Glasgow and Edinburgh, named for its high concentration of high-tech companies. (p. 305)

Silk Road *n.* the 4,000-mile route between China and the Mediterranean Sea, named for the costly silk acquired in China. (p. 375)

silt *n.* loose sedimentary material containing very small rock particles, formed by river deposits and very fertile. (p. 426)

Sinhalese *n.* an Indo-Aryan people who crossed the strait separating India and Sri Lanka in the sixth century B.C. and who created an advanced civilization there, adopting Buddhism. (p. 584)

sirocco (suh•RAHK•oh) *n.* a hot, steady south wind that blows from North Africa across the Mediterranean Sea into southern Europe, mostly in spring. (p. 279)

slash-and-burn *adj.* a way of clearing fields for planting by cutting trees, brush, and grasses and burning them. (p. 210)

smart growth *n.* the efficient use and conservation of land and other resources. (p. 178)

smog *n.* a brown haze that occurs when gases released by burning fossil fuels react with sunlight. (p. 324)

society *n.* a group that shares a geographic region, a common language, and a sense of identity and culture. (p. 71)

soil *n.* the loose mixture of weathered rock, organic matter, air, and water that supports plant growth. (p. 45)

solar system *n.* consists of the sun and nine known planets, as well as other celestial bodies that orbit the sun. (p. 27)

solstice *n.* either of two times of year when the sun's rays shine directly overhead at noon at the furthest points north or south, and that mark the beginning of summer and winter; in the Northern Hemisphere, the summer solstice is the longest day and the winter solstice the shortest. (p. 49)

South, the *n.* a region that covers about one-fourth of the land area of the United States and contains more than one-third of its population. (p. 148)

South Slav *n.* a person who migrated from Poland or Russia and settled in the Balkan Peninsula around 500. (p. 319)

Spanish conquest *n.* the conquering of the Native Americans by the Spanish. (p. 217)

sphere of influence *n.* a method of dividing foreign control in China, after the country was forced to sign a series of treaties granting special privileges to the Europeans. China was partitioned for control by Britain, France, Germany, and Russia, among others. (p. 636)

state *n.* a political term describing an independent unit that occupies a specific territory and has full control of its internal and external affairs. (p. 83)

stateless nation *n.* a nation of people that does not have a territory to legally occupy, like the Palestinians, Kurds, and Basques. (p. 526)

stateless society *n.* one in which people use lineages, or families whose members are descended from a common ancestor, to govern themselves. (p. 443)

steppe *n.* the term used for the temperate grassland region in the Northern Hemisphere. (p. 66)

Stolen Generation *n.* in Australia, what Aboriginal people today call the 100,000 mixed-raced children who were taken by the government and given to white families to promote assimilation. (p. 728)

storm surge *n.* high water level brought by a cyclone that swamps low-lying areas. (p. 562)

strategic commodity *n.* a resource so important that nations will go to war to ensure its steady supply. (p. 529)

subcontinent *n.* a landmass that is like a continent, only smaller, such as South Asia, which is called the Indian subcontinent. (p. 551)

subsistence activity *n.* an activity in which a family produces only the food, clothing, and shelter they themselves need. (p. 714)

suburb *n.* a political unit or community touching the borders of the central city or touching other suburbs that touch the city. (pp. 87, 138)

sultan *n.* a ruler of a Muslim country. (p. 585)

summer monsoon *n.* the season when winds blow from the southwest across the Indian Ocean toward South Asia, from June through September, with winds stirring up powerful storms and causing severe flooding. (p. 597)

Sunni *n.* one of the two main branches of Islam, comprising about 83 percent of all Muslims, including those in Turkey, Iraq, and Afghanistan. (p. 516)

supra *n.* Georgian (Russian) term for dinner party, with many dishes and courses, toasts, and short speeches. (p. 374)

sustainable community *n.* a community where residents can live and work in harmony with the environment. (p. 178)

sweatshop *n.* a workplace where people work long hours for low pay under poor conditions to enrich manufacturers. (p. 667)

T

taiga *n.* a nearly continuous belt of evergreen coniferous forests across the Northern Hemisphere, in North America and Eurasia. (p. 351)

Taklimakan Desert *n.* a desert located in western China between the Tian Shan and Kunlun mountains. (p. 627)

Taliban *n.* a strict Muslim group in Afghanistan that has imposed rigid rules on society, including prescribed clothing styles for both men and women, restrictions on the appearance of women in public places, and regulations on television, music, and videos. (p. 517)

Tamil *n.* a Dravidian Hindu, who arrived in Sri Lanka in the fourth century, settling in the north while the Sinhalese moved further south. (p. 584)

Taoism *n.* a philosophy based on the book *Tao Te Ching* and the teachings of Lao-Tzu, who lived in China in the sixth century B.C. and believed in preserving and restoring harmony in the individual, with nature, and in the universe, with little interference from the government. (p. 638)

taro *n.* a tropical Asian plant with a starchy root, which can be eaten as a boiled vegetable or made into breads, puddings, or a paste called poi. (p. 715)

tectonic plate *n.* an enormous moving shelf that forms the earth's crust. (p. 37)

Tenochtitlan (teh•NOH•tee•TLAHN) *n.* the ancient Aztec capital, site of Mexico City today. (p. 217)

terpen *n.* high earthen platforms used in seaworks. (p. 283)

terraced farming *n.* an ancient technique for growing crops on hillsides or mountain slopes, using step-like horizontal fields cut into the slopes. (p. 211)

terrorism *n.* the use of, or threatened use of, force or violence against individuals or property for the purpose of intimidating or causing fear for political or social ends. (p. 173)

theocratic *adj.* a form of government in which religious leaders control the government, relying on religious law and consultation with religious scholars. (p. 504)

Three Gorges Dam *n.* a dam begun in the late 20th century on the Chang Jiang in China, to help control flooding, generate power, and allow ships to sail farther into China. (p. 628)

Three Kingdoms *n.* the kingdoms formed in the peninsula of Korea by A.D. 300—Koguryo in the northeast, Paekche in the southwest, and Silla in the southeast. (p. 647)

Tigris River *n.* one of the most important rivers of Southwest Asia; it supported several ancient river valley civilizations, and flows through parts of Turkey, Syria, and Iraq. (p. 489)

tornado *n.* a powerful funnel-shaped column of spiraling air. (p. 51)

topographic map *n.* a general reference map; a representation of natural and man-made features on the earth. (p. 11)

topography *n.* the combined characteristics of landforms and their distribution in a region. (p. 36)

Transcaucasia *n.* a region that consists of the republics of Armenia, Azerbaijan, and Georgia; located between the Caucasus Mountains and the borders of Turkey and Iran. (p. 346)

Trans–Siberian Railroad *n.* a railroad that would eventually link Moscow to the Pacific port of Vladivostok; built between 1891 and 1903. (p. 355)

Treaty of Tordesillas *n.* a treaty between Spain and Portugal in 1494 that gave Portugal control over the land that is present-day Brazil. (p. 236)

Treaty of Waitangi *n.* the treaty signed by the British and Maori in 1840 giving Britain control over New Zealand. (p. 719)

tsunami (TSU•NAH•mee) *n.* a giant ocean wave, caused by an underwater earthquake or volcanic eruption, with great destructive power. (pp. 40, 662)

tuberculosis *n.* a respiratory infection spread by human contact, which often accompanies AIDS. (p. 466)

tundra *n.* the flat treeless lands forming a ring around the Arctic Ocean; the climate region of the Arctic Ocean. (p. 63)

typhoon *n.* a tropical storm, like a hurricane, that occurs in the western Pacific. (pp. 51, 625)

U

USSR *n.* the Union of Soviet Socialist Republics, or Soviet Union, formed in 1922 by the Communists and officially dissolved in 1991. (p. 363)

UNICEF (United Nations Children's Fund) *n.* an international watchdog and relief organization for children. (p. 665)

United Provinces of Central America *n.* the name of Central America after the region declared independence from Mexico in 1823. (p. 223)

upland *n.* a hill or very low mountain that may also contain mesas and high plateaus. (p. 275)

Ural Mountains *n.* the mountain ranges that separate the Northern European and West Siberian plains and used as the dividing line between Europe and Asia. (p. 346)

urban geography *n.* the study of how people use space in cities. (p. 87)

urbanization *n.* the dramatic rise in the number of cities and the changes in lifestyle that result. (p. 88)

urban sprawl *n.* poorly planned development that spreads a city's population over a wider and wider geographic area. (p. 176)

V

Vietnam War *n.* (1954–1975) the military conflict resulting from American involvement in South Vietnam to prevent its takeover by Communist North Vietnam. (p. 707)

volcano *n.* a natural event, formed when magma, gases, and water from the lower part of the crust or mantle collect in underground chambers and eventually erupt and pour out of cracks in the earth's surface. (p. 40)

voyaging canoe *n.* a large ship developed by Pacific Islanders to sail the ocean. (p. 699)

W

wadi *n.* a riverbed that remains dry except during the rainy seasons. (p. 488)

water table *n.* the level at which rock is saturated. (p. 33)

weather *n.* the condition of the atmosphere at a particular location and time. (p. 50)

weathering *n.* physical and chemical processes that change the characteristics of rock on or near the earth's surface, occurring slowly over many years. (p. 42)

West *n.* North American region, consisting of 13 states, that stretches from the Great Plains to the Pacific Ocean and includes Alaska to the north and Hawaii in the Pacific. (p. 148)

West Bank *n.* in Israel, a strip of land on the west side of the Jordan River, originally controlled by Jordan, which is part of the land set aside for Arab Palestinians. (p. 527)

Western Wall *n.* for Jews, the holiest site in Jerusalem; the only remaining portion of the Second Temple, built in 538 B.C. and destroyed in A.D. 70 by the Romans. (p. 510)

Wik Case *n.* in Australia, the court ruled in this case that Aboriginal people could claim land held under a pastoral lease. (p. 729)

winter monsoon *n.* the season when dry winds blow from the northeast across the Himalaya Mountains toward the sea from October through February, sometimes causing drought. (p. 597)

X

Xi Jiang (shee JYAHNG) *n.* also called the West River; the river that flows eastward through southeast China and joins the Pearl River (Zhu Jiang) to flow into the South China Sea, forming an estuary between Hong Kong and Macao. (p. 621)

Y

yurt *n.* a tent of Central Asia's nomads. (p. 379)

Z

Zionism *n.* a movement that began in the 19th century to create and support a Jewish homeland in Palestine. (p. 511)

Zuider Zee (ZEYE•duhr ZAY) *n.* former inlet of the North Sea in the Netherlands. (p. 283)

A

Aboriginal people [Aborígenes] *s.* gente que emigró a Australia desde Asia, hace al menos 40.000 años; los pobladores originales de la tierra. (p. 718)

absolute location [ubicación absoluta] *s.* el lugar exacto en la Tierra donde se encuentra un accidente geográfico. (p. 6)

acculturation [aculturación] *s.* el cambio cultural que ocurre cuando las personas en una sociedad aceptan o adoptan una innovación. (p. 72)

acquired immune deficiency syndrome (AIDS) [síndrome de inmunodeficiencia adquirida (SIDA)] *s.* enfermedad producida por el virus de la inmunodeficiencia humana o VIH. (p. 465)

Aksum [Aksum *s.* una importante capital comercial desde el s. I al s. VIII de nuestra era, situada en lo que hoy es Etiopía; floreció debido a su ubicación junto al Mar Rojo y el Océano Índico. (p. 431)

alluvial plain [llanura aluvial] *s.* tierra fértil para la labranza, formada por depósitos de arcilla, limo, arena o grava producidos por las aguas corrientes. (p. 553)

Amazon River [Río Amazonas] *s.* el segundo río más largo del mundo y uno de los tres principales sistemas fluviales de América del Sur. Se extiende unas 4.000 millas (6.436 km) de oeste a este y desemboca en el Océano Atlántico. (p. 203)

Andes Mountains [Cordillera de los Andes] *s.* una larga cordillera que se extiende a lo largo de la costa del Pacífico de Centroamérica y América del Sur. (p. 201)

anti-Semitism [antisemitismo] *s.* discriminación contra los judíos. (p. 315)

apartheid [apartheid] (a-par-zeid) *s.* política de separación completa de las razas, implementada por el gobierno de la minoría blanca de Sudáfrica en 1948. (p. 454)

Appalachian Mountains [Montes Apalaches] *s.* una de las dos cordilleras más importantes en la región Este de los Estados Unidos y Canadá, que se extiende 1.600 millas (2.575 km) desde Terranova (Newfoundland) hacia el sur hasta Alabama. (p. 119)

aqueduct [acueducto] *s.* estructura para transportar agua por largas distancias. (p. 292)

aquifer [acuífero] *s.* capa subterránea de roca donde se almacena agua. (p. 421)

archipelago [archipiélago] *s.* grupo de islas cercanas. (pp. 553, 689)

ASEAN [ANSA] *s.* Asociación de Naciones del Sudeste Asiático, una alianza que promueve el desarrollo económico y la paz en la región. (p. 707)

Ashanti [Ashanti] *s.* gente que vive en lo que es ahora Ghana, en África Occidental, renombrada por sus diseños artísticos de ropa asasia o kente que usa la realeza. (p. 444)

assimilation [asimilación] *s.* proceso por el cual un grupo minoritario gradualmente se desprende de su propia cultura y adopta la cultura del grupo mayoritario. (p. 728)

Aswan High Dam [La gran presa de Asuán] *s.* presa en el río Nilo de Egipto, construida en 1970, la cual aumentó las tierras arables de Egipto en un 50 por ciento y las protegió contra las sequías y las inundaciones. (p. 426)

Atlantic Provinces [Las provincias atlánticas] *s.* las provincias en la región este del Canadá: Isla Príncipe Eduardo, Nueva Brunswick, Nueva Escocia y Terranova o Newfoundland. (p. 166)

atmosphere [atmósfera] *s.* las capas gaseosas que envuelven inmediatamente la Tierra. (p. 28)

atoll [atolón] *s.* isla coralina en forma anular o un conjunto de pequeñas islas que rodean una laguna central. (pp. 553, 700)

B

balkanization [balcanización] *s.* proceso por el cual una región se fragmenta en unidades pequeñas, mutuamente hostiles. (p. 311)

Baltic Republics [Países Bálticos] *s.* los países de Latvia, Lituania y Estonia, ubicados en la costa este del mar Báltico. (p. 361)

Bantu migration [migración bantú] *s.* desplazamiento de los pueblos bantú hacia el sur a través de África, que propagaron su lengua y su cultura desde alrededor del año 500 antes de nuestra era hasta alrededor del año 1000 de nuestra era. (p. 448)

basic necessity [necesidades básicas] *s.* alimentos, ropa y vivienda. (p. 593)

Benelux [Benelux] *s.* la unión económica de Bélgica, Países Bajos (Nederland) y Luxemburgo. (p. 296)

Beringia [Behring] *s.* puente de tierra que se cree conectaba lo que son ahora Siberia y Alaska. (p. 127)

Berlin Conference [Conferencia de Berlín] *s.* una conferencia de 14 países europeos realizada en 1884-1885 en Berlín, Alemania, para establecer normas de control político de África. (p. 432)

Berlin Wall [Muro de Berlín] *s.* muro construido por Alemania Oriental en 1961 para dividir la capital de Berlín en dos, derruido en 1989. (p. 298)

Bikini Atoll [Atolón Bikini] *s.* arrecife aislado en las Islas Marshall del Pacífico central, donde se efectuaron experimentos de bombas nucleares estadounidenses, lo que contaminó el atolón con altos niveles de radiación, y ahuyentó a sus habitantes. (p. 700)

biodiversity [biodiversidad] *s.* la variedad de organismos en un ecosistema. (p. 245)

biological weapon (arma biológica) *s.* bacteria o virus que se puede utilizar para dañar o matar personas, animales o plantas. (p. 175)

biome [bioma] *s.* un ecosistema regional. (p. 65)

biosphere [biósfera] *s.* todas las partes de la Tierra donde viven plantas y animales, incluyendo la atmósfera, la litosfera y la hidrosfera. (p. 28)

birthrate [índice de natalidad] *s.* el número de nacimientos vivos por total de la población, con frecuencia expresado por miles de habitantes. (p. 78)

blizzard [ventisca] *s.* tormenta de nieve fuerte con vientos de más de 35 millas (55 km) por hora y visibilidad reducida de menos de un cuarto de milla (0.40 km). (p. 52)

Boxer Rebellion [Guerra de los bóxers] *s.* rebelión en China en 1900, producida por militantes chinos enfurecidos, o bóxers, por el control extranjero; cientos de europeos, cristianos y chinos murieron. (p. 636)

British Columbia [Columbia Británica] *s.* la provincia más occidental de Canadá en las Montañas Rocosas. (p. 169)

Buddhism [Budismo] *s.* religión originada en la India por el año 500 antes de nuestra era, que se extendió hacia China, donde se convirtió en una religión importante alrededor del año 400 de nuestra era. (p. 638)

C

calypso [calypso] *s.* estilo de música que comenzó en Trinidad y combina elementos musicales de África, España y el Caribe. (p. 227)

Canadian Shield [escudo canadiense] *s.* parte norteña de las tierras bajas interiores que es una región rocosa y plana que cubre casi dos millones de millas cuadradas (cinco millones doscientos mil kilómetros cuadrados) y encierra la Bahía de Hudson. (p. 119)

canopy [bóveda] *s.* área que comprende la parte superior de los árboles en una selva tropical, a unos 150 pies (45 metros) sobre el suelo. (p. 422)

capoeira [capoeira] *s.* arte marcial y danza que desarrollaron en Brasil los angolanos que fueron llevados allí desde el África por los portugueses. (p. 239)

Carnival [Carnaval] *s.* el día de fiesta más llamativo de Brasil. (p. 239)

carrying capacity [capacidad de soporte] *s.* número de organismos que un pedazo de terreno puede soportar sin efectos negativos. (p. 82)

Carthage [Cartago] *s.* uno de los grandes imperios de África en la antigüedad, situado en una península triangular en el Golfo de Túnez en la costa del Mar Mediterráneo. (p. 438)

cartographer [cartógrafo] *s.* persona que levanta mapas. (p. 10)

cash crop [cultivo industrial o comercial] *s.* producto cultivado para la venta directa y no para uso en una región, como café, té y azúcar en África. (p. 433)

caste system [sistema de castas] *s.* el sistema ario de clases sociales en la India y uno de los pilares del hinduismo en el cual cada persona nace dentro de una casta y sólo puede pasar a otra casta mediante la reencarnación. (p. 571)

Caucasus [Cáucaso] *s.* región que comprende el sistema montañoso del mismo nombre y se extiende entre el mar Negro y el Caspio. (p. 385)

caudillo [caudillo] *s.* dictador militar o líder político. (p. 249)

Central Asia [Asia Central] *s.* región que incluye las repúblicas de Kazajstán, Kirguistán, Tayikistán, Turkmenistán y Uzbekistán. (p. 346)

central business district (CBD) [distrito comercial central (DCC)] *s.* el centro de una ciudad, en el cual casi siempre se desarrollan actividades comerciales. (p. 89)

cerrado [cerrado] *s.* una sabana que tiene terreno plano y lluvias moderadas, lo que la hace apta para la agricultura. (p. 202)

Chang Jiang [Chang Jiang] *s.* (o Río Yang-tsé) el río más largo del Asia, que fluye unas 3.900 millas (6.275 km) desde Xizang (Tibet) hasta el mar de la China oriental. (p. 621)

Chaparral [chaparral] *s.* término, en algunos lugares, para una bioma de árboles resistentes a la sequía. (p. 66)

Chechnya [Chechenia] *s.* una de las repúblicas que continúa siendo parte de Rusia después del colapso de la Unión Soviética a pesar de los movimientos independentistas y levantamientos violentos. (p. 386)

chemical weathering [meteorización química] *s.* proceso por el cual una roca se convierte en una nueva substancia a través de la interacción entre los elementos en el aire o el agua y los minerales en la roca. (p. 43)

chernozem [quimiozen] *s.* capa superior negra del suelo, una de las tierras más fértiles del mundo. (p. 345)

cholera [cólera] *s.* enfermedad infecciosa tratable que puede ser mortal y es producida por la falta de medidas higiénicas adecuadas y de suministro de agua limpia. (p. 465)

city [ciudad] *s.* zona que es el centro de los negocios y la cultura y tiene una población numerosa. (p. 87)

city-state [ciudad-estado] *s.* una unidad política autónoma compuesta por una ciudad y los terrenos circundantes. (p. 289)

climate [clima] *s.* las condiciones atmosféricas típicas de un lugar específico que se observan con el tiempo. (p. 50)

coalition (coaliciůn) *s.* alianza. (p. 174)

Cold War [Guerra Fría] *s.* el conflicto entre los Estados Unidos y la Unión Soviética después de la II Guerra Mundial, llamada "fría" porque nunca se intensificó hasta el grado de convertirse en una guerra abierta. (p. 363)

collective farm [granja colectiva] *s.* un gran equipo de peones reunidos para trabajar juntos en enormes granjas en la Unión Soviética, durante el gobierno de Jósiv Stalin. (p. 364)

Columbian Exchange [Intercambio Colombino] *s.* el intercambio de plantas, animales y enfermedades entre el hemisferio oriental y el hemisferio occidental durante la era de las exploraciones. (p. 136)

command economy [economía dirigida] *s.* tipo de sistema económico en el cual la producción de bienes y servicios es determinada por un gobierno central, el cual usualmente es dueño de los medios de producción. Llamado también "economía planificada". (pp. 91, 364)

commodity [bien de consumo] *s.* un producto agrícola o de minería que se puede vender. (p. 462)

communism [comunismo] *s.* sistema en el cual el gobierno retiene casi todo el poder político y los medios de producción. (p. 83)

confederation [confederación] *s.* una unión política. (p. 156)

Confucianism [Confucianismo] *s.* movimiento basado en las enseñanzas de Confucio, filósofo chino que vivió alrededor del año 500 antes de nuestra era; Confucio enfatizaba la importancia de la educación en una sociedad ordenada en la cual las personas respetan a sus mayores y obedecen al gobierno. (p. 638)

coniferous [conífero] *adj.* otro término para los árboles de hojas perennes y aciculares. (p. 66)

constitutional monarchy [monarquía constitucional] *s.* sistema de gobierno en el cual los poderes del gobernante están limitados por una constitución y las leyes de la nación. (p. 580)

continent [continente] *s.* una masa de tierra firme sobre el agua en la Tierra. (p. 27)

Continental Divide [La Divisoria Continental] *s.* la línea de los picos más altos en América del Norte que marca la separación entre los ríos que fluyen hacia el este y hacia el oeste. (p. 120)

continental drift [deriva de los continentes] *s.* la hipótesis de que los continentes fueron una vez un supercontinente que se dividió lentamente a través de millones de años. (p. 29)

continentality [continentalidad] *s.* la distancia de una región de la influencia moderadora del mar. (p. 350)

continental shelf [plataforma continental] *s.* la superficie de la Tierra desde el borde de un continente hasta la parte profunda del océano. (p. 36)

convection [convección] *s.* la transferencia de calor en la atmósfera por el movimiento ascendente del aire. (p. 54)

copra [copra] *s.* la pulpa seca del coco. (p. 714)

core [centro] *s.* el núcleo de la Tierra, compuesto de hierro y niquel; el centro interior es sólido, el centro exterior es líquido. (p. 28)

crude oil [petróleo crudo] *s.* petróleo que no ha sido procesado. (p. 497)

Crusades [Cruzadas] *s.* una serie de guerras impulsadas por los cristianos europeos en 1096 para recuperar la Tierra Santa (Palestina) de los musulmanes. (p. 291)

crust [corteza] *s.* la capa delgada de rocas que compone la superficie de la Tierra. (p. 28)

cultural crossroad [cruce cultural] *s.* un lugar donde convergen varias culturas. (p. 310)

cultural hearth [centro cultural] *s.* el centro o lugar de origen de una cultura importante; un lugar de innovaciones desde el cual se difunden ideas, materiales y tecnologías fundamentales a otras culturas. (pp. 72, 222)

culture [cultura] *s.* el total de conocimientos, actitudes y comportamientos compartidos y transmitidos por los miembros de un grupo. (p. 71)

cyclone [ciclón] *s.* una tormenta violenta con vientos fuertes y mucha lluvia; el patrón climatológico más extremo del Asia Meridional. (p. 558)

czar [zar] *s.* el emperador de Rusia antes de la Revolución de 1917 y de la subsiguiente creación de la Unión Soviética en 1922. (p. 362)

D

Dead Sea [Mar Muerto] *s.* lago salado, sin salida al mar, entre Israel y Jordania, con un nivel de salinidad tan alto que casi nada puede vivir en sus aguas; se encuentra a 1.349 pies (411 m) por debajo del nivel del mar, lo que lo convierte en el lugar más bajo en la corteza expuesta de la Tierra. (p. 489)

debt-for-nature swap [Intercambio de deuda por naturaleza] *s.* acuerdo para reducir una deuda por el cual una organización acepta pagar cierta cantidad de una deuda gubernamental a cambio de protección gubernamental de cierta parte de una selva tropical. (p. 247)

deciduous [caducifolio] adj. característica de los árboles de hojas anchas, como el arce, el roble, el abedul y el Álamo de Virginia. (p. 66)

deforestation [deforestación] *s.* el corte y la eliminación de árboles y bosques. (p. 246)

delta [delta] *s.* zona de forma de abanico formada por sedimentos depositados dejados por un río que disminuye su velocidad al desembocar en el océano. (p. 43)

democracy [democracia] *s.* tipo de gobierno en el cual los ciudadanos ejercen el poder político sea directamente o mediante representantes elegidos. (p. 83)

desalinization [desalinización] *s.* la eliminación de sal del agua del océano. (p. 496)

desertification [desertización] *s.* ampliación de condiciones secas a zonas húmedas que se encuentran próximas a desiertos. (p. 424)

dialect [dialecto] *s.* una versión de un idioma que refleja cambios en patrones de habla por factores relacionados con cambios de clase, regionales o culturales. (p. 73)

dictatorship [dictadura] *s.* tipo de gobierno en el cual un individuo o grupo de individuos tienen el poder político completo. (p. 83)

diffusion [difusión] *s.* la diseminación de ideas, invenciones o patrones de comportamiento hacia otras sociedades. (p. 72)

dike [dique] *s.* muro de tierra usado para contener o desviar el curso de las aguas. (p. 282)

distance decay [deterioro de la distancia] *s.* término que se refiere al concepto de que a mayor distancia entre dos puntos, menor interacción entre los mismos. (p. 389)

diversify [diversificar] *v.* aumentar la variedad de productos en la economía de un país; promover la industria fabril y otras industrias con el propósito de lograr el desarrollo y la estabilidad. (p. 462)

Dome of the Rock [Cúpula de la Roca] *s.* un santuario en Jerusalén, ubicado en el monte del Templo, que contiene el lugar donde los musulmanes creen que Mahoma se elevó a los cielos y donde los judíos creen que Abraham preparó el sacrificio de su hijo Isaac a Dios. (p. 511)

Dominion of Canada [Dominio de Canadá] *s.* la amplia confederación de Ontario (Alto Canadá), Quebec (Bajo Canadá), Nueva Escocia y Nuevo Brunswick, creada por el Acta de la América del Norte Británica en 1867. (p. 156)

drainage basin [cuenca de drenaje] *s.* una zona drenada por un río importante y sus afluentes. (p. 33)

drip irrigation [irrigación por goteo] *s.* la práctica de usar tubos pequeños que lentamente gotean agua justo sobre el suelo para conservar agua para usarse en los cultivos. (p. 496)

drought [sequía] *s.* un largo período sin lluvia o con precipitación mínima. (p. 53)

dynasty [dinastía] *s.* una serie de gobernantes de la misma familia. (p. 635)

E

earthquake [terremoto] *s.* un movimiento a veces violento de la tierra, producido cuando placas tectónicas se tocan o deslizan una sobre otra en una falla. (p. 39)

economic system [sistema económico] *s.* la forma como la gente produce e intercambia bienes. (p. 91)

economic tiger [tigre económico] *s.* un país con rápido crecimiento económico debido al bajo coste de la mano de obra, la alta tecnología y las exportaciones agresivas. (p. 645)

economy [economía] *s.* la producción y el intercambio de bienes y servicios entre un grupo de personas. (p. 91)

ecosystem [ecosistema] *s.* una comunidad interdependiente de plantas y animales. (p. 65)

El Niño [El Niño] *s.* un patrón meteorológico creado por el calentamiento de las aguas de las costas occidentales de América del Sur, que empuja aguas cálidas y fuertes lluvias hacia el continente americano y produce condiciones de sequía en Australia y Asia. (p. 57)

entrepreneur [empresario] *s.* persona que inicia y desarrolla un negocio. (p. 575)

epicenter [epicentro] *s.* el punto en la superficie terrestre que corresponde a la ubicación en la Tierra donde comienza un terremoto. (p. 39)

equator [ecuador] *s.* la línea imaginaria que rodea la esfera terrestre, dividiendo la Tierra en las mitades norte y sur. (p. 6)

equinox [equinoccio] *s.* cada uno de los dos días del año en los cuales el día y la noche tienen la misma duración; marca el comienzo de la primavera y el otoño. (p. 49)

erosion [erosión] *s.* el resultado del desgaste de la materia producido por la acción del viento, el agua, el hielo o la gravedad. (p. 43)

escarpment [escarpa] *s.* declive empinado de un terreno con una meseta casi plana en la cima. (p. 417)

estuary [estuario] *s.* desembocadura de un río con una amplia apertura por donde las corrientes del río chocan con las mareas del océano. (p. 563)

ethnic cleansing [limpieza étnica] *s.* la política de tratar de eliminar a un grupo étnico. (p. 320)

ethnic group [grupo étnico] *s.* un grupo de personas que comparten un idioma, costumbres y una herencia común. (p. 71)

Euphrates River [Río Éufrates] *s.* un río en el Sudoeste asiático que sirvió de apoyo a varias civilizaciones antiguas, fluye a través de regiones de Turquía, Siria e Irak y desemboca en el Golfo Pérsico. (p. 489)

Eurasia [Eurasia] *s.* los continentes combinados de Europa y Asia. (p. 346)

euro [euro] *s.* moneda común propuesta por la Unión Europea para sus naciones miembros. (p. 305)

European Environmental Agency [Agencia Europea del Medio Ambiente] *s.* esta agencia proporciona a la Unión Europea información confiable sobre el medio ambiente. (p. 324)

Everglades [Everglades] *s.* una amplia zona de terrenos pantanosos subtropicales en la Florida, de cerca de 4.000 millas cuadradas (10.400 kilómetros cuadrados). (p. 126)

export [exportación] *s.* un producto o bien que se vende desde una economía a otra. (p. 140)

F

Fang sculpture [esculturas de los fangs] *s.* cajas talladas que contienen las calaveras y los huesos de los antepasados muertos, creadas por los fangs, que vivieron en Gabón, la región sur de Camerún y Guinea Ecuatorial. (p. 451)

fault [falla] *s.* una fractura en la corteza terrestre. (p. 39)

folk art [arte folclórico] *s.* artículos hechos a mano, como cerámica, objetos tallados en madera y trajes tradicionales, elaborados por habitantes de zonas rurales que llevan estilos de vida tradicionales, no por artistas profesionales. (p. 314)

federal republic [república federal] *s.* una nación cuyos poderes están divididos entre el gobierno federal o nacional y varios gobiernos estatales o locales. (p. 139)

feudalism [feudalismo] *s.* un sistema político imperante en Europa entre el *s.* IX y el *s.* XV, en el cual el rey permitía a los nobles el uso de sus tierras a cambio de servicios militares y la protección de la tierra. (p. 297)

fertility rate [índice de fertilidad] *s.* el número promedio de hijos que una mujer en edad fértil tendría durante su vida si tuviese hijos de acuerdo con el índice vigente para su país. (p. 78)

First Nations [Primeras Naciones] *s.* un grupo de indígenas del Canadá. (p. 159)

fjord [fiordo] *s.* una entrada larga, estrecha y profunda del mar en la tierra entre pendientes empinadas. (p. 273)

fossil water [agua fósil] *s.* agua bombeada desde acuíferos subterráneos. (p. 496)

free enterprise [libre empresa] *s.* sistema económico en el cual individuos privados son dueños de la mayor parte de los recursos, la tecnología y las empresas, y pueden explotarlos para obtener ganancias con poco control del gobierno. (p. 140)

frontier [frontera] *s.* la tierra libre y abierta en el Oeste Norteamericano que estaba disponible para colonización. (p. 137)

G

Ganges River [Río Ganges] *s.* río en el Sur de Asia, un importante recurso acuático que fluye más de 1.500 millas (2.415 km) desde su fuente en un glaciar del Himalaya hasta la Bahía de Bengala. (p. 560)

Gaza Strip [Franja de Gaza] *s.* territorio a lo largo del Mar Mediterráneo, justo al noreste de la Península del Sinaí; parte del territorio asignado a los palestinos y que fue ocupado por Israel en 1967. (p. 527)

Geographic Information System (GIS) [Sistema de Información Geográfica (GIS por sus siglas en inglés)] *s.* tecnología que usa información de mapas digitalizados para crear un banco de datos; diferentes "capas de datos" pueden combinarse para producir mapas especializados. El GIS permite a los geógrafos analizar diferentes aspectos de un lugar específico para resolver problemas. (p. 13)

geography [geografía] *s.* estudio de la distribución y la interacción de las características físicas y humanas de la Tierra. (p. 5)

glaciation [glaciación] *s.* cambios en los accidentes geográficos debidos al lento movimiento de los glaciares. (p. 44)

glacier [glaciar] *s.* una masa de hielo grande y duradera que se mueve debido al efecto de la gravedad. (p. 44)

global economy [economía global] *s.* la fusión de economías regionales por la cual las naciones se vuelven dependientes unas de otras para la producción de bienes y servicios. (p. 666)

global network (red mundial) *s.* grupo que se mantiene conectado alrededor del mundo. (p. 173)

global warming [calentamiento global] *s.* la acumulación de dióxido de carbono (anhídrido carbónico) en la atmósfera, lo que evita que el calor escape al espacio, aumentando las temperaturas y ocasionando cambios en las condiciones meteorológicas. (p. 246)

globe [globo] *s.* una representación tridimensional de la Tierra. (p. 10)

Gobi Desert [Desierto de Gobi] *s.* desierto ubicado en el norte de China y en el sudeste de Mongolia, zona importante para la localización de fósiles de dinosaurios. (p. 627)

Golan Heights [Altos del Golán] *s.* meseta montañosa que se eleva sobre el Río Jordán y el Mar de Galilea; un punto estratégico que ha sido sitio de conflictos en el Sudoeste asiático durante décadas. (p. 487)

Gorée Island [Isla de Gorée] *s.* isla en las costas de Senegal que sirvió como importante punto de partida de esclavos durante el tráfico de esclavos. (p. 442)

Great Barrier Reef [La Gran Barrera de Coral] *s.* una cadena de 1.250 millas (2.000 km) de más de 2.500 arrecifes e islas a lo largo de la costa noreste de Australia, que contiene unas 400 especies de coral. (p. 692)

Great Game [El Gran Juego] *s.* un conflicto entre el Imperio Británico y el Imperio Ruso por el control del Asia Central en el s. XIX. (p. 376)

Great Kanto Earthquake [El Gran Terremoto de Kanto] *s.* terremoto ocurrido en 1923 en Japón que causó la muerte de aproximadamente 140.000 personas y dejó la ciudad de Tokio en ruinas. (p. 662)

Great Lakes [Grandes Lagos] *s.* grupo de cinco lagos de agua dulce en la región central de América del Norte entre los Estados Unidos y Canadá; los lagos son el Hurón, el Ontario, el Michigan, el Erie y el Superior. (p. 121)

Great Plains [Grandes Llanuras] *s.* una amplia zona de praderas en la región central de América del Norte, carente de árboles en su mayor parte, que se eleva hasta 4.000 pies (1.200 metros) sobre el nivel del mar. (p. 119)

Great Zimbabwe [El Gran Zimbabwe]· *s.* un emplazamiento urbano en lo que es hoy Zimbabwe fundado por los shonas alrededor del año 1000; se convirtió en la capital de una próspera zona de comercio de oro. (p. 453)

greenhouse effect [efecto invernadero] *s.* la capa de gases emitidos por la quema de carbón y petróleo que atrapa la energía solar, elevando la temperatura de la Tierra. (p. 58)

Green Revolution [La Revolución Verde] *s.* programa agrícola lanzado por científicos en la década de 1960 para producir variedades de granos de mayor rendimiento y mejorar la producción de alimentos incorporando nuevas técnicas de labranza. (p. 569)

Gross Domestic Product (GDP) [Producto Interior Bruto (PIB)] *s.* el valor de sólo bienes y servicios producidos en un país durante un período determinado. (p. 95)

Gross National Product (GNP) [Producto Nacional Bruto (PNB)] *s.* el valor total de todos los bienes y servicios producidos por un país durante un período determinado. (p. 94)

ground water [agua subterránea] *s.* agua retenida debajo de la superficie terrestre, con frecuencia en y alrededor de los poros de las rocas. (p. 33)

guest worker [trabajador invitado] *s.* trabajadores poco calificados, a menudo inmigrantes del Sur y el Este de Asia, trasladados a los países productores de petróleo para ocupar puestos de trabajo que las personas nacidas en la región consideran cultural y económicamente inaceptables. (p. 525)

H

hemisphere [hemisferio] *s.* cada una de las dos mitades de la esfera terrestre. (p. 6)

high islands [Islas altas] *s.* islas del Pacífico creadas por volcanes. (p. 691)

Himalaya Mountains [Himalaya] *s.* cordillera del Sur de Asia que incluye el Monte Everest, el pico más alto del mundo. (p. 551)

Hinduism [Hinduismo] *s.* la religión dominante en la India. (p. 560)

Holocaust [Holocausto] *s.* programa de los nazis de asesinatos masivos de judíos europeos durante la II Guerra Mundial. (p. 298)

Huang He [Huang He] *s.* río del Norte de China, llamado también Río Amarillo, que nace en las Montañas Kunlun y se extiende unas 3.000 millas (4,800 km) hacia el Este, desembocando en el mar Amarillo. (p. 621)

human resources [recursos humanos] *s.* las aptitudes y los talentos de la gente que trabaja. (p. 531)

humus [humus] *s.* material orgánico en el suelo. (p. 45)

hurricane [huracán] *s.* una tormenta que se forma sobre las aguas cálidas de los océanos tropicales. (p. 51)

hydrologic cycle [ciclo hidrológico] *s.* la continua circulación de agua entre la atmósfera, los océanos y la Tierra. (p. 32)

hydrosphere [hidrosfera] *s.* las aguas que comprenden la superficie de la Tierra, incluyendo océanos, mares, ríos, lagos y el vapor en la atmósfera. (p. 28)

I

Ijsselmeer [Ijsselmeer] *s.* lago de agua dulce separado del Mar del Norte por un dique y bordeado por pólders. (p. 283)

illiteracy [analfabetismo] *s.* la incapacidad de leer o escribir. (p. 593)

Inca [Inca] *s.* miembro del pueblo quechua en América del Sur, que desarrolló una civilización en los Andes en los siglos XV y XVI. (p. 230)

Indochina [Indochina] *s.* colonia francesa compuesta por Camboya, Laos y Vietnam; obtuvo la independencia de Francia en 1954. (p. 707)

industrialization [industrialización] *s.* el desarrollo de la industria en un país o en una sociedad. (p. 730)

Indus Valley civilization [Civilización del Valle del Indo] *s.* la más grande de las primeras civilizaciones del mundo en lo que hoy es Pakistán; fue una civilización urbana altamente desarrollada, que duró desde el 2500 hasta cerca del 1500 antes de nuestra era. (p. 573)

infant mortality rate [índice de mortalidad infantil] *s.* el número de muertes de niños menores de un año, calculado por cada mil nacimientos vivos. (p. 79)

infrastructure [infraestructura] *s.* los sistemas básicos de apoyo necesarios para mantener una economía en desarrollo, que incluyen sistemas de suministro de energía, comunicaciones, transporte, aguas, servicios sanitarios y educación. (pp. 94, 177, 212)

innovation [innovación] *s.* tomar los elementos existentes en una sociedad para crear algo nuevo con el propósito de satisfacer una necesidad. (p. 72)

Institutional Revolutionary Party (PRI) [Partido Revolucionario Institucional (PRI)] *s.* partido político creado en México, en 1929, que ayudó a introducir la democracia y mantener la estabilidad política durante la mayor parte del siglo XX. (p. 218)

Islam [Islam] *s.* religión monoteísta basada en las enseñanzas del profeta Mahoma y la mayor influencia cultural y religiosa en el Norte de África. (pp. 439, 503)

J

Jakota Triangle [Triángulo de Jakota] *s.* zona de prosperidad en la década de 1980 y comienzos de la década de 1990, que comprende Japón, Corea del Sur y Taiwán. (p. 666)

Jordan River [Río Jordán] *s.* río que sirve como frontera natural entre Israel y Jordania, y fluye desde los montes de Líbano sin desembocar en el Mar Mediterráneo. (p. 489)

junta [junta] *s.* gobierno dirigido por generales después de un golpe militar. (p. 249)

K

Kashmir [Cachemira (Kashmir)] *s.* región del Norte de la India y Pakistán sobre la que se han librado varias guerras destructivas. (p. 574)

Khmer Empire [Imperio Khmer] *s.* poderoso imperio que duró aproximadamente del siglo IX al siglo XV, en lo que hoy es Camboya. (p. 706)

King Leopold II [Rey Leopoldo II] *s.* rey de Bélgica que abrió el interior del África al comercio europeo a lo largo del río Congo y para 1884 controlaba la zona conocida como el Estado Libre del Congo. (p. 449)

KLA (Kosovo Liberation Army) [ELK (Ejército de Liberación de Kosovo)] *s.* grupo que combatió contra los intentos de los serbios de controlar la región de Kosovo en la década de 1990. (p. 321)

Kunlun Mountains [Cordillera Kunlun *s.* cordillera ubicada en el Oeste de China que es la fuente de dos de los principales ríos de China, el Huang He (río Amarillo) y el Chang Jiang (Yangtzé) (p. 619)

Kurds [Kurdos] *s.* grupo étnico en el sudoeste de Asia, que ha ocupado la región de Kurdistán, ubicada en Turquía, Irac e Irán, por cerca de mil años, y que ha estado involucrado en enfrentamientos con estos tres países por recobrar tierras durante la mayor parte del siglo XX. (p. 516)

L

landfill [vertedero] *s.* método de eliminación de residuos sólidos por el cual los residuos son enterrados entre capas de tierra con el propósito de rellenar o recuperar terrenos bajos. (p. 631)

landform [accidente geográfico] *s.* una característica de la superficie terrestre formada naturalmente. (p. 33)

landlocked [sin litoral] *adj.* que no tiene salida al mar. (p. 84)

land reform [reforma agraria] *s.* proceso por el cual se dividen grandes latifundios con el propósito de lograr una distribución más equitativa de la tierra entre los agricultores. (pp. 250, 569)

Land Rights Act of 1976 [Ley de Derechos de Tierra de 1976] *s.* una ley especial promulgada en beneficio de los derechos de los aborígenes en Australia, dándoles el derecho de reclamar tierras en el Territorio Norte. (p. 728)

Landsat [Landsat] *s.* una serie de satélites que orbitan a más de 100 millas (160 km) sobre la Tierra. Cada satélite recoge información en una zona de 115 millas (185 km) de ancho. (p. 12)

latitude (lines) [latitudes (líneas)] *s.* un conjunto de líneas imaginarias que corren paralelas al ecuador, las cuales son usadas para localizar lugares al Norte y al Sur. El ecuador es denominado la línea de cero grados de latitud. (p. 6)

lava [lava] *s.* magma que ha llegado hasta la superficie terrestre. (p. 40)

lithosphere [litosfera] *s.* la capa de roca sólida de la superficie terrestre. (p. 28)

llanos [llanos] *s.* una extensa zona de praderas sin árboles de América del Sur, utilizada para pastoreo y labranza. (p. 202)

lock [esclusa] *s.* una sección de una vía acuática con puertas de entrada y salida donde se llenan o vacían de agua los espacios entre las mismas, a través de las cuales pasan los barcos. (p. 129)

loess [loess] *s.* sedimentos de limo o arcilla depositados por el viento que producen tierras muy fértiles. (p. 44)

longitude (lines) [longitud (líneas)] *s.* un conjunto de líneas imaginarias que circundan la Tierra por los polos, dividiéndola en las zonas Este y Oeste. El primer meridiano (meridiano de Greenwich) ha sido designado como la línea de cero grados para longitud. (p. 6)

Louisiana Purchase [La Compra de Louisiana] *s.* el territorio, incluyendo la región entre el río Mississippi y las Montañas Rocosas, que los Estados Unidos compró a Francia en 1803. (p. 136)

low islands [Islas bajas] *s.* islas del Pacífico formadas por arrecifes de coral. (p. 691)

M

***Mabo* Case** [el caso *Mabo*] *s.* en Australia, el proceso jurídico por el cual se declaró con lugar la reclamación de tierra del aborigen Eddie Mabo, por medio del cual el tribunal reconoció que los aborígenes eran dueños de tierras antes de la llegada de los británicos. (p. 728)

Mackenzie River [Río Mackenzie] *s.* el río más largo del Canadá, el cual es parte de un sistema fluvial que fluye a lo largo de los Territorios del Noroeste hasta el Océano Ártico. (p. 121)

magma [magma] *s.* material de roca fundida creada cuando roca sólida en el manto o corteza funde. (p. 28)

malaria [malaria] *s.* enfermedad infecciosa de los glóbulos rojos propagada por mosquitos, que se caracteriza por escalofríos, fiebre y sudor. (p. 466)

mandala [mandala] *s.* diseño geométrico usado en el budismo tibetano como símbolo del universo y que ayuda en la meditación. (p. 583)

mandala [mandala] *s.* un estado organizado como un anillo de poder alrededor de una corte central, que con frecuencia cambiaba de tamaño con el tiempo y que era usado en lugar de fronteras en los antiguos estados del sudeste asiático. (p. 705)

mantle [manto] *s.* una capa de roca de unas 1.800 millas (2.896 km) que esta entre la corteza y el centro de la Tierra. (p. 28)

Maori [Maori] *s.* los primeros pobladores de Nueva Zelanda, que emigraron de Polinesia hace más de 1.000 años. (p. 719)

Mao Zedong [Mao Zedong] *s.* líder de China comunista que derrotó a los Nacionalistas en 1949; falleció en 1976. (p. 636)

map projection [proyección cartográfica] *s.* una forma de trazar el mapa de la superficie de la Tierra que reduce la distorsión causada convirtiendo tres dimensiones en dos dimensiones. (p. 10)

map [mapa] *s.* representación gráfica bidimensional de partes selectas de la superficie de la Tierra. (p. 10)

maquiladora [maquiladora] *s.* fábrica en México que ensambla materiales importados para convertirlos en productos acabados de exportación. (p. 220)

market economy [economía de mercado] *s.* tipo de sistema económico en el cual la producción de bienes y servicios se determina por la demanda de los consumidores. Llamado también economía de demanda o capitalismo. (pp. 91, 313)

Massif Central [Massif Central] *s.* las tierras altas de Francia, que abarcan un sexto del territorio francés. (p. 275)

Mecca [Meca] *s.* la ciudad más sagrada del Islam, situada en Arabia Saudita, a la que la gente hace peregrinaciones para cumplir con deberes religiosos islámicos. (p. 503)

mechanical weathering [meteorización mecánica] *s.* proceso natural por el cual las rocas se descomponen en pedazos más pequeños. (p. 42)

megalopolis [megalópolis] *s.* una región en la cual varias ciudades grandes y las áreas circundantes se unen. (p. 146)

Melanesia [Melanesia] *s.* región en Oceanía que significa "islas negras." (p. 713)

Meseta [Meseta] *s.* la planicie central de España. (p. 275)

Mesopotamia [Mesopotamia] *s.* una región en el sudoeste asiático entre los ríos Tigris y Eufrates, donde se desarrollaron algunas de las civilizaciones más antiguas del mundo; parte del corazón cultural denominado la Media Luna de las tierras fértiles. (p. 516)

métis [métis] *s.* una persona con antepasados franco-canadienses e indígenas americanos. (p. 161)

metropolitan area [área metropolitana] *s.* área funcional que incluye una ciudad y los suburbios y exurbios que la rodean, económicamente ligados entre sí. (pp. 87, 148)

microcredit [microcrédito] *s.* un pequeño préstamo disponible a los empresarios de escasos recursos para ayudar a las empresas pequeñas a desarrollarse y elevar los niveles de vida. (p. 575)

Micronesia [Micronesia] *s.* una de las tres regiones de Oceanía, el nombre significa "islas pequeñas". (p. 713)

Midwest [El Medio-Oeste] *s.* la región que contiene los 12 estados de la zona Norte-Central de los Estados Unidos. (p. 147)

migration [migración] *s.* el desplazamiento de gente dentro de un mismo país o región. (p. 135)

Mississippi River [Río Mississippi] *s.* un importante río que fluye de norte a sur por casi todo el largo de los Estados Unidos, desde Minnesota hasta el Golfo de México y forma parte del sistema fluvial más largo del continente. (p. 121)

mistral [mistral] *s.* viento frío y seco del norte. (p. 279)

Mobutu Sese Seko [Mobutu Sese Seko] *s.* líder de Zaire, la actual República Democrática del Congo, desde su independencia en la década de 1960 hasta 1997. Puso los negocios del país bajo el control nacional, se benefició de la reorganización y utilizó el ejército para conservar el poder. (p. 450)

monarchy [monarquía] *s.* tipo de gobierno en el cual una familia gobernante dirigida por un rey o una reina, tiene el poder y puede o no compartirlo con organismos ciudadanos. (p. 83)

monsoon [monzón] *s.* viento estacional, especialmente en el Asia meridional. (p. 558)

moraine [morrena] *s.* una cadena o colina de rocas transportada y finalmente depositada por un glaciar. (p. 44)

mortality rate [índice de mortalidad] *s.* el número de muertes por cada mil. (p. 79)

mosque [mezquita] *s.* un lugar de culto islámico, donde los mahometanos rezan con el rostro orientado hacia la ciudad sagrada de la Meca. (p. 504)

Mount Kilimanjaro [Monte Kilimanjaro] *s.* un volcán en Tanzania en el Africa, es el pico más alto del Africa. (p. 417)

Mughal Empire [Imperio Mughal] *s.* el imperio musulmán establecido a comienzos del siglo XVI y que se extendió por gran parte de la India, importando nuevas costumbres que algunas veces entraban en conflicto con las de los hindúes nativos. (p. 568)

Muhammad [Mahoma] *s.* fundador y profeta del Islam, que vivió parte de su vida en la ciudad de la Meca. (p. 503)

multinational [multinacional] *s.* una compañía que realiza operaciones comerciales en todo el mundo. (p. 142)

Mutapa Empire [Imperio de Monomotapa] *s.* un estado fundado en el siglo XV por un hombre llamado Mutota y que se extendió por todo lo que hoy es Zimbabwe excepto su parte oriental. (p. 453)

N

Nagorno-Karabakh [Nagorno-Karabakh] *s.* la zona montañosa de Azerbaiján, por la cual combatieron Armenia y Azerbaiján. (p. 386)

nation [nación] *s.* un grupo de personas con una cultura común que viven en un territorio y tienen un fuerte sentimiento de unidad. (p. 83)

nationalism [nacionalismo] *s.* la creencia de que la gente tiene que ser leal con su nación y con las demás personas con la que comparte la tierra, la cultura y la historia. (p. 297)

nation–state [nación-estado] *s.* nombre de un territorio cuando una nación y un estado ocupan el mismo territorio. (p. 83)

natural resource [recurso natural] *s.* un material sobre o dentro de la Tierra, como un árbol, un pez o el carbón, que tiene valor económico. (p. 93)

needleleaf [acicular] *adj.* característica de las hojas de ciertos árboles como el pino, el abeto y el cedro, que se encuentran en las regiones del norte de América del Norte. (p. 66)

Nelson Mandela [Nelson Mandela] *s.* uno de los líderes del Congreso Nacional Africano que dirigió la lucha contra el apartheid y fue elegido presidente en 1994, en las primeras elecciones multirraciales de Sudáfrica. (p. 454)

New England [Nueva Inglaterra] *s.* los seis estados del norte en la región noreste de los Estados Unidos: Maine, Vermont, New Hampshire, Massachusetts, Rhode Island y Connecticut. (p. 145)

Niger delta [Delta del Níger] *s.* delta del río Níger y zona de Nigeria rica en depósitos de petróleo. (p. 424)

Nile River [Río Nilo] *s.* el río más largo del mundo, que recorre más de 4.000 millas (6.436 km) a través de la cuenca del Sudán, hasta Uganda, el Sudán y Egipto. (p. 416)

nomad [nómada] *s.* persona que no tiene residencia permanente y se traslada según las estaciones de un lugar a otro en busca de alimentos, agua y tierra para pastoreo. (p. 127, 378)

nonviolent resistance [resistencia pacífica] *s.* un movimiento que usa todos los medios de protesta excepto la violencia. (p. 568)

Nordic countries [países nórdicos] *s.* países del norte de Europa, entre ellos Dinamarca, Finlandia, Islandia, Noruega y Suecia. (p. 302)

NAFTA (North American Free Trade Agreement) [NAFTA (Tratado de Libre Comercio de América del Norte)] *s.* un acuerdo comercial importante que creó una amplia zona de cooperación sobre asuntos comerciales y económicos en América del Norte. (p. 220)

North Atlantic Drift [Corriente del Atlántico Norte] *s.* una corriente de agua cálida proveniente de los Trópicos. (p. 278)

Nunavut [Nunavut] *s.* uno de los territorios del Canadá, donde viven muchos de los esquimales del Canadá; fue forjado de la mitad este de los Territorios Noroestes en 1999. (p. 169)

O

oasis [oasis] *s.* un lugar donde agua de un acuífero ha llegado hasta la superficie; permite el desarrollo de vegetación y fauna. (pp. 421, 492)

Oceania [Oceanía] *s.* grupo de islas del Pacífico, que incluye Melanesia, Micronesia y Polinesia. (p. 690)

Olduvai Gorge [Garganta Olduvai] *s.* un lugar de capas fosilíferas en el norte de Tanzania, que contiene el historial más continuo que se conoce de vida humana en los últimos 2 millones de años, incluyendo fósiles de 65 homínidos. (p. 431)

oligarchy [oligarquía] *s.* un gobierno dirigido por unas cuantas personas o un pequeño grupo. (p. 249)

"one-commodity" country [país de "un solo producto"] *s.* país que depende de un producto de exportación principal para muchos de sus ingresos. (p. 462)

Ontario [Ontario] *s.* una de las Provincias más importantes del Canadá. (p. 167)

OPEC [OPEP] *s.* Organización de Países Exportadores de Petróleo, grupo establecido en 1960 por algunos países productores de petróleo para coordinar políticas sobre venta de productos de petróleo. (p. 505)

Orinoco River [Río Orinoco] *s.* río que corre principalmente por Venezuela y forma parte del sistema fluvial más hacia el norte de América del Sur. (p. 202)

outback ["outback"] *s.* zona seca y despoblada en el interior de Australia. (p. 697)

outrigger canoe [canoa con balancines] *s.* una embarcación pequeña usada en las lagunas de islas en las que se establecieron isleños del Pacífico. (p. 699)

ozone [ozono] *s.* una substancia química que se produce cuando combustibles fósiles en combustión reaccionan con la luz del sol; una forma de oxígeno. (p. 325)

P

Pacific Rim [Cuenca del Pacífico] *s.* una región económica y social que incluye los países que rodean el Océano Pacífico, la cual se extiende en el sentido de las manecillas del reloj desde Nueva Zelanda en la región occidental del Pacífico hasta Chile en la región oriental del Pacífico e incluye la costa oeste de los Estados Unidos. (p. 645)

pakehas [pakehas] *s.* término maorí para designar a las personas blancas, a los neozelandeses de ascendencia europea. (p. 722)

Palestine Liberation Organization (PLO) [Organización para la Liberación de Palestina (OLP)] *s.* grupo formado en la década de 1960 para recuperar las tierras árabes en Israel para los árabes palestinos. (p. 513)

Palestinians [Palestinos] *s.* grupo de árabes desplazados que vivían o viven todavía en la zona llamada anteriormente Palestina y ahora denominada Israel. (p. 527)

pampas [pampas] *s.* amplia zona de praderas y tierras fértiles en la región sur-central de América del Sur. (p. 202)

Panama Canal [Canal de Panamá] *s.* canal para embarcaciones a través de Panamá que conecta el Mar Caribe con el océano Pacífico. (p. 226)

pandemic [pandemia] *s.* una enfermedad que afecta a un gran número de habitantes de una amplia zona geográfica. (p. 435)

Paraná River [Río Paraná] *s.* río en la región central de América del Sur y uno de sus tres sistemas fluviales más importantes, que nace en las tierras altas del Sur del Brasil y fluye unas 3.000 millas (4.827 km) hacia el sur y el oeste. (p. 203)

parliament [parlamento] *s.* cuerpo legislativo representativo cuyos miembros son elegidos o designados y cuyas funciones legislativas y ejecutivas están combinadas. (pp. 158, 303)

parliamentary government [gobierno parlamentario] *s.* sistema en el cual las funciones legislativas y ejecutivas están combinadas en una legislatura llamada parlamento. (p. 158)

particulate [macropartícula] *s.* partícula muy pequeña de materia líquida o sólida. (p. 324)

partition [partición] *s.* separación; división en dos o más unidades territoriales con estatus político separado. (p. 574)

pastoral lease [arrendamiento pastoral] *s.* en Australia, gran extensión de terreno que todavía es propiedad del gobierno; los rancheros arriendan la tierra del gobierno. (p. 729)

PCB [PCB (policlorobifenilo)] *s.* un compuesto industrial que se acumula en el tejido animal y puede ocasionar efectos perjudiciales y defectos congénitos; el PCB fue prohibido en los Estados Unidos en 1977. (p. 631)

peat [turba] *s.* materia vegetal parcialmente descompuesta que se encuentra en las turberas. (p. 277)

penal colony [colonia penal] *s.* lugar donde son enviados los prisioneros. (p. 718)

per capita income [ingreso per cápita] *s.* la cantidad de dinero promedio que gana una persona en una unidad política. (p. 94)

permafrost [permafrost (pergelisol)] *s.* terreno permanentemente congelado. (pp. 63, 123)

polder [pólder] *s.* terreno protegido contra el mar u otra masa de agua mediante diques o drenaje. (p. 282)

Polynesia [Polinesia] *s.* una de las tres regiones de Oceanía, cuyo nombre significa, "muchas islas". (p. 713)

population density [densidad poblacional] *s.* el número promedio de habitantes de una zona mensurable, el cual se obtiene dividiendo el número de habitantes en la zona por la cantidad de tierra que ocupan. (p. 81)

population pyramid [pirámide poblacional] *s.* un dispositivo gráfico que muestra la distribución de una población por sexo y edad. (p. 79)

postindustrial economy [economía postindustrial] *s.* fase económica en la cual la manufactura no desempeña un papel dominante. (p. 142)

Prairie Provinces [Las Provincias de las Praderas] *s.* en Canadá, las provincias que se encuentran al oeste de Ontario y Quebec: Manitoba, Saskatchewan y Alberta. (p. 168)

precipitation [precipitación] *s.* gotas de agua que caen en forma de lluvia, aguanieve, nieve o granizo. (p. 50)

prevailing westerlies [vientos del oeste predominantes] *s.* vientos que soplan de oeste a este. (p. 124)

prime meridian [primer meridiano] *s.* la línea imaginaria a cero meridiano usada para medir longitud de este a oeste, y que divide la Tierra en dos mitades, este y oeste; llamado meridiano de Greenwich porque pasa por Greenwich, Inglaterra. (p. 6)

prime minister [primer ministro] *s.* la cabeza del gobierno; el líder del partido de la mayoría en el parlamento. (p. 158)

privatization [privatización] *s.* la venta de empresas propiedad del Estado a ciudadanos privados. (p. 388)

province [provincia] *s.* una unidad política. (p. 156)

pull factor [factor de atracción] *s.* un factor que atrae o arrastra a personas a otro lugar. (pp. 81, 211)

push factor [factor de empuje] *s.* un factor que hace que la gente abandone sus hogares y emigre a otra región. (pp. 81, 211, 730)

Pyongyang [Pyongyang] *s.* la ciudad más grande de Corea del Norte, con más de 2.500 millones de habitantes. (p. 650)

Q

Qin Ling Mountains [Montañas de Qin Ling] *s.* montañas de la región sudeste y este central de China; dividen la parte norte de China de la parte sur. (p. 619)

Quebec [Quebec] *s.* una de las provincias más importantes del Canadá. (p. 167)

Quechua [Quechua] *s.* idioma del Imperio Inca, hablado actualmente en las tierras de la zona andina. (p. 231)

R

rai [rai] *s.* tipo de música popular argelina compuesta en la década de 1920 por niños pobres de las zonas urbanas, con ritmos rápidos bailables; algunas veces se usó como forma de rebeldía para expresar el descontento político. (p. 440)

rain forest [selva tropical] *s.* una región selvática ubicada en la Zona Tropical con una gran concentración de diferentes especies de árboles de hojas anchas. (pp. 66, 207)

rain shadow [sombra de lluvia] *s.* la tierra del lado de sotavento de colinas o montañas que recibe muy poca lluvia del aire seco descendiente. (p. 51)

raj [raj] *s.* el período de gobierno británico en la India que duró cerca de 200 años, de 1857 a 1947. (p. 568)

Ramadan [Ramadán] *s.* práctica islámica de ayunar un mes desde que sale el sol hasta que se pone. (p. 576)

rate of natural increase [tasa de aumento natural] *s.* llamada también tasa de crecimiento demográfico; la tasa de crecimiento poblacional, que se encuentra restando la tasa de mortalidad de la tasa de natalidad. (p. 79)

recession [recesión] *s.* un período prolongado de descenso en la actividad comercial general. (p. 667)

Red Army [Ejército Rojo] *s.* nombre del ejército de la Unión Soviética. (p. 371)

refinery [refinería] *s.* lugar donde el petróleo crudo es convertido en productos útiles. (p. 497)

Reformation [Reforma] *s.* movimiento en Europa Occidental iniciado en 1517, cuando muchos cristianos se desligaron de la Iglesia Católica para fundar iglesias protestantes; esto produjo hostilidades mutuas y guerras religiosas que desgarraron a Europa. (p. 297)

reggae [reggae] *s.* un estilo de música creado en Jamaica en la década de 1960, que tiene sus raíces en la música africana, caribeña y americana, con frecuencia trata sobre problemas sociales y religión. (p. 227)

relative location [ubicación relativa] *s.* describe un lugar en relación con otros lugares que lo rodean. (p. 6)

relief [relieve] *s.* la diferencia en elevación de una forma fisiográfica, desde el punto más bajo hasta el punto más alto. (p. 36)

religion [religión] *s.* la creencia en un poder o poderes sobrenaturales que se consideran como los creadores y conservadores del universo, así como el propio sistema de creencias. (p. 75)

Renaissance [Renacimiento] *s.* época de renovado interés por la educación y las artes que duró del s. XIV al s. XVI; comenzó en los estados-ciudades italianos y se extendió hacia el norte por toda Europa. (p. 291)

representative democracy [democracia representativa] *s.* un gobierno en el cual el pueblo gobierna mediante sus representantes elegidos. (p. 139)

republic [república] *s.* gobierno en el cual los ciudadanos eligen a sus representantes para que gobiernen en su nombre. (p. 290)

reserve [reserva] *s.* terrenos públicos destinados por el gobierno para los pueblos indígenas. (p. 162)

Richter scale [escala de Richter] *s.* una forma de medir información registrada por los sismógrafos para determinar la fuerza relativa de un terremoto. (p. 40)

rift valley [Valle del Rift] *s.* un valle largo y delgado creado por la separación de las placas continentales, presente en África Oriental, el cual se prolonga por 4.000 millas (6.436 km) desde Jordania en el Sudoeste asiático hasta Mozambique en el Sur de África. (p. 416)

Ring of Fire [El Anillo de Fuego] *s.* la cadena de volcanes que bordea la cuenca del Pacífico. (pp. 41, 661)

Rocky Mountains [Las Montañas Rocosas] *s.* un importante sistema montañoso de los Estados Unidos y el Canadá que se extiende por 3.000 millas (4.827 km) desde Alaska hacia el Sur hasta Nuevo México. (p. 119)

Rub al Khali [Rub' Al Jali] *s.* conocido también como el Cuarto Vacío, uno de los desiertos arenosos más grandes del mundo, abarca cerca de 250.000 millas cuadradas (650 mil kilómetros cuadrados); ubicado en la Península Arábiga. (p. 491)

Russian Revolution [Revolución Rusa] *s.* la revuelta de 1917 por la cual el Partido Comunista Ruso dirigido por V. I. Lenin, tomó el control del gobierno de los zares. (p. 363)

runoff [escorrentía] *s.* agua de lluvia no absorbida por el suelo y que puede transportar pesticidas y fertilizantes de los campos a los ríos, poniendo en peligro la cadena alimentaria. (p. 353)

S

Sahara [Sahara] *s.* el desierto más grande del mundo, que se extiende 3.000 millas (4.827 km) por el continente africano, desde el Océano Atlántico hasta el Mar Rojo, y mide 1.200 millas (1.930 km) de norte a sur. (p. 420)

Sahel [Sahel] *s.* una banda estrecha de pradera seca, que se extiende de este a oeste en el borde sur del Sahara, usada para agricultura y pastoreo. (p. 424)

St. Lawrence Seaway [La Ruta Marítima del San Lorenzo] *s.* la ruta de barcos de aguas profundas más importante de América del Norte, la cual conecta los Grandes Lagos con el Océano Atlántico a través del Río San Lorenzo. (p. 129)

St. Petersburg [San Petersburgo] *s.* la vieja capital de Rusia, fundada por Pedro el Grande, que trasladó la capital allí desde Moscú, debido a que San Petersburgo tenía acceso directo por mar hacia Europa Occidental. (p. 362)

salt flat [salinas] *s.* terrenos planos formados por sales químicas que permanecen después de que los vientos evaporan la humedad del suelo. (p. 492)

samba [samba] *s.* danza brasileña con influencia africana. (p. 239)

samurai [samurai] *s.* soldado profesional japonés al servicio de los intereses de terratenientes y jefes de clanes. (p. 651)

satellite nation [país satélite] *s.* un país dominado por otro. (p. 312)

savanna [sabana] *s.* término para describir las llanuras herbáceas que carecen de árboles en su mayor parte, en la región de las praderas tropicales. (p. 66)

seawork [espigón] *s.* una estructura utilizada para controlar el impacto destructivo del mar en la vida humana. (p. 283)

sectionalism [faccionalismo] *s.* cuando la gente pone su lealtad a su región o sección por encima de la lealtad al país. (p. 136)

sediment [sedimento] *s.* pequeños trozos de roca producidos por la acción de los elementos. (p. 42)

seismograph [sismógrafo] *s.* un dispositivo para medir el tamaño de las ondas creadas por un terremoto. (p. 39)

Seoul [Seúl] *s.* la ciudad más grande de Corea del Sur, con una población de más de diez millones de habitantes. (p. 650)

Serengeti [Serengeti] *s.* zona de África Oriental, que tiene muchas de las mejores praderas del mundo y muchos animales de pastoreo. (p. 422)

service industry [industria de servicios] *s.* cualquier tipo de actividad económica que produce servicios en vez de productos. (p. 142)

Sherpa [Sherpa] *s.* una persona de ascendencia tibetiana en Nepal, que trabaja como guía tradicional en la región del Monte Everest. (p. 582)

Shi'ite [Shiita] *s.* una de las dos principales ramas del Islam, que incluye a la mayoría de los iraníes y parte de las poblaciones de Irak y Afganistán. (p. 516)

shogun [Shogun] *s.* el general del ejército del emperador con poderes de dictador militar, una posición creada por el emperador del Japón en 1192 después de una lucha entre dos clanes poderosos. (p. 651)

Siberia [Siberia] *s.* región del centro y la zona este de Rusia que se extiende desde los Montes Urales hasta el Océano Pacífico, conocida por sus recursos minerales y por ser un lugar de exilio político. (p. 349)

Siddhartha Gautama [Siddhartha Gautama] *s.* fundador del budismo y conocido como Buda, nacido en el Sur de Nepal en el siglo sexto antes de nuestra era. (p. 582)

Silicon Glen [Silicon Glen] *s.* sección de Escocia entre Glasgow y Edimburgo, así denominada por su alta concentración de compañías de alta tecnología. (p. 305)

Silk Road [La Ruta de la Seda] s. la ruta de 4.000 millas (6.436 km) entre China y el Mar Mediterráneo, así llamada por la costosa seda adquirida en China. (p. 375)

silt [limo] s. material sedimentario suelto que contiene partículas de roca muy pequeñas, formado por depósitos de ríos y muy fértil. (p. 426)

Sinhalese [cingalés] s. pueblo indo-ario que cruzó el estrecho que separa la India y Sri Lanka en el siglo sexto antes de nuestra era y creó una civilización avanzada, adoptando el budismo. (p. 584)

sirocco [siroco] s. viento cálido y constante del Sur que sopla desde África del Norte a través del Mar Mediterráneo hasta el Sur de Europa, usualmente en la primavera. (p. 279)

slash-and-burn [cortar y quemar] s. método para despejar los campos para plantar, que consiste en cortar y quemar árboles, arbustos y hierbas. (p. 210)

smart growth [crecimiento inteligente] s. el uso eficiente y la conservación de la tierra y otros recursos. (p. 178)

smog [smog] s. una niebla marrón que se produce cuando los gases liberados por combustibles fósiles en combustión reaccionan con la luz solar. (p. 324)

society [sociedad] s. un grupo que comparte una región geográfica, un idioma común y un sentido de identidad y cultura. (p. 71)

soil [suelo] s. la mezcla suelta de roca meteorizada, material orgánico, aire y agua que permiten el crecimiento de las plantas. (p. 45)

solar system [sistema solar] s. se compone del sol y nueve planetas conocidos, así como otros cuerpos celestes que gravitan alrededor del sol. (p. 27)

solstice [solsticio] s. cualquiera de dos épocas en el año cuando los rayos solares brillan directamente arriba al mediodía en los puntos más alejados al norte o al sur, y que marcan el comienzo del verano o el invierno; en el Hemisferio Norte, el solsticio de verano es el día más largo y el solsticio de invierno, el más corto. (p. 49)

South, the [sur, el] s. una región que cubre aproximadamente un cuarto de la superficie terrestre de los Estado Unidos y contiene más de un tercio de su población. (p. 148)

South Slav [eslavo del sur] s. una persona que emigró de Polonia y Rusia y se estableció en la Península Balcánica alrededor del año 500. (p. 319)

Spanish conquest [conquista española] s. la conquista de los pueblos indígenas americanos por los españoles. (p. 217)

sphere of influence [esfera de influencia] s. un método de dividir el control extranjero en China, después de que el país fuera obligado a firmar una serie de tratados otorgando privilegios especiales a los europeos. China fue dividida para el control por Gran Bretaña, Francia, Alemania y Rusia, entre otras potencias. (p. 636)

state [estado] s. término político para describir una unidad independiente que ocupa un territorio específico y tiene pleno control de sus asuntos internos y externos. (p. 83)

stateless nation [nación sin estado] s. un pueblo que no tiene un territorio que pueda ocupar legalmente, como los palestinos, los kurdos y los vascos. (p. 526)

stateless society [sociedad sin estado] s. una sociedad en la cual la gente usa linajes o familias cuyos miembros descienden de un antepasado común para gobernarse. (p. 443)

steppe [estepa] s. término usado para la región de praderas templadas en el Hemisferio Norte. (p. 66)

Stolen Generation [La Generación Robada] s. en Australia, término que utilizan los aborígenes actualmente para denominar a los 100.000 niños de raza mixta que fueron tomados por el gobierno y entregados a familias blancas para promover la asimilación. (p. 728)

storm surge [olas ciclónicas] s. altos niveles de agua producidos por un ciclón que inunda zonas de bajo nivel. (p. 562)

strategic commodity [recurso estratégico] s. un recurso tan importante que las naciones están dispuestas a ir a la guerra para asegurar el suministro continuo del mismo. (p. 529)

subcontinent [subcontinente] s. una masa de tierra similar a un continente, aunque de menor extensión, como Asia del Sur, denominada el subcontinente Indio. (p. 551)

subsistence activity [actividad de subsistencia] s. una actividad en la cual una familia produce únicamente los alimentos, la ropa y la vivienda que necesita. (p. 714)

suburb [suburbio] s. una unidad o comunidad política que linda con la ciudad central o con otros suburbios que lindan con la ciudad. (pp. 87, 138)

sultan [sultán] s. el gobernante de un país musulmán. (p. 585)

summer monsoon [monzón húmedo (verano)] s. la estación cuando los vientos soplan desde el sudoeste a través del Océano Índico hacia Asia del Sur, desde junio hasta septiembre, cuando los vientos producen fuertes tormentas y graves inundaciones. (p. 597)

Sunni [Suni] s. una de las dos principales ramas del Islam, la cual abarca cerca del 83 por ciento de todos los musulmanes, incluyendo los que viven en Turquía, Irak y Afganistán. (p. 516)

supra [supra] s. término georgiano (ruso) para designar una cena con muchos platos, brindis y discursos cortos. (p. 374)

sustainable community [comunidad sostenible] s. una comunidad cuyos residentes pueden vivir y trabajar en armonía con el medio ambiente. (p. 178)

sweatshop [fábrica explotadora] s. un lugar de trabajo donde se trabajan largas horas por salario bajo y en malas condiciones para enriquecer a los fabricantes. (p. 667)

T

taiga [taiga] s. una faja casi continua de bosques coníferos de hojas perennes, a través del Hemisferio Norte en América del Norte y Eurasia. (p. 351)

Taklimakan Desert [Takla-Makan] s. desierto ubicado en la región occidental de China entre las montañas de Tian Shan y Kunlún. (p. 627)

Taliban [Talibán] s. un grupo musulmán estricto en Afganistán que ha impuesto reglas muy rígidas en la sociedad, incluyendo estilos de vestuario para hombres y mujeres, restricciones en la apariencia de las mujeres en lugares públicos y reglamentos para la televisión, la música y los videos. (p. 517)

Tamil [Tamil] s. hindú dravídico que llegó a Sri Lanka en el s. IV y se estableció en el norte, mientras los sinhaleses se trasladaron más al sur. (p. 584)

Taoism [Taoísmo] s. filosofía basada en el libro Tao Te Ching y las enseñanzas de Lao-Tsé, que vivió en China en el siglo VI antes de nuestra era, quien creía en conservar y restaurar la armonía dentro del individuo, con la naturaleza y con el universo, con poca intervención del gobierno. (p. 638)

taro [taro] s. planta tropical de Asia con raíz a base de féculas, la cual se puede comer como un vegetal hervido o preparada como pan, budín o una pasta llamada "poi". (p. 715)

tectonic plate [placa tectónica] s. una enorme plataforma móvil que forma la corteza de la Tierra. (p. 37)

Tenochtitlan [Tenochtitlán] s. la antigua capital de los aztecas, donde se encuentra la Ciudad de México en la actualidad. (p. 217)

terpen [terpén] s. plataformas altas de tierra de barro usadas en trabajos de mar. (p. 283)

terraced farming [cultivo en andenes] s. una técnica antigua para cultivar la tierra en laderas o pendientes de montañas, utilizando campos horizontales a manera de peldaños, cortados en las pendientes. (p. 211)

terrorism (terrorismo) s. uso ilegal o amenazante de la fuerza, o violencia, contra individuos o propiedades, con el propÚsito de intimidar o causar temor con fines polÌticos o sociales. (p. 173)

theocratic [teocrático] adj. una forma de gobierno en la cual líderes religiosos controlan el gobierno con leyes religiosas y consultando con eruditos religiosos. (p. 504)

Three Gorges Dam [Presa de las Tres Gargantas] s. una presa que se comenzó a construir a finales del siglo. XX en Chang Jiang, China, para ayudar a controlar las inundaciones, generar energía y permitir que los barcos naveguen más hacia el interior de China. (p. 628)

Three Kingdoms [Los Tres Reinos] *s.* los reinos formados en la península de Corea por el año 300 de nuestra era: Koguryo en el norte, Paikche en el sudoeste y Silia en el sudeste. (p. 647)

Tigris River [Río Tigris] *s.* uno de los ríos más importantes del Sudoeste Asiático; sirvió de base a varias civilizaciones antiguas en el valle del río y fluye por partes de Turquía, Siria e Irak. (p. 489)

tornado [tornado] *s.* una poderosa columna de aire en espiral en forma de túnel. (p. 51)

topographic map [mapa topográfico] *s.* un mapa para referencia general; representación de características terrestres, naturales y hechas por el hombre. (p. 11)

topography [topografía] *s.* las características combinadas de formas fisiográficas y su distribución en una región. (p. 36)

Transcaucasia [Transcaucasia] *s.* una región compuesta por las repúblicas de Armenia, Azerbaiján y Georgia; situada entre el Cáucaso y las fronteras de Turquía e Irán. (p. 346)

Trans-Siberian Railroad [Ferrocarril Transiberiano] *s.* un ferrocarril que uniría Moscú con el Puerto de Vladivostok en el Pacífico; construido entre 1891 y 1903. (p. 355)

Treaty of Tordesillas [Tratado de Tordesillas] *s.* un tratado entre España y Portugal firmado en 1494, por el cual Portugal obtuvo el control de la tierra que hoy constituye el Brasil. (p. 236)

Treaty of Waitangi [Tratado de Waitangi] *s.* tratado firmado por los británicos y los maorís en 1840, por el cual Gran Bretaña obtuvo el control de Nueva Zelanda. (p. 719)

tsunami [tsunami] *s.* una ola oceánica gigantesca, producida por un terremoto o erupción volcánica subacuático, con gran poder de destrucción. (pp. 40, 662)

tuberculosis [tuberculosis] *s.* una infección respiratoria propagada a través del contacto humano, que con frecuencia acompaña al SIDA. (p. 466)

tundra [tundra] *s.* las tierras planas sin árboles que forman un aro alrededor del Océano Ártico; la región climática del Océano Ártico. (p. 63)

typhoon [tifón] *s.* una tormenta tropical, como un huracán, que se da en la región occidental del Pacífico. (pp. 51, 625)

U

USSR [URSS] *s.* la Unión de Repúblicas Socialistas Soviéticas o Unión Soviética, formada en 1922 por los comunistas y disuelta oficialmente en 1991. (p. 363)

UNICEF (United Nations Children's Fund) [UNICEF (Fondo de las Naciones Unidas para la Infancia)] *s.* organización internacional de vigilancia y ayuda para los niños. (p. 665)

United Provinces of Central America [Provincias Unidas de Centroamérica] *s.* nombre de Centroamérica después de que la región declaró su independencia de México en 1823. (p. 223)

upland [tierras altas] *s.* una colina o una montaña muy baja que también puede contener mesas y planicies altas. (p. 275)

Ural Mountains [Montes Urales] *s.* la cordillera que separa las planicies del norte de Europa y Siberia Occidental y utilizada como la línea divisoria entre Europa y Asia. (p. 346)

urban geography [geografía urbana] *s.* el estudio de cómo las personas utilizan el espacio en las ciudades. (p. 87)

urbanization [urbanización] *s.* el dramático aumento en el número de ciudades y los cambios en estilos de vida que resultan del mismo. (p. 88)

urban sprawl [expansión urbana descontrolada] *s.* desarrollo mal planificado que extiende la población de una ciudad por una zona geográfica cada vez más amplia. (p. 176)

V

Vietnam War [Guerra de Vietnam] *s.* (1954-1975) el conflicto militar producido por la intervención de Estados Unidos en Vietnam del Sur para evitar su apoderamiento por los comunistas de Vietnam del Norte. (p. 707)

volcano [volcán] *s.* un evento natural, formado cuando magma, gases y agua de la parte inferior de la corteza o capa se acumulan en cámaras subterráneas y posteriormente hacen erupción y surgen por grietas en la superficie terrestre. (p. 40)

voyaging canoe [canoas viajeras] *s.* una embarcación grande construida por habitantes de las islas del Pacífico para navegar por el océano. (p. 699)

W

wadi [wadi] *s.* lecho de un río que permanece seco excepto durante la estación lluviosa. (p. 488)

water table [nivel hidrostático] *s.* el nivel en el cual las rocas se saturan. (p. 33)

weather [clima] *s.* las condiciones atmosféricas en un lugar y tiempo específicos. (p. 50)

weathering [meteorización] *s.* proceso químico y físico que cambia las características de las rocas en o cerca de la superficie terrestre, lo cual ocurre lentamente durante el lapso de muchos años. (p. 42)

West [Oeste] *s.* región de América del Norte compuesta por 13 estados, que se extiende desde las Grandes Llanuras hasta el Océano Pacífico e incluye Alaska por el norte y Hawaii en el Pacífico. (p. 148)

West Bank [Cisjordania] *s.* en Israel, una franja de tierra en el lado oeste del Río Jordán, originalmente controlada por Jordania, que forma parte de la tierra destinada para los árabes palestinos. (p. 527)

Western Wall [El Muro de los Lamentos] *s.* para los judíos, el sitio más sagrado de Jerusalén; lo único que queda del Segundo Templo, construido en 538 antes de nuestra era y destruido en el 70 de nuestra era por los romanos. (p. 510)

Wik Case [el caso *Wik*] *s.* en Australia, los tribunales dispusieron en este caso que los aborígenes pueden reclamar tierras retenidas bajo arrendamiento pastoral. (p. 729)

winter monsoon [monzón seco (invierno)] *s.* la estación cuando los vientos secos soplan desde el noreste a través de los montes Himalaya hacia el mar desde octubre hasta febrero, algunas veces causando sequías. (p. 597)

X

Xi Jiang [Xi Jiang] *s.* llamado también el Río del Oeste; río que fluye hacia el este a través del sudeste de China y se une con el Río Perla (Zhu Jiang) para desembocar en el Mar del Sur de la China, formando un estuario entre Hong Kong y Macao. (p. 621)

Y

yurt [yurt] *s.* una tienda de nómadas del Asia Central. (p. 379)

Z

Zionism [sionismo] *s.* movimiento iniciado en el siglo. XIX para crear y apoyar una patria judía en Palestina. (p. 51)

Zuider Zee [Zuiderzee] *s.* antiguo lago interior de los Países Bajos en el Mar del Norte. (p. 283)

The U.S. Geological Survey (USGS) is the primary source for latitudes and longitudes. USGS reports these figures for any geographic feature (or political division) as averages of all the values within that feature. These averages help to locate on a map such large or extended features as continents, seas, rivers, or mountain ranges. However, one must look at a map to learn the overall shape, size, and extent of any geographic feature.

Abkhazia (43°00′N/41°00′E) A republic in northwestern Georgia in Transcaucasia, 386, *m385*

Abu Dhabi (24°28′N/54°22′E) The capital of United Arab Emirates, 484

Abuja (9°05′N/7°32′E) The capital of Nigeria, 412

Accra (5°33′N/0°13′W) The capital of Ghana, 410

Addis Ababa (9°02′N/38°42′E) The capital of Ethiopia, 433

Adriatic Sea (43°30′N/14°27′E) An arm of the Mediterranean Sea, bounded by Italy, Croatia, Yugoslavia, and Albania, 281

Afghanistan (33°00′N/65°00′E) A country in the northeast region of Southwest Asia, 516

Africa (10°00′N/22°00′E) The second largest continent; bounded by the Mediterranean Sea, the Indian Ocean, the Red Sea, and the Atlantic Ocean, 28, *m29*

Ahmadabad (23°04′N/72°38′E) A city in western India, 570, *m569*

Al Jawlan (also called the Golan Heights) (33°00′N/35°45′E) A hilly plateau in Syria overlooking the Jordan River and the Sea of Galilee, 487

Alabama (32°45′N/86°45′W) A state in the southern United States, 108

Alaska (64°00′N/150°00′W) A U.S. state that is northwest of Canada, 148

Albania (41°00′N/20°00′E) A country in Eastern Europe, 308

Albany (42°40′N/73°48′W) The capital of New York, 110

Alberta (55°00′N/115°00′W) A Prairie Province of Canada, 168

Aleutian Islands (52°06′N/173°30′W) Rugged, treeless islands that extend in an arc off the coast of Alaska, 121

Algeria (28°00′N/3°00′E) A country in North Africa, 438

Algiers (36°46′N/3°03′E) The capital of Algeria, 408

Alps (46°25′N/10°00′E) A European mountain range that arcs across France, Italy, Germany, Switzerland, Austria, and into the Balkan Peninsula, 272, *m271*

Altai Mountains (48°00′N/90°00′E) A mountain system in Central Asia, 346

Amazon rain forest A large, tropical forest located in north-central South America, 208

Amazon River (0°10′S/49°00′W) The world's second longest river; flows from northern Peru across northern Brazil to the Atlantic Ocean, 203, *m203*

American Samoa (14°21′S/170°31′W) A U.S. territory in the Pacific made up of the eastern islands of the Samoan archipelago, 112

Amman (31°57′N/35°56′E) The capital of Jordan, 484

Amsterdam (52°21′N/4°55′E) The capital of the Netherlands, 268

Amu Darya (43°40′N/59°01′E) A river that flows from the Pamir Mountains across south Central Asia to the southern Aral Sea, 347

An-Nafud (28°30′N/40°30′E) A desert in the northern part of the Arabian Peninsula, 492

Anatolia (39°00′N/35°00′E) A peninsula in northwestern Southwest Asia occupied by Turkey, 487, *m488*

Andes (20°00′S/67°00′W) A mountain range that runs down the Pacific coast of South America, 201, *m203*

Andorra (42°30′N/1°30′E) A tiny country between France and Spain in the Pyrenees, 266

Andorra la Vella (42°33′N/1°26′E) The capital of Andorra, 266

Angola (12°30′S/18°30′E) A country in Southern Africa, 453, *m454*

Ankara (39°56′N/32°52′E) The capital of Turkey, 484

Annamese Cordillera (17°00′N/106°00′E) A mountain range in Southeast Asia, 689, *m689*

Annapolis (38°59′N/76°30′W) The capital of Maryland, 110

Antananarivo (18°55′S/47°31′E) The capital of Madagascar, 410

Antarctica (90°00′S) A continent located mostly south of the Antarctic Circle; bounded by the Atlantic, Pacific, and Indian oceans, 28, *m29*

Antigua and Barbuda (17°03′N/61°48′W) A country that consists of islands in the eastern Caribbean Sea, 196

Apennines (43°00′N/13°00′E) A European mountain range that runs down the center of the Italian Peninsula from east to west, 272

Apia (13°50′S/171°44′W) The capital of Samoa, 684

Appalachian Mountains (40°00′N/78°00′W) A North American mountain chain that runs north to south about 1,600 miles from Newfoundland to Alabama, *m118*, 119

Arabian Peninsula (25°00′N/45°00′E) A peninsula separated from the continent of Africa by the Red Sea on the southwest and separated from Iran by the Persian Gulf on the east, 487

Arabian Sea (20°00′N/65°00′E) The northwest area of the Indian Ocean; lies between the Arabian Peninsula and western India, 488

Aral Sea (45°00′N/60°00′E) An inland sea in Central Asia, 348

Ararat, Mount (39°40′N/44°24′E) A mountain in Turkey, 478

Arctic Ocean (66°40′N/167°55′W) The world's smallest ocean; surrounds the North Pole between North America and Eurasia, 32

Argentina (34°00′S/64°00′W) A country in southern South America, 230, *m234*

Arizona (34°30′N/111°30′W) A state in the western United States, 108

Arkansas (34°45′N/92°30′W) A state in the southern United States, 148

Armenia (40°00′N/45°00′E) A country in Transcaucasia, 370, *m370*

Ashgabat (37°57′N/58°23′E) The capital of Turkmenistan, 342

Asia The largest continent; bounded by the Pacific Ocean, Europe, the Arctic Ocean, and the Indian Ocean, 28, *m29*

Asmara (15°20′N/38°56′E) The capital of Eritrea, 408

Astana (51°11′N/71°26′E) The capital of Kazakhstan, 342

Asunción (25°16′S/57°40′W) The capital of Paraguay, 198

Aswan High Dam (23°57′N/32°52′E) A dam on the Nile River in southern Egypt, 426, *m427*

Atacama Desert (24°30′S/69°15′W) An arid region in northern Chile, 209

Athens (37°45′N/23°30′E) The capital of Greece, 266

Atlanta (33°45′N/84°23′W) The capital of Georgia, 148

Atlantic Coastal Plain (35°00′W/79°00′W) A flat plain that begins as narrow lowland in the northeastern United States and widens as it extends southward, along the Atlantic coast, into Florida, *m118, 119*

Atlantic Ocean (10°00′N/25°00′W) The world's second largest ocean; extends from the Arctic to Antarctica and from the eastern Americas to western Europe and Africa, 32

Atlantic Provinces An area of eastern Canada that includes Prince Edward Island, New Brunswick, Nova Scotia, and Newfoundland, 166

Atlas Mountains (32°00′N/2°00′W) A mountain range in North Africa, 423

Augusta (44°20′N/69°44′W) The capital of Maine, 110

Austin (30°16′N/97°45′W) The capital of Texas, 112

Australia (25°00′S/135°00′E) The smallest continent; southeast of Asia, bounded by the Pacific and Indian oceans, and occupied by the country of Australia 28, *m29*

Austria (47°20′N/13°20′E) A country in Western Europe, 294

Azerbaijan (40°30′N/47°30′E) A country in Transcaucasia, 370, *m370*

Baffin (68°30′N/70°00′W) A large island in northern Canada, 121

Baghdad (33°20′N/44°24′E) The capital of Iraq, 484

Bahamas (24°00′N/76°00′W) A country that consists of a group of islands in the Atlantic Ocean near southeastern Florida, 203

Bahrain (26°00′N/50°30′E) A country in the Arabian Peninsula of Southwest Asia, 503

Baikal, Lake (54°00′N/109°00′E) The deepest lake in the world; located in south-central Russia, 348

Bairiki (1°19′N/172°58′E) The capital of Kiribati, 684

Baku (40°22′N/49°54′E) The capital of Azerbaijan, 371

Balkan Mountains (43°15′N/25°00′E) A European mountain range that blocks the Balkan Peninsula from the rest of Europe, 272

Balkan Peninsula (44°00′N/23°00′E) A southeastern peninsula of Europe; bounded by the Adriatic and Aegean Seas and occupied by numerous countries, *m271, 272*

Baltic States An area between Russia and the Baltic Sea that consists of Latvia, Lithuania, and Estonia, 361

Baltic Sea (56°00′N/18°00′E) An arm of the Atlantic Ocean bounded by Finland, Sweden, Denmark, Germany, Poland, Russia, Lithuanian, Latvia, and Estonia, 271, *m271*

Bamako (12°39′N/8°00′W) The capital of Mali, 410

Bandar Seri Begawan The capital of Brunei, 684

Bandung (6°56′S/107°35′E) A city in Indonesia, 732

Bangkok (13°45′N/100°31′E) The capital of Thailand, 686

Bangladesh (24°00′N/90°00′E) A country in South Asia, 573

Bangui (4°22′N/18°35′E) The capital of Central African Republic, 408

Banjul (13°27′N/16°35′W) The capital of Gambia, 410

Barbados (13°10′N/59°32′W) An island country in the eastern Lesser Antilles in the Atlantic Ocean, 196

Basseterre (17°18′N/62°43′W) The capital of Saint Kitts and Nevis, 198

Baton Rouge (30°27′N/91°09′W) The capital of Louisiana, 108

Bay of Bengal (15°00′N/90°00′E) An arm of the Indian Ocean that lies between eastern India and Southeast Asia, 552, *m554*

Beijing (39°56′N/116°23′E) The capital of China, 637

Beirut (33°52′N/35°31′E) The capital of Lebanon, 484

Belarus (53°00′N/28°00′E) A country that is west of Russia, 361

Belgium (50°50′N/4°00′E) A country in Western Europe, 294

Belgrade (44°49′N/20°28′E) The capital of Yugoslavia, 268

Belize (17°15′N/88°45′W) A country in Central America, 223

Belmopan (17°15′N/88°46′W) The capital of Belize, 196

Benelux The Western European countries of Belgium, the Netherlands, and Luxembourg, 294

Benin (9°30′N/2°15′E) A country in West Africa, 442

Berlin (52°31′N/13°24′E) The capital of Germany, 266

Bern (46°55′N/7°28′E) The capital of Switzerland, 268

Bhutan (27°30′N/90°30′E) A country in South Asia, 580

Bikini (11°35′N/165°23′E) A coral island of the Marshall Islands, 700

Bishkek (42°54′N/74°36′E) The capital of Kyrgyzstan, 342

Bismarck (46°48′N/100°46′W) The capital of North Dakota, 110

Bissau (11°51′N/15°35′W) The capital of Guinea-Bissau, 410

Black Sea (43°00′N/35°00′E) A sea situated between northern Turkey and southwestern Russia, 488, *m488*

Blanc, Mont (45°55′N/6°55′E) A mountain on the border of France and Italy, 260

Blue Ridge Mountains (35°30′N/82°50′W) A North American mountain range located in the southern part of the Appalachian system, 119

Bogotá (4°36′N/74°05′W) The capital of Columbia, 211

Boise (43°38′N/116°11′W) The capital of Idaho, 108

Bolivia (17°00′S/65°00′W) A country in central South America, 230, *m234*

Bombay (also called Mumbai) (18°59′N/72°50′W) A city in western India, *m569, 570*

Bosnia and Herzegovina (44°15′N/17°50′E) A country in Eastern Europe, 308

Bosporus Strait (41°00′N/29°00′E) A narrow waterway in northwest Turkey that connects the Black Sea and the Sea of Marmara, 488

Boston (42°18′N/71°05′W) A seaport city and capital of Massachusetts, 137, *m145*

Botswana (22°00′S/24°00′E) A country in Southern Africa, 453, *m454*

Brahmaputra River (24°02′N/90°59′E) A river starting in China that flows east, then west and south through Bangladesh where it joins the Ganges River; together they form a huge delta before entering the Bay of Bengal, 553

Brasília (15°47′S/47°55′W) The capital of Brazil, 239

Bratislava (48°09′N/17°07′E) The capital of Slovakia, 268

Brazil (10°00′S/55°00′W) A country in central South America, 236

Brazilian Highlands (18°00′S/47°00′W) A mountainous area in southeastern Brazil, 202, *m203*

Brazzaville (4°16′S/15°17′E) The capital of Republic of Congo, 408

Bridgetown (13°06′N/59°37′W) The capital of Barbados, 196

British Columbia (55°00′N/125°00′W) The Pacific Province of western Canada, 169

Brunei (4°30′N/114°40′E) A Southeast Asian country on the island of Borneo, 705

Brussels (50°50′N/4°20′E) The capital of Belgium, 266

Bucharest (44°26'N/26°06'E) The capital of Romania, 268

Budapest (47°30'N/19°05'E) The capital of Hungary, 266

Buenos Aires (34°35'S/58°40'W) The capital of Argentina, 211

Bujumbura (3°23'S/29°22'E) The capital of Burundi, 408

Bulgaria (43°00'N/25°00'E) A country in Eastern Europe, 308

Burkina Faso (13°00'N/2°00'W) A country in West Africa, 442

Burundi (3°00'S/29°30'E) A country in East Africa, 431

Cairo (30°03'N/31°15'E) The capital of Egypt, 408

California (37°15'N/119°45'W) A state in the western United States, 149

Cambodia (13°00'N/105°00'E) A country in Southeast Asia, 705

Cameroon (6°00'N/12°00'E) A country in Central Africa, 448, *m450*

Cameroon, Mount (4°12'N/9°11'E) A mountain in Cameroon, 417

Canada (60°00'N/96°00'W) A country in northern North America that consists of ten provinces and three territories, 117

Canadian Shield (55°00'N/90°00'W) A rocky, flat region that encircles Hudson Bay, *m118,* 119

Canberra (35°17'S/149°13'E) The capital of Australia, 684

Cape Verde (16°00'N/24°00'W) A country formed by a group of islands in West Africa, 442

Caracas (10°30'N/66°55'W) The capital of Venezuela, 198

Caribbean Islands Three major groups of islands: the Bahamas (in the Atlantic Ocean near southeastern Florida) and the Greater Antilles and the Lesser Antilles (in the Caribbean Sea), 203

Caribbean Sea (15°00'N/75°00'W) A body of water bounded by South America, Central America, the Gulf of Mexico, and the Greater Antilles, 191

Carson City (39°10'N/119°43'W) The capital of Nevada, 110

Carthage (36°51'N/10°20'E) A city located in northeastern Tunisia; in ancient times, the center of the Carthaginian Empire, 438

Cascade Range (44°43'N/122°03'W) A North American mountain range that runs parallel to the Pacific coastline from California to British Columbia, Canada, 120

Caspian Sea (42°00'N/50°00'E) A lake that lies between southeast Europe and western Asia, 348

Castries (14°00'N/61°00'W) The capital of Saint Lucia, 198

Catskill Mountains (42°15'N/74°15'W) A North American mountain range located in the northern part of the Appalachian system, 119

Caucasus (42°00'N/45°00'E) A region that includes the Caucasus Mountains, which stretch between the Black and Caspian seas, 385, *m385*

Caucasus Mountains (42°30'N/45°00'E) A mountain range that stretches across the isthmus that separates the Black and Caspian seas, 346

Central Africa A region of Africa that includes Cameroon, Central African Republic, Democratic Republic of the Congo, Republic of the Congo, Equatorial Guinea, Gabon, and São Tomé & Príncipe, 448, *m450*

Central African Republic (7°00'N/21°00'E) A country in Central Africa, 448, *m450*

Central America A Latin American subregion bounded by Mexico, the Caribbean Sea, the Pacific Ocean, and South America, 223

Central Asia A region that includes Kazakhstan, Kyrgyzstan, Tajikistan, Turkmenistan, and Uzbekistan, 375

Central Siberian Plateau (66°00'N/106°00'E) A plateau in central Russia, 345

Chad (15°00'N/19°00'E) A country in West Africa, 442

Chad, Lake (13°20'N/14°00'E) A lake in western Chad; on the borders of Nigeria, Niger, and Chad, 425

Chang Jiang (also called Yangtze River) (31°47'N/121°08'E) The longest river in Asia; flows from Xizang (Tibet) across China to the East China Sea, *m620,* 621

Charleston (38°21'N/81°38'W) The capital of West Virginia, 112

Charlotte Amalie The capital of the U.S. Virgin Islands, 112

Charlottetown (46°14'N/63°08'W) The capital of Prince Edward Island, Canada, 114

Chechnya (43°18'N/45°42'E) A Russian republic in the Caucasus, 385, *m385*

Chennai (also called Madras) (13°05'N/80°17'E) A city in southern India, *m569,* 570

Chernobyl (51°16'N/30°14'E) A city in north-central Ukraine, 392

Cheyenne (41°08'N/104°49'W) The capital of Wyoming, 112

Chicago (41°50'N/87°41'W) Located in northeastern Illinois; the largest city in the Midwest, 137

Chile (30°00'S/71°00'W) A country that runs along the southern Pacific coast of South America, 230, *m234*

China (35°00'N/105°00'E) A country in East Asia, 635

Chisinau (47°00'N/28°51'E) The capital of Moldova, 342

Chittagong A city in Bangladesh, 573

Chittagong Hills (23°00'N/92°15'E) A hilly region in southeastern Bangladesh, 576

Chota Nagpur Plateau (23°00'N/85°00'E) A plateau in India that is northeast of the Deccan Plateau, 552

Cincinnati (39°09'N/84°31'W) A city in southwestern Ohio, 147

Cleveland (41°29'N/81°40'W) A city in northern Ohio, 137

Colombo (6°56'N/79°51'E) The capital of Sri Lanka, 585

Colorado (39°00'N/105°30'W) A state in the western United States, 108

Colorado River (31°54'N/114°57'W) A river that rises in the Rocky Mountains, flow through the southwestern United States, and empties into the Gulf of California in northwest Mexico, 149, *m149*

Colombia (4°00'N/72°00'W) A country in northern South America, 230, *m234*

Columbia (34°00'N/81°02'W) The capital of South Carolina, 112

Columbus (39°59'N/82°59'W) The capital of Ohio, 110

Comoros (12°10'S/44°15'E) A country formed by a group of islands in Southern Africa, 453, *m454*

Conakry (9°31'N/13°43'W) The capital of Guinea, 410

Concord (43°14'N/71°34'W) The capital of New Hampshire, 110

Congo River (6°04'S/12°24'E) A river in Central Africa that flows through the Democratic Republic of the Congo and empties into the Atlantic Ocean, 416

Congo, Democratic Republic of the (0°00'N/25°00'E) A country in Central Africa, 448, *m450*

Congo, Republic of the (1°00'S/15°00'E) A country in Central Africa, 408

Connecticut (41°40'N/72°40'W) A state in New England in the northeastern United States, 145

Continental Divide The line of highest points in the Rockies that marks the separation between rivers flowing eastward and westward, 120

Copenhagen (55°40'N/12°35'E) The capital of Denmark, 266

Core Provinces An area located in east central Canada that includes Quebec and Ontario, 167

Corsica (42°00′N/9°00′E) An French-owned island in the western Mediterranean Sea, 272

Costa Rica (10°00′N/84°00′W) A country in Central America, 223

Côte d'Ivoire (8°00′N/5°00′W) A country in West Africa, 442

Crete (35°15′N/24°45′E) A Greek-owned island in the eastern Mediterranean Sea, 272

Croatia (45°10′N/15°30′E) A country in Eastern Europe, 308

Cuba (21°30′N/80°00′W) An island country in the Caribbean Sea, 226

Cyprus (35°00′N/33°00′E) A Southwest Asian island country in the Mediterranean Sea, south of Turkey, 513

Czech Republic (49°45′N/15°00′E) A country in Eastern Europe, 308

Dagestan (43°00′N/47°00′E) A Russian republic in the Caucasus, 385, m385

Dakar (14°40′N/17°26′W) The capital of Senegal, 412

Dallas–Fort Worth A metropolitan area in east central Texas formed by the rapid growth of Dallas (32°47′N/96°48′W) and Ft. Worth (32°44′N/97°19′W), 148

Damascus (33°30′N/36°18′E) The capital of Syria, 484

Damavand, Mount (35°57′N/52°07′E) A mountain in Iran, 478

Danube River (45°20′N/29°40′E) A European river that flows from southwest Germany, across southeast Europe, and into the Black Sea, 273, m273

Dardenelles Strait A narrow waterway in northwest Turkey that joins the Sea of Marmara and the Aegean Sea, 488

Dasht-e Kavir Desert A salt flat desert in central Iran, 492

Dasht-e Lut Desert A salt flat desert in eastern Iran, 492

Dead Sea (31°30′N/35°30′E) A landlocked salt lake that lies between Israel and Jordan, 489

Deccan Plateau (14°00′N/77°00′E) A large plateau in central India, 552

Delaware (39°00′N/75°30′W) A state in the southern United States (sometimes included with the Middle Atlantic states), 108

Denali (also called Mount McKinley) (63°04′N/151°00′W) North America's highest mountain; located in Alaska, 120

Denmark (56°00′N/10°00′E) A Northern European country located on the Jutland Peninsula, 300

Denver (39°44′N/104°59′W) The capital of Colorado, 108

Des Moines (41°36′N/93°37′W) The capital of Iowa, 108

Detroit (42°20′N/83°03′W) A city in southeastern Michigan, 137

Dhaka (23°43′N/90°25′′E) The capital of Bangladesh, 548

District of Columbia (38°54′N/77°02′W) A federal district in the eastern United States; occupied by the city of Washington, 108

Djibouti (11°30′N/42°30′E) A country in East Africa, 463

Djibouti, the city of (11°36′N/43°09′E) The capital of Djibouti, 408

Dnieper River (46°30′N/32°18′E) A river that flows from west-central Russia through Belarus and Ukraine to the Black Sea, 361

Dodoma (6°10′S/35°45′E) The capital of Tanzania, 412

Doha (25°17′N/51°32′E) The capital of Qatar, 484

Dom (46°06′N/7°51′E) A mountain in Switzerland, 260

Dominica (15°30′N/61°20′W) An island country in the eastern Caribbean Sea, 196

Dominican Republic (19°00′N/70°40′W) A country that occupies the eastern two-thirds of the island of Hispaniola in the Caribbean Sea, 196

Dover (39°09′N/75°31′W) The capital of Delaware, 108

Dublin (53°20′N/6°15′W) The capital of Ireland, 266

Durham (36°00′N/78°54′W) A city in North Carolina, 178

Dushanbe (38°34′N/68°46′E) The capital of Tajikistan, 342

East Africa A region in Africa that includes Burundi, Djibouti, Eritrea, Ethiopia, Kenya, Rwanda, Seychelles, Somalia, Tanzania, and Uganda, 431

East Antarctica (80°00′S/80°00′E) A major region in Antarctica lying on the Indian Ocean side of the Transantarctic Mountains, 692

East Asia A region that includes China, Japan, Mongolia, Taiwan, North Korea, and South Korea, 619

Eastern Europe A region that includes Albania, Bosnia and Herzegovina, Bulgaria, Croatia, the Czech Republic, Hungary, Macedonia, Poland, Romania, Slovakia, and Yugoslavia, 308

Eastern Ghats (14°00′N/78°50′E) A mountain range that runs along the east coast of India, 552

Eastern Mediterranean Region A region that includes Lebanon, Syria, Jordan, and Israel, 510

Ecuador (2°00′S/77°30′W) A country in northwestern South America, 230, m234

Edinburgh (55°57′N/3°12′W) A city in Scotland, 303

Edmonton (53°33′N/113°30′W) The capital of Alberta, Canada, 114

Egypt (27°00′N/30°00′E) A country in North Africa, 438

El Salvador (13°50′N/88°55′W) A country in Central America, 223

Elbe River (53°50′N/9°00′E) A European river that runs north from the Czech Republic, across Germany, and into the North Sea, 260

Elburz Mountains (36°00′N/53°00′E) A mountain range in northern Iran, 488

Ellesmere (79°00′N/82°00′W) A large island in northern Canada, 121

Equatorial Guinea (2°00′N/10°00′E) A country in Central Africa, 448, m450

Erie Canal Opened in 1825; crosses upstate New York and is used as a water link between the Atlantic Ocean and the Great Lakes; now part of the New York State Barge Canal System, 129

Erie, Lake (42°15′N/81°25′W) One of the Great Lakes of North America, m118, 121

Eritrea (15°00′N/39°00′E) A country in East Africa, 431

Estonia (59°00′N/26°00′E) A country west of Russia; one of the Baltic Republics, 361

Ethiopia (8°00′N/38°00′E) A country in East Africa, 431

Ethiopian Highlands A mountainous area in Ethiopia, 417

Euphrates River (31°00′N/47°25′E) A river that rises in central Turkey, flows southeast through Syria and Iraq, and joins the Tigris River; together they form the Shatt al Arab, which flows into the Persian Gulf, m488, 489

Eurasia The combination of Europe and Asia; some consider it to be a single continent, 346

Europe A peninsula of the Eurasian land mass; a continent bounded by Asia, the Mediterranean Sea, the Atlantic Ocean, and the Arctic Ocean, 28, m29

Everest, Mount (27°59′N/86°56′E) The world's tallest mountain; located on the border of Nepal and China, 551

Everglades (26°05′N/80°46′W) A huge swampland in southern Florida that covers about 4,000 square miles, 126

Farakka dam (24°49′N/87°56′E) A dam that crosses the Ganges River at a point just before it enters Bangladesh, 599

Feni River (22°46′N/91°26′E) A river in Bangladesh, 562

Fiji (18°00′S/178°00′E) A country that consists of an island group of Oceania in the Pacific Ocean, 712, *m713*

Finland (64°00′N/26°00′E) A country in Northern Europe, 300

Florence (43°46′N/11°15′E) A city in north-central Italy, 291

Florida (28°45′N/82°30′W) A state in the southern United States, 108

Fongafale (8°31′S/179°13′E) The capital of Tuvalu, 686

Foraker, Mount (62°58′N/151°24′E) A mountain in Alaska in the United States, 102

France (46°00′N/2°00′E) A country in Western Europe, 294

Frankfort (38°12′N/84°52′W) The capital of Kentucky, 108

Fredericton (45°57′N/66°38′W) The capital of New Brunswick, Canada, 114

Freetown (8°29′N/13°14′W) The capital of Sierra Leone, 412

French Guiana (4°20′N/53°00′W) A French overseas department in northern South America, 230, *m234*

Fuji, Mount (35°22′N/138°43′E) A volcanic mountain in Japan, 662

Gaborone (24°39′S/25°55′E) The capital of Botswana, 408

Gabon (1°00′S/11°45′E) A country in Central Africa, 448, *m450*

Galilee, Sea of (also called Lake Kinneret) (32°48′N/35°35′E) A freshwater lake in northeastern Israel, 495

Gambia (13°30′N/15°30′W) A country in West Africa, 442

Ganges River (23°22′N/90°32′E) A river that rises in the central Himalayas, flows eastward across northern India, and joins the Brahmaputra river; together they form a huge delta before entering the Bay of Bengal, 553

Ganges-Brahmaputra River delta (23°00′N/89°00′E) A triangular area of land formed by the mouth of the combined Ganges and Brahmaputra rivers, 553

Gaza Strip (31°25′N/34°20′E) A territory along the Mediterranean Sea just northeast of the Sinai Peninsula, 527

Georgetown (6°48′N/58°10′W) The capital of Guyana, 198

Georgia (42°00′N/43°30′E) A country in Transcaucasia, 370, *m370*

Georgia, the U.S. state of (32°45′N/83°30′W) A state in the southern United States, 108

Germany (51°30′N/10°30′E) A country in Western Europe, 294

Ghana (8°00′N/2°00′W) A country in West Africa, 442

Glasgow (55°50′N/4°15′W) A city in Scotland, 303

Gobi Desert (44°00′N/105°00′E) A large desert that stretches from northern China into Mongolia, 627

Godwin Austen, Mount (also called K2) (35°52′N/76°34′E) The world's second tallest mountain; located in northern Pakistan, 552

Golan Heights (also called Al Jawlan) (33°00′N/35°45′E) Located in Syria; a hilly plateau overlooking the Jordan River and the Sea of Galilee, 487

Gorèe Island (14°40′N/17°24′W) An island off the coast of Senegal; served as one of the busiest departure points for slaves during the slave trade from the mid-1500s to the mid-1800s, 442

Granada (37°11′N/3°36′W) A city in southern Spain, 291

Great Barrier Reef (18°00′S/146°50′E) A chain of more than 2,500 reefs and islands; located off the northeast coast of Australia, 692

Great Britain (54°00′N/2°00′W) An island consisting of England, Scotland, and Wales and located north of France, 272

Great Dividing Range (25°00′S/147°00′E) A mountain range near the eastern coast of Australia, 692

Great Drakensberg An escarpment in Southern Africa, 417

Great Lakes (45°41′N/84°26′W) A chain of five large lakes—Huron, Ontario, Michigan, Erie, and Superior—located in central North America, *m118*, 121

Great Plains (39°25′N/101°18′W) A largely treeless area that extends from the Interior Plains to the Rocky Mountains, *m118*, 119

Great Smoky Mountains (35°35′N/83°31′W) A North American mountain range located in the southern part of the Appalachian system, 119

Greater Antilles (20°00′N/74°00′W) A group of islands in the Caribbean Sea; includes Cuba, Jamaica, Hispaniola, and Puerto Rico, 203

Greece (39°00′N/22°00′E) A Mediterranean country of Europe, 287

Green Mountains (42°34′N/72°36′W) A North American mountain range located in the northern part of the Appalachian system, 119

Greenland (72°00′N/40°00′W) The largest island in the world; bounded by the northern Atlantic Ocean and the Arctic Ocean and owned by Denmark, 272

Greenwich (51°28′N/0°00′E) A town in England and site of the Royal Observatory, through which the prime meridian, or longitude 0°, passes, 6

Grenada (12°07′N/61°40′W) A country consisting of the island of Grenada and the southern Grenadines in the Caribbean Sea, 196

Grozny (43°18′N/45°42′E) The capital of Chechnya, *m385*, 386

Guam (13°27′N/144°44′E) A U.S. territory and island in the Pacific, 112

Guangzhou (23°07′N/113°15′E) A city in China, 637

Guatemala (15°30′N/90°15′W) A country in Central America, 223

Guatemala City (14°38′N/90°31′W) The capital of Guatemala, 196

Guiana Highlands (4°00′N/60°00′W) A mountain range in northeast South America, 202, *m203*

Guinea (11°00′N/10°00′W) A country in West Africa, 442

Guinea-Bissau (12°00′N/15°00′W) A country in West Africa, 442

Gulf Coastal Plain A broad plain that stretches along the Gulf of Mexico from Florida into Texas, 119

Gulf of Mexico (26°00′N/91°00′W) An arm of the Atlantic Ocean bordering on eastern Mexico, the southeastern United States, and Cuba, *m118*, 121

Guyana (5°00′N/59°00′W) A country in northern South America, 230, *m234*

Hagatna (13°28′N/144°45′E) The capital of Guam, 112

Hainan (19°00′N/109°30′E) An island off the coast of southern China, *m620*, 621

Haiti (19°00′N/72°25′W) A country that occupies the western one-third of the island of Hispaniola in the Caribbean Sea, 198

Halabja (35°21′N/45°54′E) A city in Iraq, 516

Halifax (44°39′N/63°36′W) The capital of Nova Scotia, Canada, 166

Hangzhou (30°15′N/120°10′E) A city in China, 637

Hanoi (21°02′N/105°51′E) The capital of Vietnam, 686

Harare (17°50′S/31°03′E) The capital of Zimbabwe, 412

Harrisburg (40°16′N/76°53′W) The capital of Pennsylvania, 112

Hartford (41°46′N/72°41′W) The capital of Connecticut, 108

Havana (23°08′N/82°22′W) The capital of Cuba, 196

Hawaii (20°45′N/156°30′W) A state in the western United States that consists of several islands in the central Pacific, 108

Hawaiian Islands (20°45′N/156°30′W) A chain of islands in the central Pacific Ocean that make up the state of Hawaii, 121

Hejaz Mountains A mountain range on the southwest corner of the Arabian Peninsula; part of the western region of Saudi Arabia, 488

Helena (46°36′N/112°02′W) The capital of Montana, 110

Helsinki (60°11′N/24°56′E) The capital of Finland, 266

Hermon, Mount (33°25′N/35°51′E) A mountain on the border between Lebanon and Syria, 478

Himalaya Mountains (28°00′N/84°00′E) The world's highest mountain range; located in Nepal, Bhutan, northern India, and southwestern China, 551

Hindu Kush (35°00′N/71°00′E) A mountain range in eastern Afghanistan and northern Pakistan, 488

Holland (52°30′N/5°45′E) Another name for the Netherlands, a country in Northern Europe, 280

Hollywood (34°06′N/118°20′W) A district of Los Angeles, California; the center of the motion picture industry in the United States, 143

Honduras (15°00′N/86°30′W) A country in Central America, 223

Hong Kong (22°15′N/114°10′E) A region on the coast of southeastern China; includes Hong Kong Island and nearby areas, 621

Honiara (9°26′S/159°57′E) The capital of the Solomon Islands, 684

Honolulu (21°18′N/157°52′W) The capital of Hawaii, 108

Honshu (36°00′N/138°00′E) The largest island of Japan, 653

Houston (31°20′N/95°25′W) A city in southeastern Texas, 148

Huang He (also called Yellow River) (37°45′N/119°05′E) A Chinese river that rises in the Kunlun Mountains, flows east for about 3,000 miles, and empties into the Yellow Sea, *m620*, 621

Hudson Bay (52°52′N/102°25′W) An extended bay located in Canada, 119

Hungary (47°00′N/20°00′E) A country in Eastern Europe, 308

Huron, Lake (44°30′N/82°00′W) The second largest of the Great Lakes of North America, *m118*, 121

Iberian Peninsula (40°00′N/5°00′W) A southwestern peninsula of Europe bounded by France, the Mediterranean Sea, and the Atlantic Ocean and occupied by Spain and Portugal, *m271*, 272

Iceland (65°00′N/18°00′W) An island country in the North Atlantic, northwest of Great Britain, 300

Idaho (44°30′N/114°15′W) A state in the western United States, 108

Ijsselmeer (52°49′N/5°15′E) A freshwater lake in the Netherlands, 281

Illinois (40°00′N/89°15′W) A state in the Midwest of the United States, 108

India (20°00′N/77°00′E) A country in South Asia, 567

Indian Ocean (10°00′S/70°00′E) The world's third largest ocean; extends from southern Asia to Antarctica and from western Australia to eastern Africa, 32

Indiana (40°00′N/86°15′W) A state in the Midwest of the United States, 108

Indo-Gangetic Plain (also called the Northern Indian Plain) (27°00′N/80°00′E) A plain in northern India and Bangladesh that lies between the Deccan Plateau and the northern mountains, 552

Indochina A peninsula located south of China; includes Myanmar, Thailand, Laos, Cambodia, Vietnam, and West Malaysia, 689

Indonesia (5°00′S/120°00′E) A Southeast Asian country that consists of several islands between the Asian mainland and Australia, 705

Indus River (24°20′N/67°47′E) A river that flows west and then south through Pakistan to the Arabian Sea, 553

Indus Valley (29°00′N/71°00′E) A valley formed by the Indus River in Pakistan, 567

Ingushetia (43°13′N/44°47′E) A Russian republic in the Caucasus, 385, *m385*

Interior Plains A lowland area that extends from the Appalachians to about 300 miles west of the Mississippi River, *m118*, 119

Iowa (42°00′N/93°30′W) A state in the Midwest of the United States, 108

Iqaluit (63°44′N/68°30′W) The capital of Nunavut, Canada, 114

Iran (32°00′N/53°00′E) A country in the northeast region of Southwest Asia, 516, *m516*

Iraq (33°00′N/44°00′E) A country in the northeast region of Southwest Asia, 516, *m516*

Ireland (53°00′N/8°00′W) A country occupying most of the island of Ireland, which is west of Great Britain, 272

Islamabad (33°42′N/73°10′E) The capital of Pakistan, 548

Israel (31°30′N/34°45′E) A country in the Eastern Mediterranean in Southwest Asia, 512, *m512*

Issyk-Kul, Lake (42°25′N/77°15′E) A lake in Kyrgyzstan, 336

Italian Peninsula A southern peninsula of Europe bounded by the Mediterranean Sea, the Adriatic Sea, France, Switzerland, Austria, and Slovenia and occupied by Italy, *m271*, 272

Italy (42°50′N/12°50′E) A Mediterranean country of Europe, 266

Jackson (32°18′N/90°11′W) The capital of Mississippi, 110

Jaffna Peninsula (9°45′N/80°10′E) A peninsula on the northern tip of the island of Sri Lanka, 585

Jakarta (6°10′S/106°49′E) The capital of Indonesia, 684

Jamaica (18°15′N/77°30′W) An island country in the Caribbean Sea, 198

Jamestown (37°19′N/78°18′W) Founded in 1607; the first permanent English settlement in the United States, 136

Japan (36°00′N/138°00′E) An East Asian country consisting of several islands in the western Pacific Ocean, 651, *m652*

Jefferson City (38°35′N/92°10′W) The capital of Missouri, 110

Jerusalem (31°47′N/35°13′E) A holy city for Jews, Muslims, and Christians; also the capital of Israel, 510, *m512*

Johannesburg (26°12′S/28°05′E) The largest city in South Africa, 457

Jordan (31°00′N/36°00′E) A country in the Eastern Mediterranean in Southwest Asia, 511, *m512*

Jordan River A river that flows south from Syria through the Sea of Galilee to the Dead Sea, 489

Juneau (58°18′N/134°25′W) The capital of Alaska, 108

Jutland Peninsula A Northern European peninsula that consists of Denmark and northern Germany, 271, *m271*

K2 (also called Mount Godwin Austen) (35°52′N/76°34E) The world's second tallest mountain; located in northern Pakistan, 552

Kabul (34°31′N/69°11′E) The capital of Afghanistan, 484

Kalahari (23°00′S/22°00′E) A desert in Southern Africa, 420

Kaliningrad (54°43′N/20°30′E) A city in western Russia, 345

Kamchatka (56°00′N/160°00′E) A peninsula of northeastern Russia bounded by Sea of Okhotsk and the Bering Sea, 346

Kampala (0°19′N/32°35′E) The capital of Uganda, 412

Kanchenjunga (27°42′N/88°08′E) A mountain on the border of India and Nepal, 542

Kansas (38°30′N/98°30′W) A state in the Midwest of the United States, 108

Kansas City (Kansas) (39°07′N/94°44′W) A city in northeastern Kansas, 147

Kansas City (Missouri) (39°05′N/94°35′W) A city in western Missouri, 147

Kara Kum (39°00′N/60°00′E) A large, black sand desert in Central Asia, 352

Karakoram Mountain Range (34°00′N/78°00′E) A mountain range in northern Pakistan, northern India, and southwestern China, 552

Karnataka Plateau A plateau in Karnataka, a state in southwestern India, 552

Kashmir A territory located at the foot of the Himalayas in northern Pakistan, northern India, and southwestern China, 600, *m601*

Kathmandu (27°43′N/85°19′E) The capital of Nepal, 581

Kathmandu Valley (27°40′N/85°21′E) A valley in Nepal, 582

Kazakhstan (48°00′N/68°00′E) A country in Central Asia, 375

Kentucky (37°30′N/85°15′W) A state in the southern United States, 108

Kenya (1°00′N/38°00′E) A country in East Africa, 431

Kenya, Mount (0°10′S/37°20′E) A volcanic mountain in East Africa, 417

Khartoum (15°45′N/32°30′E) The capital of Sudan, 425

Khyber Pass (34°04′N/71°13′E) A major land route through the Safed Koh Mountains, 552

Kiev (50°26′N/30°31′E) The capital of the Ukraine, 345

Kigali (1°57′S/30°04′E) The capital of Rwanda, 412

Kilimanjaro, Mount (3°04′S/37°22′E) Africa's highest peak; a volcanic mountain in Tanzania in East Africa, 417

Kingston (18°00′N/76°48′W) The capital of Jamaica, 198

Kingstown (13°08′N/61°13′W) The capital of Saint Vincent and the Grenadines, 198

Kinneret, Lake (also called the Sea of Galilee) (32°48′N/35°35′E) A freshwater lake in northeastern Israel, 495

Kinshasha (4°20′S/15°19′E) The capital of the Democratic Republic of the Congo, 408

Kiribati (5°00′S/170°00′W) A country that consists of an island group of Oceania in the Pacific Ocean, 712, *m713*

Kjolen Mountains (65°00′N/14°00′E) An upland area of Scandinavia, 273

Kobe (34°41′N/135°10′E) A city in Japan, 661

Kolkata (Calcutta) (22°34′N/88°22′E) A city in eastern India, *m569*, 570, 599

Kongur, Mount (38°40′N/75°21′E) A mountain in China, 611

Korea Strait (34°00′N/129°00′E) A waterway between southern South Korea and southwestern Japan that connects the Sea of Japan with the East China Sea, 647

Korean Peninsula A peninsula bounded by the Yellow Sea and the Sea of Japan and occupied by North Korea and South Korea, 620

Koror (7°20′N/134°28′E) The capital of Palau, 684

Kosovo (42°35′N/21°00′E) A province of southern Yugoslavia, 319

Kuala Lumpur (3°10′N/101°42′E) The capital of Malaysia, 709

Kunlun Mountains (36°00′N/84°00′E) A mountain range in western China, 619, *m620*

Kuril Islands (46°10′N/152°00′E) A chain of Russian-owned islands that extend off the southern tip of Kamchatka Peninsula; Japan claims ownership of some of the islands, 346

Kuwait (29°30′N/47°45′E) A country in the Arabian Peninsula of Southwest Asia, 503

Kuwait City (29°22′N/47°59′E) The capital of Kuwait, 484

Kyoto (35°00′N/135°45′E) A city in Japan, 654

Kyrgyzstan (41°00′N/75°00′E) A country in Central Asia, 375

Kyzyl Kum (42°30′N/64°30′E) A large red sand desert in Central Asia, 352

La Paz (16°30′S/68°09′W) The administrative capital of Bolivia, 196

Labrador A section of Newfoundland, Canada, 167

Lansing (42°44′N/84°33′W) The capital of Michigan, 110

Laos (18°00′N/105°00′E) A country in Southeast Asia, 705

Las Vegas (36°11′N/115°08′W) A city in southern Nevada, 149, *m149*

Latin America A region that includes Mexico, Central America, the Caribbean, and South America, 201, *m203*

Latvia (57°00′N/25°00′E) A country west of Russia; one of the Baltic Republics, 361

Lebanon (33°50′N/35°50′E) A country in the Eastern Mediterranean in Southwest Asia, 511, *m512*

Leizhou Peninsula (20°40′N/110°05′E) A peninsula in southern China between the South China Sea and the Gulf of Tonkin, 620

Lena (72°20′N/126°37′E) A river that flows through east-central Russia and empties into the Laptev Sea, 347

Lesotho (29°30′S/28°15′E) A country in Southern Africa, 453, *m454*

Lesser Antilles (15°00′N/61°00′W) A group of islands southeast of Puerto Rico; divided into the Leeward Islands and Windward Islands, 203

Liberia (6°30′N/9°30′W) A country in West Africa, 442

Libreville (0°23′N/9°27′E) The capital of Gabon, 410

Libya (25°00′W/17°00′E) A country in North Africa, 438

Libyan Desert (24°00′N/25°00′E) A desert in northeast Africa; the northeast section of the Sahara, 420

Liechtenstein (47°10′N/9°32′E) A country in Western Europe, 294

Lilongwe (13°59′S/33°47′E) The capital of Malawi, 410

Lima (12°03′S/77°03′W) The capital of Peru, 211

Lincoln (40°48′N/96°40′W) The capital of Nebraska, 110

Lisbon (38°43′N/9°08′W) The capital of Portugal, 268

Lithuania (56°00′N/24°00′E) One of the Baltic Republics, 361

Little Rock (35°45′N/92°17′W) The capital of Arkansas, 108

Ljubljana (46°03′N/14°31′E) The capital of Slovenia, 268

Llanos (5°00′N/70°00′W) Vast plains located in Colombia and Venezuela, 202, *m203*

Logan, Mount (60°34′N/140°25′W) A mountain in Canada, 102

Lombardy (45°40′N/9°30′E) A region in northern Italy, 273

Lomè (6°08N/1°13′E) The capital of Togo, 412

London (51°30′N/0°08′W) The capital of the United Kingdom, 304

Los Angeles (34°03′N/118°15′W) A major seaport city in southwestern California, 128, *m149*

Louisiana (31°00′N/92°00′W) A state in the southern United States, 148

Lowell (42°39′N/71°19′W) A city in Massachusetts that became a textile center by the 1840s, 136

Luanda (8°50′S/13°14′E) The capital of Angola, 408

Lusaka (15°25′S/28°17′E) The capital of Zambia, 412

Luxembourg (49°45′N/6°10′E) A country in Western Europe, 294

Luxembourg City (49°37′N/6°08′E) The capital of Luxembourg, 266

Macao Peninsula A peninsula in southeast China just west of Hong Kong, 620

Macedonia (41°50′N/22°00′E) A country in Eastern Europe, 308

MacKenzie River (69°20′N/134°00′W) The largest river in Canada; flows across the Northwest Territories to the Arctic Ocean, 121

Madagascar A country in Southern Africa, 453, *m454*

Madison (43°05′N/89°23′W) The capital of Wisconsin, 112

Madras (also called Chennai) (13°05′N/80°17′E) A city in southern India, *m569*, 570

Madrid (40°24′N/3°41′W) The capital of Spain, 268

Maine (45°30′N/69°15′W) A state in New England in the northeastern United States, 145

Majuro (7°06′S/171°23′E) The capital of the Marshall Islands, 684

Makalu (27°55′N/87°08′E) A mountain on the border of China and Nepal, 542

Malabo The capital of Equatorial Guinea, 408

Malawi (3°21′N/8°40′E) A country in Southern Africa, 453, *m454*

Malay Archipelago (0°00′N/120°00′E) An island group of Southeast Asia; separates the Pacific and Indian oceans and includes the Philippines, Malaysia, and the islands of Indonesia, 689

Malay Peninsula (6°00′N/102°00′E) A narrow strip of land about 700 miles long that stretches south from the Indochinese Peninsula and then curves southeast, 689

Malaysia (2°30′N/112°30′E) A Southeast Asian country that occupies part of the island of Borneo and the southern end of the Malay Peninsula, 705

Maldives (3°12′N/73°00′E) A South Asian country that occupies a chain of islands in the Indian Ocean off the southwest coast of India, 584

Male (4°10′N/73°30′E) The capital of the Maldives, 548

Mali (17°00′N/4°00′W) A country in West Africa, 442

Malta (35°55′N/14°26′E) An island country in the Mediterranean Sea, off the southern coast of Sicily, 268

Managua (12°09′N/86°25′W) The capital of Nicaragua, 198

Manama (26°14′N/50°35′E) The capital of Bahrain, 484

Manchurian Plain (44°00′N/124°00′E) A plain in northeastern China, 620, *m620*

Manila (14°35′N/121°00′E) The capital of the Philippines, 684

Manitoba (55°00′N/97°00′W) A Prairie Province of Canada, 168

Maputo (25°58′S/32°35′E) The capital of Mozambique, 410

Marrakesh (31°38′N/8°00′W) A city in Morocco, *m439*, 440

Marshall Islands (10°00′N/167°00′E) A country that consists of an island group of Oceania in the Pacific Ocean, 712, *m713*

Maryland (39°00′N/76°45′W) A state in the southern United States (sometimes included with the Middle Atlantic states), 110

Maseru (29°19′S/27°29′E) The capital of Lesotho, 410

Massachusetts (42°15′N/71°30′W) A state in New England in the northeastern United States, 145

Massif Central Uplands located in central France, 273

Mauritania (20°00′N/12°00′W) A country in West Africa, 442

Mauritius (20°18′S/57°35′E) An island country in Southern Africa, 453, *m454*

Mbabane (26°19′S/31°08′E) The capital of Swaziland, 412

McKinley, Mount (also called Denali) (63°04′N/151°00′W) North America's highest mountain; located in Alaska, 120

Mecca (21°26′N/39°50′E) The holiest city of Islam; located in western Saudi Arabia, 503

Mediterranean Europe A region that includes Spain, Italy, and Greece, 287

Mediterranean Sea (35°00′N/20°00′E) An inland sea bounded by southern Europe, northern Africa, and southwestern Asia, 277

Mekong River (10°15′N/105°55′E) A river that begins in China and crosses several Southeast Asian nations before becoming a wide delta on Vietnam's coast, *m689*, 690

Melanesia (12°00′S/160°00′E) A region in southwestern Oceania that consists of numerous Pacific islands, 713, *m713*

Meseta (41°00′N/4°00′W) A central plateau of Spain, 273

Mexico (23°00′N/102°00′W) A Latin American country bounded by the United States, the Gulf of Mexico, the Pacific Ocean, and Central America, 217

Mexico City (19°26′N/99°08′W) The largest city in Latin America and the capital of Mexico, 211

Miami (25°46′N/80°12′W) A city in southern Florida, 148

Michigan (44°15′N/85°30′W) A state in the Midwest of the United States, 110

Michigan, Lake (43°20′N/87°10′W) The third largest of the Great Lakes of North America, *m118*, 121

Micronesia (9°00′N/155°00′E) A region in northwestern Oceania that consists of numerous Pacific islands, 713, *m713*

Micronesia, Federated States of (5°00′N/152°00′E) A country that consists of an island group of Oceania in the Pacific Ocean, 712, *m713*

Mid-Atlantic Ridge (0°00′N/20°00′W) The mountain range on the ocean floor; extends for thousands of miles north to south through the middle of the Atlantic Ocean, 36

Middle Atlantic States The states of Pennsylvania, New York, and New Jersey (sometimes Maryland and Delaware are included in this group), 145

Midwest An area of the north-central United States that includes Michigan, Ohio, Indiana, Illinois, Wisconsin, Minnesota, Iowa, Missouri, Kansas, Nebraska, North Dakota, and South Dakota, 147

Milwaukee (43°04′N/87°58′W) A city in southeastern Wisconsin, 147

Minneapolis (44°58′N/93°16′W) A city in eastern Minnesota, 147

Minnesota (46°15′N/94°15′W) A state in the Midwest of the United States, 110

Minsk (53°54′N/27°34′E) The capital of Belarus, 342

Mississippi (32°45′N/89°45′W) A state in the southern United States, 110

Mississippi River (29°09′N/89°15′W) A North American river that runs from Minnesota to the Gulf of Mexico, *m118*, 121

Missouri (38°15′N/92°30′W) A state in the Midwest of the United States, 110

Missouri River (38°49′N/90°07′W) A North American river that runs from the Rocky Mountains in southwest Montana into the Mississippi River, *m118*, 121

Mogadishu (2°04′N/45°22′E) The capital of Somalia, 412

Mojave Desert (35°25′N/115°35′W) A desert in southern California, 124

Moldova (47°00′N/29°00′E) A country that lies between the Ukraine and Romania, 361

Monaco (43°44′N/7°24′E) A principality bounded by France and the Mediterranean Sea, 268

Monaco, the village of (43°44′N/7°25′E) The capital of Monaco, 268

Mongolia (46°00′N/105°00′E) A country in East Asia, 642

Mongolian Plateau A plateau in Mongolia and northeastern China, 620, *m620*

Monrovia (6°19′N/10°48′W) The capital of Liberia, 421

Montana (47°00′N/109°45′W) A state in the western United States, 110

Montevideo (34°51′S/56°10′W) The capital of Uruguay, 198

Montgomery (32°22′N/86°18′W) The capital of Alabama, 108

Montpelier (44°16′N/72°34′W) The capital of Vermont, 112

Montreal (45°30′N/73°35′W) Located in Quebec, Canada; the second largest metropolitan area in the country, 168

Morocco (32°00′N/5°00′W) A country in North Africa, 438

Moroni (11°42′S/43°14′E) The capital of Comoros, 408

Moscow (55°45′N/37°37′E) The capital of Russia, 366

Mozambique (18°15′S/35°00′E) A country in Southern Africa, 453, *m454*

Mumbai (also called Bombay) (18°59′N/72°50′W) A city in western India, *m569*, 570

Murray River (35°22′S/139°22′E) The largest river of Australia; flows into an arm of the Indian Ocean, 692

Muscat (23°37′N/58°36′E) The capital of Oman, 484

Myanmar (22°00′N/98°00′E) A country in Southeast Asia, 705

N'Djamena (12°07′N/15°03′E) The capital of Chad, 408

Nagorno-Karabakh (40°00′N/46°35′E) A mountainous republic of Azerbaijan, 386

Nagoya (35°10′N/136°55′E) A city in Japan, 630

Nairobi (1°17′S/36°49′E) The capital of Kenya, 410

Namib (23°00′S/15°00′E) A desert in southwest Africa, 420

Namibia (22°00′S/17°00′E) A country in Southern Africa, 453, *m454*

Nashville (36°10′N/86°47′W) The capital of Tennessee, 112

Nassau (25°05′N/77°21′W) The capital of the Bahamas, 196

Nasser, Lake (22°50′N/32°30′E) A lake created by the Aswan High Dam; lies in southern Egypt and northern Sudan, 426, *m427*

Nauru (0°32′S/166°55′E) An island country of Oceania in the Pacific Ocean, 712, *m713*

Nebraska (41°30′N/99°45′W) A state in the Midwest of the United States, 110

Negev (30°34′N/34°43′E) A desert area that occupies southern parts of Israel, 492

Nepal (28°00′N/84°00′E) A country in South Asia, 580

Netherlands (52°30′N/5°45′E) A country in Western Europe, 294

Nevada (39°15′N/116°45′W) A state in the western United States, 110

New Brunswick (46°30′N/66°45′W) An Atlantic Province of Canada, 166

New Caledonia (21°30′S/165°30′E) A French overseas territory that consists of an island group of Oceania in the Pacific Ocean, 691

New Delhi (28°36′N/77°12′E) The capital of India, 548

New England An area of the northeastern United States that includes Maine, Vermont, New Hampshire, Massachusetts, Rhode Island, and Connecticut, 145

New Guinea (5°00′S/140°00′E) An island north of Australia; occupied by the countries of Indonesia (west half) and Papua New Guinea (east half), 679

New Hampshire (43°40′N/71°30′W) A state in New England in the northeastern United States, 145

New Jersey (40°10′N/74°30′W) A Middle Atlantic state of the eastern United States, 145

New Mexico (34°30′N/106°00′W) A state in the western United States, 110

New Orleans (29°58′N/90°04′W) A city in southeastern Louisiana, 148

New York (43°00′N/75°30′W) A Middle Atlantic state in the eastern United States, 145

New York City (40°41′N/73°59′W) A major seaport city located in southeastern New York State, *m145*, 147

New Zealand (42°00′S/174°00′E) A country that consists of several islands (including North Island and South Island) in the Pacific Ocean off the southeast coast of Australia; part of Oceania, 691

Newfoundland (52°00′N/56°00′W) An Atlantic Province of Canada, 166

Newfoundland Island (49°00′N/56°00′W) An island that makes up part of Newfoundland, Canada, 167

Niamey (13°31′N/2°07′E) The capital of Niger, 412

Nicaragua (13°00′N/85°00′W) A country in Central America, 223

Nicosia (35°10′N/33°22′E) The capital of Cyprus, 484

Niger (16°00′N/8°00′E) A country in West Africa, 442

Niger River (5°33′N/6°33′E) A river that begins in Guinea and flows toward the Sahara (northeast); it then cuts through Nigeria and empties into the Gulf of Guinea, 416

Niger River Delta (4°50′N/6°00′E) A triangular area of land formed by the mouth of the Niger River, 425

Nigeria (10°00′N/8°00′E) A country in West Africa, 442

Nile River Delta (31°00′N/31°00′E) A triangular area of land formed by the mouth of the Nile River, 416

Nile River (l30°10′N/31°06′E) The world's longest river; flows through Uganda, Sudan, and Egypt and empties into the Mediterranean Sea, 416

Nordic countries The Northern European countries of Denmark, Finland, Iceland, Norway, and Sweden, 300

Norilsk (69°20′N/88°06′E) A Siberian mining center in Russia, 354

North Africa A region of Africa that includes Algeria, Egypt, Libya, Morocco, Sudan, and Tunisia, 438

North America The northern continent of the Western Hemisphere; bounded by the Arctic Ocean, the Atlantic Ocean, the Pacific Ocean, and the Caribbean Sea, 28, *m29*

North Carolina (35°30′N/80°00′W) A state in the southern United States, 110

North China Plain (34°00′N/116°00′E) A plain in northern China, 620, *m620*

North Dakota (47°30′N/100°00′W) A state in the Midwest of the United States, 110

North Island (37°20′S/173°30′E) The northern of the two main islands that make up New Zealand, 691

North Korea (40°00′N/127°00′E) A country in East Asia, 648, *m648*

North Ossetia (43°00′N/44°15′E) A Russian republic in the Caucasus, 385, *m385*

North Pole (90°00′N) The northern end of the earth's axis of rotation; a point located in the Arctic Ocean, 56

North Sea (55°20′N/3°00′E) An arm of the Atlantic Ocean bounded by Norway, Denmark, Germany, the Netherlands, England, and Scotland, 271, *m271*

Northeast Region of Southwest Asia A region that includes Turkey, Iran, Iraq, and Afghanistan, 516

Northern Europe A region that includes the United Kingdom, Ireland, Denmark, Finland, Iceland, Norway, and Sweden, 300

Northern European Plain A fertile plain that stretches across parts of France, Belgium, the Netherlands, Denmark, Germany, and Poland, 273

Northern Indian Plain (also called the Indo-Gangetic Plain) (27°00′N/80°00′E) A plain in northern India that lies between the Deccan Plateau and the northern mountains, 552

Northern Plains of Afghanistan A plain in northern Afghanistan, 488

Northwest Territories (65°00′N/118°00′W) A territory in north-central Canada, 169

Norway (62°00′N/10°00′E) A Northern European country that occupies the western part of the Scandinavian Peninsula, 300

Norwegian Sea (70°00′N/5°00′E) An extension of the Atlantic Ocean off the northwest coast of Norway, 271, *m271*

Nouakchott (18°06′N/15°57′W) The capital of Mauritania, 410

Nova Scotia (45°00′N/63°00′W) An Atlantic Province of Canada, 166

Nuku'alofa (21°08′S/125°12′W) The capital of Tonga, 686

Nunavut (70°00′N/90°00′W) A territory in north-central Canada; home to many of Canada's Inuit, 169

Ob River (66°45′N/69°30′E) A river in central Russia that flows into the Gulf of Ob, 347

Oceania A region that includes Australia, New Zealand, and the Pacific Islands (but not the Philippines, Indonesia, and other islands near Asia), 690

Ogallala Aquifer The largest aquifer in the United States; stretches from South Dakota to Texas, 33

Ohio (40°15′N/83°00′W) A state in the Midwest of the United States, 110

Ohio River (36°59′N/89°08′W) A North American river that runs from the Allegheny Mountains into the Mississippi River, *m118,* 121

Oklahoma (35°30′N/97°30′W) A state in the south-central United States, 110

Oklahoma City (35°28′N/97°31′W) The capital of Oklahoma, 110

Olduvai Gorge (2°58′S/35°22′E) A ravine in northern Tanzania that contains archeological sites rich in fossils, 431

Olympia (47°02′N/122°54′W) The capital of Washington, 112

Omaha (41°16′N/95°56′W) A city in eastern Nebraska, 147

Oman (21°00′N/57°00′E) A country in the Arabian Peninsula of Southwest Asia, 503

Ontario (50°00′N/86°00′W) A Core Province of Canada, 167

Ontario, Lake (43°40′N/78°00′W) The smallest of the Great Lakes of North America, *m118,* 121

Oregon (44°00′N/120°03′W) A state in the western United States, 148

Orinoco River (41°12′S/68°15′W) A river that flows through the northern part of South America, mainly in Venezuela, 202

Osaka (35°57′N/137°16′E) A city in Japan, 630

Oslo (59°55′N/10°45′E) The capital of Norway, 268

Ouagadougou (12°22′N/1°31′W) The capital of Burkina Faso, 408

outback The dry, interior region of Australia, 697

Pacific Ocean (0°00′N/180°00′E) The world's largest ocean; extends from the Arctic Circle and northeastern Asia to Antarctica and from the western Americas to eastern Asia and Australia, 32

Paektu, Mount (41°59′N/128°05′E) A mountain in Korea, 611

Pago Pago (14°17′S/170°42′W) The capital of American Samoa, 112

Pakistan (30°00′N/70°00′E) A country in South Asia, 573

Palau (7°30′N/134°27′E) A country that consists of an island group of Oceania in the Pacific Ocean, 712, *m713*

Palestine (18°30′N/73°45′W) A historical region of Southwest Asia located between the Mediterranean Sea and the Jordan River, 511

Palikir (6°55′N/158°09′E) The capital of the Federated States of Micronesia, 684

pampas (35°00′S/63°00′W) Vast plains located in Uruguay and south-central Argentina, 202 *m203*

Panama (9°00′N/80°00′W) A country in Central America, 223

Panama Canal (9°20′N/79°55′W) A canal that cuts through Panama and connects the Caribbean Sea and Pacific Ocean, 226, *m226*

Panama City (8°58′N/79°32′W) The capital of Panama, 198

Papua New Guinea (6°00′S/147°00′E) A country that consists of an island group of Oceania in the Pacific Ocean, 712, *m713*

Paraguay (22°60′S/57°60′W) A country in south-central South America, 230, *m234*

Paramaribo (5°52′N/55°10′W) The capital of Suriname, 198

Paraná River (33°43′S/59°15′W) A river that begins in the highlands of Brazil and runs south and west through Paraguay and Argentina. It then turns eastward and empties into the Atlantic, 203, *m203*

Paris (48°52′N/2°20′E) The capital of France, 266

Patagonia (44°00′S/68°00′W) A region of South America, mostly in Argentina, 209

Pearl River (also called Zhu Jiang) (22°46′N/113°38′E) A river in southeastern China that joins the Xi Jiang (or West River) and empties into the South China Sea, 622

Pennsylvania (40°45′N/77°45′W) A Middle Atlantic state of the eastern United States, 145

Persian Gulf (27°00′N/51°00′E) An extension of the Arabian Sea situated between the Arabian Peninsula and Iran, 487, *m488*

Peru (10°00′S/76°00′W) A country in western South America, 230, *m234*

Philadelphia (39°57′N/75°10′W) A city in southeastern Pennsylvania, 146, *m145*

Philippines, the (13°00′N/122°00′E) A Southeast Asian country that occupies about 7,100 islands east of the Asian mainland and northeast of Borneo, 712, *m713*

Phnom Penh (11°33′N/104°55′E) The capital of Cambodia, 684

Phoenix (33°27′N/112°4′W) The capital of Arizona, 149, *m149*

Pierre (44°22′N/100°21′W) The capital of South Dakota, 112

Pinatubo, Mount (15°08′N/120°21′E) A volcanic mountain in the Philippines, 689

Pittsburgh (40°26′N/79°60′W) A city in southwestern Pennsylvania, 137

Plateau of Tibet (33°00′N/92°00′E) A vast tableland in south-central Asia; mostly in Tibet, but extends into China, 619, *m620*

Poland (52°00′N/20°00′E) A country in Eastern Europe, 308

Polynesia (10°0′S/150°00′W) A region in central Oceania that consists of numerous Pacific islands, 713, *m713*

Port Louis (20°10′S/57°30′E) The capital of Mauritius, 410

Port Moresby (9°28′S/147°12′E) The capital of Papua New Guinea, 684

Port-of-Spain (10°39′N/61°31′W) The capital of Trinidad and Tobago, 198

Port-au-Prince (18°32′N/72°20′W) The capital of Haiti, 198

Port-Vila (17°44′S/168°19′E) The capital of Vanuatu, 686

Porto-Novo (6°29′N/2°37′E) The capital of Benin, 408

Portugal (39°04′N/8°14′W) A country located on the Iberian Peninsula; bounded by the Atlantic Ocean and Spain, 268

Prague (50°5′N/14°28′E) The capital of the Czech Republic, 312

Praia (14°55′N/23°31′W) The capital of Cape Verde Island, 408

Prairie Provinces An area located in west-central Canada that includes Manitoba, Saskatchewan, and Alberta, 168

Pretoria (25°42′S/28°14′E), **Cape Town** (33°55′S/18°25′E), **Bloemfontein** (20°08′S/26°12′E) The capital towns of South Africa, 412

Prince Edward Island (46°20′N/63°30′W) An Atlantic Province of Canada, 166

Providence (41°49′N/71°25′W) The capital of Rhode Island, 112

Puerto Rico (18°15′N/66°30′W) An island in the Caribbean Sea that is a self-governing commonwealth in union with the United States, 112

Puerto Vallarta (20°37′N/105°15′W) A city in Mexico, 213

Pyongyang (39°1′N/125°45′E) The capital of North Korea, 616

Pyrenees (42°40′N/1°00′E) A European mountain range that forms a border between France and Spain, *m271, 272*

Qatar (25°30′/51°15′E) A country in the Arabian Peninsula of Southwest Asia, 503

Qinling Shandi Mountains (33°30′N/108°36′E) A mountain range that divides the northern part of China from the southern part, 619

Quebec (54°00′N/72°00′W) A Core Province of Canada, 167

Quebec City (46°49′N/71°15′W) The capital of Quebec, Canada, 167

Quito (0°13′S/78°30′W) The capital of Ecuador, 196

Rabat (34°02′N/6°50′W) The capital of Morocco, 410

Raleigh (35°46′N/78°38′W) The capital of North Carolina, 110

Red Sea (19°00′N/39°30′E) A long, narrow sea situated between northeast Africa and the Arabian Peninsula, 487, *m488*

Regina (50°27′N/104°37′W) The capital of Saskatchewan, Canada, 114

Reykjavik (64°09′N/21°57′W) The capital of Iceland, 266

Rhine River (51°58′N/4°05′E) A European river that flows from the interior of Europe north to the North Sea, 273, *m273*

Rhode Island (41°45′N/71°30′W) A state in New England in the northeastern United States, 145

Richmond (37°33′N/77°28′W) The capital of Virginia, 112

Riga (56°57′N/24°06′E) The capital of Latvia, 342

Ring of Fire A chain of volcanoes that line the Pacific Rim, *m37*, 41, 661, *m662*

Rio de Janeiro (22°54′S/43°14′W) A city in Brazil, 239

Rìo de la Plata The name for the last stretch of the Paraná River before it empties into the Atlantic Ocean between Argentina and Uruguay, 203

Rio Grande (23°51′N/102°59′W) A river that forms part of the Mexican-U.S. border, 102

Riyadh (24°38′N/46°46′E) The capital of Saudi Arabia, 484

Rocky Mountains (43°22′N/110°55′W) A mountain system in the western United States and Canada that extends about 3,000 miles from the Arctic to the Mexican frontier, 119

Romania (46°00′N/25°00′E) A country in Eastern Europe, 308

Rome (41°54′N/12°29′E) The capital of Italy, 266

Rosa, Monte (45°55′N/7°53′E) A mountain on the border of Switzerland and Italy, 260

Roseau (15°18′N/61°24′W) The capital of Dominica, 196

Rub al-Khali (21°00′N/51°00′E) A large desert in the southern part of the Arabian Peninsula, 491

Russia An empire that extended from eastern Europe across north-central Asia to the Pacific Ocean, 361, *m362*

Russia and the Republics A region that stretches across much of eastern Europe and north-central Asia to the Pacific; consists of Russia and 14 other countries (republics), 345

Russian Far East The area of eastern Russia, 345

Rwanda, Republic of (2°00′S/30°00′E) A country in East Africa, 431

Sacramento (38°35′N/121°30′W) The capital of California, 108

Sahara (26°00′N/13°00′E) The largest desert in the world; stretches across northern Africa, from the Atlantic Ocean to the Red Sea, 420

Saint Augustine (29°54′N/81°19′W) Founded in 1565; the oldest permanent European settlement in the United States, 135

Saint Elias, Mount (60°18′N/140°56′W) A mountain located on the U.S.-Canada border, 102

Saint George's (12°03′N/61°45′W) The capital of Grenada, 196

Saint John (45°16′N/66°04′W) A city in New Brunswick, Canada, 166

Saint John's (17°07′N/61°51′W) The capital of Antigua and Barbuda, 196

Saint John's, Canada (47°28′N/52°18′W) The capital of Newfoundland, Canada, 114

Saint Kitts and Nevis, Federation of (17°20′N/62°45′W) A country consisting of the islands of Saint Kitts, Nevis, and Sombrero in the Caribbean Sea, 198

Saint Lawrence River (49°30′N/65°00′W) A Canadian river that flows from Lake Ontario to the Gulf of Saint Lawrence, *m118, 129*

Saint Lawrence Seaway (45°20′N/74°50′W) A waterway that connects the Great Lakes to the Atlantic Ocean by way of the Saint Lawrence River, 129

Saint Louis (38°38′N/90°12′W) A city in eastern Missouri, 147

Saint Lucia (13°53′N/60°58′W) An island country in the Caribbean Sea, 198

Saint Paul (44°57′N/93°06′W) The capital of Minnesota, 147

Saint Petersburg (59°54′N/30°16′E) A city in western Russia, 362

Saint Vincent and the Grenadines (13°05′N/61°12′W) A country consisting of Saint Vincent Island and the northern islets of the Grenadines in the Caribbean Sea, 198

Sakhalin Island An island, governed by a Russian Federation, off the east coast of Russia, 346

Salem (44°57′N/123°02′W) The capital of Oregon, 110

Salt Lake City (40°46′N/111°53′W) The capital of Utah, 112

Samoa, Independent State of (13°35′S/172°20′W) A country that consists of an island group of Oceania in the Pacific Ocean, 712

San Antonio (29°25′N/98°30′W) A city in southern Texas, 148

San Diego (34°43′N/117°09′W) A city in southwestern California, *m149*, 150

San Francisco (37°47′N/122°25′W) A city in western California, 150

San José (9°56′N/84°05′W) The capital of Costa Rica, 196

San Juan (18°28′N/66°06′W) The capital of Puerto Rico, 112

San Marino, Republic of (43°56′N/12°25′E) A tiny country surrounded by Italy, 268

San Marino, the city of (43°55′N/12°28′E) The capital of San Marino, 268

San Salvador (13°42′N/89°12′W) The capital of El Salvador, 196

Sanaa (15°21′N/44°12′E) The capital of Yemen, 484

Santa Fe (35°41′N/105°56′W) The capital of New Mexico, 110

Santiago (33°27′S/70°40′W) The capital of Chile, 211

Santo Domingo (18°28′N/69°54′W) The capital of the Dominican Republic, 196

São Paulo (23°32′S/46°37′W) A city in Brazil, 239

São Tomé (00°20′N/6°44′E) The capital of São Tomé and Príncipe, 412

São Tomé and Príncipe (1°00′N/7°00′E) An island country off the coast of Gabon in Central Africa, 448, *m450*

Sapporo (43°03′N/141°21′E) A city in Japan, 630

Sarajevo (43°51′N/18°23′E) The capital of Bosnia and Herzegovina, 266

Sardinia (40°00′N/9°00′E) An autonomous region of Italy; an island in the central Mediterranean Sea, 272

Saskatchewan (54°00′N/106°00′W) A Prairie Province of Canada, 168

Saudi Arabia (25°00′N/45°00′E) A country that occupies most of the Arabian Peninsula of Southwest Asia, 503

Scandinavian Peninsula (65°00′N/16°00′E) A European peninsula bounded by the Norwegian Sea, the North Sea, and the Baltic Sea; occupied by Norway, Sweden, and Denmark, 271, *m271*

Sea of Japan (43°30′N/135°45′E) An enclosed arm of the Pacific Ocean; bounded by Japan, North Korea, South Korea, and Russia, 647

Seattle (47°36′N/122°20′W) A city in northwestern Washington, 150

Senegal (14°00′N/14°00′W) A country in West Africa, 442

Seoul (37°34′N/126°60′E) The capital of South Korea, 616

Serengeti Plains (3°25′S/38°00′E) A tropical grassland in East Africa, 422

Seychelles (4°35′S/55°40′E) A country formed by a group of islands off the east coast of Africa; part of East Africa, 431

Shandong Peninsula (37°00′N/121°00′E) A peninsula in northeastern China bounded by the Bo Hai and the Yellow seas, 620

Shanghai (31°14′N/121°28′E) A city in China, 637

Siberia (60°00′N/100°00′E) A region, largely in Russia, that lies on the continent of north-central Asia, 349

Sicily (37°45′N/14°15′E) An autonomous region of Italy; an island located off the coast of southern Italy, 272

Sierra Leone (8°30′N/11°30′W) A country in West Africa, 442

Sierra Madre A mountain range that runs down Mexico, 201, *m203*

Sierra Nevada Mountains (37°42′N/119°19′W) A North American mountain range that runs parallel to the Pacific coastline from California to British Columbia in Canada, 120

Silicon Glen An area in Scotland that has many high-tech companies, 303

Silicon Valley An area in western California known for high-technology industries, 141

Sinai Peninsula (29°30′N/34°00′E) A peninsula at the north end of the Red Sea; situated between the Gulf of Suez on the west and the Gulf of Aqaba on the east, 527

Singapore (1°22′N/103°48′E) A Southeast Asian country that occupies Singapore Island and nearby smaller islands, 705

Singapore City (1°18′N/103°51′E) The capital of Singapore, 709

Skopje (42°00′N/21°26′E) The capital of Macedonia, 268

Slovak Republic (48°40′N/19°30′E) A country in Eastern Europe, 308

Slovenia, Republic of (46°15′N/15°10′E) A country in Eastern Europe, 308

Sofia (42°41′N/23°19′E) The capital of Bulgaria, 266

Solomon Islands (8°00′S/159°00′E) A country that consists of an island group of Oceania in the Pacific Ocean, 712, *m713*

Somalia (6°00′N/48°00′E) A country in East Africa, 431

Sonoran Desert An arid region in west North America, 124

South, the The south-central and southeastern area of the United States that includes the states of Maryland, Delaware, West Virginia, Virginia, North Carolina, South Carolina, Kentucky, Tennessee, Georgia, Florida, Alabama, Mississippi, Louisiana, Arkansas, Texas, and Oklahoma, 148

South Africa, Republic of (30°00′S/26°00′E) A country in Southern Africa, 453, *m454*

South America The southern continent of the Western Hemisphere bounded by the Caribbean Sea, the Atlantic Ocean, and the Pacific Ocean, 28, *m29*

South Asia A region that includes Afghanistan, India, Pakistan, Bangladesh, Bhutan, Nepal, Sri Lanka, and the Maldives, 551

South Carolina (34°00′N/81°00′W) A state in the southern United States, 112

South China Sea (15°00′N/115°00E) An arm of the Pacific Ocean bounded by southeastern China, Taiwan, Borneo, the Philippines, and Indochina, *m620*, 622

South Dakota (44°30′N/100°15′W) A state in the Midwest of the United States, 112

South Island (43°00′S/171°00′E) The southern of the two islands that make up New Zealand, 691

South Korea, Republic of (37°00′N/127°30′E) A country in East Asia, 648, *m648*

South Pole (9°S) The southern end of the earth's axis of rotation; a point located in Antarctica, 56

Southeast Asia A region that includes the countries of Brunei, Cambodia, Indonesia, Laos, Malaysia, Myanmar, the Philippines, Singapore, Thailand, and Vietnam, 705

Southern Africa A region of Africa that includes Angola, Botswana, Comoros, Lesotho, Madagascar, Malawi, Mauritius, Mozambique, Namibia, South Africa, Swaziland, Zambia, and Zimbabwe, 453, *m454*

Southern Alps (43°30′S/170°30′E) A mountain range on South Island, New Zealand, 691

Southwest Asia A region that includes Bahrain, Iran, Iraq, Israel, Jordan Kuwait, Lebanon, Oman, Qatar, Saudi Arabia, Syria, Turkey, United Arab Emirates, and Yemen, 487

Spain (40°00′N/4°00′W) A Mediterranean country in Europe, 268

Springfield (39°48′N/89°39′W) The capital of Illinois, 108

Sri Lanka, Democractic Socialist Republic of (7°00′N/81°00′E) A South Asian island country off the southeast coast of India, 584

steppe A grassland that extends from southern Ukraine through northern Kazakhstan to the Altai Mountains, 352

Stockholm (59°20′N/18°03′E) The capital of Sweden, 268

Straits of Hormuz (26°37′N/56°30′E) A narrow waterway between Oman and southern Iran that connects the Persian Gulf with the Gulf of Oman, 488

Sucre (19°03′S/65°16′W) The constitutional capital of Bolivia, 196

Sudan (15°00′N/30°00′E) A country in North Africa, 438

Suez Canal (29°55′N/32°33′E) A canal connecting the Mediterranean Sea with the Red Sea, 487

Sumatra (0°00′N/102°00′E) An island southwest of the Malay Peninsula; part of Indonesia, 678

Superior, Lake (47°38′N/89°20′W) The largest of the Great Lakes of North America, *m118,* 121

Suriname (4°00′N/56°00′W) A country in northern South America, 230, *m234*

Suva (18°08′S/178°25′E) The capital of Fiji, 684

Suzhou (33°38′N/116°59′E) A city in China, 637

Swaziland (26°30′S/31°30′E) A country in Southern Africa, 453, *m454*

Sweden (62°00′N/15°00′E) A Northern European country that occupies the eastern part of the Scandinavian Peninsula, 300

Switzerland (47°00′N/8°00′E) A country in Western Europe, 294

Syria (35°00′N/38°00′E) A country in the Eastern Mediterranean region of Southwest Asia, 511, *m512*

Syrian Desert (32°00′N/40°00′E) A desert that extends north from the An-Nafud Desert and separates the coastal regions of Lebanon, Israel, and Syria from the Tigris and Euphrates valleys, *m488,* 492

taiga (56°04′N/85°05′E) A large forest holding the world's largest timber reserve; located south of the tundra in Russia, 352

Taipei (25°01′N/121°27′E) The capital of Taiwan, 616

Taiwan (24°00′N/121°00′E) An island country off the coast of southeastern China, 642

Tajikistan (39°00′N/71°00′E) A country in Central Asia, 375

Taklimakan (39°00′N/83°00′E) A desert in western China, 627

Tallahassee (30°26′N/84°17′W) The capital of Florida, 108

Tallinn (59°26′N/24°44′E) The capital of Estonia, 342

Tampa-Saint Petersburg A metropolitan area in western Florida formed by the growth of two cities, Tampa (27°57′N/82°28′W) and Saint Petersburg (27°46′N/82°41′W), 148

Tanganyika, Lake (6°00′S/29°30′E) The longest freshwater lake in the world; forms the border between The Democratic Republic of the Congo and Tanzania, 417

Tanzania (6°00′S/35°00′E) A country in East Africa, 431

Tarim Basin (41°00′N/84°00′E) A lowland area in western China, 619

Tashkent (41°19′N/69°15′E) The capital of Uzbekistan, 342

Taurus Mountains (37°00′N/33°00′E) A mountain range in southern Turkey, 488

Tbilisi (41°43′N/44°47′E) The capital of Georgia, 342

Tegucigalpa (14°06′N/87°13′W) The capital of Honduras, 198

Tehran (35°40′N/51°25′E) The capital of Iran, 484

Tennessee (35°45′N/86°15′W) A state in the southern United States, 112

Texas (31°15′N/99°15′W) A state in the south-central United States, 148

Thailand (15°00′N/100°00′E) A country in Southeast Asia, 705

Thar Desert (27°00′N/71°00′E) A desert in southeastern Pakistan and northwestern India, 558

Thimphu (27°29′N/89°36′E) The capital of Bhutan, 548

Three Gorges Dam A dam under construction in 2001 by China; eventually it will span a valley more than one mile wide, 629

Tian Shan (42°00′N/80°00′E) A mountain range in Central Asia, 346

Tianjin (39°09′N/117°11′E) A city in China, 637

Tibesti Mountains (21°30′N/17°30′E) A mountain range in the Sahara, 417

Tierra del Fuego (54°00′S/70°00′W) The southernmost tip of South America, 201

Tigris River (31°00′N/47°25′E) A river that rises in eastern Turkey, flows southeast through Iraq, and joins the Euphrates River; together they form the Shatt al Arab, which flows into the Persian Gulf, *m488,* 489

Timor (10°08′S/125°00′E) An island of southeast Indonesia, 705

Tiranë (41°20′N/19°49′E) The capital of Albania, 266

Togo (8°00′N/1°10′E) A country in West Africa, 442

Tokyo (35°41′N/139°45′E) One of the largest cities of the world; the capital of Japan, 630

Tonga (20°00′S/175°00′W) A country that consists of an island group of Oceania in the Pacific Ocean, 712, *m713*

Topeka (39°03′N/95°41′W) The capital of Kansas, 108

Toronto (43°40′N/79°25′W) The capital of Ontario, Canada; the most populous city in the country, 168

Transantarctic Mountains (85°00′S/175°00′W) Mountain ranges in Antarctica, 692

Transcaucasia (42°00′N/45°00′E) A region bounded by Russia, the Caspian Sea, the Black Sea, Turkey, and Iran and consisting of Armenia, Azerbaijan, and Georgia, 346

Trenton (40°13′N/74°45′W) The capital of New Jersey, 110

Trinidad and Tobago (11°00′N/61°00′W) A country consisting of the islands of Trinidad and Tobago in the Atlantic Ocean near northeast Venezuela, 198

Tripoli (32°54′N/13°11′E) The capital of Libya, 410

Tucson (32°13′N/110°56′W) A city in southern Arizona, 149, *m149*

Tunis (36°48′N/10°11′E) The capital of Tunisia, 412

Tunis, Gulf of (36°58′N/10°46′E) An inlet of the Mediterranean Sea near the city of Tunis, 438

Tunisia (34°00′N/9°00′E) A country in North Africa, 438

Turkey (39°00′N/35°00′E) A country in the northwest region of Southwest Asia, 516, *m516*

Turkmenistan (40°00′N/60°00′E) A country in Central Asia, 375

Tuvalu (8°00′S/178°00′E) A country that consists of an island group of Oceania in the Pacific Ocean, 712, *m713*

U.S. Virgin Islands A U.S. territory that consists of the southwest group of the Virgin Islands, 112

Uganda (2°00′N/33°00′E) A country in East Africa, 431

Ukraine (49°00′N/32°00′E) A country that is west of Russia, 361

Ulaanbaatar (47°55′N/106°55′E) The capital of Mongolia, 616

United Arab Emirates (24°00′N/54°00′E) A country in the Arabian Peninsula of Southwest Asia, 503

United Kingdom (54°00′N/4°00′W) A Northern European nation consisting of England, Wales, Scotland, and Northern Ireland, 300

United States (38°00′N/110°00′W) A country in North America that consists of 50 states, the District of Columbia, and four territories, 117

Ural Mountains (60°00′N/60°00′E) A mountain range that runs north and south in western Russia; some consider it as the border between Europe and Asia, 345

Uruguay (33°00′S/56°00′W) A country in southern South America, 230, *m234*

Utah (39°15′N/111°45′W) A state in the western United States, 112

Uzbekistan (41°00′N/64°00′E) A country in Central Asia, 375

Vaduz (47°08′N/9°31′E) The capital of Liechtenstein, 266

Valletta (35°54′N/14°31′E) The capital of Malta, 268

Vancouver (49°15′N/123°08′W) A city in British Columbia, 169

Vanuatu (16°00′S/167°00′E) A country that consists of an island group of Oceania in the Pacific Ocean, 712, *m713*

Vatican City (41°54′N/12°27′E) An independent papal state located near Rome, Italy, 268

Venezuela (8°00′N/66°00′W) A country in northern South America, 230, *m234*

Venice (45°26′N/12°20′E) A city in northeastern Italy, 281

Verkhoyansk (67°35′N/133°27′E) A city in Siberia in Russia, 354

Vermont (44°00′N/72°45′W) A state in New England in the northeastern United States, 145

Victoria (48°26′N/123°21′W) The capital of British Columbia, Canada, 169

Victoria (4°37′S/55°27′E) The capital of Seychelles, 412

Victoria Island (71°00′N/110°00′W) A large island in northern Canada, 121

Victoria, Lake (1°00′S/33°00′E) The second largest freshwater lake in the world; lies in East Africa, 417

Vienna (48°12′N/16°22′E) The capital of Austria, 266

Vientiane (17°58′N/102°36′E) The capital of Laos, 684

Vietnam (16°00′N/106°00′E) A country in Southeast Asia, 705

Vilnius (54°41′N/25°19′E) The capital of Lithuania, 342

Vindhya Mountains (24°37′N/82°00′E) A mountain range in central India, 552

Virginia (37°30′N/78°30′W) A state in the southern United States, 148

Volga River (45°51′N/47°58′E) The longest river in Europe; rises near Moscow, flows east and then south, and empties into the Caspian Sea, 347

Warsaw (52°15′N/21°00′E) The capital of Poland, 268

Washington (47°30′N/120°30′W) A state in the northwestern United States, 148

Washington, D.C. (38°54′N/77°02′W) The capitol of the United States, *m145,* 147

Wellington (41°18′S/174°47′E) The capital of New Zealand, 684

West, the An area of the United States that stretches from the Great Plains to the Pacific Ocean and includes Alaska and Hawaii. Other states in this area are Montana, Wyoming, Colorado, New Mexico, Arizona, Utah, Idaho, Washington, Oregon, Nevada, and California, 148

West Africa A region of Africa that includes Benin, Burkina Faso, Cape Verde, Chad, Côte d'Ivoire, Gambia, Ghana, Guinea, Guinea-Bissau, Liberia, Mali, Mauritania, Niger, Nigeria, Senegal, Sierra Leone, and Togo, 442

West Antarctica A region of Antarctica; a group of islands of Antarctica linked by the ice that covers them, 692

West Bank (31°40′N/35°15′E) A strip of land on the west side of the Jordan River, 527

West Siberian Plain (60°00′N/75°00′E) A plain in west central Russia, 345

West Virginia (38°30′N/80°30′W) A state in the southern United States, 112

Western Europe A region that includes France, Germany, Austria, Liechtenstein, Switzerland, Belgium, the Netherlands, and Luxembourg, 294

Western Ghats (14°00′N/75°00′E) A mountain range that runs along the west coast of India, 552

Western Republics Countries located west of Russia; they include Ukraine, Belarus, Moldova, Latvia, Lithuania, and Estonia, 361

Whitehorse (60°43′N/135°03′W) The capital of the Yukon Territory of Canada, 114

Windhoek (22°34′S/17°05′E) The capital of Namibia, 410

Winnipeg (49°53′N/97°10′W) The capital of Manitoba, Canada, 114

Wisconsin (44°30′N/90°00′W) A state in the Midwest of the United States, 112

Wuhan (30°35′N/114°16′E) A city in China, 637

Wuxi (31°36′N/120°17′E) A city in China, 637

Wyoming (43°00′N/107°30′W) A state in the western United States, 112

Xi Jiang (also called West River) (22°48′N/113°03′E) A river that flows through southeast China, joins the Pearl River (Zhu Jiang) and empties into the South China Sea, 621, *m620*

Yalu River (39°56′N/124°19′E) A river that forms the border between North Korea and China, 622, *m620*

Yamoussoukro (6°49′N/5°17′W) The capital of Côte d'Ivoire, 408

Yangon (16°47′N/96°10′E) The capital of Myanmar, 684

Yangtze River (also called Chang Jiang) (31°47′N/121°08′E) The longest river in Asia; flows from Xizang (Tibet) across China to the East China Sea, *m620,* 621

Yaoundé (3°52′N/11°31′E) The capital of Cameroon, 408

Yellow River (also called Huang He) (37°45′N/119°05′E) A Chinese river that rises in the Kunlun Mountains, flows east for about 3,000 miles, and empties into the Yellow Sea, *m620,* 621

Yellow Sea (36°00′N/124°00′E) An arm of the Pacific Ocean between the Korean Peninsula and northeastern China, *m620,* 621

Yellowknife (62°27′N/114°21′W) The capital of the Northwest Territories of Canada, 114

Yemen (15°16′N/42°35′E) A country in the Arabian Peninsula of Southwest Asia, 503

Yenisey River (71°50′N/82°40′E) A river that flows through central Russia and empties into the Kara Sea, 347

Yerevan (40°11′N/44°30′E) The capital of Armenia, *m370,* 371

Yugoslavia (43°45′N/20°45′E) A country in Eastern Europe, 308

Yukon Territory (63°00′N/136°00′W) A territory in northwestern Canada, 169

Zagreb (45°48′N/16°00′E) The capital of Croatia, 266

Zagros Mountains (33°40′N/47°00′E) A mountain range in western Iran, 488, *m488*

Zambia (15°00′S/30°00′E) A country in Southern Africa, 453, *m454*

Zimbabwe (19°00′S/29°00′E) A country in Southern Africa, 453, *m454*

confederation, 156–157

Confucianism, 77, *i636*, 638, 648

Congo, Democratic Republic of, *i401*, *c408–409*, 417, 448, 449, 450, *i452*, 461, 469

Congo, Republic of, *c408–409*, 448, 449

Congo River, *c402*, 448

constitutional monarchies, 580, 581

Continental Divide, 120

continental drift, *i29*

continentality, 350

continental plates, 29, 661

continental shelf, 36, 620

continents, 27, *i29*, 117

convection, *i50*, 51, 54,

copper, *m93*, *m204*, 235

coral reefs, 691

core, of the earth, *i28*

Core Provinces, *m154*, 167–168

Coriolis effect, 54

Costa Rica, *c196–197*

costumes, *i716–717*

Cote d'Ivoire, *c408–409*, 418

creating a multimedia presentation, R14

creating and using a database, R15

creating a sketch map, R12

creating graphs and charts, R13

Croatia, *c268–269*, 310, 320

Croats, 314, 320, *m322*

Crusades, the, 291

crust, of the earth, *i28*

Cuba, *c94*, *c196–197*, 203, *i225*

cultural crossroads, 310

cultural hearth, 222
    defined, 72

culture, 72, 73, 75
    defined, 71

Cuzco, Peru, 210, 231

cyclones, 51, 557, 563, *i578*, *i579*

Cyprus, *c484–485*, 513

Czechoslovakia, 311, 312, 313

Czech Republic, *c268–269*, 310, 313, 314

D

dachas, 367

Dagestan, 385

Damavand, *c478*

dams, 426–427, *i562*, 563, 628, 630

dance, 456, 577, 586, *i714*

Danube River, *c262*, 275

Dardenelles Strait, 488

Dasht-e Kavir, 492

Dasht-e Lut, 492

Dead Sea, *i489*

death rate, 78

Death Valley, *i119*

debt-for-nature swap, 247

Deccan Plateau, 552, 556, 558

deforestation, 554, *i555*, 558, 587
    in Brazil, *i188*
    in Europe, 284–285
    in Latin America, *i244*, 245–246
    in Washington, *i100*

deltas, *i34*, 43

democracy, *i139*, 249–251, *i249*, *c250*, *i251*, 253, 289, *c303*, 469, 568, 569
    defined, 83

Denmark, *c224*, *c268–269*, 273, 302

Department of Homeland Security, 175

desalinization, 496

desert, 66, *i475*, *i491*, 558, 626, 627, 697
    in Africa, *c402*, 420–421
    human settlement of, *i70*
    in Latin America, *m194*, 209
    in Russia and the Republics, *m340*, 352
    in Southwest Asia, *c478*, 491–492
    in United States and Canada, 124, *m125*

desert climate region, *i60*
    defined, 62

desertification, *m107*, *i424–425*

determining cause and effect, R9

developed nations, 95

developing nations, 95

dialect, 73

diamonds, 415, 444, 456, 555

Díaz, Porfirio, 218

dictatorship
    defined, 83

didgeridoo, *i589*

disasters, *i578*, *i579*, *i640–641*, *i660*, 663, *i710*, *i711*

distinguishing fact from opinion, R11

distortion, 10

Djenné, Mali, *i398*

Djibouti, *c408–409*, 431

Dom, *c262*

Dome of the Rock, *i474*, *i511*

Dominica, *c196–197*

Dominican Republic, *c196–197*, 203

Dominion of Canada, 156–157

drawing conclusions, R5

drip irrigation, 496

drought, *i150*, *i151*, *m436*, *i437*
    defined, 53

Druze, 515

Dubai, 530

Dust Bowl, the, *m150*, *i151*

dust storms, 44, 53, *m150*, *i151*

dwellings, *i380–381*

E

earth, the, *i26*, *i28*, *i49*

earthquakes, 39–40, *i39*, *i40*, *i608*, *i660*, *m664*
    defined, 39
    detectors, *i663*
    in Ring of Fire, 41, 662
    ten most deadly, *c47*
    in Turkey, *m520*, *i521*
    in United States and Canada, *m107*

Earth Summit, 735

East Africa, 431–435, *m431*

East Asia, 606
    area by country, *c617*
    birthrate by country, *c616*
    capitals and countries of, *c616*
    cars per country, *c617*
    climate regions, 625, *m626*, 627
    doctors by country, *c617*
    economic activities in, 665–667
    expansion of Chinese empire, *m612*
    flags of, *c616*
    gross domestic product by country, *c617*
    history of, 665–666
    imports and exports by country, *c617*
    infant mortality rate by country, *c616*
    landforms in, *c611*, *c617*, 619, *m620*, 621–622
    landmass of, *c610*
    languages in, *m615*
    life expectancy by country, *c616*
    literacy rate by country, *c617*
    mountains in, *c611*, 619, *m620*
    natural resources in, *m622*, 623
    physical geography of, *c611*
    political geography of, *m612–613*
    population in, *c82*, *c610*, *m615*, *c616*, *c669*, 671
    precipitation in, *m633*
    religions of, *c614*
    rivers in, *c610*, *m620*, 621–622
    subregions of, *m634*
    televisions per country, *c617*
    total area of countries, *c617*
    vegetation of, *m614*, 625–627

Eastern Europe
    art in, 314
    Balkan conflict in, 319, *c320*, 321
    balkanization, 311
    communism in, 363
    culture in, 314
    economic activities in, 313
    ethnic and religious animosities, 314–315, 320–321
    ethnic cleansing, 320

outback, 697
outrigger canoe, 699
ozone layer, 325, *i677*, 734–737

P

Pacific Islands, 698–701
Pacific Ocean, 32, 41, 121
Pacific Provinces and Territories, *m154*, 168–169
Pacific Rim, 645
Padma River, 560
Paektu, Mt., *c611*
pakehas, 722
Pakistan, 174, *i541*, *c548–549*, *i550*, 551, 552, 554, 555, 556, 568, 573–574, *c575*, 576–577
Palau, *c684–685*, 712
Palestine, 511, 512, 527, 534
Palestine Liberation Organization (PLO), 513
Palestinians, 175, *i513*, *i527*, *m533*, 535
pampas, 66
   of Argentina and Uruguay, 202
Panama, *c198–199*, 222
pandemic, 435
Pangaea, i29, 415
Papua New Guinea, *c684–685*, 712, 714
Paraguay, *c198–199*, 203, 207, 209, 253
Paraná River, *c190*, 203
parliamentary government, 158
particulates, 324
Patagonia, *i59*, 209
PCBs, 631
Pearl Harbor, 652
Pearl River. *See* Zhu Jiang.
peninsulas, 273–274, 620, 689
Pennsylvania, 146
Pentagon, 173
Perahera, 586
per capita income
   defined, 94
permafrost, 63, 123, 280, 350, 355
Persian Gulf, 487, 489, 490, 517
Persian Gulf War, 174, 499, 517, 518
Peru, 54, *i165*, *c198–199*, 210, 211, *i717*
Philippines, *c684–685*, 689, 690, 694, 705, 709, 731, *c739*
physical maps, *i20*
Pinatuba, Mt., 689
Pinochet, Augusto, *i189*, *i232*
pipelines, 373, *m417*, 426, 497, 499
Pittsburgh, Pennsylvania, 88, 117
place
   theme of geography, 7
plains, 36, 275
   of Amazon River Basin, 202

planar projection. *See* azimuthal projection.
Plateau of Tibet, 619
plateaus, *i35*, 36, 551–552
plate tectonics, 37–39
PLO. *See* Palestine Liberation Organization.
Poland, *c270–271*, 310, 311, 312
polar zones, 56, 697
polders, 282
pollution, 324, 354, 670
   in Europe, *i260*, 285, 323–325
   along the Ganges River, 560, 561
   in Japan, 630
   in Russia and the Republics, 349, *m359*
   in Southeast Asia, 731, 732
   in Southwest Asia, 499
   in United States and Canada, 177
Polynesia, 713
Polynesians, 698, *i699*, 715
population
   in Africa, *c402*, 425
   in China, *i639*
   distribution, 80–81, *m406*
   of East Asia cities, 668–669, *c669*
   of Europe, *c262*
   of Latin America, *c190*, 238
   relocation of, 525–527, 630
   in South Asia, *c542*, *i592*
   in Southwest Asia, *c478*
population density, *m80*, 81–82, *m528*
   in Bangladesh, *i577*
   of Canada, *m107*
   in East Asia, *m615*
   of Europe, *m267*
   in India, *m594*
   along the Nile River, 416
   of South Asia, *m547*
   of United States, *m107*
   of world regions, *c82*
population growth rate, *i3*, 78–79, *c78*, *c79*, *i540*, 670, 671, *c673*
population pyramid, *c79*, *m596*
   defined, 79
Portugal, 236, *c270–271*, 274, 291, *c292*, *m404*, 449, 468
poverty, 144, *i189*, 252–253, 254, 255, *c257*, 455, 595
Powell, Lake, *i67*
Prague, Czech Republic, 314, *i315*
prairie, *i35*, 65
Prairie Provinces, *m154*, *i168*
precipitation, 735
   in Africa, 421–422
   and climate regions, 59
   in East Asia, *m633*

   in Europe, *c281*
   ocean currents and, 55
   in South Asia, 557, *m565*
   in Southwest Asia, 491–492
   types of, 50–52, *i50*
   in United States coastal mountain ranges, 124
prevailing westerlies, 124
PRI. *See* Institutional Revolutionary Party.
prime meridian, *i6*, *m357*
   defined, 6
prime minister, 158
Prince Edward Island, *c114–115*, *m157*, 166
privatization, 388
proportional circle maps, *m664*
Pueblo, 127
Puerto Rico, 203
purdah, 576
Pushkin, Aleksandr, 366
push-pull factors, 211, 730
   defined, 81
   in Latin America, 211
Putin, Vladimir, *i363*, 389
Pyongyang, North Korea, 650
pyramids, 219, *i223*, *i398*, *i509*
Pyrenees Mountains, 274

Q

qanat, *i496*
Qatar, *c484–485*, 503, 506, *c526*, *c537*
Qawwali, 577
Qinling Shandi Mountains, 619
qualitative maps, *m22*
Quebec, *c114–115*, 162, 167, 180
Quechua, 231

R

radiation, *i368*, *m368*, 377
rai, 440
rain forest, 422–423, 425, 558
   in Africa, 421
   deforestation in Brazil, *i188*
   in Latin America, 207–208, *m245*, 246, 247
   medicine from, *i205*
   vegetation in, 66
rain shadow, 51, 492
Ramadan, 504, 507, 576
ranching, *i721*
rate of natural increase
   defined, 79
ratio scale, *i16*
recession, 138, 667

Acknowledgments

This product contains proprietary property of MAPQUEST.COM.
Unauthorized use, including copying, of this product, is expressly prohibited.

TEXT ACKNOWLEDGMENTS

Unit 1, Adapted "Figure 9.51," from *Physical Geography, Second Edition.* Copyright © 1989, 1992 by West Publishing Company. Reprinted by permission of Thomson Learning.

Excerpt from "Flight of a Lifetime" by James Irwin, from *The Greatest Adventure.* Copyright © 1994 by the Association of Space Explorers.

Excerpt from "To Really See It, Leave It" by Sally Ride, from *The Greatest Adventure.* Copyright © 1994 by the Association of Space Explorers.

Unit 3, Excerpt from "Brazilian police go on trial for murder of street children" by Marina Mirabella, from CNN World News, April 26, 1996. Copyright © 1996 by Cable News Network, Inc. Reprinted by permission of Cable News Network, Inc.

Excerpt from "Hope for the no-hopers," from the *Economist,* December 23, 2000. Copyright © 2000 by the *Economist.* Reprinted by permission of the *Economist.*

Excerpt from "Rich-poor gap as wide as ever in Latin America" by Steve Gutkin, from *The Times of India Online,* September 5, 2000. Copyright © 2000 by Times Internet Limited. Reprinted by permission of Times Internet Limited. All rights reserved.

Unit 4, Excerpt from "Poland Opens Door to West, and Chills Blow Both Ways" by Edmund L. Andrews, from the *New York Times,* June 21, 1999. Copyright © 1999 by the *New York Times.* Reprinted by permission of the *New York Times.*

Excerpt from "Britain and the Single Currency," from Global Britain Briefing Note, No. 1, January 25, 1999. Copyright © 1999 by Global Britain. Reprinted by permission of Global Britain.

Unit 5, Excerpt from "Workers Bid Ill-Fated Chernobyl a Bitter Farewell" by Michael Wines, from the *New York Times,* December 15, 2000. Copyright © 2000 by the *New York Times.* Reprinted by permission of the *New York Times.*

Excerpt from "Reducing Russian Dangers," from the *New York Times,* January 21, 1999. Copyright © 1999 by the *New York Times.* Reprinted by permission of the *New York Times.*

Unit 6, Excerpt from "Cash Strapped African Leaders Beg To Be Re-Colonized" by Ron Daniels, from the *Black World Today,* August 1, 1999. Copyright © 1999 by the *Black World Today.* Reprinted by permission of the *Black World Today.*

Excerpt from "An African Success Story," from the *New York Times,* January 8, 2001. Copyright © 2001 by the *New York Times.* Reprinted by permission of the *New York Times.*

Unit 7, Excerpt from "All Sides Resist Plan by Clinton For the Mideast" by John Kifner, from the *New York Times,* December 31, 2000. Copyright © 2000 by the *New York Times.* Reprinted by permission of the *New York Times.*

Excerpt from "The Price of Peace Will Be Paid in Dreams" by John F. Kifner, from the *New York Times,* December 31, 2000. Copyright © 2000 by the *New York Times.* Reprinted by permission of the *New York Times.*

Excerpt from "A City That Echoes Eternity" by Kenneth L. Woodward, from *Newsweek,* July 24, 2000. Copyright © 2000 by Newsweek, Inc. Reprinted by permission of Newsweek, Inc. All rights reserved.

Excerpts from "City of Jerusalem," from *United Nations: General Assembly Resolution 181,* November 29, 1947. Copyright © 1947 by the United Nations. Reprinted by permission of the United Nations.

Unit 8, Excerpt from President K. R. Narayanan's state dinner toast, March 21, 2000. Copyright © 2001 by the Embassy of India, Press and Information. Reprinted by permission of the Embassy of India.

Unit 9, Excerpt from "Clinton in Hong Kong, prods China on environment," from CNN.com, July 2, 1998. Copyright © 1998 by Cable News Network, Inc. Reprinted by permission of Cable News Network, Inc.

Excerpt from "Six Billion People," from *Asiaweek.com,* October 29, 1999, Vol. 25, No. 43. Copyright © 1999 by Asiaweek. Reprinted by permission of Asiaweek.

Unit 10, Excerpt from "Record Ozone Hole Refuels Debate on Climate" by Andrew C. Revkin, from the *New York Times,* October 10, 2000. Copyright © 2000 by the *New York Times.* Reprinted by permission of the *New York Times.*

Excerpts from *Dear America, Letters Home from Vietnam* edited by Bernard Edelman. Copyright © 1985 by The New York Vietnam Veterans Memorial Commission. Reprinted by permission of Simon & Schuster.

Excerpt from "Heroes for the Planet" by Terry McCarthy, from *Time,* Apr–May 2000. Copyright © 2000 by Time, Inc. Reprinted by permission of Time, Inc.

Excerpt from "There is No Global Warming," from the American Policy Center. Copyright © 2001 by the American Policy Center. Reprinted by permission of the American Policy Center.

The editors have made every effort to trace the ownership of all copyrighted material found in this book and to make full acknowledgment for its use. Omissions brought to our attention will be corrected in a subsequent edition.

ART CREDITS

Cover **front** *background* Copyright © Orbital Imaging Corporation and processing by NASA Goddard Space Flight Center. Image provided by ORBIMAGE; *insets, top to bottom* Copyright © Hugh Sitton/Stone; Copyright © George Hunter/H. Armstrong Roberts; Copyright © James Martin/Stone; Copyright © Michael Dunning/Image Bank.

Front Matter **ii–iii** *background* Copyright © Orbital Imaging Corporation and processing by NASA Goddard Space Flight Center. Image provided by ORBIMAGE; **ii** *top, left to right* Copyright © Hugh Sitton/Tony Stone Images; Copyright © George Hunter/ H. Armstrong Roberts; Copyright © James Martin/Tony Stone Images; **iii** *right* Copyright © Michael Dunning/Image Bank; **v, vi–vii** *background* Earth from space; **viii** *top* Copyright © Schafer & Hill/Tony Stone Images; *bottom* Copyright © 1994 Jeffrey Aaronson/Network Aspen. All rights reserved; **ix** *top* SuperStock; *bottom* Copyright © Kevin Miller/Tony Stone Images; **x** *top* Copyright © Loren McIntyre; *bottom* Copyright © Ary Diesendruck/Tony Stone Images; **xi** *top* Copyright © Eye Ubiquitous/Corbis; *bottom* Ric Ergenbright Photography; **xii** *top* Copyright © Sovfoto/Eastfoto; *bottom* Copyright © David Sutherland/Tony Stone Images; **xiii** *top* Copyright © Daryl Balfour/Tony Stone Images; *center* Copyright © Mitch Reardon/Tony Stone Images; *bottom* Copyright © M. Thonig/H. Armstrong Roberts; **xiv** *top* Copyright © Ali Kazuyoshi Namachi/Pacific Press; *bottom* Copyright © John Egan/Hutchison Picture Library; **xv** *top* Copyright © Paul Harris/Tony Stone Images; *bottom* Copyright © Martin Puddy/Tony Stone Images; **xvi** *top* Copyright © David Ball/Tony Stone Images; *center* Copyright © Tony Stone Images; *bottom* Copyright © John Lamb/Tony Stone Images; **xvii** *top* Copyright © Roger Near/Tony Stone Images; *center* Copyright © Nicholas DeVore/Tony Stone Images; *bottom* Copyright © David Austen/Tony Stone Images. **xxiv** Copyright © Dani/Jeske/Animals Animals; Copyright © Patti Murray/Earth Scenes; Copyright © J. Carnemolla/Australian Picture Library; Copyright © John Cancalosi/Peter Arnold Inc.; Copyright © Norman Owen Tomalin/Bruce Coleman; Copyright © Tim Flach/Tony Stone Images; **xxv** *top* The Granger Collection, New York; *bottom* Copyright © 2001 The New Yorker Collection from cartoonbank.com. All rights reserved.

Maps pp. A1–A25, 64, 102–115, 131, 179, 190–199, 206, 248, 262–271, 281, 322, 336–343, 357, 391, 402–413, 419, 464, 478–485, 494, 528, 542–549, 559, 596, 610–617, 624, 664, 678–687, © Rand McNally & Company. All rights reserved.

Units **Unit 1, 2–3** *background* Copyright © Earth Imaging/Tony Stone Images; **2** *foreground* Copyright © Schafer & Hill/Tony Stone Images; **3** *foreground* Copyright © Damir Sagolj/Reuters/Archive Photos; **4** *background, left* MapQuest.com; **7** Copyright © Eduardo Garcia/FPG International/PictureQuest; **8** Copyright © Alan Weiner/Liaison; **10** Globe (c. 1492), Martin Benhaim. Bibliotheque Nationale, Paris/Giraudon/Art Resource, New York; **11** *background* Copyright © Paul Morrell/Tony Stone Images; *top left* National Oceanic and Atmospheric Administration/Department of Commerce; **12** *top left* Copyright © Bob Krist/ eStock Photography/PictureQuest; *top center* Copyright © PhotoDisc/Getty Images; **13** Copyright © Erwin and Peggy Bauer/Bruce Coleman Inc.; **14** *background* National Oceanic and Atmospheric Administration/Department of Commerce; *top* AP/Wide World Photos; *bottom left* Science Museum/Science & Society Picture Library, London; *bottom right* Copyright © Owen Franken/Stock Boston/PictureQuest; **26** Copyright © Paul Morrell/Tony Stone Images; **30–31** *background,* **31** Illustrations by Roberta Polfus; **32** Copyright © SuperStock; **33** Illustration by Stephen R. Wagner; **34–35** Illustration by Ken Goldammer; **36** Copyright © Earth Satellite Corporation/Science Photo Library/Photo Researchers Inc.; **38–39** Illustration by Roberta Polfus; **40** Copyright © Chip Hires/Liaison; **41** Copyright © HO/Reuters/Archive Photos; **42** Copyright © David Muench/Corbis; **43** AP/Wide World Photos; **44** Copyright © Jerryl Hout/ Bruce Coleman Inc.; **48** Copyright © SuperStock; **50** Illustration by Stephen R. Wagner; **51** National Oceanic and Atmospheric Administration/Department of Commerce; **52** *inset* Copyright © Chris Johns/Tony Stone Images; **53** Getty News Services; **59** Copyright © Vladpans/eStock Photography/PictureQuest; **60** *top* Copyright © SuperStock; *bottom* Copyright © 1994 Michael Fogden/Bruce Coleman Inc./PictureQuest; **61** *top insert* Copyright © 1999 Picture Finders Ltd./ eStock Photography/PictureQuest; *bottom insert* Copyright © Daniel J. Cox/ Liaison; **62** Copyright © Charlie Waite/Tony Stone Images; **63** Copyright © 1993 Richard Olsenius/Black Star/PictureQuest; **67** *left* Used by permission, Utah State Historical Society. All rights reserved; *right* Copyright © Tom Till Photography; **70** Copyright © 1994 David Hiser/Photographers/Aspen/PictureQuest; **72** Copyright © Adrian Arbib/Corbis; **73** Courtesy Medmaster, Inc. Miami, Florida; **77** Copyright © Werner Forman/Corbis; **81** Copyright © 1994 Jeffrey Aaronson/Network Aspen. All rights reserved; **83** Copyright © 1960 Sergio Larrain/Magnum Photos; **85** Copyright © D. E. Cox/Tony Stone Images; **87** Copyright © SuperStock; **88** Copyright © Earth Imaging/Tony Stone Images; **91** Copyright © SuperStock; **92** Photograph by Sharon Hoogstraten; **94** *top row, pots* Copyright © 1999 Stockbyte/PictureQuest; *bicycles* Copyright © Image Club/EyeWire; *middle row, kettles and sieves* Copyright © 1999 Stockbyte/PictureQuest; *televisions* Copyright © Digital Stock/Corbis; *stereos* Copyright © Jeffrey Coolidge/Image Bank; *bottom row, bicycle* Copyright © Image Club/EyeWire; *radios* Copyright © Digital Stock/Corbis; *VCR* Copyright © 1999–2001 PhotoDisc/Getty Images; **95** *top row, bicycles* Copyright © Image Club/EyeWire; *radios and telephone* Copyright

Robert Frerck/Odyssey/Chicago; **445** Copyright © Deborah Feingold/Archive Photos; **446** *clockwise from top right* Copyright © Trip/Dinodia; Copyright © 1996 Christopher Liu/ChinaStock; Copyright © Trip/H. Rogers; **447** *top* SuperStock; *bottom* Copyright © Robert Frerck/Odyssey/Chicago; **449** Cartoon by Linley Sambourne (1906). Mary Evans Picture Library, London; **451** *When There is Work, the Village Expands*, Mode Muntu. Collection of Guy de Plaen; **452** Copyright © 1995 Malcolm Linton/Liaison; **453** Robert Aberman/Art Resource, New York; **455** *from top to bottom* The Granger Collection, New York; Copyright © Hulton/ Archive Swimming Pool Database-Big Picture; The Royal Collection copyright © 2001 Her Majesty Queen Elizabeth II; Copyright © Mark Peters/Sipa Press; **456** Copyright © Robert Frerck/Odyssey/Chicago; **460** Copyright © 1968 Rene Burri/Magnum Photos; **461** Photograph by Bjorn Klingwall; **463** Copyright © Piotr Jaxa/The Rolex Awards for Enterprise; **465** Copyright © Malcolm Linton/Liaison; **467** *top* right Copyright © Wendy Stone/Liaison; **468** Corbis-Bettmann; **469** *bottom* AP/Wide World Photos; **471** Copyright © 1996 Alan King. National Archives of Canada, Ottawa, ref. No. R2905-116.

Unit 7, 474–475 *background* Copyright © 1995 WorldSat International and J. Knighton/Photo Researchers, Inc.; **474** *left* Copyright © Sylvain Grandadam/Tony Stone Images; *right* Copyright © Bernard Gerard/Hutchison Picture Library; **475** Copyright © Ali Kazuyoshi Nomachi/Pacific Press Service; **476** Copyright © John Egan/Hutchison Picture Library; **477** *top* Copyright © Robert Azzi/Woodfin Camp; *bottom* Mark Fiore. San Francisco, California. www.markfiore.com; **484–485** MapQuest.com; **486** Copyright © Peter Sanders; **487** Copyright © Richard T. Nowitz/Corbis; **489** Copyright © Roger Antrobus/Corbis; **490** AP/Wide World Photos; **491** Copyright © Alistair Duncan/DK Images; **493** Copyright © Nik Wheeler/Corbis; **495** Copyright © Alan Puzey/Tony Stone Images; **496** *background* Copyright © PhotoDisc/Getty Images; *clockwise from top left* Copyright © Richard T. Nowitz/NGS Image Collection; Copyright © Trip/H. Rogers; Copyright © Peter J. Ochs II; Copyright © Christopher Rennie/Robert Harding Picture Library; **497** Getty News Services, #372147_06; **503** Copyright © Nabeel Turner/ Tony Stone Images; **504** Scala/Art Resource, New York; **506** Copyright © 1985 Robert Azzi/Woodfin Camp; **507** Copyright © 2001 Stern Magazine/Black Star; **508–509** *background* Copyright © Hugh Sitton/Tony Stone Images; **508** SEF/Art Resource, New York; **509** *top* SuperStock; *bottom* Copyright © 1995 David Hiser/ Photographers/Aspen/PictureQuest; **510** AP/Wide World Photos; **511** Copyright © Ilene Perlman/Stock Boston/PictureQuest; **513, 514** AP/Wide World Photos; **515** Copyright © Trip/H. Rogers; **517** Copyright © Reuters New Media Inc./Corbis; **518** Copyright © Leo Touchet/Woodfin Camp; **519** Copyright © R. Ashworth/ Robert Harding Picture Library; **521** *top* Copyright © ABC Basin Ajansi/Liaison; *bottom* AP/Wide World Photos; **524** Copyright © John Egan/Hutchison Picture Library; **525** Copyright © Thomas Hartwell/TimePix; **527** Copyright © Will Yurman/Liaison; **530** *top* Copyright © Ali Kazuyoshi Nomachi/Pacific Press Service; *bottom* Copyright © Baron Wolman; **531** Copyright © David & Peter Turnley/Corbis; **532** *top* AP/Wide World Photos; *bottom left* Corbis-Bettmann; *bottom right* Copyright © Dirck Halstead/Liaison; **535** Mark Fiore. San Francisco, California. www.markfiore.com.

Unit 8, 538–539 *background* Copyright © Earth Imaging/Tony Stone Images; **538** Copyright © Paul Harris/Tony Stone Images; **539** *left* Copyright © 1997 Neal Beidleman/Network Aspen; *right* Copyright © Dominic Sansoni; **540** Copyright © James Strachan/Robert Harding Picture Library; **541** *top* Copyright © Chip Hires/Liaison; *bottom* Copyright © 1998 Carlson/Milwaukee Journal Sentinel; **550** Copyright © Jon Sparks/Corbis; **551** Illustration by Stephen R. Wagner; **552** Digital image copyright © 1996 Corbis. Original image courtesy of NASA/Corbis; **553** Copyright © E. Valentin/Photo Researchers, Inc.; **554** *inset* Copyright © Dominic Sansoni; **555** Copyright © Takeshi Takahara/ Photo Researchers, Inc.; **556** Copyright © Brian Vikander/Corbis; **558** Copyright © E. Hanumantha Rao/Photo Researchers, Inc.; **560–561** Copyright © David Sutherland/Tony Stone Images; **562** Copyright © Pablo Bartholomew/Liaison; *inset right* Copyright © St. Franklin/Magnum Photos; **568** *top* Corbis-Bettmann; *bottom left* The Granger Collection, New York; *bottom right* Copyright © Roderick Johnson/Images of India; **570** Copyright © 1978 Dilip Mehta/Contact Press Images/PictureQuest; **571** Copyright © Anthony Cassidy/Tony Stone Images; **572** The Art Archive/Victoria & Albert Museum, London/Eileen Tweedy. Ref. no. AA328654; **573** Copyright © Photobank Photo Library; **575** *left* Copyright © David Sanger/Network Aspen; *right* Copyright © Brecel/J. Hodalic/Liaison; **576** Copyright © Robert Nickelsberg/TimePix; **577** Copyright © Beatrice Kiener/ Liaison; **578–579** *background* National Oceanic and Atmospheric Administration/ Department of Commerce; **578** *bottom* Illustration by Stephen R. Wagner; **579** *top* Copyright © Topham Picturepoint; *bottom* Jim Holmes/Eye Ubiquitous; **580** Thrikheb or "throne cover." Wool, silk, and cotton, 152 cm x 70 cm. Private collection, Oltromare, Geneva, Switzerland. Photograph copyright © Erich Lessing/ Art Resource; **581** Copyright © John Callahan/Tony Stone Images; **582** *background* Illustration by Stephen R. Wagner; *top inset* Copyright © Alison Wright/ Stock Boston/PictureQuest; **583** Copyright © Barbara Bussell/Network Aspen; **584** Copyright © Nokelsberg/Liaison; **585** Copyright © Hugh Sitton/Tony Stone Images; **586** Copyright © Martin Puddy/Tony Stone Images; **587** Copyright © Pete Seaward/Tony Stone Images; **588** *left* Copyright © Greig Cranna/Stock Boston/PictureQuest; *right* Copyright © Wolfgang Kaehler/Corbis; **589** *top* Copyright © 1999 Pictor International/Pictor International, Ltd./PictureQuest *bottom* AP/Wide World Photos; **592** Copyright © James Strachan/Robert Harding Picture Library; **593** Copyright © Bruno Barbey/ Magnum Photos; **595** Copyright © Jeroen Snjdera/Images of India; **598** Illustrations by Stephen R. Wagner; **599** *top* Courtesy David Cumming/ Hodder Wayland Picture Library; *bottom* Copyright © Trip/H. Rogers; **600** *top* Copyright © Ric Ergenbright/Corbis *bottom left* Corbis-Bettmann; *bottom right* Reuters/Archive Photos; **603** Copyright © 1998 Carlson/Milwaukee Journal Sentinel.

Unit 9, 606–607 *background* Copyright © Tom Van Sant/Geosphere Project/ Planetary Visions/Science Photo Library/Photo Researchers, Inc.; **606** SuperStock; **607** *left* Copyright © David Ball/Tony Stone Images; *right* SuperStock; **608** John Pryke/Reuters/Archive Photos; **609** *top* Copyright © Hugh Sitton/Tony Stone Images; *bottom* SuperStock; **618** SuperStock; **619** Copyright © Tony Stone Images; **621** Copyright © Keren Su/Corbis; **623** Copyright © Michael S. Yamashita/Corbis; **625** Copyright © Cynthia M. Beall/NGS Image Collection; **627** Digital image copyright © 1996 Corbis. Original image courtesy of NASA/ Corbis; **628** *right* Copyright © 1997 Bob Sacha; **629** *left* NG Maps/NGS Image Collection; **630** *top to bottom* Copyright © Luo Wenfa/ChinaStock; Copyright © 1995 Wang Xinlin/ChinaStock; Copyright © ChinaStock; **631** Copyright © M. Bertinetti/White Star; **635** Copyright © Julian Calder/Tony Stone Images; **636** *left* Bibliothéque Nationale, Paris/Bridgeman Art Library, London/SuperStock; *center* By permission of The British Library, London; *right* The Granger Collection, New York; **637** *left* Copyright © ChinaStock; *right* The Granger Collection, New York; **638** *top left* Copyright © 1995 Christopher Liu/ChinaStock; *top right* The Metropolitan Museum of Art, New York. Gift of Ernest Erickson Foundation, Inc., 1985 (1985.214.99). Photograph copyright © 1986 the Metropolitan Museum of Art; *center* By permission of The British Library, London; *bottom* The Granger Collection, New York; **639** Copyright © Alain le Caromeu/Panos Pictures; **640–641** *background*, **641** *bottom* Copyright © UPI/Corbis-Bettmann; **641** *bottom* Copyright © Tom Nebbia/Corbis; **642** Illustration by Patrick Whalen; **644** Copyright © Cynthia M. Beall & Melvyn C. Goldstein/NGS Image Collection; **646** AP/Wide World Photos; **647** Copyright © Bob Thomas/Tony Stone Images; **649** Copyright © Jean-Léo Dugast/Panos Pictures; **651** Copyright © Japan Archive/TimePix; **652** *left* The Granger Collection, New York; *right* Portrait of Kisegawa of Matsubaya (c. 1796), Kitagaw Utamoro. Fitzwilliam Museum, University of Cambridge, UK/The Bridgeman Art Library, London; **653** *bottom left* The Granger Collection, New York; *bottom right* Corbis-Bettmann; **654** Copyright © 1976 Kenneth Love; **655** SuperStock; **656** *left* Manu Sassoonian/Art Resource, New York; *right* SuperStock; **657** *top* Werner Forman Archive/Private collection, New York/Art Resource, New York; *bottom* SuperStock; **660** John Pryke/Reuters/ Archive Photos; **661** AP/Wide World Photos; **663** Copyright © Bzad/ChinaStock; **665** Photograph by Manabu Watabe; **668** Copyright © John Lamb/Tony Stone Images; **671** Copyright © 2000 Nick Anderson, The Washington Post Writers Group. Reprinted with permission.

Unit 10, 674 *left* Copyright © Tony Stone Images: *right* Copyright © Roger Near/Tony Stone Images; **676** Copyright © Thad Samuels/NGS Image Collection; **677** *top* Copyright © Sergio Dorantes/Sygma; *bottom* National Oceanic and Atmospheric Administration/Department of Commerce; **687** The Granger Collection, New York; **688** Copyright © David Doubilet; **690** Illustrations by Stephen R. Wagner; **691** Copyright © David Moore/Black Star; **694** Copyright © Dani/Jeske/Earth Scenes; **695** Copyright © Denis Waugh/ Tony Stone Images; **696** Copyright © Dani/Jeske/Animals Animals; Copyright © Patti Murray/Earth Scenes; Copyright © J. Carnemolla/Australian Picture Library; Copyright © John Cancalosi/Peter Arnold Inc.; Copyright © Norman Owen Tomalin/Bruce Coleman; Copyright © Tim Flach/Tony Stone Images; **698** Copyright © Walter Edwards/NGS Image Collection; **699** Copyright © Greg Taylor; **700** Australian Picture Library; **701** Copyright © U.S. Government Air Force/NGS Image Collection; **705** Copyright © Glen Allison/Tony Stone Images; **708** Copyright © W. Robert Moore/NGS Image Collection; **709** Copyright © 1984 Jonathan Kirn/Liaison; **710–711** *bottom background* Illustration by Stephen R. Wagner; **711** *top* Copyright © Georg Gerster/Photo Researchers Inc.; **712** G. Burenhult Productions, Tjörnarp, Sweden; **714** *top* Copyright © Peter Stone/Pacific Stock; *center* Copyright © Joe Carini/Pacific Stock; *bottom* Copyright © Nicholas DeVore/Tony Stone Images; **716** *left* Copyright © Robert Frerck/Odyssey; *right* Copyright © 1991 Buddy Mays/FPG International; **717** *top* Copyright © Orion Press/Pacific Stock; *bottom* Copyright © 1988 Lee Kuhn/FPG International; **718** *left* Copyright © D. Johanson/Institute of Human Origins; *center* Detail of James Cook (1776), John Webber. Oil on canvas. The Granger Collection, New York; *right* Copyright © Douglass Bagli/Australian Picture Library; **719** *top* Australian Picture Library; *bottom* Copyright © Christopher Arnesen/Tony Stone Images; **720** Copyright © George F. Mobley/NGS Image Collection; **721** SuperStock; **722** Australian Picture Library/NZPL; **723** AP/Wide World Photos; **726** Copyright © Thad Samuels/NGS Image Collection; **727** credit to come; **729** Copyright © David Austen/Tony Stone Images; **730** Darren Whiteside/Reuters/Archive Photos; **731** Copyright © Sergio Dorantes/Sygma; **734** Copyright © Wolfgang Kaehler; **737** *top* National Climatic Data Center/ NESDIS/NOAA; *bottom* National Oceanic and Atmospheric Administration/ Department of Commerce.

1 2 3 4 5 6 7 8 9 – 09 08 07 06 05 04 03 – VEI –